What's New in This Editi[illegible]

Visual FoxPro 3.0 contains [illegible]res added since the previous version, FoxPro 2.6.

The biggest Visual FoxPro 3.0 in[illegible]mming methodology. Visual FoxPro is moving away from tradition[illegible]ard object-oriented programming. This and other key innovations [illegible]

■ **Full object-oriented programming language extensions**

Visual FoxPro 3.0 contains language extensions to support object-oriented (OO) programming (for example, the `DEFINE CLASS` command) so that you can programmatically develop OO programs. In addition to language extensions, Visual FoxPro 3.0 includes tools such as the Class and Form Designers that enable you to create classes visually.

■ **An object-oriented visual base class framework**

When you define your own user-defined classes you can base them on visual base classes that are built into Visual FoxPro. These classes support forms, form sets, and all kinds of controls, such as push buttons, tabbed page frames, and grids. Each Visual FoxPro base class defines the default behavior for all containers (forms, grids, and so forth) and controls. You can manipulate the properties, events, and access methods to customize the containers and controls to meet your own requirements.

■ **A true event-driven model**

Visual FoxPro supports a true event-driven model. This model is genuinely modeless, which allows you to coordinate multiple simultaneously active forms easily.

■ **The Form Designer**

The Form Designer allows you to visually create a form or a set of forms with a huge variety of controls, such as buttons, options, grids, tabbed page forms, toolbars, and custom OLE 2.0 controls, OLE objects, and graphics images.

■ **The Class Designer**

The Class Designer makes the process of creating and maintaining object-oriented classes easy. The classes are stored in visual class library (VCX) files. You can access classes from the visual class library programmatically or from the Form and Class Designers.

■ **Seamless connectivity to ODBC data sources**

You can visually create remote views with the View Designer or the Remote View Wizard, and you get language support for SQL pass-through to ODBC data sources.

■ **OLE 2.0 custom contr[illegible] support**

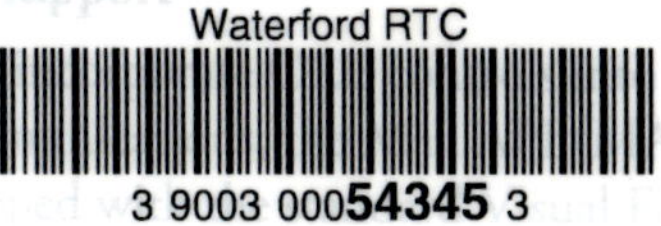

You can visually and ea[illegible]n application form. OLE custom controls that perform c[illegible]PI), and special controls such as an outline list control are s[illegible]xPro.

- **A View Designer that creates local and remote views**

  The View Designer helps you establish views, which are stored in the database. Remote views are the same as local views except that they are based on remote data such as Microsoft SQL server DBMS data. You can also create update queries.

- **The new Query Designer**

  The Query Designer is like the View Designer except that it stores queries to QPR query files.

- **The Database Designer**

  You can visually create a database consisting of tables, views, and relations. You can establish relations graphically by dragging and dropping related fields. You can establish triggers, stored procedures, and referential integrity rules. The Referential Integrity Builder helps you set up rules and it automatically establishes the rules and generates stored procedures to enforce referential integrity.

- **Complete backward compatibility with a three-way approach**

  First, FoxPro 2.*x* programs can be run, unchanged, in Visual FoxPro. Second, developers can extend existing applications to take advantage of new object-oriented features. Third, developers can use the built-in converter to transform their current FoxPro 2.*x* applications to the Visual FoxPro format. Converted forms take full advantage of Visual FoxPro object-oriented interfaces.

- **Numerous visual builder utilities to help you define visual object properties**
- **A robust DBMS with referential integrity and triggers**

  The database container (DBC) file contains information to support referential integrity, triggers, and stored procedures for tables associated with the database. It also supports extended attributes for tables, such as data validation, long field names, and default values.

- **The Data Environment Designer**

  The Data Environment Designer lets you visually create and modify the data environment of reports and object-oriented forms and form sets. The data environment defines tables, local and remote views, and relations.

- **The new Currency, DateTime, Double, and Integer data types**
- **New powerful wizard utilities**

  The Form Wizard creates a data-entry form from a single table. The One-To-Many Form Wizard creates a data-entry form from two related tables displaying fields. The Cross-Tab Wizard displays query data in a spreadsheet format. The Query Wizard creates a standard query. The View Wizard creates a view using local data and stores the data in a database container file. The Remote View Wizard creates a view using remote data from an ODBC data source. The Report Wizard creates a formatted report from a single table. The Group/Total Report Wizard creates a summary report. The One-To-Many Report Wizard creates a report that groups records from a parent table with records from a child table.

VISUAL FOXPRO® 3

Developer's Guide

Third Edition

Jeb Long
Elizabeth Long, Consulting Editor

201 West 103rd Street
Indianapolis, Indiana 46290

SAMS Developer's Guide

This book is dedicated to my wife, Elizabeth Long, my friend and partner.

THIRD EDITION

International Standard Book Number: 0-672-30653-0

Library of Congress Catalog Card Number: 94-69270

98 97 96 95 4 3 2 1

Interpretation of the printing code: the rightmost double-digit number is the year of the book's printing; the rightmost single-digit, the number of the book's printing. For example, a printing code of 95-1 shows that the first printing of the book occurred in 1995.

Composed in AGaramond and MCPdigital by Macmillan Computer Publishing

Printed in the United States of America

Trademarks

Publisher
Richard K. Swadley

Acquisitions Manager
Greg Wiegand

Managing Editor
Cindy Morrow

Acquisitions Editor
Chris Denny

Development Editor
Kelly Murdock

Software Development Specialist
Kim Spilker

Production Editor
Kitty Wilson

Copy Editors
Ryan Rader
Bart Reed

Editorial Coordinator
Bill Whitmer

Technical Edit Coordinator
Lynette Quinn

Editorial Assistants
Carol Ackerman
Sharon Cox

Technical Reviewer
Chris Capossela

Marketing Manager
Gregg Bushyeager

Assistant Marketing Manager
Michelle Milner

Cover Designer
Karen Ruggles

Book Designer
Alyssa Yesh

Vice President of Manufacturing and Production
Jeff Valler

Manufacturing Coordinator
Paul Gilchrist

Imprint Manager
Kelly Dobbs

Team Supervisor
Brad Chinn

Support Services Manager
Juli Cook

Support Services Supervisor
Mary Beth Wakefield

Production Analysts
Angela Bannon
Dennis Clay Hager
Bobbi Satterfield

Graphics Image Specialists
Becky Beheler
Steve Carlin
Brad Dixon
Teresa Forrester
Jason Hand
Clint Lahnen
Cheri Laughner
Mike Reynolds
Laura Robbins
Dennis Sheehan
Craig Small
Jeff Yesh

Production
Carol Bowers
Mona Brown
Michael Brumitt
Charlotte Clapp
Mary Ann Cosby
Terrie Deemer
Judy Everly
Donna Harbin
Michael Henry
Aleata Howard
Louisa Klucznik
Ayanna Lacey
Kevin Laseau
Shawn MacDonald
Donna Martin
Casey Price
Brian-Kent Proffitt
SA Springer
Jill Tompkins
Tina Trettin
Susan Van Ness
Mark Walche
Dennis Wesner
Michelle Worthington

Indexers
Jeanne Clark
Cheryl Dietsch
Greg Eldred

Overview

Contents

Foreword

It is a pleasure to welcome Jeb Long to the community of FoxPro authors. Jeb was present for the birth of Xbase, and as the author of JPLDIS, the immediate precursor to dBASE II, he originated many of the central language commands (`REPLACE`, `STORE`, and so forth) that we still use today. I am pleased to see him using FoxPro now.

I first became acquainted with Jeb during Ashton-Tate's abortive attempt to acquire Fox Software in 1986–1987. During those discussions I developed deep respect for Jeb as a major software engineering talent. We've been friends ever since.

It is appropriate that Jeb's new book, *Visual FoxPro 3 Developer's Guide, Third Edition,* focuses on the FoxPro language. Although Jeb covers the FoxPro power tools thoroughly, he puts most of his emphasis on using the language, whether through traditional, procedural programming or code snippets. This is an interesting contrast to most of the books published on FoxPro recently. His approach to showing how the components of the FoxPro language relate to one another is particularly lucid.

Congratulations to Jeb for *Visual FoxPro 3 Developer's Guide, Third Edition.* It is a refreshing book and should be a valuable addition to any FoxPro developer's library.

David L. Fulton

Original Creator of FoxPro

Acknowledgments

Grateful acknowledgment is extended to all the people who made this book possible with their enthusiastic support and encouragement:

The Macmillan Computer Publishing editorial and publishing staff. Special gratitude to Chris Denny, Kelly Murdock, Kitty Wilson, Bart Reed, and Ryan Rader.

I would like to extend my gratitude to Alastair Dallas, who graciously allowed me to use excerpts from the book that we coauthored.

Elizabeth Long, consulting editor. Thanks for all your assistance and encouragement in developing and preparing this manuscript.

About the Author

Jeb Long has had 30 years of experience in software design and engineering at some of the most prestigious technical organizations in the country. Mr. Long has worked as an independent consultant and author since he left Ashton-Tate Corporation in 1990. While at Ashton-Tate, he was the guru of dBASE products. In that role, he was the dBASE language architect and was responsible for the dBASE language components for all versions of dBASE III and dBASE IV, except for the initial version.

Mr. Long's relationship to dBASE dates back to 1973, when he was a software engineer at the California Institute of Technology's Jet Propulsion Laboratory. He was responsible for developing a file management program for JPL's UNIVAC 1108 mainframe computer. This program, JPLDIS, was the immediate precursor to dBASE. Later, under contract to Wayne Ratliff, Mr. Long translated and adapted the original version of dBASE II to run on the IBM PC.

In his 11 years at the Jet Propulsion Laboratory, Mr. Long was responsible for software tasks in support of our nation's planetary exploration program. Among these tasks were programs to calculate interplanetary trajectories, to process telemetry from space vehicles, to simulate spacecraft propulsion subsystems, and to support spacecraft tests and operations. He was actively involved in the Mariner and Viking missions to Mars.

A 1963 graduate of the University of Texas, Mr. Long now lives with his wife Elizabeth on a hill overlooking Los Angeles. Elizabeth has a master's degree in English and has worked as a technical writer at JPL. Jeb and Elizabeth have worked closely together in writing this book. Mr. Long has also written numerous books and articles for technical magazines. His books include *Do It Yourself Quick C for Windows*, Sams Publishing; *Do It Yourself Microsoft C/C++ 7*, Sams Publishing; *dBASE IV 1.5 Programmer's Language* (co-authored with Alastair Dallas), Sams Publishing; and *dBASE Programmer's Utilities* (co-authored with R. A. Byers and C. Wayne Ratliff), Ashton-Tate Publishing Group; and four FoxPro Developer's Guide books published by Sams Publishing. These include *FoxPro 2.5 for Windows Developer's Guide, FoxPro 2.5 for DOS Developer's Guide, FoxPro 2.6 for Windows Developer's Guide*, and this book.

Introduction

Welcome to *Visual FoxPro 3 Developer's Guide, Third Edition.* This book is designed to help you use and develop applications with Visual FoxPro. This book focuses on helping first-time FoxPro users, as well as experienced FoxPro users, master the skills necessary to develop applications in Visual FoxPro. To fully benefit from this book, it would be helpful if you have had experience with Microsoft Windows, programming, and possibly some experience with databases.

Visual FoxPro is a computer program that runs on IBM-PC and compatible microcomputer systems and operates under Microsoft Windows. Your microcomputer must have the following system components and capabilities to run Visual FoxPro:

- An 80386SX or better processor.
- A mouse.
- 640KB of conventional RAM.
- 8MB of RAM.
- Microsoft Windows 3.1 or higher.
- About 56MB of hard disk space. Disk space requirements vary depending on various installation options.

Visual FoxPro is a database management system (DBMS) with which you can create and maintain a list of data, called a *table*, or database files, such as a phone list, an inventory list, or a grocery list. In fact, you can maintain any collection of related information using FoxPro. You can sort or organize tables. You can search for and retrieve information within a table. You can generate reports, input forms, and mailing labels from tables. In a DBMS, as well as in FoxPro, you can organize information in multiple tables and retrieve the data simultaneously from any of the tables. You can relate tables that contain common information. FoxPro automatically maintains this relation so that you can manipulate or extract related information as required. This type of DBMS is loosely called a *relational DBMS.* A group of related tables is referred to as a *database.*

FoxPro uses easy-to-learn commands that create, manipulate, and retrieve data from database tables. FoxPro belongs to a category of DBMSs called Xbase. This generic term refers to languages like FoxPro, dBASE III PLUS, dBASE IV, FoxBASE+, and ARAGO. Xbase was originally derived from a mainframe DBMS called JPLDIS (*Jet Propulsion Laboratory Database-Management and Information Retrieval System*) developed in 1972 by the author of this book. Developers and programmers throughout the world have written tens of millions of Xbase code lines. It has become the language of choice for many businesses. Borland International reports that over four million people have copies of dBASE IV, one of the more popular Xbase dialects. Visual FoxPro 3.0 runs dBASE IV programs without any change except that the program runs faster under FoxPro. Since Microsoft Corporation acquired Fox Holdings, Inc., the company responsible for FoxBASE+ and FoxPro, FoxPro's market share in the Xbase market category has increased. Visual FoxPro supports commands supported by other Xbase products plus language extensions that are not included in any other Xbase product. The primary extensions to the Xbase language Visual FoxPro introduces are the object-oriented programming (OOP) extensions and programming elements that support a data dictionary.

The introduction of Visual FoxPro for Windows represents a milestone in microcomputer history, because now you can run programs written in the MS-DOS business language of the '80s—Xbase—with little or no changes, under the operating environment of the '90s—the Windows 3.1 or Windows 95 graphical user interface (GUI) in a client/server environment. Visual FoxPro supports seamless connectivity. Furthermore, you can take advantage of the powerful new object-oriented programming environment for improving the application development process.

This Book's Audience

This book is intended for a full range of FoxPro users from the programmer who is a novice in FoxPro to the expert who has used previous versions of FoxPro. Visual FoxPro 3.0 is a new product, and this book describes all its features. Because this book discusses each feature in detail, it is useful to FoxPro beginners as well as FoxPro specialists. Some books focus on how the FoxPro language can solve your problems, but this approach does not necessarily foster a thorough understanding of the FoxPro language. I wrote this book to help you better understand the Visual FoxPro 3.0 language. The better you grasp the language, the more useful Visual FoxPro will be to you.

Many FoxPro books are written for beginners who are not yet comfortable with computers. This book is not a beginner's tutorial. Although I describe all aspects of Visual FoxPro in this book, I primarily specialize in the Visual FoxPro interface, programming language, and development tools, and I provide in-depth information that cannot be found elsewhere. After beginners comprehend computer basics and wade through the tutorials, this book can then provide them with a deeper understanding of the Visual FoxPro language, the user interface, and the development tools.

This book also focuses on another audience: programmers who want to pick up the Visual FoxPro language quickly, without suffering through tutorials. This book will enable you to capture the essence of the Visual FoxPro language.

Evolution of FoxPro for Windows

FoxPro 2.5 for Windows was introduced in June 1993 and was an important milestone for Xbase for it was the first serious Xbase system that ran under the Microsoft Windows platform. This version was important because most PC developers have moved to the Microsoft

Windows platform. The message is clear—the MS-DOS market is swiftly fading away. The revenues from the Borland International dBASE IV (which runs under MS-DOS) dropped by more than 40 percent between 1993 and 1994. In 1995, Borland has plans to abandon work on any more versions of MS-DOS based dBASE.

FoxPro 2.5 for Windows was an excellent implementation of the Xbase language, and you can run your MS-DOS based dBASE III PLUS and dBASE IV 2.0 programs under FoxPro 2.5 with few changes. However, in most cases, you were required to make changes to a dBASE application before it will run under FoxPro 2.5 for Windows.

FoxPro 2.6 was introduced in March 1994. It was designed to be almost completely compatible with dBASE IV Version 2.0. The areas of incompatibility are inconsequential. In addition, FoxPro 2.6 contains a collection of *wizards* that help you do your work. A wizard is a procedure that leads you through some typical database operation. FoxPro 2.6 for Windows contained numerous wizards that would create tables and a variety of reports, labels, mail merge reports, screens, and client/server and local queries.

You could develop nice applications using FoxPro for Windows Version 2.6 using standard Windows interface control elements and dialogs. However, applications were limited because FoxPro 2.6 still used the same type of pseudo-event driven visual interfaces as the MS-DOS version of FoxPro. It was difficult to coordinate multiple forms.

Visual FoxPro, which was unveiled in the spring of 1995, solved the problems of previous versions of FoxPro. Visual FoxPro provides a truly modeless interface. You can not only easily coordinate multiple forms but you can run multiple instances of a single form at the same time. Visual FoxPro handles events for you. As a result, you can develop a slick and powerful interactive interface using an object-oriented programming environment that is superior to any interface that you could develop with previous versions of FoxPro. Furthermore, you have a choice of a large variety of visual objects that you can use with your forms, such as toolbars, grids, grids within grids, and 3-D buttons. Visual FoxPro also has a data dictionary that enforces referential integrity, triggers that can be programmed to control cross-tabular integrity, a seamless client-server database connectivity, and many powerful wizards.

What's New in Visual FoxPro 3.0 for Windows

Visual FoxPro 3.0 contains numerous major enhancements and new features. All of the existing designers and builders have been improved. There is a new type of file called a database container (DBC) file, which contains information to support referential integrity, triggers, and stored procedures for tables associated with the database. It also supports extended attributes for tables, such as data validation, long field names, and default values. The major Visual FoxPro 3.0 innovation is a reorientation of its programming methodology. Visual FoxPro is moving away from traditional procedural programming and toward object-oriented programming.

For those of you who are familiar with earlier versions of FoxPro, I have provided a list of almost all of the new features that were incorporated into the Visual FoxPro 3.0 language. Most of the new commands and functions were added to support object-oriented programming (OOP) and data integrity support:

Class Name	*Description*
`ACLASS()`	The `ACLASS()` function fills a memory variable array with an object's parent class names.
`ADATABASE()`	The `ADATABASE()` function fills a memory variable array with the names of all open databases and their paths.
`ADOBJECTS()`	The `ADOBJECTS()` function fills a memory variable array with the names of all named connections, tables, or SQL views in a database.
`ADD CLASS`	The `ADD CLASS` function appends a specified class definition to a VCX visual class library.
`ADD TABLE`	The `ADD TABLE` command adds a free table to the currently open database.
`AERROR()`	The `AERROR()` function creates a memory variable array containing information about the most recent Visual FoxPro or ODBC error.
`AINSTANCE()`	The `AINSTANCE()` function fills a memory variable array with the names of all instances of a specified class.
`ALTER TABLE`	The `ALTER TABLE` command programmatically modifies the structure of a table.
`AMEMBERS()`	The `AMEMBERS()` function fills a memory variable array with the names of properties, procedures, and member objects for an object.
`APPEND PROCEDURES`	The `APPEND PROCEDURE` command adds the procedures in a text file to the stored procedure in the currently open database.
`APRINTERS()`	The `APRINTERS()` function fills a memory variable array with the names of printers currently installed in the Windows Print Manager.
`ASELOBJ()`	The `ASELOBJ()` function fills a memory variable array with references to currently selected controls in the active Form Designer.
`AUSED()`	The `AUSED()` function fills a memory variable array with table aliases and work areas for a session.

Class Name	Description
BEGIN TRANSACTION	The BEGIN TRANSACTION command begins a transaction.
BIT...()	Eight functions were added that perform bitwise (that is, bit-at-a-time) operations on numeric values. These functions include the BITAND(), BITCLEAR(), BITLSHIFT(), BITNOT(), BITOR(), BITRSHIFT(), BITSET(), BITTEST(), and BITXOR() functions.
_BUILDER	The _BUILDER system memory variable contains a string with the name of the Visual FoxPro Builder application.
CANDIDATE()	The CANDIDATE() function returns a true (.T.) value if an index tag is a candidate index tag.
CD ¦ CHDIR	In reminiscence of the MS-DOS commands, the CD and CHDIR change the default directory to the one specified.
CLEAR EVENTS	The CLEAR EVENTS command terminates event processing that was initiated by the READ EVENTS command.
CLOSE TABLES	The CLOSE TABLES command closes all tables in the current database while leaving the database open.
COMPILE DATABASE	The COMPILE DATABASE command compiles the stored procedure in a database container (DBC) file.
COMPILE FORM	The COMPILE FORM command compiles one or more forms in the Visual FoxPro form (SCX) file.
COMPOBJ()	The COMPOBJ() function compares the properties of two objects and returns true (.T.) value if their properties and property values are identical.
_CONVERTER	The _CONVERTER system memory variable contains the name of the FoxPro converter application.
COPY PROCEDURES	The COPY PROCEDURES command copies stored procedures in the current database to a text file.
CREATE CLASS	The CREATE CLASS command opens the Class Designer, allowing you to create a class definition.
CREATE CLASSLIB	The CREATE CLASSLIB command creates a new, empty visual class library file.
CREATE CONNECTION	The CREATE CONNECTION command creates a named connection and stores it in the current database.

Class Name	*Description*
CREATE DATABASE	The CREATE DATABASE command creates a database and opens it.
CREATE FORM	The CREATE FORM command opens the new Form Designer, which generates a screen (SCX) file. The MODIFY SCREEN command performs the same function.
CREATE SQL VIEW	The CREATE SQL VIEW command displays the View Designer, from which you can create a SQL view.
CREATE TRIGGER	The CREATE TRIGGER command creates a Delete, Insert, or Update trigger for a table.
CREATEOBJECT()	The CREATEOBJECT() function creates an object from a class or subclass definition or an OLE object.
CTOT()	The CTOT() function returns a DateTime value from a character expression. The new DateTime data type contains the date and the time (for example, {12/12/95 10:34:04 am}).
CURSORGETPROP()	The CURSORGETPROP() function returns the current property settings for a FoxPro table or cursor.
CURSORSETPROP()	You can use the CURSORSETPROP() function to set a property for a FoxPro table or cursor.
CURVAL()	The CURVAL() function returns a field value directly from disk or a remote source.
DATETIME()	The DATETIME() function returns the current date and time as a DateTime value.
DBC()	The DBC() function returns the name and path of the current database.
DBGETPROP()	The DBGETPROP() function returns a property for the current database, or fields, named connections, tables, or views in the current database.
DBSETPROP()	You can use the DBSETPROP() function to set a property for the current database, or fields, named connections, tables, or views in the current database.
DBUSED()	The DBUSED() function returns a true (.T.) value if the specified database (DBC file) is open.
DECLARE - DLL	The DECLARE - DLL command registers a function in an external Windows 32-bit dynamic link library (DLL).

Class Name	*Description*
DEFINE CLASS	The DEFINE CLASS command creates a user-defined class or subclass and specifies the properties, events, and methods for the class or subclass.
DELETE CONNECTION	The DELETE CONNECTION command deletes a named connection from the current database.
DELETE DATABASE	The DELETE DATABASE command deletes a database from disk.
DELETE - SQL	The DELETE - SQL command marks records for deletion.
DELETE TRIGGER	The DELETE TRIGGER command removes a Delete, Insert, or Update trigger for a table from the current database.
DELETE VIEW	The DELETE VIEW command deletes a SQL view from the current database.
DISPLAY CONNECTIONS	The DISPLAY CONNECTIONS command displays information relating to the named connections in the current database.
DISPLAY DATABASE	The DISPLAY DATABASE command displays information about the current database, or fields, named connections, tables, or views in the current database.
DISPLAY OBJECTS	The DISPLAY OBJECTS command displays information about an object or a group of objects.
DISPLAY PROCEDURES	The DISPLAY PROCEDURES command displays the names of stored procedures in the current database.
DISPLAY TABLES	The DISPLAY TABLES command displays all tables and information about the tables contained in an open database.
DISPLAY VIEWS	The DISPLAY VIEWS command displays information about SQL views in the current database.
DO FORM	The DO FORM command executes a compiled form or form set created with the Form Designer.
DTOT()	The DTOT() function returns a DateTime value from a date expression.
END TRANSACTION	The END TRANSLATION command ends the current transaction.
ERROR	The ERROR command generates a specified FoxPro error.

Class Name	*Description*
FDATE()	The FDATE() function returns the last modification date for a file.
FTIME()	The FTIME() function returns the last modification time for a file.
GETCOLOR()	The GETCOLOR() function displays the Windows Color dialog box and returns the selected color as a numeric value.
GETCP()	The GETCP() function displays the Code Page dialog box and returns the number of the code page chosen.
GETFLDSTATE()	The GETFLDSTATE() function returns a numeric value indicating if a field in a table or cursor has been edited or the deleted status of the current record has been changed.
GETNEXTMODIFIED()	The GETNEXTMODIFIED() function returns the record number for the next modified record in a buffered cursor.
GETOBJECT()	The GETOBJECT() function activates an OLE automation object and creates a reference to the object.
GETPRINTER()	The GETPRINTER() function activates the Windows Print Setup dialog box and returns the name of the printer that you select.
HOUR()	The HOUR() function returns the hour portion from a DateTime expression.
#INCLUDE	The #INCLUDE directive instructs the Visual FoxPro preprocessor to the treat the contents of a specified file as if it appeared in a FoxPro program.
ISEXCLUSIVE()	The ISEXCLUSIVE() function returns a true (.T.) value if a table is opened for exclusive use; otherwise it returns false (.F.) value.
INDBC()	The INDBC() function returns a true (.T.) value if the designated database object is in the current database; otherwise it returns a false (.F.) value.
ISMOUSE()	The ISMOUSE() function returns a true (.T.) value if mouse hardware is present; otherwise it returns a false (.F.) value.
ISNULL()	The ISNULL() function returns a true (.T.) value if an expression evaluates to a null value; otherwise it returns a false (.F.) value.

Class Name	*Description*
LIST CONNECTIONS	The `LIST CONNECTIONS` command continuously displays information about the named connections in the current database.
LIST DATABASE	The `LIST DATABASE` command displays information about the current database.
LIST OBJECTS	The `LIST OBJECTS` command displays information about an object or a group of objects.
LIST PROCEDURES	The `LIST PROCEDURES` command displays the names of stored procedures in the current database.
LIST TABLES	The `LIST TABLES` command displays all tables and information about the tables contained in an open database.
LIST VIEWS	The `LIST VIEWS` command displays information about SQL views in the current database.
LOCAL	The `LOCAL` command creates local memory variables and memory variable arrays.
LPARAMETERS	The `LPARAMETERS` command assigns data passed from a calling program to local memory variables or arrays.
MD ¦ MKDIR	In reminiscence of the MS-DOS commands, the new `MK` and `MKDIR` commands create the specified disk directory.
MESSAGEBOX()	The `MESSAGEBOX()` function displays a user-defined dialog box.
MINUTE()	The `MINUTE()` function returns the minute portion from a DateTime expression.
MODIFY CLASS	The `MODIFY CLASS` command opens the Class Designer, allowing you to modify an existing class definition or create a new class definition.
MODIFY CONNECTION	The `MODIFY CONNECTION` command displays the Connection Designer, allowing you to modify an existing named connection stored in the current database.
MODIFY DATABASE	The `MODIFY DATABASE` command opens the Database Designer, allowing you to interactively modify the current database.
MODIFY FORM	The `MODIFY FORM` command opens the Form Designer so you can modify or create a form.

Class Name	*Description*
MODIFY PROCEDURE	The MODIFY PROCEDURE command opens the Visual FoxPro text editor, permitting you to create new stored procedures for the current database, or modify existing stored procedures in the current database.
MODIFY VIEW	The MODIFY VIEW command displays the View Designer, allowing you to modify an existing SQL view.
MOUSE	The MOUSE command clicks, double-clicks, moves, or drags the mouse. It can be used to generate demos and tutorials.
MTON()	The MTON() function returns a numeric value from a currency expression.
NTOM()	The NTOM() function returns a currency value from a numeric expression.
NVL()	The NVL() function returns a non-null value from two expressions.
OBJREF()	The OBJREF() function creates an indirect reference to an object using a memory variable or an array element as a reference to the object.
OLDVAL()	The OLDVAL() function returns the original field value for a field that has been modified but not updated.
OPEN DATABASE	The OPEN DATABASE command opens a database.
PACK DATABASE	The PACK DATABASE command removes records marked for deletion from an open database.
PRIMARY()	The PRIMARY() function returns a true (.T.) value if an index tag is a primary index tag; otherwise returns a false (.F.) value.
RD ¦ RMDIR	The RD and RMDIR commands delete the specified disk directory.
READ EVENTS	The READ EVENTS command starts event processing.
REFRESH()	The REFRESH() function refreshes a set of records in a remote, updatable SQL view.
RELEASE CLASSLIB	The RELEASE CLASSLIB command closes a VCX visual class library containing class definitions.
RELEASE PROCEDURE	The RELEASE CLASSLIB command closes a procedure file opened with the SET PROCEDURE command.
REMOVE CLASS	The REMOVE CLASS command removes a class definition from a VCX visual class library.

Class Name	Description
REMOVE TABLE	The REMOVE TABLE command removes a table from the current database.
RENAME CLASS	The RENAME CLASS command renames a class definition contained in a VCX visual class library.
RENAME CONNECTION	The RENAME CONNECTION command renames a named connection in a database.
RENAME TABLE	The RENAME TABLE command renames a table in a database.
RENAME VIEW	The RENAME VIEW command renames a SQL view in a database.
REQUERY()	The REQUERY() function repeats a data retrieval operation from a remote SQL view.
RGB()	The RGB() function returns a single color value from a set of red, green, and blue color components.
ROLLBACK	The ROLLBACK command cancels any changes made during the current transaction.
_SCREEN	You can use the _SCREEN keyword as a qualifier to manipulate the main FoxPro window as an object.
SEC()	The SEC() function returns the seconds portion from a DateTime expression.
SET CLASSLIB	The SET CLASSLIB command opens a VCX visual class library file containing class definitions.
SET COLLATE	The SET COLLATE command specifies a collation sequence for character fields in subsequent indexing and sorting operations to support international applications.
SET CPCOMPILE	The SET CPCOMPILE command specifies the code page for compiled programs.
SET CPDIALOG	The SET CPDIALOG command specifies if the Code Page dialog box is displayed when a table is opened within a program.
SET DATABASE	The SET DATABASE command specifies the current database.
SET DATASESSION	The SET DATASESSION command activates the specified form session. Each session defines a data environment for a form or report. Different sessions can be executing simultaneously.

Class Name	*Description*
SET FDOW	The SET FDOW command specifies the first day of the week.
SET FWEEK	The SET FWEEK command specifies rules for determining the first week of the year.
SET NULL	The SET NULL command determines how null values are supported by the ALTER TABLE, CREATE TABLE, and SQL INSERT commands.
SET OLEOBJECT	The SET OLEOBJECT command specifies whether Visual FoxPro searches the Windows registry when an object cannot be located.
SET PALETTE	The SET PALETTE command specifies whether BMP graphic image's palette is used.
SET SECONDS	The SET SECONDS command specifies whether seconds are displayed in the time portion of a DateTime value.
SET TOPIC ID	The SET TOPIC ID command specifies the help topic, based on the topic's context ID, to open when you invoke the FoxPro help system.
SETFLDSTATE()	The SETFLDSTATE() function assigns a field or deletion state value to a field or record in a local cursor created from remote tables.
SQLCANCEL()	The SQLCANCEL() function requests cancellation of an executing SQL statement.
SQLCOLUMNS()	The SQLCOLUMNS() function restores a list of column names and information about each column for the specified data source table to a FoxPro cursor.
SQLCOMMIT()	The SQLCOMMIT() function commits a transaction.
SQLCONNECT()	The SQLCONNECT() function establishes a connection to a data source.
SQLDISCONNECT()	The SQLDISCONNECT() function terminates a connection to a data source.
SQLEXEC()	The SQLEXEC() function sends a SQL statement to the data source, where the statement is processed.
SQLGETPROP()	The SQLGETPROP() function returns current or default settings for an active connection, data source, or attached table.
SQLMORERESULTS()	The SQLMORERESULTS() function copies another result set to a FoxPro cursor if more result sets are available.

Class Name	*Description*
`SQLROLLBACK()`	The `SQLROLLBACK()` function cancels any changes made during the current transaction.
`SQLSETPROP()`	The `SQLSETPROP()` function specifies settings for an active connection, data source, or attached table.
`SQLSTRINGCONNECT()`	The `SQLSTRINGCONNECT()` function establishes a connection to a data source through a connection string.
`SQLTABLES()`	The `SQLTABLES()` function stores the names of tables in a data source to a FoxPro cursor.
`SYS(2029)`	The `SYS(2029)` function returns a table type.
`TABLEREVERT()`	The `TABLEREVERT()` function discards changes made to a buffered row or a buffered table or cursor and restores them from the data currently on disk.
`TABLEUPDATE()`	The `TABLEUPDATE()` function commits changes made to a buffered row or a buffered table or cursor.
`THIS`	The `THIS` keyword provides a reference to an object before it is created.
`THISFORM`	The `THISFORM` keyword provides a reference to a form before it is created.
`THISFORMSET`	The `THISFORMSET` keyword provides a reference to a formset before it is created.
`TTOC()`	The `TTOC()` function returns a character value from a DateTime expression.
`TTOD()`	The `TTOD()` function returns a date value from a DateTime expression.
`TXNLEVEL()`	The `TXNLEVEL()` function returns a numeric value that denotes the current transaction level.
`UPDATE - SQL`	The SQL `UPDATE` command updates records in a table with new values.
`VALIDATE DATABASE`	The `VALIDATE DATABASE` command verifies that the location of tables and indexes are correct in the current database.
`WEEK()`	The `WEEK()` function returns a number representing the week-of-the-year from a Date or DateTime expression.
`WITH...END WITH`	The `WITH...END WITH` control structure executes multiple commands for a specified object.

Class Name	*Description*
_WIZARD	The _WIZARD system memory variable contains the name of the FoxPro wizard application.

Visual FoxPro introduces object-oriented programming language extensions to the FoxPro language. Included in these extensions are two types of classes: container classes and control classes. A container class is like a dialog box or form that contains other objects, such as control objects. An object is defined by a class. In Visual FoxPro 3.0, there are container objects and control objects that replace the controls found in earlier versions of FoxPro, plus there are new objects. The following table lists the names of the classes that define the properties, events, and methods of objects supported by Visual FoxPro:

Class Name	*Description*
CheckBox control	Creates a check box control object. Replaces the @...GET check boxes.
Column object	Creates a column in a grid that contains text box
ComboBox control	Creates a ComboBox control object. Replaces the @...GET pop-up.
CommandButton control	Creates a Command button object. Replaces the @...GET push button.
CommandGroup control	Creates a group of command buttons.
Custom object	Creates a user-defined object.
EditBox control	Creates an edit box. Replaces the @...GET edit box.
Form object	Creates a form container object, which is a high-level form of a window used as a dialog box defined in earlier versions of FoxPro.
FormSet object	Creates a FormSet object, which is a collection of forms with tabs used to choose a form.
Grid control	Creates a grid control that resembles a Browse screen.
Header object	Creates a header object, which is a heading for a grid column.
Image control	Creates an Image control, which is a graphical control that displays a BMP picture. It is similar to @...SAY BITMAP.
Label control	Creates an label object that can respond to events. It is used to display text. Replaces the @...SAY command.
Line control	Creates a line object that can respond to events and display lines. Resembles the @...TO command.
ListBox control	Creates a list box control object. Replaces the @...GET list box.
OLE control	Creates an OLE control object.

Class Name	*Description*
`OptionButton` control	Creates an option button object. Replaces the `@...GET` radio button.
`OptionGroup` control	Creates a group of option buttons. Replaces the `@...GET` radio buttons.
`Page` object	Creates a page object in a page frame. It is like a form within a form. A page object can contain control objects.
`PageFrame` control	Creates a container object that contains one or more page objects, which overlay each other.
`Shape` control	Creates a shape object such as rectangles, ovals, and circles. Similar to the `@...TO` command.
`Spinner` control	Creates a spinner control object. Replaces the `@...GET` spinner.
`TextBox` control	Creates a text box control object. Replaces the `@...GET` text box.
`Timer` control	Creates a timer object that can execute code at specified intervals.
`ToolBar` object	Creates a user-defined toolbar container object.

FoxPro commands that have been enhanced in Visual FoxPro 3.0 are presented in the following list:

Class Name	*Description*
`AFIELDS()`	A second optional argument was added to this function so that you specify a work area or table alias. Then you can insert field information for tables that are in use in a work area other than the current work area. Furthermore, the array is extended to contain the new Visual FoxPro extended field attributes.
`APPEND`	A new `IN` clause was added to the `APPEND` command so that you can specify a work area.
`APPEND FROM`	A new `AS` clause was added to the `APPEND FROM` command so that you can specify the code page of the table or file appended to the FoxPro table.
`APPEND MEMO`	A new `AS` clause was added to the `APPEND MEMO` command so that you can specify the code page of the file appended to the memo field.
`CLOSE DATABASE`	The `CLOSE DATABASE` command has been modified to close the currently open database container file, open tables in the database, and open free tables when a database is active.

Class Name	*Description*
COPY TO	A new AS clause was added to the COPY TO command that lets you specify the code page of the new table or file COPY TO creates.
CREATE TABLE	The CREATE TABLE command has been modified to support additional SQL-compliant clauses and referential integrity.
DEFINE BAR	FONT and STYLE clauses were added to these four commands to let you specify a font and font style: DEFINE BAR DEFINE MENU DEFINE PAD DEFINE POPUP
DELETE	The IN clause was added to the DELETE command so that you can specify a work area.
DELETE TAG	The IN clause was added to the DELETE TAG command so that you can specify a work area.
DOW()	Supports a new optional second argument that allows you to specify the first day of the week. This was added for international support.
EXPORT	A new AS clause was added to the EXPORT command that lets you specify the code page of the new table or file the EXPORT command creates.
EXTERNAL	The EXTERNAL command was modified to support additional file types.
GATHER	A new NAME clause was added to the GATHER command that allows you to replace field data with properties values from an object. The object is created by the SCATTER command.
HELP	You can now create your own Windows-style help system and refer to a specific help topic using a numeric context ID. The DBF type help file has also been modified to support a numeric context ID.
IMPORT	A new AS clause was added to the IMPORT command to allow you to specify the code page of the file appended to a FoxPro table.

Class Name	*Description*
`INDEX`	A new `CANDIDATE` clause was added to the `INDEX` command so that you can create candidate index tags. Candidate indexes contain no nulls or duplicate values. You are not allowed to enter a record with a duplicate or null key.
`LOCK()`	The `LOCK()` function was enhanced to support 0 as a record number, which allows you to lock the table header and prevent other users from adding new records to the table.
`MODIFY QUERY`	A new `AS` clause was added to the `MODIFY QUERY` command. The `AS` clause instructs Visual FoxPro to convert a FoxPro query created under a different code page to the current code page.
`PRTINFO()`	More information is returned by the `PRTINFO()` function.
`RELEASE ALL`	A new `EXTENDED` clause was added to the `RELEASE ALL` command that permits you to release public variables.
`RLOCK()`	You can specify 0 as a record number, which locks the table header and prevents other users from adding new records to the table.
`SCATTER`	A new `NAME` clause was added to the `SCATTER` command that creates an object with properties that are field names that contain field values.
`SET DOHISTORY`	You can designate that executing program commands be directed to a text file by specifying the new `TO` clause.
`SET PRINTER`	You can specify the new `FONT` clause with the `SET PRINTER` command to specify the default font for a printed document.
`SET PROCEDURE`	The `SET PROCEDURE` command was enhanced in Visual FoxPro 3.0 to open one or more procedure files.
`SET RELATION`	The `SET RELATION` command now supports a new `IN` clause, which permits you specify a work area or table alias.
`UNLOCK`	You can specify the new `RECORD` clause with the `UNLOCK` command to unlock a single record.
`USE`	You can now open a SQL view created with the `CREATE SQL VIEW` command with the `USE` command.

Class Name	*Description*
WAIT	You can now specify the position of the Wait window by specifying the new AT clause with the WAIT command.
ZAP	The ZAP command now supports the IN clause that permits you specify a work area.

Conventions Used in This Book

I've used the following conventions to increase the readability of this book:

- Sample programs, program fragments, keywords, functions, operators, and variables appear in a special monospace typeface that simulates the font appearing on your computer screen.
- New terms being defined appear in *italic* type.
- In syntax lines, placeholders (items for which the user substitutes) are normally enclosed in angle brackets and appear in an italic monospace typeface (*<placeholder>*).
- Access keys (or hotkeys) that you use for choosing a menu item without using a mouse, appear in bold (for example, **F**ile menu).
- Filenames and filename extensions are uppercase. For example, FOXPRO.DBF and .DBF.
- An ellipsis (...) used within a sample program indicates that a portion of the program has been omitted.

- The revised icon for Visual FoxPro 3.0 represents a language element that has been enhanced for Visual FoxPro 3.0.
- This icon represents a new feature in Visual FoxPro 3.0.
- A keystroke combination, such as Ctrl+S, indicates that you should press and hold down the Ctrl key while pressing the letter key (in this example, S).

The syntax structure for the program code in this book is Backus-Naur format, or BNF, with some additions:

- Brackets, [ ], denote optional phrases (except where noted).
- A vertical bar, |, indicates *or.*
- Braces, { }, are used only for grouping.
- ::= means *is defined as.*
- The word *list* means that the preceding phrase may be repeated, with each repetition separated by a comma. Here's an example:

  <exp list> allows *<exp>* or *<exp>*, *<exp>*, *<exp>*

  {KEY *<key list>*} allows KEY *<key>*, KEY *<key>*
- *<element>* describes a language element defined elsewhere.
- Other characters, such as ? and !, are literal.

I

Overview and Concepts

1

Introduction to Visual FoxPro

Begin at the beginning...and go on till you come to the end: then stop.

—Lewis Carroll (1832–1898)
Alice's Adventures in Wonderland

This chapter introduces the Visual FoxPro 3.0 interface. You'll see how easy it is to build a simple FoxPro database management application.

Visual FoxPro is a database management system that creates and maintains a list of data items. This list is called a *table, DBF file,* or *database file.* In the past, these three terms were used interchangeably; I prefer the term database file so that dBASE users will feel comfortable with the book's terminology. However, Visual FoxPro introduces support for a data dictionary that has a file called a *database container file,* which is often referred to in Visual FoxPro documentation as a *database.* The database container file contains information about all tables and other things used in an application. As a result, the terms DBF file and table are used interchangeably in this book.

With FoxPro you can selectively retrieve data from the table, display it, report it, reorganize it, or create a new table.

Visual FoxPro uses English words for commands that perform all operations. One command creates a table; another command displays information; and other commands edit, delete, and add new information to a table. FoxPro uses hundreds of commands to perform a variety of powerful operations. You can combine these commands into a special text file, called a *program file,* and execute the program with a single command. The art of placing a proper set of commands in a program file in the appropriate order is called *programming.* You can write a program that displays and controls a form, manipulates data items, or prints reports.

You can create an application consisting of one or more programs, information, and everything else required to perform a specific task. Microsoft Word for Windows is an application that performs word processing. Visual FoxPro 3.0 is also an application. If you create a system of programs and data using the Visual FoxPro 3.0 language, that too is an application. You can create an application that operates on one or more tables. You can relate multiple tables on common data items.

You can program an application in Visual FoxPro line by line, or you can let a *wizard* write it for you. You don't need to be a programmer to create an application in Visual FoxPro. You can use the Visual FoxPro wizards to visually create relatively complex applications with ease and without writing a single line of code. All you need to do is provide information about your proposed application.

As you learn more about Visual FoxPro, you will likely create your own complex Visual FoxPro applications. However, you still do not need to write code line by line. This is because Visual FoxPro supports a powerful, object-oriented development environment. You will use the Visual FoxPro 3.0 rapid application development (RAD) tools to generate application components visually. Most of the code is created for you automatically. The RAD tools include a Project Manager and Query, Database, Table, Class, Form, Report, and Label Designers. The Project Manager visually organizes all the components of your application.

In this chapter, I'll give you a brief guided tour of the RAD tools so that you can acquire an elementary familiarity with the overall Visual FoxPro 3.0 system. But first, I'll introduce you to the fundamentals of the Visual FoxPro 3.0 user interface.

Exploring the Visual FoxPro 3.0 Interface

I make two assumptions in this chapter. First, I assume that you know how to use the Windows interface. If you don't, you should read the "Windows Fundamentals" section in your Microsoft Windows user's guide. Then you should practice with Windows until you are comfortable using the interface. Second, I assume that you've already installed Visual FoxPro 3.0 on your computer. If this isn't the case, install it according to the instructions in the FoxPro documentation. If you have already installed Visual FoxPro 3.0, you can execute it from the Windows desktop by double-clicking the FoxPro icon. When FoxPro executes, the Visual FoxPro main window appears. Figure 1.1 shows the Visual FoxPro 3.0 main window.

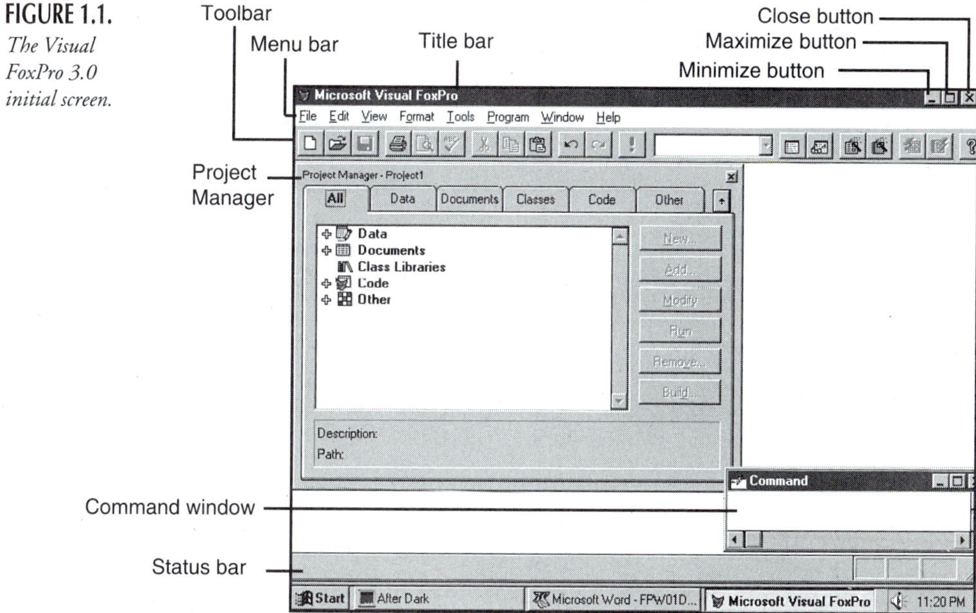

FIGURE 1.1.
The Visual FoxPro 3.0 initial screen.

When Visual FoxPro executes for the first time, the Visual FoxPro main window contains a new, empty Project Manager window and the Command window. The Project Manager organizes Visual FoxPro data and objects as a project. A *project* is a file that has a .PJX extension and contains a list of all of the files, tables, documents, classes, and programs used for a specific Visual FoxPro task as well as specific information about the files. In this chapter, you will be introduced to the Project Manager. You will be shown how to organize files with the Project Manager. If you select the Project Manager, the **P**roject menu is added to the menu bar. Chapter 22, "Project Management and Building Applications," describes the Project Manager in detail.

The Visual FoxPro 3.0 Application Window

At the top of the screen is the *title bar.* The title bar contains the application's name: Microsoft Visual FoxPro. You can point to any title bar, hold down the left mouse button, and drag the entire window to a new location.

To the left of the title bar is the *control menu box.* You can click it with the mouse or press the Alt+spacebar key combination to open it. In Windows 95, the control menu box is the traditional FoxPro Fox icon. The control menu contains options that control the window. These options enable you to restore the window to its initial size and position as well as move, size, minimize, maximize, and close the window. If you choose the **M**ove or **S**ize options, you can move or resize the window using the arrow keys. In addition, in Windows 3.1, you can choose the S**w**itch To option to execute another active Windows application.

Two controls appear to the right of the title bar. If you click the right control, called the *maximize button,* the FoxPro main window expands (maximizes) to fill the screen. If you click the maximize button when a window is maximized, the window is reduced to the size it was before you maximized it. The left control is called the *minimize* button. If you click the minimize button, the FoxPro main window reduces to an icon. You can double-click the title bar to perform the same operation as the maximize button. In Windows 95, there is a third button with an X in it. This is the *close button.* If you click on it, Visual FoxPro exits. The close button also appears on most system-type windows, and if you click on it, the window closes.

If you point the mouse to the border of a window, press and hold down the left mouse button, and drag the border to a new position, you can change the size of the window.

Below the title bar is the *menu bar,* which contains *menus.* If you click a menu, a menu with a list of options opens. You can also open a menu using the Alt key plus the underlined character in the menu. This is the *hotkey.* For example, press Alt+F to open the **F**ile menu. Figure 1.2 shows the opened **F**ile menu. Once a menu is opened, you can do the following to execute an option:

- Click an option
- Use the arrow keys to move the highlight to an option and press Enter
- Press the access key, or hotkey, which is the underlined character in the option label

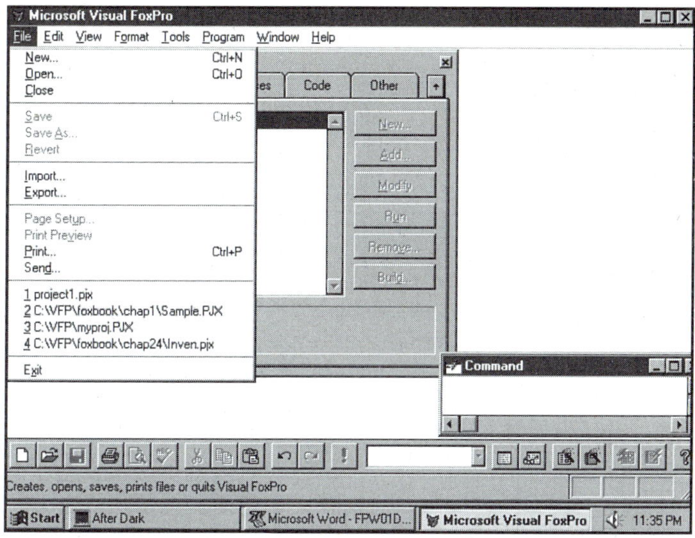

FIGURE 1.2.
The Visual FoxPro initial screen with the File menu open.

NOTE

When you first execute Visual FoxPro, the toolbar appears at the top of the Visual FoxPro window. You can click on the toolbar and drag it anywhere you want. In Figure 1.2, the toolbar has been moved to the bottom of the screen so that you can see both the toolbar and the **F**ile menu.

Occasionally, a control key label is specified to the right of a menu option, indicating a *shortcut* key for the specified option. For example, in Figure 1.2, Ctrl+S appears to the right of the **S**ave option. This is a faster way to execute the **S**ave option—by pressing Ctrl+S. Table 1.1 shows all the shortcut keys for the Visual FoxPro 3.0 menu options.

Table 1.1. Menu option shortcuts.

Option	*Shortcut Key*
File Menu	
New	Ctrl+N
Open	Ctrl+O
Save	Ctrl+S
Print	Ctrl+P

continues

Table 1.1. continued

Option		*Shortcut Key*
	Edit Menu	
Undo		Ctrl+Z
Redo		Ctrl+R
Cut		Ctrl+X
Copy		Ctrl+C
Paste		Ctrl+V
Select All		Ctrl+A
Find		Ctrl+F
Replace		Ctrl+L
	Record Menu	
Continue		Ctrl+K
	Program Menu	
Do		Ctrl+D
Resume		Ctrl+M
	Window Menu	
Cycle		Ctrl+F1
Command		Ctrl+F2
	Help Menu	
Contents		F1

You can't always choose a specific menu option because some options might not apply to the current context. For example, if the Clipboard is empty, the **E**dit menu **P**aste option is disabled. This type of menu system is a *context-sensitive* menu system. A disabled menu option displays in normal intensity and cannot be selected. Enabled menu objects display in bold intensity.

For some operations, a different set of menus appear on the menu bar. For example, the `BROWSE` command enables you to peruse data in tabular form. When it executes, a new T**a**ble menu appears on the menu bar, containing options that control the tabular display.

The Command Window

Near the bottom of Figure 1.1 is the Command window. Instead of choosing menu options, you can type Visual FoxPro commands in the Command window. Type in a command, make any required edits, press Enter, and the command executes.

You can use the up and down arrows to position the cursor on a command you have previously executed. Then press Enter and that command executes.

What Do the Menu Options Do?

Each menu option executes a different operation. The design of the Visual FoxPro menu bar layout differs from that of the FoxPro 2.*x* menu bar. The differences are due to the fact that earlier versions of FoxPro were DOS based and this version is Windows based. All Windows applications are organized in a similar manner, and Visual FoxPro 3.0 is no exception. In a standard Windows application, the first menu is **F**ile, the second menu is normally **E**dit, and the last menu is almost always **H**elp. These similarities are important because users who are familiar with one Windows application can easily learn another Windows application.

This section briefly describes each menu option. At this point in the book, you might not have the slightest idea why you would want to use some of these options. However, after reading this chapter you will, if nothing else, be aware of the existence of the options. Later, as you learn more about Visual FoxPro 3.0, you might want to refer back to this chapter.

The File Menu

The **F**ile menu provides options to create, open, save, close, and print different types of files. It also contains an option to exit FoxPro and return to Windows. Table 1.2 describes each option in the **F**ile menu.

Table 1.2. File menu options.

	Option	*Description*
	New...	Creates a table (DBF file), program, database container (DBC) file, text file, menu, index, report, label, form, menu, query, visual class library, and project file.
	Open...	Opens an existing table (DBF file), program, database container (DBC) file, text file, menu, index, report, label form, menu, query, visual class library, and project file.
	Close	Closes the active window.
	Save	Saves a file with the current name. However, if its name is Untitled, the Save As dialog box appears. You then select a directory and enter a filename, and the named file is saved.
	Save **A**s	Displays the Save As dialog box. (See Figure 1.3.) You select a directory and type a filename. The file is saved.

continues

Table 1.2. continued

Option	Description
Revert	Exits from an editing session and discards all changes.
Import	Imports data to a Visual FoxPro table from tabular information in another application such as a text file, a spreadsheet, or a table from another database management system. You can select the Import Wizard to simplify the import operation. The available formats are discussed in Chapter 12, "Data Set Operations."
Export	Exports data from a Visual FoxPro table to a format recognized by other applications. A variety of formats are available, such as a text file, an Excel or a Lotus 1-2-3 spreadsheet, and a Paradox table. The available formats are discussed in Chapter 12.
Page Set**u**p	Displays the Page Setup dialog box. You can adjust column width and page layout for reports or labels. Settings are dependent on the type of installed printer. This option is enabled when you have a report or label open.
Print Pre**v**iew	Displays the Preview window, which shows a report or labels as they would appear on a printed page. This option is enabled when you have a report or label design open.
Print...	Displays the Print dialog box. You can print the contents of an open window, a program file, a text file, or the Clipboard. From the Print dialog box, you can open the Print Setup dialog box. You can select printer options, page size, and page orientation. You can also select the Print Options dialog box, which lets you specify which table records to print.
Sen**d**	Sends e-mail through Microsoft Mail. If you are running Visual FoxPro under Windows 95 or Windows NT and have Microsoft Mail installed, this option is available.
E**x**it	Exits from FoxPro and returns to Windows.
1,2,3,4	Lists the four most recently opened project files. You can choose the project file to open.

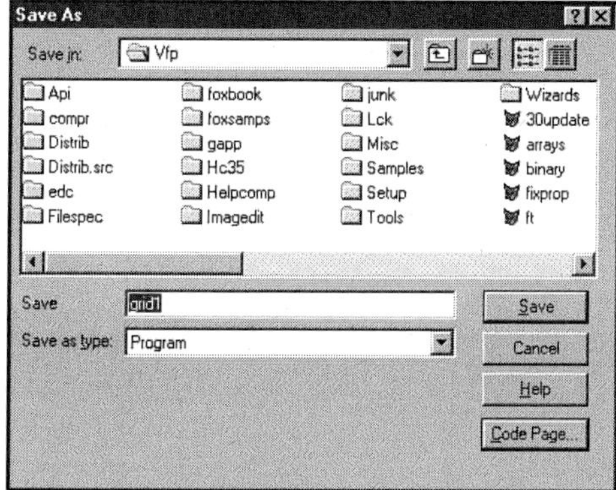

FIGURE 1.3.
The Save As dialog box.

The Edit Menu

The **E**dit menu provides options to use when you are editing text. Many of these options have shortcut keys, as shown in Table 1.3. Although it's quicker and easier to use the shortcut keys, this menu is provided to help users who haven't yet learned the shortcut keys to perform editing operations easily. Table 1.3 describes each option in the **E**dit menu. Figure 1.4 shows the **E**dit menu.

Table 1.3. Edit menu options.

	Option	*Description*
	Undo	Cancels the most recent edit operation in a text editing window or field.
	Redo	Restores an edit operation that was previously undone.
	Cu**t**	Removes selected text from a field or text editing window and places it in the Windows Clipboard.
	Copy	Copies selected text from a field or text editing window and places it in the Windows Clipboard.
	Paste	Inserts the current contents of the Clipboard into the text of the field or text editing window at the cursor position.
	Paste **S**pecial...	If a General field window is open, this option is enabled. Choose this option, and the Paste Special dialog box appears. This dialog box contains types of available OLE

continues

Table 1.3. continued

Option	Description
	objects you can either link or embed in the General field. Examples of OLE objects are sound, picture, and bitmap objects. You choose the object type and specify whether you want to link or embed the object. Then the Windows application that creates the object (for example, Microsoft Paintbrush) executes and you can create or load the object. When you exit from the application, the OLE object is either linked or embedded in the General field.
Clear	Deletes text without placing it in the Clipboard.
Select All	Selects all of the text in the active window, a field in a browse window, or all the controls on a report or form window.
Find...	Searches a text file or a memo field for the first occurrence of a search string, after first prompting you to enter the search string.
Replace	Replaces the current occurrence of a search string with a replacement string and finds the next occurrence of the search string.
Go To Line	Moves the cursor to a specified line in a text file, memo field, program file, or Command window. This command is disabled if Word Wrap mode is in effect.
Insert Object...	If a General field window is active, this option is enabled. It opens an Insert Object dialog box so that you can insert a new or existing OLE object into a General data type table field.
Object...	If a General field window is active or a bound OLE control is selected, this option is enabled. The option caption changes to reflect the type of OLE object selected. It displays a drop-down list showing the actions supported by the current object.
Link	Displays the Edit Link dialog box so that you can change or break an OLE object link.

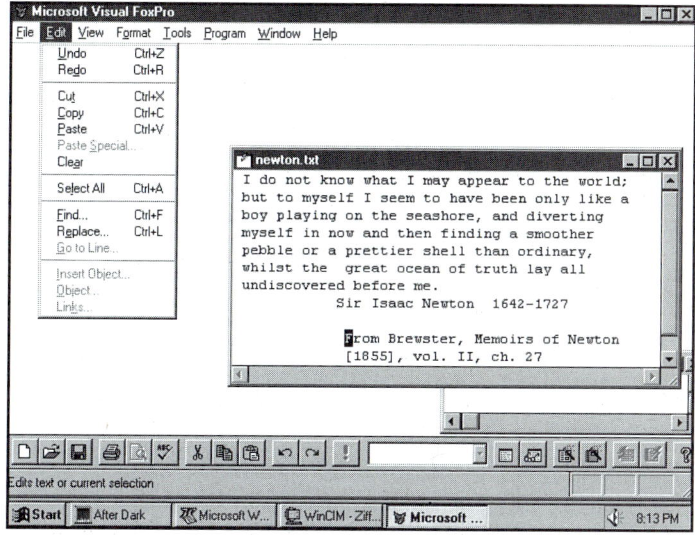

FIGURE 1.4.
The Edit menu.

The View Menu and Toolbars

The **View** menu is the most context sensitive menu in Visual FoxPro. When you first execute Visual FoxPro, it contains only the **Toolbars...** option, which displays the Toolbars dialog box, as shown in Figure 1.5. The Toolbars dialog box contains a list of all of the toolbars available in Visual FoxPro. You can select the check box next to the toolbar name in the list to force a toolbar to display. You can customize the standard toolbar by adding your own favorite controls. In Figure 1.5, all of the toolbars are open to show you how many there are. Table 1.4 describes the purpose of each toolbar. In addition, you can specify that large buttons are used in the toolbar.

You normally do not have any toolbars open, except the standard toolbar, unless you need to use them. Initially, the Visual FoxPro standard toolbar is active. When you open Visual FoxPro designers, certain toolbars are automatically opened and then hidden when the designer exits.

Table 1.4. Visual FoxPro toolbars.

Toolbar	*Description*
Color Palette	You use this toolbar to specify foreground and background colors for a control. This toolbar is available when you open the Label, Report, Form, or Class Designer.
Database Designer	You use this toolbar to execute various Database Designer actions such as adding and removing tables and views. It is available when the Database Designer is open.

continues

Table 1.4. continued

Toolbar	*Description*
Form Controls	This toolbar contains buttons that represent controls you place on forms in the Form or Class Designer. It is available only when the Form or Class Designer is active.
Form Designer	You use this toolbar to execute various Form Designer actions. This toolbar displays when you execute the Form or Class Designer.
Layout	You use this toolbar to align and size one or more selected controls in the Label, Report, Form, or Class Designer. This toolbar is active only when these designers are executing.
Print Preview	This toolbar displays when you execute the Print Preview system. You use it to move between the display pages and for zooming operations.
Query Designer	This toolbar displays when you execute the Query Designer. You use it to execute common Query Designer actions.
Report Controls	This toolbar contains buttons that represent controls you place on report forms in the Label or Report Designer. This toolbar displays when you execute the Report Designer.
Report Designer	Displays when the Report Designer executes. This toolbar contains buttons that execute frequently used operations.
Standard toolbar	This toolbar displays by default. It contains common Visual FoxPro functions.
View Designer	This toolbar displays when you execute the View Designer. You use it to execute frequently used View Designer actions.

The number of options displayed in the **V**iew menu vary depending on which operation you perform in Visual FoxPro. These options are described in Table 1.5. Some menu options are called *context sensitive*: The options are sensitive to which application is running and appear on the menu only if a certain application is running.

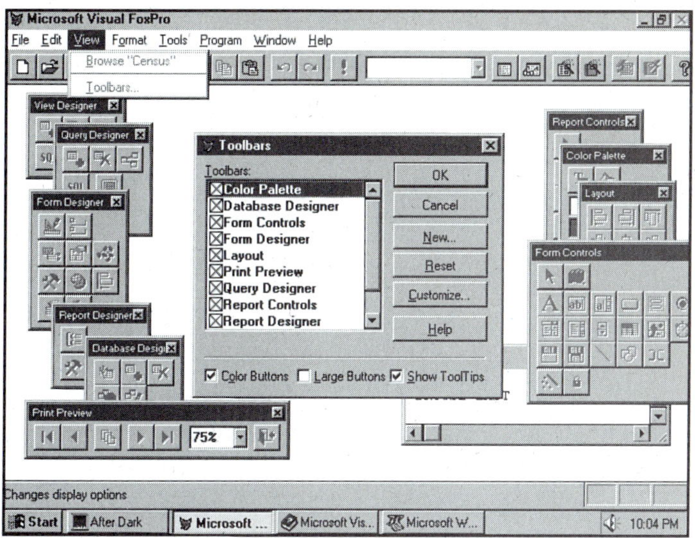

FIGURE 1.5.
The Toolbars dialog box with all toolbars open.

Table 1.5. The View menu with context-sensitive menu options.

Option	*Description*
Toolbars	You use this option to create, edit, hide, and customize toolbars. This option is always available.
Properties	This option displays the Properties window so that you can set or change the properties of forms and controls. It is available only when you open the Form or Class Designer.
Browse <*table*>	This option displays the contents of the current table horizontally in a Browse window. It is available only when a table is in use in the current work area.
Edit	The Edit option displays the contents of the selected table vertically. It is available only when a table is in use in the current work area and a Browse or Edit window is active.
Append Mode	This option automatically adds a new record to the end of the current table. It is available only when a table is in use in the current work area and a Browse or Edit window is active.
Database Designer	This option displays the Database Designer. It is available only when you use a table associated with a database container file and a Browse or Edit window is active.

continues

Table 1.5. continued

Option	*Description*
Table Desi**g**ner	This option displays the Table Designer so that you can modify the structure of a table. It is available only when you browse a table.
Grid Lines	This option removes or adds lines in various windows. It is available when you browse a table, or open the Label, Report, Form, or Class Designer.
Design	This option places a new or existing label, report, or form in Design mode. It is available only when you open the Label, Report, Form, or Class Designer.
Tab **O**rder	This option establishes the tab order for objects on a form. It is available only when you run the Form or Class Designer.
Code	This option displays the Code window so that you can write, display, and edit event code. It is available only when you open the Form or Class Designer.
Form Contro**l**s Toolbar	This option displays the Form Controls toolbar, which you use to create controls on a form. It is available only when the Form or Class Designer is open.
La**y**out Toolbar	This option displays the Layout toolbar, which you use to align, size, and position controls. It is available when the Label, Report, Form, or Class Designer is open.
Colo**r** Palette Toolbar	This option displays the Color Palette toolbar, which you use to specify foreground and background colors for a control. It is available only when the Form or Class Designer is open.
Sho**w** Position	This option toggles on and off the position display mode. When the mode is turned on, the position, height, and width of the selected object in a form, report, or label display on the status bar at the bottom of the Visual FoxPro window. It is available only when the Label, Report, Form, or Class Designer is open.
Pre**v**iew	This option displays a report or label in the Print Preview window. It is available only when you open the Label or Report Designer.

Option	*Description*
Report Controls Toolbar	This option displays the Report Controls toolbar, which you use to create controls on a report. It is available only when you open the Label or Report Designer.
General Options	This option lets you specify code for an entire menu system. It is available only when the Menu Designer is open.
Menu Options	This option lets you specify code for a specific user-defined menu. It is available only when the Menu Designer is open.
Maximize Top Pane	This option enlarges the top pane of the Query and View Designers. It is available only when you open the Query Designer or View Designer.
Minimize Top Pane	This option reduces the top pane of the Query and View Designers. It is available when you open the Query Designer or View Designer.
Data Environment	This option opens the Data Environment Designer. It is available only when you open the Form or Class Designer, Report Designer, or Label Designer.

What Is a Toolbar?

A toolbar is very useful device. It contains buttons you can click on to perform some action or activate some feature of a tool. It provides you with quick access to a tool's most frequently used features or actions.

What Is a Tooltip?

If you rest the mouse pointer on a toolbar button for one or two seconds, a little message describing its function appears. This message is called a *tooltip*. This is especially useful since the picture on the toolbar button sometimes does not reveal any clues about the operation it performs. Each Visual FoxPro designer has one or more toolbars to make the designer easier to use.

Changing the Shape of a Toolbar

You can point the mouse pointer to the border of a toolbar, and the shape of the mouse pointer changes to a double arrow. Then you can drag the border to change the shape of the toolbar. Try it.

Moving a Toolbar

You can position the mouse pointer over the gray area that surrounds the toolbar buttons, and drag the toolbar around the screen.

Docking a Toolbar

A toolbar is *docked* if it is fixed to the edge of the Visual FoxPro window. When it is docked, it has no title bar. You can double-click on the title bar or gray area of a floating toolbar to dock it. Also, you can drag a toolbar to the top, bottom, or either side of the Visual FoxPro window, and the toolbar will become docked. Try it.

Floating a Docked Toolbar

You can either double-click on the gray area of a docked toolbar or drag the toolbar away from the edge of the Visual FoxPro window to float a toolbar. A floating toolbar looks like a system window filled with buttons. It has its own title bar and close box.

The Format Menu

The F**o**rmat menu appears on the menu bar only when an editing window or the Command window is active. Use the F**o**rmat menu options to select text-formatting attributes such as font type, style, size, and line spacing. Many of the Visual FoxPro designers add additional options to the F**o**rmat menu. Table 1.6 lists the normal F**o**rmat menu options. The options added to the F**o**rmat menu by the designers are discussed in the chapters that describe the designers.

Table 1.6. Format menu options.

Option	*Description*
Font	Displays the Font dialog box. You can change the font type, size, and style for the active window.
Enlarge Font	Enlarges the font size in the active window to the next larger available font size.
Reduce Font	Reduces the font size in the active window to the next smaller available font size.
✓Single Space 1 1/2 Space Double Space	These three options designate line spacing for the active window. A check mark appears to the left of the currently selected line spacing option.
Indent	Indents selected lines of text. The lines move one tab stop to the right.
Re**m**ove Indent	Removes indentation from selected lines of text. The selected lines move one tab stop to the left.

You can change font attributes for the Visual FoxPro main window by pressing the Shift key when you choose the F**o**rmat menu. The first menu option becomes **S**creen Font… instead of **F**ont and enables you to change the font type, size, and style for the FoxPro main window. Figure 1.6 is an open Font dialog box from this menu.

FIGURE 1.6.
The Font dialog box.

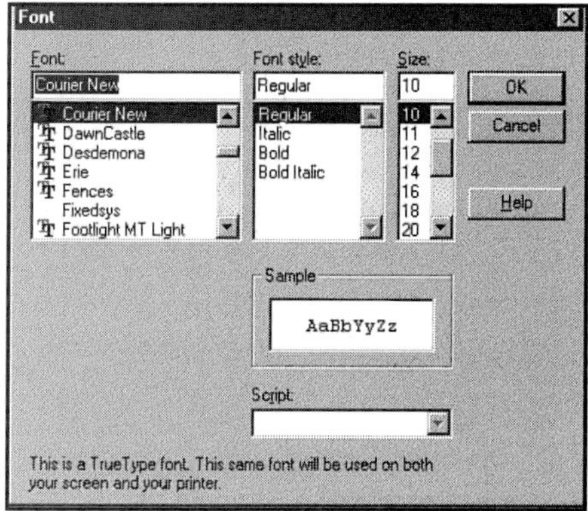

The Tools Menu

Table 1.7 lists the Tools menu options. The **T**ools menu contains options to execute Visual FoxPro tools such as the spelling checker and wizards. Visual FoxPro wizards let you visually create relatively complex applications with ease and without writing a single line of code. The **T**ools menu also has options that help you debug your program. You'll learn how to use the debugging tools in Chapter 23, "Building Visual FoxPro Applications."

Table 1.7. Tools menu options.

	Option	*Description*
	Wizards	Displays a submenu of all of the Visual FoxPro wizards, as shown in Figure 1.7. A wizard is an interactive program that helps you quickly accomplish common tasks. Wizards are discussed in Chapter 24, "Wizards."
	Spelling…	Executes the Microsoft shared spelling checker when a file or memo field window is active. You can also execute the spelling checker by executing `DO (_spellchk)` from the Command window or from a program. This option executes the FoxPro SPELLCHK.APP application.
	M**a**cros	Displays the Keyboard Macros dialog box, from which you can create and edit keyboard macros. You can also load and save a set of keyboard macros.

continues

Table 1.7. continued

Option	*Description*
Class Browser	Executes the Visual FoxPro Class Browser, which displays the relationships between classes in a visual class library (VCX). A class browser tool, named BROWSER.APP, is provided with the Professional Edition of Visual FoxPro. When you first execute it, the **C**lass Browser option is added to the **T**ools menu. The Class Browser is discussed in Chapter 15, "The Visual Class Library, the Class Designer, and the Class Browser."
Trace Window	Displays the Visual FoxPro Trace window. You can execute a program, and its source displays in the Trace window. You can execute a program a line at a time, and the line that executes is highlighted.
De**b**ug Window	Displays the Visual FoxPro debugging window. You can enter program variables or expressions in the Debug window and their corresponding values display as the program executes.
Options...	This option opens the Options dialog box so that you can establish settings for system options. The Options dialog box is shown in Figure 1.8.

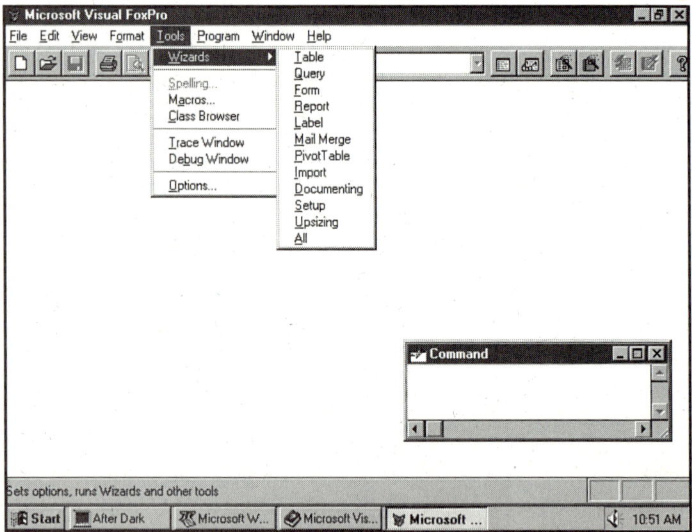

FIGURE 1.7.
The Tools menu and the Wizards submenu.

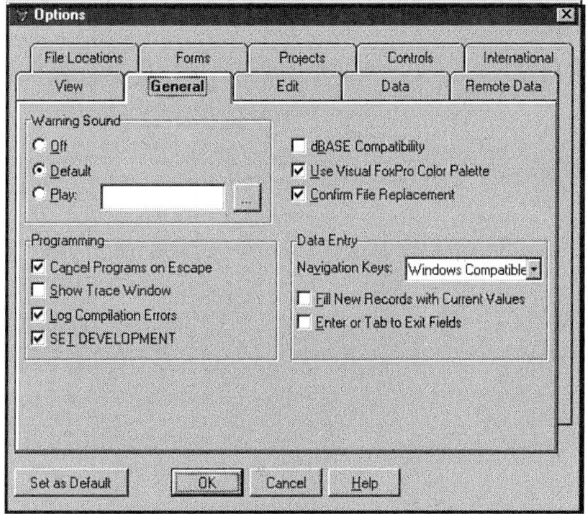

FIGURE 1.8.
The Options dialog box.

The Program Menu

Table 1.8 lists the **P**rogram menu options. With these options you can compile and run Visual FoxPro programs. You can also cancel or suspend a running program or form. Then you can debug the program using the **T**ools menu Trace and Debug options. You can also resume the execution of a suspended program. Debugging is described in Chapter 23.

Table 1.8. Program menu options.

Option	*Description*
Do	Executes a FoxPro program.
Cancel	Cancels program execution that was paused using the SUSPEND command. This option is only enabled when a program is suspended.
Resume	Resumes program execution that was paused using the SUSPEND command. This option is enabled only when a program is suspended.
Suspend	Stops the execution of a program but keeps its execution environment open at the point the program is suspended so that you can examine program parameters. To start the program again, you can either choose the **R**esume option (or RESUME command) or use the Trace window to control execution. This option is enabled only when a program is running.
Co**m**pile...	Creates an executable version of a program. Actually, if you choose the **D**o option, it compiles a program (if required) before it executes. However, with this menu option you may compile the program without executing it.

The Window Menu

The **W**indow menu provides options that control windows. You can hide a window, clear a window, and move between windows. You also can select either the View or the Command window. Table 1.9 describes each option in the **W**indow menu.

Table 1.9. Window menu options.

Option	*Description*
Arrange All	Displays all open windows so that they do not overlap.
Hide	Removes the active window from the screen.
Hide All	Removes all of the windows from view. However, the windows are still open and their names appear at the bottom of the **W**indow menu. This command only appears if you press the Shift key while choosing the **W**indow menu. It replaces the **H**ide option.
Sh**o**w All	Displays all open windows. This command appears on the **W**indow menu if you press the Shift key while choosing the **W**indow menu.
Clea**r**	Removes all displayed text in the active window. This option is equivalent to the FoxPro CLEAR command.
C**y**cle	Activates the next window in the list of open windows.
Command	Activates the Command window.
View	Activates the View dialog box, which is described in Chapter 10, "Environment." You can use the View dialog box to open files, establish relationships, and set work area properties.
1,**2**,**3**,...**9**	Displays the names of all of the open windows. When you choose one, it becomes the active window.
More Windows	Displays the Windows dialog box so that you can choose one of the open windows. When you choose one, it becomes the active window. This option appears if you have more than nine windows open.

The Help Menu

The **H**elp menu contains options for getting help. These options are described in Table 1.10.

Table 1.10. Help menu options.

Option	*Description*
Contents	Displays the FoxPro help facility.
Search for Help On...	Displays the Windows-style Search dialog box. This option is disabled unless the Windows-style help system is active.
Technical Support	Displays information about the Microsoft product support services and answers frequently asked Visual FoxPro questions.
About FoxPro...	Displays a series of windows with information about Visual FoxPro 3.0 configuration, available memory, disk space, and so on.

Visual FoxPro 3.0 offers two Help systems. If you've used FoxPro before and you're accustomed to the FoxPro 2.0-style Help system, which uses a table (FOXHELP.DBF and FOXHELP.FPT), you can still use that system. If you are accustomed to the Windows-style Help system, you can use the second available Help system, which is the default. Both systems provide speedy and context-sensitive access to Help information. Both systems furnish help relating to the current menu option, dialog box, or window when you press the F1 key. If no help topic is available for the current object, each system displays an index.

The Windows-style help system has some definite advantages, including a keyword topic search, annotated topics, and a bookmark feature. The FoxPro 2.0-style help system is useful for FoxPro 2.0 applications that use a custom FOXHELP.DBF file to support custom help.

When you install Visual FoxPro 3.0, you have the option of installing one or both of the Help systems. If you install both, you can switch back and forth between them using the `SET HELP TO` command described in Chapter 10. You can also use the Tools menu Options dialog box File Locations tab to specify which style of help system to use.

Building an Application: A Quick Tour

In this section, you'll learn how to use Visual FoxPro to create a simple application that maintains a table (DBF file). During this process, I will introduce you to the Project Manager, the Database Designer, and the Visual FoxPro Table, Form, and Report Wizards.

The Project Manager maintains all of the components of a Visual FoxPro application. It helps you keep your work organized. The Table Wizard helps you visually create a container for your data, called a table. The Form Wizard leads you through the process of creating a data entry form from which you add new data to a table or modify existing data. Throughout this process, you don't need to write a single line of FoxPro code. You shouldn't assume from the last statement, however, that writing FoxPro code is difficult, because it isn't; it's really fairly easy (as you'll learn in Part II, "The Visual FoxPro Language").

To demonstrate the procedure for building an application visually, I will show you how to create a simple application that maintains a table that contains information about your acquaintances. This guided tour will consist of the following steps:

1. Create a project file to organize your application.
2. Create a database container file so that you can use extended table properties in your form.
3. Create a data table.
4. Create a data entry form.
5. Execute your new form.
6. Create a report for your form.

Step 1: Create a Project File

When you sign onto Visual FoxPro for the first time, a new, empty Project Manager window is on the screen. You can use this project for your tour, or you can create a new project.

To begin, you will create a new project that will help you organize the components of your application. Choose the **F**ile menu **N**ew option, and the New File dialog box appears, as shown in Figure 1.9. Select the **P**roject File Type option, click on the big **N**ew File button, and the Create File dialog box appears, as shown in Figure 1.10.

Type in the name of your new project file (`Sample`), click on the Save button, and your Project Manager window appears, as shown in Figure 1.11. Notice that it contains six tabs. Each tab contains different types of files to help you organize your different types of files. The All tab contains all types of files. The example developed in this guided tour is simple enough that you can use the All tab to show all of the files with which you will be working.

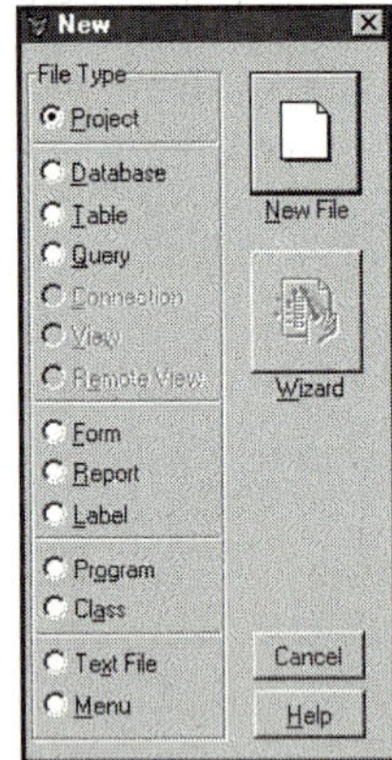

FIGURE 1.9.
The New dialog box, which you use to create a new project file.

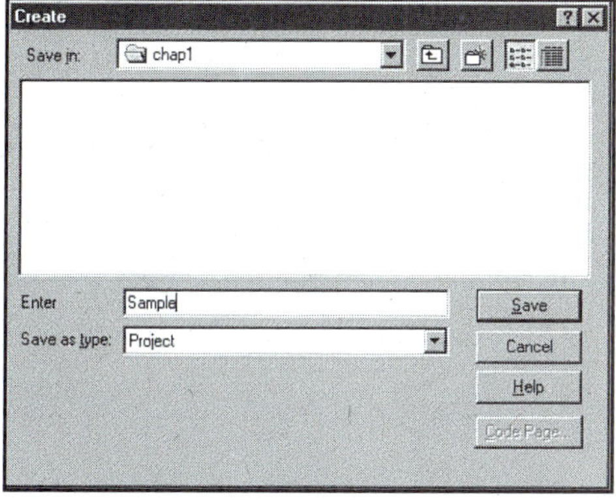

FIGURE 1.10.
The Create dialog box, which you use to give the project file a name.

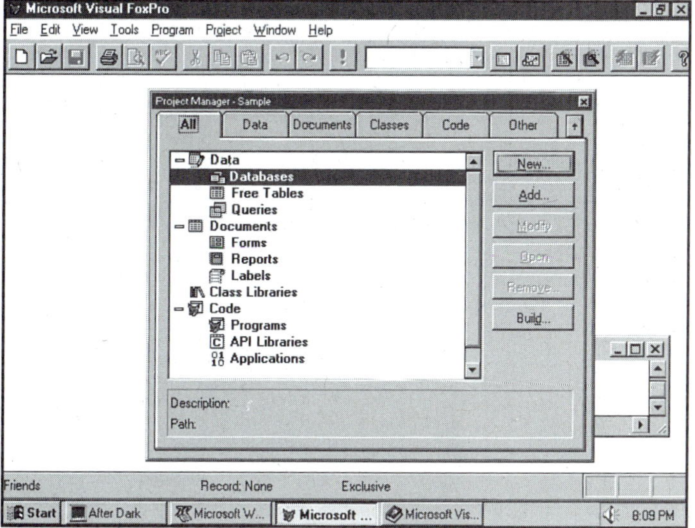

FIGURE 1.11.
The Project Manager window with the All tab open.

Step 2: Create a Database Container File

A database container is a file that has a .DBC extension and is associated with one or more tables. It contains extra table properties that were not supported by traditional FoxPro and dBASE tables (DBF files), such as validation rules, default values, and long field names. This guided tour uses the long field names, called *field caption properties*, as captions for fields in forms and report headings.

To create a database, select the Databases icon in the Project Manager, as shown in Figure 1.11, and click on the **N**ew... button. The Create dialog box appears, as shown in Figure 1.12.

Type `Sample` as the name of the database container file, as shown in Figure 1.12, and click the **S**ave button. The Visual FoxPro Database Designer window appears, as shown in Figure 1.13.

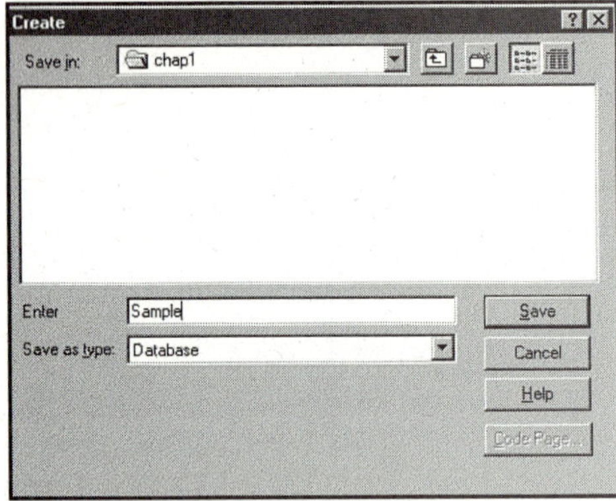

FIGURE 1.12.
The Create dialog box, in which you name your database container.

In addition to the empty Database Designer window, the **D**atabase menu is added to the menu bar, as shown in Figure 1.13.

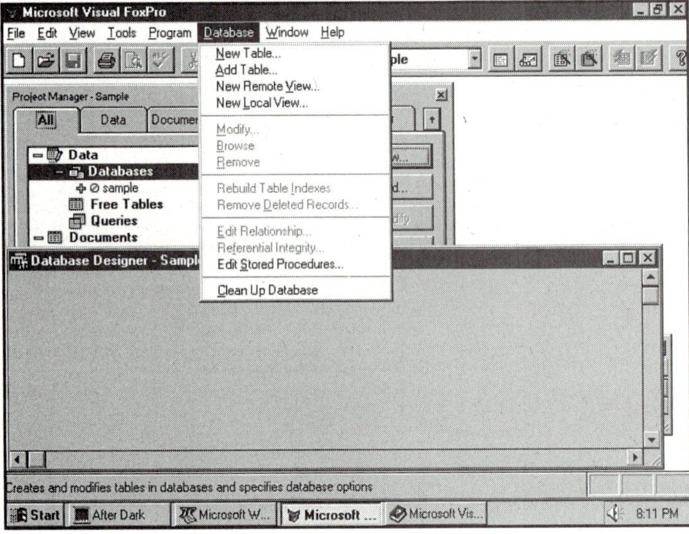

FIGURE 1.13.
The Database Designer dialog box with the Database menu open.

NOTE

The database container file is an important new feature of Visual FoxPro. It is a repository for storing information about application tables, such as record- and table-level validation rules, default values, captions, primary and candidate keys, relationships between tables, integrity rules, and stored procedures. You can also store triggers that execute when an append, a delete, or an update occurs. You can also store local and remote views. Stored procedures are programs that can be accessed by rules, index expressions, and triggers. The database container file provides the support for the seamless connectivity with remote servers.

Step 3: Create a Table with the Table Wizard

The next task is to create a table. To do this, choose the **D**atabase menu **N**ew Table option, and the New Table dialog box appears, as shown in Figure 1.14. Click on the Table Wizard button, and the Table Wizard Step 1 dialog box appears, as shown in Figure 1.15.

FIGURE 1.14.
The New Table dialog box, which you use to select the Table Wizard to create a table.

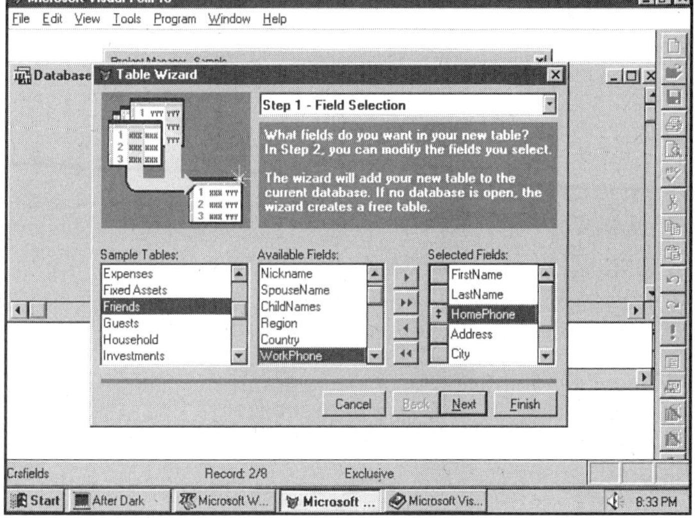

FIGURE 1.15.
The Table Wizard Step 1 dialog box, in which you select fields for your new table.

The Table Wizard performs like any other Visual FoxPro wizard. A Visual FoxPro wizard leads you through a sequence of dialog boxes that contain specific questions about the object you want to create. When the wizard obtains all the information it needs, it automatically creates that object. Wizards are described in detail in Chapter 24.

The Table Wizard Step 1 dialog box, shown in Figure 1.15, contains a list of various sample tables you can use as a model to create your own table. Choose the Friends sample table, and a list of typical fields one might use in a list of information about one's friends appears in the Available Fields list box.

Choose any fields you want to include in a table with information about your friends. You choose fields by selecting (clicking on) a field and then clicking on the button with a single, right-pointing triangle on it. The field is moved to the Selected Fields list box. When you are finished selecting fields, click on the **F**inish button and proceed to the last step, Step 4, as shown in Figure 1.16.

Note that we are skipping two steps because they are not relevant to this example.

NOTE

If you were to look at Step 2, you would see that there is information about the selected field in the table called *data field attributes*. The field attributes (Name, Caption, Type, Width, and Dec) define the contents of a data field. *Name* is used to reference the field from anywhere in FoxPro. *Caption* is used as field titles for forms, reports, and Browse tables. It can contain up to 128 characters, including blanks, to define a field. *Type* defines the type of data in a field. All of the fields shown in this example are of the Character data type. Character fields contain information consisting of any type of character (letters, numbers, and symbols). There are other types of data fields, such as Currency, Date, DateTime, Numeric, Integer, Logical, Memo, and General. For example, Numeric field values are used in numeric computations. Chapter 4, "Variables," describes the data types. *Width* specifies the width of a data field. *Dec* is the number of decimal places for a Numeric data type field. You can modify any of these field attributes in Step 2 of the Form Wizard. You can add definitions for new fields to the table structure or delete existing fields from the structure.

The Table Wizard Step 4 dialog box, shown in Figure 1.16, is the final step. Click on the **F**inish Button and the Create File dialog box appears. It is similar to the dialog box shown in Figure 1.12 except that it asks you to type the name of a table (DBF file). Type the name `Friends` and press the **S**ave button. The Table Wizard creates your table, named FRIENDS.DBF, and exits.

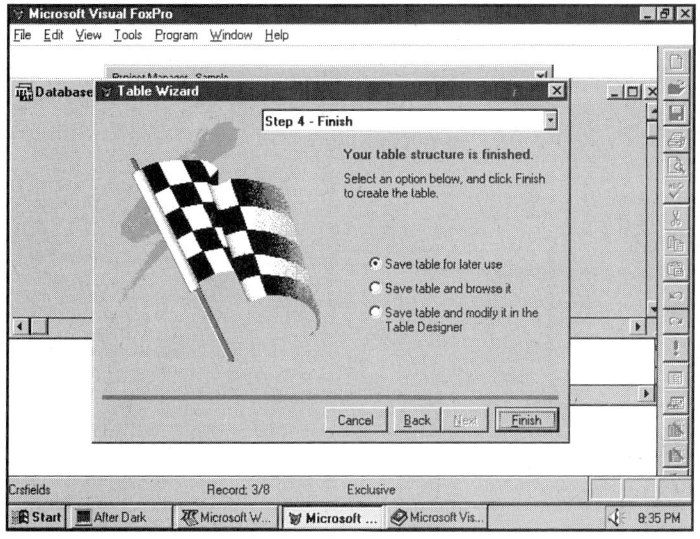

FIGURE 1.16.
The Table Wizard Step 4 dialog box, which you use to finish creating your table.

When the Table Wizard exits, a representation of your new table appears in the Database Designer window as shown in Figure 1.17. Notice that your new table, Friends, is also added to the Program Manager list under Tables.

Now, exit from the Database Designer by pressing the Esc key. If you are using Windows 95, you can click on the Close button to exit.

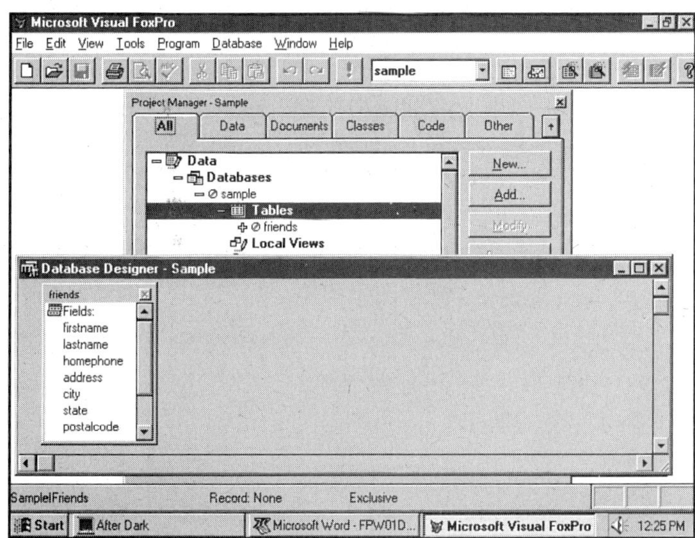

FIGURE 1.17.
The Database Designer window, which you use to look at your new table.

Step 4: Create the Data Entry Form for the Application

Now that you have created the empty FRIENDS.DBF table, you can create a data entry form that will be the foundation of the application. To create a form, select the Forms icon (click on it) and press the **N**ew button, and the New Form dialog box appears, as shown in Figure 1.18. Notice that the Forms icon in the list is highlighted. Now, click on the Form Wizard button.

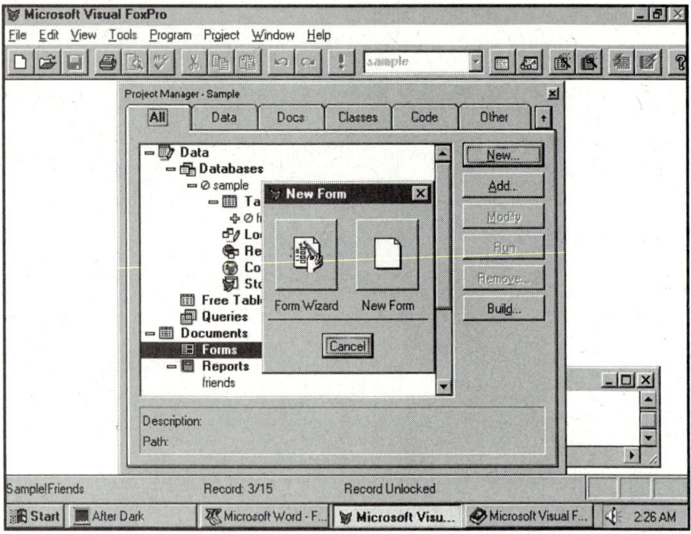

FIGURE 1.18.
The New Form dialog box, which you use to create a data entry application for your application.

When you click on the New Form Wizard button, the Wizard Selection dialog box appears, as shown in Figure 1.19. Choose the Form Wizard from the list, and the Form Wizard Step 1 dialog box appears, as shown in Figure 1.20.

Choose all of the fields in the Available Fields list box by pressing the button with two right-pointing triangles on it. All of the fields will move to the Selected Fields list box. Now, press the **N**ext button, and the Form Wizard Step 2 dialog box appears, as shown in Figure 1.21.

In this dialog box, you choose a style for your form. A graphic representation of a form in the selected style appears in the upper-left panel of the dialog box. Next, choose the Picture Buttons option from the Button Type option group. You have specified the style of your form.

Now click on the **N**ext button, and the Form Wizard Step 3 dialog box appears, as shown in Figure 1.22.

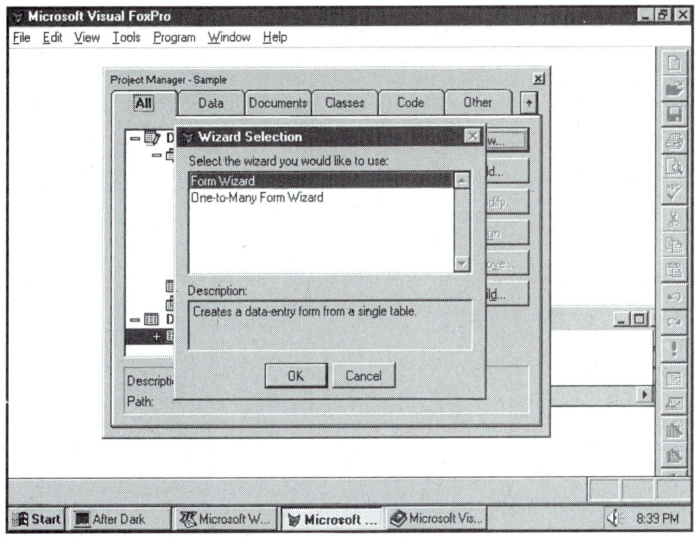

FIGURE 1.19.
The Wizard Selection dialog box, which you use to choose the Form Wizard.

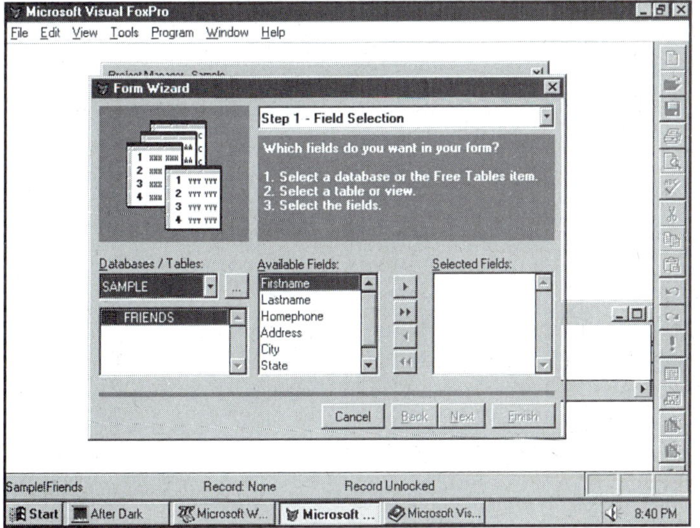

FIGURE 1.20.
The Form Wizard Step 1 dialog box, which you use to select fields for your form.

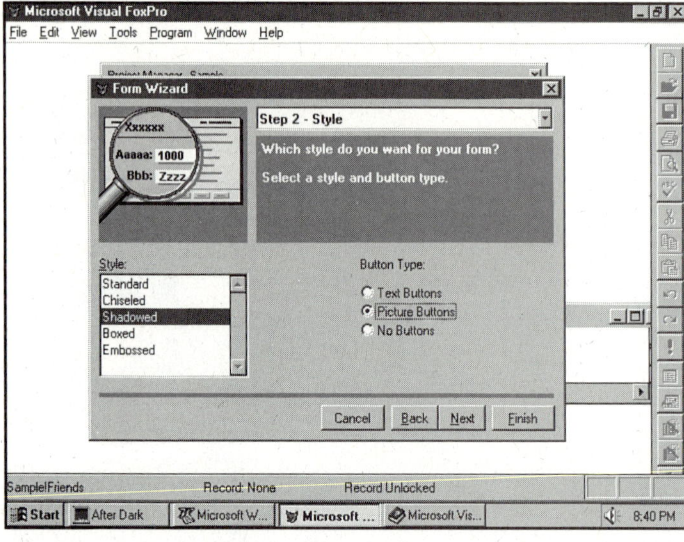

FIGURE 1.21.
The Form Wizard Step 2 dialog box, which you use to specify a style for your form.

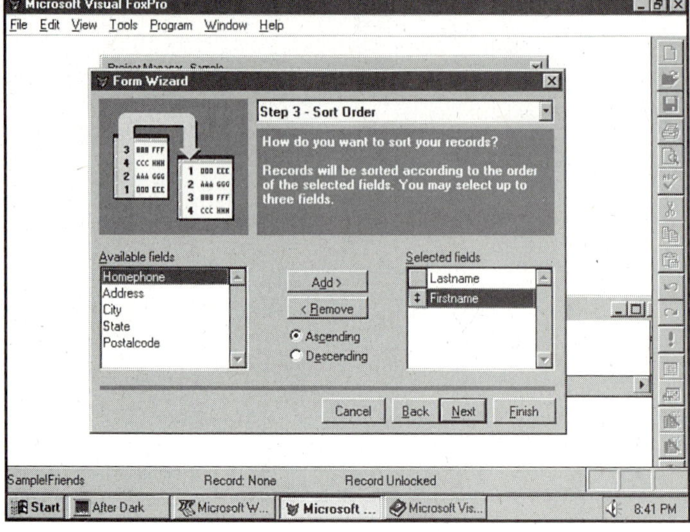

FIGURE 1.22.
The Form Wizard Step 3 dialog box, which you use to specify a sort order for your form.

You can specify the order in which records are maintained when the form is active. To designate that the records will be ordered by name, select the `Lastname` field and then press the A**d**d> button. The `Lastname` field moves to the Selected Fields list box. Repeat the process for the `Firstname` field. You add the `Firstname` field to the sort key so that the name Albert Einstein is sorted before Joe Einstein. You can also specify whether the records in the table are sorted in ascending or descending order.

When you are finished choosing the order of the records, click on the **N**ext button, and the Form Wizard Step 4 dialog box appears, as shown in Figure 1.23.

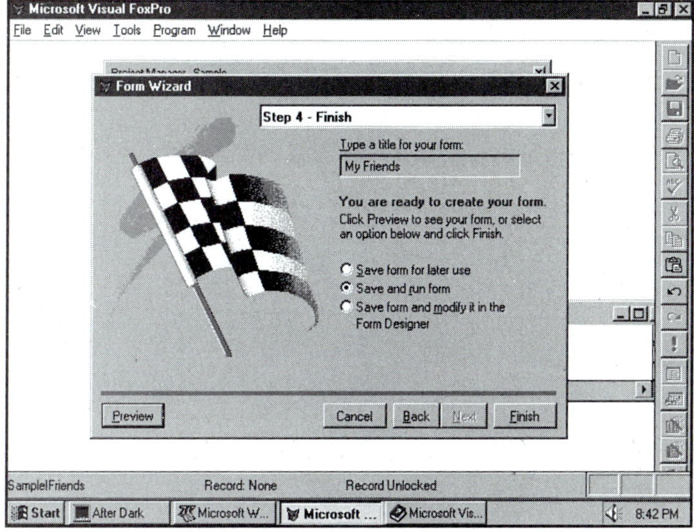

FIGURE 1.23.
The Form Wizard Step 4 dialog box, which you use to finish your form.

In the dialog box shown in Figure 1.23, you can specify a title for your form. Type the title `My Friends` in the title text box. Next, choose the option Save and **r**un form and press the **F**inish button.

Step 5: Run Your New Data Entry Form

The Form Wizard displays the Create File menu, which is similar to the one shown in Figure 1.12. You type the name of the form file, `Friends`, and the Form Wizard creates your form and runs it. Your new form displays, as shown in Figure 1.24.

Notice that all of your fields in Figure 1.24 are blank since you have not yet added any data to the fields.

At the bottom of the form is a row of buttons. The first four buttons are used to navigate through the table. You use the button on the far right to exit from the form.

Now it is time to add data. Press the button with a picture of a blank page on it. This places the form in *add new record* mode, as shown in Figure 1.25.

Notice that the picture on the Add New Record button changes to a picture of a floppy disk. The button is now used to save your changes. When you finish typing information about one of your friends, click on the floppy disk button to save your changes. Now add more records to your form so that you can play with the navigation buttons.

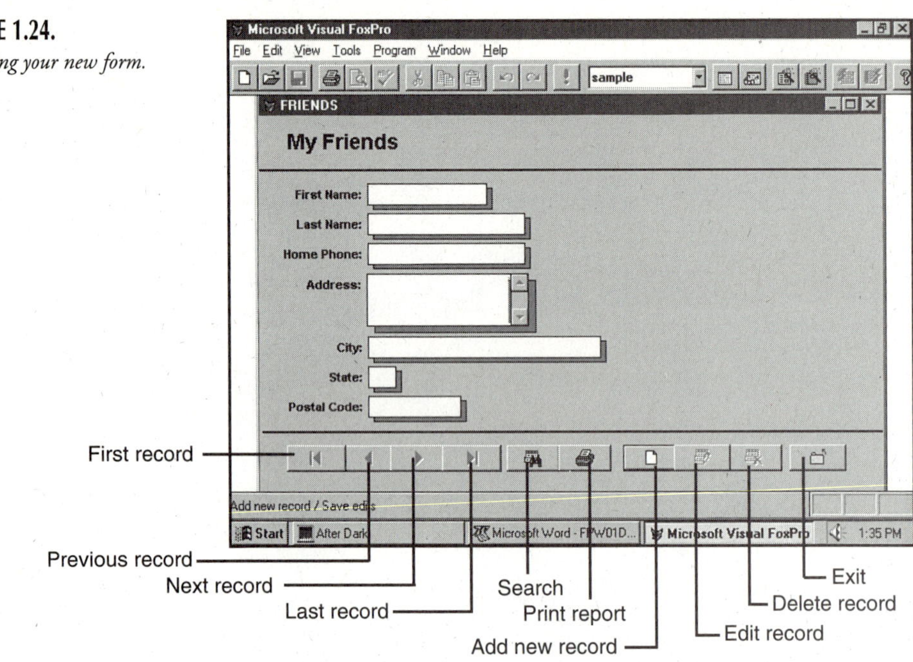

FIGURE 1.24.
Executing your new form.

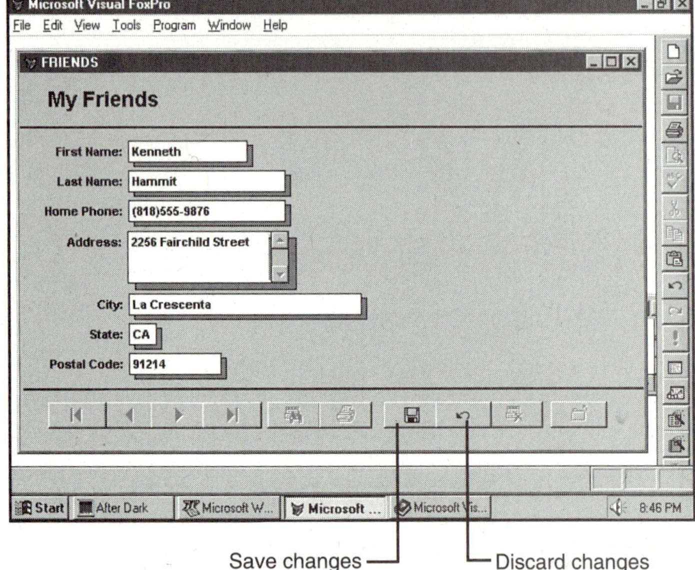

FIGURE 1.25.
Entering information into your new form.

If you want to discard changes, press the Undo button, which is to the right of the Save button, and the information you have typed is discarded.

If you click on the button with binoculars on it, the Search dialog box appears, as shown in Figure 1.26. You can specify expressions that determine which records are displayed in the form. In Figure 1.26, the search dialog box specifies that you want to view only records for friends in the state of Washington. These expressions are sometimes called *filtering expressions* because they filter out unwanted records.

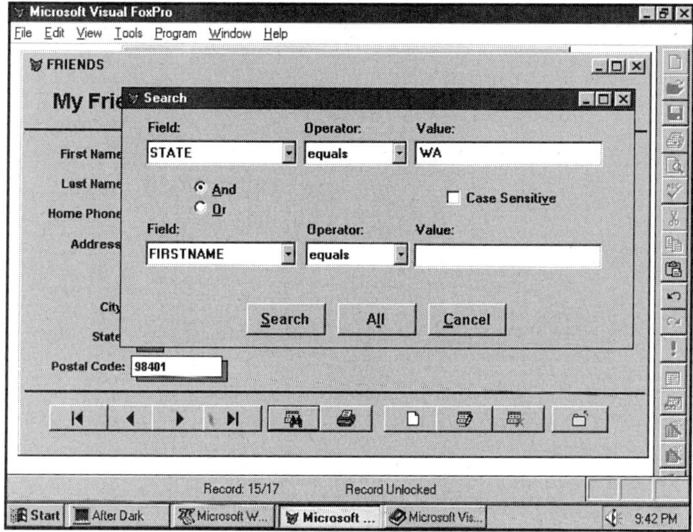

FIGURE 1.26.
Establishing a record filter.

If you click on the Print button, a report will be created before your eyes, and you have the option of customizing this report in the Visual FoxPro Form Designer. However, this is not a part of the guided tour. I will show you how to create a report form using the Report Wizard.

Now click on the Exit button and return to the Project Manager.

Step 6: Create a Report with the Report Wizard

If you have followed the instructions, and have exited your new form, the Project Manager displays on your screen. You are now going to use the Report Wizard to create a report for your application. To execute the Report Wizard, perform the following steps:

1. Select the Report icon in the Project Manager by clicking on it.
2. Click on the **N**ew button, and the Wizard Selection dialog box appears, as shown in Figure 1.27.

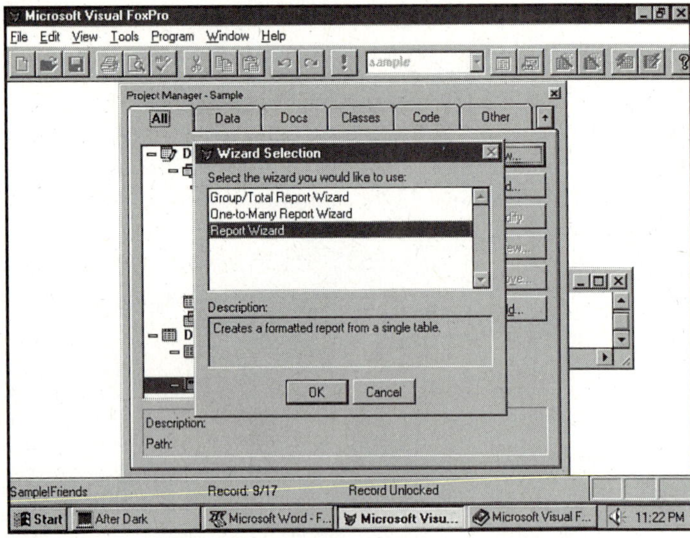

FIGURE 1.27.
Creating a report with the Report Wizard.

3. Select the Report Wizard and click on the OK button, and the Report Wizard Step 1 dialog box appears. It contains the list of fields from the FRIENDS.DBF table in the **A**vailable Fields list box.
4. Click on the button with two right-pointing triangles on it, and all of the fields will move to the **S**elected Fields list box, as shown in Figure 1.28.

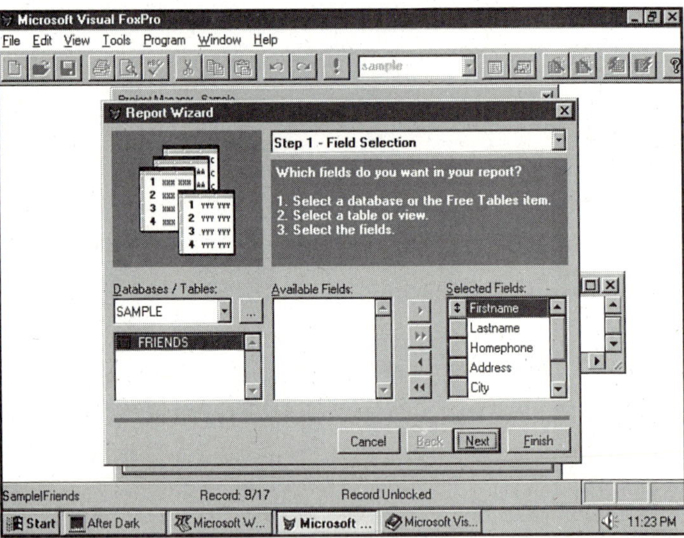

FIGURE 1.28.
The Report Wizard Step 1 dialog box, which you use to select fields for your report.

5. Click on the **F**inish button, and the Report Wizard Step 5 dialog box appears, as shown in Figure 1.29.

   Note that this quick tour is skipping the Report Wizard Steps 2 through 4 dialog boxes. You use them to specify the style, layout, and sorting order of the report. This quick tour uses the default settings defined in these dialog boxes. If you like, you can view them by pressing the **N**ext button.

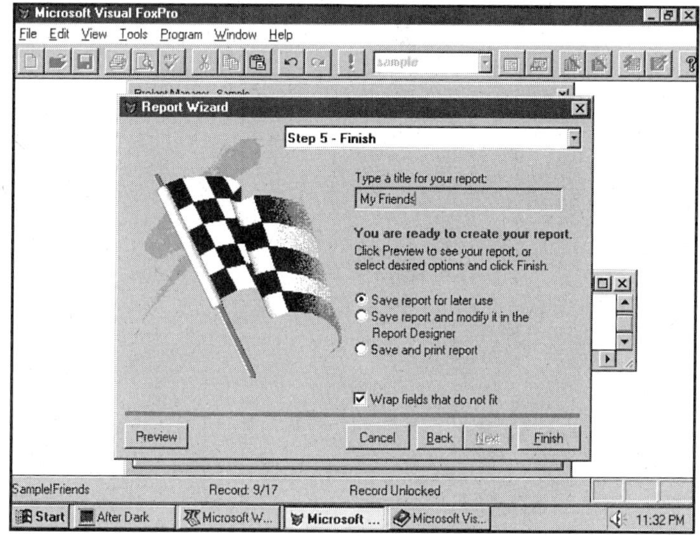

FIGURE 1.29.

The Report Wizard Step 5 dialog box, which you use to finish your report.

6. In the Step 5 dialog box, type a title for your report, as shown in Figure 1.29. You can press the Preview button to see what your report form will look like. The report will look something like what is shown in Figure 1.30.
7. Press the **F**inish button, and the Report Wizard will prompt you for a name of the report by displaying the Create File dialog box. Name your report Friends.

That is all there is to it. You have created a report. Now from the Project Manager dialog box select your new form (Friends) and click on the **R**un button to run your form.

Click on the print button with the printer icon on it, and you will be given the choice to either print your report to a printer or to display it in a preview screen.

Notice that you have the option of moving between pages of the report or zooming the report so that you can view its general layout. Press the Exit button and return to the Form Designer.

If you want to make any changes to your report form, exit from the form. From the Project Manager select your report form and click on the **M**odify button. The Visual FoxPro Report Designer activates. You can make any changes to your report that you like. The Report Designer is described in Chapter 20, "Report and Label Designers and Wizards."

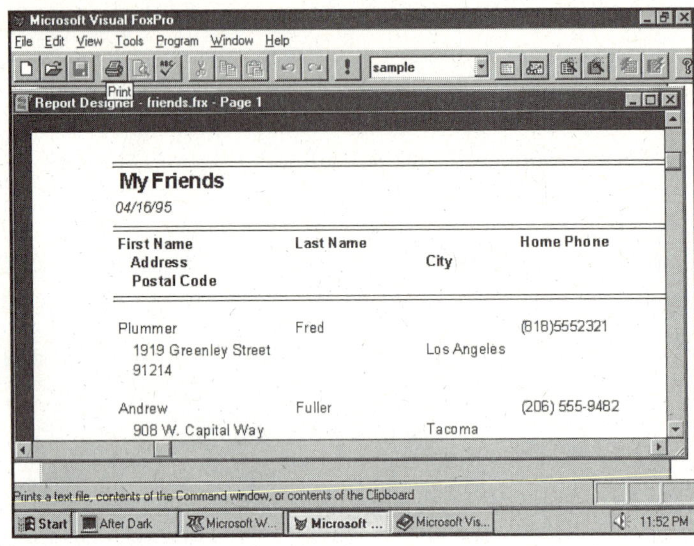

FIGURE 1.30.
Displaying your report in the Preview window.

Modifying Your Form

If you want to make any changes to your form, you will need to use the Visual FoxPro Form Designer. To modify your form, select your Friends form in the Project Manager, press the **M**odify push button, and the Form Designer appears with your form displayed, as shown in Figure 1.31. The Form Designer is described in Chapter 19, "The Form Designer."

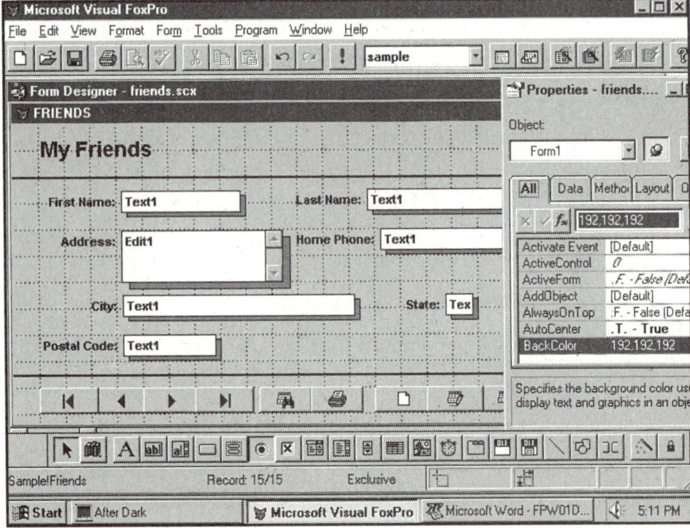

FIGURE 1.31.
Modifying your form with the Visual FoxPro Form Designer.

At this point, you are probably not familiar with powerful features of the Form Designer. However, you can do simple things such as rearranging objects on the form by dragging the objects across the form. I have rearranged some of the objects on the form (shown in Figure 1.31). I also resized the form. After you are finished experimenting with the Form Designer, you can click on the Run button (the button with the exclamation point on it) on the standard toolbar to execute your form. Figure 1.32 shows an example of the Friends form, modified using the Form Designer. If you just want to exit the Form Designer without running the form, you can choose the **F**ile menu **C**lose option or press Ctrl+End to save your changes and exit.

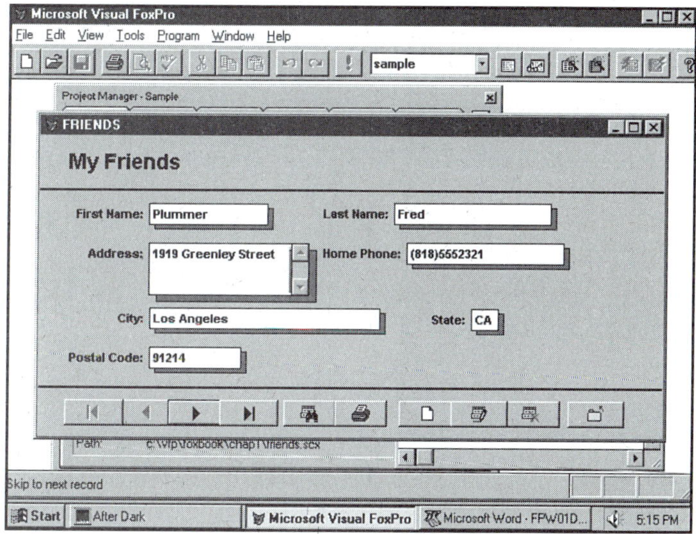

FIGURE 1.32.
The Friends form, modified with the Form Designer.

Your new application contains features for viewing and searching records, deleting records, adding and editing records in your table, and generating reports. You can execute your form from the Command window by entering the following command:

```
DO FORM FRIENDS
```

Your entire application is controlled from a Visual FoxPro form file. More complex applications can have many forms, reports, menus, queries, tables, and program files, class libraries, and other files, all of which are maintained by the Project Manager.

You can use the Project Manager Build feature to create an application (APP) file. If you have the Visual FoxPro Professional Edition, you can even create an executable file that can be executed from Windows.

Now that you have the fundamental knowledge for creating an application, you can practice by generating your own Visual FoxPro application. You can create an application to record information about your collectibles, valuables, or anything else you might want to track.

Ending a FoxPro Session

When you've finished a Visual FoxPro session, you must exit FoxPro before turning off your computer. You can exit Visual FoxPro in several ways:

- Enter `QUIT` in the Command window.
- Choose the **F**ile menu **E**xit option.
- Choose the Control menu box **C**lose command.
- If you're a Windows 95 user, you can click on the Close button.

Other than exiting, you don't need to do anything else to preserve your work. However, it's always a good idea to back up your valuable data on disks, tapes, or other permanent storage media. It doesn't matter whether valuable data consists of FoxPro tables, word processor documents, or spreadsheets. If your hard disk crashes, you'll probably lose valuable data forever.

If a catastrophe, such as a power failure, or some other disastrous event occurs that causes a FoxPro session to terminate abnormally, a number of temporary work files (with a filename extension of .TMP) are left on the disk in the Windows temporary file directory (which is usually C:\WINDOWS\TEMP). You should use the Windows File Manager or some other file utility to remove these files because they occupy disk space. When FoxPro exits normally, it deletes all temporary work files it uses in a session.

Summary

This chapter introduces the Visual FoxPro 3.0 system and describes the screen and the menu systems. It gives a brief tour through the Visual FoxPro 3.0 Project Manager and several wizards, and you create an application. After reading this chapter, you are ready to learn about database concepts and the fundamentals of the FoxPro language.

2

Database Management and the FoxPro Language

Science is organized knowledge.

—Herbert Spencer
(1820–1903)

This chapter is a bridge between abstract academic theory and a real-world implementation of such theory: FoxPro. It also presents the basic concepts of the FoxPro language. First I'll describe the relational model—the theory on which FoxPro is based—in more detail. Then I'll explain why FoxPro is controversial among database experts.

Database Concepts

Computers had been in common use for nearly 15 years before the idea of a general-purpose database management system (DBMS) became widespread. *Webster's Tenth New Collegiate Dictionary* dates the origin of the term *database* to 1967. Until then, applications programs handled their own data, often "reinventing the wheel" for each new application. Database management systems generally fall into one of three categories: hierarchical, network, and relational.

The hierarchical approach, shown in Figure 2.1, seems natural. For example, you might have three farms at the uppermost level of a tree structure. Each farm has some number of buildings: a house, a barn, a chicken coop. Each building is home to some number of people or animals. If you traverse the tree, you might arrive at a cow in the barn on Smith's farm. Each parent in a hierarchical tree can have multiple children, but each child has only one parent. Using such a tree makes it fairly easy to add a chicken to Cooper's chicken coop or to count the people living in Smith's house. It is more difficult, however, to count all cows everywhere.

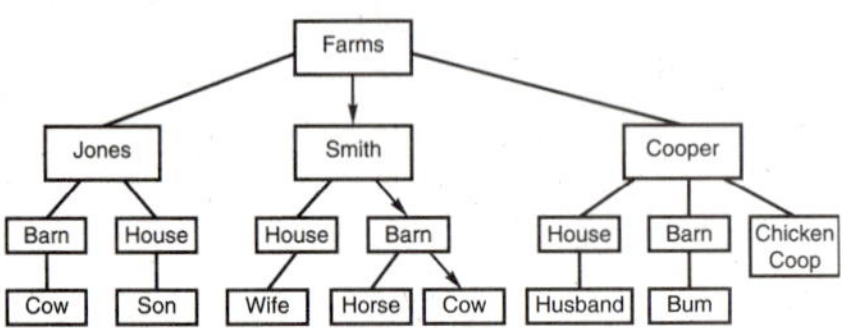

FIGURE 2.1.
The hierarchical model.

The network model, shown in Figure 2.2, is powerful but complicated. A network database is a collection of nodes and links, such that any node can be linked to any other, perhaps multiple times. The links form threads by which you can quickly answer not only how many cows are in Smith's barn but how many cows exist in the database. The links must be designed with anticipated queries and actions in mind, however, and update operations can become overly complex.

The relational model, shown in Figure 2.3 and described more fully later in this chapter in the section "The Relational Model," is powerful yet simple, both flexible and natural. Data is stored in conceptual tables in which rows are instances and columns are attributes. For example, a phone list might have columns for the name, address, and telephone number with one row for each name. The price is paid in redundancy—relational tables are sparser than other data structures, and several tables may be required to support a single set of data.

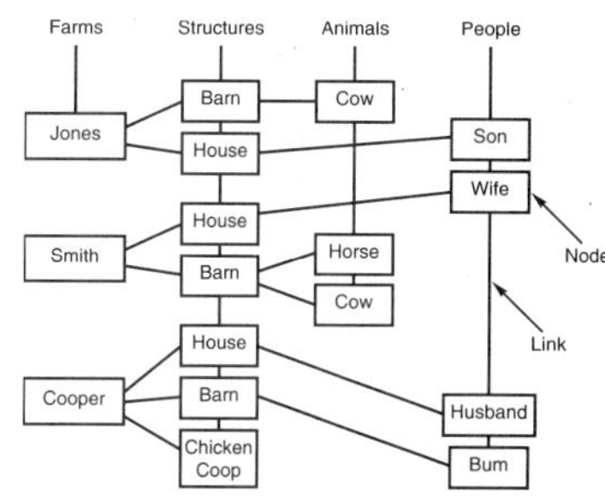

FIGURE 2.2.
The network model.

FIGURE 2.3.
The relational model.

Farms

Jones		
Smith		
Cooper		

Animals

Jones	Barn	Cow	
Smith	Barn	Horse	
Smith	Barn	Cow	
Cooper			

Structures

Jones	House		
Jones	Barn		
Smith	House		
Smith	Barn		
Cooper	House		
Cooper	Barn		
Cooper	Coop		

People

Jones	House	Son
Smith	House	Wife
Cooper	House	Husband
Cooper	Barn	Bum

Flat Files

FoxPro is *relational* because it stores data in tables and relates the tables with index keys, but its storage mechanism is more straightforward than those of other relational DBMSs. Each FoxPro table exists as a separate file with a header that describes the columns and the number of rows, followed by row after fixed-length row of the data itself. This model is called a *flat file* because data instances never contain links that would, metaphorically, leave the two-dimensional plane of the table.

Although it might be easier to think of tables as consisting of rows and columns, FoxPro defines its own terminology, as shown in Figure 2.4. Tables are files, simply because each table is stored in a separate file, usually with the .DBF extension. Databases are composed of one or more such files, so it's incorrect to refer to one file as a database unless it is the only file in the database. Tables are sometimes referred to as *relations* in the literature, but this is potentially confusing. Columns in FoxPro terminology are *fields* because they correspond to data entry fields in a screen form. Because fields have different characteristics (for example, some are numbers, some are character strings, and so on), they also are called *attributes*, but again this seems awkward. FoxPro refers to the rows of the table as *records*. Elsewhere, records are sometimes called *tuples*. (Tuple is usually pronounced to rhyme with *couple*. Believe it or not, some controversy surrounds this.)

FIGURE 2.4.
Relational model terms.

FoxPro 2	C. J. Date	SQL and others
Bunch of Files*	Database	Database
File	Relation	Table
Field	Attribute	Column
Record	Tuple	Row

*Ok, so we blew it

I use the terms *relation, attribute,* and *tuple* because I can give new terms precise technical meanings free of the connotations of more common words. For the common associations that do not conflict with the meaning, I will use both the common nomenclature (table, column, row) and the FoxPro terms (table, field, record).

Because storage mechanisms are more complicated than the flat file approach, you can more easily keep the data sorted. With FoxPro's flat file, new records are always added to the end of the file—the file is stored in entry order. (You can physically insert records when no index is in use, but this is an inefficient operation and could require rewriting the entire file.) By manipulating the links of a network or hierarchical database, it is simple to maintain any desired order. To reorder a FoxPro file, you must either rewrite the records to a new file or use an external index.

An index is like a sorted table of key values and record numbers. This table, however, is stored in a structure that is optimized for fast lookup. A simple analogy is an index in a book. Each item in the book index has corresponding page numbers. The item is analogous to a data item (called a *key value*) in the table. The page number is analogous to the record number of the record in the table that contains the key value. In 1970 Edward Meyers McCreight and Rudolf Bayer developed a new indexing method based on a multiway tree structure that they called a *B-tree.* By grouping many links into one node rather than the binary tree's two links, the B-tree optimizes disk accesses, which are practically the sole determinant of lookup speed. Three accesses (reading three nodes) can traverse a very large tree, but insert and delete operations are economical, as well. (Incidentally, all B-tree update operations consist of insert and delete operations—modification in place does not exist in an ordered tree structure.)

FoxPro uses a popular variant of the B-tree called the *B*tree* (Knuth 1973), in which only leaf nodes contain links to the database, as shown in Figure 2.5. This means that some keys are stored redundantly, but doing so makes a sequential pass through the ordered data as simple as reading all the leaf nodes.

FIGURE 2.5.
*The B*tree index.*

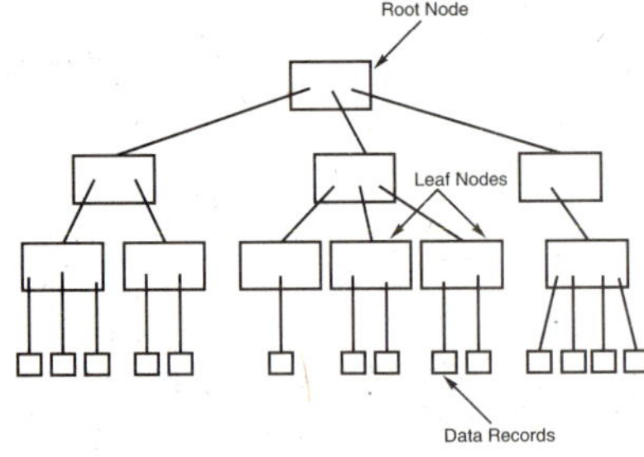

FoxPro uses external B*tree indexes to apply various orderings to the rows of entry-ordered tables. Earlier versions of dBASE supported only one index per file. Using FoxPro, a single file can contain dozens of indexes. Unlike many DBMSs, FoxPro offers almost unlimited freedom when specifying index keys. Some systems require that a key be a column in the table, but others relax this restriction to allow composite keys—one or more columns from the table. But

FoxPro allows keys to be formed with any valid expression (except logical and memo expressions). This means that FoxPro indexes are more flexible—you can index a table on the sum or product of two columns, for example, or ignore differentiations between uppercase and lowercase characters by using built-in functions such as `UPPER()`.

Enterprise Modeling

Most descriptions of database theory begin with a definition of *database* such as "a collection of stored operational data used by the application systems of some particular enterprise" (Date 1973).

This implies that the only data you need be concerned with is data under the jurisdiction of management information systems (MISs)—analog data reported by instruments, for example, is of no interest. By this definition, typical examples of databases include general bookkeeping and accounting; inventory and sales information; classes, students, and teachers; admissions at a hospital; and reservations at a hotel. Databases, in other words, are used to model real-world enterprises.

A single table of data, such as a list of names and addresses, can be quite useful; additional information in the table, such as a phone number, marital status, and so on, can be added to each record. The power of relational databases, however, comes from using several intersecting data tables to store this information.

Figure 2.6 represents a database of college classes. One table lists classes, another lists students, and a third lists teachers. Each class has one teacher and many students, each student has many classes and thus many teachers, and each teacher teaches many classes. Relationships between tables fall into three categories: one-to-many (such as teachers and classes), many-to-many (such as students and classes), and one-to-one (one teacher to each class).

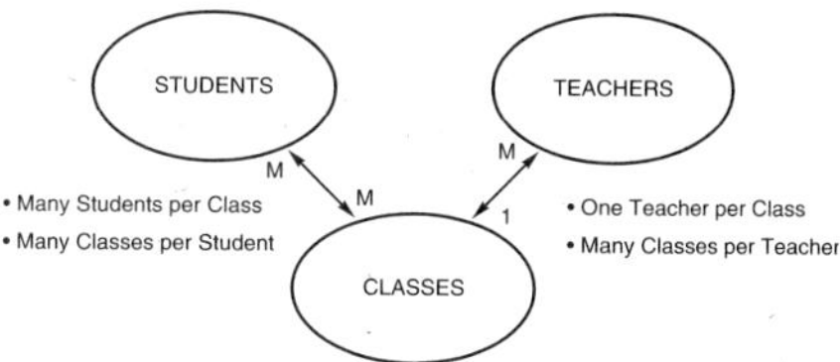

FIGURE 2.6.
The college classes database.

When a one-to-one relationship exists between two tables (such as students and their student ID numbers, for example), you can merge the two tables. Many-to-many relationships are typically treated as two one-to-many relationships: You can view students and classes either as one student having many classes or as one class containing many students. It is a simple matter of changing the ordering; dealing with both views simultaneously is usually not necessary.

How do you reduce a real-world enterprise to a model composed of a few simple tables? The process is called *database design*. Given raw data such as that illustrated in Figure 2.7, you would first normalize the data. A data table is considered normalized if each row-column intersection contains a single, unique value. When the data is laid out, each row can be identified by a unique key (the value in a single column or combination of columns), and each non-key column provides supporting information about the key. This is called *first normal form (1NF).* If the table meets certain additional criteria, it can be in second, third, or even fourth or fifth normal form. The requirements are incrementally inclusive—a table in third normal form automatically lies in second and first normal forms as well.

FIGURE 2.7.
Unnormalized (raw) data.

Student 1	Class 1 : Teacher B
	Class 2 : Teacher A
	Class 3 : Teacher C
Student 2	Class 1 : Teacher B
	Class 3 : Teacher C

Third normal form (3NF) is what the database designer generally targets when the operational data from a particular enterprise is reduced to tables. Generally, but not always, to minimize redundancy and thus minimize update difficulties, even C. J. Date admits that it is sometimes desirable to leave tables in 2NF or even 1NF. The classic example of overnormalization is a table with the columns: Name, City, State, and ZIP Code. Technically, City and State depend upon ZIP Code, but to decompose this example into two tables (Name, ZIP Code and ZIP Code, City, State) would not be worthwhile.

Figure 2.8 shows the data from Figure 2.7 in third normal form. To put a given table into third normal form, the designer simply creates new tables by duplicating the key column or columns from the original and extracting columns that depend upon columns other than the key. Column B is dependent on column A if each value in A has precisely one value in B. The value in A can be duplicated many times, but when two rows have the same A value, they must have the same B value for B to be considered dependent on A. (This definition of third normal form comes from Boyce and Codd and is sometimes referred to as *Boyce/Codd normal form,* or *B/CNF.*)

FIGURE 2.8.
Data in third normal form.

Students

Student1	Class1		
Student1	Class2		
Student1	Class3		
Student2	Class1		
Student2	Class3		

Teachers

TeacherA	Class2	
TeacherB	Class1	
TeacherC	Class3	

Classes

Class1	TeacherB		
Class2	TeacherA		
Class3	TeacherC		

Fourth, fifth, and perhaps other normal forms have been described, but they are beyond the scope of this overview. For example, any table with three or more columns can have multivalue dependencies, as well. Tables without multivalue dependencies (except on the key) are said to be in fourth normal form, which was first described by R. Fagin (Fagin 1977). Fifth normal form, also called *projection-join normal form,* concerns tables that cannot be non-loss-decomposed into two tables but can be non-loss-decomposed into three.

Functional dependencies reflect real-world conditions. A class has only one teacher, an employee has only one Social Security number, and so forth. These relationships are not discernible from the tables or even from the data. Accordingly, you can't look at a set of tables and pronounce that they are in third normal form. Therefore, no DBMS can ensure that a database remains in third normal form without a complete disclosure of the range of possible column values (called the *domain*) and the dependencies between columns and between tables. It seems that database design cannot be completely automated until the problems of artificial intelligence are solved—the solution set is large and the optimal schema is often a matter of intuition (Hubbard 1981).

The Relational Model

In 1970, E. F. Codd first described the relational model (Codd 1970). He continued to refine his concepts at IBM's San Jose Research Laboratory, where the relational model found its most prolific promoter in C. J. Date, also an IBM researcher. By the end of the decade, when dBASE II was conceived, the relational model was widely accepted as superior, at least for general purposes, to both the network (CODASYL) and the hierarchical models. (CODASYL is the Conference of Data System Languages, the organization that specified the COBOL programming language.) Codd and Date have since left IBM and formed the Relational Institute, which is dedicated to explaining the relational model.

It's important to realize that the relational model is a mathematical abstraction, designed to make it easier to talk about database issues and to design data-manipulation languages. It is also a human-interface model because tables of data are easy to understand. The relational model is not a storage or access method, however, because it does not dictate anything about how the underlying data is stored. FoxPro happens to store and present data using this tabular model, but many other commercial systems store data in more of a network style while presenting data as tables. In other words, the storage method and the presentation method may or may not be the same, and one is not indicative of the other.

The relational model has many benefits. It's intuitive and simple, and it carries a high degree of data independence, which is described shortly. Data tables and operations such as adding rows or deleting columns are easy to grasp conceptually. Operations on data tables conform to a few simple rules—mostly borrowed from set theory—that are themselves intuitive and easily understood. The idea of storing data in tables did not originate with Codd, but he has described a relational algebra consisting of eight operations and reminiscent of the four arithmetic operations. Further, he and others have invented a relational calculus, called *query optimization*, which rationalizes the steps a system takes to respond to a request for data. These rules and concepts serve to separate the stored data from the applications that manipulate the data. Such a separation, called *data independence*, is crucial to a general-purpose database management system.

Relational Terms

A *relational model* is simply a method of representing, manipulating, and retrieving information. This section examines terminology used in describing the relational model.

Schema

It's important to distinguish between the logical structure of a database and the specific instances of data. Date labels the structure as the *intension* and calls data instances the *extension*; other authors make the same distinction using different terms (Martin 1977).

The logical structure of a collection of tables that completely describes an enterprise is called a *database schema.* The schema describes the fields of each table in terms of type (character, numeric, and so on), size (each instance of a field value is the same size), name, and (in some systems) range of possible values. The schema also describes the relationships between tables. Often, a particular application deals with only a subset of the full database, called a *subschema.*

Normalization

Every table in a database must be normalized; that is, each row-column intersection must have a single, *atomic* value (which means no sets and no repeating groups). As an illustration, recall that two-toned cars were fashionable a few years ago. In a data table with a `Car_Color` field you might find it convenient to enter `Tan/Baby Blue` on one row to describe a particular classic car. You can normalize this table in three ways:

- The first way is to use two rows (records) to describe the top and bottom of the car separately. This approach fails if the table is intended as a list of cars—in this case, the number of rows should equal the number of cars. In fact, this approach is practical only if the table is a list of car colors.
- The second and preferred method is to split the `Car_Color` field into `Color_1` and `Color_2`.
- But a third (and sneaky) way out is to consider `Tan/Baby Blue` as a distinct color unrelated to `Tan`, `Baby Blue`, or `Baby Blue/Tan`.

Relational algebra requires that tables be normalized, but it does not assume any order for either the rows (records) or the columns (fields). Date explains: "A [table] is a set and sets are not ordered" (Date 1973). For practical purposes, however, the data is generally in some order, typically based on the data values themselves—for example, a table in alphabetical order by name, or ascending order by salary. FoxPro provides several mechanisms, particularly external indexes, for ordering rows. Both the `SET FIELDS` command and the `FIELDS` clause supported by various commands can produce the effect of ordering columns. Such a fields list can also hide some fields and add new, virtual columns (called *calculated fields*), but you must consider that row and column ordering are irrelevant, other than for the presentation of data.

Keys

Every table naturally includes one or more fields that compose a *primary key* that differentiates one record from all others. Because tables are sets, mathematically identical records are not permitted. However, the FoxPro language is more permissive. Some databases are designed so that redundant records are counted to determine a quantity.

A table can have more than one possible primary key. For example, Figure 2.9 shows a software inventory table with both a unique SKU number and a unique title for each software product. In this case, the `Title` and `SKU_No` fields are both candidate keys. Either one, alone, is sufficient to identify each record. Only one can be the primary key; the other is the alternate key.

FIGURE 2.9.
Two possible primary keys.

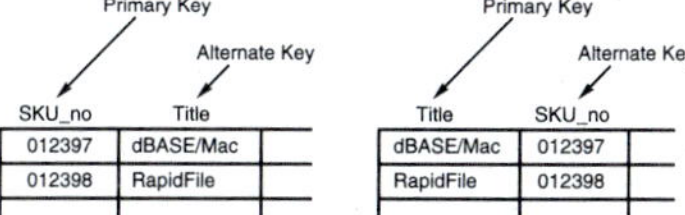

To relate two tables, the parent table must include a field containing a reference to the primary key of the subordinate, or child, table. Consider Figure 2.10, a table of employees with `Emp_No` as its primary key. A Projects table might include a `Proj_Mgr` field that was defined in the same way as the `Emp_No` field in the Employees table. To find the name and address of the project manager for a particular project, the DBMS simply looks up the number in the `Proj_Mgr` field in the Employees table. In this case, the `Proj_Mgr` field is called a foreign key because it refers to a different table.

FIGURE 2.10.
Tables are related by a foreign key.

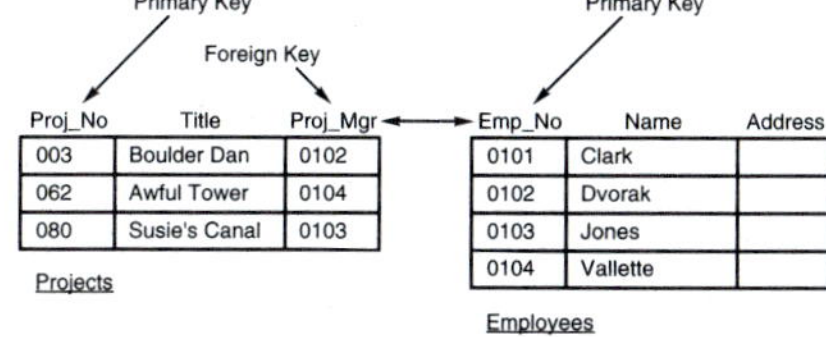

Data Integrity

The relational model imposes several data integrity rules, none of which are enforced by FoxPro. Entity integrity requires that the primary key never be null (that is, contain no value). This is mainly because primary keys must be unique. Other problems also crop up with null values. You can write applications in FoxPro that maintain entity integrity by not allowing new records or updates that result in null keys, but the system does not guarantee that primary keys are unique or that they are not null.

Referential integrity specifies that every foreign key must match some primary key in a related table. Again, this is reasonable. In earlier versions of FoxPro and other Xbase programs, you could write FoxPro applications that enforce referential integrity, but the constraint is not applied automatically. However, in Visual FoxPro, you can use the newly introduced data dictionary to enforce referential integrity. Like everything in FoxPro, you can have it if you want it. The mathematical underpinning of the relational model does not agree with the "you're the boss" attitude taken by FoxPro.

Domain integrity probably matters most to application developers. Commercial systems such as FoxPro provide a few different data types, such as character, numeric, and date, with clearly defined domains. The domain is the set of all possible values for a given field type. After you tell FoxPro that a particular field is a date, for example, the system ensures that only valid dates are stored in that field.

Frequently, however, an application needs to restrict the domain further. Instead of including all valid dates, a date field might be restricted to "no later than today's date" and "no earlier than six years ago, when the company was founded," for example. You might want to restrict the domain of a two-character field called `State` to the list of abbreviations approved by the post office. Instead of adding more field types (for example, a State type), FoxPro provides data entry mechanisms such as the `VALID` clause and user-defined *triggers* that can enforce any constraint imaginable. A trigger is an expression associated with a table that is executed whenever a record in the table is modified, deleted, or inserted. You can enforce data entry and business rules with the validation properties for each field.

Relational Algebra

Relational algebra is a set of eight operations that take one or two tables as operands and produce a table as a result. Four of the operations (union, intersection, difference, and Cartesian product) are borrowed from set theory. Because all the operators take tables as operands and produce tables as results, you can perform strings of operations, just as you can produce a string of operations in arithmetic expressions—in which one might say `(A + 4 * B - 2)`.

Extended Cartesian Product

The *extended Cartesian product* results from combining two tables such that the result features as many columns as both tables put together and enough rows to express every possible combination of the two tables. The names of the operand tables are affixed to the column names to ensure that column names remain unique, even when you're squaring a table by taking the product of A × A. Notice that two tables cannot combine to make a table larger than the extended Cartesian product.

Selection

A *selection* is a horizontal subset of a table in which only certain records are chosen. The FoxPro `SET FILTER` command is one selection mechanism; the `FOR`, `WHILE`, and `scope` clauses are others. For convenience, it's best when you can refer to only a subset of all records.

Projection

A *projection* is a vertical subset of a table in which only certain fields (columns) are displayed. The capability to choose columns implies the capability to reorder them as well. The FoxPro `SET FIELDS` command and the `FIELDS` clause support projection and reordering while extending the concept to allow the creation of virtual columns (calculated fields).

Join

A *join* is similar to a Cartesian product except that the resultant table contains only records from each table that match a particular condition. Typically, this join condition stipulates that the values be equal in a column common to both tables. This is called an *equijoin.* Relational algebra defines other possibilities as well, such as a "not equal join" or a "less than join." As defined by Date, the equijoin operation results in two identical columns (Date 1973). When one of these columns is dispensed with, the result is called a *natural join.*

The FoxPro `JOIN` command permits joins based on any valid expression, regardless of whether common columns are involved. The resulting table contains the sum of both sets of columns (unless you specify a simultaneous projection with the `FIELDS` clause). If both tables contain no common columns and all records match the condition, the result is the extended Cartesian product.

Union

The *union* of two tables is the set of all records in either table. Both tables must be *union compatible,* however, which means that the columns of each table must be identical. You can use the FoxPro `APPEND FROM` command to form the union of two tables.

Intersection

The *intersection* of two union-compatible tables is the set of all records found in both tables. FoxPro does not directly support intersection. You can perform an intersection in FoxPro, but you must use multiple commands to do it.

Difference

The *difference* between two union-compatible tables, A and B, is the set of all records found in table A that are not in table B. Notice that although union and intersection are commutative, difference is not. As in arithmetic, A – B is not the same as B – A. FoxPro does not directly support difference because it does not have a single command that performs a difference. You must write a program consisting of multiple commands.

Division

The *division* of table A by table B produces a table consisting of the columns of table A that are not common to B and the records of A that exactly match the records in table B on the common columns. The division operator is evidently included in relational algebra for completeness because it applies to few real-world situations.

Date points out that relational algebra could be used to perform updates using just the union and difference operators. But for various reasons, he concludes that data manipulation languages should include explicit insert, delete, and update operators, as well.

Extending Relational Algebra

Relational algebra is complete in that its eight operators can query, update, and maintain relational tables with no further extension. However, the algebra is a mathematical construct. To make it tangible, a real implementation such as *Structured Query Language (SQL)* or (to a less complete degree, to be sure) FoxPro is required.

Real database languages have two components, a *data definition language (DDL)* and a *data manipulation language (DML).* The DDL creates named tables and manages column (field) names and attributes. You can also use it to specify database, table, and index attributes, including physical storage, access method preferences, and password security. The DML is primarily concerned with queries and updates, but it handles addition and deletion of data instances, as well.

SQL, developed by D. D. Chamberlin and others at the IBM San Jose Research Laboratory in the 1970s, is an excellent example of both a DML and a DDL (Date 1987). It includes DDL commands such as `CREATE TABLE`, `GRANT`, and `REVOKE`, as well as DML commands such as `SELECT`, `INSERT`, `DELETE`, and `UPDATE`. SQL is relationally complete and has been quite popular on minicomputers and mainframes since its commercial introduction in 1979, which explains its inclusion in FoxPro. Unlike FoxPro, however, SQL is a complete application-development language.

Query by example (QBE), invented by Moshe Zloof while he was with IBM at their Yorktown Heights Research Laboratory (Zloof 1975), is a screen-oriented query facility based on prototype tables that a user employs to describe the desired query results. As opposed to the character-stream format of most languages, QBE uses a unique two-dimensional syntax. QBE's strength is its intuitive DML; DDL operations are handled as extensions to the concept. Visual FoxPro incorporates an implementation of relational query by example (RQBE) as a DML, which is called the Query Designer.

Is FoxPro a Relational DBMS?

One point of contention has arisen over whether FoxPro is truly relational. Of course it is. As discussed earlier in this chapter, FoxPro supports multiple-base tables and can perform selections, projections, and joins on those tables. The point is that FoxPro can hardly be classified as anything but relational. The argument, then, is over the degree to which FoxPro is relational. This argument admittedly has merit. The defense merely asks that commercial products designed for real-world use be exempt from a strict interpretation. By rigid definition, FoxPro is not fully relational because it fails to implement relational algebra without the use of loops and recursion (but it is close). It is not even semirelational because it does not enforce integrity rules.

The FoxPro language is more than a DML and a DDL. It's an application-development language with full-screen editing, exception processing, scalar variables, and control flow concepts not found in mere DDL/DMLs. (FoxPro includes several alternate DMLs, including power tools such as Database, View, Query, Report, and Label Designers.)

Visual FoxPro accomplishes both the creation of tables and the assignment of access privileges with its interactive dialog boxes. You have seen how real-world implementations such as FoxPro extend relational algebra. In addition, Codd has extended the algebra by developing a relational calculus that uses predicate calculus as a basis for optimizing database queries (Codd 1972). The calculus uses variables that act as cursors (an unfortunate overburdening of the term). *Cursor* refers to a particular record instance. Tuple variables refer to whole rows, and domain variables, a later enhancement, refer to individual data elements (Lacroix and Pirotte 1977). QBE is an example of domain calculus. A detailed discussion of these advancements lies beyond the scope of this book, however.

This section presents a synopsis of the theoretical basis for the relational model. FoxPro is an example of a real-world implementation of an academic concept. The works of Date and others contain excellent descriptions of abstract or supercomputer-based database management systems, but the literature has rarely aided directly in solving the real-world problems with microcomputers that application developers must face. Some elements of FoxPro would be different if it had been designed initially as a fully relational, full-blown DBMS, but it would never fit on a microcomputer such as the original IBM PC.

Prior to Visual FoxPro 3.0 a data dictionary was a major omission in FoxPro and all other Xbase languages. A *data dictionary* is a database that describes the data in an operational database. In Visual FoxPro, there exists a table called a *database container* that lists all known column names and the tables to which they belong, table names, and relations between tables. It is used to keep track of all tables (DBF files), columns (fields), relations, and stored procedures in an application. The Visual FoxPro database maintains persistent relations between tables, stored procedures, field- and record-level rules, and triggers.

Null values are another classic problem for which we have yet to find a good solution. A *null value* is necessary in a database system to indicate that no value is appropriate (on a handwritten form, you might write N.A.). This is particularly important with numbers, for which an unknown value is very different from zero; with dates, for which an unknown birthdate, for example, must not be confused with the beginning of the Julian calendar; and with logical values, for conditions that are neither true nor false but are unknown or indeterminate.

Xbase and earlier versions of FoxPro include the EMPTY() or ISBLANK() functions to indicate when a field contains a blank or zero value, but this function does not truly handle null values. The problem is more profound than the EMPTY() function can handle. A blank or zero value could be a valid value. For example, what should the result of an AVERAGE be when some of its values are null? *Null?* This is a problem that will not go away. As with other academic challenges, the Visual FoxPro design teams set out to implement null fields for Visual FoxPro. To do this, the FoxPro programmer devised some techniques for indicating that a field is void and provided void field handling through program control. For the sake of compatibility, they added the SET NULL ON/OFF command to support FoxPro programs that do not support null fields.

The interface with the operating system is a continuing problem as well. It is useful that FoxPro acts within the operating system, using its services for volume and file input and output. Other systems usurp control of the hardware from the operating system, leaving the user at the mercy of the DBMS for even routine services such as backup. By storing database information in MS-DOS files, however, FoxPro loses the capability to protect the user from mistakes such as unintentionally erasing a file. Of course, this is true of any MS-DOS or Windows application. Worse yet, as FoxPro's file structures become more complex, concepts such as associate files and file links appear—concepts about which the host operating system knows nothing.

Visual FoxPro, like other Xbase languages, supports a variable-length field called a *memo field*. Memo fields are stored in a separate file with the same name as the DBF file but with the .FPT extension. Putting a DBF file in use automatically opens the FPT file if memo fields are defined. When FoxPro copies a DBF file, it copies the FPT file as well. This is not so with the operating system. When you copy a file with the operating system, it doesn't copy associated files. The association between DBF and FPT exists only in the "mind" of FoxPro. It also supports binary data fields called a *general field*. This field supports OLE objects such as pictures, sound, and other multimedia data types.

A Simple Language for Database Management

FoxPro is built around a general-purpose programming language that understands database management issues. Its command-oriented syntax includes over 300 commands and over 200 built-in functions; it contains five SQL-like commands as well. (I arrived at this number of commands by considering SET ALTERNATE ON/OFF as one command and SET ALTERNATE TO as another.) These numbers may boggle the mind of a novice just learning the language. Imagine the terror one might feel confronting a test question in a FoxPro class that asks the student to list 300 FoxPro commands. Fortunately, this isn't a problem because with a small subset of fewer than 20 commands you can perform most fundamental database management operations. You can gradually learn the remaining commands as needed to develop more advanced programs.

The FoxPro programming language is conceptually simple. It is an improved implementation of the dBASE IV programming language, which Ashton-Tate Corporation originally distributed and which Borland International currently distributes. Because many vendors supply some form of the dBASE IV language, the general form of the language has been renamed *Xbase*, probably by dBASE users "talking" over a BBS. The original dBASE language owes quite a bit to the Beginner's All-Purpose Symbolic Instruction Code (BASIC), developed by John G. Kemeny and Thomas E. Kurtz at Dartmouth College in the 1960s. Like BASIC, Xbase is command oriented. Command execution is sequential unless you encounter a branching command (`IF...ELSE`), a looping command (`DO WHILE`), or a subroutine call (`DO` procedure). Although the discussion in this section pertains to the Xbase language in general, it focuses on the FoxPro language implementation in particular.

FoxPro supports some BASIC concepts such as scalar variables, arrays of scalar variables, event trapping (`ON KEY`), and user-defined functions. FoxPro implements a *high-level, nonprocedural* language—high-level because the details of management and conversion between data types such as numbers and character strings are hidden from the programmer, and nonprocedural because commands such as `SORT` and `REPORT` specify what is to be done rather than how to do it.

However, BASIC and the FoxPro language differ in many ways. For example, the controversial unconditional branch instruction (BASIC's `GOTO` command) does not appear in the FoxPro language. FoxPro also does not use line numbers. (Modern implementations of BASIC have outgrown line numbers, as well. Perhaps BASIC designers are learning from the Xbase language.) The most substantial difference between the FoxPro language and BASIC is that the FoxPro language contains higher-level, nonprocedural commands.

The FoxPro language possesses some wonderful elements that make it unique among programming languages. For example, it treats data instances (intersections of rows and columns in data tables) like scalar variables. FoxPro identifies data instances by the column name, and it bases their value on the notion of a current record number (row). Move the record number pointer to a different row, and suddenly the value of the "variable" has changed. Use a different data table, and the variable name may no longer be defined (or it may mean something different). Researchers who extend the relational model toward object-oriented databases should study the FoxPro language—it has contained persistent objects for years. (You'll find a discussion of persistence and field variables in Chapter 4, "Variables.")

The design of the original dBASE language was influenced by the interactive nature of how it would be used. For example, commands such as `USE` and `FIND` expect the name of a file to use or a string to find; they don't require an understanding of the concept of "an expression evaluating to type character." Instead, these commands support unquoted string literals, such as `USE Sales` and `FIND Smith`, which you use to type a command into the FoxPro Command window.

Likewise, the number of command verbs was originally kept small so that users had fewer commands to remember. Instead, commands such as `DISPLAY` were overloaded with secondary keywords that specify what is to be displayed. Rather than a half-dozen commands such as `STATUS`, `MEMVARS`, and `STRUCTURE`, the one `DISPLAY` command handles `DISPLAY expression-list`, `DISPLAY STATUS`, `DISPLAY MEMORY`, `DISPLAY STRUCTURE`, and so on.

Unlike most programming languages (including SQL, described in Chapter 18, "Queries Using SQL and the Query Designer"), the FoxPro language does not reserve its keywords. That is, nothing prevents you from creating a file called USE, although the documentation warns against it. This would lead to the legal statement

```
USE Use
```

In most Xbase languages, such as dBASE IV, a variable with the same name as a command, such as Count, cannot be assigned a value without the use of the STORE command

```
Count = 0
```

In dBASE IV, this results in a syntax error because COUNT is an Xbase command. But the following:

```
STORE 0 TO Count
```

is perfectly legal in dBASE IV. In FoxPro, you can even assign a value to a memory that has the same name as a command, so the FoxPro language is even less restrictive than the dBASE language.

The FoxPro language is full of surprises. All variables are global by default (that is, they're visible to the current and succeeding levels), but can be hidden to allow temporary local impostors. Arrays of variables are not monotyped. Each array element can be dynamically typed as independent of its fellows, as if it were a single variable. Each CASE in a DO CASE multiway branch has its own selector expression.

Over the years the Xbase language has evolved to support the advances in personal computer technology. The Xbase language evolved to support advances in user interface and event-driven technology. As information retrieval technology evolved, the data access evolved. Now, users can access data across multiple platforms, formats, and computers, utilizing a client/server environment. FoxPro was enhanced to support Microsoft ODBC (open database connectivity) to access data in a client/server environment. The bad news is that as Xbase becomes more complex and powerful, it also becomes more difficult to develop and maintain a complex application. The good news is that Visual FoxPro 3.0 introduces a new and advanced methodology for software design and development that makes programs easier to develop. FoxPro 3.0 introduces an *object-oriented programming* (OOP) model. OOP is introduced later in this chapter.

The Structure of a FoxPro Program

A FoxPro program is an ASCII file containing zero or more lines of text. You can join two or more physical lines into one logical line by ending all but the last line with a semicolon (;), which is the FoxPro line-continuation character.

```
program        ::= { logical line } (0 or more)
logical line   ::= <ASCII text> { ; <eol> logical line } <eol>
```

The previous notation uses *Backus-naur form (BNF)* and is described in Appendix B, "FoxPro Language Syntax." Each logical line can contain a single command verb, which can be followed by additional clauses and an end-of-line comment. You can freely intermix blank lines with lines containing commands. The `NOTE` and `*` commands begin comments that continue until the end of the logical line. The `&&` symbol starts a comment on a line already containing a command. If a comment starts on a line, continuing that line with the semicolon continues the comment as well.

With few exceptions, each command begins with a verb, such as `COPY`, `USE`, or `EDIT`. The syntax of each verb determines what clauses can follow the command verb on the line. The verb must be the first word on the line, but you may use spaces and tabs freely to lend structure to program listings. The two exceptions are the alternate forms of the `GOTO` and `STORE` commands. A numeric literal at the start of a line is an implied `GOTO` command, and an identifier followed by an equal sign (=) and an expression is an implied `STORE` command. For certain cases, you may omit the initial identifier. Other than these exceptions, a FoxPro command line always uses this form:

```
verb [ additional clauses ] [ && comment ] eol
```

Many verbs consist of two or three keywords, such as `DEFINE POPUP` or `SET ALTERNATE TO`. The clauses for any particular verb can occur in any order. In some cases, clauses can be repeated without causing any problem. Here's an example:

```
APPEND BLANK BEFORE BLANK BEFORE
```

FoxPro simply ignores duplicate clauses. Some commands, such as `ENDDO` and `ENDIF`, permit comments to follow them without the `&&` comment indicator. This inconsistency exists to retain compatibility with dBASE IV and may change in a future release. Likewise, dBASE IV programmers deliberately (and woefully) programmed dBASE IV to perpetrate this inconsistency to retain compatibility with dBASE III PLUS.

You can typically specify verb clauses and keywords, such as `FOR` *`condition`* or `TO` *`filename`*, in any order; so the following examples are identical to one another:

```
COPY TO "MyFile" ALL FOR Name = "Dvorak"
COPY ALL TO "MyFile" FOR Name = "Dvorak"
COPY FOR Name = "Dvorak" TO "MyFile" ALL
```

As a legacy of dBASE II's typing-intensive *dot prompt*, the FoxPro language has always allowed truncation of commands and other keywords to as few as four characters. For example, you can enter `DISPLAY` as `DISP`, `DISPL`, `DISPLA`, or `DISPLAY`, but the order of the characters must match the original command. (In this case, `DISPLY` is not recognized.) In other words, you can truncate, but you can't misspell.

Using the FoxPro Language

The FoxPro program makes it easy to use the FoxPro programming language as soon as the system is installed. When Visual FoxPro executes, it displays the FoxPro screen with an open Project Manager and a Command window, as shown in Figure 2.11.

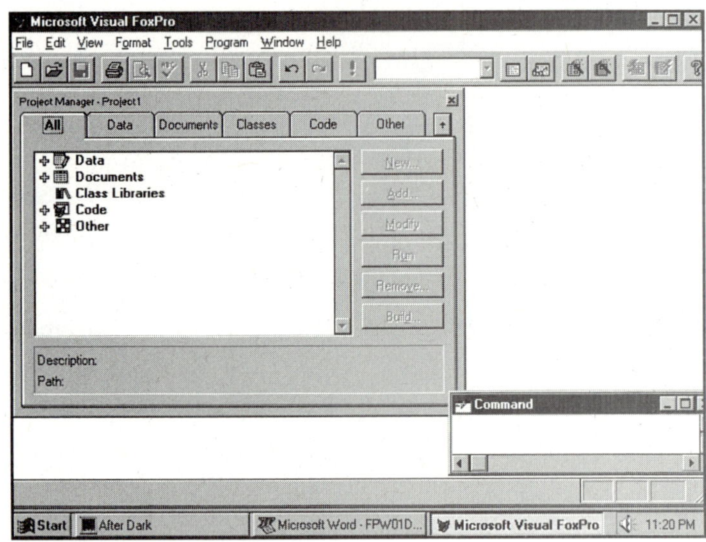

FIGURE 2.11.
The Visual FoxPro screen, with the Project Manager and the Command window.

You type a command into the Command window as follows:

```
DO <procedure>
```

and this runs any Visual FoxPro program. To create a program, either use a text editor before loading Visual FoxPro or invoke Visual FoxPro's built-in text editor by issuing this command:

```
MODIFY COMMAND <program name>
```

or select the Program Icon in the Project Manager's list and click on the **N**ew button.

To run a command as soon as FoxPro loads, you can add the command to the CONFIG.FPW configuration file. When FoxPro executes, the following CONFIG.FPW command executes:

```
COMMAND =  <command>
```

The FoxPro system not only includes a powerful program editor with mouse and menu support, but also a compiler; a debugger; Database, Table, View, Query, Report, Label, and Form Designers; and a complete set of wizards, as well as the Project Manager, which is used for linking and maintaining groups of FoxPro program files.

Object-Oriented Programming

Traditionally, Xbase programming involves writing one line of code after another to create a logical module that performs some action, combining logical modules to build an application, and focusing on the various actions that have to be performed by a program. However, in the real world, an application is composed of various forms, dialog boxes, push buttons, fields, and other objects. Each of these objects has certain properties and behaves in some manner. Object-oriented design involves breaking up a complex application into simple objects, defining the properties (position, size, color, and so forth) and behavior of each object, and programming an OOP application. For each object, you specify the properties and write procedural code to establish how the object operates or behaves. This code is called a *method* in OOP terminology. You can base (or *derive*) one object on another and use (or *inherit*) some or all of the properties of the derived object for the new object's applications, making it easier to visualize, develop, and maintain. Each object becomes a self-contained element of an application. Some properties and methods can be accessed from outside an object. Other properties and methods are *private* and can be accessed only from within an object.

In Visual FoxPro, visual objects—such as forms, dialog boxes, and controls—conform to an object-oriented model. You can create and maintain these objects through their properties, events, and methods. Since each object is a self-contained component of an application, your code that uses the object is simplified and the overall complexity of the application is reduced. In addition, objects can be reused in a current application or in other applications.

The Relationship Between a Class and an Object

Class is an object-oriented term that defines an object in the same way a set of house plans defines a house. A class is a blueprint of an object. First you define a class. Then you create an instance of an object from that class just as you would build a house from a set of house plans. (See Figure 2.12.)

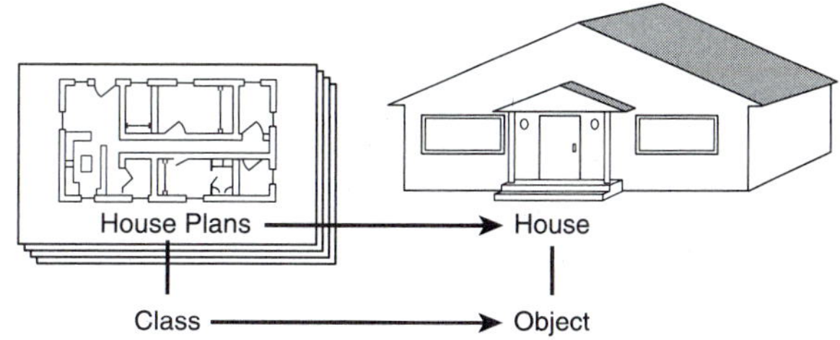

FIGURE 2.12.
Classes and objects.

Properties

Characteristics of an object are called *properties*. Properties determine attributes of an object, such as color, size, and position. For example, some of the properties of a Visual FoxPro push button include the following:

Property	*Description*
`Caption`	Text on button
`ForeColor`	Color of button text
`BackColor`	Background color
`Left,Top`	Position of top-left corner of push button
`Height`	Height of push button
`Width`	Width of push button

You establish values for the properties. You designate some properties when you design a form (*design time*). Other properties can be set when the form runs (*runtime*). But in either case, the object knows how to process the properties and how to display and manipulate the object in the desired manner.

Events and Methods

In traditional Xbase programming, you create an application with procedural code. You write code to define a set of controls and menus, as well as to anticipate whatever action is to be performed in response to user input. The problem is that applications are getting more complex, because customers want more power in their interface. The more code you write, the more complex the application gets. It becomes harder to code and maintain. Frankly, the traditional Xbase cannot compete with the modern interface standards. To meet this challenge, both Borland International and Microsoft have extended their Xbase language (dBASE 5.0 and Visual FoxPro) to support *event-driven* object-oriented language elements. With these extensions, objects can recognize various user or system initiated actions, called *events.* An event is an action such as a mouse click, mouse movement, or a timer expiring.

An object responds to the occurrence of an event by executing event-handling procedural code, called a *method.* Methods are associated with an object. A method differs from a traditional FoxPro procedure in that a method is tightly bound to an object. When you click a mouse, the method for handling an action associated with the event is called. An object also has methods that are not associated with events. These methods are explicitly called in the same manner as a FoxPro procedure is called.

So far, you have learned that an object is a self-contained (that is, *encapsulated*) unit that has properties and methods, and that can respond to events. Encapsulation is an important advantage of the object-oriented model. Once you have designed an object, all of its complexities are hidden within the object. For example, you can put a push button control object on a form and define all of its properties and methods. From then on, you do not have to concern yourself with managing its functionality.

Subclassing

You can define a class based on some existing class and add additional functionality and properties. The resulting class, called a *subclass*, benefits from all of the characteristics and functionality of the original class, plus any new functionality you have added. Using subclasses, you can reduce the amount of coding effort. In object-oriented terminology, the subclass is said to have *inherited* the characteristics and functionality of the base class. If you add any new features to the base class, all associated subclasses benefit from the new features.

For example, suppose that I want to build a house. I can hire an architect to draw the plans for the house from scratch. Alternatively, I can browse through a book containing pictures of a variety of houses. When I find one I like, I can obtain its plans. Then I can pay an architect to alter the plans to include any special requirements. I could add a deck or a new room. The original plans would correspond to a *base class,* and the plans for my house would correspond to a *subclass.* My plans are derived from the original plans, as shown in Figure 2.13.

FIGURE 2.13.
A subclass is derived from a class.

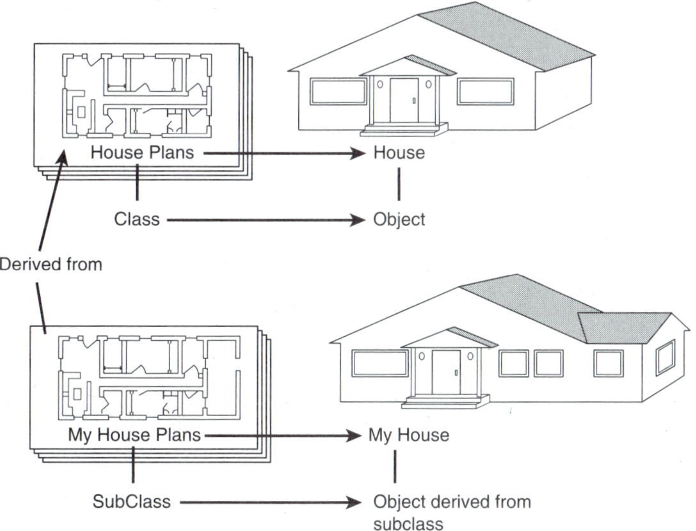

Visual FoxPro provides a built-in set of classes and subclasses arranged in a hierarchy structure (as shown in Figure 2.14) from which you can derive your own user-defined classes.

In Figure 2.14 you can see that there are *container* and *control* (or *noncontainer*) classes. Objects based on container classes can contain other objects and allow access to those objects. However, you do not have access to any of the internal elements of a control class. For example, a container form class can contain a couple push buttons (`ControlButtons`). You can access and manipulate the properties of each of the buttons within the form. However, you do not have access to any of the internal elements of the button. The control button is a self-contained or *encapsulated* system. Table 2.1 presents the types of objects that can be contained within a container class.

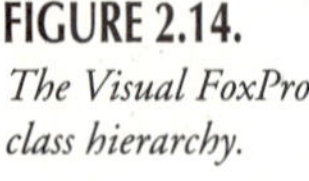

FIGURE 2.14.
The Visual FoxPro class hierarchy.

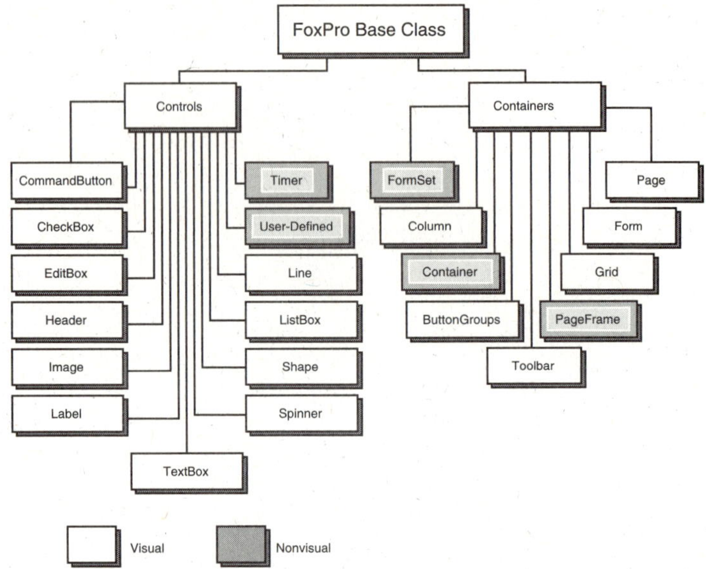

Table 2.1. Objects that can be contained within a containment class.

Container	*Can Contain*
FormSet	Forms
Forms	Page frames, any controls
PageFrame	Pages
Pages	Any controls
Toolbar	Any controls
Command button groups	Command buttons
Option button groups	Option buttons
Grids	Grid columns
Grid columns	Column headers, check boxes, combo boxes, command buttons, edit boxes, list boxes, option buttons, spinners, text boxes
User-defined objects	Any controls

The various Visual FoxPro objects are presented in Figure 2.15. This figure shows the powerful Visual FoxPro Form designer, which lets you drag and drop objects from a form to create a FormSet.

FIGURE 2.15.
Visual FoxPro objects.

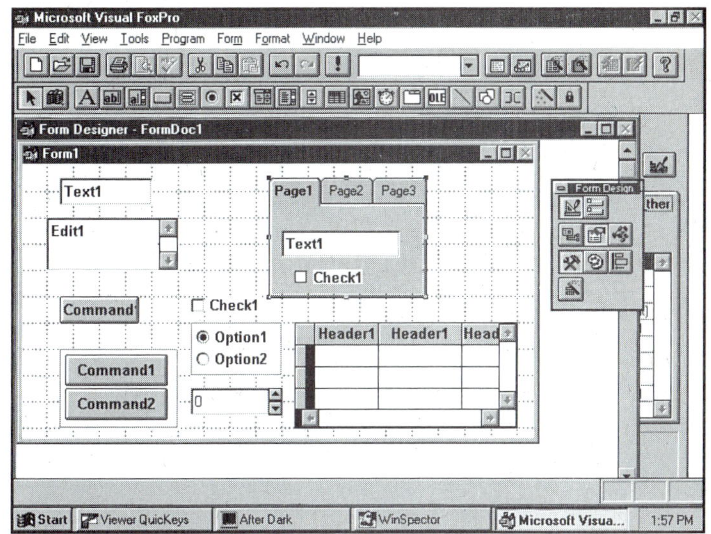

Think how difficult it would be to draw house plans and build a house if you had to design every object in the house, such as bathtubs, sinks, pipes, nails, and light fixtures. In reality, all you have to do is to specify fixtures that have already been designed and built in a factory somewhere. You specify the shape, size, and color of a bathtub and all the other objects. You design the bathroom container class, and each object in the bathroom (sink, bathtub, toilet, light figures, and so forth) is like a control object in that each is a self-contained unit. In fact, the house itself is a container object that contains a room's container objects.

Traditional Xbase programmers should not be discouraged by the new object-oriented approach introduced by Visual FoxPro. A new, powerful form designer makes it easy for you to create a variety of visual objects more advanced and powerful than you ever could with FoxPro 2.*x*. In addition, Visual FoxPro has a conversion feature that assists you in converting your old FoxPro 2.*x* forms to operate under the Visual FoxPro event-driven model. Furthermore, this model is genuinely modeless, which allows you to coordinate multiple simultaneously active forms easily.

Visual FoxPro classes and objects are presented in detail in subsequent chapters. Object-oriented language extensions are described in Chapter 14, "Object-Oriented Programming."

Summary

This chapter provided an overview of database management and Visual FoxPro language concepts. In addition, this chapter introduces you to the FoxPro language. You have learned that the FoxPro language has a lack of reserved words. You have learned about the basic command syntax, command truncation, and the & macro. You have learned how to operate the FoxPro product in the most basic sense, how to invoke it from the operating system, and how to call the built-in editor to create and modify programs written in the FoxPro programming language. You have also learned that Visual FoxPro contains object-oriented language extensions.

Academic research into database theory over the last 20 years has provided a lot of useful insight. Codd, Date, and many others have advanced the state of the art and given seed to real, but imperfect, implementations such as FoxPro. Although FoxPro advances toward the relational model with enhancements such as SQL commands, the target continues to move.

Works Cited

Codd, E. F. 1970. "A Relational Model of Data for Large Shared Data Banks," *Communications of the Association for Computing Machinery (ACM) 13* (6 June): 377-387.

———. 1972. *Data Base Systems Courant Computer Science Symposia Series,* Volume 6. Englewood Cliffs, N.J.: Prentice-Hall.

Date, C. J. 1973. *An Introduction to Database Systems,* Volume 1, Third Edition. Reading, Mass.: Addison-Wesley.

———. 1987. *A Guide to the SQL Standard.* Reading, Mass.: Addison-Wesley.

Fagin, R. 1977. "Multivalued Dependencies and a New Normal Form for Relational Databases." *ACM Transactions on Database Systems 2* 3 (September): 262-278.

Hubbard, George U. 1981. *Computer-Assisted Data Base Design.* New York: Van Nostrand Reinhold.

Knuth, Donald E. 1973. *The Art of Computer Programming, Volume 3: Sorting and Searching.* Reading, Mass.: Addison-Wesley.

Lacroix, M., and A. Pirotte. 1977. "Domain-Oriented Relational Languages." Proceedings of the 3rd International Conference on Very Large Data Bases (October).

Martin, James. 1977. *Computer Data-Base Organization.* Englewood Cliffs, N.J.: Prentice-Hall.

Zloof, M. M. 1975. "Query By Example." Proceedings of the NCC 44 (May).

3

The Referencing Environment

There are more things in heaven and earth, Horatio, than are dreamt of in your philosophy.

—William Shakespeare (1564–1616)

The following chapters describe the FoxPro commands. However, they don't tell the whole story. No command in the FoxPro language stands alone; every command is affected by the environment in which it is executed. Even the simple `?` command is affected by various printer settings and file redirection commands.

A wise man once said, "Be careful how you view your world, for that is how it is." The world in which FoxPro initially exists is defined by a file called CONFIG.FPW, manipulated by a myriad of `SET` commands, and further fine-tuned by various other contextual commands.

To work with Visual FoxPro is to manipulate the levers and knobs that are built into FoxPro: You define your world, then you live with it. FoxPro enables you to specify different colors for almost a dozen objects. You can choose a constant status readout or an on-screen clock that can display in 24-hour military format. You can also format dates and currency in many different ways.

You must request some FoxPro commands in a sequence to which the FoxPro documentation only alludes. For example, the `REPLACE` command updates data records, and the `USE` command makes DBF files accessible, but the `REPLACE` command can perform its delegated function only if a DBF file is available. Although the program prompts you to supply the name of a DBF file if none is available, it is best to place a `USE` command before the `REPLACE` command. For example, the `ACTIVATE` command is meaningful only after a `DEFINE` command. The `@...GET` command must come before a `READ` command, and the `DECLARE` command must precede any references to an array. You could say that the behavior of the `READ` command normally depends on the `@...GET` commands that set it up. The FoxPro language suffers from semantic overload—the effects of its actions depend on (and in turn control) the effects of other actions. For those of you that have never written a program in Xbase, don't be afraid if you do not understand what these commands do. The important thing is that you understand that many of the commands are interconnected.

When the environment is not strictly controlled, it's difficult for FoxPro language programmers to describe what their users should expect. For example, writing a manual for a software product is easiest when you can be sure what the screen will look like after a particular sequence of commands. If one user has `SET STATUS BAR ON` before running a program and another does not, the screen may look different to the two users. Likewise, `SET TALK`, `SET ODOMETER`, `SET DATE`, and `SET COLOR` change the display of otherwise identical FoxPro programs. Furthermore, the colors of the Visual FoxPro environment are initially determined by how the colors of the user's Windows environment are set. Normally the programmer would use `SET` commands at the beginning of a program to ensure that it always operates as intended.

The `SET COMPATIBILITY` command is one command that affects the operation of many FoxPro commands. Fox Software's primary goal was to provide the dBASE user community with a speedy alternative to Ashton-Tate's dBASE IV. To achieve this goal, Fox Software made FoxPro almost universally compatible with dBASE IV. In some circumstances, however, it was advantageous to modify the operation of a command to provide some additional capabilities.

To accomplish this, the `SET COMPATIBILITY` command was introduced to control the dBASE IV compatibility level. With the dBASE IV compatibility option set (`SET COMPATIBILITY DB4`), you can execute a program written for dBASE IV without making many changes. However, you can take advantage of the powerful FoxPro language extensions by turning off this option (`SET COMPATIBILITY OFF`). The `SET COMPATIBILITY` command alters the behavior of the commands and functions listed in Table 3.1.

Table 3.1. The commands and functions affected by the `SET COMPATIBILITY` command.

`ACTIVATE SCREEN`	`SET FIELDS`
`ACTIVATE WINDOW`	`SET MESSAGE`
`APPEND MEMO`	`STORE`
`GO/GOTO` and `SET TALK ON`	`SUM()` and `AVERAGE()`
`MENU` and `POPUP` commands	`INKEY()`
`PLAY MACRO`	`LASTKEY()`
`READ`	`LIKE()`
`RUN`	`SELECT()`
`SET COLOR TO`	`SYS(2001,"COLOR")`

You can also use the `SET COMPATIBILITY FOXPLUS` or `SET COMPATIBILITY OFF` command statements to alter the behavior of FoxPro commands so that they can run programs written specifically for FoxBASE+ and FoxPro.

Accessing Files

Some of FoxPro's built-in flexibility stems from the fact that it deals with all kinds of data files. Because all files are different—some contain text, some have data records in one form or another, this file has two million records, this one has two, and so on—FoxPro must be prepared for anything. Operating systems such as MS-DOS and Windows also permit wide latitude in the management of files and subdirectories.

File References

Windows maintains its own sense of which disk drive and subdirectory are current. It supports an environment variable called `PATH`, which defines what subdirectories to search for a given file. Rather than rely on Windows (and there are good reasons not to), FoxPro maintains its own default disk drive and file search path.

The SET DEFAULT and SET PATH commands affect every FoxPro command that opens a file, such as USE, OPEN DATABASE, DO *<program>*, and APPEND FROM. Functions that return filenames (such as the DBF(), CDX(), IDX(), and NDX() functions) can merely parrot the filename, or they can place it in the context of an absolute pathname and drive letter. The SET FULLPATH option determines the verbosity of functions that return filenames.

Many commands in FoxPro create new files—after all, FoxPro is a data file–manipulation language. What does the system do when a new file conflicts with an existing file of the same name? There are two options:

- Erase the existing file and remove the conflict.
- Ask the user if it's okay to erase the existing file.

The latter course is not necessarily better. Imagine a maintenance program with a long runtime that must be run overnight without operator supervision. Midway through the operation, the program encounters this existing file dilemma. Instead of finding results the next morning, the user encounters an on-screen error window (known as an *alert*) that asks the user if it's okay to destroy the existing file. The SET SAFETY command arbitrates between the "reckless overwriting" and the "easy does it" options.

In a multiuser environment, FoxPro automatically locks records and files to prevent users from clobbering each other's changes. It's safer to lock an entire file exclusively, but that makes the first user who accesses a file the winner and everyone else on the system the loser (until the first user is finished). The SET EXCLUSIVE command limits the amount of file sharing on a multiuser system. Likewise, SET LOCK determines whether an automatic lock should occur when a user is reading data only. For example, you can invoke the COUNT command to count records that match a defined criterion. Things go faster for everyone without the lock, but simultaneous updating of data records might invalidate the results of COUNT.

FoxPro reads files into memory, optionally modifies the data, and writes it back to the disk. For performance FoxPro often postpones writing modified data back to the disk in case more modifications occur. *Buffering*, as this technique is known, is a key method by which software improves its apparent speed. A single disk read or write is an expensive operation in terms of time relative to the speed of the CPU. MS-DOS automatically provides an uninformed type of buffering, but FoxPro performs much more extensive buffering whenever possible. FoxPro is prohibited from buffering in a multiuser situation because the nodes on a LAN cannot read each other's memory buffers; they must rely on the disk image of shared files. In addition, the SET AUTOSAVE command can cause FoxPro to cease buffering for safety purposes. Buffering is risky—if a power or media failure occurs, all changes waiting to be written to the disk are lost. SET AUTOSAVE OFF causes MS-DOS to cease buffering as well, and all disk writes are forced to the disk.

Tables (DBF Files)

A system that manages arbitrary data files depends somewhat on the idiosyncrasies of the data that it manipulates. In FoxPro, work areas control these vagaries (such as duplicate field names in different databases).

As mentioned in the previous chapter, a Visual FoxPro DBF file is a table with rows and columns. Each column has a name and is called a *field.* Each row is called a *record* and contains information relating to each field. Each field is defined by a set of *attributes.* The attributes of a field consist of its name, its width, and the data type that corresponds to the field. These are the 13 data types:

Character
Currency
Date
DateTime
Double
Numeric
Integer
Logical
Float
Memo
General
Character (binary)
Memo (binary)

General is used for Microsoft Windows object linking and embedding (OLE) objects such as pictures, documents, sound, graphics, and spreadsheets.

The *data structure* is the format of the table that defines the attributes for all the fields. The next section discusses FoxPro tables and their referencing environment.

Work Areas

At any time during a FoxPro session, only one *work area* is current. A work area is an environment that uses DBF files. Visual FoxPro provides 32767 work areas numbered from 1 to 32767. The actual number of work areas is limited by the amount of available virtual memory. In practice, you rarely need use more than half a dozen work areas. Work area 1 is the default. When a DBF file is in use in a particular work area, you can give that work area a symbolic name, or an *alias.*

The SELECT command specifies which work area is current. Many other commands support an IN clause that permits them to affect a work area that is not the current work area. In addition, many functions that return data from the current work area allow an optional work area specification. In FoxPro, it is often unnecessary to leave the default work area.

In each work area, a single DBF file is either in use or not in use. The USE command closes any existing file and then optionally opens another. The DBF file in use determines which variable names are fields and which are memory variables (or *memvars*) because DBF file fields temporarily "hide" any memvars by the same name. (For more information, see Chapter 4, "Variables.") Therefore, closing the current DBF file changes the semantics of a simple variable reference.

For example, suppose you have a memvar named LASTNAME:

Command Window	*Results*
`? LASTNAME, "is the memvar"`	`Dilbert is the memvar`

Then suppose you place a DBF file called ADDRESSES in use, which contains a data field called LASTNAME. The data field "hides" the memvar:

Command Window	*Results*
`USE ADDRESS`	
`? LASTNAME, "is a data field"`	`Smith is a data field`

As you will learn in Chapter 5, "Expressions," you can still reference a memvar by adding M. (or M->) to the name:

Command Window	*Results*
`? LASTNAME, M.LASTNAME`	
`LASTNAME = "Dilbert"`	`Smith Dilbert`

In this example Smith is a data field, and Dilbert is a memvar.

When a DBF file is in use, exactly one record is the current record. This may be any record number from 1 to the number of records plus 1. (Notice that for an empty DBF file, record 1 is the number of records plus 1.) Changing the current record is an indirect yet effective way to simultaneously change the value of all field variables. The GOTO command sets the current record number. Various commands are positioned to the first, last, next, or previous record. You can specify an ordering index that gives these relative positions a different meaning. The first record is always record 1 when no index is active, but the first record in index order depends on the index expression as well as the data found in the DBF file.

The semantics of record-positioning commands, such as GOTO and SKIP, are profoundly affected by the SET RELATION and SET SKIP commands. SET RELATION establishes a link between open DBF files in two or more work areas such that repositioning the current work area causes repositioning of related work areas, as well. SET SKIP, which works with SET RELATION, may not even reposition the current work area. A command to skip to the next record in the current work area is ignored if the next record in a related work area has the same linkage key and SET SKIP is ON. Imagine issuing a SKIP command and remaining on the same record in the current work area:

Command Window	*Results*
USE Foo	
USE Bill INDEX BillName IN 2	
SET RELATION TO Name INTO Bill	
SET SKIP TO Bill	
GOTO TOP	
? RECNO()	1
SKIP	
? RECNO()	1

Chapter 11, "DBF Files and Databases," presents the details of SET RELATION and SET SKIP.

Visual FoxPro supports a maximum of 32767 work areas. You can refer to work areas by number (1 to 32767) or by name (the ALIAS clause of the USE command or the root filename if no alias is specified). You can also refer to the first 10 work areas with the single letters A through J. You might wonder why the letters stop at the letter J. Obviously that scheme would not work with an Xbase program that supports more than 26 work areas. How would you refer to work area 27?

Not so obviously, however, a conflict would arise with the memvar disambiguator: Many FoxPro programs use M->name (or M.Name) to explicitly refer to a memory variable. The work area letters A through J are still supported to retain compatibility with dBASE. However, no other letters are supported. Simply stated, K is not work area 11. This is typical of the compatibility problems endemic to FoxPro's requirement for retaining comparability with dBASE III and IV. Notice that dBASE IV Version 1.5 released by Borland International supports 40 work areas. Like FoxPro, dBASE IV Version 1.5 supports only work area letters A through J for compatibility reasons.

Every limitation in FoxPro, no matter how reasonable it seems to the designers, eventually becomes an irritating restriction to some users. The wish list is full of requests for such things as more fields per table or more characters in a field name. Likewise, many users have expressed a desire to keep more than 26 tables open at a time.

Records

DBF file records may not be visible in the current referencing environment. Commands such as `SET DELETED` and `SET FILTER` limit the visible records to those not marked for deletion and for which a filter expression evaluates to `.T.`.

When you create indexes with the `INDEX` or `REINDEX` commands, the `SET UNIQUE` setting decides whether duplicate keys are added to the index. If `SET UNIQUE` is `ON`, duplicate keys are not added to the index. This hides records with duplicate index keys. If `SET UNIQUE` is `OFF`, all keys are added to the index.

The `SET NEAR` command affects what happens when an index is used to find a record that contains a particular key value and the key is not in the index. If `SET NEAR` is `ON`, the DBF file is positioned to the record with the nearest key after the desired key. If `SET NEAR` is `OFF`, however, and a key is not found, the DBF file is positioned at one record past the last record. In other words, the DBF file is positioned at the end of the file.

The current record affects the values of field variables; several commands and entities, such as indexes, affect the current record. The interaction between these elements is complex, yet comprehensible, and is explored in subsequent chapters.

Fields List

Every DBF file in each work area makes some field variables available to the referencing environment. Prior to FoxPro 2.6, like dBASE III PLUS, FoxPro supports the concept of a different field list for each work area that the `SET FIELDS` command establishes and manipulates. (dBASE IV and FoxPro 2.6 or later versions support the concept of one integrated fields list.)

When such a list is active, only the specified fields are visible. The `SET FIELDS` command and the `ADDITIVE` keyword add fields to the list. `SET FIELDS TO ALL` adds all the fields in the current work area to the list for a work area. `SET FIELDS TO` removes the fields from the list for the current work area. Using the `CLEAR FIELDS` command removes the restricted fields list and is essentially the same as performing a `SET FIELDS TO ALL` command in every work area.

In dBASE IV and FoxPro 2.6 or later, you can add calculated fields and read-only fields to the field list. You can also specify a wildcard specification of fields. Refer to Chapter 10, "Environment," for more information regarding the `SET FIELDS` command.

Some commands support a `FIELD` clause used to specify a fields list. Only the fields in the field list are operated on. For example, the following command copies all of the records in the current table to `newfile`. However, only fields `Name` and `Address` are copied:

```
COPY FIELDS Name,Address TO newfile
```

The following commands support a fields list:

```
APPEND FROM                  CREATE SCREEN
APPEND FROM ARRAY            DISPLAY
BLANK                        EXPORT
COPY STRUCTURE               GATHER
COPY STRUCTURE EXTENDED      JOIN
COPY TO                      LIST
COPY TO ARRAY                SCATTER
CREATE REPORT                SORTTOTAL
```

Memo Fields

Memo fields are a special case of variable-length character data. Because they are expected to be longer than the maximum character field of 254 and because their field width is not fixed as it is for other fields, memo fields are displayed on one or more lines, broken on word boundaries (word wrapped). For columnar reports, the `SET MEMOWIDTH` command enables the programmer to establish the width for a single line of a memo field display. The default is 50, but values from 8 to 255 are acceptable.

The `MEMLINES()` and `MLINE()` functions depend on the setting of `SET MEMOWIDTH`. `MEMLINES()` returns the number of lines that a memo would need to display at the current `MEMOWIDTH`. `MLINE()` returns a line from a memo field. Suppose that a particular memo field called `Sermon` in the current record contains some text (Strunk and White 1979).

If `MEMOWIDTH` is 50 and you display a memo field with the following command:

```
? Sermon
```

the screen displays this:

```
Vigorous writing is concise. A sentence should
contain no unnecessary words, a paragraph no
unnecessary sentences, for the same reason that a
drawing should have no unnecessary lines and a
machine no unnecessary parts.
```

On the other hand, if `MEMOWIDTH` is set to 12, this appears:

```
Vigorous
writing is
concise.
A sentence
should
contain
no
```

```
unnecessary
words, a
paragraph no
unnecessary
sentences,
for the same
reason that
a drawing
should have
no
unnecessary
lines and a
machine no
unnecessary
parts.
```

Although the contents of the `Sermon` memo field do not change, the visual aspect changes dramatically. The `MEMLINES()` function would return 5 in the former case and 22 in the latter case, and the value of `MLINE(4)` would be either "drawing should have no unnecessary lines and a" or "A sentence," depending solely on the setting of `MEMOWIDTH`. Clearly, when it comes to memo fields, the `MEMOWIDTH` aspect of the referencing environment matters greatly.

Database Files

The Project Manager introduced the concept of using a database (DBC) file to organize and relate tables in an application. It is used to keep track of all tables (DBF files), columns (fields), indexes, relations, and stored procedures in an application. The Visual FoxPro database file persistently maintains the relationship between tables, stored procedures, field and record-level rules, and triggers. It also maintains local and remote views. You create local and remote views with the View Designer.

You can create and utilize a new Visual FoxPro database using the `CREATE DATABASE` command. You can place and use an existing database with the `OPEN DATABASE` command. Once a database is in use, you can add tables to it with the `ADD TABLE` command or the `CREATE` command. A table not included in any database is called a *free table.* You can operate on a free table as you would with dBASE or previous versions of FoxPro. A table that has been added to a Visual FoxPro database becomes closely associated with that database. Tables added to a database can have additional properties that free tables cannot have. These properties support features such as field- and record-level rules and triggers, which support data entry and modification validation. Consequently, once you add a table to a database, it becomes a read-only file when the database is not active. This preserves the integrity of the data in the database.

A detailed discussion of Visual FoxPro databases is provided in Chapter 11.

Views and Queries

Visual FoxPro includes a Query Designer (fully described in Chapter 18, "Queries Using SQL and the Query Designer") to create views and queries. A *view* is a logical DBF file composed of one or more real DBF files, combined with SET RELATION commands, and possibly restricted by SET FILTER and other commands. The Query Designer creates a QBE or QPR file of FoxPro language commands that establishes the referencing environment by opening DBF files in different work areas, establishing relations between them, setting filters on the data, and so forth. The commands that enter the Query Designer are the following:

```
CREATE QUERY
MODIFY QUERY
```

You can establish a referencing environment by opening tables in various work areas, issuing various SET commands, and then requesting

```
CREATE VIEW <vue file> FROM ENVIRONMENT
```

After such a VUE file has been created, the SET VIEW TO command reestablishes it. The Query and View Designers are much more flexible, however.

In Visual FoxPro, you can create a view which is stored in a database container (DBC) file. If a database is open, you can execute the View Designer from the File Menu or by executing the following commands:

```
CREATE VIEW
MODIFY VIEW
```

This executes the Visual FoxPro View Designer which is just like the Query Designer except that it stores the query information in the database container file. Also, you can have access data from local or remote tables.

Input and Output

You have seen several examples of environmental settings that affect the FoxPro screen display. This makes it difficult for applications programmers to predict how their programs will look to an end user. This section describes settings that change the way data is entered and displayed.

Data Entry

Standard data entry in FoxPro is done with the APPEND or INSERT commands or with the Append mode of the CHANGE, EDIT, or BROWSE commands. By default these commands present a linear list of fields, identified by field name. The default display is utilitarian and offers no visual cues or organizational help to the person who performs data entry. Naturally, FoxPro offers an alternative. You can create forms by hand or by using the Form Designer (described in Chapter 19, "The Form Designer"). The `DO FORM` command is used to customize data entry forms to replace the lackluster default form.

The `SET FORMAT` command can alter the effect of commands such as `APPEND`, `BROWSE`, or `EDIT` by leaving out some fields and adding others, applying data validation and extra formatting, and changing colors and drawing lines and boxes on-screen.

The `SET CARRY` command further affects the appending of new records and enables you to specify fields with data that carries over from one record to the next. The default value for newly appended fields is all spaces, but if `SET CARRY` is `ON` or a field is specified in the `SET CARRY TO` list, then the previous value of the field is copied to the new record as a default value and is ready for modification.

Data entry fields are typically presented in a designed color scheme, but like nearly every other visual aspect of FoxPro, they can be changed. You can use the `SET COLOR` command to change the colors of any object, including the color of data entry fields.

Generally, typing more characters than will fit in a given data entry field simply advances the cursor to the next field in sequence. This can be a timesaving aid, such as for single-character fields. However, this also makes it easy to press two keys at once and enter the wrong data. In situations like this, the `SET CONFIRM` command forces the user to press Enter to move from field to data entry field on a form.

To edit a memo field, the FoxPro user can zoom into the memo editor by either double-clicking on the memo icon or moving the cursor to the memo icon and pressing Ctrl+Home.

Chapter 8, "Input and Output," and Chapter 9, "Full-Screen Data Editing," contain more information about data entry commands.

Output

FoxPro has two distinct output subsystems, and different environmental considerations affect each of them. The first subsystem consists of the `?`, `??`, `DISPLAY`, and `LIST` commands. The second subsystem contains `@...SAY`.

The `SET PRINTER TO` command specifies printer parameters or which shared network output device to use. With the `SET PRINTER TO FILE` command, you can specify a filename to which printer output should be directed. `SET PRINTER ON` directs all output from `?`, `DISPLAY`, and all other non-`@...SAY` sources to the printer in addition to wherever it was originally going. The `SET CONSOLE` command determines whether such output is displayed on-screen. The commands `SET PRINTER ON` and `SET CONSOLE OFF` send ordinary output to the printer and not to the screen. FoxPro defaults to the opposite configuration. The `SET ALTERNATE` command saves all non-`@...SAY` output in a text file, approximately the same as the commands `SET PRINTER TO FILE <filename>` and `SET PRINTER ON`.

All printer output is affected by the choice of a printer driver, most of the other print-system memvars, and the SET MARGIN command.

The result of @...SAY commands is redirected with this command:

```
SET DEVICE TO SCREEN ¦ PRINTER ¦ FILE <filename>
```

Unlike output in the other output subsystem, @...SAY output cannot be directed to more than one device at a time.

The DISPLAY and LIST commands are affected by the SET HEADING command and the undocumented SET LABEL command. SET HEADING OFF suppresses the field names ordinarily printed by the AVERAGE, CALCULATE, SUM, DISPLAY, or LIST commands. The SET SPACE command allows the ? command to omit the space that it generally inserts between the data items it displays.

Windows

Logical windows (described in detail in Chapter 7, "FoxPro Language Elements for Creating Windows and Menu Systems") profoundly affect many other FoxPro commands because they limit the available screen area, and conversely, allow the display outside the window to remain static while they scroll.

The Command Execution Environment

Many commands can affect the referencing environment of other commands. Certain SET commands affect the way other commands operate. The following subsections describe how set commands affect the execution environment.

String Comparisons

The SET EXACT command affects string comparisons. Here is an example:

Command Window	*Results*
SET EXACT OFF	
? "William" = "Will"	.F.
SET EXACT ON	
? "William" = "Will"	.T.

Event Trapping

Another aspect of the referencing environment is Visual FoxPro's capability to trap events, such as errors, keystrokes, or printer page ejections. If an error occurs and an ON ERROR <command> statement was previously executed, the system executes the specified command, which is typically a branch to an error-handling subroutine. If an ON ERROR statement is not provided, the system handles the error by displaying a dialog box. Alternatively, if `SET TRAP` is `ON`, an error or an Esc keypress invokes the Visual FoxPro debugger.

You can establish event trapping by executing a command such as `ON ERROR` or `ON PAGE`. Deliberate errors and commands such as `EJECT PAGE` trigger events for which event trapping has been established. For a further discussion of trapping events, see Chapter 6, "Control Flow."

Event trapping has been expanded in Visual FoxPro to the extent that you can simultaneously perform total modeless operations on multiple instances of multiple forms. Events are triggered automatically in response to some user or system action. When an event is triggered, a method associated with some object executes to perform some appropriate operation. The core set of events supported by controls in Visual FoxPro are presented in Table 3.2.

Table 3.2. The Visual FoxPro core event set.

Event	*When Is This Event Triggered?*
`Load`	Form or FormSet is loaded into memory.
`Unload`	Form or FormSet is released from memory.
`Init`	Object is created.
`Destroy`	Object is released from memory.
`Click`	User clicks on object.
`DblClick`	User double-clicks on object.
`GotFocus`	Object receives focus as a result of either user clicking on or tabbing to object or a programmatic control.
`LostFocus`	Object loses focus.
`KeyPress`	User presses and releases keyboard key.
`MouseDown`	User presses mouse button while mouse pointer is over object.
`MouseUp`	User releases mouse button while mouse pointer is over object.
`InteractiveChange`	Value of object is changed by user interaction.
`ProgrammaticChange`	Value of object is changed by programmatic control.

Program Development

Several environmental settings affect the line-by-line behavior of FoxPro programs. `SET TALK` and `SET ECHO` establish the verbosity of a FoxPro program. When `SET TALK` is `ON`, the results of commands are displayed on-screen:

Command Window	*Results*
SET TALK OFF	
A = 123	
SET TALK ON	
A = 123	123

The SET STEP and SET ECHO commands open the Trace window for debugging. You can debug your program by stepping through it a line at a time while you view the results on-screen, watch the lines of code being executed in the Trace window, and view values of program variables during execution in the Debug window. You can set breakpoints so that the program executes until it reaches a certain line of code, and then pauses. Chapter 23, "Building Visual FoxPro Applications," describes this powerful debugging tool more fully.

When the DO command executes a program, FoxPro searches for an FXP file. If no FXP file exists, the PRG file is automatically compiled and an FXP file is created. If SET DEVELOPMENT is ON, then the DO command will automatically recompile a PRG file that has been modified more recently than the FXP file with the same name.

Save and Restore Your Environment

If you execute FoxPro and run a single application during the session, you don't need to worry about any changes you make to the FoxPro environment. However, if your customer runs multiple FoxPro applications during a session, you need to save the environment at the beginning of your program and restore it at the end. This way you can designate your own working environment without interfering with the operation of other applications. If all the programs a user works with during a session are designed to change only a standard subset of the settings, you need to save and restore only that subset of settings. The following example, which saves and restores the SET TALK setting, illustrates the procedure for saving and restoring parameters:

```
SaveTalk = SET("talk")    && Fetch current SET TALK setting
IF SaveTalk = "ON"        && Is TALK ON?
   SET TALK OFF           && If so, turn it OFF
ENDIF
&& Your program goes here

SET TALK &SaveTalk        && Set it back to the way it was
RETURN
```

However, if you want to guarantee that no other program has altered the environment in a way that causes your program to malfunction, you can save and restore the current values of all the environmental settings.

Summary

This chapter briefly introduces Visual FoxPro 3.0 commands that are described more fully in the chapters that follow. At this point the detailed syntax and function of the FoxPro commands are not important. What is important is that you've learned in this chapter that commands are highly interrelated and often depend profoundly on the commands that precede them.

Work Cited

Strunk, William Jr., and E. B. White. 1979. *The Elements of Style*, Third Edition. New York: Macmillan Publishing Co., Inc.

II

The Visual FoxPro Language

Variables

That mysterious independent variable of political calculation, Public Opinion.

—Thomas Henry Huxley (1825–1895)

Variables represent the information a programming language can manipulate. *Expressions*, described in Chapter 5, "Expressions," are composed of operators (such as + or -) and functions, both of which act on operands.

Operands can be literal constants (such as `123` or `"Hello"`) or references to data objects called *scalar variables.* A programmer-assigned name (called an *identifier*) symbolically refers to these data objects. Almost every programming language includes scalar variables—so named because the range of possible values is in linear order, such as a number line. An imaginary pointer somewhere along this scale represents the current value of the variable.

The FoxPro language provides two types of scalar variables: fields and memory variables. Memory variables are also called *memvars.* Fields are the building blocks of DBF files; they store the data to be managed. Memvars are less permanent and, therefore, are more like variables in a traditional programming language such as Pascal. Although you can save them in a file, memvars are generally created when a FoxPro program is executed and disappear when the program is finished.

Memvars in FoxPro are similar to atoms in LISP (list processing language) in that they are both dynamically typed. *Dynamic typing* means that the type is assigned during program execution when a variable is created. This feature gives FoxPro an almost unintentional object-oriented flavor. FoxPro is also similar to BASIC in that derived or aggregate types (such as the `record` in Pascal or the `struct` in C) are not supported. Of course you can view DBF files as aggregate types themselves.

FoxPro supports arrays of memvars. Unlike arrays in traditional languages, however, each element in a FoxPro array is independently allocated and typed. You must declare arrays before you use them, but only to establish the size of the array, not the types of its elements.

In FoxPro you never declare the type of any variable. Although FoxPro is a strongly typed language like Pascal, it is also dynamically typed like LISP. In a more typeless language, such as HyperTalk, character strings are automatically converted to numbers when necessary. (HyperTalk is the script language for Apple Computer's HyperCard.) In the FoxPro language, the variable's current type must be appropriate for the context in which it is used, but it can be easily changed during program execution.

Data Object Attributes

Every data object, whether a field or a memvar, has certain attributes, including the following:

- An identifier (the name of the object)
- A type (such as Character or Number)
- A value (the current contents)
- A width (the number of characters in a value or the desired display width and number of decimals for numeric values)

Because the most important data objects are stored in DBF files, which are essentially unknown until runtime, the FoxPro language must be prepared for a change in an identifier's attributes while a program is executing. A field called `Name` in one DBF file might be a true-or-false field, while `Name` in another DBF file might refer to a character string. A FoxPro program such as the following must be prepared for all possible cases:

```
ACCEPT "Enter filename: " TO fname
USE (fname)
? Name
```

You won't know the attributes (particularly the type) of the DBF Name file field until the DBF file is put to use, and you won't know the name of the DBF file until the program has executed.

Memvars are similar to DBF file fields, but they have slightly different properties. Fields have a fixed width and type in the context of a particular DBF file. (Fields of the Memo and General type are a special case and are described later in this chapter.) Fields also have *permanence,* which means that their values survive between invocations of a program. The value of a field further depends on the current record of the DBF file at the time it is queried.

In contrast, memvars are *scratchpad* variables, with a life span equal to the time it takes a program or program block to execute. The width and type of a memvar is adjustable, based on its value. Memvars can be stored in a special memvar file and thus may be considered permanent, but their permanence is not inherent as is that of fields.

You can change the value of a field by using the `REPLACE` command or by editing the field with `@...GET`, `BROWSE`, or `EDIT`. You can easily change memvar values and types with the `STORE` command or with commands that automatically create memvars, such as `ACCEPT` or `CALCULATE`.

Identifiers

Programming language statements have three distinguishing features: semantic (what a statement does), syntactical (how statements are formed), and lexical (rules by which elements of the syntax, such as identifiers, are formed). *Identifiers* in the FoxPro language are subject to the following lexical rules:

- Identifiers may be any number of characters, but only the first 10 are significant.
- Identifiers must start with an alphabetic character.
- Identifiers may consist of alphabetic characters, numeric characters, or underscore characters (_).

Case is not significant: `Name` is the same as `NAME` or `nAmE`. Some languages, such as BASIC, include type-specifier characters in the syntax of the identifier. That is, `A$` refers to a character string called `"A"`, and `A%` refers to an integer variable called `"A"`. This system is not useful for FoxPro, however, because FoxPro is dynamically typed.

Furthermore, many languages specify that keywords from the language (such as `COUNT`, `USE`, `FOR`, and `TO`) may not be used as identifiers. The FoxPro language does not have such a list of reserved words, but perhaps it should. You should not use FoxPro keywords as identifiers because this may cause confusion. For example, phenomenally, the following code does not cause an error; however, it is confusing and not very readable:

```
use index
index on name to index
USE index index index
```

Code that isn't readable is bad because you cannot easily maintain it.

If FoxPro reserved keywords, the list would be quite long. Remember that you can truncate keywords to as few as four characters. Therefore, an identifier called `DECLARE` could be mistaken for the `DECL`, `DECLA`, or `DECLAR` keywords.

A special class of memvars (called *system memvars*) is used to hold system variables that contain information such as the number of copies the next report should print. You can identify system memvars by a leading underscore (for example, `_pcopies`). It's possible for users to create identifiers with leading underscores; however, you should avoid this practice because it could result in a conflict. Also, you can use system memvars in the same way you use ordinary memvars; however, because they are predefined by FoxPro, the type attribute of a system memvar is fixed. Here is an example:

```
numcopy = 2    && create type N memvar called numcopy
_pcopies = 2   && assign value to existing system memvar
```

Both are correct because `_pcopies` is of type N. But an assignment like the following is valid only for ordinary memvars:

```
numcopy = "Hello"    && change type of memvar to C
_pcopies = "Howdy"   && error-cannot change type to C
```

The lexical rules described in this section apply to all identifiers—both field and memvar names. Restricting filenames to alphabetic characters, numbers, and underscores (but limited to 8 characters, not 10) is recommended, but not strictly necessary.

Data Types

Every data object has a data type associated with it. As discussed in the preceding section, the type of a memvar may change during program execution, but at any instant the object of an identifier has only one type. FoxPro recognizes the following types:

A	Array (not accessible by users)
B	Double
C	Character
D	Date

F	Float
G	General
I	Integer
L	Logical
M	Memo
N	Numeric
P	Picture
T	DateTime
Y	Currency

The letters in the previous list are the characters used to represent the variable type in Visual FoxPro. For example, you can display memory variables with the `DISPLAY MEMORY` command. The letter appears in the list to indicate the type.

A data object's type determines the domain of values that the object may assume. The semantics of the program or built-in constraints added to a data entry form may impose further restrictions on this domain.

Character

A Character type object is a string of 0 to 254 characters from the ASCII character set. The characters denoted by binary 0 (null) and 26 (Ctrl+Z) should not be used. In certain cases, using these characters results in data loss. Ordinarily, character variables store names, addresses, and other simple text.

NOTE

In Visual FoxPro, the length of a record can be 65500 characters. That means you can have more wide character fields. In most Xbase dialects, the record length is limited to 4000 characters. Although you can have a maximum of 255 fields, the maximum of 4000 characters per record accommodates only 15 254-byte character data type fields.

Normally a well-designed database structure does not contain many wide fields. Too many wide character fields take up a lot of memory and reduce processing speed.

Date

A Date data type variable is used to hold a calendar date. Dates are stored internally as numbers, and an imaginary date such as `02/31/95` is automatically converted to `03/03/95` when it is assigned.

DateTime

A DateTime data type variable is used to hold a calendar date and time. A date-time value is stored internally as a number. However, it displays in the form `03/03/95 03:23:33 am`. This data type was introduced in Visual FoxPro 3.

Float and Numeric

Float and Numeric numbers are stored in a binary floating-point representation, which is described by the Institute of Electrical and Electronics Engineers (IEEE) as a long real binary format. Eight bytes of memory are required for each number. In a table, it can require up to 20 characters since Float and Numeric data types are stored as ASCII values in a table.

In dBASE IV, Ashton-Tate solved the round-off error problem by changing the way that Numeric (Type `N`) numbers were represented in memory. They are stored using *binary coded decimal (BCD)*, a representation that is immune to the round-off errors common to floating-point numbers. Ashton-Tate recommended use of this type of numeric representation for accounting applications. The Float (type `F`) data type was introduced in dBASE IV and was simply the binary floating-point number representation used in previous versions of dBASE. Calculations such as transcendental functions (`SIN()`, `COS()`, and so forth) are slightly faster in dBASE IV using binary floating-point arithmetic.

In order to be compatible with dBASE IV, Fox Systems added the Float data type to FoxPro. However, both type N and F numbers use identical numeric representation in memory and use the same internal arithmetic operations. Although there is no difference, the FoxPro user documentation recommends that Numeric data types be used for accounting applications and Float data types be used for scientific applications.

The value of a Float or Numeric data type can vary from –.9999999999E+19 to .9999999999E+20.

Double

A Double data type is a more accurate numeric value than a Numeric data type. It is normally used for scientific calculations. It requires 8 bytes of storage space in a table and in memory. The value is stored as a double-precision binary, floating-point number. Its value can range from `+/-4.94065645841247E-324` to `+/-1.79769313486232E308`.

Integer

An Integer data object is used for nondecimal numeric values. An integer field data type value is stored in a table as a 4-byte binary value so it requires less memory and disk space than other Numeric data types. Note that Numeric data types are stored as ASCII values. You gain improved performance when you use an Integer data object because there is no data conversion, and 32-bit integer arithmetic is much faster than floating-point arithmetic.

The Integer data type value is a 4-byte integer. It can have a range from –2,147,483,647 to 2,147,483,647 (2^{31}–1).

Logical

A Logical data object may have one of the following characters as its value:

`<space>, T, t, F, f, Y, y, N, n`

NOTE

Unlike commands and keywords, these letters are translated into foreign languages. For example, in Spanish, `Yes` and `No` are `Sí` and `No`, so the letters `S` and `N` are substituted.

Memo

Only fields can be of the Memo type. This type is actually a reference link to a variable-length stream of bytes in an associated file with the .FPT extension. Memo fields can contain any series of bytes up to 2 billion characters long. You can store any MS-DOS file in a field of a Memo type for later retrieval. More commonly, memo fields store text that exceeds the 254-character limit imposed on Character type fields. FoxPro can operate on dBASE III and FoxBASE+ memo files, which are stored in a file with a .DBT extension. FoxPro reads and writes the older form of the memo fields in their original (DBT) format so that they can be read later with FoxBASE+ or dBASE III or IV.

If you have a FoxPro table (DBF file) containing memo fields (FPT memo file), you can convert it to a FoxBASE+ table (with a DBT memo file) using the `COPY TO <filename> FOXPLUS` command.

There is a special type of Memo field type that is specially designed to contain binary data.

Number

As collections of fields, DBF files provide for the FoxPro programming language what structures provide for C or what records provide for Pascal. Other than this, FoxPro does not support aggregate types. The FoxPro language does not support user-defined types either. Such derived types are often a more restricted domain of an otherwise simple type. The FoxPro language supports this concept with the tools it provides for designing data entry forms. Sets, or enumerated types, are supported by the `PICTURE` clause of the `@...GET` command, for example. For more information, see Chapter 9, "Full-Screen Data Editing."

General

The General data type resembles a memo field, but it's used to support Microsoft OLE (object linking and embedding). General data type fields are also stored in the allocated FPT memo file, which contains any type of linked or embedded objects. You can link or embed any text, picture, sound, spreadsheet, or other object created by applications that provide OLE server support for General data type fields.

While in an external application, you can use the **E**dit menu **C**opy option to copy an OLE object to the Clipboard. Then you can use the FoxPro **E**dit menu **P**aste (or Paste **S**pecial) option to insert the object from the Clipboard into a General data type field.

Currency

The Currency data type, introduced in Visual FoxPro, should be used for specifying monetary values instead of the Numeric data type for two reasons. First, a Currency data type is stored in the field as an 8-byte binary, floating-point number. Therefore, a conversion from ASCII to a numeric value is not required, and consequently performance is improved. Second, Currency data type values are rounded to four decimal places before they are used in an expression. This provides better accuracy in monetary calculations. You can store a currency memory variable by preceding the constant number with a dollar sign (`$`). DBF fields and memory variables can be the Currency data type. Here's an example:

```
value = $23456.3345667
```

This number is stored internally as 23456.3346.

Dynamic Typing

As I've discussed, you cannot know the type of a FoxPro identifier at compile time. The FoxPro language does not require, and indeed has no mechanism for, declaring variables before they are used. (The `DECLARE` command is provided to specify the number of elements in an array, not the type of the elements.) FoxPro can manage several data tables with columns that share the same names, but not necessarily the same attributes. Because memvars are extensions of the field concept, they are dynamically typed as well. The following is an example of perfectly legal FoxPro syntax:

Command Window	*Results*
`STORE "Hello" TO A`	(Type is `C`)
`STORE 123.45 TO A`	(Contents replaced with type `N`)
`USE "Test"`	(Includes logical field `A`)
`? A`	`.T.`
`USE`	(Close file Test)
`? A`	`123.45`

Life Span

FoxPro variables that serve as fields in DBF files are active only while their DBF file is in use. This feature makes FoxPro different from other programming languages in which the scope of variables is confined to program blocks or modules. You can easily write FoxPro programs that are flexible enough to open any random DBF file and display its contents, but this flexibility has a price: It's more difficult to write an efficient compiler for a language with largely unknown variables.

Variables that are memvars behave more like variables in conventional languages, but you cannot always determine at compile time which variables are fields and which are memvars. The life of a memvar lasts until

- The FoxPro session is ended with the `QUIT` command
- The program level on which the memvar was created returns (except for `PUBLIC` memvars)
- The user explicitly releases the memvar

The life span of system memvars is the duration of the FoxPro session. System memvars are created with default values when FoxPro is first executed, may be modified initially with settings found in the CONFIG.FPW file, and exist until you execute the `QUIT` command.

Operations with Memvars

As I've mentioned before, the FoxPro language provides two types of data objects: fields and memvars. Operations with fields are more restricted than operations with memvars and are discussed more fully in Chapter 11, "DBF Files and Databases."

This section describes several FoxPro commands that act on memvars. Several commands automatically create memvars. These commands dispose of an existing memvar to re-create it with the desired attributes. Other commands dispose of memvars directly. All types of memvars may be displayed, disposed of, or written to a special memvar file.

Creating Memvars

You create a memvar by assigning it a value, invoking a command with a memvar as its target, or specifying a class for the memvar (as in `PUBLIC`).

The original memvar assignment command in dBASE II was `STORE`. The syntax is this:

```
STORE <expression> TO <identifier list>
```

The simpler approach of using an equal sign for assignment (as used in BASIC or C) was added as an option for dBASE III. It has been incorporated into all Xbase languages, including FoxBASE+ and FoxPro. This syntax is this:

```
[<identifier>] = <expression>
```

The original method of assignment—using the `STORE` command—is not archaic, however. It has two useful properties that the second form does not share. First, you may specify identifiers that are also commands. (Remember, FoxPro has no reserved words.) Second, a list of variables may be initialized at once, as in the following:

```
STORE 0 TO a, b, c, d, e
```

Notice that neither assignment method works with DBF file fields.

You can use either assignment method to initialize every element in an array by equating the name of the array without the subscripts to an expression. Here is an example:

```
DECLARE Aray[2,3]     && Create a 2 by 3 array
Aray = 3              && Assign 3 to all six elements
Store 3 to Aray       && Assign 3 to all six elements
```

All six elements of `Aray` are set to `3`. However, if the compatibility option is set for dBASE IV (`SET COMPATIBILITY DB4`), the same statement replaces the array with a memvar named `Aray` having an assigned value of `3`.

You may have noticed that the *<identifier>* for the assignment is optional. In some circumstances, you may want to call a function but you are not interested in saving the returned value. For example, suppose you call the function `CAPSLOCK()` to set a value:

```
=CAPSLOCK(OldCaps)
```

In this case, `CAPSLOCK()` sets the Caps Lock key state. The returned value is simply discarded. This language syntax is not supported by any versions of dBASE. However, Clipper and FoxPro do support it.

Several FoxPro commands assign values to memvars. Like the straightforward memvar assignment commands, if the specified memvar exists, its old definition is deleted. If it doesn't exist, it is created. The following commands create memvars:

```
ACCEPT          AVERAGE
CALCULATE       COUNT
DECLARE*        INPUT
LOCAL           LPARAMETERS*
PARAMETERS*     PRIVATE*
PUBLIC*         STORE
SUM             WAIT
```

Commands marked with an asterisk (`*`) can create memvars with unknown attributes. When the `PUBLIC` command, for example, specifies a memvar that does not yet exist, it creates a memvar of the Logical type with a value of `.F.`. These attributes will probably change the first time the memvar has a value assigned to it. The `PUBLIC` command establishes other attributes related to the life span and visibility of the memvar. (See the section "Behind the Scenes.") The `PRIVATE` and PARAMETERS commands deal with visibility, as well. The DECLARE command creates arrays of a particular size, as described in the "Arrays" section of this chapter, but each element is created as a Logical type with a value of .F., pending the first assignment.

Visual FoxPro 3.0 introduces the LOCAL and LPARAMETERS commands. The LOCAL command creates *local memory variables* and memory variable arrays. Local memory variables are visible only to the procedure or function in which they are created: They can be used and modified only within the procedure or function in which they are created. They cannot be accessed by higher- or lower-level procedures. Local memory variables are released once the procedure or function in which they are created completes execution. Like a PUBLIC variable, a local memory variable is initialized to a Logical data type variable with a value of false (.F.).

The LPARAMETER command assigns data passed from a calling program to local memory variables or arrays.

Disposing of Memvars

The RELEASE command disposes of memvars. Conceptually, RELEASE means an identifier is freed for use in naming something else. The RELEASE command has the following syntax:

```
RELEASE  ALL [EXTERNAL] [LIKE¦EXCEPT <skeleton>] ¦
   <identifier list>
```

This syntax supports disposing of one, some, or all memvars, as in the following:

```
RELEASE PhoneNo          && One
RELEASE Name, PhoneNo    && Some
RELEASE ALL LIKE N?      && Some
RELEASE ALL EXCEPT S*    && Some
RELEASE ALL              && All
RELEASE ALL EXTERNAL     && All, even if executed from within a program
```

The RELEASE ALL command disposes of all memvars visible at the current level. That is, if a subroutine issues a RELEASE ALL command, memvars defined in the Command window still exist. The CLEAR MEMORY command releases all memvars without regard to the level on which they were defined; the CLEAR ALL command includes CLEAR MEMORY. You can specify the RELEASE ALL EXTERNAL command to release all memory variables, including public memory variables, even if this command is executing from within a program.

<skeleton> is an identifier name that may contain the wildcard characters ? and *. The use of these characters is just like the use of wildcards in filenames under MS-DOS: ? matches a single character, and * matches any sequence of characters. Thus, in the preceding example, N? matches only two-letter identifiers with N as the first letter. S*, however, matches any identifier starting with S, regardless of length.

Because of the wildcard matching facility in the RELEASE command (and as you shall see, in the SAVE and RESTORE commands, as well), FoxPro programmers often choose to name their memvars starting with characters significant to how they are used. For example, all public memvars might start with `P`, and all temporary memvars might start with `T`. This not only increases the readability of a program, but it also makes it easy to periodically dispose of all temporary memvars with the following command:

```
RELEASE ALL LIKE T*
```

Listing Memvars

You can display the list of identifiers along with their attributes and current values by using the `DISPLAY MEMORY` or `LIST MEMORY` command. (`DISPLAY` pauses at each screen or window but is otherwise equivalent to `LIST`.) For example, suppose you type the following into the Command window:

```
NAME = "Smith"
amount = 3632.33
number = 2456
Value = 1/3
dollars = $32112
Date1 = {11/20/89}
DECLARE Aray[3]
Aray[2] = "Tuesday"
Aray[3] = 34
DO TEST
```

This code produces the `LIST MEMORY` display shown in Listing 4.1. Here is the TEST.PRG program:

```
PRIVATE DATE1
LOCAL lvalue
b7 = "Hello"
lValue = "Local Memory Variable"
date1 = {01/23/84}
LIST MEMORY
```

Listing 4.1. The output from the `LIST MEMORY` command.

```
NAME                    Pub        C     " Smith"
AMOUNT                  Pub        N     3632.33       (  3632.33000000)
NUMBER                  Pub        N     2456          (  2456.00000000)
VALUE                   Pub        N     0.33          (     0.33333333)
DOLLARS                 Pub        Y     32122.0000
DATE1                   (hid)      D     11/20/89   test
LVALUE                  Local      C     "Local Memory Variable"
ARAY                    Pub        A
          (   1)                   L     .F.
          (   2)                   C     " Tuesday"
          (   3)                   N     34             (     34.00000000)
B7                      Priv       C     "Hello"  test
DATE1                   Priv       D     01/23/84   test
    9 variables defined,     38 bytes used
 1015 variables available

Print System Memory Variables
```

```
_ALIGNMENT          Pub      C    "LEFT  "
_ASSIST             Pub      C    ""
_BEAUTIFY           Pub      C    ""
_BOX                Pub      L    .T.
_BUILDER            Pub      C    ""
_CALCMEM            Pub      N    0.00           ( 0.00000000)
_CALCVALUE          Pub      N    0.00           ( 0.00000000)
_CONVERTER          Pub      C    "      C:\FOX30\CONVERT.APP"
_CUROBJ             Pub      N    -1             ( -1.00000000)
_DBLCLICK           Pub      N    0.50           (  0.50000000)
_DIARYDATE          Pub      D    11/22/94
_DOS                Pub      L    .F.
_FOXDOC             Pub      C    ""
_FOXGRAPH           Pub      C    ""
_GENGRAPH           Pub      C    ""
_GENMENU            Pub      C    "      C:\FOX30\GENMENU.PRG"
_GENPD              Pub      C    ""
_GENSCRN            Pub      C    ""
_GENXTAB            Pub      C    ""
_INDENT             Pub      N    0               ( 0.00000000)
_LMARGIN            Pub      N    0               ( 0.00000000)
_MAC                Pub      L    .F.
_MLINE              Pub      N    0               ( 0.00000000)
_NEXTOBJ            Pub      N    4294967295      ( 4294967295.00000000)
_PADVANCE           Pub      C    "FORMFEED    "
_PAGENO             Pub      N    1               ( 1.00000000)
_PBPAGE             Pub      N    1               ( 1.00000000)
_PCOLNO             Pub      N    0.00            ( 0.00000000)
_PCOPIES            Pub      N    1               ( 1.00000000)
_PDRIVER            Pub      C    ""
_PDSETUP            Pub      C    ""
_PECODE             Pub      C    ""
_PEJECT             Pub      C    "NONE   "
_PEPAGE             Pub      N    32767           ( 32767.00000000)
_PLENGTH            Pub      N    66              ( 66.00000000)
_PLINENO            Pub      N    52              ( 52.00000000)
_PLOFFSET           Pub      N    0               (  0.00000000)
_PPITCH             Pub      C    "DEFAULT   "
_PQUALITY           Pub      L    .F.
_PRETEXT            Pub      C    ""
_PREVOBJ            Pub      N    4294967295      ( 4294967295.00000000)
_PSCODE             Pub      C    ""
_PSPACING           Pub      N    1               (  1.00000000)
_PWAIT              Pub      L    .F.
_RMARGIN            Pub      N    80              ( 80.00000000)
_SCREEN             Pub      O    FORM
_SHELL              Pub      C    ""
_SPELLCHK           Pub      C    ""
_STARTUP            Pub      C    ""
_TABS               Pub      C    ""
_TALLY              Pub      N    164              ( 164.00000000)
_TEXT               Pub      N    -1               ( -1.00000000)
_THROTTLE           Pub      N    0.00             ( 0.00000000)
_TRANSPORT          Pub      C    ""
_UNIX               Pub      L    .F.
_WINDOWS            Pub      L    .T.
_WIZARD             Pub      C    ""
```

continues

Listing 4.1. continued

```
_WRAP                       Pub           L     .F.

   63 System Variables Defined

Menu and Pad Definitions
    0 Menus Defined
Popup Definitions
    0 Popups Defined
Window Definitions
    0 Windows Defined
```

The `LIST MEMORY` command displays the current values of all memvars (including system memvars) and lists all menus, pads, pop-up menus, and logical windows. (See Chapter 7, "FoxPro Language Elements for Creating Windows and Menu Systems," for more information about user-defined windows, menus, pads, and pop-up menus.)

Each memvar is listed on a single line with the following attributes:

- An identifier—the name of the memvar, mapped to uppercase.
- A class—memvars are tagged with `Pub` (public), `Priv` (private), `local` (local), `(hid)` (hidden), or the array row element. Public memvars are visible to all levels; private memvars are visible only to the current level and below. (Program nesting levels are explained in more detail in Chapter 6, "Control Flow.") Memvars marked `(hid)` were defined at a higher level than the level that declared them private. Memvars that make up the elements of an array are tagged with the element number or row and column numbers.
- A type—memvar types are `A` (Array), `C` (Character), `D` (Date), `T` (DateTime), `I` (Integer), `L` (Logical), `N` (Number), or `Y` (Currency). Memvars cannot be of the Memo type.
- A value—the current value of the memvar.
- A defining block—if the memvar was defined in a program, rather than at the Command window, then the procedure name is displayed.

The value of each numeric memvar is displayed in internal form as well as conventional display format. This is important because numeric memvars have an internal binary format that is a binary approximation of the value entered. You should realize, for example, that 0.33 is stored as 0.33333333.

Memvar arrays are type `A`. The value listed for an array is its dimension, which is described in more detail in the "Arrays" section. Two-dimensional arrays, such as this:

```
DECLARE Aray[3,2]
```

are shown with both dimensions as their value, which in this case is `[3,2]`. The elements of the array are listed next as if they were separate memvars (which, internally, they are). The elements are listed in row-major order, which means that the second index varies fastest. For the array declared in the preceding example, the elements would be displayed in the following order:

Element Number	*Row, Column*
1	1,1
2	1,2
3	2,1
4	2,2
5	3,1
6	3,2

When an array is declared, a memvar is created for each element. The number of elements is equal to the dimension for one-dimensional arrays and equal to the product of both dimensions for two-dimensional arrays. Therefore, `Aray[3,2]` has six elements. These new elements, like any memvar that is created without a value, are assigned the Logical type with the value `.F.`. (I take this approach because it uses the least possible memory.) Notice that I never assigned a value to `Aray[1]` in the `LIST MEMORY` display in this section. Therefore, Listing 4.1 shows that element `[1]` is the Logical type with a value of `.F.`. As indicated previously, you can assign values other than `.F.` with an assignment statement. If the compatibility mode is off (`SET COMPATIBILITY OFF`), you can assign a value of `42.0` to all the elements in an array with either of the following two statements:

```
Aray = 42.0
STORE 42.0 TO Aray
```

Memvars that are defined in a program rather than from the Command window are classed as private by default. The memvar `B7`, for example, is automatically released when TEST.PRG returns. You probably noticed that two memvars are called `DATE1` in Listing 4.1, and each has a different value. Because the first `DATE1` was created in the Command window, it is public by default. The `PRIVATE DATE1` statement in TEST.PRG hides the first `DATE1` so that the subsequent assignment statement creates a new memvar with a different value (it could have a different type, as well). When TEST.PRG returns, this local version of `DATE1` is released (as is `B7`) and the original `DATE1` is "visible" again.

On the SAMPLES program disk, there is a program called VISIBLE.PRG that illustrates the visibility of local, private, and public memory variables. It is shown in Listing 4.2. This program creates memory variables in the main program, VISIBLE, and two lower-level procedures, `LEVEL1` and `LEVEL2`. You can see that the private memvars declared in one procedure are visible at lower-level procedures. Private and local memvars are released when the program completes its execution. `LOCAL` memvars are visible only to the procedure in which they are declared. Listing 4.3 shows the output from executing VISIBLE.PRG. Notice that `zLocal1` and `zLocal2` are not visible from the `LEVEL3` procedure. However, all public and private variables are visible.

Listing 4.2. Listing of the program VISIBLE.PRG.

```
****************************************************
* Program: Visible
* Purpose: Illustrate visibility of PUBLIC, PRIVATE,
*          and LOCAL memory variables
*****************************************************
PUBLIC zPublic1
LOCAL zLocal1
PRIVATE zPrivate1
zPublic1  = "Visible - Public variable"
zLocal1   = "Visible - Local variable"
zPrivate1 = "Visible - Private variable"
SET ALTER TO Visible
SET ALTER ON
? "Visible.prg"
DISPLAY MEMORY LIKE Z*
DO Level2
? "Return from Level2 call"
DISPLAY MEMORY LIKE Z*
SET ALTER OFF
SET ALTER TO
RETURN
********************************************
PROCEDURE LEVEL2
PUBLIC zPublic2
LOCAL zLocal2
PRIVATE zPrivate2
zPublic2  = "Level 2 - Public variable"
zLocal2   = "Level 2 - Local variable"
zPrivate2 = "Level 2 - Private variable"
? "Level 2"
DISPLAY MEMORY LIKE Z*
DO Level3
? "Return from Level3 call"
DISPLAY MEMORY LIKE Z*
RETURN
********************************************
PROCEDURE LEVEL3
PUBLIC zPublic3
LOCAL zLocal3
PRIVATE zPrivate3
zPublic3  = "Level 3 - Public variable"
zLocal3   = "Level 3 - Local variable"
zPrivate3 = "Level 3 - Private variable"
? "Level 3"
DISPLAY MEMORY LIKE Z*
?
? " Variable   Visible?"
? " zLocal1   ",TYPE("zLocal1")#"U"
? " zLocal2   ",TYPE("zLocal2")#"U"
? " zLocal3   ",TYPE("zLocal3")#"U"
? " zPrivate1 ",TYPE("zPrivate1")#"U"
? " zPrivate2 ",TYPE("zPrivate2")#"U"
? " zPrivate3 ",TYPE("zPrivate3")#"U"
? " zPublic1  ",TYPE("zPublic1")#"U"
? " zPublic2  ",TYPE("zPublic2")#"U"
? " zPublic3  ",TYPE("zPublic3")#"U"
?
RETURN
```

Listing 4.3. Output resulting from the execution of VISIBLE.PRG.

```
Visible.prg
ZPUBLIC1    Pub    C  "Visible - Public variable"
ZPUBLIC2    Pub    C  "Public variable defined in Level 3"
ZPUBLIC3    Pub    L  .F.
ZLOCAL1     Local  C  "Visible - Local variable"  visible
ZPRIVATE1   Priv   C  "Visible - Private variable"  visible
Level 2
ZPUBLIC1    Pub    C  "Visible - Public variable"
ZPUBLIC2    Pub    C  "Level 2 - Public variable"
ZPUBLIC3    Pub    L  .F.
ZLOCAL1     Local  C  "Visible - Local variable"  visible
ZPRIVATE1   Priv   C  "Visible - Private variable"  visible
ZLOCAL2     Local  C  "Level 2 - Local variable"  level2
ZPRIVATE2   Priv   C  "Level 2 - Private variable"  level2
Level 3
ZPUBLIC1    Pub    C  "Visible - Public variable"
ZPUBLIC2    Pub    C  "Level 2 - Public variable"
ZPUBLIC3    Pub    C  "Level 3 - Public variable"
ZLOCAL1     Local  C  "Visible - Local variable"  visible
ZPRIVATE1   Priv   C  "Visible - Private variable"  visible
ZLOCAL2     Local  C  "Level 2 - Local variable"  level2
ZPRIVATE2   Priv   C  "Level 2 - Private variable"  level2
ZLOCAL3     Local  C  "Level 3 - Local variable"  level3
ZPRIVATE3   Priv   C  "Level 3 - Private variable"  level3

Variable   Visible?
 zLocal1     .F.
 zLocal2     .F.
 zLocal3     .T.
 zPrivate1   .T.
 zPrivate2   .T.
 zPrivate3   .T.
 zPublic1    .T.
 zPublic2    .T.
 zPublic3    .T.

Return from Level3 call
ZPUBLIC1    Pub    C  "Visible - Public variable"
ZPUBLIC2    Pub    C  "Level 2 - Public variable"
ZPUBLIC3    Pub    C  "Level 3 - Public variable"
ZLOCAL1     Local  C  "Visible - Local variable"  visible
ZPRIVATE1   Priv   C  "Visible - Private variable"  visible
ZLOCAL2     Local  C  "Level 2 - Local variable"  level2
ZPRIVATE2   Priv   C  "Level 2 - Private variable"  level2
Return from Level2 call
ZPUBLIC1    Pub    C  "Visible - Public variable"
ZPUBLIC2    Pub    C  "Level 2 - Public variable"
ZPUBLIC3    Pub    C  "Level 3 - Public variable"
ZLOCAL1     Local  C  "Visible - Local variable"  visible
ZPRIVATE1   Priv   C  "Visible - Private variable"  visible
```

Memvar Files

You can write one, some, or all memvars to a file (with the default extension .MEM) by using the SAVE command. Conversely, the RESTORE command reads memvar descriptions from a MEM file.

The syntax of the SAVE command has several variations:

```
SAVE TO <expFN>
SAVE ALL TO <expFN>
SAVE ALL LIKE <skeleton> TO <expFN>
SAVE ALL EXCEPT <skeleton> TO <expFN>
```

The first and second variations are equivalent. Unless otherwise specified, all current memvars are written to the file specified by the TO clause. <skeleton> is an identifier with the wildcard characters * and ?, as described for the RELEASE command. If a local memvar hides another memvar that is defined at a higher level at the time the SAVE command is issued, then only the local version is saved.

The RESTORE command first performs a CLEAR MEMORY command, deleting all current memvars, then reads the memvar descriptions stored in the specified MEM file. The syntax is this:

```
RESTORE FROM <expFN> [ADDITIVE]
```

The optional ADDITIVE keyword omits the CLEAR MEMORY step. Memvars are created as if they had been defined at the program level where the RESTORE command was issued. In other words, if you RESTORE at the Command window, then the memvars described in the MEM file will be created as public. If the RESTORE command is issued by a program, then the memvars will be created as private (unless the public or private status of the identifiers is explicitly set using the PUBLIC or PRIVATE commands before the RESTORE).

Arrays

Arrays of memvars have appeared on the wish list of every Xbase programmer since the days of dBASE II. Makeshift workarounds, such as naming memvars similarly and using an ampersand macro to access one element, seem ludicrous now that arrays are supported. The following code simulates an array:

```
Month01 = "Jan"
Month02 = "Feb"
...
Month12 = "Dec"
i = 4
s = RIGHT("00"+LTRIM(STR(i)), 2)
? Month&s
```

A better workaround for fixed-length character string arrays might be this:

```
Months = "JanFebMarAprMayJunJulAugSepOctNovDec"
i = 4
? SUBSTR(Months, (i-1)*3, 3)
```

Both of these methods suffer from lack of readability, which tends to make programs harder to maintain. Both Clipper and FoxBASE+ supported arrays before dBASE. However, dBASE IV was the first version of Ashton-Tate's dBASE that supported arrays. Using FoxPro, the same code just listed can now use an array, which at least makes the line that displays the desired month more readable:

```
DECLARE Month[12]
Month[1] = "Jan"
Month[2] = "Feb"
...
Month[12] = "Dec"
i = 4
? Month[i]
```

Arrays are created using either the `DECLARE` or `DIMENSION` commands. The two command names are synonyms. The syntax is somewhat awkward in print. Brackets shown here in quotation marks are literal; unquoted brackets have the usual meaning (they denote an optional part):

```
DECLARE <identifier> "[" <expN> [, <expN>] "]"
{, <identifier> "[" <expN> [, <expN>] "]" }
```

Unlike other languages that support *n*-dimensional arrays, FoxPro's arrays may be only one- or two-dimensional. Two-dimensional arrays resemble tables of data. The first dimension is the row; the optional second dimension is the column (as shown in Figure 4.1). Each array uses a single memory variable so that you can have up to 65000 arrays—provided that you have enough memory. The total number of elements in any single array may not exceed 65000. It's just as well because it's not a good idea to push a system to its limit unless you're testing the system rather than using it.

FIGURE 4.1.
One- and two-dimensional arrays.

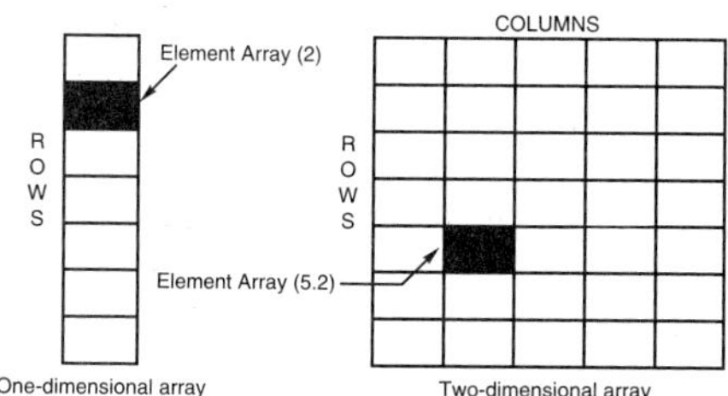

You can use the `DECLARE` (or `DIMENSION`) command to change the size and dimension of an existing array. You can change the number of dimensions from one dimension to two dimensions, or from two dimensions to one dimension. You can also increase or reduce the number of elements in an array. The contents of the original array are copied to the new, redimensioned array. The three-element array, `Aray`, is extended to two dimensions with eight elements in the following example:

Command Window	*Comments*
`DECLARE Aray[3]`	Declare an array with three elements
`Aray = 42`	Assign `42` to all three elements
`DECLARE Aray[2,4]`	Redimension the array
	Contents:
`? Aray[1,1]`	`42`
`? Aray[1,2]`	`42`
`? Aray[1,3]`	`42`
`? Aray[1,4]`	`.F.`
`? Aray[2,1]`	`.F.`
`? Aray[2,2]`	`.F.`
`? Aray[2,3]`	`.F.`
`? Aray[2,4]`	`.F.`

Several FoxPro commands support arrays. With the `TO ARRAY` clause and the `AVERAGE`, `SUM`, and `CALCULATE` commands, you can store a list of values in an array. Here is an example:

```
DECLARE Sales[4]
SUM EastSales, WestSales, NorthSales, SouthSales ;
TO ARRAY Sales
```

Following this command, the `Sales[3]` element will contain the sum of the `NorthSales` fields from every record.

The `COPY TO ARRAY` and `APPEND FROM ARRAY` commands support moving the rows and columns of DBF files to and from memvar arrays. The `COPY TO ARRAY` command fills an array with values from a DBF file. The `APPEND FROM ARRAY` command adds new records to a DBF file containing data from an array. For more information about these commands, see Chapter 12, "Data Set Operations." FoxPro provides an abundant supply of functions that you can use to manipulate arrays. They are presented in Chapter 5.

Behind the Scenes

Each memvar has additional attributes that cannot be directly modified and are not displayed by the `LIST MEMORY` command (unlike the identifier, value, and type attributes). For example, both fields and memvars are kept in the same internal list in FoxPro so that when the user issues a command, such as

```
? Fred
```

the system can quickly answer the question Do we know Fred? To keep things straight, FoxPro tags each variable with the work area where it is found. Memvars reside in an imaginary work area. Most of the memvar operations just described affect only variables tagged with this imaginary work area because a memvar has no actual work area. When you need to differentiate between a memvar and a data field of the same name, you can use `M`, the imaginary memvar work area name, as described shortly.

In the FoxPro hierarchy of variables, fields are more important than memvars. When one identifier describes both a field and a memvar, the field hides the memvar unless the operation can be done only with a memvar. Therefore, all references to this dual identifier will find the field with commands such as `?` or `@...GET`, but will find the memvar with the `=` assignment operator and the `&` macro. In the following example, the file, NEW.DBF, contains a `Name` field:

Command Window	*Results*
`USE New`	
`? Name`	`Roger`
`Name = "Charley"`	`Charley`
`? Name`	`Roger`
`? "&Name"`	`Charley`
`? M.Name`	`Charley`

The preceding example shows the use of the special work area alias, called `M` for memvar. You can think of this as the alias for the imaginary work area. This example brings up a catch-22 that arises in real-world language implementation. The letter `M` becomes a special case. You cannot use it as an alias name. What happens if you have a file named M.DBF? FoxPro will not assign the letter `M` as the alias name. It will use a work area letter such as `A` or the work area number preceded by the letter `W`. The letter `M` is useless as a work area alias. However, the number of possible alias identifiers is very large, so disallowing the use of one letter is not a significant restriction.

Nesting Levels

Another behind-the-scenes attribute of memvars that FoxPro tracks is the program level at which a memvar is created. Program levels are concerned with FoxPro programs that call other FoxPro programs. These are called *nested procedure calls* and are described in more detail in Chapter 6. The Command window is considered level 0. When you type `DO MyProg` in the Command window, `MyProg` executes in level 1. If `MyProg` includes a line such as `DO Calc`, `Calc` executes on level 2, and so on.

A memvar is visible only on the level where it's created and at deeper levels. For example, suppose that `Calc`, on level `2`, creates a memvar called `A_Var` and then calls another procedure. That procedure can refer to `A_Var` because its level, which is `3`, is deeper than the level on which `A_Var` was created, which was `2`. If `A_Var` on level `3` is declared using a `PRIVATE` or `PARAMETER` statement and changed (for example, its type or value is changed), then `A_Var` changes back when it returns to the level `2` `Calc` procedure. If `A_Var` is changed on level `3` but not declared, then its value remains in effect when it returns to the level `2` `Calc` procedure. This seems obvious, but you can make local, private copies of memvars that do not exhibit this persistence.

When one program level returns to the level that called it, all memvars defined on the departing level are automatically released. Therefore, when `Calc` returns to `MyProg`, the `A_Var` variable defined by `Calc` is discarded. When a memvar is created in the Command window (level `0`), it will never be released (until FoxPro quits). This is such a desirable property that the `PUBLIC` command was introduced just to confer permanence on memvars. (Before the introduction of FoxPro's debug window, described in Chapter 23, "Building Visual FoxPro Applications," the `PUBLIC` command made it possible to debug programs at the dot prompt in older versions of FoxPro.)

When you write `PUBLIC X` in a program, it creates a memvar called `X` as if it were created from the Command window. Not only is `X` not released, but it is available for use by every program module. A typical system written in the FoxPro language begins by calling an initialization module. If it weren't for the `PUBLIC` command, the initialization module could not create variables for use by the rest of the system.

Sometimes programmers don't want their variables visible to the rest of the system. In fact, good programming practices suggest that the use of global variables is generally a bad idea. If you write a self-contained procedure for calculating the greatest common denominator (GCD) of two numbers, for example, then you need to use temporary memvars. You also need to ensure that you don't give your memvars names that the rest of the system already uses. Otherwise your temporary values would overwrite the current values of some other memvars. Even worse, suppose you want to write your GCD procedure for use with systems that you intend to write in the future. How can you plan to avoid memvar-naming conflicts? You can't.

The `PRIVATE` command supports the notion of private local memvar names. Privacy is not an attribute of a memvar. Instead, the `PRIVATE` command sets the hidden attribute of any memvar with a name that conflicts with the new local copy.

Perhaps an example will help to illustrate this point. If you create a memvar called `A_Var` at the Command window, then issue the command

```
PRIVATE A_Var
```

in a procedure (level `1`), FoxPro simply tags the Command window version of `A_Var` as "hidden on level `1`." If level `1` creates a new memvar called `A_Var`, no conflict exists—the first, 0-level `A_Var` is hidden. Any procedure that level `1` calls will see only level `1`'s `A_Var`. When level `1` returns to the Command window, the FoxPro system searches for memvars to release. The local version of `A_Var` is released because it was defined on level `1`. The system then looks for memvars hidden on the level where it is returning and takes them out of hiding.

Chapter 6 describes levels and level transitions in more detail. It also includes an explanation of how parameters are passed to procedures. The `PARAMETERS` command does a lot with memvars, but that discussion must wait until after an explanation of expressions, which are the subject of Chapter 5.

The Memvar Storage Parameter *MVCOUNT*

Each memvar requires a certain amount of memory. In addition, space is needed to store variable-length character strings. With FoxPro, you can designate how many memory variables to assign. You should establish a goal to let knowledgeable users tune the system for the maximum number of memvars available for a FoxPro session. The default allows a maximum number of 256 memvars. You can set the MVCOUNT parameter in the CONFIG.FPW file to the maximum number of memvars for a session. You can set MVCOUNT to allow from 128 to 65000 memvars. You will probably run out of memory before you exceed the maximum value of MVCOUNT.

Summary

This chapter presents FoxPro variables, DBF file fields, and memvars. It describes various attributes of these variables and discusses commands that create and manipulate memvars. You have learned about arrays as well as about how to save memvars to MEM files. In addition, you saw some behind-the-scenes information on nesting levels, visibility, and tuning parameters that affect how much memory is used to store memvars.

5

Expressions

Of every noble work the silent part is best, Of all expression that which cannot be expressed.

—William Wetmore Story (1819–1895)

Some confusion arises in the Xbase (dBASE, FoxPro, Arago, Clipper, and so forth) literature concerning the exact nature of an expression. An *expression* in Xbase languages is nearly identical to the concept of expressions in other languages, such as BASIC, Pascal, or C.

Variables and constants are the basic data objects manipulated in a program. Operators specify what is to be done to them. Expressions combine variables and constants to produce new values (Kernighan 1978).

Expressions are constructs denoting rules of computation for obtaining values of variables and generating new values by the application of operators. Expressions consist of operators and operands (that is, variables, constants, and functions) (Wirth 1974).

In the FoxPro language, as in C, C++, Pascal, and many other programming languages, expressions consist of the following:

- Single operands (constants, variables, or functions)
- Operands combined with operators and (typically) other operands (x + y)

Functions consist of the following:

- A function name (either built in or user defined)
- Zero or more arguments, also called parameters, set inside parentheses

Functions with no arguments still have parentheses. The `DATE()` function is a good example.

The arguments to a function are themselves expressions. This is known as a *recursive* definition in computer science terms because it is a circular argument. An expression includes functions that include expressions that include functions, and on and on. Here is an example:

```
? 2           && An expression consists of a numeric constant
? 1+1         && Two numeric constants and the + operator
? SQRT(4)     && A function with one argument, a numeric constant
? SQRT(1+3)                 && The same function, but the argument
                            &&  now includes an operator
? SQRT(SQRT(1)+SQRT(9))     && The same function, but the argument
                            &&  now includes nested functions
```

The values of these four expressions are the same (2). The `SQRT()` function requires one numeric argument. That argument can be a numeric constant (4), two constants and an operator (1+3), or a numeric function call.

Differentiating among a constant, a variable, a function, and an expression is incorrect—they are all expressions.

Some FoxPro language commands require literal strings rather than expressions, such as the following:

```
FIND Fred
USE Myfile
```

The literals `Fred` and `Myfile` are not expressions because each is not a variable, and without quotation marks, each is not a constant. The syntax of the `FIND` command does not allow operators or functions. In contrast, the `SEEK` command, which performs the same duty as the `FIND` command, accepts this expression:

```
SEEK "Fred"
```

or this expression:

```
Name = "Fred"
SEEK Name
```

or this expression:

```
SEEK TRIM(UPPER(Name))
```

The `SEEK` command eliminates the need for the `FIND` command. Expressions are more flexible than simple literals. The FoxPro language is evolving steadily from literals toward full generality of expressions.

Operands

In the FoxPro language, *operands* are constants, variables, and functions. Each operand has several attributes. For example, every operand has exactly one data type. (Recall from Chapter 4, "Variables," that FoxPro's data types are Character, Currency, Date, DateTime, Float, Integer, Logical, Number, General, and Memo.) Other attributes include length and number of digits to display to the right of a decimal point.

Because they are defined recursively, expressions can be operands. For example, if you describe `2+2` as two numeric operands joined by the `+` operator, you can substitute a numeric expression for either or both operands. Accordingly, `(1+1)+(1+1)` is equivalent to `2+2`. The expression `1+1` is simply an operand in the expression. This recursive definition of an expression holds even in highly complex expressions such as this:

```
? SQRT(2+3*19/ABS(Mvar)+VAL(StrMvar))
```

Constants, expressions, and functions are ephemeral, unlike variables. Their values exist in memory for only a short time (until the next expression is evaluated), and their length attributes (unlike the length of a DBF file field) are not fixed. All operands have exactly one type; this fact is very important when using operators or functions.

Constants

Constants are sometimes called literals because their values are literally what they appear to be—they are not indirect references to other values as are variables. FoxPro supports constants of the Character, Date, Logical, and Number types.

As discussed in Chapter 4, FoxPro supports four types of numbers, `I` (Integer), `N` (Numeric), `Y` (Currency), and `F` (Float). All numeric constants are type `N` or `Y`. Memo constants are not allowed. Date and DateTime constants are supported by FoxPro. In FoxBASE+ and dBASE III PLUS, dates are created from Character constants using the `CTOD()` function.

Character Constants

Character constants (sometimes called *strings*), like Character memvars, can be up to 64KB characters and are denoted by quotation characters. FoxPro is unusual among programming languages in that it supports three different quotation characters:

```
? "This string is delimited by double quotation marks."
? 'This string is delimited by single quotation marks.'
? [This string is delimited by square brackets.]
```

A character constant must end with a quotation character that matches the character at the beginning. This flexibility allows embedded quotation characters in strings, which is often difficult to accomplish in other programming languages. Here's an example:

```
? "There's nothing you can't do between quotation marks."
? 'You can even say, "Nevermore" within a quoted string.'
? [As he said, "Nothing's impossible."]
```

Character constants can contain zero or more characters. Any character is legal. The length of a character string is determined in most Xbase languages by counting the characters until a binary `0` is read; therefore, embedding a binary `0` in a string truncates the string and loses the extra characters. However, FoxPro (even with `SET COMPATIBILITY TO DB4`) enables you to insert a binary `0` into a string. FoxPro keeps track of the actual number of characters on the string. On IBM PCs and compatibles, you can enter characters with diacritical marks and graphic characters by holding down the Alt key and entering a three-digit ASCII value on the numeric keypad. FoxPro accepts these characters in quoted strings. However, the recommended method of inserting nonprinting characters into a string is to use the `CHR()` function. For example, if you want to insert carriage returns and line feeds into a string, you can do so by using the technique illustrated in the following statement:

```
Quote = "I was gratified to be able to answer promptly," + ;
        CHR(13) + CHR(10) +    CR-LF   ;
        "and I did. I said I didn't know." ;
        CHR(13) + CHR(10) +                ;
        "           Mark Twain"
```

Date Constants

You can specify date constants with curly braces in the same way that you use quotation marks with character strings:

```
? {01/23/84}
```

Date constants are interpreted rather broadly using the following syntax:

```
date_constant ::= '{' <digits> <delimiter> <digits> <delimiter>
                  <digits>  '}'
```

NOTE

The notation used in the syntax is the Backus-Naur Format (BNF) and is described in Appendix B. The `<delimiter>` character may be just about any single non-digit, including a period, a hyphen, or an alphabetic character.

How the three integers are interpreted depends on the current setting of `SET DATE`. The meaning of the constant `{1-2-3}` varies as follows:

```
SET DATE TO AMERICAN     && 2nd day of 1st month in year 3
SET DATE TO FRENCH       && 1st day of 2nd month in year 3
SET DATE TO JAPAN        && 3rd day of 2nd month in year 1
```

In dBASE IV inappropriate values for the day or month are silently converted to their appropriate values. For example, the constant `{01/45/84}` is stored as February 14, 1984 (which would be the 45th day of January, but is actually the 14th day of February). The system handles leap years, as well. However, FoxPro, even with `SET COMPATIBILITY TO DB4`, figures that you entered an erroneous date and returns a blank (or null) date `{  /  /  }`. This is a preferred method because an erroneous value is easier to detect.

DateTime Constants

You can specify DateTime constants with curly braces just as you do with Date constants:

```
? {01/23/84 01:02:02 am}
```

Date constants are interpreted rather broadly using the following syntax:

```
DateTime_constant ::= '{' <digits> <delimiter> <digits> <delimiter>
                      <digits>  <digits> <delimiter> <digits> [<delimiter>
                      <digits>] [am ¦ pm] '}'
```

The interpretation of the six two-digit integers is dependent on the current settings of `SET DATE`, `SET HOURS`, `SET MARK`, and `SET CENTURY`. The first three two-digit integers are the same for the `Date` constant. The second three integers represent the hours, minutes, and seconds. An error is produced if the values are invalid. If the time is omitted from the expression, FoxPro adds a default time of midnight (12:00:00 A.M.). A default date of 12/30/1899 is added if the date is omitted. If the century is added and `SET CENTURY` is `OFF`, the century is ignored. Here are some examples:

```
{10/16/95 2:00 PM }
{02/12/95 14:00}
{2/17/95}           && Intrepreted as 12:00 P.M. on 2/17/95
{13:00}             && Intrepreted as 1:00 P.M. on 12/30/1899
```

Logical Values

Logical values are sometimes called *boolean values* in honor of George Boole, the mathematician who conceived boolean algebra in 1847. Although boolean values are either true or false, FoxPro permits *yes* and *no* to represent true (yes) and false (no). Therefore, this is the set of FoxPro Logical constants:

```
.T.
.F.
.Y.
.N.
```

The periods before and after the letter (which are a legacy from FORTRAN) are significant. They eliminate possible confusion between T and a memvar or a field called T. However, case is insignificant: `.T.` is the same as `.t.`.

Numeric Literals

Numeric literals are always of the `N` type, never `F`. The internal representation depends on the scale of the value—small integers are stored in a more efficient representation than the `N` type format.

But when you create a memvar by assigning a numeric literal to it:

```
Nmvar = 123.45
```

the new memvar is always type `N`. Of course, as indicated in Chapter 4, if the target is a database field of type `F` (float):

```
REPLACE Ffield WITH 123.45
```

the `N` type number, 123.45, is treated as though it is a type `N` database field because type `F` and type `N` are the same in FoxPro.

You can write numeric constants in scientific notation:

```
LightYear = 5.878E+12     && Miles
ElecVolt = 1.60E-12       && Ergs
```

Currency Literals

Currency literals are always `Y` type. They are represented internally as an 8-byte binary, floating-point number. However, they are rounded to four decimal places before they are stored or used in a calculation. You can create a memvar by assigning to it a numeric literal preceded by a dollar sign ($). Here is an example:

```
Nmvar = $123.4556789
```

This number is stored internally as 123.4557.

Null Fields

Sometimes it is significant that data associated with a field is not available. Its value is not zero or blank or anything. It is a *null* value. For example, suppose you have a survey form and the participants fail to fill in a field. Suppose they omit their ages. When you process the survey forms and compute an average age of the survey participants, you do not want to average in records with a zero age. The concept of a null field was conceived to solve this problem. Visual FoxPro has incorporated this concept. If you use `SET NULL ON`, then a table can contain null fields. If `SET NULL` is `OFF`, which it is the default, then any fields added to a table cannot contain a null value. Any field data type can be null.

You can test for a null field value using the null field literal `.NULL.`. For example, you can determine the average age for all the records in a table that do not contain null values by using the following command:

```
AVERAGE AGE FOR ISNULL(AGE)
```

The `ISNULL()` function returns a true (`.T.`) value if a field is null. You can establish a null value for a field using the null literal:

```
REPLACE city with .NULL.
```

NOTE

If a table contains any null fields, it is no longer compatible with earlier versions of FoxPro or dBASE.

When a field has a null value, it displays as a null literal (`.NULL.`). For example, this:

```
LIST Name, Age
```

displays as this:

```
Record #    Name            Age
       1    Smith, Joe       23
       2    Jones, Jack  .NULL.
```

Null fields affect certain aspects of the behavior of tables and indexes. This subject is discussed further in Chapter 11, "DBF Files and Databases."

Variables

Variables can be memvars or DBF file fields. (Chapter 4 describes variables in great detail.) Remember, when variables are used as operands in expressions, every variable has only one type.

You refer to a variable by using its identifier. When a variable is a field in another work area, or when a memvar name conflicts with a DBF file field name, you can use the special `->` operator (or a period) to resolve the situation. As described in Chapter 4, the following syntax:

```
alias->identifier
alias.identifier
```

refers to a field in another work area. An imaginary work area with the alias `M` refers to a memvar when the memvar's identifier might conflict with a field name such as `M.MyMemvar`, for example. The period operator (`->`) is something of a syntactic problem; if you call it an operator, alias names become a special kind of operand that can be used only in expressions with `->` or a period. To avoid this, treat the phrase `alias->` (or `alias.`) as a qualifier of variables.

Operators

The FoxPro language supports a full set of operators that specify actions to be performed on data objects (operands). The type of the operand often affects the semantics of the operator. Here's a simple example: In the expression `1+2` the operator is `+`, which performs arithmetic addition when used with numeric operands. The same operator in the expression `"Hello, "+"Joe"` performs character string concatenation. This aspect of a programming language is called *operator overloading.*

Types of Operators

The set of operators available in FoxPro, grouped by the type of the result, is described in the following sections.

Character Operators

The `+` operator, as you have seen, concatenates two character operands. The `-` operator performs the same service, except that any trailing blanks from the first (left) operand are moved to the end of the result. The following example illustrates this:

Command Window	*Results*
`A = "Hello     "`	`Hello`
`B = "There     "`	`There`
`? A+B`	`Hello     There`
`? LEN(A+B)`	`20`
`? A-B`	`HelloThere`
`? LEN(A-B)`	`20`

Date and DateTime Operators

The + and - operators apply to dates and DateTime expressions as well. However, only four methods are legal to combine operands and these operators:

```
<date> + <number>          && result is type <date>
<number> + <date>          && result is type <date>
<date> - <number>          && result is type <date>
<date> - <date>            && result is type <number>
<DateTime> + <number>      && result is type <DateTime>
<number> + <DateTime>      && result is type <DateTime>
<DateTime> - <number>      && result is type <DateTime>
<DateTime> - <DateTime>    && result is type <number>
```

Notice that the date must be on the left side of the - operator when the other operand is a number.

Logical Operators

Logical values result from comparing operands of various types using relational operators. Table 5.1 lists and describes the FoxPro relational operators.

Table 5.1. Logical operators.

Operator	*Description*
=	Equal
==	Exact equal (Character type only)
>	Greater than
<	Less than
>= or =>	Greater than or equal to
<= or =<	Less than or equal to
<>	Not equal
#	Not equal (Same as <>)
!=	Not equal (Same as <>)
$	Is contained in (Character and Memo only)

You may apply these operators only to operands of the same type: Only the Character, Currency, Date, DateTime, and Number (or Float) types can be compared. Comparing two numbers is a straightforward process. Dates are stored internally as a number of days, so comparing dates is the same as comparing numbers. However, date operands cannot be compared to numeric operands.

The == operator is used with character type comparisons. For two character strings to be equal, the strings must be the same length and each character in one string must be equal to the corresponding character in the other string. Simply put, the strings must be identical.

Character comparison using the = operator is less straightforward. Two character strings are equal if each character in the right string matches its corresponding character in the left string. Note the wording of the previous sentence. It helps explain the following example:

Command Window	*Results*
`A = "abc"`	`abc`
`B = "abcd"`	`abcd`
`? A = B`	`.F.`
`? B = A`	`.T.`
`? B == A`	`.F.`
`? "abc " == "abc"`	`.F.`
`? "abc " = "abc"`	`.T.`

This difference arises to accommodate the typical string comparison operation in FoxPro, which is illustrated by the following:

```
IF CField = "Mongoose"
```

Because `CField` is wider than five characters, programmers would need to write this:

```
IF CField = "Mongoose          "
```

were it not for the unusual behavior of the FoxPro string comparison operators. This behavior holds true for the other relational operators as well.

Two environmental parameters, `SET ANSI` and `SET EXACT`, affect the operation of the = operator. Both parameters are normally set to `OFF`. If `SET ANSI` is `ON`, it pads the shorter string with blanks before the comparison. If `SET EXACT` is `ON`, then characters must match character for character in order for strings to be equal. Trailing blanks in either string are ignored. Chapter 10, "Environment," discusses these two `SET` parameters.

You can apply the `$` operator to Character operands only. Sometimes called the substring operator, `$` returns `.T.` if the left string is contained within the right string. Here is an example:

Command Window	*Results*
`A = "Now is the time."`	`Now is the time.`
`? "time" $ A`	`.T.`
`? "now" $ A`	`.F.`

This example fails because the substring comparison is case sensitive. `now` is not the same as `Now`.

Two additional operators, AND and OR, combine logical expressions. Like the periods around logical constants, the periods here are significant (although probably not for any good reason in this case). The expression <expL1> AND <expL2> is .T. only if both <expL1> and <expL2> are .T.. The expression <expL1> OR <expL2> is .T. if either <expL1> or <expL2> is .T.. The other boolean algebra operator, exclusive-or, can be simulated with a more complicated expression:

```
(<expL1> OR <expL2>) AND NOT (<expL1> AND <expL2>)
```

The .NOT. operator is an example of a unary operator. The operators described so far are binary operators, so named because they are used between two operands. A unary operator such as .NOT. appears in front of a single operand. If L is .T., then .NOT. L is .F. (and vice versa). You can also use the ! character as a synonym for .NOT.. For example, ! L is equivalent to .NOT. L..

NOTE

Prior to FoxPro 2, the AND, OR, and NOT operators were enclosed by periods and had the form .AND., .OR., and .NOT.. All Xbase products support this form, including Visual FoxPro. Therefore, if portability is a consideration, you should enclose logical operators with periods. Dropping the periods certainly benefits the language syntax by making it more like standard English.

The .AND., .OR., and .NOT. forms of the logical operators date back to the genesis of the Xbase language in JPLDIS created in 1972 for a Univac mainframe computer. (JPLDIS was the original Xbase Jet Propulsion Laboratory Database Management and Information Retrieval System.) JPLDIS was written in FORTRAN, which used .AND., .OR., and .NOT..

The !, !=, and == operators were taken from the C languages. All modern Xbase programs are written in C or C++, so it was not surprising that these operator forms would find their way into the Xbase languages.

Numeric Operators

The FoxPro numeric operators, often called *arithmetic operators*, are just what you would expect from a language similar to BASIC. They are described in Table 5.2.

Table 5.2. Numeric (arithmetic) operators.

Operator	*Description*
unary -	Take the negative of the number
unary +	No effect; for symmetry with unary -

continues

Table 5.2. continued

Operator	*Description*
`+`	Addition
`-`	Subtraction
`*`	Multiplication
`/`	Division
`**` or `^`	Exponentiation
`%`	Modulus operator

The modulus operator does not operate as straightforwardly as do the numeric operators. It returns the remainder that results from dividing one numeric expression by another. A few common examples of these operators are the following:

Command Window	*Results*
`A = 123`	`123`
`? -A`	`-123`
`B = -1`	`-1`
`? +B`	`-1`
`? 2 + 234`	`236`
`? 234 - 123`	`111`
`? 4 * 8`	`32`
`? 9/3`	`3`
`? 3^3`	`27`
`? 42 % 10`	`2`
`? 91.234 % 18`	`1.234`

Operator Precedence

FoxPro expressions follow conventional precedence rules. However, not everyone remembers rules such as "multiplication is always performed before addition." The following statement:

```
? 2 + 3 * 4
```

displays `14`. If you evaluate this expression left to right, without giving the multiplication operator (`*`) higher precedence than the addition operator (`+`), the result is `20`. You can easily remember standard arithmetic precedence by memorizing the mnemonic "My Dear Aunt Sally"—M, D, A, S, for multiplication, division, addition, and subtraction, respectively.

With parentheses you can override the precedence rules and explicitly specify the order in which operations are performed. As with most programming languages, FoxPro gives the highest precedence to evaluating subexpressions within parentheses. When pairs of parentheses are nested, the innermost subexpression is evaluated first. If you want the previous example to return `20`, you would write:

```
? (2 + 3) * 4
```

Table 5.3 lists precedence rules for FoxPro. Level 1 has the highest precedence, and level 9 has the lowest precedence.

Table 5.3. FoxPro precedence rules.

Precedence Level	*Operator*
1	Parentheses
2	Unary +/-
3	Exponentiation
4	Modulus
5	Multiplication and division
6	Addition, subtraction, and string concatenation
7	Relational operators (=, <, >, and so on)
8	Unary `.NOT.`
9	Logical operators (`.AND.` and `.OR.`)

In the following example, the subexpression `3 - 1` is evaluated first because parentheses have the highest precedence:

```
? 4 * (8 - 2^3 * (3 - 1))
```

The expression is then the following:

```
? 4 * (8 - 2^3 * 2)
```

Because exponentiation has the highest precedence of the operators inside the remaining parentheses, the subexpression `2^3` is evaluated next, leaving this:

```
? 4 * (8 - 8 * 2)
```

Next comes multiplication:

```
? 4 * (8 - 16)
```

The parenthetic expression is then evaluated, leaving this:

```
? 4 * -8
```

Then the result is calculated:

```
? -32
```

This result is quite different from 7, which is the result if the expression has no parentheses:

```
? 4 * 8 - 2^3 * 3 - 1
```

Functions

Functions, like other operands, always return a particular type. Some amorphous functions, such as IIF() and LOOKUP(), return values based on their arguments, but you can usually group FoxPro functions by the type they return.

The tables in this section provide each function's syntax and description, and the data type of the returned value. Some functions can return different data types depending on the type of the arguments. The letters in Table 5.4 denote the data type of the returned value.

Table 5.4. Data types returned by functions.

Returned Value	*Data Type*
C	Character
D	Date
I	Integer
L	Logical
N	Numeric
S	Same type as the argument
T	DateTime
Y	Currency
X	Type depends on the function operation

Numeric and Mathematical Functions

Table 5.5 lists all FoxPro numeric and mathematical functions. CEILING(), FLOOR(), LOG10(), and SIGN() are standard library functions that are also available in other languages. The Return Type column is the data type of the value returned by the function.

Table 5.5. Mathematical functions.

Function	*Usage*	*Return Type*
ABS(<*expN*>)	Absolute value.	N
CEILING(<*expN*>)	Smallest integer > argument.	N

Function	*Usage*	*Return Type*	
`EXP(<expN>)`	Exponential to base E.	N	
`FIXED(<expN>)`	Returns same numeric value.**	N	
`FLOAT(<expN>)`	Returns same numeric value.**	N	
`FLOOR(<expN>)`	Largest integer < argument.	N	
`INT(<expN>)`	Truncates argument to integer.	N	
`LOG(<expN>)`	Natural logarithm of argument.	N	
`LOG10(<expN>)`	Common logarithm of argument.	N	
`MAX(<exp>, <exp>)`	Maximum value of two values.	*	
`MIN(<exp>, <exp>)`	Minimum value of two values.	*	
`MOD(<expN>, <expN>)`	Modulus.	N	
`MTON(<expY>)`	Returns a numeric value from a currency expression. (FoxPro issues an error if `<expY>` is invalid.)	N	NEW FOR VISUAL FOXPRO 3
`NTOM(<expN>)`	Returns a currency value from a numeric expression.	Y	NEW FOR VISUAL FOXPRO 3
`RAND([<expN>])`	Returns a pseudorandom number.	N	
`ROUND(<expN>, <expN>)`	Rounds first argument.	N	
`SIGN(<expN>)`	Sign of argument.	N	
`SQRT(<expN>)`	Square root.	N	
`VAL(<expC>)`	Converts string to number.	N	

* Arguments can be Character, Date, or Numeric. The type must be the same.

** dBASE IV has two types of numbers: binary-coded decimal (BCD) and floating point. FoxPro has only one type of number. In dBASE IV, `FLOAT()` converts a BCD floating number (type `N`) to an IEEE long real binary number (type `F`). `FIXED()` is simply the inverse of `FLOAT()`. It converts a type `F` number to type `N`. Normally, the conversions are transparent and these functions are not needed. FoxPro's `FLOAT()` and `FIXED()` functions are compatible with dBASE IV. They are actually dummy functions that return the numeric value of the argument. FoxPro supports two types of database structure numeric fields: Float and Numeric. FoxPro documentation suggests that you store business calculations in Numeric type fields and scientific calculations in Float type fields. However, in the current version of Visual FoxPro, the only purpose for supporting the Float and Numeric structure types is to provide compatibility with dBASE IV database files.

The RAND() function returns a pseudorandom number between 0 and 1.0. A *seed* is some arbitrary number that you feed into a random number generator in order to generate a pseudorandom number and a new random value for the seed. If the argument is a negative number, the system clock generates the seed. If the argument is a positive number, the number replaces the default seed. If no argument is provided, the current seed is used to produce the random number. If you don't provide any argument for the first call of RAND(), FoxPro uses an initial seed value of 100,001.

The FoxPro pseudorandom generator uses a multiplicative algorithm. Approximately 2^{32} numbers are generated before a pseudorandom number is repeated. This should be a sufficient number of numbers. About 1023 years are required to create a repeated sequence of pseudorandom numbers on a 386 microcomputer running at 20MHz.

To use the random number generator, call RAND() once with an argument to provide a new seed, and at the same time, call RAND() with no arguments. Listing 5.1 illustrates the RAND() function.

Listing 5.1. The source listing of the file FLIPCOIN.PRG.

```
*****************************************************
* FLIPCOIN.PRG - Illustrates the RAND() Function
*                Flip a coin
*****************************************************
=RAND(-1)  && Initialize seed value from system clock
CLEAR
Answer = 'Y'
STORE 0 to Tails, Heads
DO WHILE UPPER(Answer) = 'Y'
   IF RAND() > .5       && Call with no arguments
      @ 2,2 TO 14,22 STYLE '99' PATTERN 1 PEN 2 COLOR 'B/B'
      @ 6,7 SAY "HEADS"   color w+/B FONT "roman",24
      Heads = Heads + 1
   ELSE
      @ 2,2 TO 14,22 STYLE '99' PATTERN 1 PEN 2 COLOR 'B/R'
      @ 6,7 SAY "TAILS"   color w+/R FONT "roman",24
      Tails = Tails + 1
   ENDIF
   @ 15,4  SAY "Flip another coin? (Y/N):" GET Answer
   @ 16,4  SAY "Heads:"
   @ 16,11 SAY LTRIM(STR(Heads))
   @ 16,24 SAY "Tails: "
   @ 16,31 SAY LTRIM(STR(Tails))
   READ
ENDDO
CLEAR
RETURN
```

Figure 5.1 is sample output from the execution of the FLIPCOIN.PRG program. The program also illustrates how to draw circles.

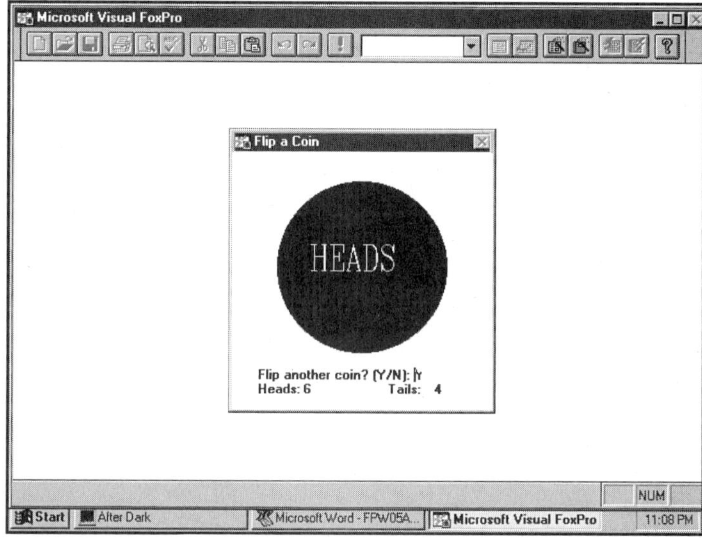

FIGURE 5.1.
The result of executing the FLIPCOIN.PRG program.

Trigonometric Functions

The functions presented in Table 5.6 are basic trigonometric functions. The arguments for `ACOS()` and `ASIN()` must be between -1.0 and 1.0, inclusive.

Table 5.6. Trigonometric functions.

Function	*Usage*	*Type*
`ACOS(`<*expN*>`)`	Arccosine $(0 > \text{acos}(x) < \pi)$*	N
`ASIN(`<*expN*>`)`	Arcsine $(-\pi/2 < \text{asin}(x) > \pi/2)$*	N
`ATAN(`<*expN*>`)`	Arctangent $(-\pi/2 > \text{atan}(x) < \pi/2)$*	N
`ATN2(`<*expN*>, <*expN*>`)`	Two argument arctangent $(-\pi > \text{atn2}(x) < \pi)$*	N
`COS(`<*expN*>`)`	Cosine**	N
`DTOR(`<*expN*>`)`	Convert degrees to radians*	N
`PI()`	Returns value of π (3.141592653589...)	N
`RTOD(`<*expN*>`)`	Converts radians to degrees	N
`SIN(`<*expN*>`)`	Sine**	N
`TAN(`<*expN*>`)`	Tangent**	N

* Results are in radians.

** Argument is in radians.

Financial Functions

FoxPro supports several functions that perform basic financial calculations. These include the `NPV()`(net present value), `FV()` (future value), `PV()` (present value), and `PAYMENT()` (a function to determine the payment schedule for a loan). The `NPV()` function is used with the `CALCULATE` command. It is described in Chapter 12, "Data Set Operations." Table 5.7 summarizes the financial functions.

Table 5.7. Financial functions.

Function	*Usage*	*Type*
FV(<*expN*>, <*expN*>, <*expN*>)	Future value*	N
PAYMENT(<*expN*>, <*expN*>, <*expN*>)	Payment for a loan**	N
PV(<*expN*>, <*expN*>, <*expN*>)	Present value*	N

* Arguments are payment, N rate, and periods, in that order.

** Arguments are N principal, rate, and number of periods, in that order.

The `FV()` function computes the compounded value of equal regular deposits into an investment that pays a given interest rate for a certain period. The future value is the amount of an annuity and is the sum of all the payments plus the accumulated compound interest. For example, assume that you invest $1 for 6 years at 8.00 percent annual interest compounded quarterly. First, compute the compounded interest rate by dividing the annual interest rate, 8.00, by the number of compounded periods per year (4). The number of periods is the number of years (6) multiplied by the number of compounded periods per year (4). Now enter these values into the `FV()` function as follows:

Command Window	*Result*
`? FV(1.0, .08/4, 6.0*4.0)`	`30.42`

The equation for computing the `FV()` in FoxPro is

$$FV=\frac{\langle payment\rangle * ((1+\langle rate\rangle\langle periods\rangle)-1)}{\langle rate\rangle}$$

<*payment*>::= constant regular payment
<*rate*> ::= compounding period interest rate
<*periods*>::= number of compounding periods

The `PV()` function computes the present value of equal regular payments invested at a constant interest rate for a given number of periods. (*Equal regular payments* means that no balloon payments or similar nonsense exists.) The payments reduce the principal, but the remaining balance continues to generate and compound interest. The present value is the amount that you must invest now to produce a known value in the future. For example, if you could afford to invest $1100 each month for a 30-year mortgage charging 12.00 percent interest (compounded monthly), the present value would be

Command Window	*Result*
`? PV (1100, .12/12, 30*12)`	`106940.16`

The FoxPro equation for computing the present value is

$$PV=\frac{\langle payment\rangle \left(1-\frac{1}{1+\langle rate\rangle\langle periods\rangle}\right)}{\langle rate\rangle}$$

`<payment>::=` constant regular payment
`<rate>   ::=` compounding period interest rate
`<periods>::=` number of compounding periods

The `PAYMENT()` function calculates the constant regular payment required to pay off a loan made for a principal amount at a certain interest rate over a particular number of periods. For example, you can use the `PAYMENT()` function to calculate the monthly payment for a 30-year $120,000 mortgage at an annual interest rate of 12.00 percent:

Command Window	*Result*
`? PAYMENT(120000.0, .12/12, 30*12)`	`1234.34`

The equation for computing the `PAYMENT()` function in FoxPro is

$$PAYMENT=\frac{\langle principal\rangle\langle rate\rangle}{(1-(1+\langle rate\rangle)\langle periods\rangle)}$$

`<principal>::=` total principal amount
`<rate>       ::=` compounding period interest rate
`<periods>    ::=` number of compounding periods

Character String Functions

The character string functions presented in Table 5.8 are used for character manipulation operations.

Table 5.8. Character string functions.

Function	Usage	Type
`ALLTRIM(<expC>)`	Returns <expC> with leading and trailing blanks removed.	C
`ASC(<expC>)`	Returns a numeric ASCII code.	N
`AT(<expC1>, <expC2> [,<expN>])`	Returns the position of the <expC1> substring in the <expC2> string. If <expN> is specified, the position of the <expN>th occurrence of <expC1> in <expC2> is returned.	N
`ATC(<expC1>, <expC2> [,<expN>])`	Returns the position of the <expC1> substring in the <expC2> string while ignoring case.	N
`ATCLINE(<expC1>, <expC2>)`	Returns the line number of the <expC1> substring in the <expC2> string while ignoring case.	N
`ATLINE(<expC1>, <expC2>)`	Returns the line number of the <expC1> substring in the <expC2> string.	N
`BETWEEN(<exp1>, <exp2>,<exp3>)`	Returns `.T.` if <exp1> is greater than or equal to <exp2> and less than or equal to <exp3>. Otherwise, it returns `.F.`.	L
`CHR(<expN>)`	Returns the ASCII character for the number.	C
`CHRSAW([<expN>])`	Returns `.T.` if a character is present in the keyboard buffer. Otherwise, it returns `.F.`. If the argument is present, it is assigned an amount of time (in seconds) to wait before it returns. If the argument is absent, `CHRSAW()` returns immediately.	L
`CHRTRAN(<expC1>, <expC2>,<expC3>)`	Translates characters in <expC1> using strings in <expC2> and <expC3> as the translation table. A character in <expC1> that matches a character in <expC2> is replaced by the corresponding character in <expC3>.	C
`DIFFERENCE(<expC>, <expC>)`	Returns the difference between two Soundex codes (1 through 4). See `Soundex()` function.	N

Function	*Usage*	*Type*
ISALPHA(<*expC*>)	Returns .T. if the first character is a letter.	L
ISDIGIT(<*expC*>)	Returns .T. if the first character is a digit.	L
ISLOWER(<*expC*>)	Returns .T. if the first character is lowercase.	L
ISUPPER(<*expC*>)	Returns .T. if the first character is uppercase.	L
LEFT(<*expC*>, <*expN*>)	Returns the specified number of characters from the left of the character string.	C
LEN(<*expC*>)	Returns the length of the character string.	N
LIKE(<*skeleton2*>, <*expC*>)	Compares the character string with the wildcard skeleton and returns .T. on a match.	L
LOWER(<*expC*>)	Converts uppercase letters to lowercase.	C
LTRIM(<*expC*>)	Removes leading blanks from the character string.	C
OCCURS(<*expC1*>, <*expC2*>)	Returns the number of times <*expC1*> occurs in <*expC2*>.	N
PADL(<*exp*>, <*expN*>[,<*expC*>])	Returns the character string containing an ASCII representation of the evaluated expression that is <*expN*> characters wide. The expression is padded with either blanks or <*expC*> on the left.	C
PADR(<*exp*>, <*expN*>[,<*expC*>])	Returns the character string containing an ASCII representation of the evaluated expression that is <*expN*> characters wide. The expression is padded with either blanks or <*expC*> on the right.	C
PADC(<*exp*>, <*expN*>[,<*expC*>])	Returns the character string containing an ASCII representation of the evaluated expression that is <*expN*> characters wide. The expression is padded with either blanks or <*expC*> on both sides (centered).	C

continues

Table 5.8. continued

Function	*Usage*	*Type*
`PROPER(<expC>)`	Returns <expC> with the first letter of each word uppercase and the remaining characters in lowercase.	C
`RAT(<expC1>, <expC2>.. [,<expN>])`	Returns the position of the <expC1> substring in the <expC2> string. The search starts from the right of <expC2>.	N
`RATLINE(<expC1>, <expC2>)`	Returns the line number of the last occurrence of the <expC1> substring in the <expC2> string.	N
`REPLICATE(<expC>, <expN>)`	Returns the character expression repeated a specified number of times.	C
`RIGHT(<expC>, <expN>)`	Returns the specified number of characters from the right of the character string.	N
`RTRIM(<expC>)`	Removes trailing blank characters from the string.	C
`SOUNDEX(<expC>)`	Converts the string to a Soundex code. A Soundex code is a four-character phonetic representation of a specified character expression. By comparing two Soundex codes, you can determine if the two expressions are phonetically similar. This means that the two expressions sound alike. For example "Smith" and "Smyth" have the same Soundex code.	C
`SPACE(<expN>)`	Returns a character string consisting of the specified number of blanks.	C
`STRTRAN(<expC1>, <expC2> [,<expC3>] [,<expN1>] [,<expN2>])`	Replaces occurrences of <expC2> in <expC1> with <expC3>. <expN1> specifies which occurrence to begin replacement. <expN2> specifies the number of occurrences to replace.	C
`STR(<expN> [,<expN> [,<expN>]])`	Converts a number to a character string.	C

Function	Usage	Type
STUFF(<expC>, <expN>, <expN>, <expC>)	Replaces a substring in a character string.	C
SUBSTR(<expC>, <expN> [,<expN>])	Extracts a substring from a string.	C
TRIM(<expC>)	Same as RTRIM().	C
UPPER(<expC>)	Converts lowercase letters to uppercase.	C

Date Functions

Functions presented in Table 5.9 are used for data operations of the Date type.

Table 5.9. Date functions.

Function	Usage	Type	
CDOW(<expD>)	Returns the day of the week (Monday, for example).	C	
CMONTH(<expD>)	Returns the name of the month in <expD>.	C	
CTOD(<expC>)	Converts a character string to a date.	D	
CTOT(<expC>)	Returns a DateTime value from a character expression.	T	NEW FOR VISUAL FOXPRO 3
DATE()	Returns today's date.		
DATETIME()	Returns the current date and time as a DateTime value.	T	NEW FOR VISUAL FOXPRO 3
DAY(<expD>)	Returns the numeric value of the day of the month.	N	
DMY(<expD>)	Converts the date to the form *DD* Month *yyyy* (28 September 1950, for example).	C	
DOW(<expD> ¦<expT> [,<expN>])	Returns the numeric day of the week. <expN> is the first day of the week. Sunday = 1 (which is the default), Monday = 2, and so on. If <expN> = 0, the "first day of week" option, in the	N	REVISED FOR VISUAL FOXPRO 3

continues

Table 5.9. continued

	Function	*Usage*	*Type*
		Tools menu, Options dialog box, is used as the first day.	
	`DTOC(<expD>[,1])`	Converts the date to a character string. Specify the second argument (1) to return a sortable value.	C
	`DTOS(<expD>)`	Converts the date to a character string in the form *CCYYMMDD* (century, year, month, day).	C
NEW FOR VISUAL FOXPRO 3	`DTOT(<expD>)`	Returns a DateTime value from a date expression.	T
NEW FOR VISUAL FOXPRO 3	`FDATE(<expFN>)`	Returns the last modification date for a file.	D
NEW FOR VISUAL FOXPRO 3	`FTIME(<expFN>)`	Returns the last modification time for a file.	C
	`GOMONTH(<expD>, <expN>)`	Returns the date that is `<expN>` months before or after `<expD>`.	D
NEW FOR VISUAL FOXPRO 3	`HOUR(<expT>)`	Returns the hour portion from a DateTime expression.	N
	`MDY(<expD>)`	Converts the date to the form *Month DD, YYYY* (June 8, 1917, for example).	C
NEW FOR VISUAL FOXPRO 3	`MINUTE(<expT>)`	Returns the minute portion from a `DateTime` expression.	N
	`MONTH(<expD>)`	Returns the number of the month for a `DateTime` expression.	N
NEW FOR VISUAL FOXPRO 3	`SEC(<expT>)`	Returns the seconds portion from a `DateTime` expression.	N
	`SECONDS()`	Returns the number of seconds elapsed since midnight.	N
	`TIME()`	Returns the current time in the form *hh:mm:ss.*	C
NEW FOR VISUAL FOXPRO 3	`TTOC(<expT>[,1])`	Returns a character value from a `DateTime` expression. Specifies the second argument (`1`) to return a sortable value.	C
NEW FOR VISUAL FOXPRO 3	`TTOD(<expT>)`	Returns a date value from a DateTime expression.	D

Function	Usage	Type
WEEK(<expD>¦<expT> [,<expN>] [,<expN>]))	Returns a number representing the week-of-the-year from a date or DateTime expression.	N
YEAR(<expD>)	Returns the year (1991, for example).	N

DBF File Functions

Table 5.10 presents functions related to DBF and DBC files. Chapter 11 discusses these functions in more depth.

Table 5.10. DBF and DBC file functions.

Function	Usage	Type
ALIAS([<expWA>])	Returns the alias name.	C
ADATABASES(<array>)	Fills the array with the names of all open databases and their paths. Returns the array's size.	N
ADBOBJECTS()(<array>, <expC>)	Fills a memory variable array with the names of all named connections, tables, or SQL views in a database.	N
AUSED(<array>,[<expN>])	Fills an array with a session's table aliases and work areas.	N
BOF([<expWA>])	Returns .T. if the record pointer of the table is positioned to the first record.	L
CURSORGETPROP(<expC> [,<expWA>])	Returns the current property (<expC>) settings for a FoxPro table or cursor.	X
CURSORSETPROP(<expC> [,<exp>][,<expWA>])	Specifies property (<expC>) settings (<exp>) for a Visual FoxPro table or cursor (<expWA>).	L
DBC()	Returns the fully qualified path and name of the current database.	C
DBF([<expWA>])	Returns the specified table (DBF file) filename.	C

continues

Table 5.10. continued

	Function	*Usage*	*Type*
NEW FOR VISUAL FOXPRO 3	`DBGETPROP(<expC1>, <expC2>,<expC3>)`	Returns a property for the current database, field, named connection, table, or view (<expC1>) in the current database. <expC2> is the type (for example, `CONNECTION`, `DATABASE`) and <expC3> is the property name.	X
NEW FOR VISUAL FOXPRO 3	`DBSETPROP(<expC1>, <expC2>,<expC3>, <expC4>)`	Sets a property for the current database, field, named connection, table, or view (<expC>) in the current database. <expC2> is the type (for example, `CONNECTION`, `DATABASE`). <expC3> is the property name.	N
NEW FOR VISUAL FOXPRO 3	`DBUSED(<expC>)`	Returns `.T.` if the current table (DBF file) is active.	L
NEW FOR VISUAL FOXPRO 3	`CURVAL(<field>,<expWA>)`	Returns a field value directly from a disk or a remote source.	X
	`DELETED([<expWA>])`	Returns `.T.` if the current record is deleted.	L
	`EOF([<expWA>])`	Returns `.T.` if the table's record pointer is positioned at the end of a file.	L
	`FCOUNT([<expWA>])`	Returns the number of fields for a table in the specified or current work area.	N
	`FIELD(<expN>[,<expWA>])`	Returns the field name of the specified field number in the table.	C
	`FILTER([<expWA>])`	Returns the `SET FILTER` expression for the current or specified table.	C
	`FLDCOUNT([<expWA>])`	Returns the number of fields in the structure of the table.	N
	`FLDLIST([<expN>])`	Returns character string containing `SET FIELDS TO` expression.	
	`FSIZE(<expC>[,<expWA)>])`	Returns the size of the specified table field in bytes. Returns the size of specified file, `FSIZE(<expFN>)`, if `SET COMPATIBILITY` is `DB4`.	N

Function	*Usage*	*Type*	
GETFLDSTATE(<expC> ¦<expN>[,<expWA>])	Returns a numeric value that indicates whether a field in a table or a cursor has been edited, or whether the deleted status of the current record has been changed.	N	NEW FOR VISUAL FOXPRO 3
GETNEXTMODIFIED(<expN> [,<expWA>])	Returns the record number for the next modified record in a buffered cursor. <expN> is the current record number.	N	NEW FOR VISUAL FOXPRO 3
HEADER([<expWA>])	Returns the size of the specified table (DBF file) header in bytes.	N	
INDBC(<expC1>,<expC2>)	Returns .T. if the specified object <expC1> of type <expC2> exists in the current database.	L	NEW FOR VISUAL FOXPRO 3
ISEXCLUSIVE(<expWA>)	Returns .T. if a table is opened for exclusive use. Returns .F. otherwise.	L	NEW FOR VISUAL FOXPRO 3
ISREADONLY([<expWA>])	Returns a logical true (.T.) value if the table in the specified work area is read only.	L	
LUPDATE([<expWA>])	Returns the date when the specified table was last updated.	D	
OLDVAL(<expC> [,<expWA>])	Returns the original field value for a field that has been modified but not updated.	N	NEW FOR VISUAL FOXPRO 3
RECCOUNT([<expWA>])	Returns the record count of the specified table.	N	
RECNO([<expWA>])	Returns the current record number of the specified table.	N	
RECSIZE([<expWA>])	Returns the length in bytes of the specified table.	N	
SELECT([0¦1¦ <expWA>])	Returns the number of the highest unused work area.	N	REVISED FOR VISUAL FOXPRO 3
SETFLDSTATE (<expC>¦<expN1>), <expN2> [,<expWA>])	Assigns a field or deletion state (<expN2>) value to a field (<expC>) or a record (<expN1>) in a local cursor created from remote tables.	L	NEW FOR VISUAL FOXPRO 3

continues

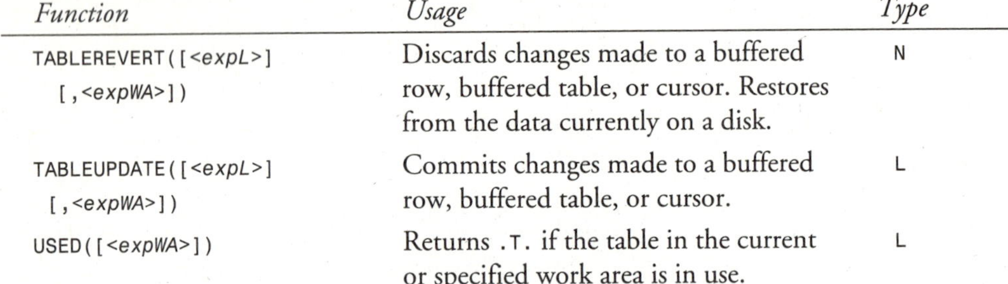

Table 5.10. continued

Function	Usage	Type
`TABLEREVERT([<expL>] [,<expWA>])`	Discards changes made to a buffered row, buffered table, or cursor. Restores from the data currently on a disk.	N
`TABLEUPDATE([<expL>] [,<expWA>])`	Commits changes made to a buffered row, buffered table, or cursor.	L
`USED([<expWA>])`	Returns `.T.` if the table in the current or specified work area is in use.	L

Memo Field Functions

Table 5.11 presents functions that are specifically related to memo fields. Some of these functions are also used with character fields; they are repeated in this section to emphasize the fact that you can use these functions with memo fields in FoxPro.

Table 5.11. Functions that operate on memo fields.

Function	Usage	Type
`AT(<expC>, <memo field name>)`	Returns the position of a substring in a memo field. The `ATC()`, `ATLINE()`, and `ATCLINE()` functions, shown in Table 5.8, also support memo fields.	N
`LEFT(<memo field name>,<expN>)`	Returns the specified number of characters from the left of the memo field.	N
`LEN(<memo field name>)`	Returns the length of a memo field.	N
`LTRIM(<memo field name>)`	Returns memo field, with leading blanks removed.	C
`MEMLINES(<memo field name>)`	Returns the number of lines in a memo field.	N
`MLINE(<field name>, <expN1> [,<expN2>])`	Returns the specified line from a memo field.	C
`RIGHT(<memo field name>,<expN>)`	Returns the specified number of characters from the right end of a memo field.	C

Function	*Usage*	*Type*
RTRIM(<*memo field name*>)	Returns a memo field, with trailing blanks removed.	C
SUBSTR(<*memo field name*>,<*expN*> [,<*expN*>])	Extracts a substring from a memo field.	C
TRIM(<*memo field name*>)	Performs the same job as RTRIM().	C

The MEMLINES() function returns the number of lines of text in a specified memo field contained within the current table. This function determines the number of lines by word wrapping the memo field contents. The width of the line is determined by the current SET MEMOWIDTH setting. (See Chapter 10.) The MLINES() function extracts a specified line from the specified memo field. For example, the following program lists the memo field, Mfield, one line at a time:

```
SET TALK OFF
SET MEMOWIDTH TO 23
Line = 0
Nolines = MEMLINES(Mfield)
DO WHILE Line < Nolines
   Line = Line + 1
   ? STR(Line,2), MLINE(Mfield, Line)
ENDDO
```

The following is the output of this program:

```
1 Once upon a midnight
2 dreary, while I
3 pondered, weak and
4 weary,
5 Over many a quaint and
6 curious volume of
7 forgotten lore
8 While I nodded, nearly
9 napping, suddenly there
10 came a tapping,
11 As of someone gently
12 rapping, rapping at my
13 chamber door.
14
15 Edgar Allen Poe, "The
16 Raven" (1845)
```

You can specify the optional third argument (<*expN2*>) with the MLINE() function to speed up the program's operation. The <*expN2*> argument specifies an offset in bytes from the beginning of the memo field to begin the search for the specified line of text. If the argument is omitted, MLINE() searches from the beginning of the memo field. Normally, the _MLINE system memory variable is specified as the third argument. Each time MLINE() is called, it extracts the specified line of text from the memo field. Then it stores the position of the memo field at the beginning of the line (following the extracted line of text) in the `_MLINE` system memory variable. Finally, it returns a character string containing the extracted line of text.

The following two examples illustrate the use of the `MLINE()` function. In the first example, `MLINE()` has two arguments. In the second, it has three arguments and runs faster. These examples produce identical results. The second example is the preferred one.

Here's an example of the two-argument `MLINE()` function:

```
SET TALK OFF
NoLines = MEMLINES( Mfield ) && Number of lines in memo field
FOR LINE = 1 TO NoLines
   ? MLINE( Mfield, LINE )
ENDFOR

*******************************************************
* Example of three argument MLINE() function usage
SET TALK OFF
NoLines = MEMLINES( Mfield ) && Number of lines in memo field
_MLINE = 0   && Always set _MLINE to zero before using it
FOR LINE = 1 TO NoLines
   ? MLINE( Mfield, 1, _MLINE )
ENDFOR
```

Data Ordering Functions

Table 5.12 shows functions that are related to index files and used to order data access. Chapter 13, "Data Ordering," discusses these topics in more detail.

Table 5.12. Table (DBF file) functions.

	Function	*Usage*	*Type*
	`CANDIDATE(<expN>, <expWA>)`	Returns true (`.T.`) if an index tag is a candidate index tag.	L
	`CDX(<expN> [,<expWA>])`	Returns the name of an index CDX file tag.	C
	`DESCENDING([[<expFN>,] <expN>[,<expWA>]])`	Returns `.T.` if the specified CDX index tag was created with the `DESCENDING` keyword. Returns a logical false (`.F.`) value otherwise.	L
	`FOR([[<expFN>], <expN>[,<expWA>]])`	Returns a character string containing the `FOR` expression specified when the CDX tag is created.	C
	`FOUND([<expWA>])`	Returns `.T.` if the index key was found.	L
	`IDXCOLLATE(<expC> [,<expN1> [,<expWA>]])`	Returns the collation sequence for an index tag or an index.	C

Function	*Usage*	*Type*	
KEY([<expC>,] <expN1> [,<expWA>])	Returns the index key expression.	C	
KEYMATCH(<exp> [,<expN1>[,<expWA>]])	Returns .T. if the specified index key is found.	L	
LOOKUP(<field1>, <exp>,<field2> [,<expC>])	Looks up the value (<exp>) from the specified field in the specified table (<field2>). If the value is found, returns the value of <field2>. If it is not found, returns a null string. If <field2> is not in the current table, then it must contain an alias specification (alias->field). (The optional fourth argument specifies a compact index tag to use in the search).	S	
MDX(<expN> [,<expWA>])	Returns the name of an index CDX file tag. Same as CDX().	C	
NORMALIZE(<expC>)	Returns a string containing an expression in the same form as a string returned by the KEY() or FOR() functions.	C	
NDX(<expN> [,<expWA>])	Returns the name of an index file.	C	
PRIMARY(<expN> [,<expWA>])	Returns .T. if an index tag is a primary index tag. Returns .F. otherwise.	L	NEW FOR VISUAL FOXPRO 3
ORDER([<expWA> [,<expN>]])	Returns the name of the primary-order index file or CDX tag.	C	
RELATION(<expN> [,<expWA>])	Returns SET RELATION for an expression in the current or specified table. <expN> specifies the relation to the return.	C	
SEEK(<exp> [,<expWA>] [,<expN> ¦ <expFN> ¦ <expC>])	Seeks the specified value in the specified indexed table. Returns .T. if the specified value is found. The third argument specifies the index file, or the index tag number or name.	L	REVISED FOR VISUAL FOXPRO 3

continues

Table 5.12. continued

Function	Usage	Type
SYS(14,<expN> [,<expWA>])	Returns an index expression.	C
SYS(21)	Returns the number of the master controlling index.	N
SYS(22)	Returns the name of the master controlling index.	C
TAG([<expC>,] <expN> [,<expWA>])	Returns the name of the specified index tag in the specified table.	C
TAGCOUNT([<expFN> [,<expWA>]])	Returns the number of index tags.	N
TAGNO([<expC> [,<expFN> [,<expWA>]]])	Returns the tag number for the specified tag name.	N
TARGET(<expN> [,<expWA>])	Returns the alias of the table that is the target table for SET RELATION (for example, INTO <alias>). <expN> specifies the relation for which the alias is returned.	C
UNIQUE([[<expFN>, <expN>[,<expWA>]])	Returns .T. if the UNIQUE flag was specified when the CDX was created.	L

Array Functions

Table 5.13 presents the functions that are related to arrays.

Table 5.13. Array functions.

Function	Usage	Type
ACOPY(<array1>, <array2> [,<expN1> [,<expN2> [,<expN3>]]])	Copies elements from <array1> to <array2>. Returns the number of elements copied. (The optional <expN1> field is the element in <array1> where copying begins. <expN2> is the number of array rows to copy. <expN3> is the element in <array2> used to begin copying.) Also deletes	N

Function	*Usage*	*Type*
	the <expN> element from the one-dimensional array.	
ADEL(<array>, <expN>[,2])	Deletes the row number <expN> from the two-dimensional array unless the third argument, 2, is specified, when <expN> is an array column number to case delete. Returns 1 if the delete is successful.	N
ADIR(<array> [,<expC> [,<expC>]])	Reads the disk directory and inserts file information (name, size, date, time, and DOS attributes) into <array>. If array does not exist, it is created. If it already exists, its size is adjusted to hold the array. <expC1> contains the MS-DOS file skeleton (*.TXT, for example). <expC2> expands the search to include additional files. It can be one or more of the following values: D for search subdirectories H for include hidden files S for include system files V for include volume names Returns the number of array elements. The columns of the resulting array contain the following file information: **Column** **Contents** **Type** 1 Name Character 2 Size Numeric 3 Date Date 4 Time Character 5 Attribute Character	N
AELEMENT(<array>, <expN1> [,<expN2>])	Returns the array element number for two-dimensional arrays that is used by ACOPY, ASCAN, and ASORT. You supply the row (<expN1>) and column (<expN2>) subscript.	N

continues

Table 5.13. continued

<table>
<tr><th>Function</th><th>Usage</th><th>Type</th></tr>
<tr><td>NEW FOR VISUAL FOXPRO 3
<code>AERROR(<array>))</code></td><td>Creates an array and fills it with information relating to the most recent FoxPro or ODBC error.</td><td>N</td></tr>
<tr><td>REVISED FOR VISUAL FOXPRO 3
<code>AFIELDS(<array> [,<expWA>])</code></td><td>Places the table structure into an array. If an array does not exist, it is created. If the array exists, its size is adjusted to fit the structure. The array contains the following table structure information:
<table>
<tr><th>Column</th><th>Information</th><th>Type</th></tr>
<tr><td>1</td><td>Field name</td><td>Character</td></tr>
<tr><td>2</td><td>Data type
C = Character
D = Date
F = Float
G = General
I = Integer
B = Double
L = Logical
M = Memo
N = Numeric
T = DateTime
Y = Currency</td><td>Character</td></tr>
<tr><td>3</td><td>Field length</td><td>Numeric</td></tr>
<tr><td>4</td><td>Decimal places</td><td>Numeric</td></tr>
<tr><td>5</td><td>Null value?</td><td>.T. or .F.</td></tr>
<tr><td>6</td><td><expL> defines a column validation rule.</td><td></td></tr>
<tr><td>7</td><td>Error text for a validation rule.</td><td></td></tr>
<tr><td>8</td><td>Character string for a default value or NULL.
<expWA> defines the work area. If omitted, the current work area is assumed.</td><td></td></tr>
</table></td><td>N</td></tr>
</table>

Function	Usage	Type
AINS(<array>, <expN>, [,2])	Inserts the new <expN> element into a one-dimensional array. Inserts the new <expN> row number into a two-dimensional array unless the third argument, 2, is specified, in which case <expN> is the array column number to insert. Returns 1 if the insertion is successful. The size of the array is not changed. The last element, row, and column are discarded and the rest are shifted to the end of the array.	N
ALEN(<array> [,<expN>])	Returns the <array> row or column subscript given the element number depending on the value of <expN2>: <expN2> = 1 = row subscript <expN2> = 2 = column subscript	N
APRINTERS(<array>)	Fills an array with the names of the printers currently installed in the Windows Print Manager.	N
ASCAN(<array> [,<exp>] [,<expN1> [,<expN2>]])	Searches the array for the value that matches the expression (<exp>). If found, returns the number of the element containing the matching value. Otherwise, this function returns 0. <expN1> is the element number of the first element to search. <expN2> is the number of elements to search.	N
ASELOBJ(<array>,[1])	Fills an array with references to currently selected controls in the active Form Designer.	N
ASORT(<array> [,<expN1> [,<expN2> [,<expN3>]]])	Sorts the <array> array in ascending (<expN3>=0) or descending (<expN3>=1) order. Returns 1 if the sort was successful; otherwise, returns -1. The optional <expN1> field is the element or row in <array> where sorting begins. <expN2> is the number of array elements or rows to sort.	N

NEW FOR VISUAL FOXPRO 3 (APRINTERS)

NEW FOR VISUAL FOXPRO 3 (ASELOBJ)

continues

Table 5.13. continued

Function	*Usage*	*Type*
`ASUBSCRIPT (<array>, <expN1>, <expN2>)`	Returns the row (<expN2> = 1) or column (<expN2> = 2) of the specified element number (<expN1>).	N

User-Defined Window Functions

Table 5.14 presents user-defined window functions. Chapter 7, "FoxPro Language Elements for Creating Windows and Menu Systems," also discusses some of them. The character-expression argument in all functions evaluates to the name of a window. If the expression is not specified, the argument assumes that the function refers to the current window.

Table 5.14. User-defined window functions.

Function	*Usage*	*Type*
`WBORDER([<expC>])`	Returns `.T.` if the window has a border.	L
`WCHILD([<expC>] ¦ <expN>])`	Returns the number and name of a child window.	N/C
`WCOLS([<expC>])`	Returns the number of columns in a window.	N
`WEXIST([<expC>])`	Returns `.T.` if the specified window has been defined.	L
`WFONT(<expN> [,<windowname>])`	Returns the current font attributes for the current or specified window: **<expN>** — **Returned Value** — **Type** 1 — Font name — C 2 — Font size — N 3 — Style — C	
`WINDOW()`	Same as the `WOUTPUT()` function.	
`WLAST([<expC>])`	Returns the name of the window that was active prior to the current window. Returns `.T.` if <expC> is specified and is the name of the window that was active prior to the current window.	C/L
`WLCOL([<expC>])`	Returns the screen column location of the top-left border of a window.	N

Function	Usage	Type
WLROW([<expC>])	Returns the screen row location of the top-left border of a window.	N
WMAXIMUM([<expC>])	Returns .T. if the specified window is maximized (enlarged to fill the screen).	L
WMINIMIZE([<expC>])	Returns .T. if the specified window is minimized (reduced to its smallest size).	L
WONTOP([<expC>])	Returns .T. if the specified window is on top. If the window is not specified, it returns the name of the window that is on top.	L/C
WOUTPUT([<expC>])	Returns .T. if the specified window is the current output window. If the window is not specified, it returns the name of the current output window.	L/C
WPARENT([<expC>])	Returns the name of a parent window or blank if no parent exists.	C
WREAD([<expC>])	Returns .T. if specified window is involved in the current READ command.	L
WROWS([<expC>])	Returns the number of rows in the specified or current window.	N
WTITLE([<expC>])	Returns the window title assigned to the current or specified window.	C
WVISIBLE([<expC>])	Returns .T. if the window is activated and is not hidden.	L

User-Defined Menu and Pop-up Functions

Table 5.15 presents user-defined menu and pop-up functions. Chapter 7 discusses them further.

Table 5.15. User-defined menu functions.

Function	Usage	Type
BAR()	Returns the pop-up menu selection bar number.	N

continues

Table 5.15. continued

Function	*Usage*	*Type*
BARCOUNT([<expC>])	Returns the number of bars in an active or specified pop-up menu.	N
BARPROMPT(<expN> [, <expC>])	Returns text that appears on a pop-up menu bar.	C
CNTBAR(<expC>)	Returns the number of bars in a pop-up. <expC> is the pop-up name.	N
CNTPAD(<expC>)	Returns the number of pads in a menu. <expC> is the pop-up name.	N
GETBAR(<expC>, <expN>)	Returns the number of bars in a specified pop-up menu. <expC> is the menu name. <expN> is the position of the bar in the menu starting from the top. When bars are rearranged (that is, the MOVER keyword is specified), the bar number can differ from the option number returned by the BAR() function.	N
NEW FOR VISUAL FOXPRO 3 GETCOLOR([<expN>])	Displays the Windows Color dialog box. <expN> is the initially selected color.	N
NEW FOR VISUAL FOXPRO 3 GETCP(<expN>, <expC>,<expC>)	Displays the Code Page dialog box and the number of the chosen code page.	N
NEW FOR VISUAL FOXPRO 3 GETPRINTER()	Displays the Windows Print Setup dialog box and returns the name of the printer selected.	C
GETDIR([<expC> [,<expC2>]])	Displays the Directory Selection dialog box and returns the name of the selected directory.	C
GETFILE([<expC1>] [,<expC2>] [, <expC3>] [, <expN>])	Displays the File Open dialog box and returns name of the selected file. <expC1> specifies extensions, <expC2> specifies the dialog caption, <expC3> specifies the Open button caption, and <expN> specifies the number of buttons.	C
GETFONT()	Displays the Font Selection dialog box so the user can select a font, font size, and font style. The selection is returned in a string containing the font, font size, and font style separated by commas (for example, Swis721 BT,12,B).	C
GETPAD(<expC>, <expN>)	Returns name of pad, given the position of the pad (<expN>) in the specified menu bar (<expC>).	C

Function	*Usage*	*Type*
`GETPICT([<expC1>] [,<expC2>] [, <expC3>])`	Displays the File Open dialog box and returns the name of the selected picture file. <expC1> specifies extensions, <expC2> specifies the dialog caption, <expC3> specifies the Open button caption.	C
`LOCFILE([<expFN> ] [,<expC1>] [,<expC2>]) [,<expC3>]`	Searches for the <expFN> file. If not found, it displays the Open File dialog box and returns name of selected file.	C
`MENU()`	Returns the active menu bar name.	C
`MRKBAR(<expC>,<expN>)`	Returns `.T.` if the pop-up bar is marked. <expC> is the pop-up name. <expN> is the named pop-up option number.	L
`MRKPAD(<expC1>, <expC2>)`	Returns `.T.` if the specified menu pad (<expC2>) of the menu bar (<expC1>) is marked.	L
`PAD()`	Returns the active menu pad name.	C
`PADPROMPT(<expC1> [,<expC2>])`	Returns the text that appears on the menu bar pad.	C
`POPUP()`	Returns the active pop-up name.	C
`PRMBAR(<expC>,<expN>)`	Returns prompt text of pop-up option. <expC> is the pop-up name. <expN> is the named pop-up option number.	C
`PRMPAD(<expC1>, <expC2>)`	Returns the prompt text of the menu pad (<expC2>) of menu bar (<expC1>).	C
`PROMPT()`	Returns the label of the most recently selected pop-up or menu bar.	C
`PUTFILE([<expC1>] [,<expFN>] [<expC2>])`	Displays the Save As dialog box and returns the name of the selected file.	C
`SKPBAR(<expC>, <expN>)`	Returns `.T.` if the pop-up option (`BAR`) is enabled; `.F.` if the pop-up option is disabled. <expC> is the name of the pop-up. <expN> is the option number.	L

NEW FOR VISUAL FOXPRO 3

continues

Table 5.15. continued

Function	*Usage*	*Type*
`SKPPAD(<expC1>, <expC2N>)`	Returns `.T.` if the menu pad is enabled, `.F.` if the menu pad is disabled. `<expC1>` is the name of the menu bar. `<expC2>` is the name of the menu pad.	`L`
`SYS(1037)`	Displays the Print Setup dialog box.	`C`
`SYS(2013)`	Returns the space-delimited character string containing the names of system menu bar, pads, pop-ups, and pop-up options.	`C`

NOTE

The `GETFILE()` and `GETFONT()` functions violate the four-unique-character rule in the FoxPro language. If you specify four characters—`GETF()`—`GETFILE()` executes. To execute `GETFONT()`, you must specify at least five characters—`GETFO()`.

Multiuser Functions

Table 5.16 presents functions related to multiuser operations. Chapter 25, "Multiuser Considerations," discusses these functions.

Table 5.16. Database multiuser functions.

Function	*Usage*	*Type*
`FLOCK([<expWA>])`	Locks a file and returns `.T.` if successful.	`N`
REVISED FOR VISUAL FOXPRO 3 `LOCK([<expC> ¦ <expN>] [,<expWA>])`	Locks specified records; returns `.T.`if successful. `<expC>` is a string containing a list of record numbers. `<expN>` is a record number.	`L`
`NETWORK()`	Returns `.T.` if Visual FoxPro for Windows is operating. In FoxPro for DOS, returns `.T.` if a multiuser system is running.	`L`
REVISED FOR VISUAL FOXPRO 3 `RLOCK([<expC> ¦ <expN>] [,<expWA>])`	Performs the same operations as `LOCK()`. If the record number is zero, the table header is locked preventing other users from adding new records to the table.	`L`

SQL Functions

Table 5.17 presents functions related to Visual FoxPro SQL commands. Chapter 18, "Queries Using SQL and the Query Designer," discusses these functions.

Table 5.17. SQL functions.

Function	*Usage*	*Type*
`REFRESH([<expN1>[,<expN2>]] [,<expWA>])`	Refreshes a set of records in a remote, updatable SQL view.	N
`REQUERY([<expWA>])`	Retrieves data again for a SQL view.	L
`SQLCANCEL(<expN>)`	Requests cancellation of an executing SQL statement.	N
`SQLCOLUMNS(<expN>,<expC1> [, FOXPRO ¦ NATIVE] [,<expC2>]))`	Stores a list of column names and column information for the specified data source table to a FoxPro cursor.	N
`SQLCOMMIT(<expN>)`	Commits a transaction.	L
`SQLCONNECT(<expC1>, <expC2>,<expC3>)`	Establishes a connection to a data source.	N
`SQLDISCONNECT(<expN>)`	Terminates a connection to a data source.	N
`SQLEXEC(<expC1>,<expC2> [,<expC3>])`	Sends a SQL statement to the data source, where the statement is processed.	N
`SQLGETPROP(<expN>¦<expC>, <expC>)`	Returns current or default settings for an active connection, data source, or attached table.	N
`SQLMORERESULTS(<expN>)`	Copies another result set to a FoxPro cursor if more result sets are available. `<expN>` is the connection handle.	N
`SQLROLLBACK(<expC>)`	Cancels any changes made during the current transaction. `<expC>` is the connection handle.	L
`SQLSETPROP((<expN>¦<expC>, <expC>[,<exp>])`	Specifies settings for an active connection, data source, or attached table.	N
`SQLSTRINGCONNECT(<expC>)`	Establishes a connection to a data source through a connection string (`<expC>`).	N

continues

Table 5.17. continued

Function	Usage	Type
`SQLTABLES(<expN>[,<expC1>] [,<expC2>)`	Stores the names of tables in a data source to a FoxPro cursor.	N

OOP Functions

Table 5.18 presents functions related to Visual FoxPro OOP methods. Chapter 14, "Object-Oriented Programming," discusses these functions.

Table 5.18. Object-oriented programming functions.

Function	Usage	Type
`ACLASS(<array>,<expC>)`	Fills array with the names of the parent class of an object. Returns the array size.	N
`AINSTANCE(<array>, <expC>)`	Fills the array with all instances of a class and returns the number of instances.	N
`AMEMBERS(<array>,<expC>)`	Fills an array with the names of properties, procedures, and member objects for an object.	N
`COMPOBJ(<expC1>,<expC2>)`	Compares the properties of two objects (`<expC>` and `<expC>`) and returns `.T.` if their properties and property values are identical.	L
`CREATEOBJECT(<expC>, <expC1>,<expC2>,...)`	Creates an object from a class or subclass definition, or an OLE object.	C
`GETOBJECT(<expFN> [,<expC>])`	Activates an OLE automation object and creates a reference to the object. `<expFN>` is the name of the file to activate. `<expC>` is the class name of the object.	O
`OBJREF(<expC>)`	Creates an indirect reference to an object using a memory variable or array element as a reference to the object.	O

Function	*Usage*	*Type*
OBJTOCLIENT(<*expC*>, <*expN*>)	Returns a position or dimension of a control or object relative to its form.<*expC*> is the object name. **<expN>** ***Position or Dimension*** 1 Top 2 Left 3 Width 4 Height	N

Functions Related to Input and Output

The functions presented in Table 5.19 are related to input and output operations. Chapter 8, "Input and Output," and Chapter 9, "Full-Screen Data Editing," discuss some of these functions in more detail.

Table 5.19. Input and output functions.

Function	*Usage*	*Type*	
COL()	Returns the current screen column position.	N	
CPCONVERT(<*expN1*>, <*expN2*>,<*expC*>)	Converts character or memo fields or character expressions to another code page.	C	NEW FOR VISUAL FOXPRO 3
CPCURRENT (1¦2)	Returns the code page setting, if available, in your Visual FoxPro configuration file, or returns the current operating system code page.	C	NEW FOR VISUAL FOXPRO 3
CPDBF(<*expWA*>)	Returns the code page with which an open table has been marked.	N	NEW FOR VISUAL FOXPRO 3
FONTMETRICS (<*expN1*> [,<*expC1*>, <*expN2*> [,<*expC2*>]])	Returns font attributes for the desktop or active output window. <*expN1*> specifies the type of attribute returned. To return an attribute for a specific font, specify the font and size (<*expC1*>, <*expN2*>) and optional font style (<*expC2*>).	C/N	

continues

Table 5.19. continued

Function	*Usage*	*Type*
`INKEY([`*<expN>*`])`	Returns the integer representing the ASCII value of a keystroke or `0` if no key has been pressed.	N
`ISMOUSE()`	Returns `.T.` if mouse hardware is present.	L
`LASTKEY()`	Returns the integer representing the ASCII value of the last key pressed.	N
`MCOL([`*<expC>*`])`	Returns the screen or window row position of the mouse. *<expC>* is the window name.	N
`MDOWN()`	Returns the state of the left mouse button. Returns `.T.` if the button is pressed.	L
NEW FOR VISUAL FOXPRO 3 `MESSAGEBOX(`*<expC1>* `[,`*<expN>* `[,`*<expC2>*`]])`	Displays a user-defined dialog box. *<expC1>* is the message. *<expC2>* is the title, and *<expN>* is the type.	N
`MROW([`*<expC>*`])`	Returns the screen or window column position of the mouse. *<expC>* is the window name.	N
`MWINDOW([`*<expC>*`]`	Returns the name of the window containing the mouse pointer if no arguments are specified. Returns `.T.` if *<expC>* (the window name) is specified and if the specified window contains the mouse pointer.	C/L
`OBJNUM(`*<expN>* `[,`*<expN>*`])`	Returns the object number of the `GET` field.	N
`OBJVAR([`*<expN1>* `[,`*<expN2>*`]])`	Returns the name of the memory variable associated with an `@...GET` object.	C
`PCOL()`	Returns the current printer column position.	N
`PRINTSTATUS()`	Returns `.T.` if the printer is ready to print output.	L
`PROW()`	Returns the current printer row position.	N
 `PRTINFO()`	Returns current Visual FoxPro printer settings.	N

Function	Usage	Type
RDLEVEL()	Returns the current nested READ level (0 through 5). Returns 0 if no READ is active.	N
READKEY()	Returns the integer value of the returned code from a full-screen, data-editing command.	N
RGB(<expN1>, <expN2>,<expN3>)	Returns a single color value from a set of red (<expN1>), green (<expN2>), and blue (<expN3>) color components.	N
RGBSCHEME(<expN1> [,<expN2>])	Returns an RGB color pair if <expN2> is specified. Otherwise, color list of 10 traditional FoxPro 2.0-type color pair RGB values are returned from the specified color scheme.	C
ROW()	Returns the current screen row position.	N
SCOL()	Returns the number of columns available on-screen.	N
SROW()	Returns the number of rows available on-screen.	N
SYSMETRICS(<expN>)	Returns the size of a window display element. The returned value is based on the value of <expN>.	N
TXTWIDTH(<expC1> [,<expC2>,<expN> [,<expC3>]])	Returns the width of a text string (<expC1>). The remaining arguments define the font, size, and style for the text string, respectively.	N
TRANSFORM(<exp>, <expC>)	Returns the PICTURE-formatted data value.	C
UPDATED()	Returns .T. if any data in the GET field was changed or if a choice was made from a GET object.	L
VARREAD()	Returns the name of the field or the memory variable currently being edited by a full-screen, data-editing command.	C

NEW FOR VISUAL FOXPRO 3

NEW FOR VISUAL FOXPRO 3

Low-Level File I/O Functions

Low-level file input and output (I/O) functions support C language type file I/O operations. See Chapter 8 for a discussion of these functions. Table 5.20 summarizes the low-level file I/O functions.

Table 5.20. Low-level file input and output functions.

Function	*Usage*	*Type*
`FCHSIZE(<expN1>, <expN2>])`	Changes the size of a file opened with a low-level I/O function. <*expN1*> is the file handle. <*expN2*> is the new size in bytes.	N
`FCLOSE(<expN>)`	Flushes and closes a low-level file. <*expN*> is the file handle.	N
`FCREATE(<expC> [,<expN>])`	Creates and opens a file. Returns the file handle used by other low-level file I/O functions. Returns `-1` if the file can't be created. <*expC*> is the filename. <*expN*> is the MS-DOS attribute.	N
`FDATE(<expFN>)`	Returns the last modification date for a file.	D
`FEOF(<expN>)`	Returns `.T.` if the file is positioned at the end of the file. <*expN*> is the file handle.	L
`FERROR()`	Returns `0` if the last file I/O operation was successful; otherwise, it returns the I/O error number.	N
`FFLUSH(<expN>)`	Flushes the buffers for the file to disk. <*expN*> is the file handle.	N
`FGETS(<expN1> [,<expN2>])`	Reads the line of information from the file. <*expN1*> is the file handle. <*expN2*> is the maximum number of bytes to read. Returns the character string containing the information read.	C
`FOPEN(<expC> [,<expN>])`	Opens an existing file for low-level file I/O. If successful, it returns a file handle that can be used by other low-level file I/O functions; otherwise, returns `-1`. <*expC*> is the filename. <*expN*> is the read/write privileges or buffer mode.	N

Function	Usage	Type
FPUTS(<expN1>, <expC> [,<expN2>])	Writes <expC> plus a carriage return and a line feed to the file. <expN1> is the file handle. <expN2> is the maximum number of bytes to write.	N
FREAD(<expN1>, <expN2>)	Reads <expN2> bytes from a file. <expN1> is the file handle. Returns the character string containing the information read.	C
FSEEK(<expN1>, <expN2> [,<expN3>])	Positions a file pointer. <expN1> is the file handle. <expN2> is the number of bytes needed to move the pointer. <expN3> is the positioning reference. Returns a new file position.	N
FSIZE(<expFN>)	Returns the size of the specified file in bytes if `SET COMPATIBLE DB4` is used.	N
FTIME(<expFN>)	Returns the last modification time for a file.	C
FWRITE(<expN1>, <expC> [,<expN2>])	Writes <expC> to a file. <expN1> is the file handle. <expN2> is the maximum number of bytes to write.	N

Bitwise Functions

Visual FoxPro 3.0 introduced *bitwise* functions. Bitwise functions are functions that operate on numeric values one bit at a time. Programmers sometimes like to save memory and disk space by packing logical type information into bits of single numeric variables. Suppose, for example, that you have the following binary-type pieces of information about a person:

1. Male or Female
2. Married: Yes or No
3. Children: Yes or No
4. US Citizen: Yes or No
5. Veteran: Yes or No
6. Employed: Yes or No
7. Retired: Yes or No
8. High School Degree: Yes or No
9. College Degree: Yes or No

You can store all this information (and more) in a single numeric value. In fact, you can store 32 pieces of logical information in a single numeric value. Suppose you have a numeric database field named `Info` and a logical memory variable array named `TRUTH`, which contain information for each item in the field. The following statements can be used to store the information in the `Info` field:

```
USE PEOPLE
m.info = 0;
FOR Item = 0 TO 8
   IF TRUTH[Item]    && Yes or No
       m.info = BITSET( m.info, Item )     && Yes (set bit to 1)
   ELSE
      m.info =  BITCLEAR( m.info, Item)          && No (Set bit to 0)
ENDFOR
REPLACE Info with m.info
```

You can use the following commands to retrieve values from the `Info` field:

```
#DEFINE SexBit       0
#DEFINE MarriedBit   1
? IIF( BITTEST(People.Info, SexBit ) , "Male", "Female" )
? IIF( BITTEST(People.Info, MarriedBit ) , "Married", "Single" )
```

Table 5.21 summarizes the bitwise functions.

Table 5.21. Bitwise functions.

Function	*Usage*	*Type*
`BITAND(<expN1>,<expN2>)`	Returns the results of a bitwise `AND` operation performed on a numeric value.	N
`BITCLEAR(<expN1>,<expN2>)`	Returns the results of setting a specified (`<expN2>`) bit or numeric value (`<expN1>`) to `0`. `<expN2>` ranged from `0` to `31`; `0` is rightmost bit.	N
`BITLSHIFT(<expN1>,<expN2>)`	Returns the results of shifting a numeric value (`<expN1>`) a specified number of bits (`<expN2>`) to the left.	N
`BITNOT(<expN>)`	Returns the results of a bitwise `NOT` operation on a numeric value. Bits in numeric value are inverted. In other words, 1 bits are set to 0, and 0 bits are set to 1.	N
`BITOR(<expN1>,<expN2>)`	Returns the results of a bitwise `OR` operation performed on two numeric values.	N

Function	Usage	Type
BITRSHIFT(<expN1>,<expN2>)	Returns the results of a shifting numeric value (<expN1>) a specified number of bits (<expN2>) to the right.	N
BITSET(<expN1>,<expN2>)	Returns the results of setting a specified bit (<expN2>) of a numeric value (<expN1>)to 1. <expN2> ranged from 0 to 31; 0 is rightmost bit.	N
BITTEST(<expN1>,<expN2>)	Returns .T. value if a specified bit in a numeric value is set to 1; otherwise it returns .F..	L
BITXOR(<expN1>,<expN2>)	Returns the result of a bitwise exclusive OR operation performed on two numeric values.	N

If you perform a bitwise logical AND operation, each bit in the first argument is compared to each bit in the second argument. If both bits equal 1, the result bit is 1. If one bit equals 0 and the other bit equals 1, the result bit is 0. If both bits equal 0, the result bit is 0. If you perform a bitwise logical OR operation, each bit in the first argument is compared to each bit in the second argument. If both bits equal 0, the result bit is 0. If either bit equals 1, the result bit is 1. If you perform a bitwise logical XOR operation, each bit in the first argument is compared to each bit in the second argument. If the bits differ, the result bit is 1. If the bits are the same, the result bit is 0. The following table illustrates the results of these three bitwise operations:

Argument	Values of Bit			
<expN1>	0	1	0	1
<expN2>	0	1	1	0
Result of bitwise AND	0	1	0	0
Result of bitwise OR	0	1	1	1
Result of bitwise XOR	0	0	1	1

A bitwise NOT operation performed by the BITNOT() function carries out a ones complement operation on the argument. A *ones complement* operation reverses the sense of each bit in the argument. Here are some examples of the bitwise functions:

```
First = 255   && 1111 1111
Second = 7    && 0000 0111
? BITAND( First, Second )  && Returns 7  or 0000 0111 binary

First  = 15  && 1111 binary
Position = 1  && 2nd bit position (0 is first bit position)
```

```
? BITCLEAR(First, Position) && Returns 13, 1101 binary

First = 6  && 0000 0110 binary
Shifter = 2  && Shift bits 2 position to the left
? BITLSHIFT(First, Shifter) && Returns 24, 0001 1000 binary

Number = 5  &&  0000 0101 binary
? BITNOT(Number) && Returns -6  ...1111 1010 binary

First  = 5  && 0101 binary
Second = 6  && 0110 binary
? BITOR(First, Second) && Returns 7, 0111 binary

First   = 7  && 0111 binary
Shifter = 2  && Shift bits 2 position right
? BITRSHIFT(First, Shifter) && Returns 1, 0001 binary

First    = 5  &&  0101 binary
Position = 2  && third bit position (0 = first bit position)
? BITSET(First, Position) && Returns 13, 1101 binary

First = 5  && 0101 binary
y = 6  && 0110 binary
? BITXOR(First, Second) && Returns 3, 0011 binary
```

Listing 5.2 illustrates how to use the `BITTEST()` function to convert a number to a binary number.

Listing 5.2. A program that illustrates the use of the `BITTEST()` function.

```
***************************************************************
*     * Description:                                          *
*     * This program illustrates BITTEST() function           *
*     * to convert number to binary value                     *
***************************************************************
CLEAR
@ 5,10 SAY "BINARY CONVERSION PROGRAM" FONT "Ariel",24
@ 9,29 TO 14,70
Number = 7
DO WHILE Number <> 0
     @ 10,30 SAY "Enter a Number" GET Number
     READ
     Binary = ""
     FOR I = 31 TO 0 STEP -1
          Binary = Binary+;
            IIF(BITTEST(Number,I),"1","0")
     ENDFOR
     @ 12,31 SAY Binary
ENDDO
```

Dynamic Data Exchange Functions

Visual FoxPro contains functions that support Windows 3.0 dynamic data exchange (DDE) operations for transferring data between FoxPro and other Windows applications. Visual FoxPro behaves both as a client and a server in the transfer of data. Chapter 17, "OLE, OLE 2.0 Controls, DDE, and Operating System Interfaces," presents these DDE functions in detail. Table 5.22 summarizes these functions. Some of them violate the four-unique-character rule for an identifier. For example, the first four characters of functions `DDEExecute()` and `DDEEnable()` are the same. Therefore, you must specify enough characters to make the function unique—`DDEEx()` and `DDEEn()`.

Table 5.22. Dynamic data exchange functions.

Function	*Usage*	*Type*
`DDEInitiate (<expC1>,<expC2>)`	Establishes a channel between FoxPro and a DDE server application. Returns a channel number or `-1` if a channel cannot be established.	N
`DDETerminate (<expN> ¦ <expC>)`	Closes a DDE channel and returns `.T.` if a channel can be closed. `<expN>` is the channel number. `<expC>` is the service name.	L
`DDERequest (<expN>, <expC>)`	Requests data from a server application. Returns data as a character string. `<expN>` is the channel number. `<expC>` specifies the item name.	C
`DDEExecute (<expN>, <expC1>) [,<expC2>]`	Sends a command to another application. Returns `.T.` if the command executes successfully.	L
`DDEAdvise (<expN1>, <expC1>, <expC2>, <expN2>)`	Establishes a warm and hot link to an item name in a server application. Returns `.T.` if the operation is successful.	L
`DDESetService (<expC1>, <expC2>, [ <exp>])`	Creates, removes, or modifies the status names in FoxPro. Returns `.T.` if successful.	L

continues

Table 5.22. continued

Function	*Usage*	*Type*
`DDESetTopics (<expC1>, <expC2> [,<expC3>])`	Establishes a topic name for a service name or releases it from the service name. Returns `.T.` if the topic name is successfully created or released.	L
`DDEEnabled (<expL1> [,<expN1> [,<expL2>]])`	Establishes a warm and hot link to an item name in a server application. Returns `.T.` if the operation is successful.	L
`DDEPoke (<expN>, <expC>, <exp>)`	Sends data between a client and a server application. Returns `.T.` if the operation is successful.	L
`DDELastError()`	Returns the last DDE error number or `0` if the last DDE function executed successfully.	N

Other Functions

Table 5.23 presents other functions and lists the chapters of this book in which they appear. This table is provided in this section to complete the list of all FoxPro functions.

Table 5.23. Other FoxPro functions.

Function	*Usage*	*Type*	*Chapter*
`CAPSLOCK([<expL>])`	Sets and returns Caps Lock key status. If the argument is `.T.`, the Caps Lock key is set.	L	17
`CURDIR(<expC>)`	Returns the current MS-DOS directory.	C	17
`DISKSPACE()`	Returns the space (in kilobytes) remaining on the disk for the current drive.	N	17
`EMPTY(<exp>)`	Returns `.T.` if the expression evaluates to an "empty" value.	L	12
`ERROR()`	Returns the error number.	C	8

Function	Usage	Type	Chapter	
`EVALUATE(<expC>)`	Evaluates `<expC>` and returns the results. The type depends on the expression evaluated.	X	5	
`FILE(<expC>)`	Returns `.T.` if the file exists.	L	17	
`FKLABEL(<expN>)`	Returns the function key label.	C	10	
`FKMAX()`	Returns the maximum number of programmable function keys.	N	10	
`FULLPATH(<expC1> [,<expN> ¦ <expC2>])`	Returns the fully qualified MS-DOS path for a specified file.	C	17	
`GETENV(<expC>)`	Returns the MS-DOS environment string.	C	17	
`HOME()`	Returns a string containing the directory in which the FoxPro executable file resides. Same as `SYS(2004)`.	C	17	NEW FOR VISUAL FOXPRO 3
`ID()`	Returns a string containing the machine number and name when FoxPro is operating in a network environment.	C	17	
`IIF(<expL>, <exp1>, <exp2>)`	Returns the evaluated value of `<exp1>` if `<expL>` is `.T.`; otherwise, returns the evaluated value of `<exp2>`.	S	6	
`INLIST(<exp1>, <exp2> [,<exp3> [,…]])`	Returns `.T.` if `<exp1>` is contained in other expressions.	L		
`INSMODE(<expL>)`	Returns or sets the insert mode. `<expL>` is `.T.` to turn on the insert mode.	L	3	
`ISBLANK(<exp>)`	Returns `.T.` if field contains an undefined value.	L	12	
`ISNULL(<exp>)`	Returns `.T.` if an expression evaluates to a null value; otherwise, returns `.F.`.	L	12	NEW FOR VISUAL FOXPRO 3

continues

Table 5.23. continued

Function	*Usage*	*Type*	*Chapter*
ISCOLOR()	Returns .T. if the computer supports colors.	L	17
LINENO()	Returns the line number of the program command about to be executed. Also used in debugging operations.	N	24
LOCFILE(<expC1> [,<expN> ¦ <expC2>])	Returns a fully qualified DOS path for a specified file. If the file is not located, the Open File dialog box appears.	C	17
MEMORY([<expN>])	Returns the remaining memory.	N	17
MESSAGE([1])	Returns an error message or the contents of the line containing the error, if available, and the optional argument is specified.	C	
NUMLOCK()	Sets and returns the Num Lock key status.	L	17
NEW FOR VISUAL FOXPRO 3 NVL(<expC1>,<expC2>)	Returns a non-null value from two expressions.	L	12
ON(<expC1> [,<expC2>])	Returns the expression for the following form of ON commands: ***Command*** — **<expC1>** ON APLABOUT — APLABOUT ON ERROR — ERROR ON ESCAPE — ESCAPE ON KEY — KEY ON PAGE — PAGE ON READERROR — READERROR <expC2> is specified for ON KEY LABEL to identify the key.	C	6
OS()	Returns the name of the operating system.	C	17

Function	*Usage*	*Type*	*Chapter*
`PARAMETERS()`	Returns the number of parameters passed to the most recently called procedure.	N	6
`PCOUNT()`	Same as `PARAMETERS()`.	N	6
`PROGRAM()`	Returns the name of the program.	C	24
`SCHEME(<expN1> [,<expN2>])`	Returns the color pair or color pair list from a specified color scheme (<*expN1*>).	C/N	10
`SET(<expC>)`	Returns the status of the specified `SET` command; returns `ON`, `OFF`, or an integer value.	C/N	10
`SYS(<expN>)`	Returns information relating to the system and certain FoxPro variables. Table 5.24 describes returned values for different numeric arguments.	C/N	5
`TXNLEVEL()`	Returns a numeric value indicating the current transaction level. 	N	
`TYPE(<expC>)`	Returns a character (`C`, `B`, `D`, `F`, `C`, `L`, `M`, `N`, `T`, or `Y`) indicating the data type of an expression; `U` is returned if the expression is undefined.		
`VERSION([<expN>])`	Returns the FoxPro version. If you provide any number, you will receive the sub-version number and the date of the version. <*expN*> can equal `0` to `3`.	C	

The `VERSION()` function is not really described in any other chapter, so it is described here. You can use the `VERSION()` function to tell what version of FoxPro is running an application and to take whatever appropriate action is required. In Visual FoxPro, the VERSION() function provides you with more information than was provided in earlier FoxPro versions. Here is what it does:

VERSION()	Returns the version only.
VERSION(1)	Returns the version and serial number.
VERSION(2)	Returns one of the following runtime types: 0 Runtime version 1 Standard version 2 Professional version
VERSION(3)	Returns the country of origin. 00 American/English 33 Spanish 49 German

If you specify any other value for the argument, Visual FoxPro issues an error.

Table 5.24 presents the system information returned by the SYS() function. The SYS() function always returns a character string.

Table 5.24. The system information returned by the SYS() function.

Syntax	*Returned Value*
SYS(0)	Returns the network machine number and name when running FoxPro/LAN.
SYS(1)	Returns the character string containing the Julian calendar system date.
SYS(2)	Returns the string containing the seconds since midnight.
SYS(3)	Returns a unique filename.
SYS(5)	Returns the SET DEFAULT drive.
SYS(6)	Returns the PRINTER device.
SYS(7 [,<expWA>])	Returns the name of the FORMAT file for the current or specified work area.
SYS(9)	Returns the FoxPro serial number.
SYS(10, <expN>)	Returns a character string containing the date in the form *mm/dd/yy* given a string containing the day number.
SYS(11, <expD> ¦ <expC>)	Converts the date or character-type date to the Julian calendar day number.
SYS(12)	Returns the remaining memory below 640KB available to run an external program.

Syntax	Returned Value
SYS(13)	Returns the printer status, OFFLINE or READY.
SYS(14,<expN> [,<expWA>])	Returns an index expression.
SYS(15, <expC1>, <expC2>)	Translates <expC1> by <expC2>. Used for foreign language character translation.
SYS(16 [,<expN>])	Returns the name of the executing program.
SYS(17)	Returns the processor in use (80286, 80386, 80486, 80586, and so on).
SYS(18)	Returns the current GET field or object.
SYS(21)	Returns the master index number.
SYS(22 [,<expN>])	Returns the master tag or index name.
SYS(23)	Returns the amount of available EMS memory in kilobytes.
SYS(24)	Returns the EMS memory limit set in the CONFIG.FPW file at startup.
SYS(100)	Returns the SET CONSOLE command to the ON or OFF setting.
SYS(101)	Returns the current SET DEVICE TO setting. The value can be SCREEN PRINT.
SYS(102)	Returns the current SET PRINTER TO command setting. Values can be ON or OFF.
SYS(103)	Returns the SET TALK command to the ON or OFF setting.
SYS(1001)	Returns the amount of memory available to FoxPro's memory manager, including memory between 640KB and 1MB.
SYS(1016)	Returns the amount of user-allocated memory remaining.
SYS(1037)	Displays the Print Setup dialog box.
SYS(2000, <expC> [,1])	Returns the name of the first file that matches a specified wildcard. If the second argument is specified, the second matched file is returned.
SYS(2001, <expC> [,1])	Returns the SET command status. This is similar to the SET() function.
SYS(2002)	Sets the cursor on and off. SYS(2002) turns the status off. SYS(2002,1) turns it on. Returns nothing.
SYS(2003)	Returns the current directory name.

continues

Table 5.24. continued

Syntax	*Returned Value*
`SYS(2004)`	Returns FoxPro's directory name.
`SYS(2005)`	Returns the currently active resource filename.
`SYS(2006)`	Returns the type of graphics card and monitor (for example, VGA/Color).
`SYS(2007, <expC>)`	Returns the checksum of `<expC>`.
`SYS(2008 [,<expC> [,<expN>]])`	Specifies the cursor shape (`<expC>`). Equals `I` for insert, and `O` for overwrite cursor. `<expN>` is `0` for underline, `1` for block, `2` for half-size block. Returns nothing.
`SYS(2009)`	Swaps the cursor shape from the overwrite to the insert cursor.
`SYS(2010)`	Returns the MS-DOS FILES setting in the CONFIG.SYS file.
`SYS(2011)`	Returns the record- or table-lock status for the current work area.
`SYS(2012 [,<expWA>])`	Returns the memo file block size for the current or specified table (DBF file).
`SYS(2013)`	Returns the character string with names of system menus, pads, pop-up menus, and pop-up options.
`SYS(2014, <expC1> [,<expC2>])`	Returns the minimum path between the specified path (`<expC1>`) and either the current or specified (`<expC2>`).
`SYS(2015)`	Returns the unique procedure name consisting of 10 characters beginning with an underscore.
`SYS(2016)`	Returns the `SHOW GETS WINDOW` name.
`SYS(2017)`	Displays the sign-on screen.
`SYS(2018)`	Returns the error message parameter, such as the name of the field or a file not found.
`SYS(2019)`	Returns the name and location of the CONFIG.FPW file.
`SYS(2020)`	Displays the total size of the default disk.
`SYS(2021 , <expN> [,<expWA>])`	Returns the filtered index expression.
`SYS(2022 [,<expC>])`	Returns the disk cluster size for the current or specified drive.

Syntax	Returned Value
SYS(2023)	Returns the temporary file drive name.
SYS(2029,<expWA>)	Returns a value corresponding to the specified table (DBF file) type (as shown in Table 5.25). The type is actually the first byte of the DBF file.
Value	*Type of File*
3	Visual FoxPro, previous versions of FoxPro, FoxBASE+, dBASE III PLUS, and dBASE IV with no memo fields.
48	Visual FoxPro with a memo field.
67	dBASE IV SQL table with no memo fields.
99	dBASE IV SQL System table with no memo fields.
131	FoxBASE+ and dBASE III PLUS with a memo field.
139	dBASE IV with a memo field.
203	dBASE IV SQL table with a memo field.
245	Previous versions of FoxPro with a memo field.

Data Type Coercion

The error, data type mismatch, occurs when the types of operands are not compatible with each other or with the operators of an expression. In some cases, FoxPro can figure out what to do. For example, when type `F` operands (database fields) are mixed with type `N` numbers, the system treats the type `F` numbers as though they are type `N` numbers. Converting a value from one type to another is called *coercion.*

Several functions support explicit type conversion as well as the friendly coercion that occurs behind the scenes. Table 5.25 lists the functions that convert between different types. In this table, the `IIF()` function converts anything to type `L` and converts type `L` to both `Character` and `Number` types. The table illustrates the flexibility of this amorphous function.

Table 5.25. Data type conversion functions.

From/ To	C	D	F	L	M	N/I/B	T	Y
C	*	CTOD()	VAL()	IIF()	*	VAL()	{}	VAL(NTOM())
D	DTOC()	*	*	IIF()	*	*	DTOT()	*
F	STR()	*	*	IIF()	*	=	*	NTOM()

continues

Table 5.25. continued

From/ To	C	D	F	L	M	N/I/B	T	Y
L	IIF	*	IIF()	*	*	IIF()	IIF()	IIF()
M	=	*	*	IIF()	*	*	()	VAL(NTOM())
I	STR()	*	REPLACE	IIF()	*	*	*	NTOM()
N	STR()	*	REPLACE	IIF()	*	*	*	NTOM()
B	STR()	*	REPLACE	IIF()	*	*	*	NTOM()
T	TTOC()	TTOD()	REPLACE	IIF()	*	MTON()	*	*
Y	STR()	*	MTON()	IIF()	*	MTON()	*	*

The `IIF()` function requires three arguments:

```
IIF( <expL>, <exp1>, <exp2> )
```

This function evaluates the first logical expression and returns the value (and type) of either `<exp1>` or `<exp2>`. If `<expL>` evaluates to `.T.`, `IIF()` returns the value of `<exp1>`; otherwise, it returns the value of `<exp2>`. It's easy to see how such a function can convert any type to logical (based on whatever rules are appropriate):

```
IIF( <operand meets condition>, .T., .F.)
```

To convert a Logical value to either Character or Numeric do the following:

```
IIF( <logical operand>, "TRUE", "FALSE")
IIF( <logical operand>, 1, 0)
```

(`1` and `0` are often used to numerically represent `TRUE` and `FALSE`.)

Memo fields, another unusual item in Table 5.25, can be converted to character memvars by simple assignment (using = or the `STORE` command). Likewise, you can convert type `F` fields to type `N` numbers using an assignment statement.

This functionality affects the `REPLACE` command as well, which supports the following:

```
REPLACE <memo> WITH <memo>
REPLACE <memo> WITH <character>
REPLACE <character> WITH <memo>
```

Even though you may read in some documents or books that the field and the `WITH` expression in the `REPLACE` command must have the same data type, this isn't actually true. Converting between memo fields and character operands is another example of the friendly coercion, which is discussed earlier in this chapter.

How Expressions Are Used

Expressions are used in a surprising number of places throughout the FoxPro language. The examples so far in this chapter have illustrated a few of the ways expressions are used in FoxPro:

```
? <expression>, @...SAY <expC>, DISPLAY <expression>
REPLACE <field> WITH <expression>
STORE <expression> TO <memvars>
GOTO <expN>
INDEX ON <expression> TO <file>
IF <expL>
DO WHILE <expL>
CASE <expL>
FOR <expL>
WHILE <expL>
NEXT <expN>
RECORD <expN>
SET DECIMALS TO <expN>
SET DELIMITERS TO <expC>
```

In addition, all filenames throughout the FoxPro language support the filename expression, or `<expFN>` in the notation of Appendix B, "FoxPro Language Syntax." A *filename expression* is identical to a character expression that is enclosed in parentheses, except a simple identifier is internally converted to a quoted string constant. Chapter 11 describes filename expressions in more detail and gives examples.

A work area expression is similar to a filename expression in that the language parser in FoxPro tries to evaluate the expression in several ways before it gives up and issues an error. Work area expressions can be numeric expressions as long as the value is between 1 and 255, inclusive. If the expression type is Character, on the other hand, it can be either a valid current alias name or a single letter from A to J. Only if the expression does not yield one of these choices is an error returned.

The FoxPro language also includes a strange language element called the *ampersand* (`&`) *macro*. The `&` macro performs a direct text substitution at runtime. Other languages do not have such a mechanism. Ampersand macros enable the programmer to write the following:

```
A = "MyFile INDEX AcctNo"
USE &A EXCLUSIVE
```

What FoxPro sees when this executes is the following:

```
USE MyFile INDEX AcctNo EXCLUSIVE
```

In fact, nothing stops a programmer from writing the following:

```
A = "QUIT"
&A
```

The `&` must be followed immediately by the name of a character memvar. At runtime, the `&` and the identifier are replaced by the current contents of the memvar, and the resulting command line is recompiled. The problems this causes for any processor of the FoxPro language are discussed in Chapter 3, "The Referencing Environment." I mention how difficult it is to categorize a feature that obviously belongs in a chapter on expressions, but is neither operand nor operator. It belongs outside both definitions because it does not return a type: It simply replaces source text. It acts like a preprocessor (like `#define` in C), but uses the dynamic values of memvars at runtime. It's difficult to pin down, but at least I managed to discuss it in this chapter.

Using Functions

Listing 5.3 is a sample program that uses some of the functions mentioned. This program is a simple scientific calculator that demonstrates how to use Visual FoxPro expressions, built-in functions, and user-defined functions. Figure 5.2 shows the calculator. You can use either the mouse or the keyboard to enter numbers and choose operations.

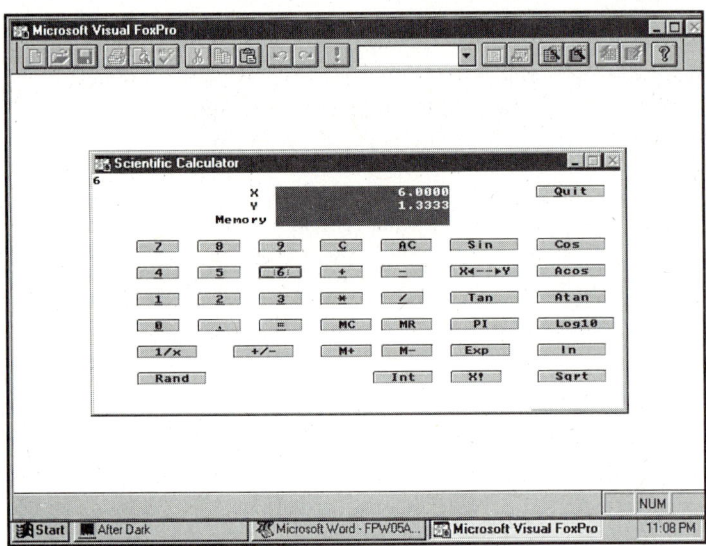

FIGURE 5.2.
The screen display generated by the scientific calculator program CALC.PRG.

The scientific calculator displays in a window and uses push buttons for the numbers and functions. The FoxPro 2.6 Screen Designer was used to create the screen elements for CALC.PRG. It uses the obsolete form of the `@...GET` command to create push button controls. `@...GET` controls have been replaced by Visual FoxPro object-oriented form creation methodology presented in Chapter 14. Then in Chapter 19, "The Form Designer," you will learn how to create object-oriented forms. In that chapter, you will learn how to recreate the scientific calculator using the Visual FoxPro Form Designer.

Listing 5.3 presents the source listing of CALC.PRG. To begin with, CALC.PRG saves some environmental parameters, defines the window, initializes some constants, and displays the screen image. It then executes the `READ CYCLE` command until you press the Quit push button t exit the program. Whenever you "push" a push button to enter a number or operation, a corresponding `@...GET` command `VALID` clause executes. The `VALID` clause consists of a call to a user-defined function (UDF). User-defined functions are discussed in Chapter 6, "Control Flow." For example, when you press the number `1` in the following statement:

```
@ 9,5 GET i1 ;
PICTURE "@*HN    \<1" ;
SIZE 1,5,1 ;
DEFAULT 1   ;
VALID VNUMBER( 1 )
```

the program calls the `VNUMBER()` UDF to process the number `1`. Incidentally, UDFs are simple procedures that can be called from within an expression. Chapter 6 discusses UDFs as well. The two characters (`\` and `<`) preceding the `1` in the `PICTURE` clause make the number `1` a hotkey. When you press a hotkey, the push button activates. Of course, you can also activate the push button with a mouse click or by pressing Enter. The `numlock()` function turns on the Num Lock mode so that the user can use the number keys and the `+`, `-`, `*`, and `/` keys on the numeric keypad. The Num Lock status returns to its original state when the program exits.

`VNUMBER()` emulates the way you enter a number in a calculator. The number is entered from right to left. Another UDF, `VOP()`, is called when you push an operator button (`+`, `-`, `*`, or `/`). It creates a character string containing an expression that consists of the previously entered operator and operands. It then calls the `EVALUATE()` function. `EVALUATE ()` evaluates the expression and returns the answer. When you push a function button (sin, cos, rand, and so forth), the `VFUNC()` UDF is called, which uses the same technique used by the `VOP()` UDF to calculate the results. The `ShowCalc` procedure displays the results.

Listing 5.3. The source listing of the file `CALC.PRG`.

```
*****************************************************************
*      * 07/09/92              CALC.PRG                 06:19:39 *
*****************************************************************
*      * Author's Name: Jeb Long                                 *
*      *                                                         *
*      * Description:                                            *
*      * This program simulates a simple scientific calculator.  *
*      *                                                         *
*****************************************************************
PRIVATE  talkstat, compstat, snumlock

IF SET("TALK") = "ON"
   SET TALK OFF
   talkstat = "ON"
ELSE
   talkstat = "OFF"
ENDIF
snumlock = NUMLOCK(.T.)         && Set the NumLock mode ON
```

continues

Listing 5.3. continued

```
compstat = SET("COMPATIBLE")
SET COMPATIBLE FOXPLUS
*
*     Window definitions
*
IF NOT WEXIST("calc")
   DEFINE WINDOW calc ;
      FROM INT((SROW()-20)/2),INT((SCOL()-63)/2) ;
      TO INT((SROW()-20)/2)+19,INT((SCOL()-63)/2)+62 ;
      TITLE "Scientific Calculator" ;
      FLOAT NOCLOSE SHADOW PANEL COLOR SCHEME 1
ENDIF
*****************************************************************
*     CALC Setup Code - SECTION 2
*
acc=0
=RAND(-1)
memory  = 0
results = 0
oldOP = "+"
Decimal = 0
*****************************************************************
*   CALC Screen Layout
*
IF WVISIBLE("calc")   && Is WINDOW calc visible?
   ACTIVATE WINDOW calc SAME
ELSE
   ACTIVATE WINDOW calc NOSHOW
ENDIF
*
*****************************************************************
*   Initialize variables
*
@ 1,18 SAY "X"
@ 2,18 SAY "Y"
@ 3,14 SAY "Memory"
DO ShowCalc WITH " "
*
*****************************************************************
*   Display the push buttons
*
   @ 11,5 GET i0 PICTURE "@*HN   \<0" ;
      SIZE 1,5,1 DEFAULT 1  VALID VNUMBER( 0 )
@ 9,5 GET i1 PICTURE "@*HN   \<1" ;
      SIZE 1,5,1 DEFAULT 1  ;
      VALID VNUMBER( 1 )
@ 9,12 GET i2 ;
      PICTURE "@*HN   \<2" ;
      SIZE 1,5,1 ;
      DEFAULT 1  ;
      VALID VNUMBER( 2 )
@ 9,19 GET i3 ;
      PICTURE "@*HN   \<3" ;
      SIZE 1,5,1 ;
      DEFAULT 1  ;
      VALID VNUMBER( 3 )
```

```
@ 7,5 GET i4 ;
     PICTURE "@*HN    \<4" ;
     SIZE 1,5,1 ;
     DEFAULT 1  ;
     VALID VNUMBER( 4 )
@ 7,12 GET i5 ;
     PICTURE "@*HN    \<5" ;
     SIZE 1,5,1 ;
     DEFAULT 1  ;
     VALID VNUMBER( 5 )
@ 7,19 GET i6 ;
     PICTURE "@*HN    \<6" ;
     SIZE 1,5,1 ;
     DEFAULT 1  ;
     VALID VNUMBER( 6 )
@ 5,5 GET i7 ;
     PICTURE "@*HN    \<7" ;
     SIZE 1,5,1 ;
     DEFAULT 1  ;
VALID VNUMBER( 7 )
     @ 5,12 GET i8 ;
     PICTURE "@*HN    \<8" ;
     SIZE 1,5,1 ;
     DEFAULT 1  ;
     VALID VNUMBER( 8 )
@ 5,19 GET i9 ;
     PICTURE "@*HN    \<9" ;
     SIZE 1,5,1 ;
     DEFAULT 1  ;
     VALID VNUMBER( 9 )
@ 11,12 GET deci ;
     PICTURE "@*HN    \<." ;
     SIZE 1,5,1 ;
     DEFAULT 1  ;
     VALID VDECIMAL()
@ 11,19 GET equals ;
     PICTURE "@*HN    \<=" ;
     SIZE 1,5,1 ;
     DEFAULT 1  ;
     VALID VEQUAL()
@ 5,26 GET CLEAR ;
     PICTURE "@*HN    \<C" ;
     SIZE 1,5,1 ;
     DEFAULT 1 ;
VALID VCLEAR()
     @ 5,33 GET ACLEAR ;
     PICTURE "@*HN  \<AC" ;
     SIZE 1,6,1 ;
     DEFAULT 1 ;
     VALID VACLEAR("AC")
@ 7,26 GET PLUS ;
     PICTURE "@*HN    \<+" ;
     SIZE 1,5,1 ;
     DEFAULT 1 ;
     VALID VOP("+")
@ 7,33 GET minus ;
     PICTURE "@*HN    \<-" ;
```

continues

Listing 5.3. continued

```
     SIZE 1,5,1 ;
     DEFAULT 1 ;
     VALID VOP("-")
@ 9,26 GET Multiply ;
     PICTURE "@*HN   \<*" ;
     SIZE 1,5,1 ;
     DEFAULT 1  ;
     VALID VOP("*")
@ 9,33 GET divide ;
     PICTURE "@*HN   \</" ;
     SIZE 1,5,1 ;
     DEFAULT 1 ;
     VALID VOP("/")
@ 13,5 GET invert ;
     PICTURE "@*HN   1/x" ;
     SIZE 1,7,1 ;
     DEFAULT 1 ;
     VALID VINVERT()
@ 13,16 GET plusminus ;
     PICTURE "@*HN   +/-" ;
     SIZE 1,7,1 ;
     DEFAULT 1 ;
     VALID VREVERSE()
@ 7,41 GET xasin ;
     PICTURE "@*HN X—Y" ;
SIZE 1,8,1 ;
     DEFAULT 1 ;
     VALID VXPOSE()
@ 11,26 GET mc ;
     PICTURE "@*HN   MC" ;
     SIZE 1,6,1 ;
     DEFAULT 1 ;
     VALID VMC()
@ 11,33 GET mr ;
     PICTURE "@*HN   MR" ;
     SIZE 1,6,1 ;
     DEFAULT 1 ;
     VALID VMR()
@ 13,26 GET MPLUS ;
     PICTURE "@*HN   M+" ;
     SIZE 1,6,1 ;
     DEFAULT 1 ;
     VALID VMEM("+")
@ 13,33 GET equals ;
     PICTURE "@*HN   M-" ;
     SIZE 1,6,1 ;
     DEFAULT 1 ;
     VALID VMEM("-")
@ 15,32 GET xint ;
     PICTURE "@*HN   Int" ;
     SIZE 1,7,1 ;
     DEFAULT 1 ;
     VALID VFUNC("Int")
@ 15,41 GET xfactor ;
     PICTURE "@*HN   X!" ;
     SIZE 1,6,1 ;
```

```
     DEFAULT 1 ;
     VALID VFACT()
@ 5,41 GET sin ;
     PICTURE "@*HN   Sin " ;
     SIZE 1,8,1 ;
     DEFAULT 1 ;
     VALID VFUNC("Sin")
@ 5,51 GET icos ;
     PICTURE "@*HN   Cos " ;
     SIZE 1,8,1 ;
     DEFAULT 1 ;
     VALID VFUNC("COS")
@ 7,51 GET xacos ;
     PICTURE "@*HN   Acos" ;
     SIZE 1,8,1 ;
     DEFAULT 1 ;
     VALID VFUNC("Acos")
@ 9,41 GET xtan ;
     PICTURE "@*HN   Tan " ;
     SIZE 1,8,1 ;
     DEFAULT 1 ;
     VALID VFUNC("Tan")
@ 9,51 GET xatan ;
     PICTURE "@*HN   Atan" ;
     SIZE 1,8,1 ;
     DEFAULT 1 ;
     VALID VFUNC("Atan")
@ 11,41 GET xpi ;
     PICTURE "@*HN   PI " ;
     SIZE 1,8,1 ;
     DEFAULT 1 ;
     VALID VPI()
@ 11,51 GET xlog10 ;
     PICTURE "@*HN  Log10" ;
     SIZE 1,9,1 ;
     DEFAULT 1 ;
     VALID VFUNC("log10")
@ 13,41 GET xexp ;
     PICTURE "@*HN   Exp " ;
     SIZE 1,7,1 ;
     DEFAULT 1 ;
     VALID VFUNC("Exp")
@ 13,51 GET xlog ;
     PICTURE "@*HN    ln " ;
     SIZE 1,8,1 ;
     DEFAULT 1 ;
     VALID VFUNC("log")
@ 15,51 GET xsqrt ;
     PICTURE "@*HN   Sqrt" ;
     SIZE 1,8,1 ;
     DEFAULT 1 ;
     VALID VFUNC("Sqrt")
@ 15,5 GET xrand ;
     PICTURE "@*HN   Rand" ;
     SIZE 1,8,1 ;
     DEFAULT 1 ;
     VALID VRAND()
```

continues

Listing 5.3. continued

```
@ 1,51 GET quit ;
     PICTURE "@*HN   \<Quit" ;
     SIZE 1,8,1 ;
     DEFAULT 1 ;
     VALID VQUIT()

IF NOT WVISIBLE("calc")
     ACTIVATE WINDOW calc
ENDIF
*
*****************************************************************
*   Activate the calculator
*

READ CYCLE
*
*****************************************************************
*   Clean things up and exit CALC.PRG
*

RELEASE WINDOW calc
IF talkstat = "ON"
     SET TALK ON
ENDIF
IF compstat = "ON"
     SET COMPATIBLE ON
ENDIF
= NUMLOCK(snumlock) && Restore original NUMLOCK status
RETURN

*****************************************************************
*         VCLEAR               CLEAR VALID                      *
*                                                               *
*         Function Origin:                                      *
*           Variable:          VCLEAR                           *
*           Called By:         VALID Clause                     *
*           Object Type:       Push button                      *
*         Purpose:  Clear registers                             *
*****************************************************************
*
FUNCTION VCLEAR     &&  CLEAR VALID
= VACLEAR("C")
Results = 0
oldOP = "+"
do ShowCalc with "Clear"
return .t.
*****************************************************************
*         VACLEAR              CLEAR ACC VALID                  *
*                                                               *
*         Function Origin:                                      *
*           Variable:          VACLEAR                          *
*           Called By:         VALID Clause                     *
*           Object Type:       Push button                      *
*         Purpose:  Clear accumulator register                  *
*****************************************************************
```

```
FUNCTION VACLEAR     &&  CLEAR ACC VALID
PARAMETER Msg
Acc = 0
Decimal = 0
do ShowCalc with Msg
return .T.

****************************************************************
*         VNumber                 # VALID                      *
*         Function Origin:                                     *
*           Variable:           I0-I9                          *
*           Called By:          VALID Clause                   *
*           Object Type:        Push button                    *
*         Purpose:  Adds digit to accumulator                  *
****************************************************************
FUNCTION VNumber
PARAMETER Number
IF Decimal = 0
     acc = acc*10 + Number
ELSE
     acc = acc + Decimal*Number
     Decimal = Decimal/10.0
ENDIF
DO ShowCalc With ltrim(str(Number))
RETURN .T.
****************************************************************
*         VDECIMAL                .  VALID                     *
*         Function Origin:                                     *
*           Variable:           deci                           *
*           Called By:          VALID Clause                   *
*           Object Type:        Push button                    *
*         Purpose:  Processes decimal point                    *
****************************************************************
FUNCTION VDECIMAL
DO ShowCalc WITH "."
IF Decimal = 0
     Decimal = .1
ELSE
     ?? chr(7)  && Ring Bell
ENDIF
RETURN .T.

****************************************************************
*         VXPOSE                   X <—> Y VALID               *
*         Function Origin:                                     *
*           Variable:           xtoy                           *
*           Called By:          VALID Clause                   *
*           Object Type:        Push button                    *
*         Purpose:  transposes registers  X and Y              *
****************************************************************
FUNCTION VXPOSE
TEMP = Results
Results = acc
acc = TEMP
DO ShowCalc WITH "X—"
RETURN .T.
```

continues

Listing 5.3. continued

```
******************************************************************
*         VMEM                     +/- Memory VALID              *
*         Function Origin:                                       *
*           Variable:              MPLUS/MMINUS                  *
*           Called By:             VALID Clause                  *
*           Object Type:           Push button                   *
*         Purpose:  Processes M+ and M- Keys                     *
******************************************************************
FUNCTION VMEM
PARAMETER MOP
Memory = EVALUATE("Memory "+ MOP + "Results")
DO ShowCalc WITH "M"+MOP
RETURN .T.
******************************************************************
*         VMR                      MR  VALID                     *
*         Function Origin:                                       *
*           Variable:              mr                            *
*           Called By:             VALID Clause                  *
*           Object Type:           Push button                   *
*         Purpose:  Retrieves Memory Register                    *
******************************************************************
FUNCTION VMR
acc = memory
DO ShowCalc WITH "MR"
RETURN .T.
******************************************************************
*         VMC                      MC VALID                      *
*         Function Origin:                                       *
*           Variable:              mc                            *
*           Called By:             VALID Clause                  *
*           Object Type:           Push button                   *
*         Purpose:  Clears memory register                       *
******************************************************************
FUNCTION VMC
memory = 0
DO ShowCalc WITH "MC"
RETURN .T.
******************************************************************
*         VReverse                 Reverses sign                 *
*         Function Origin:                                       *
*           Variable:              plusminus                     *
*           Called By:             VALID Clause                  *
*           Object Type:           Push button                   *
*         Purpose:  Reverses sign                                *
******************************************************************
FUNCTION VREVERSE
acc = - acc
DO ShowCalc WITH "+/-"
RETURN .T.
******************************************************************
*         VQUIT                    Quit                          *
*         Function Origin:                                       *
*           Variable:              quit                          *
*           Called By:             VALID Clause                  *
*           Object Type:           Push button                   *
*         Purpose:  Exits from Calculator                        *
******************************************************************
```

```
FUNCTION VQUIT
CLEAR READ
RETURN .T.
*****************************************************************
*                                                               *
*         VFUNC              Function VALID                     *
*                                                               *
*         Function Origin:                                      *
*           Variable:        Any functions (sin, cos, rand,...)*
*           Called By:       VALID Clause                       *
*           Object Type:     Push button                        *
*         Purpose:  Evaluates function                          *
*****************************************************************
FUNCTION VFUNC
PARAMETER Function     && Name of function
IF (Function = 'log' OR Function = 'log10');
     AND ACC <= 0
     WAIT WINDOW "Illegal accumulator VALUE"
     RETURN .T.
ENDIF
Results = EVAL( Function + "(ACC)")
= VACLEAR( Function )
DO ShowCalc WITH Function
RETURN .T.
*****************************************************************
*         VOP                 Operator VALID                    *
*         Function Origin:                                      *
*           Variable:         Operator: + - * / % of function  *
*           Called By:        VALID Clause                      *
*           Object Type:      Push button                       *
*         Purpose:  Evaluates math operation                    *
*****************************************************************
FUNCTION VOP
PARAMETER OP    && operation (+ - * / )
Results = EVALUATE("Results " + oldOP + " acc")
DO ShowCalc WITH OP
=VACLEAR(OP)
OldOp = OP
RETURN .T.
*****************************************************************
*         VFACT               Factorial VALID                   *
*         Function Origin:                                      *
*           Variable:         xfactor                           *
*           Called By:        VALID Clause                      *
*           Object Type:      Push button                       *
*         Purpose:  Computes factorial                          *
*****************************************************************
FUNCTION VFACT
Message = "X!"
IF acc = 0
     Results = 1
ELSE
     IF INT(acc) != ACC   && ACC Register must be int
          Message = "Error!"
     ELSE
          Results = ACC
          IF acc > 2
```

continues

Listing 5.3. continued

```
               FOR TEMP = ACC-1 TO 2 STEP -1
                    Results = Results*TEMP
               ENDFOR
          ENDIF
     ENDIF
ENDIF
=VACLEAR(Message)
DO ShowCalc WITH Message
RETURN .T.
*****************************************************************
*         VRAND                    Rand VALID                   *
*         Function Origin:                                      *
*           Variable:              xrand                        *
*           Called By:             VALID Clause                 *
*           Object Type:           Push button                  *
*         Purpose:  Calls RAND() function to computer random    *
*                   value between 0 and 1.0                     *
*****************************************************************
FUNCTION VRAND
ACC = RAND()
DO ShowCalc WITH "Rand"
OldOP = "+"
RETURN .T.
*****************************************************************
*         VPI                      PI        VALID              *
*         Function Origin:                                      *
*           Variable:              xpi                          *
*           Called By:             VALID Clause                 *
*           Object Type:           Push button                  *
*         Purpose:  Replaces acc register with PI               *
*****************************************************************
PROCEDURE VPI
acc = PI()
DO ShowCalc WITH "PI"
OldOP = "+"
RETURN .T.
*****************************************************************
*         VINVERT                  VINVERT  VALID               *
*         Function Origin:                                      *
*           Variable:              invert                       *
*           Called By:             VALID Clause                 *
*           Object Type:           Push button                  *
*         Purpose:  Divides 1 by the accumulator                *
*****************************************************************
FUNCTION VINVERT
acc = 1/ACC
DO ShowCalc WITH "1/X"
RETURN .T.
*****************************************************************
*         VEQUAL                   Factorial VALID              *
*         Function Origin:                                      *
*           Variable:              EQUALS                       *
*           Called By:             VALID Clause                 *
*           Object Type:           Push button                  *
*         Purpose:  Processes = operator                        *
*****************************************************************
```

```
FUNCTION VEQUAL
Results = EVALUATE(" Results " + oldOP + "ACC" )
=VACLEAR("=")
DO ShowCalc WITH "="
OldOP = "+"
RETURN .T.
*****************************************************************
*                                                               *
*         ShowCalc        Called to display registers           *
*                                                               *
*           Called By:    VCLEAR, VOP, VNUMBER, VACLEAR         *
*                         VXPOSE, VMEM, VMR, VMC, VREVERSE      *
*                         VFUNC, VFACE, VRAND, VPI, VINVERT     *
*           Purpose:      Displays Calculator results           *
*****************************************************************
PROCEDURE ShowCalc
PARAMETER Comment
@ 1,21 CLEAR TO 3,37 COLOR W+/BG
@ 1,21 SAY ACC ;
SIZE 1,20 ;
PICTURE "@Z 99999999999.9999" COLOR W+/BG
@ 2,21 SAY Results;
SIZE 1,20 ;
PICTURE "@Z 99999999999.9999" COLOR W+/BG

@ 3,21 SAY Memory ;
SIZE 1,20 ;
PICTURE "@Z 99999999999.9999" COLOR W+/BG
@ 0,0 CLEAR TO 0,10
@ 0,0 SAY Comment
RETURN
```

Summary

This chapter describes operands, operators, and functions that, taken together, compose the full range of FoxPro expressions. A topical grouping of the functions is also presented. This chapter describes a few of the ways expressions are used in FoxPro programs as well.

Works Cited

Kernighan, B., and D. Ritchie. 1978. *The C Programming Language.* Englewood Cliffs, N.J.: Prentice-Hall.

Wirth, Nicklaus. 1974. *Pascal Report.* New York: Springer-Verlag.

6

Control Flow

I was a-trembling because I'd got to decide forever betwixt two things, and I knowed it. I studied for a minute, sort of holding my breath, and then says to myself, "All right, then, I'll go to hell."

—Mark Twain (1835–1910)
Adventures of Huckleberry Finn

Control statements govern the flow of control in a program. A program written in the Visual FoxPro programming language takes the basic form of a sequence of command lines starting with a command verb and optionally including supporting clauses. This implies that FoxPro starts at the top of the list of commands and executes them one after the other until the list is exhausted. Although this model is basically accurate, the FoxPro language provides several mechanisms for specifying branches, loops, and subroutines.

Like BASIC, Pascal, and C, the FoxPro language supports `IF...ELSE` branching and `DO WHILE` loops. It doesn't provide an unconditional jump, or `GOTO`, command because studies have shown that it's too easy to write code that cannot be maintained using `GOTO` (Dijkstra 1968). Although not everyone is as adamantly opposed to the `GOTO` command as some structured-programming purists, the breadth of applications written in Xbase languages attests to the possibility of writing programs without an unconditional branch command. Proponents of providing the `GOTO` command in programming languages, such as Dennis Ritchie, the designer of the C programming language, point to its efficacy in extracting a program from two or more nested loops, as in the following FoxPro language example:

```
DO WHILE .T.
   DO WHILE .NOT. .F.
      IF Disaster
         BRANCH_OUT_OF_HERE
      ENDIF
   ENDDO
ENDDO
```

As described later in this chapter, a normal FoxPro language practice simply uses the `RETURN` command rather than branching out of such a situation. Because variables have a global scope by default (`PUBLIC`), the caller can test the success or failure of a procedure. The irony of the situation is that the same language designers who denounce the use of the `GOTO` command would probably decry the use of more than one `RETURN` statement from a given procedure.

In addition to the `DO WHILE` command, the FoxPro language supports the `FOR` command, which is similar to the BASIC `FOR` command. The following is an example of the FoxPro `FOR` command:

```
FOR x = 1 TO 20 STEP 2
   ? "x = ", x
ENDFOR
```

Of course, you can simulate the `FOR` command by using the `DO WHILE` command:

```
x = 1
DO WHILE x <= 20
   ? "x = ", x
   x = x + 2
ENDDO
```

The `FOR` command, however, is more efficient for this example or for almost any case that involves a loop counter. The `FOR` command is faster, and here's the proof. Listing 6.1 presents a simple program that executes a `DO` and a `FOR` loop 10000 times and prints how long it takes.

Listing 6.1. The source listing for the DOFOR.PRG program.

```
*****************************************************
* DOFOR.PRG - Demonstrates speed comparison
*             between DO and FOR
*
SET TALK OFF
start = SECONDS()
counter = 1
DO WHILE counter < 10000
   counter = counter + 1
ENDDO
DOfinish = SECONDS()
FOR counter=1 TO 10000
ENDFOR
FOR finish = SECONDS()
    ? "For 10000 iterations:"
    ? " DO WHILE loop elapsed time", DOfinish-start, "seconds"
    ? " FOR loop elapsed time     ", FORfinish-DOfinish, "seconds"
RETURN
```

Benchmark comparisons of empty loops are not very important. In the real world, the time required for looping is insignificant compared to the time required to execute what's inside the loop. Here are the results of running DOFOR.PRG on a 66MHz, 486DX2 (with 16MB RAM) microcomputer:

```
For 10000 iterations:
DO WHILE loop elapsed time    0.237 seconds
FOR loop elapsed time         0.032 seconds
```

The sections that follow discuss `DO WHILE`, `FOR`, and other FoxPro language control flow commands in more detail.

The FoxPro language also supports multiway branching like `switch...case` in the C language or `CASE...OF` in Pascal (and something like BASIC's `ON...GOSUB`). Unlike these constructs, however, the FoxPro `DO CASE` command is more generalized but less efficient. Other languages require a constant selector expression. That is, the selector expression is evaluated once and its value is used to select one of several blocks of code. This is not so with the FoxPro language. Each block of code in a FoxPro `DO CASE...ENDCASE` block contains its own selector expression. Although FoxPro selector expressions are related in practice, no constraint requires them to be even remotely connected syntactically. A pathological example might be the following:

```
DO CASE
   CASE x = 1
      && what to do if x is 1
   CASE ERROR() = 78
      && what to do if the last error was number 78
   CASE A = "Hello"
      && what to do if A is "Hello"
    OTHERWISE
      && do whatever we want
ENDCASE
```

Notice that it doesn't matter if `A` equals `"Hello"` if `x` happens to be `1` because FoxPro takes the first branch, which evaluates to `.T.`, and heads for the `ENDCASE`. Most programming languages insist that each `CASE` test the same expression. If you branch on the value of `x`, fine. Or you can choose to branch based on the current value of the `ERROR()` function, which is also fine. But you cannot mix and match in these languages as you can in FoxPro. The FoxPro `DO CASE` command is more properly classified as an `ELSEIF` construct:

```
IF x = 1
      ...
ELSEIF ERROR() = 78
      ...
ELSEIF A = "Hello"
      ...
ELSEIF
      <otherwise>
ENDIF
```

`ELSEIF` is not part of the FoxPro language. I use it in this book simply to illustrate the `DO CASE` command.

Branches and Loops

Visual FoxPro supports basic branching and looping control commands that provide an arsenal as flexible as any found in other programming languages—except for the omission of an unconditional branch statement, which most programmers can do without.

The *IF* Command

The basic decision structure in FoxPro is the `IF...ELSE...ENDIF` structure, which many other programming languages use. The following is the syntax for such a control block:

```
IF <expL>
   <one or more commands>
 [ELSE
   <one or more commands>]
ENDIF
```

The operation of the `IF` command is a straightforward process. The condition (`<expL>`) is evaluated. If it is `.T.`, the first set of commands is executed. If the condition is `.F.` and the optional `ELSE` command is present, the second set of commands is executed.

The *DO WHILE* Command

The `DO WHILE` command is one of two loop constructs in FoxPro. It is functionally equivalent to the `WHILE` statement in BASIC, C, and Pascal. The following is the syntax for a loop:

```
 [<loop control initialization>]
DO WHILE <expL>
   <one or more commands>
ENDDO
```

As long as the condition (<expL>) evaluates to .T., the loop is executed. If the condition is initially .F., the loop is not performed at all, and execution continues on the line following the ENDDO command.

Two other commands affect the control flow in a DO WHILE loop: LOOP and EXIT. The LOOP command starts the loop over again from the beginning—the loop condition is re-evaluated, and if it is still .T., the loop commands re-execute. The EXIT command branches immediately to the statement following the ENDDO command. EXIT and LOOP are typically controlled by an IF command so that the entire loop can execute under some circumstances.

The *FOR* Command

The FOR command is functionally equivalent to the FOR statement in BASIC, C, FORTRAN, and Pascal. dBASE IV is the only one of the three major Xbase languages that does not support the FOR command. The following is the syntax for a FOR loop :

```
FOR <memvar> = <expN1> TO <expN2> [STEP <expN3>]
    <one or more commands>
    [EXIT]
    [LOOP]
ENDFOR ¦ NEXT
```

<memvar>, which is called the *counter*, is initially set to <expN1>. With each loop, the counter increments by <expN3>. If the STEP clause is not specified, the counter increments by one for each loop. As long as the <memvar> is less than or equal to <expN2>, the loop is executed. If the counter is initially greater than <expN2>, the loop does not perform at all. Execution continues on the line following the ENDFOR command.

Two other commands affect the control flow in a FOR loop: LOOP and EXIT. The LOOP command starts the loop over again from the beginning after incrementing the counter—the loop condition (<memvar> <= <expN2>) is reevaluated, and if it is still .T., the loop commands execute again. The EXIT command branches immediately to the statement following the ENDFOR command. EXIT and LOOP are typically executed conditionally by an IF command so the entire loop can execute under some circumstances.

Multiway Branching

The DO CASE command in FoxPro, which I described previously, handles multiway branching in a manner similar to that of other languages. CASE commands in a DO CASE block support repeated condition tests as in the following cascading series of nested IF commands:

```
DO CASE
   CASE <expL1>
      <one or more commands>
   CASE <expL2>
      <one or more commands>
   <as many CASE commands as needed>
   [OTHERWISE
      <one or more commands>]
ENDCASE
```

The first condition (<expL1>) is evaluated. If it is `.T.`, the commands following the first `CASE` command are executed, and control moves to the statement following the `ENDCASE` command. If it is `.F.`, the condition associated with the next `CASE` in the sequence (<expL2>) is evaluated, and so on until a `CASE` condition is found that evaluates to `.T.`. If no `CASE` conditions are `.T.` and the optional `OTHERWISE` command is present, the commands in the `OTHERWISE` block are carried out.

The `IF` command could implement the `CASE` construct, as in the following example:

```
IF <expL1>
   <one or more commands>
ELSE
   IF <expL2>
      <one or more commands>
   ELSE
      <otherwise commands>
   ENDIF
ENDIF
```

When cast as a series of `IF` commands, you can easily see that not all conditional expressions are evaluated. In this example, if <expL2> evaluates to `.T.`, the commands following the `IF` would not execute if <expL1> were also `.T.`. This ordering of evaluations is not obvious when using the `CASE` command portrays the same code.

Special Cases

I'm listing two special cases of branching and looping in FoxPro here because they are useful, but not essential, shortcuts for advanced users.

The first, the `IIF()` function, has nothing obvious to do with control flow, but I describe it here because it abbreviates the common FoxPro language construct:

```
IF <expL>
   A = <expression1>
ELSE
   A = <expression2>
ENDIF
```

You can write this in the shorthand of the `IIF()` function as follows:

```
A = IIF(<expL>, <expression1>, <expression2>)
```

The `IIF()` function comes to the FoxPro language fresh from a smash engagement as the ternary `?` operator in the C language (with similar syntax: `<expL> ? <expression1> : <expression2>`). A *ternary operator* is an operator with three operands. Because `IIF()` functions (like any other expression) can be nested, they can make a single statement as powerful as at least five lines of normal FoxPro code.

The next shortcut was implemented for FoxPro because dBASE IV had it. dBASE IV designers used it because they observed that many Xbase programs included a structure such as the following:

```
GOTO TOP
DO WHILE .NOT. EOF()
   IF <record meets criterion>
      <commands>
   ENDIF
   SKIP
ENDDO
```

Many FoxPro programs need to scan through a DBF file examining every record, acting on records that meet a particular criterion. Hence the `SCAN` command, with the following syntax:

```
SCAN [<scope>] [NOOPTIMIZE] [FOR <expL>] [WHILE <expL>]
   <commands>
   [LOOP]
   [EXIT]
ENDSCAN
```

The `SCAN` command accepts `scope`, `FOR`, and `WHILE` clauses, which limit the number of records for which the `<commands>` are performed (just as the `IF` statement in the previous example limits the number of records). The default is `ALL` records. Here is an example:

```
* Nepotism check
SCAN ALL FOR LastName = "Long"
   ? FirstName, Salary, Bonus
   IF Bonus > Salary * 2
      REPLACE Bonus WITH Salary * 2
   ENDIF
ENDDO
```

The `SCAN` command is powerful for very large DBF files because, like the `CALCULATE` command, it enables you to perform several operations simultaneously during only one pass through the data. Chapter 12, "Data Set Operations," covers this subject in more detail.

You can use the `EXIT` and `LOOP` commands in a `SCAN` command structure.

Nested Blocks

You can nest the `IF`, `DO WHILE`, `DO CASE`, and `SCAN` control blocks inside other control blocks, although they may not overlap. This rule is the same in similar programming languages.

As Figure 6.1 shows, correctly nested blocks have no crossing lines. In contrast, the code example in Figure 6.2 elicits several error messages from the compiler. Figure 6.2 represents bad news for bad programmers: FoxPro does not allow any lines to cross.

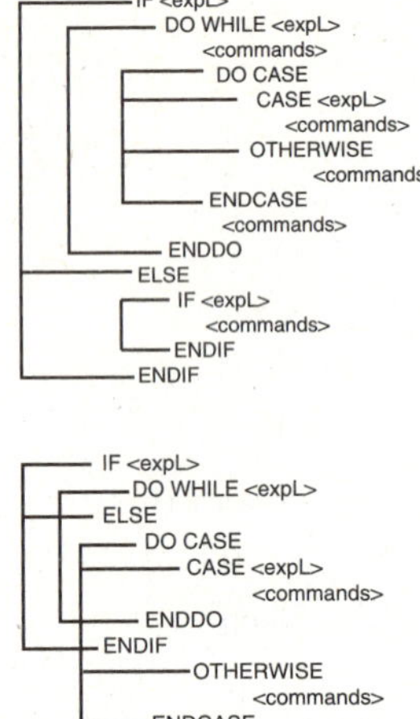

FIGURE 6.1.
A correct way to nest control blocks.

FIGURE 6.2.
An incorrect way to nest control blocks.

NOTE

You can nest structured programming commands to a maximum depth of 124 levels.

Procedures and Functions

A programming language that is more academic than FoxPro, such as Pascal, makes a clear distinction between *procedures*, which perform tasks, and *functions*, which return computed values. Functions are intended to act only upon their arguments. Procedures, although allowed to act upon global variables, are not supposed to return a value.

Procedures and functions that change the state of public variables may cause side effects. Side effects, which cannot be avoided in most practical programming languages, make programs harder to maintain. Unfortunately, the nature of the FoxPro style could cause side effects "to the max" because variables are global by default (DBF fields are available to every procedure and function) and commands that aren't procedural and that carry major ramifications (such as `REPLACE ALL`) can be performed anywhere, even in response to an error condition.

The only difference between a Visual FoxPro procedure and a Visual FoxPro function is that a function can be used in an expression and can return a value.

Procedures

FoxPro command files (PRG files) are considered procedures. You can execute a PRG file with the `DO <PRGfile>` command, which is generalized for FoxPro as follows:

```
DO <procedure name> [IN <filename>]
```

FoxPro does not execute the PRG files. Instead, it executes a binary file with the .FXP extension (FoxPro object code format). To execute a subroutine or procedure from the Command window, issue the following command:

```
DO <procedure> [IN <filename>]
```

If an FXP file by that name exists, it is read into memory and run. If no FXP file exists but a PRG file appears by that name, it is automatically compiled, and an FXP file is created. The `DO` command then loads the new FXP file and runs it. As described in the section "Procedure Files," a third possibility exists: If the procedure name is already known to the system, FoxPro circumvents the search for FXP or PRG files, loads the specified procedure, and executes it. If both an FXP file and a PRG file exist, and `SET DEVELOPMENT` is `ON`, FoxPro checks the time each file was last modified. If the PRG file was modified more recently than the FXP file, the FXP file is erased and recompiled.

You may make procedure names as long as you want, but they must be unique in their first eight characters when they refer also to MS-DOS filenames. Obviously, a procedure called `WHILE` or `CASE` would cause confusion and must be avoided. If you don't specify a filename extension, Visual FoxPro searches for and programs with the following extensions and in the following order:

1. .EXE (executable version of program)
2. .APP (application)
3. .FXP (compiled version)
4. .PRG (program)

Other types of procedure files exist, however. You can execute procedure files created by the Menu Designer (MPR), the Visual FoxPro Form Designer (SCX), a FoxPro 2.*x* screen program (SPR), or a query (QPR) by specifying the extension. For example, if you want to execute these different types of procedure files, type one of the following:

```
DO MyQuery.qpr              && Query file
DO FORM MyForm              && Visual FoxPro screen file
DO MyScreen.spr             %% FoxPro 2.x screen procedure file
DO MyMenu.mpr               && Menu procedure file
```

Notice that the `FORM` keyword is used with the Visual FoxPro screen file. Of course, the MPR, SPR, and QPR procedure files have corresponding compiled files with the same name and extensions (.MPX, .SPX, and .QPX, respectively). They are compiled and the procedure files are used in the same way as the PRG and FPX files. That is, if the compiled file is missing or out of date, it is created by compiling the corresponding procedure file. In either case, the compiled file is executed.

The optional `IN <filename>` command executes a procedure in the specified file. If you do not designate an extension, FoxPro searches for the procedure to execute in the following order: EXE, APP, FXP, and PRG. You already know about the PRG and FXP files. FoxPro programs in executable file form have an .EXE filename extension just like an MS-DOS application. An application file has an .APP extension. When searching for a procedure within an executable (EXE) or an applications (APP) file, FoxPro checks only the name of the main procedure to see if it matches the name of the procedure specified with the `DO` command. However, if `<filename>` is a PRG or FXP file, FoxPro searches all the procedures in the file for the one to execute. For example, if you execute the following statement:

```
DO THIRD IN FIRST
```

FoxPro searches FIRST.PRG for a procedure named `THIRD`. The contents of FIRST.PRG are as follows:

```
* FIRST.PRG - Program with 3 procedures
? "Who's on first"
RETURN
PROCEDURE SECOND
? "What's on second,"
RETURN
PROCEDURE THIRD
? "I Don't Know is on third."
RETURN
```

A nested procedure call occurs when one procedure includes a `DO` command that invokes another procedure. The number of levels that can be nested is set internally to 32.

Procedures start with the beginning of their PRG file (the name of which must match the procedure name) or with the `PROCEDURE` command (see the section "Procedure Files"). Procedures end with the `RETURN` command or by "falling off the end" of a PRG file. In FoxPro, a simple PRG file that contains one or more statements without `PROCEDURE` and `RETURN` commands behaves as if the compiler inserted them automatically. In the following example:

```
* PAYROLL.PRG
USE "Payroll" INDEX "EmpName"
REPLACE ALL Salary WITH Salary*1.1
```

the FoxPro compiler pretends that it sees this:

```
PROCEDURE PAYROLL
* PAYROLL.PRG
USE "Payroll" INDEX "EmpName"
REPLACE ALL Salary WITH Salary*1.1
RETURN
```

The syntax of the `DO` command enables you to specify arguments, or parameters, to send to the called procedure, as in this example:

```
DO <procedure name> [WITH <parameter list>] [IN <filename>]
```

When you use the `WITH` clause, the procedure referred to should begin with a `PARAMETERS` command, which specifies the local names for the procedure's arguments. Parameters that are simple memvars are passed by reference, which means the procedure can modify the value of the parameter. All other parameters (expressions and DBF file fields) are passed by value, which keeps the procedure from changing the original value of the parameter. To pass a simple memvar by value, enclose it in parentheses so it appears to FoxPro as a more complex expression than a single identifier. Here's an example:

Command Window	*Results and Comments*
`A = 3`	`3`
`B = "Hello"`	`Hello`
`C = 123`	`123`
`D = DATE()`	Today's date
`DO Proc1 WITH A, B, (C), D`	Execute procedure `Proc1`
`? A, B, C, D`	`4 Frank     123 A string`
`* PROC1.PRG - Arguments`	
`PARAMETERS P1, P2, P3, P4`	
`? P1, P2, P3, P4`	`3 Hello     123 03/29/89`
`P1 = 4`	Store 4 to P1
`P2 = "Frank"`	Store "Frank" to P2
`P3 = 56`	Store 56 to P3 (passed by value)
`P4 = "A string"`	Store "A string" to P4
`RETURN`	Return from procedure

I'll go through the example step by step. In the Command window, you create four memvars: `A`, `B`, `C`, and `D`. `A` and `C` are numbers, `B` is a character string, and `D` is a date. The `DO` command in this example invokes a procedure called `Proc1` and passes it four parameters. `Proc1` chooses to call these parameters `P1`, `P2`, `P3`, and `P4`. The parameters' names are local (`PRIVATE`) to `Proc1` and are unrestricted—they could be `A`, `B`, `C`, and `D` without confusion. When `Proc1` displays the values, you can see that they have not changed from the memvars created in the Command window.

The example then modifies the values of the parameters and even changes the type of the last parameter from a date to a character string. Back at the Command window, the values and types of the memvars that were passed by reference have changed. The memvar called `C`, however, was passed by value (due to the parentheses) and therefore was unaffected by the modifications made by `Proc1` to its local parameter `P3`.

NOTE

A file can have an unlimited number of procedures. However, each procedure can be only 64KB. Because an application can contain any number of procedures in one or more files, the 64KB-per-procedure limit is not a problem. Besides, a well-designed application consists of many small procedures. Large procedures are difficult to debug and maintain.

User-Defined Functions

A *user-defined function* (UDF) is a special kind of procedure with two unusual properties. First, unlike a procedure, a UDF returns a value. Second, the commands in a UDF are executed when the expression containing the function reference is evaluated rather than when an explicit DO command is executed.

A user-defined function is defined in the same way as a procedure. A reference to a UDF first looks for a file by that name with the .FXP extension. If it doesn't find the file, it looks for a PRG file and automatically compiles it and executes the FXP file. UDFs are activated by evaluating expressions rather than by using the DO command. A UDF cannot have the same name as one of the built-in functions. Remember that this also includes the abbreviated name of a built-in function. For example, you cannot have a UDF named SOUNDEX, SOUNDE, SOUND, or SOUN.

<expression> is used to return a value. In FoxPro, a UDF without a RETURN command can fall off the end of the file as procedures can. If it does, the UDF returns a logical .T. value. (FoxPro 1.02 required a RETURN.)

You can pass arguments to a UDF in the form of parameters as you would any other function. You can pass a variable, an array element, or the contents of entire arrays to UDFs. By default, parameters are passed by value to UDFs. Parameters can be passed by reference if you change the default using the SET UDFPARMS command. The SET UDFPARMS command has two forms:

```
SET UDFPARMS TO VALUE
SET UDFPARMS TO REFERENCE
```

The previous section discusses the distinction between value and reference. The form of a UDF call is as follows:

```
<udf-name>( [<parameter-list>] )
```

The *<parameter-list>* is specified if you want to pass data to a UDF. You can pass up to 24 parameters. Here are some examples of UDF calls:

```
ZIP( address )
IsRain()              && No parameters
DECLARE ARAY[3]
AINVERT( ARAY )       && Entire array is passed
IsCold( ARAY[3], x, y (z) )
```

In the last example, all four values are passed by value if you set UDFPARMS to VALUE. If UDFPARMS is set to REFERENCE, only the last parameter, (z), is passed by value.

A UDF begins with a FUNCTION command instead of the PROCEDURE command. The FUNCTION command has the following syntax:

```
FUNCTION [( <parameter-list> )]
```

Like the PROCEDURE command, the FUNCTION command is optional when the UDF is at the beginning of the file. However, functions should end with the following command:

```
RETURN <expression>
```

The optional argument list can be used in place of the PARAMETER command to specify the parameter list. For example, the FUNCTION command corresponding to the three-argument function MyFunc(amount, 2, .T.) can use either of the two following forms:

```
FUCTION MyFunc( nArgument1, nArgument2, lArgument3)
FUNCTION MyFunc
PARAMETER nArgument1, nArgument2, lArgument3
```

Here is an example of a UDF. Suppose you create a PRG file called SQUARE.PRG to calculate the square of a number. This simple function is invoked whenever the SQUARE() function occurs in an expression:

Command Window	*Results and Comments*
? SQUARE(3)	9
? "The value is "+STR(SQUARE(9))	The value is 81
? SQUARE(8)+SQUARE(7)+23	136
* SQUARE.PRG - Illustrates UDF	
FUNCTION SQUARE	
PARAMETERS x	
RETURN x * x	

User-defined functions can occur in expressions that are evaluated while other commands, such as READ or INDEX, are executing, effectively interrupting the command to perform other FoxPro commands. A potential for mayhem is present because FoxPro commands, such as LIST, are not designed to be called recursively. For example, the following code would cause unpredictable results if FoxPro allowed it:

```
LIST A, B, MyFunc()
* MyFunc - user defined function
FUNCTION MyFunc()
LIST A, B
RETURN .T.
```

UDFs can call themselves recursively, as in this textbook example:

```
FUNCTION FACT
PARAMETER x
IF x <= 1
   RETURN 1
ELSE
   RETURN FACT(x-1)*x
ENDIF
```

This function returns the factorial (!) of its argument by repeatedly calling itself. FACT(1) is 1, FACT(2) is 2, FACT(3) is 6, and so on. This function is limited to 32 recursive calls due to the nesting level limit of 32.

You'll probably use UDFs most frequently with the VALID clause of the @...GET command and with calculated fields established with the BROWSE command. In both cases, you may want to look up a value in a different DBF file. The SELECT() function is helpful in finding an unused work area. As long as you use inactive work areas, nothing is restricted on DBF commands in UDFs.

The Clipper (Summer 1987) Compiler allows a user-defined function to be used alone on a command line in place of a command verb:

```
MYFUNC()
```

This form becomes a de facto *user-defined command* (UDC). dBASE IV and Visual FoxPro do not allow this form. It can be simulated, however, as the following example shows:

```
DUMMY = MYFUNC()
```

In FoxPro you can omit the variable and the example becomes the following:

```
= MYFUNC()
```

You cannot use UDFs everywhere in FoxPro: They have restrictions. However, you can use them in almost every place you need them. Here is a current list of places in FoxPro in which you can use UDFs:

- The STORE command and assignment (=) statement
- The REPLACE command
- The control statement expressions (IF, DO WHILE, DO CASE, and FOR)
- Print statements (?, ??, and ???)
- The DISPLAY and LIST commands
- The @...SAY expression
- The VALID, DEFAULT, and WHEN expressions for @...GET and BROWSE commands
- The AVERAGE expression
- The SUM expression
- The RETURN expression
- The SCHEME expression
- The LABEL and REPORT expressions
- The INDEX ON and FOR expressions

Here is a simple, short UDF that displays a spinning symbol during some batch database operations, such as REPLACE or INDEX, so that users will know that processing is taking place:

```
* SPIN.PRG - Displays spinning symbol
FUNCTION SPIN
PARAMETER value
@ 10,40 SAY SUBSTR( "¦/-\", ( RECNO() % 4) + 1, 1)
RETURN value
```

Here are examples of the SPIN() function in use:

```
INDEX ON SPIN(Customer) TAG Customer
REPLACE ALL IDNUM1 with SPIN(IDNUM1)
```

Procedure Files

FoxPro 2.0 and later versions handle procedures differently than do previous versions. Specifically, you can define more than one procedure (or function) in any PRG file without regard to the `SET PROCEDURE` command. Therefore, you can contain an entire application in a single PRG file rather than a dozen PRG files.

In fact, the `SET PROCEDURE` command is no longer required. You can write FoxPro programs with a structure like the one shown in Listing 6.2.

Listing 6.2. An example of a program structure with multiple procedures.

```
* P1.PRG
PROCEDURE P1    && This is optional; it is implied
<commands>
DO P2
<commands>
RETURN

PROCEDURE P2
<commands>
Mvar = P3()
DO P4
RETURN

FUNCTION P3
<commands>
RETURN <expression>

PROCEDURE P4
<commands>
? P3()
DO P2
RETURN
* EOF: P1.PRG
```

Every PRG file can include extra procedures and functions in this way. If the procedure's example called a procedure named `ABC`, the ABC.PRG file would be activated along with all the additional functions and procedures defined in ABC.PRG. As file A calls file B, which in turn calls file C, FoxPro maintains an activation chain of FXP files.

Each FXP file includes a directory of the procedures and functions defined in it. When a procedure or function is referenced, the FXP directory of each file in the activation chain is searched first, starting with the most recently activated. So if two FXP files contain procedures with the same name, the procedure in the most recently activated file is found first. Only if the procedure or function is not found in any file in the activation chain does FoxPro look for an FXP file (and possibly a PRG file) to compile.

After an FXP file is loaded into memory, it tends to stay there in case it is needed again. Program execution speeds up considerably when FXP files are permitted to loiter, but if a pressing need for memory arises, inactive FXP files are some of the first items to be flushed. The CLOSE PROCEDURE command can explicitly remove all FXP files from memory (except any currently being executed).

An FXP file is limited only by the amount of available memory. Up to 32 procedure files may be active at a time. However, if you have too many procedures in memory, performance tends to degrade. The lack of available memory might become a limiting factor, as well.

Dynamic Parameter Passing

In FoxBASE+, the parameters passed to a procedure had to correspond to the number of parameters in a PARAMETER statement, as in the following example:

```
DO XYZ WITH 3,4
...
PROCEDURE XYZ
PARAMETER A,B
...
```

If this number differed, an error condition was invoked. In FoxPro, the number of parameters can be less than the number of parameters specified on the called procedure's PARAMETER statement. You can find out how many parameters are actually passed by using the PARAMETERS() function. The PARAMETERS() function is used in a called procedure or UDF to control the processing of the parameters.

In Visual FoxPro 3 you can pass parameters to functions, procedures, or methods using place-holding commas for values that will accept a default value. When you pass nothing, the function will receive .F. for that argument. In other words, you can leave parameters out of a parameter list. When you omit a parameter, the function acts as though a logical type parameter had been passed by value in its place. For example, the following statement:

```
Func(a,,b,,3)
```

would be equivalent to

```
Func(a,.F., b, .F., 3)
```

You can also omit arguments from a DO command WITH clause. Here's an example:

```
DO Proc WITH Name,,City,,Zip
```

Listing 6.3 shows an example of dynamic parameter passing. Listing 6.3 presents a FoxPro UDF, REPLACE(), which can have a variable number of parameters. The BadType() function is used to validate the type of parameters passed to the REPLACE() function. It uses the TYPE() function to verify that the parameter is the correct type. If it is not, the BadType() function returns .T..

Listing 6.3. The source listing for the REPLACE() function and the program that calls it.

```
*************************************************************
*      * 09/94               PREPLACE.PRG                   *
*************************************************************
*      * Author's Name: Jeb Long                            *
*      *                                                    *
*      * Description:                                       *
*      * This program illustrates how to process a variable *
*      * number of arguments to a user-defined function     *
*************************************************************
*************************************************************
* PREPLACE.PRG - Illustrates variable number of parameters
*
*   Note that REPLACE() UDF function can have 3 or 4 arguments.
*************************************************************
SET TALK OFF
? REPLACE("the eerie eel","e","X")        && Three arguments
? REPLACE("the eerie eel","e","X",5)      && Four arguments
? REPLACE("This will produce an error")   && One argument
? REPLACE("The eerie eel eats early","e",,9)  && Third argument is missing
? REPLACE(1,2,3)                          && Bad first three parameter types
? REPLACE("the eerie eel","e","X",9,9,9)  && Too many arguments
RETURN
*************************************************************
FUNCTION REPLACE
  *  (This UDF is similar to the FoxPro 2 strtran() function)
  *  REPLACE replaces multiple occurrences of a substring in
  *  another string.  Its syntax is
  *
  *      <string> = REPLACE(<string>,<from>,<to>,[<times>]
  *
  *  Occurrences of <from> in <string> are replaced with <to>
  *  the designated number of <times>.  If <times> is omitted,
  *  1 is assumed.
*************************************************************
PARAMETER String, From, To, Times

PCnt = PARAMETERS()  && Number of parameters
IF PCnt = 4
     NMax = Times
ELSE
     NMax = 1
     IF PCnt # 3
           ? "Error: REPLACE() must have 3 or 4 arguments"
           RETURN ""
     ENDIF
ENDIF
IF BadType("To", "C")  && Was argument omitted?
   To = ""
ENDIF
IF BadType("String", "C") OR BadType("From","C")  OR BadType ("NMax","N")
   ? " Illegal Argument Type"
   RETURN ""
ENDIF
I = 1
S = String
L= Len(From)
```

continues

Listing 6.3. continued

```
DO WHILE I <= NMax
     J = AT(From,S)
     IF J=0
           RETURN S
     ENDIF
     S = STUFF(S,J,L,To)
     I = I+1
ENDDO
RETURN S
*********************************************
* FUNCTION: BadType
* PURPOSE: This function validates the type
*          of the parameters and returns a .T.
*          if the type is bad.
*********************************************
FUNCTION BadType
PARAMETER cVariable, cType
RETURN TYPE(cVariable) != cTYPE
```

The REPLACE() UDF can have three or four arguments. Here's an example:

```
? REPLACE("the eerie eel","e","X")       && Three arguments
? REPLACE("the eerie eel","e","X",5)     && Four arguments
? REPLACE("This will produce an error")  && One argument
? REPLACE("The eerie eel eats early","e",,9)  && Third argument is missing
? REPLACE(1,2,3)                          && Bad first three argument types
? REPLACE("the eerie eel","e","X",9,9,9) && Too many arguments
```

The first five of the preceding statements produce the following five lines of output:

```
thX eerie eel
thX XXriX Xel
Error: REPLACE() must have 3 or 4 arguments
Th ri l ats arly
Illegal argument type
```

Notice that in the fourth call to the REPLACE() function, a comma placeholder is used instead of the third parameter. The REPLACE() command detects that a place-holding comma was used in place of the third parameter, and uses an empty string for the To parameter. As a result, the REPLACE() function removes the occurrence of the third character string. In the example, all occurrences of the letter e were removed from the string.

The sixth statement causes an alert box to appear, indicating that the function call contains the wrong number of parameters. This occurs when more arguments are passed than are in the PARAMETER statement.

NOTE

The PCOUNT() function was added to FoxPro for compatibility with dBASE IV. It does the same thing as the PARAMETERS() function.

One final comment—the fact that you can have a variable number of parameters in the parameter list and that you can omit parameters makes it important that you carefully count your parameters to make sure you have the correct number. Also, you need to make sure you pass the correct data type. Passing the wrong number and type of arguments to a function or procedure is one of the most common programming errors.

The *SUSPEND* and *RESUME* Commands

The only debugging available in early Xbase programs, before the advent of the FoxPro debugger (see the section on debugging in Chapter 23, "Building Visual FoxPro Applications"), was to use the `SUSPEND` and `RESUME` commands. You could see the lines of code as the Xbase program executed them by setting the `ECHO` parameter to `ON`.

The `SUSPEND` command returns to the Command window while preserving the current system state. Interrupting a program by pressing the Esc key also brings up a dialog box that offers `SUSPEND` as an option.

While a program is suspended, you can enter ad hoc commands in the Command window that describe the current state of the application (such as `DISPLAY MEMORY`). This can be an invaluable debugging aid.

To restart the program and continue from the point of the interruption, you can issue the `RESUME` command from the Command window. Executing the `CANCEL` command from the Command window clears the suspended system state information but leaves the FXP file in memory waiting to be executed again.

The FoxPro `SET STEP ON` and `SET ECHO ON` commands display in the Trace window as they execute. `ACTIVATE WINDOW TRACE` opens the Trace window so you can see your code execute.

An optional syntax for the `RETURN` command supports returning to a named procedure. This is not a good practice because it can lead to programs that are hard to maintain, but it is sometimes desirable in error recovery and debugging routines. The syntax is the following:

```
RETURN TO <procedure name>
```

or the following:

```
RETURN TO MASTER
```

The latter case, `RETURN TO MASTER`, returns control to the first procedure executed in the Command window. The former case returns from each level in turn until it encounters a level with a procedure name that matches the specified name. If no name matches, this form eventually returns to the Command window and gives up.

Event Trapping

This section describes the use of traditional FoxPro event trapping, which is still quite valid and useful in Visual FoxPro. *Event trapping*, as associated with object-oriented programming (OOP), is introduced in Chapter 2, "Database Management and the FoxPro Language," and is presented in more detail in Chapter 14, "Object-Oriented Programming." Although it's mentioned last, event trapping (or *exception handling*) is a significant form of control flow in FoxPro commands. *Events* include errors and keypresses. You can instruct FoxPro to perform a myriad of commands if any of certain events occur. This section describes the various forms of the `ON` command used for contingency processing. The `ON` command is used to set a trap that triggers a specified FoxPro command when an explicit processing event occurs. Options are available to set traps on an error condition, a keypress selection of a menu object, or a page break. Chapter 7, "FoxPro Language Elements for Creating Windows and Menus Systems," discusses menu-related events. The syntax for other forms of the `ON` command is the following:

```
ON ERROR [<command>]
ON ESCAPE [<command>]
ON MOUSE [<command>]
ON PAGE [AT LINE <expN> <command>]
ON READERROR [<command>]
ON SHUTDOWN [<command>]
```

If the triggering event occurs, the specified `<command>` is executed. In most cases, the command is `DO <program>`. After an `ON` command is executed, it remains in effect for the remainder of the session or until the `ON` command is specified without the `<command>` clause, in which case the `ON` command is disabled. Table 6.1 shows the various forms of the `ON` command and their corresponding triggering events.

Table 6.1. `ON` command triggering events.

`ON` *Command*	*Triggering Event*
`ON ERROR`	An error occurs.
`ON ESCAPE`	The Esc key is pressed.
`ON KEY`	Any key is pressed.
`ON KEY LABEL <label>`	A specific key is pressed.
`ON MOUSE`	The left mouse button is clicked anywhere in the client region.
`ON PAGE`	The page line number is passed.
`ON READERROR`	The `READ` command error occurs.
`ON SHUTDOWN`	The user exits the program from the **F**ile menu E**x**it option or the `QUIT` command.

The ON ERROR, ON ESCAPE, ON MOUSE, and ON SHUTDOWN commands can execute any command or procedure that executes any FoxPro command. This occurs because these forms of the ON command detect the contingency after a command has finished execution.

Events associated with the ON KEY and ON READERROR commands can be trapped in the execution of a command such as BROWSE, EDIT, and READ. The ON PAGE command is discussed in Chapter 8, "Input and Output."

The *ON ERROR* Command

When an error (sometimes called an *exception*) occurs, FoxPro executes the command set up by the ON ERROR command. If this command has not been issued or if no command is specified, FoxPro stops the current program and displays an error dialog box. The syntax of the ON ERROR command is the following:

```
ON ERROR [<command>]
```

Specifying an ON ERROR command without specifying a *<command>* clause disables error trapping. The associated *<command>* is most often the DO *<procedure>*, but the nature of the command is unrestricted. The error-handler procedure includes several commands and functions that help it do its job. These include the ERROR() and MESSAGE() functions and the RETRY command. The ERROR() function returns the number of the last error. The MESSAGE() function returns the character string explanation of the error. The RETRY command re-executes the line that caused the error.

You can nest ON ERROR statements, meaning that an ON ERROR procedure can contain another ON ERROR statement that is active (that is, not suspended) until the original ON ERROR procedure finishes processing. Then the new ON ERROR is discarded and the original ON ERROR statement is activated. The ON ERROR command traps FoxPro errors, but does not trap MS-DOS system errors. Windows traps MS-DOS errors, such as a full disk and a drive or printer that's not ready. The type of processing done with ON ERROR, however, is not possible for low-level MS-DOS errors.

The *ON ESCAPE* Command

The ON ESCAPE command works like the ON ERROR command and performs the specified command whenever you press the Esc key. If the ON ESCAPE command executes a program, and the program allows the return of program control to the program that was interrupted, the ON ESCAPE program must end with a RETRY command, which re-executes the command that was executing when the Esc key was pressed. If you execute a RETURN command to the interrupted program, program control returns to the line following the line of code that was about to execute or was executing when the Esc key was pressed.

NOTE

The `ON ESCAPE` command does not work unless `SET ESCAPE` is set to `ON`.

The *ON KEY* Command

The `ON KEY` command without the `LABEL` clause is used to define event processing that is triggered when any key is pressed. If `SET ESCAPE` is `ON`, the Esc key is used for interrupt processing and does not trigger `ON KEY` processing. Keyboard input can trigger event processing at the following points in FoxPro:

- Between the execution of commands in a program. Although keyboard entry is detected during the execution of most commands, it is not processed until the command completes its operation.
- During field editing. This means that a key pressed during the execution of `APPEND`, `EDIT`, `BROWSE`, and `READ` triggers `ON KEY` event processing.
- During navigation of a user-defined menu system.

You can use the `INKEY()` function to fetch an integer that represents the ASCII value of the key that triggered the event.

The *ON KEY LABEL <label>* Command

Use the `ON KEY LABEL` command to specify the label of a key that triggers event processing. The *`<label>`* clause argument is the literal name of the key. It can be a letter, number, or one of the key labels in Table 6.2. For letters, case is ignored. You can use the `ON KEY` command with or without a *`<label>`* clause, but you cannot use both forms in the same session. Using `ON KEY` without a clause resets all the `ON KEY` traps. The syntax is this:

```
ON KEY LABEL <key name> [<command>]
```

The following list catalogs the available key names. `ON ESCAPE` takes precedence over `ON KEY`; if both are in effect, the `ON ESCAPE` command is executed if the Esc key is pressed.

Table 6.2. The key names for use with the ON KEY LABEL <label> command.

Alt+0 through Alt+9	End
Alt+A through Alt+Z	Enter
Alt+F1 through Alt+F12	Esc
Alt+PgUp	F1 through F12
Alt+PgDn	Home

Backspace	Ins
Backtab	Left arrow
Ctrl+A through Ctrl+Z	PgDn
Ctrl+End	PgUp
Ctrl+F1 through Ctrl+F12	Right arrow
Ctrl+Home	Shift+F1 through Shift+F12
Ctrl+left arrow	Shift+Tab
Ctrl+PgDn	Spacebar
Ctrl+PgUp	Tab
Ctrl+right arrow	Up arrow
Del	All printable characters
Down arrow	

You can also specify the following `<key names>` with the `LABEL` clause:

`<key name>`	`<command>` *Is Executed if...*
`MOUSE`	any of the mouse buttons are pressed
`LEFTMOUSE`	the left mouse button is pressed
`RIGHTMOUSE`	the right mouse button is pressed

The mouse trapping commands do not interfere with the operation of the mouse. The `ON KEY LABEL` *<command>* executes before the designated mouse operation is performed. The `LEFTMOUSE` or `RIGHTMOUSE` button trapping commands override the `MOUSE` trapping command.

In the following examples, traps are set for `F2`, `F1`, and `Home`:

```
ON KEY LABEL F2  ? CHR(7)
ON KEY LABEL F1  DO MYHELP
ON KEY LABEL Home DO RECALC
...
PROCEDURE MYHELP
SAVE SCREEN TO X            && Save the screen
@ 8,8 TO 10,60              && Draw box
@ 9,9  SAY "This is my help message.."
@ 10,9 SAY "Press any key to continue…"
WAIT ""
RESTORE SCREEN FROM X       && Restore the screen
RETURN
```

The first `ON KEY` statement can be used to inhibit `F2` switching between `BROWSE` and `EDIT`.

The *ON MOUSE* Command

This is the syntax of the `ON MOUSE` command:

```
ON MOUSE [<command>]
```

The ON MOUSE command executes the specified command (<*command*>) when you click the left mouse button anywhere in the client region. Although this command was added to be compatible with dBASE IV, it appears to be more versatile than Borland's implementation of ON MOUSE. In dBASE IV, the ON MOUSE command is active only in the following cases:

- Outside @...GET regions when a READ or EDIT command is executing
- Outside all pads and pop-up menus
- Outside an active window client region unless the window contains a BROWSE screen

In FoxPro, the ON MOUSE command appears to be active anywhere on the screen except the FoxPro title bar.

The example presented in Listing 6.4 illustrates the use of the ON MOUSE command.

Listing 6.4. The MOUSE.PRG program source listing.

```
*********************************************
* PROGRAM: MOUSE.PRG - Demonstrates ON MOUSE
*
ON MOUSE DO MREGION
@ 10,40 TO 20,60 DOUBLE
@ 10,40 FILL TO 20,60 COLOR B+/R
dummy = space(10)
@ 22,40 SAY "Click the mouse box" GET dummy
READ
ON MOUSE
********************************************
PROCEDURE MREGION
y = MROW()
x = MCOL()
IF y > 10 AND y < 20 AND x > 40 AND x < 60
   WAIT WINDOW "You clicked the mouse box"
ELSE
   ?? CHR(7)
ENDIF
RETURN
```

The *ON READERROR* Command

The ON READERROR command is similar to ON ERROR except that it handles errors that are caused by user input during the READ command. Like the ERROR() function for use with ON ERROR, the VARREAD() function helps a READERROR procedure take context-sensitive action. Both the ON READERROR and ON KEY procedures are limited to the subset of commands that are legal in user-defined functions. The READ command and READKEY(), WLAST(), WREAD(), and other window functions can be used in harmony to enable you to create an event-driven interface similar to the FoxPro user interface. You can do this by using a single READ command, referred to as a *foundation* READ, to coordinate multiple windows each containing GET objects. A GET object can be a field, pop-up menu, menu, check box, push button, and so forth. Techniques for creating an event-driven interface are discussed in Chapter 9, "Full-Screen Data Editing."

The ON READERROR command specifies a trap procedure that is executed if a read error occurs. The ON READERROR command was a new command in FoxPro 2.5. An event is triggered for the following @...GET command field editing errors:

- Invalid date entry
- Exceeded RANGE clause limits
- Data entry fails the VALID clause condition

If the read error occurs, the specified *<command>* clause is executed. Usually the DO command is used to execute a program that performs an error recovery process.

In the following example, if the user enters an invalid date, an error message is displayed at the top of the screen:

```
ON READERROR  @ 0,0 SAY "You have entered an invalid date!!"
@ 10,10 SAY "Enter your birthday"  GET  BDATE
READ
```

The *ON SHUTDOWN* Command

The ON SHUTDOWN command executes a command when you exit Visual FoxPro by choosing E**x**it from the **F**ile menu, if you enter a QUIT command from the Command window, or if a QUIT command executes from a program. The syntax is as follows:

```
ON SHUTDOWN <command>
```

In the ON SHUTDOWN procedure, *<command>* must not contain a QUIT command. This command might be a good place to add a dialog box to remind users to back up their data.

The *ON()* Function

The ON() function returns a character string containing the *<command>* clause associated with an ON command. Its syntax is the following:

```
ON(<expC1> [,<expC2>])
```

The first argument designates for which ON command a value is returned, as presented here:

Command	*<expC1>*	*<expC2>*
ON ERROR	ERROR	
ON ESCAPE		ESCAPE
ON KEY	KEY	
ON KEY LABEL	KEY	Key label
ON PAGE	PAGE	
ON READERROR	READERROR	
ON SHUTDOWN	SHUTDOWN	

<expC2> is a key label and is specified only for the `ON KEY LABEL` to identify the key. Here is an example:

```
SaveKey = ONKEY("KEY", "CTRL+F3" )
```

The `ON()` function is a language element that is easy to forget unless you know its positive aspects. It's very useful when you need it. It is most often used to save an `ON` command action or temporarily establish another action for the same `ON` command. Consider the following code fragment:

```
**********************************************************
* ONSAVE.PRG illustrates use of ON() function
*
ON ERROR DO ERRPROC WITH 1
ON KEY LABEL CTRL+F2 DO THING1
*
*  ... Do some processing
*
ON KEY LABEL CTRL+F2 DO THING2
*
*  ...  Do some more processing
*
ON KEY LABEL CTRL+F3 DO THING3
*
* ...  Do even more processing
*
ON KEY LABEL CTRL+F2
ON ERROR
RETURN
**********************************************************
* ERRPROC - Performs error recovery operations
*
PROCEDURE ERRPROC
PARAMETER ErrLoc
SaveONerr  = ON("ERROR")  && Save the ON ERROR action
SaveCtrlF2 = ON ("KEY", "CTRL+F2")
ON KEY LABEL CTRL+F2
ON ERROR DO ERR2  && Do another error procedure
*
*  ...  Do error recovery operation
*
ON ERROR &SaveONerr      && Reestablish original ON action
ON KEY LABEL CTRL+F2 &SaveCtrlF2
RETURN
**********************************************************
```

```
* ERR2 - Secondary error recovery program
*
PROCEDURE ERR2
*   ... Process error that occurs in ERRPROC
RETURN
```

In this example, to prevent any error that may occur in the ERRPROC procedure from recalling ERRPROC, a new ON ERROR action is established. But first the original ON ERROR action is saved in the memory variable SaveONerr. When ERRPROC completes its error recovery operation, the original ON ERROR action is reestablished. By the same technique, the action for an ON KEY LABEL command is saved on entry and restored on exit to prevent an ON KEY LABEL action from being activated during the error recovery operation.

An alternative to using the ON() function and ON KEY LABEL commands to save and restore ON KEY LABEL command settings is to use the PUSH KEY and POP KEY commands. The PUSH KEY command saves all active ON KEY LABEL settings. The POP KEY command restores the settings saved with the PUSH KEY command. The syntax of the two commands is the following:

```
PUSH KEY [CLEAR]
POP KEY
```

The PUSH KEY command places all current ON KEY LABEL command settings on a stack in memory so you can nest PUSH KEY and POP KEY commands. The ON KEY LABEL command settings are placed on and removed from the stack in a last-in, first-out (LIFO) order. If you specify the CLEAR keyword, all ON KEY LABEL command settings are cleared.

The PUSH KEY and POP KEY commands could have been used in the ERRPROC procedure in the preceding example to save the ON KEY LABEL command settings, as shown in the following code fragment:

```
************************************************************
* ERRPROC - Performs error recovery operations
*
PROCEDURE ERRPROC
PARAMETER ErrLoc
SaveONerr  = ON("ERROR") && Save the ON ERROR action
PUSH KEY CLEAR
ON KEY LABEL CTRL+F2
ON ERROR DO ERR2          && Do another error procedure
*
*  ... Do error recovery operation
*
ON ERROR &SaveONerr       && Reestablish original ON action
POP KEY
RETURN
**************************************************************
```

Using Procedures and Functions

In this section an example is presented that illustrates how to use functions, procedures, and user-defined functions. The program makes use of traditional FoxPro procedure code to help you understand the how procedures and functions are called and how they are related.

Also in this section you will be treated to an example of the mortgage calculator that utilizes object-oriented form creation methodology. Although you may not understand the details of the object-oriented approach at this point, you will be able to examine a comparison between the traditional Xbase and the Visual FoxPro object-oriented methods of solving the same problem. After you become familiar with object-oriented programming, you can revisit this chapter and you will better appreciate the advantages of using an object-oriented approach.

A Mortgage Calculator Program Using the Traditional FoxPro Language Approach

The MORTGAGE.PRG program, shown in Listing 6.5, is an example of a program file containing multiple procedures and functions. The program computes home mortgage payments, given the price of the property and the down payment. It also computes the total monthly payment (or *PITI,* which is principal, interest, taxes, and insurance). You can also enter the principal and interest payment and the program will compute the price of the property.

The `PRvalid()` and `LAValid()` functions are called when the `VALID` clause evaluates. (This occurs after you type a number into one of the `@...GET` fields.) Traditionally, a `VALID` clause is used to validate data entry; however, in MORTGAGE.PRG, the `VALID` clause is used to simulate a spreadsheet. The `PRvalid()` and `LAValid()` functions call the `RECALC` procedure each time an entry field is changed to recompute and redisplay the contents of the remaining entry fields and display fields. The `PAYMENT()` function computes the payment given the principal, interest rate, and term. The `PV()` function computes the principal given the payment, interest rate, and term. You can change the interest rate and the term of the payment in MORTGAGE.PRG. Figure 6.3 shows a sample output screen for the mortgage payment calculator.

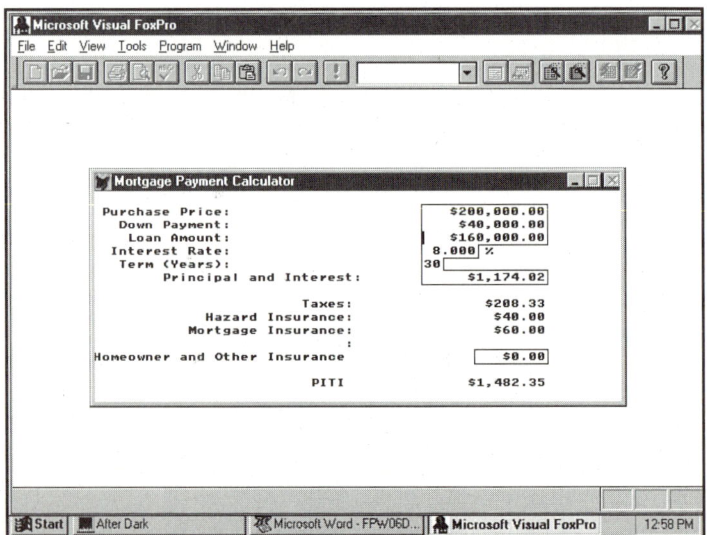

FIGURE 6.3.
A sample output screen for MORTGAGE.PRG.

Listing 6.5. The MORTGAGE.PRG source listing.

```
****************************************************************
*       * 07/09/92           MORTGAGE.PRG              06:19:39 *
****************************************************************
*       * Author's Name: Jeb Long                               *
*       *                                                       *
*       * Description:                                          *
*       * This program computes mortgage payments               *
*       *                                                       *
****************************************************************

PRIVATE m.currarea, m.talkstat, m.compstat, m.readbord

IF SET("TALK") = "ON"
   SET TALK OFF
   m.talkstat = "ON"
ELSE
   m.talkstat = "OFF"
ENDIF
m.compstat = SET("COMPATIBLE")
SET COMPATIBLE FOXPLUS
m.currarea = SELECT()
m.readbord = SET("READBORDER")
SET READBORDER ON

****************************************************************
*       *                                                       *
*       *      Window Definitions                               *
*       *                                                       *
****************************************************************

IF NOT WEXIST("mortgage")
   DEFINE WINDOW mortgage ;
      FROM INT((SROW()-18)/2),INT((SCOL()-63)/2) ;
      TO INT((SROW()-18)/2)+17,INT((SCOL()-63)/2)+62 ;
      TITLE "Mortgage Payment Calculator" ;
      FOOTER "Press Esc to Exit" ;
      NOFLOAT ;
      NOCLOSE ;
      SHADOW ;
      MINIMIZE ;
      SYSTEM ;
      COLOR SCHEME 8
ENDIF
****************************************************************
*       *                                                       *
*       *      Setup Mortgage parameters                        *
*       *                                                       *
****************************************************************
*
STORE 0 TO Price, DownPayment,LoanAmt, pi, taxes,hi,mi,hoi,piti
STORE 30 TO term  && Payment term in years
Rate = 8.0        && Annual mortgage rate in percent
TaxRate = .0125   && Tax rate
MTR = TaxRate/12  && Monthly Tax rate (impound)
HIR = .003        && Hazard insurance rate
MHI = .8*HIR/12   && Monthly hazard insurance impound
```

continues

Listing 6.5. continued

```
MIR = .0045       && Mortgage insurance rate
MMI = MIR/12      && Monthly mortgage insurance impound
IR = Rate/1200.   && Monthly interest rate
Tmonth = 12*term  && Term in months

***************************************************************
*     *                                                        *
*     *      MORTGAGE SCREEN LAYOUT                            *
*     *                                                        *
***************************************************************

IF WVISIBLE("mortgage")
   ACTIVATE WINDOW mortgage SAME
ELSE
   ACTIVATE WINDOW mortgage NOSHOW
ENDIF
@ 1,1  SAY "Purchase Price:"
@ 2,3  SAY "Down Payment:"
@ 3,4  SAY "Loan Amount:"
@ 4,2  SAY "Interest Rate:"
@ 5,3  SAY "Term (Years):"
@ 6,8  SAY "Principal and Interest:"
@ 8,24 SAY "Taxes:"
@ 9,13 SAY "Hazard Insurance:"
@ 10,11 SAY "Mortgage Insurance:"
@ 12,0 SAY "Homeowner and Other Insurance:"
@ 14,25 SAY "PITI:"
@ 4,45 SAY "%"
DO SHOWCALC  && Display Screen
@ 1,38 GET price PICTURE "@$ 999,999,999.99"  VALID PRvalid()
@ 2,38 GET DownPayment PICTURE "@$ 999,999,999.99" VALID PRvalid()
@ 3,38 GET loanamt PICTURE "@$ 999,999,999.99" VALID LAvalid()
@ 4,38 GET rate PICTURE "99.999"  VALID PRvalid()
@ 5,38 GET term PICTURE "99" VALID PRvalid()
@ 6,38 GET pi PICTURE "@$ 999,999,999.99" VALID PIvalid()
@ 12,40 GET hoi PICTURE "@$ 9,999.99" VALID PRvalid()

IF NOT WVISIBLE("mortgage")
   ACTIVATE WINDOW mortgage
ENDIF
READ CYCLE

RELEASE WINDOW mortgage
SELECT (m.currarea)


IF m.talkstat = "ON"
   SET TALK ON
ENDIF
IF m.compstat = "ON"
   SET COMPATIBLE ON
ENDIF
IF m.readbord = "OFF"
   SET READBORDER OFF
ENDIF
```

```
*************************************************************
*      *                                                    *
*      *   PRvalid              price VALID                 *
*      *                                                    *
*      *   Function Origin:                                 *
*      *                                                    *
*      *   From Screen:         MORTGAGE,                   *
*      *   Variable:            price                       *
*      *   Called By:           VALID Clause                *
*      *   Object Type:         Field                       *
*      *   Snippet Number:      1                           *
*      *                                                    *
*************************************************************

FUNCTION PRvalid     &&  price VALID
DO RECALC
CLEAR GETS
RETURN .T.
*************************************************************
*      *                                                    *
*      *   LAvalid              loanamt VALID               *
*      *                                                    *
*      *   Function Origin:                                 *
*      *                                                    *
*      *   From Screen:         MORTGAGE,                   *
*      *   Variable:            loanamt                     *
*      *   Called By:           VALID Clause                *
*      *   Object Type:         Field                       *
*      *   Snippet Number:      2                           *
*      *                                                    *
*************************************************************
*
FUNCTION LAvalid        &&  loanamt VALID
downpayment  = price-loanamt
DO RECALC
CLEAR GETS
RETURN .T.

*************************************************************
*      *                                                    *
*      *   LAvalid              PI principal and Interest VALID*
*      *                                                    *
*      *   Function Origin:                                 *
*      *                                                    *
*      *   From Screen:         MORTGAGE,                   *
*      *   Variable:            pi                          *
*      *   Called By:           VALID Clause                *
*      *   Object Type:         Field                       *
*      *   Snippet Number:      3                           *
*      *                                                    *
*************************************************************
*
FUNCTION PIvalid        &&  PI VALID
LoanAmt = PV(PI, IR, Tmonth)
Price = LoanAmt + DownPayment
RETURN LAvalid()
```

continues

Listing 6.5. continued

```
*****************************************************************
*     *                                                         *
*     *   RECALC                 Recomputes payment, etc.       *
*     *                                                         *
*     *   Function Origin:                                      *
*     *                                                         *
*     *   Called By:             PRvalid, LAvalid               *
*     *                                                         *
*****************************************************************
PROCEDURE RECALC
LoanAmt = Price - DownPayment
Tmonth = 12*term          && Term in months
Taxes    = MTR*Price      && Monthly Impound for Real Estate Taxes
HI       = MHI*Price      && Monthly Impound for Hazard Insurance
MI       = MMI*LoanAmt    && Monthly Impound for Mortgage Insurance
PI = PAYMENT(LoanAmt, IR, Tmonth)
PITI = PI + HI + MI + HOI + Taxes
IR = Rate/1200.           && Monthly interest rate
DO SHOWCALC
RETURN
*****************************************************************
*     *                                                         *
*     *   SHOWCALC               Displays variables             *
*     *                                                         *
*     *   Function Origin:                                      *
*     *                                                         *
*     *   From Screen:           MORTGAGE,                      *
*     *   Called By:             MORTGAGE, RECALC               *
*     *                                                         *
*****************************************************************
PROCEDURE SHOWCALC
@ 14,38 SAY piti PICTURE "@$ 999,999,999.99"
@ 8,38  SAY taxes PICTURE "@$ 999,999,999.99"
@ 9,38  SAY hi PICTURE "@$ 999,999,999.99"
@ 10,38 SAY mi PICTURE "@$ 999,999,999.99"
SHOW GETS
RETURN
```

A Mortgage Calculator Program Using the Visual FoxPro Object-Oriented Form Creation Methodology Language Approach

The MORTCLAS.PRG program is another example of the Mortgage Calculator application. The difference is that this example was created visually using the Visual FoxPro Form Designer.

The Form Designer creates a form (SCX) file that contains all of the information required to create a form. This information consists of a class definition of the form and all the controls contained in the form. A class definition is used to create a form object. A class definition contains definitions for properties, event code, and methods for an object. All classes that you define in Visual FoxPro are based on Visual FoxPro base classes, which are sometimes called *superclasses.*

Method is an object-oriented term that refers to a procedure associated with an object. A property is like a variable except that it is associated with an object. The properties define the behavior of an object. For example, the `Height` and `Width` properties define the height and width of a form or control. Most of the properties for a control have default values and you do not have to change their value. Others, such as the `Position` and `Size` properties, are set visually when you place a control on the form and change its size. To change a property, you just change its value in the Form Designer Properties window.

The objects are fully event driven, which means that when some event—such as a mouse click—occurs, event code executes to perform whatever action is required. All of this is discussed in detail in Chapter 14.

When you want to specify some action other than the operations handled by the superclasses, you write code for the event that your want your action to respond to. In the Class Designer, you add code to the Code window for the appropriate event. Just double-click on a control, and the Code window appears. Then you choose the event to which you want to respond, and you add code. The Form Designer is described in Chapter 19, "The Form Designer." Figure 6.4 shows the Mortgage Calculator program being designed with the Form Designer.

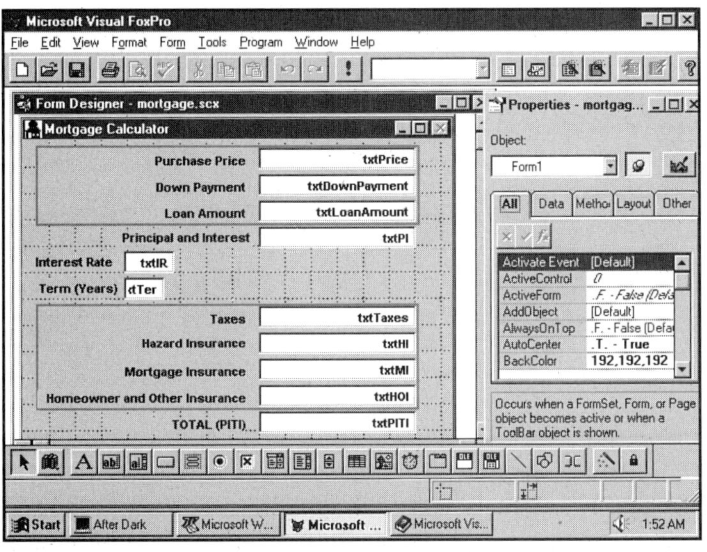

FIGURE 6.4.
Designing the Mortgage Calculator with the Form Designer.

When you create a form visually, you do not have to do anything in any special order, as long as you add all the right controls and code. So you might decide to use the following procedure to create the Mortgage Calculator form using the Form Designer:

1. Execute the Form Designer by selecting the Form icon in the Project Manager and clicking on the **N**ew button.

2. Add a text box control to the form. Set the properties that will be common to all the text box controls, as shown in Listing 6.6. (Text box controls display values.)
3. Add a label control to the form and set the properties that will be common to all of the label controls, as shown in Listing 6.6. These properties include such items as background color (`BackColor`), font size (`FontSize= 8`), and so on. Label controls display static text, such as `"Purchase Price"`.
4. Align and arrange the two controls as shown in Figure 6.4.
5. Select both controls and copy them to the Clipboard using the Ctrl+C key combination.
6. Press the Ctrl+V key combination to paste a copy of the two controls. Position the new pair of controls so that they line up under the original text box and label controls.
7. Repeat Steps 5 and 6 for all the fields you need for the Mortgage Calculator form.
8. Add the appropriate title to each label.
9. Change the names of the text box controls to names that will be easy to remember when you add code.
10. Add the user-defined properties shown in Listing 6.6 by using the For**m** menu New **P**roperty option.
11. Add the user-defined `ReCalc` method shown in Listing 6.6 by using the For**m** menu New **M**ethod option. At this point all you enter is the name `ReCalc`.
12. Click on the form and set its properties, such as background color (`BackColor`) and `AutoCenter`, to correspond with the settings in Listing 6.6.
13. Double-click on the form and add the code in the Code window for the `Init` event, as shown in Listing 6.6. This code initializes all the user-defined properties.
14. Select your user-defined `ReCalc` method from the Procedures combo box in the Code window. Then add the code for the `ReCalc` method that is shown in Listing 6.6.
15. Add the `LostFocus` event code for the text box controls, as shown in Listing 6.6. (The `LostFocus` event occurs when the user clicks on another field.)
16. Optionally, you can add other objects on the screen, such as a rectangle to separate parts of the form and other properties in the Properties window. You can use the F**o**rmat menu tools to help you align and position any of the controls as required.
17. Now press the Exclamation point (!) button on the Visual FoxPro standard toolbar and watch your new form run.

Listing 6.6. A listing of the Mortgage Calculator form class definition code.

```
**************************************************
*  PROGRAM MORTCLAS.PRG
*  Purpuse: Computes mortgage payments
oMortGage = CREATEOBJECT("Form1")
oMortGage.Show
```

```
READ EVENTS
RETURN
**************************************************
*— Form:          form1
*    \vfp\foxbook\chap6\mortgage\mortgage.scx)
*— ParentClass:  form
*— BaseClass:    form
*
DEFINE CLASS form1 AS form
   Height = 275
   Width = 394
   DoCreate = .T.
   AutoCenter = .T.
   BackColor = RGB(192,192,192)
   Caption = "Mortgage Calculator"
   FontSize = 8
   Icon = "mortgage.ico"
   LockScreen = .F.
   Name = "Form1"
*
*  User-Defined Properties
   nrate = 8              &&— Interest rate in percent
   ntaxrate =   0.0125    &&— Annual Property Tax Rate . decimal
   nhir = 0       &&— Hazard Insurance Rate
   nmhi = 0       &&— Monthly Hazard insurance rate
   nmir = 0       &&— Mortgage Insurance Rate
   nmmir = 0      &&— Monthly Mortage Insurance rate
   ir = 0         &&— Monthly interest Rate in decimal
   ntmonth = 0    &&— Number of payments  12&&term
   pi = 0         &&— Principal and interest
   ntaxes = 0     &&— Taxes
   nhoi = 0
   nmtr = 0

ADD OBJECT shape2 AS shape WITH ;
      BackColor = RGB(192,192,192), ;
      BorderWidth = 2, ;
      BorderColor = RGB(128,128,128), ;
      Height = 73, ;
      Left = 12, ;
      Top = 5, ;
      Width = 353, ;
      Name = "Shape2"

   ADD OBJECT shape1 AS shape WITH ;
      BackColor = RGB(192,192,192), ;
      BorderWidth = 2, ;
      BorderColor = RGB(128,128,128), ;
      Height = 97, ;
      Left = 12, ;
      Top = 149, ;
      Width = 352, ;
      Name = "Shape1"

   ADD OBJECT label1 AS label WITH ;
      FontShadow = .T., ;
      FontSize = 8, ;
      Alignment = 1, ;
```

continues

Listing 6.6. continued

```
    BackColor = RGB(192,192,192), ;
    BorderStyle = 0, ;
    Caption = "Purchase Price", ;
    Height = 17, ;
    Left = 84, ;
    Top = 12, ;
    Width = 121, ;
    Name = "Label1"

 ADD OBJECT txtprice AS textbox WITH ;
    FontSize = 8, ;
    Alignment = 1, ;
    Value = 0, ;
    ControlSource = "", ;
    Format = "R", ;
    Height = 20, ;
    InputMask = "$99,999,999.99", ;
    Left = 216, ;
    Top = 7, ;
    Width = 145, ;
    Name = "txtPrice"

 ADD OBJECT label2 AS label WITH ;
    FontSize = 8, ;
    Alignment = 1, ;
    BackColor = RGB(192,192,192), ;
    BorderStyle = 0, ;
    Caption = "Down Payment", ;
    Height = 17, ;
    Left = 84, ;
    Top = 36, ;
    Width = 121, ;
    Name = "Label2"

 ADD OBJECT txtdownpayment AS textbox WITH ;
    FontSize = 8, ;
    Alignment = 1, ;
    Value = 0, ;
    Format = "R", ;
    Height = 20, ;
    InputMask = "99,999,999.99", ;
    Left = 216, ;
    Top = 31, ;
    Width = 145, ;
    Name = "txtDownPayment"


 ADD OBJECT label3 AS label WITH ;
    FontShadow = .T., ;
    FontSize = 8, ;
    Alignment = 1, ;
    BackColor = RGB(192,192,192), ;
    BorderStyle = 0, ;
    Caption = "Loan Amount", ;
    Height = 17, ;
    Left = 84, ;
```

```
    Top = 60, ;
    Width = 121, ;
    Name = "Label3"

ADD OBJECT txtloanamount AS textbox WITH ;
    FontSize = 8, ;
    Alignment = 1, ;
    Value = 0, ;
    Format = "R", ;
    Height = 20, ;
    InputMask = "99,999,999.99", ;
    Left = 216, ;
    Top = 55, ;
    Width = 145, ;
    Name = "txtLoanAmount"


ADD OBJECT label4 AS label WITH ;
    FontShadow = .T., ;
    FontSize = 8, ;
    Alignment = 1, ;
    BackColor = RGB(192,192,192), ;
    BorderStyle = 0, ;
    Caption = "Interest Rate", ;
    Height = 17, ;
    Left = -1, ;
    Top = 104, ;
    Width = 84, ;
    Name = "Label4"


ADD OBJECT txtir AS textbox WITH ;
    FontSize = 8, ;
    Alignment = 1, ;
    Value = 0, ;
    Format = "R", ;
    Height = 20, ;
    InputMask = "99.99", ;
    Left = 93, ;
    Top = 101, ;
    Width = 46, ;
    Name = "txtIR"


ADD OBJECT label5 AS label WITH ;
    FontShadow = .T., ;
    FontSize = 8, ;
    Alignment = 1, ;
    BackColor = RGB(192,192,192), ;
    BorderStyle = 0, ;
    Caption = "Term (Years)", ;
    Height = 17, ;
    Left = 9, ;
    Top = 128, ;
    Width = 79, ;
    Name = "Label5"
```

continues

Listing 6.6. continued

```
ADD OBJECT txtterm AS textbox WITH ;
   FontSize = 8, ;
   Alignment = 1, ;
   Value = 0, ;
   Format = "R", ;
   Height = 20, ;
   InputMask = "99", ;
   Left = 93, ;
   Top = 125, ;
   Width = 37, ;
   Name = "txtTerm"


ADD OBJECT label6 AS label WITH ;
   FontShadow = .T., ;
   FontSize = 8, ;
   Alignment = 1, ;
   BackColor = RGB(192,192,192), ;
   BorderStyle = 0, ;
   Caption = "Principal and Interest", ;
   Height = 17, ;
   Left = 88, ;
   Top = 82, ;
   Width = 121, ;
   Name = "Label6"


ADD OBJECT txtpi AS textbox WITH ;
   FontSize = 8, ;
   Alignment = 1, ;
   Value = 0, ;
   Format = "R", ;
   Height = 20, ;
   InputMask = "$99,999,999.99", ;
   Left = 216, ;
   Top = 79, ;
   Width = 145, ;
   Name = "txtPI"


ADD OBJECT label7 AS label WITH ;
   FontShadow = .T., ;
   FontSize = 8, ;
   Alignment = 1, ;
   BackColor = RGB(192,192,192), ;
   BorderStyle = 0, ;
   Caption = "Taxes", ;
   Height = 17, ;
   Left = 84, ;
   Top = 156, ;
   Width = 121, ;
   Name = "Label7"


ADD OBJECT txttaxes AS textbox WITH ;
   FontSize = 8, ;
```

```
   Alignment = 1, ;
   Value = 0, ;
   Format = "R", ;
   Height = 20, ;
   InputMask = "99,999,999.99", ;
   Left = 216, ;
   ReadOnly = .T., ;
   Top = 151, ;
   Width = 145, ;
   Name = "txtTaxes"

ADD OBJECT label8 AS label WITH ;
   FontShadow = .T., ;
   FontSize = 8, ;
   Alignment = 1, ;
   BackColor = RGB(192,192,192), ;
   BorderStyle = 0, ;
   Caption = "Hazard Insurance", ;
   Height = 17, ;
   Left = 84, ;
   Top = 178, ;
   Width = 121, ;
   Name = "Label8"

ADD OBJECT txthi AS textbox WITH ;
   FontSize = 8, ;
   Alignment = 1, ;
   Value = 0, ;
   Format = "R", ;
   Height = 20, ;
   InputMask = "99,999,999.99", ;
   Left = 216, ;
   ReadOnly = .T., ;
   Top = 175, ;
   Width = 145, ;
   Name = "txtHI"


ADD OBJECT label9 AS label WITH ;
   FontShadow = .T., ;
   FontSize = 8, ;
   Alignment = 1, ;
   BackColor = RGB(192,192,192), ;
   BorderStyle = 0, ;
   Caption = "Mortgage Insurance", ;
   Height = 17, ;
   Left = 84, ;
   Top = 204, ;
   Width = 121, ;
   Name = "Label9"


ADD OBJECT txtmi AS textbox WITH ;
   FontSize = 8, ;
   Alignment = 1, ;
   Value = 0, ;
   Format = "R", ;
   Height = 20, ;
```

continues

Listing 6.6. continued

```
      InputMask = "99,999,999.99", ;
      Left = 216, ;
      ReadOnly = .T., ;
      Top = 199, ;
      Width = 145, ;
      Name = "txtMI"


   ADD OBJECT label10 AS label WITH ;
      FontShadow = .T., ;
      FontSize = 8, ;
      Alignment = 1, ;
      BackColor = RGB(192,192,192), ;
      BorderStyle = 0, ;
      Caption = "Homeowner and Other Insurance", ;
      Height = 17, ;
      Left = 13, ;
      Top = 228, ;
      Width = 192, ;
      Name = "Label10"


   ADD OBJECT txthoi AS textbox WITH ;
      FontSize = 8, ;
      Alignment = 1, ;
      Value = 0, ;
      Format = "R", ;
      Height = 20, ;
      InputMask = "99,999,999.99", ;
      Left = 216, ;
      Top = 223, ;
      Width = 145, ;
      Name = "txtHOI"


   ADD OBJECT label11 AS label WITH ;
      FontShadow = .T., ;
      FontSize = 8, ;
      Alignment = 1, ;
      BackColor = RGB(192,192,192), ;
      BorderStyle = 0, ;
      Caption = "TOTAL (PITI)", ;
      Height = 17, ;
      Left = 84, ;
      Top = 252, ;
      Width = 121, ;
      Name = "Label11"


   ADD OBJECT txtpiti AS textbox WITH ;
      FontSize = 8, ;
      Alignment = 1, ;
      Value = 0, ;
      Format = "R", ;
      Height = 20, ;
      InputMask = "$99,999,999.99", ;
```

```
      Left = 216, ;
      Top = 247, ;
      Width = 145, ;
      Name = "txtPITI"
***********************************************************
* User-Defined Method which computes mortgage values
***********************************************************
   PROCEDURE recalc
      WITH THISFORM
      .txtLoanAmount.Value = ;
              .txtPrice.Value ;
            - .txtDownPayment.Value
        .nTmonth = 12*.txtTerm.Value   && term in months
        .txtTaxes.Value = .nMTR*.txtPrice.Value    && Monthly Impound for Real
Estate Taxes
        .txtHI.Value    = .nMHI*.txtPrice.Value    && Monthly Impound for Hazard
Insurance
        .txtMI.Value    = .nMMIR*.txtLoanAmount.Value  && Monthly impound for
mortgage insurance
        .txtPI.Value    = PAYMENT(.txtLoanAmount.Value, ;
                               .IR, .nTmonth)
        .txtPITI.Value = .txtPI.Value ;
                           + .txtHI.Value ;
                           + .txtMI.Value ;
                           + .txtHOI.Value  ;
                           + .txtTaxes.Value
        .Refresh
      ENDWITH
   ENDPROC
**************************************************************
* Code for Form's Init Event.
**************************************************************
   PROCEDURE Init
      WITH THISFORM
        .txtIR.Value = 8.0    && Annual mortgage rate in percent
        .txtTerm.Value = 30   && Term in Years
        .nTaxRate = .0125     && Tax Rate
        .nMTR = .nTaxRate/12  && Monthly Tax rate (impound)
        .nHIR = .003          && Hazard insurance rate
        .nMHI = .8*.nHIR/12   && Monthly hazard insurance impound
        .nMIR = .0045         && Mortgage insurance rate
        .nMMIR= .nMIR/12      && Monthly mortgage insurance impound
        .IR = .nRate/1200.    && monthly interest rate
        .nTmonth = 12*.txtTerm.Value   && term in months
      ENDWITH
   ENDPROC
******************************************************************
*  Destroy Event for Rorm Form1
******************************************************************
PROCEDURE Destroy
        CLEAR EVENTS
ENDPROC
*********************************************************************
*      Price of Property
* Control: TxtPrice object based on TextBox control
* Event:   LostFocus
*  This code executes when the user moves to another field
*********************************************************************
```

continues

Listing 6.6. continued

```
   PROCEDURE txtprice.LostFocus
      THISFORM.Recalc
   ENDPROC

**********************************************************************
*        Down Payment text box
* Control: TxtDownPayment object based on TextBox control
* Event:   LostFocus
*  This code executes when the user moves to another field
**********************************************************************
   PROCEDURE txtdownpayment.LostFocus
      THISFORM.Recalc
   ENDPROC
**********************************************************************
*    Amount of Loan field
* Control: TxtLoanAmount object based on TextBox control
* Event:   LostFocus
*  This code executes when the user moves to another field
**********************************************************************
   PROCEDURE txtloanamount.LostFocus
      WITH THISFORM
        .txtDownPayment.Value = .txtPrice.Value ;
                                - .txtLoanAmount.Value
        .Recalc
      ENDWITH
   ENDPROC
**********************************************************************
*    Interest Rate Text box
* Control: TxtIR object based on TextBox control
* Event:   LostFocus
*  This code executes when the user moves to another field
**********************************************************************
   PROCEDURE txtir.LostFocus
      WITH THISFORM
         .IR = .txtIR.Value /1200.     && monthly interest rate
         .Recalc
      ENDWITH
   ENDPROC
**********************************************************************
*      Term of Loan in Years
* Control: TxtTerm object based on TextBox control
* Event:   LostFocus
*  This code executes when the user moves to another field
**********************************************************************
   PROCEDURE txtterm.LostFocus
      WITH THISFORM
         .nTmonth = 12*.txtTerm.Value   && term in months
         .Recalc
      ENDWITH
   ENDPROC
**********************************************************************
*       Principal and Interest
* Control: TxtPI object based on TextBox control
* Event:   LostFocus
*  This code executes when the user moves to another field
**********************************************************************
```

```
   PROCEDURE txtpi.LostFocus
      WITH THISFORM
         .txtLoanAmount.Value = PV(.txtPI.Value, .IR, .nTmonth)
         .txtPrice.Value = .txtLoanAmount.Value ;
                         +  .txtDownPayment.Value
         .txtLoanAmount.LostFocus
      ENDWITH
   ENDPROC
ENDDEFINE
*
*— EndDefine: form1
*************************************************************************
```

I think the mortgage calculator operates much better this way than it does when you create it using the traditional Xbase approach. It was definitely easier to code and it looks much better. (See Figure 6.5.)

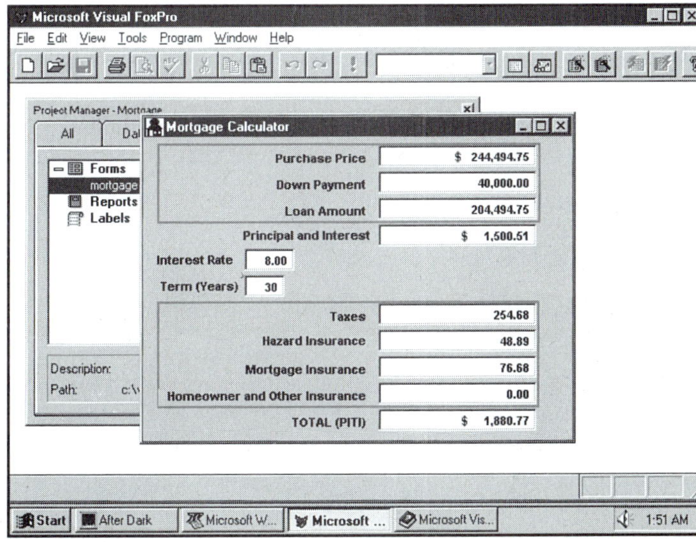

FIGURE 6.5.
The Mortgage Calculator created with the Form Designer.

The coding technique used in the Form Designer–created Mortgage Calculator application is different. You reference values and procedures differently. For example, if you want to store a zero in the `txtDownPayment` text box control in a method, you store a zero in the `Value` property using the following statement:

```
THISFORM.txtDownPayment.Value = 0
```

If you want to call the `Recalc` method to recompute all of the values in the form, you use the following statement in the method code:

```
THISFORM.Recalc
```

The mortgage calculator is stored in a form file, MORTGAGE.SCX. You can execute it from the Project Manager by opening the form file outline, selecting mortgage, and clicking on the **R**un button. You can execute it from the Command window using the following command:

```
DO FORM MORTGAGE
```

You might wonder where I got Listing 6.6 if all the class definition information is hidden in the MORTGAGE.SCR form file. I executed the Visual FoxPro Class Browser (BROWSER.APP), opened the MORTGAGE.SCR screen file, and pressed the View Class File button. A window appeared, containing most of the code shown in Listing 6.6. I saved it in a program file named MORTCLAS.PRG and added a couple statements to create and show the form. You can execute MORTCLAS.PRG with the `DO` command to run the mortgage calculator.

Summary

This chapter presents the various control flow commands in the FoxPro language: branches and loops, procedures and functions, and several shortcuts and special cases associated with these concepts. The chapter also touches on event trapping, the method by which you preprogram FoxPro to respond to future events that may or may not occur.

Works Cited

Dijkstra, Edsger. 1968 "`GOTO` Statement Considered Harmful." Communications of the ACM. (March).

7

FoxPro Language Elements for Creating Windows and Menu Systems

It is only the modern that ever becomes old-fashioned.

—Oscar Wilde (1854–1900)

As microcomputer applications become more sophisticated, the need for an advanced user interface is more important. Menu bars and pop-up menus are an essential part of any Windows application. Software vendors paste all types of menus and pop-ups into their products. When Apple introduced the Macintosh computer, a new design standard was established—the graphical user interface. Unfortunately, the Macintosh interface doesn't run on an IBM PC. Then Microsoft Corporation introduced Windows, which quickly became the standard interface for the IBM PC and compatibles. Every software publisher has either developed a Windows product or is in the process of developing one. The appearance of MS-DOS products has been like a character-based version of the Windows interface for years. FoxPro 2 is one of these products. If you know how to use FoxPro 2.*x*, you'll have little trouble moving to Visual FoxPro. In fact, your FoxPro 2.*x* programs will run under Visual FoxPro with few changes, and FoxPro 2.5 and FoxPro 2.6 screen, menu, project, and report files are automatically converted to run on Visual FoxPro.

The Visual FoxPro OOP user-interface language extensions antiquate many of the traditional FoxPro 2.*x* visual language elements. However, since millions of lines of FoxPro 2.*x* and dBASE IV code exist, no one even would suggest that the old-fashioned commands be deleted from the FoxPro language. Even if you only use Visual FoxPro OOP to build your user interface, you will need to know about the obsolete commands if you ever need to upgrade old FoxPro 2.*x* applications. For that reason, this chapter describes the functionality and utilization of the FoxPro 2.*x* procedural type commands and functions that create and manipulate the FoxPro user-defined window subsystem.

To compete with today's sophisticated user-interface standards, your applications must possess a modern user interface. Microsoft Windows is the most popular graphical user interface (GUI). All applications designed to operate under Windows, including Visual FoxPro, have a common user interface (CUI). Therefore, after a user is trained to use one Windows application, that person will require much less training to learn another Windows application. If you develop your application with Visual FoxPro and incorporate user-defined windows, menus, and dialog boxes, your potential customers will already know how to interface to your application.

What Are Windows?

You can generate Visual FoxPro code that creates windows on-screen. You can designate one of the on-screen windows as the *active window*. All subsequent screen output is then confined to the interior of that active window. You can use a window to display help information, reports, or error messages. You can view multiple records in a table in a Browse window, or you can edit text or a memo field inside a window. You can make the window disappear and the text or windows covered by a window reappear.

In FoxPro, a *window* is a rectangular portion of the screen that is associated with names, borders, titles, color schemes, sizes, and coordinates. A single window is referred to as a *window object*.

When a window is active, all subsequent output is directed to the window. Displayed text scrolls within a window. In addition to normal text display, the following commands can operate within a window:

- `@`
- `BROWSE`
- `MODIFY` file or programs
- `EDIT` memo fields

Only the amount of available memory limits the number of window objects that you can define and display on-screen at one time.

Before you can use a window object, you must first define it. The `DEFINE` command is used for this purpose:

```
DEFINE WINDOW <window-name1>
  FROM <expN1>,<expN2> TO <expN3>,<expN4>
  ¦ AT <expN5>,<expN6>  SIZE <expN7>,<expN8>
  [IN [WINDOW] <window-name2> ¦ SCREEN ¦ IN DESKTOP]
  [NAME <object-name>]
  [TITLE <expC2>] [FOOTER <expC3>]
  [DOUBLE ¦ PANEL ¦ NONE ¦ SYSTEM ¦ <border-definition-string>]
  [CLOSE ¦ NOCLOSE] [FLOAT ¦ NOFLOAT] [GROW ¦ NOGROW]
  [MDI ¦ NOMDI] [ZOOM ¦ NOZOOM]  [MINIMIZE ¦ NOMINIMIZE] [SHADOW]
  [HALFHEIGHT]
  [FILL <expC4> ¦ FILE <expFN1>]
  [COLOR [<standard>][,<enhanced>][,<border>] ¦
  [COLOR SCHEME <expN9>] ¦
  [COLOR RGB(<color-value-list>)]
  [FONT <expC5> [,<expN10>] [STYLE <expC6>]
  [NAME <expC7>]
  [ICON FILE <expFN2>]
```

Defining Windows

Each window is given a name, which is used to reference the window object. The name conforms to the same conventions as those for memory variables.

Coordinates

The `FROM` and `TO` clauses define the row and column coordinates of the top-left (`<expN1>,<expN2>`) and bottom-right (`<expN3>,<expN4>`) corners of the window's screen area, respectively. The coordinates can define a window that is bigger than the screen. The row and column coordinates for the `FROM` and `TO` clauses are based on the size of the font of the defined window's parent window. The parent window can be the FoxPro main window or another window if the `IN WINDOW` clause is specified. The size of the window is therefore based on the size of the font of the parent window. For example, a window defined as 20 characters wide and 30 rows high (`SIZE 30, 20`) is larger if the text's point size is 10 than if its point size is 8.

NOTE

You define the coordinate position for the corner of a window (or any other object) in Xbase by specifying two numeric values, separated by commas, that represent the row and column of the displayed text. In Visual FoxPro, you can specify a fractional value to precisely position any object (for example, windows, menus, controls, GET objects). Here's an example:

```
DEFINE WINDOW W1 FROM 2.3,4.25 TO 14.25,78.5
```

FoxPro for MS-DOS does not permit precise positioning. If you execute the previous command in FoxPro for MS-DOS, the fractional portion of the number is ignored and interpreted as follows:

```
DEFINE WINDOW W1 FROM 2,4 TO 14,78
```

Rather than use the FROM and TO clauses, you can use the AT and SIZE clauses to specify the position and size of a defined window. The AT *<expN5>*,*<expN6>* clause defines the coordinates of the top-left corner of the window, and the SIZE *<expN7>*,*<expN8>* clause defines the height and width of the window, respectively, based on the font of the defined window. The following two DEFINE statements are equivalent:

```
DEFINE WINDOW W1 FROM 4,4 TO 15,45
DEFINE WINDOW W1 AT 4,4 SIZE 10,40
```

Assuming that the font of the FoxPro main window is not 24-point Roman typeface, the following commands define windows of different sizes:

```
DEFINE WINDOW W1 FROM 4,4 TO 15,45 FONT "Roman",24
DEFINE WINDOW W1 AT 4,4 SIZE 10,40 FONT "Roman",24
```

The size of the window for the first command is based on the font of the FoxPro main window. The size of the second window is based on the font of the window itself.

Borders

You can designate the border that frames the window you define by specifying the NONE, BORDER, SYSTEM, or PANEL keywords or the *<border definition string>* clause. If you omit any of these options, the last border type specified by the SET BORDER command will frame the window. Incidentally, if you have not issued any SET BORDER commands, the default single-line border type is used. The DOUBLE keyword designates a double-line border. If you specify the NONE keyword, the window has no border at all, and the area normally occupied by the border becomes part of the display area. The PANEL keyword uses a block character for the window border to resemble a solid panel. You can simulate the look of a Visual FoxPro System window if you specify the SYSTEM keyword.

If these options are not sufficient, you can designate your own custom border definition by specifying the `<border definition string>`, which consists of a list of up to 16 border characters. The first eight characters in the list define the window border when a window is displayed but not active. The next eight border characters define the window border when the window is the currently active window. The discussion of SET BORDER in Chapter 10, "Environment," describes the border definition strings. After you define window objects, the SET BORDER command cannot change the borders.

NOTE

If you specify the NONE keyword, there are no borders to click or double-click with the mouse to zoom, minimize, size, or move the window. You must use keyboard commands to perform these operations.

In the following examples, the window frame is a double line, a system-like window, a blank, a block character, and a border string, respectively:

```
DEFINE WINDOW MyWindow  FROM 3,3 TO 20,60  DOUBLE
DEFINE WINDOW MyWindow  FROM 3,3 TO 20,60 SYSTEM ;
    GROW CLOSE MINIMIZE ZOOM
DEFINE WINDOW MyWindow  FROM 3,3 TO 20,60  PANEL
DEFINE WINDOW MyWindow  FROM 3,3 TO 20,60  " "
DEFINE WINDOW MyWindow  FROM 3,3 TO 20,60  ;
    "T","B","L","R","*","*","*","*"
```

In FoxPro for MS-DOS, you can enhance the active window border to simulate a 3-D effect by specifying the SHADOW keyword. When you specify SHADOW, a darkened image (or shadow of the window) appears below the window. Any object or text covered by the shadow is still visible. Once you specify the SHADOW keyword when defining a window, you can turn the shadow display on and off with the SET SHADOW command. By default, the SET SHADOW option is set to ON. No shadowing exists for Windows. In Visual FoxPro, you can specify the SHADOW keyword and SET SHADOW command, but they are ignored.

Colors

The COLOR clause defines the color of a character, the background displayed for the standard and enhanced characters, and the color of the border. In the following example, the standard character is bright blue on white, the enhanced character is white on blue, and the border is red on white:

```
DEFINE WINDOW MyWindow  FROM 3,3 to 10,10 ;
COLOR B+/W,W/B,R/W
```

You can specify the COLOR SCHEME clause to select one of the FoxPro (or your own) color-scheme definitions. If you don't specify a color, COLOR SCHEME 1 is used for the defined window. You can set a color-scheme number (<expN9>) from 1 to 24. Each scheme has 10 color pairs. Each pair describes a foreground color (color of the character) and a background color. The color pairs for a scheme that designates the color for a window element are the following:

Color Pair	*Window Element*
1	The @...SAY expression
2	The @...GET field
3	The window border
4	The title when the window is active
5	The title when the window is idle
6	A selected object in the window
7	The clock when displayed in the window
8	The window shadow
9	The enabled control displayed in the window
10	The disabled control displayed in the window

In Visual FoxPro, you can also use the COLOR RGB(<color-value-list>) clause to specify colors. <color-value-list> consists of a list of three to six numbers separated by commas. The numbers represent the color values described in the discussion of the SET COLOR TO command in Chapter 10.

Displaying a Window Inside Another Window

You can define one window to reside inside another window using the optional IN [WINDOW] clause. You specify <window-name> where the defined window resides.

NOTE

Notice that the WINDOW keyword is optional, so you can omit it. For example, both of the following statements define window A inside window B:

```
DEFINE WINDOW A FROM 3,3 TO 10,23 IN B
DEFINE WINDOW A FROM 3,3 TO 10,23 IN WINDOW B
```

The preferred form is to specify the IN WINDOW clause because someday designers may add an option to FoxPro that enables you to put an object inside some other object, and the IN clause won't work anymore.

The defined window is called the *child window*, and the window designated by the IN WINDOW clause is called the *parent window*. The coordinates of the child window are relative to the top-left corner of the parent window. A child window that is defined and activated inside a parent window cannot be moved outside the parent window and cannot be larger than the parent window. When the parent window moves, the child window moves with it. You can change the parent of a child window when the child window is activated.

You can specify the SCREEN keyword to designate that the window is placed on-screen rather than in the window. The screen becomes the parent. This is the default state.

In Visual FoxPro, you can specify the IN DESKTOP clause to place the defined window on the Windows desktop. In this case, the window is outside the FoxPro main window, and the window coordinates are relative to the Windows desktop. However, the current font for the FoxPro main window determines the size of the window.

The *TITLE* and *FOOTER* Clauses

The optional TITLE clause displays the specified character string centered on the top border. A specified character string is truncated if it is wider than the window.

Visual FoxPro ignores the optional FOOTER clause. In FoxPro for MS-DOS, the FOOTER clause displays the specified character string centered on the bottom border. A specified character string is truncated if it is wider than the window.

The Fill Character

By default, when you clear a window or when you scroll, the new lines are filled with blanks. You can specify another fill character instead of a blank with the FILL *<expC4>* clause. If the character string, *<expC4>*, contains more than one character, only the first character is used as the fill character.

Wallpaper and the *FILL FILE* Clause

With the FILL FILE *<expFN>* clause you can specify the background (or *wallpaper*) of a window to be filled with a bitmap picture (BMP) file. If you don't supply a filename extension, .BMP is assumed.

The *FONT* and *STYLE* Clauses

The optional FONT clause specifies the name and size of a font for text that is output. *<expC5>* defines the font and *<expN10>*, the optional numeric expression, defines the point size. Here are some examples:

```
DEFINE WINDOW .... FONT "Roman",24
DEFINE WINDOW .... FONT "MS Serif",14
DEFINE WINDOW .... FONT "Times New Roman",12
DEFINE WINDOW .... FONT "Wingdings"
DEFINE WINDOW .... FONT "Script"
DEFINE WINDOW .... FONT "symbol", 8
```

The first command defines a window containing text in 24-point Roman font.

You can also specify the font style with the STYLE <expC6> clause. Windows displays the style for the font if it's available. Some styles cannot be displayed for certain fonts. The character expression <expC6> specifies one or more of the characters that correspond to styles shown in Table 7.1.

Table 7.1. STYLE clause characters that designate font styles.

<expC6>	*Style*
B	Bold
I	Italic
O	Outline
S	Shadow
-	Strikethrough
T	Transparent
U	Underline

Here are some examples of STYLE clauses:

```
STYLE 'BI'   && Bold and italic font
STYLE 'U'    && Underlined font
STYLE "BS"   && Shadowed bold font
```

The STYLE clause applies only to Visual FoxPro. FoxPro for MS-DOS ignores this clause.

The *ICON FILE* Clause

You use the ICON FILE clause to specify an icon that displays when the window is minimized for Windows 3.1. You must include the MINIMIZE keyword with the DEFINE WINDOW command. You must specify an icon (ICO) file. No other type of image file is accepted. For Windows 95, if you specify the SYSTEM and CLOSE keywords, the icon appears at the left of the title bar whether it is minimized or not. In the following example, the TEST.ICO icon appears when the file is minimized for Windows 3.1 and at the left of the title bar for Windows 95:

```
DEFINE WINDOW  Wind1 FROM 10,10 TO 15,60 SYSTEM  ;
    MINIMIZE CLOSE ICON FILE "\vfp\foxbook\chap7\test.ico"
ACTIVATE WINDOW  Wind1
```

The *NAME* Clause

You specify the NAME clause to create an object reference for the window. This lets you manipulate the window with object-oriented properties and methods for the form object. See Chapter 14, "Object-Oriented Programming," for more information. Use help to get information regarding the form object properties and methods. In the following example, the window MyWindow is defined and named oMyWindow. Then it is manipulated using the form object methods. Also, property values are displayed:

```
DEFINE WINDOW MyWindow ;
   FROM 10,10 TO 15,60 ;
   SYSTEM  NAME "oMyWindow"    && Object reference is OMyWindow
oMyWindow.show    && Show the Window
WAIT WINDOW TIMEOUT 4
oMyWindow.move(0,35,490,180)      && Move window to 0,0 and change size
? "Left:     ", oMyWindow.Left    && Displays:  Left:    0
? "Top:      ", oMyWindow.Top     && Displays:  Top:     6
? "Height:   ", oMyWindow.Height  && Displays:  Height: 20
? "Width:    ", oMyWindow.Width   && Displays:  Width:  70
oMyWindow.move(90,35)             && Move to row 10, column 5
WAIT WINDOW TIMEOUT 4
oMyWindow.hide                    && Hide window
oMyWindow.Release                 && Release window
```

You can also use the _SCREEN system memory variable to reference the active form object. _SCREEN is a reference to the Visual FoxPro main window. One of the _SCREEN properties is the ActiveForm property, which is a reference to the active form (or active window). When a user-defined window is the active window, you can refer to it using this referencing technique. For example, if you want to set the background color of an active user-defined window named MyWindow to light gray, you can use the following statements:

```
DEFINE WINDOW  MyWindow FROM 10,10 to 25,80 SYSTEM
ACTIVATE WINDOW  MyWindow
_SCREEM.ActiveForm.BackColor=RGB(192,192,192)
```

The BackColor property and any property that is available for a form object is available for a user-defined window.

Window Control

With FoxPro, you can specify how the user can manipulate a window. Table 7.2 presents the keywords that grant or revoke from the user control of a window.

Table 7.2. Options that grant or revoke from the user control of a window.

Keyword	*Description*
CLOSE	If you specify the CLOSE keyword, you allow a window to be closed. You can close a window by choosing the **F**ile menu **C**lose option. You can close a window by choosing the window's Close Box menu **C**lose option. If you are using Windows 95, you can click on the Close button (with an X on it) at the upper-right corner of the System or Halfheight title bar. Closing a window permanently removes it from memory. If you want to use it again, you must issue another DEFINE WINDOW command. (See Figure 7.1.)

continues

Table 7.2. continued

Keyword	*Description*
NOCLOSE	If you specify the NOCLOSE keyword or do not specify the CLOSE keyword, you designate that the defined window cannot be closed. The only ways to remove a window defined with a NOCLOSE keyword are to issue DEACTIVATE WINDOW, RELEASE WINDOWS, CLEAR WINDOWS, or CLEAR ALL commands. If CLOSE is activated, you can close a window by clicking on the Close Box at the top-left corner of the window.
FLOAT	If you specify the FLOAT keyword, you can change the location of a window on the screen. To move a window with the mouse, point to the window's title bar, hold down the left mouse button, and drag the window to a new location. Also, you can move a window by choosing the window's Close Box menu **M**ove option or by pressing Ctrl+F7. Then use the arrow keys to move the window to a new location. Press a key other than an arrow key to stop the move operation.
NOFLOAT	If you specify the NOFLOAT keyword or you don't specify the FLOAT keyword, you cannot move a window. Therefore, NOFLOAT is the default.
GROW	If you specify the GROW keyword, you can change the size of the window. To change the size of a window with the mouse, point to the window border or corner, hold down the left mouse button, and drag the border or corner. The opposite border or corner remains anchored to its position and the window shrinks or grows as you move the mouse. (See Figure 7.1.) Also, you can size a window by choosing the window's Close Box menu **S**ize option or by pressing Ctrl+F8. Use the arrow keys to change the size of the window. Press a key other than an arrow key to finish the sizing operation.
NOGROW	If you specify the NOGROW keyword or you don't specify the GROW keyword, you cannot size a window.
MDI	In Visual FoxPro you can specify the MDI keyword to designate that the text in the defined window complies with the *multiple-document interface* (MDI) format. MDI is a format for text windows used in Microsoft Windows. The specification for MDI describes the structure and behavior of multiple-document windows. An MDI window can have child windows.
NOMDI	If you specify the NOMDI keyword, you designate that the defined window does not comply with MDI. If neither MDI nor NOMDI is specified, the defined window complies with MDI.

Keyword	*Description*
`ZOOM`	If you specify the `ZOOM` keyword, you can maximize (or zoom) the size of the window to fill the screen, or if the window is enlarged, you can shrink it to its defined size. To zoom a window with the mouse, click the Maximize button at the top-right of the window border. You can also maximize the window by double-clicking on the title bar. You can zoom a window also by choosing the window's Close Box menu Ma**x**imize option or by pressing Ctrl+F10.
`NOZOOM`	If you specify the `NOZOOM` keyword or you don't specify the `ZOOM` keyword, you cannot zoom a window.
`MINIMIZE`	If you specify the `MINIMIZE` keyword, you can reduce the window to its minimum size (minimize) and dock it in the bottom-left corner of the screen. You can minimize a window by clicking on the Minimize button at the top of the window. You can also minimize a window by choosing the window's Close Box Mi**n**imize option or pressing Ctrl+F9. If the `MINIMIZE` option is not specified, you cannot minimize a window.
`NOMINIMIZE`	If the `NOMINIMIZE` option is specified, you cannot minimize a window.
`HALFHEIGHT`	If you specify the `HALFHEIGHT` keyword, you can create windows with half-height title bars. Half-height title bars provide compatibility for applications created with FoxPro for MS-DOS that are imported into Visual FoxPro. Half-height title bars are used for user-defined windows unless the `SYSTEM` keyword or the `FONT` clause are specified. Half-height title bars always display if you specify the `HALFHEIGHT` keyword.

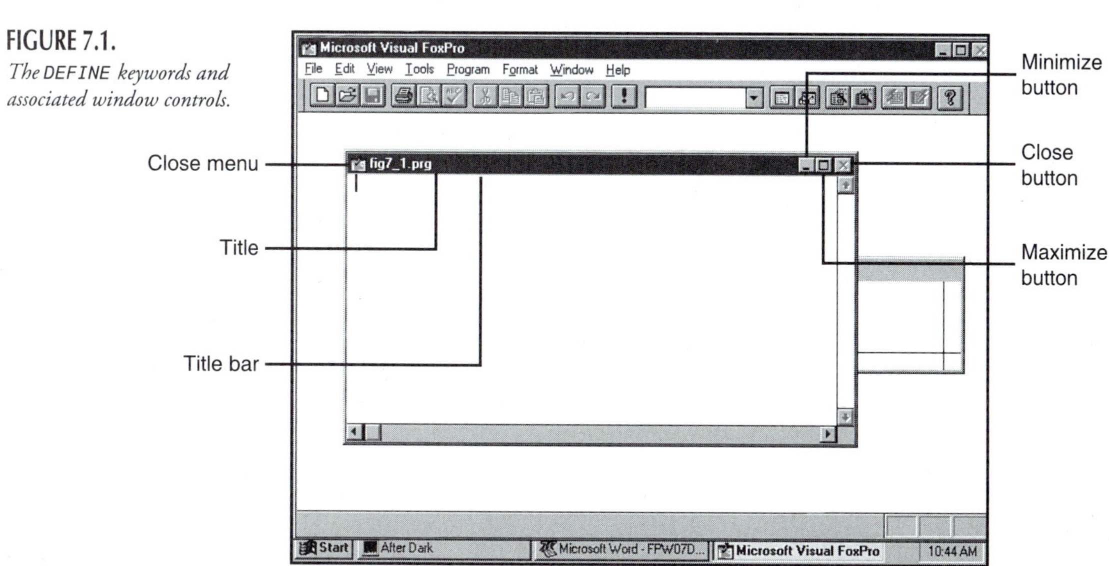

FIGURE 7.1.

The `DEFINE` keywords and associated window controls.

The example shown in Listing 7.1 illustrates different types of window borders and options. Eight windows, W1 through W8, are defined in the WINTYPES.PRG program. Each window has a different border type.

Listing 7.1. The source listing for the program WINTYPES.PRG.

```
****************************************************************
*     * 07/12/92             WINTYPES.PRG              11:18:19 *
****************************************************************
*     * Description:                                           *
*     * This program illustrates types of window boundaries    *
*     *                                                        *
****************************************************************
SET TALK OFF
SET COLOR TO n/W,w/n
CLEAR
Top        =  CHR(205)    && Define custom border characters
Side       =  CHR(179)
UpperLeft  =  CHR(213)
UpperRight =  CHR(184)
LowerLeft  =  CHR(212)
LowerRight =  CHR(190)

SET COLOR TO W/B,b+/w, n
DEFINE WINDOW W1 FROM 1,0   TO 10,19  TITLE "default"
DEFINE WINDOW W2 FROM 12,0  TO 20,19  NONE   TITLE "None"
DEFINE WINDOW W3 FROM 1,20  TO 10,39  DOUBLE TITLE "Double";
   FILL FILE TREE.BMP
DEFINE WINDOW W4 FROM 12,20 TO 20,39  PANEL  TITLE "Panel";
   COLOR SCHEME 3
DEFINE WINDOW W5 FROM 1,40  TO 10,59 ;
   ,,,,,,,,top,top,side,side,UpperLeft,;
UpperRight,LowerLeft,LowerRight ;
   TITLE "Characters"
DEFINE WINDOW W6 FROM 12,40 TO 20,59  "A"    TITLE " Letter "
DEFINE WINDOW W7 FROM 1,60   TO 10,77  SYSTEM TITLE "System"
DEFINE WINDOW W8 FROM 5,5 TO 13,20  SYSTEM    TITLE " System ";
   MINIMIZE SHADOW FLOAT ZOOM GROW FOOTER "Shadow"
ACTIVATE WINDOW ALL
USE CENSUS
BROWSE
CLEAR ALL
CLEAR
```

Figure 7.2 is the output from WINTYPES.PRG. Notice that window W8 is active and contains a BROWSE display. Window W3 contains a background picture (wallpaper) because the FILL FILE TREE.BMP clause is specified. All the windows have titles displayed except window W2; it's the one with BORDER type NONE. Its defined title exists internally, but it is not displayed because W2 has no borders. However, you can retrieve it with the WTITLE() function. Notice that in Visual FoxPro, the DOUBLE, PANEL, and SYSTEM border types create the same type of borders and that the SHADOW keyword and FOOTER clause are ignored. When you run the same program on FoxPro 2.5 and 2.6 for MS-DOS, these language elements operate as they do in FoxPro 2.0. Therefore, you don't need to make any changes to your programs when you run them on different platforms.

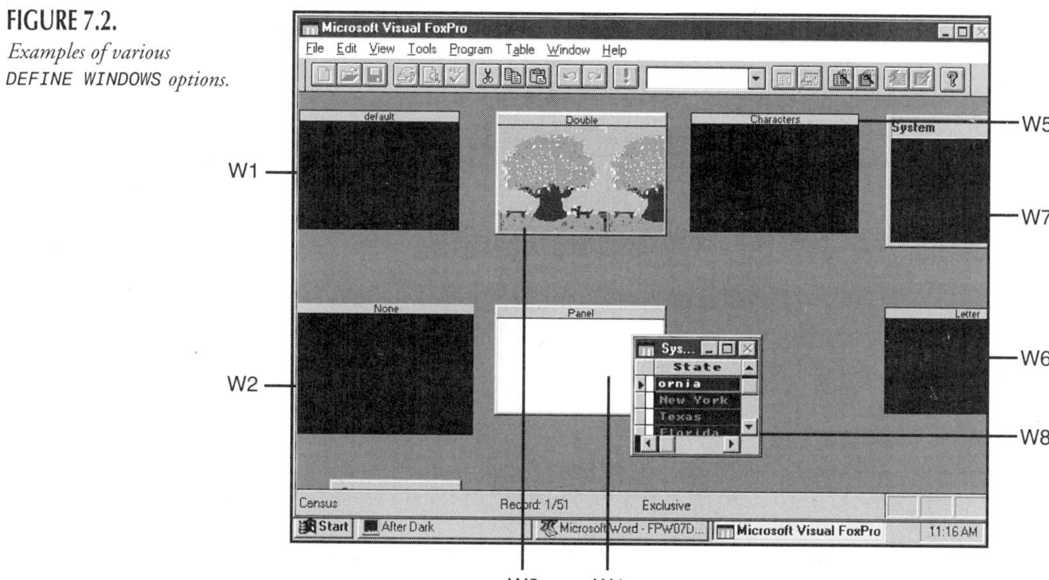

FIGURE 7.2.
Examples of various `DEFINE WINDOWS` *options.*

Activating Windows

After you define a window object you can activate it, and all output is directed to the window. Use the `ACTIVATE` command to activate a window. The syntax is

```
ACTIVATE WINDOW <window-name-list> ¦ ALL
   [IN [WINDOW] <window-name2>] ¦ SCREEN ]
   [BOTTOM ¦ TOP ¦ SAME] [NOSHOW]
```

If `<window-name-list>` contains more than one window object, all windows are displayed on-screen in the order specified by the list. The last window specified is the most recently activated window, and it becomes the active window—the window to which output is directed.

If you specify the `ALL` keyword, all defined window objects are activated in the order in which they were defined, and output is directed to the last defined window. Here's an example:

```
DEFINE WINDOW  Wind_1  FROM 1,10  TO  20,90
DEFINE WINDOW  Wind_2  FROM 5,5   TO  30,60
DEFINE WINDOW  Wind_3  FROM 10,1  TO  40,30
ACTIVATE WINDOW ALL
```

All three windows are activated (as shown in Figure 7.3). Output, however, is directed to `Wind_3`.

If `Wind_2` is activated as follows:

```
ACTIVATE WINDOW Wind_2
```

`Wind_2` becomes the most recently activated window and it receives output. `Wind_3` remains displayed on-screen. (See Figure 7.4.)

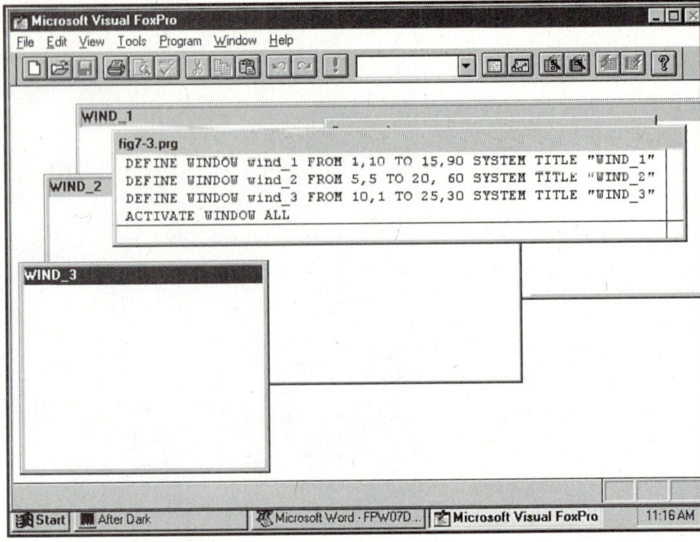

FIGURE 7.3.
The `ACTIVATE WINDOWS` example.

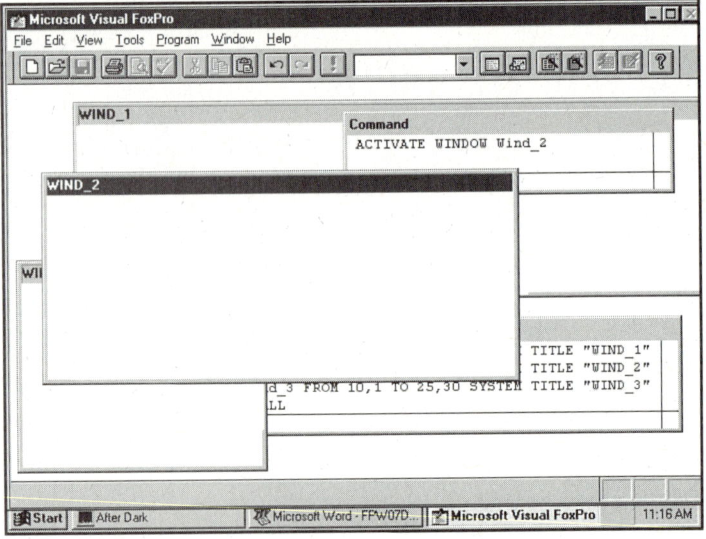

FIGURE 7.4.
The `ACTIVATE WINDOW Wind_2` example.

You can activate one window inside another window with the `IN` *`<window-name>`* clause. To activate `Wind_1` inside `Wind_3`, type the following command:

```
ACTIVATE WINDOW Wind_1 IN Wind_3
```

Wind_1 becomes the most recently activated window, and output is now directed to it. However, Wind_1 is inside Wind_3, as shown in Figure 7.5. Its coordinates are relative to the top-left corner. Wind_2 and Wind_3 remain on-screen. Wind_1 is the child window and Wind_3 is the parent window. You can use the IN SCREEN clause with the ACTIVATE command to place a child window on-screen. After a child window is placed on-screen, it is no longer related to its former parent window.

FIGURE 7.5.
The ACTIVATE WINDOW Wind_1 IN Wind_3 example.

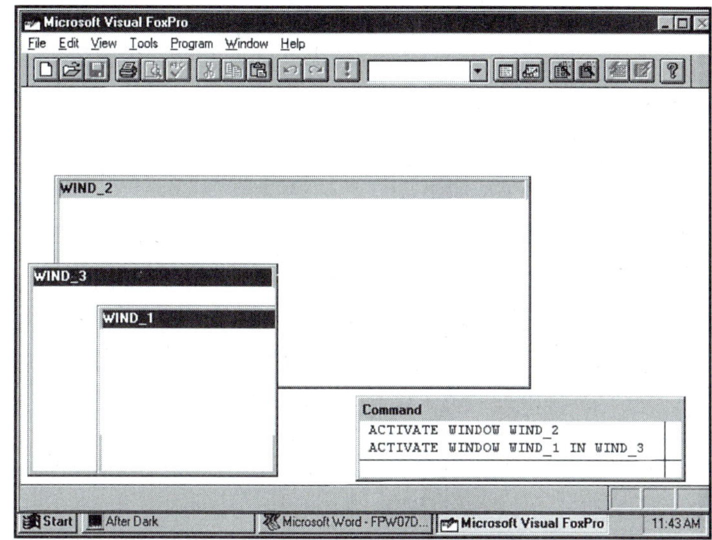

When you activate a window, it remains on-screen until a DEACTIVATE WINDOW or HIDE WINDOW command is executed to remove it from the screen. The window remains in memory, and you can execute an ACTIVATE WINDOW or SHOW WINDOW command to display the window again.

You can use the CLEAR WINDOWS, CLEAR ALL, and RELEASE WINDOWS commands to remove windows from the screen and memory. After a window is removed from Windows, you must redefine it using the DEFINE WINDOW command before you can redisplay it on-screen with the SHOW WINDOW or ACTIVATE WINDOW command.

When you activate a window, you can place it on-screen on top of other windows (the default position), place it beneath other windows, or leave it where it is even if it's beneath a stack of windows. You can activate a window and not display it. Whichever display positioning option you use, subsequent output is still directed to the active window. Table 7.3 summarizes these options.

Table 7.3. The front-to-back window positioning options.

Keyword	*Description*
BOTTOM	Activates window and places it beneath all other windows.
SAME	Activates window, but leaves it at the same position in the stack of windows.
TOP	Activates window and places it on top of other windows. This is the default option.
NOSHOW	Activates window, but does not display it.

The screen coordinates used by the @ command and DEFINE MENU, DEFINE POPUP, and DEFINE PAD commands are relative to the top-left corner of an activated window object. Here's an example:

```
@ 0,0  Say  "Text is in window"
```

The message this command outputs is positioned in the top-left corner of an active window.

The *SHOW WINDOW* Command

With the SHOW WINDOW command, you can display a window that already has been defined but has been hidden or has never been displayed. SHOW WINDOW also enables you to change the front-to-back display positioning. This command displays a window but does not activate it. In other words, you can display a window with SHOW WINDOW, but you cannot direct output to it. For that you need the ACTIVATE WINDOW command. The syntax of the SHOW WINDOW command is the following:

```
SHOW WINDOW <window-name-list> ¦ ALL
   [IN [WINDOW] <window-name2> ¦ SCREEN ]
   [BOTTOM ¦ TOP ¦ SAME]
   [SAVE] [REFRESH]
```

If <window-name-list> contains more than one window object, all windows are displayed on-screen in the order that the list specifies. If you specify the ALL keyword, all defined window objects stored in memory are displayed in the order in which they were defined.

You can specify the front-to-back positioning using the BOTTOM, TOP, and SAME keywords. The BOTTOM keyword places the window beneath all other currently displayed windows. The TOP keyword places the window on top of all displayed windows. The SAME keyword displays the window at the same front-to-back position it displayed the last time it was on the screen. If you don't specify the BOTTOM, TOP, or SAME keywords, TOP is assumed.

If you specify the SAVE keyword, the image of the window remains on-screen (or in a window) whenever the window is hidden. You can clear the image with the CLEAR command.

The *HIDE WINDOW* Command

You can hide one or more windows displayed on-screen with the HIDE WINDOW command. The windows are placed in memory, and you can redisplay them with the ACTIVATE WINDOW or SHOW WINDOW command. If the active window is hidden, output is still directed to it. The syntax of the HIDE WINDOW command is the following:

```
HIDE WINDOW [<window-name-list> ¦ ALL ]
    [IN [WINDOW] <window-name2> ¦ SCREEN ]
    [SAVE] [BOTTOM ¦ TOP ¦ SAME]
```

If <window-name-list> contains more than one window object, all windows in the list are hidden. If you specify the ALL keyword, all displayed window objects are removed from the screen and stored in memory. If the HIDE WINDOW command is used without any specified windows, the active window is hidden.

If you specify the SAVE keyword, the image of the window remains on-screen (or in a window) whenever the window is hidden. You can clear the image with the CLEAR command.

You can also hide a window using the **W**indow menu **H**ide command. You can redisplay a hidden window by choosing its name from the **W**indow menu.

Deactivating Windows

You can deactivate windows with the DEACTIVATE command. The syntax is the following:

```
DEACTIVATE WINDOW <window-name-list> ¦ ALL
```

The specified windows are deactivated. They are cleared from the screen but remain in memory. You can subsequently activate any of them. The contents of a window are saved when the window is deactivated.

The RELEASE WINDOWS and CLEAR WINDOWS commands deactivate windows, erase them from the screen, and remove them from memory. The syntax is the following:

```
RELEASE WINDOWS [<window-name-list>]
CLEAR WINDOWS
```

RELEASE WINDOWS removes the specified list of window objects from the system; CLEAR WINDOWS removes all defined window objects from the system. The CLEAR ALL command clears all windows, tables, and memory variables. If a database is open, the CLEAR ALL command leaves it open but it closes all of its associated tables. You have to use the CLOSE DATABASES or CLOSE ALL command to close the active database.

The *MODIFY WINDOW* Command

The MODIFY WINDOW command modifies the attributes of an existing user-defined window or the FoxPro main window. However, you cannot modify the attributes of FoxPro system windows (Command, Browse, Filer, and others). Before you can modify a window, you must create it with the DEFINE WINDOW command. The syntax of the MODIFY WINDOW command is the following:

```
MODIFY WINDOW <window-name> ¦ SCREEN
   FROM <expN1>,<expN2> TO <expN3>,<expN4>
   ¦ AT <expN5>,<expN6>  SIZE <expN7>,<expN8>
   [TITLE <expC2>] [FOOTER <expC3>]
   [DOUBLE ¦ PANEL ¦ NONE ¦ SYSTEM]
   [CLOSE ¦ NOCLOSE] [FLOAT ¦ NOFLOAT] [GROW ¦ NOGROW]
   [MDI ¦ NOMDI] [ZOOM ¦ NOZOOM]  [MINIMIZE ¦ NOMINIMIZE] [SHADOW]
   [HALFHEIGHT]
   [FILL <expC4> ¦ FILE <expFN1>]
   [COLOR [<standard>][,<enhanced>][,<border>] ¦
   [COLOR SCHEME <expN9>] ¦
   [COLOR RGB(<color-value-list>)]
   [FONT <expC5> [,<expN10>] [STYLE <expC6>]
   [ICON FILE <expFN2>]
```

<window-name> specifies the name of a window that has been created using the DEFINE WINDOW command. You can modify the FoxPro main window using the SCREEN keyword instead of *<window-name>*. After you've modified the FoxPro main window, you can return it to its original configuration with the following command:

```
MODIFY WINDOW SCREEN
```

The remaining clauses and keywords are the same ones that you can specify with the DEFINE WINDOW command described earlier in this chapter.

Here is an example of the MODIFY WINDOW command in use. Assume that you have defined a window with the following statement:

```
DEFINE WINDOW MyWindow FROM 10,10 TO 30,90 FLOAT GROW ZOOM
```

You can move, size, and zoom MyWindow. With the following command, you can change the MyWindow window attributes so that you cannot move it, change its size, or zoom it:

```
MODIFY WINDOW MyWindow NOFLOAT NOGROW NOZOOM
```

The *WINDOW* Clause

You can also activate a window object when the WINDOW clause is specified with the BROWSE, CHANGE, EDIT, MODIFY COMMAND, and MODIFY FILE commands. When the WINDOW clause is specified with the BROWSE, CHANGE, or EDIT commands, the editing operation occurs inside the window. When the command exits, the window is deactivated. Here's an example:

```
DEFINE WINDOW BR1 FROM 4,3 to 30,40 COLOR SCHEME 8
BROWSE WINDOW BR1
```

Figure 7.6 shows the `BROWSE` command executing in window `BR1`. Incidentally, if a window is active when the `BROWSE`, `CHANGE`, or `EDIT` commands are executed, the commands execute within the active window.

You can specify a `WINDOW` clause with the `@` command also, which specifies a window where memo-field editing is performed. The window is not activated, however, until the memo field is edited. The format of the `WINDOW` clause is this:

```
<command>...WINDOW <window-name>
```

You can also define a window in which memo-field editing is performed by using the following command:

```
SET WINDOW OF MEMO TO <window-name>
```

The `WINDOW` clause for the `@` command follows the `GET` clause. You can precede it with the `OPEN` keyword. When you supply the `OPEN` keyword, the memo field is displayed in the window as soon as a command such as `READ`, `EDIT`, or `APPEND` executes. Otherwise, only a memo-field icon is displayed until the text editor is activated to edit the memo field. At that time, the designated window is activated and memo-field editing is performed inside the window. Chapter 9, "Full-Screen Data Editing," provides detailed information regarding the `@` command.

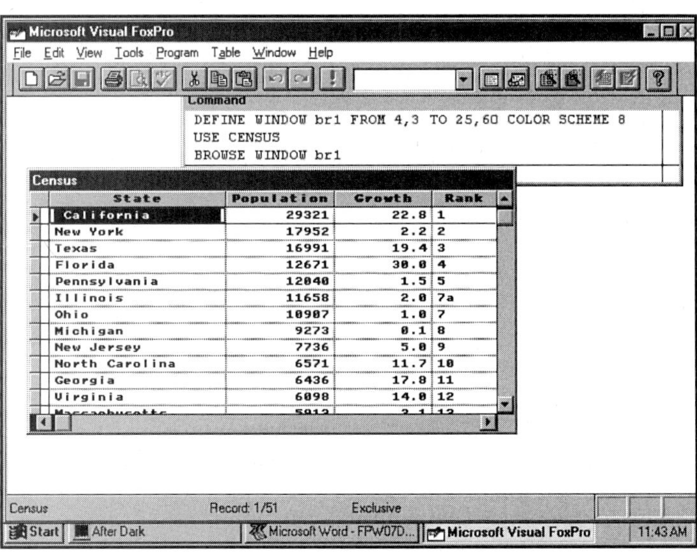

FIGURE 7.6.
Activating a window with the `BROWSE` command.

You can use the `MODIFY MEMO` command to edit a memo field. You can specify the `IN WINDOW <window-name>` clause with this command to specify a window in which to edit a memo field.

Saving and Retrieving Windows

You can save window objects to disk using the SAVE WINDOW command. Use the following syntax:

```
SAVE WINDOW <window-name-list> ¦ ALL
   TO <filename> ¦ TO MEMO <memo field>
```

The specified window objects are written to a disk file or saved in a memo field. If a filename extension is not specified, the default extension of the disk file is .WIN. The existing window display is not affected.

You can retrieve window objects from a disk file using the RESTORE WINDOWS command. Use the following syntax:

```
RESTORE WINDOW <window-name-list> ¦ ALL
   FROM <filename> ¦ FROM MEMO <memo field>
```

The specified window objects are retrieved from the specified disk file or memo field and stored in memory. If you specify ALL, all window objects in the disk file or memo field are restored. If the names of any window objects in the disk file or memo field already exist in memory, the window object in memory is replaced by the one retrieved from the disk or memo field. If the filename extension of the file to be restored is not .WIN, you must supply the extension.

If you supply *<window-name-list>*, the windows are restored in the listed order regardless of how they are ordered on disk.

The *ACTIVATE SCREEN* Command

When a window object is active, all output is written inside the window. Sometimes it's useful to display information outside the window without disturbing the window configuration. With the ACTIVATE SCREEN command, you can place output anywhere on-screen without redrawing any window objects. Use the following syntax:

```
ACTIVATE SCREEN
```

When a window is active and you issue the ACTIVATE SCREEN command, output is directed to the screen. The window remains on-screen. When the output operation is complete, you can reactivate the window with the ACTIVATE WINDOW command.

Saving Screen Contents

You can transfer the contents of an entire screen to a memory variable with the following command:

```
SAVE SCREEN [TO <memory variable>]
```

The screen buffer is saved to a memory variable or an array element. They are given a data type `S`, which you can observe if you list memory variables with the `LIST MEMORY` or `DISPLAY MEMORY` commands, as in this example:

```
SAVE SCREEN TO ScreenSave
DISPLAY MEMORY LIKE Scr* && Display memory variable, scr*
```

The previous statements produce the following output:

```
SCREENSAVE Pub    S   80 by 25
```

You cannot use type `S` memory variables in expressions. The maximum number of screen memory buffers that you can save to memory variables depends on the amount of available memory. Each screen memory buffer requires about 4KB of memory.

If you omit the `TO` clause, the screen contents are saved in an unnamed buffer and can be restored only if you issue the `RESTORE SCREEN` command. When you restore the screen, the unnamed buffer is released.

You can move a screen memory buffer saved in a memory variable (memvar) back to the screen by using the following command:

```
RESTORE SCREEN FROM <memory variable>
```

Screen memory buffers saved in memory variables remain in memory until they are removed with the following command:

```
RELEASE ALL [LIKE ¦ EXCEPT <skeleton>] ¦ <memory variable list>
```

The memory variables named in the list are removed from memory, and the memory is released to the system. You can remove all memory variables from memory if you specify the `ALL` keyword or use one of two forms of the `CLEAR` command:

```
CLEAR MEMORY
```

```
CLEAR ALL
```

Suppose an application requires a help screen. It takes a quarter second or so to draw the help screen, and perhaps another quarter second to restore the original screen. You can design an application that uses the `SAVE SCREEN` and `RESTORE SCREEN` commands to make the help screen access appear instantaneously.

In Listing 7.2, the help screen displays when you press F1. The first time you press F1, the help screen is generated and displayed, and the screen contents are saved. On subsequent calls to the `HELPER` procedure, the original screen is saved in a screen buffer called `ORIGINAL`, and the screen containing the help box is restored. Just before `HELPER` exits, the original screen is restored.

Listing 7.2. A custom help screen.

```
*****************************************************************
*- Name....: YOURPROG.PRG - Your Program
*- Date....: 7-12-92
*- Version.: FoxPro

*****************************************************************
*... (your code)
PUSH KEY
ON KEY LABEL F1 DO HELPER
*… (your code)
Char = ' '
DO WHILE Char # 'x'
@ 10,10 SAY "Press F1 for help" GET Char
READ
ENDDO
POP KEY
RETURN
*****************************************************************
*- Name.…: HELPER
*- Date.…: 7-12-92
*- Version.: FoxPro
*****************************************************************
PROCEDURE HELPER
PUBLIC FIRSTHELP, HELP1
SAVE SCREEN TO ORIGINAL
IF .not. FIRSTHELP
FIRSTHELP=.T.
*
*   Draw help screen
*
@ 2,5 CLEAR TO 14,58
@ 2,5 TO 14,58 DOUBLE
@ 4,8 SAY "The syntax of the ACTIVATE WINDOW command is:"
@ 7,10 SAY  "ACTIVATE WINDOW [<window-name1>"
@ 8,15 SAY  "  [, <window-name2> … ]] ¦ ALL"
@ 9,15 SAY  "  [IN [WINDOW] <window-name3>"
@ 10,15 SAY "  ¦ SCREEN]"
@ 11,15 SAY "  [BOTTOM ¦ TOP ¦ SAME] [NOSHOW]"
*  Save current screen
SAVE SCREEN TO HELP1
ELSE
RESTORE SCREEN FROM HELP1
ENDIF
*   Wait for user response, restore original screen, and exit
AChar = ' '
@ 13,15 SAY "Press any key to continue" Get AChar
READ
RESTORE SCREEN FROM ORIGINAL
RELEASE ORIGINAL
RETURN
```

Moving Windows

You can move window objects on-screen with the MOVE command. You can change the location of any user-defined window object, even if it is covered by an active window. The syntax is the following:

```
MOVE WINDOW <window-name> TO <expN1>,<expN2>
¦ BY <expN3>,<expN4> ¦ CENTER
```

If you supply the TO clause, the named window is moved to a new location. The TO clause defines the new row and column coordinates of the top-left corner of the window. The BY clause defines the number of rows and columns to move the window. The BY clause arguments can be positive or negative integers. If the row or column argument is a negative integer, the window moves up or backward. If you specify the following command:

```
MOVE WINDOW <window-name> CENTER
```

the named window moves to the center of its parent window.

Listing 7.3 is the BOUNCE.PRG program, which illustrates the use of the MOVE command. This program defines and activates the Bounce window, then executes the MOVE command to randomly move the window around the screen. It also randomly changes the color of the window. It uses the RAND() function (which returns a pseudorandom number between 0 and 1.0) to pick a random direction each time the window moves and changes its color scheme. If you enter any character, the program terminates. The argument for the INKEY() function is .1, which limits the speed of the loop to one cycle every tenth of a second. Without this time delay, the window moves too fast to see. The expression containing nested IIF() function calls computes the direction that the window moves. If the bouncing window bounces too close to the edge of the screen, the window moves away from the edge. Otherwise, it moves in a random direction.

Listing 7.3. The source listing for the BOUNCE.PRG program.

```
*****************************************************************
*      * 07/11/92            BOUNCE.PRG               10:10:29 *
*****************************************************************
*      *                                                        *
*      * Description:                                           *
*      * This program illustrates MOVE command                  *
*      *                                                        *
*****************************************************************
SET TALK OFF
=RAND(-1)
CLEAR
DEFINE WINDOW Bounce FROM 10,10 TO 14,20 ;
COLOR W+/R FILL FILE BALL PANEL
ACTIVATE WINDOW Bounce
```

continues

Listing 7.3. continued

```
DO WHILE  INKEY(.1) = 0
   mcol =    IIF(WLCOL() < 16 ,  10,  ;
   IIF(WLCOL() > 60 , -10,  ;
   IIF(rand()  > .5 , 10, -10 )))
   mrow =    IIF(WLROW() <  5 ,  4,  ;
   IIF(WLROW() > 18 , -4,  ;
   IIF(rand()  > .5 , 4, -4 )))
   MOVE WINDOW Bounce BY mrow,mcol
   @ 0,0 FILL TO 13,19 COLOR SCHEME INT(23*rand())+1
ENDDO
RELEASE WINDOW Bounce
RETURN
```

The *ZOOM WINDOW* Command

The `ZOOM WINDOW` command is used to alter the size and position of system- and user-defined windows. With the `ZOOM WINDOW` command, you can reduce a window to an icon, expand it to fill the main FoxPro window, or resize it to any size in between. If you create a user-defined window with the `DEFINE WINDOW` command and you specify the `IN DESKTOP` clause, the window you create can be enlarged to fill the entire Windows desktop. The syntax of the `ZOOM WINDOW` command is the following:

```
ZOOM WINDOW <window name> MIN ¦ MAX ¦ NORM
      [AT <row1, column1> [ SIZE <row2, column2> ]]
    ¦ [FROM <row1, column1> [TO <row2, column2>]]
```

You can use the `ZOOM WINDOW` command to resize all system windows except the Filer and the Project Manager. If you want to zoom a Visual FoxPro system window, enclose the entire system menu name in quotation marks. For example, if you want to minimize the Command window, specify the following command:

```
ZOOM WINDOW 'Command Window' MIN
```

You must use the `<window name>` expression to specify the name of the window operated on by this command plus you must specify one of the three keywords `MIN`, `MAX`, or `NORM`.

If you specify the `MIN` keyword, the window is reduced in size to an icon, which makes it easy to place many windows on the desktop, the main FoxPro window, the Windows desktop, or in a user-defined window simultaneously and still have sufficient space to do work. All system windows can be reduced to icons. However, before you can reduce a system window to an icon, it must be open. A user-defined window can be minimized after it is defined. It doesn't have to be activated before you change its size. When you specify the `MIN` keyword, the window displays as an icon in the lower portion of the Windows desktop, which is the same operation performed when you press a window's Minimize button.

You can specify the MAX keyword to expand a window to fill the main FoxPro window, the Windows desktop, or a user-defined window. The MAX keyword performs the same action as performed when you click on a window's Maximize button. If a child window is placed in a parent window and the child window is expanded to its maximum size, it expands to fill its parent window. If you specify the MAX keyword, the AT, SIZE, TO, or FROM clauses are ignored if specified. Only user-defined windows can be zoomed to maximum size.

You can specify the NORM keyword to instruct FoxPro to restore a window to its original size after it has been minimized or maximized. In addition, the NORM keyword must be used to move or resize a window with the ZOOM command.

You can specify the AT or FROM clauses to reposition a window. You can specify the placement of a window by including the optional AT or FROM clauses. If the MAX keyword is specified, the AT and FROM clauses are ignored. If you specify the NORM keyword, the left edge of the window is placed in the main FoxPro window at the location specified by the AT clause. In the following example, the window, cwin, is initially defined, maximized, and then normalized (restored to its original size of 10 by 10), but it is placed in a new location:

```
DEFINE WINDOW cwin AT 10,10 SIZE 30,30
ACTIVATE WINDOW cwin
ZOOM WINDOW cwin MAX                ; MAXIMIZE IT
ZOOM WINDOW cwin NORM AT 50,50      ; Normalized but moved
```

If you define a user-defined window and specify the IN DESKTOP clause, the left edge of the window is placed in the Windows desktop at the location specified using the AT or FROM clauses. If either the MIN or MAX keyword is specified, the AT and FROM clauses are ignored.

The arguments for the AT, SIZE, FROM, and TO clauses have the same function as they do when used with the DEFINE command: They define positions and sizes of windows. For example, the AT and FROM clauses have *<row1>*, *<column1>* coordinates that specify where the upper-left corner of the window is placed. The AT and SIZE clauses are paired together as well as the FROM and TO clauses. The SIZE and TO clauses are optional if you do not want to resize a window. You can also use MOVE WINDOW to reposition a window.

Scrolling the Window or Screen Contents

You can use the SCROLL command to scroll any rectangular region of information on-screen or in a window vertically or horizontally. The syntax is this:

```
SCROLL <expN1>,<expN2>,<expN3>,<expN4>,<expN5>[,<expN6>]
```

The first two numeric expressions define the row and column of the top-left corner of the rectangular region to be scrolled. The second two expressions define the row and column of the bottom-right corner of the region to be scrolled. *<expN5>* and *<expN6>* specify the number of lines to scroll vertically and horizontally, respectively. If *<expN5>* is positive, the rectangular region scrolls up; if <expN5> is negative, the rectangular region scrolls down. Similarly, if <expN6> is positive, the region scrolls right; if <expN6> is negative, the region scrolls left. In the following examples of the use of the SCROLL command, a region extending from row 3, column 4 to row 16, column 60 is scrolled:

```
SCROLL 3,4,16,60,2        && Scroll up two lines
SCROLL 3,4,16,60,-2       && Scroll down two lines
SCROLL 3,4,16,60,0,3      && Scroll right three columns
SCROLL 3,4,16,60,0,-4     && Scroll left four columns
SCROLL 3,4,16,60,2,3      && Scroll up 2 lines, right 3 columns
```

Window Functions

The FoxPro language contains functions that return information about windows. Each of these functions contains the name of a window as its optional field.

Certain window functions return a parameter associated with either the current window or the specified window. These are the functions and the values they return:

Function	*Value Returned*
SCOLS()	The number of columns in the FoxPro main window
SROWS()	The number of rows in the FoxPro main window
WCOLS([<expC>])	The number of columns in a window
WFONT(<expN> [,<expC>])	The font attributes of text in a window
WLCOL([<expC>])	The screen column location of the left window border
WLROW([<expC>])	The screen row location of the top window border
WROWS([<expC>])	The number of rows in a window
WTITLE([<expC>])	The title assigned to a window

The screen lies underneath all the user-defined windows. It is sometimes called the *desktop*. If no window is active, the WCOLS(), WROWS(), WLCOL(), and WLROW() functions return their respective parameters for the screen. Even if a window is active, you can retrieve the screen parameters by passing these functions a null string ("").

You can move windows off-screen. Furthermore, a window can be on-screen initially but positioned off-screen when a SET DISPLAY command changes the number of screen rows. As a result, the WLCOL() and WLROW() functions can return a value that is off the screen. If the window is off the top or left of the screen, the WLROW() and WLCOL() functions return a negative number.

The SROWS() and SCOLS() functions, which return the number of rows and columns in the FoxPro main window, are more useful in Visual FoxPro applications because a FoxPro window can be any size. You should take this into consideration when writing your application.

The WFONT(<expN> [,<expC>]) function returns font attributes of the current font for either the current window or the specified window if <expC> is specified. You specify a numeric value to indicate the type of font attribute that is returned. The numeric values are the following:

`<expN>`	*Value Returned*
1	Name of the current font
2	Point size of the current font
3	One or more characters denoting the style of current font (See Table 7.1.)

Certain window functions return a logical value for either the currently active window or the window named in the `<expC>`. The following functions return a true value (`.T.`) if one of the following is true:

- `WBORDER([<expC>])`—The window has a border.
- `WEXIST(<expC>)`—The named window has been defined.
- `WMAXIMUM([<expC>])`—The window is enlarged to fill the screen.
- `WMINIMIZE([<expC>])`—The window is reduced to its minimum size.
- `WVISIBLE([<expC>])`—The window is activated and is not hidden.
- `WREAD([<expC>])`—The window is the current Read window.

Otherwise, these functions return a false value (`.F.`).

The `WOUTPUT()`, `WLAST()`, and `WONTOP()` functions can return either a logical value or a character string. The syntax of the `WOUTPUT()` function is the following:

```
WOUTPUT([<expC>])
```

The `<expC>` argument is the name of a window. If an argument is supplied, `.T.` is returned if the specified window is the current output window. If you don't specify an argument, the `WOUTPUT()` function returns the name of the current output window. If the output is directed to the screen, it returns a null string.

NOTE

> The `WINDOW()` function is supported for dBASE IV compatibility. However, the `WINDOW()` function returns only the name of the active window, which is the window that currently has input focus. The `WOUTPUT()` function is more powerful.

The syntax of the `WLAST()` function is the following:

```
WLAST([<expC>])
```

If the name of the window (`<expC>`) is specified, this function returns `.T.` if the named window was the active window before the currently active window became active. If you supply no argument, this function returns the name of the window that was active prior to the current window.

You use the `WONTOP()` function to determine if the active or specified window is in front of all other windows. This is the syntax:

```
WONTOP([<expC>])
```

If the name of the window (<*expC*>) is specified, this function returns `.T.` if the window is on top of the stack of windows. If you supply no argument, this function returns the name of the window that is on top.

You can have a window inside a window inside a window, and so forth. A window inside another window is called a *child window.* A child window is inside a parent window. If the desktop is active, all windows are children of the screen. You can use the `WPARENT()` function to retrieve a character string containing the name of a parent window. If no parent window exists, `WPARENT()` returns a null string, which implies that the desktop is the parent. The syntax of the `WPARENT()` function is this:

```
WPARENT([<expC>])
```

If you don't specify the name of a window (<*expC*>), the currently active window is assumed.

Inside a window you can have a stack of child windows. The child windows are referred to by numbers. The child on the bottom of the stack is the number `0`. The window on top of child `0` is child `1`, and so forth. You can use the `WCHILD()` function to retrieve either the number of child windows or the name of a child window. The syntax is this:

```
WCHILD([<expC>] ¦ <expN>])
```

If you pass the number (<*expN*>) of a child window, the name of the child window for the active window is returned. If you specify the name of a window, the number of its child windows is returned. If you specify no arguments, the number of child windows for the active window is returned. Here's an example:

```
DEFINE WINDOW W1 FROM 1,1 TO 20,70
DEFINE WINDOW W2 FROM 1,1 to 5,5 IN W1
DEFINE WINDOW W3 FROM 8,8 TO 15,15 IN W1
ACTIVATE ALL
ACTIVATE W1
? WCHILD()      && Displays: 2 (number of child windows)
? WCHILD(0)     && Displays: W2 (window on bottom of stack)
? WCHILD(1)     && Displays: W3 (Top of stack)
? WCHILD(2)     && Displays null string (no more child windows)
```

The WINFUN.PRG program, shown in Listing 7.4, illustrates the use of most window functions. A table displays in window `W8` that shows status information relating to the window on top of the stack. The `ShowStat` procedure displays the table whenever either mouse button is pressed. The `ON KEY LABEL MOUSE` command establishes an event trap that is triggered whenever either mouse button is pressed and `ShowStat` is called. You can choose any of the windows to be on top. You can size, minimize, move, or zoom them, and then click the window to see the updated status information. Finally, you can press the Exit button to terminate the program.

Listing 7.4. The WINFUN.PRG program.

```
*****************************************************************
*      * 07/16/92            WINFUN.PRG                 12:18:19 *
*****************************************************************
*      *                                                         *
*      * Description:                                            *
*      * This program illustrates use of window functions        *
*      *                                                         *
*****************************************************************
SET TALK OFF
CLEAR
IF .NOT. WEXIST("W1")   && Only define it if it does not exist
DEFINE WINDOW W1 FROM 1,0   TO 10,19  TITLE "default" ;
    FILL chr(176) FLOAT
ENDIF

DEFINE WINDOW W2 FROM 12,0  TO 20,19  NONE  ;
    FLOAT GROW MINIMIZE ZOOM FONT "MS Serif",8
DEFINE WINDOW W3 FROM 1,21  TO 10,39  DOUBLE TITLE "Double";
    FLOAT GROW MINIMIZE ZOOM FONT "MS Serif",8
DEFINE WINDOW W4 FROM 12,21 TO 20,39 PANEL   TITLE "Panel";
    COLOR SCHEME 3 FLOAT GROW MINIMIZE ZOOM FONT "MS Serif",8
DEFINE WINDOW W5 FROM 1,41  TO 10,59 SYSTEM;
    TITLE "System2" FLOAT GROW MINIMIZE ZOOM FONT "MS Serif",8
DEFINE WINDOW W6 FROM 12,41 TO 20,59  "A"    TITLE " Letter ";
    FLOAT GROW MINIMIZE ZOOM FONT "MS Serif",8
DEFINE WINDOW W7 FROM 1,61   TO 10,77 SYSTEM  TITLE "System";
    FILL FILE TREE.BMP FLOAT GROW MINIMIZE ZOOM FONT "MS Serif",8
DEFINE WINDOW W8 FROM 5,5 TO 18,40  SYSTEM    TITLE " System ";
    MINIMIZE SHADOW FLOAT ZOOM GROW FOOTER "Shadow" ;
    COLOR SCHEME 8
ACTIVATE WINDOW ALL  && Note that W8 will be current active
ON KEY LABEL MOUSE DO SHOWSTAT
DO SHOWSTAT
choice = 1
@ 11,14 GET choice FUNCTION "*  \<Exit"
READ CYCLE
CLEAR ALL
ON KEY
RETURN
*****************************************************************
*      * PROCEDURE: ShowStat                                     *
*      * Description:                                            *
*      * Display window status information                       *
*****************************************************************
PROCEDURE SHOWSTAT
@ 0,1 SAY "Output Window: "+ WOUTPUT()
WOT = WONTOP()
@ 1,1 SAY "Parameters for Window: "+ WOT
@ 2,1 SAY "  Title:                "+ WTITLE(WOT)+"  "
@ 3,1 SAY "  Prior active window: "+ WLAST()
@ 4,1 SAY "  Output Window?        "+;
IIF( WOUTPUT(WOT), "Yes","No ")
@ 5,1 SAY "  Border?               "+;
IIF( WBORDER(WOT), "Yes","No ")
```

continues

Listing 7.4. continued

```
@ 6,1 SAY "  Minimized?           "+;
IIF( WMINIMUM(WOT), "Yes","No ")
@ 7,1 SAY "  Maximized?           "+;
IIF( WMAXIMUM(WOT), "Yes","No ")
@ 8,1 SAY "  Is it visible?       "+;
IIF( WVISIBLE(WOT), "Yes","No ")
@ 9,1 SAY "  Current READ Window? "+;
IIF( WREAD(WOT), "Yes","No ")
@ 10,1 SAY "Location: "+N2C(WLROW(WOT))+;
","+N2C(WLCOL(WOT))+;
" Size: "    +N2C(WROWS(WOT))+;
","+N2C(WCOLS(WOT)) + "     "
RETURN
*****************************************************************
*      * PROCEDURE: N2C                                         *
*      * Description:                                           *
*      * Converts number to trimmed string                      *
*****************************************************************
FUNCTION N2C
PARAMETER Number
RETURN LTRIM(STR(Number))
```

Figure 7.7 shows a sample output from the execution of WINFUN.PRG. Notice that window `W7` has been moved and resized and is filled with TREE.BMP, which is a picture of a tree that has been duplicated to fill the window.

The `SYSMETRIC()` function returns the size of Microsoft Windows display elements. Its syntax is this:

```
SYSMETRIC(<expN>)
```

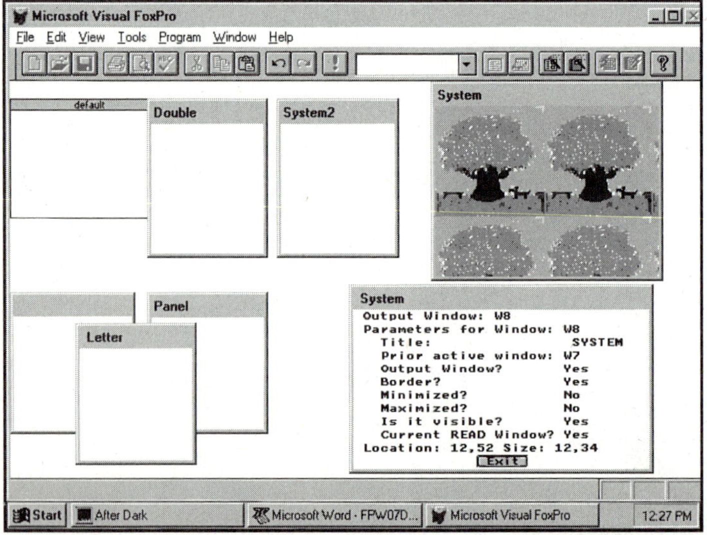

FIGURE 7.7.

The sample output resulting from executing WINFUN.PRG.

The numeric argument specifies the display element for which the size is returned. Table 7.4 describes which value is returned for each Microsoft Windows display element. The returned values are in pixels unless otherwise stated.

Table 7.4. Visual FoxPro display element values.

<expN>	*Display Element*
1	Width of window screen
2	Height of window screen
3	Width of sizable window frame
4	Height of sizable window frame
5	Width of scroll arrows on vertical scroll bar
6	Height of scroll arrows on vertical scroll bar
7	Width of scroll arrows on horizontal scroll bar
8	Height of scroll arrows on horizontal scroll bar
9	Height of window table
10	Width of nonsizable window frame
11	Height of nonsizable window frame
12	Width of `DOUBLE` or `PANEL` window frame
13	Height of `DOUBLE` or `PANEL` window frame
14	Scroll box width on horizontal scroll bar in text editing window
15	Scroll box height on horizontal scroll bar in text editing window
16	Minimized window icon width
17	Minimized window icon height
18	Maximum insertion point cursor width
19	Maximum insertion point cursor height
20	Single-line menu bar height
21	Maximized menu width
22	Maximized menu height
23	Kanji window height
24	Minimum sizable window width
25	Minimum sizable window height
26	Minimum window width
27	Minimum window height

continues

Table 7.4. continued

<expN>	*Display Element*
28	Width of window controls
29	Height of window controls
30	1 if mouse hardware present; otherwise, 0
31	1 for Windows debugging version; otherwise, 0
32	1 if mouse buttons are reversed; otherwise, 0

Menu, Pad, Pop-up, and Dialog Objects

Visual FoxPro 3.0 introduces object-oriented programming into the Xbase language. You are going to learn all about visual class objects for containers and controls in Chapter 14 and Chapter 19, "The Form Designer." You probably would expect that Visual FoxPro would support menu objects, too. This is not the case. Visual FoxPro still uses the FoxPro 2.*x* menu definition commands. In a way, it is a good thing because it reduces the number of new things that you have to learn if you already know how to program in FoxPro 2.*x*. However, as Visual FoxPro evolves, menu classes will probably be incorporated. You can, however, prepare for the future by always using the Menu Designer to build your user-defined interfaces. Then it will be easier to upgrade your applications when OOP is used to define menu objects.

One of the dynamic features of FoxPro is user-defined menus that support menu bars and pop-up menus. The internal support for the menu system is the same as the support for the FoxPro full-screen commands and main interface. This ensures that any FoxPro user-defined menu system interface is consistent with the rest of Visual FoxPro.

It is really easy to create a user-defined menu system. You define a menu, menu pads, pop-ups, and selection bars for the pop-up menus. Then you create code to activate the menu system. Finally, you add code to perform some operation when a menu is selected. An even easier way to generate a menu interface is to use the Visual FoxPro Menu Designer which is described in Chapter 16, "The Visual FoxPro Menu Designer."

The following sections describe the commands used to generate a menu system. If you understand how to use the commands to create a menu-driven interface, you will be better prepared to use the FoxPro Menu Designer and better able to make custom changes to the menu interface code.

These sections discuss different types of menu objects that Visual FoxPro supports.

The Menu Bar

A user-defined menu bar object consists of one or more prompt pad objects, as shown below the system menu bar in Figure 7.8. A prompt pad object is simply an identifying label. You can define more than one menu bar object and each one can have its own set of prompt pad objects. Then, during processing, any one of the menu bars can be activated. When a menu bar is activated, the *current pad* is highlighted. You can select a pad by clicking on it with the mouse. You also can use the keyboard to move from pad object to pad object by pressing either the ← or → key. If no pop-up menu is attached to a menu pad, you can use the ↑ and ↓ keys to move between the pads. You select a pad by pressing Enter.

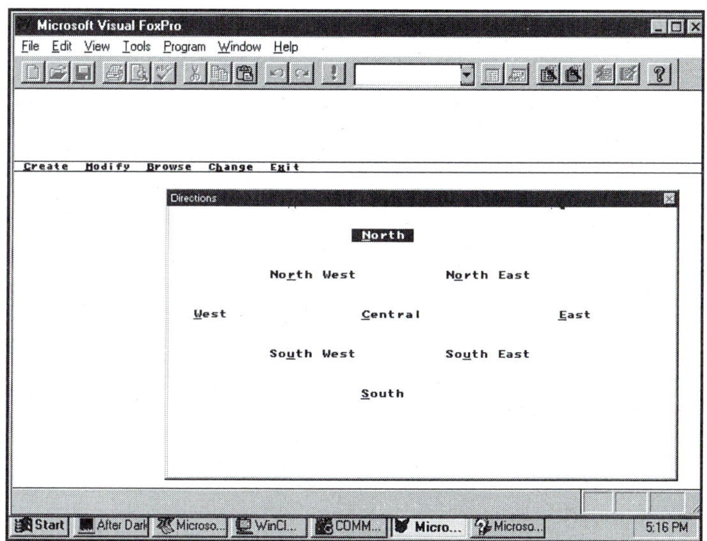

FIGURE 7.8.
Menu objects.

When you select a prompt pad object, a specified action is performed. An action can be any FoxPro command.

You can supply an optional explanation message with any object. This message displays centered on the bottom line of the screen if `SET STATUS` is `ON`. If the Windows-style status bar is active (`SET STATUS BAR ON`), the message displays at the left of the status bar. The message supplied with the menu object displays only if a message is not provided with the pad object.

Another way to select a prompt pad object is to use the Alt key with the hotkey. The hotkey is either the first letter of the prompt pad object label or the character in the label preceded by a backslash character and a left angle bracket (`\<`). For example, the letter t is the hotkey for the following label:

```
Ho\<t key
```

The hotkey character is underlined in the label. In Figure 7.8, Alt+C activates the action associated with the **C**reate prompt pad, and the Alt+H hotkey activates the C**h**ange prompt pad action.

By default, a menu bar displays horizontally. If no coordinates are supplied, the menu bar displays on the first line of the screen. A space is added to the beginning and end of the label. However, you can place pad objects anywhere on the screen by supplying coordinates with the AT clause. An example of a scattered layout is provided inside the Directions window in Figure 7.8.

Pop-up Objects

A pop-up object is a rectangular box containing a list of selection bar objects. The current selection bar is highlighted. You can choose a selection bar by clicking on it. Using the keyboard, you can position the pop-up cursor with the ↑, ↓, PgUp, PgDn, Home, and End keys or by typing the selection bar hotkey. You press Enter to select an entry.

When a selection bar object is chosen, a specified action is performed. An action can be any FoxPro command. The Esc, ←, and → keys deactivate the pop-up object without making any selection and without performing any action.

If the number of selection bar objects exceeds the height of the pop-up, the pop-up scrolls. The four types of pop-up objects are shown in Figure 7.9. The first type is a *menu pop-up object.* It consists of a pop-up window object containing user-defined selection bar objects.

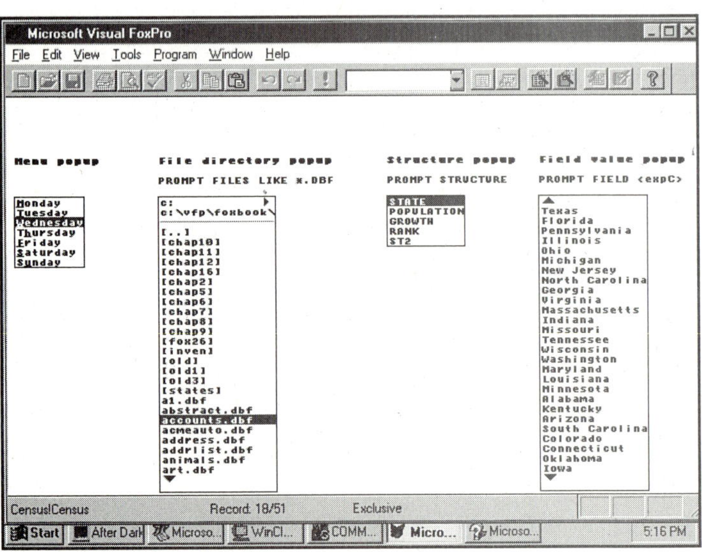

FIGURE 7.9.
Pop-up objects.

The second type of pop-up object is a *file directory pop-up object.* This pop-up enables users to select a disk drive, directory, or file. The directory pop-up object is powerful. It enables users to select files anywhere in the directory tree on any drive. If the current drive is selected, a disk drive pop-up object is displayed, and a new drive can be selected. Bar labels enclosed in square brackets ([ ]) are disk directories. The [. .] label represents the parent directory for the current directory. If you select a directory bar object, it becomes the current directory, and its files are displayed in the directory pop-up object.

The third type of pop-up object is a *table structure pop-up object.* It contains the structure of the table in use in the currently selected work area.

The fourth type of pop-up object is a *field value pop-up object.* This pop-up contains values of fields in the table in either the currently selected work area, or if an alias name is specified, in the specified work area. The rightmost pop-up in Figure 7.9 is a field value pop-up for a field named STATE.

Dialog Box Objects

Several functions display a dialog box and return the user's response. Table 7.5 describes these functions and commands.

Table 7.5. The functions and commands that display dialog boxes.

Function or Command	*Type of Dialog Box*	*Value Returned in Character String*	
FILER	MS-DOS File Utility	Nothing	
GETFILE()	File Open dialog box	User-selected filename	
GETDIR()	Directory dialog box	User-selected directory	NEW FOR VISUAL FOXPRO 3
GETPICT()	Open File dialog box	User-specified BMP file	
LOCFILE()	File Open dialog box if file is not found	User-selected filename	
GETCP()	Code Page dialog box	User-selected code page number	NEW FOR VISUAL FOXPRO 3
GETPRINTER()	Windows Print Setup dialog box	User-selected printer name	
MESSAGEBOX()	System dialog box that returns pad number	N/A	NEW FOR VISUAL FOXPRO 3
PUTFILE()	Save As dialog box	User-specified filename	
GETFONT()	Font dialog box	User-selected font type, size, and style	
GETEXPR	Expression Builder dialog box	User-specified expression expression	
WAIT WINDOW	Wait message	User-entered character	

The FILER command is used to execute the Visual FoxPro Filer MS-DOS File utility. This command provides MS-DOS file maintenance operations. You can copy, move, or delete one or more files, view and change file attributes, and create and view directories. Here is the syntax:

```
FILER [LIKE <skeleton>] [NOWAIT]
    [IN [WINDOW] <window-name> ¦ SCREEN]
```

You can specify the LIKE clause to instruct the **F**iler to display only those files designated by the wildcard specification. *<skeleton>* can contain the * and ? wildcard characters. You can specify that the FILER command window reside inside another window (*<window-name>*) using the optional IN [WINDOW] clause. The Filer window becomes the child window to the specified parent window. If the parent window moves, the Filer window moves with it. If you execute the FILER command from a program, the Filer window displays and program execution pauses until the user finishes performing file utility operations and closes the file. However, if you specify NOWAIT, the window opens, returns immediately to your program, and executes the line of code following the FILER NOWAIT statement.

An example of the Open File dialog box displayed by the GETFILE() function is shown in Figure 7.10. The GETFILE(), LOCFILE(), and PUTFILE() functions all display a dialog box with drive, directory, and filename list controls. Each of these functions returns a string containing a filename. The syntax of all three of these commands is similar. Here are examples:

```
GETFILE([<expC1>] [,<expC2>] [, <expC3>][, <expN>])
GETPICT([<expC1>] [,<expC2>] [, <expC3>])
LOCFILE([<expFN>] [,<expC1>] [, <expC2>] [, <expC4>])
PUTFILE([<expC2>] [,<expFN>] [, <expC1>])
```

<expC1> is the file name extension string that displays in the Directory list box when the All File check box is not checked. It can have any of the following forms:

- A single file extension (for example, .DBF).
- A list of file extensions separated by semicolons (for example, EXE;COM;BAT). If two files have the same name but different extensions, only the first name appears in the list.
- A list of file extensions separated by the vertical bar (¦) character (for example, EXE¦COM¦BAT). If two files have the same name but different extensions, they both appear in the list.
- A string containing a semicolon, in which case every file without an expression is displayed.
- All strings are displayed in the list if a null string is used.
- A string containing wildcard characters (* and ?).

<expC2> is used to specify a caption for the dialog box. *<expN>* specifies the number and type of buttons that appear in the Open dialog box. If you omit this option or you specify 0 for *<expN>*, the Open and Cancel push buttons appear in the box. If you specify 1 for *<expN>*, the Open, New, and Cancel buttons appear. If you specify 2 for *<expN>*, the Open, None, and Cancel buttons appear. In any case, if the None, New, or Cancel button is pressed, a blank string is returned by the GETFILE() function.

The GETPICT() function is similar to the GETFILE() function except that it lets you select a graphics image file (BMP). Also, it contains a Preview button that lets you view the currently selected bitmap.

<expFN> is used with the PUTFILE() function to specify the default filename displayed in the dialog text box. *<expFN>* is used with the LOCFILE() function to specify the name of the file to locate. If *<expFN>* includes only a filename, LOCFILE() searches the Visual FoxPro default directory or folder first. If the file isn't found in the default directory or folder, the Visual FoxPro path is then searched. If *<expFN>* includes a path and a filename, the specified location is searched. If the file can't be found in the specified location, LOCFILE() searches the Visual FoxPro default directory or folder and then the Visual FoxPro path.

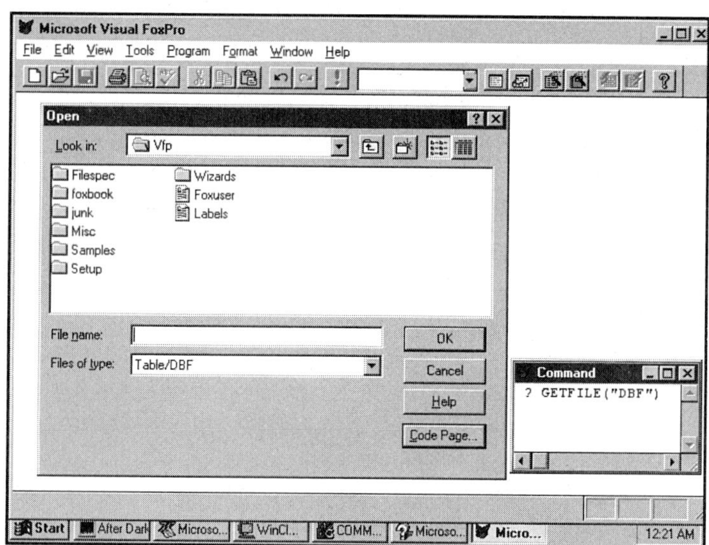

FIGURE 7.10.
The dialog box generated by the GETFILE() command.

The GETDIR() function returns a selected directory path. Here is the syntax:

```
GETDIR([[<expC1> [,<expC2>])
```

You can specify the initially displayed directory with *<expC1>*, and you can specify the caption of the dialog box with *<expC2>*. An example of the Directory dialog box generated by the GETDIR() command is provided in Figure 7.11.

The GETEXPR command opens the Expression Builder window so that your application can use the same Expression Builder program that is available to the Visual FoxPro designers. Here is the syntax:

```
GETEXPR [<expC1>] TO <memvar>  [TYPE <expC2>]
   [DEFAULT <expC4>]
```

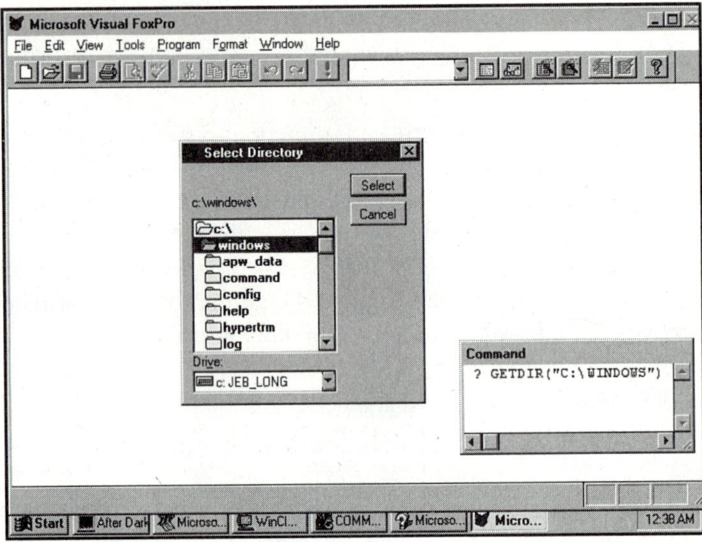

FIGURE 7.11.
The Select Directory dialog box generated by the `GETDIR()` *command.*

You can provide your own dialog box title with the `<expC1>` clause so that you can instruct users as to the type of expression to build. You are required to supply the name of a memory variable. Visual FoxPro stores the resultant expression as a character string in the named memory variable (`<memvar>`). You use the `TYPE <expC2>` clause to specify the data type of the expression and an error message that displays if the user supplies an illegal expression. `<expC2>` evaluates a single letter denoting the data type (`C`, `D`, `T`, `N`, `F`, `B`, or `Y`) followed optionally by a semicolon (;) and an error message. The error message displays in an alert box if the expression entered by the user is invalid. Here is an example: `"C;Expression is invalid. Try again."`.

You can specify a default expression with the `DEFAULT` clause. Remember that you can use alternate delimiters (`[]`, `''`, `""`) to enclose a Character expression within a Character expression. Here is an example:

```
GETEXPR  "Specify a Character expression ", ;
     TO SaveExpr TYPE "C;Illegal character expression. ";
     DEFAULT "Employee = [O'Brian]"
```

In the previous example, after the Expression Builder window displays, the user enters an expression and presses the OK button. The resultant character string is stored in memory variable `SaveExpr`.

The `GETCOLOR()` function opens the Color dialog box and returns the color number in an RGB form that the user chooses. Here is the syntax:

```
GETCOLOR ([<expN>])
```

The optional argument specifies the initially selected color when the Color dialog displays. If it is omitted, black is initially selected. If you provide a bogus value, the first color in the Color dialog is initially selected. The color number is returned unless the user presses an Esc key, in which case, `-1` returns.

The GETCP() function opens a Code Page dialog box with a list of code pages. You choose a code page, and a number is returned that indicates which code page you chose. Here is the syntax:

```
GETCP ([<expN1>][,<expC1>  [,<expC2>]])
```

The optional first argument, <expN>, specifies the initially selected code page number. The second optional argument specifies the caption that displays in the dialog box. If you omit it, the Please select a code page for cross-platform data sharing message displays. The third optional argument is the title for the dialog box. If you omit it, Code Page displays.

The GETPRINTER() function opens the Windows Print Setup dialog box with a list of installed printers. You choose a printer and the setup options. It returns the name of the selected printer. Here is the syntax:

```
GETPRINTER()
```

If you press the Esc key, the Print Setup dialog box exits and returns an empty string.

The MESSAGEBOX() function opens a system dialog box that contains menu pads and returns a number that indicates which push button was selected by the user. Here is the syntax:

```
MESSAGEBOX(<expC1> [,<expN>  [,<expC2>]])
```

The first argument, <expC1>, specifies the text that appears in the dialog box. You can insert carriage returns (CHR(13)) in the message to display multiple lines. Here is an example:

```
"This is first line"+CHR(13)+"This is second line"
```

The second argument, <expN>, specifies the buttons and icons that appear in the box. Its value is composed of the sum of three numbers: the button code, the icon code, and the default button code. These codes are presented in Tables 7.6 through 7.8. For example, if you want to create a system dialog box that displays the Abort, Retry, and Ignore push buttons and a stop sign icon, and you want the second button to be the default button, then you supply 274 (2 + 16 + 256) as the second argument.

Table 7.6. The button types for the MESSAGEBOX() command.

Type of Button	*Value*
OK	0
OK and Cancel	1
Abort, **R**etry, and **I**gnore	2
Yes, **N**o, and Cancel	3
Yes and **N**o	4
Retry and Cancel	5

Table 7.7. The icon types for the MESSAGEBOX() command.

Type of Icon	*Value*
Stop sign	16
Question mark	32
Exclamation point	48
Information	64

Table 7.8. The default buttons for the MESSAGEBOX() command.

Default Button	*Value*
First	0
Second	256
Third	512

The third argument, `<expC2>`, specifies a title for the dialog box.

The `MESSAGEBOX()` function returns a number that indicates which push button the user selects as shown in Table 7.9.

Table 7.9. Values returned by the MESSAGEBOX() function.

Push Button Selected	*Returned Value*
OK	1
Cancel	2
Abort	3
Retry	4
Ignore	5
Yes	6
No	7

Figure 7.12 illustrates the use of the `MESSAGBOX()` function.

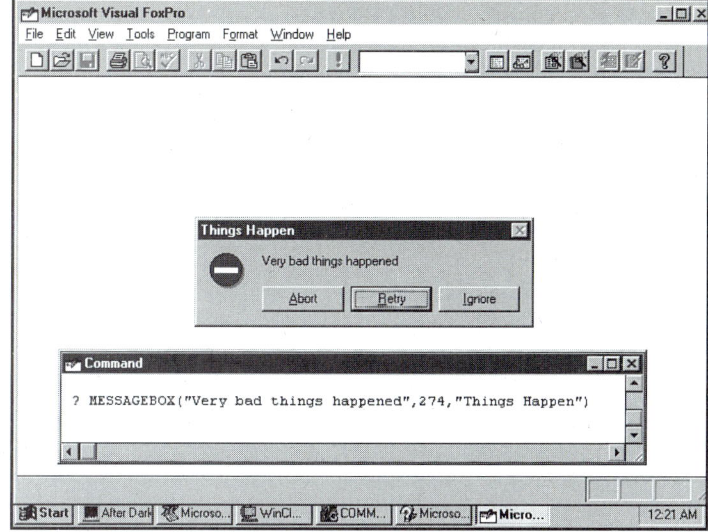

FIGURE 7.12.
A dialog box generated by the MESSAGEBOX() *function.*

Other Objects

There are other objects used in FoxPro that have no counterpart in the menu system. They can be simulated, however, by using multiple commands.

A *system dialog box* appears when FoxPro encounters an anomaly. A system dialog box consists of an icon, a prompt message, and a menu bar, as shown in Figure 7.13. You select the desired pad by pressing the pad label hotkey or by using the → and ← keys to highlight the desired pad and then pressing Enter. An error box can be simulated using the `MESSAGEBOX()` function.

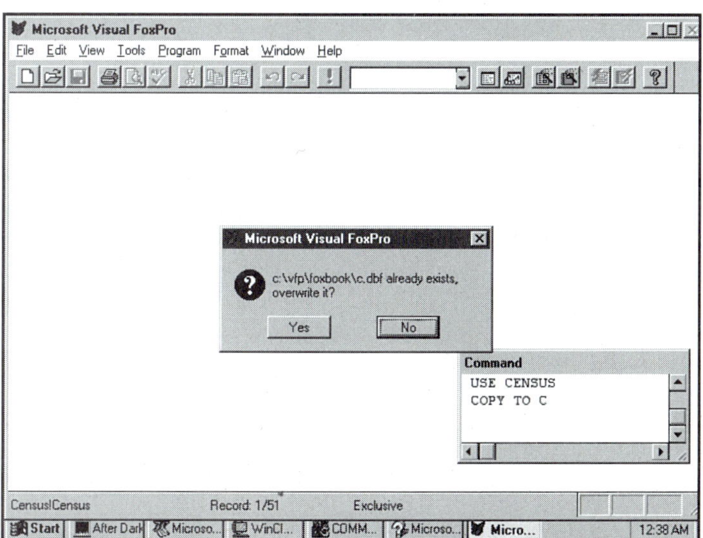

FIGURE 7.13.
A system dialog box.

Other objects include an *alert box* and a *system message box*. An alert box contains an error or warning message and an icon, as shown in Figure 7.14. Whn you click the ouse button or press any key other than a function key, the alert box disappears. A *system message box* is similar to an alert box except that it contains informative text instead of an error or warning message.

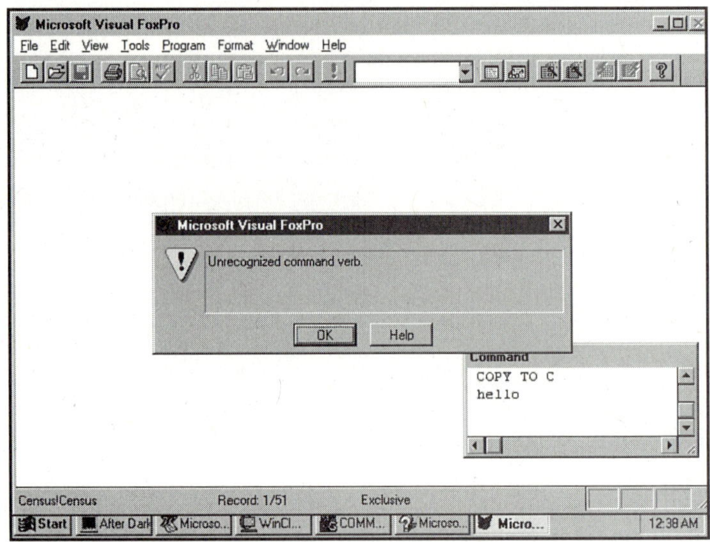

FIGURE 7.14.
An alert box.

Menu System Commands and Functions

The menu system commands are summarized in Table 7.10.

Table 7.10. A summary of the user-defined menu commands.

Command	*Usage*
`ACTIVATE MENU ¦ POPUP`	Activates a menu system
`CLEAR MENUS ¦ POPUPS`	Removes menus or pop-ups from the system
`DEACTIVATE MENU ¦ POPUP`	Deactivates a menu or pop-up system
`DISPLAY MEMORY`	Displays active pop-up and menu object usage, among other things
`DEFINE MENU ¦ PAD ¦ POPUP ¦ BAR`	Defines objects
`HIDE MENU ¦ POPUP`	Makes a menu bar or pop-up disappear
`ON BAR ¦ PAD`	Activates a pop-up for the current pad

Command	*Usage*
`ON SELECTION MENU ¦ POPUP ¦ PAD ¦ BAR`	Specifies what action is performed when an object is selected
`POP MENU`	Restores the specified menu bar definition that was placed on the stack with the `PUSH MENU` command
`PUSH MENU`	Places a menu bar definition in a stack of menu bar definitions in the menu
`RELEASE MENU ¦ POPUP ¦ PAD ¦ BAR`	Removes menus or pop-ups from the system
`SET MARK OF`	Controls the check mark on pads or bars
`SET SKIP OF`	Enables or disables menu objects
`SHOW MENU ¦ POPUP`	Displays an inactive menu or pop-up on-screen

The *DEFINE* Command

Before any objects can be used, you must define them with the `DEFINE` command. Objects include menu bars, menu prompt pads, pop-up menus, pop-up selection bars, and windows. For a snappy interactive interface, it is a good idea to define all objects at the beginning of a program and then use them as needed.

The *DEFINE MENU* Command

The menu bar object consists of one or more prompt pads. Here is the syntax of the command to define the menu object:

```
DEFINE MENU <menu name>
  [BAR [AT LINE <expN1>]]
  [IN [WINDOW] <window name> ¦ IN SCREEN]
  [KEY <key label>]
  [MESSAGE <expC2>]
  [NOMARGIN]
  [FONT <expC3> [, <expN2>]]
     [STYLE <expSTYLE>]
  [COLOR <color pair list>
  ¦ COLOR SCHEME <expN3>
  ¦ COLOR RGB (color value list)]
```

The name associated with the menu object, or any other defined object, follows the same convention as memory variables. The `MESSAGE` clause, which can be supplied for any object, is displayed either below the traditional Xbase status line or on the Windows-style status bar.

The `BAR [AT LINE <expN1>]` clause modifies the behavior of the menu such that it acts like the FoxPro system menu bar. If there are too many menu pads to fit on the menu bar, it scrolls. The `AT LINE` clause specifies the line on which the defined menu bar displays.

The `IN [WINDOW] <window name>` clause designates that the menu bar appears in a named window. Otherwise, the menu bar is placed on the screen unless an output window is active. If the `IN SCREEN` is specified, the menu bar is always placed in the main FoxPro window. You can specify the `IN` clause with the `DEFINE MENU`, `DEFINE POPUP`, and `DEFINE WINDOW` commands.

The `KEY <key label>` clause specifies a key or key combination used to activate the defined menu bar. You can specify special characters using the same notation as used with the `ON KEY LABEL` command and keyboard macros, for example, Alt+M. (See Table 7.11.) The `KEY` clause is equivalent to using the `ON KEY LABEL` command to activate the menu. If you have a keyboard set to the same `<key label>` specified with the `KEY` clause, the keyboard macro has precedence, and the menu bar cannot be activated by pressing the keystroke specified by `<key label>`.

Table 7.11. Key names for use with the `ON KEY LABEL` command.

Alt+0 through Alt+9	End
Alt+A through Alt+Z	Enter
Alt+F1 through Alt+F12	Esc
Alt+PgUp	F1 through F12
Alt+PgDn	Home
Backspace	Ins
Backtab	Left arrow
Ctrl+A through Ctrl+Z	PgDn
Ctrl+End	PgUp
Ctrl+F1 through Ctrl+F12	Right arrow
Ctrl+Home	Shift+F1 through Shift+F12
Ctrl+Left arrow	Shift+Tab
Ctrl+PgDn	Spacebar
Ctrl+PgUp	Tab
Ctrl+Right arrow	Up arrow
Del	*<All printable characters>*
Down arrow	

The `MESSAGE <expC2>` clause displays the message `<expC2>` whenever any pad is highlighted. The message appears centered on the screen under the traditional Xbase status line if `SET STATUS` is `ON`. If the Windows-style status bar is active (`SET STATUS BAR ON`), the message appears to the left of the status bar. The MESSAGE <expC2> clause can be specified with the DEFINE MENU, DEFINE POPUP, DEFINE PAD, and DEFINE BAR commands. A MESSAGE clause specified with the DEFINE PAD and DEFINE BAR commands overrides any MESSAGE clause specified with the DEFINE MENU and DEFINE POPUP commands, respectively.

Normally, extra spaces are inserted to the left and right of a pad label. However, if the optional NOMARGIN keyword is specified, these extra spaces are omitted.

You can specify COLOR clauses with all forms of the DEFINE command. This is discussed in Chapter 10 in the section "The COLOR Clauses."

You can specify a font type, size, and style with the FONT and STYLE clauses. The FONT and STYLE clauses have the following form:

```
FONT <expC> [, <expN>] STYLE <expSTYLE>
```

<expC> is the name of the font (Roman, Times, and so on). <expN> is the size of the font in points (10 point, 12 point, and so on). A 10-point font is used if <expN> is omitted. Microsoft Windows maintains the fonts so the accessible fonts, sizes, and styles vary from system to system. A list of available fonts is shown when you choose the **T**ext menu **F**ont option. <expSTYLE> is Character expression that contains one or more style codes as shown in Table 9.4.

The *DEFINE PAD* Command

DEFINE MENU must be placed in a program to execute before any pads are defined. You define menu pads with the DEFINE PAD command. A DEFINE PAD command is required to define each menu pad. Here is the syntax:

```
DEFINE PAD <pad name1>
  OF <menu name> PROMPT <expC1>
  [AT <row>, <column>]
  [BEFORE <pad name2> ¦ AFTER <pad name3>]
  [NEGOTIATE LEFT ¦ NEGOTIATE MIDDLE ¦ NEGOTIATE RIGHT]
  [KEY <key label> [, <expC2>]]
  [SKIP [FOR <expL>]]
  [MESSAGE <expC4>]
  [FONT <expC5> [, <expN1>]]
     [STYLE <expSTYLE>]
  [COLOR <color pair list>
  ¦ COLOR SCHEME <expN2>
  ¦ COLOR RGB (<color value list>)]
```

Each pad is given a unique name, <pad name>, which is subsequently used to reference the menu pad. You must specify the OF clause also to designate the name of the menu bar to which the pad belongs. This is required because you can have more than one menu bar defined at one time.

The PROMPT expression contains the label for the PAD. The convention is to begin the first character of the label with an uppercase letter. You can designate a hotkey by placing a backslash and a left angle bracket (\<) in front of the character that you assign as the hotkey.

The optional `AT` clause defines the row and column screen or window position. If you omit the `AT` clause, the first pad begins at the first column of the top row of the screen or active window. By default, menu bars are horizontal. You can place menu pads for a menu bar anywhere you like by specifying the `AT` clause.

If you leave out the optional `BEFORE` and `AFTER` clauses, menu pads appear on the menu bar and are highlighted in the order in which the `DEFINE PAD` statements are executed. You can change this order by specifying the `BEFORE` and `AFTER` clauses. For example, if you specify the `AFTER <pad name2>` clause, `<pad name2>` is the name of the menu pad activated before the menu pad you're defining is activated; the `BEFORE` clause specifies the name of the menu pad activated after the menu pad you're defining is activated.

The optional `NEGOTIATE LEFT`, `NEGOTIATE MIDDLE`, and `NEGOTIATE RIGHT` keywords designate location in the Visual FoxPro systems menu bar when OLE visual editing occurs. The following is the location of the menu title for each keyword:

`NEGOTIATE LEFT`	Left of the file group
`NEGOTIATE MIDDLE`	Left of the container group after the Edit menu
`NEGOTIATE RIGHT`	Left of the window group

The `KEY <key label> [, <expC2>]` clause specifies a shortcut key for the menu pad or a pop-up menu bar. You press the shortcut key or key combination and the menu pad or pop-up bar executes. The shortcut key is specified with the `<key label>` field. The key label convention is the same one used with `ON KEY LABEL` command and keyboard macros as defined in Table 7.11. You must choose a key that does not conflict with a keyboard macro because keyboard macros have precedence. The `<key label>` displays at the right of the menu pad or selection bar. For example, if you specify `Quit` for a menu pad label and `Ctrl+X` for a shortcut key, the menu pad displays as follows:

```
Quit  Ctrl+X
```

You can specify the optional `<expC2>` Character expression to replace the `<key label>` text. For example, you can specify the `KEY CTRL+X, "^X"` clause and `^X` displays to the right of the menu pad label instead of `CTRL+X`. You can specify a null string (`""`) for `<expC2>` to eliminate the display of the shortcut key.

You can specify the `SKIP` clause with both the `DEFINE PAD` and `DEFINE BAR` commands. The `SKIP [FOR <expL>]` clause enables or disables a menu pad or a pop-up menu selection bar based on the specified Logical expression. If you specify the `SKIP` keyword without the `FOR` clause, the pad or bar is always disabled (or skipped). If the `SKIP FOR <expL>` clause is specified, FoxPro evaluates the Logical condition `<expL>` right before the cursor moves to the pop-up. If the results evaluate to a true (`.T.`) value, the pad or bar is enabled, and you can select it. If the results evaluate to a false (`.F.`) value, the pad or bar is disabled and cannot be selected. You can also place a backslash character in front of a pad or bar label. For example, `PROMPT "\Names:"` disables a pad or bar.

The following examples use the DEFINE MENU and DEFINE PAD commands:

```
DEFINE MENU Food
DEFINE PAD Breakfast OF Food PROMPT "Breakfast" AT 0,10 ;
MESSAGE "Tasty breakfast menu selections"
DEFINE PAD Lunch OF Food PROMPT "Lunch" AT 0,30 ;
MESSAGE "Savory lunch menu selections"
DEFINE PAD Dinner OF Food PROMPT "Dinner" AT 0,50 ;
MESSAGE "Luxurious dinner menu selections"
```

The *DEFINE POPUP* Command

You use the DEFINE POPUP command to create a pop-up menu. A pop-up menu contains a list of options. The various options are illustrated in Figure 7.9. As for the menu bar and its menu pads, you must DEFINE a pop-up menu before you can use it. When you display and activate the pop-up menu with the ACTIVATE POPUP command, you can choose an option from the list. When the option is chosen, a procedure can be executed or another pop-up can be activated. A pop-up that activates another pop-up or menu bar when you choose an option is called a *hierarchical pop-up*. You use the ON BAR command to create a hierarchical pop-up.

Here is the general DEFINE POPUP syntax:

```
DEFINE POPUP <popup name>
   [FROM <row1>, <col1>] [TO <row2>, <col2>]
   [IN [WINDOW] <window name> ¦ IN SCREEN]
   [FOOTER <expC1>]
   [KEY <key label>]
   [MARGIN]
   [MESSAGE <expC3>]
   [MOVER]
   [MULTISELECT]
   [PROMPT FIELD <expr>
   ¦ PROMPT FILES [LIKE <skeleton>]
   ¦ PROMPT STRUCTURE]
   [RELATIVE] [SCROLL] [SHADOW]
   [TITLE <expC4>]
   [FONT <expC5> [, <expN1>]]
      [STYLE <expSTYLE>]
   [COLOR SCHEME <expN2>
   ¦ COLOR  <color pair list>
   ¦ COLOR RGB (<color value list>)]
```

The IN, KEY, MESSAGE, and COLOR clauses serve the same purpose in both the DEFINE MENU and DEFINE POPUP commands.

The FROM clause defines the row and column of the upper-left corner of the pop-up. The TO clause defines the row and column of the lower-right corner of the pop-up window. If you omit the TO clause, FoxPro automatically computes the height and width based on the number of lines and the width of the longest line.

You can specify the optional FOOTER clause and the SHADOWS keyword, but Visual FoxPro ignores them because the Windows-style interface does not support these features.

If you specify the `MARGIN` keyword, extra space is added to the left and right of each pop-up option label. This option is necessary if you display check marks using the `SET MARK OF POPUP` command. The extra space on the left is needed to display the check mark. If you don't specify `MARGIN`, the check mark overwrites the first character of the option label. Furthermore, if you have an additional hierarchical pop-up object, an arrow displays to the right of the option label. You need an extra space at the right of the label for the arrow, or the arrow may overwrite the last character of the option label.

If you specify the `MOVER` keyword, you can rearrange the order of the pop-up options when the pop-up is activated. When the pop-up activates, push buttons display to the left of each option. To move an option with the mouse, click on one of these push buttons and a vertical double-headed arrow appears. Then you can drag the option up and down to a new position. From the keyboard, use the arrow keys to highlight the option you want to move. Then use the Ctrl+↑ and Ctrl+↓ key combinations to reposition the option. The `GETBAR()` function returns the bar number from a position in a pop-up. You can use this function to determine where each option is positioned in the list.

You can specify the `MULTISELECT` keyword to choose a mode in which multiple pop-up menu options can be selected. When you choose an option from a pop-up, a check mark character appears at the left of the option. You choose multiple options with the mouse by holding down the Shift key and clicking on multiple options. You can choose multiple options with the keyboard by holding down the Shift key and selecting the options by pressing the Spacebar or Enter. By default, the "check mark" character is a small diamond symbol (✦). You can use the `MRKBAR()` function to determine which options are selected. It returns a true (`.T.`) value if an action is selected. One final point—if you specify the `MULTISELECT` keyword, you will probably want to include the `MARGIN` option to keep the check mark from overwriting the first character of the option labels.

The `RELATIVE` keyword controls the order in which options are placed in a pop-up list when options are defined using the `DEFINE BAR` command. More information regarding this keyword is provided in the discussion of the `DEFINE BAR` command.

NOTE

You cannot rearrange options or do multiple selections in pop-up menus when the `PROMPT` clause is specified. In other words, if you specify the `PROMPT` clause, you cannot specify the `MULTISELECT`, `MOVER`, or `RELATIVE` keywords.

If you specify the `SCROLL` keyword, a scroll bar is attached to the right of a pop-up. The scroll bar displays only when the pop-up list is too large to fit in the pop-up.

You can use the optional `TITLE` *<expC4>* clause to specify a message that appears centered in the title bar.

The pop-up objects operate differently depending on the type of PROMPT clause or whether the PROMPT clause is omitted. Each of the four types is described in the following sections.

No *PROMPT* Clause

If you omit the PROMPT clause, you must define selection bars. Here is the syntax of the DEFINE BAR command:

```
DEFINE BAR <expN1> ¦ <System option name>
        OF <popup name> PROMPT <expC1>
        [BEFORE <expN2>
        ¦ AFTER <expN2>]
        [KEY <key label> [, <expC2>]]
        [MARK <expC3>]
        [MESSAGE <expC4>]
        [SKIP [FOR <expL>]]
        [FONT <expC5> [, <expN2>]] [STYLE <expSTYLE>]
        [COLOR <color pair list>
        ¦ COLOR SCHEME <expN3>
        ¦ COLOR RGB (<color value list>) ]
```

The KEY, MARK, and COLOR clauses serve the same purpose as they do for the DEFINE PAD command.

You must define the pop-up before you can define any bar objects. The *<expN1>* is an integer that represents the pop-up object line number. This number identifies the bar object. If a bar is not defined for a line in the pop-up, the line is left blank and cannot be selected.

If you use the SKIP keyword, FoxPro skips the bar object when you navigate with the ↑ and ↓ keys. If you specify the SKIP FOR *<condition>*, the bar is skipped if the results of the Logical expression are true. Skipped bar objects cannot be selected. You can also skip a bar by placing a backslash (\) character in front of the bar label.

It is sometimes useful to divide a pop-up menu into groups and separate each group with a separation bar. You can define a separating bar between two options by using a backslash and a dash (\-) in a PROMPT clause *<expC1>* Character expression. This enables you to group options together. For example, the following command:

```
DEFINE BAR 5 PROMPT '\-'
```

in a pop-up definition creates a separator between the fourth and sixth options.

You can define the pop-up shown in Figure 7.15 using the following commands:

```
CLEAR
DEFINE POPUP POP1 FROM 1,1
DEFINE BAR 1 OF POP1 PROMPT " \<Table"
DEFINE BAR 2 OF POP1 PROMPT " \<Program"
DEFINE BAR 3 OF POP1 PROMPT "\-"         && Separation bar
DEFINE BAR 4 OF POP1 PROMPT " \<Report"
DEFINE BAR 5 OF POP1 PROMPT " \<Label"
DEFINE BAR 6 OF POP1 PROMPT "\-"          && Separation bar
DEFINE BAR 7 OF POP1 PROMPT " \<Application"
```

The RELATIVE keyword controls the order in which options are placed in a pop-up list. If you create a pop-up without the RELATIVE clause, the options are positioned in a pop-up list in an order determined by the option's bar number. Space is reserved in the pop-up for options that have yet to be defined. For example, if you define the first and fourth items of pop-up named Pop as this:

```
DEFINE POPUP Pop FROM 1,1
DEFINE BAR 1 OF Pop PROMPT "One"
DEFINE BAR 4 OF Pop PROMPT "Four"
```

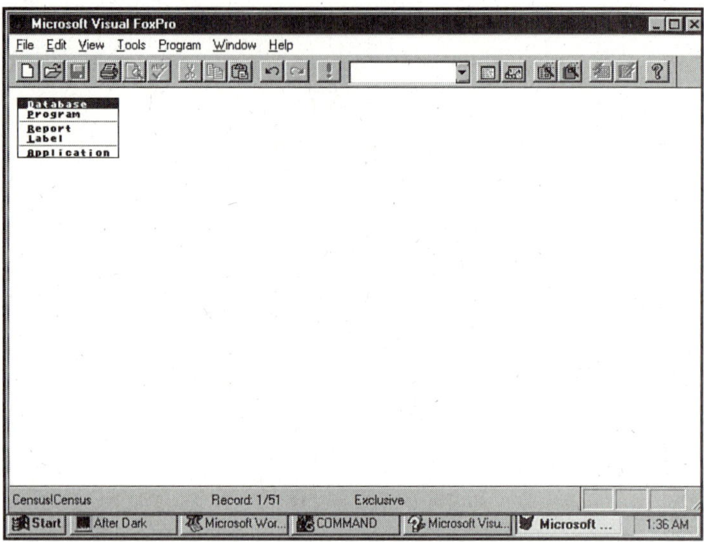

FIGURE 7.15.
An example of the DEFINE POPUP and DEFINE BAR commands.

When the pop-up activates, the second and third options in the list of four options are blank because the space is reserved for the second and third options in the pop-up. If you specify the RELATIVE keyword with the DEFINE POPUP command, options appear in the pop-up in the order they are defined, and space is not reserved for options that have yet to be defined. Here is an example:

Without RELATIVE	*With* RELATIVE
DEFINE POPUP Z FROM 1,1	DEFINE POPUP Z FROM 1,1 RELATIVE
DEFINE BAR 5 OF Z PROMPT "Five"	DEFINE BAR 5 OF Z PROMPT "Five"
DEFINE BAR 2 OF Z PROMPT "Two"	DEFINE BAR 2 OF Z PROMPT "Two"
DEFINE BAR 3 OF Z PROMPT "Three"	DEFINE BAR 3 OF Z PROMPT "Three"
DEFINE BAR 1 OF Z PROMPT "One"	DEFINE BAR 1 OF Z PROMPT "One"
Popup options will appear as:	Popup options will appear as:
One	Five
Two	Two
Three	Three
	One
Five	

If you specify the RELATIVE keyword with the DEFINE POPUP command, you can use the BEFORE and AFTER clauses in the DEFINE BAR command to place options in the pop-up relative to other options. In contrast, if you define a pop-up without the RELATIVE keyword and specify either the BEFORE or AFTER clause in a DEFINE BAR command, you will be confronted with a syntax error. The Numeric argument for the BEFORE clause (*<expN2>*) specifies the pop-up menu bar number.

The Directory Pop-up Object

The following form of the DEFINE POPUP command defines a file directory pop-up object. Here is its syntax:

```
DEFINE POPUP <popup name> PROMPT FILES [LIKE <skeleton>]
   [FROM <row1>, <col1>] [TO <row2>, <col2>]
   [IN [WINDOW] <window name> ¦ IN SCREEN]
   [KEY <key label>]
   [MARGIN]
   [MARK <expC2>]
   [MESSAGE <expC3>]
   [MOVER]
   [MULTISELECT]
   [RELATIVE]
   [SCROLL] [TITLE <expC4>]
   [FONT <expC4> [, <expN1>]] [STYLE <expSTYLE>]
   [COLOR SCHEME <expN2>
   ¦ COLOR  <color pair list>
   ¦ COLOR RGB (<color value list>)]
```

You can use the LIKE clause to restrict the types of files to choose from. The following example demonstrates how to define a directory pop-up that displays tables (DBF). This pop-up is similar to the pop-up in Figure 7.9:

```
DEFINE POPUP ShowFiles FROM 10,20 PROMPT FILES LIKE *.DBF
```

The Table Structure Pop-up Object

The next form of the DEFINE POPUP command defines a table field structure pop-up. Here is the syntax:

```
DEFINE POPUP <popup name> PROMPT STRUCTURE
...
```

The names of the fields in the table in the current work area are displayed in the pop-up window. The following example defines a table structure pop-up window similar to the one shown in Figure 7.9:

```
DEFINE POPUP STRU1 FROM 10,50 PROMPT STRUCTURE
```

The Field Value Pop-up Object

The last form of the DEFINE POPUP command defines table field value pop-up objects. Here is the syntax:

```
DEFINE POPUP <popup name> PROMPT FIELD <field expr>
...
```

The PROMPT clause defines the name of the field. The field's values are displayed in the pop-up window. You can specify all type fields. However, it does make sense to include Memo and General type fields because only an icon (Memo and Gen) appears for each option. You can specify an alias name with the field name. The table containing the data doesn't have to be the one currently in use because when the pop-up is activated, the proper work area is selected. In addition, the *<Field exp>* expression can be a field, or it can contain multiple field names and expressions concatenated with the addition (+) operator. The *<Field exp>* expression can be a user-defined function (UDF).

If you don't specify the TO clause, the width is either the width of the field or the width of the window or screen, whichever is smaller. Rushmore optimization is used if you set a filter on the PROMPT field used in the pop-up.

You can have a maximum number of 32767 options in a pop-up created with the PROMPT FIELD clause. If the table has more records than this, an alert—Pop-up too big, first *nnnnn* entries shown—is displayed. From a practical point of view, however, if you include more than 200 records, performance may be substantially degraded.

An example of a pop-up defined with the PROMPT FIELD clause is shown in Figure 7.9. Here is the command used to define this pop-up:

```
DEFINE POPUP Flds FROM 10,70 PROMPT FIELDS State
```

ON Command Events

After you've defined the menu objects, you need to specify what happens when a menu object is selected. Several things can happen. For example, a FoxPro command can be executed or another menu can be drawn. To set up the linkage between a menu selection and an action, you specify the ON SELECTION command. You can link the pad of a menu bar to a pop-up menu or another menu bar using the ON PAD command. This way, when a menu pad is highlighted (or chosen if the BAR keyword is specified with DEFINE MENU command) a pop-up menu or another menu bar displays and is activated.

The *ON SELECTION* Command

The ON SELECTION command specifies a FoxPro command that is executed when a menu pad or pop-up option is chosen. Here is its syntax:

```
ON SELECTION BAR <expN> OF <popup name> [<command>]
ON SELECTION MENU <menu name> ¦ ALL [<command>]
ON SELECTION PAD <pad name> OF <menu name> [<command>]
ON SELECTION POPUP <popup name> ¦ ALL [BLANK] [<command>]
ON EXIT BAR <expN> OF <expC> [<command>]
ON EXIT POPUP <expC1> [<command>]
```

If you supply the `ALL` keyword instead of a pop-up or menu name, the supplied *<command>* is executed when any bar of any defined pop-up or pad of any menu object is chosen.

Normally, the `DO` command is used with the `ON SELECTION` command to execute a procedure when a pad or pop-up bar object is selected.

The `ON SELECTION BAR` command has precedence over any `ON SELECTION POPUP` commands. In the following example, when the first option in `MyPopup` is chosen, the `OneBar` procedure executes. For the second and third options in the pop-up chosen, function `AllBars` executes. Here is the example:

```
DEFINE POPUP MyPopup FROM 10,10
DEFINE BAR 1 OF MyPopup PROMPT "Apples"
DEFINE BAR 2 OF MyPopup PROMPT "Oranges"
DEFINE BAR 3 OF MyPopup PROMPT "Bananas"
ON SELECTION BAR 1 OF MyPopup Do OneBar
ON SELECTION POPUP MyPopup DO AllBars
```

Likewise, the `ON SELECTION PAD` command has priority over the `ON SELECTION MENU` command.

If you specify any form of the `ON SELECTION` command without the *<command>* clause, the previously specified *<command>* clause is deactivated for the specified menu object. In the previous example, to release the `ON SELECTION` action for the first option of `MyPopup`, you must specify the following statement:

```
ON SELECTION BAR 1 OF MyPopup
```

Then the `AllBars` procedure executes for all three options.

The `BLANK` keyword was added to the `ON SELECTION POPUP` command in FoxPro 2.6 to acquire compatibility with dBASE IV. When you specify the `BLANK` keyword, the pop-up is hidden while *<command>* executes. In other words, the pop-up disappears before *<command>* executes and reappears after *<command>* is executed. This command is equivalent to using the `HIDE POPUP` and `ACTIVATE POPUP` commands to provide equivalent functionality.

The only problem with the `BLANK` keyword is that it does not work. The keyword is simply ignored in Visual FoxPro. This becomes a compatibility issue. To make a pop-up disappear, you have to add the `HIDE` and `ACTIVATE` commands to your dBASE IV code before the pop-up menu will work the same as it did running under dBASE IV.

The *ON PAD* Command

In menu systems, it is customary to have both a pad and a pop-up object active at the same time. The ON PAD command is provided to support this function. Here is the syntax:

```
ON PAD <pad name> of <menu name1>
  ACTIVATE POPUP <popup name>
  | ACTIVATE MENU <menu name2>
ON PAD <expC1> OF <expC2> [<command>]
```

When the current pad of the specified menu is chosen, the specified pop-up or menu bar object activates. If you specify the BAR keyword with the DEFINE MENU command, the menu bar navigation is altered to operate like the Visual FoxPro system menu bar and the Windows interface. If you don't specify the BAR keyword, the menu bar navigation works like it does with the FoxPro 2.0 interface. For example, if BAR is not specified, the ON PAD command activates the pop-up *<popup name>* or menu bar *<menu name2>* when you use the arrow keys to move the highlight to the specific menu pad. If BAR is specified, the associated menu object activates after you use the arrow keys to move the highlight to the specified menu bar and choose the pad by pressing Enter.

In FoxPro 2.5, the ON PAD command specifies a menu bar or pop-up menu that activates when you choose a pad (*<expC1>*) from a specified menu bar (*<expC2>*). It was designed to allow a pop-up menu or another menu bar to activate when a menu bar pad is highlighted. However, in Visual FoxPro, the ON PAD command allows any command (*<command>*) to be executed by the ON PAD command. *<command>* executes when you position the cursor to the designated pad (*<expC1>*) for the designated menu bar (*<expC2>*).

When the Plants pad object is highlighted (active), the pop-up P_Plants is activated in the following example:

```
ON PAD Plants OF Things ACTIVATE POPUP P_Plants
```

Use the ↑ and ↓ keys to navigate through the pop-up selection bars and the ← and → keys to navigate through the pad objects.

Likewise, when the Animals menu pad is highlighted (active), the menu bar named M_Animals is activated in the following example:

```
ON PAD Animal OF Things ACTIVATE MENU M_Animals
```

After menu bar M_Animals activates, you can move between its menu pads using the arrow keys.

The *ON BAR* Command

When you choose an option from a pop-up, some action occurs. If an ON SELECTION command exists for the pop-up or the option, a command executes. If the ON BAR command was issued for a pop-up menu option, a hierarchical pop-up or a menu bar displays and is activated. An arrow is placed to the right of a pop-up option that has an associated ON BAR assignment. The arrow indicates that an additional pop-up or menu bar is available for the option. The arrow is called a *hierarchical arrow* because it indicates that a hierarchical menu is available for the option.

When you define a pop-up menu that has a hierarchical pop-up or menu bar, you should specify the MARGIN keyword, so that the hierarchical arrow doesn't overwrite the rightmost character of the option. Here is the syntax of the ON BAR command:

```
ON BAR <expN1> of <popup name1>
        [ACTIVATE POPUP <popup name2> ¦
         ACTIVATE MENU <menu name>]
ON BAR <expN> OF <expC> [<command>]
```

When you choose the pop-up menu *<popup name1>* option identified by the number *<expN1>*, either the pop-up menu *<popup name2>* or the menu bar *<menu name>* displays and becomes active. If you choose the second option of pop-up Things, the Animals pop-up menu displays and activates in the following example:

```
ON BAR 2 OF Things ACTIVATE POPUP Animals
```

In FoxPro 2.5, the ON BAR command specifies a menu bar or pop-up menu that is activated when you choose an option (*<expN>*) from a pop-up menu (*<expC>*). It was designed to allow one pop-up menu to activate another pop-up menu. However, in FoxPro 2.6 and later versions, you can specify any command (*<command>*) to be executed by the ON BAR command. If you specify a command other than the ACTIVATE command, *<command>* is executed when you position the cursor on the designated bar (*<expN>*) for the designated pop-up menu (*<expC>*). To reiterate, if *<command>* is ACTIVATE POPUP or ACTIVATE MENU, you must select the designated pop-up menu bar before the menu pop-up or menu activates.

The example presented in Listing 7.5 illustrates how to use the ON BAR and ON EXIT BAR commands. Pop-up menu x has three options. If you position the cursor on the first option, the MODIFY FILE Notes.txt command executes. Then when you position the cursor on another pop-up menu bar, the ON EXIT BAR 1 command executes a command that deactivates the NOTES.TXT window. The third pop-up menu bar operates differently from the first two options. You have to select the third option before pop-up menu y activates.

Listing 7.5. The source listing for the DROPDOWN.PRG program.

```
*************************************************
* PROGRAM: DROPDOWN.PRG - Demonstrates: ON BAR
*                                       ON EXIT BAR
*
DEFINE POPUP x
DEFINE BAR 1 OF x PROMPT "\<Edit Notes"
DEFINE BAR 2 OF x PROMPT "\<Greeting"
DEFINE BAR 3 OF x PROMPT "\<Files"
ON BAR 1 OF x MODIFY FILE NOTES.TXT NOWAIT
ON BAR 3 OF x ACTIVATE popup y
ON BAR 2 OF x DO Greet
ON EXIT BAR 1 OF x DEACTIVATE WINDOW "NOTES.TXT"
ON EXIT BAR 2 OF x DEACTIVATE WINDOW J
DEFINE POPUP y FROM 3,12 PROMPT FILES
ACTIVATE POPUP x
```

continues

Listing 7.5. continued

```
CLEAR ALL
************************************************
* Procedure Greet - Executed by ON BAR 2
PROCEDURE Greet
DEFINE WINDOW J FROM 0,0 TO 4,30 PANEL
MOVE WINDOW J CENTER
ACTIVATE WINDOW J
@ 1,8 SAY "Good Morning"
RETURN
```

Figure 7.16 is the sample output screen resulting from the execution of the DROPDOWN.PRG program.

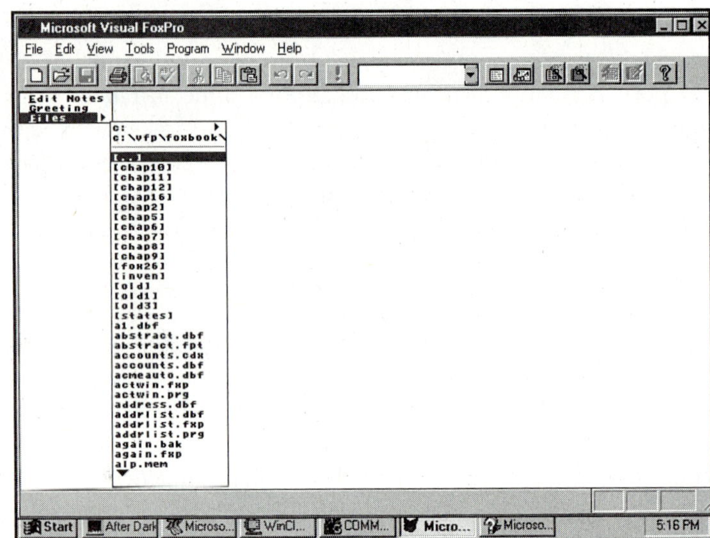

FIGURE 7.16.
The sample output screen resulting from the execution of the DROPDOWN.PRG program.

The *ON MENU* Command

The ON MENU command specifies a command (<*command*>) that executes when you move the cursor to any of the pads in the designated menu bar (<*expC*>) for which there is no ON PAD command(s) assigned.

If you execute the ON PAD or ON MENU commands and omit the <*command*> clause, any previously established <*command*> is disabled. Here is the syntax:

```
ON MENU <expC> [<command>]
```

The *ON POPUP* Command

The ON POPUP command is used to specify a command (*<command>*) that executes when you move the cursor to any bar in the designated pop-up menu (*<expC>*) for which there is not an ON BAR command assigned.

If you execute the ON BAR or ON POPUP command and omit the *<command>* clause, any previously established *<command>* is disabled. Here is the syntax:

```
ON POPUP <expC> [<command>]
```

The *ON EXIT BAR* and *ON EXIT POPUP* Commands

The ON EXIT BAR command executes the specified *<command>* whenever the user moves the cursor off the specified bar (*<expN>*) in the specified pop-up menu (*<expC>*). The ON EXIT POPUP command is used to specify a command (*<command>*) that executes when you move the cursor off any bars in the designated pop-up menu (*<expC>*) for which there is not an ON EXIT BAR command assigned associated with a bar in the pop-up menu *<expC>*.

You can move the cursor off a bar using any of the following methods:

- Press the up or down arrow key
- Press the hotkey of another bar
- Click or double-click another bar
- Drag the mouse cursor from the designated bar
- Deactivate the current pop-up menu

If you execute the ON EXIT BAR or ON EXIT POPUP command and omit the *<command>* clause, any previously established *<command>* is disabled. Here is the syntax:

```
ON EXIT BAR <expN> OF <expC> [<command>]
ON EXIT POPUP <expC1> [<command>]
```

Listing 7.5 presents a program that illustrates the usage of the ON EXIT BAR command.

The *ACTIVATE* and *DEACTIVATE* Commands

After you've defined all the objects and established the actions, it's time to activate a menu bar. This is done with the ACTIVATE MENU command. Here is its syntax:

```
ACTIVATE MENU <menu name> [PAD <pad name>] [NOWAIT]
```

This command activates a menu object. The pad objects are displayed. If you specify the *<pad name>* clause, that pad becomes the current pad and is highlighted. Otherwise, the first pad object defined for the menu becomes the current pad. If you specify the optional NOWAIT keyword, the menu bar displays, activates, and continues execution with the command following the ACTIVATE command.

The menu remains active until you press Esc, activate another menu object, or execute the `DEACTIVATE MENU` command. When a menu is deactivated, it is erased from the screen, and the original text covered by the menu objects is restored. When a menu is deactivated, all descendent pop-up and menu objects are also deactivated.

When an object is selected, a procedure is executed. The `DEACTIVATE` command can be in that procedure. When the `DEACTIVATE` command is executed, the procedure exits and returns control to the command following the `ACTIVATE` command. Here is the syntax:

```
ACTIVATE POPUP <popup name> [AT <row>,<column>] [NOWAIT] [REST]
     [BAR <expN>]
DEACTIVATE POPUP <popup name>
```

The first command activates pop-up objects and displays the pop-up on the screen. When activated, the first selection bar object is highlighted. You use the ↑ and ↓ keys to navigate. The ←, →, and Esc keys and the `DEACTIVATE POPUP` command deactivate the pop-up.

If you specify the optional `NOWAIT` keyword, the pop-up displays, activates, and continues execution with the command following the `ACTIVATE` command. You can use the `BAR` clause to specify the number *<expN>* of the bar to initially highlight when the pop-up activates.

When you define a pop-up menu with the `PROMPT FIELD` clause, you can specify the optional `REST` keyword with the `ACTIVATE` command to initially highlight the option in the pop-up that corresponds to the current record.

When the action of one pop-up causes another pop-up to be activated, the parent pop-up object is suspended. When the descendent pop-up is deactivated, the parent pop-up object is reactivated.

The following simple example illustrates how to activate a file directory pop-up:

```
DEFINE POPUP Filer FROM 10,10 PROMPT FILE
   ON SELECTION POPUP Filer WAIT WINDOW PROMPT()
   ACTIVATE POPUP Filer
```

The directory pop-up named `Filer` is defined. The `ON SELECTION POPUP` command designates what happens if you select a pop-up option. Specifically, a wait box displays containing the file selected. Incidentally, the pop-up contains a list of all filenames in the current directory. When you choose a filename, the `PROMPT()` function returns the fully qualified filename.

Menu System Functions

In the procedures associated with the `ON SELECTION` commands, several functions return parameters associated with the menu and pop-up objects. User-defined menu and pop-up functions are presented in Table 7.12.

Table 7.12. User-defined menu functions.

Function	*Usage*	*Type*
BAR()	Returns the pop-up selection bar number.	N
BARCOUNT([<expC>])	Returns the number of bars in an active or specified (<expC>) pop-up.	N
BARPROMPT(<expN> [, <expC>])	Returns the text that appears on the specified (<expC>) pop-up.	C
CNTBAR(<expC>)	Returns the number of bars in a pop-up. <expC> is the pop-up name.	N
CNTPAD(<expC>)	Returns the number of pads in a menu. <expC> is the pop-up name.	N
GETBAR(<expC>,<expN>)	Returns the number of bars in the specified pop-up. <expC> is the pop-up name. <expN> is the position of the bar in the pop-up, starting from the top. When bars are rearranged (the MOVER keyword is specified), the bar number can differ from the option number returned by the BAR() function.	N
GETPAD(<expC>,<expN>)	Returns the position (<expN>) for a given menu name and pad position in the specified menu bar (<expC>).	C
MENU()	Returns the active menu bar name or a null string if none is active.	C
MRKBAR(<expC>,<expN>)	Returns .T. if the pop-up bar is marked. <expC> is the pop-up name. <expN> is the named pop-up option number.	L
MRKPAD(<expC1>,<expC2>)	Returns .T. if the specified menu pad <expC2> of menu bar <expC1> is marked (with SET MARK OF).	L
PAD()	Returns the active menu pad name as an uppercase string.	C
PADPROMPT(<expN> [, <expC>])	Returns the text that appears on the specified (<expC>) menu pad.	C

continues

Table 7.12. continued

Function	*Usage*	*Type*
POPUP()	Returns the active pop-up name.	C
PRMBAR(<expC>,<expN>)	Returns the prompt text of the pop-up option. <expC> is the pop-up name. <expN> is the named pop-up option number.	C
PRMPAD(<expC1>,<expC2>)	Returns the prompt text of menu pad <expC2> of menu bar <expC1>.	C
PROMPT()	Returns the label of the most recently selected pop-up or menu bar.	C
SKPBAR(<expC>,<expN>)	Returns .T. if the pop-up option (BAR) is enabled; .F. if the pop-up option is disabled. <expC> is the name of the pop-up. <expN> is the option number.	L
SKPPAD(<expC1>,<expC2N>)	Returns .T. if the menu pad is enabled; .F. if menu pad is disabled. <expC1> is the name of the menu bar. <expC2> is the name of the menu pad.	L
SYS(2013)	Returns the space delimited character string, which contains the names of the system menu bar, pads, pop-ups, and pop-up options.	C

The BAR() function returns the integer BAR number of the last selected bar object from the last selected pop-up bar. It returns 0 if no pop-up objects are defined, or if you press the Esc, ←, or → key to deactivate a pop-up.

The MENU(), PAD(), and POPUP() functions return character strings that consist of the name of the most recently selected menu, pad, or pop-up object, respectively. If no menu objects are active, the MENU() and PAD() functions return a null string. Similarly, if no pop-up objects are active, the POPUP() function returns a null string.

The BARCOUNT([<expC>]) function returns the number of bars in an active or specified (<expC>) pop-up. This function is most often used to retrieve the number of elements in a pop-up menu with either the PROMPT FIELD, PROMPT FILES, or PROMPT STRUCTURE clauses specified.

You can retrieve the text that appears on a pop-up menu bar with the BARPROMPT(<*expN*> [, <*expC*>]) function. You specify the bar number (<*expN*>). If the pop-up is defined and active, you do not have to specify the optional pop-up menu name (<*expC*>). However, if you want to retrieve the pop-up menu bar text for a pop-up that is defined but not active, you must specify the pop-up name. The following example displays the text associated with the 28th bar in a pop-up menu named Cities.

```
DEFINE POPUP Cities PROMPT FIELD City
? BARPROMPT( 28, "Cities" )
ON SELECTION POPUP CITIES ? BARPROMPTS(28)
ACTIVATE POPUP CITIES
```

You can retrieve the text that appears on a menu bar pad with the PADPROMPT(<*expC1*> [, <*expC2*>]) function. You specify the pad name (<*expC1*>). If the menu bar is defined and active, you do not have to specify the optional menu bar name (<*expC*>). However, if you want to retrieve the text of a menu bar pad for a menu that is defined but not active, you must specify the menu bar name. The following example displays the text associated with the menu pad named Pad4 for the menu bar named MyMenu:

```
? PADPROMPT( "PAD4", "MyMenu" )
```

PROMPT() returns a character string that consists of the pad or bar object label that was last selected. PROMPT() returns the values shown in Table 7.13.

Table 7.13. The returned value type for objects.

Object Type	*Returned Value*
Pad objects	PROMPT clause label
Pop-up objects	
No PROMPT clause	DEFINE BAR PROMPT label
Directory	Fully qualified filename
Table structure	Field name
Field value	Table field contents

The CNTBAR(<*expC*>) function is useful for determining how many options are in the named pop-up <*expC*>. The PRMBAR(<*expC*>, <*expN*>) returns the prompt label for the <*expN*> option in pop-up <*expC*>. The MRKBAR(<*expC*>,<*expN*>) function is useful for determining whether a bar (<*expN*>) in pop-up <*expC*> is marked. You can mark or unmark a pop-up bar using the SET MARK OF BAR command.

When pop-up menu bars are rearranged in a pop-up menu, the `GETBAR(<expC>,<expN>)` function is useful for returning the bar number given the name of the pop-up and the position of the bar in the pop-up menu. The POPDEMO.PRG program, shown in Listing 7.6, illustrates the use of all these functions. The program creates a pop-up menu that can be rearranged. You can press F3 to retrieve and display the pop-up options in their new order. POPDEMO.PRG also demonstrates how to retrieve the check mark status.

Listing 7.6. The source listing for the POPDEMO.PRG program.

```
************************************************************
*     * 10/22/92             POPDEMO.PRG           18:12:10 *
************************************************************
*     *                                                    *
*     * Description:                                       *
*     *  Illustrates use of CNTBAR() PRMBAR(), BAR(), and    *
*     *  GETBAR(), MRKBAR() functions and SET MARK OF command*
*     *                                                    *
************************************************************
CLEAR
*
**** The first order of business is to define the popup.
*     The MOVER keyword specifies that popup can be rearranged.
*
DEFINE POPUP  pop1 FROM 10,1 MARGIN MOVER
DEFINE BAR 1 OF pop1 PROMPT "Mary Jones   "
DEFINE BAR 2 OF pop1 PROMPT "Tom Smith    "
DEFINE BAR 3 OF pop1 PROMPT "John Doer    "
DEFINE BAR 4 OF pop1 PROMPT "Sam Lazy     "
DEFINE BAR 5 OF pop1 PROMPT "Alvin Simmons"
DEFINE BAR 6 OF pop1 PROMPT "Jane Jeane   "
DEFINE BAR 7 OF pop1 PROMPT "Joe Heart    "
*
*** Now designate that F3 key executes showpop1 procedure
*
ON KEY LABEL f3 DO showpop1
*
*** Establish action: Choose any option and procedure
*** togmark is called to toggle check mark
*
ON SELECTION POPUP pop1 DO togmark
*
*** Now, it is time to activate the popup!
*
ACTIVATE POPUP pop1
**************************************************************
* ShowPop1 - Displays table of options for popup pop1
*
PROCEDURE showpop1
COUNT = CNTBAR("Pop1")
@ 30,10 SAY "Order of popup Pop1 options"
FOR i = 1 TO COUNT
@ 30+i,10 SAY STR(i) + IIF(MRKBAR("Pop1", GETBAR("Pop1",i)), ;
" <Marked> ", "          ") ;
+ PRMBAR("PoP1", GETBAR("Pop1",i));
+ STR(GETBAR("Pop1",i))
```

```
ENDFOR
RETURN
*****************************************************************
* Procedure TogMark     - Toggle check mark
PROCEDURE togmark
SET MARK OF BAR BAR() OF pop1 TO NOT MRKBAR("Pop1", BAR() )
DO showpop1
RETURN
```

Figure 7.17 shows a sample output screen resulting from the execution of POPDEMO.PRG. Notice that the options in the pop-up are rearranged and the bar number differs from the position number.

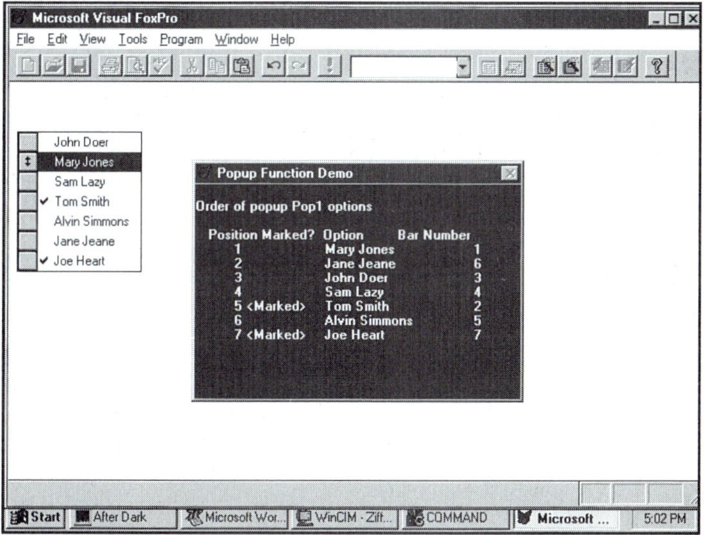

FIGURE 7.17.
An example of the functions that support DEFINE POPUP *and* DEFINE BAR *commands.*

The GETPAD(<expC>,<expN>) function returns the pad name in the specified menu bar and the specified position on the menu bar. The MRKPAD(<expC1>,<expC2>) function indicates if the specified menu pad (<expC2>) in the specified menu bar (<expC1>) has a check mark. The PRMPAD (<expC1>,<expC2>) function returns the prompt label for the specified pad. The CNTBAR(<expC>) function is useful for determining how many menu pads are in the named menu bar (<expC>). The following example illustrates how to use the CNTBAR(), GETPAD(), and PRMPAD() functions to search for the Text menu on the system menu bar:

```
FOR padno = 1 TO CNTPAD('_msysmenu')  && Number of pads
     IF PRMPAD('_msysmenu', GETPAD('_msysmenu', padno)) = 'Text'
          ?  (GETPAD('_msysmenu', padno)) ,padno
          EXIT
     ENDIF
ENDFOR
```

The program compares the pad text for each pad in the FoxPro system menu bar with the character string `"Text"` until a match is found. Then it displays the pad name and pad number:

```
_MSM_TEXT    6
```

The menu object names for the system menu bar are discussed in this chapter in the section "The System Menu Bar." You can also use the `SYS(2013)` function to return a character string containing all of the system menu bar object names. For example, the statement

```
? SYS(2013)
```

outputs the following:

```
_MFIRST _MLAST _MSYSMENU _MSM_SYSTM _MSM_FILE
_MSM_EDIT _MSM_DATA _MSM_RECRD _MSM_PROG
_MSM_WINDO _MSM_VIEW _MSM_TOOLS _MSM_FORMAT
_MSYSTEM _MST_OFFICE _MST_HELP _MST_HPSCH
_MST_HPHOW _MST_MACRO _MST_SP100 _MST_FILER
_MST_CALCU _MST_DIARY _MST_SPECL _MST_ASCII
_MST_CAPTR _MST_PUZZL _MST_SP200 _MST_DBASE
_MST_SP300 _MST_TECHS _MST_ABOUT _MFILE _MFI_NEW
_MFI_OPEN _MFI_CLOSE _MFI_CLALL _MFI_SP100
_MFI_SAVE _MFI_SAVAS _MFI_REVRT _MFI_SP200
_MFI_SETUP _MFI_PRINT _MFI_SP300 _MFI_QUIT
_MFI_PREVU _MFI_PGSET _MFI_IMPORT _MFI_EXPORT
_MFI_SP400 _MFI_SEND _MEDIT _MED_UNDO _MED_REDO
_MED_SP100 _MED_CUT _MED_COPY _MED_PASTE
_MED_PSTLK _MED_CLEAR _MED_SP200 _MED_INSOB
_MED_OBJ _MED_LINK _MED_CVTST _MED_SP300
_MED_SLCTA _MED_SP400 _MED_GOTO _MED_FIND
_MED_FINDA _MED_REPL _MED_REPLA _MED_SP500
_MED_PREF _MDATA _MDA_SETUP _MDA_BROW _MDA_SP100
_MDA_APPND _MDA_COPY _MDA_SORT _MDA_TOTAL
_MDA_SP200 _MDA_AVG _MDA_COUNT _MDA_SUM _MDA_CALC
_MDA_REPRT _MDA_LABEL _MDA_SP300 _MDA_PACK
_MDA_RINDX _MRECORD _MRC_APPND _MRC_CHNGE
_MRC_SP100 _MRC_GOTO _MRC_LOCAT _MRC_CONT
_MRC_SEEK _MRC_SP200 _MRC_REPL _MRC_DELET
_MRC_RECAL _MPROG _MPR_DO _MPR_SP100 _MPR_CANCL
_MPR_RESUM _MPR_SP200 _MPR_COMPL _MPR_GENER
_MPR_SP300 _MPR_BEAUT _MPR_DOCUM _MPR_GRAPH
_MPR_SUSPEND _MWINDOW _MWI_ARRAN _MWI_HIDE
_MWI_HIDEA _MWI_SHOWA _MWI_CLEAR _MWI_SP100
_MWI_MOVE _MWI_SIZE _MWI_ZOOM _MWI_MIN _MWI_ROTAT
_MWI_COLOR _MWI_SP200 _MWI_CMD _MWI_DEBUG
_MWI_TRACE _MWI_VIEW _MVI_TOOLB _MVIEW _MVI_TOOLB
_MTOOLS _MTL_SPELL _MTL_WZRDS _MTL_SP100
_MTL_SP200 _MTL_SP300 _MTL_OPTNS _MREPORT _MLABEL
_MBROWSE _MBR_MODE _MBR_GRID _MBR_LINK _MBR_CPART
_MBR_SP100 _MBR_FONT _MBR_SZFLD _MBR_MVFLD
_MBR_MVPRT _MBR_SP200 _MBR_GOTO _MBR_SEEK
_MBR_DELET _MBR_APPND _MMACRO _MDIARY _MFILER
_MSCREEN _MMBLDR _MMB_GOPTS _MMB_MOPTS _MMB_SP100
_MMB_PREVU _MMB_SP200 _MMB_INSRT _MMB_DELET
_MMB_SP300 _MMB_QUICK _MMB_GENER _MPROJ _MRQBE
```

```
_MSM_TEXT _MWIZARDS _MWZ_TABLE _MWZ_QUERY
_MWZ_FORM _MWZ_REPRT _MWZ_LABEL _MWZ_MAIL
_MWZ_PIVOT _MWZ_IMPORT _MWZ_FOXDOC _MWZ_ALL
_MTABLE _MTB_PROPS _MTB_SP100 _MTB_GOTO _MTB_APPND
_MTB_DELRC _MTB_SP200 _MTB_DELET _MTB_RECAL
_MTB_SZFLD _MTB_MVFLD _MTB_MVPRT _MTB_SP300
_MTB_LINK _MTB_CPART _MTB_SP400
```

The FILESHOW.PRG program, shown in Listing 7.7, demonstrates the use of the `ON POPUP` command and the `BLANK` option of the `ON SELECTION POPUP` command.

Listing 7.7. The source listing for the FILESHOW.PRG program.

```
*************************************************
* Program: fileshow.prg - demonstrates ON BAR
*
SET COMPATIBLE TO DB4
DEFINE WINDOW fw FROM 0,0 TO 8,40 PANEL TITLE "Files"
ACTIVATE WINDOW fw
MOVE WINDOW fw CENTER
ACTIVATE SCREEN
DEFINE POPUP files PROMPT FILES LIKE *.* ;
     FROM 0,0 TO 30,20
ON POPUP files DO ShowIt WITH PROMPT()
ON SELECTION POPUP files BLANK DO ShowSele WITH PROMPT()
ACTIVATE POPUP files
CLEAR ALL
RETURN
PROCEDURE ShowIt
PARAMETER fn
ACTIVATE WINDOW fw
CLEAR
IF "["$fn
     @ 4,5 SAY "Directory: "+fn
ELSE
     @ 1,5 SAY "Filename: "+fn
     @ 2,5 SAY "    Size: "+STR(FSIZE(fn))
     @ 3,5 SAY "    Date: "+DTOC(FDATE(fn))
     @ 4,5 SAY "    Time: "+FTIME(fn)
ENDIF
@ 6,5 SAY "Directory contains "+ ;
ALLTRIM(STR(BARCOUNT("files"))) + ;
     " entries"
RETURN
PROCEDURE ShowSele
PARAMETER fn
ACTIVATE WINDOW Fw
CLEAR
@ 4,1 SAY "Selected File: "+fn
WAIT WINDOW "Select more files? (Y/N): " TO Answer
IF UPPER(Answer) = "N"
     DEACTIVATE WINDOW fw
     DEACTIVATE POPUP  files
ENDIF
RETURN
```

Figure 7.18 shows a sample output screen resulting from the execution of the FILESHOW.PRG program.

FIGURE 7.18.
A sample output screen resulting from the execution of the FILESHOW.PRG program.

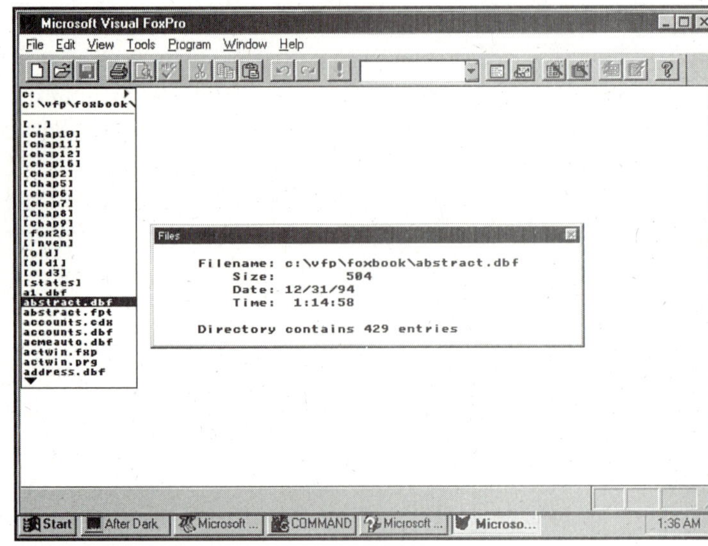

The *SHOW* Command

You can display defined menu and pop-up objects simply by using the `SHOW` command. Here is the syntax:

```
SHOW MENU <menu name list> ¦ ALL [PAD <pad name>] [SAVE]
SHOW POPUP <popup name list> ¦ ALL [SAVE]
```

You can use the `SHOW` command to display one or more objects on the screen even though the object is not activated. One occasion for doing this is if all available options must be visible. One way to have several pop-up objects displayed at the same time is to use the `SHOW POPUP` command.

The `ALL` keyword causes all menus or pop-ups to display. If you specify the `SAVE` command, the images of the pop-up remain on the screen, and you must use the `CLEAR` command to erase them.

The *HIDE* Command

The `HIDE` command enables you to hide defined and activated menus and pop-up objects. Here is the syntax:

```
HIDE MENU <menu name list> ¦ ALL [SAVE]
HIDE POPUP <popup name list> ¦ ALL [SAVE]
```

The HIDE command removes one or more menu bars or pop-ups from the screen. It is often useful to cause a menu bar or pop-up to disappear while the action procedure (which is invoked when you choose a menu pad or pop-up menu option) executes. When the action procedure exits, the pop-up reactivates. You can also make the pop-up reappear with the SHOW MENU and SHOW POPUP commands. In the following example, when you choose a file from the Pop1 pop-up, the procedure Action executes. The pop-up disappears as soon as the HIDE command executes in procedure Action:

```
DEFINE WINDOW FEdit FROM 10,30 TO 40,90
DEFINE POPUP Pop1 FROM 10,10 PROMPT FILES LIKE *.TXT ;
MESSAGE "Choose a file to view and edit"
ON SELECTION POPUP Pop1 DO Action
ACTIVATE POPUP Pop1
PROCEDURE Action
HIDE POPUP Pop1
MODIFY FILE PROMPT() WINDOW FEdit
RETURN
```

When Action returns, the Pop1 pop-up reappears, and you can choose another file. Press Esc to exit from the pop-up.

The ALL keyword designates that all menu bars or pop-ups are hidden. If you specify the SAVE command, the images of the pop-up remain on the screen, and you must use the CLEAR command to erase them.

The *PUSH* and *POP* Commands for Menus and Pop-ups

You can save a menu bar definition on a stack with the PUSH MENU command. (In computer terminology, a *stack* is a last-in, first-out buffer type used to store information. The verb *push* means to place an item on a stack, and the verb *pop* means to retrieve the most recently pushed item from the *stack.* After you push a menu bar definition on the stack, you can establish a new menu bar definition. Later on, you can restore the menu you saved on the stack with the POP MENU command. In fact, you can place multiple menu bar definitions on the menu stack with the PUSH MENU command. Then you can restore the previously saved menu bar definitions you placed on the stack with the POP MENU command. Here is the syntax for these two commands:

```
PUSH MENU <menu bar name>
POP MENU <menu bar name> [TO MASTER]
```

<menu bar name> is the name of the menu. The menu bar can be either a user-defined menu bar or the Visual FoxPro system menu bar. If you want to return the first menu bar definition you saved on the stack, you can specify the TO MASTER clause.

For example, you can push the Visual FoxPro system menu bar on the stack and modify it to display just the File menu. Later on, when you want to restore the original system menu bar, you can use the POP MENU command. Here are the commands to do this:

```
PUSH MENU _MSYSMENU          && Save the Visual FoxPro system menu
SET SYSMENU TO _MFILE        && Establish a new menu
...
POP MENU _MSYSMENU           && Restore the system menu
```

In a similar manner, you can save a menu definition on the stack with the PUSH POPUP command. You can modify the menu anyway you like and, later on, restore the menu definition with the POP POPUP command. Here is the syntax:

```
PUSH POPUP <popup name>
POP POPUP <popup name>
```

In the example shown in Listing 7.8, two copies of a menu are placed on the stack. A menu named MyPopup is defined and activated. The two PUSH commands push the menu definition to the stack twice. Next, the menu is modified. Then a POP command executes to pop the original menu off of the stack. A new menu bar is added. Finally the second copy of the original menu is restored by popping it off of the stack.

Listing 7.8. The source listing for the MENUDEMO.PRG program.

```
**********************************************
*  Procedure: PUSHPOP.PRG
*  Description: Illustrates PUSH POPUP and POP
*               POPUP commands
CLEAR
DEFINE POPUP MyPopup FROM 10,10
DEFINE BAR 1 OF MyPopup PROMPT 'Blue'
DEFINE BAR 2 OF MyPopup PROMPT 'Green'
DEFINE BAR 3 OF MyPopup PROMPT 'Red'
DEFINE BAR 4 OF MyPopup PROMPT 'White'
DEFINE BAR 5 OF MyPopup PROMPT 'Black'
ACTIVATE POPUP MyPopup NOWAIT
PUSH POPUP MyPopup
PUSH POPUP MyPopup
WAIT WINDOW 'Popup MyPopup is PUSHed twice'
RELEASE BAR 4 OF MyPopup && Remove last 2 menu items
RELEASE BAR 5 OF MyPopup
WAIT WINDOW 'Popup is modified'
POP POPUP MyPopup
WAIT WINDOW 'Original popup is POPed from stack'
DEFINE BAR 6 OF MyPopup PROMPT 'Gray'
WAIT WINDOW 'Popup is modified again '
POP POPUP MyPopup
WAIT WINDOW 'Second PUSHed popup is POPed from stack'
DEACTIVATE POPUP MyPopup
RELEASE POPUP MyPopup
```

The *CLEAR* and *RELEASE* Commands for Menus and Pop-ups

You can remove all pop-up or menu objects from the system by using the CLEAR command. Here is the syntax for this form of the CLEAR command:

```
CLEAR MENUS ¦ POPUPS
```

You can remove one or more of the pop-up or menu objects from the system by using the RELEASE command. Here is the syntax for these forms of the RELEASE command:

```
RELEASE POPUP <popup name list> [EXTENDED]
RELEASE BAR <expN> OF POPUP <popup name>
RELEASE BARS ALL OF <popup name>
RELEASE MENUS <menu name list> [EXTENDED]
RELEASE PAD <pad name> OF <menu name>
RELEASE PAD ALL OF <menu name>
```

Here is an example of the RELEASE POPUP command:

```
RELEASE POPUP POP1,POP2,POP3
```

If you specify the EXTENDED keyword with the RELEASE MENU command, the specified menu bars are released and all dependent pads, pop-ups, and ON procedures are released. Likewise, if you specify the EXTENDED keyword with the RELEASE POPUP command, the specified pop-up menus are released and all dependent pop-ups, bars, and ON procedures are released.

You can use the RELEASE PAD command to remove a pad from a user-defined menu bar or the system menu bar (**F**ile, **E**dit, and so on) by including the <*pad name*> clause. For example, to remove the **F**ormat and **W**indows pads (menus) from the system menu bar, you can use the following commands:

```
RELEASE PAD _MSM_FORMAT OF _MSYSMENU
RELEASE PAD _MSM_WINDO OF _MSYSMENU
```

You can use the RELEASE BAR command to remove options from the system menu pop-ups that appear under the system menu bar. To release a system menu pop-up, include the name of the system menu pop-up (_MFILE, _MEDIT, _MVIEW, _MTOOLS, _MPROG, _MFORMAT, _MWINDOW, and _MSYSTEM). Here are two examples:

```
RELEASE BAR _mwi_hide OF _MWINDOW
RELEASE BAR _mtl_spell OF _MTOOLS
```

You can restore the default system menu bar and system menu pop-ups by executing the SET SYSMENU TO DEFAULT command. See Chapter 10 for more information regarding the SET SYSMENU command. The names of the menu objects for the system menu bar are discussed in this chapter in the section "The System Menu Bar."

The *DISPLAY MEMORY* Command

The DISPLAY MEMORY command, in addition to displaying memory variables, displays the amount of memory used by the menu system. Here is the menu system portion of the display:

```
Menu and Pad Definitions

Menu Name
<menu name> <number of bytes> Bytes
Pad name:
<name of first pad object> <number of bytes> Bytes
```

```
Menu Name
<menu name> <number of bytes> Bytes
Pad names:
<name of first pad object> <number of bytes> Bytes
...
<number of menus> Menu Defined

Popup Definition
<popup file name> <number of bytes>  Bytes
...
<number of popups> Popup Defined
```

In addition to the space taken up with the message and labels, memory space is required for the menu, pad, and pop-up objects. However, when a menu or pop-up is activated, additional memory is needed to retain the text covered by the menu object display.

Putting It All Together

Now that I've discussed all the user-defined menu commands, I can present a sample case, shown in Figure 7.19. In this example, the menu definition is hard coded. Be aware that it is much easier to use the Menu Designer program to create menus than it is to hard code them.

This example contains a menu object with four pad objects. A pop-up object is attached to the File pad; when File is highlighted, the pop-up is activated. If you select the Use a Table… or Use a Form… bar object, a descendent directory pop-up is activated.

If the Edit pad is selected, the program edits the table currently in use. If the Report pad is selected, the user is prompted to enter a filename. If the Exit pad is selected, the menu is deactivated, and the program exits to the Command window. The program, MENUDEMO.PRG, is shown in Listing 7.9.

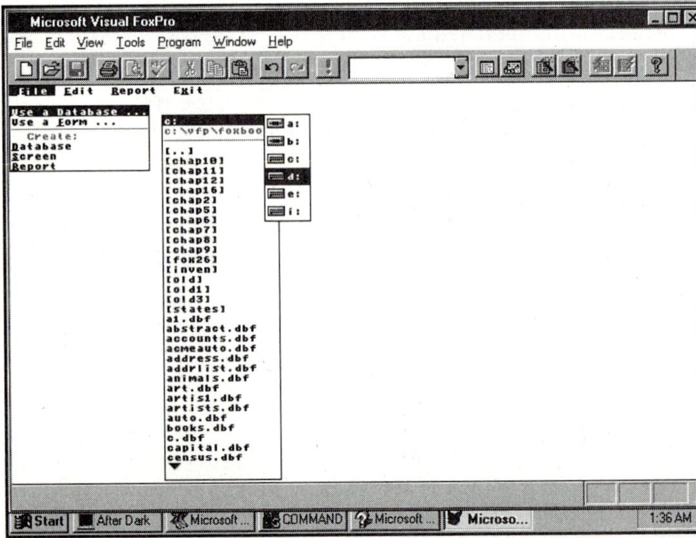

FIGURE 7.19.
An example of a menu program screen.

Listing 7.9. The source listing for the MENUDEMO.PRG program.

```
*************************************************************
*     * 8/20/92           MENUDEMO.PRG           11:02:20 *
*************************************************************
*     *                                                   *
*     * Description:                                      *
*     *  This program is a simple example of the use of the *
*     *  FoxPro user-defined menu system commands         *
*     *                                                   *
*************************************************************
*
SET TALK OFF
SET STATUS BAR ON
*
*  Now, define all the objects.
*
*     First define the menu bar
DEFINE MENU Sample
*
*     Define the prompt pad objects for the Sample menu.
*
DEFINE PAD Files OF Sample PROMPT "\<File"
DEFINE PAD Edit OF Sample PROMPT "\<Edit" ;
     MESSAGE "Edit table data" KEY CTRL+E, ""
DEFINE PAD Report OF Sample PROMPT "\<Report";
     MESSAGE "Generate a report"
DEFINE PAD Exit OF Sample PROMPT "E\<xit";
     MESSAGE "Exit the application"
*
*     Now, define all popup objects.
*
*     Note that because the TO clause is omitted,
*     the height and width are computed. The height
*     is 9 rows high (7 bars + borders). The width
*     is determined by the width of the widest bar
*     object, BAR 3. Each bar object is DEFINEd.
*
DEFINE POPUP Pop_File FROM 1,0 COLOR SCHEME 4
DEFINE BAR 1 OF Pop_File PROMPT "\<Use a Table ..."
DEFINE BAR 2 OF Pop_File PROMPT "Use a \<Form ..."
DEFINE BAR 3 OF Pop_File ;
     PROMPT "\-"
DEFINE BAR 4 OF Pop_File PROMPT "  Create:" SKIP
DEFINE BAR 5 OF Pop_File PROMPT "\<Table";
     MESSAGE "Create a table"
DEFINE BAR 6 OF Pop_File PROMPT "\<Screen"    ;
     MESSAGE "Create or modify a screen file"
DEFINE BAR 7 OF Pop_File PROMPT "\<Report"   ;
     MESSAGE "Create or modify a report form"

DEFINE POPUP Use_Dbf PROMPT FILE LIKE *.DBF FROM 3,10 ;
     COLOR SCHEME 4
DEFINE POPUP Use_Form PROMPT FILE LIKE *.FRM FROM 4,10 ;
     COLOR SCHEME 4
```

continues

Listing 7.9. continued

```
*
*  Now, establish actions.
*     The POP_File popup displays whenever the cursor is
*     on the File pad; it is never selected. There is an ON
*     SELECTION for the other PAD objects: Edit, Report,
*     and Exit.
*
ON PAD Files OF Sample ACTIVATE POPUP POP_File
ON SELECTION PAD Edit OF Sample EDIT
ON SELECTION PAD Report OF Sample DO Do_Report
ON SELECTION PAD Exit OF Sample Do Quitter
*
ON SELECTION POPUP Pop_File DO P_File with BAR()
ON SELECTION POPUP Use_Dbf  DO U_Dbf with PROMPT()
ON SELECTION POPUP Use_Form DO U_Form with PROMPT()
*
*  Everything is defined and established.
*  Now activate the menu system
*
ACTIVATE MENU SAMPLE

RETURN
**********************************************************
*  Procedure Do_Report performs the actions for the Report
*  pad object.
*
PROCEDURE Do_Report
fn = GETFILE()
IF NOT EMPTY(fn)
     REPORT FORM fn
ENDIF
RETURN
**********************************************************
*  Procedure P_File performs the actions for the POP_File
*  popup object.
*

PROCEDURE P_File
PARAMETER Bar_Number        && Bar_number is the number of
&& the bar object
SET MESSAGE TO
@ 12,30 SAY ""
DO CASE
*
*  Use a table. This is done by activating a
*  directory popup, then using the selected file.
*
     Case Bar_Number = 1
          ACTIVATE POPUP Use_Dbf
*
*     Set up a format file.
*
     CASE Bar_Number = 2
          IF '' = dbf()
               WAIT WINDOW ;
               "Table must be in use. Press any key to continue."
          ELSE
               ACTIVATE POPUP Use_Form
```

```
          ENDIF
*
*     Create a form, and report files
*
     CASE Bar_Number = 5
          CREATE
     CASE Bar_Number = 6
          CREATE SCREEN
     CASE Bar_Number = 7
          CREATE REPORT
ENDCASE
RETURN
*********************************************************
*  Procedure U_Dbf puts a file in use. It is executed when
*  a filename is selected from a directory popup object.
*
PROCEDURE U_Dbf
PARAMETER FileName          && FileName is the name of the
&& selected file
USE (FileName)
DEACTIVATE POPUP
RETURN
*********************************************************
*  Procedure U_Form establishes a format file.
*  The filename is selected from a directory popup object.
*

PROCEDURE U_Form
PARAMETER FileName          && FileName is the name of the
&& selected file
SET FORMAT TO (FileName)
RETURN

**********************************************************
*  Procedure Quitter removes the menu bar and exits
*
PROCEDURE Quitter
DEACTIVATE MENU Sample        && Deactivate menu before
&& you release it
RELEASE MENU Sample EXTENDED  && Release entire menu system
RETURN
```

The System Menu Bar

You can modify the system menu bar and its associated pop-up menus. For example, suppose that you want to build your own system menu bar. In the program shown in Listing 7.10, pads are removed from the system menu bar and three new pads are added. When you choose any of the three pads, a pop-up is activated. Before you can create any new menu pads, you must save the current system menu bar in memory with the `SET SYSMENU SAVE`. (Incidentally, the name of the system menu bar is `_SYSMENU`.) You remove all of the system menu pads with the `SET SYSMENU TO` command. If you just want to add a new pad to the system menu, then don't use the `SET SYSMENU TO` command.

Next, you create the new menu system. You probably will want to use color scheme 3 when you define a menu pad, and you will probably want to use color scheme 4 when you define a pop-up to conform with the color scheme normally used with the system menu. You need to use the `ON PAD` command to link the new menu pads to the new pop-ups. The system menu normally remains displayed after the `SYSPOPUP` program exits. As a result, you must specify the `IN SYSPOPUP` clause with the `DO` command so that FoxPro knows where the pop-up action procedure (`Action`) resides. Finally, you don't need to activate the menu system because the system menu bar is active already.

Listing 7.10. The source listing for the SYSPOPUP.PRG program.

```
***************************************************************
*     * 09/22/92          SYSPOPUP.PRG              9:14:11   *
***************************************************************
*     *                                                       *
*     * Description:                                          *
*     *  This program illustrates how to replace the FoxPro   *
*     *  system menu bar with your own "system menu bar"      *
*     *  using the user-defined menu system commands          *
*     *                                                       *
***************************************************************
*
CLEAR
SET SYSMENU SAVE    && Save the Systems menu bar
SET SYSMENU TO      && Remove the system menu bars
*
*** Now define a new PAD for the system menu bar

DEFINE PAD Bpad OF _MSYSMENU PROMPT '\<Breakfast' COLOR SCHEME 3 ;
KEY ALT+B, ''
DEFINE PAD Lpad OF _MSYSMENU PROMPT '\<Lunch' COLOR SCHEME 3 ;
KEY ALT+L, ''
DEFINE PAD Dpad OF _MSYSMENU PROMPT '\<Dinner' COLOR SCHEME 3 ;
KEY ALT+D, ''

ON PAD Bpad OF _MSYSMENU ACTIVATE POPUP Breakfast
ON PAD Lpad OF _MSYSMENU ACTIVATE POPUP Lunch
ON PAD Dpad OF _MSYSMENU ACTIVATE POPUP Dinner

DEFINE POPUP Breakfast MARGIN RELATIVE COLOR SCHEME 4
DEFINE BAR 1 OF Breakfast PROMPT '\<Eggs'
DEFINE BAR 2 OF Breakfast PROMPT '\<Toast'
DEFINE BAR 3 OF Breakfast PROMPT '\<Pancakes'
DEFINE BAR 4 OF Breakfast PROMPT '\-'
DEFINE BAR 5 OF Breakfast PROMPT '\<Ham'
DEFINE BAR 6 OF Breakfast PROMPT '\<Bacon'
DEFINE BAR 7 OF Breakfast PROMPT '\-'
DEFINE BAR 8 OF Breakfast PROMPT '\<Coffee'
DEFINE BAR 9 OF Breakfast PROMPT 'Te\<a'

DEFINE POPUP Lunch MARGIN RELATIVE COLOR SCHEME 4
DEFINE BAR 1 OF Lunch PROMPT '\<Caesar Salad'
DEFINE BAR 2 OF Lunch PROMPT '\<Santa Fe Spinach Salad'
DEFINE BAR 3 OF Lunch PROMPT 'C\<obb Salad'
DEFINE BAR 4 OF Lunch PROMPT 'So\<up du Jour'
DEFINE BAR 5 OF Lunch PROMPT '\-'
DEFINE BAR 6 OF Lunch PROMPT '\<Hamburger'
```

```
DEFINE BAR 7 OF Lunch PROMPT 'Ch\<eese Burger'
DEFINE BAR 8 OF Lunch PROMPT '\<Grilled Chicken Sandwich'
DEFINE BAR 9 OF Lunch PROMPT '\-'
DEFINE BAR 10 OF Lunch PROMPT 'Co\<la'
DEFINE BAR 11 OF Lunch PROMPT 'Co\<ffee'
DEFINE BAR 12 OF Lunch PROMPT '\<Ice Tea'

DEFINE POPUP Dinner MARGIN RELATIVE COLOR SCHEME 4
DEFINE BAR 1 OF Dinner PROMPT '\<Caesar Salad'
DEFINE BAR 2 OF Dinner PROMPT 'C\<obb Salad'
DEFINE BAR 3 OF Dinner PROMPT '\<Soup du Jour'
DEFINE BAR 4 OF Dinner PROMPT '\-'
DEFINE BAR 5 OF Dinner PROMPT '\<Top Sirloin Steak'
DEFINE BAR 6 OF Dinner PROMPT '\<Fresh Fish'
DEFINE BAR 7 OF Dinner PROMPT 'Chicken \<Barbacoa'
DEFINE BAR 8 OF Dinner PROMPT 'Chicken \<Marsala '
DEFINE BAR 9 OF Dinner PROMPT 'Fett\<ucine Alfredo'
DEFINE BAR 10 OF Dinner PROMPT '\-'
DEFINE BAR 11 OF Dinner PROMPT 'Coff\<ee'
DEFINE BAR 12 OF Dinner PROMPT 'Te\<a'
DEFINE BAR 13 OF Dinner PROMPT '\-'
DEFINE BAR 14 OF Dinner PROMPT 'E\<xit';
KEY CTRL+X , "^X"

ON SELECTION POPUP ALL;
DO Action IN syspopup WITH PROMPT(), POPUP(), BAR()

**********************************************************
*
*** Procedure Action is called whenever you choose any
*   popup options
*
PROCEDURE Action
PARAMETERS p_prompt, p_popup, p_bar

WAIT WINDOW 'You chose ' + p_prompt + ;
     " (Bar Number: "+ LTRIM(STR(p_bar)) +;
     ") from popup " + p_popup NOWAIT
IF p_prompt = 'Exit'
     WAIT WINDOW "The Restaurant Menu bar terminates" NOWAIT
     SET SYSMENU TO DEFAULT
ENDIF
```

Figure 7.20 is the sample output screen showing the system menu bar created by SYSPOPUP.PRG. When an option is chosen from the pop-up, the pop-up menu action procedure (`Action`) is called to execute the option. When you choose the Exit menu, the system menu bar pads and pop-ups, created in the SYSPOPUP.PRG procedure system, are deactivated and then released. Finally, the original system menu is restored with the `SET SYSMENU TO DEFAULT` command.

In Listing 7.10, you may have noticed the `RELATIVE` keyword is specified with the `DEFINE POPUP` commands for pop-ups associated with the system menu bar. The `RELATIVE` keyword enables you to insert a new option anywhere in a pop-up. For example, you can use the following command to insert a Milk option after the Coffee option in the Breakfast pop-up:

```
DEFINE BAR 99 OF Breakfast AFTER 8 PROMPT "\<Milk"
```

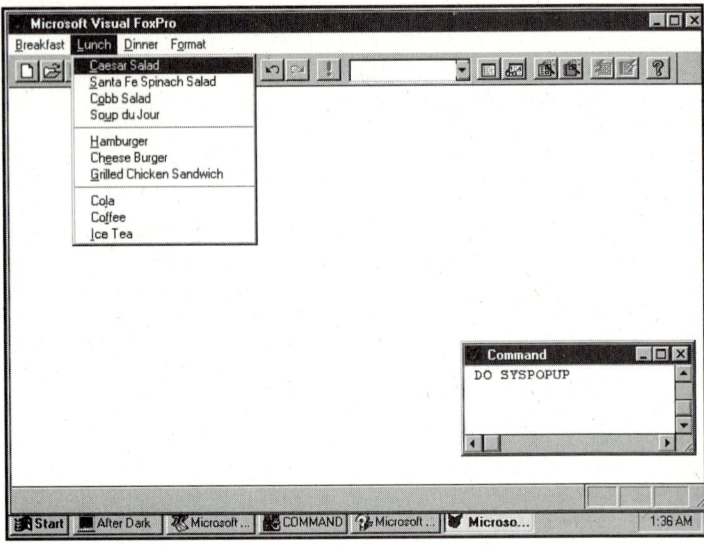

FIGURE 7.20.
A sample output screen resulting from the execution of the SYSPOPUP.PRG program.

The **M**ilk option is placed after the **C**offee option. You can also dispose of any of the options using the `RELEASE` command. Here is an example:

```
RELEASE BAR 5 OF Breakfast && Option "Ham" is released
```

In the same way, you can add options to the system menu. For example, you can execute the following statements to add a pop-up option, Word Count, to the system menu bar **T**ools pop-up following the **S**pelling… option:

```
DEFINE BAR 99 OF _MTOOLS AFTER _MTL_SPELL  PROMPT "\<Word Count"
ON SELECTION BAR 99 OF _MTOOLS WAIT WINDOW NOWAIT;
LTRIM(STR(OCCURS(" ", _CLIPTEXT)+1))+" Words in Clipboard"
```

Because the pop-up option number is relative, the bar number can be any arbitrary value. I picked 99. The `AFTER` clause instructs FoxPro to place the **W**ord Count option after the **S**pelling… option. This option determines roughly the number of words in the Clipboard by counting the blank characters. The word count displays in the Wait window.

FoxPro assigns names to all the system menu bar objects. In the preceding example, `MSM_SPELL` is the bar number of the **S**pelling… option in the **T**ools menu. `_MTOOLS` is the name of the system menu bar.

You can also use the `RELEASE` command to remove any of the system menu bar options. For example, to remove the **S**pelling… option from the **T**ools menu, you can type this statement:

```
RELEASE _MTL_SPELL OF _MTOOLS
```

Tables 7.14 through 7.20 provide the names of pads in system menu bar, system menu pop-up names, option labels, and system menu pop-up option names.

Table 7.14. Names for the system menu bar File menu.

Menu Pad	*Pad Name*	*Pop-up Name*	*Option Label*	*Option Name*
File	_MSM_FILE	_MFILE	**N**ew...	_MFI_NEW
			Open...	_MFI_OPEN
			Close	_MFI_CLOSE
			Separator 1	_MFI_SP100
			Save	_MFI_SAVE
			Save **A**s...	_MFI_SAVAS
			Revert	_MFI_REVRT
			Separator 2	_MFI_SP200
			Import	_MFI_IMPORT
			Export	_MFI_EXPORT
			Separator 3	_MFI_SP300
			Page Set**u**p...	_MFI_SETUP
			Pre**v**iew	_MFI_PREVUE
			Print...	_MFI_PRINT
			Separator 4	_MFI_SP400
			E**x**it	_MFI_QUIT

Table 7.15. Names for the system menu bar Edit menu.

Menu Pad	*Pad Name*	*Pop-up Name*	*Option Label*	*Option Name*
Edit	_MSM_EDIT	_MEDIT	**U**ndo	_MED_UNDO
			Re**d**o	_MED_REDO
			Separator 1	_MED_SP100
			Cu**t**	_MED_CUT
			Copy	_MED_COPY
			Paste	_MED_PASTE
			Paste **S**pecial	_MED_PSTLK
			Cle**a**r	_MED_CLEAR
			Separator 2	_MED_SP200
			Se**l**ect All	_MED_SLCTA
			Separator 3	_MED_SP300

continues

Table 7.15. continued

Menu Pad	*Pad Name*	*Pop-up Name*	*Option Label*	*Option Name*
			Find...	_MED_FIND
			Replace...	_MED_REPL
			Go To Line...	_MED_GOTO
			Separator 4	_MED_SP400
			Insert Object	_MED_INSOB
			Object...	_MED_OBJ
			Links...	_MED_LINK
			Convert to Static	_MED_CVTST

Table 7.16. Names for the system menu bar View menu.

Menu Pad	*Pad Name*	*Pop-up Name*	*Option Label*	*Option Name*
View	_MSM_VIEW	_MVIEW	Toolbars...	_MVI_TOOLB

Table 7.17. Names for the system menu bar Tools menu.

Menu Pad	*Pad Name*	*Pop-up Name*	*Option Label*	*Option Name*
Tools	_MSM_TOOLS	_MTOOLS	Wizards	_MTL_APPND
			Separator 1	_MTL_SP100
			Spelling...	_MTL_SPELL
			Macros...	_MST_MACRO
			Separator 2	_MTL_SP200
			Trace Window	_MWI_TRACE
			Debug Window	_MWI_DEBUG
			Separator 3	_MTL_SP300
			Options...	_MTL_OPTNS

Table 7.18. Names for the system menu bar Program menu.

Menu Pad	*Pad Name*	*Pop-up Name*	*Option Label*	*Option Name*
Program	_MPROG	_MSM_PROG	**D**o...	_MPR_DO
			Cancel	_MPR_CANCL
			Resume	_MPR_RESUM
			Suspend	_MPR_SUSPEND
			Separator 1	_MPR_SP100
			Compile	_MPR_COMPL

Table 7.19. Names for the system menu bar Window menu.

Menu Pad	*Pad Name*	*Pop-up Name*	*Option Label*	*Option Name*
Window	_MSM_WINDO	_MWINDOW	**A**rrange All	_MWI_ARRAN
			Separator 1	_MWI_SP100
			Hide	_MWI_HIDE
			Hide All	_MWI_HIDEA
			Sho**w** All	_MWI_SHOWA
			Clea**r**	_MWI_CLEAR
			C**y**cle	_MWI_ROTAT
			Separator 2	_MWI_SP200
			Command Window	_MWI_CMD
			View Window	_MWI_VIEW

Table 7.20. Names for the system menu bar Help menu.

Menu Pad	*Pad Name*	*Pop-up Name*	*Option Label*	*Option Name*
Help	_MSYSTEM	_MSM_SYSTM	**C**ontents	_MST_HELP
			Search for Help on...	_MST_HPSCH
			Separator 1	_MST_SP100
			Technical Support	_MST_TECHS
			Separator 1	_MST_SP200
			About Microsoft Visual FoxPro	_MST_ABOUT

Summary

This chapter describes commands to control the Visual FoxPro user-defined window subsystem, user-defined menus, and the FoxPro 2.*x* dialog objects that have been made obsolete by the Visual FoxPro OOP language extensions. You have learned about the following commands:

```
ACTIVATE SCREEN
ACTIVATE WINDOW
CLEAR ALL
CLEAR SCREEN
CLEAR WINDOWS
DEACTIVATE WINDOW
DEFINE WINDOW
FILER
HIDE WINDOW
MODIFY WINDOW
MOVE WINDOW
RELEASE WINDOWS
RESTORE WINDOWS
SAVE WINDOWS
SCROLL
SHOW WINDOWS
```

You have learned how to use the following functions:

```
SCOLS()
SROWS()
SYSMETRICS()
WCHILD()
WCOLS()
WEXIST()
WFONT()
WINDOW()
WLAST()
WLCOL()
WLROW()
WMAXIMUM()
WMINIMUM()
WONTOP()
WOUTPUT()
WPARENT()
WREAD()
WROWS()
WTITLE()
WVISIBLE()
```

This chapter also discusses the use of the `WINDOW` keyword with the `BROWSE` and `@` commands.

In addition, this chapter describes the FoxPro user-defined menu system. The commands used to create a menu system have not been replaced with object-oriented elements. You can use the commands presented in this chapter to add a sophisticated advanced user interface to a FoxPro application. Furthermore, this FoxPro user-defined interface is consistent with the rest of the Visual FoxPro user interface. You can build a user-defined menu interface visually by using the Menu Designer which is described in Chapter 18.

The commands described in this chapter include the following:

```
ACTIVATE MENU ¦ POPUP
CLEAR MENUS ¦ POPUPS
DEACTIVATE MENU ¦ POPUP
DISPLAY MEMORY
DEFINE MENU ¦ PAD ¦ POPUP ¦ BAR
HIDE MENU ¦ POPUP
ON BAR ¦ PAD
ON EXIT PAD <expC1> OF <expC2> [<command>]
ON EXIT MENU <expC2> [<command>]
ON MENU <expC> [<command>]
ON SELECTION MENU ¦ POPUP ¦ PAD ¦ BAR
POP MENU <expC> TO MASTER
PUSH MENU
RELEASE MENU ¦ POPUP ¦ PAD ¦ BAR
SET MARK OF
SET SKIP OF
SHOW MENU ¦ POPUP
```

The following functions are discussed in this chapter:

```
BAR()
BARCOUNT([<expC>])
BARPROMPT(<expN> [,<expC>])
CNTBAR(<expC>)
CNTPAD(<expC>)
GETBAR(<expC>,<expN>)
GETPAD(<expC>,<expN>)
MENU()
MRKBAR(<expC>,<expN>)
MRKPAD(<expC1>,<expC2>)
PAD()
PADPROMPT(<expC1> [, <expC2>])
POPUP()
PRMBAR(<expC>,<expN>)
PRMPAD(<expC1>,<expC2>)
PROMPT()
SKPBAR(<expC>,<expN>)
KPPAD(<expC1>,<expC2N>)
SYS(2013)
```

Chapter 8, "Input and Output," describes commands that allow FoxPro to communicate with the outside world.

8

Input and Output

It takes two to speak the truth—
one to speak, and
another to hear.

—Henry David Thoreau
(1817–1862)
A Week on the Concord and
Merrimack Rivers

This chapter and Chapter 9, "Full-Screen Data Editing," explore the realm in which the world communicates with Visual FoxPro. In particular, these chapters explore commands used to input data to FoxPro and to produce visual and printed output. Information presented in these two chapters is organized in two categories: line-oriented input and output and screen-oriented input and output.

This chapter examines the first category, which includes commands and functions related to line-oriented input and output. Line-oriented output always starts at the current screen cursor position or printer line and column, and is the mode of output of all output commands except the `@` command. Line-oriented output commands are `?`, `??`, `???`, `DISPLAY`, `LIST`, `LABEL`, and `REPORT`. Line-oriented input commands are `ACCEPT`, `INPUT`, and `WAIT`. The `INKEY()` function and `KEYBOARD` command are also discussed.

Chapter 9 covers the second category, which is screen-oriented input and output, characterized by the `@` command. In addition, data editing commands, such as `APPEND`, `BROWSE`, `EDIT`, and `READ`, and format files are discussed in the next chapter because they relate to screen-oriented input and output.

This chapter also discusses the *typeahead buffer* (an internal memory buffer that traps keyboard input as it is entered), `ON` command contingency processing, and system memory variables that relate to printer operations.

Input Operations

This section discusses the `ACCEPT`, `INPUT`, and `WAIT` commands. These commands originated early in the infancy of dBASE before dBASE supported full-screen editing. The `INKEY()` function, `ON` command, and typeahead buffers are also discussed.

The *ACCEPT* and *INPUT* Commands

The `ACCEPT` and `INPUT` commands are used to input data from the keyboard. Both commands output an optional prompt message that prompts the user to enter data. The user ends data entry by pressing Enter. The value is stored in a memory variable or in an element of a predeclared array.

Data entry for the `ACCEPT` command is treated as a literal character string, and the resultant memory variable or array element is a Character data type. Data entry for the `INPUT` command is interpreted as an expression that is evaluated and stored in the memory variable or array element. Its data type, which can be Character, Date, Logical, or Numeric, is determined by the expression. The following is the syntax for these commands:

```
ACCEPT [<expC>] TO <memvar-name> ¦ <array-element>
INPUT [<expC>] TO <memvar-name> ¦ <array-element>
```

If you omit the <expC> prompt message, no prompt message is output. For the INPUT command if you enter an illegal expression, an error message is displayed and the prompt message is redisplayed. Here's an example:

Command Window	*Results*
`ACCEPT 'Enter a name: ' TO AName`	`Enter a name:` **`Joe Smith`**
`INPUT 'Enter a name: ' TO BName`	`Enter a name:` **`"Joe Smith"`**
`? ANAME,BNAME`	`Joe Smith` **`Joe Smith`**
`INPUT 'Enter a date: ' TO ADate`	`Enter a date:` **`{03/04/90}+3`**
`? ADate`	**`03/07/90`**
`INPUT "Enter a number:" TO ANUM`	`Enter a number:` **`SQRT(77)`**
`INPUT 'Enter a number:' TO BNUM`	`Enter a number:` **`3*3`**
`? ANUM, BNUM`	`8.77 9`

In the example, ADate is a Date data type, and ANUM and BNUM are both Numeric data types.

It is preferable to use ACCEPT, @...GET, or WAIT for requesting character string input so that the user doesn't have to enclose the character string in quotation marks.

> **NOTE**
>
> The ACCEPT and INPUT commands have been around since the earliest version of Vulcan (1979). Vulcan was the predecessor of dBASE II. In the early days of microcomputers, only a few full-screen interfaces were available. The model for interfaces for most early microcomputer programs was *line-at-a-time terminals*, called TTYs. The ACCEPT and INPUT commands are obsolete, but they have been kept in Xbase languages to maintain backward compatibility. The @...GET command, described in Chapter 9, is normally used for input.

The *WAIT* Command

The WAIT command halts processing until a key is pressed. You can supply a prompt message; if you don't, the message Press any key to continue... displays. Here's the syntax:

```
WAIT [<expC>] [TO <memvar-name> ¦ <array-element>]
```

```
    [WINDOW [NOWAIT]] [TIMEOUT <expN>] [AT  <expN>,<expN>]
WAIT [CLEAR]
```

If you supply the `TO` clause, a Character data type memory variable is created to receive the character entered by the user. The user's entry can also be saved in an array element. The array must be declared already. If the user presses Enter, the length of the character string is zero. The following example:

```
WAIT
```

displays the message Press any key to continue...

You can use the following code to prompt the user for a yes-or-no answer:

```
WAIT "Delete the file? (Y/N)" TO Answer
IF UPPER(Answer) = 'Y'
   ERASE FILE
ENDIF
```

If the `TO` clause is not specified, the keystroke is discarded. If you specify the `WINDOW` keyword, the `WAIT` message displays in a small window in the top-right corner of the screen and execution pauses. When you press any key or click the mouse on the window, the window disappears, and execution continues. If you click on the window, a null string is returned. The optional `AT` clause specifies the position that the wait window displays.

If you specify `WINDOW NOWAIT`, the window containing the `WAIT` message appears but execution continues. When you press any key or move the mouse, the window disappears. This mode of the `WAIT` command operates like FoxPro system messages. You can use this mode for an information message that displays while some other operation is in progress. Here's an example:

```
*********************************************************
* WAIT.PRG - Demonstrates WAIT ... WINDOW NOWAIT
*********************************************************
WAIT "Indexing in progress, please wait" WINDOW NOWAIT
INDEX ON ACCOUNT TAG ACCOUNT
WAIT CLEAR
RETURN
```

The wait window remains on-screen until indexing is complete. The `WAIT WINDOW NOWAIT` form of the `WAIT` command always returns a null string. It does not extract a character from keyboard input. The `WAIT CLEAR` command clears a system window or a `WAIT WINDOW NOWAIT` message from the screen.

You can specify the `TIMEOUT` clause to specify how long the `WAIT` is in effect. The *<expN>* Numeric expression designates how many seconds elapse without any mouse or keyboard input before the `WAIT` command terminates. The numeric expression may include fractions of a second. If you specify a `TO` clause, and `WAIT` terminates because the `TIMEOUT` interval expires, a null string is returned.

```
*********************************************************
* TIMEWAIT.PRG - Demonstrates WAIT TIMEOUT
```

```
********************************************************
WAIT "Enter Spacebar to stop" WINDOW TIMEOUT 3.25 TO CHAR
IF ASC(CHAR) = 32       && Was spacebar entered?
   ? "You entered a SpaceBar"
ELSE
   IF LEN(CHAR) = 0   && Null string?
      ? "You did not enter a spacebar for 3-1/4 seconds"
   ENDIF
ENDIF
```

You can have multiple-line `WAIT` messages. All you have to do is insert a carriage return, `CHR(13)`, after each line of the multiple-line message. Here's an example:

```
WAIT WINDOW "First line"+CHR(13)+"Second Line"
```

The *INKEY()* Function

Instead of the `WAIT` command, the `INKEY()` function can be used to wait indefinitely for keyboard input or for a specified duration. It can also be used to detect a mouse click. The `INKEY()` function returns an integer value that corresponds to the ASCII value of the most recently entered key; if no key is pressed, `INKEY()` returns `0`.

The typeahead buffer is an internal memory buffer that traps keyboard input as it is entered. If FoxPro is busy executing a command, keyboard entries are saved in this buffer. You can specify the size of the buffer using the `SET TYPEAHEAD` command, described in Chapter 10, "Environment." If characters are already in the typeahead buffer, the `INKEY()` function returns the first character in the buffer and clears the remaining characters from the buffer. The next section further discusses the typeahead buffer. The syntax of the `INKEY()` function is as follows:

```
<integer> ::= INKEY([<expN>] [,<expC>]
```

The first optional numeric argument (`<expN>`) specifies the number of seconds to wait for a keyboard entry before returning to the user. The argument may include fractions of a second. `INKEY()` traps all characters except Shift+F10 and Alt+F1 through Alt+F10, which are used by keyboard macros. Table 8.1 lists integer values returned by the `INKEY()` function.

Table 8.1. Integer values returned by the `INKEY()` function.

Key Label	*Key Alone*	*Shift+*	*Ctrl+*	*Alt+*
F1	28	84	94	104
F2	-1	85	95	105
F3	-2	86	96	106
F4	-3	87	97	107
F5	-4	88	98	108
F6	-5	89	99	109

continues

Table 8.1. continued

Key Label	*Key Alone*	*Shift+*	*Ctrl+*	*Alt+*
F7	-6	90	100	110
F8	-7	91	101	111
F9	-8	92	102	112
F10	-9	93	103	113
F11	133	135	137	139
F12	134	136	138	140
1	49	33	—	120
2	50	64	33	121
3	51	35	—	122
4	52	36	—	123
5	53	37	—	124
6	54	94	30	125
7	55	38	—	126
8	56	42	—	127
9	57	40	—	128
0	48	41	—	19
a	97	65	1	30
b	98	66	2	48
c	99	67	3	46
d	100	68	4	32
e	101	69	5	18
f	102	70	6	33
g	103	71	7	34
h	104	72	127	35
i	105	73	9	23
j	106	74	10	36
k	107	75	11	37
l	108	76	12	38
m	109	77	13	50
n	110	78	14	49
o	111	79	15	24
p	112	80	16	25

Key Label	*Key Alone*	*Shift+*	*Ctrl+*	*Alt+*
q	113	81	17	16
r	114	82	18	19
s	115	83	19	31
t	116	84	20	20
u	117	85	21	22
v	118	86	22	47
w	119	87	23	17
x	120	88	24	45
y	121	89	25	21
z	122	90	26	44
Ins	22	22	146	162
Home	1	1	29	151
Del	7	7	147	163
End	6	6	23	159
PgUp	18	18	31	153
PgDn	3	51	30	161
UpArrow	5	5	141	152
RightArrow	4	4	2	157
LeftArrow	19	19	26	155
DownArrow	24	24	145	160
Esc	27	27	27	1
Enter	13	13	10	28
Backspace	127	127	127	14
Tab	9	15	148	165
Mouse click	151	151	151	151

The second optional argument (`<expC>`) is a character string. Use this argument if you want to hide or display the cursor when `INKEY()` executes. You can also use this argument to instruct `INKEY()` to detect a mouse click. If you want to hide the cursor, specify `H`. If you want to show the cursor, specify `S`. If you specify this argument and don't specify the first argument, omit the preceding comma. If you want to detect a single mouse click, specify `M`. Here are some examples:

```
INKEY(.6,"MH")    && Hide cursor and detect mouse
```

```
                    &&  and wait for.6 seconds.
INKEY("S")          && Show cursor. Ignore mouse.
INKEY(.6, "MS")     && Show cursor and detect mouse clicks.
INKEY("M")          && Detect mouse clicks and show cursor.
INKEY(3)            && Show cursor and ignore mouse clicks.
```

The `INKEY()` function suppresses the action of the `ON KEY` and `ON ESCAPE` commands. It ignores the state of the `SET ESCAPE` flag. `INKEY()` also traps the ASCII value of the Esc key and the Ctrl+S key combination.

In the following example, a prompt message appears for five seconds. If the user doesn't respond, the program rings a bell and continues to wait for the user's response. The program can easily be modified to display additional instructions if the user doesn't respond after 5½ seconds.

```
CLEAR
SET TALK OFF
@ 10,10 TO 12,40
@ 11,13 SAY "Exit to DOS? (Y/N)"
DO WHILE .T.
   Response = UPPER(CHR(INKEY(5.5)))  && Wait 5-1/2 seconds
   DO CASE
      CASE Response = "Y"
         QUIT
      CASE Response = 'N'
         EXIT
      CASE Response = ""    && No data was entered
         ? CHR(7)  && Ring Bell
   ENDCASE
ENDDO
```

Another use for the `INKEY()` command is to fetch the key that was pressed. Here's an example:

```
*********************************************************
*  INKEY.PRG - Illustrates INKEY() usage
*********************************************************
ON KEY DO KEYTRAP
…
* The KEYTRAP procedure is executed whenever
* a key is pressed.
PROCEDURE KEYTRAP
j=INKEY()    && Fetch the key just pressed and
&& clear the typeahead buffer
IF J = 83    && Is the character S?
   DO SPROCESS
ENDIF
RETURN
```

The program example presented in Listing 8.1 is a game that revisits the bouncing window. This program has up to 20 bouncing windows. The object of the game is to click on as many bouncing windows as you can in 60 seconds. You get a point if you successfully click on a little window and lose a point if you miss. `INKEY()` is the function that traps mouse clicks.

Listing 8.1. The MBOUNCE.PRG program.

```
************************************************************
*      * 07/28/92           MBOUNCE.PRG           9:15:02 *
************************************************************
*      *                                                  *
*      * Description:                                     *
*      * This program is a primitive game.The entire      *
*      * purpose is to illustrate how to capture          *
*      * mouse clicks with INKEY.                         *
************************************************************
SET TALK OFF
************************************************************
* Get old top score
IF FILE("MBOUNCE.MEM")
   RESTORE FROM MBOUNCE
ELSE
   TOPSCORE = 0
ENDIF
************************************************************
*  Initialize Arrays, memory variables, RAND() and ON ESCAPE
=RAND(-1)
CLEAR
DECLARE WinNames[20], WINDEX[20]
FOR I = 1 TO 20     && Create window names
   STORE "W"+LTRIM(STR(I)) TO  WinNames[I]
ENDFOR
DontStop = .T.
ON ESCAPE DontStop=.F.
Score = 0
StopTime = SECONDS() + 60
************************************************************
*  Start the game
DO WHILE DontStop .AND. SECONDS() < StopTime
   DO MakeWindow   && Make new windows sometimes
   FOR I = 1 TO 20 && MOVE defined windows
      IF WINDEX[I]
         DO Bounce WITH I
      ENDIF
   ENDFOR
ENDDO
DO ENDGAME  && Game's over, man - Print closing screen

Safety = SET("SAFETY")  && Save value of SET SAFETY
SET SAFETY OFF
SAVE TO MBOUNCE ALL LIKE TOPSCORE
SET SAFETY &Safety   && Restore original SET SAFETY value
CLEAR ALL
************************************************************
*  Make a new window or Destroy old one 20 percent of the time
*
PROCEDURE MakeWindow
IF Rand() < .2
   Wndx = ASCAN( WINDEX, .F. )
   IF Wndx = 0
      Wndx = INT(RAND()*19))+1  && Kill off a random Window
      WINDEX[Wndx] = .F.
      RELEASE WINDOWS WinNames[Wndx]
```

continues

Listing 8.1. continued

```
   ELSE
      * Pick a random position on the screen
      row1=INT(Rand()*20)
      col1=INT(Rand()*80)
      DEFINE WINDOW ( WinNames[Wndx] );
         FROM row1,col1 TO row1+2,col1+3 ;
         COLOR W+/R FILL CHR(176) PANEL
      ACTIVATE WINDOW ( WinNames[Wndx])
      WINDEX[Wndx] = .T.
   ENDIF
ENDIF
RETURN
**************************************************************
* Bounce: Move a window
PROCEDURE Bounce
PARAMETER WinIndex
Char = INKEY(.1,"HM")  && Hide the cursor; Wait 1/10 second
IF (Char = 27 )
   DontStop = .F.
ELSE
   IF Char = 151   && Mouse entry
      InWindow = MWINDOW() && Name of window clicked on
*            Field is Empty if it is a null string ("").
*            If InWindow is a null string, mouse has
*            clicked on screen
      IF .NOT. EMPTY(InWindow))
         ?? CHR(7)   && Ding
         WAIT "Mouse is in the window" WINDOW NOWAIT
         SCORE = SCORE + 1
*               Returns non-zero value if name is in array
         Wndx = ASCAN(  WinNames , InWindow )
         IF Wndx > 0
             WINDEX[Wndx] = .F.  && Zap Window
             WOld = WLAST()
             RELEASE  WINDOWS WinNames[Wndx]
             ACTIVATE SCREEN
             xrow=WLROW(InWindow) && Get left corner
             xcol=WLCOL(InWindow)
             @ xrow,xcol FILL TO xrow+2,xcol+3 COLOR R/R
             ACTIVATE WINDOW (WOld)
         ENDIF
      ELSE
         WAIT "You missed" WINDOW NOWAIT
         SCORE = SCORE - 1
      ENDIF
   ENDIF
ENDIF
WName =  WinNames[WinIndex]
** Pick a random direction to move.
mcol =    IIF(WLCOL(Wname) < 10 ,  5,  ;
IIF(WLCOL(Wname) > 70 , -5,  ;
IIF(rand()  > .5 ,  5, -5 )))
mrow = IIF(WLROW(Wname) <  5 ,  4,  ;
       IIF(WLROW(Wname) > 18 , -4,  ;
       IIF(rand()  > .5 , 4, -4 )))
MOVE WINDOW ( WinNames[WinIndex]) BY mrow,mcol
```

```
   *@ 0,0 FILL TO 13,19 COLOR SCHEME INT(23*rand())+1
RETURN
************************************************************
* End Game: Prints the closing window
**  (This screen was created using CREATE SCREEN)
*
PROCEDURE EndGame
DEFINE WINDOW endgame ;
   FROM INT((SROW()-13)/2),INT((SCOL()-50)/2) ;
   TO INT((SROW()-13)/2)+12,INT((SCOL()-50)/2)+49 ;
   SHADOW PANEL COLOR SCHEME 7
ACTIVATE WINDOW endgame
@ 1,18 SAY "GAME OVER!!!!"
@ 3,12 SAY "Your score is: "
@ 3,28 SAY Score PICTURE "@B"
@ 5,9  SAY "The top score is:"
@ 5,28 SAY TopScore PICTURE "@B"
IF TopScore < Score
   @ 8,1 SAY "Congratulations, You have the new TOP SCORE"
   TopScore = Score
ENDIF
=INKEY(10,"H")  && Hide cursor and wait 10 seconds
RELEASE WINDOW ENDGAME
RETURN
```

The MBOUNCE.PRG program consists of a main program, the `MBOUNCE` procedure, and other procedures such as `MakeWindow`, `Bounce`, and `EndGame`. The `MBOUNCE` procedure does some initialization and then drops into a `DO WHILE` loop that loops repeatedly for one minute. Each time it loops, it calls `MakeWindow` and `Bounce`. The initialization process involves creating some variables and declaring and initializing two arrays: `WINDEX[]` and `WinNames[]`. `WinNames[]` contains the names of the windows (`W1` through `W20`). Each element in `WINDEX[]` contains a `.T.` or `.F.` value. A `.T.` value indicates that the corresponding window in `WinNames[]` is defined. `MakeWindow` creates a window 20 percent of the time it's called. If 20 windows are active, `MakeWindows` destroys one of the windows. When a window is defined, a random position is determined. The `Bounce` procedure determines a random direction for the window to move and moves the window. The program also calls `INKEY()` to check if the mouse has been clicked in a window. If it has been clicked, the window is released, the bell rings, and a `WAIT` message displays. `Bounce` also keeps score. The `EndGame` procedure prints the Game Over box.

The Typeahead Buffer

The typeahead buffer is a first in, first out (FIFO) memory buffer that stores keystrokes. In a FIFO buffer, the first data item stored is the first item retrieved. Whenever FoxPro is busy doing calculations or a disk operation, keyboard entries are saved in the typeahead buffer. If the buffer fills up and `SET BELL` is `ON`, the bell sounds whenever another key is pressed. After FoxPro finishes its task and requests more keyboard input, characters saved in the typeahead buffer are passed to the input routine. When the typeahead buffer is empty, the input routine waits for more keyboard input.

The size of the typeahead buffer is normally 20 characters. You can change the size with the SET TYPEAHEAD command or the CONFIG.FPW TYPEAHEAD= command. (See Chapter 10.)

The INKEY() function gets the first character in the typeahead buffer and discards the remaining characters. Sometimes, you might want to disregard the contents of the typeahead buffer. You can do this with the INKEY() function or the following command:

```
CLEAR TYPEAHEAD
```

The *KEYBOARD* Command

The KEYBOARD command replaces the contents of the typeahead buffer with a string, simulating keyboard input. It's used with commands that accept user input or control information, such as the ACCEPT, INPUT, ACTIVATE POPUP, and READ commands. The syntax is as follows:

```
KEYBOARD <expC> [PLAIN] [CLEAR]
```

The character expression can be any valid character string and can contain any ASCII character except null, CHR(0). Here's an example:

```
KEYBOARD "Happy" + CHR(13) + "Birthday" + CHR(13)
```

When you execute the KEYBOARD command, the character string is stuffed into an internal keyboard buffer. Characters from the keyboard buffer are input to FoxPro as though they were typed from the keyboard. The keyboard buffer can hold up to 128 characters. If <expC> is longer than 128, an alert box appears containing the message Key string too long.

If you specify the CLEAR keyword with the KEYBOARD command, the *keyboard buffer* is emptied before any new characters in the character expression (<expC>) are stuffed into it.

You can specify special characters using the notation used with the ON KEY LABEL command and keyboard macros. (See Table 6.2.) These symbols are embedded in the character string specified with the KEYBOARD command. The symbols consist of the key label enclosed in braces. Here's an example:

```
KEYBOARD "I will now press the F2 Key. {F2}"
KEYBOARD "{ALT+S}cc123*321=Q{Ctrl+W}? _CALCVALUE{ENTER}"
```

In FoxPro, the keyword names often elucidate their actions. When I see the PLAIN keyword, I think of "plain old" characters like A or B. For the REPORT command, PLAIN instructs FoxPro to print a plain report—a report without headings on each page. However, if the PLAIN keyword is specified with the KEYBOARD command, the literal values of any characters in the character expression that are not plain are stuffed into the keyboard buffer. A character is *not plain* if it has a corresponding keyboard macro or if it is to be trapped because it was assigned to a procedure with the ON KEY LABEL command. Here's an example.

```
*****************************************************
*  KYPLAIN.PRG: Illustrates use of PLAIN with KEYWORD
ON KEY LABEL x WAIT "X was trapped" WINDOW
```

```
KEYBOARD "? 'Texas'{Enter}" PLAIN
KEYBOARD "? 'Texas'{Enter}"
RETURN
```

Program KYPLAIN.PRG inserts `"? 'Texas'{Enter}"` into the keyboard buffer twice. The first time `PLAIN` is specified. Then the program exits. In the Command window, the first `?` command is entered literally and `Texas` displays. Next, the second command is entered. However, the `x` is trapped by `ON KEY LABEL` and the `WAIT` command executes. The a is used to clear the `WAIT`. As a result, only `Tes` displays.

Listing 8.2 demonstrates the use of the `KEYBOARD` command. A value selected from a pop-up menu is stuffed into the typeahead buffer, which is subsequently processed by the `READ` command.

Listing 8.2. An example of the use of the KEYBOARD command.

```
***********************************************************
*  Program: KEYBOARD.PRG
*  This program demonstrates the use of the KEYBOARD
*  function. A prompt is issued requesting that a
*  filename be entered. If you press Enter, a popup
*  of filenames appears. When you select a file, the
*  filename is stuffed into the typeahead buffer, which
*  is read into the input field by the READ command.
*
CLEAR
SET TALK OFF
DEFINE POPUP GetFile FROM 6,30 PROMPT FILES LIKE *.DBF
ON READERR ?? ""   && Suppress read error intercept
ON SELECTION POPUP GetFile DO action
dbffile='                                    '
TestFile= ' '
@ 5,1 SAY "Enter name of a DBF file (or press Enter)" ;
GET dbffile valid testx(dbffile)
READ
WAIT "The filename is: " + dbffile WINDOW NOWAIT
RETURN
***********************************************************
*
*  Function:  Testx(filename)
*  Description: UDF activates directory popup to select
*               the filename if the user did not enter a
*               filename.*
*  Input:  Filename character string
*  Output: Logical true value if filename was entered.
*          Otherwise, a logical false is returned.
*
FUNCTION Testx
PARAMETER filename
IF .NOT. EMPTY(filename)
   RETURN .T.         && User entered filename, return valid
ENDIF
ACTIVATE POPUP GetFile
TestFile = PROMPT()     && Fetch selected filename
DEACTIVATE POPUP
```

continues

Listing 8.2. continued

```
IF TestFile = ' '
   ?? CHR(8)          && Filename was not selected…
ELSE
   KEYBOARD TestFile  && Stuff filename into typeahead
   && buffer with filename that will
   && be read by the GET command
ENDIF
RETURN .F.
************************************************************
*
*   POPUP menu action procedure
*
PROCEDURE action
testfile = PROMPT()   && Fetch the filename
DEACTIVATE POPUP
RETURN
************************************************************
```

NOTE

In dBASE IV, the size of the character string exceeds the size of the typeahead buffer (default of 20 characters). The remaining characters are ignored. If you want `KEYBOARD` to insert more than 20 characters, you need to use the `SET TYPEAHEAD TO` command to change the size of the typeahead buffer. In FoxPro, however, you can stuff 128 characters by using `SET COMPATIBILITY DB4`, regardless of the size of the typeahead buffer.

The *ON PAGE* Command

Chapter 6, "Control Flow," discusses commands that initiate event trapping. One such command is `ON PAGE`. The `ON PAGE` command initiates a trap procedure that is executed after a specified line has been printed or when the `EJECT PAGE` command is executed. The syntax is as follows:

```
ON PAGE [AT LINE <expN> <command>]
```

The line number is specified with the `AT LINE` clause. The purpose of the `ON PAGE` command is to support the printing of headers and footers on reports that are printed with the `?` and `??` commands. If you use the `ON PAGE` command without a clause, any trap procedures established by previous commands are disabled.

This form of the `ON` command has more power than you may realize. It was devised to support the printing of reports in dBASE IV. The designers of FoxPro 2.0 decided that this command would be useful for two reasons. First, without this feature, FoxPro would not be compatible with dBASE IV because you cannot execute dBASE IV report files (.FRG) without supporting the `ON PAGE` command, system memory variables, and other language elements used in dBASE

IV reports. The second, more important, reason for including this feature is its usefulness for providing custom headers and footers using the `LIST` command or other commands. In Listing 8.3, the `ON PAGE` command is used with the `LIST` command to generate custom headers and footers. After each line is printed, the current line number system memory variable, `_PLINENO`, is compared with the `ON PAGE AT LINE` argument. If they are the same, the `ON PAGE` procedure is triggered.

Listing 8.3. An example of the use of the `ON PAGE` command.

```
*****************************************************
* Program:        ONPAGE.PRG
* Description:    Displays
ON PAGE AT LINE 60 DO Break
SET HEADINGS OFF
_PAGENO = 1             && Initialize page number system memvar
DO Header
USE Customer
LIST OFF Customer, CustNo, Address TO PRINTER
ON PAGE               && Disable ON PAGE processing
RETURN
*
PROCEDURE Break       && Do a page break
DO Footer
DO Header
RETURN
PROCEDURE Footer      && Print the footer
?
? Date(),"            Company Confidential    "
RETURN
*
PROCEDURE Header      && Print the header
EJECT PAGE
? "       ACME Company Customer List    Page #";
   ,STR(_PAGENO, 3)
?
? "     Customer      Customer No    Address"
?
RETURN
```

The Output Commands

This section discusses line-oriented output commands, which include the `?`, `??`, `???`, `DISPLAY`, and `LIST` commands. System memory variables used for control of line-oriented output are also discussed in this section.

The ? and ?? Commands

The `?` and `??` commands display a list of expressions. Some people call these the *calculator commands* because they enable FoxPro to be used as a desktop calculator. They were originally derived from the short form of the BASIC language `PRINT` statement.

In dBASE IV, the `?` command was extended to support the requirements of the dBASE IV Report Generator. FoxPro also supports these extensions. With these extensions to the `?` and `??` commands, you can define the font and style of printed results and specify the beginning display column. In addition, you can specify a `PICTURE` template (as with the `@` command). Special display functions are available, as well. Here's the syntax:

```
? [<exp-list>]
? <exp> [PICTURE <expPIC1>] [FUNCTION <expFUNC1>]
[AT <expN>] [STYLE <expSTYLE> [, <exp>…]
?? [<exp-list>]
?? <exp> [PICTURE <expPIC>] [FUNCTION <expFUNC>]
[AT <expN>] [STYLE <expSTYLE> [, <exp>…][,]

<expFUNC1> ::= <expC> (which evaluates to a <Func_chars>)
<expPIC1>  ::= <expC> (which evaluates to a <picture>)

<picture> ::=[ @<Func_chars><space>] [<any characters>]
<stringPIC> ::= <dbl_quote_strPIC>
<single_quote_strPIC>
<Func_chars> ::= <Func_char1> [<Func_char1>]…
<Func_char1> ::= ; ¦ ! ¦ ^ ¦ ( ¦ $ ¦
   B ¦ C ¦ D ¦ E ¦ I ¦
   J ¦ L ¦ T ¦ V<digits>¦
   X ¦ Z ¦
<expSTYLE> ::= <expC> (which evaluates to <Style_chars>)

<Style_char> ::= B ¦ I ¦ U ¦ R ¦ L ¦
   1 ¦ 2 ¦ 3 ¦ 4 ¦ 5
```

The only difference between the `?` command and the `??` command is that the `?` command outputs a carriage return and a line feed before it displays the results. In other words, `?` starts outputting at the first column on the next line, whereas `??` starts outputting at the current screen and printer column. If no expressions are specified with the `?` command, a blank line is printed.

The first form of the `?` and `??` commands in FoxPro is the same as in FoxBASE+, dBASE III PLUS, and Clipper, and expressions are simply separated by commas, as in the following example:

```
?  COST*RATE, NAME, Date
??  Address
```

The resultant display is as follows:

```
993433.33 Joe Smith     01/12/90   2233 First Street
```

The second form is similar but allows you to supply the new `PICTURE`, `FUNCTION`, `AT`, and `STYLE` clauses for each expression, as in the following example:

```
? COST*RATE  PICTURE "@$ 999,999.99" STYLE "B", ;
NAME, DATE FUNCTION "E"
?? Address
```

The resultant display is as follows:

```
993,433.33 Joe Smith     12/01/90   2233 First Street
```

The definition of each syntax clause is discussed in the following sections.

The *PICTURE* Clause

All `PICTURE` templates used with the `@...SAY` command can be used with the `?` or `??` commands. (See Chapter 9.) The syntax is as follows:

```
PICTURE <expC>
```

`<expC>` is a character expression that evaluates to a `PICTURE` template.

The *FUNCTION* Clause

In the `FUNCTION <expC>` clause, the `<expC>` argument is a character expression that defines a special code called the *display function*, which determines how the expression is displayed. For example, a `$` display function instructs FoxPro to add a currency marker to a numeric display. The display function can be specified with the `?` and `??` commands to modify the display of expressions, as shown in Table 8.2. All display functions in Table 8.2—except the semicolon, `H`, and `V`—can be used with the `@` command also.

Table 8.2. Display functions used with the ? and ?? commands.

Function	*Usage*
!	Converts lowercase to uppercase
^	Displays numbers in scientific notation (for example, 1.23E+09)
(	Displays negative values in parentheses (for example, (99.99))
$	Displays a currency sign
;	Treats a semicolon embedded in text as a carriage return
B	Aligns text to the left of a field
C	Displays credit notation (CR) after a positive number
D	Displays dates in current SET DATE format
E	Displays dates in European format
I	Centers text within a field
J	Adjusts text right within a field
L	Displays leading zeros
T	Trims leading and trailing blanks from a field
V<n>	Allows a field to stretch vertically
X	Displays debit notation (DB) after a negative number
Z	Displays zero numeric value as a blank string

The display functions `B`, `I`, `J`, and `T` are used with `PICTURE` templates that are wider than the field. The following examples show the effect of these display functions. In the first example, the text is centered:

```
Animal = 'Mongoose'
? "<", Animal PICTURE "@I XXXXXXXXXXXXXXX", ">"
```

The resultant display is as follows:

```
<      Mongoose     >
```

Next, the text is right aligned:

```
Animal = 'Mongoose'
? "<", Animal PICTURE "@J XXXXXXXXXXXXXXX", ">"
```

The resultant display is as follows:

```
<         Mongoose >
```

In the following, the text is first trimmed, then left aligned:

```
Animal = "     CAT      "
? "<", Animal PICTURE "@TB XXXXXXXXXXXXXXX", ">"
```

The resultant display is as follows:

```
<CAT                >
```

In the final example, the text is trimmed, then right aligned.

```
Animal = "     CAT      "
? "<", Animal PICTURE "@TJ XXXXXXXXXXXXXXX", ">"
```

The resultant display is as follows:

```
<                CAT>
```

The `B`, `I`, and `J` display functions override the alignment system memvar `_ALIGNMENT`. The `B`, `I`, `J`, and `T` display functions can be used with the `@...SAY` command also.

The semicolon display function provides dBASE III compatibility for printing reports and labels; a carriage return is printed whenever a semicolon is encountered. Here's an example:

```
Addr = "Joe Smith" + CHR(59)+"2222 First Street";
   + CHR(59) + "New York, NY"
? Addr
Joe Smith;2222 First Street;New York, NY
? Addr  FUNCTION CHR(59)
```

The resultant display is as follows:

```
Joe Smith
2222 First Street
New York, NY
```

Note that the semicolon is ASCII character 59.

The V display functions are the vertical field stretch display functions. If it is not specified, the display width is determined by the width of the field or the width of the PICTURE template, whichever is smaller. If the template is smaller, the data is truncated.

The V display function forces an expression to wrap in a vertical column. It simulates the column wrapping in the FoxBASE+, FoxPro, and dBASE III PLUS Report Generators. The numeric argument defines the width of the column. If a PICTURE template is used and the V display function's numeric argument is less than the template width, the data wraps in columnar fashion using the PICTURE template to format the data. If the V display function's numeric argument is larger than the template width, the column width is defined by the numeric argument and is blank filled. The following example

```
? Author, Title FUNCTION "V20", ;
Abstract FUNCTION "V20",Pdate
```

displays as this:

```
Joseph Starbuck   Wildflowers in     This article tells 12/20/27
Upstate New York  about the species
of wildflowers
that are of
considerable
botanical interest
and frequent the
Northern region of
New York state.
```

NOTE ON COMPATIBILITY

In dBASE IV, if the V display function's numeric argument is zero or not specified, the memo field is displayed as it appears in the word wrap editor and is aligned to the left margin. The following example:

```
? Author,  Abstract FUNCTION "V",Pdate
```

displays as this:

```
Joseph Starbuck
This article tells about the species of wildflowers that are of
considerable botanical interest and frequent the Northern region of
New York state. 12/20/27
```

However, in FoxPro, if the argument for V is zero or omitted, the SET MEMOWIDTH value is assumed.

The *AT* <*expN*> Clause

You use the AT <*expN*> clause to specify the column where an expression is displayed. The results are always displayed in the designated column even if they overwrite previously displayed information.

The *STYLE* <expC> Clause

The STYLE clause defines the various styles or fonts in which the expression is printed. The STYLE clause is ignored when output is directed to the screen or a window. The character expression consists of numbers 1 through 5 and one or more of the following letters:

Character	*Style*
B	Bold
I	Italic
O	Outline
Q	Opaque
S	Shadow
-	Strikethrough
T	Transparent
U	Underline

The numbers indicate the font numbers that are defined in CONFIG.FPW. See the discussion of the PRINTER= CONFIG.FPW command in Chapter 10. Here's an example:

```
? "This is in Bold" STYLE "B",;
"This is italic and underlined"  Style "IU"
```

The resultant printed output is as follows:

```
This is in Bold
This is Italic and Underlined
```

The ??? Command

The ??? command outputs a character expression directly to the printer. It provides a means of sending print control codes to the printer.

For all other commands, output directed to the printer is processed and in some cases filtered by the printer drivers, and the internal printer row and column positions are modified. For the ??? command, output directed to the printer does not display on the screen, does not pass through the print drivers, and does not change the printer row and column. It goes directly to the printer. The syntax is as follows:

```
???  [<expC>]
```

If you omit the character expression, ??? performs no function. The character expression contains printable characters, CHR() functions, and symbols enclosed in curly braces, {}, representing control codes. The symbols are converted to their ASCII representation before being output to the printer. The symbols and their corresponding ASCII representation are presented in Table 8.3.

Table 8.3. Control code symbols for the ??? command.

Code	*Symbol*	*Code*	*Symbol*	*Code*	*Symbol*
0	{NULL}	11	{Ctrl+K}	22	{Ctrl+V}
1	{Ctrl+A}	12	{Ctrl+L}	23	{Ctrl+W}
2	{Ctrl+B}	13	{RETURN}	24	{Ctrl+X}
3	{Ctrl+C}	14	{Ctrl+N}	25	{Ctrl+Y}
4	{Ctrl+D}	15	{Ctrl+O}	26	{Ctrl+Z}
5	{Ctrl+E}	16	{Ctrl+P}	27	{ESC} or {ESCAPE}
6	{Ctrl+F}	17	{Ctrl+Q}	28	{Ctrl+\}
7	{BELL}	18	{Ctrl+R}	29	{Ctrl+]}
8	{BACKSPACE}	19	{Ctrl+S}	30	{Ctrl+^}
9	{TAB}	20	{Ctrl+T}	31	{Ctrl+_}
10	{LINEFEED}	21	{Ctrl+U}	32	{DEL} or {DELETE}

Codes can be sent to the printer before the printing starts and after printing ends. _PSCODE and _PECODE are directed to the printer before printing starts and after printing ends, respectively.

System Memory Variables

System memory variables, or SMVs, were originally designed to control line-oriented output to support a comprehensive report generator in dBASE IV. However, the concept is continually expanding to support other Visual FoxPro features. This section covers all existing SMVs, with the focus on SMVs that are used for document and printer control.

SMVs work like normal memory variables. You can use them in expressions, as well as to store, retrieve, and display values. Anything that you can do with memory variables you can do with SMVs, except to release them from memory. You can use the PRIVATE command to make SMVs private, so that they revert to their original value when the program is finished. SMVs differ from normal memory variables in that their first character is an underscore (_), and they control internal system functionality or modify some internal system control parameter.

The syntax, default value, and allowable range of values of SMVs used for print control are presented in Table 8.4.

Table 8.4. System memory variables used for print control.

Syntax	*Values*	*Default*	*Description*

`_ALIGNMENT = <expC>`	`LEFT`
	`CENTER`
	`RIGHT`
		`LEFT`	Paragraph alignment

`_BOX = <expL>`	`.T.` `.F.`	`.T.`	`DEFINE BOX` print control (active only if `_WRAP=.T.`)
`_INDENT = <expN>`	`0-254`	`0`	Paragraph indent (active only if `_WRAP=.T.`)
`_LMARGIN = <expN>`	`0-254`	`0`	Left margin offset (active only if `_WRAP=.T.`)
`_PADVANCE = <expC>`	`FORMFEED` `LINEFEEDS`	`FORMFEED`	Type of printer advance
`_PAGENO = <expN>`	`1-32767`	`1`	Page number
`_PBPAGE = <expN>`	`1-32767`	`1`	Print job beginning page number
`_PCOLNO = <expN>`	`0-255`		Current column number
`_PCOPIES = <expN>`	`1-32767`	`1`	Number of copies to print for print job
`_PDSETUP`	`Null`		Printer driver setup
`_PECODE = <expC>`	`Null`		Print job ending control code

`_PEJECT = <expC>`	`BEFORE`
	`AFTER`
	`BOTH`
	`NONE`
		`BEFORE`	Page eject control

`_PEPAGE = <expN>`	`1-32767`	`32767`	Print job ending page
`_PLENGTH = <expN>`	`1-32767`	`66`	Output page length
`_PLINENO = <expN>`	`0 to _PLENGTH-1`	0	Current line number
`_PLOFFSET = <expN>`	`0-254`	0	Offset from left of printed page

Syntax	*Values*	*Default*	*Description*
`_PPITCH = <expC>`	`DEFAULT` `CONDENSED` `PICA` `ELITE`	`DEFAULT`	Currently defined printer pitch
`_PQUALITY = <expL>`	`.T.` `.F.`	`.F.`	Printer mode (`.T.` for letter quality; `.F.` for draft mode)
`_PSCODE = <expC>`	Null		Print job starting control code
`_PSPACING = <expN>`	`1-3`	`1`	Output spacing
`_PWAIT = <expL>`	`.T.` `.F.`	`.F.`	Pause after printing page control
`_RMARGIN = <expN>`	`_LMARGIN+1 to 255`	`80`	Right margin offset (active only if `WRAP=.T.`)
`_TABS = <expC>`	Null		Printed output tab locations
`_WRAP = <expL>`	`.T.` `.F.`	`.F.`	Word wrapping control mode

All the SMVs presented in Table 8.4 are discussed in the following paragraphs because they relate to printing and print control. Other SMVs are discussed in Table 8.5.

Page and Paragraph Layout Control

Some SMVs are used for defining page and paragraph layout parameters. These parameters affect printed output using the `?` and `??` commands. (See Figure 8.1.)

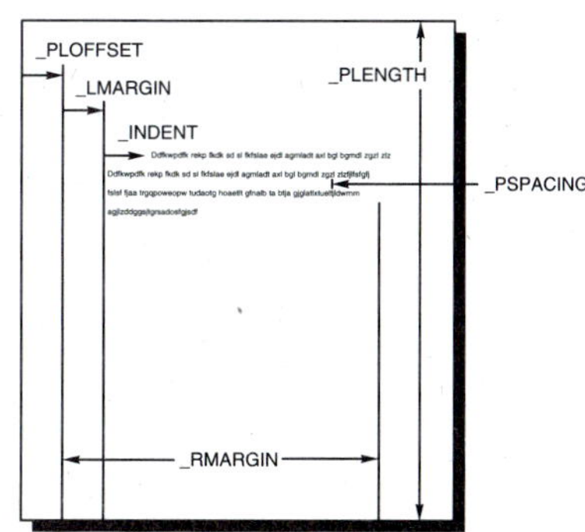

FIGURE 8.1.
Page layout parameters.

The following are the page layout parameters:

`_ALIGNMENT`	Controls the alignment of the text between the left and right margins of the output generated by the `?` and `??` commands. The assignment can be `LEFT`, `RIGHT`, or `CENTER` (centered). It is especially useful for headers and footers.
`_INDENT`	Defines the number of characters to use for the indent for the first line of each paragraph.
`_LMARGIN`	Defines the left margin. It is the number of characters between the page offset (`_PLOFFSET`) and the beginning of a paragraph. `_LMARGIN` must be less than 255 characters, and `_INDENT` plus `_LMARGIN` must be less than `_RMARGIN`.
`_PLENGTH`	Stores or retrieves the total number of lines in a page.
`_PLOFFSET`	Stores or retrieves the offset measured in columns from the left edge of the page where printing begins. If `_PLOFFSET` is 10, printing begins at column 11. This relates to printed output only. Storing a value to this SMV is identical to using the `SET MARGIN TO` command, which is described in Chapter 10.
`_PSPACING`	Sets or retrieves the number of line feeds output for each line printed. In other words, `_PSPACING` is used to specify whether the output is single, double, or triple spaced.
`_RMARGIN`	Defines the right margin. It is the number of characters between the page offset (`_PLOFFSET`) and the right side of a paragraph. `_RMARGIN` must be less than 256 characters.
`_WRAP`	Sets or retrieves the word-wrapping mode. While in word-wrapping mode, text is displayed in the boundaries defined by the left margin, `_LMARGIN`, and the right margin, `_RMARGIN`. Any word that would extend past the right boundary is output on the next line. `_ALIGNMENT`, `_LMARGIN`, `_INDENT`, and `_RMARGIN` are operational only in word-wrapping mode (`_WRAP=.T.`).

Line-Oriented Output Control

Certain SMVs affect all line-oriented output. In addition to the items presented in this section, `_PLENGTH` also affects line-oriented output:

`_BOX`	Notifies FoxPro that it's time to output a box defined with the `DEFINE BOX` command. As soon as `_BOX` is set to `.T.`, the box is output.
`_PAGENO`	Displays the page number in the heading or footing. It's updated as pages are printed.
`_PCOLNO`	Defines the column number of the next output to be printed using the `??` command.

_PDSETUP — This system memory variable isn't used in Visual FoxPro. It is used in dBASE IV and FoxPro for DOS to define printing parameters.

_PLINENO — Stores or retrieves the current line number. It is maintained by FoxPro as it directs output to the print device. It can range between 0 and one less than _PLENGTH. The row tracked by the PROW() function increments only when output is actually being directed to a print device—it is not incremented when SET PRINTER is OFF. On the other hand, _PLINENO is always incremented regardless of where output is directed.

_TABS — Stores or retrieves the current tab stop character string. The string contains a list of integer column numbers in ascending order separated by commas (for example, _TABS = "5,10,15,20,60"). Whenever an ASCII tab character is output, blank characters are output until the printer column is positioned to the next tab stop. If the value of _TABS is a null string, tabs are spaced every eight characters.

PRINTJOB Output Control

Some SMVs are active only when the PRINTJOB command is executing. These system memory variables are the following:

_PBPAGE — The page number of the first page to be printed for a print job. When FoxPro is processing output, it does not start directing any output to the printer until _PBPAGE equals _PAGENO.

_PCOPIES — Sets the number of copies to be printed for a print job.

_PECODE — Sets a character string that is output to the printer when a print job ends. In other words, the string is output when the ENDPRINTJOB command is encountered. This SMV exists to reset the printer to its original state.

_PEJECT — Controls page ejecting operations. It supports page ejection BEFORE a PRINTJOB, AFTER a PRINTJOB, BOTH, or NONE (no page ejection).

_PEPAGE — Is assigned with the value of the page number of the last page printed. When page number _PEPAGE has finished printing, the print job ends. When _PAGENO reaches a value that is one greater than _PEPAGE, printing stops.

_PSCODE — Sets a character string that is output to the printer before a print job begins. In other words, when the PRINTJOB command is executed, the _PSCODE character string is output directly to the printer.

Printer Control

The following system memory variables control printer operations:

`_PADVANCE` Stores or retrieves a character string that indicates the method FoxPro uses to perform a page eject operation. `_PADVANCE` is a character string data type. It can have two values. If `_PADVANCE = "FORMFEED"`, a form feed character is used to advance the paper to a new page. If `_PADVANCE = "LINEFEEDS"`, the process of advancing to a new page is accomplished by outputting line feed characters. The number of line feeds sent to the printer is computed by subtracting `_PLINENO` from `_PLENGTH`.

`_PPITCH` Sets the printer pitch setting to pica, elite, condensed, or the default, or it retrieves the setting. Default is the normal state corresponding to the printer hardware configuration. When `_PPITCH` is set, the appropriate ASCII escape sequence is sent to the printer so the next output to the printer is printed using the specified pitch.

`_PQUALITY` Sets and retrieves the value of the quality flag. When the value is changed and the printer supports quality or draft mode, the appropriate escape sequence is sent to the printer to change the mode.

`_PWAIT` Supports single-sheet feed printers. If `_PWAIT` is set to `.T.` and the printer finishes printing a page, it outputs a line feed and prompts the user to press any key to continue before printing the next page.

The *PRINTJOB* and *ENDPRINTJOB* Commands

Before a typical report generator prints a report, it carries out certain housekeeping tasks, such as initializing line counts and setting up fonts. It also does cleanup work after a printing operation. To support these activities in the dBASE IV Report Generator, a structured construct to the language, `PRINTJOB`, was added. FoxPro also supports the `PRINTJOB` concept for compatibility purposes, but FoxPro doesn't use it with its Report Writer. The syntax of the `PRINTJOB` construct is as follows:

```
PRINTJOB
<report generation commands>
ENDPRINTJOB
```

A print job provides a means of initializing print parameters and performing initialization functions before the report is printed and performing deinitialization procedures after the report is finished. A print job also controls multiple-copy printing. You use the `PRINTJOB` command to begin a print job. When FoxPro encounters the `PRINTJOB` command, the following actions are performed:

- Outputs the starting print codes to the printer, as defined by `_PSCODE`
- Outputs a page eject if `_PEJECT` equals `BEFORE` or `BOTH`

The ENDPRINTJOB command signals the end of a print job. It performs the following actions:

- Outputs the ending print codes to the printer, as defined by _PECODE
- Outputs a page eject if _PEJECT equals AFTER or BOTH
- Repeats the print job commands until the desired number of copies are printed

The two rules for using PRINTJOB and ENDPRINTJOB are use them only in a program, and do not nest them.

Table 8.5 contains system memory variables that don't relate to printing or print control.

Table 8.5. Other system memory variables.

Syntax	*Values*	*Default*	*Description*
_ASSIST = <expC>		Null string	Executes a program run with the ASSIST command
_BUILDER = <expC>		BUILDER.APP	The name of Visual FoxPro's builder application
_CALCMEM = <expN>		0.0	Value stored in calculator memory
_CALCVALUE = <expN>		0.0	Value displayed by calculator
_CLIPTEXT = <expC>	0 to 65504 characters	Null string	Returns or assigns the contents of the Clipboard
_CONVERTER = <expC>		CONVERTER.APP	The name of Visual FoxPro's conversion application
_CUROBJ = <expN>		-1	The number of the currently selected GET object
_DBCLICK = <expN>	0.05 to 5.5 seconds	0.5	The time interval FoxPro uses to detect a double or triple mouse click
DIARYDATE = <expD>	Any valid date	Current date	The date selected in the calendar/diary

continues

Table 8.5. continued

Syntax	*Values*	*Default*	*Description*
_DOS	.F.	.F.	.T. if FoxPro for DOS is running
_FOXDOC = <*expFN*>		FOXDOC.EXE	Specifies the name and location of FoxDoc
_FOXGRAPH = <*expFN*>		FOXGRAPH.EXE	Specifies the name and location of FoxPro Graphics Package
_GENGRAPH = <*expFN*>		GENGRAPH.PRG	Specifies the program used by FoxGraph for RQBE results
_GENMENU = <*expFN*>		GENMENU.PRG	Specifies the program used by FoxPro to generate menu code
_GENPD = <*expFN*>		GENPD.APP	Specifies the program used by FoxPro for print driver interface
_GENSCRN = <*expFN*>		GENSCRN.PRG	Specifies the program used by FoxPro to generate screen code
_GENXTAB = <*expFN*>		GENXTAB.PRG	Specifies the program used by FoxPro to generate cross-tab reporting code
_MAC	.F.	.F.	.T. if FoxPro for Mac is running
_MLINE = <*expN*>		0	Contains offset in memory field of last MLINE() call
_PRETEXT = <*expC*>		Null	Character expression output before a TEXTMERGE text line is output
_SCREEN = <*Object Reference*>		N/A	Used to reference the Visual FoxPro main window object so you can reference active form properties and methods

Syntax	*Values*	*Default*	*Description*
`_SHELL = <expFN>`		Null string	Specifies program shell
`_SPELLCHK = <expFN>`		`SPELLCHK.APP`	Specifies Visual FoxPro text editor spelling checker
`_STARTUP = <expFN>`		`FOXSTART.APP`	Specifies FoxPro startup application
`_TALLY = <expN>`		0	Contains number of records processed after command finishes executing
`_TEXT = <expC>`		Null	Character expression used to output before a text line with `SET TEXTMERGE`
`_THROTTLE = <expN>`	0 to 5.5 seconds	0	Specifies **T**race window execution speed
`_TRANSPORT = <expC>`		`TRANSPORT.PRG`	Converts FoxPro for DOS screens and reports to Visual FoxPro format
`_UNIX`	`.F.`	`.F.`	`.T.` if FoxPro for UNIX is running
`_WINDOWS`	`.T.`	`.T.`	`.T.` if Visual FoxPro is running
`_SPELLCHK = <expFN>`		`SPELLCHK.APP`	Specifies Visual FoxPro Text Editor spelling checker
`_WIZARDS`		`WIZARD.APP`	The name of FoxPro Wizard application

Most SMVs presented in Table 8.5 are discussed in other places in this book. `_CUROBJ` is discussed in Chapter 9. `_THROTTLE` is discussed in Chapter 23, "Building Visual FoxPro Applications," `_TALLY` is discussed in Chapter 12, "Data Set Operations," and `_MLINE` is discussed in Chapter 5, "Expressions."

The *DISPLAY* and *LIST* Commands

The traditional DISPLAY and LIST commands in FoxPro are similar to those in FoxBASE+ and dBASE III PLUS. In FoxPro, more information is displayed by commands such as LIST STATUS and LIST MEMORY than was displayed in FoxBASE+ and dBASE III PLUS. You can direct output from the LIST and DISPLAY commands to a file using the TO FILE clause; the generated file is given a default filename extension of .TXT if you don't supply one. You can still use the TO PRINTER clause to route output to a printer.

For all forms of the DISPLAY and LIST commands (except DISPLAY FILES), you can specify the NOCONSOLE keyword to suppress output to the screen or a window. This option enables you to direct output to a file or printer without displaying it on the screen.

The NOOPTIMIZE keyword disables the Rushmore index optimization. (See Chapter 13, "Data Ordering.") *Rushmore* is the name FoxPro developers gave to a technology that improves data access performance.

The DISPLAY command is similar to the LIST command except that it displays one screen (or window) full of information and the WAIT box appears, containing this message:

```
Press any key to continue...
```

Because all output is line oriented, scrolling output from all forms of the DISPLAY and LIST commands can be paused using Ctrl+S and halted by pressing Esc. Interruption of scrolling output is optional as long as SET ESCAPE is set to ON.

Features such as ON PAGE, COLOR OF HEADINGS, and SET LABELS TO can affect the display. (See the section "The ON PAGE Command.") COLOR OF HEADINGS and SET LABELS are discussed in Chapter 10. The display is affected also by certain system memory variables. (See the section "System Memory Variables.")

NOTE

Are you familiar with the dBASE III or FoxBASE+ LIST HISTORY command? FoxPro does not have a LIST HISTORY command. It simply is no longer needed. You can view or execute any of the old commands in the Command window. You can copy commands in the Command window to a program you are editing.

DISPLAY and *LIST* Data

The LIST and DISPLAY commands display the contents of a selected group of records and fields. The following is the syntax:

```
DISPLAY  [[FIELDS] <exp-list>] [OFF] [NOCONSOLE] [NOOPTIMIZE]
   TO PRINTER [PROMPT] ¦ TO FILE <expFN>]
```

```
   [<scope>] [FOR <expL>] [WHILE <expL>]

LIST  [[FIELDS] <exp-list>] [OFF]
   TO PRINTER [PROMPT] ¦ TO FILE <expFN>]
   [<scope>] [FOR <expL>] [WHILE <expL>]
```

The <scope>, FOR, and WHILE clauses restrict the number of displayed records. The default scope for DISPLAY is NEXT 1 unless FOR or WHILE is specified, in which case the default scope is ALL. The default scope for LIST is ALL. The records selected are also restricted by the SET FILTER TO and SET DELETED commands.

If you don't specify a FIELDS clause, all the fields are displayed, except the contents of memo fields. The Memo memo field icon is displayed if the record contains data for that memo field. If the memo field is empty, the memo icon is displayed.

If you do specify a FIELDS clause, only the specified expressions are displayed. If one of the items in the list is a memo field, that field is displayed in a column determined by the value of SET MEMOWIDTH TO.

If the SET FIELDS TO command is active, only the fields specified in the command can be displayed. If the FIELDS clause is omitted, all SET FIELDS TO fields are displayed. LIST also displays fields in a relation and is governed by the SET SKIP command.

If the width of the LIST display is greater than the screen or window width, the information wraps to the next line. The OFF keyword suppresses the display of the record number.

If SET HEADINGS is ON, column headings are printed. A column heading consists of a field name or an expression. The following example:

```
LIST FNAME, BDATE, City, ZIP, COST*QUANTITY
```

displays as this:

```
Recno#    FNAME     BDATE     City        COST*QUANTITY
1         Albert    03/11/68  Phoenix     343.32
2         Bert      01/22/71  Boston      123.45
3         Harvey    01/23/45  Port Arthur 22.33
```

Directory Display Commands

The DISPLAY FILES, LIST FILES, DIR, and DIRECTORY commands all display a file directory. Here is the syntax of the commands:

```
DISPLAY FILES [[LIKE] <skeleton>]
   TO PRINTER [PROMPT] ¦ TO FILE <expFN>]

LIST FILES [[LIKE] <skeleton>]
   TO PRINTER [PROMPT] ¦ TO FILE <expFN>]

DIR [[ON] <letter>:] [[LIKE] [<path>] <skeleton>]

DIRECTORY [[ON] <letter>:] [[LIKE] [<path>] <skeleton>]
```

If you don't supply the `<skeleton>` argument, only the following directory information for tables is displayed:

- Table names
- Number of records
- Date that tables were last updated
- Size in bytes of tables
- Number of files
- Total number of bytes in all tables
- Number of bytes remaining on the drive

If you specify the `<skeleton>` argument, only the filenames, total space used by the files, number of files displayed, and space left on the disk are displayed. If you don't specify a `<path>` argument, files in the current directory are displayed.

The following statement:

```
DIR *.FXP
```

displays as follows:

```
INVEN.FXP     CUSTOMER.FXP     NAMES.FXP     SUPPLY.FXP
PAYROLL.FXP
```

The following command:

```
DIR
```

displays only DBF files:

```
Database Table/DBF files    # Records    Last Updated    Size
CUSTOMER.DBF                     300     07/13/92       47041
INVENT.DBF                      1122     07/11/92       73726

120767 bytes in    2 Files
91322121 bytes remaining on drive
```

Displaying Status Information

You can use the `DISPLAY` and `LIST` commands to display internal system information. The keywords `MEMORY`, `STATUS`, and `STRUCTURE` designate the status information to display. The following is the syntax of the various forms of these commands:

```
DISPLAY CONNECTIONS
    TO PRINTER [PROMPT] ¦ TO FILE <expFN>] [NOCONSOLE]

DISPLAY DATABASES
     TO PRINTER [PROMPT] ¦ TO FILE <expFN>] [NOCONSOLE]
```

```
DISPLAY MEMORY LIKE <skeleton>
    TO PRINTER [PROMPT] ¦ TO FILE <expFN>] [NOCONSOLE]

DISPLAY OBJECTS LIKE <skeleton>
    TO PRINTER [PROMPT] ¦ TO FILE <expFN>] [NOCONSOLE]

DISPLAY PROCEDURES
    TO PRINTER [PROMPT] ¦ TO FILE <expFN>] [NOCONSOLE]

DISPLAY STATUS TO PRINTER [PROMPT] ¦ TO FILE <expFN>] [NOCONSOLE]

DISPLAY STRUCTURE [IN <expWA>]
    TO PRINTER [PROMPT] ¦ TO FILE <expFN>] [NOCONSOLE]

DISPLAY TABLES
    TO PRINTER [PROMPT] ¦ TO FILE <expFN>] [NOCONSOLE]

LIST CONNECTIONS
    TO PRINTER [PROMPT] ¦ TO FILE <expFN>] [NOCONSOLE]

LIST DATABASES
     TO PRINTER [PROMPT] ¦ TO FILE <expFN>] [NOCONSOLE]

LIST MEMORY LIKE <skeleton>
TO PRINTER [PROMPT] ¦ TO FILE <expFN>] [NOCONSOLE]

LIST OBJECTS LIKE <skeleton>
    TO PRINTER [PROMPT] ¦ TO FILE <expFN>] [NOCONSOLE]

LIST PROCEDURES
     TO PRINTER [PROMPT] ¦ TO FILE <expFN>] [NOCONSOLE]

LIST STATUS TO PRINTER [PROMPT] ¦ TO FILE <expFN>] [NOCONSOLE]

LIST STRUCTURE [IN <expWA>]
TO PRINTER [PROMPT] ¦ TO FILE <expFN>] [NOCONSOLE]

LIST TABLES
    TO PRINTER [PROMPT] ¦ TO FILE <expFN>] [NOCONSOLE]
```

In a consistent manner, the `TO PRINTER`, `TO FILE`, and `NOCONSOLE` clauses are supported in all of these forms of the `DISPLAY` command. The `LIKE` clause on the `DISPLAY MEMORY` and `DISPLAY OBJECTS` commands lets you specify wildcard characters (`*` and `?`) to selectively display active memory variables and objects, respectively. The `DISPLAY STATUS` and `LIST STATUS` commands are described in Chapter 10. Table 8.6 summarizes the output from each of these commands.

Table 8.6. Forms of the DISPLAY command used to show status.

Command	*Output*	*Chapter*
`DISPLAY CONNECTIONS` `LIST CONNECTIONS`	Displays named connection in the current database	11

continues

Table 8.6. continued

Command	*Output*	*Chapter*
`DISPLAY DATABASES` `LIST DATABASES`	Displays contents of current database table (DBF file) including field names, named connections, tables, or views	11
`DISPLAY MEMORY` `LIST MEMORY`	Displays the memory variable, system memory variables, and other memory objects	8
`DISPLAY OBJECTS` `LIST OBJECTS`	Displays OOP object information	8
`DISPLAY PROCEDURES` `LIST PROCEDURES`	Displays a list of stored procedures in the current database	8
`DISPLAY STATUS` `LIST STATUS`	Displays environmental parameters, the current database, and table and index file information	10
`DISPLAY STRUCTURE` `LIST STRUCTURE`	Displays the structure of the current table	8
`DISPLAY TABLES` `LIST TABLES`	Displays information about tables in the current database	11

The `DISPLAY MEMORY` and `LIST MEMORY` commands display memory variables, system memory variables, and information relating to internal memory use of the following objects:

- Memory variables and array elements
- Symbol tables
- Menu and pad objects
- Pop-up menu objects
- User-defined windows
- Available memory

The following values are displayed for memory variables, array elements, and print system memory variables:

- Name
- Public or private status, or array element identification
- Data type (`C`, `D`, `F`, `L`, `N`) or `A` for array
- Value

An example of the output from the LIST MEMORY command is provided in Listing 4.1 in Chapter 4, "Variables." You can use a wildcard specification to display some of the memory variables using the LIKE clause. The following example:

```
DISPLAY MEMORY LIKE AMO*
```

displays all memory variables that begin with AMO. Here are examples:

```
AMOUNT      Pub    N        3632.33   (       3632.33000000)
AMOUNT1     Pub    N        3   (       3.00000000)
AMOUNT2     Pub    N        0   (       0.00000000)
```

The DISPLAY STRUCTURE and LIST STRUCTURE commands display the field structure of the table (DBF file) currently in use. They display the table name, number of records, date of last update, and structure. The structure consists of the field name, type, width, number of decimal fields for a numeric field, and index indicator flag.

If SET FIELDS is active, the > character is displayed before the field name for each field included in the field list. An example of output from the DISPLAY STRUCTURE command follows:

```
Structure for database: D:\DB\ARTICLES.DBF
Number of data records:     1321
Date of last update    : 03/20/89
Field  Field Name  Type        Width    Dec     Index  Collate                 Nulls
  1    ARTICLE     Character     20                                             No
  2    MAGAZINE    Character     20                                             No
  3    AUTHOR      Character     20                                             No
  4    DATE        Date           8                                             No
  5    VOLUME      Character      8                                             No
  6    ABSTRACT    Memo          10                                             No
  7    PICTURE     General       10                                             No
** Total **                      87
```

The DISPLAY DATABASE and LIST DATABASE commands display the information contained in the open database, which includes the names of tables, fields, indexes, persistent relations, and stored procedures. The following listing presents a partial display of output from the LIST DATABASE command:

```
NWIND

   1    1 Database    Database
                      * Version          8
   2    1 Database    TransactionLog
   3    1 Database    StoredProceduresSource
   4    1 Database    StoredProceduresObject
   5    1 Table       customer
                      * SYSTEM PROPERTY *
                      * Path               customer.dbf
                      * PrimaryKey         cust_id
   6    5 Field       cust_id
   7    5 Field       company
   8    5 Field       contact
 ...
  19    1 Table       contact
                      * SYSTEM PROPERTY *
                      * Path               contact.dbf
```

```
 20  19 Field        cust_id
 21  19 Field        emp_id
  ...
* SYSTEM PROPERTY *
                     * Path             behindsc.dbf
                     * PrimaryKey       screen_top
123 122 Field        screen_id
124 122 Field        feature_id
    ...
131 122 Field        codetoshow
132   5 Index        cust_id
                     * Unique           TRUE
...
136  19 Index        cust_id
                     * Unique           FALSE
137  19 Relation     cust_id
                     * RelatedTable     customer
                     * RelatedTag       cust_id
                     * RelatedChild     cust_id
...
```

The DISPLAY TABLES and LIST TABLES commands display the name and location (path) and type of tables in the currently active database (DBC). Information displays for all tables in the current database even for tables that are not in use. The type can be native or a remote connection. If you execute the following commands:

```
OPEN DATABASE NWIND
LIST TABLES
```

the following output displays:

```
Tables in Database  nwind:

  Name             Type       Source
  customer         native    c:\fox30\samples\data\customer.dbf
  contact          native    c:\fox30\samples\data\contact.dbf
  userlevl         native    c:\fox30\samples\data\userlevl.dbf
  supplier         native    c:\fox30\samples\data\supplier.dbf
  shippers         native    c:\fox30\samples\data\shippers.dbf
  products         native    c:\fox30\samples\data\products.dbf
  orditems         native    c:\fox30\samples\data\orditems.dbf
  orders           native    c:\fox30\samples\data\orders.dbf
  employee         native    c:\fox30\samples\data\employee.dbf
  category         native    c:\fox30\samples\data\category.dbf
  busrules         native    c:\fox30\samples\data\busrules.dbf
  behindsc         native    c:\fox30\samples\data\behindsc.dbf
```

The DISPLAY OBJECTS and LIST OBJECTS commands display the information about all or selected existing OOP objects. It displays the following object-related characteristics:

- Properties and corresponding values of properties
- Methods (procedures)
- Member objects and the class or subclass on which they are based
- The class or subclass on which objects are based
- The class hierarchy for objects

The *REPORT* Command

The REPORT command prints a report based on a selected group of records from the currently active database table (DBF file) or view. The format of the report is controlled by the specified report form file. Form files are created using the CREATE REPORT or MODIFY REPORT commands. (See Chapter 20, "Report and Label Designers and Wizards.") FoxPro has a powerful and comprehensive report generator that satisfies almost all reporting requirements. The following is the syntax of the REPORT command:

```
REPORT [FORM <expFN>] ¦ ?
   [ENVIRONMENT] [HEADING <expC>]
   [NOCONSOLE] [NOEJECT] [NOOPTIMIZE]
   [PDSETUP] [PLAIN] [PREVIEW] [SUMMARY]
   [<scope>] [FOR <expL>] [WHILE <expL>]
   TO PRINTER [PROMPT] ¦ TO FILE <expFN>]
```

The *FORM* Clause

The *<expFN>* argument in the FORM clause is a filename expression representing the report form file. If *<expFN>* is not specified or a question mark is specified, an Open File dialog box containing files with the .FRX extension appears, from which a file can be selected.

The *ENVIRONMENT* Keyword

The ENVIRONMENT keyword instructs the REPORT command to restore the environment stored in the report definition file before printing the report. The environment consists of the names of all open tables (DBF files), index files, the index order, and any relationship between the tables. When you create a report using the MODIFY REPORT command, you are given the option of saving the environment in the report definition table.

The *HEADING* Clause

The HEADING clause defines an extra heading line that is printed on the first line of each page of the report.

The *NOCONSOLE* Keyword

The NOCONSOLE keyword instructs the REPORT command to not display the output on the screen.

The *NOEJECT* Keyword

If the report form is designed to output a line feed before printing the first page, the NOEJECT keyword suppresses outputting of that line feed.

The *NOOPTIMIZE* Keyword

The NOOPTIMIZE keyword instructs the REPORT command not to use the Rushmore technology to optimize data retrieval. Commands that use the FOR clause can use the Rushmore technology to improve performance. Rushmore technology is discussed in Chapter 13.

Normally you have no reason to disable the Rushmore technology. However, if you have a report application that modifies the FOR expression dynamically during reporting, the record set selected by Rushmore is not valid. You will need to disable Rushmore using the NOOPTIMIZE keyword.

The *PDSETUP* Keyword

If the PDSETUP keyword is specified, the print driver setup associated with the report is used.

The *PLAIN* Keyword

The PLAIN keyword forces the REPORT command to print headers and footers on only the first page.

The *PREVIEW* Keyword

The PREVIEW keyword instructs the REPORT command to display the report on the screen so that you can view it before you print it.

The *SUMMARY* Keyword

The SUMMARY keyword suppresses the printing of detail lines. Only subtotals and totals are printed.

The *TO PRINTER* and *TO FILE <expFN>* Clauses

You can use the TO clause to direct REPORT output to a printer or a text file. If the filename extension is not specified, .TXT is used. Incidentally, if an alternate file is active output is directed to the alternate file also. (See Chapter 10.)

The *LABEL* Command

The LABEL command prints labels derived from a selected group of records in the current table (DBF file). The format of the generated labels is controlled by a specified label form file. Label form files are created with the CREATE/MODIFY LABEL command. The following is the syntax for the command:

```
LABEL FORM [ <expFN>] ¦ ?
   [ENVIRONMENT] [HEADING <expC>]
   [NOCONSOLE] [NOEJECT] [NOOPTIMIZE]
   [PDSETUP] [PLAIN] [PREVIEW] [SUMMARY]
   [<scope>] [FOR <expL>] [WHILE <expL>]
   TO PRINTER [PROMPT] ¦ TO FILE <expFN>] [SAMPLE]
```

The *FORM* Clause

The `<expFN>` argument in the `FORM` clause is a filename expression representing the label form file. If `<expFN>` is not specified or a question mark is specified, an Open File dialog box containing files with the .LBX extension appears, from which a file can be selected.

All keywords and clauses serve the same purpose for the `LABEL` command as for the `REPORT` command except the `SAMPLE` keyword. The `SAMPLE` keyword forces the `LABEL` command to print test labels, which are used to verify the correct alignment of labels. When the row of labels is printed, the label fields are filled with `x` characters rather than label values.

Prerecorded Input

The word *macro* can be confusing because the term relates to several things. The three types of macros in FoxPro are command macros and two types of macros you can use to preprogram the keyboard. A command macro, which appears in FoxPro programs, consists of an ampersand symbol (`&`) followed by a memory variable. This type of macro is replaced by the literal contents of the memory variable in the command line. Command macros are discussed in Chapter 5.

The second type of macro in FoxPro, the keyboard macro, is discussed in this section. The third type, the `SET FUNCTION` macro, is similar to the keyboard macro, but you can preprogram only F2 through F10 and Shift+F1 through Shift+F10. This type is described in Chapter 10 in the discussion of `SET FUNCTION`.

What Are Keyboard Macros?

You can use keyboard macros anywhere in FoxPro to capture keystrokes, save the keystrokes in a macro buffer, assign that buffer to a key, and play the captured keystrokes back. They are especially useful for capturing keystrokes for repetitive processes associated with full-screen operations.

Basic Recording and Playback Operations

The basic operation is as simple as using a tape recorder. At the point in your session where you want to start recording keystrokes, press Shift+F10. The dialog box shown in Figure 8.2 appears.

The Defined Key edit field is selected. You press a key that you use to call the macro. You can press any of the keys shown in Table 8.7. Then you enter the macro name. Initially, it is set to the name of the key you pressed, but you can enter any name you like.

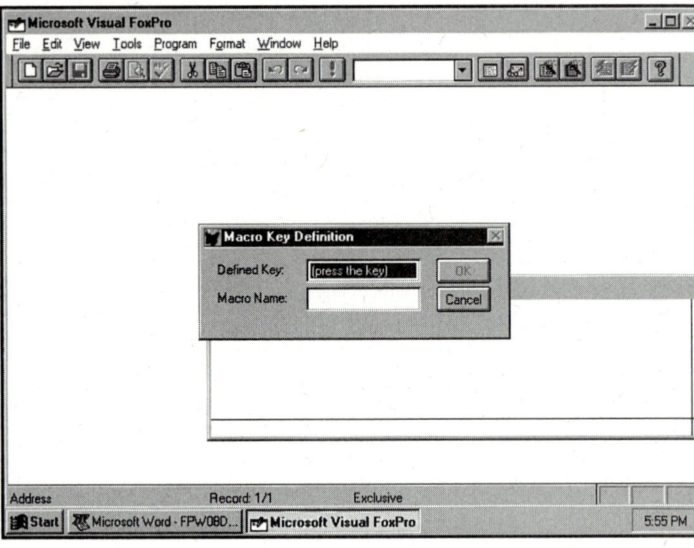

FIGURE 8.2.
The Macro Key Definition dialog box.

Table 8.7. Macro key definition.

Key Label	*Key Alone*	*Shift+Key*	*Ctrl+Key*	*Alt+Key*
F1–F9	Yes		Yes	Yes
F10	Yes	No	Yes	Yes
A–Z			Yes	Yes
F10, A–F10, Z	Yes	Yes		
Ins	Yes	Yes		
Del	Yes	Yes		
Home	Yes	Yes	Yes	
End	Yes	Yes	Yes	
PgUp	Yes	Yes	Yes	
PgDn	Yes	Yes		
Up Arrow	Yes	Yes		
Left Arrow	Yes	Yes	Yes	
Right Arrow	Yes	Yes	Yes	
Down Arrow	Yes	Yes		

Next, press the OK push button. The dialog box disappears. If a macro already exists for the specified key, the Overwrite Macro dialog box (shown in Figure 8.3) appears and gives you the option to overwrite the existing macro, add more keystrokes to the existing macro, or abandon the operation.

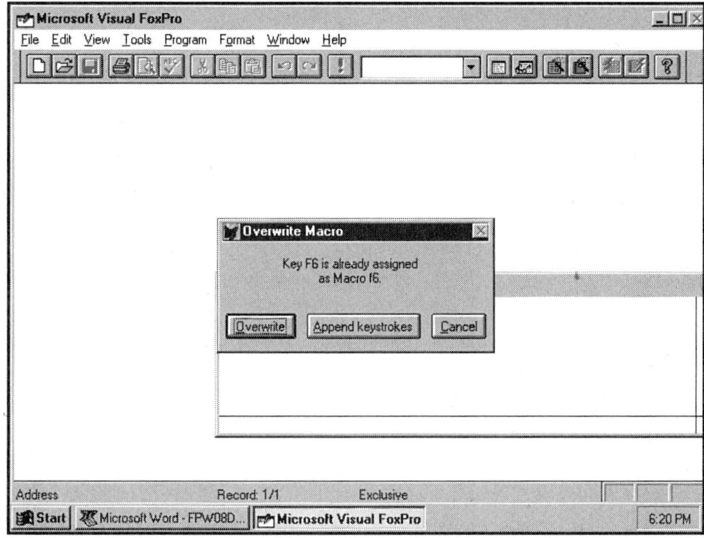

FIGURE 8.3.
The Overwrite Macro dialog box.

If you choose to continue, the dialog box disappears. Then, any keystrokes that are typed are captured in the macro buffer. When you have completed your keystroke recording session, press Shift+F10, and the dialog box shown in Figure 8.4 appears.

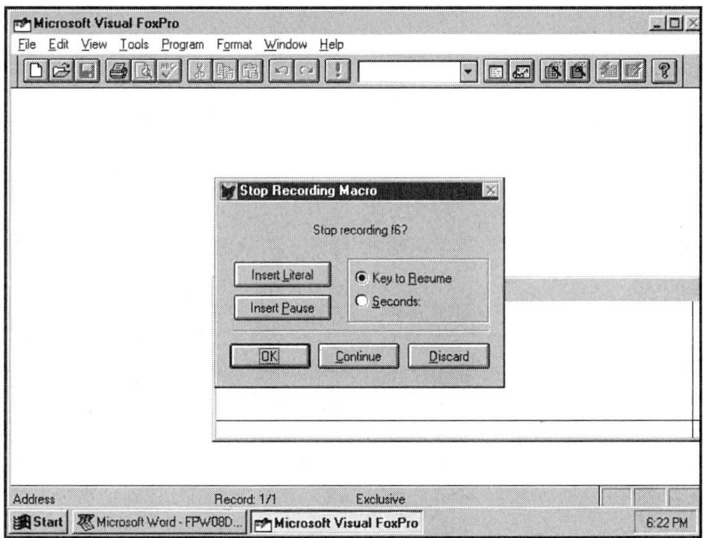

FIGURE 8.4.
The Stop Recording Macro dialog box.

From the Stop Recording Macro dialog box, you have the following options:

Insert **L**iteral	Records the literal meaning of the next keystroke. This means if the keystroke is a keyboard macro, it inserts the keystroke, not the macro contents, and then returns to normal macro recording.
Insert **P**ause	Records a pause in the macro, then returns to normal macro recording. You can use this option if you reach a point in the recording session where you want to solicit user input during playback or you want a timed pause.
Key to **R**esume	If selected, macro playback is suspended when a pause is encountered. You can type characters from the keyboard. When you are ready to resume playback, press a certain key. `SET MACKEY` defines the key.
Seconds	This check box is an alternative to the Key to Resume check box. When you select this option, you also specify an elapsed time. If specified, a macro pause suspends the macro playback for the designated elapsed time.
OK	Stops recording and makes the keyboard macro available for use.
Continue	Continues macro recording at the point the Stop Recording Macro dialog box was activated. Select this option if the Stop Recording Macro dialog box was activated by mistake and you do not want to end a recording session.
Discard	Cancels macro recording operation.

The *PLAY MACRO* Command

You can execute keyboard macros from the command language using the `PLAY MACRO` command. The syntax is as follows:

```
PLAY MACRO <macro name> [TIME <expN>]
```

`<macro name>` is the name associated with the macro. This name is assigned when you create the macro. You can vary the speed of the macro playback by specifying the `TIME` clause. The *`<expN>`* expression specifies the time in seconds.

The following example plays back the macro that was created in the previous section:

```
PLAY MACRO Appointments TIME 1.3
```

During playback, each macro character is played back every 1.3 seconds.

The Macros Menu

You can do other things with keyboard macros. To access this additional functionality, choose the **M**acros option in the **T**ools menu, as shown in Figure 8.5. A **M**acros menu pad also appears on the menu bar. The **M**acros menu contains the same options available in the Macros dialog box.

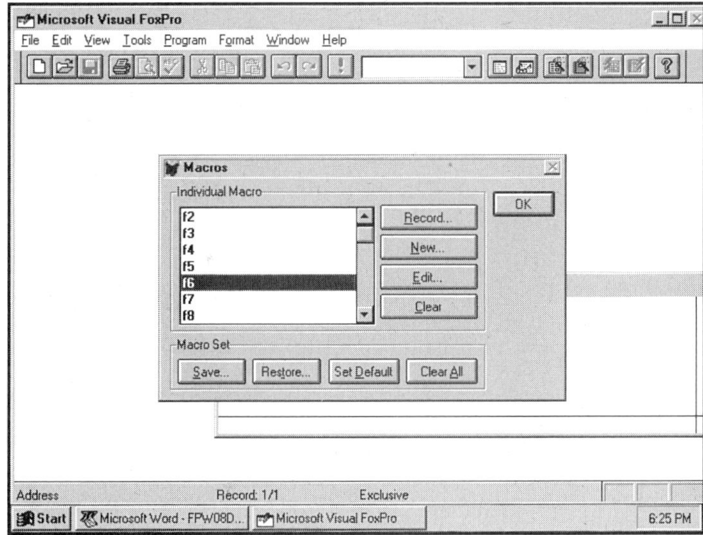

FIGURE 8.5.
The Macros dialog box with the Macros menu open.

On the left of the Keyboard Macros table is a list of the names of all of the existing macros. You can select one of the names, and the Macro Edit dialog box appears, as shown in Figure 8.6.

The contents of the macro appear in the edit window. From here you can make any required changes to the macro. For nonprintable characters use the labels in Table 8.8.

Table 8.8. Macro keystroke labels.

`{Alt+<key>}`*	`{Backspace}`	`{Ctrl+<key>}`*
`{Del}`	`{DownArrow}`	`{End}`
`{Enter}`	`{Esc}`	`{F1}` through `{F10}`
`{Home}`	`{Ins}`	`{LeftArrow}`
`{PgDn}`	`{PgUp}`	`{PrtSc}`
`{RightArrow}`	`{SHIFT+<key>}`*	`{Tab}`

*`<key>` indicates that another keycap symbol follows (for example, `{Alt+F3}`, `{Ctrl+F3}`, and `{Shift+F3}`).

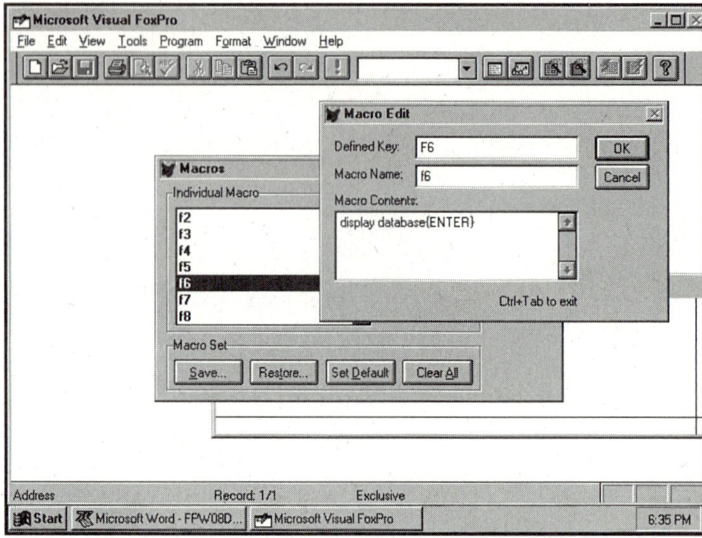

FIGURE 8.6.
The Macro Edit dialog box.

The Macros dialog box, shown in Figure 8.5, contains the following options to operate on keyboard macros:

Save	Saves current macro set to a file. A menu appears and you select a file with an .FKY extension or type in the name of a new file.
Res**t**ore	Restores macro set from a macro file. The file is selected from the Restore Macros dialog box.
Set **D**efault	Saves current macros set in the DEFAULT.FKY file in the same directory as your FOXUSER file.
Clear **A**LL	Clears all macros from current macro set.
Record	Displays the Macro Key Definition dialog box. You enter the macro key and type the macro name and recording begins.
New	Defines or edits a new macro.
Edit	Activates Macro Edit dialog box to edit highlighted keyboard macro.
Clear	Removes highlighted keyboard macro for the current macro set.

Load Macros and Save Macros

The current set of keyboard macros can be saved and restored from the Macros dialog box, as described in the previous section. In the command language, the current set of macros is saved and restored by using the following commands:

```
SAVE MACRO TO <expFN>
RESTORE MACRO FROM <expFN>
```

The `SAVE` command creates a new macro FKY file and stores the existing macros in the file. The `RESTORE` command loads the specified macro file.

Low-Level File Input and Output

FoxPro has a group of functions that support C-language type low-level file input/output (I/O) operations. These functions have the same functionality and parameters as Microsoft's file I/O library. These functions are the following:

`FCHSIZE()`	Changes the size of an MS-DOS file
`FCLOSE()`	Closes an MS-DOS file
`FCREATE()`	Creates an MS-DOS file
`FDATE()`	Returns the date when the specified file was last modified
`FEOF()`	Returns the end-of-file status
`FERROR()`	Returns the file I/O error status
`FFLUSH()`	Flushes MS-DOS file buffers and directory entry
`FGETS()`	Reads a string terminated with an ASCII carriage return
`FOPEN()`	Opens an existing MS-DOS file
`FPUTS()`	Writes an ASCII string to an MS-DOS file
`FREAD()`	Reads the specified number of characters from an MS-DOS file
`FSEEK()`	Seeks a specified position in an MS-DOS file
`FSIZE()`	If `SET COMPATIBLE` is `ON`, returns the size in bytes of the specified file as a numeric data value
`FTIME()`	Returns the time when the specified file was last modified
`FWRITE()`	Writes the specified number of characters to an MS-DOS file

The `FOPEN()` and `FCREATE()` functions return a numeric file handle that is used by the other functions as an argument to reference the MS-DOS file. This handle is an important integer and can be used from the time you open or create a file until the time you close it. Then you can forget about it, release it, or trash it. However, you can no longer use the handle to reference the file.

FoxPro maintains a table of the handles used for low-level file I/O operations. Thus, if a reference is made to a file handle that does not belong to the low-level file I/O subsystem, an error condition is triggered. This prevents users from manipulating files for other subsystems using the low-level file I/O subsystem.

The `CLOSE ALL` command closes all files related to the low-level file I/O subsystem. The `DISPLAY/LIST STATUS` command displays the opened low-level files as well as all related information.

In addition, you can use the FoxPro low-level file I/O functions to perform communications port input and output operations. All you need to do is open the file with the name of the communications port (`COM1`, `COM2`, `COM3`, and `COM4`). You use `FOPEN()` to open the communications port; `FGETS()`, `FREAD()`, `FPUTS()`, or `FWRITE()` for I/O; and `FCLOSE()` to close the communications port. Before you run FoxPro, you must initialize the communications port to the proper baud rate, number of data bits, number of stop bits, and parity byte. You can do this with the MS-DOS MODE program.

The FTIME(<*expFN*>) and FDATE(<*expFN*>) functions return the time and date, respectively, that the specified file (<*expFN*>) was last modified. The time is returned as a character string in the form *hh*:*mm*:sss and the date is returned as a date data type. FSIZE(<*expFN*>) returns the size in bytes of a file. <*expFN*> specifies the filename and can include the full pathname. However, it does not support wildcard characters. FSIZE() searches the current directory and the directories specified by the SET PATH command.

The *FCHSIZE()* Function

The FCHSIZE() function changes the size of an MS-DOS file. It is used in conjunction with low-level file I/O functions. The final size in bytes is returned if the operation is successful. Otherwise, -1 is returned. The syntax is as follows:

```
<expN1> = FCHSIZE(<expN2>, <expN3>)
```

<*expN2*> is the MS-DOS file handle assigned by the FOPEN() or FCREATE() function. <*expN3*> is an integer value in bytes that specifies the new size of the file. If the original file is larger than <*expN3*>, the file is truncated. If the value of the pointer is larger, the file is expanded.

In the following example, the size of DEMO.TXT is changed to 99 bytes:

```
Handle = FOPEN("DEMO.TXT")
IF Handle > 0
   IF ( FCHSIZE(Handle, 99 ) != 99 )
      ? "Operation was unsuccessful"
   ENDIF
   =FCLOSE(Handle)
ENDIF
```

The *FCLOSE()* Function

The FCLOSE() function closes an MS-DOS file that was opened using the FOPEN() function or created using the FCREATE() function. The syntax is as follows:

```
<expL> = FCLOSE(<expN>)
```

The <*expN*> argument is the MS-DOS file handle, assigned by the FOPEN() or FCREATE() function. The FCLOSE() function returns .T. if the file close operation is successful; otherwise, it returns .F..

An example of the FCLOSE() function follows:

```
Handle = FOPEN("DEMO.TXT")
IF Handle > 0
   <do file I/O>
   = FCLOSE(handle)
ENDIF
```

The *FCREATE()* Function

The `FCREATE()` function creates a new MS-DOS file. The syntax is as follows:

```
<expN1> = FCREATE(<expFN> [,<expN2>])
```

`<expFN>` is a character string containing the filename and extension of the file to create. (You must supply the filename extension.) If the file to be created is not on the default drive, the filename must be preceded with its drive and directory location.

`<expN2>` is an optional argument for setting the MS-DOS attributes for the file. If `<expN2>` is not specified, the file is opened with read and write privileges. No attributes are set. The allowed values for this argument follow:

<expN2>	*Description*
0	Read and Write (no attributes set)
1	Read-Only attribute
2	Hidden attribute
3	Read-Only and Hidden attributes
4	System attribute
5	Read-Only and System attributes
6	System and Hidden attributes
7	Read-Only, Hidden, and System attributes

If you use `FCREATE()` to create a file with the MS-DOS Read-Only attribute set (`1`), you can write to the file until you close it. The next time you open the file using `FOPEN()` you can read the file only if you use some MS-DOS utility to remove the Read-Only attribute. Files with a hidden attribute will not display in a file directory and cannot be implicitly accessed.

`FCREATE()` creates an MS-DOS file that is operated on by other low-level file functions. If a file with the same name already exists, it is overwritten. That is, the length of the file is truncated to zero, effectively deleting its contents.

If `FCREATE()` is successful, it returns a numeric file handle that is used by the other low-level file I/O functions to identify the file to process. If `FCREATE()` is not successful, it returns `-1` and the handle is not set. The reason for the failure can be discovered by examining the value returned by the `FERROR()` function.

NOTE

It is important that every time you open an existing file with `FOPEN()` or create a file with `FCREATE()` you check the returned value to ensure that it's greater than zero before you use it for any low-level file I/O operations. When FoxPro is unable to create or open a file, it returns `-1`.

An example of `FCREATE()` follows:

```
Handle = FOPEN('DEMO.TXT')  && Open file
IF Handle < 0               && If file does not exist…
   Handle = FCREATE('DEMO.TXT')    && create it
ENDIF
IF Handle < 0
   WAIT "Cannot create file"
   RETURN                   && Exit
ENDIF
<do file I/O operations>
=FCLOSE(Handle)
CANCEL
```

The *FEOF()* Function

The `FEOF()` function returns `.T.` if the file pointer for the specified file is positioned at the end of the file. Otherwise, `FEOF()` returns `.F.`. The syntax is as follows:

```
<expL> = FEOF(<expN>)
```

<expN> is a valid MS-DOS file handle assigned by the `FOPEN()` or `FCREATE()` function. An example of `FEOF()` follows:

```
FileName = "DEMO.TXT"
Handle = FOPEN(FileName)
Temp = FSEEK(Handle, 0)  && Position to beginning of file
IF FEOF(Handle)
   ? "File:", FileName, " is empty."
ENDIF
```

The *FERROR()* Function

The `FERROR()` function is used to determine the success of a low-level file I/O function by returning its I/O error status. The syntax is as follows:

```
<expN> = FERROR()
```

There are no arguments. `FERROR()` returns `0` if the previously executed low-level I/O function was successful. Otherwise, it returns one of the following positive integers, which represent standard MS-DOS file I/O errors:

I/O Error Code	*Description*
2	File does not exist
3	Path not found
4	Too many open files (no handles left)
5	Access denied (file is read-only, directory, and so on)
6	Invalid file handle
8	File queue is full

25	Seek error
29	Disk full
31	Error opening file or general failure

An example of `FERROR()` follows:

```
PROCEDURE SHOWERROR
ERRNO = FERROR()
DO CASE
   CASE ERRNO = 0
      m.msg= "Not file error: "
   CASE ERRNO = 2
      m.msg = "File does not exist"
   CASE ERRNO = 3
      m.msg = "Path not found"
   CASE ERRNO = 4
      m.msg = " Too many open files (no handles left)"
   CASE ERRNO = 5
      m.msg = "Access denied (file is read only or directory)"
   CASE ERRNO = 6
      m.msg = "Invalid file handle"
   CASE ERRNO = 8
      m.msg = "File queue is full"
   CASE ERRNO = 25
      m.msg = "Seek error"
   CASE ERRNO = 29
      m.msg = "Write fault-disk full"
   CASE ERRNO = 31
      m.msg = "Error opening file or general failure"
ENDCASE
WAIT m.msg WINDOW
CANCEL
```

The *FFLUSH()* Function

The `FFLUSH()` function writes out the MS-DOS buffers and directory entry for the specified file. It returns `.T.` if the operation is successful. The syntax is as follows:

```
<expL> = FFLUSH(<expN>)
```

<expN> is a valid MS-DOS file handle assigned by the `FOPEN()` or `FCREATE()` function. While writing a file, MS-DOS stores data in internal buffers and writes to disk during a pause in CPU activity. As each block of data is written to disk, the cluster address is stored in a directory entry maintained in RAM. The directory entry is written to disk only when the file is closed. If a power outage or some other calamity causes your computer to crash, all data written to disk can be lost. If you are writing valuable data to disk using low-level file I/O operations, you can call `FFLUSH()` periodically to save your data.

The following is an example of `FFLUSH()`:

```
FileName = "DEMO.TXT"
Handle = FOPEN(FileName)
<MS-DOS file I/O>
```

```
IF FFLUSH(Handle)
   ? "Operation was successful"
ENDIF
...
```

The *FGETS()* Function

The `FGETS()` function reads a string of characters terminated by a carriage return from an MS-DOS file and returns them as a character string. The syntax is as follows:

```
<expC> = FGETS(<expN1> [,<expN2>])
```

`<expN1>` is the MS-DOS file handle assigned by either the `FOPEN()` or `FCREATE()` function.

`<expN2>` is an optional numeric expression that is a positive number representing the number of bytes to read, beginning at the current character position. The number must be greater than 0 and less than 255. If you omit `<expN2>`, 254 is assumed.

Beginning at the current position of the file pointer, the `FGETS()` function reads either a specified number of characters or until it encounters a carriage return. After the read operation, the pointer is positioned after the last character read or after the carriage return. `FGETS()` ignores line feeds.

`FGETS()` returns a character string containing the information read from the file. If the read operation is unsuccessful (for example, the pointer is positioned at the end of the file), a null string is returned. To find out why the function returned a null string, check the `FEOF()` or `FERROR()` function.

An example of the `FGETS()` function follows:

```
Handle = -1
ON ERROR DO ShowError               && See FERROR() function
Handle = OPEN("BOOK")               && Open to read
If (Handle > 0)
   DO WHILE .NOT. FEOF(Handle)
      Line = FGETS(Handle)  && Read a line from the file "Book"
      ? Line                && Display the line
   ENDDO
ENDIF
= FCLOSE(Handle)
RETURN
```

The *FOPEN()* Function

The `FOPEN()` function opens an MS-DOS file. The syntax is as follows:

```
<expN1> = FOPEN(<expFN> [,<expN2>])
```

`<expFN>` is a character string containing the filename and extension of an existing file. (You must include the filename extension.) If the file to be opened is not in the default directory on the default drive, in the `SET PATH TO` path, or the MS-DOS path, you must precede the filename with its drive and directory location.

<expN2> is an optional argument that specifies the file access privileges and buffering scheme used. If you do not include <expN2>, the file is opened with read-only privileges. The allowed values for this argument follow:

<expN2>	*Read/Write Privileges*	*Buffered?*
0	Read-only (default)	Buffered
1	Write-only	Buffered
2	Read and write	Buffered
10	Read-only	Unbuffered
11	Write-only	Unbuffered
12	Read and write	Unbuffered

The FOPEN() function opens an MS-DOS file for reading and writing by the low-level file I/O functions. If the file does not exist or the file cannot be opened, error processing is invoked and the handle is not returned. If FOPEN() can open the file, the function returns a positive integer representing the MS-DOS file handle.

If the file is opened as read-only (0 or 10), write operations cannot be performed. If the file has only write privileges (1 or 11), read operations cannot be performed, but its existing contents can be overwritten. If the file is opened with read and write privileges (2 or 12), you can read or write information. If you want to update a record, however, you must use FSEEK() after the record is read to properly reposition the file pointer before writing to the file. In all of these cases, when the file is opened, it is initially positioned at the beginning of the file.

If you want to append data to the end of the file, you must first position the file pointer to the end of the file using the FSEEK() function.

The CLOSE ALL command closes all files related to the low-level file I/O subsystem.

An example of FOPEN() follows:

```
Handle = FOPEN("DEMO.TXT",2)     && Read and write privileges
IF Handle < 0
   RETURN                       && Error occurred
ELSE
   <do file I/O>
Handle  = .T.
Handle = FCLOSE(Handle)
IF Handle
   ? "File was closed"
ELSE
   ? "Unable to close file"
RETURN
ENDIF
Handle = FOPEN('DEMO.DOS') && Read only
IF Handle < 0              && Did file open okay?
   ? "Unable to open file. File error #:",FERROR()
ELSE
   DO WHILE .NOT.FEOF()
      String = FGETS(Handle)
      ? String
```

```
   ENDDO
ENDIF
RETURN
```

The *FPUTS()* Function

The FPUTS() function writes a character string to an MS-DOS file or communication port. Also, FPUTS() outputs a carriage return and a line feed to the output file. The syntax is this:

```
<expN1> = FPUTS(<expN2>, <expC> [,<expN3>])
```

<*expN2*> is the MS-DOS file handle assigned by FOPEN() when the file is opened or FCREATE() when the file is created.

<*expC*> is the character string written to the file. <*expN3*> is an optional numeric value that specifies the number of characters to write to the file. <*expN3*> characters are written to the file if <*expN3*> is less than or equal to the number of characters in <*expC*>. If <*expN3*> is greater than the length of <*expC*>, then all characters in <*expC*> are written to the file.

The FPUTS() function writes the specified character string to the file identified by the file handle. The writing begins at the current position of the file pointer.

After the characters have been output to the file, a carriage return and a line feed are output to the file. The FWRITE() function does not output the carriage return and line feed.

The function returns a numeric value representing the number of bytes written to the file. If the write operation is unsuccessful, 0 is returned. You can use the FERROR() function to determine the type of error.

An example of FPUTS() follows:

```
DEMOFILE = "C\DEMO\DEMO.TXT"
ON ERROR DO ShowError             && See FERROR() function
Handle = FOPEN(DEMOFILE,"A")      && Open file to append data
IF Handle < 0
   WAIT "File doesn't exist. It will be created" WINDOW
   Handle = FCREATE(DEMOFILE)
   If Handle < 0
      WAIT " ... File cannot be created. Error #"+;
      STR(FERROR()) WINDOW
      RETURN
   ENDIF
ENDIF
USE ADBF
NumBytes=0
SCAN
   NumBytes = FPUTS(Handle, RTRIM(Customer)) +Numbytes
ENDSCAN
m.msg = LTRIM(STR(NumBytes));
        + " characters were output to file:" + DEMOFILE
WAIT m.msg WINDOW
= FCLOSE(Handle)
RETURN
```

The *FREAD()* Function

The FREAD() function reads a specified number of bytes from an MS-DOS file into a character string. The syntax is as follows:

```
<expC> = FREAD(<expN1>, <expN2>)
```

<expN1> is the MS-DOS file handle assigned by the FOPEN() or FCREATE() function. *<expN2>* is a numeric expression that must evaluate to a positive integer. It specifies the number of bytes to read from the file.

The FREAD() function reads the specified number of characters from the designated file, beginning at the current file pointer position. FREAD() returns the characters read as a character string.

The file pointer is repositioned after the last character is read. If the end of the file is encountered, FREAD() returns a string containing those characters already read, if any, even though the number of characters returned may be less than *<expN2>*.

The function returns a character string that contains the characters read from the file. Its length is the same number as specified with *<expN2>* unless the end of the file or a disk-read error is encountered.

The following is an example of FREAD():

```
ON ERROR DO ShowError            && See FERROR() function
Handle = FOPEN("DEMO.TXT")
IF Handle < 0
  ? "Cannot open file: DEMO.TXT. Error #",FERROR()
RETURN
ENDIF
USE ADBF
ZAP
DO WHILE .not. FEOF(Handle)   && Loop until end of file
   Manuf = FREAD(Handle, 30) && Read a line
   IF Len(Manuf) = 30
      APPEND BLANK    && Add record to table
      REPLACE Company WITH Manuf
   ENDIF
ENDDO
= FCLOSE(Handle)
RETURN
```

The *FSEEK()* Function

The FSEEK() function positions the file pointer anywhere in an MS-DOS file. The next file I/O operation takes place at the new location. The syntax is as follows:

```
<expN1> = FSEEK(<expN2>, <expN3> [,<expN4>])
```

<expN2> is the MS-DOS file handle assigned by the FOPEN() or FCREATE() function. *<expN3>* is an integer value that specifies the number of bytes to move the file pointer. If the value is positive, the pointer is moved toward the end of the file. If the value is negative, the pointer is moved toward the beginning of the file.

<expN4> is an optional numeric expression that evaluates to an integer value of 0, 1, or 2. If you omit <expN4>, 0 is assumed. The following values designate the reference point for positioning:

<expN4>	*Positioning Reference*
0	Beginning of the file (default)
1	Current pointer position
2	End of the file

FSEEK() moves the file pointer in a file. The displacement is defined by <expN2> and is referenced from the beginning of the file, the current position, or the end of the file, depending on the value of <expN3>. FSEEK() returns an integer numeric value that is the position of the file pointer relative to the beginning of the file after the repositioning operation is completed. Listing 8.4 illustrates how to use the FSEEK() function.

Listing 8.4. Source listing of the FSEEK.PRG program.

```
************************************************************
*      * 07/26/94            FSEEK.PRG               9:31:22 *
************************************************************
*      *                                                     *
*      * Description:                                        *
*      *   This program illustrates how to use the FSEEK     *
*      *   low-level I/O function                            *
************************************************************
SET TALK OFF
CLOSE ALL    && Close all files, etc. including low-level files
STORE 0 TO BEGIN
STORE 1 TO CURRENT
STORE 2 TO END
*************************************************************

ON ERROR DO FileError                  && Set error trap
Handle = FOPEN("DEMO.TXT",2)           && Open file for read/write
IF Handle < 0
   DO FileError
   RETURN
ENDIF
NewLoc = FSEEK(Handle, 0, END)         && Move to end of file
DO ShowAnswer WITH NewLoc, "Move to end of file"
NewLoc = FSEEK(Handle, 0, BEGIN)       && Move to beginning of file
                                       &&   (rewind)
DO ShowAnswer WITH NewLoc, "Move to beginning of file"
NewLoc = FSEEK(Handle, 50, BEGIN)      && Move to before 51st byte
DO ShowAnswer WITH NewLoc, "Move to 51st byte"
NewLoc = FSEEK(Handle, 5, CURRENT)     && Move 5 characters forward
                                       &&   from current position
DO ShowAnswer WITH NewLoc, "Move 5 characters forward"
NewLoc = FSEEK(Handle, -15, CURRENT)   && Move 15 characters
                                         &&   backward from
                                         &&   current position
DO ShowAnswer WITH NewLoc, "Move 15 characters backwards"
NewLoc = FSEEK(Handle, 0, CURRENT)   && Determine current position
DO ShowAnswer WITH NewLoc, "Determine current position"
```

```
NewLoc = FSEEK(Handle, 0)           && Move to beginning of file
DO ShowAnswer WITH NewLoc, "Move to beginning of file"
************************************************************
* Now exchange all occurrences of "cat" with "dog" in file
DO WHILE .NOT. FEOF(Handle)
   Position = FSEEK(Handle, 0, CURRENT)   && Save position
   String = FGETS(Handle)
   Position = FSEEK(Handle, Position, BEGIN )   && Move back
   String = STRTRAN(String, "cat", "dog", 1, 99)
   = FPUTS(Handle, String)
ENDDO
ON ERROR
= FCLOSE( Handle )
*******************************************************************
PROCEDURE FileError
WAIT "File I/O Error #"+STR(FERROR()) WINDOW
RETURN
*******************************************************************
PROCEDURE ShowAnswer
PARAMETER Position, Message
WAIT Message + "   New file position: " ;
   +LTRIM(STR(Position)) WINDOW
RETURN
```

The *FWRITE()* Function

The `FWRITE()` function writes characters from a character string to an MS-DOS file. The syntax is as follows:

```
FWRITE(<expN1>, <expC> [,<expN2>])
```

<expN1> is the MS-DOS file handle assigned by the `FOPEN()` or `FCREATE()` function. *<expC>* is the character string written to the file.

<expN2> is an optional numeric expression that must evaluate to a positive integer. It specifies the number of bytes to write to the file. If you do not specify *<expN2>*, the entire string is written to the file.

`FWRITE()` writes the specified character string to the file identified by the file handle. The writing begins at the current file pointer position. When the writing operation is completed, the file pointer is repositioned after the last character written. The entire character string is output to the file unless you specify the optional *<expN2>* argument. In this case, only *<expN2>* characters are output to the file if *<expN2>* is less than the number of characters in the string. Of course, if *<expN2>* is greater than the number of characters, the entire string is output.

The function returns a numeric value that represents the number of bytes output to the file. If the write operation is unsuccessful, `0` is returned. You can use the `FERROR()` and `FEOF()` functions to determine the type of error.

In the following example, the low-level `FWRITE()` function is used to output contents of a table field to a file for every record in the table:

```
Handle = FCREATE("DEMO.TXT")
IF Handle < 0
   DO ShowError       && See FERROR() function
   RETURN
ENDIF
USE ADBF
SCAN
   IF FWRITE(Handle, Customer) = 0
   *        We have a problem. Display error.
      DO ShowError           && See FERROR() function
      = FCLOSE(Handle)
      RETURN
   ENDIF
ENDSCAN
= FCLOSE(Handle)
RETURN
```

Summary

This chapter presents the various aspects of the FoxPro line-oriented input and output commands. System memory variables, keyboard macros, and low-level file I/O functions are also discussed.

9 Full-Screen Data Editing

Thunder is good, thunder is impressive; but it is lightning that does the work.

—Mark Twain (1835–1910)
Letter to an unidentified person

This chapter continues the exploration of Visual FoxPro and focuses specifically on old-fashioned, screen-oriented input and output characterized by the @ command. Data editing commands, such as APPEND, BROWSE, CHANGE, and READ, and format files are also examined as they relate to screen-oriented input and output. (The EDIT command is not included in this discussion because it is identical to CHANGE.)

The @ Command

When you think about screen-oriented user interface, forget about the INPUT, ACCEPT, ?, and ?? commands. Old-time Xbase experts will instruct you to use the @ command for screen input and output. In general, the @ command displays and inputs information at a designated position on-screen. In FoxPro for Windows Version 2.5, the @ command became even more powerful and sophisticated. You can do the following operations with the @ command:

- Output an expression at a specified location on-screen
- Define a data input field at some location on-screen
- Draw a box
- Erase a portion of the screen
- Color a rectangular box
- Create text edit boxes
- Create menu objects (including check boxes, list boxes, control buttons, invisible buttons, option buttons, spinners, and combo boxes)
- Display bitmap (BMP) files
- Display General type files

It was only a couple of years ago that FoxPro for Windows Version 2.5 gave all the new power to the ubiquitous @ command. And now, the mighty @ command has become antiquated for Windows. It has been replaced by the Visual FoxPro object-oriented programming elements. However, until you have upgraded all of your old FoxPro applications, you will still need to know about the @ command. Also, the @ command is useful when learning the FoxPro procedural language. Remember, you need the FoxPro procedural language to write methods for your OOP classes.

In dBASE II days, dBASE programmers had to determine the placement of the @ command's SAY and GET statements by drawing the form on a piece of paper and coding each @ command to create the form. This process was improved by third-party developers and (later) by dBASE III PLUS with the introduction of a *screen designer* (also called a *screen builder* or *screen painter*). With this program, you paint your form by placing text, fields, lines, boxes, and special characters on-screen. When you're finished defining your form, the program generates a FORMAT file. Most Xbase languages use the MODIFY SCREEN command to generate forms. Fortunately, screen painters have improved and can be activated with the MODIFY SCREEN command, although the Visual FoxPro Form Designer is activated by the `MODIFY FORM` command. The Visual FoxPro Form Designer no longer creates a screen program file (SPR) containing procedural FoxPro commands. The FoxPro 2.*x* Screen Designer creates a screen program file (with an .SPR filename extension) that can be directly executed or incorporated in an application. The Visual FoxPro Form Designer generates a screen file (SCX) containing definitions for the properties and methods of all of the objects that constitute a form.

With the Visual FoxPro Form Designer, you can design a form that contains not only text and edit fields, but also other objects such as check boxes, control buttons, option buttons, spinners, combo boxes, list boxes, toolbars, and edit boxes. It even generates a form containing multiple tab forms, called a *formset*. I recommend that you always use the Visual FoxPro Form Designer to create all your forms for your applications.

In this chapter, you'll learn to use the various forms of the obsolete `@` commands and how these commands behave. You must understand these commands if you are going to work with or upgrade existing FoxPro 2.*x* applications or make advanced coding changes to the forms you generated with the FoxPro 2.*x* Screen Designer.

Basic @...*SAY*...*GET* and *READ* Commands

Before I become involved with all the complications of the powerful features of the `@` command, I'll first examine the basic concepts of the `@` command's `SAY` and `GET` clauses and the `READ` command. Note the following simplified syntax of the `@` command and the `READ` command:

```
@ <row>,<col>  SAY <exp> GET <variable>
READ [SAVE]
```

The *<row>* and *<col>* Expressions

The numeric expressions *<row>* and `<col>` define the position relative to the upper-left corner of the active window where the values are output. If no windows are active, these expressions define the position relative to the upper-left corner of the screen. The screen is sometimes referred to as the *global window*.

If the conventional Xbase status line is not active, the global window extends from the first line on-screen (row 0) to the bottom line of the screen. If the status line is active, the bottom of the global window is the line above the status line. *<row>* can have any value between 0 and the bottom line of the window. `<col>` can have any value between 0 and the right boundary of the window or the main FoxPro window.

The *SAY* *<exp>* Clause

The `SAY <exp>` clause defines any type of expression displayed at the specified row and column position, as in the following example:

```
@ 3,4 SAY "Hello, World"
@ 4,4 SAY DATE()
@ 5,4 SAY  Rate*Time + 3.0
```

These three fields are displayed on-screen at the designated row and column locations.

The *GET <variable>* Clause

The GET clause is used to define an input field on-screen. The variable can be an existing memory variable, an element from a declared array, or a table field (DBF file) from the currently active table or view. Enter @...GET commands for the input fields that you want to input together, then issue the READ command. In the following example, the SAY and GET clauses are combined to create a simple input form:

```
USE CUSTOMER   && .dbf has fields used in GET clauses
@ 0,20 SAY "Customer Input Form"
@ 3,0  SAY "Customer name" GET Customer
@ 4,0  SAY "Street address " GET Address
@ 5,0  SAY "City           " GET City
@ 6,0  SAY "State          " GET State
@ 7,0  SAY "Zip code" GET Zip
READ
```

As the @ commands are executed, the SAY expression and the values of the GET variables are displayed on-screen at the designated locations. The SAY and GET values are displayed in the color specified by SET COLOR OF NORMAL and SET COLOR OF FIELD, respectively. The FIELD color is displayed in reverse video. You can also set the color scheme using the SET COLOR OF SCHEME command. (See Chapter 10, "Environment," for more information on the forms of the SET COLOR command.)

The purpose of the READ command is to activate GET objects. GET objects are GET fields, control buttons, text-editing fields, option buttons, combo boxes, check boxes, and list boxes. You should be familiar with fields and control buttons. All GET objects issued since the last READ command (unless SAVE was specified) or CLEAR GETS command was executed are activated. After a READ command begins executing, GET objects are activated for input in the order that their @ command is executed. The cursor is placed on the first character of the first specified GET field. You can move the cursor in the confines of the input fields using the arrow and control keys and make any required changes to the data. To navigate through the GET objects, you can press Enter, Tab, or ↓ to move to the next object, or press Shift+Tab or ↑ to move to the previous object. You can select any of the GET objects with a mouse click. When a GET field or text-editing region is selected, you can use any of the standard FoxPro editing operations. (See Table 9.1 for more information regarding navigation.) To exit from a READ command, use the following methods:

- Move forward past the last GET object
- Move back to before the first GET object
- Press Ctrl+W or Ctrl+End (to save results)
- Press Esc or Ctrl+Q (to abandon changes)

Navigation

This is a good time to concentrate on the navigation keystrokes for the full-screen commands. In FoxPro, all full-screen commands that edit fields use the standard FoxPro navigation conventions. These commands are APPEND, BROWSE, CHANGE, EDIT, INSERT, and READ. The conventions are used also by data entry fill-in fields and the Command window.

Table 9.1 describes the function of each control key used for editing input data fields. Keystrokes for editing memo fields using the word wrap editor are also included in the table.

Table 9.1. The keystrokes used for editing input data fields.

Key Label	*Function*
↑	Moves up one row, line, or field
→	Moves one position to the right
←	Moves one position to the left
↓	Moves down one row, line, or field
Ctrl+→	Moves right one word (for BROWSE, moves right one field)
Ctrl+←	Moves left one word (for BROWSE, moves left one field)
PgUp	Moves up one screen or window
PgDn	Moves down one screen or window
Ctrl+PgUp	In BROWSE and CHANGE, moves to the first record in the file; in text, moves to the start of the file (no action in READ)
Ctrl+PgDn	In BROWSE and CHANGE, moves to the last record in the file; in text, moves to the end of the file (no action in READ)
Home	In BROWSE, CHANGE, and READ, goes to the first field; in text, goes to the start of the line
End	In BROWSE, CHANGE, and READ, goes to the last field; in text, goes to the start of the line
Tab	Tabs to the next field, column, or tab stop
Shift+Tab	Tabs to the previous field, column, or tab stop
Backspace	Deletes the previous character
Ctrl+Backspace	Deletes the previous word in the text editor (also used for *outdenting*, which removes indents from selected lines of text)
Del	Deletes the currently selected item
Ins	Toggles between insert and overtype mode
Esc, Ctrl+Q	Escapes from CHANGE, BROWSE, READ, or APPEND without saving changes

continues

Table 9.1. continued

Key Label	*Function*
Enter	Moves to the next line or field
Ctrl+End, Ctrl+W	Exits from the full-screen edit command and saves the results

Visual FoxPro requires a mouse, and you'll find that many navigation operations are performed more efficiently using a mouse. You can select a field or text, scroll records and text, delete a record in BROWSE and CHANGE, and select menu objects, to name just a few operations that you can accomplish using the mouse.

The *SAVE* Keyword

The SAVE keyword causes the READ command to save the GET information after it exits. When each @ command is executed, information associated with its GET clauses is saved in a memory buffer. When the READ command executes, it uses the information to process each GET clause. When READ exits, the memory buffer containing the GET information is normally cleared. If the SAVE keyword is specified with the READ command, the GET information remains in memory and can be used again by a subsequent READ command. Later in this chapter, the section "The Mighty READ Command" describes the full syntax and operation of the READ command. You can clear the GET information by using the CLEAR GETS or CLEAR ALL commands.

Full-Screen Editing

In addition to the READ command, APPEND and CHANGE can edit an input form. The READ command exits when you attempt to move backward off the first field or forward off the last field. Under the same circumstances, the CHANGE and APPEND commands move the cursor to the first field of the previous or next record, respectively. All these full-screen commands exit when you press Ctrl+End or Ctrl+W. You can press Esc or Ctrl+Q to exit (changes are not made to the current record).

Advanced @...*SAY*...*GET* Command Options

The @ command in Visual FoxPro is embellished with many data validation and display enhancements. Note the following complete syntax:

```
@ <row>,<col>
   [SAY <exp1> ¦ <expC1> BITMAP [CENTER] [ISOMETRIC ¦ STRETCH]
   [PICTURE <expPIC1>] [FUNCTION <expFUNC1>]
   [SIZE <expN1>, <expN2>]
   [VERB <expN3>]
   [FONT <expC3> [, <expN4>]]
   [STYLE <expSTYLE>]
   [COLOR SCHEME <expN5>
   ¦ COLOR [<color attribute>][,<color attribute>]
   ¦ COLOR RGB(<color value list>) ]]
```

```
    [GET <variable>
    [[OPEN] WINDOW <window name>]
    [PICTURE <expPIC2>] [FUNCTION <expFunc2>]
    [RANGE [<exp2>] [,<exp3>]]
    [ENABLE ¦ DISABLE]
    [VALID <expL1> ¦ <expN1> [ERROR <expC5>]]
    [WHEN <expL2>] [DEFAULT <exp4>]
    [MESSAGE <expC6>]]
    [SIZE <expN1>, <expN2>]
    [FONT <expC3> [, <expN3>]]
    [STYLE <expSTYLE>]
    [COLOR SCHEME <expN5>
    ¦ COLOR [<color attribute>][,<color attribute>]
    ¦ COLOR RGB(<color value list>)]]

<expSTYLE> ::= <expC> (which evaluates to <Style_chars>)

<Style_char> ::= B ¦ I ¦ N ¦ O ¦ Q ¦ S ¦ - ¦ T ¦ U

<expFunc>::= <expC> (which evaluates to a <Func_chars>)

<expPIC>  ::= <expC>(which evaluates to a <picture>)

<picture> ::= [@<Func_chars><space>][<picture symbol>]

<stringPIC> ::= <dbl_quote_strPIC>¦<single_quote_strPIC>

<picture symbol> ::= ! ¦ # ¦ $ ¦ * ¦ + ¦ - ¦ , ¦
   . ¦ 9 ¦ A ¦ L ¦ N ¦ X ¦ Y ¦
   <other symbols>

<other symbols> ::= Overrides the data character for
                     character type data (See PICTURE)

<Func_chars> ::= <Func_char> [<Func_char>]…

<Func_char> ::= ! ¦ ^ ¦ ( ¦ $ ¦ A ¦
                B ¦ C ¦ D ¦ E ¦ I ¦ J ¦
                K ¦ L ¦ M <string> ¦ R ¦
                S<digits> ¦ T ¦ X ¦ Z ¦

<color attribute> ::= <foreground>/<background>
<foreground> ::= <color character>[<color character>]…
<background> ::= <color character>[<color character>]…
<color character> ::= B ¦ G ¦ I ¦ N ¦ R ¦
                      U ¦ W ¦ X ¦ * ¦ +
<row>  ::=  <expN>
<col>  ::=  <expN>
```

The <row> and <col> Numeric Expressions

As noted, `<row>` and `<col>` are numeric expressions that define the position relative to the upper-left corner of the active window where the values are output. Output can be directed to a printer or a file using the `SET DEVICE TO PRINTER[PROMPT]/FILE <expFN>` command. In such a case, the row can range from 0 to 32768 and the column can range from 0 to 255. Normally `SET DEVICE TO SCREEN` is in effect and the row and column values are bounded by the limits of the defined window or the global window.

The coordinate position of a corner of an `@` command (or any other object) is defined in Xbase by specifying *<row>* and *<col>* separated by commas, which represents the position of the displayed text. In Visual FoxPro, you can specify a fractional value to precisely position any object (windows, menus, controls, `GET` objects, and so on). Note the following example:

```
@ 2.3,4.25 SAY "Hello, there"
```

Precise positioning is not permitted in FoxPro for DOS. If you execute the preceding command in FoxPro for DOS, the fractional portion of the number is ignored and interpreted as follows:

```
@ 2,4 SAY "Hello, there"
```

Figure 9.1 illustrates the `@...SAY` command with fractional *<row>* and *<col>* values.

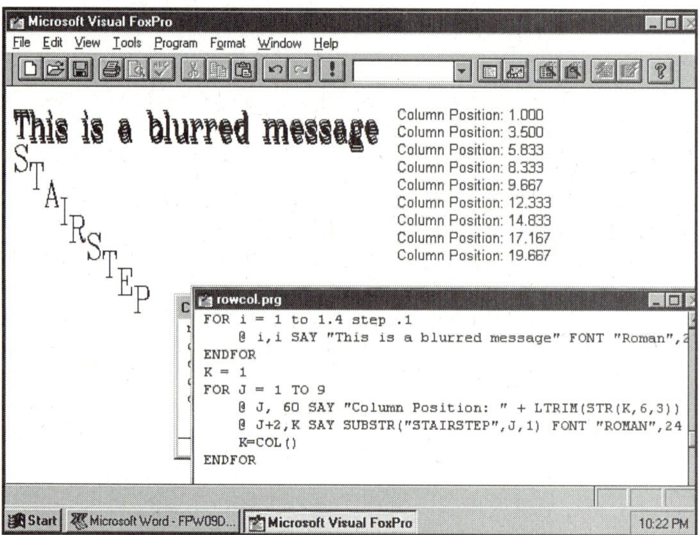

FIGURE 9.1.
An example of fractional <row> and <col> values.

The *SAY* and *GET* Clauses

The `SAY` clause displays the value of the expression. This value can be modified with a `PICTURE` or `FUNCTION` clause. `GET` *<variable>* displays the value of *<variable>* as a data input field. Its display can be enhanced by the `PICTURE` or `FUNCTION` clauses. When you enter the full-screen editing mode, the *<variable>* can be edited. The following sections describe each of the keywords and clauses for the `SAY` clause.

The *PICTURE <expPIC>* Clause

The `PICTURE` clause formats data to be displayed and restricts input. It normally contains an input or output template. The template is composed of a symbol for each character that is input or output. Each symbol is described in Table 9.2. The FUNCTION clause can be included in a PICTURE clause (see the syntax description for <*picture*>).

Table 9.2. The PICTURE clause template symbols.

Symbol	*Description*
!	Converts lowercase letters to uppercase letters
#	Allows only digits, blanks, and signs to be entered
$	Displays current SET CURRENCY string with numeric value (see Chapter 10)
*	Fills a numeric value with asterisks (*)
,	Displays a comma for numeric values if digits are to the left of the comma (for example, PICTURE "99,999.99")
.	Specifies the position of decimal point in numeric display
9	For a character type data entry, allows only digits to be entered; for any numeric type data, allows only digits and signs to be entered
A	Allows only letters to be entered
L	Allows only logical type data (T, F, Y, and N) to be entered
N	Allows only letters and digits to be entered
X	Allows any character to be entered
Y	Allows only Y, y, N, or n to be entered

The symbols !, #, 9, A, N, and X can be used with both the SAY and GET clauses. The symbols 9, #, A, N, and X allow only certain categories of characters to be entered into a data field. These symbols, however, do not restrict the display of data. In other words, invalid values are still displayed. Note the following examples:

```
SET CURRENCY TO " $"
@ 3,3  SAY 234567.89 PICTURE "$999,999,999.99"
@ 4,3  SAY 4567.89 PICTURE "*999,999,999.99"
@ 5,3  SAY "hello, there" PICTURE "!!!!!!!!!!!!!!!"
```

The results are displayed as follows:

```
$234,567.89
***4,567.89
HELLO, THERE
```

The main characteristic of a template is that each character in the template corresponds to a displayed character. Templates are sometimes used to indicate the width of a data field. Here's an example:

```
Name = ' '
Cost = 1234.5
```

```
@ 3,3 SAY "Enter name:" GET Name PICTURE REPLICATE("X",20)
@ 5,3 SAY "Enter cost:" GET Cost PICTURE "999,999.99"
```

The first input data field displayed is 20 characters wide. The second data field is as wide as the template: "999,999.99". The input form appears as follows:

```
Enter Name: Joe Smith

Enter Cost: 1,743.99
```

The *FUNCTION* <expFunc> Symbols

A FUNCTION symbol is a single character that affects the display or the manner in which data is input into the field. Table 9.3 lists and describes each FUNCTION symbol and indicates which data types can be used with the function. FUNCTION symbols used with menu objects are presented in the section "What Are GET Objects?"

Table 9.3. The FUNCTION symbols.

Symbol	*Type*	*Description*
!	Character	Converts all lowercase letters to uppercase letters (works only when displaying data).
^	Numeric, Float, Double, or Integer	Displays numbers in scientific notation (for example, 1.3E+06).
$	All numeric data types*	Displays data in currency format. (The currency symbol is displayed immediately before or after the number depending on the value of SET CURRENCY TO LEFT/SET CURRENCY TO RIGHT.)
(	Numeric or Float or all numeric data types*	Encloses negative numbers in parentheses.
A	Character or all numeric data types*	Allows only alphabetic letters for input.
B	All numeric data types*	Left aligns a field within a PICTURE template or a table field (display only).
C	All numeric data types*	Displays the credit symbol (CR) after a positive number.
D	Date	Uses the current SET DATE format for dates.
E	Date	Displays and inputs the date in European format.
I	Character or all numeric data types*	Centers text within a PICTURE Numeric or Float template or table field (display only).
J	Character or all numeric data types*	Right aligns data within a PICTURE Numeric or Float template or table field.

Symbol	*Type*	*Description*
`K`	All types	Selects an entire field for editing when the cursor moves into the field. (If you enter any noncursor movement character, the contents of the field are erased and replaced with the new character; if you use a → to move to a character in the field, you can edit its original contents.)
`L`	All numeric data types*	Displays leading zeros instead of spaces (for example, `000009345`).
`M`<*list*>	Character	Selects a value from a list of choices with the `GET` clause. (See the discussion in the text that follows this table.)
`R`	Character	Forces the display of literal characters in the template. (They are not entered into the data field; this display function is used with a `PICTURE` template.)
`S`<*n*>	Character	Initiates horizontal scrolling while a Character data type `GET` variable is being edited.
`T`	Character	Trims leading and trailing blanks from the field.
`X`	All numeric data types*	Displays the debit symbol (DB) after a negative number.
`Z`	All numeric data types*	Displays a zero numeric value as a blank setting.

*All numeric data types includes Currency, Double, Float, Integer, and Numeric.

The `M` <*list*> function symbol specifies that values for the `GET` field are selected from a <*list*>. The following is the syntax:

```
M <list>
```

If the `GET` variable value is not in the list, the first value in the list is displayed. Press the space bar to cycle through the list. Pressing Enter selects a value and moves to the next field. You can select an item by pressing the character key for the first letter of the item. If two or more items in the list have the same first letter, the next item matching on the first letter is selected:

```
FUNCTION "M Mon,Tue,Wed,Thu,Fri,Sat,Sun"
```

The `S`<*n*> function symbol initiates horizontal scrolling while a Character data type `GET` variable is being edited. A literal positive integer, <*n*>, is specified with the `S` function symbol. <*n*> limits the width of the input field; it must be narrower than the character field. Data scrolls horizontally in the field. The string starts scrolling when the cursor moves to the right edge of the scrolling window, enabling the user to view and edit the entire field. The →, ←, Home, and End keys bring text into view. Note the following example:

```
@ 10,10 GET Name FUNCTION "S30"
```

Certain display functions can be combined to add more flexibility for display and input. You can combine the `T` and `I` display functions, for example, to trim spaces from both ends of a character string and then center it for display. Certain functions such as `Z` and `$`, however, are mutually exclusive.

The *SIZE* Clause

The `SIZE` clause specifies the height (`<expN1>`) in rows and width (`<expN2>`) in columns of a rectangular region in which data displays for the `SAY` command. The `SIZE` clause can also be used to specify the height and width of a `GET` object. The `<row>` and `<col>` values define the position of the upper-left corner of the region. In other words, the region extends to the right and below the coordinate position of the `@` command. If a `SIZE` clause is not specified, a default region that is one row high is used for text. The width of the default region is determined by the displayed value or the `PICTURE` clause. Note the following example of `SIZE` clause usage:

```
@ 1,2 SAY "Here is a message" SIZE 3,4
```

The preceding statement displays the character expression within the region defined by the `SIZE` clause:

```
Here
is a
mess
```

Any information outside the region is clipped. In the preceding example, "age" was truncated from the word "message." When text displays, it is word wrapped.

If you specify a `PICTURE` template and the picture is not as wide as the `SIZE` region, `PICTURE` width takes precedence. Note the following example:

```
@ 1,2 SAY "Here is a message" SIZE 3,4 PICTURE "AA"
```

The preceding statement displays the character expression within the region defined by the `SIZE` clause. However, because the `PICTURE` template is two characters wide, only two characters of each line display:

```
He
is
me
```

You can also specify the `SIZE` clause with a `GET` object or variable. When the `@...GET` command executes, the variable contents display within the `SIZE` region. If the variable is a Character data type field or memvar, and a `READ` command executes, you can move into the `GET` field and edit its contents within the region. However, you must move through the region with the left and right arrow keys. If you press the up and down arrow keys, the cursor doesn't move to the next or previous row of the region—it moves to the next or previous field.

In Visual FoxPro, the SIZE clause region also bounds the display of a graphic picture (bitmap file) and an OLE object, as described in the next section.

Displaying Bitmap Files and OLE Objects

In Visual FoxPro you can display bitmap and OLE objects using the @...SAY command. You can display a graphics bitmap file (BMP) by specifying a character expression containing the name of the bitmap file followed by the BITMAP keyword. Here's an example:

```
@ 10,10 SAY "C:\BMP\GRAPHIC.BMP" BITMAP
```

In the preceding example, the bitmap file (GRAPHICS.BMP) displays to the right and below the coordinates specified, which define a default rectangular SAY region. You must specify the entire filename (including the filename extension .BMP). If the file is not in the current default directory, you must supply the full path. The default SAY region for bitmap display is bound on the right and bottom by either the main FoxPro window or a user-defined window.

The SIZE *<expN1>*,*<expN2>* clause can be specified to define the size of the SAY region. The SIZE clause defines a rectangular region in which the bitmap picture displays. *<expN1>* defines the height in rows and *<expN2>* defines the width in columns based on the type and size of the window font.

You can also display an OLE object from a General data type field in a table with the @...SAY command. The OLE object also displays in the SAY region. However, if you don't specify the SIZE clause, the general field icon gen displays. In other words, you must specify the SIZE clause if you want the OLE object to display.

The layout of the bitmap or OLE picture within the SAY region depends on the following factors:

- If the CENTER, ISOMETRIC, or STRETCH keywords are not specified, and the bitmap or OLE picture is smaller than the SAY region, the picture displays in the upper-left corner of the region. If the picture is larger than the region, the picture is clipped to fit in the region. The picture of a tree drawn in the upper-left corner of the single line box in Figure 9.2 illustrates this mode. I used the following commands to draw the box and picture:

  ```
  @ 10,10 TO 20,50
  @ 10,10 SAY "tree.bmp" BITMAP SIZE 10,30
  ```

- If you specify the CENTER keyword and the bitmap or OLE picture is smaller than the SIZE clause region, the picture is centered within that region. An example of how to use the CENTER keyword is shown in Figure 9.2 (note the picture in the center of the drawn box). I used the following command to center the picture:

  ```
  @ 10,10 SAY "tree.bmp" BITMAP SIZE 10,40 CENTER
  ```

- If you specify the `STRETCH` keyword, the bitmap or OLE picture expands or contracts to fit within the region. The picture is scaled horizontally, vertically, or both to fit inthe region. The picture of a tree on the right side of Figure 9.2 is distorted because it was stretched to fit into the specified `SIZE` region. I used the following command to scale the picture:

  ```
  @ 1,52 SAY "tree.bmp" BITMAP SIZE 20,10 STRETCH
  ```

- If the `CENTER` and `STRETCH` keywords are both specified, the `CENTER` keyword is ignored.
- If you specify the `ISOMETRIC` keyword, the bitmap or OLE picture expands or contracts so that the proportions of the picture are retained. I drew the picture of the tree in the upper-left corner of Figure 9.2 with the `ISOMETRIC` keyword specified. This picture was reduced to fit into a rectangular region (`SIZE 5,10`). However, its proportions were maintained. Incidentally, `STRETCH` and `ISOMETRIC` are mutually exclusive. I used the following command to proportionally size the picture:

  ```
  @ 1,10 SAY "tree.bmp" SIZE 5,10 ISOMETRIC
  ```

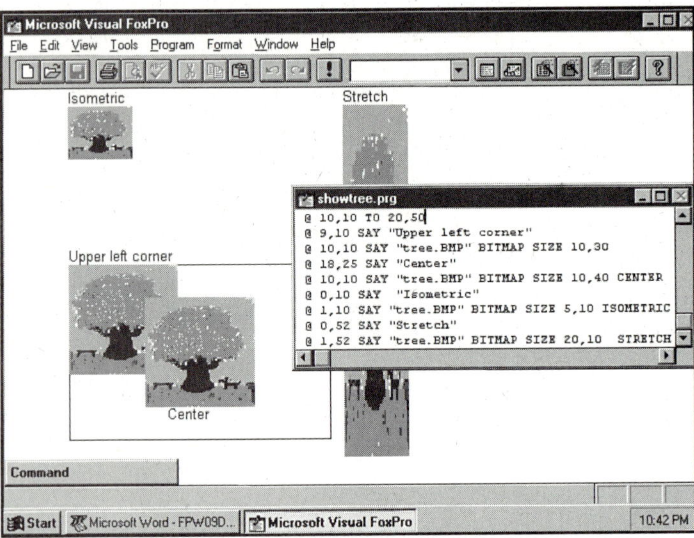

FIGURE 9.2.
An example of the @...SAY command used to display bitmaps.

The *VERB* <expN3> Clause

Associated with certain OLE objects is a list of commands that perform on the object certain operations, such as playing or recording an OLE sound object. These commands, called *verbs*, are referenced in Visual FoxPro using numeric values. The `VERB` clause can be specified with an `@...SAY` command to cause a specified verb to operate on the General data type field instead of displaying the field. For example, if the command to play an OLE sound object is `3` and the object is stored in a General data type field named `Music`, you can play the music (if you have a properly configured sound board) using the following command:

```
@ 10,10 SAY Music VERB 3
```

The Microsoft Sound Recorder application appears on-screen and plays the OLE sound object contained in the General data type field named `Music`. Nothing displays. You can play music or sounds without displaying the Sound Recorder by specifying a WAV file with the `SET BELL TO` command and by sounding the WAV file with the `?? CHR(7)` command. For example, to sound the "chime" WAV file, enter the following commands:

```
SET BELL TO "CHIME.WAV"
?? CHR (7)
```

Of course, you must have a sound board installed.

The *FONT* and *STYLE* Clauses

You can specify a font type, size, and style with the `FONT` and `STYLE` clauses. The `FONT` clause has the following form:

```
FONT <expC3> [, <expN4>]
```

<expC3> is the name of the font (for example, Roman, Helvetica). *<expN4>* is the size of the font in points (for example, 10 point, 12 point). A 10-point font is used if *<expN4>* is omitted. Because Microsoft Windows maintains the fonts, the accessible fonts, sizes, and styles vary from system to system. A list of available fonts is shown when you choose the **T**ext menu F**o**rmat option.

The form of the `STYLE` clause is as follows:

```
STYLE <expC4>
```

<expC4> is character expression that contains one or more style codes. (See Table 9.4.)

Table 9.4. Text STYLE codes.

Code	*Style*
B	Bold
I	Italic
N	Normal (default)
O	Outline
Q	Opaque
S	Shadow
-	Strikethrough
T	Transparent
U	Underline

You can specify these two clauses with the following forms of the @ command:

```
@ ... SAY/GET
@ ... GET  (for Menu objects)
@ ... EDIT
```

The following examples illustrate the use of the FONT and STYLE clauses:

```
*          24 Point Roman font displayed in Bold Italic.
@ 1,1 SAY LNAME FONT "Roman",24 STYLE "BI"
*          14 point script
@ 5,5 SAY FNAME FONT "Script", 14
*          10 point bold System font
@ 20,40 SAY "This is a 10 point font"  FONT "System" STYLE "B"
*          12 point Bold Courier Font
@ 17,30 GET FNAME FONT "courier",12  STYLE "B"
```

The *[OPEN] WINDOW <window name>* Clause

Use the optional WINDOW clause to specify the name of a user-defined window in which to edit a memo field. If you don't define the WINDOW clause, the memo field is edited either in a window defined by the SET WINDOW OF MEMO TO command (see Chapter 10) or in the full screen. If you supply the OPEN keyword, the contents of the memo field are always displayed. If you don't supply OPEN, an icon is displayed at the position designated by the @ command coordinates. If the memo field contains data, the icon displays as MEMO. If the memo field is empty, the icon displays as MEMO. In either case, while you're editing a form, the cursor moves to the OPEN window or the icon; press Ctrl+Home to enter the memo field editor. Note the following example:

```
DEFINE WINDOW Wind1 FROM 4,4  TO 9,20
DEFINE WINDOW Wind2 FROM 11,1 TO 15,60
@ 1,1 GET Mymemo OPEN WINDOW Wind1
@ 2,1 GET Memo2 WINDOW WIND2
```

The *RANGE [<exp2>][,<exp3>]* Values

RANGE specifies a minimum value (first expression) and maximum value (second expression) for entering data into a Character, Currency, Double, Float, Integer, Numeric, or Date type data variable for a GET. The initial value and entered data must be in the specified range. The minimum or maximum limit can be omitted. If you supply only the upper limit value, however, it must be preceded by a comma. If a value outside the specified range is entered, a system message box appears in the upper-right portion of the screen containing the following message:

```
RANGE <lower limit> to <upper limit>
```

If the ON READERROR command is active, ON READERROR processing overrides RANGE error processing. In effect, the range error message is not displayed, leaving the ON ERROR procedure to handle the range limit error. If you enter a field with an invalid value, you can move to another field without correcting it. However, after you change the value it must be within the range. Note the following examples:

```
@ 10,10 SAY "Enter date:" GET ADate RANGE {3/3/84},DATE()
@ 11,10 SAY "Enter Cost:" GET Cost RANGE 100,300
@ 11,10 SAY "Enter Quantity" GET Qty RANGE 1
@ 11,10 SAY "Enter Hours" GET Hours RANGE ,40
```

The *ENABLE* and *DISABLE* Keywords

You can prevent access to a GET variable using the DISABLE keyword (later you can enable a GET field with the SHOW GET ENABLED). If DISABLED is not specified or ENABLE is specified, the GET field is initially enabled. When a field is enabled, it displays using COLOR SCHEME 6. If it is disabled, its display is controlled by COLOR SCHEME 1. These keywords are principally used when the GET field displays control buttons, check boxes and other GET objects discussed in the section "@ Command Dialog Objects."

The *VALID* and *ERROR* Clauses

The VALID clause validates data input to the GET variable. You can specify either a logical (*<expL1>*) or numeric (*<expN1>*) expression. If you specify a logical expression and it evaluates to true (.T.), the data is considered valid, the input is accepted, and the cursor moves to the next GET field. If the logical expression evaluates to false (.F.), a system message box appears in the upper-right portion of the screen containing the message Invalid Input.

If an ERROR clause is supplied, the user-supplied message rather than the preceding message is displayed in the system message box.

The VALID condition is evaluated whenever an attempt is made to exit the field. This is true even if the existing GET variable is not changed. This differs from the RANGE clause, which enables you to leave the field if it contains an invalid value—as long and you do not change the value. The only way to escape from a GET variable with a VALID clause without validating the field is to press Esc.

In the following example, data input to the Code GET variable is checked to see if it is A, B, or C:

```
Code = 'A'
@ 10,10 SAY "Enter A, B, or C" GET Code;
    VALID Code='A' .OR. Code='B' .OR. Code='C';
    ERROR "Illegal code value was entered"
READ
```

In the following example, the Account GET field is checked for validity against the chart of accounts table, CHART.DBF.

```
USE CHART ORDER Account IN 3
Account="                  "
@ 10,10 SAY "Enter account:" GET Account;
    VALID SEEK(Account,"CHART");
    ERROR "Account:"+TRIM(Account)+" is invalid."
READ
```

If account number A333444 is entered and it is not in the chart of accounts, the following error message is displayed in a system message box in the upper-right portion of the screen:

```
Account: A333444 is invalid.
```

In the following example, a user-defined function (UDF) is used to check the ACode data input GET variable:

```
ACode = 0
@ 10,10 SAY "Enter Code" GET ACode VALID Check()
...
FUNCTION Check
IF Bcode = 3
   If ACode < 4 .OR. ACode > 9
      RETURN .F.   && ACode is invalid
   ELSE
      IF ACode < 1 .OR. ACode > 17
         RETURN .F.   && ACode is invalid
   ENDIF
ENDIF
RETURN .T.           && ACode is valid
```

The CHECK() user-defined function is called to validate the value of ACode. If ACode is valid, CHECK() returns .T. Otherwise, it returns .F.. If it is false, the standard VALID error message is displayed (centered) at the bottom of the screen.

If you specify a numeric expression (<*expN1*>) with the VALID clause, the action is determined by the value of the evaluated numeric expression. If the expression evaluates to zero, FoxPro assumes a validation error has occurred, the system message box appears, and the cursor remains on the GET field. If the expression evaluates to a nonzero value, FoxPro assumes the GET field data entry is valid. This value is then used to determine how many fields to move. If the number is positive, it indicates how many fields to advance. If the field is negative, the number specifies how many fields to move backward. This option is extremely useful if you want to skip over fields based on a value that was input.

The *WHEN* <expL2> Clause

Use the WHEN clause to specify a condition that determines whether the GET variable can be edited. The expression is evaluated before the GET variable is edited. If the result is .F., the GET variable cannot be edited and the cursor skips to the next field. If the result is .T., the cursor moves to the GET variable data input field to allow normal editing operations.

The *DEFAULT* <exp4> Clause

The DEFAULT clause sets a value that is inserted in the field when the record is appended to the table (unless the value is changed by the user). The expression must match the data type of the GET variable. The expression is evaluated by the APPEND command when the GET value is displayed. The value can be changed by the input process, but if the value is not changed, the default expression result is stored in the table. Because APPEND uses @...GET commands only when they are in a format file, the DEFAULT clause is functional only in a format file.

The MESSAGE <*expC6*> Clause

The MESSAGE clause defines a message that appears while the GET variable is being edited. The message displays under the control of the APPEND, EDIT, CHANGE, INSERT, or READ commands. When the cursor moves to a field with an associated MESSAGE clause, the associated message is displayed. This message normally displays on the bottom line, even if the status line is turned off. You can use the SET MESSAGE TO command to redefine the message display line. You can also designate that a message is displayed in a window by using the SET MESSAGE WINDOW command. (See Chapter 10.) Only the first 79 characters are displayed—the remaining characters are truncated.

The *SIZE* <*expN1*>,<*expN2*> Clause

Normally, a GET field editing region is one row high and wide enough to hold the field. Its width is determined by the width of the field or a PICTURE clause. You can modify this edit region into a multiple-row rectangle with the SIZE clause. *<expN1>* specifies the height of the region and *<expN2>* specifies the width of the region in columns. The width of the GET variable and the PICTURE clause control how editing is performed in the region.

If you have a PICTURE, and the PICTURE clause is smaller than the editing region, the PICTURE has precedence. If the PICTURE template is larger than the size of the editing region, the data scrolls within the region.

If there is no PICTURE clause, certain rules govern the way editing is done in a region. These rules are based on the width and type of the variable. If a variable is a table field and its width is less than the size of a region, editing occurs only in the area covered by the field. When you move past the end of the table field, the cursor moves to the next field. Because you are in the middle of a region, the sudden movement of the cursor to the next field can be perplexing. Therefore, you should use the SIZE clause to specify an edit region that is either smaller than or equal to the size of a table field. If the table field width is greater than the size of the region, text scrolls in the edit region.

If the GET field is a memory variable, and the width of the field is less than the size of the edit region, you can edit in the entire edit region. If you make any changes, the memory variable becomes the width of the edit region. On the other hand, if the memory variable is wider than the edit region, the memory variable text scrolls inside the window.

The rectangular edit regions specified by GET and SIZE provide a nice little window for editing text inside of a window.

The *COLOR, COLOR SCHEME,* and *COLOR RGB()* Clauses

You can specify a COLOR clause to override the current color of text output to the screen by the @ command. Visual FoxPro supports the two forms of color supported by other versions of

FoxPro and adds a third method for specifying colors. The following is the syntax for the forms of the `COLOR` clause:

```
[COLOR SCHEME <expN5>
 ¦ COLOR [<color attribute>][,<color attribute>]
 ¦ COLOR RGB(<color value list>)]]
```

In the first form, you can choose one of 24 FoxPro color schemes. The second form is the traditional Xbase `COLOR` clause. Use it to specify color attributes for the output from the `@` command. The first `<color attribute>` defines the color of the `SAY` display. The second `<color attribute>` defines the color of the `GET` data input field. You can define the foreground attribute (the color of the character) and the background attribute for either one. If you don't specify the `COLOR` clause, the `COLOR OF NORMAL` and `COLOR OF FIELD` color attributes define the color of the `SAY` and `GET` displays, respectively.

The third form of the `COLOR` clause is used exclusively with Visual FoxPro. It contains the `RGB()` function, which contains a list of up to six numeric values ranging from 0 to 255. The first three numbers represent the intensity of red, green, and blue color displays, respectively, for the foreground color; the second three represent the intensity of these same colors for the background colors. You can specify a list of up to ten `RGB()` functions. Each item in the list defines the colors for one of the ten FoxPro color pairs. Note the following examples:

```
@ 1,20 SAY "ACME IMPORT FORM"  COLOR  R+/B

@ 3,3 SAY "Enter Date:" GET ADate COLOR  GR+/B,B/GR+
@ 4,3 SAY "Enter Name and Address" COLOR GR+/B
@ 5,4 GET Name COLOR ,B/GR
@ 6,4 GET Address COLOR ,B/GR
@ 7,4 GET City COLOR SCHEME 4
@ 8,4 GET State COLOR RGB(255,0,0,255,255,255),255(0,255,0,0,0,0)
```

You can learn more about color settings by reading the discussion about `SET COLOR` command forms in Chapter 10.

Relative Addressing

I once saw dBASE III code that used the antiquated dBASE II `$` relative operator with the `@` command, and I thought that I should say something about it in this book because it is still supported in Visual FoxPro. The `<row>` or `<col>` numeric expression can contain the `$` relative addressing operator. The `$` operator denotes the current row when used in the `<row>` expression and the current column when used in the `<col>` expression. For example, in the following code, the second message appears at row 4, column 8:

```
@ 3,3 SAY "Hello"
@ $+1 ,$ SAY "there"
```

I mention the `$` operator in this book only because it is supported by the language and some people are using it in their applications. It is cryptic, however, and most people agree that it should not be used. It is not documented in dBASE III and FoxPro. A general rule in the software industry is that undocumented features may not be supported in future versions. You should use the `ROW()` and `COL()` functions for relative addressing because the code is more readable and these functions will always be supported. The following code is the preferred form of the preceding example:

```
@ 3,3 SAY "Hello"
@ ROW()+1,COL() SAY "there"
```

Note that relative addressing does not work from the Command window because the coordinates are set to `21,0`.

The @...*CLEAR* Command

The `@...CLEAR` form of the `@` command clears a rectangular portion of the screen. Here is the syntax for this form:

```
@ <row>,<col> [CLEAR [TO <row>,<col>]]
```

If you omit the `TO` clause, the command clears from the specified *<row>* and *<col>* position to the end of the screen. If you omit the `CLEAR` keyword and the `TO` clause, the specified *<row>* is cleared, beginning at the specified *<col>*. Like all other forms of the `@` command, the coordinates are relative to the upper-left corner of the currently active window. The currently active window can be the global window or a user-defined window. Coordinates must be inside the window—otherwise, an error message box appears.

If you specify the `TO` clause, the first coordinates define the upper-left corner of the rectangular region of the window to be cleared, and the `TO` clause coordinates define the lower-right corner. To erase a box that begins at row 3, column 10, and extends to row 9, column 53, enter the following command:

```
@ 3,10  CLEAR TO 9,53
```

To erase the entire contents of row 7, enter this:

```
@ 7,0
```

To erase row 7, beginning at column 10 (and the rest of the window as well), enter this:

```
@ 7,10 CLEAR
```

The @...*FILL* Command

The `@...FILL` form of the `@` command changes the color of a rectangular region of the screen without changing its contents. The syntax for this form is as follows:

```
@ <row>,<col> FILL TO <row>,<col>
   [COLOR <color attribute>
   ¦ COLOR SCHEME <expN>]
   ¦ COLOR RGB(<color value list>)]
```

The first `<row>,<col>` is the coordinate of the upper-left corner of the rectangle. The `TO` clause defines the lower-right corner of the rectangle. You can change the foreground and background colors of the rectangular region. For example, to change the color of a box to red letters on a blue background, enter the following:

```
@ 3,3 FILL TO 9,60 COLOR R/B
```

The @...*TO* Command

The `@...TO` form of the `@` command draws a box with single-line, double-line, or panel borders. You can also define the border color. The following is the syntax for this form:

```
@ <row>,<col> TO <row>,<col>
   DOUBLE ¦ PANEL ¦ NONE ¦ <border definition string>
   [PATTERN <expN1> ]
   [PEN <expN2> [, <expN3> ]]
   [STYLE <expC> ]
   [COLOR <color attribute>
   ¦ COLOR SCHEME <expN4>]
   ¦ COLOR RGB(<color value list>)]
```

The first `<row>,<col>` is the coordinate of the upper-left corner of the box. The `TO` clause defines the lower-right corner of the box. The following define the border definition values:

Keyword	*Border Type*
(None)	A single-line border unless a different border was set with the `SET BORDERS TO` command.
`DOUBLE`	Creates double-line border characters. If the `PATTERN`, `PEN`, or `STYLE` clause is included, the `DOUBLE` keyword is ignored.
`PANEL`	Creates a block character, `ASCII 219`. If the `PATTERN`, `PEN`, or `STYLE` clause is included, the `PANEL` keyword is ignored.
<border definition string>	See the section "The `SET BORDER TO` Command" in Chapter 10 for a discussion of this value.

You can also define the color of the border character (the foreground) and the color of the background. If you don't supply the `COLOR` *<color attribute>* clause, the border is colored according to the `SET COLOR OF NORMAL` setting.

In Visual FoxPro you can specify the `PATTERN`, `PEN`, and `STYLE` clauses. The `PEN` clause specifies the width of the border of the object to be drawn and the type of pen used to draw it. Numeric values are used to specify these items. The first item, *<expN2>*, is the width of the pen in points (as shown in Table 9.5). Table 9.6 presents the optional second numeric value, *<expN3>*, which defines pen types. If you specify both *<expN2>* and *<expN3>*, the pen type *<expN3>* overrides the pen width *<expN2>*.

Table 9.5. PEN style numeric values.

<expN2>	PEN *Style*
0	Hairline (the default)—some video hardware with lower resolutions displays hairline as 1 point
1	1 point
2	2 points
3	3 points
4	4 points
5	5 points
6	6 points

Table 9.6. PEN clause pen types.

<expN3>	Pen *Type*
0	None
1	Dotted
2	Dashed
3	Dash-dot
4	Dash-dot-dot

You are not restricted to boxes and rectangles in Visual FoxPro—unlike in FoxPro 2.0—when you use the `@...TO` command. You can draw boxes with rounded corners, circles, and ellipses. To do this, specify a number between 0 and 99 in `<expC>` to designate the corner curvature of an object; 0 denotes no curvature (a box or rectangle), 99 specifies the maximum curvature, which draws a circle or an ellipse. By default, objects drawn with the Visual FoxPro `@...TO` command are opaque. If you include the letter `T` in `<expC>`, the `@...TO` command draws a transparent object, as in the following examples:

```
@ 10,10 to 20,70 STYLE "99T" && Draw an ellipse
@ 10,10 to 20,20 STYLE "99T" && Draw a circle
@ 10,10 TO 20,20 STYLE "16T" && Draw a box with round edges
```

The numeric argument specified with the `PATTERN` clause ranges from 0 to 7. This number specifies the displayed pattern, as shown in Figure 9.3.

Program ATTO.PRG, presented in Listing 9.1, contains usage examples of the `@...TO` command. The output from this program is shown in Figure 9.3.

Listing 9.1. The source listing of ATTO.PRG.

```
*       ***********************************************************
*       *
*       * 10/09/94              ATTO.PRG                 19:48:22
*       *
*       ***********************************************************
*       *
*       * Description:
*       * This program illustrates the @…TO command.
*       *
*       ***********************************************************
SET TALK OFF
CLEAR
*** Ellipse
@  1, 5 TO 13,45 PATTERN 7 PEN 2, 8 STYLE "99";
        COLOR RGB(,,,0,0,0)
@ 14,6.800 SAY '        STYLE "99" PATTERN 7 PEN 2, 8' ;
        FONT "MS Sans Serif", 8 STYLE "T"
*
*** Patterns
@  6,72 TO  8,100 PEN 1, 8
@  8,72 TO 10,100 PATTERN 1 PEN 1, 8 ;
        COLOR RGB(,,,0,0,0)
@ 10,72 TO 12,100 PATTERN 2 PEN 1, 8 ;
        COLOR RGB(,,,0,0,0)
@ 12,72 TO 14,100 PATTERN 3 PEN 1, 8 ;
        COLOR RGB(,,,0,0,0)
@ 14,72 TO 16,100 PATTERN 4 PEN 1, 8 ;
        COLOR RGB(,,,0,0,0)
@ 16,72 TO 18,100 PATTERN 5 PEN 1, 8 ;
        COLOR RGB(,,,0,0,0)
@ 18,72 TO 20,100 PATTERN 7 PEN 1, 8 ;
        COLOR RGB(,,,0,0,0)
@ 20,72 TO 22,100 PATTERN 6 PEN 1, 8 ;
        COLOR RGB(,,,0,0,0)
@  5,66 SAY "< expN1>  " ;
        FONT "MS Sans Serif", 8 STYLE "T"
@  5,81 SAY "Pattern Fill" ;
        FONT "MS Sans Serif", 8 STYLE "T"
@  6.5,68 SAY "0"
@  8.5,68 SAY "1"
@ 10.5,68 SAY "2"
@ 12.5,68 SAY "3"
@ 14.5,68 SAY "4"
@ 16.5,68 SAY "5"
@ 18.5,68 SAY "6"
@ 20.5,68 SAY "7"

@ 16,3 TO 20,40 ;
        PATTERN 3 PEN 6, 8 STYLE "16" ;
        COLOR RGB(,,,0,0,0)
@ 21,7 SAY 'STYLE "16" PATTERN 2  PEN 6, 8' ;
        FONT "MS Sans Serif", 8 STYLE "T"
FOR Styles = 0 TO 99 STEP 9
     @ 5,50 TO 15,65 STYLE LTRIM(STR(Styles))
ENDFOR
@ 16,50 SAY "STYLE ranging"
```

```
@ 17,50 SAY "from 0 TO 99"
READ CYCLE
CLEAR
RETURN
```

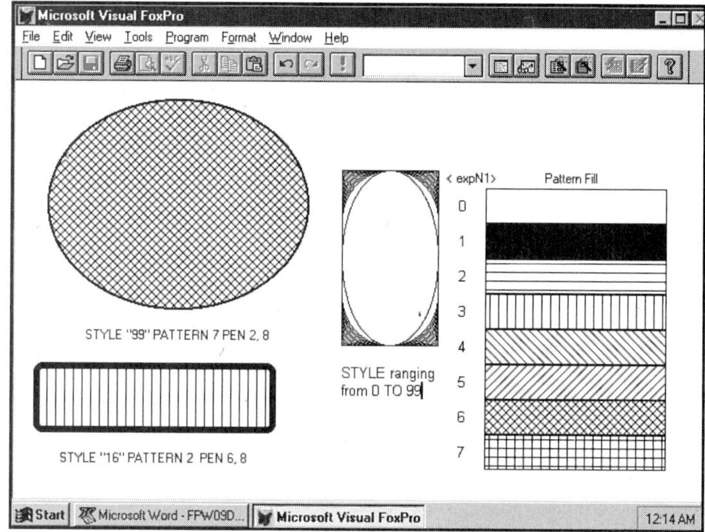

FIGURE 9.3.
Output examples from the @...TO command.

Drawing a Box

The FoxPro language contains a special form of the `@` command for drawing a box. The following is the syntax for this form:

```
@ <expN1>,<expN2>, <expN3>,<expN4> BOX [<expC>]
```

`<expN1>,<expN2>` defines the row and column coordinates of the upper-left corner of the rectangle to be drawn. `<expN3>,<expN4>` defines the row and column coordinates of the lower-right corner of the rectangle to be drawn. The optional `<expC>` field defines a character that is used to draw the box. If the field is not specified, the `SET BORDER TO` border definition is used. Note the following example:

```
* Draw a box using SET BORDER TO borders
@ 10,10 20,60 BOX
* Draw a box using small block (ASCII 254) as border
@ 11, 9, 21,49 BOX CHR(254)
```

The @...*EDIT* Command

You can use a `GET` command with the `SIZE` clause to edit a Character data type variable in a rectangular region. However, this form of the `@` command is weak. If you press the down arrow key, for example, the cursor moves to the next field. You can disable this action by including a

UDF with the VALID clause. A better solution, however, is to use the @...EDIT command, which also edits text in a rectangular region and provides superior editing capabilities. The @...EDIT command behaves like any other GET object, except that you are required to press Tab (or Ctrl+Tab if the TAB keyword is specified) to move to the next field. The following is the syntax for this form:

```
@ <row>,<col> EDIT <variable>
   [FUNCTION <expC1>] [DEFAULT <exp>]
   SIZE <expN1>, <expN2> [, <expN3>]
   [MESSAGE <expC2>]
   [VALID <expL1> [ERROR <expC3>]] [WHEN <expL2>]
   [ENABLE | DISABLE] [NOMODIFY] [SCROLL] [TAB]
   [FONT <expC4> [, <expN4>]]
   [STYLE <expSTYLE>]
   [COLOR SCHEME <expN5>
   |    COLOR [<color attribute>][, <color attribute>]
   |    COLOR RGB()]
```

The <row>,<col>, DEFAULT, MESSAGE, VALID, ERROR, WHEN, FONT, STYLE, and COLOR clauses and ENABLE and DISABLE keywords behave the same way for this command as for other forms of the @ command. This command displays a rectangular text-editing region that you use to edit a variable. The <variable> field can be any Character data type variable, including a memory variable, an array element, a table field, or a memo field. However, memo fields are most often edited (and all FoxPro text-editing features are supported) with this command.

When the @...EDIT command executes, the contents of the variable display in the field. After the READ command executes and the cursor moves into the field, editing begins. After you finish editing, press Tab (or Ctrl+Tab) to save changes—at this point the cursor moves to the next GET field or object. If you press Esc, the changes will not be saved, with one exception: If you are editing a memo field with a VALID clause specified and you press Esc, the changes to the memo field are saved only if the VALID clause evaluates to .T..

The *FUNCTION* <expC2> Clause

Only two function symbols are permitted with the FUNCTION <expC2> clause: I and J. If FUNCTION I is specified, text is centered in the editing region. If FUNCTION J is specified, text is right aligned in the field.

The *SIZE* <expN1>, <expN2> *[*, <expN3>*]* Clause

The SIZE clause specifies the size of the rectangle region. The <expN1> and <expN2> numeric expressions designate the height in rows and width in columns, respectively, of the editing region. The optional <expN3> expression specifies the maximum number of characters that can be edited.

The *NOMODIFY* Keyword

The NOMODIFY keyword causes the text-editing region to display (however, you cannot edit in this region).

The *SCROLL* Keyword

If you specify the SCROLL keyword, a scroll bar is placed to the right of the text-editing region in case the text won't fit in the text-editing region.

The *TAB* Keyword

You normally use Tab and Shift+Tab to move to the next or the previous GET field or GET object, respectively. However, sometimes you might want to insert a Tab character in the text you are editing. If you specify the TAB keyword, tabs are inserted into the edited text. You press Ctrl+Tab to save your changes, exit the text-editing region, and move to the next GET field or GET object. (You can still press Shift+Tab to move to the previous field.)

The @ Command Dialog Objects

In the early days of Xbase, one of the most difficult and time-consuming tasks for an Xbase programmer was creating an input form. FoxPro introduced Screen Builder in FoxPro 2.0, which made this task easy. The task was further simplified by *controls*, such as control buttons, check boxes, and option buttons. In FoxPro 2.*x*, these controls are referred to as GET *objects*. A GET object is a special form of the @ command GET clause. The @ command initially displays the GET object just as it displays a GET field. The READ command provides input control over a GET object in the same manner that it operates on a GET field. Using GET objects, you can include controls as part of a form. The READ command cycles through the GET objects in the same manner that it cycles through GET fields.

With the FoxPro 2.*x* Screen Builder you were able to place a control anywhere on the form and define all its attributes without concerning yourself with its syntax. In fact, it was recommended that you not edit the screen program (SPR) files. You were encouraged to make any changes to the form using the FoxPro 2.*x* Screen Builder. Therefore, you never needed to become an expert at writing code for the various GET objects. However, as with everything in life, exceptions occurred. Sometimes you had to write or modify code involving GET objects. For example, you are required to write code snippets that interpret input from GET objects and perform operations based on this input. As a result, you still needed to understand the interaction between GET objects, the READ command, and the snippets.

With Visual FoxPro Form Designer, you still place controls on the form. However, GET objects are not created and there is no procedural screen program created. The Visual FoxPro Form Designer employs advanced object-oriented technology. The screen (SCX and SCT) files that are created contain definitions of the properties, events, and methods, the formset, the forms, and control objects. Furthermore, the controls are much more powerful and there are more of them. There are only three reasons that GET objects are presented in this book:

- You might need to upgrade FoxPro 2.*x* applications to run under Visual FoxPro.
- The GET objects are still supported by Visual FoxPro.

- You can use the GET objects to write simple FoxPro procedural applications until you learn to use and understand OOP.

The names of the various controls used in FoxPro 2.*x* do not exactly correspond to the names used for the same controls in Microsoft Windows. To remedy this, the names of the various controls were changed in Visual FoxPro to match the terminology used in Microsoft Windows. Table 9.7 compares names used for the same controls in FoxPro 2.*x* and Visual FoxPro.

Table 9.7. A comparison between FoxPro 2.*x* and Visual FoxPro control terminology.

FoxPro 2.x Controls	*Visual FoxPro Controls*
`@...GET Text box`	`TextBox`
`@...GET Check box`	`CheckBox`
`@...GET List`	`ListBox`
`@...GET Popups`	`ComboBox`
`@...GET Push buttons`	`ControlButtons`
`@...GET Radio buttons`	`OptionButtons`
`@...GET Spinner`	`Spinner`
`@...GET Text edit box`	`EditBox`

This section provides you with a reference of the syntax used to generate the various GET objects.

What Are *GET* Objects?

The GET objects available in Visual FoxPro are described in Table 9.8. Visual FoxPro 3.0 terminology is used in this section. FoxPro 2.*x* terminology in Table 9.8 is enclosed in parentheses.

Table 9.8. Types of GET objects.

FoxPro 3.0 GET *Object (FoxPro 2.x Object)*	*Description*
Check box (Check box)	A check box is a small square box that is either blank or contains an × symbol, which indicates if an option is on or off, true or false, and so forth. At the right of the box is text (called the

FoxPro 3.0 GET *Object (FoxPro 2.x Object)*	*Description*
	prompt). The associated logical GET variable is set to .T. if the check box contains an × symbol; otherwise, it is set to .F..
Invisible button	An invisible button is a rectangular region of the screen or a window that you can select. You can use @...SAY to place characters over the rectangular button region. When you select an invisible button, the characters in the button are highlighted.
List box (List)	A list box is a rectangular box that contains options (and a scroll bar on the right). You can choose any one of the values in the list box, and the GET variable is set to that value.
Combo box (Pop-up)	A combo box is a box with a scroll bar arrow on the right. You can enter a value directly or you can click on the arrow to drop down a list of options from which you can choose a value. The GET variable is set to the selected value.
Control button (Push button)	A control button is a rectangular box that contains text or a bitmap picture. If you press the control button, an action is triggered.
Option button (Radio button)	A option button is a small circle that resembles a round control button and is followed by text. Normally, a single GET object consists of more than one option button. One of the option buttons usually is selected and marked with a bullet symbol inside the small circle. With option buttons, you can choose one of several related objects. You can select another option button, and the bullet symbol moves to the newly selected option button. The GET variable is set to the number of the option button. The first option button is number 1, the second is number 2, and so forth.
Spinner	You can "spin" through a set of numbers displayed in a text box by clicking on the up and down arrows at the right of the text box. If you click on the up or down arrow, the number gets larger or smaller, respectively. You can still type a number directly into the text box. In either case, the GET variable is set to the text box value.

The Syntax for *GET* Fields

The forms of the `@` command are similar for all the `GET` objects. The clauses specified with the `@` command for each type of `GET` object are indicated in Table 9.9. The following is the general form of the `@` command, used to create a `GET` object:

```
@ <row>, <column> GET <var>
     [SPINNER <expN1>[,<expN2>[, <expN3>]]]
     [FUNCTION <expC1>] [PICTURE <expC2>]
     [FONT <expC3> [, <expN4>]]
     [STYLE <expC4>]
     [DEFAULT <expr>]
     [SIZE <expN5>, <expN6> [,<expN7>]]]
     [ENABLE ¦ DISABLE]
     [POPUP <popup-name>]
     ¦ [FROM <array> [ RANGE <expN8>[,<expN9> ]]]
     [MESSAGE <expC5>]
     [VALID <expL1> ¦ <expN10> [ERROR <expC6>]]
     [WHEN <expL2>]
     [COLOR SCHEME <expN11>
           ¦ COLOR <color pair list>
           ¦ COLOR RGB (<color value list>)]
```

Table 9.9. The `@` command clauses used with `GET` objects.

Clause	*Check Box*	*Invisible Box*	*List Box*	*Combo Box*	*Control Button*	*Option Button*	*Spinner*
<row,column>	✓	✓	✓	✓	✓	✓	✓
GET	✓	✓	✓	✓	✓	✓	✓
Data type:	L,N	N	N,C	N,C	N,C	N	N
SPINNER							✓
FUNCTION ¦ PICTURE	✓	✓	✓	✓	✓	✓	✓
FONT	✓	✓	✓	✓	✓	✓	✓
STYLE	✓	✓	✓	✓	✓	✓	✓
DEFAULT	✓	✓	✓	✓	✓	✓	✓
SIZE	✓	✓	✓	✓	✓	✓	✓
ENABLE ¦ DISABLE	✓	✓	✓	✓	✓	✓	✓
MESSAGE	✓	✓	✓	✓	✓	✓	✓
POPUP			✓				
FROM *<array>* RANGE			✓	✓			
RANGE							✓

Clause	*Check Box*	*Invisible Box*	*List Box*	*Combo Box*	*Control Button*	*Option Button*	*Spinner*
VALID	✓	✓	✓	✓	✓	✓	✓
ERROR							✓
WHEN	✓	✓	✓	✓	✓	✓	✓
COLOR	✓	✓	✓	✓	✓	✓	✓

GET objects are placed on the screen when the @ command executes. When the READ command executes, GET objects are activated one at a time in the order the @ commands were executed, regardless of whether the GET object is a GET field, a control button, an edit box, an option button, a combo box, a check box, a list box, or a spinner. All the GET objects issued since the last READ (unless SAVE was specified) or CLEAR GETS command was executed are activated. Either the cursor is placed on the first character of the first specified GET field or the GET object activates. To navigate through the GET objects, you can press Enter, Tab, or ↓ to move to next object. Press Shift+Tab or ↑ to move to the previous object. You can select any GET object also by clicking on it.

Each of the clauses used with the @ command to create GET objects is described in the following sections.

The *<row>, <column>* Elements

The *<row>* and *<column>* elements are numeric expressions that designate the coordinate position of the upper-left corner of the GET object. The row can have a value from zero (top of window) to one less than the maximum height of the window. The column can have a value from zero (left of the window) to one less than the maximum width of the window.

The *GET <var>* Clause

You must specify a GET clause for all types of GET objects. The variable can be a memory variable, an array element, or a table field where the value of GET object is stored. Depending on the type of GET object, the resulting value is stored to *<var>*. If Esc is pressed, *<var>* remains unchanged. Table 9.10 describes the usage of the variable for GET objects.

Table 9.10. Description of the GET clause variable for GET objects.

GET *Object*	GET *<var> Description*
Check box	If *<var>* is a Logical variable, a true value (.T.) is stored if the box is checked. If *<var>* has a nonzero Numeric value, the box is checked. If *<var>* has a zero Numeric value, the box is not checked.

continues

Table 9.10. continued

`GET` *Object*	`GET <var>` *Description*
Invisible Button	`<var>` must be a Double, Float, Integer, or Numeric data type that contains a number corresponding to the choice. If initial value is less than one or greater than the number of objects, no object is initially selected.
List Box	`<var>` must be a Double, Float, Integer, Numeric, or Character data type. If its initial value corresponds to a value in the list box, the option is selected.
Combo Box	`<var>` must be a Double, Float, Integer, Numeric, or Character data type. If `<var>` is a Character data type, the prompt of the item you choose is stored to `<var>`. If `<var>` is a Numeric data type, the number representing the position of the chosen item in the combo box is stored to `<var>`. Initially the value of `<var>` determines which combo box option displays. If the initial value does not correspond to any value, the value of `<var>` initially displays on the face of the combo box and is added as a temporary option at the end of the combo box.
Control button	`<var>` must be a Double, Float, Integer, Currency, Double, Float, Integer, Numeric, or Character data type. If `<var>` is a Numeric data type, a number corresponding to your control button choice is stored to `<var>`. The first control button is number `1`, and so forth. If `<var>` is a Character data type, the text of the chosen prompt is stored to `<var>`.
Option button	`<var>` must be a Double, Float, Integer, or Numeric value. If the initial value corresponds to one of the option buttons, the option button is initially selected.
Spinner	`<var>` must be a Currency, Double, Float, Integer, or Numeric data type. When you choose or type in a value, it is stored to `<var>`.

The *[SPINNER <expN1>[,<expN2>[, <expN3>]]]* Clause

The `SPINNER` clause is specified only for the spinner object. The numeric expression, `<expN1>`, designates how much the value in the text box is incremented or decremented each time you click on the up or down arrows. If you omit `<expN1>`, the value is incremented or decremented by 1.

<expN2> and *<expN3>* specify the minimum and maximum value, respectively, that can be displayed in the spinner when you change the spinner value with the mouse. However, with the keyboard you can enter a value in the text box that lies outside the range specified by *<expN2>* and *<expN3>*. You need to use the `VALID` or `RANGE` clauses to validate a value entered in the text box with the keyboard.

The *[FUNCTION <expC1>]* and *[PICTURE <expC2>]* Clauses

The most substantial difference between the specification of a traditional `GET` field and a `GET` object is the specification of the `PICTURE` and `FUNCTION` clauses. Historically, the `GET` objects that FoxPro supports are extensions of the concept introduced in dBASE IV that have a display function (`M`) that allows users to choose one value from a list of values. Here's an example:

```
FUNCTION "M Monday,Tuesday,Wednesday,Thursday,Friday"
```

The section "The `FUNCTION` *<expFunc>* Symbols" has a discussion of the `M` (multiple choice) display function. All the `GET` objects, except the spinner, use this concept for defining an object. That is, each type of `GET` object has a unique display function. The prompt text associated with a `GET` object is also specified as part of the `FUNCTION` expression. A space separates the display function codes and the prompt text. In addition, you can specify a function with a `PICTURE` expression by placing an `@` character in front of the display function code. Display functions can be specified using either a `PICTURE` clause, a `FUNCTION` clause, or both. For example, the following three specifications are equivalent:

```
Choice = 1
@ 10,10 GET Choice FUNCTION "^ Monday;Tuesday;Wednesday"
@ 10,10 GET Choice PICTURE  "@^ Monday;Tuesday;Wednesday"
@ 10,10 GET Choice FUNCTION "^" ;
PICTURE "Monday;Tuesday;Wednesday"
```

The preceding example illustrates a display function code for a combo box `GET` object. The text to the right of the display function code specifies three options separated by semicolons (;). The options are `Monday`, `Tuesday`, and `Wednesday`. You can disable an option or prompt by placing two backslash characters (`\\`) in front of the text. Also, you can specify a hotkey by placing the `\<` characters in front of the hotkey character. In the following example, three hotkeys are specified (`M`, `u`, and `W`), and the combo box option `Tuesday` is disabled:

```
Choice = 1
@ 10,10 GET Choice FUNCTION ;
"^ \<Monday;\\T\<uesday;<\Wednesday"
```

In Table 9.11, only the `FUNCTION` clause is used. However, you could use the `PICTURE` clause or a combination of the `FUNCTION` and `PICTURE` clauses. The display function code used to specify which type of `GET` object is created, the supplied prompt, and the option text are described in Table 9.11.

Table 9.11. Description of the GET clause display function codes for GET objects.

GET *Object*	*Code*	*Description*
Check box	*C	Specifies that the object is a single check box. Also specifies the prompt text in the following form: FUNCTION "*C <*prompt text*>".
	B	Displays the contents of a bitmap (BMP) picture file in a check box. You can display three pictures: one when the check box is enabled, one when the check box is selected, and one when the check box is disabled. The names of the three files are specified following the display function code and are separated by a comma. The form is FUNCTION ; "*CB <*enabled*>,<*selected*>,<*disabled*>"
	N	The check box does not terminate READ. (This is the default.)
	T	The check box terminates READ, as in the following examples: FUNCTION "*CT \\<Orange" && O is hotkey FUNCTION "*C A\\<pple" && p is hotkey
Invisible button	*I	Specifies that the object is an invisible box. Also specifies the prompt text for each invisible box. Prompts are separated by semicolons. Here is the general form: FUNCTION ; "*C <*prompt text 1*>;<*prompt text 2*>;..."
	N	The invisible box does not terminate READ. (This is the default.)
	T	Selects a box and READ terminates.
	H	Horizontal buttons.
	V	Vertical buttons. Here are examples: FUNCTION "*ITV Red;Blue;Green" FUNCTION "*IH Apples;Orange;Plum"
List box	&	Specifies that the object is list box object. The prompt text is specified for each list box object. Options are separated by semicolons. The general form is as follows: FUNCTION ; "& <*option text 1*>;<*option text 2*>;..."

GET Object	Code	Description
		Alternatively, you can specify option text with the FROM clause.
	N	Chooses an option and READ does not terminate. (This is the default.)

	T	Chooses an option and READ terminates. Here are examples:
		`FUNCTION "&T Red;Blue;Green"`
		`FUNCTION "& Apples;Orange;Plum"`

Combo box	^	Denotes that the combo box object is specified. Also specifies the option text for each combo box object. Options are separated by semicolons. Here is the general form:
		`FUNCTION`
		`"& <option text 1>;<option text 2>;…"`
		Alternatively, you can specify option text with the FROM <array> and POPUP clauses.

	N	User chooses an option and READ does not terminate. (This is the default.)

	T	User Chooses an option and READ terminates.
		Here are examples:
		`FUNCTION "&T Red;Blue;Green"`
		`FUNCTION "& Apples;Orange;Plum"`

Control button	*	Specifies control button objects. Also specifies the prompt text for each control button. Prompts are separated by semicolons. Here is the general form:
		`FUNCTION;`
		`"* <prompt text 1>;<prompt text 2>;…".`

	B	Displays the contents of bitmap (BMP) picture file in control buttons. You can display three pictures in each control button: one when the button is enabled, one when button is selected, and one when button is disabled. The names of the three files are specified following the display function code and are separated by a comma. Here is the general form:
		`FUNCTION ;`
		`"*B <enabled>,<selected>,<disabled>;…"`

continues

Table 9.11. continued

GET *Object*	*Code*	*Description*
		You can specify up to three BMP files for each push button.
	N	The control button does not terminate READ.
	T	The user chooses the control button and the READ terminates. (This is the default.)
	H	Horizontal buttons.

	V	Vertical buttons. Here are examples:
		`FUNCTION "*NV Red;Blue;Green"`
		`FUNCTION "*H Apples;Orange;Plum"`

Option button	*R	Specifies option button objects and the prompt text for each control button. Prompts are separated by semicolons. Here is the general form:
		`FUNCTION ;`
		`"*R <prompt text 1>;<prompt text 2>;…".`

	B	Displays contents of bitmap (BMP) picture file in option buttons. You may display three pictures in each option button. (See the control button description.)
	N	The Option button does not terminate READ.
	T	The user chooses the Option button and READ terminates. (This is the default.)
	H	Horizontal buttons.

	V	Vertical buttons. Here are examples:
		`FUNCTION "*NV Red;Blue;Green"`
		`FUNCTION "*H Apples;Orange;Plum"`

Spinner		The same display function codes and PICTURE template codes used with numeric GET fields are used with the spinner objects. See Tables 9.2 and 9.3.

You can specify bitmap pictures in check boxes, control buttons, and option buttons. Bitmap pictures are stored in disk files with the filename extension .BMP. These buttons, sometimes called *picture buttons*, behave like check boxes or option buttons. You can specify three pictures for each control. You can specify one picture that displays when a control is selected, another picture that displays when a control is enabled and not selected, and a third picture that displays when a control is disabled. For example, suppose you have three pictures—ENABLED.BMP, DISABLED.BMP, and SELECTED.BMP—and you want to display them in a check box. You specify them, separated by commas, where you would display the prompt text. Here's an example:

```
@ 20,20 GET Choice ;
FUNCTION "*CB enabled.bmp,selected.bmp,disabled.bmp"
```

The display function code B denotes that a bitmap picture file will be specified. It might seem obvious, but don't forget to separate the display function codes and the specification of the first filename with a space. Also implied in the preceding example is the order in which the bitmap files are specified. If you want to specify a set of two control buttons containing pictures, you can specify up to three pictures for each control button. Here is an example:

```
@ 10,30 GET Choice FUNCTION
"*BV en1.bmp,se1.bmp,di1.bmp; en2.bmp,se2.bmp,di2.bmp"
```

The *[FONT <expC3> [, <expN4>]]* and *[STYLE <expC4>]* Clauses

You can specify FONT and STYLE clauses for the values, prompts, and options displayed in the GET objects.

The *[DEFAULT <expr>]* Clause

The value associated with a GET object is stored in the variable specified by the GET clause. If the GET variable is a memory variable that doesn't exist, and the DEFAULT clause is specified, Visual FoxPro creates the memory variable and assigns it the value specified with the DEFAULT clause. If the variable is a table field, an array element, or an existing memory variable, the DEFAULT clause is ignored.

The *[SIZE <expN5>, <expN6> [, <expN7>]]* Clause

In general, the SIZE clause defines the height (*<expN5>*) in rows and the width (*<expN6>*) in columns of a GET object. When appropriate it defines the spacing between controls (*<expN7>*) in columns. The height and width are based on the font size of the text displayed on or in the control. The SIZE clause values for GET objects are discussed in Table 9.12.

Table 9.12. Description of the SIZE clause variable for GET objects.

GET *Object*	SIZE *Clause Description*
Check box	The check box height is always 1, so the first numeric expression (<*expN5*>.) is ignored. The width is determined by either the width of the prompt or the second numeric expression (<*expN6*>), whichever is greater. <*expN7*> is not specified.
Invisible	You specify the height and width of each button with the numeric expressions <*expN5*> and <*expN6*>. You specify the spacing between the buttons with the third numeric expression, <*expN7*>. The default for the height and width of invisible buttons is 0.
List box	You specify the height and width of a list box with <*expN5*> and <*expN6*>, respectively. <*expN7*> is not specified.
Combo box	You should always specify 1 for the height (<*expN5*>) of a combo box. <*expN5*> specifies width of combo box. By default, the width of the combo box is determined by the length of the longest option. The SIZE clause is optional. If you want to type a value into the combo box's text box that is longer than any option, however, you can specify the SIZE clause to designate the height (1) and width.
Control button Option button	The height of the control button or option button object is always 1. By default, the width of each individual button is determined by the length of the control button prompt. However, if you want wider buttons, you can specify <*expN6*> to designate a new width. The third numeric expression (<*expN7*>) specifies the spacing between buttons.
Spinner	You can specify the height of the spinner using the numeric expression (<*expN5*>). The height of the spinner is a multiple of the current font or the font you specify when you create the spinner. For example, if <*expN5*> is 2, the height of the spinner is twice the height of the current font or the font you specify. You can specify the width of a spinner with the numeric expression (<*expN6*>). The width of the spinner is a multiple of the average width of the current font or the font you specify when you create the spinner.

The *[ENABLE | DISABLE]* Clause

If you want your controls to be enabled, you can ignore these keywords because, by default, controls defined by the @ command are enabled when READ executes. However, if you want controls to be disabled, specify the DEFAULT keyword.

The *FROM <array>* and *RANGE <expN8> [, <expN9>]* Clauses

As an alternative to providing a list of options for combo box and list box controls with the FUNCTION clause, you can instruct FoxPro to build an option list from an array. The array can be one or two dimensional. If the array is one dimensional, the first array element is the first option in the list box, the second array element is the second option, and so forth. If the array is two dimensional, the elements in the first column of the array are used to build the list of options.

If the FROM clause is specified, any options specified in the PICTURE or FUNCTION clauses are ignored. You are still required to specify the display function code, however. In the following example, list box and combo box objects are created, and the options are built from array elements:

```
Choice = 1
DECLARE Aray[3]
Aray[1] = "<\Apple"
Aray[2] = "<\Orange"
Aray[3] = "A<\pricot"
@ 10,10 GET Choice FUNCTION "^" FROM Aray && List Box object
@ 10,40 GET Choice FUNCTION "&" FROM Aray && Combo box object
```

You can specify the RANGE clause with the FROM *<array>* clause to designate different starting elements in the array. Here's the syntax:

```
RANGE <expN8> [, <expN9>]
```

The numeric expressions *<expN8>* and *<expN9>* specify the row and column, respectively, of the element containing the first option to transfer.

The *POPUP <popup name>* Clause

You may specify the POPUP clause when creating a list box object. This clause specifiesn option list using the options from a pop-up menu created with the DEFINE POPUP command.

The *COLOR* Clause

The `COLOR` clause overrides the current color scheme by specifying a different predefined color scheme, or by specifying a list of color pairs. If you don't specify any form of the `COLOR` clause, colors are derived from the color scheme of the desktop or the current output window for all `GET` objects. A more complete discussion of color schemes is provided in Chapter 10 in the section "The `COLOR` Clauses." This section describes coloring information that relates specifically to `GET` objects.

A color scheme is a set of 10 color pairs that describe the color characteristics of the window or desktop. You can override the current color scheme by specifying a different predefined color scheme, a list of color pairs, or a set of RGB color values. *<color pair list>* is a list of 10 color pairs separated by commas. The first half of a pair specifies the foreground color. The second half of a pair specifies the background color. When you skip a color pair, you must include a comma where the color pair would have been. The color pairs that color the various elements of control buttons, option buttons, check boxes, and spinners are presented in Table 9.13.

Table 9.13. Color pair descriptions for the elements of control buttons, option buttons, check boxes, and spinners.

Color Pair	*Control Element*
1	Not used
2	Not used
3	Not used
4	Not used
5	Message
6	Selected control prompt
7	Hot keys
8	Not used by control
9	Enabled control prompt
10	Disabled control prompt

The color pairs that color various elements of a list box are presented in Table 9.14.

Table 9.14. Color pair descriptions for the elements of the list box.

Color Pair	*List Box Control Element*
1	Disabled option
2	Enabled option

Color Pair	*List Box Control Element*
3	Border and scroll bar (Controls are drawn in the background color. Bars are drawn in a dimmer shade of the foreground color.)
4	Not used by list box
5	Message
6	Selected list item
7	Not used by list box
8	Not used by list box
9	Enabled list box
10	Disabled list box

The `COLOR` *`<color pair list>`* clause can be specified for a combo box object. However, *`<color pair list>`* controls only the color of the face of the combo box when the combo box is selected, enabled, or disabled, and the color of the message (combo box color attributes are controlled by color scheme `<expN11>`). You must specify two color schemes (`COLOR SCHEME <expN11>, <expN12>`) to specify all the colors associated with a combo box. The second color scheme, `<expN12>`, determines the color of the combo box options and the border of the box that contains the options. Incidentally, the `COLOR SCHEME` clause for all other `GET` objects has only one numeric expression (`<expN11>`).

Table 9.15 lists the color pairs for both color schemes and their corresponding combo box elements.

Table 9.15. Color pair descriptions for the elements of the combo box object.

Color Pair Element	`<expN11>` *Combo Box Element*	`<expN12>` *Combo Box*
1	Not used by combo box	Disabled options
2	Not used by combo box	Enabled options
3	Not used by combo box	Border
4	Not used by combo box	Not used by combo box
5	Message	Not used by combo box
6	Selected combo box	Selected option
7	Not used by combo box	Hotkeys
8	Not used by combo box	Not used by combo box
9	Enabled combo box	Not used by combo box
10	Disabled combo box	Not used by combo box

Here are some examples of GET clauses with the COLOR clause specified:

```
Choice = 1
@ 7,0 GET Choice FUNCTION '*C Paid' COLOR SCHEME 4 && Check box

*  Specify check boxes color combinations
*     Selected box- bright white prompt on blue background (W+/B)
*     Hot key      - red on a blue background (R/B)
*     Enabled      - yellow prompt on a blue background (GR+/B)
*     Disabled     - white prompt on a blue background (W/B)
@ 5,0 GET choice FUNCTION '*C \<Paid';
   COLOR ,,,,,W+/B,R/B,,GR+/B,W/B       && Enabled Check box
@ 9,0 GET choice FUNCTION '*C \\Paid';
   COLOR ,,,,,W+/B,R/B,,GR+/B,W/B       && Disabled Check box
*
* Override combo box colors
color = 1
@ 15,20 GET color FUNCTION '^ Red;Blue;Green' ;
   COLOR SCHEME 4,5
* Specify push and option button color combinations
*   Selected button  - bright white prompt on blue
*                      background(W+/B)
*   Hot key          - red on blue background (R/B)
*   Enabled buttons  - yellow prompt on blue background (GR+/B)
*   Disabled buttons - white prompt on blue background (W/B)
STORE 1 TO choice
@ 5,0 GET choice FUNCTION '* \<OK;\<CANCEL;\\DISABLED';
   COLOR ,,,,,W+/B,R/B,,GR+/B,W/B  && Control buttons
@ 5,0 GET choice FUNCTION ;
   "*R \<Small;M\<edium;\\Large';
   COLOR ,,,,,W+/B,R/B,,GR+/B,W/B  && Option buttons
```

Other Clauses

The VALID clause is described in detail earlier in this chapter in the section "The VALID and ERROR Clauses." The VALID clause evaluates an expression when a control is selected. This expression may be a UDF that executes some action when a control is selected. The VALID clause is normally used to trigger an action when a control button is pressed.

The MESSAGE, ERROR, and WHEN clauses perform the same service for the GET objects as they do for GET fields. They are discussed in detail earlier in this chapter.

A Final Word Regarding *GET* Objects

As the discussion of GET objects indicates, the syntax of GET objects is relatively simple, but some aspects of GET fields syntax are difficult to code by hand. For example, getting a control in the correct position is more difficult to do if you hand code it. The display function syntax is also cryptic and hard to remember. In FoxPro 2.*x*, it is easy to do if you used Screen Builder. However, the FoxPro 2.*x* Screen Builder is no longer available. In Visual FoxPro, you can use Form Designer or Form Wizard to build your interfaces. However, @ commands are no longer used. Controls are defined by control objects that are instances of subclasses. In fact, the Visual FoxPro forms and controls have many more properties than GET objects so you can create a much more interesting and powerful interface. You no longer have to worry about the `GET` objects—you just have to learn OOP.

The Visual FoxPro Form Designer and Form Wizards enable you to paint controls and fields on the screen and execute them. The Form Designer saves a screen design in two files. The files have the same name but different extensions, .SCX and .SCT. The files contain all of the information for defining all formset, form, and control properties, events, and methods. You can execute an SCX file using the `DO FORM` command. If you want to execute a form file named EXAMPLE.SCX, enter the following command:

```
DO FORM EXAMPLE
```

You can execute a form also by choosing the **P**rogram menu **D**o option. There are other ways to run a form and operate on its properties at runtime. These are discussed in Chapter 14, "Object-Oriented Programming."

Format Files

In Visual FoxPro format files are obsolete, thanks to the Visual FoxPro Form Designer. The Form Designer builds a form (SCX) file that you can execute as a complete form-oriented application. You can use the Form Designer to build a complex application consisting of a complex set of forms, which is called a formset. Support for format files is retained so that existing applications that use them can still operate. A format file is a special form of the FoxPro program file used to support custom input forms in conjunction with the `APPEND`, `BROWSE`, `EDIT`, `CHANGE`, `INSERT`, and `READ` commands. It contains `@` commands that define a custom form. You can create a format file only using `MODIFY COMMAND`, which brings you to the program editor. To activate a format file, use the `SET FORMAT TO` command. Once activated, the file can be used by the full-screen editing commands. The format file in Listing 9.2, for example, defines a custom form.

Listing 9.2. An example of a format file.

```
*********************************************************
*     * Format File: PARTLIST.FMT                       *
*     *                                                 *
*********************************************************
@ 0,0  SAY "              ACME Company Part List Entry Form"
@ 0,50 SAY date()   && Display today's date
@ 2,0 TO 7,50
@ 3,1 SAY "Enter part number: "
@ 3,20 GET partno PICTURE "999" ;
  VALID partno > 100 AND partno < 500 ;
  ERROR "Invalid part number entered";
  MESSAGE "Enter a valid part number"
@ 4,1 SAY "Part description: "
@ 4,20 GET descript
@ 5,1 SAY "Enter quantity:   "
```

continues

Listing 9.2. continued

```
@ 5,20 GET qty PICTURE "999999"
@ 6,1 SAY  "Enter new price:   "
@ 6,20ET price PICTURE "@$ 9999,999.99"
```

To use PARTLIST.FMT, you need the following code:

```
USE PARTLIST
SET FORMAT TO PARTLIST
CHANGE
```

The `SET FORMAT TO` command establishes a form for the currently used table (DBF file) or view. When executed, FoxPro searches for a format object file with the .PRX filename extension. If the format object file is found and the `SET DEVELOPMENT` option is `ON`, a check is made to see if the file is older than the format source file. If it is, the source file is recompiled.

If the format object file is not found, FoxPro looks for a format source file that has the .FMT filename extension. If found, the format source file is compiled to generate a new format object file.

In either case, the format object file is opened. If a catalog is active and the format file is not in the catalog, it is added to the catalog. The following is the syntax for this form:

```
SET FORMAT TO [<expFN> ¦ ?]
```

If you specify `SET FORMAT TO` without any arguments, the format file in the current work area is closed. `CLOSE FORMAT` closes format files in all work areas. A format file is also closed when the active table in the same work area is closed.

If you specify a question mark instead of a filename, an Open file dialog box containing FMT files appears. When you select one of the files, it becomes active.

Full-Screen Data-Editing Commands

All the screen-editing commands share some functionality. For example, `APPEND`, `BROWSE`, `CHANGE`, and `INSERT` share the same cursor navigation for all the commands as presented in Table 9.1. In addition, the **T**able menu is added to the system menu bar whenever any of these commands execute, and additional options are added to the **V**iew menu. You can suppress the **T**able menu by specifying the `NOMENU` keyword with any one of the full-screen editing commands. The **V**iew menu options that relate to the editing command, shown in Figure 9.4, and the options presented in the **T**able menu, shown in Figure 9.5, are described in Table 9.16. The characters preceded by a Ctrl+ character (that is, H, T, and N) that appear under the menu options denote shortcut keys. For example, you can press Ctrl+Y to enter append mode in `BROWSE` or `CHANGE`.

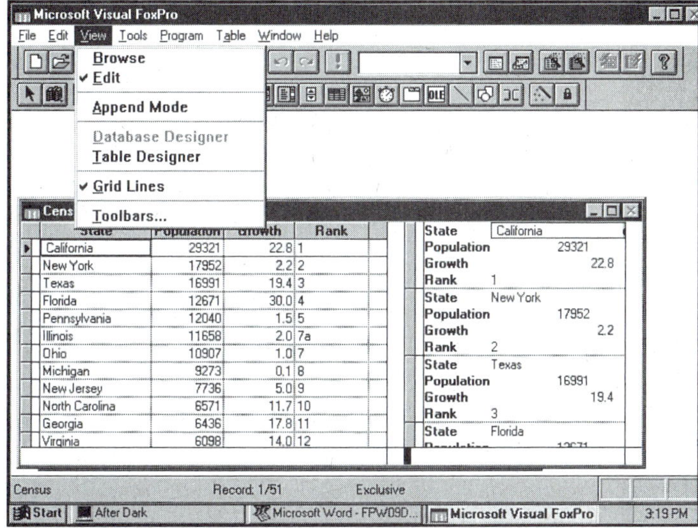

FIGURE 9.4.
The Browse window with the View menu open.

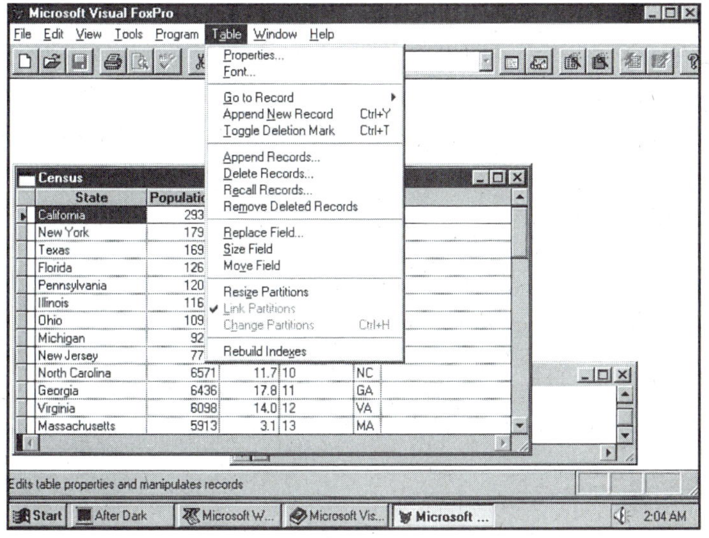

FIGURE 9.5.
The Browse window with the Table menu open.

Table 9.16. View and Table menu options.

Menu Option	*Description*
View Menu	
B rowse **E**dit	Toggles between Browse window and Edit window mode. When the Edit window is active, the **E**dit option is checked. When the Browse window displays, the **B**rowse option is checked.
Append Mode	Use this option to enter append mode. A check mark appears next to the option to indicate that you are in append mode. A blank record appears at the bottom of the window. You can enter a new record for as long as you remain in append mode.
Database Designer	Either the Browse or the Edit window disappears and the Database Designer window appears in its place. In Database Designer you can modify the properties of a database. This option is only enabled if a database is active.
Table Designer	Either the Browse or the Edit window disappears and the Table Designer window appears in its place. In Table Designer you can modify the structure of the table.
G rid Lines	This option either removes vertical lines (**G**rid Lines is not preceded with a check mark) or turns on vertical lines (**G**rid Lines is preceded with a check mark) between data in the Browse window.
Table Menu	
Properties...	The Work Area dialog box appears. In it you can modify the structure of a table, select index files and fields, define data filters, and set data buffering options.
Font...	The Font dialog box appears. You can set the font, font size, and font style of the text in the Browse or Edit window. See the section "The `GETFONT()` Function" for more information about the Font dialog box.
Go To Record	Use this option to go to the first, last, or a specified record in the Browse or Edit window. You can also skip over a specified number of records.
Append **N**ew Record Ctrl+Y	Use this option to append a record to the table. A blank record appears at the bottom of the window. You can enter a new record.

Menu Option	*Description*
Toggle Deletion Mark Ctrl+T	Use this option to mark or unmark the selected record for deletion. A black column displays to the left of a selected record when a record is marked.
Append Records...	Displays the Append From dialog box. You can choose the name of a table. Records from the selected table are appended to the current table. (Same as the APPEND FROM command.)
Delete Records...	Displays the Delete dialog box. You can select scope and selection criteria for a set of records to be marked for deletion. (Same as the DELETE command.)
R**e**call Records...	Displays the Recall Records dialog box. You can select scope and selection criteria for a set of records to be unmarked for deletion. (Same as the RECALL command.)
Re**m**ove Deleted Records	Removes all of the records marked for deletion from the table in the current work area. (Same as the PACK command.)
Replace Field...	Changes the value of a field in one record or in a range of records. (Same as the REPLACE command.)
Size Field	Use this option to size a field from the keyboard. When you choose this option, the column header in which the cursor resides becomes highlighted. Use the → and ← keys to size the field; press Enter to terminate the sizing process. You can also size a field column by pointing to the vertical line that divides the two columns, then dragging the line horizontally to expand or contract the column size.
Mo**v**e Field	Use this option to move a field with the keyboard. Move the cursor into the field you want to move, choose the Move Field option, and use the ← and → keys to move the field to a new location. You can move a field also by dragging the field header with the mouse to a new location.
Resi**z**e Partitions	Use this option to resize partitions from the keyboard. You can use it also to split the window into two partitions. In addition, the small black rectangle that appears to the left of the horizontal scroll bar can be dragged to a new location to size a partition or to split a window into two partitions.

continues

Table 9.16. continued

Menu Option	*Description*
Link Partitions	This option is active only if you have split the Browse or Change screens into two partitions. The three ways to split a window into two partitions are to use the **R**esize Partition menu option; specify the PARTITION clause with the BROWSE or CHANGE command; or drag the black rectangle that appears to the left of the horizontal scrollbar to the right. An example of a Browse window split into two partitions is shown in Figure 9.5. The partitions can be linked on the record number. When you highlight a record in one partition, the same record is highlighted in the other partition. You can toggle on and off this linkage with this option. When partitions are linked, the option is preceded with a check mark.
C**h**ange Partitions Ctrl+H	This option is used to make an active partition window inactive and an inactive partition window active. You can also perform this operation by clicking on the inactive window with the mouse or by pressing Ctrl+H. This option is enabled only when a Browse window is split.
Rebuild Inde**x**es	Rebuilds the active indexes for the current table. (Same as the REINDEX command.)

The *APPEND* Command

Use the APPEND command to add records to the end of the currently active table (DBF file) in full-screen mode. If any indexes are active, they are updated. The following is the syntax for this command:

```
APPEND [BLANK]
```

The APPEND command with the BLANK keyword specified is used in a program to append a blank screen without initiating a full-screen append. If the BLANK keyword is omitted, the full-screen APPEND window appears. If a format file is not active, a default form displays. Data is entered into the form one record at a time. The data entry process ends if you press Esc when a blank form is displayed for a new record. You can use Ctrl+End also to end data entry. If Ctrl+End is entered as the first key entry to a blank record form, however, a blank record is added to the file.

When the cursor is moved to the previous record, FoxPro moves out of append mode and into change mode. In change mode, records can be edited. By pressing Ctrl+Y or by choosing the Table menu Append New Record option, you can re-enter the append mode. Figure 9.6 shows an append screen split into two partitions. The left partition contains the append form. The right partition displays records in browse mode.

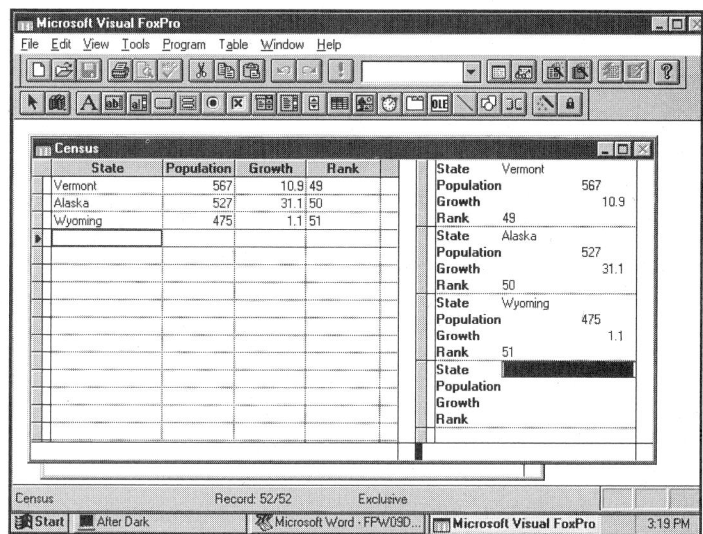

FIGURE 9.6.
An append screen with open partitions.

The *BROWSE* Command

The `BROWSE` command displays records in tabular form and enables you to edit fields in the form. The table is confined to a window. The records in the table are displayed in their logical order. You can use the mouse to navigate through the records. In addition, you can use the keyboard to move between records with the ↑ and ↓ keys, to page through a page of records with the PgUp and PgDn keys, and to move to the next and previous fields using the Tab and Shift+Tab keys, respectively. Table 9.1 presents other navigation keys. You can edit a memo field by placing the cursor on the Memo icon and pressing Ctrl+PgDn or by double-clicking on the Memo field icon with the mouse.

If no user-defined window is active, `BROWSE` displays its own window and uses its "normal" attributes (`COLOR SCHEME 10`, `GROW`, `FLOAT`, `ZOOM`, and so on). If a user-defined window is active and foremost or a window is specified with the `WINDOW` clause, `BROWSE` displays in that window and inherits its color size, position, and window control options.

If a `SET FIELDS` list is active, the `BROWSE` table contains only the fields in the list. The cursor highlights the field to be edited. You can append records by pressing Ctrl+Y or by choosing the

Append New Record option in the Table menu. BROWSE switches into the append mode and you can add records to the file.

The BROWSE table displays in the Browse window unless you specify a window with the WINDOW clause. The following is the syntax for BROWSE:

```
BROWSE [FIELDS <browse field list>]
   [FORMAT] [FOR <expL1>] [FREEZE <field name>]
   [KEY <exp1> [, <exp2>]]
   [LAST] [LEDIT] [REDIT] [LPARTITION]
   [LOCK <expN1>]
   [NOAPPEND] [NOCLEAR] [NODELETE] [NOEDIT ¦ NOMODIFY]
   [NOLGRID] [NORGRID]  [NOLINK] [NOMENU] [NOOPTIMIZE]
   [NOREFRESH]  [NORMAL] [NOWAIT] [NOINIT]
   [PARTITION <expN2>] [PREFERENCE <expC1>]
   [REST] [SAVE]
   [TIMEOUT <expN3>] [TITLE <expC2>]
   [VALID [:F] <expL2> [ERROR <expC3>]]
   [WHEN <expL3>]  [WIDTH <expN4>]
   [[WINDOW <window name1>]
   [IN [WINDOW] <window name2> ¦ IN SCREEN]]
   [FONT <expC4> [, <expN5>]]
   [STYLE <expSTYLE>]
   [COLOR SCHEME <expN6>
   ¦  COLOR [<color attribute>][, <color attribute>]
   ¦  COLOR RGB()]

<browse field list> ::= <field name1> [:R] [:<column width>]
[:V = <expL1> [:F] [:E = <expC1>]]
[:P = <expC2>]
[:B = <exp1>, <exp2> [:F]]
[:H = <expC3>]
[:W = <expL2>]
[, <field name2> [:R]  ... ]
¦  <calculated field exp>
[, <field name> [:R] [:<column width>]  ¦
   <calculated field exp>]...]

<calculated field exp> ::=  <field name> = <exp>
<column width> ::= <positive integer>
```

If the syntax seems to be too complex, don't worry. You can simply type BROWSE, press Enter, and go on to edit fields in a table. If you want to take advantage of the power of the FoxPro BROWSE command, however, continue reading. The following section describes each keyword and clause.

The *FIELDS* <browse field list> Clause

The FIELDS clause defines the fields displayed in the BROWSE table. The fields are displayed in the order specified by the *<browse field list>* argument.

You can specify options along with the field names to request some form of special handling of the field. These options are preceded by a colon (:) and are presented in Table 9.17.

Table 9.17. Browse field options.

Option	*Purpose*
:R	Field is read-only; you cannot edit it.
:<column width>	You can specify the width of the field column with this option. If the display heading is wider than the specified <column width>, the heading is truncated. This option is ignored for logical and memo fields.
:V = <expL1>	This option enables you to specify a validation clause for the field. It is just like VALID specified with the @...GET command. This option is ignored for memo fields.
:F	This option is specified with either the :R or the :V clause and forces the validation. Any time the cursor leaves the field, the validation is performed (for example, :V = X < 3:F).
:E = <expC1>	This option specifies an error message used with the :V option.
:P = <expC2>	Specifies a PICTURE for the field.
:B = <exp1>,<exp2>	Specifies a range of values used to validate the field. This operates like the @...GET command RANGE clause.
:H = <expC3>	Specifies the column heading for the field.
:W = <expL2>	Specifies a condition for which entry to a field is allowed or prohibited. This operates like the @...GET command WHEN clause.

The following example shows you how to use the display options with the FIELD clause:

```
BROWSE FIELD Name :10,Salary:R, Occupation :R :20
```

You can include a calculated field in the BROWSE field list. Here is its form:

```
<calculated field exp> ::=  <field name> = <exp>
```

<field name> follows the normal field naming conventions. It is displayed as the browse table display heading. The value resulting from the evaluation of the calculated field expression is displayed in the browse table columns. Note the following example of a BROWSE command with calculated fields. In this example, GETTAX() is a user-defined function:

```
BROWSE FIELDS  Name, Pay = Hours*Salary, ;
Tax = GETTAX(Pay), Total_Pay = Pay - Tax
```

The *FONT* and *STYLE* Clauses

In Visual FoxPro, you can specify a font type, size, and style with the FONT and STYLE clauses for all text in the Browse window. The FONT clause has the following form:

```
FONT <expC4> [, <expN5>]
```

<expC4> is the name of the BROWSE window font. <expN5> is the size of the font in points. A 10-point font is used if <expN5> is omitted. Because Microsoft Windows maintains the fonts, the accessible fonts, sizes, and styles vary from system to system. A list of available fonts is shown when you choose the T**a**ble menu **F**ont option. The form of the STYLE clause is as follows:

```
STYLE <expSTYLE>
```

<expSTYLE> is a character expression that contains one or more style codes, as shown in Table 9.4.

The *FORMAT* Keyword

The FORMAT keyword directs BROWSE to use the @...GET variables from the currently active form file. All parameters, except the row and column positioning parameters, are used. This is an important feature because the BROWSE command supports conditional editing (WHEN clause), data validation (VALID and RANGE clauses), and PICTURES and FUNCTIONS classes.

You can also support this level of functionality with the FIELDS clause. For example, consider the following format file:

```
* Format file: ORDERS.FMT
@ 0,0 GET Name PICTURE "XXXXXXXXXXXXXXXX"
@ 0,0 GET AccNO VALID FetchAccts()
@ 0,0 GET Price PICTURE "@$ 999,999.99"
@ 0,0 GET Quantity RANGE 1,200
@ 0,0 SAY Price*Quantity PICTURE "@$ 999,999.999"
```

Because the rows and columns are not used by BROWSE, they can all be set to any legal value. In this example, both the row and column are set to 0. The following example uses this format file:

```
****************************************************************
*     * 07/30/92            BFORMAT.PRG                 4:42:02 *
*     * Description:                                            *
*     * This program illustrates BROWSE with FORMAT keyword     *
*     * and with FIELDS clause by contrast                      *
****************************************************************
SET TALK OFF
USE ORDERS
USE ACCOUNTS IN 2 ORDER ACCOUNT
DEFINE POPUP GetAccount FROM 3,60 PROMPT FIELD ACCOUNTS->ACCOUNT
ON SELECTION POPUP GetAccount DO Action
SET FORMAT TO ORDERS
BROWSE FORMAT
*...
RETURN
*****************************************************
* PROCEDURE: FetchAccts - Executed to validate AcctNo field entry
FUNCTION FetchAccts
IsValid = .T.
```

```
IF NOT SEEK(AccNo, "ACCOUNTS" )
ACTIVATE POPUP GetAccount
ENDIF
RETURN
*****************************************************
* PROCEDURE: Action - executed when popup option is
*            selected. Fetches selected account
PROCEDURE Action
IF BAR() # 0
REPLACE AccNO WITH PROMPT()
ELSE
IsValid = .F.
ENDIF
DEACTIVATE POPUP GetAccount
RETURN
```

You can use a complicated `FIELDS` clause to accomplish the same action performed by the format file. You could replace the `BROWSE` statement in the preceding example with the following code:

```
BROWSE FIELDS ;
Name :P= "XXXXXXXXXXXXXXXX",   ;
AccNO :V= FetchAccts():F,      ;
Price :P= "@$ 999,999.99",     ;
Quantity :B= 1,200,            ;
Total = Price*Quantity :P="@$ 999,999.99"
```

You can also discard the `SET FORMAT` statement. Both forms of the `BROWSE` command produce similar results. (See Figure 9.7.) The only difference is the column title. For the format file, the column title is `PRICE*QUANTITY`, and for the `BROWSE` fields, the column title is `Total`.

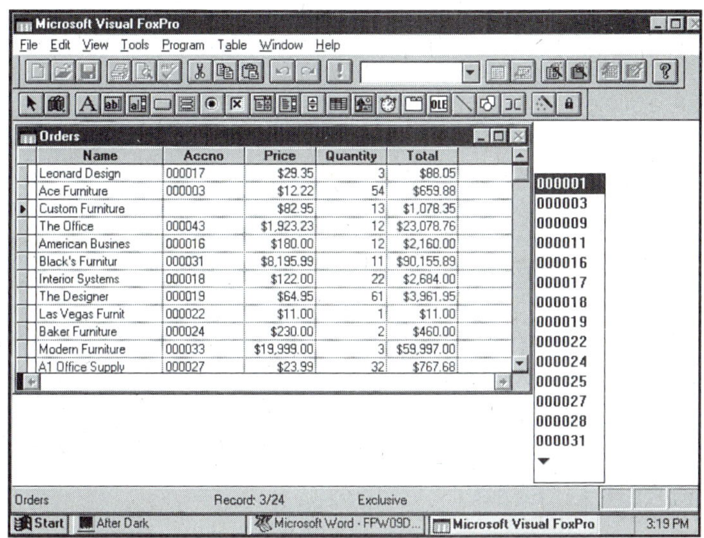

FIGURE 9.7.
An example of the BROWSE *command with the* FORMAT *keyword specified.*

In the example shown in Figure 9.7, the validation clause for the table field AccNo calls FetchAccts() to validate the account number entry. If the value of AccNo is invalid, a pop-up list appears. When you select an account number from the pop-up list, procedure Action is called. It replaces the table field, AccNo, with the selected value and deactivates the pop-up list.

The *FREEZE <field name>* Clause

The FREEZE clause limits editing to a specified field in the browse table. With this clause, all other fields become display-only fields. The field cursor remains in the frozen field. The *<field name>* argument is the literal name of the field to freeze.

The *KEY <exp1> [, <exp2>]* Clause

The KEY clause is used to limit the scope of records displayed. You can either specify a single index key value *<exp1>* that corresponds to the records to browse, or you can specify a range of key values. If you specify a range, *<exp1>* is the lower limit of the range and *<exp2>* defines the upper limit of the range. In the following example, records are browsed for employees who earn from $30000 to $35000:

```
USE EMPLOYEE
INDEX ON SALARY TAG SALARY
BROWSE KEY 30000,35000
```

If you want to BROWSE records for employees who earn $22000, type this:

```
BROWSE KEY 22000
```

The *LAST* and *NOINIT* Keywords

If you specify the LAST keyword and SET RESOURCE is ON, the Browse window opens in the same configuration that was last saved in the FOXUSER file. This configuration includes the size and position of the Browse window, field list information, and so on. The LAST and NOINIT keywords are synonyms. The NOINIT keyword was added for compatibility with dBASE IV Version 2.0.

The *LEDIT* and *REDIT* Keywords

The LEDIT and REDIT keywords instruct BROWSE to place the left and right partitions in CHANGE mode. You can specify either or both keywords.

The *LOCK <expN1>* Clause

The LOCK clause specifies the number of display columns that are placed in their own partition in the Browse window. The *<expN1>* argument must be a positive integer number less than the number of fields that display on-screen.

The *LPARTITION* Keyword

When you specify the PARTITION clause to split the Browse window into two partitions, the cursor is initially placed in the first field of the right partition. However, if you specify the LPARTITION keyword, BROWSE places the cursor in the first field in the left partition.

The *NOAPPEND* Keyword

The NOAPPEND keyword suppresses the append mode. That is, records cannot be appended. The Table menu Append New Record option is disabled.

The *NOCLEAR* Keyword

The NOCLEAR keyword instructs BROWSE to leave an image of the Browse window on-screen after BROWSE exits.

The *NODELETE* Keyword

The NODELETE keyword suppresses deletion operations. Records cannot be deleted using Ctrl+T. The Table menu Toggle Deletion Mark option is dimmed.

The *NOEDIT* and *NOMODIFY* Keywords

Both the NOEDIT and NOMODIFY keywords suppress table editing by the BROWSE command.

The *NOLGRID* and *NORGRID* Keywords

The NOLGRID and NORGRID keywords instruct BROWSE to not display vertical field grid lines in the left and right partitions, respectively.

The *NOLINK* Keyword

The NOLINK keyword instructs BROWSE not to link partitions. This means that if you move between records in one partition, the record selection in the other partition does not change.

The *NOMENU* Keyword

The NOMENU keyword suppresses access to the menu bar and the display of the Table menu pad on the system menu bar.

The *NOOPTIMIZE* Keyword

When you specify the NOOPTIMIZE keyword, Rushmore technology is disabled.

The *NOREFRESH* Keyword

The REFRESH keyword instructs BROWSE not to update the BROWSE data at the refresh rate specified by the SET REFRESH command while running in a multiuser environment. The only time this option is useful is when you are viewing a read-only file in a multiuser file and you want to improve performance.

The *NORMAL* Keyword

If you specify the NORMAL keyword, BROWSE displays using its "normal" attributes, including COLOR SCHEME 10, ZOOM, SIZE, FLOAT, and so on. (This is the way it displays if no user-defined windows are active and the WINDOWS clause is not specified.) If the NORMAL keyword is not specified and a user-defined window is active or the WINDOWS clause is specified, the Browse window inherits its colors, size and position, title, and control options (GROW, FLOAT, ZOOM, and so on) from this window.

The *NOWAIT* Keyword

If you specify the NOWAIT keyword, the program activates the Browse window, displays its contents, and continues executing the user program.

The *PARTITION* <expN2> Keyword

The PARTITION clause splits the Browse window into two partitions. The numeric expression (<*expN2*>) specifies the column where the window splitter—a bullet character between the horizontal scroll bars for the two partitions—is located.

The *PREFERENCE* <expC1> Clause

The PREFERENCE clause saves the attributes and options of a Browse window for later use. The PREFERENCE state is saved in the resource file. <*expC1*> is a name associated with a PREFERENCE state. When the name is first specified with BROWSE, it is saved in the resource file. After that point, every time a PREFERENCE clause with the same name is specified with BROWSE, the Browse window is restored to the saved PREFERENCE state. If you exit BROWSE by pressing Esc, the PREFERENCE state is not saved.

The *REST* Keyword

The REST keyword is specified in conjunction with the FOR clause to instruct BROWSE to start processing records beginning with the current record. It instructs BROWSE to process the remaining records in the table (DBF file) when searching for records that satisfy the FOR condition.

The *SAVE* Keyword

You can specify the SAVE keyword from within a program to force BROWSE to leave the Browse window and the associated memo field window on-screen when BROWSE exits.

The *TIMEOUT <expN3>* Clause

The TIMEOUT clause specifies how long BROWSE waits without user input before automatically closing the Browse window. The numeric expression <expN3> specifies the number of seconds. You can use the TIMEOUT clause only in programs.

The *TITLE <expC2>* Clause

You can specify a custom title for the Browse window by using the TITLE clause—the title is centered in the top border of the Browse window. The character expression <expC2> is used as the title. If this clause is not specified, the name of the table is used as the title.

The *VALID <expL2> [ERROR <expC3>]* Clause

The VALID clause operates exactly like the @ command's VALID clause except that it operates at a record level instead of at a field level. It is evaluated when you attempt to move from one record to another to ensure that the record you've just edited satisfies a condition. The validation is performed only if you make changes to any of the fields in the current record and attempt to move to another record. The validation is not performed if the only fields changed are memo fields. If the VALID clause returns a false value (.F.), you are prevented from proceeding to the next record, an Invalid Input system message appears, and the cursor is returned to the current field of the current record. You can specify the ERROR clause to replace the Invalid Input message with your own custom message.

You can also place :F after the VALID keyword (for example, VALID:F CHECK()) to force the validation even if you do not change any fields in the current record. In the following example, the SHOWPOP() UDF is called whenever you move from one record to another to display the 1980 population in a window. CENSUS.DBF contains 1989 population statistics for each state. Listing 9.3 is an example of the BROWSE command with a VALID clause.

Listing 9.3. An illustration of the BROWSE command with a VALID clause.

```
*************************************************************
*      * 07/30/92            BVALID.PRG              8:42:02  *
*      * Description:                                         *
*      * This program illustrates a VALID clause for BROWSE   *
*************************************************************
DEFINE WINDOW VALID FROM 6,60 to 11,79
USE CENSUS
BROWSE VALID:F SHOWPOP()
```

continues

Listing 9.3. continued

```
RELEASE WINDOW VALID
RETURN
PROCEDURE SHOWPOP
ACTIVATE WINDOW VALID
@ 0,2 SAY STATE
@ 2,0 SAY "Old Population:"
@ 3,1 SAY TRIM(STR(Population/(1+GROWTH/100)))
ACTIVATE WINDOW (WLAST())
RETURN .T.
```

The *WHEN <expL3>* Clause

You use the WHEN clause to specify a condition that determines whether the current record can be edited. The expression is evaluated before the cursor variable is edited. If the result is .F., the current record cannot be edited. However, the cursor is placed on the record. If the result is .T., the cursor moves to the record and normal editing operations are allowed. Listing 9.4 is a variation of the example shown in Listing 9.3. In this example, the state and population display for the current record before the cursor enters the record. The SHOWPOP() UDF returns .T. unless you move to record 3. If you move to record 3, .F. returns. As a result, the cursor moves to record 3, although you cannot edit any fields in record 3.

Listing 9.4. An illustration of a BROWSE command with a WHEN clause.

```
*************************************************************
*     * 07/30/92            BRWHEN.PRG              8:53:12  *
*     * Description:                                         *
*     * This program illustrates a WHEN clause for BROWSE    *
*************************************************************
DEFINE WINDOW VALID FROM 6,60 to 11,79
USE CENSUS
BROWSE WHEN SHOWPOP()
RELEASE WINDOW VALID
RETURN
PROCEDURE SHOWPOP
ACTIVATE WINDOW VALID
@ 0,2 SAY STATE
@ 2,0 SAY "Old Population:"
@ 3,1 SAY TRIM(STR(Population/(1+GROWTH/100)))
ACTIVATE WINDOW (WLAST())
RETURN RECNO() <> 3
```

The *WIDTH <expN4>* Clause

The WIDTH clause defines the maximum width of each BROWSE table column. The *<expN4>* argument evaluates to a positive integer that must be greater than 1. (Anything wider than the width of the window is impractical.) Normally, you should specify a width that is small enough to display multiple fields. If the actual width of a character field is wider than the specified width, the contents of the field scroll horizontally during editing. If the specified maximum width is less than the field name header, the header is truncated. The width of a field specified with the `FIELD` clause (for example, `FIELDS NAME:10`) overrides the `WIDTH` clause for that field.

The *WINDOW* Clause

The `WINDOW` clause causes the `BROWSE` table to be drawn inside a previously defined window instead of in the Browse window. (See Chapter 7, "FoxPro Language Elements for Creating Windows and Menu Systems," for a description of `DEFINE WINDOW`.) `BROWSE` activates the named window on entry; the browse table occupies the window during processing. The window is deactivated and erased from the screen when `BROWSE` exits. If you specify the `NOCLEAR` keyword, the window is not erased. Here's an example of a window that is active when `BROWSE` is executed (for example, `BROWSE` operates inside the active window).

```
DEFINE WINDOW WIND1 FROM 3,3 to 16,79
BROWSE WINDOW WIND1
```

The *IN WINDOW <window name2> | SCREEN* Clause

If you specify the optional `IN WINDOW` clause, the Browse window or a defined window displays inside the other window. In the following example, the Browse window is displayed inside of a window named Little. The Little window displays inside a window named Big, as shown in Figure 9.8. If you move Big, the Browse window (Little) moves with it:

```
DEFINE WINDOW Big FROM 2,2 TO 30,78 ;
TITLE "Big" PANEL FLOAT
DEFINE WINDOW Little FROM 4,4 TO 20,50;
TITLE "Little" COLOR SCHEME 10
ACTIVATE WINDOW Big
BROWSE WINDOW Little IN BIG
```

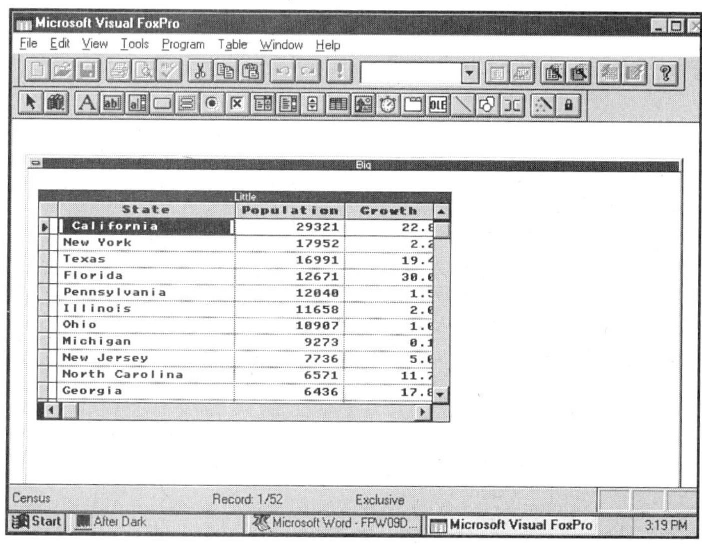

FIGURE 9.8.
An example of a `BROWSE` command with a `WINDOW` clause.

The *COLOR* Clause

You can use the COLOR clause to specify a color scheme to display in the Browse window or display a list of color attributes. Normally, the Browse window display is controlled by COLOR SCHEME 10. This default scheme has been chosen to best display the Browse window. Remember that if the BROWSE command displays in another active window, it assumes the attributes of that window, including the colors of the Browse window elements (scroll bar, size box, and so on). For this reason, if you display the browse table in a window other than the Browse window, you might want to consider specifying COLOR SCHEME 10.

The *CHANGE* Command

The CHANGE command provides full-screen support for viewing and editing fields in a table record in the active table (DBF file) or view. The CHANGE and EDIT commands are the same. Whereas BROWSE displays records in table form, CHANGE displays records in a vertical form with a field occupying a line. If a format file is not active, the display is arranged vertically with the field names on the left and the data values on the right. This is called the *default form.* When a format file is active, the form can have any arrangement.

Figure 9.9 illustrates an example of a CHANGE command with fields displayed in 24-point Times font. The following is the command that activates this display:

```
CHANGE FONT "Times",24
```

Here is the syntax:

```
CHANGE
  [FIELDS <edit field list>]
  [<scope>]
  [FOR <expL1>]
  [WHILE <expL2>]
  [FREEZE <field>]
  [KEY <exp1> [, <exp2>]]
  [LAST]
  [LEDIT] [REDIT]
  [LPARTITION]
  [NOAPPEND]
  [NOCLEAR]
  [NODELETE]
  [NOEDIT ¦ NOMODIFY]
  [NOLINK]
  [NOMENU]
  [NOOPTIMIZE]
  [NORMAL]
  [NOWAIT]
  [PARTITION <expN1>]
  [PREFERENCE <expC1>]
  [REST]
  [SAVE]
```

```
    [TIMEOUT <expN2>]
    [TITLE <expC2>]
    [VALID [F:] <expL3>     [ERROR <expC3>]]
    [WHEN <expL4>]
    [WIDTH <expN3>]
    [[WINDOW <window name1>]
      [IN [WINDOW]
      <window name2> ¦ IN SCREEN]]
    [FONT <expC4> [, <expN4>]]
      [STYLE <expSTYLE>]
    [COLOR SCHEME <expN6>
     ¦ COLOR [<color attribute>][, <color attribute>]
     ¦ COLOR RGB(<color value list>)]

<edit field list> ::= <field name1> [:R] [:<column width>]
[:V = <expL1> [:F] [:E = <expC1>]]
[:P = <expC2>]
[:B = <exp1>, <exp2> [:F]]
[:H = <expC3>]
[:W = <expL2>]
[, <field name2> [:R]  ... ]
¦  <calculated field exp>
[, <field name> [:R] [:<column width>]  ¦
<calculated field exp>]...]

<calculated field exp> ::=  <field name> = <exp>
<column width> ::= <positive integer>
```

You can use the `<scope>`, `FOR`, and `WHILE` clauses to define which records are processed. If no scope is supplied, `ALL` is assumed. All other keywords and clauses have the same function as they do for the `BROWSE` command.

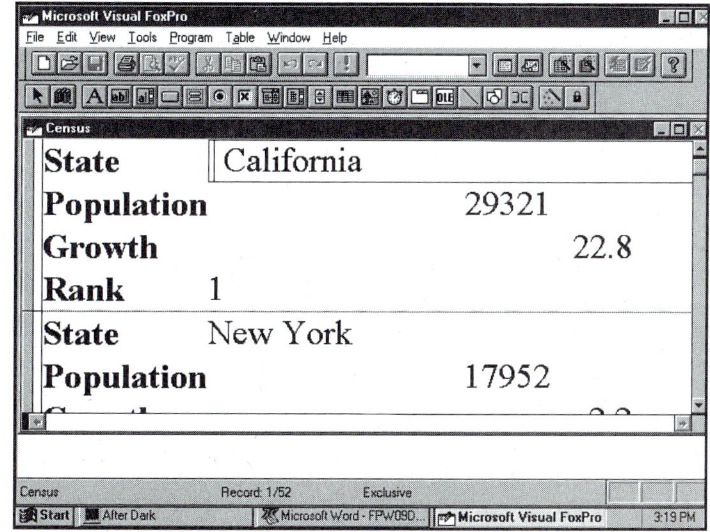

FIGURE 9.9.
The CHANGE command window with large font size.

The *INSERT* Command

The INSERT command adds a single record after the current record, if a master index is not active. If a master index is active, INSERT enters the APPEND command and records are added to the end of the file (that is, the indexes are updated). The following is the syntax for this command:

```
INSERT [BEFORE] [BLANK]
```

The full-screen INSERT command blanks the screen, displays the field list, and prompts the user to edit the field values. The INSERT BLANK command, however, adds a blank record to the table (DBF file) without any comment. The full-screen INSERT command works exactly like the APPEND command. (In fact, it uses the same internal code.)

If a master index is not active, the record is inserted in the file after it has been filled in and the user exits by pressing Ctrl+End or moving off the end of the last field. The other records in the table (DBF file) are physically repositioned from the position of the insertion to the end of the file, and the new record is written to its designated location. This is a slow process; most knowledgeable people recommend that you not use this command to insert a record in large tables (DBF files).

If the BEFORE keyword is specified, the record is added before the current record instead of after it. If you specify the BLANK keyword, the INSERT command inserts a blank record before or after the current record.

The *MODIFY MEMO* Command

The MODIFY MEMO command is similar to the MODIFY COMMAND command except that it edits one or more memo fields in the current record in any active tables. The following is the syntax for this command:

```
MODIFY MEMO <memo field list>
     [NOEDIT] [NOWAIT] [SAVE] [SAME]
     [RANGE <expN1>, <expN2>]
     [WINDOW <window name 1>]
     [IN [WINDOW] <window name2> ¦ IN SCREEN]
```

This program opens editing windows for each of the memo fields specified in the memo field list. You can edit more than one memo field in a single table or you can edit memo fields in different tables. If NOEDIT is specified, the memo field displays although you cannot edit it.

The NOWAIT keyword works as it does for other full-screen commands, and it works only inside a program. When MODIFY MEMO is executed without the NOWAIT keyword, program execution is suspended until memo field editing is finished. If you specify the NOWAIT keyword, the memo field editing windows display and program execution continues with the statement immediately following the MODIFY MEMO command.

The RANGE expression defines a range of characters in the memo field that are already selected for editing. <expN1> defines the position of the first character in the memo field selected. <expN2> defines the position of the character that follows the last character selected. If <expN1> equals <expN2>, no characters are selected and the cursor is positioned at <expN1>.

If a program, text, or memo editing window is open and the MODIFY MEMO command executes with the SAME keyword specified, the editing window will not come forward and will not become the active window. If the editing window is hidden, it displays but does not become the active window.

Note the following examples:

```
USE BOOKS
USE Magazine IN 2
* Edit two memo fields in different work areas
MODIFY MEMO Books.Notes, Magazine.Notes

* Edit memo field My_Memo and place cursor on third character
MODIFY MEMO My_Memo RANGE 3,3

* Edit memo My_Memo with characters 3 through 5 selected
MODIFY MEMO My_Memo RANGE 3,6
```

The WINDOW clause and the SAVE keyword behave exactly like the other full-screen editing commands. You can close an open memo field using the CLOSE MEMO command. The following is the syntax for this command:

```
CLOSE MEMO <memo-field-list> ¦ ALL
```

The specified open memo field edit windows are closed. If ALL is specified, all open memo field edit windows in all work areas are closed. This command closes memo field edit windows regardless of how they were opened. The MODIFY MEMO, BROWSE, CHANGE, and @...EDIT commands can open memo field edit windows.

The *MODIFY GENERAL* Command

Visual FoxPro supports Microsoft Windows object linking and embedding (OLE). The MODIFY GENERAL command is a full-screen command that is part of the OLE support. MODIFY GENERAL edits a general field in the current record in any active table. The following is the syntax for this command:

```
MODIFY GENERAL <general field list>
     [NOEDIT] [NOWAIT] [SAVE] [SAME]
     [RANGE <expN1>, <expN2>]
     [WINDOW <window name 1>] [IN [WINDOW] <window name2> ¦ IN SCREEN]
```

This program opens an edit window for the specified general fields, <general field list>, in the current record in an active table. When a window is open, you can insert, modify, or delete linked or embedded objects (sound, pictures, spreadsheets, and so on). You can paste an object that has been copied to the Clipboard by another application that supports OLE. (OLE is discussed in detail in Chapter 17, "OLE, OLE 2.0 Controls, DDE, and Operating System Interfaces.") If a general field contains an OLE object, you can double-click on the window and the application associated with the object is executed and you can operate on the object.

The Mighty *READ* Command

The traditional Xbase READ command reads through a set of @...GET commands starting with the first GET in the list and continues until you move off the last GET or move backward past the first GET. Then READ exits. In FoxPro, the READ command still operates in its rudimentary form, but it is endowed with magnificent improvements that have come about since Wayne Ratliff designed READ in 1980 for Vulcan Version 1.6. (Vulcan was the immediate precursor to dBASE II.) With the vastly enhanced FoxPro READ command, you can create more versatile, powerful, and flexible interfaces with less coding.

The FoxPro READ command supports the following complex operations without complex programming:

- Performs a multiple window READ
- Reads within READ commands (nested READ commands)
- Incorporates non–form window applications such as Browse, text editing, and system windows
- Controls window activation and deactivation
- Supports menu control objects
- Provides conditional entry and exit control

Before I discuss the details of implementing these features, it is important that you understand each of the following elements of the READ command syntax:

```
READ
    [EVENTS]
    [CYCLE]
    [ACTIVATE <expL1>]
    [DEACTIVATE <expL2>]
    [MODAL]
    [WITH <window title list>]
    [SHOW <expL3>]
    [VALID <expL4> ¦ <expN1>]
    [WHEN <expL5>]
    [OBJECT <expN2>]
    [TIMEOUT <expN3>]
    [SAVE]
    [NOMOUSE]
    [LOCK ¦ NOLOCK]
    [COLOR SCHEME <expN4>]
    ¦ [COLOR [<color attribute>][, <color attribute>]]
    ¦ [COLOR RGB(<color-value-list>)]
```

In Chapter 14 you learn how to apply OOP techniques to create visual objects (forms and controls.) Once you start using the Form Designer to create your forms, the only form of the READ EVENTS command that you will normally need is this:

```
READ EVENTS
```

When a READ EVENTS command executes, Visual FoxPro starts event processing. When a CLEAR EVENTS command executes, Visual FoxPro terminates event processing and program execution continues with the line following the READ EVENTS command. For example, suppose you have a form named Planets and you want to execute it from program SOLARSYS.PRG. In the Destroy event code, you add a CLEAR EVENTS statement. To create and display the Planets object, you would include the following code:

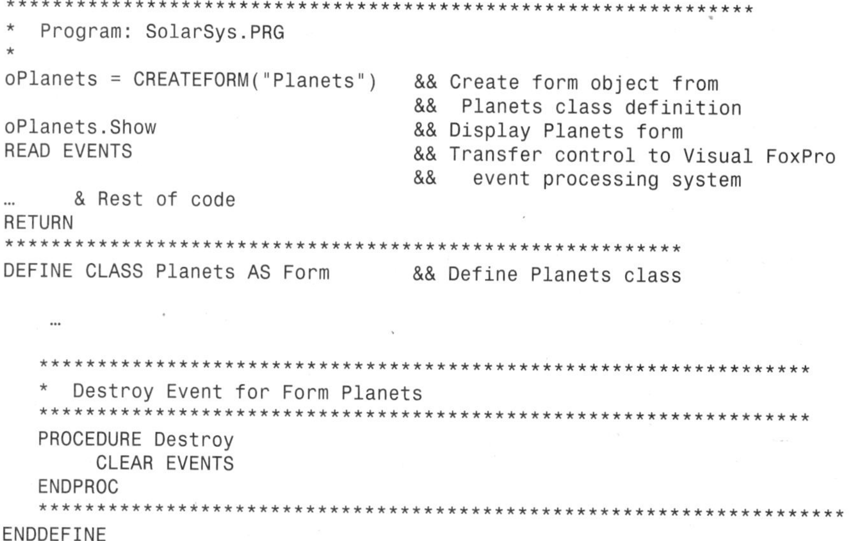

```
****************************************************************
*  Program: SolarSys.PRG
*
oPlanets = CREATEFORM("Planets")   && Create form object from
                                   &&  Planets class definition
oPlanets.Show                      && Display Planets form
READ EVENTS                        && Transfer control to Visual FoxPro
                                   &&   event processing system
...     & Rest of code
RETURN
**********************************************************
DEFINE CLASS Planets AS Form       && Define Planets class

    ...

   *****************************************************************
   *  Destroy Event for Form Planets
   *****************************************************************
   PROCEDURE Destroy
        CLEAR EVENTS
   ENDPROC
   ********************************************************************
ENDDEFINE
```

The following sections describe each of the clauses and keywords for the READ command.

The *COLOR* Clause

You can specify the color of the current READ object by including the optional COLOR clause. When an object is selected, it assumes the colors of the second color attribute. All other colors in the color attribute list are ignored. You can omit the first attribute, but you must still include the comma.

The *COLOR SCHEME* <expN4> Clause

If you include a COLOR SCHEME clause instead of the COLOR clause, the color pair 2 of the specified color scheme determines the color of the current field. By default, the color of the current

READ field is determined by color pair 2 of color scheme 1 (user windows). The colors of READ objects are not affected by this color clause.

The *COLOR RGB()* Clause

The COLOR clause contains the RGB() function, which has a list of up to six numeric values ranging from 0 to 255. The first three numbers represent the intensity of red, green, and blue color displays, respectively, for the foreground; the next three numbers represent the intensity of the same three colors for the background.

The *CYCLE* Keyword

When you specify the CYCLE keyword, the READ command exits only when the user presses Esc, Ctrl+W, or Ctrl+End; when the CLEAR READ command executes; or the elapsed timer feature expires. The TIMEOUT clause initiates the timer.

Traditionally, Xbase programmers write code that controls what happens when you move forward past the last GET object or backward past the first GET object. Normally, when the READ command exits under these circumstances, traditional programs simply reinitiate the READ command and loop it until Ctrl+End or Esc is pressed. It then exits as illustrated in the following example:

```
USE EMPLOYEE
SCATTER TO SaveRecord
DO WHILE .T.
    @ 1,40 SAY "ACME Employee Information List"
    @ 4,3  SAY "Last name:"  GET LastName
    @ 5,3  SAY "First name:" GET FirstName
    ...
READ
Key = READKEY()
IF Key = 12     && Esc key pressed and no update
    EXIT
IF Key = 268    && Esc key pressed & record was updated
    GATHER FROM TEMP   && Restore original contents
    EXIT
IF Key = 270  && Ctrl+W or Ctrl+End was pressed
    EXIT               && Update record and exit
ENDDO
```

With the CYCLE keyword you don't need to add the DO WHILE loop and all the associated code. When the cursor moves to the last GET object and you press Tab, Enter, or the down arrow, the cursor moves to the first GET object. Likewise, if the cursor is positioned on the first GET object and you press Shift+Tab or the up arrow, the cursor moves to the last GET object. The preceding example can be simplified if you specify the CYCLE keyword as follows:

```
USE EMPLOYEE
SCATTER TO SaveRecord
@ 1,40 SAY "ACME Employee Information List"
```

```
@ 4,3  SAY "Last name:"  GET LastName
@ 5,3  SAY "First name:" GET FirstName
...
READ CYCLE
Key = READKEY()
IF Key = 268   && Esc key pressed & record was updated
    GATHER FROM Save Record   && Restore original contents
ENDIF
```

The SCATTER command transfers data from table fields to arrays, memory variables, or named objects. The GATHER command transfers data from arrays, memory variables, or named objects to fields in a table. These commands are discussed in Chapter 12, "Data Set Operations."

The *OBJECT* Clause

The OBJECT clause enables you to designate which GET object is initially selected when a READ command executes. This feature solves a problem that has inflicted grief on Xbase programmers for years. Prior to the introduction of this feature, some programmers reordered the GET objects. Others used the KEYBOARD command to insert down-arrow keystrokes into the input stream.

The value of *<expN2>* is a positive number that specifies which GET object is initially activated for input. The order in which the GET objects are executed determines the number. Note the following example:

```
@ 4,1 SAY " Last Name:" GET LastName
@ 5,1 SAY "First name:" GET First Name
@ 6,1 SAY "   Address:" GET Address
READ OBJECT 3
```

When READ executes, the third GET field (variable Address) is selected. However, a GET that produces control buttons, invisible buttons, and option buttons produces more than one object. In the following example, the fifth object—the second control button, Cancel—is selected:

```
USE ADDRLIST
STORE 1 to PushButton
@ 4,1 SAY " Last Name:" GET LastName   && Object # 1
@ 5,1 SAY "First name:" GET FirstName  && Object # 2
@ 6,1 SAY "   Address:" GET Address    && Object # 3
*                        Object  #4  #5    #6
@ 8,1 GET PushButton PICTURE "@*H OK;Cancel;Panic"
READ OBJECT 5
```

The Cancel control button is the fifth object, and it is selected initially.

The *NOMOUSE* Keyword

If you specify the NOMOUSE keyword, you cannot use the mouse to move from object to object; you must use the keyboard. However, you may use the mouse to position the cursor within a field or select text for cut-and-paste operations.

The *TIMEOUT* Clause

Sometimes you might want to interrupt an application input form if the user does not enter data after a certain period of time. For example, consider a library search application. A customer searches for a topic, finds some articles, requests a printout, and walks away. It would be nice if the library search program returned to its main menu after 10 or 15 minutes. Other applications can benefit from a READ command time-out. FoxPro supports this category of functionality with the READ command's TIMEOUT *<expN3>* clause.

The TIMEOUT clause specifies a length of time that the READ command waits without any user input before the READ command automatically exits. The value of the *<expN3>* Numeric argument specifies the number of seconds that must elapse without input before the READ command terminates.

You can use the READKEY() function to determine whether any changes were made to fields when the time-out occurred. When a READ command is terminated with a time-out and no changes have been made to any GET fields, the READKEY() function returns 20. If any changes were made when the time-out occurs, the READKEY() function returns 276. In the following example, the user is given help if no information is entered in 60 seconds:

```
DO WHILE .T.
     CLEAR
     @ 10,10 SAY "    Company:" GET Company
     @ 11,10 SAY "Date Range"
     @ 12,10 SAY "   Starting:" GET SDate
     @ 13,10 SAY "     Ending:" GET EDate
     @ 15,10 SAY "Quarterly Gross Range"
     @ 16,10 SAY "    Minimum:" GET MinGross
     @ 17,10 SAY "    Maximum:" GET MaxGross
     READ TIMEOUT 60  && Exit if READ is idle 60 seconds
     IF READKEY() = 20
          DO HELPER && Display help screen
          WAIT WINDOW
     ELSE
     *       Process entry
     *       ...
     ENDIF
ENDDO
```

Conditional Clauses

The READ command optionally executes conditional clauses at certain logical points in its internal logic to provide more control over full-screen operations. For example, if you specify the WHEN clause, the READ command executes it before activating full-screen editing. You can supply a logical expression or a UDF that usually returns a logical true or false value. These conditional clauses make the FoxPro READ command sufficiently powerful and versatile to support multiple window, nested, and Foundation READ operations. These conditional clauses are summarized in Table 9.18.

Table 9.18. READ command conditional clauses.

Conditional Clause	*When the Clause Is Called*
ACTIVATE <*expL1*>	The current READ window changes
DEACTIVATE <*expL2*>	Another window becomes the active window
SHOW <*expL3*>	The SHOW GETS command is issued
VALID <*expL4*>, <*expN1*>	After you exit READ
WHEN <*expL3*>	Before you enter READ

When an active window is the current output window and an @...GET command executes, the GET object becomes attached to that window. GET objects attached to different windows can be processed by a single READ command. When a READ command executes, it activates all windows that are attached to the GET object. The window attached to the first GET object becomes the current output window. It also becomes the forward window in the stack of windows. When you move to a GET object that is in another window, the new window becomes the forward output window. Note the following example:

```
DEFINE WINDOW A FROM 3,3 TO 8,40
DEFINE WINDOW B FROM 10,3 TO 15,40
ACTIVATE WINDOW A
@ 1,1 SAY "    Name:" GET Name
@ 2,1 SAY "     Age:" GET Age
ACTIVATE WINDOW B
@ 1,1 SAY "Company:" GET Company
@ 2,1 SAY "Address:" GET Address
@ 3,1 SAY "    City:" GET City
@ 4,1 SAY "   State:" GET State
@ 5,1 SAY "     Zip:" GET Zip
READ
```

The GET fields Name and Age are attached to Window A, and the others (Company, Address, City, State, and Zip) are attached to Window B. When the READ command executes, both windows are activated; Window A becomes the output window and is placed on top of Window B. When you move from Age to Company, Window B becomes the output window. When the READ command first executes, the WHEN clause executes. Whenever you leave one window, the DEACTIVATE clause is called. When you enter another window, the ACTIVATE clause is called. When READ first displays the GET objects, the SHOW clause executes. The READ command flow diagram shown in Figure 9.10 illustrates when the READ-level conditional clauses are called. In Figure 9.10 the SHOW clause is not shown. It is called whenever a SHOW GETS command executes from within the READ command. The READ command ignores the value of <*expL3*>. The logical expression is usually a UDF call that can be used to refresh @...SAY commands or to enable or disable GET objects.

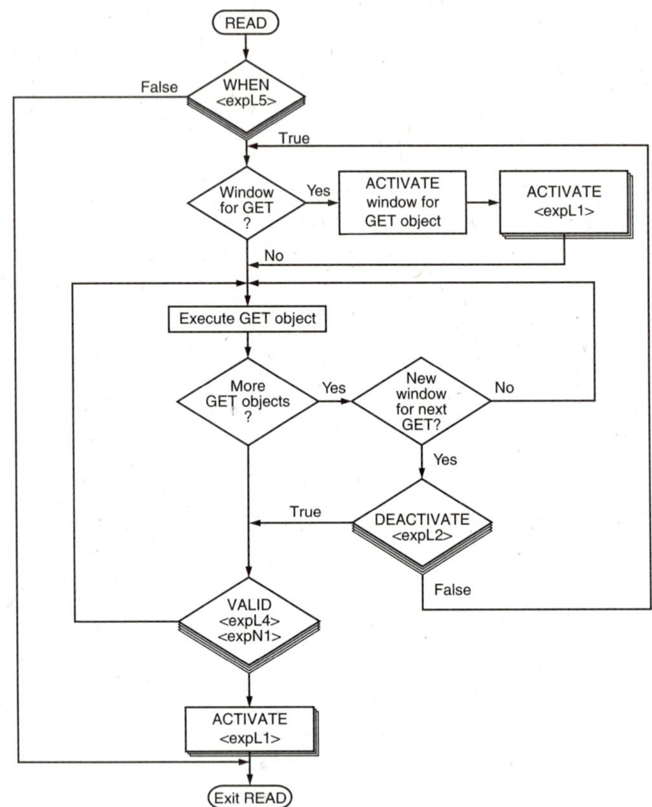

FIGURE 9.10.
A flow diagram for the READ command.

As illustrated in Figure 9.10, if the optional `WHEN` *`<expL5>`* clause is specified, the first thing the `READ` command does is call the `WHEN` clause. If the logical expression *`<expL5>`* evaluates to `.T.`, the `READ` command continues to execute. If *`<expL5>`* evaluates to `.F.`, the `READ` command immediately exits and program execution continues with the command immediately following the `READ` command.

In Figure 9.10 you can see that the `ACTIVATE` *`<expL1>`* clause executes whenever the current `READ` window changes. The Logical expression *`<expL1>`* is normally a UDF. The UDF can use the `WOUTPUT()` function to retrieve the name of the current output window. You can use the function `WREAD()` to determine whether a specific window is participating in the current `READ`. It returns `.T.` if the window is participating. Note the following examples of operations that are typically performed with UDFs:

- Disable `GET` objects in other windows
- Display messages
- Hide windows

READ executes the DEACTIVATE <expL2> clause whenever you attempt to bring any other window forward. You might view the DEACTIVATE clause as a window-level VALID clause. The Logical expression <expL2> is normally a UDF that can validate the contents of fields in a window before enabling you to bring another window forward. You can discover which window was just brought forward by calling the WONTOP() function. You can call the WLAST() function to get the name of the window that was formerly the window on top of the stack. If <expL2> evaluates to .T., the READ terminates. If <expL2> evaluates to .F., the READ does not terminate.

If the VALID clause is specified, it is called any time you attempt to exit the READ command. It is also called when the elapsed timer times out. The elapsed timer is established with the optional TIMEOUT clause. The VALID clause expression can evaluate to either a Logical (<expL4>) or Numeric (<expN1>) value. Because the expression normally consists of a call to a UDF, the UDF can return either type of value. If the expression evaluates to .T., the READ command terminates. If it evaluates to .F., the cursor remains positioned on the same GET field or object that it was on when the exit attempt was initiated. If the VALID clause evaluates to a number, the cursor is moved to the corresponding object number. If no object number corresponds to the evaluated number, the READ command terminates. If the clause evaluates to a value that is not a Logical or Numeric type, the READ command terminates.

Listing 9.5 is a simple example of a multiple window READ operation. Some GET objects that participate in the READ operation are associated with Window A and others are attached to Window B. The READ command contains ACTIVATE and DEACTIVATE clauses.

Whenever a window is about to be activated, the ACTIVATE clause is called. Its expression contains a call to the ShowPrompt() functions that instruct the user to make corrections. The READ command calls the DEACTIVATE clause before you leave a window.

The DEACTIVATE clause consists of a call to function CheckExit(). If the user initiates some action that results in the cursor moving from a field in Window A to a field in Window B, the CheckExit() function displays Window C with a prompt message asking the user to confirm that editing is complete. Window C also contains Yes and No control buttons. The READ statement in the CheckExit() function statement activates the GET objects in Window C. This READ command is an example of a READ within a READ, also called a *nested* READ. If the user responds in an affirmative manner by pressing the Yes control button, the nested READ exits and the CheckExit() function returns .T. and the top-level READ command exits. Otherwise, the function returns .F. and editing continues.

Listing 9.5. An example of a multiple window READ with ACTIVATE and DEACTIVATE clauses specified.

```
****************************************************************
*     * 07/31/92          MULTWIND.PRG            9:12:22     *
****************************************************************
*     *                                                        *
*     * Description:                                           *
*     * This program illustrates multiple window READs         *
****************************************************************
```

continues

Listing 9.5. continued

```
SET TALK OFF
CLEAR ALL
CLEAR
USE INFOFILE
STORE 2 TO CHOICE
DEFINE WINDOW A FROM 3,3 TO 8,45 TITLE "Personal Data";
FLOAT SHADOW DOUBLE COLOR SCHEME 5
DEFINE WINDOW B FROM 10,3 TO 18,45 TITLE "Company Info";
FLOAT SHADOW DOUBLE COLOR SCHEME 5
DEFINE WINDOW C FROM 10,30 TO 16,70 TITLE "Confirmation";
FLOAT SHADOW COLOR SCHEME 10
ACTIVATE WINDOW A
@ 1,1 SAY "    Name:" GET Name
@ 2,1 SAY "     Age:" GET Age
ACTIVATE WINDOW B
@ 1,1 SAY " Company:" GET Company
@ 2,1 SAY " Address:" GET Address
@ 3,1 SAY "    City:" GET City
@ 4,1 SAY "   State:" GET State
@ 5,1 SAY "     Zip:" GET Zip
READ CYCLE DEACTIVATE CheckExit() ;
ACTIVATE ShowPrompt()
CLEAR ALL
RETURN
***************************************************
FUNCTION CheckExit
IF WONTOP() = "A"
     Choice = 1
     ACTIVATE WINDOW C
     @ 1,3 SAY "Have you finished making changes?"
     @ 3,5 GET Choice PICTURE '@*H Yes;No' SIZE 1, 8, 12
     READ MODAL CYCLE
     DEACTIVATE WINDOW C
     RETURN (Choice = 1)
ENDIF
RETURN .F.
**************************************************
FUNCTION ShowPrompt
WAIT WINDOW NOWAIT "Please correct the information"
RETURN .T.
```

Figure 9.11 shows the screen during execution of the MULTWIND.PRG, Listing 9.5. In this example, all three windows (A, B, and C) are displayed.

If a READ command is executing and the program issues an @...GET command and another READ command, you create a new level of READ that exists and operates independently of the first READ command. While the second READ executes, you can create more GET objects and activate them with a third READ command. However, you can have only 10 READ commands nested. This is referred to as a *nesting level.* You can nest READ commands to a maximum depth of 10 levels. (The number of allowable nested READ commands in FoxPro 2.*x* is 5.) This is an extremely useful extension to the Xbase language. The only problem is that you must be careful not to exceed the 10-level limit. FoxPro provides you with the RDLEVEL() function that returns the current READ level. You must test the READ level before you issue a new READ command to keep from exceeding the level. When you find that you are about to exceed a READ level, you can either prevent the execution of the next READ or you can execute the READ CLEAR command to dispose of a READ that is currently active.

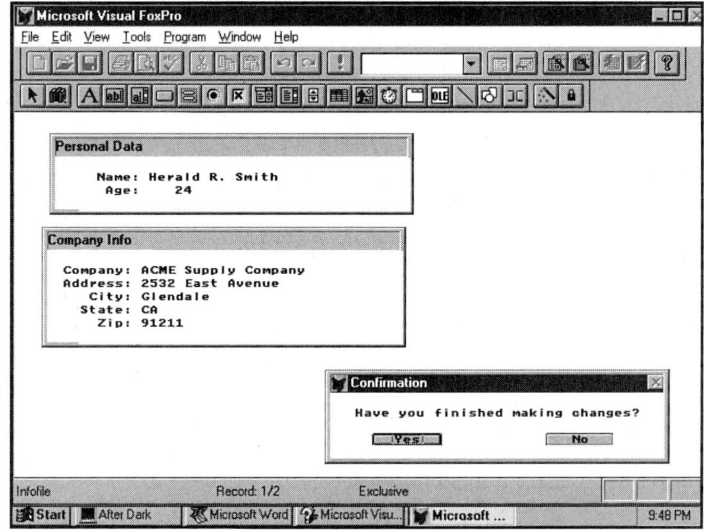

FIGURE 9.11.
An example of a multiple window READ screen.

Listing 9.6 presents an example of a program that illustrates nested READ commands. The main program calls function Nester(). Nester() defines a window, then issues a couple of @ commands and a READ command. The READ command contains a WHEN clause that does a recursive call to Nester(). As a result, nested READ commands are created until the level limit of 10 is exceeded. Figure 9.12 shows what happens when the level limit is exceeded.

Listing 9.6. Source listing of a program that exceeds the maximum nested READ level.

```
**********************************************************
* PROGRAM READLVL.PRG illustrates what happens if maximum
*   READ nesting level is exceeded.
*
= NESTER()
WAIT WINDOW
CLEAR ALL
RETURN
**********************************************************
FUNCTION Nester
Index = RDLEVEL()+1
Name = CHR(64 + Index)
set talk off
R = Index*3
DEFINE WINDOW (Name) FROM R,10+R TO R+3,30+R
STORE Index TO &Name
ACTIVATE WINDOW (Name)
```

continues

Listing 9.6. continued

```
@  0,0  SAY "Window:"  GET Name
@  1,0 SAY "Level: "+ LTRIM(STR(RDLEVEL()))
READ WHEN Nester()
RETURN .F.
```

> **NOTE**
>
> The `Nester()` function calls itself. It is referred to as a *recursive function.*

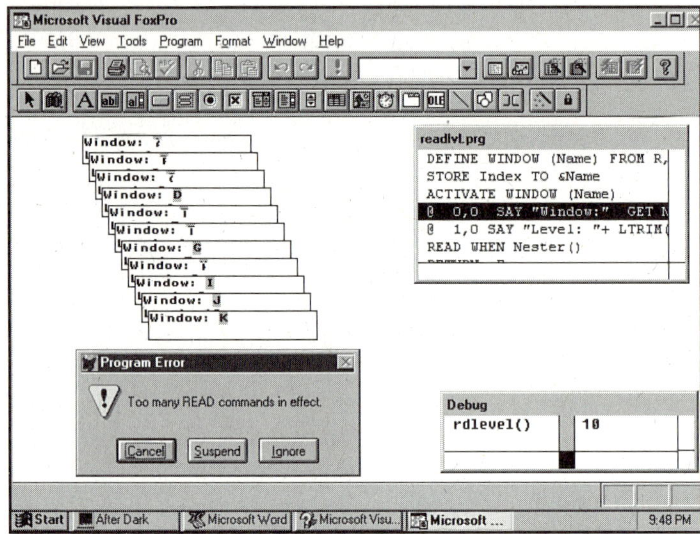

FIGURE 9.12.
An example of a condition in which the maximum READ *nesting level is exceeded.*

The *MODAL* Keyword

In the example presented in Listing 9.5, the window defined as C (the `Confirmation` window) has two control button `GET` objects attached to it. The `READ` command that activates the control buttons contains the `MODAL` keyword. The `MODAL` keyword prevents all windows from being activated except those windows that are involved in the `READ`. You cannot activate or access any window that is not involved in a `READ` operation when the `READ` command that contains the `MODAL` keyword executes. In the example shown in Listing 9.5, you cannot select any `GET` object in Window A and Window B. The only action that you can perform is to choose either the Yes or No control button or press Esc. You normally use a modal type `READ` to force the user to complete some action in one window before proceeding to other tasks in other windows.

The *WITH* Clause

You can use the WITH clause to include other windows not normally involved in a READ operation. The WITH clause contains a list of titles of windows that will be involved in the read. You can include in *<window title list>* a Browse window, a text editing window, memo field editing windows, and even FoxPro system windows such as Calendar/Diary and Calculator.

GET objects associated with a READ command and all the windows that are specified in the WITH *<window title list>* clause are participants in an implicit modal read. No other windows can be accessed during the READ operation.

The rule for specifying a title in the *<window title list>* is that it can contain only letters, numbers, and underscore characters. If the title includes other characters, you can use the characters in the title up to, but not including, the disallowed character. For example, if you are including the FoxPro system window Calendar/Diary, specify Calendar. As a further example, the title in the Browse window is, by default, the name of the table. In that case, include the filename without the .DBF characters. For example, if the Browse window title is CLIENTS.DBF, specify CLIENTS in the *<window title list>*. However, the READ command does not activate the windows in *<window title list>*. You must activate them yourself.

Another method of specifying a title in the window title list is to enclose the entire name in quotes. For example, if the window title is BIG FILE, specify "BIG FILE" in the *<window title list>*. Note the following example of a READ command with a WITH clause:

```
READ WITH "BIG FILE", Calendar, Calculator, CLIENTS
```

If you do not specify a WITH clause, all interactive windows such as the Browse window, Change window, FoxPro system windows, and windows opened with MODIFY FILE, MODIFY COMMAND, and so on can participate in a READ operation. The WITH limits the windows that can be accessed.

The *LOCK* and *NOLOCK* Keywords

You can designate that automatic locking of GET fields is enabled or disabled by specifying the optional LOCK or UNLOCK keywords, respectively. If neither LOCK nor UNLOCK is specified, LOCK is assumed. The LOCK and UNLOCK keywords are used when Visual FoxPro is operating in a multiuser mode. If either one is specified with the single-user version, it is ignored. If you specify the LOCK keyword, the READ command attempts to lock all records associated with GET fields. If the locking operation is successful, you can edit the records. The SET REPROCESS command specifies how many times the locking operation will be tried. If you specify NOLOCK, the records associated with the GET fields are not locked and they become read-only. In other words, if you specify NOLOCK, you cannot edit GET fields associated with table records.

The SHOW GETS command honors the LOCK and NOLOCK state specified with the READ command. SHOW GETS attempts to lock records associated with GET FIELDS if LOCK is specified. An optional LOCK keyword can be specified with the SHOW GETS command to override a NOLOCK keyword specified with the READ command.

Event-Driven Interfaces

An event-driven system is a system that continually executes a loop while waiting for some event to take place. It checks for a keystroke, a mouse click, or even an elapsed timer to expire. When an event occurs, the event is handled and control is returned to the loop. This type of loop works effectively if it is running in a single-tasking system. However, if the program is running in a multitasking environment such as Windows, no other task can run concurrently because the program is hogging the CPU. With the READ command and the READKEY(), WLAST(), and WREAD() functions, you can enable a traditional Xbase event-driven interface without taking up CPU resources. You no longer need to have a DO WHILE .T. event loop. In Visual FoxPro, you do not even need the READ command or the functions.

You've already seen how a single READ statement can be used to support multiple windows. You can also include windows such as Browse, Change, text editing, memo field, and FoxPro system windows that are not traditionally supported by READ statements.

FoxPro supports another type of READ, called a GET-less or *Foundation* READ, in which there are no GET fields. This type of READ command is used to manage multiple READ commands and window applications in a single interactive system. The Foundation READ normally has a VALID clause. The clause expression can be a UDF that activates and maintains control over its subordinate READ commands. The VALID clause is activated by any event that normally terminates a READ command. The event is analyzed in the UDF and terminates only if the event is specifically intended to terminate the Foundation READ. To terminate the system, the UDF returns .T.. The UDF returns .F. if the Foundation READ is to remain active.

You can use the FoxPro READKEY() function to assist in the management of subordinate READ commands. You supply any numeric value as the argument to the READKEY() function, and it returns a value that indicates how the last READ was terminated. The returned values are presented in Table 9.19. If you specify the READKEY() function with no argument, it returns the traditional Xbase READKEY() function values as discussed in the section "Functions Used with the READ Command."

Table 9.19. Values returned by the READKEY() function indicating why the last READ was terminated.

Returned Value	*Description*
1	None of the following
2	A CLEAR READ command was issued
3	A terminating control was chosen
4	The READ window was closed

Returned Value	Description
5	The READ command DEACTIVATE clause returned .T.
6	The READ TIMEOUT clause timed out

The following example demonstrates a simple Foundation READ that controls the execution of two FoxPro 2.*x* screen program files, SCREEN1.SPR and SCREEN2.SPR:

```
QuitIt = .F.
DO SETUP      && Set up variables, save environment, etc.
ON KEY LABEL F3 DO SCREEN1.SPR
ON KEY LABEL F4 DO SCREEN2.SPR
ON KEY LABEL F7 DO StopIt
READ VALID QuitIt    && Foundation Read
CLEAR ALL
DO FINISH            && Cleanup
RETURN
PROCEDURE Stopit
CLEAR READ ALL  &&  Exits any active READs
QuitIt = .T.    &&  Make Foundation read exit
RETURN
```

When either F3 or F4 is pressed, a screen file is activated. When you press F7, the program calls the StopIt procedure, which clears all the active READ commands (except the Foundation READ), sets QuitIt to false, and returns control to the VALID clause of the Foundation READ.

The Foundation READ was created as an attempt to support an event-driven interface in FoxPro 2.*x*. It is clumsy and hard to use. Many developers do not understand how to effectively use a Foundation READ. The only reason it is even discussed in this chapter is to provide a background if you need to upgrade a FoxPro 2.*x* application to run under Visual FoxPro 3. Visual FoxPro easily supports totally modeless operations. It is extremely simple to use Visual FoxPro to develop applications that coordinate multiple active forms and multiple instances of a form, concurrently. I promise—you will never need to use a Foundation READ in Visual FoxPro.

The *SHOW* Command

Forms of the SHOW command exist to display GET objects. The SHOW GETS command redisplays all the GET objects; the SHOW GET and SHOW OBJECT commands redisplay an individual GET object. The following is the syntax of these three forms of the SHOW command:

```
SHOW GETS [ ENABLE ¦ DISABLE ] [LEVEL <expN1>] [LOCK]
     [OFF ¦ ONLY ] [WINDOW <window-name>]
     [COLOR SCHEME <expN4>
          ¦ COLOR [<color attribute>][,<color attribute>]
          ¦ COLOR RGB(<color value list>)]

SHOW GET <variable> [, <expN1> [PROMPT <expC>]]
     [ ENABLE ¦ DISABLE ] [LEVEL <expN2>]
     [COLOR SCHEME <expN5>
     ¦ COLOR [<color attribute>][,<color attribute>]
     ¦ COLOR RGB(<color value list>)]]
```

```
SHOW OBJECT <expN1> [ ENABLE ¦ DISABLE ]
     [LEVEL <expN2>] [PROMPT <expC>]
     [COLOR SCHEME <expN5>
     ¦ COLOR [<color attribute>][,<color attribute>]
     ¦ COLOR RGB(<color value list>)]
```

With these commands you can redisplay GET objects for the current READ level, or if you specify the LEVEL clause, you can redisplay GET objects for any other READ level. You can enable, or disable and change, the color of GET objects with these commands. These commands are often used in VALID clauses to redisplay objects after they are changed. It is used to redisplay the GET field values when the table record changes.

With the SHOW GET or SHOW OBJECT commands, you can specify the variable of a GET object. For the GET OBJECT command you can specify the number of a GET object. The GET object number is based on the order in which you specify the @...GET commands. Each control object (control button, option button, and so on) has a unique number.

Incidentally, you can use the GETOBJ() function to determine the object number for an object. The _CUROBJ system memory variable contains the number of the current GET object. You can retrieve its value or change its value to reposition the cursor to another GET object.

You can also change the prompt of an individual control type GET object using the PROMPT clause. For example, to change the eighth prompt object in the preceding list from Top to Hop, issue either of the two following commands:

```
SHOW OBJECT 8 PROMPT "Hop"
SHOW GET Choice,3 PROMPT "Hop"
```

The first command changes the eighth object. In the second command, the number (3) is the number of the control button for the *<variable>* named Choice.

The SHOW GETS command executes the SHOW clause on the READ statement. SHOW GET and SHOW OBJECT do not execute the SHOW clause. If you can specify the OFF keyword with the SHOW GETS command, the READ command SHOW clause is executed (the GET objects, however, are not refreshed). However, if you specify the ONLY keyword with the SHOW GETS command, the GET objects are refreshed and the SHOW clause is not executed.

The SHOW GETS command also supports a WINDOW clause. If you have a READ command that is associated with GET objects in different windows, you can specify the WINDOW clause to refresh only the GET objects in the designated window. You can use the SYS(2016) function to retrieve the name of the window specified with the SHOW GETS command. The SYS(2016) function returns "*" if no WINDOW clause is specified with the SHOW GETS command. Furthermore, this function returns a null string unless it is executed in a UDF specified with the READ command SHOW clause.

Functions Used with *READ* Commands

The READKEY() function returns values that indicate what causes a full-screen editing command to exit. As discussed earlier in this chapter, READKEY() has been enhanced to support sophisticated user interfaces. The enhanced version has a Numeric argument and returns the values shown in Table 9.20. The value of the Numeric argument can be any numeric value—0, 42, 100,000, or any number. However, if you don't specify a Numeric argument, the value returned indicates which keystroke causes the APPEND, BROWSE, CHANGE, CREATE, EDIT, INSERT, MODIFY, or READ full-screen data-editing commands to exit. The READKEY() function returns values indicating which key was pressed and whether a field has been changed. If the returned value is greater than 255, the field has been updated. The READKEY() function returned values are shown in Table 9.20. The *No Update Code* and *Update Code* columns in the table indicate which value READKEY() returns if GET fields were not updated or were updated, respectively. The ASCII codes in Table 9.20 are the same values returned by the INKEY() and LASTKEY() functions.

Table 9.20. Values returned by the READKEY() function.

Key	*ASCII Code*	*No Update Code*	*Update Code*	*Description*
Backspace	128	0	256	Move back
←	19			one character
Ctrl+H	128			
Ctrl+S	19			
→	4	1	257	Move forward
Ctrl+D*	4			one character
Ctrl+L	12			
Home	1	2	258	Move back
Ctrl+A*	1			one word
End	6	3	259	Move forward
Ctrl+F	6			one word
↑	5	4	260	Move back
Ctrl+E*	5			one field
Shift+Tab	15			
Ctrl+K*	11			
↓	24	5	261	Move forward
Ctrl+X*	24			one field
Tab	9			
Ctrl+Enter	10			
Ctrl+I	9			
Ctrl+J	10			

continues

Table 9.20. continued

Key	*ASCII Code*	*No Update Code*	*Update Code*	*Description*
PgUp	18	6	262	Page up
Ctrl+R*	18			
PgDn	3	7	263	Page down
Ctrl+C	3			
Ctrl+←	26	8	264	Filled
Ctrl+Q	17	12	268	Exit and abandon
Esc changes	27			
Ctrl+End	23	—	270	Exit and save changes
Ctrl+W	23			
Enter	13	15	271	Return or filled
Ctrl+→	2			
Ctrl+M	13			
TIMEOUT	0	20	276	Elapsed timer expires (`TIMEOUT` clause)
Ctrl+Home	29	33	289	Toggle menu display
Ctrl+]	29			
Ctrl+PgUp	31	34	290	Zoom out
Ctrl+-	31			
Ctrl+PgDn	30	35	291	Zoom in
Ctrl+^	30			
F1	28	36	292	Help function key
CTRL+\	28			

*The `READKEY()` function returns values for Ctrl+A, Ctrl+D, Ctrl+E, Ctrl+K, Ctrl+R, and Ctrl+X, as indicated in the table only if `SET SYSMENU` is `OFF` or the default FOXPLUS.FKY macro key file is loaded. The FOXPLUS.FKY file is in the \FOXPRO2\GOODIES\MISC directory.

Other functions used with the READ command are summarized in the following list:

OBJNUM(<*variable*>[,<*expN1*>])	Returns the object number of the specified GET object. If the object is a group of controls (control buttons, option buttons, and so on), <*expN1*> is the control number.
OBJVAR(<*expN*> [,<*expN2*>]])	Returns the name of the memory variable associated with a GET object.
RDLEVEL()	Returns the READ level number 0 through 10, which indicates the depth that READ commands are nested.
SYS(2016)	Returns the name of the window included in the last SHOW GETS windows.
UPDATED()	Returns .T. if a field has been updated.
VARREAD()	Returns the name of the current GET object in uppercase.
WLAST([<*window name*>])	Returns the name of the window that was active prior to the current window if you specify no arguments. If you specify an argument, WLAST() returns a true or false value, depending on whether the specified window name was active prior to the current window.
WONTOP([<*window name*>])	Returns .T. if the window is the foremost window. Returns the name of the foremost window if a window name is not specified.
WOUTPUT([<*window name*>])	Returns .T. if the specified window is the current output window. Returns the name of the current output window if a window name is not specified.
WREAD([<*window name*>])	Returns .T. if the specified window is involved in a current READ operation. Returns the name of the window that is involved in the current READ if a window name is not specified.

In FoxPro, controls, which are created with the @...GET and @...EDIT commands, are referred to as *objects.* Objects can be fields, check boxes, lists, pop-ups, invisible buttons, push buttons, option buttons, spinners, and text-editing regions. You can refer to an object with a number that corresponds to the order in which the object is created by the @ command.

You can use the OBJNUM() function to obtain the current object. You supply the object number (<*expN1*>) as an argument to the OBJVAR() function, and OBJVAR() returns the name of the corresponding object. If you omit <*expN1*>, the OBJVAR() returns the name of the object for the currently active object. You can use the _CUROBJ system memory variable to determine the currently active object.

Memory variable and array element names returned by the OBJVAR() function are prefaced with the letter M and a period (M.). Field names returned by the OBJVAR() function are prefaced by the table alias and a period.

The OBJVAR() function returns a null string if <*expN1*> is greater than the number of objects.

Nested READ commands are created by issuing an @...GET command and a READ command in a routine called during a READ command. You can nest READ commands to 10 levels. You can retrieve the name of a memory variable or an array element for an object at a READ level other than the current READ level by specifying the optional READ level number <*expN2*>. If <*expN2*> is omitted, the OBJVAR() function returns memory variable and array element names for objects at the current READ level.

Fonts and Styles

Microsoft Windows is a *graphical user interface*, and MS-DOS is a *character-based interface*. In MS-DOS, characters are all the same size, although you have the option of changing the number of lines of fixed sized characters (25, 43, or 50 lines of characters that appear on-screen). However, in Windows you can have different sizes of characters and different fonts and styles.

A font is a graphic design for a collection of characters, numbers, and symbols. Windows supplies various standard fonts. Other vendors can supply other fonts. Three categories of fonts are available in Windows: bitmap fonts, Microsoft TrueType fonts, and printer fonts. Bitmap fonts consist of a fixed-size pattern for each character in the font. Bitmap fonts come in a fixed number of sizes and styles. In contrast, TrueType fonts are scaleable—they can be scaled to any size. They are printed exactly as they appear on-screen. Most TrueType fonts support standard Normal, Italic, and Bold styles. Printer fonts are built into the printer. Some printers have built-in PostScript fonts that are scaleable, like TrueType fonts. When you use printer fonts and the exact font is not available in Windows, Windows displays characters in a font that closely resembles the printer font. However, the font used by Windows may look different on-screen than it does on the printed page.

When you purchase a new font set from a vendor, you must install it to make it available for use. Also, you can remove little-used fonts to save memory and disk space. For additional information on installing or removing Windows fonts, refer to the "Control Panel" chapter in your *Microsoft Windows User's Guide*. Special fonts used with Visual FoxPro are automatically installed when you install FoxPro.

Visual FoxPro supplies a special font, the FoxFont font, that emulates the character mode interface. If you run a FoxPro 2.0 application without converting it to Visual FoxPro, FoxPro uses the FoxFont font so that your application looks good when you run it under Visual FoxPro.

In FoxPro for DOS, the fonts, font sizes, and styles are not supported. However, Visual FoxPro supports fonts and styles. In FoxPro 2.5 and 2.6 for DOS, the FONT and STYLE statements are simply ignored.

The *FONT* and *STYLE* Clauses

Visual FoxPro provides menu and programmatic controls for fonts and styles. In order to define which font, font size, and style to use for text, the following commands contain FONT and STYLE clauses:

```
@...SAY/GET
@...GET - Check boxes
@...GET - Lists
@...GET - Popups
@...GET - Control buttons
@...GET - Option buttons
@...GET - Spinners
@...EDIT - Text edit regions
BROWSE
CHANGE
DEFINE WINDOW
```

The FONT and STYLE clauses are described in the section "Advanced @...SAY...GET Command Options." Here is the syntax of these clauses for supported commands:

```
[FONT <expC> [, <expN>]] [STYLE <expSTYLE>]
```

Font Support Functions

Visual FoxPro supports several functions to assist you in developing applications that take advantage of fonts.

AFONT()	Retrieves information for available fonts.
FONTMETRICS()	Returns font attributes.
GETFONT()	Displays the font selection dialog box and returns the user's choice.
SYS(1037)	Displays the Print Setup dialog box. In this dialog box you can make adjustments to printer settings such as page sizes and orientations.
TXTWIDTH()	Returns the character expression width given the font, font size, and style.
WFONT()	Returns the current font name, size, or style for a window.

The *AFONT()* Function

The `AFONT()` function retrieves information relating to the available fonts. Here is the syntax for this function:

```
AFONT( <array-name>, [<expC> ,<expN>]] )
```

This function performs different operations depending on how many arguments are specified. It always returns `.T.` or `.F.`. However, the meaning of the returned value also depends on the number of arguments.

If you specify only the name of an array, the array is filled with the names of the available fonts. If the array does not have enough elements to hold all the fonts, it is expanded. If it has two dimensions, it's changed into a one-dimensional array. If `AFONT()` successfully completes this operation, it returns `.T.`; otherwise, it returns `.F.`.

The second argument (*<expC>*) is the name of a font. If you supply it, `AFONT()` fills the specified array with the sizes available for each font. If a font is scaleable, a single element in the specified array is filled with `-1`. If the specified font name is not available, `AFONT()` returns `.F.`; otherwise, it returns `.T.`. The following example illustrates the use of the `AFONT()` function. This program lists the font names and sizes of each font:

```
DECLARE Fonts[1]
IF  AFONT( Fonts )
     FontCnt = ALEN( Fonts )
     ? "The number of available fonts is:", FontCnt
     ? "Names of the Fonts:"

     FOR Ft = 1 TO FontCnt
          ? Fonts[Ft]
          DECLARE SizeFont[1]
          IF AFONT( SizeFont, Fonts[Ft] )
               IF SizeFont[1] = -1
                    ?? "  - Font is scalable"
               ELSE
                    FOR S = 1 TO ALEN( SizeFont )
                         ?? SizeFont[S]
                    ENDFOR
               ENDIF
          ENDIF
          RELEASE SizeFont
     ENDFOR
ELSE
     ? "Unable to retrieve fonts."
ENDIF
```

The third form of the `AFONT()` function has three arguments. The third argument is the font size. This function returns `.T.` if the font size (*<expN>*) for the specified font (*<expC>*) is available. A single array element is set to `.T.` if the font size is available. In the following example, the `?` command displays `.T.` if a 10-point Roman font is available:

```
DECLARE Exists[1]
? AFONT( Exists,"Roman",10 )
```

The *FONTMETRICS()* Function

The `FONTMETRICS()` function returns font attribute information for available fonts. Here is the syntax for this function:

```
FONTMETRIC(<expN1> [,<expC1> ,<expN2> [,<expC2>]])
```

If the optional arguments are not specified, this function returns attributes for the current font in the active output window. If the optional arguments are specified, you must specify both the font name (*<expC1>*) and font size in points (*<expN2>*) for an installed font. Then the specified font attribute is returned for the specified font and size. You can optionally specify the font style in *<expC2>* to return an attribute for a specific font style. If *<expC2>* is omitted, the attribute is returned for the normal font style. The font style code can be one character or a combination of the characters listed in Table 9.4.

Now it is time to talk about the first argument (*<expN1>*). This argument is the numeric value you specify to designate which font attribute is returned by `FONTMETRIC()`. Table 9.21 lists values for *<expN1>* and the corresponding font attribute that it returns.

Table 9.21. Values returned by the `FONTMETRICS()` function.

<expN1>	*Font Attribute*
1	Character height in pixels
2	Character ascent (units above baseline) in pixels
3	Character descent (units below baseline) in pixels
4	Leading (the space between lines) in pixels
5	Extra leading in pixels
6	Average character width in pixels
7	Maximum character width in pixels
8	Font weight
9	Italic (`0` = no)
10	Underlined (`0` = no)
11	Strikeout (`0` = no)
12	First character defined in the font
13	Last character defined in the font
14	Default character (substituted for characters not in the font)
15	Word break character
16	Pitch and family
17	Character set

continues

Table 9.21. continued

<expN1>	*Font Attribute*
18	Overhang (extra added width)
19	Horizontal aspect for the font device
20	Vertical aspect for the font device

If any of these attributes puzzle you and you want to delve deeper into the subject, refer to the chapter that describes the `TEXTMETRIC()` function in the *Microsoft Windows Programmer's Reference*, or visit your local technical library for more information.

The *PRTINFO()* Function

The `PRTINFO()` function returns the current Visual FoxPro printer settings. This is the syntax:

```
PRTINFO(<expN>,<expC>)
```

Visual FoxPro printer settings are established by using the FoxPro Print Setup dialog box. Choose the Print Setup... option from the **F**ile menu, and the Print Setup dialog box appears, as shown in Figure 9.13. You also can activate the Print Setup dialog box by executing the `SYS(1037)` function.

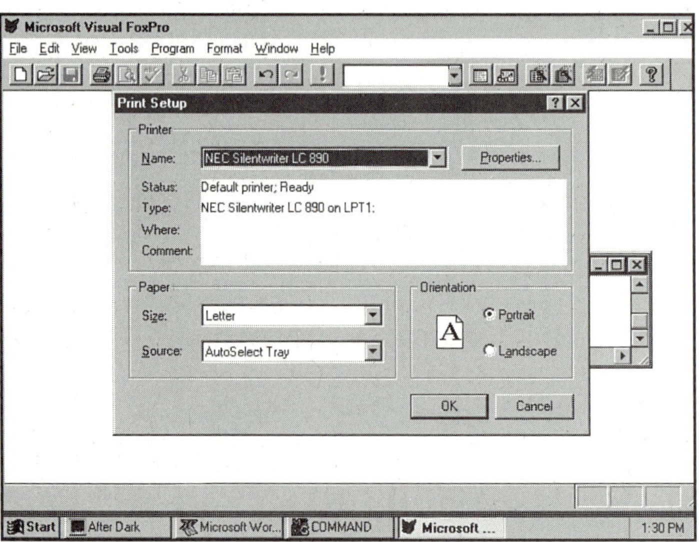

FIGURE 9.13.
The FoxPro Print Setup dialog box.

You designate which printer setting is returned by specifying the Numeric expression `<expN>`. Table 9.22 lists the values for `<expN>` and the corresponding printer setting return values. If you execute `PRTINFO(2)` and it returns `-1`, use `<expN> = 3` and `<expN> = 4` to determine the paper size. If PRTINFO(2) returns a value from Table 9.23, then PRTINFO(3) and PRTINFO(4) return -1. The optional second argument, <expC>, specifies the name of a printer for which the PRTINFO() function returns information. If the second argument is omitted, PRTINFO() returns information for the default printer.

TIP

There is a special type of Visual FoxPro file called an *include file,* which has the extension .H. This file usually contains various #DEFINE statements that provide a symbolic reference to commonly used constants. You can include this file in your program with an #INCLUDE statement and use the parameter names instead of constants. The FOXPRO.H include file is supplied with Visual FoxPro and contains #DEFINE statements for commonly used Visual FoxPro parameters. FOXPRO.H includes define statements for parameters that can be used as the first PRTINFO() argument. These parameter are also presented in Table 9.22. Here's an example:

```
#INCLUDE "FOXPRO.H"
    ...
    ? PRTINFO(PRT_PAGESIZE)
```

Table 9.22. Values returned by the PRTINFO() function.

<expN>	FOXPRO.H #DEFINE	Return Value	Description
1	PRT_ORIENTATION	-1	Information unavailable
		0	Portrait
		1	Landscape
2	PRT_PAPERSIZE	(Described in Table 9.14.)	
3	PRT_PAPERLENGTH	Paper length	In tenths of a millimeter
4	PRT_PAPERWIDTH	Paper width	In tenths of a millimeter
5	PRT_SCALE	Output print scaling	
6	PRT_COPIES		
7	PRT_DEFASOURCE	Default paper source	(See Table 9.24.)

continues

Table 9.22. continued

<expN>	FOXPRO.H #DEFINE	Return Value	Description
8	PRT_PRTQUAL	Print quality or values in Table 9.25	Dots per inch
9	PRT_COLOR	1 — Color 2 — Monochrome	Print color
10	PRT_DUPLEX	1 — Simplex printing 2 — Vertical duplex 3 — Horizontal duplex	Duplex mode
11	PRT_YRESOLUTION	Vertical resolution -1	Dots per inch If not available
12	PRT_TTOPTION	True Type font print mode 1 — Print as bitmapped graphics 2 — Download as soft fonts 3 — Substitute device font	
13	PRT_COLLATE	0 — No collation 1 — Collation	Collation

Table 9.23. Values returned by `PRTINFO(2)`.

Returned Value	Description	Dimensions
-1	Information unavailable	
1	Letter	$8^1/_2 \times 11$ in.
2	Letter small	$8^1/_2 \times 11$ in.
3	Tabloid	11×17 in.
4	Ledger	17×11 in.
5	Legal	$8^1/_2 \times 14$ in.
6	Statement	$5^1/_2 \times 8^1/_2$ in.
7	Executive	$7^1/_4 \times 10^1/_2$ in.
8	A3	297×420 mm
9	A4	210×297 mm

Returned Value	Description	Dimensions
10	A4 small	210 × 297 mm
11	A5	148 × 210 mm
12	B4	250 × 354 mm
13	B5	182 × 257 mm
14	Folio	$8^1/_2$ × 13 in
15	Quarto	215 × 275 mm
16	10 × 14 in	
17	11 × 17 in	
18	Note	$8^1/_2$ × 11 in
19	Envelope #9	$3^7/_8 \times 8^7/_8$ in
20	Envelope #10	$4^1/_8 \times 9^1/_2$ in
21	Envelope #11	$4^1/_2 \times 10^3/_8$ in
22	Envelope #12	$4^1/_2$ × 11 in
23	Envelope #14	$5 \times 11^1/_2$ in
24	C size sheet	
25	D size sheet	
26	E size sheet	
27	Envelope DL	110 × 220 mm
28	Envelope C5	162 × 229 mm
29	Envelope C3	324 × 458 mm
30	Envelope C4	229 × 324 mm
31	Envelope C6	114 × 162 mm
32	Envelope C65	114 × 229 mm
33	Envelope B4	250 × 353 mm
34	Envelope B5	176 × 250 mm
35	Envelope B6	176 × 125 mm
36	Envelope	110 × 230 mm
37	Envelope Monarch	$3^7/_8$ × 7.5 in
38	6 $^3/_4$ Envelope	$3^5/_8 \times 6^1/_2$ in
39	US Std Fanfold	$14^7/_8$ × 11 in
40	German Std Fanfold	$8^1/_2$ × 12 in
41	German Legal Fanfold	$8^1/_2$ × 13 in

Table 9.24. Values returned by `PRTINFO(7)`.

Returned Value	*Default Paper Source Setting*
1	Upper bin
2	Lower bin
3	Middle bin
4	Manual feed
5	Envelope bin
6	Manual feed envelope
7	Auto select
8	Tractor feed
9	Small format
10	Large format
11	Large capacity
14	Cassette

Table 9.25. Values returned by `PRTINFO(8)`.

Returned Value	*Print Quality Setting*
-1	Draft
-2	Low
-3	Medium
-4	High

The *GETFONT()* Function

The `GETFONT()` function displays the Visual FoxPro Font dialog box. It displays font names, sizes, and styles of available fonts. You can choose a font, a size, and a style; the `GETFONT()` function returns your choices as a character string containing the font name, size, and style separated by commas. For example, if you choose a 14-point, bold Roman font as shown in Figure 9.14, the `GETFONT()` function returns the following:

```
Roman,10,B
```

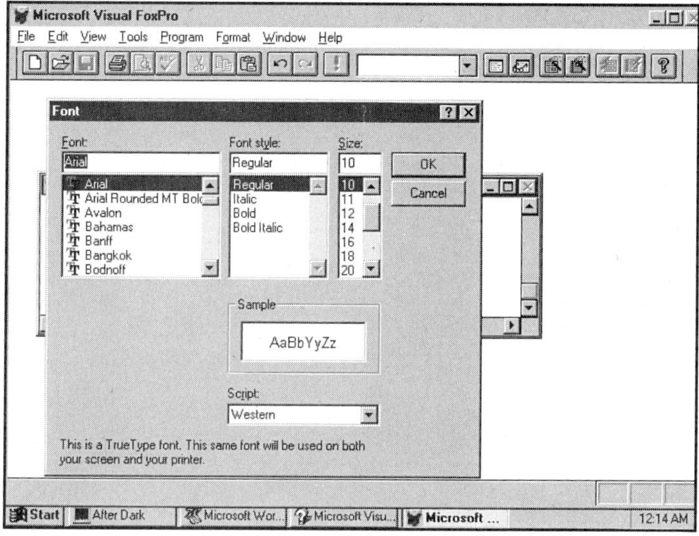

FIGURE 9.14.
The Visual FoxPro Font dialog box.

The *SYS(1037)* Function

The `SYS(1037)` function displays the Print Setup dialog box shown in Figure 9.13. In this dialog box you can make adjustments to printer settings such as page sizes and orientations. You can also choose the **F**ile menu P**r**int Setup... option to display the Print Setup dialog box.

The `SYS(1037)` always returns a null string.

The *TXTWIDTH()* Function

Positioning text is easy when you're using a character-based application that has fixed-size text. However, the characters of many Windows fonts have different widths. Different styles of the same character have different widths. You can no longer rely on the `LEN()` function to determine the width of a string. FoxPro provides you with the `TXTWIDTH()` function that provides the precise width of a string based on its font, font size, and style. Here is the syntax for this function:

```
TXTWIDTH( <expC1> [, <expC2>, <expN> [,<expC3> ]])
```

The first argument (`<expC1>`) contains the text string. The text string's width is returned. If you don't specify any of the optional arguments, the current font of the active window is assumed. If you specify the font name (`<expC2>`), you must specify the font size argument (`<expN>`).

You can optionally specify the font style in <*expC2*> to return a width based on a specific font style. If <*expC2*> is omitted, the returned width is based on the normal font style. The font style code can be one character or a combination of characters. (See Table 9.4.)

The program in Listing 9.7 illustrates a typical use of the `TXTWIDTH()` function. In the program, the `prtline()` function displays a line in the specified font, size, and font style. It also returns the position of the next display column.

Listing 9.7. Source listing of a program that illustrates the use of the `TXTWIDTH()` function.

```
************************************************************
* Program TEXTDEMO.PRG illustrates use of TXTWIDTH()
************************************************************
tstart = prtline("Text displays in ","Roman",14,"N",10,1)
tstart = prtline("Bold","Roman",14,"B",10,tstart)
tstart = prtline(", ","Roman",14,"N",10,tstart)
tstart = prtline("Italics","Roman",14,"I",10,tstart)
tstart = prtline(", and","Roman",14,"N",10,tstart)
tstart = ;
prtline("Bold and Italics","Roman",14,"BI",10,tstart)
tstart = prtline(".","Roman",14,"N",10,tstart)
******************************************************
* PRTLINE() Displays text in specified font and style
******************************************************
PROCEDURE prtline
PARAMETER TEXT, tfont, tsize, tstyle, LINE, start
@ LINE,start SAY TEXT FONT TFont,tsize STYLE tstyle
RETURN start + TXTWIDTH(TEXT,tfont, tsize, tstyle)
```

The following is the output from program TEXTDEMO.PRG:

`Text displays in` **`BOLD`**`,` *`Italics`*`, and` **`BOLD`** `and` *`Italics`*`.`

Another way to display text of different widths is to use the `COL()` function for the `@` command column position. The `COL()` function always contains the precise position of the column cursor. For example, to obtain identical results, you could replace TEXTDEMO.PRG with the following:

```
@ 10,1 "Text displays in " FONT "Roman",14 STYLE "N"
@ 10,COL() SAY "Bold" FONT "Roman",14 STYLE "B"
@ 10,COL() SAY ", " STYLE "Roman",14 STYLE "N"
@ 10,COL() SAY "Italics" FONT "Roman",14 STYLE "I"
@ 10,COL() SAY ", and" FONT "Roman",14 STYLE "N"
```

However, there are circumstances in which you want to determine the width of a text line before you display it. For example, you might want to create a user-defined window that is wide enough to display a line of multifont text. The `TXTWIDTH()` function is ideal for this purpose.

The *WFONT()* Function

The `WFONT(<expN> [,<expC>])` function returns font attributes for the current font for either the current window or the specified window if `<expC>` is specified. The `<expN>` argument specifies the type of attribute to return. The `WFONT()` function is described in Chapter 7.

Summary

This chapter presents the various aspects of the traditional FoxPro full-screen input and output commands that are still supported by Visual FoxPro. The topics this chapter discusses concentrate on screen-oriented commands, controls, data editor commands, and fonts. In Chapter 10 you will learn more about the environment setting comman

10

Environment

"Then you should say what you mean," the March Hare went on. "I do," Alice hastily replied; "at least—at least I mean what I say—that's the same thing, you know." "Not the same thing a bit!" said the Hatter. "Why, you might just as well say that 'I see what I eat' is the same thing as 'I eat what I see!'"

—Lewis Carroll (1832–1898)
Alice's Adventures in Wonderland

Environmental parameters, discussed in this chapter, control the internal operations of Visual FoxPro. These parameters initially are assigned default values. By using the `SET` command or the initial configuration commands in the CONFIG.FPW file, you can change the parameters. A configuration parameter retains its original value for the remainder of the Visual FoxPro session or until you issue another `SET` command. A `SET` command is useful for reviewing and changing current settings.

This chapter also describes how to view, set, and fetch system memory variables and configuration parameters.

Displaying Environmental Parameters

You can display the current settings of environmental parameters using the `DISPLAY STATUS` and `LIST STATUS` commands. Here is the syntax:

```
DISPLAY STATUS [TO PRINTER [PROMPT] ¦ FILE <expFN>] [NOCONSOLE]
LIST STATUS [TO PRINTER [PROMPT] ¦ FILE <expFN>] [NOCONSOLE]
```

Listing 10.1 shows the environmental settings for `DISPLAY STATUS`. If any database tables are in use, the open database table and index files, index tags, and key expressions are displayed. The master index is flagged. Index types (descending, unique, and so on) are displayed when appropriate.

Listing 10.1. The `DISPLAY STATUS` listing.

```
Processor is 80386
Currently Selected Table:
Select area:  2, Table in Use: C:\VFP\FOXBOOK\CITIES.DBF  Alias: CITIES
            Code page:   0
  Structural CDX file:   C:\VFP\FOXBOOK\CITIES.CDX
     Master Index tag:   STATE   Collate: Machine   Key: STATE
       Lock(s): Exclusive USE

Select area:  1, Table in Use: C:\VFP\FOXBOOK\CENSUS.DBF Alias: CENSUS
            Code page:   0
  Structural CDX file:   C:\VFP\FOXBOOK\CENSUS.CDX
    Index tag:   STATE       Collate: Machine Key: STATE
    Index tag:   GROWTH      Collate: Machine Key: GROWTH
    Index tag:   RANK        Collate: Machine Key: RANK
    Index tag:   POP80       Collate: Machine Key: POPULATION/(1+(GROWTH/100))
    Index tag:   DELETED     Collate: Machine Key: DELETED()
    Index tag:   USTATE      Collate: Machine Key: STATE Unique
    Index tag:   BACKSTATE   Collate: Machine Key: STATE Unique   (Descending)
       Lock(s): Exclusive USE
         Related into:   Cities
             Relation:     STATE

File search path:
Default directory: C:\VFP\FOXBOOK
Print file/device:  PRN
Work area               =    2
```

```
Margin                  =    0
Decimals                =    2
Memowidth               =   50
Typeahead               =   20
Blocksize               =   64
Reprocess               =        0
Refresh                 = 0,5 SECONDS
DDE Timeout             =     2000
DDE Safety              = on

Code page:    1252
Collating sequence:  Machine
Compiler code page:    1252
Date format: American
Macro Hotkey =  SHIFT+F10
UDF parameters are passed by:   VALUE
Textmerge Options
          Delimiters:  Left =  <<  Right =  >>
          Show

Alternate         - off               Fullpath         - on
ANSI              - off               Heading          - on
Bell              - on                Help             - on
Blink             - on                Intensity        - on
Brstatus          - off               Lock             - off
Carry             - off               Logerrors        - on
Century           - off               Mouse            - on
Clear             - on                Multilocks       - off
Color             - on                Near             - off
Compatible        - off               Null             - off
Confirm           - off               Optimize         - on
Console           - on                Print            - off
Cursor            - on                Readborder       - off
Debug             - on                Safety           - on
Deleted           - off               Space            - on
Device            - scrn              Status           - on
Echo              - off               Sysmenus         - on
Escape            - on                Talk             - off
Exact             - off               Textmerge        - off
Exclusive         - on                Title            - off
Fields            - off               Unique           - off
Fixed             - off
```

The environmental parameters of the DISPLAY STATUS listing are shown in Table 10.1.

Table 10.1. Parameters used by the DISPLAY STATUS command.

Displayed Item	*Description*
File search path: <*path*>	The Visual FoxPro search path. FoxPro searches the directories in the path when looking for a FoxPro file. Change the path with the SET PATH TO command.

continues

Table 10.1. continued

Displayed Item	*Description*
`Default directory: C:\VFP\...`	Default drive and path are displayed if none are specified with a filename. Change the disk drive with the `SET DEFAULT TO` command.
`Print file/device: PRN`	Destination of printed output. Change with the `SET PRINTER TO` command.
`Work area = 2`	Current work area.
`Margin = 0`	Left margin value. Change the value with the `SET MARGIN` command.
`Decimals = 2`	Current number of decimal places to the right of the displayed decimal. Change the value with the `SET DECIMAL TO` command.
`Memowidth = 50`	Width of memo field output line. Change the value with the `SET MEMOWIDTH TO` command.
`Typeahead = 20`	Size of the typeahead buffer. Change the value with the `SET TYPEAHEAD TO` command.
`Blocksize = 64`	Size of an index node in bytes. Change the value with the `SET BLOCKSIZE TO` command.
`Reprocess = 0`	Number of times to retry a lock. Change the value with the `SET REPROCESS TO` command.
`Refresh = 0,5 SECONDS`	`SET REFRESH TO` value. Specify whether, or how often, a Browse window is updated with changes made by other users on the network.
`DDE Timeout = 2000`	Number of milliseconds that DDE functions wait for the server application to respond.
`DDE Safety = on`	Indicates whether (`on`) or not (`off`) a dialog box displays when you establish a channel with a server application that does not respond.
`Code Page: 1252`	Current code page setting.
`Collating sequence: Machine`	Correlation sequence for sorting and indexing operations.
`Compiler code page: 1252`	Code page used by the compiler.
`Date format: American`	Specifies date format. Change the value with the `SET DATE` command.
`Macro Hotkey = SHIFT+F10`	This is followed by the key set that activates macro recording. Change the value with the `SET MACKEY TO` command.

Displayed Item	*Description*
`UDF parameters are passed by: VALUE`	Indicates how parameters are passed to a user-defined function (UDF). Parameters can be passed by value or by reference. Change the mode with the `SET UDFPARMS TO` command.
`Textmerge Options Delimiters: Left = << Right = >> Show`	Change with the `SET TEXTMERGE` command.

The middle portion of the `DISPLAY STATUS` listing contains the configuration parameters that can be set `ON` or `OFF`. The exception is `SET DEVICE`, which can have a value of `SCREEN`, `PRINT`, or `FILE`. If `FILE` is used, the following appears above the file search path item:

```
Device file:  <filename>
```

The *SET* Command and the View Dialog Box

In previous versions of FoxPro, the `SET` command was used to review and change many of the environmental parameter settings. In Visual FoxPro, the `SET` command only provides an easy way to open tables and indexes and establish relations. This command displays the View dialog box. Other environmental parameters can be examined or set using the **T**ools menu **O**ptions item. You can also use the `SET VIEW` command. To execute this command, enter either of the following:

```
SET
```

or

```
SET VIEW
```

You can also invoke the View dialog box by choosing the **W**indow menu **V**iew Window item. You can open free tables and attached tables, establish indexes and relations, and even view the results in a Browse table. Free and attached tables are discussed in Chapter 11, "DBF Files and Databases." Figure 10.1 shows the View window. In this figure, tables Transact.DBF, Clients.DBF, and Inven.DBF and their associated indexes are open. Notice that the relationships are presented graphically.

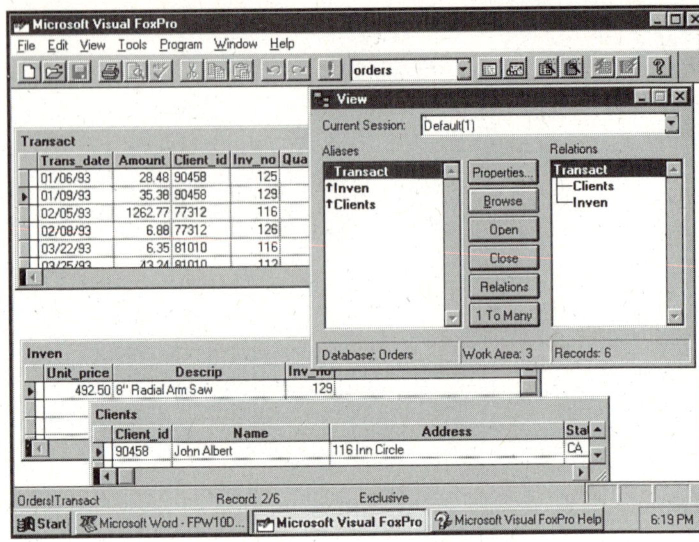

FIGURE 10.1.
A sample View window.

Table 10.2 summarizes the View dialog box controls.

Table 10.2. A description of the View dialog box controls.

Control	*Description*
Properties...	Activates the Work Area Properties window, from which you can establish the data environment for a work area, as shown in Figure 10.2. You can enable data buffering mode and options. You can specify a data filter (`SET FILTER TO`) and a field filter (`SET FIELDS TO`). You can modify the structure of a table and establish indexes (`SET ORDER TO`).
Browse	Used to review selected database contents in the Browse window. You can also position the cursor on a table (DBF file) in the Aliases list and press Enter to execute the `BROWSE` command.
Open	Displays the Open dialog box for selection of a table to be opened in an unused work area.
Close	Closes the selected table and any associated files in the current work area.
Relations	Used to establish a relationship between databases.

Control	*Description*
1-**T**o-Many	Displays the 1-To-Many dialog box. You can use this dialog box, which executes the `SET SKIP TO` command, to establish a one-to-many relationship between databases.
Aliases list	Displays aliases for open databases. Indexed databases are preceded by an up- or down-arrow symbol. (See Figure 10.1.)
Relations area	Displays any relationships that exist between tables in work areas.

Once you establish a view with the View window, you can save it to a view file (VUE) with the **F**ile menu **S**ave or Save **A**s options. You can also save a view with the `CREATE VIEW FROM ENVIRONMENT` command. Anytime you would like to reestablish the same view, you can do so with the `SET VIEW TO` command.

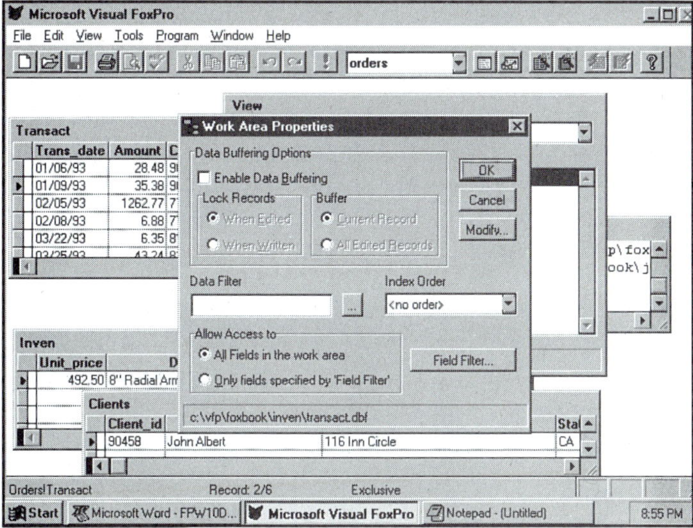

FIGURE 10.2.
The View window with the Work Area Properties dialog box displayed.

The Options Dialog Box

Various environmental parameters can be examined and set using the **T**ools menu **O**ptions item, which displays the Options dialog box. The Options menu, shown in Figure 10.3, contains 10 overlaying tab forms with the Data tab displayed on top.

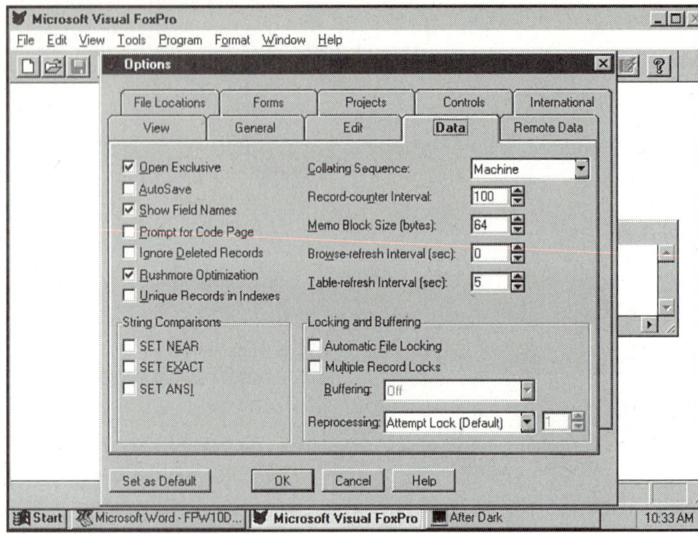

FIGURE 10.3.
The Options dialog box with the Data tab displayed.

The Options Dialog Box Data Tab

In Figure 10.3 there are check boxes that indicate the value of environmental parameters that can be set `ON` or `OFF`, such as `SET EXCLUSIVE ON`. If a box is checked, the parameter is set `ON`. Some of the `ON`/`OFF` parameters don't appear in the window because no one is likely to change them outside a program. For example, `SET CONSOLE OFF` isn't supported. Also, there are settings that do not correspond to any environmental parameter settings. The Options dialog box Data tab contains options for manipulating data and tables. Table 10.3 describes the Data tab options and correlates them with the `SET` commands.

TIP

If you want all of the settings that you modify with the Options dialog box to be converted to `SET` commands and echoed in the Command window, hold the Shift key down when you click on the OK button to exit the Options dialog box.

Table 10.3. A description of the Data tab controls in the Options dialog box.

Control	*Description*
	Main Tab Group
Open Exclusive	`SET EXCLUSIVE ON/OFF`—When you check this option, tables are opened exclusively. Corresponds to the `SET EXCLUSIVE` command.

Control	*Description*
AutoSave	SET AUTOSAVE
Show Field Names	SET HEADINGS ON/OFF—When you check this check box, a field name appears as a column heading above each field in the output of the AVERAGE, CALCULATE, DISPLAY, LIST, and SUM commands.
Prompt For Code Page	SET CPDIALOG—When you check this check box, Visual FoxPro prompts you to attach a code page when opening a table that does not already have one attached.
Ignore Deleted Records	SET DELETED ON/OFF—When you check this option, Visual FoxPro processes records marked for deletion and if they are available for use in other commands.
Rushmore Optimization	SET OPTIMIZE—You can specify whether the Rushmore index optimization is used.
Unique Records In Indexes	SET UNIQUE—You use this option to specify whether records with duplicate index key values are maintained in an index file.
Collating Sequence	SET COLLATE—You check this option to specify a collation sequence for character fields in indexing and sorting operations.
Record-counter Interval	SET ODOMETER—You use this option to specify the reporting interval in number of records.
Memo Block Size	SET BLOCKSIZE—You use this option to specify the block size in which disk space for memo fields is allocated.
Browse-refresh Interval	SET REFRESH—You can specify how often (in seconds) the display of an active BROWSE window is updated in a multiuser environment.
Table-refresh Interval	SET REFRESH—You can specify how often (in seconds) the display of an active table is updated in a multiuser environment.
	String Comparisons Group
SET NEAR	SET NEAR—When you check this option, Visual FoxPro positions the record pointer on the closest matching record if a record match is unsuccessful.

continues

Table 10.3. continued

Control	*Description*
SET EXACT	SET EXACT—You check this option to indicate that expressions must match character for character to be equivalent when comparing two strings of different lengths. Trailing blanks are ignored.
SET ANSI	SET ANSI—You check this option to indicate that when comparing two strings of unequal length with the = operator in FoxPro SQL commands, the shorter string is padded with blank characters to match the length of the longer string.
	Locking and Buffering Group
Automatic File Locking	SET LOCK ON/OFF—When you check this option, Visual FoxPro performs automatic file locking.
Multiple Record Lock	SET MULTILOCKS—When you check this option, Visual FoxPro allows you to lock multiple records.
Buffering	Sets Row and Table Buffering mode: ■ Set buffering off ■ Set pessimistic row buffering on ■ Set optimistic row buffering on ■ Set pessimistic table buffering on ■ Set optimistic table buffering on
Reprocessing	SET REPROCESS—You can specify the number of times Visual FoxPro attempts to lock a record or file after an initial unsuccessful attempt.

The Options Dialog Box International Tab

You can use the International tab to examine and set options for date, time, and numerical formatting. You can temporarily or permanently override system settings in Visual FoxPro. The controls that perform the same function as the SET command are presented in Table 10.4. Figure 10.4 shows the Options dialog box with the International tab displayed.

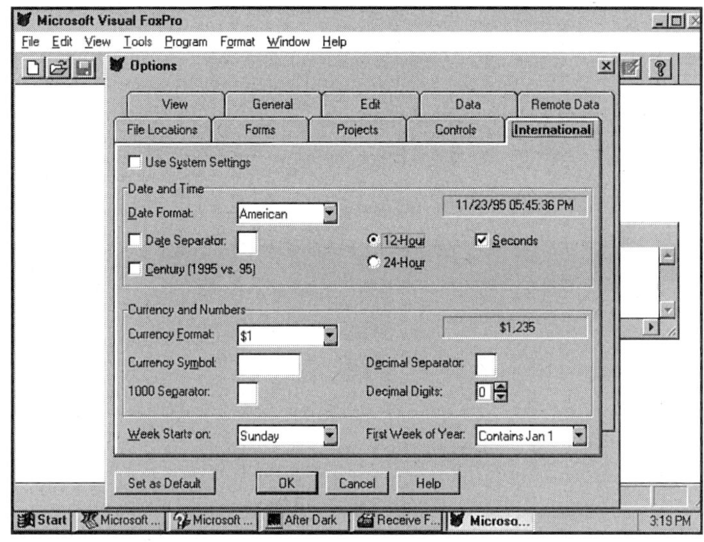

FIGURE 10.4.
The Options dialog box with International tab displayed.

Table 10.4. A description of the Options dialog box International tab controls.

Control	*Description*
	General Options
Use System Settings	When you check this option, all of the options on this tab are read from the system—the display settings match those in the Windows Control Panel. In this mode, most of the options are read-only. When you uncheck this option, you can override the system settings for Visual FoxPro. This setting corresponds to the `SET SYSFORMATS` command.
Week Starts On	`SET FDOW TO`—You specify which day the week starts on with this option.
First Week Of Year	`SET FWEEK TO`—You specify where a yearly calendar begins with this option.
Date and Time Group (The settings specified in this options group are visually updated in the top-right box of the options group.)	
Date Format	`SET DATE TO`—You specify a date format with this option.
Date Separator	`SET MARK`—When this is checked, you can specify a different character in the box that separates month, day, and year.

continues

Table 10.4. continued

Control	*Description*
Century (1995 vs. 95)	`SET CENTURY TO`—When you check this one, the numerical format for the year is four digits long (that is, 1995). Otherwise, it is two digits long (that is, 95).
12 Hour	`SET HOUR TO 12`—You set the time to a 12-hour format that displays AM or PM with this option.
24 Hour	`SET HOUR TO 24`—You set the time to a 24-hour format with this option.
Seconds	`SET SECONDS ON/OFF`—You can check this option to instruct Visual FoxPro to display seconds with the DateTime format. Otherwise, seconds are not displayed.
Currency and Numbers Group (The settings specified in this options group are visually updated in the top-right box of the options group.)	
Currency Format	`SET CURRENCY TO`—You use this option to instruct Visual FoxPro to display the currency symbol before or after the number string.
Currency Symbol	`SET CURRENCY TO`—You use this option to specify the currency symbol.
1000 Separator	`SET SEPARATOR TO`—You use this option to specify a character that is inserted at every third digit left of the decimal separator.
Decimal Separator	`SET POINT TO`—You use this option to specify a character that is used to indicate the decimal.
Decimal Digits	`SET DECIMAL TO`—You use this option to specify the number of digits to follow the decimal separator.

The Options Dialog Box File Locations Tab

The File Locations tab specifies the locations of different files used by Visual FoxPro. If you select the File Locations tab, you can establish an alternate file or select a procedure or help, resource, and other files. You can type a path and filename into a text box, or you can click on the push button to the right of the text box and an Open File or a Create File dialog box appears from which you select or enter the drive, directory, and filename. The controls are described in Table 10.5.

Table 10.5. A description of the Options dialog box File Locations tab controls.

Control	*Description*
Default Directory	`SET DEFAULT TO`—You can specify the default Visual FoxPro directory.
Search **P**ath	`SET PATH`—You can specify the directory where FoxPro should search for a file if it does not find the file in the default directory. Directories for paths are separated by commas or semicolons. You can use the button to the right of the box to automatically insert semicolons when specifying multiple directories.
Temporary Files	You can specify the directory in which Visual FoxPro saves temporary files.
Help **F**ile	`SET HELP`—You can specify the file that Visual FoxPro uses for help support. The check box to the left sets help on and off (`SET HELP ON/OFF`). If the extension is .HLP, Visual FoxPro uses Windows graphical help. If the extension is .DBF, Visual FoxPro uses DBF-style help. If no extension is used, the default is graphical help.
Resource File	`_BUILDER` and `SET RESOURCE`—You can specify the file that Visual FoxPro uses for saving resource settings. The check box to the left of the text box sets resources on and off.
Convertor	`_CONVERTOR`—You can specify the file that is used for the Convertor application.
Menu Builder	`_GENMENU`—You can specify the file that is used for the Menu Designer program.
Spell Checker	`_SPELLCHK`—You can specify the file that is used for the Spell Checker application.
Builders	`_BUILDER`—You can specify the file that is used for the Builder application.
Wizards	`_WIZARD`—You can specify the file that is used for the Wizard application.

The Options Dialog Box View Tab

The View Tab contains `SET` options that control the display of certain FoxPro elements. Table 10.6 presents the controls for the View tab.

Table 10.6. A description of the Options dialog box View tab controls.

Control	*Description*
	Show Group
Status Bar	`SET STATUS`—Displays and hides the status bar at the bottom of the main FoxPro window.
Clock	`SET CLOCK`—Displays and hides the clock on the status bar.
Command Results	`SET TALK`—Designates whether command results are displayed.
System Messages	`SET NOTIFY`—Turns on and off the display of certain system messages.
Recently Used Project List	Turns on and off the File 1, 2, 3, 4 display in the Project menu.
Open Last Project on Startup	Designates whether on startup FoxPro opens the project that was opened when FoxPro last exited.

The Options Dialog Box General Tab

The General tab contains miscellaneous options, such as sound and programming, that were not included on other tabs. The options are described in Table 10.7.

Table 10.7. A description of the Options dialog box General tab controls.

Control	*Description*
Warning Sounds	`SET BELL`—Establishes sound and other options.
Off	No sound is used.
Default	Uses Windows default sound for a bell or error sound.
Play	Establishes a WAV file to be used for the error sound. Type the file name in the text box or click the button to the right of the text box to select an existing WAV file.
dBASE Compatibility	`SET COMPATIBLE`—Specifies compatibility with FoxBASE+ and other Xbase languages.
Use FoxPro Color Palette	`SET COLOR TO`
Confirm File Replacement	`SET SAFETY ON/OFF`—Specifies whether you are prompted to confirm whether existing file should be overwritten.

Control	Description
	Programming Group
Cancel Programs on Escape	`SET ESCAPE ON/OFF`—Specifies whether a user is allowed to exit the program by pressing the Esc key.
Show Trace	`SET TRACE ON/OFF`—Initiates debugging Window trace.
Log Compilation Errors	`SET LOGERRORS ON/OFF`—Designates whether compilation errors are written to a text (LOG) file.
Set Development	`SET DEVELOPMENT ON/OFF`—Instructs FoxPro to compare the creation date of a program with the creation date of the program's compiled objects when the program is run.
	Data Entry Group
Navigation Keys	`SET KEYCOMP TO`—Sets the navigation keys to conform to FoxBASE+ or Windows standards.
Fill New Records with current values	`SET CARRY ON/OFF`—Carries forward values from fields in current record to a newly appended record.
Enter or Tab to Exit Fields	`SET CONFIRM ON/OFF`

The Options Dialog Box Edit Tab

The Edit Tab, described in Table 10.8, contains options for designating saved files, compatibility, and text manipulation. You can set any of these options only when you are editing text in programs, the code window, and text files.

Table 10.8. A description of the Options dialog box Edit tab controls.

Control	Description
Edit Options for the Command Window Group	
Drag-and-Drop Editing	Enables or disables drag-and-drop text editing for manipulating text with the mouse.
Word Wrap	Specifies whether lines wrap within the window.
Automatic Indent	Specifies whether lines are indented automatically in the window display according to the first line's indentation.

continues

Table 10.8. continued

Control	*Description*
Alignment	Specifies whether text is left-, right-, or center-aligned in the edit window.
Tab Width (characters)	Specifies the number of characters used for a tab.
Show Line/Column Position	Specifies whether line and column positions display on the left side of the status bar.
Make Backup Copy	When you check this option, Visual FoxPro creates a backup copy each time you save a file. The backup copy has the extension .BAK.
Compile Before Saving	When you check this option, Visual FoxPro automatically compiles the program and checks for syntax errors when the file is saved. This option only applies when editing program files.
Save With End-Of-File Marker	When you check this option, Visual FoxPro places a Ctrl+Z at the end of a file when the file is saved.
Save With Line Feeds	When you check this option, Visual FoxPro saves files with the line feeds that have been entered into the file. When unchecked, Visual FoxPro removes the line feeds when the file is saved.
Save Preferences	Saves preferences of this group for editing only the current file. Or, if not checked, saves preferences for all files.
Save as Default for `<files>`	Save the current settings as the default for all new files of this type. For example, save the current settings for all .PRG files.

The Options Dialog Box Forms Tab

You can use the Forms tab to specify options for the Form Designer program. The controls are described in Table 10.9.

Table 10.9. A description of the Options dialog box Forms tab controls.

Control	*Description*
	Grid Group
Grid Lines	You can specify whether Visual FoxPro displays grid lines in the Form Designer.

Control	*Description*
Sn**a**p to Grid	You can specify whether the initial setting of the Snap to Grid option is set on or off.
Hori**z**ontal Spacing (pixels)	Specifies the width of the space between horizontal grid lines. The width is based on the Scale Units option.
Vertical Spacing (pixels)	Specifies the height of the space between vertical grid lines. The height is based on the Scale Units option.
Show **P**osition	Specifies whether the position and dimensions of the selected object display on the status bar.
Tab Ordering	Specifies the procedure used to order tabs in the form control tab ordering.
S**c**ale Units	Sets the default scale mode for the form and class designers. Specifies pixels or characters (Foxels).
Ma**x**imum Design Area	Specifies a maximum size of the form for design time. FoxPro will not let you size a form that is bigger than the specified resolution. It is a good idea to specify the smallest resolution that your users will need so that your forms will be viewable by all your users. Options are 800×600, 640×480, 1024×768, and 1280×1024.
Template Classes	You can specify a class library and class on which to base your new forms and form sets. If none is selected, FoxPro uses the base class. Specifying classes makes it easy to give your forms a consistent look and feel.
Form Set	The Registered Library drop-down list contains class libraries that you have registered. You can register class libraries in the Controls tab of the Options dialog box. The Class Name drop-down list contains form set classes in the selected registered library.
For**m**	The Registered Library drop-down list contains class libraries that you have registered. The Class Name drop-down list contains form classes in the selected registered library.

The Options Dialog Box Projects Tab

You can use the Projects tab to specify options for the Project Manager. The Projects tab is described in Table 10.10.

Table 10.10. A description of the Options dialog box Projects tab controls.

Control	*Description*
Project Double-Click Action	You can specify whether FoxPro runs or modifies a file when you double-click it in Project Manager.
Prompt For Wizards	You can specify whether Visual FoxPro automatically prompts you to use a wizard when you click on the **N**ew button or choose the **P**roject menu **N**ew File button.

The Options Dialog Box Controls Tab

You use the options on the Controls tab to register libraries for specifying template classes on the Forms tab. These options also specify what can be selected from the View Classes button on the Form Controls toolbar so that adding custom controls to forms is easy. Each of the controls on the Controls tab is described in Table 10.11.

This tab operates a little differently than other tabs on the Options dialog box. The following steps are required to make a library appear on the View Classes button menu:

1. Select one of the two radio buttons at the top of the dialog box to choose either a Visual Class Library or an OLE Control. Select the **V**isual Class Library button.
2. Click on the **A**dd button and the Open dialog box appears. Select a visual class library file. The selection appears in the **S**elected list box.
3. Select one of the libraries in the **S**elected list box.
4. Click on the OK button and the setting is saved.
5. Choose OK and the settings are saved.

The items that appear in the **S**elected list appear on the shortcut menu when you click the View Classes button on the Form Controls toolbar. The View Classes button makes it easy to access different libraries.

Table 10.11. A description of the Options dialog box Controls tab controls.

Control	*Description*
Visual Class Libraries	Updates the display in the Selected list box and Controls tab to display the class libraries related information, which includes the **L**abel Name, Library, and **A**dd and **R**emove controls.
OLE Controls	Updates the display in the Controls tab so that the Selected list box contains OLE controls and the Controls tab contains the **I**nsertable Objects, **C**ontrols, and **A**dd controls.
Selected	List box that shows either OLE controls or visual class library (VCX) files.
Label Name	Shows the label name of the selected visual class library (VCX option).
Library	The text box that displays the selected visual class library (VCX option).
Add	If the **V**isual Class Libraries option is selected, press this button and the Open File dialog box appears containing VCX visual class libraries. You select a visual class library to add. If **O**LE Controls is selected, press this button, and the OLE Control Selection dialog box appears. You can select OLE controls to add to the **S**election list.
Remove	Push this button and the visual class libraries selected in the **S**elected list box are removed (VCX option).
	Show Group (OLE Controls option only)
Insertable Objects	Shows registered OLE applications that are insertable objects in the **S**elected list box.
Controls	Shows registered OLE controls in the **S**elected list box.

The Options Dialog Box Remote Tab

The Options dialog box Remote tab contains options for remote (ODBC) view and connection default values. Table 10.12 describes the Options dialog box Remote tab control.

Table 10.12. A description of the Options dialog box Remote tab control.

Control	*Description*
	Remote View Defaults Group
Share Connection	You use this check box to specify whether the current shared connection can be used for new views. Default value is unchecked.
Fetch Memo	You use this check box to specify whether Memo fields are not fetched from the data source until a Memo field is activated in the view output. The default value is checked because you normally do not want to transfer large volumes of data, such as a memo field, unless you really want to use it.
SQL Updates: **C**riteria	This combo box is used to designate which type of field you check to determine the user on a remote server before you attempt to perform an update. The update fails if the data in the remote fields specified by the selected criterion has been changed. The types of fields are key and modified fields (which is the default), key fields only, key and updatable fields, and key and timestamp fields.
SQL Updates: **M**ethod	You use this combo box to specify how information is updated on the remote server. These combo box options determine which SQL commands are used in the update statement sent to the remote server or source tables when records are updated.
Records To Fetch At A Time	You use this spinner control to specify how many records are returned at a time from the remote data source. The default is 100 records.
Ma**x**imum Records To Fetch	You use this spinner control to designate the maximum number of records that are returned by a view.
Use Memo For Fields >=	You use this spinner control to specify when you want to convert long Character type data fields to Memo fields in the output of your view.
Records To Batch Update	You use this spinner to specify the number of records to update with a single command. For more information, see the `REPLACE` command and `Scope` clauses.
	Connection Defaults Group
Asynchronous **E**xecution	You select this check box if you want to enable asynchronous processing.

Control	*Description*
Displa**y** Warnings	You select this check box to enable the display of warning messages.
Batch **P**rocessing	You select this check box to enable batch processing. If you select this check box, Visual FoxPro does not return results from the `SQLEXEC()` call until all individual result sets have been retrieved. This option corresponds to setting the `BatchMode` option in the `SQLSETPROP()` function.
Automatic **T**ransactions	This check box specifies how the connection manages transactions on the remote table. Selecting this check box is equivalent to setting the `Transactions` property of the `SQLSETPROP()` function to `1`. When this check box is not checked, it is equivalent to setting the `Transactions` property of the `SQLSETPROP()` function to `2`.
Show Lo**gi**n	You use this combo box to specify how often login prompts display. The choices are Only when necessary, Always, and Never. Login prompts display only when login information is not specified in the connection or view definition.
Co**n**nection Timeout (sec)	You use this spinner to specify how many seconds to wait for a connection to be established with the remote server. If the connection cannot be established within the specified time, Visual FoxPro issues an error. The default is `15 seconds`.
Idle Timeout (min)	You use this spinner control to specify how many minutes of idle time is allowed before Visual FoxPro terminates the connection. If a request to the server is not made within the specified time, Visual FoxPro terminates the connection. However, Visual FoxPro attempts to reconnect automatically if a request to the server is made after the connection has timed out. The default is `0 seconds`.
Query Timeout (sec)	You use this spinner control to specify how many seconds to wait for the server to respond to a request. If the server takes longer than the specified number of seconds to process the query, Visual FoxPro issues an error. The default is `0 seconds`.

continues

Table 10.12. continued

Control	*Description*
Wait Time(ms)	You use this spinner control to specify how many milliseconds to wait between request completion checks.

Setting Environmental Parameters

This section describes the `SET` command. dBASE II had only 21 `SET` commands. Visual FoxPro has about 118. Only the environmental parameters that directly relate to the operational environment are covered in detail in this chapter. The others are mentioned with references to the chapters where each is discussed.

You can execute FoxPro without setting environmental parameters. With the `SET` commands, however, you can customize Visual FoxPro to your requirements and turn on additional functionality. Here is the general form of a `SET` command:

```
SET <set keyword> <TO ¦ ON ¦ OFF ¦> <definition parameters>
```

Here is the equivalent CONFIG.FPW file command:

```
<set keyword> = <definition parameters>
```

By convention, the default value for `SET` commands with an `ON` or `OFF` keyword is indicated by uppercase. The alternative is lowercase.

The remainder of this section describes each form of the `SET` command in alphabetical order. Table 10.13 presents forms of the `SET` command, organized by function.

Table 10.13. `SET` command forms.

Data Editing	*Display*	*Output*
BRSTATUS	BLINK	CONSOLE
CARRY	BORDER	DATE
CENTURY	CLEAR	DECIMALS
CONFIRM	CLOCK	HEADING
CURRENCY	COLOR OF	HOURS
DELIMITERS	COLOR SET	MARGIN
FDOW	COLOR TO	MEMOWIDTH
FWEEK	CURSOR	ODOMETER

Data Editing	*Display*	*Output*
MARK OF	DEVICE	PDSETUP
MARK TO	FIXED	PRINTER
MARK TO	INTENSITY	SECONDS
POINT	MESSAGE	SPACE
READBORDER	NOTIFY	TALK
SEPARATOR	PALETTE	
	WINDOW OF	
Files	*Other*	*Input*
ALTERNATE	BELL	ESCAPE
DEFAULT	COMPATIBLE	FUNCTION
FULLPATH	HELP	KEYCOMP
PATH	HELPFILTER	MACKEY
RESOURCE	SESSION	TYPEAHEAD
SAFETY	TEXTMERGE	
DIRECTORY	TOPIC	
	TOPIC ID	
Database	*Programming*	*Multiuser*
ANSI	CLASSLIB	AUTOSAVE
BLOCKSIZE	DEBUG	EXCLUSIVE
COLLATE	DEVELOPMENT	LOCK
CPDIALOG	DOHISTORY	MULTILOCKS
DELETED	ECHO	REFRESH
DATABASE	LIBRARY	REPROCESS
EXACT	LOGERRORS	
FIELDS	PROCEDURE	
FILTER	SCOREBOARD	
FORMAT	SYSMENU	
INDEX	TRBETWEEN	
KEY	UDFPARMS	
MBLOCK	STATUS	
NULL	OLEOBJECT	
OPTIMIZE		

continues

Table 10.13. continued

Database	*Programming*	*Multiuser*
ORDER		
NEAR		
RELATION		
SKIP		
STEP		
UNIQUE		
VIEW		

The *SET ALTERNATE* Command

The `SET ALTERNATE` command generates an ASCII file containing all output from Visual FoxPro except `@` command output. Here is the syntax:

```
SET ALTERNATE TO [<expFN> [ADDITIVE]]
SET ALTERNATE on ¦ OFF
```

Here is the equivalent CONFIG.FPW file command:

```
ALTERNATE = [<filename> [ADDITIVE]]
ALTERNATE = on ¦ OFF
```

If you omit the filename extension, .TXT is used. If you supply `ADDITIVE`, the text is appended to the end of the specified file. If you don't supply a filename, the open alternate file is closed. The `ON ¦ OFF` form regulates the output to the alternate file. Here is an example:

```
SET ALTERNATE TO TEXT         && Filename will be TEXT.TXT
SET ALTERNATE ON
DISPLAY STATUS                && Generate output
?  "This message is output to alternate file"
SET ALTERNATE OFF
SET ALTERNATE TO              && Close alternate file
```

The *SET ANSI* Command

The `SET ANSI` command determines how the Visual FoxPro SQL commands do comparisons between strings of different lengths when the = operator is used. Here is the syntax:

```
SET ANSI ON ¦ off
```

Here is the equivalent CONFIG.FPW file command:

```
ANSI = ON ¦ off
ALTERNATE = on ¦ OFF
```

If SET ANSI is ON, the = operator is equivalent to the == operator when making comparisons in Visual FoxPro SQL commands. When SET ANSI is OFF, the string is compared character for character until the end of the shorter string is reached, at which time if the strings match, the strings are equal. In other words, the = operator functionality for SQL commands is the same as the functionality in FoxPro commands.

The term *ANSI* is an acronym for *American National Standards Institute*, which is the standardization committee for SQL. The ANSI in the SET ANSI command connotes that if SET ANSI is ON, SQL command comparisons operate as specified in the SQL standards.

The *SET AUTOSAVE* Command

You can use the Visual FoxPro SET AUTOSAVE feature to reduce data loss due to system or power failure. If this feature is activated, the data record buffers, DOS directory, and file allocation table (FAT) are written to disk after a record is changed. When activated, the feature is used by the APPEND, BROWSE, EDIT, PACK, INDEX, and REINDEX commands. For performance reasons, this option is initialized to OFF. Here is the syntax:

```
SET AUTOSAVE on ¦ OFF
```

Here is the equivalent CONFIG.FPW file command:

```
AUTOSAVE = on ¦ OFF
```

This function works by using the DOS DUP function to open a duplicate file handle. Then the file with the duplicate file handle is closed. The file close operation causes the buffers, DOS directory, and FAT to be written to disk. This technique is much faster than a traditional file close operation followed by a file open operation because the file remains open for the original file handle, eliminating a time-consuming directory search for the filename.

If AUTOSAVE is OFF, the buffers are flushed every five minutes, after exiting a READ, or when control returns to the Command window.

The *SET BELL* Command

The SET BELL command controls the bell sound. You can turn the bell sound on or off and vary the frequency (in hertz or cycles per second) and duration (in ticks). You can also set a WAV sound file that plays instead of the Windows bell sound. Here is the syntax:

```
SET BELL ON ¦ off
SET BELL TO [<expN> , <expN>]
SET BELL TO <expC>,<expN>
```

Here is the equivalent CONFIG.FPW file command:

```
BELL = ON ¦ OFF ¦ <integer constant>,<integer constant>
BELL =  <WAV sound file>, <integer constant>
```

The first argument is the frequency and the second is the duration. The frequency range is 19 through 10000 hertz. The duration can be from 1 to 19 ticks. (One tick equals about .0549 seconds.) The default values for frequency and duration are 512 hertz and 2 ticks. The following program emits a pleasant sounding three-tone bell:

```
*****************************************************
* Ding: A program that emits a three-tone bell sound
PROCEDURE DING
SET BELL TO 300,1
?? CHR(7)
SET BELL TO 499,1
?? CHR(7)
SET BELL TO 700,1
?? CHR(7)
SET BELL TO 512,2  && Set to default value
RETURN
```

If your computer contains a sound board, you can play waveform files in Windows. In Visual FoxPro, you can specify a waveform sound to play when the bell rings. You specify a Character expression (`<expC>`), which is the name of a waveform sound (WAV) file to play or an entry in the sounds section of your WIN.INI file. If the sound cannot be found, the default sound specified by the `SystemDefault` entry in the sounds section of your WIN.INI file is played. No sound plays if there isn't a `SystemDefault` entry, the default sound cannot be located, or you don't have a sound board in your computer.

If you specify a waveform sound, you must also include a value for the `<duration>` argument. A syntax error occurs if the duration value is omitted. The duration value you specify is ignored and the entire sound is played. The following example plays the CHIME.WAV waveform file when the bell sounds:

```
SET BELL TO 'C:\WINDOWS\CHIME.WAV', 0
```

The *SET BLINK* Command

If you use a VGA or EGA video adapter card, you can choose whether the brightness of background colors can be changed or the foreground display blinks. You can't do both at the same time. You can specify the `SET BLINK` command to control which mode you want, as in the following example:

```
SET BLINK ON ¦ off
```

Here is the equivalent CONFIG.FPW file command:

```
BLINK = ON ¦ off
```

If you use `SET BLINK ON`, the foreground (character) blinks. You use the asterisk (`*`) attribute to specify that a screen element displays with either a bright background or a blinking foreground:

```
SET BLINK ON  && The following text will now blink
@ SAY 10,10 "This text either blinks or has a " +
```

```
" bright white background"  COLOR R*/W
WAIT WINDOW
SET BLINK OFF && Now the text will display a bright background
```

If you set `BLINK` to `OFF`, you can actually increase the number of available colors.

The *SET BLOCKSIZE* Command

REVISED FOR VISUAL FOXPRO 3

The `SET BLOCKSIZE` command is used to change the size of the data block for memo (FPT file). Here is the syntax:

```
SET BLOCKSIZE TO <expN>
```

Here is the equivalent CONFIG.FPW file command:

```
BLOCKSIZE = <integer constant>
```

The Numeric expression can be a number between 1 and 32, which is multiplied by 512 bytes to achieve the actual block size. The default value is 1 (512 bytes). In most cases, this block size is sufficient for optimum performance. If the memo fields will be large and many text searches will be performed, you improve performance by creating a memo field that uses larger buffers.

The `SET BLOCKSIZE` command affects memo file buffer sizes only if the file is created using the `CREATE`, `COPY`, `TOTAL`, or `IMPORT` commands. Other commands are unaffected by the value of `BLOCKSIZE`. The new block size remains in effect for the life of the FPT file because the block size is in the file header. For most applications, the default block size for FPT files doesn't need to be changed.

If you want to change the block size for a memo field, simply `SET BLOCKSIZE` to a new value and create a new database table with the `COPY` command.

If you set the block size to 0 (`SET BLOCKSIZE TO 0`), disk space is allocated in blocks of one byte each. In this way, you can have much more compact memo files because you waste no space in the memo field. For example, if you have 512-byte blocks (`SET BLOCKSIZE TO 32`) and have 100 records with each one averaging about 32 bytes, you use up 51,200 bytes of disk space to store 3200 bytes of data. However, if you `SET BLOCKSIZE to 0`, you only use 3200 bytes of disk space.

The *SET BORDER TO* Command

The `SET BORDER TO` command defines the type of borders surrounding boxes, pop-up menus, menus, and window objects. Here is the syntax:

```
SET BORDER TO [SINGLE ¦ DOUBLE ¦ PANEL ¦ NONE ¦
<border definition string1>, <border definition string2>]
```

Here is the equivalent CONFIG.FPW file command:

```
BORDER =  SINGLE ¦ DOUBLE ¦ PANEL ¦ NONE ¦
<border definition string2> [, <border definition string2>]
```

The border types are defined in Table 10.14.

Table 10.14. The border type keywords.

Keyword	*Border Composition*
`SINGLE`	Single-line ASCII line-drawing characters
`DOUBLE`	Double-line ASCII line-drawing characters
`PANEL`	ASCII block character, `CHR(219)`
`NONE`	No border drawn
(No value)	Resets to default border types

The default value for the border type is `DOUBLE` for FoxPro-style pop-up menus and `SINGLE` for boxes, menus, and window objects. `SET BORDER` doesn't change the border type for the systems and pop-up menus or for any object in which the `BORDER` clause is specified.

The border can also be two border definition strings. Each consists of a list of up to eight integer or character string values and defines the four sides and corners of the border. The first border definition string defines the border for boxes, menus, pop-up menus, and the currently active window. The optional second border definition string defines the border for the inactive window.

Here is the form:

```
border string ::= <top>,<bottom>,<left side>,<right side>,
<upper-left corner>,<upper-right corner>,
<lower-left corner>,<lower-right corner>
```

Integers can be used to represent the ASCII code for a character. If only the first border character is defined, it is used for all sides and corners. The SETBORD.PRG program shown in Listing 10.2 provides some examples.

Listing 10.2. A program that illustrates the use of the `SET BORDER` command.

```
***************************************************************
*      * 08/13/92              SETBORD.PRG           21:34:46 *
***************************************************************
*      *                                                      *
*      * Description:                                         *
*      *  Illustrates the use of the SET BORDER command       *
*      *                                                      *
***************************************************************
CLEAR
SET BORDER TO "*"
@ 1,0 TO 10,38          && Draw a box
SET BORDER TO "A","B","C","D","E","F","G","H"
@ 12,0 TO 22,38         && Draw a box
SET BORDER TO PANEL, DOUBLE
@ 1,40 TO 10,78         && Draw a box
```

```
*
* Following statement also provides borders for Windows.
* The ASCII character 178 is for <border definition string2>.
* It becomes the border for the inactive window
SET BORDER TO 205,205,179,179,213,184,212,190,178
DEFINE WINDOW Wind1 FROM 6,20 TO 18,60
DEFINE WINDOW Wind2 FROM 8,25 TO 20,65
@ 12,40 TO 22,78        && Draw a box
SET BORDER TO DOUBLE
ACTIVATE WINDOW Wind1
ACTIVATE WINDOW Wind2
@ 2,2 TO 10,10          && Draw a box inside of the window
WAIT WINDOW
CLEAR ALL
```

The result of running the program shown in Listing 10.2 is shown in Figure 10.5.

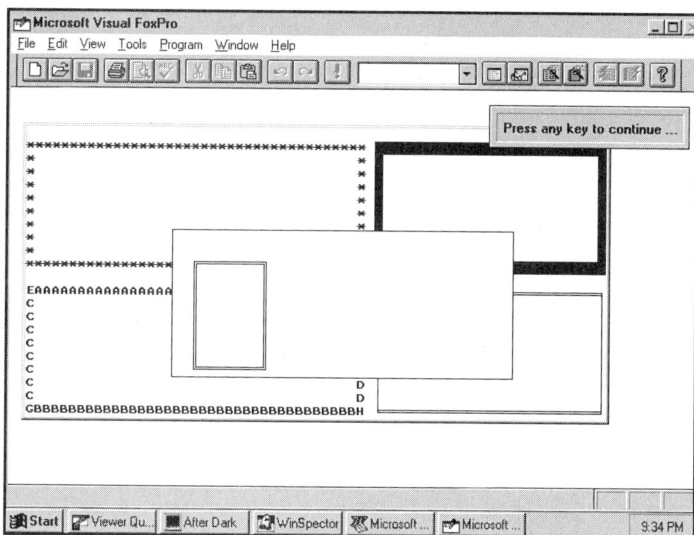

FIGURE 10.5.
Examples of border types.

The *SET BRSTATUS* Command

When BROWSE executes, the SET BRSTATUS command controls the status display on the third line from the bottom of the screen. When BROWSE executes and SET BRSTATUS is ON, the status line appears. The status line also appears if SET STATUS is ON. See the section "The SET STATUS Command" for more information regarding the status line. Here is the syntax:

```
SET BRSTATUS on ¦ OFF
```

Here is the equivalent CONFIG.FPW file command:

```
BRSTATUS = on ¦ OFF
```

Most FoxPro programmers don't use the status line in their applications because it uses up a line of the screen. However, the status line is supported to maintain compatibility with dBASE III, dBASE IV, and FoxBASE+ applications. Visual FoxPro has a Windows-style status bar that appears at the bottom of the display. This status bar resembles those of Windows applications such as Word for Windows. When you develop Visual FoxPro applications, you probably will want to use the Windows-style status line. See the section "The SET STATUS Command."

The *SET CARRY* Command

The SET CARRY command initializes all fields or selected fields with the values of the previously entered record. Here is the syntax:

```
SET CARRY ON ¦ off
SET CARRY TO [<field name list> [ADDITIVE]]
```

Here is the equivalent CONFIG.FPW file command:

```
CARRY = ON ¦ off ¦ <field name list>
```

If a field list is supplied, only the specified fields are initialized. The SET CARRY field list is cleared unless you supply the ADDITIVE keyword, in which case the specified fields are added to the existing list. This command is discussed in detail in Chapter 11.

The *SET CENTURY* Command

The SET CENTURY command controls the display and input of date fields and variables. By default, CENTURY is set OFF, and the year is displayed as a two-digit number, 12/03/91. If CENTURY is set ON, the year is displayed as a four-digit number, 12/03/1991. Here is the syntax:

```
SET CENTURY on ¦ OFF
```

Here is the equivalent CONFIG.FPW file command:

```
CENTURY = on ¦ OFF
```

The *SET CLASSLIB* Command

The SET CLASSLIB command establishes a visual class library from which objects can be created. A *visual class library file* is a table-like file with a VBX extension that contains multiple class definitions. Here is the syntax:

```
SET CLASSLIB TO <expFN> [ADDITIVE] [ALIAS <expC>]
```

Here is the equivalent CONFIG.FPW file command:

```
CLASSLIB = <expFN> [ADDITIVE] [ALIAS <expC>]
```

<expFN> is the name of a visual class library file. If you don't specify a filename extension, .VCX is assumed. If you don't specify the ADDITIVE keyword and any visual class libraries are open,

they are closed before the specified visual class library file is opened. If the ADDITIVE keyword is specified, the designated visual class library is opened without closing any visual class libraries that are already open. You can remove all visual class libraries from memory by specifying the SET CLASSLIB TO command without naming a file. You can remove an individual visual class library with the RELEASE CLASSLIB <*expFN*> command. You can add a class to a visual class library with the ADD CLASS <*expFN*> command.

The ALIAS clause specifies an alias name for the visual class library. You can refer to the visual class library by its alias. For example, you can use the following commands to open a VCX visual class library named YourClass, assign it the alias YourButtonClass, and then create a control named YourButton:

```
SET CLASSLIB TO YourClass ALIAS YourButtonClass
mYourButton = CREATEOBJ("YourButtonClass.BigButton")
```

When you execute the CREATEOBJECT() function or the ADD OBJECT command, Visual FoxPro searches for the class definition for the object to be created in the following locations and order:

1. The current program
2. VCX visual class libraries opened with SET CLASSLIB
3. Procedure files opened with SET PROCEDURE
4. Programs in the FoxPro program call chain

When Visual FoxPro searches the program's call chain, it begins its search with the most recently executed program and continues searching until it encounters the first executed program. If the class definition cannot be located, Visual FoxPro generates a class definition not found error message.

The *SET CLEAR* Command

Suppose you want to prepare a background display and then execute a SET FORMAT TO <*expFN*> command. The SET FORMAT command clears the screen and displays the @...SAY and @...GET commands. Your background display is gone. If you execute the SET CLEAR OFF command before you prepare the background display, the problem is eliminated. The SET CLEAR command designates whether a window or screen is cleared when the SET FORMAT TO and QUIT commands execute. By default, SET CLEAR is ON, so the SET FORMAT TO and QUIT commands clear the screen before they execute. If SET CLEAR is OFF, the screen isn't cleared by these two commands. Here is the syntax:

```
SET CLEAR ON ¦ off
```

Here is the equivalent CONFIG.FPW file command:

```
CLEAR = ON ¦ off
```

When SET CLEAR is OFF, you can quit FoxPro and leave your custom sign-off display on-screen after FoxPro exits.

The *SET CLOCK* Command

Using the SET CLOCK command, you can display a clock in the form *hh*:*mm*:*ss* anywhere on-screen. Here is the syntax:

```
SET CLOCK on ¦ OFF ¦ STATUS
SET CLOCK TO [<expN>,<expN>]
```

Here is the equivalent CONFIG.FPW file command:

```
CLOCK = on ¦ OFF ¦ <row>,<column> ¦ STATUS
```

The Numeric arguments represent row and column screen coordinates. If you don't specify coordinates, the clock is placed in the top-right corner of the screen. The default for the clock is OFF. For full-screen commands, the clock always appears in the top-right corner, regardless of the SET CLOCK setting.

Here is the form for a 12-hour display:

```
11:31:33 pm
```

Here is the form for a 24-hour display:

```
23:31:33
```

The SET CLOCK STATUS form is supported by Visual FoxPro. When you execute this command, the clock is turned on and placed at the right of the Windows-style status bar. See the section "The SET STATUS Command."

The *SET COLLATE TO* Command

The SET COLLATE TO command specifies a collation sequence for character fields in subsequent indexing and sorting operations. If you are developing applications that will be used internationally, you need to be concerned with the collation sequence. This command lets you index tables containing accented characters that are used in many foreign languages. When you index or sort a file, the current setting of SET COLLATE TO is used. Visual FoxPro uses this setting for the lifetime of the index. For example, if an index is created with SET COLLATE TO set to GENERAL and the SET COLLATE TO setting is later changed to SPANISH, the index retains the GENERAL collation sequence. Here is the syntax:

```
SET COLLATE TO <expC>
```

Here is the equivalent CONFIG.FPW file command:

```
COLLATE = cSequenceName
```

The supported collation sequence options are provided in the following list:

Option	*Language*
CZECH	Czech
DUTCH	Dutch
GENERAL	English, French, German, Modern Spanish, Portuguese, and other Western European languages
GREEK	Greek
HUNGARY	Hungarian
ICELAND	Icelandic
MACHINE	Machine (the default collation sequence for earlier FoxPro versions)
NORDAN	Norwegian, Danish
POLISH	Polish
RUSSIAN	Russian
SLOVAK	Slovak
SPANISH	Traditional Spanish
SWEFIN	Swedish, Finnish
UNIQWT	Unique weight

The argument `<expC>` is a character string. Therefore, you must enclose the option in quotation marks, as in the following example:

```
SET COLLATE TO "SPANISH"
```

`MACHINE` is the default collation sequence option and is the most familiar sequence to Xbase users. Characters are ordered as they appear in the current code page.

`GENERAL` may be the preferable sequence for U.S. and Western European users. Characters are ordered as they appear in the current code page. In FoxPro versions earlier than 2.5, you might have used `UPPER()` or `LOWER()` on character fields when you created indexes. In FoxPro versions later than 2.5, you can instead specify the `GENERAL` collation sequence option and omit the `UPPER()` conversion.

Note that if you specify a collation sequence option other than `MACHINE` and create an IDX file, a compact IDX is always created.

Use `SET("COLLATE")` to return the current collation sequence.

If you include the following line in your Visual FoxPro configuration file (CONFIG.FPW), a collation sequence is specified when you start Visual FoxPro:

```
COLLATE = GENERAL
```

Choosing Colors in FoxPro

Interface design is an art that has rapidly evolved in the short history of the highly interactive microcomputer system, and color is an important element of interface design. Many talented artists have contributed to interface design and to the choice of colors for interface elements. Products with well-designed interfaces are more likely to be accepted by the user community than those with poorly designed interfaces.

The Visual FoxPro designers used this design knowledge base when they designed the interface and chose the default colors for the interface elements. Professional Xbase developers reviewed the choice of colors during beta testing, and their feedback improved the interface even further. As a result, you will probably be satisfied with the color choices provided with the FoxPro default color set for your application. If you decide to change the colors of certain elements, this section contains instructions for doing so. FoxPro provides commands with which you can change the color of virtually every interface element. The following are the methods for changing colors:

- The Form Designer's Colors dialog box
- The `SET COLOR TO` command (traditional Xbase command)
- The `SET COLOR OF` command (dBASE IV color command)
- The `COLOR` clauses specified with certain commands
- The `SET COLOR OF SCHEME` command
- The `SET COLOR SET` command
- The `CREATE COLOR SET` command

When you choose colors for interface elements, you should follow a few basic guidelines.

Be careful with the use of bright colors. They are good for window and screen titles, but too many bright screen elements make the screen busy and are distracting. The background should be a pale color, such as light blue, white, or green—never bright red unless a particular element, such as an alert message, demands the user's attention. However, you should never rely on color to communicate information. That should be done with text. Some people are color-blind, and some monitors are monochrome. Foreground characters and background should contrast enough to make the display easy to see. Remember that you view a screen for a relatively short time while developing an application, but the user might spend hours each day viewing the screen while using your application.

You should use colors consistently. If the user is accustomed to looking at a table in a certain color scheme, all instances of that table should use the same colors. Before choosing colors for an application, browse through some computer magazines and notice the color combinations others have chosen. However, don't use the screen shot of the old FoxPro 1.0 advertisement as a model. It is a good example of a poorly designed screen. The screen is too busy, bright colors are overused, and every table employs a different color scheme. It is advertising copy. Its purpose was probably to illustrate that you can have several tables on-screen at the same time and each table can have a different color scheme.

You can even look at noncomputer applications, such as a calculator, a toaster, or the dashboard of an automobile, to help you determine how to coordinate colors for a good interface design.

The *SET COLOR TO* Command

The `SET COLOR TO` command controls the colors of the standard text, enhanced text, and border display. Here is the form:

```
SET COLOR TO [ [<standard color attribute>]
[,[<enhanced color attribute>]
[,[<border color attribute>] ]]]
```

Here is the equivalent CONFIG.FPW file command:

```
COLOR = ON ¦ OFF ¦ [[<standard color attribute>]
[,[<enhanced color attribute>]
[,[<border color attribute>]
```

Here is the format of each color attribute:

```
<color attribute> ::= <foreground>/<background>

<foreground> ::= <color character>][<color character>]...
<background> ::= <color character>][<color character>]...
```

Use this form for color monitors:

```
<color character> := B ¦ G ¦ N ¦ R ¦ W ¦ X  ¦ * ¦ +
```

Use this form for monochrome monitors:

```
<color character> := I ¦ N ¦ U ¦ W ¦ X ¦ * ¦ +
```

The vertical bar is used as a delimiter. Text color is specified by one or two characters representing the color and a third character that activates the bright attribute (a plus sign) or the blinking attribute (an asterisk). The `*` character has two display modes, which are determined by the `SET BLINK` setting. Table 10.15 lists the codes for color displays.

Table 10.15. The color character codes.

Character	*Color*
N (or blank)	Black
W	White
B	Blue

continues

Table 10.15. continued

Character	*Color*
G	Green
R	Red
BG or GB	Cyan
RG or GR	Brown
RG+	Yellow (bright brown)
BR or RB	Magenta
X	Blank

In the following example, standard text characters are bright white on a blue background. The enhanced text (@... GET prompts) has blue characters on a white background, and the border around the screen is blue:

```
SET COLOR TO W+/B,B/W,B
```

If you omit any attributes, the color of the corresponding item is unchanged. If you omit all attributes, the colors are changed to the system defaults, which are W/N,N/W,N.

The color attributes for monochrome displays are defined in Table 10.16.

Table 10.16. The monochrome character codes.

Character	*Color*
I	Reverse video
N (or blank)	Black
U	Underline
W	White
X	Blank

The *SET COLOR OF* Command

The purpose of this command is to maintain compatibility with dBASE IV. Visual FoxPro has implemented a more comprehensive way of saving colors for various objects using the SET COLOR OF SCHEME command. Nevertheless, the COLOR OF command affects the colors of COLOR SCHEME 1 (colors for user-defined windows) and COLOR SCHEME 2 (colors for user-defined menus).

WARNING

If you are starting a new application, use the `COLOR SCHEME` system (`SET COLOR OF SCHEME` and `SET COLOR SET` commands). To simplify the task of converting a program from dBASE IV, you might want to retain the existing `SET COLOR` commands. Be aware, however, that this form of the `SET COLOR` command, as well as the `SET COLOR TO` command, changes the color in the currently active color set and can affect the color of elements you didn't intend to change. If you can, use the FoxPro `COLOR SCHEME` system. This book discusses the older forms of the `SET COLOR` commands because they are often used in the immense multimillion-line Xbase code.

In dBASE IV, objects in full-screen applications are divided into seven screen categories. The color of each category can be assigned by using the `SET COLOR OF` command. Here is the syntax:

```
SET COLOR OF HIGHLIGHT ¦ MESSAGES ¦ TITLES ¦ BOX ¦
INFORMATION ¦ NORMAL ¦ FIELD
TO [<color attribute>]
```

Here is the equivalent CONFIG.FPW file command:

```
COLOR OF HIGHLIGHT ¦ MESSAGES ¦ TITLES ¦ BOX ¦
INFORMATION ¦ NORMAL ¦ FIELD = <color attribute>
```

By default or if the `SET COLOR TO` command is specified, `MESSAGES`, `TITLES`, `BOX`, and `NORMAL` are set to the color of the standard attribute whereas `HIGHLIGHT`, `INFORMATION`, and `FIELDS` are set to the color of the enhanced attribute. If you omit the color attribute, it is set to black on black (`N/N`), resulting in an invisible display.

Here are two examples:

```
SET COLOR TO BOX TO B+/W
SET COLOR OF INFORMATION TO R+/W
```

The following is a list of color categories and their associated elements:

`NORMAL`	Any command that outputs static text, such as the `?` and `@...SAY` commands.
`FIELDS`	`GET` fields (`@...GET`).
`MESSAGES`	Text appearing on message lines, unselected user-defined window menus and pop-up titles, and enabled options.
`TITLES`	Headings for `LIST`, `DISPLAY`, `SUM`, and `AVERAGE`, and titles for active user-defined pop-up menus and menus.
`BOX`	User-defined menus, pop-up menus, and prompt box borders.
`HIGHLIGHT`	Selected text and other items.
`SET COLOR OF INFORMATION`	Defines the color of the clock (see the section "The `SET CLOCK` command") and the status line.

The *COLOR* Clauses

You can specify a COLOR clause to override the current color of an object output to the screen.

Visual FoxPro supports the two forms of COLOR clauses supported by other versions of FoxPro and includes a third method for specifying colors. The following are sample uses of the COLOR clause:

```
@ 10,10 SAY "It is not easy being green" COLOR G+/W
@ 10,10 SAY "Here is a better color scheme" COLOR SCHEME 3
```

The color clause can be added to the following commands:

```
@...EDIT - text edit regions   BROWSE
@...GET/SAYCHANGE
@...GET - check boxes    DEFINE BAR
@...GET - invisible buttons    DEFINE MENU
@...GET - lists    DEFINE PAD
@...GET - popup menus    DEFINE POPUP
@...GET - push buttons   DEFINE WINDOW
@...GET - radio buttons EDIT
@...GET - FILL TO READ
@...GET - TO       SHOW GET
      SHOW GETS
      SHOW OBJECT
```

The following is the syntax for the three forms of the COLOR clause:

```
[COLOR SCHEME <expN5>
  ¦ COLOR [<color attribute>][,<color attribute>]
  ¦ COLOR RGB(<color value list>)]]

<color attribute> ::= <foreground>/<background>
<foreground> ::= <color character>[<color character>]...
<background> ::= <color character>[<color character>]...
<color character> ::= B ¦ G ¦ I ¦ N ¦ R ¦
U ¦ W ¦ X ¦ * ¦ +
```

In the first form (COLOR SCHEME <expN5>) you can choose one of the 24 FoxPro color schemes. You can also use the traditional Xbase COLOR clause (second form) to specify color attributes for the object that is output. The first <*color attribute*> defines the color of text display, such as output from an @...SAY command. The second <*color attribute*> defines the color of an input field display, such as the GET data input field. You can define the foreground attribute (the color of the character) and the background attribute for both the text and input field displays.

The third form of the COLOR clause is used exclusively with Visual FoxPro. It contains the RGB() function, which has a list of up to six numeric values ranging from 0 to 255. The first three numbers represent the intensity of red, green, and blue for the foreground color, and the second three represent the intensity of the same three colors for the background color. You can specify a list of up to 10 RGB() functions. Each item in the list defines the colors for one of the 10 FoxPro color pairs. (A color pair consists of a pair of color attributes, one for the foreground color and one for the background color, such as GR/B.) When you skip an item in the list, you should specify a comma in place of a missing item. The RGB() function values that are equivalent to the traditional Xbase color attributes follow:

RGB(<red>,<green>,<blue>)	Color Attributes Foreground	Background
RGB(255, 0, 0)	R+	R*
RGB(0, 255, 0)	G+	G*
RGB(0, 0, 255)	B+	B*
RGB(0, 0, 0)	N	N*
RGB(255, 0, 255)	W+	W*
RGB(0, 255, 255)	BG+	BG*
RGB(255, 0, 255)	RB+	RB*
RGB(255, 255, 0)	GR+	GR*

Here are some examples:

```
@ 1,20 SAY "ACME IMPORT FORM"  COLOR  R+/B
@ 3,3 SAY "Enter Date:" GET ADate COLOR  GR+/B,B/GR+
@ 4,3 SAY "Enter Name and Address" COLOR GR+/B
@ 5,4 GET Name COLOR ,B/GR @ 6,4 GET Address COLOR ,B/GR
BROWSE COLOR SCHEME 4
@ 8,4 GET State COLOR RGB(255,0,0,255,255,255),255(0,255,0,0,0,0)
```

The *SET COLOR OF SCHEME* Command

`SET COLOR OF SCHEME` is the preferred command for setting colors in Visual FoxPro. It establishes a set of 10 color attribute pairs that comprise a color scheme. Each color pair is the color of a specific screen object. Here is the syntax:

```
SET COLOR OF SCHEME <expN1> TO
[<color attribute list> ¦ SCHEME <expN2>]
```

Here is the equivalent CONFIG.FPW file command:

```
COLOR OF SCHEME <expN> = <color attribute>
```

Unless you change the color scheme in the CONFIG.FPW file, FoxPro executes with the default color scheme. You can change the colors in any of the color schemes with this command. The Numeric expression `<expN1>` designates which of the 24 color schemes you can change. It can be any value from 1 through 10, and 17 through 24. Each color scheme has up to 10 color attribute pairs. You don't have to specify all 10 color pairs. However, you can't omit a comma from the list for those color pairs not specified. In the following example, only color pairs 2 and 6 are specified for color scheme 3:

```
SET COLOR OF SCHEME 3 TO ,W+/G,,,,R+/W
```

Here are more examples:

```
SET COLOR TO SCHEME 2 TO ;
BG/W,N/W,N/W,B/W,W/N,N/BG,W+/W,N+/N,B/W,W/N
```

```
SET COLOR OF SCHEME 3 TO
BG/W,,BG/N,,BG/N,,W+/W,N+/N,BG/N,BG/N
```

You can use the `SCHEME()` function, which has two Numeric arguments, to retrieve the color attribute pairs. The first argument is the color scheme number. The second argument is optional and defines which color attribute pair to return. Here are examples:

Command Window	*Results*
`? SCHEME(2)`	`BG/W,N/W,N/W,B/W,W/N,N/BG,W+W/,N+/N,B/W,W/N,+`
`? SCHEME(3,3)`	`BG/W`

You can also assign the color set of one color scheme to another using this command. For example, use the following command to assign the color scheme 3 to color scheme 2:

```
SET COLOR SCHEME 2 TO SCHEME 3
```

If you specify `SET COLOR OF SCHEME <expN1> TO` with no other argument, the color reverts to the last-named color set established for that color scheme. The default color set is used if no color set is specified in the CONFIG.FPW file (`COLOR SET =`). You also can establish a named color set with the `SET COLOR SET TO` command. Table 10.17 describes the color attribute pairs for each of the 12 standard color schemes.

Table 10.17. Color schemes.

Color Scheme	*Color Pair*	*Object Colored*
User-	1	`SAY` field
defined	2	`GET` field
windows	3	Border
	4	Title for active window
	5	Title for inactive window and message
	6	Selected item
	7	Clock and hotkeys
	8	Shadow
	9	Enabled control
	10	Disabled control
User-	1	Disabled
defined	2	Enabled options
menus	3	Border
	4	Menu titles
	5	Message
	6	Selected options

Color Scheme	Color Pair	Object Colored
	7	Hotkeys
	8	Shadow
	9	Enabled control
	10	Disabled control
Menu	1	Disabled pads
bar	2	Enabled pads
	3	Border
	4	Title
	5	Message
	6	Selected pad
	7	Hotkeys
	8	Shadow
	9	Enabled control
	10	Disabled control
Pop-up	1	Disabled options
menus	2	Enabled options
	3	Border
	4	Title
	5	Message
	6	Selected options
	7	Hotkeys
	8	Shadow
	9	Enabled control
	10	Disabled control
Dialog	1	Normal text
boxes	2	Text box
	3	Border
	4	Title
	5	Message
	6	Selected options
	7	Hotkeys
	8	Shadow

continues

Table 10.17. continued

Color Scheme	*Color Pair*	*Object Colored*
	9	Enabled control
	10	Disabled control
Pop-up	1	Disabled options
dialog	2	Enabled options
boxes	3	Border and scrollable lists (However, if you select a bright foreground, it is changed to the normal color for a scrollable list border.)
	4	Title
	5	Message
	6	Selected item
	7	Hotkeys
	8	Shadow
	9	Enabled control
	10	Disabled control
Alerts	1	Normal text
	2	Text box
	3	Border
	4	Title
	5	Message
	6	Selected item
	7	Hotkeys
	8	Shadow
	9	Enabled control
	10	Disabled control
Windows	1	Normal text (In addition, displays static text in View and Label Layout windows. The background color is used for the Label Layout window label dimension lines and arrows.)
	2	Text box for the View and Label Layout windows
	3	Border
	4	Title for active window
	5	Title for inactive window

Color Scheme	*Color Pair*	*Object Colored*
	6	Selected text
	7	Hotkeys
	8	Shadow
	9	Enabled control and the lines and arrows that show the label dimension for the Label Layout window
	10	Disabled control
Pop-up	1	Disabled option
windows	2	Enabled option
	3	Border (This is also the color of a scrollable list. However, the foreground is of normal intensity even when the color bright attribute (+) is present.)
	4	Title
	5	Message
	6	Selected option
	7	Hotkeys
	8	Shadow
	9	Enabled control
	10	Disabled control
Browse	1	Other records and background for grid lines
	2	Current field
	3	Borders and foreground for grid lines
	4	Active title
	5	Idle title
	6	Selected text
	7	Current record and background for bullet used for record deletion mark
	8	Shadow
	9	Enabled control
	10	Disabled control
Report	1	Text and Band B when full of text
	2	Report field

continues

Table 10.17. continued

Color Scheme	*Color Pair*	*Object Colored*
	3	Border
	4	Active title
	5	Inactive title
	6	Selected item
	7	Empty Band A region
	8	Shadow
	9	Full Band A
	10	Empty Band B
Pop-up	1	Disabled option
alerts	2	Enabled option
	3	Border and scrollable list (Scrollable lists always appear in normal color even if bright (+) attribute is present.)
	4	Title
	5	Message
	6	Selected option
	7	Hotkeys
	8	Shadow
	9	Enabled control
	10	Disabled control

The *SET COLOR SET TO* Command

You can use the `SET COLOR SET TO` command to load a predefined color set. You can define a color set with the `SET COLOR OF SCHEME` command. You can save the current color set configuration using the `CREATE COLOR` *<color set name>* command. Here is the syntax of the `SET COLOR SET TO` command:

```
SET COLOR SET TO [<color set name>]
```

Here is the equivalent CONFIG.FPW file command:

```
COLOR SET = <color set name>
```

If you don't include the optional argument (*<color set name>*) with the `TO` clause, the color scheme reverts to the last named color set. A default color set is used if no color set is specified in the CONFIG.FPW file (`COLOR SET =`).

The *SET CONFIRM* Command

`SET CONFIRM` controls the action of the cursor when it moves past the end of a field as data is entered in the field. When `CONFIRM` is `OFF`, the cursor moves to the next field. When `CONFIRM` is `ON`, the cursor remains on the last character of the field, and if `SET BELL` is `ON`, the bell sounds. You must press Enter to move to the next field. You can't move past the end of a field without confirmation. Many programmers feel that the data entry process is more reliable if `SET CONFIRM` is `ON`. Here is the syntax:

```
SET CONFIRM on ¦ OFF
```

Here is the equivalent CONFIG.FPW file command:

```
CONFIRM = on ¦ OFF
```

The *SET COMPATIBLE* Command

Millions of lines of Xbase code have been written, especially for dBASE III and dBASE IV. You can run any dBASE III or dBASE IV program under Visual FoxPro and probably will not need to make any changes at all. You only need to add the `SET COMPATIBLE ON` command to your program. This command is required because the Visual FoxPro language contains extensions to the Xbase language that operate differently than they do in dBASE III, dBASE IV, and other Xbase languages. For example, array initialization operates much differently under FoxPro than it does under dBASE IV. Here is the syntax:

```
SET COMPATIBLE on ¦ OFF ¦ db4 ¦ FOXPLUS [PROMPT ¦ noprompt]
```

Here is the equivalent CONFIG.FPW file command:

```
COMPATIBLE = on ¦ OFF ¦ db4 ¦ FOXPLUS [PROMPT ¦ noprompt]
```

The `ON` option is equivalent to the `DB4` option and `FOXPLUS` is equivalent to the `OFF` option. If `SET COMPATIBLE` is `ON`, or `DB4`, certain commands behave more like dBASE IV commands than Visual FoxPro commands so that programs written in dBASE III and dBASE IV run with little or no change.

The `PROMPT` and `NOPROMPT` keywords were added to the `SET COMPATIBLE` command. The `PROMPT` and `NOPROMPT` keywords determine whether or not, respectively, a dialog box displays when you open a dBASE IV database file with a memo field.

By default, whenever you open a dBASE database file that contains a memo field, the Convert Memos dialog box displays, prompting you to designate whether you want FoxPro to convert the dBASE memo file to a FoxPro format. You must convert the memo field to a FoxPro format to open the database table (DBF file) in FoxPro.

At any time, you can translate a FoxPro memo file to dBASE IV format by specifying the TYPE FOXPLUS option with the COPY command. You can specify the PROMPT keyword with the SET COMPATIBLE command to display the Convert Memos dialog box.

If you specify the NOPROMPT keyword with the SET COMPATIBLE command, the Convert Memos dialog box does not display when you open a dBASE database file that contains a memo field. The dBASE memo file is automatically converted to a FoxPro format.

If you want the maximum compatibility with dBASE IV, execute the following command:

```
SET COMPATIBLE DB4
```

If SET COMPATIBLE is OFF in FoxPro and you assign a value to a declared array name, the value is assigned to every element in the array. With SET COMPATIBLE DB4, if you assign a value to a declared array name, the array name is released, and a memory variable with the same name is created. If you assign new dimensions to an array, it acts differently depending on the state of SET COMPATIBLE. If SET COMPATIBLE is OFF and you use the DECLARE command or an array function to assign new dimensions to an array, the existing values in the array are retained. If SET COMPATIBLE is ON, values are replaced with .F.. Here are some examples:

Command Window	*Results*
SET COMPATIBLE OFF	(FoxPro compatible)
DECLARE ARY1[3], ARY3[2]	(Declare three-element array)
ARY1 = "Cat"	(Initialize all three values)
ARY3 = "Dog"	(Initialize both elements)
DECLARE ARY3[3]	(Redimension array)
SET COMPATIBLE ON	(Set for dBASE IV compatible)
DECLARE ARY2[3]	
ARY2 = "Bat"	(Replace array with memvar)
DISPLAY MEMORY LIKE ARY*	ARY1 Pub A (1) C "Cat" (2) C "Cat" (3) C "Cat" ARY2 Pub C "Bat" ARY3 Pub A (1) C "Dog" (2) C "Dog" (3) L .F.
DECLARE ARY1[5]	(Redimension array in DB4 mode)

```
DISPLAY MEMORY LIKE ARY1          ARY1      Pub A
                                            (  1)   L  .F.
                                            (  2)   L  .F.
                                            (  3)   L  .F.
                                            (  4)   L  .F.
                                            (  5)   L  .F.
```

In the preceding example, the dBASE IV program actually releases the `ARY1` array and declares a new array with the same name and a different position. *Array redimension* is a new feature in FoxPro with Version 2.5. If you have an existing FoxPro 1.2 program that relies on arrays maintaining their original dimension, you might need to modify your program.

The `SET COMPATIBLE DB4` command changes the behavior of certain FoxPro commands and functions to correspond with the way they behave in dBASE IV. When you convert a dBASE IV program to run under Visual FoxPro, even though you definitely will want to change the interface, you can get the dBASE IV application up and running quickly and easily if you add the `SET COMPATIBLE DB4` command to the beginning of your program.

When you are operating in the Catalog Manager mode, `SET COMPATIBLE DB4` is the default. Table 10.18 lists commands affected by the `SET COMPATIBLE` command.

Table 10.18. The commands and functions affected by `SET COMPATIBLE`.

```
@...GET with a RANGE clause
@...SAY with CHR(7)
@...SAY scrolling
@...SAY when STATUS is ON
@...SAY...PICTURE
ACTIVATE SCREEN
ACTIVATE WINDOW
APPEND MEMO
DECLARE
DIMENSION
GO ¦ GOTO with SET TALK ON
FSIZE()
INKEY()
LASTKEY()
LIKE()
```

continues

Table 10.18. continued

`MENU and POPUP commands`
`PLAY MACRO`
`READ with an @...GET VALID clause`
`READ with a numeric PICTURE clause`
`READ (Nested READs)`
`RUN ¦ !`
`SET COLOR TO`
`SET("BORDER")`
`SET DEFAULT TO`
`SET FIELDS`
`SET MESSAGE`
`SET PRINT TO <file>`
`STORE`
`SUM`
`TRANSFORM( ) with a numeric PICTURE clause`
`SELECT( )`
`SYS(2001, "COLOR")`

Other commands affected by the `SET COMPATIBLE` command are described in the *Visual FoxPro User's Guide.*

The *SET CONSOLE* Command

The `SET CONSOLE` command suppresses all displays to the screen except output generated by the `@` command, menus, prompt boxes, and error messages. Here is the syntax:

```
SET CONSOLE ON ¦ off
```

`SET CONSOLE` can't be used in the Command window and isn't provided in the full-screen `SET` command. It can be used only in a program.

Here is the equivalent CONFIG.FPW file command:

```
CONSOLE = on ¦ OFF
```

The *SET CPCOMPILE* Command

The `SET CPCOMPILE` command sets the code page for compiled programs. The syntax is this:

```
SET CPCOMPILE TO [<expN>]
```

The equivalent CONFIG.FPW file command is this:

```
CPCOMPILE = <code page number>
```

The argument `<expN>` is the code page number for the code page that is used while compiling source code. If you omit `<expN>`, the code page reverts to the current code page.

The *SET CPDIALOG* Command

The `SET CPDIALOG` command designates whether the Code Page dialog box displays when a table is opened within a program.

```
SET CPDIALOG ON ¦ OFF
```

Here is the equivalent CONFIG.FPW file command:

```
CPDIALOG = ON ¦ off
```

If `SET CPDIALOG` is `OFF`, the display of the Code Page dialog box is always suppressed. If `SET CPDIALOG` is `ON`, the Code Page dialog box displays when a table is opened from within a program and the following conditions are true:

- The table is opened exclusively.
- The table is not marked with a code page.
- `CODEPAGE = AUTO` is included in your Visual FoxPro configuration file.

The Code Page dialog box always displays if the above conditions are true, regardless of the `SET CPDIALOG` setting, if you open a table interactively from within the Command window or from the File menu.

The *SET CURRENCY* Command

The `SET CURRENCY` command controls where the currency symbol is displayed when using the dollar picture function. By default, the currency symbol is displayed on the left side of the number.

You can also use `SET CURRENCY` to change the currency symbol, which can be up to nine characters. If you omit the symbol, the default value is used. For the U.S. version of Visual FoxPro, a dollar sign is the default. Here is the syntax:

```
SET CURRENCY LEFT ¦ right
SET CURRENCY TO [<expC>]
```

Here is the equivalent CONFIG.FPW file command:

```
CURRENCY = LEFT ¦ RIGHT
CURRENCY = <string>
```

The following are examples:

```
SET CURRENCY RIGHT
SET CURRENCY TO "DM"
?  amount  PICTURE  "@$ 999,999.99"
@ 5,5 SAY  amount  PICTURE  "@$ 999,999.99"
SET CURRENCY LEFT
@ 5,5 SAY  amount  PICTURE  "pi"@$ 999,999.99"
```

Here is the displayed value for the first two output statements:

```
12,345.67 DM
```

Here is the displayed value for the third output statement:

```
DM12,345,67
```

The `SET CURRENCY` command is often used with the `SET PERIOD TO` and `SET SEPARATOR TO` commands.

The *SET CURSOR* Command

The `SET CURSOR` command is used to control the display of the cursor. Normally, the cursor appears as a blinking underline character. Here is the syntax:

```
SET CURSOR ON ¦ off
```

Here is the equivalent CONFIG.FPW file command syntax:

```
CURSOR = ON ¦ off
```

If you specify `SET CURSOR OFF`, the cursor is turned off during a pending `GET` command, an `INKEY()` function call, and the execution of a `WAIT` command.

The *SET DATABASE* Command

The `SET DATABASE` command specifies the name of the database to be made the current database. A *database*, sometimes called a *database container*, is a special type of table with a .DBC extension. It contains all of the information about a database including the names of tables, table fields, procedural files, and objects associated with a database. Many database containers can be open at the same time, but only one can be the current database. You open a database container with the `OPEN DATABASE` command. Commands and functions, such as `ADD TABLE`, `DBC()`, `DBSETPROP()`, and `DELETE TABLE`, that manipulate databases, operate on the current database. Here is the syntax:

```
SET DATABASE TO [<expFN>]
```

Here is the equivalent CONFIG.FPW file command syntax:

```
DATABASE = <Filename>
```

`<expFN>` specifies the name of the database. If you omit `<expFN>`, no database is made the current database.

The *SET DATASESSION* Command

In older versions of FoxPro and other Xbase systems, the term *session* represents the time between when FoxPro first executes and when FoxPro exits (`QUIT`) and returns control to the operating system. In Visual FoxPro, a session means something entirely different. A *session* in FoxPro is the data environment description for a form or a formset. This data environment describes work areas, cursors (tables), indexes, and relations. Visual FoxPro automatically creates a distinct session for each instance of a form or formset. Then multiple instances of a form in a project can access separately the same data environments. Visual FoxPro can create a separate session each time an instance of a form or formset is loaded. You can force Visual FoxPro to use the default session, session 1, by executing the `SET SESSION TO 1` command. Here is the syntax:

```
SET SESSION TO [<expN>]
```

`<expN>` specifies the session to activate. If `<expN>` is omitted, session 1 is activated.

Session 1 is the Visual FoxPro global session and is activated when Visual FoxPro executes.

One of the properties of a form is `MultiSession`. You use the `MultiSession` property to designate whether a form possesses its own unique session when created. If you set `MultiSession` to true (`.T.`), the form has its own session. If you set `MultiSession` to false (`.F.`), a session is not created for the form. You can fetch the session number for a form by examining the value of its read-only `SessionId` property. If a form's session is not the default session, the session is released when the form closes.

There is a group of `SET` commands that are associated with a data session. Each data session can have its own values for this group of `SET` command. The following `SET` commands scope to the current data session:

```
SET ANSI
SET AUTOSAVE
SET BLOCKSIZE
SET CARRY
SET CENTURY
SET COLLATE
SET CONFIRM
SET CURRENCY
SET DATABASE
SET DATE
SET DECIMALS
SET DELETED
SET DELIMITERS
SET EXACT
SET EXCLUSIVE
SET FIELDS
SET FIXED
SET LOCK
SET MARK TO
SET MEMOWIDTH
SET MULTILOCKS
SET NEAR
```

```
SET NULL
SET PATH
SET POINT
SET REFRESH
SET REPROCESS
SET SAFETY
SET SEPARATOR
SET SYSFORMATS
SET TALK
SET UNIQUE
```

The *SET DATE* Command

The `SET DATE` command is used to change the date display form. Here is the syntax:

```
SET DATE [TO] AMERICAN ¦ ansi ¦ British ¦ French
¦ German ¦ Italian ¦ Japan ¦ USA ¦ mdy ¦ dmy ¦ ymd
```

Here is the equivalent CONFIG.FPW file command:

```
DATE = AMERICAN ¦ ansi ¦ British ¦ French ¦ German
¦ Italian ¦ Japan ¦ USA ¦ mdy ¦ dmy ¦ ymd
```

The date display forms and corresponding keywords are presented in Table 10.19. In the table, *yy* denotes the year, *mm* denotes the month, and *dd* denotes the day of the month.

Table 10.19. Date display forms.

Keyword	*Form*
AMERICAN	*mm/ dd/ yy*
ANSI	*yy.mm.dd*
BRITISH	*dd/ mm/ yy*
FRENCH	*dd/ mm/ yy*
GERMAN	*dd.mm.yy*
ITALIAN	*dd-mm-yy*
JAPAN	*yy/ mm/ dd*
USA	*mm-dd-yy*
MDY	*mm/ dd/ yy*
DMY	*dd/ mm/ yy*
YMD	*yy/ mm/ dd*

The *SET DEBUG* Command

The `SET DEBUG` command controls menu access to the Debug and Trace windows. Here is the syntax:

```
SET DEBUG ON ¦ off
```

Here is the equivalent CONFIG.FPW file command:

```
DEBUG = ON ¦ off
```

If `SET DEBUG` is `ON`, you can open the Debug or Trace windows by choosing the **D**ebug or **T**race options in the **P**rogram menu. If `SET DEBUG` is `OFF`, you can't access either option. However, if `SET DEBUG` is `OFF`, you can access the Trace window by executing either the `SET STEP ON` or `ACTIVATE WINDOW TRACE` commands and the Debug window with either the `SET ECHO ON` or `ACTIVATE WINDOW DEBUG` commands. More information regarding debugging is provided in Chapter 23, "Building Visual FoxPro Applications."

The *SET DECIMALS TO* Command

The `SET DECIMALS TO` command specifies the number of decimal places displayed to the right of the decimal point. The maximum number of decimal places is 18, and the default is 2. The number of decimal places for the result of a Numeric expression is usually determined by the `SET DECIMALS TO` command. Here are the only exceptions:

- No decimal places are displayed for integer numbers.
- If the expression contains only a database field, the number of decimal places is determined by the field structure.

Here is the syntax:

```
SET DECIMALS TO <expN>
```

Here is the equivalent CONFIG.FPW file command:

```
DECIMALS = <integer constant>
```

The *SET DEFAULT TO* Command

The `SET DEFAULT TO` command is used to define either the current disk drive, current directory, or both. Here is the syntax:

```
SET DEFAULT TO [<expC>]
```

Here is the equivalent CONFIG.FPW file command:

```
DEFAULT = [<expC>]
```

The `SET DEFAULT TO` command changes the current drive or the current drive and directory. If you don't specify a drive and directory with a filename after you execute this command, the newly selected drive and directory are used. A `SET DEFAULT TO` command with a directory specified is equivalent to logging on another drive in MS-DOS and doing an MS-DOS change directory command:

```
SET DEFAULT TO D:\FOXPRO\ACCOUNTS
SET DEFAULT TO C:..\ORDERS
SET DEFAULT TO \INVOICE\APRIL
SET DEFAULT TO E:
```

In dBASE IV, you can change only the default drive with the `SET DEFAULT TO` command. However, you can use the dBASE IV `SET DIRECTORY TO` command to change the current directory.

The *SET DELETED* Command

The `SET DELETED` command controls access to deleted records. A record can be marked as deleted by using the `DELETE` command or by using Ctrl+T in the full-screen `BROWSE`, `EDIT`, `INSERT`, and `APPEND` commands. The record remains in the database table (DBF file)until the file is packed. If `SET DELETED` is `OFF`, all deleted records can be accessed. If `SET DELETED` is `ON`, deleted records are ignored. Here is the syntax:

```
SET DELETED on ¦ OFF
```

Here is the equivalent CONFIG.FPW file command:

```
DELETED = on ¦ OFF
```

When `SET DELETED` is `ON` the following things occur:

- `LIST` and `DISPLAY` ignore deleted records unless you specify a scope clause.
- `GOTO` *<record #>* still moves to a specified record, even though that record is deleted.
- `RECALL` doesn't recall any records.
- `INDEX` and `REINDEX` process all records.
- `FIND`, `SEEK`, and `SEEK()` don't find deleted records.
- Commands such as `COPY`, `SORT`, `EDIT`, `BROWSE`, and `LOCATE` ignore deleted records.
- Deleted records in child relations are ignored. In dBASE III, deleted records in child relations are processed.

The *SET DELIMITERS* Command

The `SET DELIMITERS` command is used to turn `ON` and `OFF` characters that enclose input fields (`@...GET` fields) during full-screen `APPEND`, `CHANGE`, `EDIT`, `INSERT`, and `READ` commands. It is also used to change the delimiter characters.

If the `SET DELIMITERS` command is `ON`, subsequent input fields are enclosed by colons. A colon is the default delimiter. If the `SET DELIMITERS` command is `OFF`, which is the default, no delimiters are displayed. Arguments to change delimiters can consist of one or two characters. If you specify two characters, the first character becomes the left delimiter and the second character becomes the right delimiter. For example, the command statement

```
SET DELIMITERS ON
```

```
SET DELIMITERS TO "<>"
```

causes GET fields to appear with the field enclosed with the <> delimiters. If you specify the DEFAULT keyword, a colon is used as the delimiter. Here is the syntax:

```
SET DELIMITERS on ¦ OFF
SET DELIMITERS TO <expC> ¦ DEFAULT
```

Here is the equivalent CONFIG.FPW file command:

```
DELIMITERS = on ¦ OFF
DELIMITERS = <one or two characters>
```

The SET DELIMITERS command is a carryover from dBASE II days when not all terminals had reverse video mode.

The *SET DEVELOPMENT* Command

When SET DEVELOPMENT is ON (the default), the creation dates of the program file and the object file are compared. If the object file is older, it is deleted, and the newly modified program is recompiled. This eliminates the frustration that results from the unintentional execution of an out-of-date object file. It takes extra time to open the source file, however, because the DOS directory is read when a file is opened. After the applications developer has completed a system, DEVELOPMENT can be set to OFF so that the dates aren't checked and the application runs a little faster.

Here is the syntax:

```
SET DEVELOPMENT ON ¦ off
```

Here is the equivalent CONFIG.FPW file command:

```
DEVELOPMENT = ON ¦ off
```

Regardless of the status of the SET DEVELOPMENT command, a program is recompiled if you modify it with the MODIFY command. However, if you use your own external editor, the program isn't recompiled. You must either use SET DEVELOPMENT ON or execute the CLEAR PROGRAM command to force the program to recompile.

In the Visual FoxPro **P**rogram menu, the **C**ancel option can be used to cancel program execution during a READ. This menu is enabled when SET DEVELOPMENT is ON and disabled when SET DEVELOPMENT is OFF. This feature eliminates the problem encountered in FoxPro 2.0 of being hung up in a READ command with the system menu turned off.

The *SET DEVICE TO* Command

The SET DEVICE TO command controls the destination of the @ command's SAY output. It can be directed to the screen (the default), the printer, or a file. If you omit the filename extension, .TXT is used:

```
SET DEVICE TO SCREEN ¦ printer ¦ file <expFN>
```

The *SET DIRECTORY* Command

Here is the syntax for the SET DIRECTORY command:

```
SET DIRECTORY TO <expC>
```

You can use the SET DIRECTORY command to set the operating system directory. The system path (<expC>) can be a drive name followed by a colon, a directory name, or both. Do not terminate <expC> with a slash.

This function operates exactly the same way as SET DEFAULT TO in FoxPro. When Ashton-Tate first designed dBASE IV, it extended the SET DEFAULT TO command to include a directory. Unfortunately, this ran into some obscure code-breaking, backward-compatibility problems, and a new SET function had to be added: SET DIRECTORY. This command was added to FoxPro to support compatibility with dBASE IV.

The *SET DISPLAY TO* Command

The SET DISPLAY TO command specifies the display mode supported by various display adapters. This command was important for MS-DOS versions of FoxPro because there were so many types of display devices. However, in Windows, the display device is controlled by the operating environment. Visual FoxPro establishes different sizes of fonts and numbers of lines to simulate the various display adapters modes. The syntax is

```
SET DISPLAY TO CGA ¦ EGA25 ¦ EGA43 ¦ VGA25 ¦ VGA50
```

Here is the equivalent CONFIG.FPW file command:

```
DISPLAY = CGA ¦ EGA25 ¦ EGA43 ¦ VGA25 ¦ VGA50
```

The following list describes the font size used to simulate different display modes:

Display Mode	*Font Size*	*Number of Lines*
CGA	9-point	25
EGA25	9-point	25
EGA43	7-point	50
VGA25	9-point	25
VGA50	7-point	50

The *SET DOHISTORY* Command

The SET DOHISTORY command displays commands from an executing program to be placed in the Command window or a file. Here is the syntax:

```
SET DOHISTORY on ¦ OFF ¦ TO <expFN> [ADDITIVE]
```

Here is the equivalent CONFIG.FPW file command:

```
DOHISTORY = on ¦ OFF
```

If SET DOHISTORY is ON, commands from executing programs are placed in the Command window. You can edit and execute any of these commands as you do any other command.

The SET DOHISTORY command is another legacy left by dBASE III. It remained in FoxPro even though it was used rarely because FoxPro already had a marvelous full-screen debugger (Trace window). Visual FoxPro breathed new life into this command with the addition of the TO clause. You can redirect the stream of commands from an executing program to a text file with the TO <*expFN*> clause. If you do not specify the file extension, .TXT will be used. Visual FoxPro automatically creates the file if the specified file (<*expFN*>) does not exist. If the file exists, you omit the ADDITIVE keyword, and if SET SAFETY is ON, a dialog box appears delegating to you the responsibility for determining the fate of the existing file. If the ADDITIVE keyword is specified, the output is appended to the file if it exists.

CAUTION

The SET DOHISTORY command slows down your program. Furthermore, if you forget that the history is being written to a file while you are running a complex program, you might create a rather large history file.

The *SET ECHO* Command

The SET ECHO command opens the Trace window for debugging. Here is the syntax:

```
SET ECHO on ¦ OFF
```

Here is the equivalent CONFIG.FPW file command:

```
ECHO = on ¦ OFF
```

If you execute the SET ECHO ON command, the Trace window displays. You can debug a program using the Trace window as described in Chapter 23. You can't close the window by executing SET ECHO OFF. You can close the Trace window by clicking its close box or executing the DEACTIVATE WINDOW TRACE command. When the Trace window closes, SET ECHO is automatically set to OFF.

NOTE

SET STEP ON and SET ECHO ON perform essentially the same operation. If you are a newcomer to the Xbase language, you might wonder why two commands do the same thing. In dBASE II, dBASE III, and FoxBASE+, when SET ECHO is ON, each program command line displays on-screen as it executes. After a command line in a program executes when SET STEP is ON, execution pauses, and you are given the options of executing another line of code, terminating the program, or suspending execution. With the Visual FoxPro full-screen debugging system, the functionality of both the SET ECHO and SET STEP commands is incorporated into the Trace window operations. Either of the commands could have been eliminated. However, the decision was made to retain both commands for backward compatibility.

The *SET ESCAPE* Command

The SET ESCAPE command controls the function of the Esc key. If SET ESCAPE is ON and you press Esc, program execution is interrupted and the ***INTERRUPTED*** message displays. Here is the syntax:

```
SET ESCAPE ON ¦ off
```

Here is the equivalent CONFIG.FPW file command:

```
ESCAPE = ON ¦ off
```

In addition, if SET ESCAPE is ON, you can use Ctrl+S to stop and start screen scrolling. If ESCAPE is OFF, the functions of the Esc and Ctrl+S keys and the ON ESCAPE command are disabled.

The *SET EXACT* Command

The SET EXACT command controls string comparison evaluations. If SET EXACT is OFF, two strings are compared; if the string on the left of the expression is shorter than the string on the right but all characters match, the comparison results in a logical true value (that is, the strings match). If SET EXACT is ON, the content and length of the strings must match before the comparison is true. For example, the result of the evaluation of the condition "Friday" = "Friday morning" is .T. if SET EXACT is OFF, and .F. if SET EXACT is ON. The INDEX and REINDEX commands and index updating always use exact comparisons. The FIND and SEEK commands and the SEEK() function honor the SET EXACT setting. Here is the syntax:

```
SET EXACT on ¦ OFF
```

Here is the equivalent CONFIG.FPW file command:

```
EXACT = on ¦ OFF
```

The *SET EXCLUSIVE* Command

The SET EXCLUSIVE command controls the method of opening database tables (DBF files) when running in a multiuser environment. If SET EXCLUSIVE is ON, all files accessed in a multiuser environment are opened in exclusive mode. This means that after a database table is opened by the user, no other user can access the file. If SET EXCLUSIVE is OFF, database tables are opened in a shared mode and can be accessed simultaneously by many users. The CREATE, MODIFY, COPY, EXPORT, IMPORT, JOIN, TOTAL, and SAVE commands always open the target files in exclusive mode. More information is provided in Chapter 25, "Multiuser Considerations." Here is the syntax:

```
SET EXCLUSIVE on ¦ OFF
```

Here is the equivalent CONFIG.FPW file command:

```
EXCLUSIVE = on ¦ OFF
```

The *SET FDOW* Command

The SET FDOW command establishes the number returned by the DOW() function. By default, DOW() returns 1 for Sunday, 2 for Monday, and so forth. With this command you can specify a number to represent which day is considered the first day of the week by the DOW() function. Here is the syntax:

```
SET FDOW TO <expN>
```

The equivalent CONFIG.FPW file command is

```
FDOW = <number>
```

where <expN> evaluates to an integer between 1 and 7 that represents a day of the week. 1 is Sunday, 2 is Monday, and so on. In the following example, assume that today is Wednesday:

```
 SET FDOW TO 1                 && Sunday is first day of week
? DOW(DATE())                  && Returns 4 since Wed. is fourth
                               && day of week if Sunday is first.
SET FDOW TO 2                  && Monday is first day of week
? DOW(DATE())                  && Returns 3
```

Any value you set FDOW to in the CONFIG.FPW file (for example, FDOW = 1) overrides the setting in the registry. It does not change the registry.

The *SET FWEEK* Command

The SET FWEEK command establishes the rule used to determine whether a day of the week is in the first week of a year. It affects the value returned by the WEEK() function. Here is the syntax:

```
SET FWEEK TO [<expN>]
```

The equivalent CONFIG.FPW file command is

```
FWEEK = <number>
```

where <expN> indicates which rule is used to determine the requirement for a week to be the first week of the year. <expN> can have the following values:

<expN>	*First week requirement*
1	The first week contains the first of January. (This is the default.)
2	Four days of the first week must be in the current year.
3	The first week has seven days in the current year.
Omitted	Same as 1.

The *SET FIELDS* Command

The SET FIELDS command establishes a Logical view. Here is the syntax:

```
SET FIELDS on ¦ OFF [PROMPT ¦ noprompt] [GLOBAL ¦ LOCAL]

SET FIELDS TO [<field name1> [,<field name2> [,…]]]

SET FIELDS TO ALL [LIKE <skeleton>] [EXCEPT <skeleton>]
```

If you specify the TO clause with no arguments, the command deletes any existing SET FIELDS TO list, and the field list reverts to all the fields in the current work area. The SET FIELDS TO command is additive. That is, any fields specified using the SET FIELDS TO command are added to the existing SET FIELDS TO list.

In FoxPro, as well as in dBASE III+, the SET FIELDS command limits you to fields in the current work area. Furthermore, the command will not let you specify the order of a field list. You can also establish a field list in each active work area. You can even have a field list consisting of fields from different work areas. Here is an example:

```
USE CENSUS
SET FIELDS TO STATE,POPULATION
DISPLAY
```

Here is the output from the last command:

```
Record# STATE       POPULATION
1 California       29321
```

However, in dBASE IV, the SET FIELD command was extended so that you can specify fields in other work areas and can designate field order. In dBASE IV, you can specify a new type of field called a *calculated field*.

FoxPro 2.6 for Windows and later versions support both styles of SET FIELDS if you issue one of the following two commands:

```
SET COMPATIBLE DB4
SET FIELDS ON GLOBAL
```

By default, if you issue

```
SET FIELDS ON LOCAL
```

and SET COMPATIBLE is set to FOXPLUS, FoxPro 2.6 and later versions support the dBASE III PLUS style of SET FIELDS.

The SET FIELDS TO command is additive. Each time you execute a SET FIELDS TO command with a field list, the specified fields are added to those currently in the field list. If you specify no fields with the SET FIELDS TO command, the field list is cleared.

Table 10.20 describes the clauses and keywords for the SET FIELDS command.

Table 10.20. A description of the clauses and keywords for the SET FIELDS command.

Clause	*Description*
ON	When the SET FIELDS option is set to ON, you can access only the fields specified in the field list.
OFF	When the SET FIELDS option is set to OFF, all the fields in the current database table are accessible. SET FIELDS OFF is the default setting.
LOCAL	You can access only the fields in the current work area listed in the fields list (dBASE III+ style).
GLOBAL	You can access all fields in the field list, including fields in other work areas. With the SET FIELDS GLOBAL command, you can access fields in other work areas without issuing the SET COMPATIBLE TO DB4 command (dBASE IV style).
TO <*field1*>, <field2>,...	The following are the TO clause elements: Names of the fields to be accessed. You can specify fields from database tables open in other work areas if the fields are prefaced with their alias names. However, these fields cannot be accessed until you execute either the SET FIELDS GLOBAL or SET COMPATIBLE DB4 commands. Note that if two or more fields in the field list have the same name, the alias names must be used when referencing them.
ALL	All fields in the current work area are added to the field list.
LIKE <*skeleton*>	Fields that match the wildcard skeleton specification are included in the field list.
EXCEPT <*skeleton*>	Fields that match the wildcard skeleton specification are excluded from the list.

You can add statements for creating calculated fields to the field list. A calculated field contains read-only data created with an expression. This expression can take any form, but it must be a valid FoxPro expression. Here is the format of the statement you use to create a calculated field:

```
<calculated field name> = <exp>
```

You can reference the `<calculated field name>` as you would any other field in the field list. For example, you can add the calculated field named `Cost` to the field list with the following statement:

```
SET FIELDS TO Cost = UnitPrice * Quantity
```

Here are other examples:

```
FullName =  ALLTRIM(FirstName)+" "+ALLTRIM(MidName)+;
ALLTRIM(LastName)
DueDate  =  OrdDate + 30
```

The example presented in Listing 10.3 illustrates how to use the `SET FIELD TO` command to form a field list. In this example, three tables are placed in use: `TRANSACT.DBF`, `CLIENTS.DBF`, and `ITEM.DBF`. `TRANSACT.DBF` is related to `CLIENTS.DBF` on the field `Client_id` and `ITEM.DBF` on the field `Inv_no`. The field list consists of fields from all three tables and a calculated field. Listing 10.4 presents sample output that results from executing the program INVEN.PRG. Notice that the fields included in the field list are marked with a right angle bracket (>) character in the `DISPLAY STRUCTURE` output.

Listing 10.3. The INVEN.PRG program source listing.

```
************************************************
* PROGRAM: INVEN.PRG - Demonstrates SET FIELDS
SET COMPATIBLE DB4
SET TALK OFF
CLEAR ALL
SET ALTER TO Z
SET ALTER ON
USE transact IN 1
USE clients  IN 2 ORDER Client_id
USE item     IN 3 Order Inv_no
SET RELATION TO Client_id INTO Clients, ;
Inv_no    INTO Item
SET FIELDS TO Inv_no, Quantity, ;
Clients.Name, item.Descrip,;
Amount = Quantity * item.Unit_Price
DISPLAY STRUCTURE IN 1
DISPLAY STRUCTURE IN 2
DISPLAY STRUCTURE IN 3
LIST OFF
```

Listing 10.4. Sample output that results from executing INVEN.PRG.

```
Structure for table:          c:\VFP\transact.dbf
Number of data records:       44
```

```
Date of last update:          11/20/92
Code Page:                    0
Field   Field Name  Type        Width   Dec   Index  Collate
1   TRANS_DATE  Date            8
2   AMT         Numeric         8       2
3   CLIENT_ID   Character       5             Asc   Machine
4  >INV_NO      Character       5
5  >QUANTITY    Numeric         6
** Total **                         33


Structure for table:          c:\VFP\clients.dbf
Number of data records:       3
Date of last update:          11/17/92
Code Page:                    0
Field   Field Name   Type       Width   Dec   Index  Collate
1   CLIENT_ID    Character      5             Asc     Machine
2  >NAME         Character     20
3   ADDRESS      Character     30
4   CITY         Character     15
5   STATE        Character      2
6   ZIP          Character      5
7   AREACODE     Character      3
8   PHONE        Character      8
9   EXTENSION    Character      5
10   STARTBAL     Numeric        8     2
11   BALDATE      Date           8
** Total **                       110

Structure for table:       c:\VFP\item.dbf
Number of data records:      20
Date of last update:         11/17/92
Code Page:                   0
Field   Field Name   Type        Width   Dec   Index  Collate
1   UNIT_PRICE   Numeric         8      2
2  >DESCRIP      Character      30
3   INV_NO       Character       6            Asc     Machine
** Total **                          45


INV_NO QUANTITY NAME         DESCRIP                   AMOUNT
114           7 John Albert  8" Radial Arm Saw         923.30
119           3 Joe Hubbarz  30" Bathroom Sink #31     400.68
115           6 Joe Hubbarz  32" Bathroom Sink Jet      14.10
121           5 Pete Wilsoz  1" Roofing Nails  1 Lb 768.75
116          34 Herb Amzirm  8' - 1"x12" Pine Board     75.48
```

No CONFIG.FPW file command corresponds to `SET FIELDS`. However, you can use `VIEW =` to establish a field list.

The *SET FILTER* Command

The `SET FILTER` command defines a condition used to select records for processing in the currently active file. Each work area can have a separate `SET FILTER` command. This command is described in Chapter 11. Here is the syntax:

```
SET FILTER TO [<expL>]
```

The <expL> argument specifies the filter condition. If you specify the TO clause without <expL>, the filter is disabled. There is no equivalent CONFIG.FPW file command.

The *SET FIXED* Command

The SET FIXED command affects the number of displayed decimal digits. Here is the syntax:

```
SET FIXED ON ¦ off
```

If SET FIXED is OFF, the number of digits displayed depends on the constants, variables, functions, and operators in an expression. If SET FIXED is ON, the number of decimal places displayed depends on the SET DECIMAL setting. SET FIXED is scoped to the current data session. In other words, each data session can have its own SET FIXED setting. Here are some examples:

Command Window	*Comments and Results*
SET FIXED OFF	(This is the default)
? 3.12*4.23	13.1987
SET FIXED ON	(Use SET DECIMAL setting)
SET DECIMAL TO 2	(This is the default)
? 3.12*4.23	13.20

The *SET FORMAT* Command

SET FORMAT is described in Chapter 9, "Full-Screen Data Editing." Here is the syntax:

```
SET FORMAT TO [<expFN> ¦ ?]
```

The *SET FULLPATH* Command

The SET FULLPATH command controls the composition of the filename returned by certain Visual FoxPro functions. If SET FULLPATH is ON, the DBF(), CDX(), and IDX() functions return a file specification that includes the drive and complete path of the file. If SET FULLPATH is OFF, the functions return only the drive and filename. Here is the syntax:

```
SET FULLPATH on ¦ OFF
```

Here is the equivalent CONFIG.FPW file command:

```
FULLPATH = on ¦ OFF
```

Here are some examples:

Command Window	*Comments and Results*
`USE MYDBF`	(Places table in use)
`SET FULLPATH ON`	(This is the default value)
`? DBF()`	`C:\FOX\MYDBF.DBF`
`SET FULLPATH OFF`	
`? DBF()`	`C:MYDBF.DBF`

The *SET FUNCTION* Command

The `SET FUNCTION` command programs function keys with a specified character string. The string can be up to 238 bytes. When a programmed function key is pressed, the character string contents are directed to the input as if they had been typed. A semicolon inserted into the character stream is treated as a carriage return. For example, you can use the following statement to program the F6 key to execute the `USE`, `COPY`, and `LIST` commands:

```
SET FUNCTION F6 TO "USE MYFILE;COPY TO NEWFILE;LIST;"
```

In Visual FoxPro, programmed function keys can't be used with `EDIT` and `BROWSE` because the function keys are used for extended `EDIT` and `BROWSE` options that conform to the full-screen command interface standard. However, the function keys work with the `READ` command and within the Command window. The function keys are preprogrammed with the values shown in Table 10.21. Here is the syntax:

```
SET FUNCTION <expN> ¦ <expC> ¦ <key label> TO <expC>

<expC> results in a <key label>
<expN> results in a value from 1 to 10

<key label>::=
F2 ¦ F3 ¦ F4 ¦ F5 ¦ F6 ¦ F7 ¦ F8 ¦ F9 ¦ F10 ¦
SHIFT-F1 ¦ SHIFT-F2 ¦ SHIFT-F3 ¦ SHIFT-F4 ¦
SHIFT-F5 ¦ SHIFT-F6 ¦ SHIFT-F7 ¦ SHIFT-F8 ¦
SHIFT-F9 ¦ CTRL-F1  ¦ CTRL-F2  ¦ CTRL-F3  ¦
CTRL-F4  ¦ CTRL-F5  ¦ CTRL-F6  ¦ CTRL-F7  ¦
CTRL-F8  ¦ CTRL-F9  ¦ CTRL-F10
```

Here is the equivalent CONFIG.FPW file command syntax:

```
FUNCTION <key number> =  <string>

<key label> ::= <string>
<key number> ::= 1 ¦ 2 ¦ 3 ¦ 4 ¦ 5 ¦ 6 ¦ 7 ¦ 8 ¦ 9 ¦ 10
```

Table 10.21. Function key values.

Function Key	*Value*
F1	`HELP`
F2	`SET;`
F3	`LIST;`
F4	`DIR;`
F5	`DISPLAY STRUCTURE;`
F6	`DISPLAY STATUS;`
F7	`DISPLAY MEMORY;`
F8	`DISPLAY;`
F9	`APPEND;`
F10	System menu bar

The *SET HEADING* Command

The `SET HEADING` command controls the display of column headings for the `AVERAGE`, `CALCULATE`, `DISPLAY`, `LIST`, and `SUM` commands. If `SET HEADING` is `ON`, headings are displayed. Because column width is determined by the width of the heading or the field display (whichever is larger), the width of the display line is also affected by `SET HEADING`. Here is the syntax:

```
SET HEADING ON ¦ off
```

Here is the equivalent CONFIG.FPW file command:

```
HEADING = ON ¦ off
```

The *SET HELP* Command

The `SET HELP` command controls the availability of the help facility or specifies a different help file. Here is the syntax:

```
SET HELP ON ¦ off
SET HELP TO [<expFN>]
```

Here is the equivalent CONFIG.FPW file command:

```
HELP = ON ¦ off
```

The `SET HELP ON` command enables the FoxPro help facility, and the `SET HELP OFF` command disables it. You can change the name of the help file using the `SET HELP TO` command. You can restore the FoxPro help facility by specifying the `SET HELP TO` command without specifying the filename. The FoxPro help database table (DBF file) is named FOXHELP.DBF, and FoxPro looks for it in the FoxPro base directory.

Visual FoxPro offers two help systems. Those who use Windows applications and are accustomed to the way the Windows help system operates can use the Windows-style help for Visual FoxPro. Those who prefer the FoxPro DBF-style help system can use that option. When you install Visual FoxPro, you have the option of installing either the Windows-style FOXPRO.HLP file, the FoxPro DBF-style FOXPRO.DBF and FOXPRO.FPT files, or both. You must install the proper file before you can use it. If files for both options are loaded, you can switch between them with one of the following forms of the `SET HELP TO` command:

```
SET HELP TO FOXPRO.DBF    && Use FoxPro DBF-style help
SET HELP TO FOXPRO.HLP    && Use Windows-style help
```

You can also specify the default startup help file by placing one of the two commands in the CONFIG.FPW configuration file:

```
HELP = FOXPRO.DBF    && FoxPro DBF-style help
HELP = FOXPRO.HLP    && Windows-style help
```

You can also create your own help facility. The CD-ROM shipped with this book contains a Windows-type help authoring tool that you can use to create Windows-style help. If you want to create a DBF-style help file, the technique is described in the following paragraphs.

All you need to do is create a file with at least two fields: The first must be a character field that contains the topic, and the second must be a memo field that contains the contents of the Help window. Your help database table must have fewer than 32776 records.

To learn how the help file works, take a look at the FoxPro FOXHELP.DBF help file:

```
SET HELP OFF
USE FOXHELP
LIST NEXT 20
```

Listing 10.5 shows the output from the `LIST` statement, which is a listing of the first 20 records.

Listing 10.5. The first 20 records of the FOXHELP.DBF help file.

```
Record#  TOPIC                                  DETAILS       CLASS
      1  Commands, Functions, and Operators     Memo
      2  ACLASS() Function                      Memo
      3  ADATABASE() Function                   Memo
      4  ADD CLASS Command                      Memo
      5  ADD TABLE Command                      Memo
      6  AERROR() Function                      Memo
      7  ALTER TABLE Command                    Memo
      8  AMEMBERS() Function                    Memo
      9  APRINTERS() Function                   Memo
     10  ASELOBJ() Function                     Memo
     11  ATABLES() Function                     Memo
     12  AUSED() Function                       Memo
     13  BEGIN TRANSACTION Command              Memo
     14  _BUILDER System Memory Variable        Memo
     15  CANDIDATE() Function                   Memo
     16  CLEAR EVENTS Command                   Memo
     17  CLOSE TABLES Command                   Memo
```

continues

Listing 10.5. continued

```
   18  COMPILE DATABASE Command                        Memo
   19  COMPILE FORM Command                            Memo
   20  COMPOBJ() Function                              Memo
```

FOXHELP.DBF contains three fields. The first, named TOPIC, contains the help topics for the FoxPro help facility and is used in the help index. The second, named DETAILS, is a memo field that contains the text displayed in the help window for a selected topic. The FoxPro help facility contains a third field, CLASS, which is used to categorize help topics. The CLASS field contains two-letter codes, which you can use to group different fields. For example, the code wn means What's New in FoxPro. You can use the

```
SET HELPFILTER TO "wn" $ CLASS
```

command to show only those topics in the index that describe some new feature in FoxPro.

The *SET HELPFILTER* Command

The SET HELPFILTER command controls which help file records are available in the help facility. Here is the syntax:

```
SET HELPFILTER [AUTOMATIC] TO [<expL>]
```

The TO *<expL>* clause specifies a Logical expression used to select a subset of the records that display in the Help window. If you specify the AUTOMATIC keyword, the filter is removed after the Help window is closed. The HELP filter can be removed also by specifying the SET HELPFILTER TO without specifying a Logical expression. The Logical expression involves the TOPIC or CLASS fields from the FOXHELP.DBF database table.

The CLASS field includes a general category and multiple instances of two-character codes. The codes are used to group a subset of topics that have something in common. For example, the two-character code db is in the CLASS field for every topic relating to database tables. The general categories are shown in Table 10.22.

Table 10.22. General categories in the help file CLASS field.

Category	*Description*
General	General information
Commands	FoxPro commands
Functions	FoxPro functions
Sysmemvar	System memory variables
Interface	FoxPro user interface

The two-character codes used to group common topic elements are presented in Table 10.23.

Table 10.23. A description of two-character codes in the help file CLASS field.

Category	*Code*	*Category*	*Code*
Character	ch	Logical	lo
Compatibility	cm	Low-level	ll
Configuration	cf	Memory variables	mv
Data conversion	dc	Menus, interface	me
Database	db	Menus and pop-up menus	mp
Date and time	dt	Multiuser	mu
Desk accessories SMV	da	New in FoxPro 2.5, 2.6	nx
Dialogs, interface	di	Numeric	nu
Enhanced Foxpro 2.5,2.6	ex	Operations, interface	in
Environment	en	Printing	pr
Error messages	em	Program execution	pe
Errors and debugging	er	SQL	sq
Event handlers	eh	Structured programming	sp
File I/O	fi	System menu names SMV	sn
File management	fm	Text merge	tm
General interface	ge	What's new	wn
Indexing	ix	Windows	wi
Keyboard and mouse	km		

Some sample uses of the `SET HELPFILTER` command follow:

```
* Select help topics about commands that start with SET
SET HELPFILTER TO topic = "SET"
* Select only topics about windows and remove
* filter when Help window is closed
SET HELPFILTER TO AUTOMATIC "wi"  CLASS
* Select topics about functions enhanced in FoxPro 2.5 and 2.6
SET HELPFILTER TO "en" $ class AND "Function" $ class
* Select topics about multiuser commands
SET HELPFILTER TO "Command" $ class AND "mu" $ class
* Remove help filter
SET HELPFILTER TO
```

The *SET HOURS* Command

The SET HOURS command selects either a 12- or 24-hour clock for the full-screen and SET CLOCK commands. The argument is one of the keywords, 12 or 24, not an integer value. Because the SET() function returns an integer value of 12 or 24, the output of SET() must be converted to a string before it can be used as an argument. Here is an example:

```
SAVEHOUR = STR(SET("HOURS"))
...
SET HOURS TO &SAVEHOUR      && Restore clock display
```

If you don't supply an argument, the clock display reverts to its default value, which is 12 for the U.S. version of FoxPro software. Here is the form for a 12-hour display:

```
1:31:33 pm
```

Here is the form for a 24-hour display:

```
13:31:33
```

Here is the syntax:

```
SET HOURS TO [12 ¦ 24]
```

Here is the equivalent CONFIG.FPW file command:

```
HOURS =   12 ¦ 24
```

The *SET INDEX* Command

The SET INDEX command opens and establishes NDX or CDX index files for the current database table (DBF file). Chapter 13, "Data Ordering," contains more information on the SET INDEX command. Here is the syntax:

```
SET INDEX TO [? ¦ <filename list>
[ORDER <expN>  ¦
<expFN1> ¦
[TAG]  <expTN1> [OF <expFN3>]]
[ASCENDING ¦ DESCENDING]]]
[ADDITIVE]

<filename list> ::= <expFN2> ¦ <expTN2> [OF <expFN3>],

<expFN4> ¦ <expTN3> [OF <expFN5>],...
```

<expFN2> and <expFN4> evaluate to IDX filenames. <expTNx> evaluates to an index tag for a compound index (CDX) filename. The OF clause specifies a CDX file other than the structural CDX file. As usual, the filename and tag name can be a name or a character expression. If ? is used, files can be selected from a directory pop-up menu. If no arguments are specified with the SET INDEX TO command, all indexes are closed for the current database.

The ORDER clause defines the master index and can be either the CDX file tag name, an index filename (<expFN1>), or the index order number (<expN>). The index order number is based on either the order in which IDX files are specified in <filename list> or the order in which an index tag was created in a CDX file. The master index is determined by the following:

ORDER <expN>	Order number of the index tag or IDX file
ORDER <expFN1>	Name of the IDX index file
ORDER <expTN>	Tag name from a structural index
ORDER <expTN> OF <expFN3>	Tag name of a specific CDX file

With the ASCENDING or DESCENDING keywords, you can designate whether records are accessed in ascending or descending order. The keyword follows the ORDER clause. Incidentally, the order of the database table isn't changed in any way—only the order in which the index is accessed and displayed.

If a structural CDX file exists when you open a database table (DBF file), it too is opened. In addition, you can specify that other CDX and IDX files be opened when you open an index file with the USE command. You can use the SET INDEX file to open more index files by specifying the ADDITIVE keyword. If you don't specify the ADDITIVE keyword, all open indexes, except the structural index files, are closed before the specified indexes are opened.

NOTE

Because of the lack of standards and the proprietary nature of Xbase, different vendors create their own terms for elements of Xbase. In Visual FoxPro, an index file containing more than one index is called a *compound index file* (CDX file). A CDX file associated with a table (same filename, different extension) is called a *structural index file*. In dBASE IV and Arago, a file containing more than one index is called a *multiple index file* (MDX file). An MDX file associated with a database table (DBF file) is called a *production index*. The Xbase language needs to be standardized.

The *SET INTENSITY* Command

The SET INTENSITY command controls the color attributes of the data input fields. If SET INTENSITY is ON, the FIELDS color category (see the section "The SET COLOR OF Command) displays the data input field. If INTENSITY is OFF, the NORMAL color category is used. If you specify the COLOR clause with @...GET, the value of SET INTENSITY is ignored. This command affects the APPEND, EDIT, INSERT, and READ full-screen commands. Here is the syntax:

```
SET INTENSITY ON ¦ off
```

Here is the equivalent CONFIG.FPW file command:

```
INTENSITY = ON ¦ off
```

The *SET KEY TO* Command

The `SET KEY TO` command lets you control access to a set of records based on their index keys. You normally use the `SET KEY` command to restrict the access of records in an indexed table. The syntax is this:

```
SET KEY TO  [<exp1> ¦ RANGE <exp2> [,<exp3>]] [IN <expWA>]
```

The `<expN1>` expression evaluates to a single key value and only those records with a key value that corresponds to that value. The `RANGE` clause specifies a range of values. Records with key values that fall within that range can be accessed.

If you do not specify any arguments with the `SET KEY TO` command, access is restored to all records in the table.

The *SET KEYCOMP TO* Command

The `SET KEYCOMP TO` command specifies which set of keystrokes is used to navigate your application's interface. You can select keystrokes that adhere to the Microsoft Windows interface conventions or the FoxPro 2.0 interface conventions. Here is the syntax:

```
SET KEYCOMP TO DOS ¦ WINDOWS
```

Microsoft Windows and FoxPro 2.0 user interfaces evolved independently. Windows evolved from a combination of Microsoft products, such as Word for DOS, and the Apple Macintosh interface. FoxPro 2.0 evolved from dBASE IV with influence from the Apple Macintosh interface as a result of the FoxPro for Mac product. Although the keystrokes that FoxPro 2.0 uses to navigate its interface are similar to the keystrokes used by Windows, they aren't identical. Visual FoxPro enables you to choose which of the two keystroke navigation conventions your application supports. If your users are familiar with the FoxPro 2.0 interface convention and are moving up to Windows, you might want to select the FoxPro 2.0 convention by executing the following command:

```
SET KEYCOMP TO DOS
```

If your users are familiar with Windows applications and prefer that convention, you can use the following command:

```
SET KEYCOMP TO WINDOWS
```

The Windows keystroke navigation convention is the default setting. You can override the default setting by placing the following command in the CONFIG.FPW configuration file.

```
KEYCOMP = DOS
```

The *SET LIBRARY TO* Command

Visual FoxPro is an open architecture system. You can seamlessly integrate an external library of functions into FoxPro with the SET LIBRARY command. You can write a library in C or assembly language that accesses internal FoxPro functionality using the FoxPro External Routine Application Program Interface (API). You then use the SET LIBRARY TO command to open your custom (FLL) library. You can call functions from this external library as you would any other FoxPro function. You can extend the language as well as the user interface. Here is the syntax:

```
SET LIBRARY TO [<expFN>] [ADDITIVE]
```

Here is the equivalent CONFIG.FPW file command:

```
SYSPROC = <filename> [ADDITIVE]
```

<expFN> is the name of an API library file. If you don't specify a filename extension, .FLL is assumed. If you don't specify the ADDITIVE keyword and any API libraries are open, they are closed before the specified library file is opened. If the ADDITIVE keyword is specified, the designated API library is opened without closing any API libraries that are already open. You can remove all API libraries from memory by specifying the SET LIBRARY TO command without naming a file. You can remove an individual API library with the RELEASE LIBRARY *<expFN>* command.

Suppose you have an API library named REVERSE.FLL, and you want to open it. You enter the following command:

```
SET LIBRARY TO REVERSE
```

Suppose that the newly opened REVERSE API library is a REVERSE function that reverses the characters in a string. After it's open, you can use the REVERSE() function as you would any other FoxPro function:

```
RString = REVERSE(String)
```

You can display open API libraries with the DISPLAY STATUS command. The following is an example of a segment of the DISPLAY STATUS command showing the REVERSE.PLB API library:

```
API library                  Segment
F:\FOXPRO\REVERSE.FLL        45CB

Function                     Address
REVERSE                      45CB:011C
```

You will learn how to build your own external library in Chapter 21, "Extending the Visual FoxPro Language."

In dBASE IV you can establish a second procedure library using the SET LIBRARY command. To be compatible with dBASE IV, the Visual FoxPro SET LIBRARY command supports procedure files as well as application program interface (API) libraries.

API routine libraries extend the capabilities of the FoxPro language and user interface. Once an external API routine library is opened, you can use the API functions as if they were FoxPro functions. The `SET LIBRARY` command and API libraries are discussed in Chapter 21.

If you use the `SET LIBRARY` command to open a procedure file, all open API libraries are closed. Likewise, if you use the `SET LIBRARY` command to open API libraries, any procedure file opened with the `SET LIBRARY` function is closed. Of course you can circumvent this problem by using the `SET PROCEDURE` function to open a procedure file to prevent API libraries from being unloaded.

If you specify a procedure file, the procedures within the procedure file are made available to all programs and are also available interactively through the Command window.

You use the filename (`<expFN>`) to specify an API library or procedure file to open. Visual FoxPro assumes an .FLL extension for libraries. If the library has an .FLL extension, you don't have to include the extension with the filename. If a library has an extension other than .FLL, you must include the extension with the filename. Visual FoxPro assumes a .PRG extension for a procedure file.

Once a procedure file is established, you can execute any of the procedures in the file with the `DO` command. When you execute a procedure, FoxPro searches for the procedure in the following order:

1. The file containing the executed procedure.
2. The procedure in the procedure library file, if established, opened with the `SET PROCEDURE` command.
3. Programs in the execution chain starting with the most recently executed program and continuing back to the first executed program.
4. The procedure in the procedure library file, if established, opened with the `SET LIBRARY` command.
5. A standalone program file. If a program file with the same name as the filename specified with `DO` is found, the program is executed.

If after searching through all these possibilities a matching program filename is not found, FoxPro displays the File does not exist error message.

You can open additional API libraries by successively issuing the `SET LIBRARY` command and specifying the `ADDITIVE` keyword after `<expFN>`. However, Visual FoxPro ignores the `ADDITIVE` keyword when you use the `SET LIBRARY` command to open a procedure file.

You can remove a procedure file or all API libraries from memory by executing the `SET LIBRARY TO` command without including `<expFN>`. You can remove an individual API library file with the `RELEASE LIBRARY <expFN>` command.

NOTE

It is common practice to place FLL API library files in the same directory in which the Visual FoxPro VFP.EXE file resides. Then when you use the `SET LIBRARY` file, you use the `SYS(2004)` function to specify that directory and use a command such as the following:

```
SET LIBRARY TO SYS(2004) + "FOXTOOLS.FLL".
```

However, when you execute a Visual FoxPro compact file (an executable that just contains your Visual FoxPro code but executes VFP300.ESL), it cannot find the library that resides in the Visual FoxPro home directory because `SYS(2004)` returns the directory in which VFP300.ESL resides and not the location of the compact EXE file. VFP300.ESL happens to reside in the Windows system directory (\WINDOWS\SYSTEM??).

If you want to fetch the compact EXE file directory, use the `SYS(16)` or `HOME()` functions. For example, if you place the FOXTOOLS.FLL library in the same directory as your compact EXE, the `SET LIBRARY TO` command will find it if you specify the following command:

```
SET LIBRARY TO HOME()+"\FOXTOOLS.FLL"
```

The *SET LOCK* Command

The `SET LOCK` command controls automatic file and record locking in a multiuser environment. Automatic locking is used for the `AVERAGE`, `SUM`, `CALCULATE`, `COPY`, `COUNT`, `DISPLAY`, `JOIN`, `LABEL`, `LIST REPORT`, `TOTAL`, `SORT`, and `INDEX` commands. Detailed information relating to `SET LOCK` is provided in Chapter 25. Here is the syntax:

```
SET LOCK ON ¦ off
```

Here is the equivalent CONFIG.FPW file command:

```
LOCK = ON ¦ off
```

The *SET LOGERRORS* Command

The `SET LOGERRORS` command controls the printing of error log files during the compilation of programs. If `LOGERRORS` is `ON`, errors that occur when a program is compiling are written to an error file. The filename is the same as the name of the program with the extension .ERR. Here is the syntax:

```
SET LOGERRORS ON ¦ off
```

Here is the equivalent CONFIG.FPW file command:

```
LOGERRORS = ON ¦ off
```

The *SET MACKEY* Command

The SET MACKEY command specifies the keystroke or combination of keystrokes that activates the Keyboard Macro dialog box. By default, Shift+F10 initiates the Keyboard Macro dialog box. The keystroke or combination of keystrokes is called the *macro hotkey*. You can assign any key to serve as the macro hotkey. Here is the syntax:

```
SET MACKEY TO [<expC>]
```

Here is the equivalent CONFIG.FPW file command:

```
MACKEY =  <expC>
```

The <expC> character expression specifies the label of the macro hotkey. Key labels are the labels used with the ON KEY LABEL command shown in Table 10.24. This command differs from other SET commands in that if you specify the command without <expC>, it doesn't revert to the default value. It simply assigns no macro hotkey, and the capability is disabled.

Table 10.24. Key names for use with the ON KEY LABEL command.

Alt+0 through Alt+9	End
Alt+A through Alt+Z	Enter
Alt+F1 through Alt+F12	Esc
Alt+PgUp	F1 through F12
Alt+PgDn	Home
Backspace	Ins
Backtab	Left arrow
Ctrl+A through Ctrl+Z	PgDn
Ctrl+End	PgUp
Ctrl+F1 through Ctrl+F12	Right arrow
Ctrl+Home	Shift+F1 through Shift+F12
Ctrl+Left arrow	Shift+Tab
Ctrl+PgDn	Spacebar
Ctrl+PgUp	Tab
Ctrl+Right arrow	Up arrow
Del	*<All printable characters>*
Down arrow	

For example, the following command assigns Shift+F6 as the macro hotkey:

```
SET MACKEY TO Shift+F6
```

The *MARGIN* Command

The `SET MARGIN` command specifies the distance from the paper edge for the left margin of all Visual FoxPro printed output. The value ranges from 0 to 254 characters. The `SET MARGIN` command provides the same functionality as assigning a value to the `_PLOFFSET` system memory variable. The `_WRAP` and `_LMARGIN` system memory variables also affect the `SET MARGIN` value. If `_WRAP` is true (`.T.`), the left margin offset is determined by adding `_LMARGIN` and `_LPLOFFSET`. If `_WRAP` is false (`.F.`), `_LMARGIN` doesn't affect the margin. Here is the syntax:

```
SET MARGIN TO <expN>
_PLOFFSET = <expN>
```

Here is the equivalent CONFIG.FPW file command:

```
MARGIN =  integer constant
```

The *SET MARK TO* Command

The `SET MARK TO` command redefines the character that separates the month, day, and year. For the U.S. version of Visual FoxPro, the default character is a slash. Here is an example:

Command	*Result*
`? DATE()`	`12/25/89`
`SET MARK TO "."`	
`? DATE()`	`12.25.89`

Here is the syntax:

```
SET MARK TO [<expC>]
```

Here is the equivalent CONFIG.FPW file command:

```
MARK =  <expC>
```

The *SET MARK OF* Command

The `SET MARK OF` command designates whether the check mark at the left of a menu pad displays. There are various forms of this command for menus and pop-up menus. Here is the syntax of the forms:

```
SET MARK OF MENU <menu name> TO <expL1>
SET MARK OF PAD <pad name> OF <menu name> TO <expL2>
SET MARK OF POPUP <popup name> TO <expL3>
SET MARK OF BAR <expN> OF <popup name> TO <expL4>
```

The logical expressions (<*expL1*> through <*expL4*>) designate whether a check mark displays. If the expression evaluates to a logical true value (`.T.`), the check mark displays; if not, it doesn't display.

A different form of the `SET MARK OF` command controls its display of one or more menu objects. Table 10.25 lists the menu objects affected by the `SET MARK OF` command.

Table 10.25. Menu objects affected by the `SET MARK OF` command forms.

Command Form	*Menu Object Affected*
`SET MARK OF MENU` <*menu name*> `TO...`	Every pad in the specified menu
`SET MARK OF PAD` <*pad name*> `OF MENU` <*menu name*> `TO...`	Specified pad in the specified menu
`SET MARK OF POPUP` <*popup name*> `TO...`	Every bar in the specified pop-up menu
`SET MARK OF BAR` <*bar number*> `OF POPUP` <*popup name*> `TO...`	Specified bar in the specified pop-up menu

In the example presented in Listing 10.6, a new menu pad, labeled **B**ackground, is added to the system menu. If you choose the Background menu options, you can change the background color. The option for the current background color is marked. Commands for defining menus are described in Chapter 7, "FoxPro Language Elements for Creating Windows and Menu Systems." The purpose of MARK.PRG is to illustrate the use of the `SET MARK OF` command.

Listing 10.6. The MARK.PRG program, which illustrates the `SET MARK OF` command.

```
****************************************************************
*     * 08/17/92             MARK.PRG              23:56:33   *
****************************************************************
*     * Description:                                          *
*     *  Illustrates how the SET MARK OF command operates     *
*     *                                                       *
****************************************************************
CLEAR
SET TALK OFF
PUBLIC m._bar_cur, m._Bright
m._bar_cur = 2
m._Bright = .F.
*
**** Add new menu pad to systems menu
*
DEFINE PAD ycolor OF _MSYSMENU PROMPT '\<Background';
```

```
KEY ALT+B, 'ALT+B'
*
**** Create new Popup for menu pad ycolor
*
ON PAD ycolor OF _MSYSMENU ACTIVATE POPUP zcolor
DEFINE POPUP zcolor MARGIN RELATIVE SHADOW COLOR SCHEME 4
DEFINE BAR 1 OF zcolor  PROMPT '\<Black'
DEFINE BAR 2 OF zcolor  PROMPT 'B\<lue'
DEFINE BAR 3 OF zcolor  PROMPT 'Br\<own'
DEFINE BAR 4 OF zcolor  PROMPT '\<Cyan'
DEFINE BAR 5 OF zcolor  PROMPT '\<Green'
DEFINE BAR 6 OF zcolor  PROMPT '\<Magenta'
DEFINE BAR 7 OF zcolor  PROMPT '\<Red'
DEFINE BAR 8 OF zcolor  PROMPT '\<White'
DEFINE BAR 9 OF zcolor  PROMPT 'Br\<ight'
ON SELECTION POPUP zcolor DO zcolorpop IN MARK.PRG

SET BLINK OFF          && Turn off blinking
SET COLOR TO W+/B
*
*  Turn Mark On for the second bar in Popup zcolor
SET MARK OF BAR 2 OF zcolor TO .T.
*
CLEAR
RETURN
*****************************************************************
* Procedure called when popup menu bar is selected
PROCEDURE zcolorpop
IF BAR() != 9
*
***** Mark bar selected and unmark previous bar
*
SET MARK OF BAR m._bar_cur OF zcolor TO .F.
SET MARK OF BAR BAR() OF zcolor TO .T.
m._bar_cur = BAR()
ENDIF
DO CASE
CASE BAR() = 8
SET COLOR TO ( IIF( m._Bright, "N*/W", "N/W" ) )
CASE BAR() = 9
m._Bright = ! m._Bright
SET MARK OF BAR 9 OF zcolor TO m._Bright
OTHERWISE     && Bars 1-8
SET COLOR TO ( IIF(m._Bright, "W*/", "W/") + ;
SUBSTR("N  B  GR BG G  RB R  W  ", ( 3*BAR() ) - 2, 3))
ENDCASE
CLEAR
RETURN
```

Figure 10.6 shows the result of executing program MARK.PRG. The pop-up menu, named `zcolor`, associated with the **B**ackground menu pad displays.

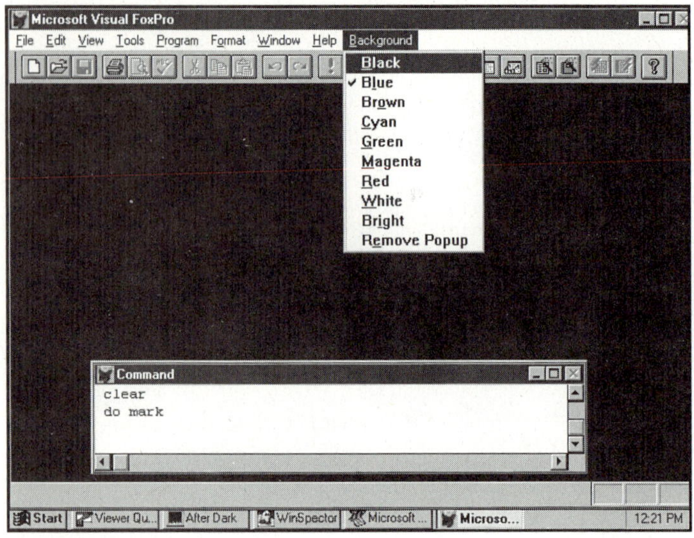

FIGURE 10.6.
An example of a check marked bar in the Background pop-up menu.

The *SET MBLOCK TO* Command

Here is the syntax for the `SET MBLOCK TO` command:

```
SET MBLOCK TO <expN>
```

The `SET MBLOCK TO` function controls the memo field block size. It is nearly identical to the `SET BLOCKSIZE` command, except that it sets memo fields of 64 bytes when the value of `<expN>` is less than 257. Above that, it works like the `SET BLOCKSIZE` command.

The *SET MEMOWIDTH TO* Command

The `SET MEMOWIDTH TO` command modifies the column width of memo field output. The default value is 50; the minimum value is 8; the maximum value is 254. The command affects the column display width of memo fields for the `?`, `??`, `DISPLAY`, and `LIST` commands, as well as the width of the string returned by the `MLINE()` function and the number returned by the `MEMLINES()`, `ATLINE()`, and `ATCLINE()` functions.

You also can alter the memo field column-width display with the vertical stretch picture function, `@V`. See the description of the `?` command `PICTURE` clause in Chapter 8, "Input and Output." Here is the syntax:

```
SET MEMOWIDTH TO <expN>
```

Here is the equivalent CONFIG.FPW file command:

```
MEMOWIDTH =  <integer constant>
```

The *SET MESSAGE TO* Command

The SET MESSAGE TO command specifies a user-defined menu message that appears centered on the message line (the bottom line of the screen), on the Windows-style status bar, or optionally, on another specified line. After a message is established, it is displayed either when SET STATUS is ON or under the following conditions:

- A READ command executes a GET object with a MESSAGE clause.
- A user-defined pop-up menu or menu is active.

Here is the syntax:

```
SET MESSAGE TO [<expC> ]

SET MESSAGE TO [ <expN>] [ LEFT ¦ CENTER ¦ RIGHT ]

SET MESSAGE WINDOW [ <window name> ]
```

There is no equivalent CONFIG.FPW file command.

The <expC> character expression specifies the message that displays on the message line if SET STATUS is ON.

The numeric expression <expN> specifies the line where the message appears. If the form of SET MESSAGE with a numeric expression is never executed, the message displays on the message line (line 24). The LEFT, CENTER, and RIGHT keywords specify whether the message is left aligned, right aligned, or centered. If none of the three keywords is specified and any line other than 24 is specified, the message is left aligned. Under the same circumstances in FoxPro 1.2, the message is centered. If no expression is specified, any active message is deleted. If the message is currently being displayed, the line containing the message is cleared.

The SET MESSAGE WINDOW command designates the window where the message appears. The window name is that of a defined window. If messages have been directed to a window and you want them to display on-screen, specify the SET MESSAGE WINDOW command without <window name>.

Here is an example of the SET MESSAGE command:

```
SET MESSAGE TO 20 CENTERED
SET MESSAGE "This message is centered on line 20"
```

The length of a message can be up to 79 characters. If a message is longer, the extra text is truncated. When using the user-defined menu system, the message is overwritten by the menu object messages and is restored upon exit.

The *SET MOUSE* Command

The SET MOUSE command controls the sensitivity of the mouse in FoxPro 2.0. However, in Visual FoxPro, this command isn't supported. If it is encountered in a program, it is ignored. If you want to change the mouse sensitivity, use the Windows Control Panel.

The *SET MULTILOCKS* Command

The SET MULTILOCKS command enables or disables multiple-record locking. Here is the syntax:

```
SET MULTILOCKS on ¦ OFF
```

Here is the equivalent CONFIG.FPW file command:

```
MULTILOCKS = on ¦ OFF
```

In Visual FoxPro you have the option of locking one record at a time using the RLOCK() and LOCK() functions when MULTILOCKS is OFF. When you lock one record, any other locked record is unlocked. You can lock multiple records simultaneously with the RLOCK() and LOCK() functions if SET MULTILOCKS is ON. If you need more details regarding multiple-record locking, see Chapter 15, "The Visual Class Library, the Class Designer, and the Class Browser."

The *SET NEAR* Command

The SET NEAR command controls the positioning of the record pointer following an unsuccessful FIND or SEEK. If SET NEAR is OFF and the record search is unsuccessful, the record pointer is positioned at the end of the database table (DBF file). However, if SET NEAR is ON under the same circumstances, the record pointer is positioned on the closest matching record. SET NEAR is described in Chapter 13. Here is the syntax:

```
SET NEAR on ¦ OFF
```

Here is the equivalent CONFIG.FPW file command:

```
NEAR = on ¦ OFF
```

The *SET NOCPTRANS TO* Command

The SET NOCPTRANS TO command prevents code page translation for a specified list of fields in a table. This is the syntax:

```
SET NOCPTRANS TO <field list>
```

No code page translation is performed for the fields in the field list *<field list>*. If you specify SET NOCPTRANS TO without any other arguments, the code page translation is performed for all characters and memo fields in the table.

The *SET NOTIFY* Command

The SET NOTIFY command enables and disables the display of certain system messages. System messages display in a window in the top-right corner of the screen. Here is the syntax:

```
SET NOTIFY ON ¦ off
```

Here is the equivalent CONFIG.FPW file command:

```
NOTIFY = ON | off
```

If `SET NOTIFY` is `OFF`, certain system messages don't display. System messages that provide operational information, such as `DO Canceled`, are affected by this command.

The *SET NULL* Command

The `SET NULL` command designates how null values are supported by the `ALTER TABLE`, `CREATE TABLE`, and SQL `INSERT` commands. `SET NULL` only affects how null values are supported by `ALTER TABLE`, `CREATE TABLE`, and SQL `INSERT`. Other commands are unaffected by `SET NULL`. Here is the syntax:

```
SET NULL ON | off
```

If you set `NULL` to `ON`, all columns in a table created with `ALTER TABLE` and `CREATE TABLE` will allow null values. You can override null value support for columns in the table by specifying the `NOT NULL` clause in the column definitions or by not checking the Null button for a field in the Table Designer. By setting `NULL` to `ON`, you can allow the SQL `INSERT` command to insert null values into any columns not included in the SQL `INSERT` command `VALUE` clause. The SQL `INSERT` command only inserts null values into columns that allow null values.

If you set `NULL` to `OFF`, all table columns created with the `ALTER TABLE` and `CREATE TABLE` commands will not allow null values. You can designate null value support for columns in the table by including the `CREATE TABLE` command `NULL` keyword in the definition of a column. In addition, when you set `NULL` to `OFF`, the SQL `INSERT` command will insert blank values into any columns not included in the `VALUE` clause of the SQL `INSERT` command.

The *SET ODOMETER* Command

The `SET ODOMETER` command controls the value of the increment used each time the record counter display is incremented. If `TALK` is `ON`, the `APPEND`, `AVERAGE`, `CALCULATE`, `CONVERT`, `COPY`, `COUNT`, `EXPORT`, `IMPORT`, `JOIN`, `MODIFY`, `PACK`, `REPLACE`, `SUM`, `TOTAL`, and `UPDATE` commands display a record counter while records are being processed. Records are processed much faster than the incremented record count is displayed. Therefore, processing is slower when the record count displays each time a record is processed. One approach to solving this problem is to set `TALK` to `OFF` and suppress the record count display. If you don't want to look at an inactive screen while you're processing a large database table (DBF file), use the `SET ODOMETER` command to change the record count display increment. Its value can range from 1 to 32768; its default value is 100.

Here is the syntax:

```
SET ODOMETER TO [<expN>]
```

Here is the equivalent CONFIG.FPW file command:

```
ODOMETER = <integer constant>
```

The *SET OLEOBJECT* Command

The `SET OLEOBJECT` command specifies whether Visual FoxPro searches the Windows Registry when an object cannot be located. This is the syntax:

```
SET OLEOBJECT ON ¦ off
```

This is the equivalent CONFIG.FPW file command:

```
OLEOBJECT  = ON ¦ off
```

If `SET OLEOBJECT` is set to `ON`, Visual FoxPro searches for an OLE object in the Windows Registry when the OLE object cannot be located. Otherwise, Visual FoxPro does not search the Windows Registry.

When Visual FoxPro creates an object with the `CREATEOBJECT()` or `GETOBJECT()` functions, Visual FoxPro searches for the object in the following locations:

- Visual FoxPro base classes.
- Class definitions in memory in the order in which they are loaded.
- Class definitions in the current program.
- Class definitions in the visual class libraries (VCX) opened with the `SET CLASSLIB` command.
- Class definitions in procedure files opened with `SET PROCEDURE`.
- Class definitions in the Visual FoxPro program execution chain.
- The Windows Registry.

There are times during a development process when you are creating classes and you are not using OLE objects. If you misspell the name of an object, you have to wait for Visual FoxPro to search the Windows Registry before you get an error message. If `SET OLEOBJECT` is `OFF`, you will not have to wait. OLE objects in General fields and OLE objects used in forms are not affected by the `SET OLEBOJECT` command setting.

The *SET OPTIMIZE* Command

The `SET OPTIMIZE` command enables and disables the FoxPro Rushmore index optimization technology. (Rushmore technology is explained in Chapter 13.) Here is the syntax:

```
SET OPTIMIZE ON ¦ off
```

Here is the equivalent CONFIG.FPW file command:

```
OPTIMIZE = ON ¦ off
```

If you use a `FOR` clause or the `SET FILTER TO` command to access a subset of records, Rushmore technology enhances performance. Certain commands operate on a set of database records and exhibit improved performance if `SET OPTIMIZE` is `ON`. These include the following:

AVERAGE	BROWSE	CALCULATE	CHANGE	COPY TO
COUNT	DELETE	DISPLAY	EDIT	EXPORT
JOIN	LABEL	LIST	LOCATE	RECALL
REPLACE	REPORT	SCAN	SORT	SUM
TOTAL				

An alternative to the `SET OPTIMIZE` command is to specify the `NOPTIMIZE` keyword with any of the preceding commands to disable the Rushmore technology.

The `SET OPTIMIZE OFF` command instructs FoxPro not to use the Rushmore technology to optimize data retrieval. See Chapter 13 for more on Rushmore technology.

Normally, you have no reason to disable the Rushmore technology. However, if you have an application that modifies the `FOR` expression dynamically during processing, the record set selected by Rushmore is not valid. You must disable Rushmore.

The *SET ORDER TO* Command

The `SET ORDER TO` command designates which of the opened indexes for the current database table (DBF file) is the master index. The master index controls the access sequence of records. This command is discussed in detail in Chapter 13.

The *SET PALETTE* Command

NEW VISUAL FOXPRO

The `SET PALETTE` command designates whether (`ON`) or not (`OFF`) the Visual FoxPro default color palette is used. Each bitmap can contain its own color palette, which defines a specific set of colors used to display the bitmap. If `SET PALETTE` is `OFF`, the Visual FoxPro default palette color is replaced with the color palettes from the first BMP graphics or OLE object displayed. When other bitmaps are displayed, they use the color palette from the first bitmap. In some cases, if the color palette for the first palette is strange, the colors of the other graphics objects may look bizarre. For most cases, you will find that the best color display can be achieved by setting the `SET PALETTE` command to `ON` (which is the default) and use the Visual FoxPro default color palette to display all graphics objects. This is the syntax:

```
SET PALETTE ON ¦ off
```

This is the equivalent CONFIG.FPW file command:

```
PALETTE = ON ¦ off
```

The *SET PATH* Command

The SET PATH command specifies the file search path for Visual FoxPro files. This file search path is referred to as the *FoxPro path*. FoxPro first searches the current directory for a file. If the file isn't found and a path established by SET PATH exists, Visual FoxPro searches each directory in the path in the order specified. If the file still isn't found, Visual FoxPro displays a File not found system message in a window. Visual FoxPro doesn't search according to the DOS path. The DIR command displays only those files in the current or specified directory. Here is the syntax:

```
SET PATH TO [<path list>]
```

Here is the equivalent CONFIG.FPW file command:

```
PATH = <path string>
```

The argument consists of a series of directories separated by commas or semicolons. Here is an example:

```
SET PATH TO C:\dbase\dbdata;D:\dbsample;c:\
```

The *SET POINT* Command

The SET POINT command redefines the decimal point character. The argument consists of a single character. The default value for U.S. versions of Visual FoxPro is a period. Some international versions use a comma instead of a period. If you don't specify an argument, the default value is restored. Numeric and blank characters aren't allowed.

Changing the value of SET POINT affects the display and input of numbers using PICTURE templates. The character codes used in the PICTURE templates, however, are unchanged. SET POINT is used with the SET SEPARATOR command. Here is the syntax:

```
SET POINT TO [<expC>]
```

Here is the equivalent CONFIG.FPW file command:

```
POINT = <character>
```

The *SET PRINTER FONT* Command

You can use the SET PRINTER FONT command to specify the default font and style for printed output. If you do not execute this command, the default printer font and font style are used. Here is the syntax:

```
SET PRINTER FONT <expC> [,<expN>]  [STYLE <expStyle>]
```

Here is the equivalent CONFIG.FPW file command:

```
PRINTER FONT = <font name> [,<font size>]
PRINTER STYLE = <style>
```

<expC> specifies the name of the font. <expN> specifies the size of the font. <expStyle> consists of one or more characters that specify the style. If <expStyle> is omitted, normal font style is used. The following is a list of available font styles:

Character	*Font Style*
B	Bold
I	Italic
N	Normal (default)
O	Outline
Q	Opaque
S	Shadow
-	Strikethrough
T	Transparent
U	Underline

You can specify one or more characters to designate a combination of styles. Here's an example:

```
SET PRINTER FONT "Arial",8 STYLE "BI"
```

The *SET PRINTER ON* Command

The `SET PRINTER ON` command causes all console output, except that from full-screen and `@` commands, to echo to the printer device or a file. The `SET PRINTER OFF` command ends the routing of output to the printer. Ctrl+P toggles the same internal printer flag controlled by `SET PRINTER ON ¦ OFF`. Here is the syntax:

```
SET PRINTER on ¦ OFF
```

Here is the equivalent CONFIG.FPW file command:

```
PRINTER = on ¦ OFF
```

The *SET PRINTER TO* Command

The `SET PRINTER TO` command redirects printed output to a print device or a file. The syntax of the various forms of the `SET PRINTER TO` command is as follows:

```
(1)  SET PRINTER TO
(2)  SET PRINTER TO <DOS device>
(3)  SET PRINTER TO \\<computer name>\
       <printer name>=<destination>
(4)  SET PRINTER TO \\SPOOLER [\NB]
          [\F = <expN1>] [\B = <expC1>]
          [\C = <expN2>] [\P = <expC2>]
          [\S = <server>] [\Q = <queue>]
```

```
 (5)  SET PRINTER TO [ FILE <expFN> [ADDITIVE] ¦ <port>

<DOS device>  ::= PRN ¦ lpt1 ¦ lpt2 ¦ lpt3 ¦ com1 ¦ com2
<destination> ::= LPT1 ¦  LPT2   ¦  LPT3
```

If no arguments are specified, as in form 1, the destination print device reverts to the default MS-DOS device, PRN. When running on a network, `SET PRINTER TO` and form 2, `SET PRINTER TO <DOS device>`, can be used to redirect printed output to a local printer and to print spooled output on a network spooler.

Forms 3 and 4 are used for printing on a network. Form 3 is used for 3-Com and IBM networks. `<computer name>` and `<printer name>` are assigned by the network shell. `<destination>` defines the installed shared printer device, which can be at the logged workstation or a remote site. Form 4 is used on Novell networks to redirect printed output to the network spooler.

NOTE

The term *spool* is an old mainframe term. Mainframe printed output was printed offline. It was written, or *spooled*, to eight-inch magnetic tape. The tape was then unmounted and taken to a separate minicomputer with an attached high-speed printer. The sole purpose of this minicomputer was to print spooled output.

For the Novell network, output is spooled to a disk file on the server and then printed. For example, to direct report output to a network spooler, you can enter the following commands:

```
SET PRINTER TO \\SPOOLER\          && Direct output to spooler
REPORT FORM MYREPORT TO PRINTER  && Generate report
SET PRINTER TO                     && Print spooled output
```

For form 4, you can take advantage of network services. The options described in Table 10.26 can be used to access network services. When specifying these options, don't insert any spaces between them.

Table 10.26. The syntax for accessing network printing services.

Option	*Description*
`[\N]`	You can specify that the printing of a banner be suppressed with this option. A banner is a page that is printed before the first page of a listing and is used to identify the listing. The banner message is printed in large letters.
`[\F = <expN1>]`	You can specify a form number from 0 to 255. This form number identifies the type of form containing the printed output.

Option	Description
[\B = <expC1>]	You can specify a character string of up to 12 characters that is printed in large letters on the banner page.
[\C = <expN2>]	With this option you can specify the number of copies of the listing that is printing. You can specify a number from 1 to 255. The default is 1.
[\P = <expC2>]	Use this option to specify a character string that identifies the network printer.
[\S = <server>]	Use this option to specify the name of the server to which the printer receiving output is connected. <server> must be the literal name of the server. It can't be a character string.
[\Q = <queue>]	Use this option to specify the name of the queue that is assigned to the printer receiving output. <queue> must be the literal name of the queue. It can't be a character string.

In the following example, output is directed to printer number 3 on the network server, then redirected to the local printer. The server will print a banner. The first line of the banner contains `Joe's List` in large letters.

```
SET PRINTER TO \\Server\P=3\B="Joe's List"
LIST
SET PRINTER TO
```

Form 5 directs printed output to a file or a communications port. Here is an example:

```
SET PRINTER TO FILE POUT              && Redirect printed output to
                                      &&   a file
REPORT FORM INVEN TO PRINTER [PROMPT] && File and generate report
SET PRINTER TO                        && Close POUT.PRT print file
SET PRINTER TO FILE POUT              && Redirect printed output to
REPORT FORM CUST TO PRINTER [PROMPT]  &&   a file and generate report
SET PRINTER TO                        && Close POUT.TXT print file
```

The *SET PROCEDURE* Command

The `SET PROCEDURE` command establishes one or more procedure files. A *procedure file* is a program file that contains multiple procedures. The actual limit is determined by available memory. The size of the procedure file can't be greater than 65KB. When `SET PROCEDURE` is executed and `SET DEVELOPMENT` is `ON`, each procedure (.PRG) file and its associated object (.FXP) files are opened, and their creation dates are compared. If the object file is older or doesn't exist, the source file is compiled and a new object file is generated and opened. If `SET DEVELOPMENT` is `OFF`, the creation dates aren't compared.

Each procedure in a procedure file begins with a PROCEDURE or FUNCTION statement that defines the name of the procedure and is used with the DO command to execute the procedure. Procedure names are then added to the procedure table. If the first procedure doesn't contain an explicit PROCEDURE statement, that procedure is given the same name as the file. For more information regarding procedures, consult Chapter 6, "Control Flow."

Here is the syntax:

```
SET PROCEDURE TO [<expFN1> ][, <expFN2>,…] [ADDITIVE]
```

The arguments consist of the procedure filenames. If no filename extension is designated, .PRG is assumed. There is no equivalent CONFIG.FPW file command. If the ADDITIVE keyword is specified, the existing procedures remain open and the procedures in the new procedure files are opened.

The *SET READBORDER* Command

You use the SET READBORDER command to specify whether borders are placed around editing regions that are created using the @…GET command. If SET READBORDER is ON, single-line borders are drawn around all GET field editing regions. If SET READBORDER is OFF, the single-line border is not drawn. The default for SET READBORDER is OFF. Here is the syntax:

```
SET READBORDER on ¦ OFF
```

Here is the equivalent CONFIG.FPW command:

```
READBORDER = on ¦ OFF
```

If the SET READBORDER command is ON when the first @…GET for a READ level is issued, all subsequent @…GET commands created in the same READ level also have borders. Likewise, if the SET READBORDER command is OFF when the first @…GET command executes, no borders will be drawn around the editing regions for any of the subsequent GET fields created in the same READ level. In the following example, a border is drawn around all GET field editing regions for the first READ level and not drawn around the GET field for the second READ level:

```
SET BORDER ON
WithBord=  "This GET has a border"
AlsoBord = "This GET also has a border"
NoBorder="This GET does not have a a border"
@ 1,1 GET WithBord    && This get has a border
SET BORDER OFF
@ 6,2 GET AlsoBord    && This also has a border
READ                  && First read level
@ 8,2 GET NoBord      && This does not have a border
READ                  && Second read level
```

The *SET REFRESH* Command

The `SET REFRESH` command is used in a multiuser environment to specify how often a database table (DBF file) is interrogated to see if any records have changed during `BROWSE`, `CHANGE`, and `EDIT` commands and memo field editing (`MODIFY MEMO`). Here is the syntax:

```
SET REFRESH TO <expN1> [,<expN2>]
```

Here is the equivalent CONFIG.FPW file command:

```
REFRESH = <integer constant>
```

Refresh processing works differently in `BROWSE` than in `EDIT`. In `BROWSE`, all records displayed on-screen are reviewed to see if any have been changed by another user on the network. If any record has changed, the entire screen is redisplayed. In `EDIT`, only the current record is reviewed. The <*expN1*> numeric expression is the number of seconds between refresh operations. The value of <*expN1*> can be from 0 to 3600 seconds. The default is 0. If the value is 0, the screen isn't periodically refreshed.

Part of the data is buffered in the local memory in the user's workstation. You can specify the second optional Numeric argument, <*expN2*>, to designate how often the local buffers are updated. The value of <*expN2*> can range from 0 to 3600 seconds. The default is 0. If the value is set to 1, the local buffers are refreshed every second.

The *SET RELATION* Command

The `SET RELATION` command establishes a relation between files based on an index key expression or a record number. The current database table (DBF file) or one in the work area specified with the optional `IN` <*expWA2*> clause can be related to one or more tables. Here is the syntax:

```
SET RELATION TO  [IN <expWA2>]
SET RELATION TO <exp> [IN <expWA2>]
SET RELATION TO <exp> INTO <expWA>
     [,<exp> INTO <expWA>]… [ADDITIVE]  [IN <expWA2>]
```

The `INTO` clause specifies an active work area of the child database tables. If the database table designated by the `INTO` clause contains an active master index, <*exp*> is used to relate the value of the expression with a corresponding index key value in the child database. If the child doesn't have an active master index, <*exp*> must be a numeric expression. Its value is assumed to be a record number and is used to position the child database to the corresponding record. For a record-to-record link between parent and child databases, <*exp*> can be the `RECNO()` function.

The clause group <*exp*> `INTO` <*expWA*> can be repeated for each child of the parent. If the `ADDITIVE` keyword is specified, all existing relations in the current work area are retained and the new relation is created. If the `ADDITIVE` keyword is omitted, any existing relations for the current work area are deleted before the new relation is created.

Figure 10.7 illustrates the following example that relates one database table to other database tables:

```
USE PARENT IN 0
USE Child1 IN 0 ORDER Name
USE Child2 IN 0 ORDER Class
SET RELATION TO Name INTO Child1, Class INTO Child2  IN PARENT
```

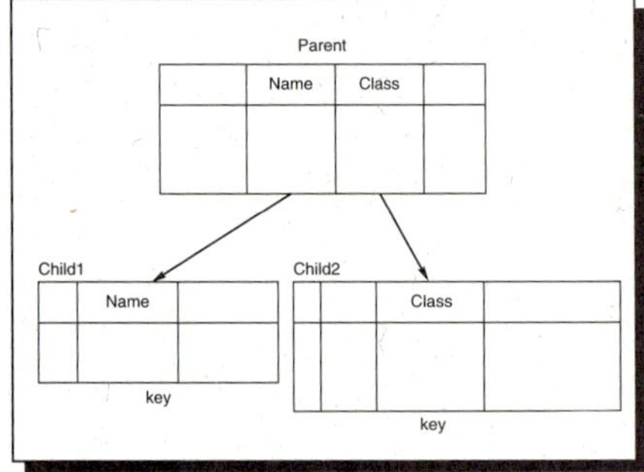

FIGURE 10.7.
Related files.

If no arguments are specified with the `SET RELATION TO` command, all relations in the active work area are closed. You can remove a single relation using the following form of the `SET RELATION` command:

```
SET RELATION OFF INTO <expWA>  [IN <expWA2>]
```

Any other existing relations associated with the current work area remain active. For detailed information relating to `SET RELATION`, see Chapter 11. You can graphically set relations through the View window.

The *SET REPROCESS* Command

The `SET REPROCESS` command is used in a multiuser environment to designate how many times Visual FoxPro attempts a command or function that results in a network error before returning an error condition. It is normally used with the `USE` command, the `RLOCK()` and `LOCK()` record locking functions, and the `FLOCK()` file locking function. Detailed information is provided in Chapter 25. Here is the syntax:

```
SET REPROCESS TO <expN> [SECONDS] ¦ [TO AUTOMATIC]
```

Here is the equivalent CONFIG.FPW file command:

```
REPROCESS = <integer constant>
```

The argument is an integer value, ranging from -2 to 32000. The -1 value directs the system to continually reprocess the operation forever. The default value is 0, which suppresses the reprocess. If the optional `SECONDS` keyword is specified, `<expN>` designates how many seconds the system waits following an unsuccessful lock attempt before it retries.

If you specify a numeric value of -2 or specify the TO AUTOMATIC clause, the system repeatedly attempts to lock a record or file until the lock is successful or until you press Esc. While attempting to lock a record, FoxPro/LAN displays the system message Attempting to lock...Press ESC to Cancel.

When you press Esc and an ON ERROR command is active, it is executed. If no ON ERROR procedure is active, an alert box appears, containing the message Record is in use by another.

The *SET RESOURCE* Command

The SET RESOURCE command establishes or updates the resource file for the remainder of your FoxPro session. A *resource file* is a FoxPro database table that contains information on the FoxPro system and user-defined resources such as the following:

- Color sets
- Keyboard macros
- System window location and size
- Preferences
- Calendar/diary entries
- Print driver setups

Here is the syntax:

```
SET RESOURCE TO [<expFN>]
SET RESOURCE ON ¦ off
```

Here is the equivalent CONFIG.FPW file command:

```
RESOURCE = [<filename>]
RESOURCE = ON ¦ off
```

By default, or if you specify the SET RESOURCE TO command without specifying a filename, the resource file is named FOXUSER.DBF. An associated memo file is named FOXUSER.FPT. However, you can specify the name of a custom resource file, which becomes the resource database table (DBF file). If the file doesn't exist, an alert box displays the system error message Cannot open file.

You should set up the FOXUSER.DBF resource file to support the specific needs of your custom application. Then rename both the FOXUSER.DBF and FOXUSER.FPT files using names that you choose. For example, rename FOXUSER.DBF to MYRES.DBF and FOXUSER.FPT to MYRES.FPT. When your application executes, it issues the SET RESOURCE TO MYRES command to establish your custom resource file as the system resource file.

By default, RESOURCE is set to ON, and any changes made to the FoxPro environment are saved in the resource file. If RESOURCE is OFF, changes aren't saved.

You can retrieve the name of the current resource file using either the `SYS(2005)` or `SET("RESOURCE",1)` function.

The *SET SAFETY* Command

The `SET SAFETY` command controls the file overwrite warning system. If `SET SAFETY` is `ON`, the prompt box in Figure 10.8 is displayed before the contents of an existing file are overwritten by another file with the same name.

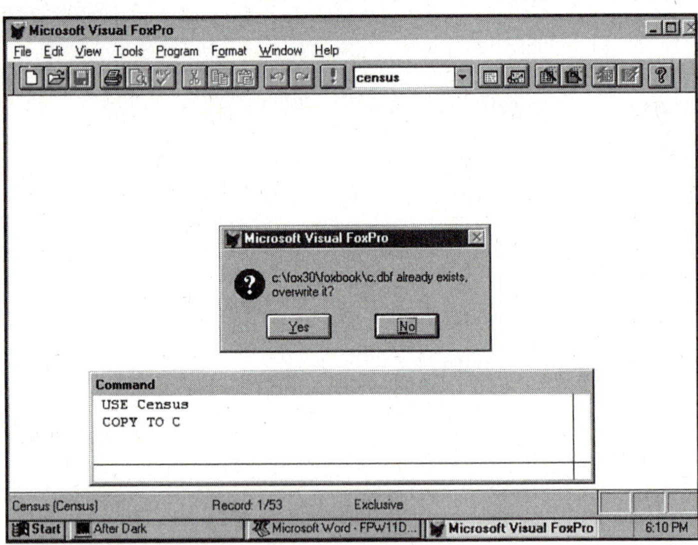

FIGURE 10.8.
The overwrite confirmation box.

If you select the **Y**es prompt, the existing file is overwritten. If `SET SAFETY` is `OFF`, the existing file is overwritten without any warning. The `ZAP` command also honors the `SET SAFETY` command. If `SET SAFETY` is `ON`, the system message `ZAP: <filename>?` appears in an alert box.

Here is the syntax:

```
SET SAFETY ON ¦ off
```

Here is the equivalent CONFIG.FPW file command:

```
SAFETY = ON ¦ off
```

The *SET SCOREBOARD* Command

The `SET SCOREBOARD` command has no function in Visual FoxPro. Its syntax is retained to keep compatibility with previous versions of Xbase.

The *SET SECONDS* Command

The `SET SECONDS` command designates whether seconds display in the time portion of a DateTime value. Here is the syntax:

```
SET SECONDS ON ¦ off
```

If `SET SECONDS` is `ON`, seconds display in DateTime values. `ON` is the default. If `SET SECONDS` is `OFF`, seconds do not display. Here is an example:

```
SET SECONDS ON
? DATETIME() && Displays 9/23/95 10:13:14am
SET SECONDS OFF
? DATETIME() && Displays 9/23/95 10:13am
```

Here is the equivalent CONFIG.FPW file command:

```
SECONDS = ON ¦ off
```

The *SET SEPARATOR* Command

The `SET SEPARATOR` command redefines the thousands separator character. The argument consists of a single character. The default value for U.S. versions of Visual FoxPro software is a comma. For some international numeric displays, a period is used instead of a comma. If no argument is specified, the default value is restored. Numeric and blank characters are not allowed.

Changing the value of `SET SEPARATOR` affects the display and input of numbers using `PICTURE` templates. However, the character used in the `PICTURE` template codes is unchanged. `SET SEPARATOR` is used in conjunction with the `SET POINT` command. Here is the syntax:

```
SET SEPARATOR TO [<expC>]
```

Here is the equivalent CONFIG.FPW file command:

```
SEPARATOR = <character>
```

The following example demonstrates the use of `SET SEPARATOR` and `SET POINT`:

Command	*Results*
`SET POINT TO ","`	
`SET SEPARATOR TO "."`	
`? 1234567.89 PICTURE "999,999,999.99"`	1.234.567,89

Notice that the `PICTURE` function's separator and point characters remain unchanged. This makes the program language independent.

The *SET SHADOWS* Command

The `SET SHADOWS` command controls the display of shadows for user-defined windows in FoxPro for MS-DOS. Visual FoxPro does not support this command. Visual FoxPro ignores it. It affects only FoxPro for MS-DOS user-defined windows that have been defined with the `SHADOW` keyword. If `SET SHADOWS` is `ON`, hadows display; if `SET SHADOWS` is `OFF`, shadows don't display. Here is the syntax:

```
SET SHADOWS ON ¦ off
```

Here is the equivalent CONFIG.FPW file command:

```
SHADOWS = ON ¦ off
```

Microsoft Windows does not support shadowed windows. As a result, Visual FoxPro doesn't support shadowed windows. You can still develop an application in FoxPro that runs on both Visual FoxPro and FoxPro for DOS and uses shadows in the DOS version. Although Visual FoxPro doesn't display shadows, it doesn't issue an error if you specify the `SET SHADOWS` command or specify a `SHADOW` keyword with a `DEFINE WINDOW` command. Visual FoxPro just ignores any instance of the `SET SHADOW` command and any `SHADOW` keywords.

The *SET SKIP* Command

The `SET SKIP` command controls record positioning of relationships set by the `SET RELATION TO` command to support multiple-detail line processing. It converts a one-to-one relationship to a one-to-many relationship. If `SET SKIP` isn't specified, only the first record that matches the relation key in a child database table is selected.

`SET SKIP` establishes a list of child databases in an existing relation chain for which multiple occurrences of records that match the parent record are selected. Detailed information for `SET SKIP` is provided in Chapter 11. Here is the syntax:

```
SET SKIP TO [<expWA> [, <expWA>]… ]
```

The argument list designates work areas in a relation chain. If you want to convert a one-to-many back to a one-to-one relation, issue a `SET SKIP TO` command without any arguments.

The following example demonstrates the use of the `SET SKIP` command:

```
USE Classes
USE Students IN 2 ORDER Classno
SET RELATION TO Classno INTO Students
SET SKIP TO Students
LIST Class, Student.Name  NEXT 7
```

Here is the output from the `LIST` command:

```
Recno#  Class               Student.Name
1   Thermodynamics 633  Rick Leonard
1   Thermodynamics 633  Lisa Martin
```

```
1  Thermodynamics 633  George Daniels
1  Thermodynamics 633  John Goetz
1  Thermodynamics 633  Jim Rash
2  Philosophy 667      Luke Hobbes
2  Philosophy 667      Mary Socrates
```

The *SET SKIP OF* Command

You can selectively enable or disable menus, pads, and pop-up menu options with the SET SKIP OF command. You can operate on menu objects for user-defined menus as well as the FoxPro system menu bar. Here are the forms of the command:

```
SET SKIP OF MENU <menu name> <expL>

SET SKIP OF PAD <pad name> OF <menu name> <expL>

SET SKIP OF POPUP <popup name> <expL>

SET SKIP OF BAR <expN> | <system-option-name>
OF <popup name> <expL>
```

With any form of the SET SKIP OF command, if the Logical expression <*expL*> evaluates to a true (.T.) value, the menu control or the controls specified with SET SKIP OF are disabled. They are grayed out and can't be selected. *Grayed out* means that each disabled control is colored with a dim attribute (color pair 10). The menu, menu pad, pop-up menu, or pop-up option included in SET SKIP OF is disabled and appears in the disabled colors. If the logical expression <*expL*> evaluates to a false (.F.) value, the control or controls are enaled. They can be selected. Enabled controls display in the enabled color attributes (color pair 9).

The SET SKIP OF PAD command enables or disables a designated menu pad on the designated menu bar. The SET SKIP OF MENU command enables or disables all menu pads on the designated menu bar. The SET SKIP OF BAR command enables or disables a designated option in a pop-up menu. The SET SKIP OF POPUP command enables or disables all options in the designated pop-up menu.

You can selectively enable or disable a FoxPro system menu pad. To disable the **C**alculator option in the **S**ystem menu, use the following command:

```
SET SKIP OF BAR _MST_CALCU OF _MSYSTEM  .T.
```

Here is the command to disable the entire System pop-up menu:

```
SET SKIP OF POPUP _MSYSTEM .T.
```

Here is the command to disable the **S**ystem menu pad:

```
SET SKIP OF PAD _MSM_SYSTM OF _MSYSMENU .T.
```

Here is the command to disable the entire FoxPro menu bar:

```
SET SKIP OF MENU _MSYSMENU .T.
```

After the system menu bar is disabled, you can enable the entire FoxPro menu bar with the following command:

```
SET SKIP OF MENU _MSYSMENU .F.
```

Chapter 7 describes this command in detail and gives a complete listing of the FoxPro system menu bar objects.

The *SET SPACE* Command

The SET SPACE command controls the printing of a space between expressions displayed with the ? and ?? commands. Visual FoxPro programs always output a space to separate the display of ? and ?? command expressions. If SET SPACE is set to OFF, the output of this space is suppressed. Both settings are illustrated the following example:

Command	*Results*
SET SPACE ON	
? "Dog","Cat"	Dog Cat
SET SPACE OFF	
? "Dog","Cat"	DogCat

Here is the syntax:

```
SET SPACE ON ¦ off
```

Here is the equivalent CONFIG.FPW file command:

```
SPACE = ON ¦ off
```

The *SET STATUS* Command

Visual FoxPro contains two status bars. The character-based status bar is similar to the one in FoxPro 2.0 and other Xbase products. The Windows-style status bar displays at the bottom of the main FoxPro window. It is similar to the status bar in many Windows applications and resembles the status bars in the Microsoft File Manager, Word for Windows, Excel, and other Windows products. The only purpose for retaining the character-based, dBASE-style status bar is to retain compatibility with dBASE IV, FoxBASE+, and FoxPro 2.0 without making any changes to your program. Only one status bar can be active at a time. When you turn on the character-based status bar, the Windows-style status bar is turned off, and vice versa.

The Traditional Character-Based Status Bar

The SET STATUS command controls the display of the character-based status bar on the third line from the bottom of the display. The status line is displayed if SET STATUS is ON. Here is the syntax:

```
SET STATUS on ¦ OFF
```

Here is the equivalent CONFIG.FPW file command:

```
STATUS = on ¦ OFF
```

The following items are displayed on the status line:

- Name of currently executing program (if any)
- Current active database and table name
- Current record number
- Number of records in the table
- Lock type:
  `ExclLock` (Exclusive lock)
  `File Lock` (File lock is active)
  `ReadOnly` (File is read-only)
  `RecLock` (Current record is locked)
- Current record is deleted (Del or blank)
- Num Lock key status (Num or blank)
- Caps Lock key status (Caps or blank)
- Insert mode status (Ins or blank)

The Windows-Style Status Bar

The `SET STATUS BAR` command controls the display of the Windows-style status bar that displays at the bottom of the main FoxPro window. The status line is displayed if `SET STATUS BAR` is `ON`. Here is the syntax:

```
SET STATUS BAR on ¦ OFF
```

Here is the equivalent CONFIG.FPW file command:

```
STATUS BAR = ON ¦ off
```

The following items are displayed on the Windows-style status bar:

- Menu pad or menu option
- Information messages
- `SET MESSAGE TO` message
- Status information for the following commands when `SET TALK` is `ON`:

APPEND FROM	COUNT	PACK	SORT
AVERAGE	DELETE	REINDEX	SUM
CALCULATE	INDEX	REPLACE	TOTAL
COPY TO	JOIN	SELECT (SQL)	UPDATE

- Name of open database (DBC) if active
- Alias name for the current work area if active
- The current record number and the number of records in the database
- Lock type:
  `Exclusive` (Exclusive lock)
  `File Lock` (File lock is active)
  `Read Only` (File is read-only)
  `Record Lock` (Current record is locked)
- Key lock status
  `NUM` (Num Lock key is set)
  `CAPS` (Caps Lock key is set)
  `OVR` (Insert mode is active)
- Clock if you execute the `SET CLOCK STATUS` command

When objects with an associated `MESSAGE` clause (`DEFINE MENU`, `DEFINE POPUP`, `DEFINE BAR`, `@...GET`) are active, the messages always appear in the Windows-style status bar.

System messages and command results appear on the Windows-style status bar and remain displayed for a designated time. Then the messages disappear. You can specify the length of time these messages remain using the `SET STATUS TIMEOUT` command. Here is the syntax:

```
SET STATUS TIMEOUT TO [<expN>]
```

The numeric value `<expN>` specifies the number of seconds that messages and command results are displayed in the Windows-style status bar. If you specify 0, messages and results remain displayed until you press a key or click the mouse. The `SET STATUS TIMEOUT` default value is five seconds. If you omit the Numeric argument, the default setting is restored.

The *SET STEP* Command

The `SET STEP ON` command, like the `SET ECHO ON` command, opens the Trace window for debugging. Here is the syntax:

```
SET STEP on ¦ OFF
```

Here is the equivalent CONFIG.FPW file command:

```
STEP = on ¦ OFF
```

When you execute the `SET STEP ON` command, the Trace window appears. Debugging a program using the Trace window is described in Chapter 23. You can't close the window by executing `SET STEP OFF`. You close the Trace window by clicking on its close box or by executing the `DEACTIVATE WINDOW TRACE` command. When the Trace window closes, `SET STEP` is automatically set to `OFF`.

The *SET STICKY* Command

The `SET STICKY` command controls the display of FoxPro 2.0 System menu output. Visual FoxPro doesn't support `SET STICKY` and ignores it when it is present in an application. Here is the syntax:

```
SET STICKY ON ¦ off
```

NOTE

In FoxPro 2.0, when `SET STICKY` is `ON`, the mouse menu selection interface works like the Microsoft Windows Interface and other SAA/CUA-compliant interfaces. (*SAA/CUA* stands for IBM *System Applications Architecture/Common User Interface.*) When `SET STICKY` is `OFF`, the mouse menu selection interface operates as the Macintosh interface does. In Windows, you click on a menu option to open a pop-up menu and the pop-up menu remains open. In the Macintosh interface, you must point to a menu pad to open a pop-up menu, and the pop-up menu remains open for as long as you hold down the button.

The *SET SYSFORMATS* Command

The `SET SYSFORMATS` command specifies whether Visual FoxPro system settings are updated with the current Windows system settings when the Windows system settings are changed. This is the syntax:

```
SET SYSFORMATS on ¦ OFF
```

This is the equivalent CONFIG.FPW file command:

```
SYSFORMATS = on ¦ OFF
```

If `SET SYSFORMATS` is set to `ON`, the Visual FoxPro settings are updated when the Windows system settings are changed. Otherwise the Visual FoxPro system settings are not updated when the Windows system settings are changed. Incidentally, this setting is set to `ON` if you check the Use Systems Settings check box in the International tab in the Options dialog box. This command affects the following environment setting commands:

```
SET CENTURY
SET CURRENCY
SET DATE
SET DECIMALS
SET HOURS
SET MARK TO
SET POINT
SET SEPARATOR
```

The *SET SYSMENU* Command

The SET SYSENU command controls access to the FoxPro System menu bar. Here is the syntax:

```
SET SYSMENU ON ¦ off ¦ AUTOMATIC ¦ SAVE ¦ NOSAVE
     TO [ <System menu popup list>] ¦
     <System menu pad list>]    ¦
     DEFAULT ]
```

Here is the equivalent CONFIG.FPW file command:

```
SYSMENU = ON ¦ off
```

If SET SYSMENU is OFF, you can't execute the FoxPro system menu while a program is executing. If SET SYSMENU is ON and the system is waiting for input while in BROWSE, CHANGE, or READ, you can access the menu bar during program execution. However, the menu bar doesn't appear unless you press Alt or F10 or double-click the right mouse button. If you specify SET SYSMENU AUTOMATIC, the system menu is not only active during program execution but is also displayed. Menu options are enabled when appropriate for the command executing.

You specify the SET SYSMENU TO DEFAULT command to restore the FoxPro system menu to its default state. The SET SYSMENU SAVE command makes the current system menu configuration the default. If you issue a SET SYSMENU SAVE command and change the system menu, you can reinstate the saved menu with the SET SYSMENU TO DEFAULT command. If you specify the SET SYSMENU NOSAVE command, the menu bar is restored to the standard FoxPro configuration. If you specify SET SYSMENU TO with no other arguments, the system menu is completely disabled. You specify a TO *<System menu popup list>* or a TO *<System menu pad list>* clause to designate a subset of system menu objects to be displayed on the System menu bar.

For example, you can specify that only the Help menu pad appears on the FoxPro menu bar with the following command:

```
SET SYSMENU TO _MSM_HELP
```

Here is another example:

Table 10.27 contains a representation of the System menu bar contents after each SET SYSMENU command in the following examples executes.

```
* (1) Modify system menu to only display System and File pads
SET SYSMENU TO _MSM_HELP, _MSM_FILE
* (2) Now save the configuration
SET SYSMENU SAVE
* (3) Modify system menu to only display File menu pad
SET SYSMENU TO _MSM_FILE
* (4) Restore system menu to display System and File menu pads
SET SYSMENU TO DEFAULT
* (5) Now restore system menu to its standard startup
*     configuration.
SET SYSMENU NOSAVE
```

```
* (6) Disable system menu bar
SET SYSMENU TO DEFAULT
* (7) Restore system menu bar
```

Table 10.27. Representation of the System menu bar for the preceding example.

Command	*Menu*
	File **E**dit **V**iew F**o**rmat **T**ools **P**rogram **W**indow **H**elp
(1)	**F**ile **E**dit
(2)	**F**ile **E**dit
(3)	**F**ile
(4)	**F**ile **E**dit
(5)	**F**ile **E**dit
(6)	
(7)	**F**ile **E**dit **V**iew F**o**rmat **T**ools **P**rogram **W**indow **H**elp

A complete list of system menu names is provided in Chapter 7.

The *SET TALK* Command

The SET TALK command controls output from commands. If TALK is ON, the output displays. If TALK is OFF, no output displays. Here is the syntax:

```
SET TALK ON ¦ off ¦ WINDOW [<Window>] ¦ NOWINDOW
```

<Window> is the name of a user-defined window into which output is directed. If you specify the NOWINDOW keyword, output is directed to the main Visual FoxPro window. If you do not specify NOWINDOW, output is directed to the active user-defined window. Here is the equivalent CONFIG.FPW file command:

```
TALK = ON ¦ off
```

The following commands generate output only if TALK is ON:

- AVERAGE, COUNT, CALCULATE, STORE, SUM, and MEMVAR assignments display results.
- APPEND, AVERAGE, BLANK, CALCULATE, CONVERT, COPY, COUNT, EXPORT, IMPORT, JOIN, MODIFY, PACK, REPLACE, SUM, TOTAL, and UPDATE display a record counter while records are being processed.
- INDEX, REINDEX, and SORT display processing statistics.
- COMPILE, DEBUG, and DO display the line counter.
- FIND and SEEK display messages if unsuccessful.
- LOCATE and CONTINUE display status information.

When SET TALK is ON, messages and results display in the specified window (WINDOW *<expC>*), active window, or main FoxPro window unless the Windows-style status bar is active. If the Windows-style status bar is active, the output from commands such as COUNT and DELETE appears there. (See the section "The SET STATUS BAR Command.")

The *SET TEXTMERGE* Command

The Menu Designer generates code based on a *template*, which is just another FoxPro program that incorporates FoxPro text merge language extensions. The template is simply a blueprint for a generated program. It contains normal FoxPro commands plus special expressions enclosed in text merge delimiters. The expressions are replaced with values during the code generation process. The expressions consist of variables that are established when you create a screen or menu design. The code generated is standard FoxPro language code. The GENMENU.PRG program is an example of templates using the text merge features to generate menu code from menu (MNU) files.

The text merge extension to the FoxPro language consists of the following four commands:

```
SET TEXTMERGE ON TO <filename>
SET TEXTMERGE DELIMITERS TO <delimiter characters>
\   && Output line of text merge output followed by CR-LF
\\  && Output line of text merge output without CR-LF
```

The first command defines the file into which text-merged output is directed. It also turns on text merge processing. The second command defines the characters used to enclose database fields, memory variables, expressions, or functions. By default, the left delimiter is << and the right delimiter is >>. The last two commands direct text merge output to the file. If the line contains expressions enclosed in text merge delimiters, the expression is evaluated, and the results become part of the text output. For example, Listing 10.7 illustrates how to use the text merge features to create mail merge letters.

Listing 10.7. An example of the text merge feature.

```
*****************************************************************
*     * 08/21/92              LETTER.PRG              12:27:21 *
*****************************************************************
*     * Description:                                           *
*     *  This program illustrates how to use the text merge    *
*     *  features of FoxPro.                                   *
*     *  Program outputs mail merge letter to file, Let.TXT    *
*****************************************************************
CLEAR
m.From = "Joe Jones"
SET TEXTMERGE ON TO LET.TXT
USE CUSTOMERS
SCAN
\ <<REPLICATE(" ",50)>>
\\<<MDY(DATE())>>
\<<Company>>
\<<Address1>>
```

```
\
\Dear Mr. <<Company>>
\
\Enclosed is the information you requested.
\
\                   Sincerely
\                   <<m.From>>
\<<CHR(12>>
ENDSCAN
SET TEXTMERGE TO     && Close LET.TXT
```

The output from this program is directed to a file named LET.TXT. The following is a sample page of output from LET.TXT:

```
August 21, 92
DataTech Inc.
480 Village St.

Dear Mr. DataTech Inc.

Enclosed is the information you requested.

Sincerely
Joe Jones
```

Here is the syntax of the `SET TEXTMERGE` command:

```
SET TEXTMERGE [ on ¦ OFF] [TO [ <expFN> ] [ ADITIVE]]
[WINDOW <window name>] [SHOW ¦ NOSHOW]
SET TEXTMERGE DELIMITERS [TO <expC1> [,<expC2> ]]
```

Here is the equivalent CONFIG.FPW file command:

```
TEXTMERGE = on ¦ OFF
```

If `SET TEXTMERGE` is `ON`, expressions enclosed in text merge delimiters are evaluated before the command line is executed.

You can direct text merge output to a file, the screen, or a window. When you direct text merge output to a file, it is displayed to the screen or window unless the `NOSHOW` keyword is specified. If screen or window output is suppressed, you can start screen or window display by specifying the `SET TEXTMERGE SHOW` command. You can append output to an existing file by specifying the `ADDITIVE` keyword.

You specify two character expressions, *<expC1>* and *<expC2>*, to specify the left and right text merge delimiters. For example, if you want both delimiters to be a single ampersand (`&`) character, enter this:

```
SET TEXTMERGE DELIMITERS TO "&","&"
```

If you specify the `SET TEXTMERGE DELIMITERS TO` command with no arguments, the default delimiters (`<<` and `>>`) are reinstated.

The *SET TOPIC* Command

The `SET TOPIC` command is used to specify a help topic to display when the `HELP` command executes with no arguments or when you press the F1 key with no text selected. Here is the syntax:

```
SET TOPIC TO <expC>
```

The Character expression, `<expC>`, defines the help topic. This command is used along with the `SET HELP TO` command when you create a custom help system.

The *SET TOPIC ID* Command

The `SET TOPIC ID` command specifies the help topic to display when you invoke the FoxPro help system. The help topic is based on the topic context ID. Here is the syntax:

```
SET TOPIC ID TO <expN>
```

`<expN>` is the context ID of the help topic to display.

You have two options for making a help system for your FoxPro application. You can use the Windows-style help system (`SET HELP TO FOXHELP.HLP`), or you can use the DBF-type help system. If you are using the DBF-type help system, you can add a new Numeric (N) type field named `CONTEXTID`. Then you can assign a help context ID number from 1 to 32767 to each help topic. At a place in your application where a particular help topic is appropriate, you can use the `SET TOPIC ID TO` command to assign a context help ID for that topic. If the user activates help (presses F1 or clicks on a Help button), the appropriate context-sensitive help topic displays. Here is an example:

```
save_help = SET("HELP",1)        && Fetch current help file
SET HELP TO C:\MYAPP\MYHELP.DBF  && Establish your help file
...
* Establish context sensitivity to a topic id of 8
SET TOPIC ID TO 8
... && User gets help for CONTEXTID = 8 when help activates

...
SET HELP TO (save_help)   && Restore original help file
```

If you want context-sensitive help for a form or formset, include a command that establishes the `HelpContextID` property in the `Init` event procedure of the form. For example, if `CONTEXTID = 8` for the appropriate help topic, you can insert the following statement in the form's `Init` event procedure:

```
this.SETALL("HelpContextID",8)
```

Next you add a command button with the caption Help on the form. Add the following statement in the click event procedure for the command button:

```
HELP ID This.HelpContextID
```

When the user clicks on the help button, the appropriate help topic displays.

The *SET TRBETWEEN* Command

The `TRBETWEEN` keyword is shorthand for "trace between breakpoints." When you debug a program using the Trace window, you can single-step through the program one command line at a time, or you can force the program to continue executing until a breakpoint is encountered. In the latter mode, you have two display options: You can specify that every line of code is highlighted as it is executed with `SET TRBETWEEN ON`, or you can specify that the program run at full speed until a breakpoint is reached with `SET TRBETWEEN OFF`. Only the line containing the breakpoint is highlighted if `SET TRBETWEEN` is `OFF`. Here is the syntax:

```
SET TRBETWEEN ON ¦ off
```

Here is the equivalent CONFIG.FPW file command:

```
TRBETWEEN = ON ¦ off
```

The *SET TYPEAHEAD TO* Command

The `SET TYPEAHEAD TO` command specifies the maximum size of the typeahead buffer. The argument defines the number of characters that can be held in the buffer. The default value is 20; the range is from 0 to 128. Here is the syntax:

```
SET TYPEAHEAD TO <expN>
```

Here is the equivalent CONFIG.FPW file command:

```
TYPEAHEAD = <integer constant>
```

If `SET ESCAPE` is `OFF`, the Esc character is stuffed in the typeahead buffer each time you press Esc. This can cause problems because Esc becomes just another character in the input stream. When Esc is eventually encountered, it could cause certain commands such as `BROWSE` and `EDIT` to exit, producing unexpected results.

When `SET TYPEAHEAD` is `0`, the `INKEY()` function and the `ON KEY` command are disabled.

The *SET UDFPARMS TO* Command

The `SET UDFPARMS TO` command specifies whether variables are passed to user-defined functions by value or by reference. When a parameter is passed *by value*, its contents are transferred to a temporary memory variable. The user-defined function uses the temporary variable. You can change the value of the temporary variable, but the original parameter isn't changed.

When a parameter is passed *by reference*, its value can be changed because the actual variable is passed to the user-defined function. Incidentally, if you call a procedure (`DO <procedure>`), variables are passed by reference unless they are part of an expression. The easiest way to make a variable part of an expression is to enclose it in parentheses. Here is the syntax for the `SET UDFPARMS TO` command:

```
SET UDFPARMS TO VALUE ¦ REFERENCE
```

Here is the equivalent CONFIG.FPW file command:

```
UDFPARMS = VALUE ¦ REFERENCE
```

By default, database fields, memory variables, and array elements are passed to a user-defined function (UDF) by value (`SET UDFPARMS VALUE`). If you use `SET UDFPARMS TO REFERENCE`, variables are passed by value. Notice that when you pass an entire array as an argument, it is always passed by reference. You can also pass an individual variable in a parameter list by reference if you use the (`@`) character as a prefix. Here are some examples:

```
V=3
R=3
S=3
SET UDFPARMS VALUE          && Arguments are passed by value
? MYUDF( V )                && Pass by value; Displays 4
? MYUDF( @R )               && Pass by reference; Displays 4
? "V=",V, "R=",R            && Displays: V=  3  R=  4
SET UDFPARMS REFERENCE      && Arguments are passed by reference
? MYUDF( V )                && Pass by reference; Displays 4
? MYUDF( S )                && Pass by reference; Displays 4
? MYUDF( (R) )              && Pass by value; Displays 5
? "V=",V, " S=",S," R=",R  && Displays: V=  4 S=  4 R=  4
RETURN
FUNCTION MYUDF
PARAMETER X
X = X + 1
RETURN X
```

The *SET UNIQUE* Command

The `SET UNIQUE` command controls the unique indexing mode. When `SET UNIQUE` is `ON`, all subsequent `INDEX` commands generate a unique index. A *unique index* contains only one value for each key value in the index, regardless of the number of records in the file with the same key value. If `SET UNIQUE` is `OFF`, a key is generated for all records in a database table being indexed. After an index is created, the unique index mode is stored in the index header. `REINDEX` and index updates ignore the value of `SET UNIQUE`. The unique mode can be activated also by specifying the `UNIQUE` keyword with the `INDEX` command. See Chapter 13 for more information regarding unique indexes. Here is the syntax:

```
SET UNIQUE on ¦ OFF
```

Here is the equivalent CONFIG.FPW file command:

```
UNIQUE on ¦ OFF
```

The *SET VIEW TO* Command

The SET VIEW TO command establishes a view. A Visual FoxPro view consists of the following elements:

- Tables opened in designated work areas
- Established indexes for the tables
- All established relations (SET RELATION) between open tables
- All field lists (SET FIELD TO)
- All active filters for open tables (SET FILTER TO)
- Established format files (SET FORMAT TO)
- The SET SKIP TO status
- The SET DEFAULT and SET PATH settings
- The active alternate file
- The status bar state (SET STATUS)
- The SET PROCEDURE file setting
- The current help file (SET HELP TO)
- The current resource file

The views are stored in a binary file with a .VUE extension. You can create a view file with the CREATE VIEW <*expFN*> command. When SET VIEW executes, Visual FoxPro searches for a VUE file. If found, a view is established from the VUE file. If you specify a question mark as the argument, the Open File dialog box displays with the VUE files listed. More information is provided in Chapter 11.

You can open the View window to establish a view with the SET VIEW ON or ACTIVATE VIEW commands. If the View window is open, you can close it with the SET VIEW OFF or DEACTIVATE VIEW command. The View window is discussed in this chapter in the section "The SET Command and the View Dialog Box." Here is the syntax:

```
SET VIEW ON ¦ OFF

SET VIEW TO <expFN> ¦ ?
```

Here is the equivalent CONFIG.FPW file command:

```
VIEW = <filename>
```

The *SET WINDOW OF MEMO* Command

The SET WINDOW OF MEMO command designates the name of a window object where the memo field will be edited. The only reason FoxPro supports this command is to retain backward compatibility. When you edit a memo field, it is best to use the @...EDIT command. The WINDOW clause specified with the `@...GET` command overrides the `SET WINDOW OF MEMO` command specification. Windows are described in Chapter 7. Here is the syntax:

```
SET WINDOW OF MEMO TO <window name>
```

There is no equivalent CONFIG.FPW file command.

CONFIG.FPW Commands

The CONFIG.FPW commands in this section don't correspond to any `SET` command options presented in the previous sections. Most commands in this section determine the system configuration performed at initialization. These commands are presented in Table 10.28.

Table 10.28. CONFIG.FPW commands not related to `SET` commands.

Item	*Value*	*Default*	*Description*
`COMMAND`	*<command>*	""	Specifies an initial command to be executed by FoxPro. Any command can be specified.
`EDITWORK`	*<directory>*	Startup directory	Specifies where the editor directly places its work files.
`F11F12`	`ON ¦ OFF`	`ON`	Specifies `F11F12=OFF` if you don't have F11 and F12 keys. The cursor doesn't appear in the Command window when you start FoxPro.
`GENGRAPH`	*<program>*	GENGRAPH.PRG	Specifies the program used by relational query by example (RQBE) to output results to FoxGraph.
`GENMENU`	*<program>*	GENMENU.PRG	Specifies the Menu Designer template program.
`_GENPD`	*<application>*	GENPD.APP	Specifies the name of the printer setup interface application.

Item	*Value*	*Default*	*Description*
`_GENSCRN`	<*program*>	GENSCRN.PRG	FoxPro 2.6 screen generator program name. Not used in Visual FoxPro but retained for backward compatibility.
`_GENXTAB`	<*program*>	GENXTAB.PRG	Specifies the program used by RQBE to output results to FoxGraph when the cross-tabulation option is chosen.
`INDEX`	<*extension*>	IDX	Specifies the extension for FoxPro index files.
`LABEL`	<*extension*>	LBX	Specifies the extension for FoxPro label definition files.
`MVCOUNT`	`128-65000`	`256`	Specifies the maximum number of variables.
`OUTSHOW`	`ON ¦ OFF`	`ON`	Disables the feature that hides all windows in front of the current output window when you press Shift+Ctrl+Alt.
`OVERLAY`	<*directory*> [`OVERWRITE`]	FoxPro directory	Specifies where FoxPro places its overlay (.OVL) file.
`PROGWORK`	<*directory*>	Startup	Specifies where the directory program cache file is placed.
`REPORT`	<*extension*>	FRX	Specifies the extension for FoxPro report definition files.
`RESOURCE`	<*pathname*>	FOXUSER startup directory	Specifies where FoxPro finds the FOXUSER resource file. <*pathname*> can be a directory or a fully qualified pathname.

continues

Table 10.28. continued

Item	*Value*	*Default*	*Description*
SORTWORK	<*directory*>	Startup directory	Specifies where commands such as SORT and INDEX place their temporary work files.
TEDIT	[/<*expN*>] <*editor* name>	""	Specifies the external text editor used when you edit program files with MODIFY COMMAND. Optional clause /<*epN*> specifies the amount of memory FoxPro makes available for an external text editor.
TIME	1-1000000	6000	Specifies the amount of time that FoxPro waits for the print device to accept a character.
TMPFILES	<*drive:*>	Startup	Specifies the drive directory where the EDITWORK, SORTWORK, and PROGWORK files are stored.

The *SET()* Function

The SET() function returns the current status of selected SET commands. A single integer or the ON or OFF argument returns the status for any SET command. The "ON" or "OFF" character string or an integer value is returned. The argument of the SET() function is a character string containing the set option keyword. Here are examples:

Command Window	*Results*
? SET ("TALK")	ON
? SET("HOURS")	12
? SET ("BELL")	ON

The following SET() function arguments return YES or NO values:

ALTERNATE	CURSOR	HELP	SCOREBOARD
ANSI	DEBUG	INTENSITY	SHADOWS

AUTOSAVE	DELETED	LOCK	SPACE
BELL	DELIMITERS	LOGERRORS	SKIP
BLINK	DEVELOPMENT	MARGIN	STATUS
BRSTATUS	ECHO	MULTILOCKS	STATUS BAR
CARRY	ESCAPE	NEAR	STEP
CENTURY	EXACT	NOTIFY	SYSMENU
CLEAR	EXCLUSIVE	OPTIMIZE	TALK
CLOCK	FIELDS	PRINTER	TEXTMERGE
COLOR	FIXED	READBORDER	TITLE
COMPATIBLE	FULLPATH	RESOURCE	TWBETWEEN
CONFIRM	HEADINGS	SAFETY	UNIQUE
CONSOLE			

The following `SET()` function arguments return integer values:

BLOCKSIZE	MBLOCK	ODOMETER	REPROCESS
DECIMALS	MEMOWIDTH	POINT	TYPEAHEAD
HOURS	MOUSE	REFRESH	
MARGIN			

The `SET()` function also returns a character string containing the value of the environmental parameters shown in Table 10.29.

Table 10.29. The `SET()` function forms that return a character string.

BORDER	The `SET BORDER TO` string, which can be `SINGLE`, `DOUBLE`, `PANEL`, `NONE`, or digits representing border characters separated by commas
DATE	The international date type such as `AMERICAN`, `FRENCH`, or `JAPAN`
DEFAULT	The current disk drive and directory
DEVICE	The name of the device or file to which screen output is directed
DIRECTORY	The operating system directory (Same as `SYS(5)+SYS(2003)`)
DISPLAY	The type of video adapter mode (for example, `VGA25`)
FILTER	The filter expression
INDEX	The active index filename list
LIBRARY	The library filename
MARK	The date separation character
ORDER	The master index tag name
PATH	The FoxPro path

continues

Table 10.29. continued

`POINT`	The decimal point character
`PROCEDURE`	The procedure filename
`RELATION`	The `SET RELATION TO` argument in the form: `<key> INTO alias,...`
`SEPARATOR`	The Numeric thousands separation character
`SKIP`	The `SET SKIP TO` field list

The `SET("ATTRIBUTE")` function returns a string reflecting the color attributes set by the `SET COLOR` and `SET COLOR OF` commands. The format of the string is in the following form:

```
<att1>,<att2>,<att3> && <att4>,<att5>,<att6>, <att7>,<att8>
```

The attributes are defined in the following list:

Attribute	`SET COLOR OF`
`<att1>`	Normal
`<att2>`	Highlight
`<att3>`	Perimeter of the border of the screen (only applies to certain monitors)
`<att4>`	Messages
`<att5>`	Titles
`<att6>`	Boxes
`<att7>`	Information
`<att8>`	Fields

The following is sample output from `? SET("ATTRIBUTES")`:

```
N/W*,W+/RB,N/N && N/W*,W+/RB,N/W*,W+/RB,N/W*
```

Here are some examples:

Command Window	*Results*
`? SET("PATH")`	`C:\FOXPRO\SAMPLES`
`? SET("ATTRIBUTES")`	`W+/B,RG+/GB,N/N && RG+/B,W/B,RG+/GB,R+/W,N/GB`
`SET BORDER TO DOUBLE`	
`? SET("BORDER")`	`DOUBLE`

`SET BORDER TO ,,,,,,,200`	
`? SET("BORDER")`	`205,205,186,186,201,187,200,200`
`? SET("RELATION")`	`EMPNO INTO EMPLOYEE, MANFNO INTO MANUF`

You can use the `SET()` function to save an environmental state and restore it later in a program, as shown in the following example:

```
SaveColor = SET("ATTRIBUTE")
SaveStatus= SET("STATUS")='YES'

SET COLOR TO &SaveColor
IF SaveStatus
SET STATUS ON
ELSE
SET STATUS OFF
ENDIF
```

Some `SET` commands have multiple forms. The `SET()` function can have any numeric value as a second argument. You can use this second form of the `SET()` function to retrieve the value established by the second form of a multiple-form `SET` command. Table 10.30 presents environmental parameters for which the `SET()` function returns two values.

Table 10.30. The two-argument `SET()` function usage.

First Argument	*`SET(<expC>)` Returned Value*	*`SET(<expC>,1)` Returned Value*
`alternate`	`"ON"` or `"OFF"`	Alternate filename
`clock`	`"ON"` or `"OFF"`	Character string containing coordinates of clock (for example, `"69,0"`)
`currency`	`"LEFT"` or `"RIGHT"`	Character string containing currency symbol (for example, `"$"`)
`delimiters`	`"ON"` or `"OFF"`	Character string containing delimiters (for example, `"::"`)
`fields`	`"ON"` or `"OFF"`	Character string containing field list
`help`	`"ON"` or `"OFF"`	Filename of help file
`message`	message line number	Character string message
`printer`	`"ON"` or `"OFF"`	Filename or port designating where printed output is directed (for example, `"PRN:"`)

The SET() function is most commonly used to save an environmental setting at the beginning of a program or procedure and then restore it when the program exits. In this example, the SET EXACT setting is saved when you enter the program. Then when you exit from the program, you restore the value.

```
PROCEDURE YourProg
LOCAL llSetExact
llSetExact = SET("EXACT")== "ON"
SET EXACT OFF
  ... <code here>
IF llSetExact
   SET EXACT ON   && Restore original value
ENDIF
ENDPROC
```

The preceding example illustrates the traditional method of saving environmental settings. On the book's accompanying CD-ROM, there is an object-oriented program, ENVLIB.PRG. You use ENVLIB whenever you want to save an environmental setting, change it, and restore it. Most often, we need to do this with Visual FoxPro SET and ON commands and open table settings. The ENVLIB.PRG program's object-oriented design lets you do what you need in most cases with just one line of code. Once you get used to it, you'll never want to use the traditional method of saving environmental parameters again. ENVLIB.PRG contains programmatic definitions of ENV classes. You load the classes with the following command:

```
SET LIBRARY TO EnvLib.prg ADDITIVE
```

Then, anytime you want to save an environmental setting, change it, and restore it to its original value, you do so as shown in the following example:

```
PROCEDURE MyProg
LOCAL loSetExact
loSetExact = CREATEOBJECT("SetExact", "Off")
   <code goes here>
ENDPROC
```

All ENV classes save the current setting and set the new one in their Init events. The saved setting is restored in their Destroy event, so this happens automatically when the procedure returns and its object variable goes out of scope. To reset within the procedure, you can simply execute the RELEASE command to release the object variable.

NOTE

The ENV class definitions are stored in ENVLIB.PRG and ENV.VCX visual class libraries. They contain exactly the same information. The ENVLIB.PRG file is the programmatic definition and the ENV.VCX file is the visual definition. You only need one or the other to instantiate an object from the ENV class. Both of the definition files require the named constant file, the TRUE.H include file, at compile time. ENV.VCX is not on the CD-ROM. You can use the TRUE PrgToVcx program to convert ENVLIB.PRG to a visual class library, ENV.VCX. The PrgToVcx.PRG program is also on the book's accompanying CD-ROM.

The ENVLIB.PRG class library was contributed by Tom Rettig of Rettig Micro Corporation. You can freely use the library for whatever purpose you like. See the documentation in file ENV.DOC on the CD-ROM for more information.

Tom Rettig's Utility Extensions (TRUE) were developed by Rettig Micro Corporation; designed, implemented, and documented by Tom Rettig, and tested and quality assured by Tom Rombouts.

Summary

This chapter discusses the use and purpose of environmental parameters. Descriptions of the many varied forms of the `SET` command are scattered throughout the book; this chapter describes how to view, set, ad fetch all environmental parameters and CONFIG.FPW parameters.

Now that an environment has been established, it is time to focus on the Visual FoxPro database container and DBF file, which are described in Chapter 1.

11

DBF Files and Databases

Knowledge is of two kinds.
We know a subject ourselves, or
we know where we can
find information upon it.

—Dr. Samuel Johnson
(1709–1784)

This chapter describes the data files that Visual FoxPro creates and maintains. These files are called *DBF* files because they typically have the .DBF extension. DBF files are a standard in the personal computer industry. Many software products other than FoxPro and dBASE can read files (and some can write to files) in this format. FoxPro refers to DBF files as *tables.* I describe the DBF file format in some detail, not because you need to understand the data file structure to use the FoxPro programming language, but because the file format is a bridge between the FoxPro language and other languages and systems.

Next, I discuss the commands for creating, opening, and closing a DBF file and accessing individual records. Be prepared to turn back to Chapter 2, "Database Management and the FoxPro Language," to the section on logical views, because that section explains how you can use the FoxPro language to create virtual tables from simple DBF files.

Finally, I will tell you all about the *database container* file, which is a fascinating innovation introduced with the release of Visual FoxPro 3.0. The database container is a flat file that contains all information related to a database, which includes the names of tables, fields, objects, relationships between tables, triggers, stored procedures, and extended field properties. Visual FoxPro uses a database container to control the relationships between tables in a database.

The DBF File Format

FoxPro programs use the *flat file* format, as shown in Figure 11.1. Conceptually, the file format has not changed since the first version of the dBASE language was written in 1979. In fact, the JPLDIS format designed in 1972 is similar to the FoxPro flat file format.

A flat file is a sequential file of fixed-length records. The advantage of using fixed-length records is that finding the *n*th record (starting with 0) is simply a matter of positioning:

```
<header size> + (n * <record size>)
```

In specific instances, however, dBASE II, dBASE III, dBASE IV, FoxPro 2.0, and Visual FoxPro data file formats differ subtly.

All DBF files begin with a header that describes the file, as shown in Figure 11.2. In FoxPro, you call a DBF file a *table.* The first portion of the header, which some people refer to as the *prologue,* has a fixed length of 32 bytes. Following the prologue is a list of field descriptors. Because the number of fields can vary, the number of field descriptors varies as well. The total header size is stored in the prologue to make it easier to calculate the offset of any given record.

The Header Prologue

In older versions of dBASE and FoxPro the first byte of the prologue, called the *signature,* indicates the version of Xbase software that created the file. For dBASE II, this byte is 02H; for FoxBASE+, dBASE III, and FoxPro, it is 03H. FoxBASE+ and dBASE III, however, also set the high-order bit (making it 83H) when one or more memo or general fields are defined.

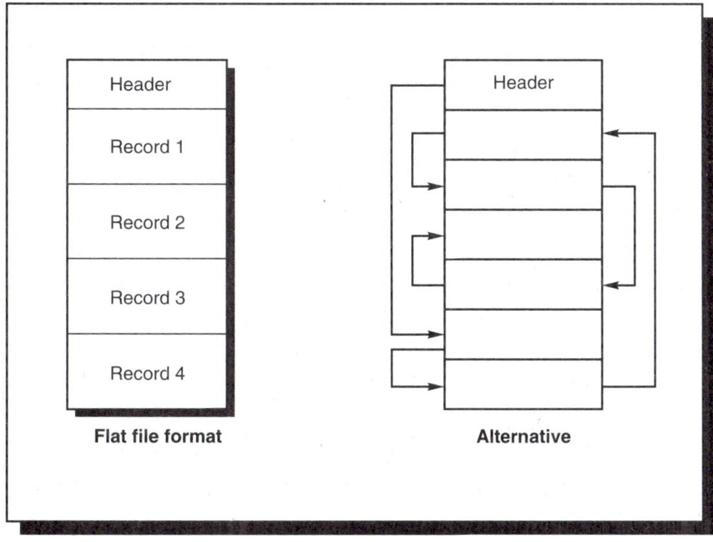

FIGURE 11.1.
A simple flat file format and the alternative file format.

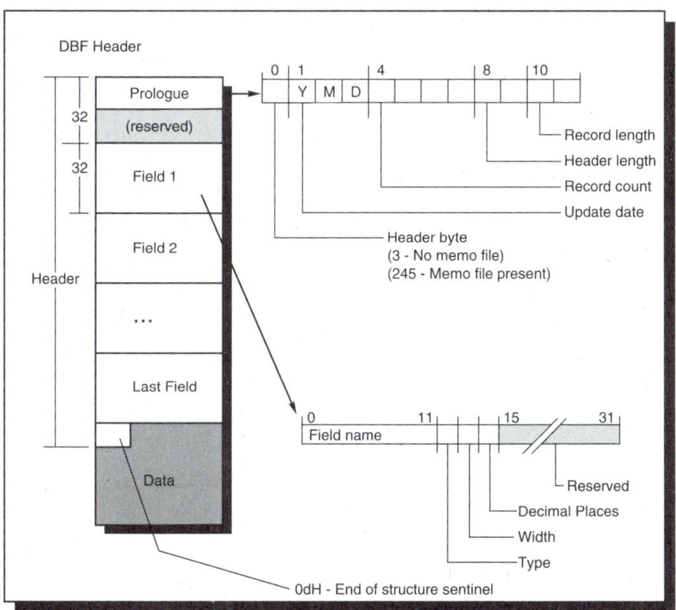

FIGURE 11.2.
The DBF file header structure.

Because the format of FPT (memo and general field) files was changed for FoxPro, the signature byte is changed to F5H to indicate that FoxPro created the memo file. FoxPro then looks for the associated FPT file. If the signature byte is 83H, FoxPro assumes that FoxBASE+ or dBASE III generated the memo file. The signature byte for all DBF files created by Visual FoxPro has a value of 0×30 hex (or 48 decimal). Although FoxPro can read all these formats, FoxBASE+

cannot read FoxPro or Visual FoxPro formats. So again, changing the contents of the signature byte has the effect of denying access to versions earlier than FoxPro.

The next three bytes are an anachronism. It is the date of the last update in *YY MM DD* format. It is an anachronism because modern operating systems, such as MS-DOS, maintain this information down to 1/30 of a minute. After the date, the number of records in the table is stored as an Intel 4-byte integer (a long integer in C).

Because signed long integers can express values up to 2^{31}, the maximum number of records FoxPro can support is 2,147,483,647. Luckily, no FoxPro user has a single disk that large before that limit would ever be reached, both the operating system and FoxPro would probably be bogged down.

After the number of records is a 2-byte integer that describes the total length of the header (`<header size>`), including the prologue, and another integer that describes the record length. The record length is the sum of the field lengths plus a 1-byte delete flag, which is discussed shortly.

`<header size>` defines the length of the field dictionary, prologue, field descriptors, and if the table is attached to a database, space (263 bytes) for the path of the database container (DBC) file.

The remainder of the 32-byte prologue consists of undocumented fields in reserved space. For example, the flag at offset 28 (29th byte) contains certain flag bits that have the following meanings:

- The DBF file has production MDX fields (for FoxPro and dBASE files)
- The DBF file has memo fields (for Visual FoxPro only)
- The DBF file has database container (DBC) fields (for Visual FoxPro only)

The fact that the header and field descriptors are 32 bytes each is another anachronism: Powers of 2 (32, 64, 128, and so on) could be read and written to disk faster than odd sizes under primitive operating systems.

Field Descriptors

Once upon a time, the 32-byte field descriptor was simply a copy of the structure used to describe a field or memvar in memory; in effect, several bytes of the descriptor were stored needlessly (but harmlessly) for convenience. With Visual FoxPro, this is no longer the case—the structure in memory is quite different from the structure stored on disk.

As shown in Figure 11.2, the following important information is stored in the field descriptor:

- Name (10 bytes, uppercase, terminated with \0)
- Type (a single letter `B`, `C`, `D`, `I`, `L`, `M`, `N`, `F`, `G`, `Y`, or `T`)

- Width (a single byte)
- Number of decimal places (for type `B`, `F`, or `N` only)

Type `F` and type `N` numbers are the same. By recognizing type `F` as a synonym for type `N`, external programs that access dBASE III and FoxBASE+ DBF files can be made compatible with FoxPro tables.

Field descriptors are stored sequentially in all versions. The signature byte of the last descriptor is 0DH, another anachronism due to the need in dBASE II for a sentinel byte to mark the last defined field.

If a DBF file (table) is associated with a database container, you can have additional field descriptors, and the extended field descriptors (called *field properties*) are stored in the database container file. These are the field properties:

- Long field names
- Default values for data in a field
- Field level rules (for example, the `@...GET VALID` clause)
- Primary and candidate key designation

These extended attributes are discussed in the section "The Database Container File."

In Visual FoxPro, the 19th byte in each of the field descriptors is a flag byte. Bits in this flag byte designate information about the field. Here is a description of the meaning of the bits:

- Bit 0 (low-order bit) indicates that the field is a system field that is invisible. You cannot access or view this field from within Visual FoxPro. In Visual FoxPro 3.0 there is one type of system field, called a *nullable field,* that is used to contain the null flags for fields that are allowed to have a null value. This field is sized to contain 1 bit for each preceding field that is marked as nullable.
- Bit 1 denotes whether a field is nullable. If this bit is set, the field is a nullable field. This means that this field can contain null values. Null values are indicated by the presence of 1 bit in the appropriate position of the system field. When the null bit is set on, the contents of the field are ignored because the field contains a null value.
- Bit 2 denotes whether a field is translatable. If this bit is set, the field is a `NOCPTRANS` field. This means that this field contains binary information and that Visual FoxPro must not be translated to or from the system's code page when reading or writing.

The Database Container Filename

If the table is attached to a database container (DBC) file, the name of the database container is stored in the tables following the field descriptor signature byte (0DH). Only the DBC filename is stored if the database container file is in the current directory. However, if the DBC file is in another directory, the relative path of the DBC file is stored in the database container.

Data Records

Data records consist of a 1-byte delete flag (set to `*` if the record is marked for deletion) followed by fixed-length fields stored in the order in which they are described in the header. Fields have different characteristics based on their type, as shown in the following list:

- Character fields are stored verbatim, without the \0 terminator.
- Date fields are stored as 8-byte ASCII numbers in *YYYYMMDD* format.
- DateTime fields are stored as 8-byte binary numbers.
- Float numbers, like `N` numbers, are stored in ASCII numbers.
- Logical fields are `.T.` or `.F.` (which translate to appropriate characters for display in different languages).
- Memo and general fields are 4-byte binary integers that refer to blocks in the associated FPT file.
- Number fields are stored in ASCII format.
- Double and Currency fields are stored as 8-byte (64-bit) IEEE binary floating-point format.
- Integer fields are stored in 4-byte binary integer format.

It is unusual that numbers and dates are stored in ASCII format: They are kept as binary numbers in memory and must be converted whenever they are used. (Internally, type `N` and `F` numbers are in 64-bit IEEE floating-point format.) One reason to use ASCII files is that they are easier to read when you use a debugger to try to recover a damaged data file. Another advantage is that the ASCII file format is easier for software vendors to decipher. This has resulted in the proliferation of support for the DBF file format throughout the software industry. Most software publishers support the DBF format in their products.

Visual FoxPro is the first Xbase product that has deviated from the traditional ASCII file format for DBF data. The Double, Integer, DateTime, General, and Memo fields are stored as binary values. By storing these fields as binary values, speed performance should be greatly improved because ASCII to binary conversion will not be required when accessing data in a Visual FoxPro table.

Data records follow the 0DH field descriptor signature byte, or appear immediately after the database container (DBC) filename if the table is attached to a database, and continue sequentially. The last byte of the DBF file is 1AH, or ASCII EOF. This is an anachronism due to the lack of a difference between physical and logical file length in primitive operating systems.

Creating Tables

Everything you need to know to create a table (DBF file) is in the list of field descriptors. The number of fields establishes the size of the header, and each field has a fixed width, so you can calculate the record size.

The CREATE command displays the Table Designer, which is a dialog box designed to support the creation of such a list. (See Figure 11.3.) The MODIFY STRUCTURE command uses the same screen form as the CREATE command, except the MODIFY STRUCTURE command enables you to edit an existing DBF file's list of fields.

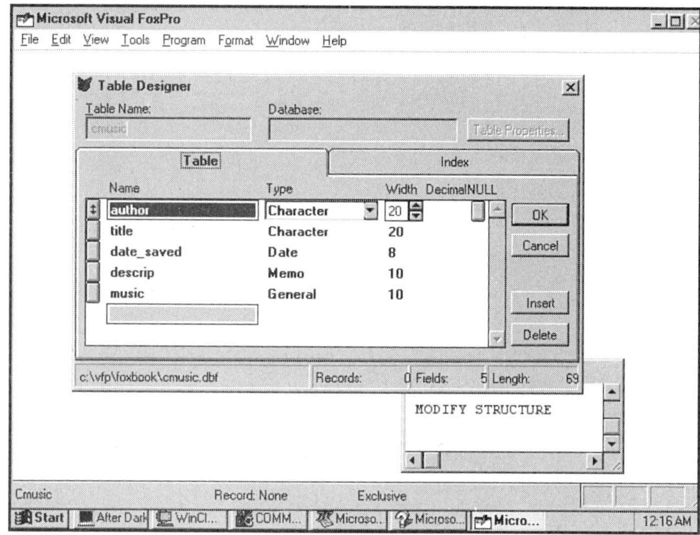

FIGURE 11.3.
The CREATE command database screen.

A list of field descriptors looks very much like a data file with the fields shown in Table 11.1. The traditional Xbase way to create a DBF file is to use the interactive CREATE command. However, you can use the Visual FoxPro language to create a DBF file out of thin air—you use the CREATE TABLE command described in the section "The CREATE TABLE and ALTER TABLE Commands." Remember that FoxPro refers to DBF files as tables. It is similar to the SQL CREATE TABLE command described in Chapter 18, "Queries Using SQL and the Query Designer." Using the CREATE TABLE command, you can create the table shown in Figure 11.3 using the following:

```
CREATE TABLE Cmusic FREE ;
   (Author C(20), ;
    Title C(20),  ;
    Date_Saved D, ;
    Descrip M,    ;
    Music G )
```

You can modify a DBF file using the ALTER command described later in this chapter. For example, here is how to add a new 12-character-wide Numeric field, Cost, to the Cmusic.DBF file:

```
ALTER TABLE Cmusic ;
    ADD Cost N(12,2)
```

There also exists a traditional Xbase technique for programmatically creating a DBF file. You use any existing DBF file to create another by using

```
USE <any file>
COPY TO Temp STRUCTURE EXTENDED
USE Temp
ZAP
```

for each field desired. Here are examples:

```
APPEND BLANK
REPLACE Field_Name WITH <field name>, ;
Field_Type WITH <field type>, ;
Field_Len WITH <field length>, ;
Field_Dec WITH <field decimals>
CREATE New FROM Temp
```

Table 11.1. A table created with the COPY STRUCTURE EXTENDED command.

Name	*Type*	*Length*	*Decimal*
`Field_Name`	Character	10	
`Field_Type`	Character	1	
`Field_Len`	Numeric	3	0
`Field_Dec`	Numeric	3	0

More generally, you can use structure extended tables to examine and modify the structure of any given DBF file using FoxPro language commands.

Accessing DBF Files

You access a DBF file in a context called a *work area.* (See Chapter 3, "The Referencing Environment.") FoxPro 2.0 has 25 work areas available, and you can refer to them using the numbers 1 through 25. You can refer to the first 10 work areas using the letters *A* through *J,* for historical reasons. In Visual FoxPro, the number of work areas has increased from 225 to 32767. You will definitely exhaust memory resources before you ever reach the 32767 work area limit.

Only one work area is current at any time. A DBF file can be accessed in another work area explicitly or in the current work area by default. Work areas with active DBF files have names called *aliases.* If the alias is not specified explicitly when the DBF file is put into use, the name of the DBF file is used as a default alias. For example, if the PAYROLL.DBF table is active in a work area, you can refer to that work area by the alias `PAYROLL` unless the default alias is explicitly overridden. If the filename is GL0208.DBF, an explicit alias, such as `LEDGER`, might make the program more readable.

When a DBF file is put into use, its header is read into memory, and the work area's data changes to reflect the new active status. The DBF header indicates whether an FPT or a CDX file is associated with the DBF file; if so, these files are opened as well. A buffer equal to the size of a single record is created, and the first record is read into memory. The work area keeps track of the current record number; the format file (if any); relationships between DBF files, filters, access privileges, and locks; and other data specific to a particular DBF file session.

If associated files cannot be found, action must be taken before Visual FoxPro allows access to the DBF file. If the FPT file is missing, you must disable general and memo fields for the duration of the session or create an empty FPT file, wiping out all previous general and memo field information in the DBF file. If the structural CDX index file is missing, you must remove the reference to it in the DBF file header before proceeding. Visual FoxPro displays a message box that prompts you for a choice between canceling the `USE` command and deleting the missing CDX file reference indicator from the DBF file header.

If dBASE IV created the DBF file and the file has a production index (MDX), FoxPro converts this index to a CDX index. Likewise, if a DBT file was created by FoxBASE+, dBASE III, or dBASE IV, FoxPro converts this file to an FPT memo file. You can always create a DBT memo file again using the `COPY TO` command with the `FOXPLUS` conversion type keyword specified.

Opening a Table (DBF File)

Using the `USE` command is the only way you can access a table with the FoxPro language. `USE` can perform several other functions at one time, such as opening index files and naming the work area something other than the DBF filename. Here is the syntax for opening a table:

```
USE <expFN> ¦ <sqlViewName> ¦ ?
[AGAIN]
[INDEX <index list> ¦ ? ]
[ORDER [TAG] <tag name> [OF <.cdx file>] [ASCENDING ¦ DESCENDING] ]
[ALIAS <expWA1>]
[EXCLUSIVE ¦ SHARED] [NOUPDATE] [NOREQUERY] [NODATA]
[<data session number>]
[IN <expWA2> ¦ 0 ]
```

This command opens the table referred to by `<expFN>` in the current work area or the work area specified by the `IN` clause. In Visual FoxPro, you also can open a SQL view file (`<expFN>`) that was created using the `CREATE` command. If the work area is not explicitly named by an `ALIAS` clause, the filename is used, if possible.

Aliases must conform to the rules for other FoxPro identifiers. They must start with an alphabetic character, and the remaining characters must be alphanumeric or underscores (_). Because the single letters *A* through *J* are reserved for use by FoxPro and because filenames are not restricted to the rules for FoxPro identifiers, filenames cannot always be used as aliases. If a default alias is needed and the filename is not suitable, one of the single letters *A* through *J* already assigned to the work area does double duty as an alias. You can specify an alias of `0`, which selects the lowest available work area before it places the file in use. In the following example, Visual FoxPro tables are placed in use in work areas 1 through 3; the fourth statement places the MYFILE file in use in the lowest available work area, which is work area 4:

```
USE ONE IN 1
USE TWOFILE IN 2
```

```
USE THREE IN 3
USE MYFILE IN 0
```

Although the structural compound index (CDX) file (if it exists) is opened automatically, you can use the INDEX clause (described further in Chapter 13, "Data Ordering") to activate particular CDX tags or old-fashioned IDX indexes. The ORDER clause specifies which tag or IDX file determines the logical record ordering. You can also specify whether indexes are accessed in ASCENDING or DESCENDING order. The EXCLUSIVE clause denies other users on a network access to the table. (This is described in more detail in Chapter 25, "Multiuser Considerations.") You can specify the NOUPDATE keyword to prevent modification of data or structure in a Visual FoxPro table.

The AGAIN keyword relaxes the restriction against opening the same table in two different work areas. When a table is open in one work area, and you specify the AGAIN keyword when you open the table in another work, the table in the new work area takes on the attributes of the table in the original work area. For example, if a table is opened for read-only or exclusive access and is opened again in another work area, the table is opened for read-only or exclusive access in the new work area. This restriction is necessary because FoxPro is not set up to deal with the conflicts that might arise from misuse.

You might wonder why you would want to open a table twice. Here is an example. Suppose that you wanted to access employee records and you would like to list all of the employees who made more money than their bosses. Consider the following table, EMPLOYEE.DBF:

```
Structure for table:    C:\VFP\FOXBOOK\CHAP11\EMPLOYEE.DBF
Field  Field Name  Type        Width  Dec  Index  Collate Nulls
    1  LNAME       Character     20                         No
    2  FNAME       Character     20                         No
    3  EMPNO       Numeric        8                         No
    4  SALARY      Numeric       10    2                    No
    5  POSITION    Character     10                         No
    6  BOSS_ID     Numeric        8                         No
```

The EMPLOYEE.DBF table contains the following data records:

```
Record#  LNAME    FNAME  EMPNO    SALARY POSITION  BOSS_ID
      1  Zort     Mort   2233   29000.00 Salesman  2222
      2  Johnson  Jane   5132   30000.00 Salesman  2222
      3  Altman   Robert 2341   27000.00 Engineer  2222
      4  Clinton  Joe    2222   28000.00 VP        4122
      5  Smith    Roger  4122   78000.00 President    0
```

In table EMPLOYEE.DBF, there is a field, BOSS_ID, that contains the employee number (EMPNO) for the employees' boss. You need to do what is called a *self-join.* A self-join is when you establish a relation between a table and itself. FoxPro will not allow you to relate a table to itself. You can get around this by opening the table twice and relating the first instance of the table to the second.

Listing 11.1 presents the source code for a program (AGAIN.PRG) that illustrates the use of the AGAIN keyword and illustrates how to display information about employees who make more money than their bosses.

Listing 11.1. The source listing of a program that illustrates the use of the AGAIN keyword.

```
****************************************************************
*     * 10/10/95            AGAIN.PRG               20:50:16 *
****************************************************************
*     *                                                      *
*     * Description:                                         *
*     *  Illustrates how to use the AGAIN command to         *
*     *  perform a "self join"                               *
****************************************************************
CLEAR ALL
USE Employee
INDEX ON EmpNo TAG EmpNo
USE Employee AGAIN ALIAS Boss ORDER EmpNo IN 0
SET RELATION TO Boss_ID INTO Boss
LIST FIELDS EmpNo, Employee.LName,  Salary, ;
            Boss.Lname, Boss.Salary ;
             FOR Salary > Boss.Salary AND FOUND("Boss")
```

Notice that the `ALIAS Boss` clause provides a way of referencing the EMPLOYEE.DBF table the second time it is placed in use. The `IN 0` clause places the table in use in an unused work area. Here is the resultant output from the execution of the AGAIN.PRG program:

```
Record#  EMPNO Employee.LNAME   SALARY     Boss.LNAME  Boss.SALARY
      1   2233 Zort            29000.00    Clinton        28000.00
      2   5132 Johnson         30000.00    Clinton        28000.00
```

FILENAME AND WORK AREA EXPRESSIONS

A typical programming language, such as BASIC, uses the following syntax for a file open command:

`OPEN <filename>`

`<filename>` is defined as an expression of type Character. Quotation marks are required to enter a literal name.

For reasons explained in Chapter 2 the FoxPro language was designed to accept an unquoted string literal for the `USE` command. This makes it difficult for the user to amend the syntax to allow the use of scalar variables, Character operators, and built-in functions. It was accomplished in FoxPro, while maintaining backward compatibility, by specifying the syntax of a filename expression as a Character expression, with one exception. The exception is that if the Character expression is formed by a single identifier (which would ordinarily be taken as a scalar variable or memvar), you can assume that it is a quoted string literal:

```
USE A         && Treated as USE "A"
USE "A"       && Refers to a file called A
USE A+B       && Concatenates two memvars, A and B
USE "A+B"     && Refers to a file called A+B
USE (A)       && Refers to the value of memvar A
```

```
USE UPPER(A)  && Refers to the value of memvar A
USE A+""      && Refers to the value of memvar A
```

Filename expressions are acceptable to FoxPro wherever the FoxBASE+ and dBASE III syntax specifies unquoted string literals.

A work area expression is similar. In addition to a Numeric expression evaluating to an integer value from 1 to 25, the expression can be of type Character, evaluating to either a valid alias name (not case sensitive) or to a letter from *A* to *J*. The expression parser tries all possibilities before giving up.

Closing a Table (DBF File)

The `USE` command also closes tables, which ensures that the disk image of the file is sound. Until the file is closed, the data is not guaranteed safe. The `SET AUTOSAVE ON` feature essentially closes and reopens the table whenever its contents change, effectively guaranteeing its safety. Here is the syntax for closing files:

```
USE [IN <expWA> ]
```

Both forms of the `USE` command first close any table open in the current or specified work area. If you specify a filename, the table is opened as described in the preceding section. If you do not specify a filename, the work area is left inactive. Placing a table in use twice closes and re-opens the table to ensure that it is safely written to disk. However, `SET AUTOSAVE ON` is more effective for this purpose because it is ubiquitous and much faster. To *checkpoint* (as the operation is called) only at program-controlled times, set `AUTOSAVE` to `OFF` and reuse the file as you like.

The worst thing a FoxPro program can do is lose data; everything is organized to fight that possibility. Therefore, all open tables are automatically closed by the `QUIT` command, and an `ABORT` command is not available to circumvent this feature. You can turn off your computer to simulate an `ABORT` command, but it cannot be done using the FoxPro language.

The `CLOSE DATABASES` and `CLOSE ALL` commands also safely close all open tables. When a table is closed, any associated DBT, CDX, IDX, or FMT files are safely closed as well.

Accessing DBF Header Information

The FoxPro programming language provides several built-in functions for extracting information about open tables. For example, the `DBF()` function returns the name of the table, and the `ALIAS()` function returns the alias name. Both functions take an optional work area expression argument (`<expWA>`) that specifies a work area other than the current work area. The current work area is the default. Other functions make available the information stored in the table header:

- `FIELD()` returns the name of a particular field.
- `FCOUNT()` returns the number of fields.
- `FLDCOUNT()` returns the number of fields as does `FCOUNT()`.
- `ISREADONLY()` returns a Logical true value if the Visual FoxPro table in the specified work area is read-only.
- `LUPDATE()` returns the date of the last update.
- `RECCOUNT()` returns the number of records.
- `RECSIZE()` returns the size of a single record in bytes.

For all these functions, you can include a work area expression argument (`<expWA>`) to specify a different work area.

You can use the `ISREADONLY()` function to determine if a Visual FoxPro table in the specified work area is a read-only table. You can open a Visual FoxPro table as read-only by specifying the `NOUPDATE` keyword with the `USE` command. You can also open a Visual FoxPro table as read-only by checking the **R**ead Only check box when opening the Visual FoxPro table from the Open dialog box. When the MS-DOS read-only attribute is set for a Visual FoxPro table, the file is opened in read-only mode. Note that a cursor created with the SQL `SELECT` command is always in read-only mode.

The `FLDLIST(<expN>)` function returns a character string containing the fields and calculated field expressions of a `SET FIELDS TO` command. You specify the Numeric argument (`<expN>`) to designate which field to return. If you specify `1`, the first field is returned; if you specify `2`, the second field is returned; and so forth. If `<expN>` exceeds the number of fields in the list, a null string is returned. If `<expN>` is omitted, a character string is returned containing all the field names, separated by commas. The `FLDLIST()` function returns a field name preceded by the alias name and a period.

NOTE

In dBASE IV, the `FLDLIST()` function returns a string containing the alias and field name separated by `->`. FoxPro uses a period as a separator. Here is an example:

dBASE IV	`alias->fieldname`
Visual FoxPro 3.0	`alias.fieldname`

Also, the read-only field indicator (/R) recognized by dBASE IV is ignored by FoxPro.

Record Operations

At any time, an open table has only one current record. References to fields act on the data instances for the current record only. When a table is first put into use, the current record is the first record in the file or the first record in index order if an index was specified. Using the SKIP command, however, you can create a situation in which there is no current record, as I shall discuss.

The GOTO command (which can be abbreviated GO) and the SKIP command change the current record directly. Other commands, particularly data set operations (see Chapter 12, "Data Set Operations"), can alter the current record as well. Relations, which are discussed shortly, alter the current record in related work areas.

It is useful to think in terms of a moving record pointer that points to one record at a time. This pointer can be moved to a particular physical record by specifying the record number; it can be moved logically by going to the TOP or BOTTOM of the file; or it can be moved relative to the current record.

The GOTO command positions this pointer to a particular record or to the TOP or BOTTOM. Its syntax has several forms:

```
GO <expN> [IN <expWA>]
GOTO <expN> [IN <expWA>]
<expN>

GO TOP [IN <expWA>]
GOTO TOP [IN <expWA>]

GO BOTTOM [IN <expWA>]
GOTO BOTTOM [IN <expWA>]
```

When you use the <*expN*> argument, pointer movement is to the absolute record number indicated. The GOTO TOP and GOTO BOTTOM commands are more abstract because they refer to index order if an index is in use. GOTO TOP is the same as GOTO 1 if no index is in use. Likewise, GOTO BOTTOM is equivalent to GOTO RECCOUNT() when there is no index. When an index controls record order, however, the GOTO TOP and GOTO BOTTOM commands refer to the first and last records, in index order, which are usually quite different records. You can optionally specify which active database is positioned by specifying the IN clause.

The SKIP command positions the record pointer relative to the current record in either the current or a specified work area. Here is the syntax:

```
SKIP <expN> [IN <expWA>]
```

If <*expN*> is positive, the record pointer moves forward; If it is negative, the record pointer moves backward. That is, SKIP moves to the next or previous record. It can also move by more than one record at a time, although this is rarely necessary. The commands for first (TOP), last (BOTTOM), next, and previous work differently if an index is in use. This is shown in Table 11.2.

Table 11.2. The effects of GOTO and SKIP with and without an index.

Action	*FoxPro Command*	*Without Index*	*With Index*
First	`GO TOP`	`GOTO 1`	`GOTO <first>`
Last	`GO BOTTOM`	`GOTO RECCOUNT()`	`GOTO <last>`
Next	`SKIP`	`GOTO RECNO()+1`	`GOTO <next>`
Previous	`SKIP -1`	`GOTO RECNO()-1`	`GOTO <prev>`

If an index is in use, terms like *first* and *next* refer to index order. Without an index, the position is physical and absolute; with an index, the position is logical and relative. Full-screen commands, such as `CHANGE` and `BROWSE`, use these positioning commands conceptually as well, to present records in physical (sometimes called *natural*) or logical (indexed) order. Data set operations, described in Chapter 12, also support these concepts.

Skipping past the last record is an important condition. Typically, a program that skips through records wants to detect the last record in order to end a loop. In other cases, skipping too far is a result of user misunderstanding and an error message should be displayed. Therefore, FoxPro supports an imaginary sentinel record following the last record, called the *end-of-file marker.* When the database is positioned to this record (for example, with `GO BOTTOM` followed by `SKIP`), all fields are blank, and the `EOF()` function returns `.T.`. Skipping past the last record sets `EOF()` to `.T.`, but no error occurs. If an attempt is made to skip past this imaginary record, however, an error occurs. In this manner, loop operations can detect the end of the file in an orderly fashion without generating an error condition.

To detect skipping backward from the first record, the `BOF()` function is provided. Some elegance is lost, however, because there is no sentinel record number 0. Instead, attempts to skip backward from the first record leave the pointer on the first record and set the `BOF()` function to `.T.`. The second attempt returns an error.

Deleting Records

Because physically removing a record is a relatively time-consuming operation, FoxPro programs have long supported a batch delete facility in which records are tagged for removal with the `DELETE` command. Tagging records takes almost no time, and as a side effect, allows for recovery (with the `RECALL` command) before the record is erased. The `PACK` command erases all records tagged for deletion at one time.

The *delete flag* is a built-in field at the start of every record. The field is one character wide. It contains an ASCII space if the record is active, an asterisk if the record is tagged for deletion, or an ASCII EOF (1AH) if the record is the end-of-file marker. The EOF tag is an anachronism that probably will not be supported in future versions, but its absence should go unnoticed because there is no programmatic access to the EOF tag. The DELETED() function returns .T. if the current record has been tagged for deletion.

Removing a record is more difficult than it sounds. In theory, the only way to erase records is to rewrite the entire table and copy only the records that are not tagged for deletion. In practice, the PACK command uses a shortcut, as shown in Figure 11.4. The PACK command shifts records in place, taking advantage of the fact that a PACK never expands the table, but only potentially shrinks it. It's still time-consuming—to remove record 10 from a 20-record table, records 11 through 20 must be rewritten.

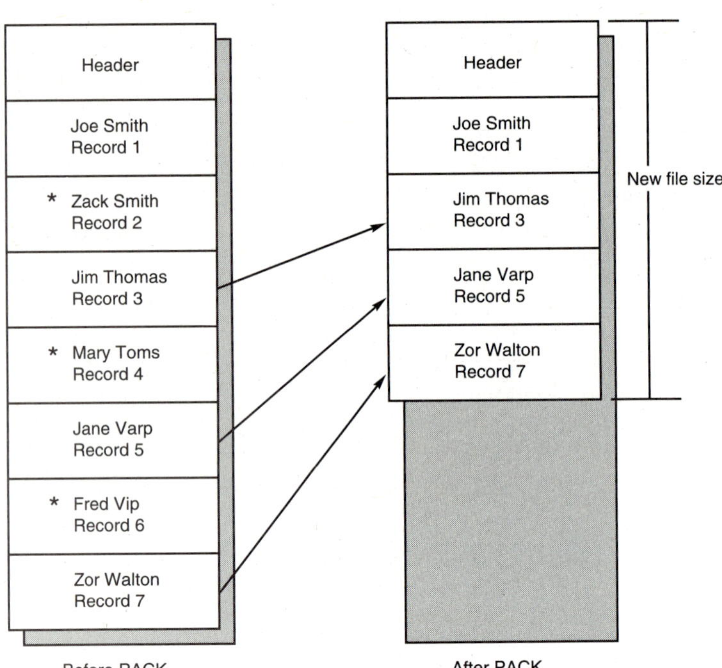

FIGURE 11.4.
The operation of the PACK *command operation.*

With dBASE II programmers occasionally needed to mark all of the records in a table as deleted (DELETE ALL) and remove all of the records marked as deleted from the file (PACK). This operation required reading and writing each record to tag each for deletion, then rewriting the table. In dBASE III, the DELETE ALL and PACK commands were combined into the useful, but dangerous, ZAP command. ZAP truncates the table just past the header and clears the record count stored in the header. Obviously, ZAP is considerably faster than deleting and packing. The ZAP command is used in all Xbase languages, including Visual FoxPro. When you execute ZAP, FoxPro prompts you to confirm that you really intend to destroy your data. Of course, this confirmation prompt does not protect you if you have disabled the safety feature with the SET SAFETY OFF command. Here is the syntax of the ZAP command:

```
ZAP [IN <expWA>]
```

Visual FoxPro lets you specify with the IN clause the work area for the table that is to be zapped.

Adding Records

Initially, a new table contains no records, so that both the EOF() and BOF() functions return .T.. Records are added with the APPEND command either interactively, one at a time, or in batch mode from another data file. APPEND BLANK adds a new, empty record to the end of the file. The interactive form of APPEND is equivalent to APPEND BLANK followed by EDIT.

The INSERT command physically inserts a new record after the current record, moving all subsequent records as necessary. Options include INSERT BLANK, which forgoes the edit, and INSERT BEFORE, which inserts the record before the current record rather than after. If an index is in use, INSERT is identical to APPEND; the record is positioned in index order anyway, so it is simply added to the end of the physical file.

When a new record is added, it is filled with spaces. Accordingly, the screen form that the APPEND command displays is empty. The SET CARRY ON command, however, causes the step in which the record is filled with spaces to be left out so that the record contains its previous values. The SET CARRY TO command was introduced in dBASE IV and cloned by FoxPro 1.2. It extends the concept on a field-by-field basis; only some fields are carried over while others are filled with blank spaces. Both CHANGE and BROWSE have append modes in FoxPro and respect SET CARRY as well.

Logical Views

A *logical view* is the exact table of data needed for the task at hand. It may be the same as the physical table, but more often the view is needed in index order with some records filtered out. Sometimes a single logical view consists of more than one physical table.

Logical tables are more important than the physical file (called a *base table*), because the natural order (or entry order) of the records probably does not reflect the order that is appropriate for a particular application. A list of names and addresses should be in order by name, regardless of entry order. An index accomplishes this handily. Furthermore, commands that affect the physical file, such as INSERT, PACK, or SORT, are slow operations that can be avoided by using logical views.

Several elements of the FoxPro language come together to create a logical view from one or more physical tables. As you may recall from Chapter 2, a *selection* is a horizontal subset of the table; that is, only certain records are selected, or visible. The FoxPro language implements selection with the SET FILTER TO command: Only records for which the *filter expression* is true are visible. The GOTO and SKIP positioning commands respect the filter, so that SKIP continues skipping until a record that matches the filter expression is found. Issuing the command SET FILTER TO .F. hides all records and sets EOF() and BOF() to .T..

The delete flag is a form of selection as well. Deleted records can be hidden from view with the `SET DELETED ON` command. Positioning commands respect this setting, but an explicit `GOTO <record number>` command ignores both the `SET DELETED` and `SET FILTER` settings. Another way to perform a selection using the FoxPro language is to specify a scope that limits a command to certain records. A scope allows a command to act on a subset of records. Scope is described in more detail in Chapter 12.

The FoxPro language includes a mechanism to define a projection. A *projection* is a vertical subset of columns that can include a reordering of columns. (See Chapter 2.) The `SET FIELDS` command specifies which columns are visible. Fields that are not on this list are not accessible by any means. The `SET FIELDS` command in Visual FoxPro supports reordering of columns. Commands such as `LIST`, `CHANGE`, and `BROWSE` respect the subset and the specified order of the fields even though they also support a `FIELDS` clause, which defines a subset of fields for the duration of the command. Here is an example:

Command Window	*Results*		
LIST	Record #	SALES	COSTS
	1	4000.00	2000.00
	2	5000.00	5001.00
	3	39900.00	2300.00
	4	45000.00	42300.00
SET FIELDS TO Costs			
LIST	Record #	COSTS	
	1	2000.00	
	2	5001.00	
	3	2300.00	
	4	42300.00	
? sales	Variable	'SALES' not found	

In addition to choosing and reordering the fields, FoxPro allows *calculated fields* for the `BROWSE` and `CHANGE` commands. Calculated fields are virtual, read-only fields defined by an expression that is recalculated for each record. Calculated fields can be dependent on DBF data, as in the following example:

```
BROWSE FIELDS SALES, COSTS, PROFITS = SALES - COSTS
```

One of the most significant differences between Visual FoxPro and FoxPro 2.5 (and earlier versions of FoxPro) support for the `SET FIELDS TO` command is that Visual FoxPro supports a global mode that has one fields list for all work areas. However, FoxPro 2.5 supports a separate fields list for each work area. The ramifications are subtle, but it is important to be able to specify a global fields list because screen forms can include fields from tables open in different work areas.

The tables in two work areas can be synchronized so that positioning to a new record in one work area repositions the other work area. The two tables are said to be *related.* This is an extremely powerful concept because it allows a foreign key in the current, or parent, work area to reference additional information in the related, or child, work area. For example, suppose that a name and address DBF is in use in work area B and an invoice table is in use in work area A, as shown in Figure 11.5. The command

```
SET RELATION TO Name INTO B
```

establishes a relation between work areas A and B in such a way that B is always positioned to the record corresponding to the `Name` field of A. If A is indexed by invoice number, the clients' names are in near-random order. The name and address list in B is in order by name. Positioning A to a particular invoice automatically positions B to the record whose `Name` field matches the `Name` field in A, so that a command to print

```
? InvNo, Date, Name, B.Address, B.Phone
```

provides more detailed information about each invoice than is stored in the invoice table. Notice also that `Fred` doesn't appear in the logical view because `Fred` has no invoices.

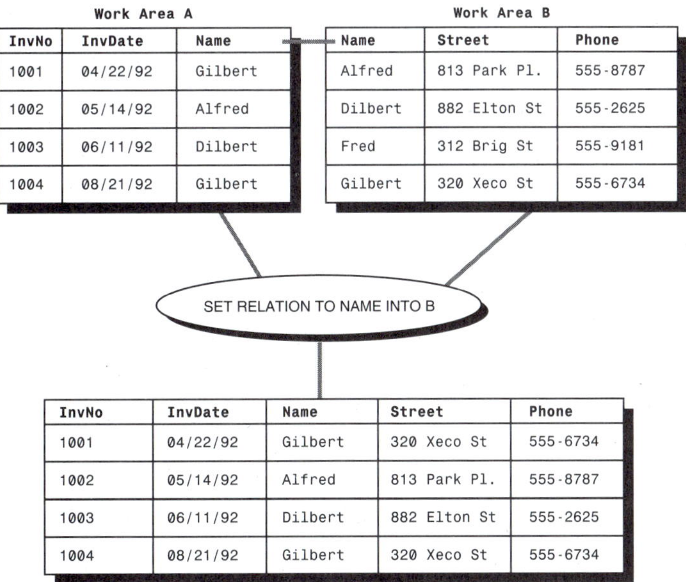

FIGURE 11.5.
An illustration of the `SET RELATION` *command.*

The `SET RELATION` command is more powerful than a simple selection of rows or columns because it provides a mechanism for expressing one-to-many relationships. In the preceding example, each client is probably referenced by many invoices, and yet only the name (the foreign key) is duplicated for each invoice. Although the client's address and phone number appear redundantly in the logical view, they are stored only once in the physical file.

Visual FoxPro supports *multichild relations*, which means that any work area can be related to up to nine other work areas. Because each work area can be related to any other and one parent can be related to many children, repositioning the table in the current work area could have the effect of automatically repositioning all other open tables. Through a series of relations, it is possible that a command to reposition the current work area results in the work area also repositioning itself automatically, which would send the computer into an endless loop. FoxPro detects this and issues a Cyclic relation error.

The child work area must be indexed on the expression specified unless you use the `SET RELATION TO RECNO()` variation. This variation is for one-to-one relationships; it specifies that tables in two work areas should always be positioned to the same record number.

The `SET SKIP` command handles cases in which more than one record in the child table matches the foreign key in the parent table. The `SET SKIP` command hides or makes visible the extra matching child records, which are called *detail records*, making it possible to support many-to-many relationships. Figure 11.6 presents an example of the `SET SKIP` command.

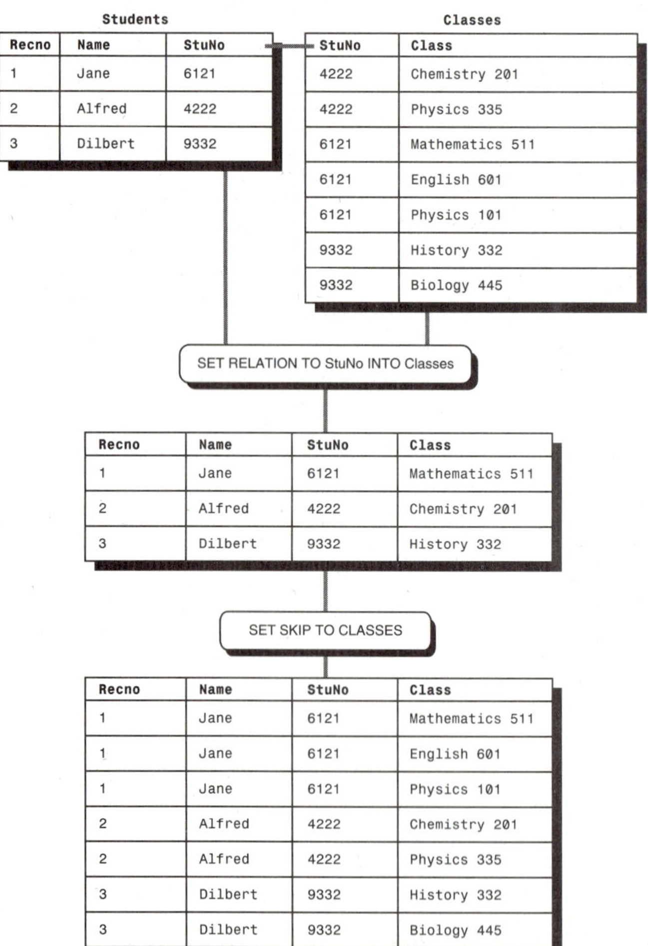

FIGURE 11.6.
An illustration of the `SET SKIP` command.

Notice that with SET SKIP and SET RELATION active, the SKIP command may reposition related work areas but leave the record position in the current work area as is, leading to the following head-scratching situation:

Command	*Results*
? RECNO()	148
SKIP	
? RECNO()	148

When an index is active, it determines which records are visible in addition to specifying their order. If a record is not in the index, it is not accessible. The SET UNIQUE ON command specifies that no duplicate keys should be stored in a new index; this has the effect of hiding records that have duplicate keys.

Too much raw data obscures the overall meaning. One solution offered by computer science is called *information hiding*. Because this is an increasingly important topic, it is not surprising that converting raw data tables into a knowledge base would involve selection, projection, and relationships between tables. All the various mechanisms that FoxPro makes available—SET FILTER, SET FIELDS, SET DELETED, SET RELATION, SET SKIP, SET UNIQUE—create subsets of the data. No operation creates more records; each summarizes or hides information that is not germane at the time.

Logical views make more sense than physical tables. Actions that change logical views are instantaneous compared to actions applied to physical tables. The time required to physically sort a data table is roughly the same as the time required to index it (the two operations share common code), but the insert, delete, query, and update times for an indexed file are considerably faster. The capability to switch between multiple indexes imparts a high degree of data independence to applications.

Applications written in the FoxPro programming language that assume familiarity with the physical table structure are more difficult to convert to future FoxPro systems, which may not support the table format. If you write applications using logical tables today, you can expect forward compatibility tomorrow.

The Database Container File

In Visual FoxPro, a database is defined as an assortment of related data and objects. A database can contain one or more tables (DBF files), plus related queries, forms, reports, and programs. In Visual FoxPro, a list of all of the database components is automatically maintained in the *database container file*.

A Physical Description of the Database Container File

Before I describe the use and behavior of a database container file, it would be useful to describe its physical characteristics. There is no mysterious format associated with a database container file. It is just another DBF type file with a .DBC extension. It has a *signature byte* of 0×01. The signature byte is the first byte of a DBF-type file, as discussed earlier in this chapter, that identifies the type of table. A DBC file is not manipulated in the same way as a table. You do not make any direct changes to a DBC file. Visual FoxPro automatically updates the DBC file when appropriate. The database container also has a memo field file with a .DCT extension and a structural compound index file with a .DCX extension. Here is the DBC structure:

Field Name	*Type*	*Width*	*Description*
OBJECTID	I	4	Specifies a unique value for identifying each object.
PARENTID	I	4	Specifies the OBJECTID of the object's container.
OBJECTTYPE	C	10	Specifies the type of the object.
OBJECTNAME	C	128	Specifies the name of the object.
PROPERTY	M	4	This field contains properties of the objects in binary.
CODE	M	4	Contains source code or compiled code for stored procedures.
RIINFO	C	6	Data that is used by the Referential Integrity Builder.
USER	M	4	This field is reserved for the user. You can use it for whatever you like.

The OBJECTID field always corresponds to the record number and is used to identify the object. Visual FoxPro adds new records to the end of a DBC file so that the record number always corresponds to the OBJECTID field. Database container manipulation commands simply mark records for deletion when an object is removed or modified. If you perform many operations that make changes to your DBC file, you may want to pack the file using the PACK DATABASE command to save disk space.

The OBJECTTYPE field is the type of object defined by a given record. The types can be Database, Table, System, Relation, Index, Record, and Field. Records that contain the Database type of OBJECTTYPE have the different subtypes of objects associated with the database. The value indicating the subtype of database objects such as `StoredProcedureSource`, `StoredProceduresObject`, `TransactionLog`, and `Database`, is stored in the `OBJECTNAME` field. The `OBJECTNAME` for Field, Table, and Index type records is the name of the Field, Table, and Index tag, respectively.

The `PARENTID` field value corresponds to the `OBJECTID` of the parent object. For example, a Table type object has a `PARENTID` that corresponds to the `OBJECTID` (or record number) of the associated Database type record. The `PARENTID` value of a record with an `OBJECTTYPE` value of Field corresponds to the `OBJECTID` of its associated Table object type.

The `PROPERTY` field is used to store object properties. For example, records with an `OBJECTTYPE` value of Field store field-level rules, captions, and other extended field properties in the `PROPERTY` memo field. Records with an `OBJECTTYPE` value of Table store record-level rules in the `PROPERTY` memo field. The database stored procedures are stored in the `CODE` memo field.

You can use the `USER` field for whatever you like. It is unused by Visual FoxPro. However, you must ensure that the values you store in the `USER` field are up-to-date following any changes that Visual FoxPro makes to the DBC file. You are not allowed to add any records to the DBC file or any indexes to the DCX file. However, you can add more fields. When you add a field, you must begin its name with `U_` (for example, `U_MyProp`).

That should be enough information to demystify the DBC file. Now I'll explain how to use it and show some good uses for it.

Creating a Database Container Visually

There are three ways to create a database container:

- Use the **F**ile menu **N**ew option
- Use the Project Manager window Data tab
- Use the `CREATE DATABASE` command

You should use Program Manager to create a database container if you are building an application. (See Chapter 23, "Building Visual FoxPro Applications.") From the Project Manager window Data tab, you highlight the Databases item in the outline and press the **N**ew push button, as shown in Figure 11.7. The Create File menu appears, and you enter the name of the new database.

When you enter the name of the new database and choose the OK button, the Database Designer window displays and looks like the Database Designer window shown in Figure 11.8 except that there are no tables shown in the client area.

In Figure 11.8, the **D**atabase menu is open, showing options for adding objects to the named database. With Database Designer you can do any of the following database management operations:

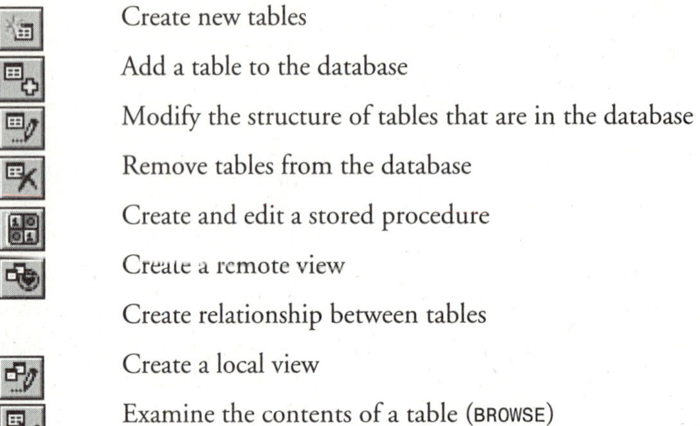

Create new tables

Add a table to the database

Modify the structure of tables that are in the database

Remove tables from the database

Create and edit a stored procedure

Create a remote view

Create relationship between tables

Create a local view

Examine the contents of a table (`BROWSE`)

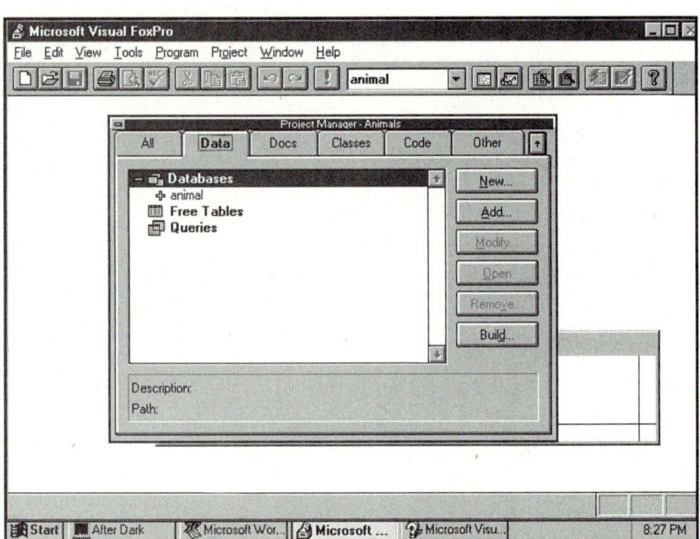

FIGURE 11.7.
The Project Manager window Data tab.

The Database Designer toolbar shown in Figure 11.8 appears when the Database Designer is active. It contains commonly used database operations and provides a convenient way to perform operations. For example, if you want to add an existing table to the database, you click on the Add Table button. If you right-click on the Database Designer window, the shortcut menu appears. It also contains many of the most commonly used **D**atabase menu options.

Table 11.3 summarizes the options in the **D**atabase menu that appear on the menu bar when the Database Designer is active. You must first select a table (click on it) before you can choose an option that operates on a table, such as **M**odify, **B**rowse, or Rebuild Table **I**ndexes.

FIGURE 11.8.
The Database Designer window.

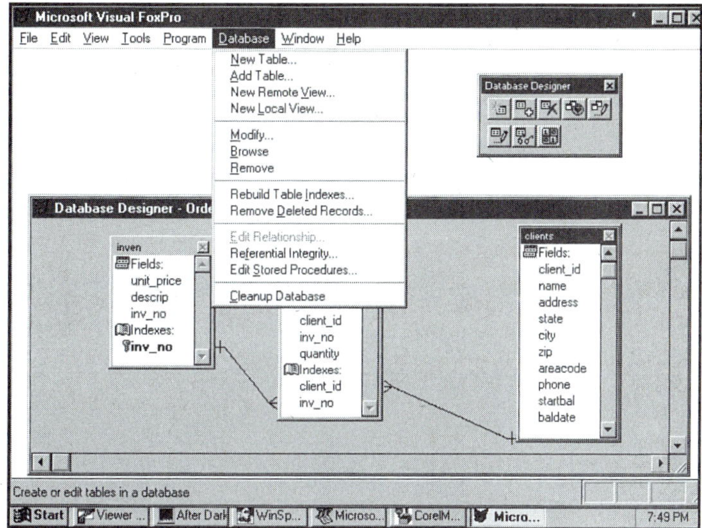

Table 11.3. Database menu options.

Option	*Function*
New Table	Creates a new table using a wizard or Table Designer.
Add Table	Adds an existing table to a database.
New Remote **V**iew	Creates a new remote view using a wizard or a View Designer.
New **L**ocal View	Creates a new local view using a wizard or a View Designer.
Modify	Opens the selected table in the Table Designer.
Browse	Displays the selected table in the Browse window for editing.
Remove	Removes the selected table from the database or deletes it from the disk.
Rebuild Table **I**ndexes	Generates keys and rebuilds indexes for the selected table.
Remove **D**eleted Records	Permanently removes all records from the active table that are marked for deletion.
Edit Relationship…	Alters the relationship between tables. You must first select the line drawn between two indexes to enable this option. Also, you can double-click on the line to execute this option.

continues

Table 11.3. continued

Option	*Function*
Referential Integrity	Displays the Referential Integrity Builder, in which you set up rules to control how records are inserted, updated, or deleted in related tables. (See Figure 11.13.)
Edit **S**tored Procedures	Displays a Visual FoxPro procedure in an editing window.
Clean Up Database	Runs the PACK command to decrease the size of the database by removing rows that have been marked for deletion.

Although this section focuses on the programmatic creation of a database, it is easy to create a database visually. Once the Database Designer is active, you can create new tables, or view or add existing tables or views to the database. When you add a new table or view, you have the choice of using a wizard or a designer to create the table or view. (Wizards are discussed in detail in Chapter 24, "Wizards.") You can also establish index tags using the Table Designer.

You can also visually create persistent relationships between tables by linking their indexes. It is extremely simple. All you have to do is drag an index from one table to the matching index in another table. When you do this, the Edit Relationship dialog box appears. From this dialog box, you can establish a one-to-one or one-to-many relationship. After you have established a relationship between two tables, a line is drawn between the indexes in the two tables.

If you want to modify a relation, you can click on a line drawn between two indexes and the line *thickens.* Then you can choose the **D**atabase menu **E**dit Relationship menu, and the Edit Relationship dialog box displays. You can also invoke the Edit Relationship dialog box by double-clicking on the line.

Creating a Database Container Programatically

You can programmatically create a database using the CREATE DATABASE command. Here is the syntax:

```
CREATE DATABASE [<expFN> | ?]
```

<expFN> specifies the name of the database to create. If you don't specify a filename extension, a .DBC extension is assumed. If you specify a question mark (?) character instead of a filename, Visual FoxPro displays the Save As dialog box and you specify the name of the database to create. If you execute the CREATE DATABASE command without any other argument, the Create dialog box displays and you specify a name for the database.

The CREATE DATABASE command creates the designated database with a .DBC extension and opens it exclusively, regardless of the setting of the SET EXCLUSIVE command. As a consequence, you do not have to execute a subsequent OPEN DATABASE command. When the CREATE DATABASE command creates the DBC table file, a DBT memo field file and a DCX structural compound file are created.

Opening a Database Container

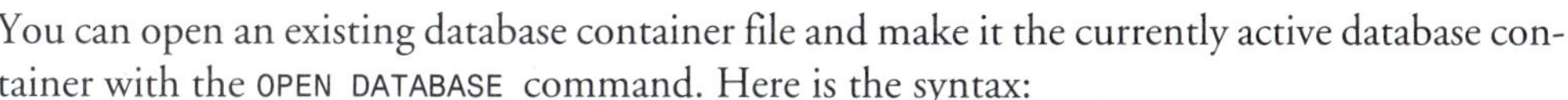

You can open an existing database container file and make it the currently active database container with the `OPEN DATABASE` command. Here is the syntax:

```
OPEN DATABASE  [<expFN> ¦ ?]
[EXCLUSIVE ¦ SHARED]
[NOUPDATE]
[VALIDATE]
```

<expFN> is the name of an database container file. If you don't specify a filename extension, a .DBC extension is assumed. If you omit *<expFN>* or specify a question mark (`?`) character, the Open dialog box appears. You can choose an existing DBC file or enter the name of a new DBC file to create. If you specify the `EXCLUSIVE` keyword or if `SET EXCLUSIVE` is `ON`, other users cannot access the file. If you specify the `SHARED` keyword, the file is opened in shared mode and other users can access the file. If you specify the `NOUPDATE` keyword, the DBC file is opened in read-only mode and you cannot make any modifications to the file. However, any tables associated with the database container can be updated.

Once you open a database container, all tables attached to it are made available for use. You still must utilize the `USE` command to open a table. Incidentally, if you open a table that is attached to a database, Visual FoxPro automatically opens its database container file. The table's associated database does not become the currently active database. But it is open. You can also specify a database qualifier. The database qualifier operator is an exclamation point (`!`). You specify the table filename with its associated database container filename and the exclamation point (`!`) character prepended. For example, suppose a table, tiger.DBF, is associated with an unopened or inactive database named animals.DBC. You can place the table in use with the following command:

```
USE animals!tiger
```

Tables that are not attached to a database container are called *free tables.* You can always open a free table with the `USE` command. When a database is in use and the `USE` command executes, it searches through the database container for the table. If the table is not found, it looks for the file outside the database container.

When you open a database container file, its name appears in the list box on the toolbar, as shown in Figure 11.9. If you open another DBC file, the name of the new DBC file appears in the toolbar list box and the new DBC file becomes the currently active database container. The list box contains the names of the active DBC files. The currently active database container is displayed. You can change the currently active database container by either selecting another DBC file from the database list box or by using the `SET DATABASE TO [`*<expFN>*`]` command. For example, suppose you opened two database containers with the following statements:

```
OPEN DATABASE Cats        && Cats.DBC becomes current DBC
OPEN DATABASE Dogs        && Dogs.DBC becomes current DBC
                          &&  and Cats.DBC is still active
```

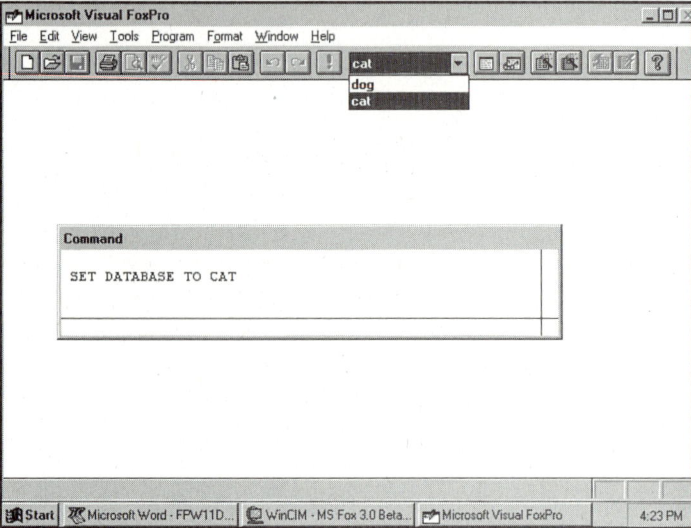

FIGURE 11.9.
Selecting a currently active database.

If you want `Cats.DBC` to become the currently active database container again, execute the following command:

```
SET DATABASE TO Cats
```

The exclamation point (`!`) character is used as a special operator, called a *database qualifier operator*, used to distinguish which database is associated with a table. It is needed only when the database is not the active database. Although you may have more than one database container file open at one time, only one can be active. In other words, you can reference a table in an existing database by prefixing the table name with the name of the database and the database qualifier (`!`). The following example illustrates this point:

```
OPEN DATA Cats            && contains table CENSUS.DBF
OPEN DATA Dogs            && Contains table CITIES.DBF
USE Cats!Census IN 0
USE Dogs!Cities IN 0
USE Rats!Countrys IN 0
DISP Census.State, Cities.State
```

In this example, the database Dogs is open and active. However, you can still use the database qualifier to make it clear to which database table Cities belongs. If you specify a database that is not open, it is opened but it is not made the currently active database. In the above example, the database Rats was opened when the `USE Rats!Countrys IN 0` statement executed. However, the database Dogs remains the active database.

Now that you have an open database container, it is time to use it. You can manage an open database container using Database Designer (as discussed in the previous section). You also can use any of the commands described in Table 11.4.

Table 11.4. Commands for manipulating a database.

NEW FOR VISUAL FOXPRO 3

Command	*Function*
`ADD TABLE`	Adds a free table to a database.
`ALTER TABLE`	Programmatically modifies the structure of a table.
`APPEND PROCEDURE`	Appends a stored procedure in a text file to the stored procedure in the currently active database.
`CLOSE DATABASE`	Closes all open databases, tables, indexes, and format files in all work areas and selects work area 1.
`CLOSE TABLES`	Closes all tables in the currently active database and leaves the database open.
`COMPILE DATABASE`	Compiles the stored procedure in a database.
`COPY PROCEDURE`	Copies the stored procedure in the currently active database to a text file.
`CREATE CONNECTIONS`	Creates a named connection and stores it in the currently active database.
`CREATE DATABASE`	Creates a database and opens it.
`CREATE TABLE`	Programmatically creates a table.
`CREATE TRIGGER`	Programmatically creates a delete, insert, or update trigger for a table in a database.
`CREATE VIEW`	Creates a view from the FoxPro environment.
`DELETE CONNECTIONS`	Deletes a named connection from the currently active database.
`DELETE DATABASE`	Deletes a named database from the disk. Optionally, this command deletes tables contained in the database from the disk.
`DELETE TRIGGERS`	Removes a delete, update, or insert trigger for the specified table in the currently active database.
`DELETE VIEW`	Removes a SQL view from the currently active database.
`MODIFY CONNECTION`	Displays the Connection Designer from which you can modify an existing named connection in the currently active database.
`MODIFY DATABASE`	Displays the Database Designer from which you can modify the currently active database. (See Figure 11.8.)

continues

Table 11.4. continued

Command	*Function*
`MODIFY STRUCTURE`	Displays the Table Structure dialog box from which you can modify the structure of a table in the current work area.
`MODIFY VIEW`	Displays the View Designer from which you can modify an existing SQL view.
`OPEN DATABASE`	Opens the named database and makes it the currently active database.
`PACK DATABASE`	Removes from the currently active database records that are marked for deletion. The database must be open exclusively, and tables associated with the database cannot be open.
`REMOVE TABLES`	Removes a specified attached table from the database and makes it a free table or, optionally, deletes it from the disk. The table can be added to other databases.
`RENAME CONNECTION`	Renames a specified named connection in the currently active database.
`RENAME TABLE`	Renames a specified table in the currently active database.
`RENAME VIEW`	Renames a SQL view in the currently active database.
`VALIDATE DATABASE`	Verifies that the location of tables and indexes is correct in the currently active database.

The Visual FoxPro automated database provides you with a multitude of services that make it easier for you to develop applications. Once you have designed a database, it is easier to implement it. For example, you can incorporate field-level and record-level validation rules into the database. Then you no longer have to concern yourself with writing code to validate data every time you implement a new procedure or object. Visual FoxPro automatically takes care of validation operations. You can think of the database container file as the knowledge base, or *data dictionary*, that knows all about your database, its tables, and the relationship between the tables. With the various graphic tools and procedural commands, you can extend the information that a data dictionary possesses regarding your data. You can create and maintain any of the following database elements in a data dictionary:

- Long field names of up to 128 characters
- Default values for fields
- Field-level and record-level rules for data validation
- Primary and candidate keys
- Triggers

- Persistent relations between database tables
- Stored procedures
- Connections to remote data sources
- Remote and local views

Adding Tables to a Database Container

A free table does not support extended attributes such as long fields and field-level rules. A free table needs to be associated with a database to become an *attached table*. Once it is attached, you take advantage of the extended attributes. If you have an open database, you can add a free table to that database with the `ADD TABLES` command. You cannot add an attached table to another database—in other words, a table can be attached to only one database. Here is the syntax of this command:

```
ADD TABLE <expFN> ¦ ? [NAME <expTable>]
```

`<expFN>` specifies the name of the table (DBF file) that you want to add to the currently active database. If you specify a question mark (`?`), the Open dialog box appears and you choose the name of a table from the dialog box. (See Figure 11.10.) You can use the `NAME` clause to specify a long filename of up to 128 characters. You can use long filenames to reference the table.

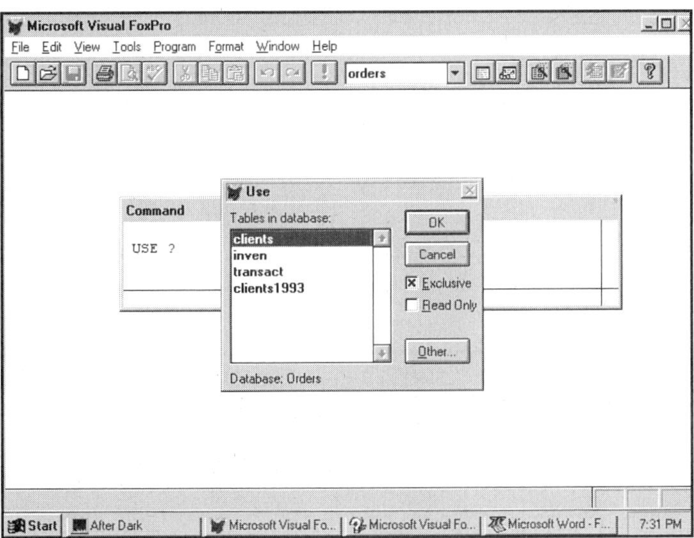

FIGURE 11.10.
The Use dialog box.

You can perform any operation on an attached table that you can perform on any other table. However, you cannot place an attached table in use unless its associated database is available. When you open a table and its associated database is not open, its database file is opened. However, its database file does not become the currently active database. You can make an attached table into a free table by executing the REMOVE TABLE command as described in the next section.

Any valid table can be added to a database as long as it does not have the same name as a table already attached to the database. Or you can assign the table a unique long name. Here is an example:

```
OPEN DATABASE MyData
ADD TABLE c:\acme\Clients
ADD TABLE d:\amc\Clients NAME Clients1993
```

In this example, both Clients' tables are added to the database named MyData.DBC. However, if you access the second one, you must use the name Clients1993. Here is an example:

```
USE MyData!Clients1993
```

Or, since MyData.DBC is active, you can use

```
USE Clients1993
```

Incidentally, if you execute USE ?, the Use dialog box appears, showing long filenames in its list box, as shown in Figure 11.10.

The *REMOVE TABLE* Command

You can remove an attached table from the currently active database and make it a free file with the REMOVE TABLE command. Here is the syntax:

```
REMOVE TABLE  <expTable> ¦ ? [DELETE]
```

<expTable> specifies the name of the table to remove from the currently active database. You can use the long table name. If you specify the question mark (?) character, the Remove dialog box appears and you can choose the name of a table to remove. When a table is removed from the database, it becomes a free table and can be added to another database. If the SET SAFETY setting is ON, a confirmation dialog appears that asks if you are sure you want to delete the table from the database.

CAUTION

It is important for you to be aware that the REMOVE TABLE command also removes all validation rules, primary indexes, constraints, default values, and specifications associated with the specified table. Furthermore, any rules and relations associated with the table being removed and any other table in the currently active database are no longer valid when the specified table is removed from the database.

If you specify the optional DELETE command, the specified table is not only removed from the database, it is removed from the disk—it is erased.

> **CAUTION**
>
> If you specify the `DELETE` keyword, the `REMOVE TABLE` command deletes the specified table from the disk without warning even if the `SET SAFETY` setting is `ON`.

The *CREATE TABLE* and *ALTER TABLE* Commands

Now it is time to start investigating the mechanism that is used for dealing with extended properties in tables attached to a database. You can create and modify the structure and the extended properties of a table with the `CREATE TABLE` and `ALTER TABLE` commands. Both of these commands are more similar to SQL than to Xbase. However, they provide a powerful programmatic approach to managing the structure of a table. The SQL syntax uses commas to separate certain clauses. Be careful to note the placement of commas in the syntax.

Because these two commands are similar, I'll explain the complicated and cryptic syntax of both commands at the same time. Here is the syntax of the command that creates a new table:

```
CREATE TABLE ¦ DBF <expFN> 1 [NAME  <expTable1> ] [FREE]
 (<field1>  <FieldType> [(<expN1>  [, <expN2> ])
                [NULL ¦ NOT NULL]
                [CHECK <expL1>  [ERROR <expC1> ]]
                [DEFAULT <exp1> ]
                [PRIMARY KEY ¦ UNIQUE]
                [REFERENCES <expTable2> [TAG <tag name1>]
                [NOCPTRANS]]
        [, <field2> ...]])
                [, PRIMARY KEY <exp2> TAG <tag name2>
                ¦, UNIQUE <exp3>  TAG  <tag name3>]
                [, FOREIGN KEY <exp4>  TAG <tag name4>
                     REFERENCES <expTable3>  [TAG <tag name5>]]
                [, CHECK <expL2>  [ERROR <expC2> ]]
        ¦ FROM ARRAY ArrayName
```

Here is the syntax of the command that modifies an existing attached table:

```
ALTER TABLE <expTable1>
   [ADD ¦ ALTER [COLUMN] <field1>
                 <FieldType> [(<expN1> [,<expN2> ]])
                [NULL ¦ NOT NULL]
                [CHECK <expL1> [ERROR <expC1> ]]
                [DEFAULT <exp1>]
               [PRIMARY KEY ¦ UNIQUE]
                [REFERENCES <expTable2> [TAG <tag name1> ]]
                [NOCPTRANS]]
        [ALTER [COLUMN] <field2>
                [SET DEFAULT <exp2>]
                [SET CHECK <expL2> [ERROR <expC2>]]
                [DROP DEFAULT]
                [DROP CHECK]]
        [DROP [COLUMN] <field3>]
        [SET CHECK <expL3> [ERROR <expC3>]]
        [DROP CHECK]
        [ADD PRIMARY KEY <exp3> TAG <tag name2>
```

```
[DROP PRIMARY KEY]
[ADD UNIQUE <exp4> TAG <tag name3>]
[DROP UNIQUE TAG <tag name4>]
[ADD FOREIGN KEY [<exp5>] TAG <tag name4>
      REFERENCES <expTable2> [TAG <tag name5>]]
[DROP FOREIGN KEY TAG <tag name6> [SAVE]]
¦
[RENAME COLUMN <field4> TO <field5>]
[NOVALIDATE]
```

In general, you can create a table with the `CREATE TABLE` command and change an existing table with the `ALTER TABLE` command. The `CREATE TABLE` command creates a table exclusively in the next available unused work area. The following paragraphs discuss each of the keywords and clauses for these two commands. Table 11.5 summarizes the `CREATE TABLE` and `ALTER TABLE` command syntax elements.

Table 11.5. A summary of `CREATE TABLE` and `ALTER TABLE` syntax elements.

Syntax Element	*Description*
CREATE TABLE ¦ DBF <*expFN1*>	Name of table file
[NAME <*expTable1*>]	Long file name
[FREE]	Creates a free table
(<*field1*>	Field name
<*FieldType*>	Data type
[(<*expN1*>	Field width
[, <*expN2*>])	Number of decimal places
[NULL ¦	Allows null values in field
NOT NULL]	Doesn't allow null values in field
[CHECK <*expL1*>	Field-level validation rule
[ERROR <*expC1*>]]	Validation error message
[DEFAULT <*exp1*>]	Default value for field
[PRIMARY KEY ¦	Declares primary key for field
UNIQUE]	Unique key for field
[REFERENCES <*expTable2*>	Related parent table
[TAG <*tag name1*>]	Index used for relation
[NOCPTRANS]]	No code page translation
[, <*field2*> ...]])	Name of second field to create
[, PRIMARY KEY <*exp2*>	Primary key expression
TAG <*tag name2*>	Name of primary key tag
¦, UNIQUE <*exp3*>	Unique key expression
TAG <*tag name3*>]	Name of primary key tag

Syntax Element	*Description*
[, FOREIGN KEY <exp4>	Foreign key expression
TAG <tag name4>	Name of primary key tag
REFERENCES <expTable3>	Reference to parent relation
[TAG <tag name5>]]	Name of index key tag
[, CHECK <expL2>	Record-level validation rule
[ERROR <expC2>]]	Error message for rule
¦ FROM ARRAY ArrayName	Creates table from named array
ALTER TABLE <expTable1>	Name of table to be modified
[ADD ¦ ALTER [COLUMN] <field1>	Field to alter or add
<FieldType>	Data type
[(<expN1>	Field width
[,<expN2>]])	Number of decimal places
[NULL	Allows null values in field
¦ NOT NULL]	Does not allow null values in field
[CHECK <expL1>	Field-level validation rule
[ERROR <expC1>]]	Validation error message
[DEFAULT <exp1>]	Default value for field
[PRIMARY KEY	Declares primary key for field
¦ UNIQUE]	Unique key for field
[REFERENCES <expTable2>	Related parent table name
[TAG <tag name1>]]	Name of tag used in relation
[NOCPTRANS]]	Does not allow translation of code page
[ALTER [COLUMN] <field2>	Name of existing field to modify
[SET DEFAULT <exp2>]	New default value
[SET CHECK <expL2>	New validation rule
[ERROR <expC2>]]	New error message for rule
[DROP DEFAULT]	Removes default value
[DROP CHECK]]	Removes validation rule
[DROP [COLUMN] <field3>]	Removes named field from table structure
[SET CHECK <expL3>	Specifies table validation rule
[ERROR <expC3>]]	Error message for rule
[DROP CHECK]	Removes table validation rule
[ADD PRIMARY KEY <exp3>	Adds new primary key expression

continues

Table 11.5. continued

Syntax Element	*Description*
TAG *<tag name2>*	Tag name for new primary key
[DROP PRIMARY KEY]	Removes new table primary key
[ADD UNIQUE *<exp4>*	Adds unique key expression
TAG *<tag name3>*]	Tag name for new unique key
[DROP UNIQUE TAG *<tag name4>*]	Removes unique key
[ADD FOREIGN KEY [*<exp5>*]	Adds foreign key expression
TAG *<tag name4>*	Tag name for new foreign key
REFERENCES *<expTable2>*	Specifies new parent table
[TAG *<tag name5>*]]	Tag name for relation key
[DROP FOREIGN KEY TAG *<tag name6>*	Removes foreign key tag
[SAVE]]	Doesn't allow removal of tag from CDX file
¦	
[RENAME COLUMN *<field4>*	Renames field
TO *<field5>*]	
[NOVALIDATE]	Doesn't allow validation of ALTER changes

Specifying the Table Name

You can create and alter both free and attached tables. However, if you operate on a free table, none of the extended properties contained in a database can be specified. In other words, if a database is not active and you create or alter a table, it must be a free table and you cannot specify the NAME, CHECK, DEFAULT, FOREIGN KEY, PRIMARY KEY, REFERENCES, UNIQUE, and SET clauses. If you attempt to do so, Visual FoxPro displays an error message.

<expFN> specifies the name of the database to create. If you don't specify a filename extension, the .DBF extension is assumed. For the CREATE TABLE command, the NAME *<expTable1>* clause specifies an optional long table name for the table to be created. For the ALTER TABLE command, *<expTable1>* specifies the table name or filename for the table whose structure is to be altered. Here is the syntax for specifying table names:

```
CREATE TABLE ¦ DBF <expFN> 1 [NAME  <expTable> ] [FREE] …
ALTER TABLE <expTable1> …
```

The TABLE and DBF keywords are interchangeable. You can specify either CREATE TABLE or CREATE DBF. If you specify the FREE keyword with the CREATE TABLE command, a free table is created.

Creating and Altering the Structure of a Table

You can create a structure with the CREATE TABLE command by specifying a list of field definition clauses. The entire list is enclosed in parentheses. Here is the syntax for describing the entire structure:

```
(<field1>  <FieldType> [(<expN1> [,<expN2> ]])
              [NULL | NOT NULL]
              [CHECK <expL1> [ERROR <expC1> ]]
              [DEFAULT <exp1>]
              [PRIMARY KEY | UNIQUE]
              [REFERENCES <expTable2> [TAG <tag name1> ]]
              [NOCPTRANS]]
      [, <field2> ...]] )
```

The first clause defines the field name (<field1>), field type (<FieldType>), field width (<expN1>), and number of decimal places (<expN2>). The field type (<FieldType>) consists of a single character, which denotes the type of field, as shown in Table 11.6. The field width and number of decimal places are ignored for D, T, Y, L, M, G, and P types. If you do not specify the number of decimal places (<expN2>) for field types N, F, or B, zero is assumed.

Table 11.6. Field types for the CREATE TABLE and ALTER TABLE commands.

Field Type	*Field Width*	*Decimal Places*	*Description*
C	*n*	-	Character field of width *n*
D	-	-	Date
T	-	-	DateTime
I	-	-	Integer
N	*n*	*d*	Numeric field of width *n* with *d* decimal places
F	*n*	*d*	Floating Numeric field of width *n* with *d* decimal places
B	-	*d*	Double
Y	-	-	Currency
L	-	-	Logical
M	-	-	Memo
G	-	-	General
P	-	-	Picture

In the following example, the table named CLIENTS.DBF with a long filename of Clients1994 is created. It will be attached to the `Orders` database. The code for this example is as follows:

```
OPEN DATABASE Orders
CREATE TABLE Clients  NAME Clients1994 ;
  (     Client_ID      C(5),  ;
        Name           C(20), ;
        StreetAddress  C(30), ;
        State          C(2),  ;
        City           C(15), ;
        ZIP            C(10), ;
        Approved       L,     ;
        Picture        G,     ;
        Areacode       C(3),  ;
        PhoneNumber    C(8),  ;
        StartBalance  N(8, 2),;
        BalanceDate    D    )
```

Notice that some field names are longer than the traditional Xbase maximum of 10 characters. In Visual FoxPro you can have field names of up to 128 characters provided they are attached to a database. Free tables cannot have field names of more than a 10 characters.

The long field names are stored in the database container (DBC) file. The first 10 characters are stored in the DBF file structure. In the above example, the names that are longer than 10 characters are stored in the DBF structure as `STREETADDR`, `PHONENUMBE`, and `STARTBALAN`. In the event that names are not unique in the first 10 characters, the rightmost character is replaced with a number:

Long Name	*Stored in DBF Structure As*
`AutomobileRadio`	`Automobile`
`AutomobileRadioTape`	`Automobil1`
`AutomobileRadioCD`	`Automobil2`

You can add or modify an existing field in a table with the `ALTER TABLE` command. The form of the field clause is the same. The only difference is that you need to precede the field clause with an `ADD [COLUMN]` or `ALTER [COLUMN]` clause. The `COLUMN` keyword is optional. Here is the field clause syntax for the `ALTER` command:

```
ALTER TABLE <expTable> ADD [COLUMN] <field1>
                <FieldType> [(<expN1> [,<expN2> ]]) ...
```

NEW FOR VISUAL FOXPRO 3

```
ALTER TABLE <expTable> ALTER [COLUMN] <field1>
                <FieldType> [(<expN1> [,<expN2> ]]) ...
```

Notice that the field clause is not enclosed in parentheses for the `ALTER TABLE` command. Here is an example of a Numeric field that is added to the Clients table:

```
OPEN DATABASE Orders
ALTER TABLE Clients ADD CurrentBalance N(8,2)
```

In the following example, the width of the field `Name` will be increased to 40 characters:

```
OPEN DATABASE Orders
ALTER Table Clients ALTER  Name C(40)
```

You can also alter or remove other properties of a field with the following form of the ALTER TABLE command:

```
ALTER <expTable> ALTER [COLUMN] <field1>
              [NULL ¦ NOT NULL]
              [CHECK <expL1> [ERROR <expC1> ]]
              [DEFAULT <exp1>]
              [PRIMARY KEY ¦ UNIQUE]
              [REFERENCES <expTable2> [TAG <tag name1> ]]
              [NOCPTRANS]]
       [ALTER [COLUMN] <field2>
              [SET DEFAULT <exp2>]
              [SET CHECK <expL2> [ERROR <expC2>]]
       [DROP DEFAULT]
       [DROP CHECK]]
       [DROP [COLUMN] <field3>]
```

Suppose you want to specify a default value and impose the restriction that users cannot enter any birthdays earlier than 1900 into the field. Here's an example:

```
OPEN DATABASE Orders
ALTER TABLE Clients ALTER  Birthday
     SET DEFAULT {1/1/95} ;
     SET CHANGE Birthday > {01/01/1900} ;
     ERROR "No clients over 95 are permitted"
```

You can remove a column entirely with the DROP clause. Here is the syntax:

```
ALTER TABLE <expTable> DROP [COLUMN] <field1>
```

The following example demonstrates how to remove the column Birthday from the table Clients:

```
OPEN DATABASE Orders
ALTER TABLE Clients DROP  Birthday
```

You can remove a field-level rule or a default-value property of a field from the structure of a table using the following forms of the ALTER TABLE command:

```
ALTER TABLE  <expTable> ALTER  [COLUMN] <field1>  DROP CHANGE
ALTER TABLE  <expTable> ALTER  [COLUMN] <field1>  DROP DEFAULT
```

The other components of the field clause are discussed in a little more detail in the following sections.

Default Values and Null Fields

You can use the DEFAULT clause to specify a value that is automatically stored in a field when a new record is added to a table using the APPEND, APPEND BLANK, or INSERT commands. Default values are also applied to new records when the APPEND FROM WITH DEFAULTS and SQL INSERT commands execute. However, default values do not overwrite fields that have existing values in corresponding fields in the source file. In the following example, the source file Table_B has only one field, F1:

```
OPEN DATABASE MyData
CREATE TABLE Table_A     ;
   (F1 C(10)    DEFAULT "JUNK" ,    ;
    F2 N(8,2)   DEFAULT 4 )
APPEND BLANK
APPEND FROM Table_B WITH DEFAULTS     && Table_B only has field F1
```

The first record contains default values (`Junk` and `4`) for both fields. The remaining records contain default values for field `F2` and values from `Table_B` field `F1`.

The type of the `DEFAULT` expression, *<exp1>*, must evaluate to the same type as its associated field. The expression can even contain a user-defined function (UDF). If the expression does not evaluate to the same type as the field, Visual FoxPro displays an error message. You can supply default values for all field types except the General (`G`) type. If you do not supply a `DEFAULT` clause for a field, the value inserted into the field is one of the following:

- Filled with blanks if `SET NULL` is `OFF`
- Set to a null value if `SET NULL` is `ON`
- Set to a null value if the `NULL` keyword is specified

NOTE

Regardless of the `SET NULL` setting, the `APPEND BLANK` command always inserts blanks into fields unless the `DEFAULT` clause is specified. The specified default value can be `.NULL.` if you want to insert null values in the fields of new records.

If you specify the `NULL` keyword for a field, null values can be inserted into the field. If you specify the `NOT NULL` keyword for a field, Visual FoxPro prohibits null values from being placed into that field. The `NULL` and `NOT NULL` keywords explicitly designate whether the contents of a field can have a null value regardless of the value of the `SET NULL` command.

For fields with the `PRIMARY KEY` or `UNIQUE` clause specified, null values are never allowed regardless of the `SET NULL` setting.

NOTE

A null value has no explicitly assigned value. A null value is not equivalent to zero or blank. It is used to indicate that no value has ever been entered into a field. A value of null is not considered to be greater than, less than, different from, or equivalent to any other value, including another value of null. Any expression that contains a null value theoretically evaluates to a value of null. However, in many cases, it is necessary to use the `ISNULL()` function to test a variable to determine if it has a null value prior to using that value in an expression.

In the following example, the field `CurrentBalance` is added to the structure of the table Clients and is allowed to have null values:

```
OPEN DATABASE Orders
ALTER Table Clients ADD CurrentBalance N(12,2) NULL
```

In the following example, the field `Birthday` is added to the structure of the table Clients, and null values cannot be entered into the new field:

```
OPEN DATABASE Orders
ALTER TABLE Clients ADD  Birthday D  NOT NULL
```

The following example demonstrates how to remove a `DEFAULT` value property from the field `Birthday` from the structure of the table Clients:

```
OPEN DATABASE Orders
ALTER TABLE Clients ALTER Birthday DROP DEFAULT
```

Field-Level Data Validation Rules

You can enforce data entry by adding field-level or record-level entry rules with the `CREATE TABLE` and `ALTER TABLE` commands. All of these rules operate like the `@...GET` command `VALID` clause. That is, a specified expression is evaluated and Visual FoxPro allows the user to proceed if the expression evaluates to a true (`.T.`) value. If the expression evaluates to false (`.F.`), the process will not be allowed to proceed. Specifically, if you enter an invalid value in the field, you will not be allowed to move out of the field until you enter a valid value. To specify field-level rules when you modify a field structure, you use the following clause:

```
CHECK <expL1> [ERROR <expC1> ]]
```

The `ERROR` clause displays when the table validation rule is violated. Also, it only displays when data is changed within a `BROWSE` or `CHANGE` command.

When you only modify the `CHECK` expression for a field, use the following syntax:

```
ALTER <expTable> ALTER <Field2> SET CHECK <expL2> [ERROR <expC2> ]]
```

When you make a change to the value of a field and attempt to move the cursor out of a field, the expression *<expL1>* is evaluated. If the expression *<expL1>* evaluates to a true (`.T.`) value, the data is considered valid and you can proceed to the next object. Otherwise, the `ERROR` *<expL1>* message displays, and the cursor returns to the field. If you move the cursor into a field with field-level rule and make no change to the field, the expression is not evaluated.

Visual FoxPro evaluates field-level validation rules any time the data in the field is about to be changed by any of the following commands:

```
APPEND
APPEND BLANK
INSERT
INSERT-SQL
REPLACE
```

In the following examples, field-level rules that prohibit you from entering a birthday earlier than January 1, 1900, and a starting balance of less than $1000 are added to the `Birthday` and `StartBalance` fields.

```
OPEN DATABASE Orders
ALTER TABLE Clients ALTER  Birthday ;
     SET CHANGE Birthday > {01/01/1900} ;
        ERROR "No clients over 95 are permitted"
```

In this example, if the table contains records with a `Birthday` field value less than 1/2/1900, Visual FoxPro displays the error message Field birthday validation rule is violated and does not add or change the field-level rule:

```
ALTER TABLE Clients ALTER  StartBalance ;
    SET CHANGE StartBalance >=1000.0 ;
       ERROR "You cannot enter starting balance less than $1,000"
```

The following example demonstrates how to remove a field-level rule property from the field `Birthday` from the structure of the table Clients:

```
OPEN DATABASE Orders
ALTER TABLE Clients ALTER Birthday DROP CHANGE
```

The following example demonstrates how to use a UDF to make sure that a user enters the correct two character state abbreviation for the `State` field. To add this field-level rule, you can specify the following:

```
ALTER TABLE Clients ALTER  State ;
    SET CHANGE ChkState(State) ;
       ERROR "Illegal State value"
```

The UDF for validating the `State` field is presented in Listing 11.2.

Listing 11.2. The UDF for validating abbreviations in the `State` field.

```
FUNCTION chkstate
PARAMETER TState
SaveAlias = ALIAS()
IF USED("STATES")
     SELECT STATES
ELSE
     USE STATES ORDER Abbrev IN 0
ENDIF
ret = SEEK( TState )
IF NOT ISBLANK(SaveAlias)
    SELECT (SaveAlias)
ENDIF
RETURN ret
```

You can insert the UDF, `ChkState`, in the database's *stored procedure*. In fact, you can store any functions that you need for supporting database table–related services such as data validation and triggers in the stored procedure. You use the `MODIFY PROCEDURE` command to create or edit the stored procedure for a database. This command opens the Visual FoxPro text editor to edit the stored procedure in the currently active database. Here is an example:

```
OPEN DATABASE Orders
MODIFY PROCEDURE
```

A useful command for programmatically creating a database is the APPEND PROCEDURE command. For example, you can append procedures from a text file into the stored procedure in the currently active database using the APPEND PROCEDURE command. Here is the syntax:

```
APPEND PROCEDURE FROM <expFN> [AS <expN>] [OVERWRITE]
```

The FROM clause specifies the name of the text file from which the procedure is appended. The AS clause specifies the code page of the text file from which the procedure is appended. See the COPY TO command described earlier in this chapter for a discussion of the code page. If you specify the OVERWRITE keyword, the existing stored procedure in the database is overwritten by the appended procedure. Otherwise, the appended procedure is added to the existing stored procedure.

The COPY PROCEDURE command copies the stored procedure in the database to a text file. Here is the syntax:

```
COPY PROCEDURE TO <expFN> [AS <expN>] [ADDITIVE]
```

If you specify the ADDITIVE keyword, the stored procedure in the currently active database is appended to the text file (TO <expFN>). If you omit the ADDITIVE keyword and the target text file exists, the stored procedure is overwritten. The AS clause specifies the code page of the target text file.

You can maintain a library of text files that contain commonly used stored procedures. You can use the APPEND PROCEDURE command to transfer the appropriate stored procedure to a database. Once you have checked out a stored procedure in a database, you can use the COPY PROCEDURE command to add it to your stored procedure library.

You can list the names of stored procedures for the currently active database with the DISPLAY PROCEDURES or LIST PROCEDURES command. Here is an example:

```
OPEN DATABASE Orders
LIST PROCEDURES
```

The previous example displays this:

```
Stored Procedures in Database Orders
 cascadedelete
 cascadeinsert
 cascadeupdate
```

Record-Level Data Validation Rules

You can use the CREATE TABLE and ALTER TABLE commands CHECK clause to add record-level entry rules. These rules control the type of data that you can enter into a record of an attached table. Before Visual FoxPro adds a record to a table, the CHECK expression is evaluated. The record is added or updated if the expression evaluates to a true (.T.) value. If the expression evaluates to a false (.F.) value, the candidate record entries are rejected and the record is not added or updated. Normally, you use the record-level validation when you want to determine whether to add a record or upgrade it based on an expression involving several fields in the candidate record. The following CHECK clause is specified with the CREATE TABLE command to specify a record-level validation rule:

```
[SET CHECK <expL3> [ERROR <expC3>]]
```

The ERROR clause displays when the table validation rule is violated. Also, it only displays when data is changed within a BROWSE or CHANGE command.

The following example creates the structure for a table of stock quotes. The CHECK clause in the example imposes the restriction that records are added to this table only when the value of the stock changes during the trading session and the volume of the stock exceeds 1000 shares:

```
CREATE TABLE Stocks  NAME StockQuotes ;
   (Stock      C(10),         ;
    Volume     N(8),          ;
    Open       N(8,2),        ;
    High       N(8,2),        ;
    Low        N(8,2),        ;
    Last       N(8,2) ),       ;
    Check  Last <> Open  AND  Volume  > 1000 ;
      ERROR "Stock "+ Stock+ ;
    " did not change or volume is less than 1000 shares."
```

You use the following form of the ALTER TABLE command to specify record-level rules:

```
ALTER TABLE <expTable1>  SET CHECK <expL3> [ERROR <expC3>]
```

You use the following form of the ALTER TABLE command to remove a record-level rule:

```
ALTER TABLE <expTable1>  DROP CHECK
```

The Primary and Candidate Keys

A *primary key* is a field or group of fields whose value uniquely identifies a record. There are no duplicate or null values in a primary index. There can only be one primary index for a table. That is not to say that there cannot be other indexes for a table that do not have duplicate keys or null values. A candidate index meets these requirements. In fact, a candidate index can be used as a primary index because it contains no null values or duplicate values.

When you create a table with the CREATE TABLE command or modify an existing table with the ALTER TABLE command, you can specify that a field be a primary key by specifying the PRIMARY KEY clause. Likewise, you can designate that a field be a candidate key by specifying the UNIQUE clause. The following example creates the Clients table. The ClientID field becomes the primary key, and the Soc_Sec_No field becomes the candidate key:

```
OPEN DATABASE Orders
CREATE TABLE Clients  NAME Clients1994      ;
  (     Client_ID      C(5)   PRIMARY KEY,  ;
        Soc_Sec_No     C(9)    UNIQUE,        ;
        Name           C(20), ;
        StreetAddress  C(30), ;
```

```
State          C(2),  ;
City           C(15), ;
ZIP            C(10), ;
Approved       L,     ;
Picture        G,     ;
Areacode       C(3),  ;
PhoneNumber    C(8),  ;
StartBalance   N(8, 2),;
BalanceDate    D    )
```

NOTE

Indexes that are created with the INDEX command UNIQUE keyword, as discussed in Chapter 13, are different from candidate index keys created by the CREATE TABLE or ALTER TABLE commands. The INDEX command's unique indexes can have duplicate records, whereas candidate indexes cannot.

Persistent Relationships

You can define a relationship between two tables and store it in a database. This is called a *persistent relationship.* In Visual FoxPro you can define a persistent relationship using the Database Designer. In addition, you can programmatically create persistent relationships by using the REFERENCES clause with the CREATE TABLE or ALTER TABLE commands. Here is the syntax of this clause:

```
[REFERENCES <expTable2> [TAG <tag name1> ]]
```

<expTable2> is the parent table name. If you do not specify the TAG clause, the relationship is established using the parent table's primary index. Visual FoxPro displays an error if the parent table does not have a primary index. However, if you specify a TAG clause, the named index tag is used to establish the relationship. The named index tag must exist in the parent table.

The example shown in Listing 11.3 demonstrates the use of the REFERENCES clause to generate a relationship between files. When you execute the MODIFY DATABASE command, the persistent relationships are presented graphically in the Database Designer window. Figure 11.11 shows the Database Designer window for the Orders database created by this example.

Listing 11.3. An example of the use of the CREATE TABLE command REFERENCE clause.

```
*****************************************************************
*     * 12/94               INVEN.PRG                           *
*****************************************************************
*     * Author's Name: Jeb Long                                 *
*     *                                                         *
*     * Description:                                            *
*     * This program illustrates the use of CREATE TABLE        *
*     * to create persistent relationships                      *
*     *                                                         *
*****************************************************************
```

continues

Listing 11.3. continued

```
SET SAFETY OFF
CLOSE DATABASES
CLEAR ALL
CREATE DATABASE Orders


CREATE TABLE Clients  ;
  (     Client_ID  C(5)   PRIMARY KEY,        ;
        Name      C(20),     ;
        Address    C(30),     ;
        State      C(2),      ;
        City       C(15),     ;
        ZIP        C(5),      ;
        Areacode   C(3),      ;
        Phone      C(8),      ;
        StartBal   N(8, 2),   ;
        BalDate    D    )


CREATE TABLE Inven ;
  (     Unit_Price  N(8,2), ;
        Descrip     C(30),       ;
        Inv_No      N(5)  PRIMARY KEY)

CREATE TABLE Transact       ;
  (     Trans_Date  D(8),       ;
        Amount    N(8,2),       ;
        Client_ID   C(5) REFERENCES Clients,       ;
        Inv_No      N(5) REFERENCES Inven,      ;
        QUANTITY    N(6) )
```

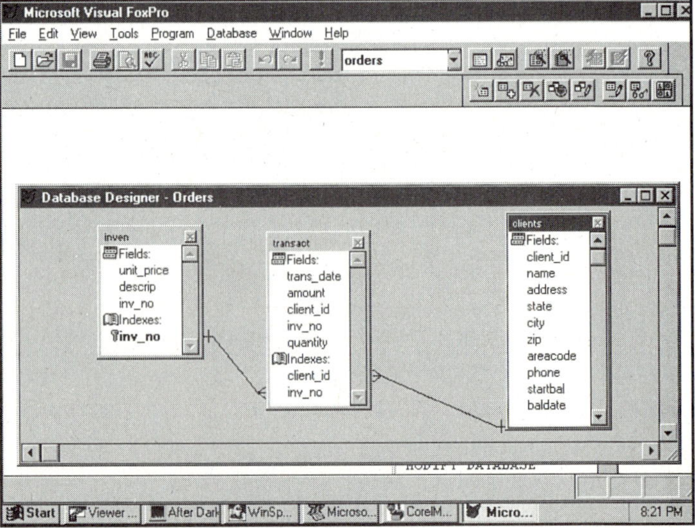

FIGURE 11.11.
The Database Designer window showing persistent relations.

In this example, the table Transact contains a record for each transaction. There would normally be multiple Transact records for each customer and multiple records for each inventory item. The field `ClientID` in the Clients table and the `Inv_No` in the Inven table are primary keys for their tables. The `ClientID` and `Inv_No` fields in the Transact table are referred to in database terminology as *foreign keys.* A foreign key can have duplicate records as it does in the example shown in Figure 11.11. A table can have only one primary key, but it can have multiple foreign keys as it does in this example.

You can also have primary, candidate, and foreign keys based on a complex expression. You can use these indexes to create persistent expressions. Here are some examples:

```
CREATE TABLE Author ;
  (      LastName      C(30),    ;
         FirstName     C(30),    ;
         MI            C(1),     ;
         ADDRESS        C(30) )  ;
   , PRIMARY KEY (FirstName + MI + LastName) TAG Name

ALTER TABLE Supplies ADD PRIMARY KEY MfgCode + PartNo ;
    TAG InvCode

ALTER TABLE Boats REFERENCE MfgCode + PartNo ;
```

You can specify a foreign key based on a complex expression with the `CREATE TABLE` command `FOREIGN KEY` clause. Here is the syntax:

```
[, FOREIGN KEY <exp4>  TAG <tag name4>
        REFERENCES <expTable3>  [TAG <tag name5>]]
```

You can add or remove a foreign key based on an expression with the `ALTER TABLE` command `ADD FOREIGN KEY` clause. Here is the syntax:

```
[ADD FOREIGN KEY [<exp5>] TAG <tag name4>
        REFERENCES <expTable2> [TAG <tag name5>]]
[DROP FOREIGN KEY TAG <tag name6> [SAVE]]
```

Adding Records to Tables

The traditional Xbase method of programmatically adding records to a table is to use the `APPEND BLANK`, `GATHER`, `APPEND FROM`, and `APPEND FROM ARRAY` commands. These commands are discussed elsewhere in this book. Normally, you enter data using a form or simply using the append or browse window. A rarely used technique for entering data in FoxPro is to use the `APPEND BLANK` command to add a blank record followed by one or more `REPLACE` commands to store constant values. The following example of this technique is presented to show an Xbase command set that is equivalent to the SQL `INSERT` command:

```
SaveAlias = ALIAS()
IF USED( Clients )
        SELECT Clients
ELSE
        USE  Clients IN 0
ENDIF
```

```
APPEND BLANK
REPLACE    Client_ID    WITH "90458",
           Name         WITH "John Albert",    ;
           Address      WITH "116 Inn Circle",          ;
           City         WITH "San Jose",       ;
           State        WITH "CA",             ;
           ZIP          WITH "95131"
IF  NOT ISBLANK( SaveAlias )
     SELECT (SaveAlias)
ENDIF
```

The Xbase commands in the previous example can be replaced by a single `INSERT INTO` command. The `INSERT INTO` command is often used to insert data into SQL databases. It can also be used to insert data into a Visual FoxPro table. Here is the syntax of the `INSERT INTO` command forms:

```
INSERT INTO <expFN> [(<field1> [, <field2>, ...])]
      VALUES (<value1> [, <value2>, ...])
INSERT INTO <expFN> FROM ARRAY <Array> ¦ FROM MEMVAR
```

`<expFN>` specifies the name of the table to which the new record is appended. If the specified table is not open, it is opened exclusively in a new work area. If the specified table is in use, the SQL `INSERT` command appends the new record to the table. The current work area is not changed by the `INSERT INTO` command operation.

The `[(<field1> [, <field2>, ...])]` clause specifies the name of the fields in which the values in the `VALUE` clause are inserted in the new record. If you omit the field name list, you must specify the field values in the order of the fields in the structure of the table.

The `FROM ARRAY` clause specifies the name of an array that contains values that are inserted into the new record. The order of the elements in the array corresponds to the order of the fields in the table structure.

The `FROM MEMVAR` clause designates that the values of the memory variables with the same name as the name of the fields in the table are inserted into the new table record. If no memory variable exists that corresponds to a field name, the field is left empty or the default value is used.

The example shown in Listing 11.4 demonstrates the use of `INSERT INTO` command to add data to the tables created in the example shown in Listing 11.3.

Listing 11.4. An example of the use of the `INSERT INTO` command.

```
OPEN DATABASE Orders
INSERT INTO Clients ;
   (Client_ID, Name, Address, City, State, ZIP)  ;
   VALUE ( "90458","John Albert","116 Inn Circle",;
           "San Jose","CA","95131" )
INSERT INTO Clients ;
   (Client_ID, Name, Address, City, State, ZIP)  ;
   VALUE ( "81010","Sam Haldeman","229 Dank St.",;
           "San Diego","CA","92115")
INSERT INTO Clients ;
   (Client_ID, Name, Address, City, State, ZIP)  ;
```

```
   VALUE ( "77312","Horach Grumm","54 Alta St",;
          "San Jose","CA","92334" )

INSERT INTO Transact ;
   ( Trans_Date, Amount, Client_ID, Inv_No, Quantity );
   VALUE ( {01/06/93},  28.48, "90458", 125, 2 )
INSERT INTO Transact ;
   ( Trans_Date, Amount, Client_ID, Inv_No, Quantity );
   VALUE ( {01/09/93},  35.38, "90458", 129, 2 )
INSERT INTO Transact ;
   ( Trans_Date, Amount, Client_ID, Inv_No, Quantity );
   VALUE ( {02/05/93},1262.77, "77312", 116, 34 )
INSERT INTO Transact ;
   ( Trans_Date, Amount, Client_ID, Inv_No, Quantity );
   VALUE ( {02/08/93},   6.88, "77312", 126, 10 )
INSERT INTO Transact ;
   ( Trans_Date, Amount, Client_ID, Inv_No, Quantity );
   VALUE ( {03/22/93},    6.35,"81010", 116, 67 )
INSERT INTO Transact ;
   ( Trans_Date, Amount, Client_ID, Inv_No, Quantity );
   VALUE ( {03/25/93},  43.24,"81010", 112,  4 )

INSERT INTO Inven (Unit_Price, Descrip, Inv_No );
      VALUE (2.22,    [8' x 2"x4" Pine Board],       116 )
INSERT INTO Inven (Unit_Price, Descrip, Inv_No );
      VALUE (6.44,    [2"x10"x14   Pine Board],      125 )
INSERT INTO Inven (Unit_Price, Descrip, Inv_No );
      VALUE (2.35,    [1" Roofing Nails  1 Lb. Box],126 )
INSERT INTO Inven (Unit_Price, Descrip, Inv_No );
      VALUE (492.50, [8" Radial Arm Saw],            129 )
INSERT INTO Inven (Unit_Price, Descrip, Inv_No );
      VALUE (3.21,    [12'x2"x4" Pine Board],        120 )
INSERT INTO Inven (Unit_Price, Descrip, Inv_No );
      VALUE (108.10, [Wooden Door   # 12334],        112 )
```

TIP

The APPEND FROM ARRAY and INSERT INTO commands add records much faster to a table than does the APPEND BLANK command, subsequently used with the REPLACE command. This is especially true in multiuser applications.

Triggers

A *trigger* is a record-level event expression or procedure that executes whenever data is inserted into a table, a record is deleted, or a record is modified. You can bind a different trigger to a each of these three table maintenance events. Visual FoxPro executes triggers after it executes record-level rules and does not execute triggers for buffered updates.

You can use triggers any time you want to do some processing following a record-level event. You can use triggers for transaction logging, for ensuring referential integrity, or for a bizarre application such as issuing an alarm if a customer buys an excessive amount of spray paint. However, triggers are most frequently used to ensure cross-table integrity. You can create a set of up to three triggers for each table with the `CREATE TRIGGER` command. Here is the syntax:

```
CREATE TRIGGER ON <expTable> FOR DELETE ¦ INSERT ¦ UPDATE  AS <exp>
```

You use the `ON` clause to specify the name of a table in the currently active database. Note that the table must be associated with a database. The `AS` clause specifies an expression that executes when an event specified by the `FOR` clause occurs. When a record is marked for deletion, the `FOR DELETE` trigger executes. When a new record is about to be added to the specified table, the `FOR INSERT` trigger executes. If you make any changes to fields in a record of the specified table, the `FOR UPDATE` trigger executes. Visual FoxPro evaluates the `<exp>` trigger expression and if it evaluates to true (`.T.`), the command or operation that was responsible for triggering the event is allowed to proceed. If the expression evaluates to false (`.F.`), Visual FoxPro issues a trigger failed error message and the operation is not allowed to proceed—the record is not updated, added, or deleted depending on the type of trigger. You can trap the error processing with an `ON ERROR` command, and, if you like, you can perform some form of recovery processing.

If a trigger of the corresponding type exists and the `SET SAFETY` setting is `ON`, Visual FoxPro asks if you are sure that you want to overwrite the existing trigger. If the `SET SAFETY` setting is `OFF`, the existing trigger is overwritten without warning.

The trigger expression (`<exp>`) can be a UDF. The UDF is called a stored procedure because it is stored in the database. You can create and edit stored procedures with the `MODIFY PROCEDURE` command. Table 11.7 lists commands that triggers events.

Table 11.7. The commands that trigger events.

Trigger Type	*Command or Operation*
`DELETE`	`DELETE`
	Marks a record for deletion from the Browse or Change window
`INSERT`	`APPEND BLANK`
	`APPEND FROM`
	`APPEND FROM ARRAY`
	Appends a record to a table from the Browse or Change window
	`IMPORT`
	SQL `INSERT`
	`RECALL`
	Toggles the delete record mark off from the Browse or Change window

Trigger Type	Command or Operation
UPDATE	GATHER
	REPLACE
	SQL UPDATE

The INSERT command cannot be applied to a table with a trigger. No trigger is activated when you execute the PACK command or if you update a record that is marked for deletion.

When the transaction-processing buffering mode is operational, an UPDATE trigger is not activated until you commit the buffered modifications to the target table by executing the TABLEUPDATE() function. The UPDATE trigger is activated as each buffered record is updated in the target table. If the buffering mode is not in effect, an UPDATE trigger is activated when a record is modified.

NOTE

Transaction processing was introduced in Visual FoxPro. It is done by making updates to a temporary buffer during the transaction. Then, at the appropriate time, the target table is updated from the buffer using the TABLEUPDATE() function or rejected using the TABLEREVERT() function. You can establish a buffering mode using the CURSORSETPROP() function. This topic is discussed in Chapter 25.

You can remove a trigger from the table designer with the DELETE TRIGGER command. Here is the syntax:

```
DELETE TRIGGER ON <expTable> FOR DELETE ¦ INSERT ¦ UPDATE
```

The only way you can modify a trigger is by using the Table Designer. Programmatically, if you want to change a trigger, you must delete it first and then re-create it. Here is an example:

```
DELETE TRIGGER ON Inven  FOR DELETE
CREATE TRIGGER ON Inven  FOR DELETE AS Cascade("Inven")
```

The following example involves the Transact and Inven tables that are associated with the Orders database. The source code for creating these tables is presented in Listing 11.3. In this example, DELETE, INSERT, and UPDATE triggers are created for the Inven table. These triggers are designed to make sure that cross-table integrity is maintained when data in the Inven table is changed. Specifically, when you change an inventory number (Inv_No) in the inventory table (Inven.DBF), the corresponding inventory number (Transact.InvNo) is automatically changed for all the records in the transaction table (Transact.DBF) with a matching inventory number. When you delete or recall a record in the inventory file, the corresponding records in the transaction table are deleted or recalled, respectively. The triggers in this example are created with the following code:

```
OPEN DATABASE Orders
CREATE TRIGGER ON Inven FOR DELETE AS CasDelete("Inven")
CREATE TRIGGER ON Inven FOR INSERT AS CasInsert ("Inven")
CREATE TRIGGER ON Inven FOR UPDATE AS CasUpdate ("Inven")
USE Inven IN 0 ORDER Inv_No
USE Transact IN 0
SELECT Transact
SET RELATION TO Inv_No INTO Inven
*   Shows that UPDATE triggers are working
CHANGE  FIELDS   Transact.Trans_Date,   ;
                 Transact.Quantity,     ;
                 Inven.Inv_No,          ;
                 Transact.Inv_No,       ;
                 Inven.Descrip
```

Listing 11.5 presents the listing of the stored procedure for the Orders database, which contains the `CasDelete()`, `CasInsert()`, and `CasUpdate()` stored procedures. Whenever you change the `Inv_No` field in the Inven table, you need to make sure that the related records with the foreign key `Inv_No` field value in the Transact table are handled properly.

The `CasDelete()` stored procedure marks for deletion the records in the Transact table with a value of `Inv_No` that correspond to the record in the Inven table that was deleted. The `CasUpdate()` stored procedure replaces the value of `Inv_No` for records in the Transact table with the updated value of the `Inv_No` field in the Inven table. The `CasInsert()` stored procedure removes the deletion marks from records in the Transact table to account for a `RECALL` operation performed on the Inven table.

Listing 11.5. A listing of the stored procedures for the Orders database.

```
*****************************************************
*   CasDelete - Do cascading Deletes
*      Delete any records in Transact that relate on Inv_No
*      to a record just deleted in Inven.
*
FUNCTION CasDelete
PARAMETER FName
DO ToggleIt WITH .T.   && DELETE records
RETURN .T.
*****************************************************
*   CasInsert - Do cascading Insert (Recall)
* Recall any records in Transact that relate on Inv_No
* to a record just recalled in Inven.
*
FUNCTION CasInsert
PARAMETER FName
DO ToggleIt WITH .F.    && RECALL records
RETURN .T.
*****************************************************
*   CasUpdate - Do cascading Updates
```

```
* replace values of Inv_No in Transact records that relate on
* Inv_No to a value of Inv_No just upgraded in Inven.
*
FUNCTION CasUpdate
PARAMETER FName
IF FName = "inven"
        OldValue = OLDVAL("Inven.Inv_No")
        NewValue = inven.Inv_No
        IF OldValue != NewValue  && Did value change?
               SaveWA = ALIAS()
               SELECT Transact
               REPLACE Transact.Inv_No WITH NewValue ;
                       FOR OldValue == Transact.Inv_No
               SELECT (SaveWA)
        ENDIF
ENDIF
RETURN .T.
*************************************************
* ToggleIt - Delete or Recall records corresponding
*            to deleted records in table inven
PROCEDURE ToggleIt
PARAMETER DoDELETE
IF FName = "inven"  AND LEFT( GETFLDSTATE(-1) , 1 ) == "2" )
        OldValue = OLDVAL("Inven.Inv_No")
        SaveWA = ALIAS()
        SELECT Transact
        IF DoDELETE
               DELETE FOR OldValue == Transact.Inv_No
        ELSE
               RECALL FOR OldValue == Transact.Inv_No
        ENDIF
        SELECT (SaveWA)
ENDIF
```

Here is an example for using the triggers for the Inven table, which executes the code in the stored procedures shown in Listing 11.5:

```
OPEN DATABASE Orders
USE Inven IN 0
USE Transact IN 0
SELECT Transact
BROWSE
SELECT Inven
EDIT
```

When you modify a value of the inventory number (`Inv_No`) in the inventory table (Inven.DBF), the `Inv_No` value for all the records that correspond to the changed Inven.DBF table `Inv_No` field are also changed. You can delete a record in the Inven.DBF table, and all the records in the Transact.DBF table that correspond to the deleted Inven.DBF table record are automatically deleted, as illustrated in Figure 11.12. In this figure, the Edit and Browse windows are resized and moved so that both are visible. Then the Inven.DBF table record with an `Inv_No` value of `116` is deleted and all records in the transaction file with a value of `116` are also deleted. In database terminology, the changes are said to *cascade* through the relation.

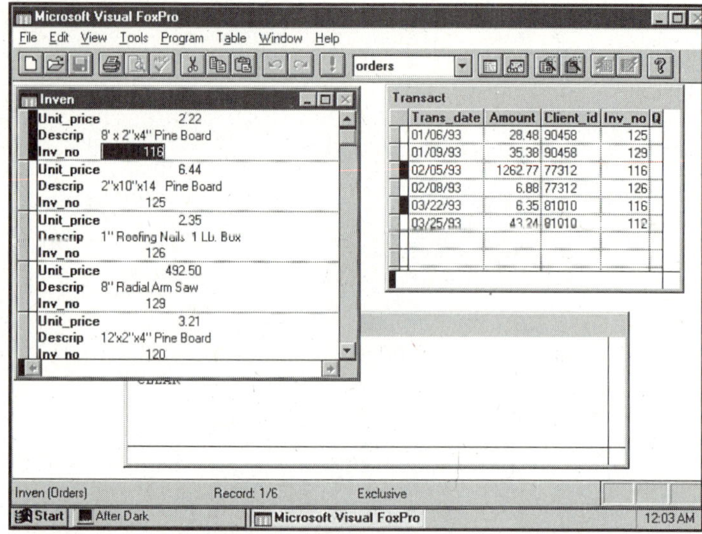

FIGURE 11.12.
An example of a `DELETE` *trigger operation.*

Establishing Referential Integrity Visually

You have learned how to programmatically use triggers to enforce referential integrity. You can also establish triggers using the Referential Integrity Builder, which is very easy to do.

There are several ways to run the Referential Integrity Builder when the Database Designer is active. Here are three ways to run the Referential Integrity Builder:

- Use the Database menu Referential Integrity option.
- Right-click on the Database Designer window relation line and choose the shortcut menu Referential Integrity option. (See Figure 11.13.)
- Double-click on a relation line to display the Edit Relationship dialog box. Then click on the Referential Integrity button. (See Figure 11.14.)

Regardless of the manner in which you invoke the Referential Integrity Builder, it appears as shown in Figure 11.15. A grid at the top of the window contains a list of all of the relations. It shows the parent and child tables, parent and candidate index tags, and the action employed for handling child records when a record in the parent table is modified. The lower panel is a tabbed page form containing tabs for each type of trigger (update, deletion, and insertion). The Rules for Updating tab is shown in Figure 11.15. You can specify which of the following rules to apply when the key value in the parent table changes:

- All related records in the child table are updated with the new key value.
- Updates are not allowed if there are related records in the child table.
- Ignore the updates and perform no action on the related records in the child table if its corresponding key is changed in the parent table.

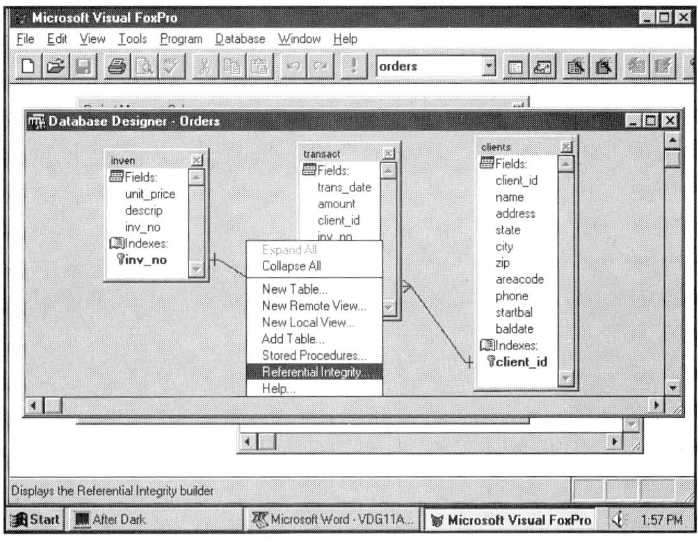

FIGURE 11.13.
The Database Designer window with the shortcut menu open.

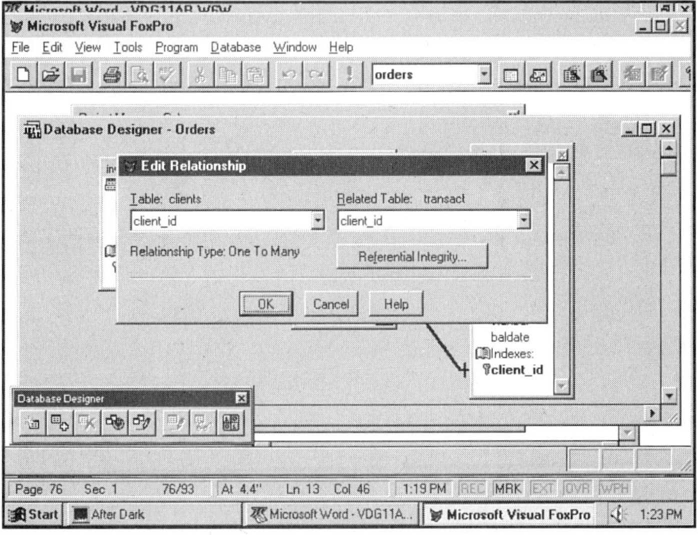

FIGURE 11.14.
The Edit Relationship dialog box.

You specify which referential integrity rule should apply for all the relations in the database. Your choice appears in the Update grid columns. You can choose the Rules for Deleting tab (see Figure 11.16) and specify rules for deletion of child table records in response to the deletion of a related record in the parent table. The Rules for Inserting tab, as shown in Figure 11.17, lets you specify which rule to apply to the child table when you insert a record in the parent table.

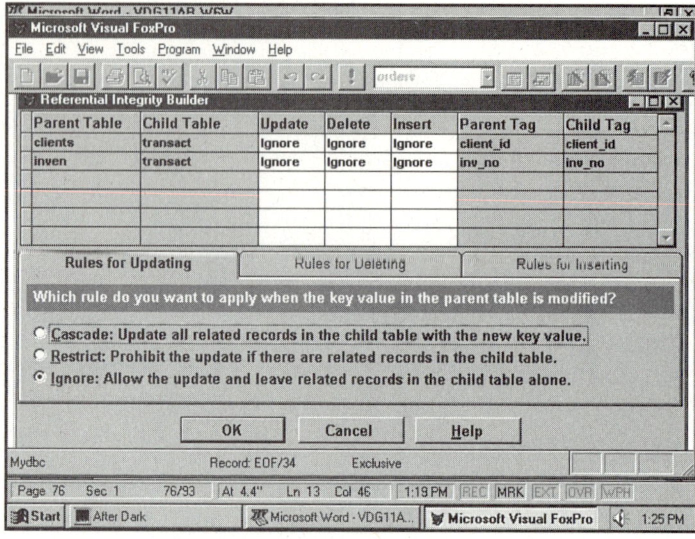

FIGURE 11.15.
The Rules for Updating tab of the Edit Relationship dialog box.

When you have finished specifying which rules you want to apply, press the OK button and the Referential Integrity Builder will do the rest automatically. It establishes trigger conditions and adds stored procedure code that enforces referential integrity rules.

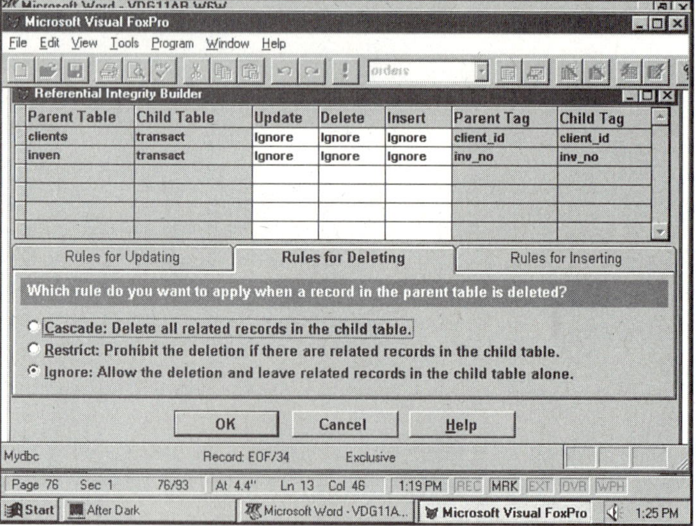

FIGURE 11.16.
The Referential Integrity Builder window with the Rules for Deleting tab displayed.

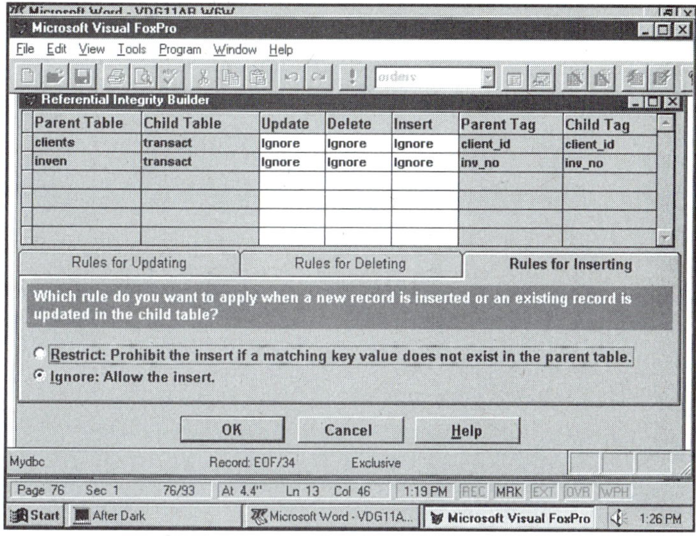

FIGURE 11.17.
The Referential Integrity Builder window with the Rules for Inserting tab displayed.

Functions That Retrieve Database Information

This section presents commands and functions used to retrieve information relating to database and database components. The following functions are useful for returning information relating to databases and tables.

The *ADATABASE()* Function

The `ADATABASE(<array>)` function inserts the names of the open databases and their paths into the named array (`<array>`). If the array does not exist, it is created. If the array exists but is the wrong size, its size is adjusted to be large enough to hold the database names. The array is two-dimensional. The first column contains the names of the open databases. The second column contains the paths to the databases.

The *ADBOBJECTS()* Function

The `ADBOBJECTS(<array>,<expC>)` function inserts the names of named connections, tables, or SQL views in the currently active database into the named array (`<array>`). If the array does not exist it is created. If the array exists but is the wrong size, its size is adjusted to be large enough to hold the names of the objects. The array is two-dimensional. The first column contains the names of the objects, the second column contains the paths to the objects. The type of names to be placed in the memory variable array is determined by `<expC>`. These are the types (`<expC>`) and the corresponding objects to be placed in the array:

<expC>	*Names Placed in Array*
CONNECTION	Connection names
TABLE	Table names
VIEW	View names

The values of <*expC*> cannot be abbreviated. Here is an example:

```
OPEN DATABASE Orders
? ADBOBJECTS(Aray, "TABLES" )
```

The *AERROR()* Function

You can use the `AERROR()` function with `ON ERROR` processing to determine if you have encountered a trigger error. Here is the syntax:

```
AERROR(<array>)
```

The `AERROR()` function creates a one-dimensional named array (<*array*>) with five elements. When a Visual FoxPro error occurs, the `AERROR()` function adds the following value types in the elements:

Element	*Description*	*Type*
1	Contains the number of the error. This value is identical to the value returned by the `ERROR()` function.	N
2	Contains the text of the error message. This string is identical to the value returned by the `MESSAGE()` function.	C
3	This element contains either `.NULL.` or the text of an additional error message returned by certain error conditions. For example, if you reference a memory variable that does not exist, the name of the memory variable is included in the error message. This array element can contain error message parameters that normally are names of memory variables and files. These values are identical to the value returned by the `SYS(2018)` function.	C

4	This element either contains .NULL. or the number of the work area in which the error occurred.	N
5	This element contains either .NULL. or, if a trigger fails (Error 1539), one of the following Numeric values: 1—Insert trigger failed 2—Update trigger failed 3—Delete trigger failed	N

If an ODBC error occurs, the array returns a different set of five values:

Element	*Description*	*Type*
1	Contains the remote number of the error.	N
2	Contains the text of the remote error message.	C
3	Contains the connection handle number if a SQL call fails.	N
4	Unused.	NULL
5	Unused.	NULL

The *CANDIDATE()* and *PRIMARY()* Functions

You can use the PRIMARY() and CANDIDATE() functions, respectively, to determine whether an index tag is a primary or secondary index tag. This is the syntax of these two commands:

```
CANDIDATE([<index number>][,<expWA>])
PRIMARY([<index number>][, <expWA> ])
```

The CANDIDATE (function returns true (.T.) if the index tag is a candidate index tag; otherwise, it returns false (.F.). *<index number>* is the order of the index tags in the structural compound index. If it is omitted, the master controlling index tag is chosen. If there is no controlling index tag, the CANDIDATE() function returns false (.F.). Since a candidate index can be a primary index, you can use this function to find out if you can use an index tag as a primary index.

The PRIMARY() function returns true (.T.) if the index tag is a primary index tag; otherwise, it returns false (.F.).

The *CURVAL()* and *OLDVAL()* Functions

The CURVAL() function returns a value of the specified field from the disk. The OLDVAL() function returns the original value for the specified field that has been updated. This is the syntax of these commands:

```
CURVAL(<field1>[, <expWA>])
OLDVAL(<field1>[, <expWA>])
```

These two functions return the same data type as the specified field. The CURVAL() and OLDVAL() functions can be compared to determine if a record on the network changed while the field was being edited. However, they can only return different values when *optimistic* row or table buffering is enabled. The CURSORSETPROP() function is used to establish buffering modes. Row and table buffering is presented in Chapter 25.

The *DBC()* Function

The DBC() function returns the name and path of the currently active database. If there is no currently active database, the DBC() function returns an empty string.

The *DBGETPROP()* Function

The DBGETPROP() function returns a property for the currently active database, or for fields, named connections, tables, or views in the currently active database. You can set values of some of the database object properties with the DBSETPROP() function. The syntax of these two functions is

```
DBGETPROP(<expC1>,<expC2>,<expC3>)
DBSETPROP(<expC1>,<expC2>,<expC3>,<expC4>)
```

<expC1> is the name of the database, field, and so forth for which you want the property returned. If <expC2> is a field, you must prepend the name of the associated table or view to the field. For example, to specify field duck in table fowl, you must specify fowl.duck. <expC2> is the type of property based on the value of <expC1>. <expC3> is name of the property for which a value is returned. Some <expC2> values are shown in Table 11.8. You use the <exp> argument with the DBSETPROP() function to specify a new value. If you attempt to set a property that is read-only, Visual FoxPro displays the Property is read-only error message. Those properties that cannot be changed (read-only) are marked with an asterisk (*) in Table 11.8. The other properties are read-write.

Table 11.8. The types of properties (<expC3>) for the DBGETPROP() and DBSETPROP() functions.

Type <expC2>	*Property* <expC3>	*Return Type*	*Description of Property*
CONNECTION			(Table 11.9 describes the properties for the CONNECTION type.)

Type <expC2>	*Property* <expC3>	*Return Type*	*Description of Property*
DATABASE	Comment	C	The text of the database comment.
	Version	C	The database version number.*
FIELD			The FIELD object type for tables.
	Comment	C	The text of the field comment.
	DefaultValue	C	The default value.*
	RuleExpression	C	The rule expression for the field (CHECK clause).
	RuleText	C	The ERROR clause text.
FIELD			The FIELD object type for views.
	Comment	C	The text of the field comment.
	DefaultValue	C	The default value.*
	KeyField	L	.T. if the field is specified in any key expression.
	ODBCName	C	The name of the field on the remote table.*
	RuleExpression	C	The rule expression for the field (CHECK clause).
	RuleText	C	The ERROR clause text.
	Updatable	L	.T. if the field can be updated.
	UpdateName	C	The field name used when the data of the field is updated to a remote table.
TABLE	Comment	C	The text of the table comment.
	DeleteTrigger	C	Deletes the trigger expression.*
	InsertTrigger	C	Updates the trigger expression.*
	Path	C	The path to the table.*
	RuleExpression	C	The row rule (CHECK clause) expression.*
	RuleText	C	The row rule (ERROR clause) text.*
	UpdateTrigger	C	Updates the trigger expression.*

continues

Table 11.8. continued

Type <expC2>	*Property* <expC3>	*Return Type*	*Description of Property*
VIEW	BatchUpdateCount	N	The number of update statements that are sent to the back end for views. The default value is 1. You can adjust this value to increase update performance.
	Comment	C	The text of the view comment.
	ConnectName	C	The name of the named connection used when the view is opened.*
	FetchMemo	L	If memo fields are fetched with the view results, this value is .T.; otherwise, this value is .F.(which is the default value).
	FetchSize	N	The number of records that are fetched at a time from the remote tables when you enable progressive fetches. The default is 100 records. You can set FetchSize to -1 to retrieve the complete result set. (The maximum number is limited by the MaxRecords setting.)
	MaxRecords	N	The maximum number of rows fetched when result sets are returned. The default is -1 (all rows are returned). A value of 0 specifies that the view is executed but no results are fetched.
	RuleExpression	C	The row rule expression.
	RuleText	C	The rule text expression displayed when an error occurs when data is edited in a browse or edit window.
	SendUpdates	L	Contains .T. if a SQL update query is sent to update remote tables; otherwise, contains .F..

Type <expC2>	Property <expC3>	Return Type	Description of Property
	ShareConnection	L	Contains .T. if the view can share its connection handle with other connections; otherwise, contains .F..
	SourceType	N	The view source.* SourceType can assume the following values: 1—Source is local tables. 2—Source is remote tables.
	SQL	C	The SQL statement is executed when the view opens.*
	Tables	C	The list of the names of the tables (comma delimited).*
	UpdateType	N	The type of update. Here are the valid values: 1—The old data is deleted and the new data is inserted. 2—The old data is updated. (2 is the default value.)
	UseMemoSize	N	The minimum size of the result column in bytes before result column is returned in memo fields. UseMemoSize can vary from 1 to 255; the default value is 255.
	WhereType	N	The WHERE clause updates remote tables. WhereType can have the following values: 1—The WHERE clause consists of only the primary fields specified with the KeyFieldList property. 2—(DB_KEYANDUPDATABLE) 3—The WHERE clause consists of primary fields specified with the KeyFieldList property and any other fields that are updated. 4—(DB_KEYANDTIMESTAMP)

*Read-only properties.

Table 11.9. Connection properties (<expC3>) for the DBGETPROP() and DBSETPROP() functions.

Property <expC3>	*Return Type*	*Description of Property*
Asynchronous	L	Designates whether the connection mode is a synchronous (.T., the default) or asynchronous connection (.F.).
BatchMode	L	Designates the batch processing mode that indicates whether (.T., the default) or not (.F.) the connection operates in batch mode.
Comment	C	Contains the connection's comment text.
ConnectString	C	Contains the login connection string.
ConnectTimeout	N	Contains the connection timeout interval in seconds. The default is 0, which indicates that you wait indefinitely.
DataSource	C	Contains the name of the data source as defined in the ODBC.INI file.
DispLogin	N	Contains a numeric value that determines when the ODBC Login dialog box displays. It can have the following values to indicate when the ODBC Login dialog box displays: 1—Some required information is missing (default). 2—Always. 3—Never (error is generated).
DispWarnings	L	Contains a logical value that indicates whether (.T., the default) or not (.F.) nontrappable warnings from the remote table, ODBC, or Visual FoxPro are displayed.
IdleTimeout	N	Contains the idle timeout interval in seconds. Active connections are deactivated after the specified time interval. The default value is 0, which indicates an indefinite wait.
PacketSize	N	Contains the size of the network packet used by the connection. Adjust this value to improve performance. The default value is 4096 bytes (4KB).

Property <expC3>	*Return Type*	*Description of Property*
PassWord	C	Contains the connection password.
QueryTimeout	N	Contains the query timeout interval in seconds. The default value is 0, which indicates an indefinite wait.
Transactions	N	Contains a numeric value that indicates whether transaction processing from a remote table is automatically handled or is handled through SQLCOMMIT() and SQLROLLBACK() functions.
UserId	C	Contains the user identification.
WaitTime	N	Contains the amount of time in milliseconds that elapses before Visual FoxPro checks whether the SQL statement has completed executing. The default is 100 milliseconds.

Here are examples of the use of the DBGETPROP() function:

```
? dbgetprop("Clients.startbal", "FIELD", "RuleExpression")
? dbgetprop("Clients.startbal", "FIELD", "RuleText")
? dbgetprop("Clients", "TABLE", "Path")
? dbgetprop("inven", "TABLE", "DeleteTrigger")
```

Here is the resultant output from the preceding commands:

```
Clients.startbal=>1000.0
"Starting Balance must be greater than 1000"
clients.dbf
cascadedelete("Inven")
```

The *GETFLDSTATE()* and *SETFLDSTATE()* Functions

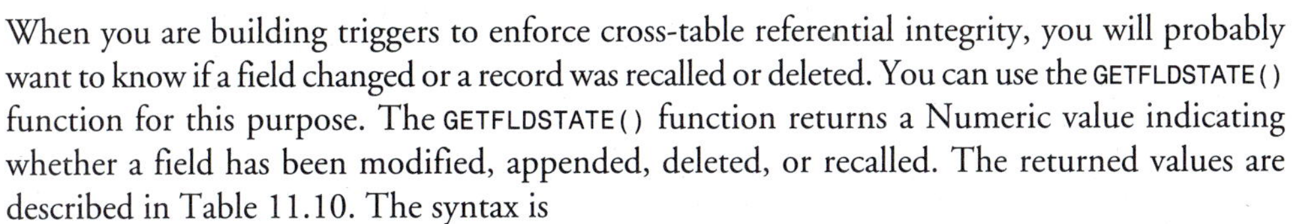

When you are building triggers to enforce cross-table referential integrity, you will probably want to know if a field changed or a record was recalled or deleted. You can use the GETFLDSTATE() function for this purpose. The GETFLDSTATE() function returns a Numeric value indicating whether a field has been modified, appended, deleted, or recalled. The returned values are described in Table 11.10. The syntax is

```
SETFLDSTATE(<expC> ¦ <expN>, <expN> [, <expWA> ])
GETFLDSTATE( <expC> ¦ <expN> [, <expWA> ] )
```

You can either specify the name of a field (<expC>) or the order number of the field (<expN>) in the structure of the database file in use in the specified (<expWA>) work area.

Table 11.10. The types of properties (<*expC3*>) for the GETFLDSTATE() and SETFLDSTATE() functions.

Value Returned	*Edit or Deletion Status*
1	The field has not been edited or deletion status has not changed.
2	The field has been edited or deletion status has changed.
3	The field in an appended record has not been edited and deletion status has not changed.
4	The field in an appended record has been edited or deletion status has changed.

Once you have detected that the deletion status has changed, you can use `DELETED([<expWA>])` to determine the current deletion status of a record. The `DELETED()` function returns true (`.T.`) if the current record is deleted.

If you set `-1` for the field order number (<*expN*>), the `GETFLDSTATE()` function returns a string with the deletion status of the record followed by the status code for each field. For example, if you change the second field for a table with four fields, the `GETFLDSTATE()` function returns `11211`. Notice that the first number indicates the deletion status of the record; in this case the deletion status has not changed.

The `SETFLDSTATE()` function assigns a field edit or deletion state (<*expN*>) in a local cursor created from remote tables. With this function you can control which fields are updated by Visual FoxPro even though no changes are actually made to the record. The assigned state (<*expN*>) can have a value from `1` to `4`. The values correspond to the same numbers returned by the `GETFLDSTATE()` function.

The *ISEXCLUSIVE()* Function

The `ISEXCLUSIVE([ <expWA> ])` function returns true (`.T.`) if the table in the current or specified (<*expWA*>) work area was opened in exclusive mode. Otherwise, it returns false (`.F.`).

Displaying Database Information

The Visual FoxPro language contains several forms of the `DISPLAY` and `LIST` command. These commands display information about components in the currently active database, as summarized in Table 11.11.

Table 11.11. The commands that display database information.

Command	*Displayed Information*
`DISPLAY CONNECTIONS` `LIST CONNECTIONS`	The named connection information in the currently active database.

Command	Displayed Information
DISPLAY DATABASE LIST DATABASE	All object types in the currently active database, including fields, named connections, tables, and views.
DISPLAY PROCEDURES LIST PROCEDURES	The list of stored procedures in the currently active database.
DISPLAY TABLES LIST TABLES	List of all tables in the current database.
DISPLAY VIEWS LIST VIEWS	The SQL view information in the currently active database.

Here is the generalized form of the DISPLAY and LIST commands shown in Table 11.11:

```
DISPLAY <keyword>  [TO PRINTER [PROMPT] ¦ TO FILE <expFN>] [NOCONSOLE]
LIST <keyword>  [TO PRINTER [PROMPT] ¦ TO FILE <expFN>] [NOCONSOLE]
```

You can direct output to a printer or a named file (<expFN>). If you do not specify a file extension, .TXT will be used. You can also suppress output to the current window or screen with the NOCONSOLE keyword.

Listing 11.6 and 11.7 present examples of sample output from the LIST TABLES and LIST DATABASE commands, respectively.

Listing 11.6. An example of output from the DISPLAY TABLES command.

```
Tables in Database  Orders:

  Name              Type              Source
  clients           native           c:\fox30\foxbook\chap11\clients.dbf
  inven             native           c:\fox30\foxbook\chap11\inven.dbf
  transact          native           c:\fox30\foxbook\chap11\transact.dbf
  author            native           c:\fox30\foxbook\chap11\author.dbf
   ORDERS
```

Listing 11.7. An example of output from the DISPLAY DATABASE command.

```
   1 Database     Database
                      * Version          8
   2    1 Database    TransactionLog
   3    1 Database    StoredProceduresSource
   4    1 Database    StoredProceduresObject
   5    1 Table       clients
                      * SYSTEM PROPERTY *
                      * Path             clients.dbf
                      * PrimaryKey       client_id
   6    5 Field       client_id
   7    5 Field       name
```

continues

Listing 11.7. continued

```
  8    5 Field       address
  9    5 Field       state
 10    5 Field       city
 11    5 Field       zip
 12    5 Field       areacode
 13    5 Field       phone
 14    5 Field       startbal
 15    5 Field       baldate
 16    5 Index       client_id
                     * Unique            TRUE
 17    1 Table       inven
                     * SYSTEM PROPERTY *
                     * Path              inven.dbf
                     * PrimaryKey        inv_no
                     * DeleteTrigger     cascadedelete("Inven")
                     * InsertTrigger     cascadeinsert("Inven")
                     * UpdateTrigger     cascadeupdate("Inven")
 18   17 Field       unit_price
 19   17 Field       descrip
 20   17 Field       inv_no
 21   17 Index       inv_no
                     * Unique            TRUE
 22    1 Table       transact
                     * SYSTEM PROPERTY *
                     * Path              transact.dbf
 23   22 Field       trans_date
 24   22 Field       amount
 25   22 Field       client_id
 26   22 Field       inv_no
 27   22 Field       quantity
 28   22 Index       client_id
                     * Unique            FALSE
 29   22 Relation    Relation 1
                     * RelatedChild      client_id
                     * RelatedTable      clients
                     * RelatedTag        client_id
 30   22 Index       inv_no
                     * Unique            FALSE
 31   22 Relation    Relation 2
                     * RelatedChild      inv_no
                     * RelatedTable      inven
                     * RelatedTag        inv_no
 32    1 Table       author
                     * SYSTEM PROPERTY *
                     * Path              author.dbf
 33   32 Field       lastname
 34   32 Field       firstname
 35   32 Field       mi
 36   32 Field       address
```

Summary

This chapter describes the basic unit of the Visual FoxPro programming language—the table and the database container (DBC) file. The formats of these files are presented, as are the Visual FoxPro commands that give access to these types of file.

This chapter introduces the concept of a current record pointer and describes the FoxPro commands that position this pointer at the first, last, next, and previous records. These concepts are different for physical and logical (indexed) files. I also discuss the FoxPro selection, projection, and relationship commands, which are used to create logical views of base tables. The mechanism for physically deleting records is described, too.

In this chapter you are shown how to create and use a database container file and how to create and use triggers, data validation, and other database properties.

Chapter 12 expands on these concepts. It explains how FoxPro commands act on an entire set of records at once and elaborates on the critically important FoxPro concept called *scope*.

12

Data Set Operations

Why can't somebody give us a list of things that everybody thinks and nobody says, and another list of things that everybody says and nobody thinks.

—Dr. Oliver Wendell Holmes (1809–1894)

The Visual FoxPro commands that act on data records can be applied to one, many, or all records in a table. The set of records on which a command acts is the *scope* of the command. A scope selects a subset of records and is viable only for the duration of the command. This chapter describes the FoxPro commands that support data set operations by acting in a specified scope.

Included in these commands are commands that move data sets from one file to another, including the `APPEND`, `COPY`, `EXPORT`, `IMPORT`, `SCATTER`, `GATHER`, and `INSERT` commands. This chapter also discusses the use of `COPY` and `APPEND` to transfer data between arrays and tables. The `COPY` and `APPEND` commands serve almost as systems inside a system. Briefly expressing the cornucopia of features incorporated in these commands is difficult. The `COPY` and `APPEND` commands transfer data. The `SCATTER` command transfers data from table fields to arrays, memory variables, or a named object. The `GATHER` command transfers from arrays, memory variables, or a named object to fields in a table. The `IMPORT` and `EXPORT` commands transfer data between FoxPro DBF files and external format files. However, the `COPY` and `APPEND` commands also perform this function. Table 12.1 describes which command performs which type of transfer.

Table 12.1. File transfer commands.

TYPE *Keyword*	*Format*	*IMPORT*	*EXPORT*	*APPEND*	*COPY TO*
FOXPLUS	FoxBASE+ table	Yes		Yes	Yes
DELIMITED	ASCII file			Yes	Yes
DIF	VisiCalc 1.0 spreadsheet		Yes	Yes	Yes
FW2	Framework II	Yes		Yes	
MOD	Multiplan spreadsheet	Yes	Yes	Yes	Yes
PDOX	Borland Paradox database file	Yes		Yes	
RPD	RapidFile data file	Yes		Yes	
SDF	ASCII file			Yes	Yes
SYLK	SYMBOLIC link interchange format used by Microsoft Multiplan		Yes	Yes	Yes
WK1	Lotus 1-2-3, Version 2.*x*	Yes	Yes	Yes	Yes

TYPE Keyword	Format	IMPORT	EXPORT	APPEND	COPY TO
WK3	Lotus 1-2-3, Revision 3.*x*	Yes		Yes	
WKS	Lotus 1-2-3, Release 1A	Yes	Yes	Yes	Yes
WR1	Lotus Symphony spreadsheet Version 1.1	Yes	Yes	Yes	Yes
WRK	Lotus Symphony spreadsheet Version 1.01	Yes	Yes	Yes	Yes
XLS	Excel spreadsheet Version 2.*x*	Yes	Yes	Yes	Yes
XL5	Excel spreadsheet Version 5.*x*	Yes	Yes	Yes	Yes

Scope

The scope of a command is specified by one or more scope clauses such as the following:

```
<scope>         ::=  <scope clause>
                        [FOR <expL>]
                        [WHILE <expL>]

<scope clause> ::=  ALL
          ¦ NEXT <expN>
          ¦ RECORD <expN>
          ¦ REST
```

Notice that FOR and WHILE clauses can coexist with any one of the other scope clauses for a particular command. Many explanations of the Xbase language incorrectly separate FOR and WHILE from the discussion of scope.

The ALL keyword specifies all records, respecting any current filter. This is the default for many commands, but it overrides single record defaults when necessary. NEXT specifies the current record and subsequent records (in index order, respecting the filter), up to a total number of records specified with <expN>. RECORD restricts the scope to a particular record, and REST refers to all records from the current one to the end of the file. In the following examples, records are selected using a scope:

Command Window	*Results*	
`LIST`	`Record#`	`STATE`
	`1`	`California`
	`2`	`New York`
	`3`	`Texas`
	`4`	`Florida`
	`5`	`Pennsylvania`
	`6`	`Illinois`
	`7`	`Ohio`
	`8`	`Michigan`
`LIST RECORD 5`	`Record#`	`STATE`
	`5`	`Pennsylvania`
`LIST NEXT 2`	`Record#`	`STATE`
	`5`	`Pennsylvania`
	`6`	`Illinois`
`LIST REST`	`Record#`	`STATE`
	`6`	`Illinois`
	`7`	`Ohio`
	`8`	`Michigan`
`LIST FOR Name < "M"`	`Record#`	`STATE`
	`1`	`California`
	`4`	`Florida`
	`6`	`Illinois`

`FOR` is a single-command filter. The `SET FILTER` is often called the Super-`FOR`, because a filter acts like a multiple-command `FOR` clause. `FOR` examines all records in the file, starting with an implicit `GOTO TOP`, and specifies all records for which the `FOR <expL>` expression evaluates to `.T.`.

The `WHILE` clause behaves the same as the `FOR` clause, but without the `GOTO TOP`—that is, `WHILE` starts with the current record. `FOR .T.` is the same as `ALL`, while`.T.` is the same as `REST`, and `RECORD RECNO()` is the same as `NEXT 1`. The scope of commands such as `DELETE` and `LIST` is affected by the specification of these clauses. If either `ALL` or `FOR` is specified, the first action is `GOTO TOP`; otherwise, processing starts at the current record. A record is acted on if both the `WHILE` expression and the `FOR` expression (if specified) evaluate to `.T.`. These commands stop processing when they reach the *end of scope*, at which point skipping to the next record either puts the pointer past `EOF`, puts the pointer past the record specified, or increases the count beyond what was requested by a `NEXT` clause. `FOR` and `ALL` march on to the end of the file, as they must, but the other clauses can reach the end of scope sooner. For example, the command

```
LIST FOR RECNO() < 5000
```

reads all 100,000 records in a 100,000-record data file and lists the first 5000. The last 95000 read operations are useless. Unless an index is in use, it is smarter to use the following:

```
LIST FOR .T. WHILE RECNO() < 5000
```

The FOR clause forces an implicit GOTO TOP, but the WHILE clause reaches the end of scope and thus stops reading records at record 5000.

Some commands assume you want all records, whereas others act only on the current record, unless a broader scope is specified. See Table 12.2 for specific information. For example, DELETE and LIST work differently. LIST displays all records, unless a more limited scope is requested. DELETE, on the other hand, deletes only the current record.

Table 12.2. Data set commands.

Command	*Default Scope*	*Notes*
APPEND FROM	ALL	Allows only FOR
AVERAGE	ALL	
BROWSE	ALL	Allows navigation and only FOR
CALCULATE	ALL	
CHANGE	ALL	NEXT 1, allows navigation
COPY TO	ALL	
COUNT	ALL	
DELETE	NEXT 1	
DISPLAY	NEXT 1	
EDIT	ALL	NEXT 1, allows navigation
EXPORT	ALL	
JOIN	ALL	Allows only FOR
LABEL	ALL	
LIST	ALL	
LOCATE	ALL	Affects subsequent CONTINUE commands
RECALL	NEXT 1	
REPLACE	NEXT 1	
REPORT	ALL	
SCAN	ALL	
SORT	ALL	
SUM	ALL	
TOTAL	ALL	

All commands in Table 12.2, except APPEND, take advantage of the famous FoxPro *Rushmore technology* to optimize the operation of FOR clauses and the SET FILTER TO command by using indexes to speed up record access. (Designers of FoxPro use the name Rushmore for a technology that uses available indexes to optimize data retrieval of commands using the FOR clause.) The Rushmore technology is used when the filter clause contains fields with indexes. You can suppress the use of Rushmore technology by specifying the NOPTIMIZE keyword with the commands in Table 12.2 or by specifying the SET OPTIMIZE OFF command. If SET OPTIMIZE is OFF, you can enable Rushmore technology for a single command by specifying the OPTIMIZE keyword with these commands. However, you rarely need to suppress Rushmore technology. See Chapter 13, "Data Ordering," for more information.

Commands that use scopes can move the current record pointer. Except in the case of the RECORD clause, specifying a scope leaves the pointer on the first record that ended the scope (or EOF), which can be useful for stepping through a file.

Consider a file sorted on a field called State. The following code displays the records with a Ctrl+Break on State:

```
SET HEADINGS OFF
GOTO TOP
DO WHILE .NOT. EOF()
        A = State
        ?
        ? "Here are the records for "+A+":"
               DISPLAY WHILE State = A
ENDDO
```

I'll discuss more efficient ways to accomplish this using the SCAN command, but the result is as follows:

```
Here are the records for AZ:
1     AZ Phoenix
2     AZ Tempe

Here are the records for CA:
3     CA San Jose
4     CA Laguna Beach
5     CA Los Gatos

Here are the records for CO:
6     CO Denver
```

This example takes advantage of the fact that the end of scope for the first DISPLAY is exactly where I want to start the next DISPLAY.

Special Cases

I should mention a few unusual instances of scopes in the FoxPro syntax. APPEND FROM, BROWSE, and JOIN support a FOR clause for selecting records but permit no other scope clauses.

The EDIT and CHANGE commands display a single record but allow navigation from record to record using the Page Up and Page Down keys. In this case, scope clauses do not affect the single-record orientation, but they profoundly influence record navigation.

LOCATE is another special case. The scope of LOCATE lives on past the single command and affects all subsequent CONTINUE commands as well.

The following example requires some explanation:

Command Window	*Results*
USE CENSUS	
LOCATE FOR RECNO() < 5	Record = 1
DISPLAY RECORD 15	Record# STATE POPULATION RANK
	15 Missouri 5159 15
CONTINUE	End of LOCATE scope.
GOTO 2	CENSUS: Record
CONTINUE	Record = 3

The first LOCATE performs a GOTO TOP because a FOR clause is specified. This puts you at record 1. The DISPLAY command has its own scope, which positions the current record pointer to record 15. The CONTINUE command moves the current record pointer forward and tests the original LOCATE scope; in this case, you have reached the end of the LOCATE scope. That is not the end of it, however, because the LOCATE scope is kept until another LOCATE statement is issued. When you position the pointer to record 2, the next CONTINUE command moves forward (to record 3) and tests the LOCATE scope again. This time, record 3 is found to be in the scope.

By the way, contrary to some accounts, LOCATE without a scope is legal syntax, but the FOR keyword cannot be implied. Like other commands that default to ALL, a simple LOCATE is equivalent to LOCATE FOR .T., as in the following example:

```
LOCATE             && Same as LOCATE FOR .T.
LOCATE <expL>      && Error: FOR keyword is required
```

This is a good place to point out that the FOR clause of the DEFINE BAR command has nothing to do with record-level scoping.

The *DISPLAY* and *LIST* Commands

Both the DISPLAY and LIST commands display data records, calculated fields, and miscellaneous expressions. The most discussed difference between these commands is that DISPLAY pauses after each screenful, but LIST is designed more for listing output to a printer (LIST TO PRINTER [PROMPT]) or a file (LIST TO FILE). Digging deeper, you see that the default scope of DISPLAY is the current record, but the default scope of LIST is ALL. However, the distinction is trivialized by the fact that you can simulate the LIST command with

```
DISPLAY ALL        && Still pauses at each screenful
```

and simulate the `DISPLAY` command with

```
LIST NEXT 1        && Current record only
```

While I discuss `LIST`, I also want to elaborate on something not always mentioned. Regardless of the expressions listed, the scope of the list governs the number of rows of data in the current work area. This can have strange effects. Consider the following situation:

```
SELECT 1
USE "fileA"
USE "fileB" IN 2
GOTO 50 IN 2
```

Suppose `fileA` contains 10 records and `fileB` contains 100 records. The following examples are interesting:

```
LIST
```

The result is what you would expect. FoxPro displays all 10 records of `fileA`, leaving `fileA` at the end of the file.

```
LIST B.field1, B.field2
```

Does FoxPro display all 100 records in `fileB`? No, it displays `field1` and `field2` from records 50 to 60 of `fileB`, leaving `fileB` on record 61. Here is another example:

```
LIST "Tuesday", field1
```

FoxPro displays all 10 records of `fileA`, repeating the word `"Tuesday"` in front of each of them.

Empty Fields

Data can include known and unknown values. For example, suppose you have an employee table with a field for birthdays, but the birthdays of some employees are unknown. A program designed to calculate the average age of employees is confused by the following code:

```
AVERAGE DATE() - Birthday
```

FoxPro provides better support for the concept of a blank field (extending the concept of the `APPEND BLANK` command). The `EMPTY()` function returns a true value if the expression argument contains only blank characters or a `NULL` string. Its primary function is to evaluate table field values, but you can use it on any expression. Its syntax is

```
<logical> = EMPTY(<exp>)
```

<exp> can be any type of expression, but it is usually a table field. The preceding example works better as

```
AVERAGE DATE() - Birthdate FOR .NOT. EMPTY(Birthdate)
```

One limitation of the `EMPTY()` function is that a character field can legitimately contain all spaces without being *blank* in this sense. But the `EMPTY()` function returns `.T.`, because any special blank processing for character fields is not backward compatible. Other field types, however, are amenable to the concept of blank values. Numbers, for example, treat as a blank value all spaces that are not 0 (even though they display and evaluate as 0). Logical values that consist of spaces display and evaluate as `.F.`, but `EMPTY()` returns `.T.`.

If you want to know whether data has been added to a field since an `APPEND` or `APPEND BLANK`, you can use the `EMPTY()` function. Table 12.3 defines `EMPTY()` operations for different data types.

Table 12.3. The usage of the `EMPTY()` function.

Field Type	*Table Field Contents*	*`EMPTY()` Returns*	*Display Example*
Character	Nulls or all blank characters	`.T.`	
Character	At least one nonblank character	`.F.`	`Joe Smith`
Logical	Blank character	`.T.`	`.F.`
Logical	T or Y	`.F.`	`.T.`
Logical	F or N	`.F.`	`.F.`
Numeric/Float	All blank characters	`.F.`	`.F.`
Numeric/Float	0	`.T.`	`0`
Numeric/Float	Any numeric value	`.F.`	`12345.67`
Date	Blank characters	`.T.`	`"  /  /  "`
Date	Any date	`.F.`	`"02/24/92"`
Memo	All blank characters	`.T.`	`memo`
Memo	Nonblank numerics	`.F.`	`MEMO`

Here is an example of three records displayed using the `LIST` command:

```
Record#    CHAR      NUMERIC    MEMO    DATE      LOGICAL    FLOAT
1        Apple        33       MEMO   12/01/91    .T.        1000
2                      0       memo     /  /      .F.        0
3        Oranges       0       memo     /  /      .F.        0
```

The following are the values returned by `EMPTY()` for each field and record:

Record Number	*EMPTY (CHAR)*	*EMPTY (NUMBER)*	*EMPTY (MEMO)*	*EMPTY (DATE)*	*EMPTY (LOGICAL)*	*EMPTY (FLOAT)*
1	.F.	.F.	.F.	.F.	.F.	.F.
2	.T.	.T.	.T.	.T.	.T.	.T.
3	.F.	.F.	.T.	.T.	.T.	.T.

Blank Fields

There are many applications in which you do not want values in a table record to be included in a process, because a data value is unknown and, consequently, no value was entered into the corresponding data field. Data can include known and unknown values. For example, suppose that an employee table has a field for birthdate, but the birthdate of some employees is not known. A program to calculate the average age of employees will be confused by this:

```
AVERAGE DATE()-Birthdate
```

The results would be invalid. To resolve this problem and acquire compatibility, the designers of FoxPro borrowed the `ISBLANK()` function from dBASE IV. This function provides better support for the concept of a blank field. Using the `ISBLANK()` function, the preceding statement becomes

```
AVERAGE DATE()-Birthdate FOR NOT ISBLANK(Birthdate)
```

Only the records for known employee birthdates are used in computing the average age of employees. If no value for a birthdate has been entered in a field, the record is not included in the calculation.

The `ISBLANK()` function takes advantage of the fact that all data fields in an appended blank record contain blank characters, even if they are Numeric, Date, Memo, or Logical data type fields. So when you execute an `APPEND BLANK` command, all fields have null values. When any value is entered into a field, the field is no longer a null field.

This is the syntax of the `ISBLANK()` function:

```
ISBLANK(<exp>)
```

The `ISBLANK()` function returns a logical true (`.T.`) value if the expression *<exp>* is blank, or the function returns false (`.F.`) if the expression evaluates to a nonblank value. *<exp>* is usually a field in a table (DBF) file. It also can be a memory variable, array element, or expression.

NOTE

The `ISBLANK()` function differs from `EMPTY()`. The `EMPTY()` function returns a logical true value if a character expression contains any combination of nulls, spaces, tabs, carriage returns, or line feeds. The `ISBLANK()` function returns true if a character expression contains only the null string or spaces.

The `ISBLANK()` function returns logical true (`.T.`) or false (`.F.`) values if the table field contains the values indicated in Table 12.4.

Table 12.4. `ISBLANK()` returned values.

Field Type	*Contents*	`ISBLANK()`	*Example*
Character	Null string or spaces	.T.	
Character	At least one nonblank character	.F.	"Apple"
Logical	Blank spaces	.T.	
Logical	F or N	.F.	.F.
Logical	T or Y	.F.	.T.
Numeric or Float	Blank spaces	.T.	
Numeric or Float	0	.F.	0
Numeric or Float	Any numeric value	.F.	3241
Date	Blank characters	.T.	" / / "
Date	Any date	.F.	"2/2/95"
Memo	No memo entry	.T.	memo
Memo	At least one character	.F.	MEMO
General	Empty (no OLE object)	.F.	general
General	OLE link	.T.	GENERAL

For a Character or Date type memory variable, array element, or expression, the `ISBLANK()` function returns a logical true (`.T.`) value if the character contains the following values:

Type	*Contents*
Character	Null string or spaces
Date	Blank date ({ / / })

One limitation of the `ISBLANK()` function is that a Character field can legitimately contain all spaces without being a null or blank field in this sense. This is because the `ISBLANK()` function returns a logical true (`.T.`) value even if you replace its value with blank characters. However, all other field types are amenable to the concept of null fields. Numeric fields, for example, initially contain blank spaces even though they display and evaluate as 0. Initially, logical data fields contain spaces but display and evaluate as `.F.`.

Some developers never use the `PACK` command to remove deleted records from a table. They simply reuse deleted records. To be able to reuse records, there must be a capability of restoring one using the `BLANK` command. You can make any table field blank using the `BLANK` command. Its syntax is

```
BLANK [FIELDS <field list>] [<scope>] [NOOPTIMIZE]
```

If the optional `FIELDS` clause is specified, only the fields in the `FIELDS` list are blanked. If this clause is not specified, all fields are blanked. You can also specify fields in other work areas. Note that the field list can contain a list of fields or the `ALL [LIKE <skeleton> EXCEPT <skeleton>]` clause.

The `<scope>` clauses are `ALL`, `NEXT <expN>`, `RECORD <expN>`, `REST`, `FOR <expL>`, and `WHILE <expL>`. The records that are selected by the `<scope>` clause are blanked. If none of the `<scope>` clauses are specified, only the current record is blanked.

If you specify the `NOOPTIMIZE` keyword, the Rushmore optimization is suppressed.

The program BLANKER.PRG, presented in Listing 12.1, demonstrates the use of the `BLANK` command.

Listing 12.1. The BLANKER.PRG program source listing.

```
************************************************
* BLANKER - Example of ISEMPTY() and BLANK usage
*
USE SAMPLES
? "LIST Initial Database Table"
LIST
BLANK RECORD 2
? "LIST with Record 2 BLANKed"
LIST
LIST ISBLANK(CHARACTER),;
ISBLANK(NUMERIC),;
ISBLANK(MEMO)
LIST ISBLANK(DATE),;
     ISBLANK(LOGICAL)
```

The output that results from executing BLANKER.PRG is as follows:

```
LIST Initial Database Table
Record#  CHARACTER  NUMERIC MEMO   DATE      LOGICAL
```

```
1  Apples           33 Memo    12/01/95  .T.
2  Grapes         2345 Memo    12/04/95  .F.
3  Oranges           0 memo      /  /    .F.

LIST with Record 2 BLANKed
Record#  CHARACTER     NUMERIC MEMO    DATE       LOGICAL
1  Apples              33 Memo    12/01/95  .T.
2                         memo      /  /    .F.
3  Oranges              0 memo      /  /    .F.

Record# ISBLANK(character)  ISBLANK(numeric) ISBLANK(memo)
1   .F.                  .F.               .F.
2   .T.                  .T.               .T.
3   .F.                  .F.               .T.

Record# ISBLANK(date) ISBLANK(logical)
1   .F.           .F.
2   .T.           .T.
3   .T.           .F.
```

Null Values

First there were *empty* fields. Then there were *blank* fields. And now, introduced by Visual FoxPro, there are `.NULL.` fields. Confused? Well don't be. This is just another example of Xbase evolution. The only problem is that the obsolete semantic elements are still maintained. After all, there are millions of lines of Xbase code that must be supported.

A null value has no explicitly assigned value. A null value is not equivalent to zero or blank. It is used to indicate that no value has ever been entered into a field. A value of null is not considered to mean greater than, less than, equal to, different from, a member of a group, or any other value, including another value of null. Any expression that contains a null value theoretically evaluates to a value of null. In fact, any expression or condition that contains a null value in most cases evaluates to a null value. However, in many cases, it is necessary to use the `ISNULL()` function to test a variable to determine whether it has a null value prior to using that value in an expression.

There are many applications in which you do not want values in a table record to be included in a process because a data value is unknown and consequently no value was entered into the corresponding data field. Data can include known and unknown values. For example, suppose that an employee table has a field for birthdate, but the birthdate of some employees is not known. A program to calculate the average age of employees will be confused by this:

```
AVERAGE DATE()-Birthdate
```

The results would be invalid. To resolve this problem and acquire compatibility, Visual FoxPro introduced the null value. (See Chapter 11, "DBF Files and Databases.") Visual FoxPro also incorporated the `ISNULL()` and `NVL()` functions into the FoxPro language. Using the `ISNULL()` function, the preceding statement becomes

```
AVERAGE DATE()-Birthdate FOR NOT ISNULL (Birthdate)
```

Only the records for known employee birthdates are used in computing the average age of employees. If no value for a birthdate has been entered in a field, the record is not included in the calculation.

You can also use the .NULL. constant, which is used to create a null value for a field or memory variable, as in the following example:

```
STORE .NULL. TO NullValuc
REPLACE COST WITH .NULL.
```

The ISNULL() function can detect null fields for all data type fields. This is the syntax of the ISNULL () function:

```
ISNULL(<exp>)
```

The ISNULL() function returns a logical true (.T.) value if the expression *<exp>* is null, or the function returns false (.F.) if the expression contains any null elements. There is more. An expression that evaluates to a null value returns a value called .NULL.. This is a special null data type that, in reality, is not a data type at all because unknown values have no data type.

You can create a null memory variable using the STORE .NULL. TO *<memvar>* command. Then you can use it in expressions to see how a null value used in an expression always returns a .NULL. constant value, as in the following example:

```
STORE .NULL. To NULLValue      && Create null memvar
? NullValue                  && Displays .NULL.
? ISNULL(NullValue)            && Displays  .T.
```

The NVL() function returns a non-null value from two expressions. You can use this function to exchange some default value for any unknown or null value in a field. The syntax is

```
NVL(<exp1>, <exp2>)
```

The NVL() function returns *<exp2>* if *<exp1>* evaluates to .NULL.. Otherwise, the NVL() function returns *<exp1>*.

The following example uses the SUM command to sum the values in the COST field in the SALES table. Because the COST field can contain null values, the NVL() function is used to return a zero when a record contains a .NULL. value. In the following example, .NULL. values in the cost field are replaced by a 0 value.

```
USE SALES
SUM  NVL(cost,0) TO TOTSALES
```

The SET NULL command determines how null values behave when you use the ALTER TABLE, CREATE TABLE, and INSERT INTO commands. You can specify that all fields in a table created with the CREATE TABLE and modified with the ALTER TABLE command can accept null data with the SET NULL ON command. If you specify the NOT NULL clause for a field, that field will not be affected by the SET NULL ON command. Also, when SET NULL is ON, the INSERT INTO command inserts null values into any columns not included in the `INSERT INTO VALUE` clause. In the following example, the table PEOPLE1.DBF is created:

```
SET NULL ON


CREATE TABLE People1 ;
 ( Name   C(20),        ;
   Age    N(3) NO NULL,        ;
   Height N(4),         ;
   BirthDate  D         )
INSERT INTO People1 (Name) VALUES ("Smith")
```

The `INSERT INTO` command causes Visual FoxPro to issue an error because you attempted to add a record with null values into the `Age` field. The `Age` field does not allow null values because the `NO NULL` clause was specified when it was created.

By default, `SET NULL` is `OFF` and all fields in a table that are created with `ALTER TABLE` and `CREATE TABLE` will not allow null values. You can designate null value support for fields by specifying the `NULL` keyword for the field with the `ALTER TABLE` and `CREATE TABLE` commands. Also, when `SET NULL` is `OFF`, the `INSERT INTO` command inserts blank values in fields that are not included in the `INSERT INTO VALUE` clause.

Index key values that are null appear at the beginning of the index, before any index keys with non-null values. Note that primary and unique index tags do not contain any records with null key values.

NOTE

There is a physical difference between null and blank fields. A field containing blank characters can be a valid value, so it is not necessarily null. Furthermore, a field can have any value. So there is really no value that you can place in a field that would indicate that the field is null. Therefore, the designers of Visual FoxPro decided to add an invisible field as the last field in the structure of a table that can have null values. This field, named `_NullFlags`, contains a bit for each field. If a bit in this invisible field is set, the corresponding field value is null. You cannot directly access the `_NullFlags` field.

Data Set Calculations

Single records cannot be put into perspective by analysis. Data sets, however, are open to the imagination. You can discover how many records a data set specification yields, find the mean and standard deviation of a set of numeric fields, and calculate the maximum value of a field in the context of a selection. It is easy to justify the need to incorporate commands that work on data sets.

The simplest calculation is a COUNT of the number of data records. Using scope clauses, the COUNT command can return the number of records that match particular criteria. Other simple calculations are SUM, which totals one or more numeric fields, and AVERAGE, which divides the sum by the count.

If an AVERAGE command were not available, an Xbase programmer would have to use COUNT on the records, use SUM on them, and then perform the division. The penalty would be that the COUNT command, like the SUM command, would need to read every record in the file. So COUNT followed by SUM reads every record twice. AVERAGE reads them once, which provides a 50 percent savings in time.

As you probably expect, an ever-increasing variety of data set operations are added to the Xbase language, some of which have not evolved from the original set. The CALCULATE, SCAN, and SQL-type commands are recent additions, and subsequent versions will no doubt offer even more powerful tools for dealing with sets of data at one time. When I worked on the dBASE IV design team at Ashton-Tate, we wanted to extend this savings to the broad range of statistical commands we had planned. Instead of a new MAX command or a command to determine standard deviation, we added to dBASE IV the CALCULATE command, which incorporates eight functions and reads each data record only once. The FoxPro designers, in their desire to retain compatibility with dBASE IV, incorporated the CALCULATE command. They raised the level of abstraction even higher by incorporating the powerful SELECT command into FoxPro. (See Chapter 18, "Queries Using SQL and the Query Designer.")

In addition to a scope specifying which records are of interest, the CALCULATE command accepts any combination of the functions listed in Table 12.5.

Table 12.5. The functions supported by CALCULATE.

Function	*Description*
CNT()	Counts the number of records
SUM(<*expN*>)	Computes the sum of the values of the numeric expression <*expN*>, for records in the data set
AVG(<*expN*>)	SUM() divided by CNT()
MIN(<*exp*>)	Minimum value of expression in data set (expressions can be Character, Date, or Numeric)
MAX(<*exp*>)	Maximum value of expression in data set (expressions can be Character, Date, or Numeric)
VAR(<*expN*>)	Population variance
STD(<*expN*>)	Standard deviation, SQRT(VAR())
NPV(<expN>, <expN>, <*expN*>)	Net present value

The CALCULATE command can perform complex analysis in one pass through the data file. Using just one command, you can count the number of records selected, total a numeric field, find the average of another numeric field, determine the latest date in a date field, and compute the standard deviation of three unrelated fields. The COUNT, SUM, and AVERAGE commands are internally converted to CALCULATE commands for processing.

Examples of the CALCULATE command are shown in Listing 12.2. In this example, stock market statistics are computed for different companies.

Listing 12.2. The CALC2.PRG program, which illustrates the CALCULATE command.

```
***************************************************************
*     *                      CALC2.PRG                        *
***************************************************************
*     *                                                       *
*     * Description:                                          *
*     *   This program illustrates how to use the CALCULATE   *
*     *   command                                             *
***************************************************************
SET TALK OFF
USE d:STOCKS
DO CalcStock WITH "IBM"
DO CalcStock WITH "MSFT"   && Microsoft Corporation
DO CalcStock WITH "BORL"   && Borland International
DO CalcStock WITH "LOTS"   && Lotus Development
RETURN
*******************************************************************
*  Print Stock statistics
PROCEDURE CalcStock
PARAMETER SName  && Stock symbol
?
CALCULATE FOR Name=SName;
MIN(Date),MAX(Date) TO FirstDate,LastDate
?
? "Stock: ", SName, " Stock Performance Statistics for last: "
?? LastDate-FirstDate, " days"
? "Starting Date:", FirstDate, "  Ending Date: ", LastDate
?
CALCULATE FOR Name = SName ;
        MAX(High),MIN(Low),AVG(Last),STD(Last),;
        MAX(Volume), MIN(Volume);
        TO H,L,AVL,STDL, HV, LV
DO ShowStat
   ? "Today's Date: ", DATE(), "- Statistics for Previous 30 Days"

CALCULATE FOR Name = SName .AND. Date > DATE()-31 ;
        MAX(High),MIN(Low),AVG(Last),STD(Last), ;
        MAX(Volume), MIN(Volume);
        TO H,L,AVL,STDL, HV, LV
****************************************************************
DO ShowStat
Procedure ShowStat
? "High:          ", H,   " Low:              ", L
```

continues

Listing 12.2. continued

```
? "Average:          ", AVL, " Standard Deviation:", STDL
? "Maximum Volume: ", HV,   " Minimum Volume:    ", LV
?
RETURN
```

CALC2.PRG calls procedure `CalcStock`, which calls the `CALCULATE` command to compute statistics based on daily stock values. It computes the high, low, and average stock values; the standard deviation; and the minimum and maximum values of the stock sales volume. The records in the STOCKS.DBF table are processed. Listing 12.3 presents the structure of the STOCKS.DBF table.

Listing 12.3. The structure of the STOCKS.DBF table.

```
Structure for table: D:\STOCKS.DBF
Number of data records:    11830
Date of last update    : 08/21/92
Field  Field Name  Type        Width    Dec    Index
1      NAME        Character     5              Asc
2      VOLUME      Numeric      11
3      LAST        Numeric       8       3
4      CHANGE      Numeric       8       3
5      HIGH        Numeric       8       3
6      LOW         Numeric       8       3
7      DATE        Date          8
8      SVALUE      Numeric       9       2
** Total **                       66
```

Each record in STOCKS.DBF contains a daily summary for selected stocks. It contains the daily volume, the high and low stock values, the last stock quote for the day, and the stock symbol. Listing 12.4 is the output resulting from executing the program CALC1.PRG.

Listing 12.4. The output from CALC1.PRG.

```
Stock:  IBM Stock Performance Statistics for last: 1254  days
Starting Date: 03/16/89   Ending Date:  08/21/92

High:                 139.75  Low:                       81.75
Average:              101.56  Standard Deviation:        12.07
Maximum Volume:  5007000.00  Minimum Volume:        341300.00

Today's Date:  08/24/92 - Statistics for Previous 30 Days
High:                  95.50  Low:                       85.75
Average:               90.34  Standard Deviation:         3.13
Maximum Volume:  3431700.00  Minimum Volume:        634800.00


Stock:  MSFT Stock Performance Statistics for last: 1254  days
Starting Date: 03/16/89   Ending Date:  08/21/92
```

```
High:                   133.25  Low:                        45.00
Average:                 87.07  Standard Deviation:         22.28
Maximum Volume:     4712000.00  Minimum Volume:         188200.00

Today's Date:  08/24/92 - Statistics for Previous 30 Days
High:                   74.75  Low:                        68.00
Average:                71.61  Standard Deviation:          1.50
Maximum Volume:    4539800.00  Minimum Volume:         857300.00

Stock:  BORL Stock Performance Statistics for last: 1254  days
Starting Date: 03/16/89   Ending Date:  08/21/92

High:                   86.75  Low:                        36.50
Average:                58.25  Standard Deviation:         13.82
Maximum Volume:    2981600.00  Minimum Volume:          84900.00

Today's Date:  08/24/92 - Statistics for Previous 30 Days
High:                   48.00  Low:                        39.00
Average:                42.85  Standard Deviation:          2.42
Maximum Volume:    1960000.00  Minimum Volume:         154100.00

Stock:  LOTS Stock Performance Statistics for last: 1254  days
Starting Date: 03/16/89   Ending Date:  08/21/92

High:                   38.75  Low:                        15.50
Average:                28.07  Standard Deviation:          6.01
Maximum Volume:    3000500.00  Minimum Volume:         124200.00

Today's Date:  08/24/92 - Statistics for Previous 30 Days
High:                   19.50  Low:                        16.75
Average:                17.90  Standard Deviation:          0.53
Maximum Volume:    1357800.00  Minimum Volume:         159900.00
```

The *SCAN* Command

You have already learned how the CALCULATE command improves performance by handling a variety of operations during only one pass through the data set. The SCAN command (also described in Chapter 6, "Control Flow") offers the advantage of a pass through the data file for any purpose.

Commands bracketed by SCAN and ENDSCAN are performed for each record in the scope. The SCAN syntax is

```
SCAN [<scope>]
        <commands>
ENDSCAN
```

The SCAN command is nearly, but not quite, equivalent to the following:

```
GOTO TOP                  && If <scope> is ALL or FOR
DO WHILE .NOT. EOF()
        <commands> <scope>
        SKIP
ENDDO
```

It is certainly possible to perform the same task using older Xbase commands, but SCAN is more elegant and concise. SCAN uses the same *looper* engine designed for the CALCULATE command, so it is slightly faster than discrete commands.

Just as SET FILTER expands the FOR clause beyond a single command (and thus becomes a Super-FOR), the SCAN command allows any kind of scope to affect multiple commands. SCAN should rightly be called *super-scope.*

The *UPDATE* Command

The UPDATE command uses a related transaction file to create a subset of the pertinent records in a master file. UPDATE is not widely understood by dBASE language users, and perhaps it doesn't need to be. UPDATE dates back to JPLDIS, when no SET RELATION command existed.

Suppose you have a general ledger data file containing an account number and a balance. You have a transaction file also, with fields that include an account number and an amount field:

```
LEDGER.DBF
Acct_no     Balance    <other fields>

TXN.DBF
Acct_no     Amount     <other fields>
```

You want to adjust the balances in the ledger based on the transactions in the TXN table. The following code accomplishes that:

```
USE "TXN" INDEX "T_ANO"
USE "LEDGER" INDEX "L_ANO" IN B ALIAS Master
SET RELATION TO Acct_no INTO Master
REPLACE ALL Master.Balance WITH ;
Master.Balance + Amount
```

This code is equivalent to

```
USE "LEDGER" INDEX "L_ANO"
USE "TXN" INDEX "T_ANO" IN B ALIAS Txn
UPDATE ON Acct_no FROM Txn ;
REPLACE Balance WITH Balance + Txn.Amount
```

Although the latter example uses fewer lines of code, it does not appreciably improve the speed, nor does the syntax improve the UPDATE command's popularity.

The *COPY TO* and *EXPORT* Commands

The COPY TO and EXPORT commands copy a selected set of Visual FoxPro table records from the current view or table to another file. The TYPE clause determines the other file. The syntax is as follows:

```
COPY TO <expFN>  [FIELDS <field name list>]
        [[WITH] CDX ] ¦ [[WITH] PRODUCTION ]
```

```
        [[TYPE] ¦ DIF ¦ FOXPLUS ¦ FOX2X ¦ MOD ¦ SDF ¦ SYLK ¦ WK1
        ¦ WKS ¦ WR1 ¦ WRK ¦ XLS ¦ XL5 [SHEET <expC>] ¦
         DELIMITED [WITH BLANK ¦ <delimiter>¦ WITH TAB ]]
        [<scope>] [FOR <expL>] [WHILE <expL>] [NOOPTIMIZE]
        [AS <expN>]


EXPORT TO <expFN>  [FIELD <field name list>]
        [TYPE] ¦ DIF ¦  MOD ¦ SYLK ¦ WK1
        ¦ WKS ¦ WR1 ¦ WRK ¦ XLS ¦ XL5 [SHEET <expC>]
         [<scope>] [FOR <expL>] [WHILE <expL>] [NOOPTIMIZE]
        [AS <expN>]

<field name list> ::= <field name> [,<field name>]...
<delimiter>       ::= <any character>
```

You don't really ever need to use the EXPORT command because the COPY TO command incorporates all export operations. Designers added it to the FoxPro language only to add compatibility with dBASE IV. The only reason dBASE IV has an EXPORT command is to provide symmetry with the IMPORT command.

The scope (ALL, NEXT *<expN>*, REST, RECORD *<expN>*) defines the group of records copied. If you don't specify a scope keyword, ALL is assumed and all records are copied. When you specify the FOR clause, all records in the defined scope that satisfy the supplied condition are copied. If you specify the WHILE clause, records are copied beginning with the current record until the supplied condition is no longer satisfied, as in the following example:

```
COPY NEXT 100 FOR Name = "Smith" TO NEWFILE
```

Any of the next 100 records with the field NAME containing the value "Smith" are copied to the NEWFILE.DBF file.

In the following example, copying begins with the first record and continues until POPULATION is less than one million people:

```
Command Window                     Results and Comments
LIST County, Population                Record#   COUNTY              POPULATION
                                                 1 Los Angeles       8700000
                                                 2 San Diego         2373000
                                                 3 Orange            2271000
                                                 4 Santa Clara       1448000
                                                 5 Alameda           1260000
                                                 6 Riverside          982000
                                                 7 San Francisco      750000
GO TOP COPY WHILE POPULATION >;
    1000000 TO NEWFILE                 5 Records Copied
```

The following example demonstrates the use of the COPY TO command with various *<scope>* clauses:

```
COPY RECORD 3 TO NEWF   && Only record 3 is copied
COPY TO NEWF            && All records are copied
COPY NEXT 3 TO NEWF     && Three records are copied
                        && beginning with the current record
```

```
COPY REST TO NEWF       && Current and remaining records in
                        && the table are copied
```

The `FIELDS` clause defines a list of fields in the active table. The new file is created with only those fields in the field list. Alias names cannot be specified with field names in the field lists. If a `SET FIELDS` command field list is active, only those fields can be copied. If a `SET FIELDS` command field list is active, only those fields in the `SET FIELDS` list can be specified with the `FIELDS` clause, as in the following example:

```
USE SALARY
SET FIELDS TO Employee, Empno, Hours
COPY TO FILE1           && Employee, Empno, hours
COPY FIELDS Employee, EmpNo  TO FILE1
```

If the new file already exists, it will be overwritten. If the `SET SAFETY` flag is `ON`, however, a prompt box appears requesting confirmation before the file can be overwritten. If the `NOOPTIMIZE` keyword is specified, Rushmore technology is disabled.

You can specify either the `[[WITH] CDX ]` or the `[[WITH] PRODUCTION ]` clause to generate an identical structural index (CDX) file for the target file. dBASE IV uses the term *production indexes* for structural index files. FoxPro does not actually generate a dBASE IV production multiple index (MDX) file; it just uses the `WITH PRODUCTION` clause for compatibility. The following statements produce the same results. The NEWFILE.DBF table and its associated structural index file, NEWFILE.CDX, is generated:

```
USE CENSUS   && This has an associated CDX file
COPY TO NEWFILE CDX
COPY TO NEWFILE WITH CDX
COPY TO NEWFILE WITH PRODUCTION
COPY TO NEWFILE PRODUCTION
```

The `TYPE` clause is used to specify the type of output file. `MEMO` type files are not copied to any exported files. Output types are defined in the following sections.

The *DELIMITED* Keyword

For the `DELIMITED` keyword, the resulting file contains ASCII records. Each record is terminated with a carriage return and a line feed. Fields are separated by commas. Character fields are enclosed in quotation marks. The default extension is .TXT.

Command Window	*Results and Comments*
USE POP	
DISPLAY	Record# COUNTY POPULATION CCODE CDATE 1 Los Angeles 8700000 .T. 06/05/89
COPY TO ASCFILE; DELIMITED FOR ; POPULATION<1000000	
TYPE ASCFILE.TXT	ASCFILE.TXT 06/06/88 "Los Angeles",8700000,T,19890605

```
"San Diego",2373000,T,19890304
"Orange",2271000,T,19890104
"Santa Clara",1448000,T,1989326
"Alameda",1260000,T,19890504
```

In this example, the ASCFILE.TXT ASCII file is generated. It contains Character, Numeric, Logical, and Date type fields. The quotation marks enclose the Character fields.

The *DELIMITED WITH <character>* Clause

The `DELIMITED WITH <character>` clause specifies the generation of an ASCII file. However, the specified `<character>`, which consists of any single printable character, is used instead of quotation marks. In the preceding example, if the `COPY` command was

```
COPY TO ASCFILE DELIMITED WITH *
```

the generated records would be

```
*Los Angeles*,8700000,T,19890605
*San Diego*,2373000,T,19890304
*Orange*,2271000,T,19890104
*Santa Clara*,1448000,T,1989326
*Alameda*,1260000,T,19890504
```

The *DELIMITED WITH BLANK* Clause

The `DELIMITED WITH BLANK` clause also generates an ASCII file. However, fields are separated by a blank character, and Character fields are not enclosed by delimiters. In the previous example, if the `COPY` command was

```
COPY TO ASCFILE DELIMITED WITH BLANK
```

the generated records would be

```
Los Angeles 8700000 T 19890605
San Diego 2373000 T 19890304
Orange 2271000 T 19890104
Santa Clara 1448000 T 1989326
Alameda 1260000 T 19890504
```

The `DELIMITED WITH TAB` clause is exactly like `DELIMITED WITH BLANK` except that a Tab character separates each field.

The *DIF* Keyword

The `DIF` keyword is used to export the currently active table or view to VisiCalc Version 1.0 DIF files. The default filename extension is .DIF. The file is transferred in row major order: Fields are converted to VisiCalc columns, and records are converted to rows. The Visual FoxPro field names are output as DIF column header records.

The *FOXPLUS* Keyword

The FOXPLUS keyword is used to copy a Visual FoxPro table with a memo field to a new file with a memo file, DBT, compatible with FoxBASE+. Why is this necessary? FoxBASE+ and dBASE III tables with memo fields are upwardly compatible with Visual FoxPro, but the reverse is not true. FoxBASE+ cannot read tables generated by Visual FoxPro.

Visual FoxPro memo field data blocks have changed so that they can support non-ASCII type data. The size of the memo field is stored at the beginning of the memo field on the disk, and the filename extension is .FPT. If Visual FoxPro uses a FoxBASE+ or dBASE III PLUS table with a DBT memo, the memo file remains unchanged. FoxPro reads and writes to the DBT memo file without converting it to a FoxPro FPT memo file. However, if you create a table with FoxPro 2.*x* or 3, the table cannot be used by FoxBASE+ or dBASE III PLUS; if this is attempted, the Not a FoxBASE+ file error message is issued.

When you use the FOXPLUS keyword with the COPY TO command TYPE clause, a FoxBASE+-compatible table with DBT memo file is generated.

The *FOX2X* Keyword

The FOX2X keyword copies a Visual FoxPro table to a new file that is compatible with FoxPro 2.*x* versions. This form converts Visual FoxPro field types as indicated in Table 12.6.

Table 12.6. Field conversion using the COPY TO command with the FOX2X keyword specified.

Visual FoxPro Field Type	*FoxPro 2.x Field Type*
Currency	Float
DateTime	Date
Double	Float

If you associate a table with a database (ADD TABLE) or create an attached table with Visual FoxPro, the table cannot be used by earlier versions of FoxPro or dBASE; if attempted, the Not a FoxBASE+ file error message is issued. The header of a Visual FoxPro attached table is 265 bytes larger than an ordinary free FoxPro table. The extra space contains the name of an attached table's associated database container (DBC) file.

The *MOD* Keyword

The MOD keyword transfers the currently active table or active view to a Microsoft Multiplan spreadsheet Version 4.01 file. The default filename extension is .MOD.

The *RPD* Keyword

The RPD keyword transfers the currently active table or view to a RapidFile table. The default filename extension is .RPD.

The *SDF* Keyword

The SDF keyword copies the currently active table or view to a system data format (SDF) file. An SDF file is an ASCII text file with the following characteristics:

- Each record is terminated with a carriage return and a line feed.
- The record is the same length as the data record.
- Data is laid out field-for-field in the record.
- Character type fields are not delimited.
- No blanks or separator characters exist between fields.
- Memo fields are not output.
- Date type fields are output in the form *YYYYMMDD*.
- The default filename extension is .TXT.

In the following example, the fields COUNTY and POPULATION are exported to a text (SDF) file, ASCFILE.TXT:

```
USE POP
COPY TO ASCFILE SDF FIELDS County,Population
TYPE ASCFILE.TXT
```

Here is the resulting output:

```
ASCFILE.TXT 06/06/89

Los Angeles       8700000
San Diego         2373000
Orange            2271000
Santa Clara       1448000
Alameda           1260000
Riverside          982000
San Francisco      750000
```

The term SDF came from JPLDIS days. It was used with the JPLDIS COPY command for the same function as in dBASE programs. The UNIVAC 1100 Mainframe EXEC-8 operating system term for text files was System Data Format, or SDF, files.

The *SYLK* Keyword

The SYLK keyword exports the currently active table or view to a Multiplan spreadsheet. The default filename extension is blank. The file is transferred in row major order. The Visual FoxPro field names are output as a Multiplan spreadsheet column headers record.

The *WKS, WK1, WR1,* and *WRK* Keywords

The WKS and WK1 keywords export the currently active table or view to a Lotus 1-2-3 spreadsheet. The default filename extension for 1-2-3 Version 1.0 Release 1A WKS files is .WKS. The default filename extension for 1-2-3 Version 2.0 and 2.1 WK1 files is .WK1. The file is transferred in row major order. The Visual FoxPro field names are output as Lotus 1-2-3 column headers. WKS files can be used also by Lotus Symphony and other products similar to 1-2-3, such as Quattro Pro. Nevertheless, the WR1 and WRK options were provided to export Lotus Symphony spreadsheet Versions 1.01 and 1.10, respectively.

The *XLS* Keyword

The XLS keyword exports the currently active table or view to an Excel spreadsheet Version 2. The default filename extension is .XLS. The file is transferred in row major order. The Visual FoxPro field names are output as an Excel column headers record.

The *XL5 [SHEET <expC>]* Clause

The XL5 clause exports the currently active table or view to an Excel spreadsheet Version 5. The default filename extension is .XLS. The file is transferred in row major order. The Visual FoxPro field names are used to create the Excel column headers record. You can export data to a specific Excel worksheet with the SHEET clause in which *<expC>* is the name of the sheet. If you omit the SHEET clause, Visual FoxPro exports data to the Excel worksheet Sheet1.

The *AS* Clause and Code Pages

As the software business becomes more globalized, international data exchange becomes more prevalent. There is more demand for internationalized applications. Visual FoxPro enables you to transfer data stored under one code page to another code page. The AS *<expN>* clause specifies the code page of the file that the COPY TO or EXPORT commands create. As Visual FoxPro transfers data, it automatically translates the data to the specified code page. If you specify a code page that is not supported, Visual FoxPro issues an error. If you specify code page 0, Visual FoxPro performs no code page translation during the data transfer operation.

Visual FoxPro does not perform any code page conversion if you omit the AS clause. When possible, Visual FoxPro stores the code page into the header of the table that is created by the COPY TO or EXPORT command.

The *APPEND FROM* Command

The APPEND FROM form of the APPEND command adds records to the end of the current table from an existing table or foreign file. The syntax is

```
APPEND FROM <expFN> ¦ ? [FIELDS <field list>] [FOR <expL>]
   [[TYPE] [DELIMITED [WITH TAB ¦ WITH <delimiter> ¦ WITH BLANK]
   ¦ DIF ¦ FW2 ¦ MOD ¦ PDOX ¦ RPD ¦ SDF ¦ SYLK
   ¦ WK1 ¦ WK3 ¦ WKS ¦ WR1  ¦ WRK ¦ XLS ¦ XL5 [SHEET <expC>]]]
   [AS <expN>]
```

If any index files or index tags are active, they are updated each time a record is appended.

If you specify a question mark (?) instead of a filename for appending records from a Visual FoxPro table, a directory pop-up menu appears, from which you can choose a table to append.

The *APPEND* Command

If you omit the TYPE clause, the source table is assumed to be a FoxPro table. Data is appended for only those fields whose names exist in the currently used table. Field types don't necessarily have to match. Field types are converted as indicated in Table 12.7.

Table 12.7. Field conversion using APPEND.

FROM/TO	*Character*	*Numeric*	*Float*	*Logical*	*Memo*	*Date*
Character	Yes	Yes	Yes	No	No	Yes
Numeric	Yes	Yes	Yes	No	No	Yes
Float	Yes	Yes	Yes	No	No	Yes
Logical	Yes	No	No	Yes	No	No
Memo	No	No	No	No	No	Yes
Date	Yes	Yes	Yes	No	No	Yes

When Character fields are converted to Numeric fields, only a sign, numerals, a decimal point, and an exponent are allowed; for example, 1.234E+7 is valid. For Character-to-Date field conversion, the date must be in the date display format; in the United States, the form is *MM/DD/YY*. Date-to-Numeric conversion converts the date to a Julian date value. When numbers are converted to a Character field and the numeric value is too wide to fit, the character field is filled with asterisks.

If the FROM field is wider than the corresponding field in the file currently in use, Character field data values are truncated.

If you supply the FOR clause, only those records that satisfy the condition are appended. The condition is evaluated after a candidate record is fabricated. Therefore, the condition must contain only those fields present in the currently used table.

You can specify the optional FIELDS clause to designate a list of fields to receive data. Any fields not included in the field list are blanked out.

The *DELIMITED* Keyword

When you specify `DELIMITED`, data from an ASCII text file is appended to the table currently in use. If you don't supply the filename extension, .TXT is assumed. Each record contains field values separated by commas, and the record is terminated with a carriage return and a line feed. Character fields are enclosed with quotation mark delimiters. The following is a typical example of a delimited record, with the Character field enclosed in quotation marks:

```
"Los Angeles",8700000,T,19890605
```

The *DELIMITED WITH* Clause

The `DELIMITED WITH` form of the `APPEND` command functions exactly like `DELIMITED`, except that Character fields are delimited with a user-supplied character instead of quotation marks. Assuming that records are delimited with asterisks, in the command

```
APPEND FROM Population DELIMITED WITH *
```

FoxPro would expect a record to look like this:

```
*Los Angeles*,8700000,T,19890605
```

The *DELIMITED WITH BLANK* and *DELIMITED WITH TAB* Clauses

The `DELIMITED WITH BLANK` form of the `APPEND` command functions exactly like `DELIMITED WITH`, except fields are separated by a single blank character and Character fields are not delimited. The `APPEND` command expects a `DELIMITED WITH BLANK` record to appear as follows:

```
Pasadena 8700000 T 19890605
```

The `DELIMITED WITH TAB` form of the `APPEND` command is exactly like `DELIMITED WITH BLANK`, except that a Tab character separates each field.

The *DIF* Form

The `DIF` form appends VisiCalc Version 1.0 DIF files to Visual FoxPro tables. The default filename extension is .DIF. The DIF file must be in row major order. VisiCalc spreadsheet columns are mapped to Visual FoxPro fields, and rows are mapped to records, as in the following example:

```
USE CENSUS
APPEND FROM POP1 TYPE DIF
```

The *FW2* Keyword

Use the `FW2` form to append a Framework II table to the currently active table. The default filename extension is .FW2.

The *MOD* Keyword

The MOD keyword is used to append a Microsoft Multiplan Version 4.01 spreadsheet file to the currently active table. The default filename extension is .MOD.

The *PDOX* Keyword

The PDOX keyword is used to append a Borland International Paradox Version 3.5 table to the currently active table. The default filename extension is .DB.

The *RPD* Keyword

The RPD keyword is used to append a RapidFile file to the currently active table. The default filename extension is .RPD.

The *SDF* Keyword

The SDF keyword is used to append a system data format (SDF) file to the currently active table. An SDF file is an ASCII text file with the following characteristics:

- Each SDF record is terminated with a carriage return and a line feed.
- Data is appended character by character, beginning with the first field.
- Memo fields are not appended.
- Date type fields are expected to be in the form *YYYYMMDD*.
- The default filename extension is .TXT.

The *SYLK* Keyword

The SYLK keyword appends a Multiplan spreadsheet to the currently active table. The default filename extension is blank. The file is assumed to be in row major order.

The *WKS, WK1, WK3, WR1,* and *WRK* Keywords

The WKS, WK1, and WK3 forms of the APPEND command append a Lotus 1-2-3 spreadsheet to the currently active table. The default filename extension for Lotus 1-2-3 Version 1.0 Release 1A WKS files is .WKS. The default filename extension for Lotus 1-2-3 Versions 2.0 and 2.1 is .WK1. The default filename extension for Lotus 1-2-3 Version 3.*x* files is .WK3. The file is assumed to be in row major order. The WR1 form appends a Symphony spreadsheet Version 1.1 or 1.2. The WRK form appends a Symphony spreadsheet Version 1.0.

The *XLS* Keyword

The XLS keyword appends a Microsoft Excel worksheet Version 2.0 to the currently active table. The default filename extension is .XLS. The file is assumed to be in row major order.

The *XL5 [SHEET <expC>]* Clause

The XL5 keyword appends an Excel worksheet Version 5 to the currently active table or view. The default filename extension is .XLS. The file is transferred in row major order. The Visual FoxPro field names are derived from the Excel column headers record. You can append data from a specific Excel worksheet with the SHEET clause in which <*expC*> is the name of the sheet. If you omit the SHEET clause, data from Sheet1 is appended.

The *AS* Clause

The AS <*expN*> clause specifies the code page conversion of the appended table or file. As Visual FoxPro appends data, it automatically translates the data to the specified code page. If you specify a code page that is not supported, Visual FoxPro issues an error. If you specify code page 0, Visual FoxPro performs no code page translation during the data transfer operation.

If you omit the AS clause and Visual FoxPro is unable to determine the code page of the appended table or file, it automatically converts the data to the current code page. If SET CPDIALOG is ON, Visual FoxPro stores the current code page into the header of the table in the current work area. If you attempt to append data from a table whose header does not contain a code page indication, the Code Page dialog box displays and you can choose a code page. If Visual FoxPro can determine the code page of the table or file that is to be appended, it automatically translates the data, if necessary, as it appends records to the current table.

The *APPEND FROM SDF* Example

The form of the APPEND FROM command with the specified SDF keyword might be the most frequently used Xbase import command. Here is an example. I have always had a problem with stock quotes listed in the newspaper. A single daily stock quote doesn't tell me much. If I look at one of the financial newspapers, I find stock quotes plotted over time, but the stock that interests me is not always available. I subscribed to Prodigy for the exclusive purpose of downloading stock quotes, appending them to a table, and plotting them. You can also download stock quotes from other telecommunications services such as CompuServe. Picking through the Prodigy menus to access the stock quotes takes time. Therefore, I use a batch file that executes one of the available shareware keyboard macro programs so that I call up Prodigy and get my list of stock quotes. I also use a shareware program that redirects printed output to a text file, STOCK.TXT. In Prodigy, you can create a list of up to 30 stocks (JUMP QUOTE TRACK 1). Listing 12.5 shows the batch file, and Listing 12.6 shows the keyboard macro file.

Listing 12.5. The STOCK.BAT batch file for retrieving stock quotes.

```
d:
cd \
erase stock.txt
prn2file stock.txt
key /mc
key prodigy /ml
```

Listing 12.6. The PRODIGY.MAC SuperKey keyboard macro script.

```
<BEGDEF><alt.>
<AUTO>
<ENTER>
pr<ENTER>
 (user-id)<ENTER>
 (password)<ENTER>
j<ENTER>
Quote Track 1<ENTER>
C<ENTER>
j<ENTER>
Quote Track 2<ENTER>
C<ENTER>
<ENDDEF>
```

The keyboard macro signs on to Prodigy and prints the stock quotes. Actually, in September 1992, Prodigy added a new feature that dumps the quotes directly to a text file in the same format. Listing 12.7 shows an example of the resulting text file (STOCK.TXT).

Listing 12.7. An example of a STOCK.TXT daily stock quote file.

```
PRODIGY (R) interactive personal service   09/22/1992     01:01 PM
QUOTE TRACKsm


Change/    Open/                                   Volume/
Stock      Last       Bid        Asked       High        Low         Date
-----------------------------------------------------------------------------
CMK        11 7/8        +0      11 3/4      11 7/8      11 3/4        36500
GE         78 1/2 *  -  1/2          79      79 1/4      78 1/2       715800
LTR           115        +0         115         115     114 1/2        53800
MCD        44 3/4    +  1/8      44 3/4      45 1/8      44 1/2       390700
MFM         9 1/2        +0       9 1/2       9 5/8       9 1/2        76300
NMA            16    -  1/8      16 1/8      16 1/4          16        43900
VIT             8        +0           8           8       7 7/8        28100
WX         16 1/4    -  1/8      16 1/4      16 3/8      16 1/8       434200

7-Day      Average          7-Day
Security     Net Asset     Offering    Average    Maturity         Effective
Symbol       Value         Price       Yield      (in Days)/Date   Yield
------------------------------------------------------------------------------
ACRNX          49.40         49.40
```

continues

Listing 12.7. continued

```
EFBVX        *13.39        13.39
FMAGX         65.57        67.60
GTGEX          8.85         9.29
PCTEX          8.40         8.82
PTFIX         15.07        15.07
SLSUX         14.68        14.68

Change/   Open/                           Volume/
Stock     Last       Bid        Asked      High       Low       Date
--------------------------------------------------------------
BORL      41 3/8    - 1/2          42          42     39 3/8   1178000
IBM       84 3/8    + 7/8      83 7/8      84 1/2     83 7/8   1256300
LOTS      20 5/8    + 7/8      19 3/4      20 3/4     19 1/2   2054900
MSFT      79 1/8    - 3/4      78 3/4      79 1/2     78 1/4    994100
NQC       15 3/8    - 1/8      15 3/8      15 1/2     15 3/8     27900
NXC       15 1/8    + 1/8      15 1/8      15 1/8     15 1/8       500
ORCL      19 3/4    - 1/2          20      20 1/8     19 5/8    365300

7-Day     Average        7-Day
Security    Net Asset    Offering    Average   Maturity          Effective
Symbol      Value        Price       Yield     (in Days)/Date    Yield
---------------------------------------------------------------------
JAVLX       22.84        22.84
SRSPX       21.10        21.10
TWCGX       23.97        23.97
TWCVX       10.84        10.84
USGIX       10.91        11.36
```

Next, FoxPro executes and STOCK.PRG (shown in Listing 12.8) runs. The STOCK.PRG procedure first appends the STOCK.TXT text file to the STOCK1.DBF table. Stock quotes are presented as a whole number plus a fraction of a quote. These are converted to a decimal number. For example, `16 1/4` is converted to `16.25`. Mutual fund values appear as decimal numbers, so no conversion is necessary.

Listing 12.8. A source listing for STOCK.PRG.

```
**************************************************************
* STOCK.PRG - Imports Prodigy DOW Jones stock quotes into a  *
* dbf table                                                  *
* Version 1.0 1/25/90                                        *
**************************************************************
CLOSE ALL
SET SAFETY OFF
SET TALK OFF
USE stock1
ZAP
APPEND FROM stock SDF
*
**** Retrieve stock symbols from portfolio file, PORT.DBF.
SELECT 2
USE Port ORDER Symbol
COUNT TO NSymbols
```

```
DECLARE SymTable[NSymbols,2]
COPY TO ARRAY SymTable FIELDS Symbol,Descrip ALL
SELECT 1
*
**** Now, reformat stock quotes
*
SCAN
        I = 1
        found = .F.
        FOR L = 1 TO NSymbols
           Company = rtrim(SymTable[L,1])
           IF Name = Company
               do FindValues && Reformat stock quote values
                              && For example: 3 1/4 -> 3.25
               REPLACE Date WITH DATE()
               found = .t.
           ENDIF
        ENDFOR
        IF NOT found
               DELETE
        ENDIF
ENDSCAN
PACK
*
**********************************************************
* Now append records from STOCK1 to archive file
*
USE STOCKS              && Archive stock quote file
APPEND FROM stock1      && Today's Quotes
DO GETVALUES            && Update current portfolio values
DO PLOT                 && Plot stocks
RETURN
*
************************************************************
*    Name: Extract values from stock quotes and convert them
*       to a numeric form
*
PROCEDURE FindValues
IF Volume < 13
*
****** Format encountered for mutual funds
*
        ast = at("*",cchange)
        IF ast>0
               REPLACE cchange WITH STUFF(cchange,ast,1," ")
        ENDIF
        REPLACE last   WITH  val(cchange) ;
               high   WITH  val(copen)    ;
               change WITH  val(chigh)
ELSE
*
**** Standard stock quote format
*
        REPLACE last   WITH Convert(clast), ;
               change WITH Convert(cchange), ;
               high   WITH Convert(chigh), ;
               low    WITH Convert(clow)
```

continues

Listing 12.8. continued

```
ENDIF
RETURN
*
*****************************************************************
* Name: Convert - Converts a stock price in fraction form      *
*                 like "87 3/4" to a decimal stock price       *
* Version:  1.0 1/25/90                                        *
*****************************************************************
*
FUNCTION Convert
PARAMETER stockvalue
ast = AT("*",stockvalue)  && Remove any asterisks
IF ast>0
        stockvalue = stuff(stockvalue,ast,1," ")
ENDIF
slash = AT('/',stockvalue)
IF slash > 0
        value = val(substr(stockvalue,slash-1))/ ;
        val(substr(stockvalue,slash+1));
               + val(substr(stockvalue,1,slash-2))
ELSE
        value =  val(stockvalue)
ENDIF
IF value >=0 AND at('-',stockvalue)#0  && Negative value?
        value=-value
ENDIF
RETURN value
*
***********************************************************
*
PROCEDURE GETVALUES
SET RELATION TO Name INTO 2
SCAN for FOUND(2) .and. Date=date()
        xvalue = b->volume*IIF(last=0,change,last)
        REPLACE svalue WITH xvalue, ;
               b->amount with xvalue ;
               b->date with dtoc(date())
        ENDSCAN
RETURN
```

The contents of STOCK1.DBF are appended to the STOCKS.DBF table, which contains the stock quotes that have accumulated over a period of time. A third table, PORT.DBF, contains a record for each stock symbol that contains fields such as the stock symbol, the name of the stock, and the number of shares in the user's portfolio. The stock symbols from PORT.DBF are copied to an array and used to identify the quotes extracted from the STOCK1.DBF text file and choose stocks for plotting. Figure 12.1 shows the field names and sample contents of these three DBF files.

Finally, STOCK.PRG executes the PLOT.PRG program to plot the stock quotes. Each stock is plotted over time, as Figure 12.2 shows.

One line is displayed for each daily stock quote. A white bar displays the value of the stock at the end of the trading day. A yellow bar indicates the daily trading range for the day. At the right of the screen, a brown bar indicates the daily volume. The three columns that display at the left of the screen are the stock price, the dollar portfolio value, and the date. Listing 12.9 is the source listing of PLOT.PRG.

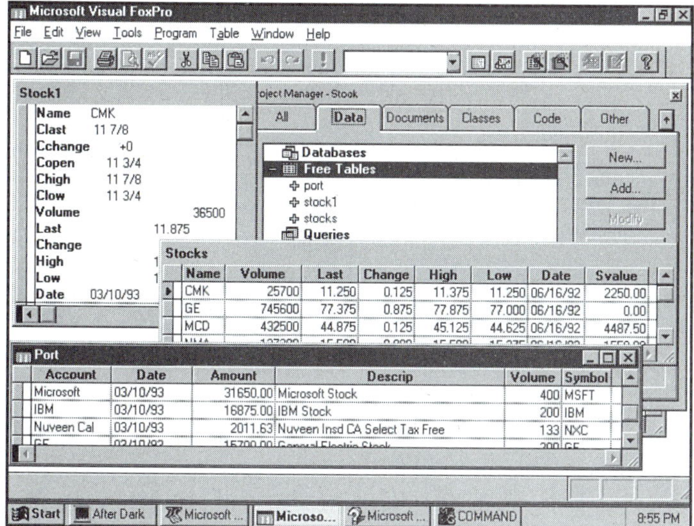

FIGURE 12.1.
The tables used by the STOCK.PRG and PLOT.PRG programs.

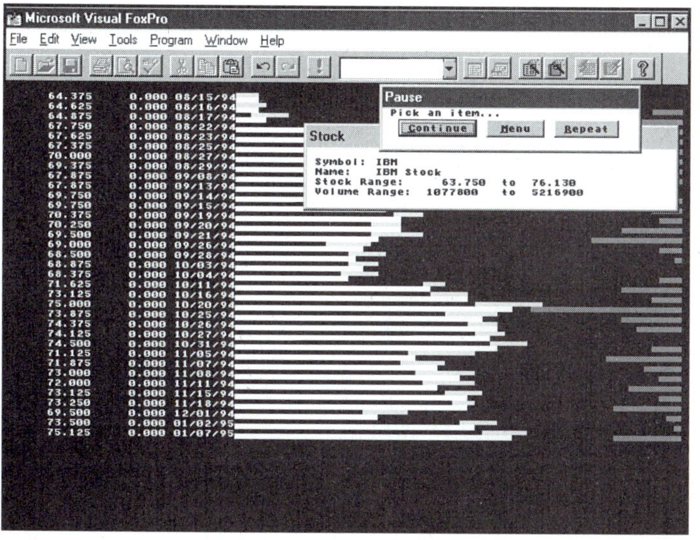

FIGURE 12.2.
An example of output from the program PLOT.PRG.

Listing 12.9. A source listing for PLOT.PRG.

```
*************************************************************
* NAME: PLOT
* PURPOSE:
*     Plots stocks loaded from Prodigy stock quote service
*
* This version averages values to display on a single screen
*
**************************************************************
CLEAR ALL
MyPath = ""   && Used if executed outside of local directory
SET STATUS OFF
SET SCOREBOARD OFF
SET TALK OFF
SET COLOR TO w+/b
DEFINE WINDOW HEADER FROM 4,40 TO 11,90 SYSTEM ;
      COLOR SCHEME 8 TITLE "Stock"
CLEAR
PDisplay = TYPE("quick")='L'
USE MyPath+"Stocks" ORDER name
USE MyPath+"PORT" ORDER symbol IN 2
*
***** Fetch the symbols
*
SELECT 2
COUNT TO NSymbols
DECLARE SymTable[NSymbols,2]
COPY TO ARRAY SymTable FIELDS Symbol,Descrip ALL
SELECT 1

PrtFlag = SET("PRINT")="ON"
PCHAR =IIF(PrtFlag,CHR(242), chr(220))
L=1
*
***** Plot all of the stocks and mutual funds ***
*
FOR L = 1 TO NSymbols
        DO Plotter WITH TRIM(SymTable[L,1])
        IF Prtflag
               ?
        ELSE
               Answer = Prompter()
               CLEAR
               IF Answer = 2
                       EXIT
               ELSE
                       IF Answer = 3
                           L = L - 1
                       ENDIF
               ENDIF
        ENDIF
ENDFOR
DEACTIVATE WINDOW HEADER
IF PrtFlag
        SET PRINTER OFF
        EJECT
        ? "Printer was turned off"
```

```
ELSE
        DO CHOOSE  && Plot selected stocks
ENDIF
RETURN
*
********************************************************
* WAITER - Does a Wait and returns results in upper case
*
FUNCTION WAITER
PARAMETER Message
WAIT WINDOW Message TO Ans
RETURN UPPER(Ans)
*
*****************************************************
* Procedure that does the plot for a stock
*
PROCEDURE Plotter
PARAMETER Symb
ACTIVATE SCREEN
StartVolume =SCOLS()-21
CLEAR
@ 0,0
SELECT 2
SEEK TRIM(Symb)
desc=IIF(FOUND(),descrip,"")
SELECT 1
SEEK symb
CALCULATE min(iif(volume < 13, last, low)), ;
          max(iif(volume < 13, last, high)), ;
         cnt(), min(volume) ,max(volume);
         TO min1,max1,cnt1,vmin1,vmax1 WHILE name=symb
Increment  = IIF(max1=min1, 0, 40/(max1-min1))
VIncrement = IIF(vmax1=vmin1, 0, 20/(vmax1-vmin1))
NAVERAGE   = int(cnt1/35)

DO ShowHead

STORE 0 TO i,v,vol
hilo='  '
SEEK symb
SCAN WHILE NAME=Symb
        IF PDisplay AND naverage > 1 && Display page at a time
               i=i+1
               IF i <= NAVERAGE
                       v1   = IIF(last=0, change, last)
                       V    = V + v1
                       vol  = max(vol,volume)
                       hilo = IIF(v1=max1,"Hi",IIF(v1=min1,"Lo",hilo))
                       amount = svalue
               ELSE
                       DO PlotALine WITH v/NAverage,vol,amount,0,0
                       hilo = '  '
                       v=0
                       vol=0
                       i=0
                ENDIF
        ELSE
```

continues

Listing 12.9. continued

```
                v1= IIF( last=0, change, last )
                hilo = IIF( v1=max1, "Hi", IIF(v1=min1, "Lo", "  "))
                amount = svalue
                DO PlotALine WITH v1,volume,amount,high,low
                hilo='  '
        ENDIF
        if inkey()#0 AND upper(chr(inkey(0))) = "S"
                EXIT
        ENDIF
ENDSCAN
IF i>0
        DO PlotALine WITH v/i,vol/i,amount,0,0
ENDIF
RETURN
*
*************************************************************
* ShowHead - Displays stock symbol and minimum and maximum
*            stock price and volume
*
PROCEDURE ShowHead
ACTIVATE WINDOW Header
clear
   @ 1,1 SAY "Symbol: "+Symb
   @ 2,1 SAY "Name:   " + desc
   @ 3,1 SAY "Stock Range:"
   @ 3,17 SAY min1 picture "###.###"
   @ 3,26 SAY "to"
   @ 3,29 SAY max1 picture "###.###"
IF vmax1 > 13
        @ 4,1 SAY "Volume Range:"
        @ 4,15 SAY vmin1 Picture "########"
        @ 4,26 SAY "to"
        @ 4,29 SAY vmax1 PICTURE "########"
ENDIF
ACTIVATE SCREEN
RETURN

*************************************************************
* PlotALine - Plots a line
*
PROCEDURE PlotALine
PARAMETER v, vol,amt1,hi,lo
J =INT((V-min1)*Increment)+1
k =StartVolume-INT((vol-vmin1)*vIncrement)

IF hilo='Hi'
        SET COLOR TO w+/r
ENDIF
IF hilo='Lo'
        SET COLOR TO w+/bg
ENDIF

? hilo,STR(V,9,3),str(amt1,9,3),DATE
zcol=col()
@ row(),zcol SAY repli(PCHAR,J)
```

```
IF hilo#'  '
        SET COLOR TO w+/b
ENDIF

IF k<StartVolume AND vmax1>13
        @ ROW(),k+20  SAY REPLICATE(PCHAR,StartVolume-k);
              STYLE "T" COLOR w/rg
ENDIF
IF hi#lo .and. vmax1>13
        ilow  = INT((lo-min1)*Increment)+zcol
        ihigh = INT((hi-min1)*Increment)+zcol
        @ ROW(),ilow SAY REPLICATE(CHR(223),;
                ihigh+1-ilow) STYLE "T" COLOR rg+/rb
ENDIF
RETURN
*
************************************************************
* Choose - Displays popup menu of stock quotes
*          User selects a popup bar and ACTION is called
*
PROCEDURE Choose
DEFINE POPUP Stock FROM 5,2 MESSAGE "Select a stock" COLOR SCHEME 9
FOR ISYM = 1 TO NSymbols
  DEFINE BAR ISYM OF Stock ;
        PROMPT SYMTABLE[ISYM,1]+" - "+ SYMTABLE[ISYM,2]
ENDFOR
DEFINE BAR NSymbols+1 OF Stock Prompt "Z - Toggle PLOT display mode"
DEFINE BAR NSymbols+2 OF Stock Prompt "Quit"

ON SELECTION POPUP Stock DO Action
ACTIVATE POPUP Stock
RELEASE POPUP Stock
RETURN
********************************************************************
*  Action -  Action procedure for popup Stock
*
PROCEDURE Action
HIDE POPUP Stock
prmpt = PROMPT()
DO CASE
        CASE 'Z -'$prmpt
                PDisplay = NOT PDisplay
        CASE prmpt = 'Quit'
                RELEASE WINDOW Header
                CLOSE ALL
                DEACTIVATE POPUP

        OTHERWISE
                DO Plotter WITH TRIM(SUBSTR(prmpt,1,5))
                WAIT WINDOW
                CLEAR
ENDCASE
RETURN
********************************************************************
*  Prompter
*
FUNCTION Prompter
```

continues

Listing 12.9. continued

```
DEFINE WINDOW Prompter FROM 0,50 TO 5,85 SYSTEM COLOR SCHEME 9 TITLE "Pause"
ACTIVATE WINDOW Prompter
@ 0,1 SAY "Pick an item..."
choice = 1
@ 1,2 GET Choice FUNCTION "*TH \<Continue;\<Menu;\<Repeat" SIZE 2,8
READ
RELEASE WINDOW Prompter
RETURN Choice
```

You can use the STOCKS.DBF stock quote table to perform a variety of analysis operations. In this example, the data is simply plotted. The PLOT.PRG program plots all the stocks. However, you can access a menu to plot a single stock. Figure 12.3 shows the pop-up menu.

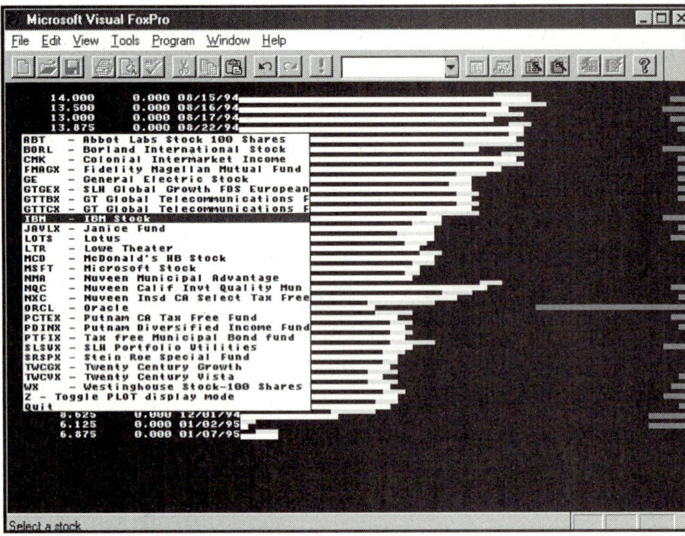

FIGURE 12.3.
The PLOT program pop-up menu for choosing stocks to plot.

If the printer is on when the PLOT.PRG program executes, the PLOT program directs output to a printer and changes the characters used to draw the graph to improve the appearance of the printout.

The `PLOTTER` procedure uses the `CALCULATE` command to compute the minimum and maximum values for plot scaling. Then it calls the `PlotALine` procedure to plot a line. The `ShowHeader` procedure displays the name and minimum and maximum stock quote and volume values.

The `CHOOSE` procedure displays a pop-up menu containing a selection bar for each stock symbol. When the user selects an option, the `ACTION` procedure is called that either quits the PLOT program or generates a plot for the selected stock. The program also features an option (`Z`) that toggles between two plot display modes. One mode displays all the available quote entries in the table for a stock. If the number of entries to plot is more than the number of lines on-screen, the display scrolls. The second mode compresses the plot so that all data for a stock displays on a single screen.

The *IMPORT* Command

The IMPORT command creates a new Visual FoxPro table, puts it in use, and appends data to it. The generated Visual FoxPro file has the same name as the imported file, but the filename extension is .DBF. The syntax is

```
IMPORT FROM <expFN> [TYPE]  FW2 ¦ MOD ¦ PDOX ¦ RPD ¦ WK1
        ¦ WK3 ¦ WKS ¦ WR1 ¦ WRK ¦ XLS  ¦ XL5 [SHEET <expC>]  [AS <expN>]
```

Notice that the specification of the TYPE clause is mandatory, but the TYPE keyword itself is optional.

The Visual FoxPro field names are derived from the field names used by Paradox, RapidFile, and Framework files. Field names are created by Visual FoxPro for file types PFS and WK1. Field names for tables imported from PFS are in the form FIELD01, FIELD02, and so on. Field names for tables imported from WK1 files correspond to the spreadsheet column headings: A,B,...AA,AB,....

AS *<expN>* defines a code page number.

The *APPEND BLANK* Command

The APPEND BLANK command adds one blank record to the table currently in use. The syntax is

```
APPEND BLANK  IN <expWA>
```

If index tags are active, the index is updated.

In the past, programmers used this command heavily in applications because they could not perform data validation with the full-screen APPEND command. They used the @...GET and READ commands to input data into memory variables. The memory variables were validated, and if all were okay, a blank record was appended to the table and the table field values were replaced with the memory variables. Visual FoxPro added the WHEN and VALID clauses to the @...GET command. As a result, this category of application might not need the APPEND BLANK command.

The full-screen APPEND command, however, still appends records only to the active table. Consequently, APPEND BLANK—when used with @...GET and READ—still plays a predominant role in applications in which records are appended to multiple tables. Blank records are appended to each file in the relation, and the READ command updates data in all the files.

The IN <expWA> clause specifies the work area of the table to which the blank record is appended.

Remember that the APPEND FROM ARRAY and INSERT INTO commands add records much faster to a table than does the combination of APPEND BLANK and REPLACE.

The *COPY STRUCTURE* Command

The COPY STRUCTURE command creates a new file and copies the structure of the active table to the new file. No data is transferred to the file. The syntax is

```
COPY STRUCTURE TO <expFN> [FIELDS <field name list>]
        [[WITH] CDX ] ¦ [[WITH] PRODUCTION ]
```

If you specify a FIELDS clause, only the specified files are transferred. If a SET FIELDS field list is active, only the fields in that list are copied. If the new file already exists, it is overwritten. If the SET SAFETY flag is on, however, a prompt box appears requesting confirmation before the file can be overwritten.

If you specify either the [[WITH] CDX] or the [[WITH] PRODUCTION] clause, an identical structural index (CDX) file for the target file is generated.

The *COPY STRUCTURE EXTENDED* and *CREATE FROM* Commands

The COPY STRUCTURE EXTENDED command creates a new table, called an *extended structure table*, which consists of the structure of the active table as records. You can create a table with the CREATE FROM command. These two commands, used together, provide a means of generating a table in a Visual FoxPro program. The syntax of the two commands is

```
COPY TO <expFN> STRUCTURE EXTENDED [FIELD <field list>]
        CREATE <expFN> FROM <expFN>
```

The structure of the new extended structure table is as follows:

Field Name	*Type*	*Width*	*Description*
FIELD_NAME	Character	10	Field name
FIELD_TYPE	Character	1	Data type (C, N)
FIELD_LEN	Numeric	3	Field width
FIELD_DEC	Numeric	3	Number of decimal places
FIELD_IDX	Character	1	Index flag (Y or N value)

A record is created for each field. You can change the structure as required; you can create a new file with the CREATE FROM command. The newly created file is placed in use. The first filename expression defines the table that will be created. The FROM clause filename expression defines the name of the extended structure file used to define the structure of the new file.

The following example demonstrates the use of the COPY STRUCTURE EXTENDED and CREATE FROM commands:

```
Command Window                   Results and Comments
USE Phones
DISPLAY STRUCTURE                Structure for table: C:\PHONES.DBF
COPY TO Phone1 ;                 Number of Data records: 1000
STRUCTURE EXTENDED               Date of last update   :  09/04/92
                                 Field Field Name  Type       Width Dec Index
                                 1     NAME        Character    30      Asc
                                 2     PHONE       Character    14      Asc
                                 ** Total **                    45

USE Phone1
GO 2
? FIELD_NAME                     PHONE

REPLACE Field_name;
WITH "PHONE_NO"                  && Change field name
REPLACE Field_len;
WITH 13                          && Change field width
CREATE newphone FROM Phone1
DISPLAY STRUCTURE                Structure for table: C:\NEWPHONE.DBF
                                 Number of Data records: 0
                                 Date of last update   :  09/04/91
                                 Field Field Name  Type       Width Dec Index
                                 1     NAME        Character    30      Asc
                                 2     PHONE_NO    Character    13      Asc
                                 ** Total **                    44
```

The *COPY FILE* Command

The COPY FILE command creates a new file and transfers the contents of the source file into the new file. The syntax is

```
COPY FILE <expFN> TO <expFN>
```

The FILE clause defines the source file; the TO clause defines the destination file. No default filename exists for either file. This command uses the large buffering technique, which results in an outstanding performance improvement. The COPY FILE command is much faster than the MS-DOS COPY command.

Transferring Data Between Tables and Arrays

The COPY TO ARRAY command copies one or more table records to an existing array. The APPEND FROM ARRAY command adds one or more records to the active table. The appended records contain the contents of the specified array. If the array has a single dimension, data for a single record is transferred. The SCATTER command transfers fields in a table to an array, memory variables, or a named object. The GATHER command transfers data from an array, memory variables, or a named object to a table.

The *COPY TO ARRAY* Command

The COPY TO ARRAY command replaces the value of the array elements with the contents of a selected set of table records and fields. The first field replaces the contents of the first array element, the second field replaces the second element, and so forth, until all the fields have been transferred or the maximum dimension of the array is reached. If the array is two dimensional, the contents of each record are copied to each array row. The syntax is

```
COPY TO ARRAY <array name> [FIELDS <field name list>]
        [<scope>] [FOR <expL>] [WHILE <expL>] [NOOPTIMIZE]
```

Memo fields are not transferred to arrays. If you specify a FIELD clause, the specified fields are copied to array column elements. If a SET FIELDS field list is active, those fields are transferred to the array. The FOR and WHILE clauses as well as *<scope>* determine which records are selected for transferring to an array. If the NOOPTIMIZE keyword is specified, Rushmore technology is disabled.

In the following example, three fields of the CUST table replace the first three elements of the VALUES array:

```
Command Window                      Results and Comments
DECLARE VALUES[5]                   && Declare an array
USE CUST                            Record#  CUSTOMER      CUSTNO  DATE
DISPLAY NEXT 2                         1     Smith, Joe    00222   12/01/91
                                           2     Jones, Jack  00334   11/03/91
COPY TO ARRAY VALUES                && One record is copied
                                          1 Record copied
? VALUES[1]                         Smith, Joe
? VALUES[2]                         00222
? VALUES[3]                         12/01/91
? VALUES[4]                         .F.
```

If an array has two dimensions, the first index represents the row and the second index represents the column. Table fields are copied to array columns and records are copied to array rows. In the following example, table records are copied to a two-dimensional array.

```
Command Window                            Results and Comments
DECLARE Ary[3,5]                          && Declare an array
USE CUST
COPY TO ARRAY Ary                         && Three records are copied
                                                   3 records copied
? Ary[1,1], Ary[1,2]                      Smith, Joe   00222
? Ary[1,3], Ary[1,4]                      12/01/91   .F.
? Ary[2,1], Ary[2,2]                      Jones, Jack  00334
? Ary[1,3], Ary[2,4]                      11/03/91 .F.
? Ary[3,1], Ary[3,2]                      Doe, John    00418
? Ary[3,3], Ary[3,4]                      11/14/91   .F.
```

The number of records transferred is either the row dimension or the number of records selected, whichever is smaller.

The *APPEND FROM ARRAY* Command

The APPEND FROM ARRAY command adds records to a table from an array. The syntax is

```
APPEND FROM ARRAY <array name> [FOR <expL>]
```

The APPEND FROM command adds a record for each array row that satisfies the optional FOR condition. The first column array element is transferred to the first field, the second is transferred to the second field, and so forth. If there are more fields than column array elements, the remaining fields are left blank. If there are more array elements than fields, the extra array elements are ignored. No array data is transferred to memo fields. In the following example, the three rows of the Ary array are appended to three records of the CUST table as follows:

```
Command Window                      Results and Comments
APPEND FROM ARRAY ARY                   1 Record added
DISPLAY ALL                             Record#  CUSTOMER     CUSTNO  DATE
                                           1     Smith, Joe   00222   12/01/91
                                           2     Jones, Jack  00334   11/03/91
                                           3     Doe, John    00418   11/14/91
                                                  ...
                                           8     Smith, Joe   00222   12/01/91
                                           9     Jones, Jack  00334   11/03/91
                                          10     Doe, John    00418   11/14/91
```

The last three records were appended. If the data type of an array element differs from the data type of the corresponding field in the active table, conversion is performed, if possible.

The *SCATTER* and *GATHER* Commands

The SCATTER command transfers field values from a single record to an array or memory variable. Its syntax is

```
SCATTER [FIELDS <field list>] [MEMO] TO <array name> [BLANK]
SCATTER [FIELDS <field list>] [MEMO] NAME <object name>
SCATTER [FIELDS <field list>] [MEMO] MEMVAR [BLANK]
```

If the FIELDS clause is not specified, data is transferred from all the fields in the table. If the MEMVAR keyword is specified, all table field values for the current record are copied to memory variables. The memory variables receive the same name as the table field. Because the names of the table fields and the memory variable are the same, you need to specify a memory variable in its fully qualified form: You must precede the memory variable name with the M. qualifier. If the memory variables don't exist, they are created.

CAUTION

Invariably there are semantic quirks in most languages that people often trip over. This is true of the SCATTER command. You should be careful that you do not specify the TO keyword with the MEMVAR keyword. If you do, Visual FoxPro creates an array named MEMVAR. The TO clause is only used to scatter fields to array elements.

You can use the form of the SCATTER command with the NAME clause to create an object that contains properties that have the same names as fields in the table. Each of the properties for the object has a value that corresponds to the contents of the fields in the table. No properties are created for memo, general, or graphics fields in the table. For example, suppose you have a table named Parts.DBF with the fields Item, Quantity, and Cost, and you use the following SCATTER command to create an object named OParts.

```
Command                     Results
USE Parts
SCATTER NAME Oparts
DISPLAY                     Record#  ITEM       QUANTITY     COST
                                  1  Widget           42     1.98

DISPLAY OBJECTS             Object: OPARTS   Pub    O      EMPTY
                            Class Tree:
                                    EMPTY
                            Properties:
                                    COST          Y      1.9800
                                    ITEM          C      "Widget"
                                    QUANTITY      N      42   (42.00000000)
```

You will create an object with three properties. You can reference the properties of an object, OPARTS, by using the name of the object as the qualifier as illustrated in the following example:

```
? OParts.Cost
```

If the name of the object is the same as an open table, you can preface the property name with the M. qualifier as illustrated in the following example:

```
? M.OParts.Quantity
```

In the following example, the table named ABSTRACT.DBF has four fields, AUTHOR, TITLE, DATE, and INFO. INFO is a memo field.

```
Command Window               Results and Comments
USE ABSTRACT                 && Fields: AUTHOR, TITLE, DATE, and INFO
SCATTER MEMVAR               && Copy 3 fields to memory variables
DISPLAY MEMORY               AUTHOR  Pub   C  "Joe Starbuck                "
                             TITLE   Pub   C  "Wild Flowers                "
                                DATE    Pub   12/12/73
                                3 variables defined, 19 bytes used
                ...
SCATTER MEMO MEMVAR          && Copy all fields to memory variables
DISPLAY MEMORY               AUTHOR  Pub   C  "Joe Starbuck                "
                                TITLE   Pub   C  "Wild Flowers                "
                                DATE    Pub   D 12/12/73
                                INFO    Pub  C "This article tells about the
                                   of wildflowers that are cons
                                   botanical interest and frequ
                                   Northern region of the US
                                4 variables defined, 169 bytes used
SCATTER NAME MyObject        && Copy 3 fields to named object, MyObject
DISPLAY OBJECTS
                             Object: MYOBJECT     Pub     O     EMPTY
                             Class Tree:
                                  EMPTY
```

```
                                  Properties:
                                           AUTHOR      C     "Joe Starbuck"
                                           DATE        D     12/12/73
                                           TITLE       C     "Wild Flowers "
                                       ...
? M.TITLE                         Wild Flowers       (From MEMVAR)
? TITLE                           Wild Flowers       (From table)
? TITLE                           Wild Flowers       (From table)
? MyObject.TITLE                  Wild Flowers       (From named object)
```

If you specify a TO clause, table field values for the current record are copied to array elements. If the array does not exist, it is created. If the array contains too few elements to hold data for all the fields, the array is expanded. On the other hand, if the array has more elements than the number of fields copied, the remaining elements are unchanged.

Normally, memo fields are not transferred to an array. However, if the MEMO keyword is specified, memo fields are copied to memory variables or array elements.

If the BLANK keyword is specified, no data is actually copied. However, blank array elements or memory variables are created with field widths and types that correspond to the fields in the current table. If the field list is specified, a memory variable or array element is created for each field in the list. Otherwise, a memory variable or array element is created for each field in the structure. Here are some examples:

```
SCATTER MEMVAR             && Copy all of the fields to memory variables
                           && except memo fields
SCATTER MEMO MEMVAR         && Copy all of the fields to memory variables
*                               Only copy fields LASTNAME and FIRSTNAME
*                               to memory variables
SCATTER MEMVAR FIELDS LASTNAME, FIRSTNAME
SCATTER TO ARAY            && Copy all of the fields to the array ARAY
                           && except memo fields
SCATTER MEMO TO ARAY       && Copy all of the fields to array ARAY
*
*                        Only copy fields LASTNAME and FIRSTNAME
*                        to array ARAY
SCATTER TO ARAY FIELDS LASTNAME, FIRSTNAME
```

The GATHER command transfers the contents of array elements or memory variables to the fields of the current table record. The syntax is

```
GATHER [FIELDS <field list>] FROM <array name> [MEMO]
GATHER [FIELDS <field list>] MEMVAR [MEMO]
GATHER [FIELDS <field list>] NAME <Object-name> [MEMO]
```

If you do not specify the FIELDS clause, all the fields in the current record of the table are replaced with array elements or memory variables. If you specify the MEMVAR keyword, all table field values for the current record are replaced with memory variables that have the same name as the table fields. If you specify an object with the NAME clause, all table field values for the current record are replaced with the properties that have the same name as the table fields. If you specify the FROM clause, the fields for the current data record are replaced with the named array. The first field is replaced with the value of the first array element. The second field is replaced with the second array element. This process continues until you run out of fields or array elements. Memo fields are skipped unless the MEMO keyword is specified. The SCATTER and GATHER commands are normally used together to edit records, as in the following example:

```
USE AFILE
SCATTER MEMO TO ARAY   && All fields are copied to ARAY
*
* … Edit the elements of array ARAY
*
GATHER MEMO FROM ARAY  && Replace fields with elements of ARAY
```

In the example shown in Listing 12.10, the current record contents are transferred to memvars. The memvars are edited, and if the user does not press the Esc key to exit the READ, the changed values are saved.

Listing 12.10. The source code of the program SALES1.PRG.

```
****************************************************************
*      * 09/07/92           SALES1.PRG                  19:00:56 *
****************************************************************
*      *                                                       *
*      * Description:                                          *
*      *  Illustrates use of SCATTER and GATHER commands       *
*      *                                                       *
****************************************************************
SET TALK OFF
CLEAR
USE SALES
WAIT WINDOW "Append or Edit? (E/A): " TO DoWhat
DoWhat = UPPER(DoWhat)
DO CASE
        CASE DoWhat = "E"
               SCATTER MEMVAR && Copy fields to memory variables
               IF ReadData()
                       GATHER MEMVAR  && Move memvars to record
               ENDIF
        CASE DoWhat = "A"
               SCATTER MEMVAR BLANK && Fill memory variables with blanks
               IF READDATA()
                       APPEND BLANK
                       GATHER MEMVAR  && Move memvars to record
               ENDIF
        OTHERWISE
               WAIT WINDOW "Bad Choice! Bye…"
ENDCASE
RETURN
FUNCTION ReadData
@ 1,10 SAY "Monthly Sales"
@ 3,3  SAY ' Last name: '  GET m.lastname
@ 5,3  SAY 'First name: '  GET m.firstname
@ 7,3  SAY '     Sales: '  GET m.sales
@ 9,3  SAY '      Rank: '  GET m.rank
@ 11,3 SAY ' Hire date: '  GET m.hiredate
READ
RETURN LASTKEY() != 27 AND UPDATED()
```

If you prefer to use arrays instead of memvars, you can. Listing 12.11 illustrates the use of arrays with the SCATTER and GATHER commands.

Listing 12.11. The source code of the program SALES2.PRG.

```
*****************************************************************
*      * 09/07/92           SALES2.PRG                 19:00:56 *
*****************************************************************
*      *                                                        *
*      * Description:                                           *
*      *  Illustrates use of SCATTER and GATHER commands        *
*      *                                                        *
*****************************************************************
SET TALK OFF
CLEAR
USE SALES
WAIT WINDOW "Append or Edit? (E/A): " TO DoWhat
DoWhat = UPPER(DoWhat)
DO CASE
        CASE DoWhat = "E"
               SCATTER TO ARY && Copy all fields to array
               IF ReadData()
                       GATHER FROM ARY  && Move array elements to record
               ENDIF
        CASE DoWhat = "A"
               SCATTER TO ARY BLANK && Fill array elements with blanks
               IF READDATA()
                       APPEND BLANK
                       GATHER FROM ARY  && Move array elements to record
               ENDIF
        OTHERWISE
               WAIT WINDOW "Bad Choice! Bye..."
ENDCASE
RETURN
FUNCTION ReadData
@ 1,10 SAY "Monthly Sales"
@ 3,3  SAY ' Last name: '  GET ARY[1]
@ 5,3  SAY 'First name: '  GET ARY[2]
@ 7,3  SAY '     Sales: '  GET ARY[3]
@ 9,3  SAY '      Rank: '  GET ARY[4]
@ 11,3 SAY ' Hire date: '  GET ARY[5]
READ
RETURN LASTKEY() != 27 AND UPDATED()
```

Transferring Memo Fields

APPEND MEMO transfers any type of file into a specified memo field in the current record of the active table. COPY MEMO transfers a specified memo field to an external file. The default filename extension of the external file is .TXT. The syntax of the memo field transferred commands is

```
APPEND MEMO <field name> FROM <expFN> [OVERWRITE] [AS <expN>]
COPY MEMO <field name> TO <expFN> [ADDITIVE] [AS <expN>]
```

`<field name>` specifies the memo field involved in the transfer operation. `<expFN>` is the filename expression that defines the name of the file. The `AS` clause specifies the code page.

If you specify the `OVERWRITE` keyword with the `APPEND MEMO` command, the current contents of the memo file are erased before the new data is added. Otherwise, the data is appended at the end of the current contents of the memo field.

If you specify the `ADDITIVE` keyword with the `COPY MEMO` command, the contents of the memo field are appended at the end of the external file, as in the following example:

```
APPEND MEMO Abstract FROM Abstract
COPY MEMO Letter TO Mail ADDITIVE
```

In the first example, the ABSTRACT.TXT file is appended to a memo field named `ABSTRACT`. In the second example, the contents of the memo field are appended to the MAIL.TXT file.

NOTE

The `APPEND GENERAL` command imports OLE objects from a file and places them into a General data type field. It is discussed in Chapter 17, "OLE, OLE 2.0 Controls, DDE, and Operating System Interfaces."

Using Menus for Import and Export

You might sometime want to perform a one-time import or export operation. The simplest way to do this is through the menu system.

Importing a Table

From the menu system, you can append an external file format to an existing FoxPro table or you can create a new table from imported data. Choose the **F**ile menu **I**mport option. When the Import dialog box appears. You have two methods to import data. You can specify the type, name, and location of the file to import, as well as the name of the target table, and the import operation is performed. The second method is to use the Import Wizard, which is much more flexible. To run the Import Wizard, click on the Import Wizard button. The Import Wizard appears as shown in Figure 12.4. Follow the simple instructions provided by the Import Wizard to import data in a variety of formats to your specified table. The Import Wizard is discussed in detail in Chapter 24, "Wizards."

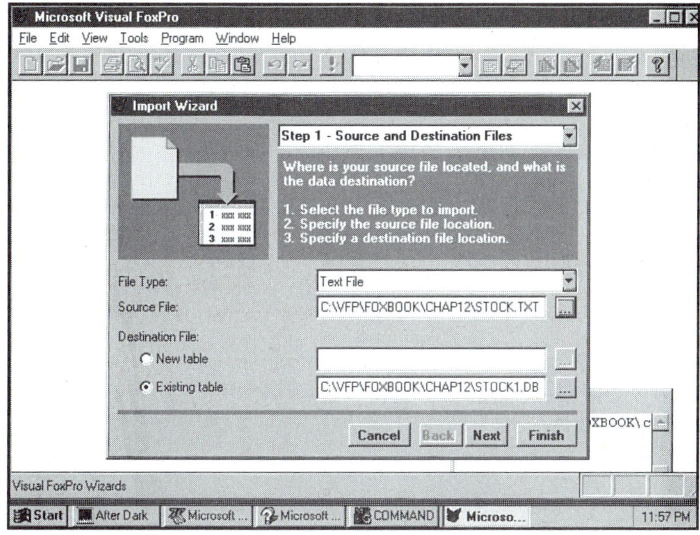

FIGURE 12.4.
Importing a file.

Exporting a Database Table

To export a file, choose the **F**ile menu **E**xport option. The Export dialog box appears, as shown in Figure 12.5. Choose the file type from the Type list box. Specify the name of the table to be exported in the T**o** text box. Then type the name of the target file in the **F**rom text box. You can use the Browser button (…) to the right of the text boxes to use the Open dialog box (or Save As) to choose a directory and filename. Finally, press the OK button in the Export menu, the target export file is created, and records from the selected table are exported to the target file.

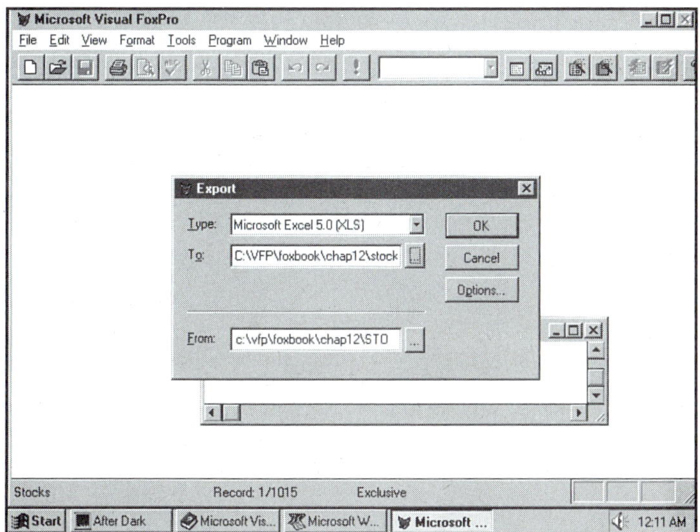

FIGURE 12.5.
The Export dialog box.

Summary

This chapter discusses the FoxPro commands with syntax that allows scope clauses. Scopes extend commands to support sets of data. Special cases in the syntax and the (possibly unexpected) behavior of `DISPLAY` and `LIST` are discussed.

You have also learned about the `CALCULATE` command and how it can perform several simple (`COUNT` and `SUM`) and complex (statistical and financial) functions with a single pass through a data file. I mentioned the `UPDATE` command, and touched on the `SCAN` command and arrays. The `SCAN` command and arrays are covered in more detail in other chapters.

This chapter also explores the use and functionality of commands that move a data set from one file to another. It also describes how to transfer data from tables to arrays and memo fields, and vice versa. The following commands were presented: `APPEND`, `COPY`, `EXPORT`, `IMPORT`, `INSERT`, `SCATTER`, and `GATHER`.

The current record pointer concept makes the FoxPro language easier to understand, but the capability to refer to more than one record at a time using data set operations makes a single command very powerful.

13

Data Ordering

Physics is experience, arranged in economical order.

—Ernst Mach (1838–1916)
The Economical Nature of Physical Inquiry

After you create a DBF file, you can access your records in record-number sequence. The first record is record number 1, the second record is record number 2, and so forth. The order in which data is stored in a FoxPro DBF file is referred to as the *physical order* of the DBF file. Each time a record is appended, it is added to the end of the file.

You can rearrange the physical order of a file with the SORT command. SORT creates a new file containing the rearranged records. The INDEX command builds a separate file containing one or more indexes, but the physical order of the file remains unchanged.

Although a table (DBF file) can have as many indexes as will fit in available memory, only a single index—called the *master* or *controlling index*—determines the order in which records are accessed. Any one of the indexes can be made the controlling index. When a controlling index is active, it controls the order in which records are accessed. This is called *logical order.*

Sort or Index?

The application determines whether to use SORT or INDEX. The SORT command reorders data so that it can be sequentially accessed in the desired order. But if new records are added or the sequence field is changed, the file has to be re-sorted. The INDEX command provides fast access to data with the FIND and SEEK commands, and unlike sorts, indexes are updated automatically as data is changed or new records are added.

Most programmers don't want to re-sort their data every time they want to add or edit data or access the data in a different order. Consequently, SORT is rarely used in favor of INDEX. How you specify keys for the INDEX and SORT commands differs. To specify the SORT command keys, you use a list of field names. You can specify ascending, descending, and case-sensitivity sorting attributes for each sort key field. For the INDEX command, you define the sorting key with a single expression, which can consist of multiple fields.

Using *SORT*

The SORT command creates a new DBF file containing the records arranged in a new order. You can use a list of up to 10 sort keys to determine the order of the sorted DBF file. This is the syntax:

```
SORT TO <expFN>
        ON <field name> [/A] [/C] [/D]
        [, <field name> [/A] [/C] [/D]]...
        [ASCENDING ¦ DESCENDING] [<scope>] [FOR <expL>]
        [WHILE <expL>] [NOOPTIMIZE]
SORT TO <expFN>
        ON ALL [LIKE <skeleton>] [ EXCEPT <skeleton>]
        [ASCENDING ¦ DESCENDING] [<scope>] [FOR <expL>]
        [WHILE <expL>] [NOOPTIMIZE]
```

The selected set of records from the currently active DBF file is sorted in the order designated by the `ON` clause field list. The DBF file defined by the `TO` clause is created and receives the sorted records; this DBF file contains the same structure as the currently active DBF file.

The `ON` clause field list cannot contain Logical or Memo type fields. The first field in the list is the most significant sort key, also called the *major key*. The last field is the least significant sort key, or the *minor key*. If a Character type key field is followed by `/C`, case is ignored—that is, `SORT` treats uppercase and lowercase characters as the same characters. This is called a *dictionary order sort*. If `/C` is not specified, the field is sorted in ASCII order. See Table 13.1.

Table 13.1. The sequencing order for the `SORT` command.

Order	*Character Sequence Order*
ASCII ascending	0, 1,...9, A, B,...Z, a, b,...z
Dictionary ascending	0, 1,...9, A, a, B, b,...Z, z
ASCII descending	Z,...B, A, z,...b, a, 9,...1, 0
Dictionary descending	Z, z...A, a, 9,...1, 0

Sorting is normally in ascending order. A field followed by `/A` or `/D` is sorted in ascending or descending order, respectively. The `ASCENDING` and `DESCENDING` keywords determine the sorting order for all fields that are not followed by `/A` or `/D`. You can combine `/C` with `/A` or `/D` as follows: `/AC` or `/DC`. Table 13.2 is the sample file used as the basis for examples in the remainder of this section.

Table 13.2. The physical ordering of the sample file.

Record#	*Lastname*	*Firstname*	*City*	*Sales*	*Rank*	*Hiredate*
1	Brown	Joe	Boston	29366.00	3	09/12/85
2	Smith	Howard	Glendale	48323.00	1	05/12/73
3	Black	Hamil	Greenview	2841.00	5	11/12/88
4	Green	Jim	Austin	19221.00	4	05/14/90
5	Brook	Jerry	GREENVIEW	32381.00	2	02/03/81

Enter the following command to sort the file on `City` in ascending ASCII order:

```
SORT ON City TO Newfile1
```

The result is shown in Table 13.3.

Table 13.3. The NEWFILE.DBF file sorted by city, using ASCII sort.

Record#	Lastname	Firstname	City	Sales	Rank	Hiredate
4	Green	Jim	Austin	19221.00	4	05/14/90
1	Brown	Joe	Boston	29366.00	3	09/12/85
5	Brook	Jerry	GREENVIEW	32381.00	2	02/03/81
2	Smith	Howard	Glendale	48323.00	1	05/12/73
3	Black	Hamil	Greenview	12841.00	5	11/12/88

You really don't want an ASCII sort for the cities, because GREENVIEW is not in the order that you want. To remedy this, sort the file on `City` and specify dictionary order:

```
SORT ON City/C TO Newfile
```

Note in Table 13.4 that the two records for the city of Greenview are adjacent because case is ignored.

Table 13.4. The NEWFILE.DBF file sorted by city, ignoring case.

Record#	Lastname	Firstname	City	Sales	Rank	Hiredate
4	Green	Jim	Austin	19221.00	4	05/14/90
1	Brown	Joe	Boston	29366.00	3	09/12/85
2	Smith	Howard	Glendale	48323.00	1	05/12/73
5	Brook	Jerry	GREENVIEW	32381.00	2	02/03/81
3	Black	Hamil	Greenview	12841.00	5	11/12/88

Now, sort on the `Sales` field in descending order:

```
SORT ON Sales/D TO Newfile
```

Table 13.5 shows the results.

Table 13.5. The NEWFILE.DBF file sorted in descending order by sales.

Record#	Lastname	Firstname	City	Sales	Rank	Hiredate
2	Smith	Howard	Glendale	48323.00	1	05/12/73
5	Brook	Jerry	GREENVIEW	32381.00	2	02/03/81
1	Brown	Joe	Boston	29366.00	3	09/12/85
4	Green	Jim	Austin	19221.00	4	05/14/90
3	Black	Hamil	Greenview	12841.00	5	11/12/88

Records in the following `SORT` command are sorted in ascending dictionary order by `Lastname`, and descending order by `Sales` and `Hiredate`:

```
SORT ON LastName/AC,Sales,HireDate TO Newfile DESCENDING
```

The `SORT` command supports the `LIKE` and `EXCEPT` clauses. For example, if you want all fields that begin with `NA` to be sort keys, you can specify

```
SORT FIELDS ALL LIKE NA* TO newfile
```

You can also specify both the `LIKE` and `EXCEPT` clauses if you want to include some fields and exclude others. For example, if you want to sort records to a new file, and you want to sort only on fields that begin with `X` and not on fields that begin with `XZ`, you specify

```
SORT ON ALL LIKE X* EXCEPT XA* TO newfile
```

Index Files

FoxPro has two types of index files. The first type of file is called an IDX file and contains a *single index.* The second type is a *compound index file.* In dBASE IV, an index file containing up to 47 multiple indexes is called a *multiple index file* (MDX). The number of indexes in a compound index file (CDX) is limited only by the amount of available memory; each index is called a *tag.* A compound index file that has the same filename as the DBF file and is tightly coupled with that DBF file is called a *structural compound index file.*

CDX files are great because you use up file handles when you open IDX files. The number of files that you can have open at one time in MS-DOS and Windows is limited. Furthermore, because it takes time to open a file, especially if the directory is large, opening a database table (DBF file) with many traditional IDX files can take several seconds. Structural CDX files provide a means of assuring index integrity by tightly coupling a DBF file with its associated indexes.

An IDX file contains an anchor record node (B*tree node zero) and remaining B*tree nodes, as shown in Figure 13.1. The anchor node contains the index key expression, the `UNIQUE` status flag, and other parameters, and indicates whether the index is compact.

A compound index file contains a header record and an anchor node and B*tree nodes for each index tag. (See Figure 13.2.) The header contains the block size parameter, the name of each tag, and a pointer to each tag's anchor node.

Each index tag has an anchor node similar to the IDX file anchor node. The tag anchor node, however, contains additional information such as a code indicating whether the index is sorted in ascending or descending order and whether the tag is a `UNIQUE` type index.

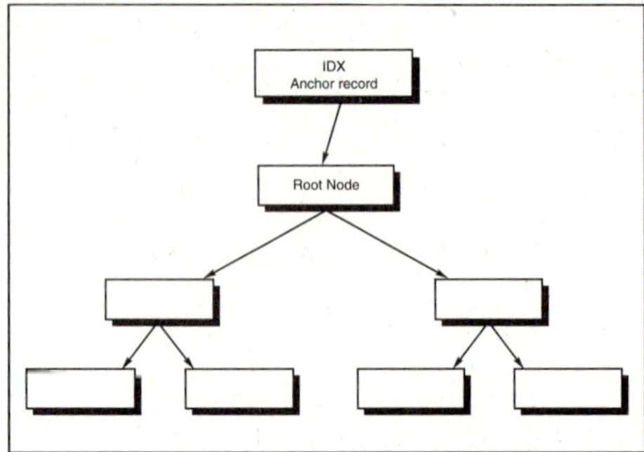

FIGURE 13.1.
An IDX file diagram.

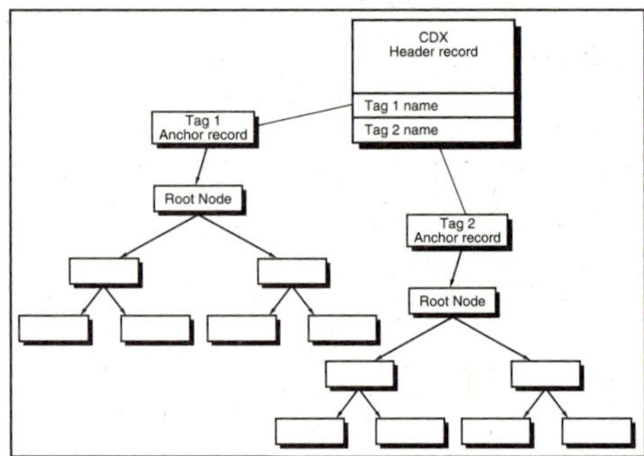

FIGURE 13.2.
The CDX file structure.

A special form of the compound index file is called the structural compound index file. It has the same filename as its associated DBF file and the .CDX filename extension. When a DBF file with a structural compound index file is placed in use, its structural compound index file is also placed in use. This is done to always enforce the integrity of the index tags. The index tags are always updated whenever any data in the DBF file changes.

Creating Indexes

You can create an index with the `INDEX` command, and you can re-create a damaged or outdated index with the `REINDEX` command.

The *INDEX* Command

The `INDEX` command creates an index. The syntax for an IDX file is

```
INDEX ON <expKEY> TO <expFN> [UNIQUE] [COMPACT] [ADDITIVE]
```

The syntax for a CDX (compound index) file is

```
INDEX ON <expKEY> TAG <expTN> [OF <expFN>]
        [UNIQUE] [DESCENDING] [FOR <expL>]
        [ASCENDING ¦ DESCENDING ] [ADDITIVE] [CANDIDATE]
```

The currently active DBF file is indexed in the order designated by the ON clause key expression, <expKEY>. The key expression can be any Character, Logical, Numeric, Float, or Date data type expression—well, almost any expression. A few restrictions apply. A memo field cannot be referenced alone in an index expression; it must be an element of an expression, such as SUBSTR(memofld). A user-defined function can be referenced in an index expression, but its presence can substantially slow down indexing operations. If you reference a memory variable or fields in other DBF files and they are no longer active, the Variable not found error message appears.

NOTE

When you specify an ON clause expression, it's best to never specify an alias name with a field unless you really intend to reference a field in another work area. Here is why: Rushmore internal optimization technology uses indexes to optimize performance. However, Rushmore does not use indexes with an alias name specified. To ensure that you don't forget, FoxPro displays a warning message when you specify an alias with a field name. For example, if you specify `INDEX ON SALES.CITIES TO CITIES`, FoxPro displays `Warning: Index expression contains aliased fields.`

The maximum length of a key is 100 characters for IDX files and 240 characters for CDX files. Index expressions should be a fixed type. Character data type expressions should be a fixed length. If the type or length changes, no error message is issued, but the index might not function correctly.

If you specify the TO clause, an IDX file is created. If you specify the TAG clause, an index tag is added to a compound index file. If you specify the OF clause, the index tag is created and written to the designated compound index file; the file is made active. If you do not specify the OF clause, the index tag is written to the structural compound index file. In either case, if the compound index file does not exist, it is created. The default filename extension for a compound index file is .CDX.

In FoxPro 1.2 and FoxBASE+, only IDX files exist. After you create an index, you must always keep it open whenever the DBF file is open and you update the field associated with the index or the index goes out of date. However, the index tags in the structural CDX file are always maintained. When you are creating an index that you plan to use frequently, it's best to create structural CDX index tags, but if you create a temporary index, it's best to create an IDX index and delete it afterward. Furthermore, the IDX index should be a COMPACT IDX index to save disk space and speed up access. In the following three examples, the destination files are different for each example:

```
INDEX ON Last_Name TAG SKEY OF X  && Tag is added to CDX file
INDEX ON Last_Name TO SKEY        && IDX file is created
INDEX ON Last_Name TAG SKEY       && Tag is added to
                                  &&   structural CDX file
```

If you specify the FOR clause, only records that satisfy the FOR clause condition are included in the index. The resulting index contains only records that satisfy the condition. Whenever a DBF file is updated or records are appended, the record is included in an index tag with a FOR clause if the FOR clause condition is satisfied. The FOR clause can be specified only when creating a compound index file tag. The FOR clause condition can contain memory variables, user-defined functions, and fields from work areas other than the current work area.

Whenever you create an index, any open IDX or CDX file (except the structural CDX file) closes. However, if you specify the ADDITIVE keyword, any open index files remain open.

The newly created index becomes the controlling index and defines the order in which records are accessed. The following examples demonstrate the use of the INDEX command:

```
USE MYFILE EXCLUSIVE
INDEX ON Name TO Myindex        && Myindex IDX file created
File1 = "Myindex"
INDEX ON Name TO (File1)        && Myindex IDX file created
INDEX ON Name TAG Name          && Structural CDX tag, Name,
                                &&  created for structural CDX
                                &&  file, MYFILE.CDX
INDEX ON Name TAG Name OF File1 && CDX tag, Name, created for
                                &&  CDX file, MYINDEX.CDX
```

NOTE

You must open a file in EXCLUSIVE mode before you can index it.

By default, indexes are arranged in ascending order. To produce an index in descending order, specify the DESCENDING keyword with a compound index file only. The DESCENDING keyword cannot be used when creating an IDX file. The ASCENDING keyword is available, but obviously its use is redundant and unnecessary as far as the program is concerned. The only reason to specify ASCENDING is as a reminder that the index is arranged in ascending order.

All CDX index tags are compact. A compact index is one that has been compressed using FoxPro Compact Index Technology. Compact indexes are smaller, as the name implies. Commands and functions that use compact indexes access data faster. The two types of IDX files are normal IDX files, which are compatible with FoxBASE+, and compact IDX files, which are smaller than normal IDX files.

TIP

The structural CDX indexes are preferred over nonstructural CDX and IDX indexes because the structural CDX files automatically open when the DBF is placed in use.

If you specify the UNIQUE keyword, only the first occurrence of records having the same key expression value are included in the index; the resulting index is known as a *unique index*. After a unique index is created, it remains unique for the life of the index, whether or not it is re-indexed or updated. If you don't specify the UNIQUE keyword, an index is created using all records in the database table (DBF file), even if they have the same key expression value. The UNIQUE keyword has the same effect as the SET UNIQUE ON command, discussed in Chapter 10, "Environment." You can specify the CANDIDATE keyword to create a tag that does not allow duplicate or NULL keys. If you attempt to add a record with a key value that already exists in a table, you get the error message Uniqueness of Index <*field name*> violated, and you are not allowed to add the record. Candidate indexes are discussed in Chapter 11, "DBF Files and Databases."

NOTE

The indexes created with the INDEX command and the UNIQUE option are different from the candidate indexes created with CREATE TABLES or ALTER TABLES or by specifying the CANDIDATE keyword. The candidate indexes do not allow a duplicate index key and reject any attempt to add a record that has a duplicate key. Index keys created with the INDEX command using the UNIQUE option, called *Xbase Unique Indexes*, allow duplicate keys. Xbase unique indexes contain the first occurrence of a duplicate key value.

When a DBF file is indexed, all records in the file are processed. The SET FILTER expression is ignored. All records marked for deletion are also included, regardless of the SET DELETED flag setting.

Because Visual FoxPro is inherently a multiuser product, the currently active DBF file must be in EXCLUSIVE mode before INDEX can be executed.

If a DBF file is indexed on a character field, the file will be in ASCII order, as in the following example:

```
INDEX ON Name TAG Name
```

If you want to index a file in dictionary order, the UPPER() function can be used to force the INDEX, as in the following example:

```
USE SALES
LIST
INDEX ON UPPER(City) TAG City
LIST
```

This is the output:

```
Record#  Lastname  Firstname  City       Sales     Rank  Hiredate
1        Brown     Joe        Boston     29366.00   3    09/12/85
2        Smith     Howard     Glendale   48323.00   1    05/12/73
3        Black     Hamil      Greenview  12841.00   5    11/12/88
4        Green     Jim        Austin     19221.00   4    05/14/90
5        Brook     Jerry      GREENVIEW  32381.00   2    02/03/81
```

```
5 Records indexed

Record#  Lastname  Firstname  City       Sales     Rank  Hiredate
4        Green     Jim        Austin     19221.00   4    05/14/90
1        Brown     Joe        Boston     29366.00   3    09/12/85
2        Smith     Howard     Glendale   48323.00   1    05/12/73
3        Black     Hamil      Greenview  12841.00   5    11/12/88
5        Brook     Jerry      GREENVIEW  32381.00   2    02/03/81
```

The `City` field is indexed in dictionary order, and a structural compound index tag named `City` is created.

You can use functions to convert Numeric and Date type fields to Character type fields. Thus, in effect, an index key can consist of multiple field types, as in the following example:

```
INDEX ON Last_Name + STR(ACCNO) + DTOS(TDate) TO SKEY
```

Notice that all the elements of the preceding `ON` clause expression are Character type. This is no accident. As you've already learned, you cannot mix data types in an expression. The only way you can create a key consisting of fields with different data types is to convert them to the same data type.

If you prefer to use the Visual FoxPro menus to create your indexes, you can. And there are several ways to do it. One way is to first choose the **F**ile menu **O**pen option. The File Open dialog box appears. Choose a database container (DBC) file, and the Database Designer window appears, as shown in Figure 13.3. Then click the right mouse button on a table and the shortcut menu appears, showing table properties. Figure 13.3 shows the shortcut menu for the table CENSUS.DBF. This table contains population statistics for all 50 states.

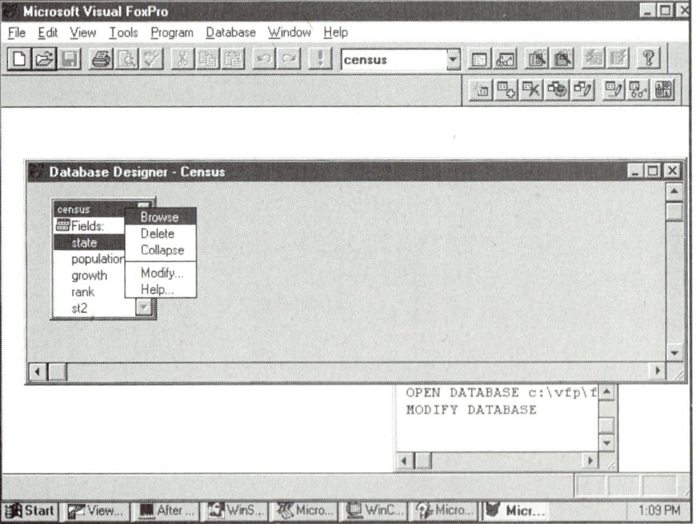

FIGURE 13.3.
The Database Designer window.

Next, select the **M**odify option, and the Table Designer window (`MODIFY STRUCTURE`) appears. It has two tabs. Choose the Index tab as shown in Figure 13.4.

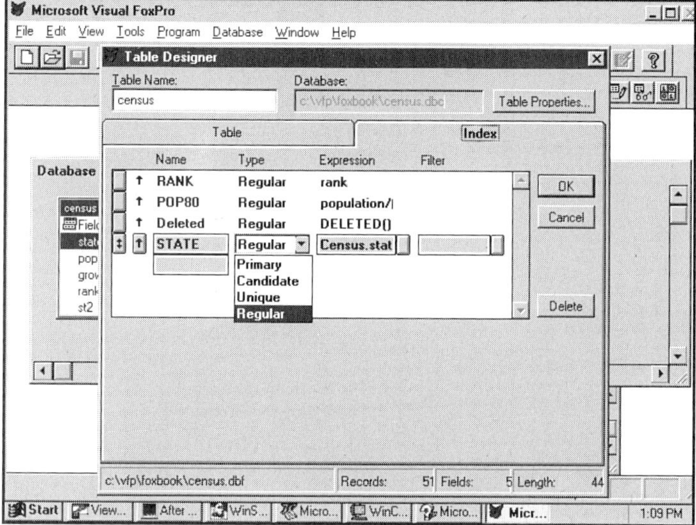

FIGURE 13.4.
The Table Designer with the Index tab selected.

Next, specify an index using the following steps:

1. Specify a tag name.
2. Choose the type of index. The types are shown in the open drop-down list in Figure 13.4.
3. Specify the `KEY` expression.
4. Optionally specify a filter (`FOR` expression).
5. Press the OK button when you finish adding indexes.

When the Table Designer window disappears and uncovers the Database Designer window (as shown in Figure 13.5), note that the `State` index is in the index section of the list for the Census table.

You can choose an existing index as the controlling index. To do this, you choose the T**a**ble menu **I**ndex Table option when a change or Browse window is active, as shown in Figure 13.6. You can execute the Browse window from the table properties list (shown in Figure 13.6), which appears on the Database Designer window when you click on a table using the right mouse button.

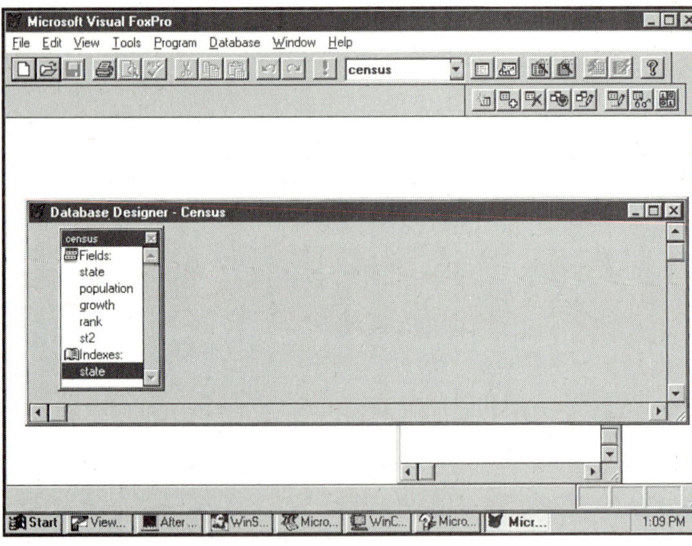

FIGURE 13.5.
The Database Designer window with the newly created Census table index highlighted.

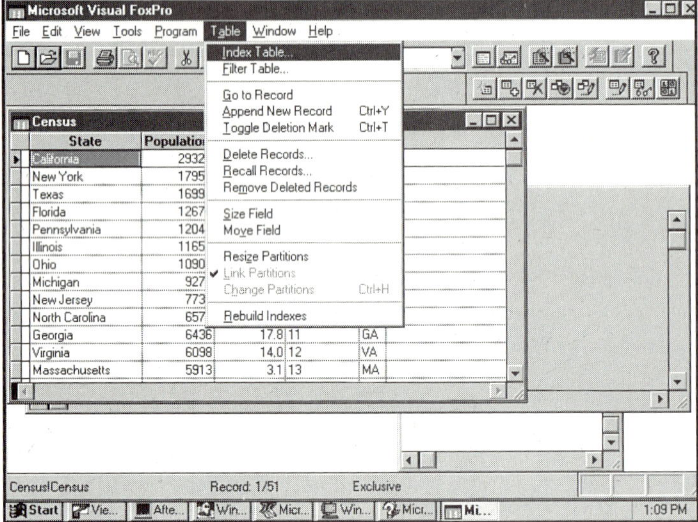

FIGURE 13.6.
The Browse window and Table menu.

Types of Indexes

In Chapter 11 you learned about primary and candidate files. In this chapter, you have learned about regular and Xbase unique indexes.

A regular index is the type of index created with the `INDEX` command without the `UNIQUE` keyword. Regular indexes can have any number of duplicate records, as in the following example:

```
USE Cities
INDEX ON City TAG City
```

Index keys created with the `INDEX` command using the `UNIQUE` option, called Xbase unique indexes, allow duplicate keys. Xbase unique indexes contain the first occurrence of duplicate key values. Xbase unique indexes are created with the `INDEX` command with the `UNIQUE` option. You can create this type of index by specifying the `UNIQUE` keyword with the `INDEX` command or by setting the `SET UNIQUE` command to `ON` prior to creating the index The following example shows how to use `SET UNIQUE ON` to create an Xbase-style unique index.

```
USE Cities
SET UNIQUE ON
INDEX ON City TAG City
```

The following example illustrates the use of the `UNIQUE` keyword with the `INDEX` command:

```
USE Cities
INDEX ON City TAG City UNIQUE
```

A *primary index* is an index that never allows the insertion of any duplicate values on its key field or expression. Primary indexes are normally used with primary tables for enforcing referential integrity in a persistent relationship. There is only one primary key for a table; it is the one that is referenced from another table when a persistent relationship is established.

A *candidate index* does not allow duplicate values on its key fields or expressions, making it similar to a primary key. In fact, its name denotes the characteristics of the index—it is a candidate for a primary key. It can become the primary key for a table. For example, an employee table can have an index on the employee ID field that is its primary index. It can also have an index on its social security number field that is its candidate index. When needed, you can make the social security number index into the table's primary index. You can have more than one candidate index for a table. You can use a candidate index as either the referenced or referencing index to enforce referential integrity.

When you attempt to create a primary or candidate index on an existing table, the creation processes fail if the table contains duplicate keys. You get an error message and the record is rejected if you attempt to add a record with a duplicate key to a primary or candidate index. Also, null values are not allowed in primary and candidate indexes. Primary and candidate indexes can only be created for tables that are associated with a database. You can create these indexes with the `INDEX`, `CREATE TABLE`, `ALTER TABLE`, and `MODIFY STRUCTURE` commands.(See Chapter 11.) The following example uses the `ALTER TABLE` command to add primary and candidate indexes to table Employee.DBF:

```
OPEN DATABASE Company                                        && Create:
ALTER TABLE Employee  ADD PRIMARY KEY EmployID TAG EmployID  &&   Primary index
ALTER TABLE Employee  ADD UNIQUE SocSecNo TAG SocSecNo       &&   Candidate index
```

Primary and candidate indexes are always stored in a structural CDX index for its associated table.

The *REINDEX* Command

The REINDEX command re-creates all active IDX indexes and all the tags of active compound index files for the DBF file in the current work area. If an index is not active when index keys are modified in its associated table, the index can become outdated and you need to reindex it the next time you use it. In addition, indexes can be damaged due to a power failure or some other disaster. When this happens, you can use the REINDEX command to rebuild your indexes. The syntax is simply

```
REINDEX [COMPACT]
```

REINDEX salvages the tag name, the key expression, the blocksize parameter, the UNIQUE status, the tag types of all active indexes, and any FOR conditions. It throws away all the index nodes and releases the disk space. All the indexes are then re-created from scratch. If you specify the COMPACT keyword, standard IDX index files are converted to a compact IDX file.

The key expressions and other parameters are stored in the header of the index file. If the header is damaged (a rare occurrence in FoxPro), you have to use the INDEX command to re-create the index file.

Because Visual FoxPro is a multiuser product, the currently active DBF file must be in EXCLUSIVE mode before REINDEX can be executed, as in the following example:

```
USE Myfile INDEX MyIndex EXCLUSIVE
REINDEX
```

Using Indexes

If an index already exists, you can make it active with the USE and SET INDEX commands. The structural compound index file is automatically activated when its corresponding DBF file is placed in USE. All other CDX files and all IDX files are activated with the INDEX clause on the USE command or with the SET INDEX command.

When an index is active, it is updated whenever data in the database table (DBF file) is modified. In addition, you can assign an index to be the controlling index with any of the following:

- The USE command ORDER clause
- The SET ORDER TO command
- The USE command INDEX clause (IDX file only)
- The SET INDEX TO command (IDX file only)

A detailed discussion of the USE command syntax is provided in Chapter 11.

The *SET INDEX TO* Command

The SET INDEX TO command establishes IDX and nonstructural compound index files. You can also use this command to establish an IDX file as the controlling index. This is the syntax:

```
SET INDEX TO [? ¦ [<filename list>
        [ORDER <expFN> ¦ <expN> ¦ [TAG] <expFN>
        ¦ <expTN> [OF <expFN>]]] [ASCENDING ¦ DESCENDING ]]
        [ADDITIVE]

<filename list> ::= <expFN1> ¦ <expTN1> [OF <expFN2>],
    <expFN3> ¦ <expTN>  [OF <expFN4>],…
```

<filename list> can contain an arbitrary combination of compound index and IDX files. As usual, the filename and tag names can be a name or a character expression. If ? is used, index files can be selected from the directory pop-up.

If you use the SET INDEX TO command with no arguments, all indexes are closed for the current database table (DBF file), except the structural compound index file. An IDX file can be established as the controlling index by placing it first in the <filename list> argument.

In FoxPro, the best way to establish the controlling index is with the ORDER clause. The ORDER clause defines the controlling index and can be either a compound index file tag name or an index filename. You must use the OF clause to specify the CDX file, as long as it is not the structural CDX filename. The numeric value, <expN>, refers to the index in the order that the indexes are specified. Forget the form of the ORDER clause that uses a numeric expression (<expN>). It can be too difficult to figure out. Use the IDX or CDX index names instead.

The SET INDEX TO command first closes all currently opened index files except the structural compound index file in the current work area. The index files are then opened in the order specified. If the first index file opened is an IDX file, it becomes the controlling index file. The number of CDX and IDX files that can be opened simultaneously for each active DBF file are limited by the number of available file handles.

After the ORDER clause, you can specify the ASCENDING or DESCENDING keyword that specifies the order in which records are displayed or accessed. This keyword doesn't affect the index. It only indicates the access direction.

Whenever you establish existing indexes with the SET INDEX TO command, any open IDX or CDX is closed, except the structural CDX file. However, if you specify the ADDITIVE keyword, any open index files remain open.

The *SET ORDER TO* Command

The SET ORDER TO command designates which of the indexes that are open for the current DBF file will become the controlling index. The controlling index controls the access sequence of the records. This is the syntax:

```
SET ORDER TO [<expN> ¦ <expFN1> ¦ [TAG] <expTN>
        [OF <expFN2>] [ASCENDING ¦ DESCENDING]] [ADDITIVE]
```

The <*expN*> argument specifies an IDX filename or CDX tag that becomes the controlling index. The `OF` clause is required only if it is needed to establish a unique choice. In other words, if more than one open CDX tag or IDX file has the same name as the one specified, the `OF` clause is required to distinguish which tag to establish as the controlling index.

The `TO` clause can be any one of the following:

- A numeric expression, which can be used only when IDX files are open. FoxPro supports this option only for the sake of FoxBASE+ and dBASE III compatibility. The range of values is from `0` to `25`. A `0` is the same as no argument. The selected index corresponds to the order in which index files are specified with the `USE` command `INDEX` clause or the `SET INDEX` command.
- A literal IDX filename (<*expFN1*>).
- A literal CDX tag name (used only if a CDX file is open). The `TAG` keyword is optional (`[TAG] <expTN>[OF <expFN2>]`).
- A Character type expression that results in a tag or index filename when evaluated (used only when a CDX file is open).
- No argument, which designates no controlling index, in which case record positioning follows a natural order (by record number). Open index files and tags are still updated.

The `ASCENDING` and `DESCENDING` keywords specify the order in which records are displayed or accessed. These keywords don't affect the index. They only indicate the access direction.

The following examples demonstrate methods of establishing indexes:

Command Window	*Results and Comments*
`USE SALES EXCLUSIVE`	
`INDEX ON FIRSTNAME`	`(Structural CDX Tag FIRSTNAME)`
`TAG FIRSTNAME`	`5 Records Indexed`
`INDEX ON LASTNAME`	`5 Records Indexed`
`TO LASTNAME (LASTNAME.IDX)`	
`INDEX ON RANK TO RANK`	`5 Records Indexed (RANK.IDX)`
`INDEX ON CITY TO CITY`	`5 Records Indexed (CITY.IDX)`
`SET INDEX TO LASTNAME, RANK,CITY`	`(LASTNAME.IDX is master index)`
`SET ORDER TO 3`	`Master index: CITY.IDX`
`IDXno = 2`	
`SET ORDER TO IDXno`	`Master index: RANK.IDX`
`SET ORDER TO CITY`	`Master Index: City.IDX`
`tag1 = "CITY"`	`CITY`
`SET ORDER TO (tag1)`	`Master Index: CITY.IDX`
`SET ORDER TO`	`(Table is in natural order)`
`SET ORDER TO 1`	`Master Index: LASTNAME.IDX`

```
SET ORDER TO 2                    Master Index: RANK.IDX
SET ORDER TO 3                    Master Index: CITY.IDX
SET ORDER TO 4                    Master Index: SALES.CDX
                                  Tag: LASTNAME
```

You can establish index files (CDX, IDX, or both) using the following:

```
USE SALES INDEX City IN 3                && Use DBF and IDX file in
                                         && work area 3; City
                                         && becomes master index
USE SALES INDEX IDXFILE OF CDXFILE IN 3  && Establish indexes
                                         && and IDXFILE becomes
                                         && the master index
SET ORDER TO 0 IN 3                      && Positioning is in natural order
```

If the CDXFILE index file has three tags—`LASTNAME`, `SALES`, and `RANK`—you make the `SALES` tag the controlling index as follows, using either of the two commands:

```
USE MyDbF INDEX IDXFILE,CDXFILE ORDER SALES
SET ORDER TO SALES
```

The *SEEK* Command

The `SEEK` command performs an indexed search for the evaluated expression value in the currently active DBF file controlling index. If a match is found, the record pointer is repositioned to the record with the index key that matches the expression value. This is the syntax:

```
SEEK <exp>
```

If the search is not successful and `SET TALK` is `ON`, the message `No find` appears and the `FOUND()` function returns `.F.`. If the search is not successful and `SET NEAR` is `OFF`, the record pointer is positioned to the end of the file record and the `EOF()` function returns `.T.`. If `SET NEAR` is `ON`, the record is positioned on the first record that has a higher logical sequence of the two records that bound the value of the search key.

If the search is successful, `FOUND()` returns `.T.` and `EOF()` returns a false value (`.F.`).

Look at the following example:

```
USE Sales
INDEX ON UPPER(City) TAG City
SEEK "GREENVIEW"
IF FOUND()
        DISPLAY WHILE UPPER(City) = "GREENVIEW"
ELSE
        ? "Record was not found"
ENDIF
```

The resulting output is the following:

Record#	LASTNAME	FIRSTNAME	CITY	SALES	RANK	HIREDATE
3	Black	Hamil	Greenview	12841.00	5	11/12/88
5	Brook	Jerry	GREENVIEW	32381.00	2	02/03/81

The `SEEK` command respects any restrictions imposed by the `SET FILTER`, `SET EXACT`, and `SET DELETED` commands. For `SET EXACT`, this means that if `SET EXACT` is `ON`, the expression value must match the complete string. If `SET EXACT` is `OFF`, the search value must match only the index key, character for character, beginning at the left up to the length of the search value.

The *FIND* Command

The `FIND` command works like the `SEEK` command, except that a literal string is specified instead of an expression. For program applications, `SEEK` is more efficient than `FIND`. Here's why. The only way you can use a variable to designate a literal value is with a macro. Command lines containing macros have to be recompiled in FoxPro. Compiling a line of code slows down performance, and as a result, programs containing macros run slowly.

One use for the antiquated `FIND` command does remain: doing ad hoc queries from the Command window. This is the syntax:

```
FIND [<left string delimiter>]<character string>
       [<right string delimiter>]

<character string>       ::= Any number of characters
<left string delimiter>  ::= " | ' | [
<right string delimiter> ::= " | ' | ]
```

The `FIND` command trims blank spaces from the character string. Therefore, if you search for a key that begins with spaces, enclose the character string in quotation marks, as in the following example:

Command Window	*Results and Comments*
`USE Sales ORDER Lastname`	`&& ordered by Lastname`
`SET NEAR OFF`	`&& The default setting`
`FIND Green`	
`? Firstname, Lastname`	`Jim Green`
`? FOUND(), EOF()`	`.T. .F.`
`FIND Blue`	`No find.`
`? Firstname, Lastname`	`( End of file record)`
`? FOUND(), EOF()`	`.F.  .T.`
`Find "Green"`	
`? Firstname, Lastname`	`Jim Green`
`? FOUND(), EOF()`	`.T.  .F.`
`SET NEAR ON`	
`FIND Brough`	`No find.`
`? Firstname, Lastname`	`Jerry Brook`
`? FOUND(), EOF()`	`.F.  .F.`

The *SEEK()* Function

The SEEK() function performs an index search in a specified work area. It returns .T. if the index key is found and .F. if the index key is not found. This is the syntax:

```
SEEK(<exp> [,<expWA>]  [,<expN> ¦ <expFN> ¦ <expC>] )
```

If no work area is defined, the current work area is used. The SEEK() function evaluates the specified expression and tries to find its value in the controlling index. The SEEK() function works like the SEEK command, except that it returns the same value as the FOUND() function. The third argument defines either an index tag number (<expN>), an index file name (<expFN>), or the name of an active tag (<expC>). If specified, the index is used for the seek operation and after the seek operation is complete, the original controlling index is restored.

The *LOOKUP()* Function

You might decide not to use the powerful LOOKUP() function because it appears to be complicated. If you look at it closely, however, you probably will use it. The LOOKUP() function searches for a record in the specified DBF file and if the record is found, returns the value of a field. This is the syntax:

```
LOOKUP(<field name1> , <exp> , <field name2> [,<expTag>])
```

The <*field name1*> argument is the name of a database field. If the search is successful, the value of that field is returned. If the search is not successful, values are returned as follows:

- Character fields return a null value.
- Logical fields return .F..
- Float and Number fields return the largest number.
- Date fields return { / / }.

The data type of the value returned is the same as the type for this field. If this field is not in the current work area, it must contain the alias name in the field specification (for example, alias->field or alias.field).

The <*exp*> argument is an expression that is evaluated and compared with the values for <*field name2*> in the look-in database table, the DBF file in which the search is performed. It must evaluate to the same data type as <*field name2*>.

The <*field name2*> argument is the name of the field in the look-in database table. If this field is not in the current work area, it must contain an alias name in the field specification for the look-in database table (for example, alias.field).

The LOOKUP() function searches the look-in database table for a value of <*exp*> that is equal to the value of <*field name2*>. If this is found, it positions the record pointer in the look-in database table to the record in which the value was found, and then returns the value of <*field name1*>. The FOUND() flag in the look-in database table is set to reflect the outcome of the search.

LOOKUP() is a smart function. It searches the active indexes of the look-in database table for an index key equal to *<field name2>*. If it finds this key, it establishes it as the controlling index and does a SEEK operation to find the value. LOOKUP() then reestablishes the original controlling index for the look-in database table. If LOOKUP() can't find a key, it searches sequentially for the target value in the look-in database table. It operates like the LOCATE command, and Rushmore optimization is used, if possible.

If you provide LOOKUP() with the fourth argument (the tag name), it doesn't need to search for index tags; it finds the record by using the index tag specified as the fourth argument. If the tag name is specified, the Rushmore index optimization isn't used because an indexed seek is performed.

You can use the returned value of the LOOKUP() function in an expression in the same way that you can with any other function, as in the following example:

```
?  3.0 + Time * LOOKUP( Table.Rate,  Value*3,  Table.X)
?  IIF(LOOKUP(ABC.Value, X*Y, ABC.CNO) = XNO), ;
       "I Found it","Sorry, Charlie")
?  LOOKUP(Cust.Firstname, Cno, Cust.Custno) ;
       + " "+ Cust.Lastname
```

The output is the following:

```
767.33
Sorry, Charlie
Charlie Brown
```

The LOOKUP() function is useful for looking up a value in a table. It is often used in a UDF (user-defined function) that is called from an @ command VALID clause. It can replace many other commands. In the following example, the state tax rate lookup function is performed without using the LOOKUP() function:

```
USE DlySALES   && Daily Sales DBF
SELECT 0
USE ST_TAX ORDER State
REPLACE All Total WITH Cost*( 1 + STATE_TAX( State))
RETURN

FUNCTION STATE_TAX
PARAMETER TheState
PRIVATE Save_Alias, Tax
Save_Alias = ALIAS()  && Save current work area
SELECT ST_TAX         && Select the work area for ST_TAX.DBF
SEEK TheState         && Search for state
*
*  The tax rate is returned state is found.
Tax = IIF ( FOUND(), Tax_Rate, 0 )
SELECT (Save_Alias)
RETURN TAX
```

The preceding example is a fairly simple and straightforward operation. However, it can be much simpler. You can discard the STATE_TAX function and replace the STATE_TAX function call in the REPLACE command. Here is the same program using the LOOKUP() function:

```
USE DlySALES  IN 2 && Daily Sales DBF
USE ST_TAX ORDER State
REPLACE ALL Total WITH Cost*(1.0 + ;
LOOKUP( ST_TAX.Tax_Rate, DYLSALES.State, ST_TAX.State ) )
RETURN
```

Incidentally, the structures of the two database tables used in the previous examples are the following:

```
Structure for table: F:\FOXPRO\DLYSALES.DBF
Number of data records:        5
Date of last update    : 08/27/92
      Field  Field Name    Type        Width     Dec     Index
      1      LASTNAME      Character     15
      2      FIRSTNAME     Character     15
      3      ADDRESS       Character     15
      4      CITY          Character     15
      5      STATE         Character     15
      6      COST          Numeric       10      2
      7      TOTAL         Numeric       10
** Total **                              96

Structure for table: F:\FOXPRO\ST_TAX.DBF
Number of data records:        4
Date of last update    : 08/27/92
Field  Field Name  Type        Width     Dec     Index
      1      STATE       Character     15
      2      TAX_RATE    Numeric       10      3
** Total **                            26
```

The *SET NEAR* Command

The SET NEAR command controls the positioning of the record pointer following an unsuccessful FIND or SEEK. In FoxBASE+ and dBASE III PLUS, the record pointer is always positioned at the end of the file if a key value was not located. In FoxPro, if SET NEAR is OFF (the default), FIND and SEEK work the same as they do in FoxBASE+.

But if SET NEAR is ON and a FIND or SEEK operation is unsuccessful, the record pointer is positioned to the record that has a key expression value that is nearest the pursued target value. The record pointer is positioned to the first encountered record with an index key higher in the index sequence than the pursued value. If no value is higher, the record pointer is positioned at the end of the file. When NEAR is ON and the seek is unsuccessful, the EOF() function returns .F., provided the pursued value is not higher than any key value in the DBF file. The FOUND() function determines whether SEEK was successful.

This is the syntax:

```
SET NEAR on ¦ OFF
```

In the CONFIG.FPW file, this is the syntax:

```
NEAR =  on ¦ OFF
```

The *CLOSE INDEX* Command

Although you can use the SET INDEX TO and USE commands to close an index in the current work area, the CLOSE INDEX command closes the IDX and nonstructural compound index files in all 10 work areas. This is the syntax:

```
CLOSE INDEX
```

The *DELETE TAG* Command

As you add more index tags, more processing time is required to update indexes. Consequently, your program slows down. Therefore, removing any index tags that you don't need is advantageous. Because index tags are stored in a compound index file, they are not actually files and cannot be removed using the ERASE command. To remove a tag from a CDX file, use the DELETE TAG command. You can use it also to close, but not delete, an IDX file. This is the syntax:

```
DELETE TAG <expFN1> ¦ <expTN1> [OF <expFN2>]
              [, <expFN3> ¦ <expTN2> [OF <expFN4>] ]… IN <expWA>

DELETE TAG ALL [OF <expFN>] IN <expWA>
```

If you specify the TAG clause, an index tag is deleted from a compound index file. If you specify the OF clause, the index tag is deleted from the designated compound index file. If you don't specify the OF clause, the index tag is deleted from the structural compound index file. If all the tags are removed from a compound index file, the compound index file is deleted.

The DELETE TAG command accepts the specification of IDX files if they are active. However, the command closes the IDX files and does not delete them.

If you specify the ALL keyword, all index tags in the specified CDX file are deleted. If you don't specify a CDX filename, all index tags are deleted from the structural CDX file.

The IN *<expWA>* clause specifies the work area of the table to which the blank record is appended.

In a multiuser environment, the DBF file must be in EXCLUSIVE use mode before this command is executed. If it is not and this command is executed, an error message appears.

Copying Indexes and Tags

The COPY INDEXES command transfers IDX index files to compound index files. The COPY TAG command transfers multiple file index tags to IDX index files.

The *COPY INDEXES* Command

The COPY INDEXES command copies a list of active IDX files to a CDX file. This is the syntax:

```
COPY INDEXES <expFN1> [,<expFN2> ]… [TO <expFN2>]
```

```
COPY INDEXES ALL [TO <expFN>]
```

The INDEX clause specifies a list of active index files. The TO clause specifies the name of the compound index file to which the index is transferred. If you don't specify the TO clause, the indexes are transferred to the structural compound index file. If the target compound index file doesn't exist, it is created. The value of SET SAFETY is respected.

If the target compound index file is active, the new tag is added and the file remains active. If the target index file is not active, it is opened, the new tag is added, and the target index is closed.

The process of adding a new tag involves adding the tag name and key to the compound index file tag directory and then creating a whole new index for the tag.

The *COPY TAG* Command

The COPY TAG command copies an active compound index file tag to an IDX file. This is the syntax:

```
COPY TAG <expTN> [OF <expFN>] TO <expFN>
```

The TAG clause defines an active compound index file tag name. If the tag name is not unique among the active indexes, you must supply the OF clause to define the compound index file. The TO clause is the name of the IDX file that will be created. The value of the SET SAFETY flag is respected. If the target file is an active index, the *<filename>* already exists error message appears and the operation is canceled.

Index Functions

FoxPro supports a group of functions that relate to index files and indexed data access. These functions are presented in this section.

The *DESCENDING()* Function

This is the syntax:

```
DESCENDING([[<expFN>],<expN>[,<expWA>]])
```

The DESCENDING() function returns a logical true (.T.) value if the specified CDX index tag was created with a DESCENDING keyword. Otherwise, it returns a logical false (.F.) value.

The *FOR()* Function

This is the syntax:

```
FOR([[<expFN>],<expN>[,<expWA>]])
```

The `FOR()` function returns a character string containing the `FOR` expression specified when a CDX tag is created. It returns a null string in the following cases:

- When the tag does not exist
- When no `FOR` expression was specified when the CDX tag was created

The *FOUND()* Function

The `FOUND()` function returns `.T.` if the `FIND`, `LOCATE`, `SEEK`, and `CONTINUE` commands perform a successful search operation. If the operation is unsuccessful, `.F.` is returned. Each work area in FoxPro has an internal variable that is set to true as the result of a successful search. The `FOUND()` command simply returns that value. This is the syntax:

```
FOUND([<expWA>])
```

If you don't specify an alias name, the current work area is assumed.

When the `SET RELATION TO` command links DBF files, you can use the `FOUND()` function with the `SET FILTER TO` command to exclude parent records from a view if no corresponding record is in the subordinate file. This makes it easy to support inner joins. For example, given a customer and an order DBF file, the following example establishes an inner join:

```
SELECT 1
USE CUSTOMER
USE ORDERS IN 2 ORDER Custno
SET RELATION TO Custno INTO ORDERS
SET FILTER TO FOUND(2)
```

Records in the `CUSTOMER` DBF file do not display unless a corresponding record exists in the `ORDERS` DBF file.

The *KEYMATCH()* Function

This is the syntax of the `KEYMATCH()` function:

```
KEYMATCH(<exp>[,<expN1>[,<expWA>]])
```

The `KEYMATCH()` function searches the specified index tag for an index key (<*exp*>) and returns `.T.` if the index key is found. If it is not found, `.F.` is returned. This function does not reposition the pointer or change the controlling index. It provides a fast method to determine whether a duplicate record exists in a DBF file. For example, during an `APPEND` command, before you add a record, you can use the KEYMATCH() function with a VALID clause to determine whether a matching index key already exists in the file. If KEYMATCH() returns .T., you can prevent the user from appending a new record.

The KEYMATCH() function does not read records; it only examines the actual index keys. Consequently, it ignores the SET DELETED, SET FILTER, and SET KEY commands.

The example presented in Listing 13.1 illustrates the use of the KEYMATCH() function to restrict the entry of records with duplicate FIRSTNAME and LASTNAME fields.

Listing 13.1. The KEYFIND.PRG program source listing.

```
*******************************************************
* PROGRAM - keyfind.prg - append nonduplicate record
*
USE address
INDEX ON Firstname and Lastname TAG Name
DEFINE WINDOW  WAPPEND FROM 0,0 TO 8,40 PANEL
ACTIVATE WINDOW  WAPPEND
MOVE WINDOW  WAPPEND CENTER
DO WHILE .T.
        SCATTER MEMVAR BLANK
        @ 0,0 SAY "First Name" GET M.Firstname
        @ 1,0 SAY " Last Name" GET M.Lastname
        @ 2,0 SAY "   Address" GET M.Address
        @ 3,0 SAY "      City" GET M.City
        @ 4,0 SAY "     State" GET M.State
        @ 5,0 SAY "       Zip" GET M.Zip
        @ 6,0 SAY "     Phone" GET M.Phone
        READ
        IF READKEY() < 255
               EXIT
        ENDIF
*
* KEYMATCH() returns .T. if index key value is found
*
        IF KEYMATCH(M.Firstname+M.Lastname, TAGNO("name"))
               WAIT WINDOW "Duplicate entry"
        ELSE
*
* Append record since no duplicate record exists for name
*
               APPEND BLANK
               GATHER MEMVAR
        ENDIF
ENDDO
RELEASE WINDOW WAPPEND
```

Index File Parameter Functions

FoxPro has a group of functions that return index names, tags, and keys. These are shown in Table 13.6.

Table 13.6. Index file parameter functions.

Function	*Returned Character String*
`FOR()`	`FOR` expression of a specified CDX index tag.
`IDXCOLLATE()`	Correlation sequence of IDX file or CDX index tag.
`KEY()`	Key expression of a specified IDX file or CDX index tag.
`CDX()`	Name of a specified CDX file.
`MDX()`	Name of a specified CDX file (same as `CDX()`).
`NDX()`	Name of a specified IDX file.
`ORDER()`	Name of a controlling index file or CDX tag; this index is the primary order key.
`TAG()`	Name of specified IDX file or CDX tag.
Function	*Other Types of Values Returned*
`TAGCOUNT()`	The number of active index tags for the specified CDX file or work area. If no arguments are specified or if the CDX file is not specified, `TAGCOUNT()` returns the total number of active indexes in the specified work area. This count also includes active IDX files.
`TAGNO()`	The index tag number for the specified name of an index tag.
`UNIQUE()`	Logical true (`.T.`) value if the CDX key is a unique key; otherwise, it returns `.F.`.

The syntax for the index file parameter functions is the following:

```
FOR([[<expFN>],<expN>[,<expWA>]])
KEY([[<expFN> ], <expN> [, <expWA>]])
CDX([<expN> [, <expWA>]])
IDXCOLLATE(<expC> [,<expN1>[,<expWA>]])
MDX([<expN> [, <expWA>]])
NDX([<expN> [, <expWA>]])
ORDER([<expWA> [,1]])
TAG([[<expC> ], <expN> [, <expWA>]])
TAGCOUNT([<expFN>[,<expWA>]])
TAGNO([<expC>[,<expFN>[,<expWA>]]])
UNIQUE([[<expC>, ] <expN> [, <expWA>]])
```

The optional `<expWA>` argument defines a work area containing a DBF file with active index files. If it's not specified, the current work area is assumed.

The optional <expC> argument specified with the functions is supplied only if the designated index is a nonstructural compound index file tag.

The <expN> argument specified with the `KEY()`, `TAG()`, and `UNIQUE()` functions represents the order number of the IDX file or index tag in the index directory. The <expN> argument specified with the `CDX()` and `NDX()` functions represents the order number of the index files. For all of these functions, the order is established by the order in which the indexes were specified using the `USE` or `SET INDEX TO` commands. In general, IDX files are ordered first, followed by structural CDX files, which are followed by any specified CDX files.

If the order number is invalid, a null string is returned. If an invalid alias name is specified, the Alias not found message is displayed.

In the following example, a DBF file has a structural index with two index tags—`FIRSTNAME` and `LASTNAME`. Two IDX files named `PHONE` and `ZIP` and an additional CDX file named `MINDEX` are established using the `SET INDEX TO` command. `MINDEX` contains two index tags—`CITY` and `STATE`. Here is an example:

```
SET INDEX TO PHONE,ZIP, MINDEX
```

This command results in the following index order:

Index File	*Tag Name*	*Tag Order*	*CDX Number*	*IDX Number*
Index file: PHONE.IDX	`phone`	1		1
Index file: ZIP.IDX	`zip`	2		2
Structural CDX	`firstname`	3	1	
Structural CDX	`lastname`	4	1	
CDX file: MINDEX.CDX	`city`	5	2	
CDX file: MINDEX.CDX	`state`	6	2	

Listing 13.2 shows the active index tags and associated attributes for a DBF file in the current work area.

Listing 13.2. The INDLIST.PRG program source listing.

```
*************************************************
*  Program: INDLIST - Lists index tag attributes
*
USE address INDEX phone,zip,mindex
SET TALK OFF
I = 1
?  "Number of Tags", TAGCOUNT()
?  "Tagno()  A/D  U  Tag Name"
?? "Key expression" AT 30
?? "For Expression" AT 50
```

continues

Listing 13.2. continued

```
DO WHILE i <= TAGCOUNT()
        ? STR(TAGNO(TAG(I)),6)
        ?? DESCENDING() AT 10
        ?? UNIQUE() AT 13
        ?? TAG(I) AT 17
        ?? KEY(I) AT 30
        ?? FOR(I) AT 50
        I = I + 1
ENDDO
? "Controlling index: ", ORDER()
SET TALK ON
```

When you execute INDLIST.PRG, the following is displayed:

```
Number of Tags            6
Tagno()  A/D  U  Tag Name     Key expression     For Expression
1     .F..F. PHONE        PHONE
2     .F..F. ZIP          ZIP
3     .F..F. FIRSTNAME    FIRSTNAME
4     .F..F. LASTNAME     LASTNAME
5     .F..F. CITY         CITY
6     .F..F. STATE        STATE
Controlling index:  PHONE
```

You can retrieve the name of the controlling index with the `ORDER()` function. You can retrieve the name of the file containing the controlling index by adding the optional numeric arguments that follow:

Command Window	*Results and Comments*
`USE Sales ORDER Lastname`	Master index: F:\SALES.CDX, Tag: Lastname
`? ORDER()`	Lastname
`? ORDER("Sales", 1)`	F:\SALES.CDX

The *NORMALIZE()* Function

When you execute certain functions such as `KEY()` or `FOR()` that return a character string containing an expression, you'll notice that the expression is not necessarily in the form in which it was originally specified. It is in *normalized* form. The following changes are made to an expression to convert it to a normalized form:

- The character expression is converted to uppercase. However, embedded strings are not changed. An example of an embedded string is `"Elephant"` in the character expression `"LEFT('Elephant',1)"`.
- Any abbreviated FoxPro keywords in the character expression are expanded to their full length. For example, `"ALLT(TEXT)"` is expanded to `"ALLTRIM(TEXT)"`.
- Any `->` operators separating aliases from field names are converted to periods.

Many times you need to compare an expression with one of these normalized expressions. You can use the `NORMALIZE()` function to translate a character string containing an expression to a normalized form. Then you can compare that expression with the character string returned by some function such as `KEY()`, `FOR()`, or `SET("FILTER")`. This is the syntax:

```
NORMALIZE(<expC>)
```

In addition, the `NORMALIZE()` function checks the syntax of any FoxPro command or function within the character expression although the expression is not evaluated. If the syntax is incorrect, a syntax error is generated.

The `NORMALIZE()` function does not check for the existence of any fields, tables, memory variables, user-defined functions, or other references in the character expression.

For example, the `KEY()` function returns a character string containing a normalized expression. Use `NORMALIZE()` to convert a character expression supplied by a user into a normalized form that can be compared with the value returned by the `KEY()` function. The following code is an example of the use of the `NORMALIZE()` function:

```
Expr = "uppe(z->fname)+uppe(z->lname)"
IF KEY() = NORMALIZE( Expr )
```

The character string returned by the `NORMALIZE(Expr)` function is

```
"UPPER(Z.FNAME)+UPPER(Z.LNAME)"
```

Rushmore Data Access Technology

One feature supported by Visual FoxPro that sets it apart from other Xbase systems is its internal optimization data access technology, known as *Rushmore.* The name comes from Mount Rushmore National Memorial, near Keystone, South Dakota. Likenesses of the heads of Presidents Washington, Jefferson, Lincoln, and Theodore Roosevelt are carved on the face of Mount Rushmore. These sculptures were done by Gutzon Borglum and his sons. Although all this information might interest tourists visiting the Black Hills, it has nothing to do with the technology, and it has nothing to do with the fact that the mountain appeared in the Alfred Hitchcock movie *North by Northwest.* The relevance is that this movie appeared on TV the night before the FoxPro development team decided what to name its high-speed data access internal project, and the name Rushmore was adopted. Although the Rushmore technology has been around since FoxPro, the fact that Visual FoxPro is a 32-bit system means that it can access much larger memory buffers and, as a result, Rushmore is much more efficient in Visual FoxPro.

The nicest thing about the Rushmore technology is that it is automatic. You do not have to do anything. You run your programs without any changes. Rushmore does the rest. However, under rare circumstances, Rushmore might cause you grief. If you understand what these circumstances are, it is easy to avoid potential problems.

The Rushmore technology efficiently accesses sets of records at a speed comparable to that of sequential record access. The `SET FILTER TO` command, `LOCATE` command, and `FOR` clauses weren't used to access data records in extremely large database tables before Rushmore technology was available. This is because the `FOR` condition was tested for every single record in the file. `SEEK` was used instead of `LOCATE`. Before Rushmore, if you wanted to process a set of records in a large database table, you generally used the following code:

```
USE BIGFILE ORDER Account
Seek ACTNO
REPLACE QUANTITY WITH QTY+QUANTITY WHILE ACCOUNT = "1254-01"
```

You can do the same thing using Rushmore and the `FOR` clause, assuming an active `ACCOUNT` index key exists, using the following statement:

```
REPLACE QUANTITY WITH QTY+QUANTITY FOR ACCOUNT = "1254-01"
```

Rushmore uses the existing `ACCOUNT` index key to locate all records having an `ACCOUNT` field with a value of `"1254-01"`. Then the records are accessed many times faster than a sequential access.

With Rushmore, some complex database operations run hundreds of times faster than before. FoxPro enables personal computers to handle extremely large database tables, containing millions of records. The `FOR` expression doesn't need to be a simple expression. For example, if you also have an index on `STATE`, FoxPro uses Rushmore technology to optimize complex queries such as the following:

```
LIST FOR ACCOUNT = "1254-01" AND STATE = "Idaho"
LIST FOR ACCOUNT <> "1254-01" AND STATE != "Idaho"
AVERAGE Receipts FOR STATE = "OHIO" OR  STATE = "IDAHO"
SUM TOTAL FOR (ACCOUNT = "1254-01" AND STATE = "Idaho") AND ;
(ACCOUNT = "1745-99" AND STATE = "Kansas")
COUNT FOR ACCOUNT > "1254-01" .AND. STATE = "Vermont"
COUNT FOR NOT STATE = "OHIO"
```

In statements containing the `NOT` or `!` logical operators, as in the last statement, FoxPro doesn't look for an index containing a logical `NOT` operator. In the last example, FoxPro looks for an index key `STATE`. Then FoxPro chooses those records for the data set that do not satisfy the `STATE = "OHIO"` condition.

Table 13.7 lists the FoxPro operators that can be optimized.

Table 13.7. The operators that Rushmore can optimize.

Operator	*Description*
<	Less than
>	Greater than
=	Equal to
<=	Less than or equal to

Operator	*Description*
>=	Greater than or equal to
<>	Not equal to
#	Not equal to
!=	Not equal to

Rushmore uses almost any available, active indexes. This includes the CDX files and IDX files. An IDX file can be a standard IDX file used in earlier versions of FoxPro or compact IDX indexes used in FoxPro. Compressed IDX files access data much faster than standard IDX files because they are smaller and fewer disk accesses are required to read an index. In fact, a compressed IDX file can be as small as 1/16 the size of the standard IDX files. All CDX index files are compressed. Compression is part of the new index technology incorporated into FoxPro.

Rushmore doesn't use the controlling index or indexes that are unique or have a filter (INDEX ... FOR <*expL*>) for optimization. If the controlling index refers to a key that is needed for a query expression, you should issue the SET ORDER TO command to change the controlling index or restore the natural order before you do an optimized query. Whenever you index a file, the indexed file becomes the controlling index. If you index on a key only for a query, be sure to issue a SET ORDER TO command before you do the query, as in the following example:

```
USE STATE
INDEX ON POPULATION TAG POPULATION
SET ORDER TO   && Sequential access
CALCULATE MAX(POPULATION), MIN(POPULATION) FOR POPULATION > 2000
```

The Rushmore technique for rapid data access is to use the index to locate every record satisfying the condition and build in memory a table of record numbers. The table is used to access records. The more records included in a data set, the more memory required. If you have a huge data set that exceeds 500,000 records, you need at least 8MB before you can realize substantial speed improvements through the use of Rushmore. In fact, Visual FoxPro really needs 8MB for acceptable operating speed. If FoxPro doesn't have enough memory to optimize a query, the warning message Not enough memory for optimization appears. The query is then performed without the benefit of Rushmore—it uses the same slow technique used in FoxBASE+, FoxPro, and dBASE IV.

Rushmore improves performance of commands of single database operations with a FOR clause, which includes commands listed in Table 13.8. However, optimization is applied only to the commands with NEXT and ALL scope clauses, or if the command's default scope is ALL. Rushmore optimization is applied to data set operations that are filtered when a filter established by the SET FILTER TO is active.

Table 13.8. The data set commands that Rushmore can optimize.

APPEND FROM	LOCATE	REPLACE
AVERAGE	RECALL	REPORT
BROWSE	DELETE	SCAN
CALCULATE	DISPLAY	SORT
CHANGE	EDIT	SUM
COPY TO	EXPORT	TOTAL
COPY TO ARRAY	LABEL	
COUNT	LIST	

If the `WHILE` clause is specified in any of the commands in Table 13.8, Rushmore optimization is not performed.

The only way to benefit from Rushmore when you operate with multiple database tables is to use FoxPro's SQL `SELECT` command. This command is covered in detail in Chapter 18, "Queries Using SQL and the Query Designer." The SQL facility uses Rushmore to support multiple-database table query optimization. When you perform a query with the `SELECT` command, Rushmore not only uses existing indexes, but it creates new ad hoc temporary indexes as needed.

The `FOR` clause expression must be either a *basic optimizable expression* or a *complex optimizable expression.* A basic optimizable expression has one of the two following forms:

```
<index expression> <relational operator> <constant expression>

<constant expression> <relational operator> <index expression>
```

The *<index expression>* must match the expression on which an index is constructed, and it cannot contain aliased fields. You must use one of the operators listed in Table 13.7 as the *<relational operator>*. The *<constant expression>* can be any expression consisting of constants, memory variables, and fields from other unrelated database tables. It cannot contain any fields from the database table in the current work area on which the optimized query is performed. In the following example, a query is performed on the CENSUS.DBF table with index tags, `STATE`, `POPULATION`, and `GROWTH`. Here are some examples of commands using `FOR` with basic optimizable expressions:

```
USE Census
USE Cities IN 2 ORDER City
COUNT FOR STATE = "New York"
COUNT FOR GROWTH > 10
LIST FOR Population > ;
LOOKUP( Cities.Pop80, "New York", Cities.City )
ST = "Ohio"
COUNT FOR STATE != ST
COUNT FOR STATE < "O"
```

Here are some examples of commands containing a FOR clause that are not optimizable:

```
COUNT FOR RANK < 10   && There is no index key RANK
COUNT FOR Census.State  && ALIAS is used
* There is no Population/(1+Growth) index key
COUNT FOR Population/(1+Growth) > 200
COUNT FOR "N"$State     && Disallowed operator
```

Suppose the current database table is Cities.dbf, and you have a key on both CITY and STATE. The widths of the State and City fields are 14 and 20 respectively. Is the following command optimizable?

```
*                      12345678901234
LIST FOR STATE+CITY = "New York      New York"
```

The command displays the proper record if SET EXACT is OFF. However, Rushmore optimization is not used because no STATE+CITY index key is present. The two ways to gain Rushmore optimization are to create a STATE+CITY index key, or preferably, to change the query to

```
LIST FOR STATE = "New York" AND CITY = "New York"
```

As shown in the last example, you can combine simple and complex expressions with an AND or OR logical operator to form a complex expression. In addition, you can apply a unary NOT operator to an expression to form a complex expression. If a complex expression contains both optimizable and nonoptimizable expressions, it is referred to as a *partially* optimizable complex expression. The resulting complex expression may or may not be optimizable. Complex expressions formed by optimizable expressions are always optimizable. Don't think that you can't achieve improved performance from partially optimizable expressions. For example, suppose you have a database table that contains all engineers in the United States, and you have indexes on the State and City fields. You could form a partially optimizable FOR expression to display engineers in Santa Clara, California, named Smith, as follows:

```
USE ENGINEER
LIST FOR State = "California" AND ;
City = "Santa Clara" AND LNAME = "Smith"
```

Rushmore data retrieval optimization uses the STATE and CITY index keys to select the data set. Then the LIST command uses the resulting data set to select engineers named Smith to display. The query is completed much faster than if FoxPro 1, FoxBASE+, or dBASE had done it. You can also use parentheses to group basic expressions, as in the following example:

```
USE ENGINEER
LIST FOR State = "California" AND ;
        City = "Santa Clara" AND ;
        (LNAME = "Smith" OR LNAME = "Jones")
```

Table 13.9 presents rules for forming FOR expressions. The table indicates that a complex expression formed by other expressions can be optimizable, partially optimizable, or fully optimizable. This distinction has no effect on the operation of a command. It affects only the speed with which the command performs its operation.

Table 13.9. Rules for combining FOR expressions.

Basic Expression	*Operator*	*Basic Expression*	*Results*
Optimizable	AND	Optimizable	Fully Optimizable
Optimizable	OR	Optimizable	Fully Optimizable
Optimizable	AND	Not Optimizable	Partially Optimizable
Optimizable	OR	Not Optimizable	Not Optimizable
Not Optimizable	AND	Not Optimizable	Not Optimizable
Not Optimizable	OR	Not Optimizable	Not Optimizable
	NOT	Optimizable	Fully Optimizable
	NOT	Not Optimizable	Not Optimizable
Complex Expression	*Operator*	*Complex Expression*	*Results*
Fully Optimizable	AND	Fully Optimizable	Fully Optimizable
Fully Optimizable	OR	Fully Optimizable	Fully Optimizable
Fully Optimizable	AND	Partially Optimizable	Partially Optimizable
Fully Optimizable	OR	Partially Optimizable	Partially Optimizable
Fully Optimizable	AND	Not Optimizable	Partially Optimizable
Fully Optimizable	OR	Not Optimizable	Not Optimizable
	NOT	Fully Optimizable	Fully Optimizable
Partially Optimizable	AND	Partially Optimizable	Partially Optimizable
Partially Optimizable	OR	Partially Optimizable	Partially Optimizable
Partially Optimizable	AND	Not Optimizable	Partially Optimizable
Partially Optimizable	NOT	Not Optimizable	Not Optimizable
	NOT	Partially Optimizable	Partially Optimizable
Not Optimizable	AND	Not Optimizable	Not Optimizable
Not Optimizable	OR	Not Optimizable	Not Optimizable
	NOT	Not Optimizable	Not Optimizable

When a command that utilizes Rushmore executes, Rushmore uses the indexes to determine which records satisfy the FOR clause condition and includes them in a data set. The command manipulates the records in the data set. Here is where the problem occurs. Commands rarely modify index keys while they are executing. But if you ever encounter this situation, be sure to disable Rushmore before you execute the command. For example, look at the following line:

```
REPLACE ALL ZDate WITH ZDate + 90 FOR ZDATE < {12/1/93}
```

NOTE

If the command alters any of the index keys in the `FOR` clause expression while processing the data set, the data set becomes obsolete—that is, it is no longer valid.

You can disable Rushmore by including the `NOOPTIMIZE` keyword with an individual command. You can globally disable or enable Rushmore with the `SET OPTIMIZE OFF` or `SET OPTIMIZE ON` commands, respectively. The default setting is `ON`.

Improving Rushmore Optimization Performance

You can take certain steps to improve the performance of Rushmore operations. If you understand these techniques, you will better appreciate the power of Rushmore technology:

1. Avoid the use of the `INDEX` command index clause.

   Rushmore does not use index keys containing a filter. For instance, Rushmore does not use the following index key for optimization in the following example:

   ```
   INDEX ON City FOR Population > 100000 TAG City
   LIST FOR City > 200000  && Rushmore not used
   ```

2. Set index order to sequential order whenever possible using the `SET ORDER TO 0` command.

   As you probably know, when you list a file in sequential order, the speed of the display is much faster than if you list a file with an indexed order. With Rushmore technology, this is also true. Unless you need a report generated or records processed in a specific order, it is best to use `SET ORDER TO 0` before you execute a command that uses Rushmore optimization so the command executes faster.

3. If you use `SET DELETE ON`, you need to create a `DELETED()` tag.

   If you are processing a database table using Rushmore, and you use `SET DELETE ON`, FoxPro must look at each record as it builds an internal table of records from the indexes. This slows down processing. You can improve processing by creating an index tag with a key of `DELETED()`. Rushmore detects the tag and uses it to determine whether a record is deleted rather than having to read the data record, which speeds up processing considerably.

4. Do not use the `NOT` logical operator for index tags.

   Perhaps you never use the `NOT` keyword in an expression. Other Xbase programs do not allow logical index tags. However, FoxPro does and users have found them useful especially for the `DELETED()` key. But if you use the `NOT` logical operator, Rushmore ignores the key. For example, use an index key such as `DELETED()` and do not use `NOT DELETED()` to speed up performance. You can use the `DESCENDING` keyword when you issue a `SET ORDER TO` command. For example, the following two code fragments are equivalent:

```
* Fragment 1 (LIST runs slowest - No Rushmore)
USE AFile
SET DELETED ON
INDEX ON NOT DELETED() TAG DEL
REPLACE ALL Salary WITH 1.1*Salary WHILE DELETED()
SET ORDER TO
LIST
* Fragment 2 (LIST runs faster with Rushmore)
USE AFile
SET DELETED ON
INDEX ON DELETED() TAG DEL
SET ORDER TO DEL DESCENDING
REPLACE ALL Salary WITH 1.1*Salary WHILE DELETED()
SET ORDER TO
LIST
```

5. Be aware that simple expressions might run more slowly with Rushmore.

   Rushmore is most powerful when you use a complex expression. You can examine specific procedures, and with a little analysis and testing, you'll find certain operations run faster without Rushmore. In the following example, the record selection condition is a basic expression, `STATE = "New York"`. For example, consider the following two code fragments:

```
* Fragment 1 (runs slowest with Rushmore)
USE Salesman  && No order
REPLACE ALL Pay WITH Salary + Comm ;
FOR STATE = "New York"
...

* Fragment 2 (runs faster - no Rushmore)
USE Salesman ORDER State
SEEK "New York"
REPLACE ALL Pay WITH Salary + Comm ;
WHILE STATE = "New York"
...
```

The second fragment runs faster, especially if you're processing a very large file. This is because Rushmore uses memory to hold the record reference for the data set; therefore, less memory is available for I/O buffering and processing is consequently slowed down. On the other hand, the data access method between the two cases is approximately equivalent. However, if the `FOR` clause expression is complex (`STATE = "New York" AND City = "Brooklyn"`), the first code fragment runs faster. What is important is that if you're attempting to speed up an application, you should try different techniques to discover the fastest method.

Summary

This chapter discussed the physical and logical ordering of DBF files—in particular, the function and use of the following commands: `SORT`, `INDEX`, `REINDEX`, `SEEK`, `FIND`, `COPY INDEXES`, `COPY TAGS`, `CLOSE INDEX`, `DELETE TAG`, and `SET ORDER TO`.

The chapter explains FoxPro Rushmore technology, and it covers the following FoxPro functions that are used with indexes: `DESCENDING()`, `FOUND()`, `KEY()`, `LOOKUP()`, `CDX()`, `KEYMATCH()`, `NDX()`, `ORDER()`, `SEEK()`, `TAG()`, `TAGCOUNT()`, `TAGNO()`, and `UNIQUE()`.

You have now learned about most of the procedural components of the FoxPro language. In Chapter 14, "Object-Oriented Programming," you will be reoriented. You'll learn about object-oriented programming (OOP), but you will still need most of the procedural language commands to program the OOP methods.

III

Object-Oriented Programming

14

Object-Oriented Programming

Inanimate objects are classified scientifically into three major categories—those that don't work, those that break down and those that get lost.

—Russell Baker (b. 1925)

This chapter teaches you about the object-oriented elements of Visual FoxPro. You will learn about classes, objects, properties, methods, and events and how to use them and how they are all related. You will learn how to define a class and how to use that class to create an object.

Naming Conventions

Throughout this book, I have used the name conventions that are fairly standard in the FoxPro 2.*x* and dBASE IV world. Along with the reorientation from procedural Xbase code to Visual FoxPro object-oriented programming (OOP), you will also be introduced, in this chapter, to new naming conventions for objects, classes, and even program variables.

Microsoft has decided to adopt a new standard set of naming conventions and to introduce them with Visual FoxPro 3. If these conventions are accepted and used by all developers, it will be easier to develop, maintain, and exchange software. The naming conventions proposed by Microsoft are based on recommendations by the Microsoft staff and other experienced developers in the Visual Basic user community. Since Visual FoxPro's object-oriented model and methodology are generally derived from Visual Basic, naming conventions that are similar to other Microsoft products, such as Access and Visual Basic for Windows, were adopted.

Microsoft's Object Naming Conventions

The Visual Basic standards designate that each object name begin with a three-character, lowercase prefix that designates the type of object. Each distinct word in the name should be capitalized without underscores. Table 14.1 provides a list of prefix values for different types of objects.

Table 14.1. Standard naming convention prefixes for Visual FoxPro objects.

Keyword	*Object*	*Prefix*	*Example*
`CheckBox`	Check box	`chk`	`chkMarried`
`ComboBox`	Combo box	`cbo`	`cboLanguage`
`CommandButton`	Command button	`cmd`	`cmdOK`
`CommandGroup`	Command button	`cmg`	`cmgNavigation`
`Control`	Control	`ctl`	`ctlMyControl`
	Directory list box	`dir`	`dirSourceFiles`
	Drive list box	`drv`	`drvTargetFiles`
`Custom`	User-defined class	`udc`	`udcBirthday`
`DataEnvironment`	Database environment	`dbe`	`dbeInventory`

Keyword	*Object*	*Prefix*	*Example*
`EditBox`	Edit box	`edb`	`edbComments`
	File list box	`fil`	`filSource`
	Frame	`fra`	`fraGeneralOptions`
`Form`	Form [1]	`frm`	`frmDataEntry`
`FormPage`	Form page	`frp`	`frmDataEntry`
`FormSet`	Form [1]	`frs`	`frmDataEntry`
	Graph/chart	`gra`	`graWeeklyProfits`
`Grid`	Grid	`grd`	`grdBrowser`
`Column`	Grid column	`grc`	`grdBrowser`
`Header`	Grid header	`grh`	`grdBrowser`
`Image`	Image	`img`	`imgBitmap`
`Label`	Label	`lbl`	`lblHelpMessage`
`Line`	Line [2]	`lin`	`linHorizontal`
`ListBox`	List box	`lst`	`lstCities`
	Menu	`mnu`	`mnuEdit`
`OLEControl`	OLE bound control	`ole`	`oleObject`
`OLEBoundControl`	OLE bound control	`ole`	`oleObject`
`OptionButton`	Option button	`opt`	`optChoices`
`OptionGroup`	Option button group	`opg`	`opgChoices`
`Page`	Page	`lin`	`linHorizontal`
`PageFrame`	Page frame	`lin`	`linHorizontal`
`Relation`	Two table relation	`rel`	`relView`
`Separator`	Toolbar separator	`sep`	`sepBar`
`Shape`	Shape [3]	`shp`	`shpRectangle`
`Spinner`	Spinner	`spn`	`spnNumberOfCopies`
`TextBox`	Text box	`txt`	`txtInformation`
`Timer`	Timer	`tmr`	`tmrAlarmClock`
`Toolbar`	Toolbar button	`btn`	`btnPrevious`

[1]You can add an s or an m character to the `frm` prefix to denote a subform or MDI form.

[2]A line can be vertical, horizontal, or diagonal.

[3]A shape can be a circle, a square, an oval, a rectangle, a rounded rectangle, or a rounded square.

Microsoft's Variable Naming Conventions

Variables are used less often in Visual FoxPro than in traditional FoxPro. The capability of using and manipulating object names directly without the need of assigning a variable to each object will reduce variable use. The naming conventions proposed by Microsoft adopt the use of Hungarian notation. Every variable begins with a two-character, lowercase prefix. The first character designates the variable scope. The second character designates the variable type. Each keyword in the variable name is capitalized without underscores. Only one character, `o`, is used to designate an object instance. An object name contains the object's scope and type. Microsoft's naming convention for variable scope types is presented in Table 14.2. The naming convention for variable data types is presented in Table 14.3.

Table 14.2. Microsoft's naming convention prefix characters for Visual FoxPro variables scope types.

Scope Type	*Keyword*	*Prefix*	*Example*
Private	`PRIVATE`	`p`	`pcCity`
Public	`PUBLIC`	`g`	`gcTemperature`
Local	`LOCAL`	`l`	`lnIndicator`
Form		`f`	`fnInstance`
Form Set		`t`	`tOpened`
Object Instance	`o`	`o`	`MyNiceObject`
Class		*<none>*	`CheckBox`
Constant (`#DEFINE`)	`ALLCAPS`	`TRUE`	

Table 14.3. Naming convention prefix characters for Visual FoxPro variables data types.

Data Type	*Prefix*	*Example*
Array	`a`	`aMyArray`
Character	`c`	`cCustomer`
Currency	`y`	`ySalary`
Date	`d`	`dSold`
DateTime	`t`	`tRecorded`
Double	`b`	`bValue`
Float	`f`	`fResults`
General	`g`	`gWaveSound`
Logical	`l`	`lJointReturn`

Data Type	*Prefix*	*Example*
Memo	`m`	`mAbstract`
Numeric	`n`	`nAge`
Picture	`p`	`pLandscape`

Tell Me Again—What Is a Class?

As you recall from Chapter 2, "Database Management and the FoxPro Language," a class is a template or a pattern for an object. It defines an object's properties (color, size, position, and so on), methods, and event code. *Methods* are blocks of code (procedures and functions) that are called from other methods or events to perform some operation on an object. For example, one of the methods supported by a `ListBox` object is `AddItem`. The method is called to add an item to the list box. *Event code* is code that executes when an event occurs. Event code can also be called from a program.

A subclass is a new class definition for an object that uses another class definition as a starting point. The subclass definition inherits properties, methods, and events from its parent class. When you define your own class in Visual FoxPro, it is derived from built-in base classes in Visual FoxPro.

How Do I Define a Class?

You can create a class or subclass visually by using the Class Designer or the Form Designer utility, or you can create a class programmatically. You will find that it is a lot easier to define a class with Form Designer or Class Designer. However, you have to learn so many unrelated things that you can lose sight of the basic fundamentals of creating classes and objects. In this chapter you will learn how to use Class Designer to design a class. Chapter 19, "The Form Designer," describes how to use Form Designer to define a class. But first, I will show you how to define a class programmatically and use that class to create and use an object.

How Do I Write a Program to Define a Class?

When you define a class or subclass in a program, you use the `DEFINE CLASS` code structure, which consists of a group of commands that are placed at the end of a procedure. The code that defines a class is not executed. Its purpose is to define the properties, events, and methods for the class or subclass. Executable code is placed at the beginning of the procedure. The executable code is normally very simple. It sets things up, creates objects by using the

CREATEOBJECT() command, and activates the objects. The objects do the rest. The code in the object's event code executes in response to events, and the object's properties and methods govern how the object behaves. The objects are self-contained. Furthermore, most code is defined within the Visual FoxPro built-in base classes. User-defined classes are derived from these base classes. You only need to write methods and event code related to the specific needs of your application. Also, you set properties of your user-defined, derived subclasses to meet the specific needs of your application. For example, you need to define the size, position, and caption of a button control. You also need to define what action takes place when an event, such as the user clicking on the button, occurs. Everything else is taken care of by the Visual FoxPro base class.

Here is the syntax of the basic DEFINE CLASS shell:

```
DEFINE CLASS ClassName1 AS cBaseClass
    [[PROTECTED PropertyName1, PropertyName2 ...]
    PropertyName = eExpression ...]
    [ADD OBJECT [PROTECTED] ObjectName
          AS ClassName2 [NOINIT]
          [WITH cPropertylist]]...
    [[PROTECTED] FUNCTION ¦ PROCEDURE Name
      cStatements
    [ENDFUNC ¦ ENDPROC]]
         ...
ENDDEFINE
```

The Name of the Class or Subclass

To start, ClassName1 is the name of your class or subclass. It is the name to which you refer when you create an object with the CREATEOBJECT() function. Here is an example:

```
oMyObject = CREATEOBJECT("MyClass")
DEFINE CLASS MyClass AS Custom
...
ENDDEFINE
```

The *AS cBaseClass* Clause

You specify the name of the parent class with the AS cBaseClass clause, which is the class on which the defined class or subclass is based. The AS cBaseClass clause can be another user-defined class or subclass or it can be one of the Visual FoxPro base classes listed in Table 14.4.

Table 14.4. A description of the Visual FoxPro base classes.

Base Class	*Description*
CheckBox	Creates a check box.
ComboBox	Creates a combo box.
CommandButton	Creates a command button (push button).
CommandGroup	Creates a group of command buttons.

Base Class	*Description*
Container	Creates an object that contains other objects and allows access to the objects they contain. For example, if a Container object, A, which contains a control (,) is placed on a form, you can access the properties and methods of the B control.
Control	Creates a control object that can contain protected objects.
Cursor	Created when a table or view is added to the data environment for a form, formset, or report.
Custom	Creates a custom, user-defined object.
DataEnvironment	Creates a data environment when a form, formset, or report is created.
EditBox	Creates an edit box.
Form	Creates a form.
FormSet	Creates a form set (a collection of forms).
Grid	Creates a grid that is a container object and displays data in rows and columns. A grid is similar in appearance to a browse window.
Column	Creates a column in a grid control.
Header	Creates a header for a column in a grid.
Image	Creates an image control that displays a BMP picture.
Label	Creates a label control that you use to display text that users cannot change. It is similar to a FoxPro 2.6 @...SAY command.
Line	Creates a horizontal, vertical, or diagonal graphic line control.
ListBox	Creates a list box control that displays a list of items. You can select one or more of the items.
OLEControl	Creates an OLE 2 control. OLE 2 controls are external 32-bit DLLs with specialized functionality. Examples are Outline, Picture Clip, and communications shipped with Visual FoxPro.
OLEBoundControl	Creates an OLE bound control. These controls are bound to a General field in a table. You can access objects from other applications, such as Excel, Word, and Lotus 1-2-3, with an OLE bound control.

continues

Table 14.4. continued

Base Class	*Description*
OptionButton	Creates an option button (radio button).
OptionGroup	Creates a set of option buttons.
Page	Creates a page in a page frame.
PageFrame	Creates a page frame to contain pages. Page frames can contain tabbed pages.
Relation	Created when you establish relationships from within the Data Environment Designer for a form, formset, or report.
Separator	Creates a separator object that you use to place space between controls in a toolbar.
Shape	Creates a shape control that displays a rectangle, circle, or ellipse.
Spinner	Creates a spinner control that you use to choose a range of numeric values.
TextBox	Creates a text box in which you can edit the contents of a memory variable, an array element, or a field.
Timer	Creates an invisible timer control that executes code at specified time intervals.
ToolBar	Creates a custom toolbar.

All of the Visual FoxPro Base classes contain a complete definition of visual class objects. For example, when you create a form object based on a Visual FoxPro `Form` base class, you get a default form object. Then, you just change its properties and call its methods to make it behave and appear like you want it to. Try this:

1. Create a default Form object by typing the following statement into the Command window:

   ```
   oFirstForm = CREATEOBJECT("Form")
   ```

   A `Form` object named `oFirstForm` is created in memory.

2. Use the `Show` method to display your new form object by typing the following statement into the Command window:

   ```
   oFirstForm.Show
   ```

   Your form object appears in the Visual FoxPro main window. It is about 375 pixels wide and 250 pixels high. These values are the default `Width` and `Height` properties of a default form object.

3. Now let's change the `Width` property of your `oFirstForm` object, color it blue, and move it by typing the following three statements into the command window:

   ```
   oFirstForm.Width = 100
   oFirstForm.BackColor = RGB(0, 0, 255)
   oFirstForm.Move(50,50)
   ```

   Notice that your form gets narrower, turns blue, and moves to a new position. The details are not important, but you get the idea. The only thing left to do now is dispose of the form by releasing the object type memory variable.

4. Type the following statement into the Command window to clear the form from the screen and release it from memory:

   ```
   Release.oFirstForm
   ```

Here is a very simple program that contains the definition of a subclass, `MyForm`, which is based on the Visual FoxPro `Form` base class. Because none of the properties are used, the default size and position of the base class are used. The object, `oMyform`, is based on the user-defined class, `MyForm`, and is created with the `CREATEOBJECT()` function. The following listing contains the source of the program that creates and displays the `oMyform` object:

```
* Form1: Simple example of the creation of object oMyForm
PUBLIC  oMyForm     && Keep object around after program exit
oMyForm = CREATEOBJECT("MyForm")
oMyForm.Show()
DEFINE CLASS MyForm AS Form
   PROCEDURE CLICK
      RELEASE oMyForm
   ENDPROC
ENDDEFINE
```

When the object type memory variable, `oMyForm`, goes out of scope, the object is released. It is made public so that it will remain in scope when the program exits. The `Show()` function is a method in the `Form` base class and displays the `oMyForm` object. The `Click` procedure is a method that is called when you click on the `oMyForm` form. When the `Click` method executes to process a `Click` event, the object type memory variable is released, and the object is automatically destroyed. The `Form` base class also handles the destruction of the class.

NOTE

The memory variable, `oMyForm`, of type `O`, is actually a reference to an object of type `MyClass`. You can visualize an object as an internally encapsulated entity. You use a memory variable as an instrument to interface to the object. When a memory variable loses scope or is released (`RELEASED` *<memvar>*), the object is released from memory. As a result, the `Destroy` event fires and executes the `Destroy` method when the object is released.

Properties

Properties consist of similar memory variables. They have a name and an associated value like a memory variable. Also, you use an equals sign (=) to assign a default value to a property. However, a property is an element of a class. Properties are used to define the characteristics or attributes of a class and define how a class behaves. Classes and subclasses can have no properties or many properties. The Visual FoxPro base classes have many properties. In the following example, the `MyStuff` user-defined class is defined. It has four user-defined properties: `cItem`, `yCost`, `dDateBought`, and `nQuantity`. These properties are initialized to default values. Here is the class definition:

```
DEFINE CLASS MyStuff AS Custom
        cItem = ""
    yCost = $0.00
    dDateBought = { /  /  }
    nQuantity = 0
ENDDEFINE
```

Next, I can create an object defined by the `MyStuff` class by using the `CREATEOBJECT()` function:

```
oMyObject = CREATEOBJECT("MyStuff")
```

Now, I can access the object properties for `oMyObject` to store actual values using the following statements:

```
oMyObject.cItem = "RCA VCR"
oMyObject.yCost = $299.95
oMyObject.dDateBought = {12/23/34}
oMyObject.nQuantity = 1
```

You can even create an array of objects defined by the `MyStuff` user-defined subclass. Also, you can store the items in the properties of the objects for each array element. In the following example, field values from records in a table containing personal property inventory information is transferred to the user-defined properties of the `MyStuff` class objects. Each class object is referred to by an array element. The following program illustrates how to create an array of objects and store data in the user-defined properties of the objects:

```
********************************************************
* Program  MYSTUFF.PRG  - Illustrates how to create an array
*                         of objects. It stores data from
*                         a table in array of objects.
********************************************************
USE MyThings  && Table containing personal property
*                inventory
DIMENSION oMyObjects[RECCOUNT()]
nI=1
SCAN WHILE  !EOF()
    oMyObjects[nI]  = CREATEOBJECT("MyStuff")
    oMyObjects[nI].cItem       = MyThings.ItemName
    oMyObjects[nI].yCost       = MyThings.ItemCost
    oMyObjects[nI].dDateBought = MyThings.BoughtDate
    oMyObjects[nI].nQuantity   = MyThings.Quantity
    nI=nI+1
ENDSCAN
...
```

```
DEFINE CLASS MyStuff AS Custom
    cItem = ""
    yCost = $0.00
    dDateBought = { / / }
    nQuantity = 0
ENDDEFINE
```

In the preceding example, you can add methods that retrieve values, display values, and so forth. However, the purpose of the example is to illustrate how to create and access user-defined properties.

The Visual FoxPro built-in base classes have many properties. For example, Table 14.5 lists the available properties for the `Form` class. The list is fairly representative of the number of properties available for other base classes. When you are writing your own classes, you can use the Visual FoxPro help to find out which properties are available and how to use them. When you use Class Designer or Screen Designer, the properties are listed along with their default values. In many cases, you can change properties visually. Normally, you only have to change a few properties because the default values will be used for those properties you don't change.

Table 14.5. A list of the `Form` class properties.

ActiveControl	Controls	ForeColor	ParentClass
ActiveForm	ControlCount	FontTransparent	Movable
AlwaysOnTop	CurrentX	FontUnderline	Name
AutoCenter	CurrentY	HalfHeightCaption	ParentClass
BackColor	DataEnvironment	Height	Picture
BaseClass	DataSession	HelpContextID	RecordLocks
BorderStyle	DataSessionID	Icon	RecordSelector
BufferMode	Desktop	KeyPreview	ReleaseType
Caption	DrawMode	Left	ScaleMode
Class	DrawStyle	LockScreen	ShowTips
ClassLibrary	FillStyle	MaxButton	TabIndex
ClipControls	FontBold	MaxHeight	TabStop
Closable	FontItalic	MaxLeft	Top
FillColor	FontName	MaxTop	Visible
DrawWidth	FontOutline	MDIForm	Width
Enabled	FontShadow	MinButton	Window
Comment	FontSize	MinHeight	WindowState
ControlBox	FontStrikeThru	MinWidth	WindowType

There is no reason for you to memorize lists of properties. You can look them up in the Visual FoxPro Language Reference manual or the Visual FoxPro Help when you need to use them. A minimum set of Visual FoxPro base class properties are described in Table 14.6. You do not have to remember that list either. It is presented to make you aware of the existence of these properties.

Table 14.6. A minimum set of Visual FoxPro base class properties.

Property	*Description*
`Class`	Type of class.
`BaseClass`	The base class from which the class or subclass was derived. Some examples are `Form`, `Custom`, and `CommandButton`.
`ClassLibrary`	The class library to which the class belongs.
`ParentClass`	The name of the user-defined class from which the object was derived. If the object was derived directly from a Visual FoxPro base class, the `ParentClass` property is an empty string.

Referencing Object Properties

You can reference properties by specifying the object name, which is followed by a period, followed by the property name. However, the general form to set a value is this:

```
[<parent name>.]<objectname>.<property name> = <exp>
```

To access a value, the form is this:

```
<lvalue> = [<parent name>.]<objectname>.<property name>
```

To manipulate an object, you need to specify it in relationship to its container hierarchy. It is analogous to describing how to reference your location by specifying your office address. You specify your name, company, mail stop, street address, city, state, country, planet, and so forth.

For example, suppose you want to enable an option button (`Option1`). To do this, you set the `Enable` property for the button to a logical true (`.T.`) value. If you want to reference the `Enable` property for an option button, `Option1`, in the following container hierarchy:

```
Formset1
    Form1
    ControlGroup1
        Option1
        Option2
...
```

you specify the following statement:

```
Formset1.Form1.ControlGroup1.Option1.Enable = .T.
```

The system memory variable `_SCREEN` refers to the Visual FoxPro main window object. It has the same properties as a form object. For example, you can customize the Visual FoxPro title bar text with the following command:

```
_SCREEN.Caption = "Widget Maker Company Ordering System "
```

You can use the `ActiveForm` property of the `_SCREEN` variable to provide an absolute reference to the active form. For example, if you want to change the background color of the active form, use the following statement:

```
_SCREEN.ActiveForm.BackColor = RGB(255,255,255)
```

Relative referencing is an important feature of the Visual FoxPro OOP model. Special keywords are provided to support relative referencing of objects within the container hierarchy. These keywords are described in Table 14.7.

Table 14.7. Keywords for relative referencing.

Keyword	*Reference*
`Parent`	The immediate container of the object
`THIS`	The current object
`THISFORM`	The form that contains the current object
`THISFORMSET`	The form set that contains the current object

If you want to change the caption property of a control from within its method or event code, you can use the following statement:

```
THIS.Caption = "Off"
```

If you want to disable a control (`Control1`) from the event or method code of another control (`Control2`) in the same form, you can set the `Enable` property of `Control1` with the following statement:

```
THISFORM.Control1.Enable = .F.
```

Suppose you have a form set (`frsMyFormSet`) that consists of a toolbar (`MyToolbar`), and a dialog type form (`frmMyDialog`) that has the following class hierarchy:

`frsMyFormSet`	This is the form set
`frmMyDialog`	This is the dialog box
`cmdButton1`	A control button
...	Other controls
`MyToolbar`	Toolbar container
`cmdPrevious`	Toolbar button

`cmdNext`	Toolbar button
...	More toolbar buttons

Suppose that you want to enable a control button (`CmdNext`) on the toolbar from one of the `cmdButton1` object's methods. You can do this by adding the following statement to the method:

```
THISFORMSET.MyToolBar.CmdNext.Enabled = .T.
```

The following example shows a class definition that uses the `THIS` keyword to refer to properties. In this example, method `SetClient` is called to set the properties to new values. Method `GetBirthDay` retrieves the value of the `dBirthDay` property. Here is an example:

```
DEFINE CLASS Client AS CUSTOM
    cName = "Albert Elkman"
    dBirthday = {03/11/68}
    PROCEDURE dGetBirthDay
       RETURN This.dBirthDay
    ENDPROC
    PROCEDURE SetClient
    PARAMETER cNewName, dNewDate
       This.dBirthDay = dNewDate
       THIS.cName     = cNewName
    ENDPROC
ENDDEFINE
```

Protected Members

If you specify the `PROTECTED` keyword, the associated property, object, procedure, and function are designated as *protected.* A protected item can be accessed only by other methods within the class definition. A protected property, method, or object is invisible to external methods. It is the objective of OOP design to hide all data and methods not specifically required by external methods. Here is one question you might ask yourself when you are designing a class and are adding a new property, method, or object: Is there any reason an external object would need to access this new property, method, or object? If you cannot think of any reason, declare it `PROTECTED`. Here is an example of the syntax for the `PROTECTED` keyword:

```
DEFINE CLASS ClassName1 AS cBaseClass
    [[PROTECTED PropertyName1, PropertyName2 ...]
    PropertyName = eExpression ...]
    [ADD OBJECT [PROTECTED] ObjectName
          AS ClassName2 [NOINIT]
          [WITH cPropertylist]]...
    [[PROTECTED] FUNCTION | PROCEDURE Name
      cStatements
    [ENDFUNC | ENDPROC]]
       ...
ENDDEFINE
```

In the following example, if you do not want anyone who might access an object created from the `Client` class to change the birthday of a client, you make the client's birthday protected with the PROTECTED command. Then it cannot be accessed from an external method. However, if you want to allow users to access the client's birthday, you can provide a method, GetBirthDay, that can be accessed. It returns the birthday. A method used for this purpose is sometimes called a *wrapper method* in object-oriented (OO) terminology. The following code shows the definition of the Client class:

```
DEFINE CLASS Client AS CUSTOM
PROTECTED dBirthDay
    cName = "Albert Elkman"
    dBirthday = {03/11/68}
    PROCEDURE GetBirthDay
        RETURN This.dBirthDay
    ENDPROC
ENDDEFINE
```

Scope and Visibility Revisited

In the traditional Xbase language, the PUBLIC and PRIVATE commands define the scope and visibility of memory variables and arrays. A PUBLIC variable or array is visible to all procedures in an application and exists until it is released or the application exits. A PRIVATE command hides a variable from all higher-level programs. The PRIVATE variable is visible to all procedures or functions it calls. A PRIVATE variable exists as long as the procedure or function in which it is designated as PRIVATE is executing. As soon as this procedure returns control to its calling, or the variable is explicitly released, the variable goes out of scope (is released from memory).

A PUBLIC command creates an array or variable and initializes it with a logical false (.F.) value. A PRIVATE command does not create a variable, it simply hides a variable from higher-level programs.

The LOCAL command was introduced in Visual FoxPro. It creates local variables or arrays and initializes them to a false (.F.) value. A local variable or array is only visible within the procedure or function in which it is specified. It cannot be accessed by higher- or lower-level programs. It is released once its procedure or function completes execution.

Here is the syntax of these commands:

```
LOCAL <memvar list>

LOCAL [ARRAY] <array name1> (<rows1> [, <Columns1>])
    [, <array name2> (<rows2> [, <columns2>])] ...

PRIVATE <memvar list>

PRIVATE ALL LIKE <skeleton> ¦ EXCEPT <skeleton>]

PUBLIC <memvar list>

PUBLIC [ARRAY] <array name1> (<rows1> [, <Columns1>])
    [, <array name2> (<Rows2> [, <columns2>])] ...
```

Adding Objects

Container classes contain other objects. You can add an object to a container class by specifying the ADD OBJECT clause with the DEFINE CLASS command. Here is an example of the syntax:

```
DEFINE CLASS ClassName1 AS cBaseClass
    [[PROTECTED PropertyName1, PropertyName2 ...]
    PropertyName = eExpression ...]
    [ADD OBJECT [PROTECTED] ObjectName
          AS ClassName2 [NOINIT]
          [WITH cPropertylist]]...
    [[PROTECTED] FUNCTION ¦ PROCEDURE Name
      cStatements
    [ENDFUNC ¦ ENDPROC]]
       ...
ENDDEFINE
```

Suppose that you want to create a form with a big command button in it. You can use the ADD OBJECT clause to add the command button to the form, as shown in Figure 14.1.

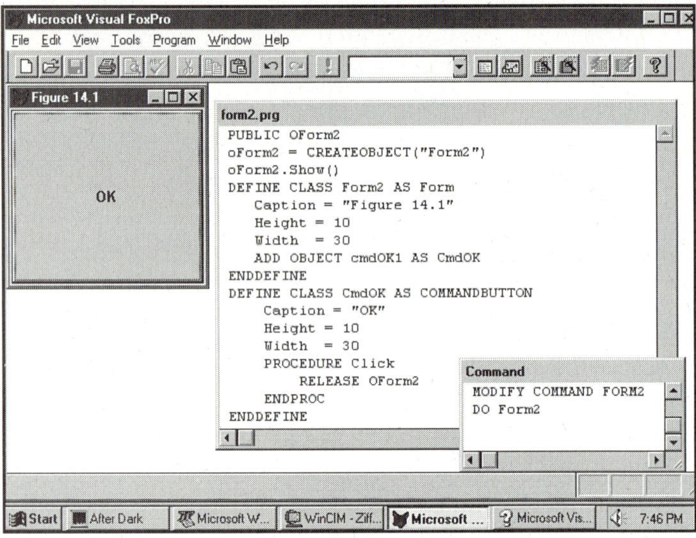

FIGURE 14.1.
An example of the ADD OBJECT clause.

In this example, the object cmdOK1 is created from the CmdOK subclass and is added to the container class, Form1 using the following statement:

```
ADD OBJECT cmdOK1 AS CmdOK
```

You can add as many objects as you like to a container class by using the ADD OBJECT clause. There are other ways to add objects to a class. One of the characteristics of a container class is that it has an AddObject() method. You can use this method to add objects to a container object after it has been created. Here is an example:

```
oForm1 = CREATEOBJECT("Form")     && Create Form object
oForm1.AddObject("cmdExit","COMMANDBUTTON")
```

In this example, a command button object, `cmdExit`, is added to a form object, `oForm1`.

In the example shown in Figure 14.1, the definition of the `CmdOK` class was required to assign initial values to the `Caption`, `Width`, and `Height` properties. An alternative is shown in Figure 14.2. You can add a method that contains code for the `Form1` class `Init` event. When the form is created, the `Init` event code is triggered. You can add code that initializes the properties for the `oCmdOK` object to the `Init` event code. You can also specify `Click` event code that is triggered when the `Click` event for the `CmdOK` object occurs. Listing 14.1 provides the source listing for a program that illustrates the use of the `ADD OBJECT` clause.

Listing 14.1. A program that illustrates the use of the ADD OBJECT clause.

```
**********************************************************************
* FORM3.PRG - Illustrates the use of the ADD OBJECT clause
oForm2 = CREATEOBJECT("Form2")
oForm2.Show()
READ EVENTS
DEFINE CLASS Form2 AS Form
   Caption = "Figure 14.1"
   Height = 90
   Width  = 210
   ADD OBJECT oCmdOK AS COMMANDBUTTON
   PROCEDURE Init
      This.oCmdOK.Caption = "OK"
      This.oCmdOK.Height = 90
      This.oCmdOK.Width  = 210
   ENDPROC
   PROCEDURE oCmdOK.Click
        CLEAR EVENTS
   ENDPROC
ENDDEFINE
```

In the example shown in Listing 14.1, the `READ EVENTS` command executes once the form, `Form1`, displays. When Visual FoxPro encounters a `READ EVENTS` command, it starts event processing, which means that Visual FoxPro returns to the Visual FoxPro event processing loop until the `CLEAR EVENTS` command executes. The `Click` event code for the `oCmdOK` object contains the `CLEAR EVENTS` statement. When a `Click` event occurs, the `CLEAR EVENTS` command executes. The `CLEAR EVENTS` command stops event processing. Then program execution continues with the line immediately following the `READ EVENTS` command. At that time, program FORM3.PRG exits, the form object reference variable, `oForm2`, goes out of scope, the form disappears from the screen, and the form is released from memory.

Here is another example of the use of the `AddObject()` method. In this example, when a class is initialized, the `Init` event occurs which executes the `Init` event method for an object. At that time, you can add objects to a container as shown in the following class definition:

```
DEFINE CLASS Form1 AS Form
    ...
    PROCEDURE INIT        && Code executes when Init event fires
         THIS.AddObject("cmdExit","COMMANDBUTTON")
     ENDPROC
ENDDEFINE
```

Methods and Events

A class or subclass contains procedures and functions that are actually methods and events. When you need to write event code that executes in response to the occurrence of an event, such as a mouse click, you write event functions or procedures within the class or subclass definition. Likewise, you can create method functions or procedures within a class or subclass definition. A method is a procedure that operates on the object. A method resides within the class or subclass definition that defines that object. Here is an example of the syntax:

```
DEFINE CLASS ClassName1 AS cBaseClass
         ...
    [[PROTECTED] FUNCTION ¦ PROCEDURE Name
          cStatements
    [ENDFUNC ¦ ENDPROC]]
        ...
ENDDEFINE
```

The Visual FoxPro base classes contain code for methods and events. You can write code for as many additional methods as you like to support your application. In addition, when you derive a class or subclass from another class that you have created, you can write code to override or replace the code for the method and event that already exist in the class on which the class is based. In this case, your new event or method code is called instead of the code in the class on which the class is based. In the following example, the `Click` event code in the `CmdButton` class is overridden by the derived class, `Button1`, `Click` event code:

```
DEFINE CLASS Button2 AS Button1
     Caption = "OK"
     Left = 9
     PROCEDURE Click     && Overrides Class Button1 Click command
          WAIT WINDOW "Someone clicked the OK button"
     ENDPROC
ENDDEFINE
DEFINE CLASS Button1 AS CmdButton
     Height = 72
     Width  = 56
     Caption = "My Button"
     PROCEDURE Click     && Does not overwrite anything because
                         && Visual FoxPro Base event methods
                         && are automatically called
         WAIT WINDOW "Mouse button was pressed"
     ENDPROC
ENDDEFINE
```

On the other hand, Visual FoxPro base class event code is automatically called even if you write your own event method. If you want to suppress the calling of the Visual FoxPro base class event code, you can specify the `NODEFAULT` statement in your event code.

Here is the set of rules that governs the writing of code for methods and events:

- The set of events supported by Visual FoxPro base classes is fixed and cannot be extended.
- Visual FoxPro base classes recognize a fixed set of default events. The minimum set of events is composed of the `Init`, `Destroy`, and `Error` events. Here is a description of each event:

  The `Init` event occurs when an object is created. In the `Init` event code for your class or subclass, you can add code to initialize the object.

  The `Destroy` event occurs when an object is released from memory. You can add cleanup code in the `Destroy` event code.

  The `Error` event occurs whenever an error is encountered in one of the methods or the event code.
- When you create a method for a class definition that has the same name as an event that the class can recognize, the code in the method executes when the event occurs. Here is an example:

```
DEFINE CLASS Button1 OF COMMANDBUTTON
   * The following method is event code for click event
   PROCEDURE Click
      WAIT WINDOW "Someone clicked on this button"
   ENDPROC
ENDDEFINE
```

- You create a method for a class when you write a procedure or function within the class definition.

The Scope Resolution Operator

If you derive one class from another and override code for one of its events, but you still want to execute code derived from the class, you can use the *scope resolution operator* (::). For example, suppose you derive a new subclass, `Button2`, from Class `Button1` (see the previous example). Then you override the `Click` event and call the `Button1 Click` procedure using the scope resolution operator. In this example, if you click on the `Button2` control, the `Button2 Click` event code executes and displays a message dialog box, as shown in Figure 14.2. If you click on the Yes button, the `Button1 Click` event code executes and closes `Form1` using the `RELEASE THIS FORM` command.

Incidentally, the scope resolution operator can be used any time you want to explicitly execute any method or event code for some other control or container.

Listing 14.2 is the source listing of an example that illustrates the use of scope resolution operator.

Listing 14.2. Listing for the `Button2` function that illustrates the use of the scope resolution operator.

```
******************************************************************
* Function: Button2  illustrates use of scope resolution operator
FUNCTION Button2
oForm2 = CREATEOBJECT("Form2")      && Create the form2 object
oForm2.SHOW()                       && Display form
RETURN oForm2                       && Return reference to Form2 object
******************************************************************
*   Class definition of Form2
DEFINE CLASS Form2 AS Form
     Caption = "Figure 14.2"        &&  Assign Title bar text for form
     Height = 72                    &&  Assign form height property in Foxels
     Width  = 210                   &&  Assign form width property in Foxels
     ADD OBJECT cmdButton2 AS Button2    &&  Add Button2 object to form
ENDDEFINE
*******************************************************************************
*   Class definition of Button1 command button
DEFINE CLASS Button1 AS COMMANDBUTTON
     Height = 72                    &&    Assign height property of command button
     Width  = 210                   &&    Assign width property of command button
     Caption = "My Button"          &&    Assign
     PROCEDURE Click                && Overrides code for
                                    && COMMANDBUTTON Class Click event
         WAIT WINDOW "Button1: Mouse button was pressed"
         RELEASE THIS FORM          && Deactivate and destroy the form.
     ENDPROC
ENDDEFINE
******************************************************************
* Class definition of Button2
DEFINE CLASS Button2 AS Button1
     Caption = "My Button2"         &&  Assign button caption
     PROCEDURE Click                && Click event code overrides
                                    &&   Button1 Click event code
         IF MESSAGEBOX('Do you want to call Button1 Click Code?' ;
                  ,36,'Exiting?') = 6
            Button1::Click          && Call Click function in Class Button1
                                    &&   using global resolution operator
         ENDIF
     ENDPROC
ENDDEFINE
```

In the example shown in Listing 14.2, a reference to the object is returned by the `Button2` function. You execute this function using the following command:

```
oForm2 = Button2()
```

The program defines a class, creates an object from that class, displays the form, and returns a reference to the class. The returned value is stored in a memory variable, `oForm2`, that is a reference to the `Form2` object. You can cause the form to be destroyed and released from memory using the following command:

```
RELEASE oForm2
```

If you like, you can create a reference to the control button object, `cmdButton2`, and change its caption using the following commands:

```
cmdButton = oForm2.cmdButton2
cmdButton.Caption = "New Caption"
```

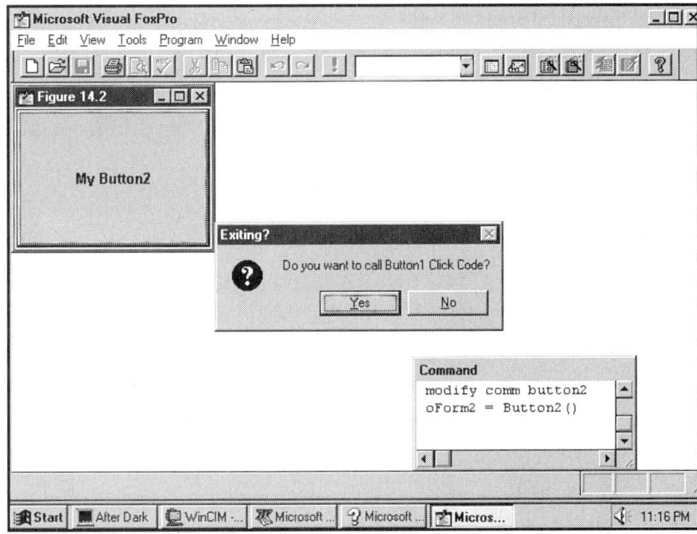

FIGURE 14.2.
The output resulting from the execution of the `Button2` *function.*

Once you have created a reference to any object contained in the form, it is not as easy to destroy the form with the `RELEASE` command. First, you must release any references to any objects that belong to the form. For example, once you create `cmdButton`, you must release both references to destroy the form and remove the form from memory using the following commands:

```
RELEASE oForm2
RELEASE cmdButton
```

The *NODEFAULT* Keyword

The call to the Visual FoxPro base class event method happens automatically in the Visual FoxPro object-oriented model. I have discussed this point already, but it is important, so I will go over it again. You can specify the `NODEFAULT` keyword in your event method when you want to prevent a Visual FoxPro base class method from being automatically called. For example, you might want to gobble up a keystroke or mouse click. When you explicitly call the Visual FoxPro base class event method, you are forcing that event method to be executed at a time when you want it executed. In the example shown in Listing 14.3, suppose that you want only numeric values to be placed in the text box object named `txtNumbers`, which is an instance of the `Numbers` class. (`Numbers` a subclass derived from the base class event, `TextBox`.)

Listing 14.3. A function that illustrates the use of the `NODEFAULT` keyword.

```
************************************************************
* Program: Numbers.prg illustrates use of NODEFAULT keyword
*                      and use of global scope resolution
*                      operator (::) to call VFP base class
*                      event method
************************************************************
frmEnterNumbers = CREATEOBJECT("EnterNumbers")
frmEnterNumbers.Show
DEFINE CLASS EnterNumbers AS FORM
       ADD OBJECT txtNumbers AS Numbers
       PROCEDURE DESTROY
           CLEAR EVENTS
       ENDPROC
ENDDEFINE
DEFINE CLASS Numbers AS TextBox
    PROCEDURE KeyPress    && KeyPress event Method
            PARAMETERS nKeyCode, nShiftAltCtrl    && Required parameters
        NODEFAULT        && Suppress base class call to
                && its KeyPress event method
        IF BETWEEN(nKeyCode, 48, 57)    && Between "0" and "9"
        TextBox::KeyPress(nKeyCode,nShiftAltCtrl)
        ELSE
               ?? CHR(7)  && Ring bell
            ENDIF
    ENDPROC
ENDDEFINE
```

In the example shown in Listing 14.3, the `NODEFAULT` keyword prevents the base class event method, `KeyPress`, from being called automatically by Visual FoxPro when the user presses a key. The `BETWEEN()` function returns a true (`.T.`) value if `nKeyCode` (the character entered by the user) is a number. If so, you call the `KeyPress` base class event method using the scope resolution operator; otherwise, you ring the bell.

You can use the `NODEFAULT` keyword when you want to set a property in an event method before the Visual FoxPro base class event method executes.

If you do not believe that Visual FoxPro always calls its base class event methods, try removing the `NODEFAULT` keyword from the example shown in Listing 14.3. Then, when you type a number, you'll see double numbers in the text box since the Visual FoxPro base class event method, `KeyPress`, gets called once explicitly and once automatically.

The important thing to remember is that you add the `NODEFAULT` keyword to prevent the automatic call by Visual FoxPro.

Using Arrays with Objects

You can define an array in a class definition. One use of an array in a class definition is to refer to objects added to the class. Suppose you create a form that contains some controls, and you want to use array elements to refer to the controls. This type of array is called a *control array*. A control array is a collection of controls that share a common name, type, and event procedure. Each control has a unique index. When an event occurs for one of the controls in the array, Visual FoxPro calls the event procedure for the group and passes the index as an argument. You use this index in your event method to determine which control recognizes the event. The example shown in Listing 14.4 illustrates the use of a control array and how to process the index parameter for the `Click` event method.

Listing 14.4. A listing of a program that illustrates the use of a control array.

```
***********************************************
*  Program: ARRAYS.PRG
*  Purpose: Illustrates how to a use control array
***********************************************
frmArray = CREATEOBJECT("Form5")
frmArray.show
READ EVENTS
DEFINE CLASS Form5 AS Form
   DIMENSION aControl[4]     && declare control array
   ScaleMode = 0             && Foxels screen mode
   Height = 2               && Height of form
   Width  = 55               && Width of form
   AutoCenter = .T.           && Automatically center form
   *  Add four control objects
   ADD OBJECT aControl[1] AS CommandButton ;
     WITH Left = 1,  Height =2, Caption = "Panic"
   ADD OBJECT aControl[2] AS CheckBox ;
     WITH Left = 20, Caption = "Reverse"
   ADD OBJECT aControl[3] AS OptionButton ;
     WITH Left = 35, Width = 9, Caption = "On"
   ADD OBJECT aControl[4] AS OptionButton ;
     WITH Left = 45, Width = 9, Caption = "Off"
   PROCEDURE aControl.CLICK
      PARAMETERS nIndex
      Wait Window "index: "+ LTRIM(STR(nIndex)) TIMEOUT 1
      DO CASE
          CASE nIndex = 1     && Panic
             RELEASE THISFORM && Exit form
          CASE nIndex = 2      && Reverse checkbox inverts background
                                && and foreground color of form
             ThisForm.ForeColor = BITNOT(ThisForm.ForeColor)
             ThisForm.BackColor = BITNOT(ThisForm.BackColor)
             ThisForm.Refresh
          CASE nIndex = 3     && On
             aControl[4].Value = 0
          CASE nIndex = 4     && Off
             aControl[3].Value = 0
      ENDCASE
   ENDPROC
   PROCEDURE Destroy
       CLEAR EVENTS
   ENDPROC
ENDDEFINE
```

The `aControl[]` array members are assigned references to four control objects. Then, when you click on any of the controls, Visual FoxPro calls the `Click` event method and passes it the index number of the control. The case statement executes different code depending on which control was clicked. Figure 14.3 shows the results from the execution of the ARRAYS.PRG program.

FIGURE 14.3.
An example of the form generated by executing the ARRAYS.PRG program.

The Event Model

The programming model in FoxPro has changed with Visual FoxPro. Programs have evolved from a single long list of commands to a whole collection of little procedures and functions associated with objects. Each of these little procedures is an event method and is triggered by the occurrence of some event. This is the *event model.* Other methods and properties are available to modify the behavior of objects. Visual FoxPro is not quite as radical as it may seem since all of the old FoxPro commands are still available. You can still program the old-fashioned way. At the same time, you can ease into Visual FoxPro OOP until you finally master it.

There is a basic collection of Visual FoxPro events that are supported by most controls. You can obtain a complete description of the syntax and use of each Visual FoxPro event from help. A list of the core set of Visual FoxPro events is provided in Table 14.8.

Table 14.8. A basic collection of Visual FoxPro events.

Event	*The Event Is Triggered When...*
`Click`	The user clicks the object using the primary (left) mouse button.
`DblClick`	The user double-clicks the object using the primary (left) mouse button.
`Destroy`	An object is released from memory.
`GotFocus`	An object receives input focus by the user clicking on the object, tabbing to the object, or pressing the access key, or by program code that executes the `SetFocus()` method.
`Init`	An object is created. The `Init` event method for all of the controls executes before the `Init` method of the form. As a result, you can add code in the `Init` event method to manipulate any control it contains. You also can add controls using the `AddObject()` method in the form's `Init` event method.

Event	*The Event Is Triggered When...*
`InteractiveChange`	The value of the object changes as a result of user interaction (for example, someone changes the value of a check box by clicking on it).
`KeyPress`	The user presses and releases a key.
`Load`	A `Form` or a `FormSet` object is loaded into memory. This is the first event that occurs when you load a form or form set. At this point, none of the controls have been loaded so you cannot add any code to manipulate or define a control in the `Load` event method. However, you can establish the database environment in the `Load` event method.
`LostFocus`	An object loses input focus by the user clicking on the object, tabbing to the object, pressing the access key, or by program code that executes the `SetFocus()` method to change the focus to another object.
`MouseDown`	The user presses a mouse button while the mouse pointer is over the object.
`MouseMove`	The user moves the mouse pointer over the object.
`MouseUp`	The user releases the mouse button while the mouse pointer is over the object.
`ProgrammaticChange`	The value of the object is changed programmatically.
`RightClick`	The user clicks the object using the secondary (right) mouse button.
`Unload`	A `Form` or a `FormSet` object is released from memory.

How the Class Hierarchy Is Related to the Execution of Event Methods

Visual FoxPro does not trigger event code for container objects for events that are associated with its control objects. For example, if you click on a control button, the `Click` event method for the control button is called. However, the `Click` event method for the form that contains the control button is not called. In fact, when you interact with a control by clicking on it, moving the mouse over it, tabbing to it, an so on, any corresponding form event method is not called. This is illustrated in the program shown in Listing 14.5.

On the other hand, if there is an event that occurs that is not associated with a control, Visual FoxPro looks for an event method associated with the event for a control higher up the class hierarchy.

In the example shown in Listing 14.5, a class is defined for a form with three control buttons, `Button1`, `Button2`, and `Button3`. All three are derived from the `Button` class. The definition for the `Button` class contains an event method for the `Click` event. Also, there exists a `Click` event method for the `Button1` control button object. If you click on either `Button2` or `Button3`, the `Click` event code for the `Button` class executes since neither button has its own `Click` event method. If you click on `Button1`, its `Click` event method executes. Its `Click` event method overrides the `Click` event method in the `Button` class definition. The only way you can get the `Click` event method for the `Form4` class to execute is to click on the form. When you click on the form, the `Click` event in the `Form4` class definition executes. This results in the form being cleared from the screen and removed from memory.

Listing 14.5. A listing of a program that illustrates how Visual FoxPro traverses class hierarchy to find event code.

```
*************************************************
* Program: FORM4.PRG
* Purpose: Illustrates that if Visual FoxPro does
*          not find event method for a class it
*          executes event method higher up the
*          class hierarchy.
*
frmTEST = CREATEOBJECT("Form4")
frmTEST.SHOW
READ EVENTS
DEFINE CLASS Form4 AS FORM
  ADD OBJECT Button1 AS Button
  ADD OBJECT Button2 AS Button WITH Top= 2
  ADD OBJECT Button3 AS Button WITH Top= 4
  PROCEDURE Button1.Click
      WAIT WINDOW "Button1 was clicked" TIMEOUT 1
  ENDPROC
  PROCEDURE Click
     WAIT WINDOW "Form will be destroyed" TIMEOUT 1
     RELEASE THISFORM
  ENDPROC
  PROCEDURE DESTROY
     CLEAR EVENTS
  ENDPROC
ENDDEFINE
DEFINE CLASS Button AS COMMANDBUTTON
  PROCEDURE Click
   WAIT WINDOW THIS.Caption TIMEOUT 1
  ENDPROC
ENDDEFINE
```

Exceptions to the Rule

The `CommandGroup` and `OptionGroup` classes are the exceptions to the rule. They are a special type of container class. If you do not provide an event method for one of the controls contained by a `CommandGroup` or an `OptionGroup` object, and the corresponding group event method exists, then the group event method executes in response to its corresponding event. In the example shown in Listing 14.6, the BGROUP class is derived from the CommandGroup base class. The cmgButtons object is created from the BGROUP class. In the BGroup class definition, four buttons are added. Only the cmdLast button has its own Click event method since cmdLast is derived from class LBUTTON. When you click on the other three buttons, the Click event method for the cmgButtons group object executes.

This differs from the rule because the BGroup class is definitely not in the class hierarchy of the classes for the buttons in the group. However, this is the way group containers work. It works this way so that you can process a group of buttons or options from a single event method. This is important when you are interested in which one of a group of options is selected.

Listing 14.6. An example of event handling by the CommandGroup class object.

```
************************************************
* Program: GROUP.PRG
* Purpose: Illustrates how group container class
*          event methods are executed if there
*          are no corresponding event methods
*          for the controls it contains.
************************************************
frmTEST = CREATEOBJECT("Form5")
frmTEST.SHOW
READ EVENTS
DEFINE CLASS Form5 AS FORM
  AutoCenter = .T.
  ScaleMode  = 0
  Height = 12
  Width = 22
  ****************************************************
  * Add command group object
  ADD OBJECT cmgButtons AS BGroup
  **************************************************
  *  Form5 event methods
  PROCEDURE Click
     WAIT WINDOW "Form will be destroyed" TIMEOUT 1
     RELEASE THISFORM
  ENDPROC
  PROCEDURE DESTROY
     CLEAR EVENTS
  ENDPROC
ENDDEFINE
DEFINE CLASS BGROUP AS COMMANDGROUP
  Left = 2
  Top = 2
  Height = 8
  Width = 20
  ****************************************************
  * Add buttons to command group
  ADD OBJECT cmdFirst    AS COMMANDBUTTON ;
      WITH Caption = "First", Height = 2, Top = 0
  ADD OBJECT cmdPrevious AS COMMANDBUTTON ;
      WITH Caption = "Previous", Height = 2, Top = 2
```

continues

Listing 14.6. continued

```
  ADD OBJECT cmdNext     AS COMMANDBUTTON ;
      WITH Caption = "Next", Height = 2, Top = 4
  ADD OBJECT cmdLast     AS  LButton ;
      WITH Top = 6
*******************************************************
*  Command group Click event method
*  For a command group:
*    THIS.Value - Index on the button clicked
*    THIS.Buttons() is array of button object references
*    THIS.Buttons(THIS.Value).Name   - Name of clicked
*                                      button object.
*    THIS.Buttons(THIS.Value).Caption   - Caption of clicked
*                                      button object.
********************************************************
  PROCEDURE Click
WAIT WINDOW TIMEOUT 1 ;
      "Button number " ;
      + LTRIM(STR(This.Value));
      + " which is named " + ;
      + THIS.BUTTONS(THIS.Value).Name ;
      + " with caption " ;
      + THIS.BUTTONS(THIS.VALUE).Caption ;
      + " was pressed."
  ENDPROC
ENDDEFINE
DEFINE CLASS LBUTTON AS COMMANDBUTTON
   Caption = "Last"
   Height = 2
   PROCEDURE Click
      WAIT WINDOW "The Last button was pressed" TIMEOUT 1
   ENDPROC
ENDDEFINE
```

Figure 14.4 shows the form created by the program in Listing 14.6. Notice that there are four buttons inside the box. The box is the container group object, `cmgButtons`. If you click on one of the First, Previous, or Next buttons, the `cmgButtons` group object click method executes. For example, if you click on the Next button, the Wait window displays the message shown in Figure 14.4. If you click on the Last button, the Wait window displays the following message:

```
The Last button was pressed
```

If you click on the group box at the right of the buttons, and the Previous button currently has the focus, the Wait window displays the following message:

```
Button number 2 which is named Button2 with caption Previous  was pressed
```

If you click on the form, the form disappears and is removed from memory after displaying the Form is being destroyed message in the Wait window.

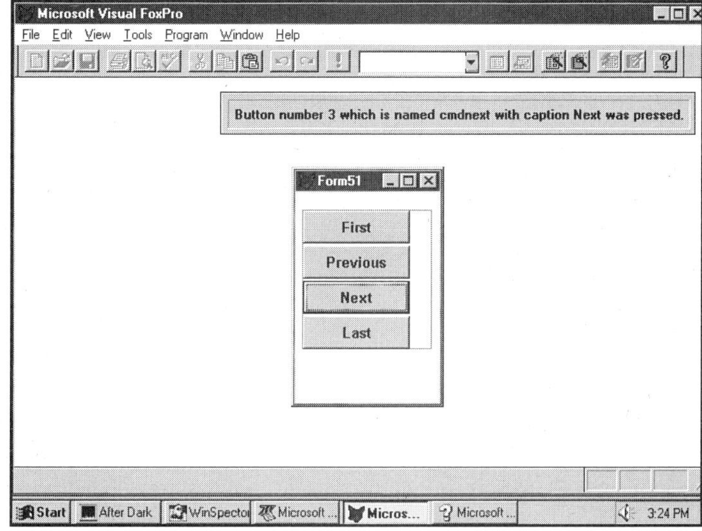

FIGURE 14.4.
An example of the use of the `CommandGroup` *event methods.*

Viewing Events as They Occur

You have learned about events and now know when and how they occur. You know how to write event methods to respond to the events. In this section, you will be able to see a trace of events as they occur by executing the program shown in Listing 14.7. This program contains a method, `ShowObject`, that displays the name of the event as the event occurs and the name of the object that responds to the event. This method is defined in the `MyForm` class. As you can see by examining the code, the `ShowObject` method is called by the event methods of the form and the controls using the following statement:

```
THISFORM.ShowObject(<event name>, THIS )
```

Listing 14.7. A program, VEVENTS.PRG, that lets you view some basic events as they occur.

```
*************************************************
* Program: VEvents.PRG lets you view events.
*
ERASE EVENTS.TXT
SET ALTERNATE TO Events
SET ALTERNATE ON
oMyForm = CREATEOBJECT("MyForm")
oMyForm.Show()
READ EVENTS
*********************************************
*  Define Form Class, MyForm
DEFINE CLASS MyForm AS Form
   ScaleMode = 0
```

continues

Listing 14.7. continued

```
   Height = 3
   AutoCenter = .T.
   ADD OBJECT oCheckbox AS MyCheckBox
   ADD OBJECT oTextBox AS MyTextBox
   ADD OBJECT oLabel AS Label ;
     WITH Caption = "Text Box:", Left=25, Width = 10
   **************************************
   * Event Code
   PROCEDURE Init
      THISFORM.ShowObject("Init", THIS )
   ENDPROC
   PROCEDURE Load
      THISFORM.ShowObject("Load", THIS )
   ENDPROC
   PROCEDURE Unload
      THISFORM.ShowObject("Unload", THIS )
   ENDPROC
   PROCEDURE Destroy
      THISFORM.ShowObject("Destroy", THIS )
      CLEAR EVENTS
      SET ALTER OFF
      SET ALTER TO
   ENDPROC
   ********************************************
   * ShowObject: Displays Event and object name
   FUNCTION ShowObject
   PARAMETERS cEventName, oObject
      WAIT WINDOW cEventName +": " + oObject.Name TIMEOUT 1
      ACTIVATE SCREEN
      ? cEventName +": " + oObject.Name
   RETURN .T.
   ENDFUNC
ENDDEFINE
*********************************************
* Definition of MyCheckBox
DEFINE CLASS MyCheckBox AS CheckBox
   PROCEDURE INIT
      THIS.Left = 2            && Position left corner 2 foxels
                              &&  from left border of form
      THIS.Caption = "Checkbox"
      THISFORM.ShowObject("Init", THIS)
   ENDPROC
   PROCEDURE CLICK
      THISFORM.ShowObject("Click", THIS )
   ENDPROC
   PROCEDURE Destroy
      THISFORM.ShowObject("Destroy", THIS )
   ENDPROC
   PROCEDURE DblClick
      THISFORM.ShowObject("DblClick", THIS )
   ENDPROC
   PROCEDURE InteractiveChange
      THISFORM.ShowObject("InteractiveChange", THIS )
   ENDPROC
   PROCEDURE MouseUp
      PARAMETERS nButton, nShift, nXCoord, nYCoord
      THISFORM.ShowObject("MouseUp", THIS )
   ENDPROC
```

```
   PROCEDURE DragDrop
      THISFORM.ShowObject("DragDrop", THIS )
   ENDPROC
   PROCEDURE DragOver
      THISFORM.ShowObject("DragOver", THIS )
   ENDPROC
   PROCEDURE LostFocus
      THISFORM.ShowObject("LostFocus", THIS )
   ENDPROC
   PROCEDURE KeyPress
        PARAMETER nKeyCode, nKeyCode2
       THISFORM.ShowObject("KeyPress", THIS )
   ENDPROC
   PROCEDURE RightClick
      THISFORM.ShowObject("RightClick", THIS )
      RELEASE THISFORM
   ENDPROC
   PROCEDURE GotFocus
      THISFORM.ShowObject("GotFocus", THIS )
   ENDPROC
   PROCEDURE MouseDown
      PARAMETERS nButton, nShift, nXCoord, nYCoord
      THISFORM.ShowObject("MouseDown", THIS )
   ENDPROC
   PROCEDURE Valid
      THISFORM.ShowObject("Valid", THIS )
   ENDPROC
   PROCEDURE When
      THISFORM.ShowObject("When", THIS )
   ENDPROC
ENDDEFINE

*********************************************
* Definition of MyTextBox
DEFINE CLASS MyTextBox AS TextBox
   PROCEDURE INIT
      THIS.Left = 40
      THISFORM.ShowObject("Init", THIS )
   ENDPROC
   PROCEDURE CLICK
      THISFORM.ShowObject("Click", THIS )
   ENDPROC
   PROCEDURE DblClick
      THISFORM.ShowObject("DblClick", THIS )
   ENDPROC
   PROCEDURE Destroy
      THISFORM.ShowObject("Destroy", THIS )
      SET ALTER OFF
      SET ALTER TO
   ENDPROC
   PROCEDURE InteractiveChange
      THISFORM.ShowObject("InteractiveChange", THIS )
   ENDPROC
   PROCEDURE MouseUp
      PARAMETERS nButton, nShift, nXCoord, nYCoord
      THISFORM.ShowObject("MouseUp", THIS )
   ENDPROC
   PROCEDURE DragDrop
```

continues

Listing 14.7. continued

```
      THISFORM.ShowObject("DragDrop", THIS )
   ENDPROC
   PROCEDURE KeyPress
   PARAMETER nKeyCode, nKeyCode2
         THISFORM.ShowObject("KeyPress", THIS )
   ENDPROC
   PROCEDURE DragOver
      THISFORM.ShowObject("DragOver", THIS )
   ENDPROC
   PROCEDURE LostFocus
      THISFORM.ShowObject("LostFocus", THIS )
   ENDPROC
   PROCEDURE RightClick
      THISFORM.ShowObject("RightClick", THIS )
      CLEAR EVENTS
   ENDPROC
   PROCEDURE GotFocus
      THISFORM.ShowObject("GotFocus", THIS )
   ENDPROC
   PROCEDURE MouseDown
      PARAMETERS nButton, nShift, nXCoord, nYCoord
      THISFORM.ShowObject("MouseDown", THIS )
   ENDPROC
   PROCEDURE Valid
      THISFORM.ShowObject("Valid", THIS )
   ENDPROC
   PROCEDURE When
      THISFORM.ShowObject("When", THIS )
   ENDPROC
ENDDEFINE
```

Figure 14.5 shows an example execution of the VEVENTS.PRG program.

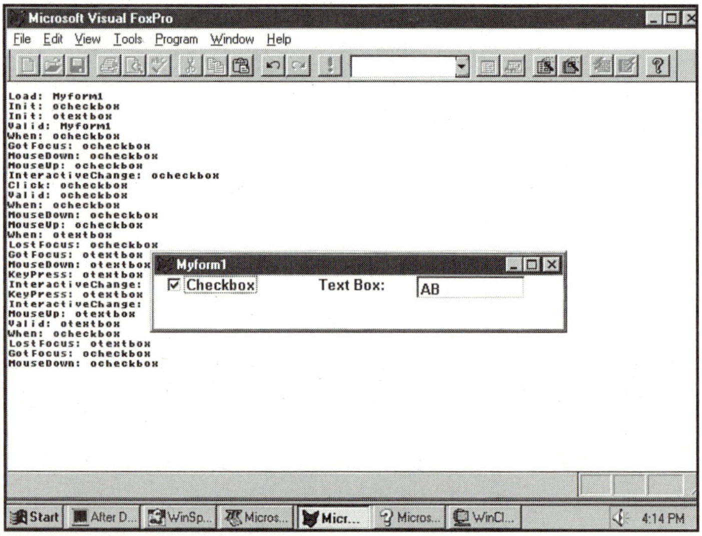

FIGURE 14.5.
A form created by the VEVENTS.PRG program.

Table 14.9 shows some output from the execution of the VEVENTS.PRG program. The first column shows the event trace output that is directed to the alternate file (EVENT.TXT) as the program executes. The other column describes the action that caused the event or group of events to occur.

Table 14.9. A list and description of events as they occur in the VEVENTS.PRG program.

Event: Object	*The Action That Caused the Event to Occur*
`Load: Myform1`	`DO VEVENTS` (the user executes the program).
`Init: ocheckbox`	
`Init: otextbox`	
`Init: Myform1`	
`When: ocheckbox`	
`GotFocus: ocheckbox`	
`MouseDown: ocheckbox`	User clicks on the check box.
`MouseUp: ocheckbox`	
`InteractiveChange: ocheckbox`	
`Click: ocheckbox`	
`Valid: ocheckbox`	
`When: ocheckbox`	
`MouseDown: ocheckbox`	
`KeyPress: ocheckbox`	The Tab key is pressed (focus moves to the text box).
`LostFocus: ocheckbox`	
`When: otextbox`	
`GotFocus: otextbox`	
`KeyPress: otextbox`	The letter A is typed in the text box.
`InteractiveChange: otextbox`	
`KeyPress: otextbox`	The letter B is typed in the text box.
`InteractiveChange: otextbox`	
`MouseUp: ocheckbox`	User clicks on the check box.
`InteractiveChange: ocheckbox`	
`Click: ocheckbox`	
`Valid: ocheckbox`	
`When: ocheckbox`	

continues

Table 14.9. continued

Event: Object	*The Action That Caused the Event to Occur*
`Valid: otextbox`	
`When: ocheckbox`	
`LostFocus: otextbox`	
`GotFocus: ocheckbox`	
`MouseDown: ocheckbox`	User clicks on the check box with right mouse button (causes the form to close).
`MouseUp: ocheckbox`	
`RightClick: ocheckbox`	
`MouseDown: ocheckbox`	
`Destroy: Myform1`	
`Destroy: otextbox`	
`Destroy: ocheckbox`	
`Unload: Myform1`	

This event trace viewing program is very simple. It only has two controls. It was designed to be tolerably brief so that you will have little difficulty following the code.

If you are really interested in viewing event traces for all types of supported controls as they are executed, you can execute the EVENTS.SCX sample program supplied with Visual FoxPro. It is quite instructional. It creates an elaborate set of forms you can manipulate. At the same time, it displays event traces for almost every type of control supported by Visual FoxPro. EVENTS.SCX resides in directory \VFP\SAMPLES\CONTROLS\EVENTS.SCX. Figure 14.6 shows the EXAMPLE.SCX form set. You can choose an option that displays event traces on the screen. If you like, you can direct the event traces to a window. The toolbar in the figure controls the event trace display mechanism.

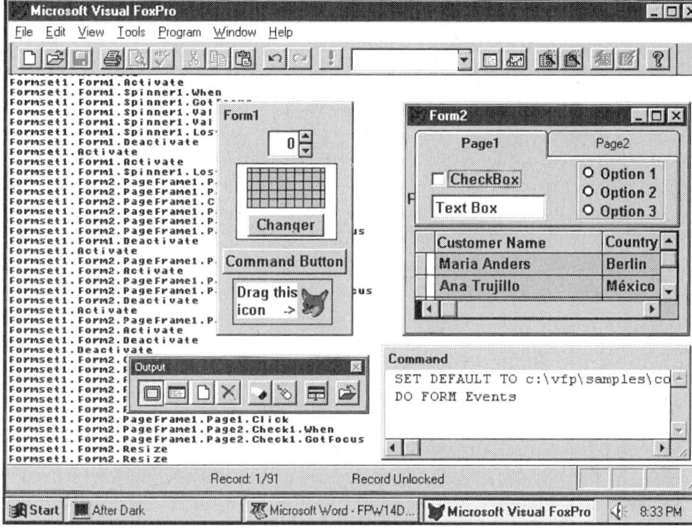

FIGURE 14.6.
The EVENTS.SCX form.

Designing a Sample Form

In this section you will learn how to create the Address Book form shown in Figure 14.7. This form has a set of VCR-type control buttons that are used to navigate through a table containing names, addresses, and phone numbers.

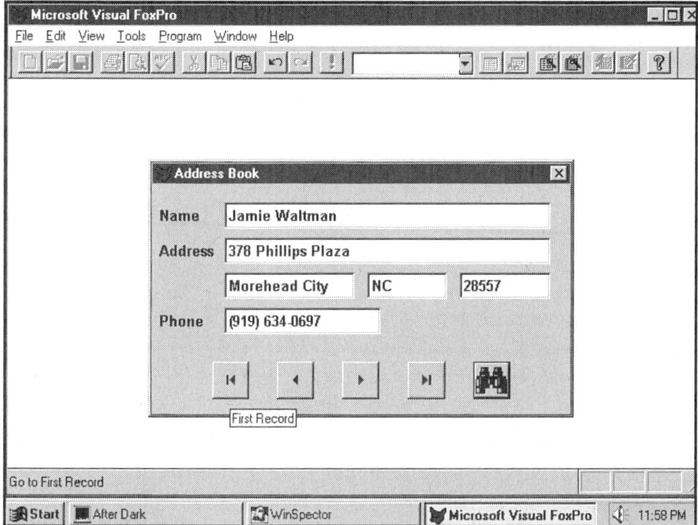

FIGURE 14.7.
The Address Book form.

When you are planning to design such a form, figure that you need some `TextBox` objects to display the data, some `Label` objects for headings, and a set of control buttons to navigate through the database. When you design objects, you look for common characteristics among groups of controls. Since the size and top position of all the navigation buttons are the same, it makes sense to define a generalized navigation class that contains the common properties and methods and then derive all the other buttons from this class.

The classes for the other buttons will inherit the properties and methods of the generalized navigation button class. Listing 14.8 shows the class definition of the generalized navigation button. In this example, The `Caption`, `Top`, `Height`, and `Width` properties are common to all the navigation buttons. You override the `Picture` and `Left` properties when you define a subclass. However, the generalized navigation button assigns default properties. A `Click` event method is provided to assure that the ADDRESS.DBF table work area is the current work area.

Listing 14.8. The source listing for the definition of the generalized navigation button class.

```
*****************************************************
*  Define Generalized Navigation button class
DEFINE CLASS NavButton AS COMMANDBUTTON
   Caption = ""   && No caption since we are using pictures
   Top =     10        && Top of button
   Left =    9        && Default left side of button
   Height =  2.3    && Height of button
   Width =   6        && Width of button
   Picture = "\VFP\Fox.dbf"   && Default Picture
   ************************************************************
   * Generalized Navigation button Click class
   PROCEDURE Click
     IF ALIAS() != THISFORM.DBFAlias
         SELECT (THISFORM.DBFAlias)
     ENDIF
   ENDPROC
ENDDEFINE
```

Once you have defined the generalized navigation control buttons, you can derive the other buttons from them. Listing 14.9 shows the definition of the Previous Record control button.

Listing 14.9. A source listing for definition of the Previous Record command button subclass.

```
****************************************************************
* Define Previous Record Navigation Button
DEFINE CLASS PrevButton AS NavButton
   Left =  19
   Picture = "prvrec_s.bmp"
   ToolTipText = "Previous Record"
   StatusBarText = "Skip to Previous Record"
   PROCEDURE Click
       NavButton::Click
       SKIP -1
       IF BOF()
          =MessageBox("Beginning of file encountered",64)
```

```
        GO TOP
      ENDIF
      THISFORM.Refresh
   ENDPROC
ENDDEFINE
```

The `PrevButton` control button subclass is derived from the generalized navigation control button class, `NavButton`. All you need to do is to define the `Click` event method and the following properties:

Property	*Purpose*
`Left`	This property specifies the position of the left side of the control in foxels. (See the Note box that follows this list.)
`Picture`	This property specifies a graphics bitmap file or field that displays on a control. You are required to enter the complete path of the bitmap image (for example, `Picture = C:\VFP\MYDIR\ZOO.BMP`).
`ToolTipText`	This property specifies the text that appears as `ToolTip` for a control. You can only set the `ToolTipText` property if the `ShowTips` property is set to true (`.T.`) for the form or toolbar that contains the control. In the `AddressForm` class definition, the `ShowTips` property is set to true (`.T.`). In Figure 14.7, the mouse pointer (not visible) is over the button to the far left, and the `ToolTipText` message First Record is displayed.
`StatusBarText`	This property specifies the text that appears in the status bar when a control has the focus. Notice in Figure 14.7 that the Go to First Record message is displayed on the status bar, and the mouse pointer (not visible) is hovering over the `cmdFirst` object. (The `cmdFirst` object has the focus.)

NOTE

For all of the examples in this chapter, values for position and size properties are specified in a scaling mode called a foxel. *Foxel* is a term that was dreamed up by the FoxPro development team. It refers to a scaling mode that facilitates the conversion of programs between character-based and graphical platforms. A foxel is equivalent to the average height and width of a character in the current font.

The `Click` event method uses the global resolution operator (::) to call the `Click` event method for the `NavButton` class, and then selects the previous record in the ADDRESS.DBF table. A message box displays if the record pointer is already positioned on the first record. The `Click` event methods for the `cmdFirst`, `cmdNext`, and `cmdLast` subclasses are similar to the class definition for `cmdPrev`.

The `THISFORM.Refresh` method is called in all navigation buttons after the table is repositioned to repaint the Address Book form and refresh all of the data values.

Listing 14.10 shows the `Click` event method for the `cmdSearch` subclass, which is much different from the other navigation buttons. This button has a picture of a pair of binoculars on it. The picture suggests that this button is used to *look* for something. When you choose the search button, the `SearchForm` form displays as shown in Figure 14.8. You enter some characters in a text box, and the `LOCATE` command searches for one of the `address.name` fields that contains the typed text. This is a simple search mechanism, but its purpose is to illustrate how you can create a new form from within another. Also, the `SearchForm` form is modal, which means that it is active and retains the focus until you explicitly close it with the OK button. In other words, you cannot access another window in Visual FoxPro until you choose the OK push button. If the argument passed to the form's `Show()` method is `1`, the form is modal. If you omit the argument or set it equal to `0`, the form becomes modeless. Listing 14.10 presents the source listing for the `cmdSearch` subclass `Click` event method and the class definition for the `SearchForm` class.

Listing 14.10. The source listing for the `cmdSearch` subclass `Click` event method and the `SearchForm` class definition.

```
PROCEDURE Click
       LOCAL frmSearch
       NavButton::Click
       frmSearch = CREATEOBJECT("SearchForm")     && Prompt for string
       frmSearch.Show(1)            && Display as a modal form
       GO TOP
       LOCATE FOR __TempString$Name
       RELEASE __TempString
       IF EOF()
          GO TOP
          =MessageBox("Name was not found",64)
       ENDIF
       RELEASE frmSearch
       THISFORM.Refresh
   ENDPROC

****************************************************************
*  This form prompts user for search string
*  It must be made a 'Modal' form. That means that other
*  disabled until the form is destroyed.
 DEFINE CLASS SearchForm AS FORM
   Caption = "Search for Record"
   ScaleMode =  0    &&  Foxels screen mode
   MaxButton = .F.   && No Maximum button
   MinButton = .F.   && No Minimize button
   ControlBox= .F.   && No control box in left-upper corner
   WindowType= 2
   Top    =   2
   Left   =   2
   Height =  6.75
   Width  =  36
   AutoCenter = .T.
```

```
    BackColor = RGB(192,192,192)
    ADD OBJECT txtSearch AS TextBox ;
       WITH Top = 2.25, Left =   4.00, ;
            Height = 1.50, Width =  28, ;
            Value = ""
    ADD OBJECT label1 AS Label ;
        WITH Caption = "Enter Name to search for:", ;
             Top = 0.75, Left = 6, Height = 1,      ;
             Width = 28, BackColor = RGB(192,192,192)
    ADD OBJECT cmdOK AS CommandButton ;
        WITH Caption = "OK", Top = 4.5, Left =  12, ;
        Height = 1.5, Width =  12
    ************************************************************
    * Methods
    PROCEDURE cmdOK.Click
         RELEASE THISFORM
    ENDPROC
    PROCEDURE cmdOK.Destroy
         PUBLIC __TempString
         __TempString = ALLTRIM(THISFORM.txtSearch.Value)
    ENDPROC
ENDDEFINE
```

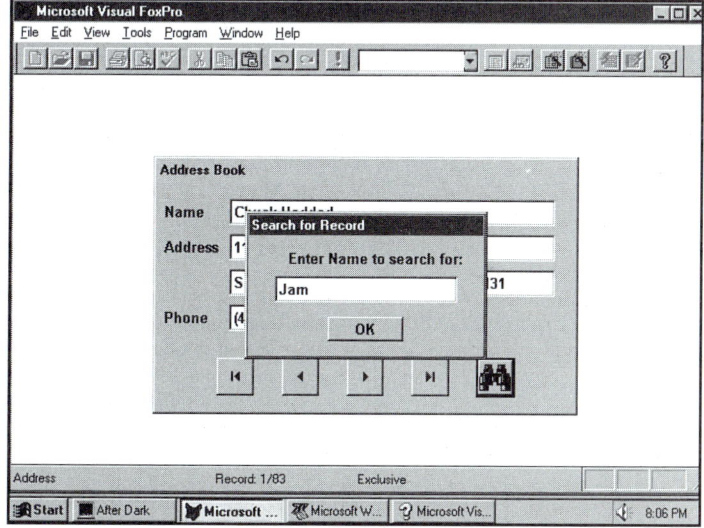

FIGURE 14.8.
The Search for Record form.

When you exit from the `SearchForm` form, the contents of the text box are stored in a public variable, `_TempString`, when the form is destroyed. The `Destroy()` event method for the `cmdOK` object contains the following commands:

```
PUBLIC __TempString
__TempString = ALLTRIM(THISFORM.txtSearch.Value)
```

`txtSearch` is the `TextBox` object on the form. Note that the `Value` property contains the contents of a `TextBox` control. When a modal form returns, program control returns to the statement, which follows the `frmSearch.Show(1)` statement, that activated the form.

Now that you have all your buttons defined, it is time to define the AddressBook form class and add the labels, TextBox, and navigation button objects. The following properties were set:

Property Assignment	*Description*
`ScaleMode = 0`	Sets scale mode to foxels. (`ScaleMode = 3` is for pixel scale mode, which is normally used in Form Designer.)
`MaxButton = .F.`	Suppresses the Maximize button.
`MinButton = .F.`	Suppresses the Minimize button.
`Caption = "Address Book"`	Establishes the form caption.
`ScaleMode = 0`	Establishes the scale mode. It determines whether position and size values for properties are specified in Foxels (0) or Pixels (3, the default).
`Height = 13`	The height of the form.
`Width = 64`	The width of the form.
`BackColor = RGB(192,192,192)`	Sets the background color to gray.
`AutoCenter = .T.`	Automatically centers the form in the screen.
`ShowTips = .T.`	Shows `Tiphelp` when the mouse pointer is over the control.

The `ADD OBJECT` statement is used to add all the controls to the form. You should examine the `ADD OBJECT` statements in Listing 14.11 to make sure you understand them. There is one property specified for the `TextBox` objects that you have not seen before. It is the `ControlSource` property. This property sets a field or expression that displays in the text box. The `ControlSource` property is used to specify the source of data to which a control is bound. Here is the syntax:

```
Object.ControlSource[ = <expC>]
```

For controls, `<expC>` specifies a variable or field. For a text box control, the `ControlSource` property is normally set to a field. However, it also can be set to an expression. If it is set to an expression, it becomes read-only. When a `ControlSource` property is established, the object's `Value` property contains a data value which is the same data type as the `ControlSource` variable or field.

The `AddressBook` class definition contains three event methods: the `Init`, `Load`, and `Destroy` event methods. You can access the contained objects from within the `Init` event method of the container since the `Init` events for all the objects contained in a container object are triggered before the `Init` event of the container. For this reason, the form's `Init` event method is a good place to initialize the objects it contains. Consequently, the `AddressBook` class `Init` event method establishes the `Top` property for the navigation buttons relative to the height of the Address Book form.

The `Load` event for the form occurs before any of the objects it contains are initialized. Many of the controls contained in the form need to define data properties. Therefore, the `Load` event method is a good place to establish the data environment used by the form. The `AddressBook` class `Load` event method places the ADDRESS.DBF table in use.

The `Destroy` event method terminates the `READ EVENTS` command by executing a `CLEAR EVENTS` command. The complete listing of the Address Book application is provided in Listing 14.11.

Listing 14.11. The source listing for the Address Book application.

```
*************************************************************
* Program: ADDRESS.PRG
* Purpose: Form that displays address book entries
*************************************************************
frmAddresses = CREATEOBJECT("AddressBook")    && Create the form
frmAddresses.Show                       && Display the form
READ EVENTS
*************************************************************
* Define Addressbook form
*
DEFINE CLASS AddressBook AS FORM
   ScaleMode  = 0    && Set Scale mode to Foxel.
                     && (ScaleMode=3 is for Pixel scale mode)
   MaxButton = .F.   && No Maximum button
   MinButton = .F.   && No Minimize button
   Caption    = "Address Book"
   Height     = 13                  && Height of form
   Width      = 64                  && Width of form
   BackColor  = RGB(192,192,192)    && Gray background color
   AutoCenter = .T.    && Automatically centers form in screen
   ShowTips   = .T.    && Show Tiphelp when cursor is over control
   DBFAlias   = "ADDRESS"
   ***********************************************************
   * Add Navigation buttons to form
   ADD OBJECT cmdFirst  AS FirstButton
   ADD OBJECT cmdPrev   AS PrevButton
   ADD OBJECT cmdNext   AS NextButton
   ADD OBJECT cmdLast   AS LastButton
   ADD OBJECT cmdSearch AS Search
   ***********************************************************
   * Add text fields to Form
   ADD OBJECT txtName  AS TextBox      ;
      WITH Top = 1.0,  Left =  11.0,   ;
      Height = 1.5,    Width =  50.0,  ;
      ControlSource = "address.name"
   ADD OBJECT txtAddress  AS TextBox   ;
      WITH Top = 3.0,  Left =  11.0,   ;
        Height = 1.5,  Width =  50.0,  ;
        ControlSource = "address.address"
   ADD OBJECT txtCity  AS TextBox      ;
      WITH Top = 5.0, Left =  11.0,    ;
        Height = 1.5, Width = 20.0,    ;
        ControlSource = "address.city"
   ADD OBJECT txtState  AS TextBox     ;
      WITH Top =  5.0,   Left =  33.0, ;
         Height = 1.5 ,  Width = 12.0, ;
         ControlSource = "address.state"
   ADD OBJECT txtZip  AS TextBox       ;
```

continues

```
frmAddress1 = CREATEOBJECT("AddressBook")
frmAddress1.Show
frmSearch = CREATEOBJECT("SearchRecord")
frmSearch.Show
```

Four important characteristics that the object-oriented programming language must support are reusability, encapsulation, extendibility, and polymorphism. Visual FoxPro supports all four of these characteristics.

Listing 14.12. The source listing for the derived Address Book application, ADDRESS1.PRG.

```
****************************************************************
* Program: ADDRESS1.PRG
* Purpose: Illustrates how to create a Grid control and how to
*          derive a subclass from an existing user-defined class
*****************************************************************
SET PROCEDURE TO ADDRESS.PRG ADDITIVE
use address
frmAddr1 = CREATEOBJECT("NewAddressBook")
frmAddr1.Show
READ EVENTS
****************************************************************
* Define NewAddressBook subclass derived from Addressbook
DEFINE CLASS NewAddressBook AS AddressBook
    Height = 21    && Make form taller to make room for the
                       && grid
    ************************************************************
    * Init Event code - Add the grid and move buttons
    PROCEDURE Init
       AddressBook::Init
       THISFORM.AddObject("grdAddress","AddressGrid")
       THISFORM.grdAddress.Visible = .T.
       THISFORM.grdAddress.Height = 8.5
ENDPROC
ENDDEFINE

****************************************************************
* Definition for Grid class, AddressGrid
DEFINE CLASS AddressGrid AS Grid
    Caption = "Address Book"
    Top = 9        && Position of top of grid
    Left = 0        && Position of left side of grid
    Width = 64        && Width of grid
    ColumnCount = 6    && Number of columns in grid
    Visible = .T.    && Required to make grid visible
    ************************************************************
    *  Specify column data fields for grid
    Column1.ControlSource = "Address.Name"
    Column2.ControlSource = "'('+Address.AreaCode+') '+Address.Phone"
    Column3.ControlSource = "Address.Address"
    Column4.ControlSource = "Address.City"
    Column5.ControlSource = "Address.State"
    Column6.ControlSource = "Address.Zip"
    ************************************************************
    *  Grid Init Event Method - Good place to setup Headings
    *                           and other properties for columns
    Procedure Init
      WITH THIS.Column1
```

```
         .Width = 20            && Width of first column
         .Header1.Caption = "Name"    && Column label grid
      ENDWITH
      WITH THIS.Column2
         .Width = 15
         .Header1.Caption = "Phone Number"
      ENDWITH
      WITH THIS.Column3
         .Width = 20
         .Header1.Caption = "Address"
      ENDWITH
      WITH THIS.Column4
         .Width = 15
         .Header1.Caption = "City"
      ENDWITH
      WITH THIS.Column5
         .Width = 8
         .Header1.Caption = "State"
      ENDWITH
      WITH THIS.Column6
         .Width = 6
         .Header1.Caption = "Zip"
      ENDWITH
   ENDPROC
   ***********************************************************
   *  BeforeRowColChange - Event Method that fires when
   *                 the selected row or column changes.
   *  (Code refreshes form when new row is selected)
   Procedure BeforeRowColChange
      PARAMETERS nColumnChange
      THISFORM.Refresh
   ENDPROC
ENDDEFINE
```

Creating a Custom Toolbar

Sometimes you have operations in an application that are used frequently, and you want to provide your users a convenient and fast method of executing these operations. Custom toolbars are ideal for this purpose. This section illustrates how to create a custom toolbar programmatically. Of course, it is easier to create a custom toolbar with Form Designer or the Class Designer. However, the point of this chapter is to illustrate OOP language extensions.

The program presented in Listing 14.13, TOOLBAR.PRG, is a great example that demonstrates how to take advantage of the powerful functionality of the Visual FoxPro `ToolBar` base class. In this example, the `NavigateToolBar` custom toolbar is defined. It is based on the `ToolBar` base class and inherits all of its power.

The `oToolBar` variable is a reference to the object created from the `NavigateToolBar` class. It is declared a `PUBLIC` variable, so it will still exist after the TOOLBAR.PRG program finishes executing. As long as `oToolBar` exists, the custom toolbar remains active. The `oToolBar` variable exists until you release it with the `RELEASE oToolBar` or `CLEAR ALL` commands.

Listing 14.13. The source listing for the custom toolbar program TOOLBAR.PRG.

```
***************************************************************
* TOOLBAR.PRG
* Description: Create a custom toolbar
***************************************************************
#INCLUDE "FOXPRO.H"
PUBLIC oToolBar
oToolBar= CREATEOBJECT("NavigateToolBar")
oToolBar.Show

***************************************************************
* Define class of menu buttons for toolbar
DEFINE CLASS ToolButton AS COMMANDBUTTON
   Left = 0
   Caption= ""      && No caption, picures are used
   Height =  1.8     && Height of button
   Width =   4.0    && Width of button
   PROCEDURE Click
        LOCAL cName
        IF EMPTY( DBF())  && Is there an active table?
           cFilename=GETFILE("DBF")
           IF ( EMPTY(cFileName) )
               RETURN
           ENDIF
           USE (cFileName)
        ENDIF
        cName = UPPER(THIS.Name)
        DO CASE
          CASE cName = "FIRST"
             GO TOP
          CASE cName = "PREV"
             SKIP -1
             IF BOF()
                 =MessageBox ;
                 ("Beginning of file encountered")
                 GO TOP
             ENDIF
          CASE cName = "NEXT"
             SKIP
             IF EOF()
                GO BOTTOM
                =MessageBox("End of file encountered")
             ENDIF
          CASE cName = "LAST"
             GO BOTTOM
          CASE cName = "DELETE"
             IF DELETED()
                =MESSAGEBOX("Record is already Deleted")
             ELSE
                DELETE
             ENDIF
          CASE cName = "NEW"
             APPEND BLANK
             GO BOTTOM
      ENDCASE
      DISPLAY
   ENDPROC
ENDDEFINE
```

```
* Define class of NavigateToolbar toolbar
*  place it below system menu
*
DEFINE CLASS NavigateToolBar AS Toolbar
   ScaleMode= SCALEMODE_USER
   Caption= "Navigate"
   Left= 0          && Make sure custom toolbar
   Top = 0            && docks at the left of the
                       && standard toolbar
   BackColor  = COLOR_GRAY    && from FOXPRO.H
   ControlBox = .F.    && No control box (with Close, etc.)
   Movable    = .T.    && Make it so it can be moved
   Sizable    = .T.     && Make it so its size can be changed

   ***************************************************************
   * Add buttons to toolbar
   ***************************************************************
   ADD OBJECT btnTop AS ToolButton ;
         WITH Name= "FIRST", ;
              Picture = "frsrec_s.bmp", ;
              ToolTipText= "Go to First record"

   ADD OBJECT btnPrev AS ToolButton ;
         WITH Name= "PREV", ;
              Picture = "prvrec_s.bmp",;
              ToolTipText= "Go to Previous Record"

   ADD OBJECT btnNext AS ToolButton ;
         WITH Name= "NEXT", ;
              Picture = "nxtrec_s.bmp", ;
              ToolTipText= "Go to Next record"

   ADD OBJECT btnLast AS ToolButton ;
         WITH Name= "LAST", ;
              Picture = "lstrec_s.bmp", ;
              ToolTipText= "Go to Last record"

   ADD OBJECT sep3 AS Separator
   ADD OBJECT sep4 AS Separator

   ADD OBJECT btnSave AS ToolButton ;
         WITH Name= "DELETE", ;
              Picture= "remov_s.bmp", ;
              ToolTipText= "Mark for deletion"

   ADD OBJECT btnNew AS ToolButton ;
         WITH Name= "NEW", ;
              Picture = "new_s.bmp", ;
              ToolTipText= "Add new record"

   PROCEDURE Init
       THIS.Dock(TOOL_TOP)  && Dock toolbar at top
   ENDPROC
ENDDEFINE
```

The ToolButton class is based on the CommandButton base class and defines a generalized button for the toolbar. It contains code for the Click event method, which performs table navigation functions for all the other buttons. It operates on the table in the current work area. If you do not have a table in use in the current work area, the GETFILE() function is called to display the Open File dialog box so that you can select a table. When you do a navigation operation, the new record displays.

The other button objects are created from the ToolButton class. They inherit all the properties and methods from the ToolButton class. You only need to override the Name, Picture and ToolTips properties when you create the buttons and add them to the custom toolbar. The Name property is the name that you use to refer to an object in code. It is supplied only so that it can be used in the Init event method to determine which navigation operation to perform. For example, the object named First positions the database to the first record in the table.

The NavigateToolBar class is based on the Visual FoxPro Toolbar base class. As you can see in Listing 14.13, several of the properties are overwritten. The only ones that are significant are the Left=0 and Top=0 properties which force the NavigateToolBar object to be placed at the beginning of the Visual FoxPro standard toolbar.

If you wish, you can make the standard toolbar disappear when your custom toolbar activates by placing the following code in the Init event method of your custom toolbar:

```
IF WEXIST("")  && Check to see if Standard Toolbar is present
    HIDE WINDOW Standard
ENDIF
```

You can make the standard toolbar reappear when your application exits by placing the SHOW WINDOW Standard command in the Destroy event method of your custom toolbar.

The toolbar base class DOCK() method, called in the Init event method, forces the custom toolbar to be docked at the top of the main window. Here is the syntax of the DOCK() function:

```
oToolBar.DOCK(<expN>[,nX,nY])
```

The Numeric argument designates how the custom toolbar is docked and can have the following values:

<expN>	*Constant*	*Description*
-1	TOOL_NOTDOCKED	Undocks the toolbar
0	TOOL_TOP	Docks the toolbar at the top of the window
1	TOOL_LEFT	Docks the toolbar at the left side of the window
2	TOOL_BOTTOM	Docks the toolbar at the bottom of the window
3	TOOL_RIGHT	Docks the toolbar at the right side of the window

The optional `nX` and `nY` arguments specify optional horizontal and vertical coordinates of the docked position.

NOTE

The constants listed in the table are defined in the FOXPRO.H header file. To use this file, you include it at the beginning of your program with the `#INCLUDE "FOXPRO.H"` statement. The `#DEFINE` statements in a header file are read into the `#DEFINE` table in memory as though they were part of your program. FOXPRO.H resides in the home directory and contains useful constants that are used throughout Visual FoxPro. The `COLOR_GRAY` and `SCALEMODE_USER` constants in Listing 19.1 are defined in FOXPRO.H.

Incidentally, header files typically have an .H file name extension. The only statements that are recognized in header files are the `#DEFINE`, `#UNDEF`, and `#IF…#ENDIF` preprocessor directives. Comments and Visual FoxPro commands included in a header file are ignored.

The `ADD OBJECT` statements in the `NavigateToolbar` class definition add the button objects to the custom toolbar. In addition to the buttons, a couple `SEPARATOR` type objects are added to the toolbar to put space between the two groups of buttons. These objects are based on the Visual FoxPro `SEPARATOR` base class.

Figure 14.10 shows the custom toolbar, `NavigateToolbar`, that is defined and created by the TOOLBAR.PRG program. You can undock, resize, or redock this toolbar by dragging it around the screen the same way you can any other Visual FoxPro toolbar. Notice that when you dock a toolbar, its title bar disappears and its border changes to a single line. You can resize a toolbar from a single row of buttons to multiple lines of buttons.

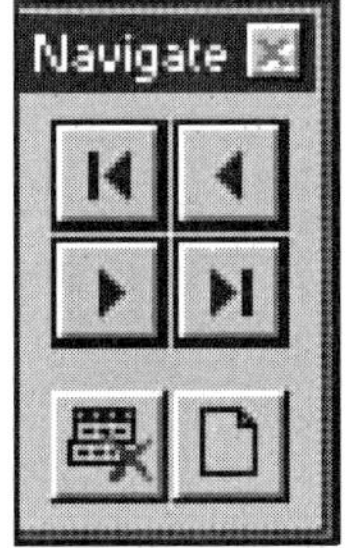

FIGURE 14.10.
Example output resulting from the execution of the TOOLBAR.PRG program.

TIP

You can use the `SetAll()` method to set all of the grid `Header` object's foreground and background colors to red on blue in the grid shown in Figure 14.10. Simply add the following two lines of code to the Form's `Init` method:

```
THISFORM.grdAddress.SetAll('ForeColor',;
        RGB(255,0,0),'header')
THISFORM.grdAddress.SetAll('BackColor',;
        RGB(0,0,255),'header')
```

You can use the `Grid` class `SetAll` method to set other column and header properties.

It is easier to describe how the various Visual FoxPro OOP programming elements operate by showing you code that programmatically creates and uses classes. However, it is not the easiest way to generate classes. You normally use the Class Designer to create classes and class libraries visually. You normally use the Form Designer to create forms and form sets visually. In Chapter 15, "The Visual Class Library, the Class Designer, and the Class Browser," you will learn how to create classes and class libraries using Class Designer.

Summary

This chapter explores the use and functionality of the object-oriented programming (OOP) language extensions incorporated in the Visual FoxPro language. I show how Visual FoxPro supports the fundamental characteristics of OOP, such as inheritance, subclassing, encapsulation, and polymorphism. I show how to programmatically define classes and subclasses that inherit properties and methods from Visual FoxPro base classes and user-defined classes. I show how properties and methods are encapsulated into an object. I show how encapsulation allows you to restrict access to objects so that users can only refer to the methods and properties you designate. I also show how Visual FoxPro takes advantage of polymorphism to allow you to have different object types with methods of the same name but behave differently depending on the type of object that is referenced.

15

The Visual Class Library, the Class Designer, and the Class Browser

In general, the art of government consists in taking as much money as possible from one class of citizens to give to the other.

—Voltaire (1694–1778)
Dictionnaire Philosophique

Chapter 14, "Object-Oriented Programming," showed you how to define classes and reuse them in various applications. Visual FoxPro provides a mechanism that allows you to store class definitions in a library, called a *visual class library,* and to access these definitions as needed for applications. In this chapter, you will learn what visual class libraries are, how to create them, how to add class definitions to them, how to maintain them, and how to use them.

In addition, you will learn how to use the Class Designer to visually create class definitions. Classes that are created by the Class Designer are stored in visual class libraries. You will also learn all about the Class Browser and how to use it.

Visual FoxPro Class Libraries

When you are designing an application, you break it into many elements. Many of the elements are the same. They just appear on different forms (for example, OK buttons, different parts of the application). Suppose you had an application with 30 different forms. Many of the controls used on the various forms are common to most of the forms. You might have, for example, buttons labeled OK, Exit, and Help that appear on most of the forms. In the old days of traditional programming, you would program an OK button every time you needed it for a form.

With the Visual FoxPro object-oriented programming (OOP) model, you can create your own user-defined classes that define commonly used objects, and you can store them in a class library. Then, whenever you need one, you can pick a user-defined class out of the library and place it on your form at the appropriate place. For example, you could have in your class library a class that defines a big picture button with a big red check mark on it that signifies to the user OK, I am ready to exit the form. It might even contain a `RELEASE THISFORM` command in its `Click` event method to exit the form. Then, whenever you want to use this button, you can pick it out of the class library and place it on your form. This is really easy to do in the Form and Class Designers. You have the option to select any class library and have its classes appear as buttons on the Form Control toolbar. You can pick one of these buttons and place it on the form. Of course, an object defined in the class library can be a single button or a whole collection of objects, such as a toolbar containing table record navigation controls.

Also, you might have certain application components, such as a sign-on screen, that are used with all of your applications. You might have a query tool, a company phone book, or even a form that looks like a mail box that appears whenever you receive e-mail. Application components are good candidates for inclusion in a class library.

You may want to maintain a certain naming convention or your own interface standards for your class library. For example, you can develop a library of classes that contains a standardized set of interface elements for your company. In addition, the names of your user-defined subclasses and any user-defined properties and methods can conform to a standard. If you can get your programming staff to use a standardized library, you will benefit from the increased productivity of your staff and the improved maintainability and updatability of your software base.

In addition to building your own user-defined Visual FoxPro class libraries, you can purchase Visual FoxPro class libraries from third-party developers. In addition, you can download Visual FoxPro class libraries from online service libraries such as the CompuServe forum library, FoxForum. (See Appendix D.) These class libraries are contributed to the user community by generous Visual FoxPro developers. If a third-party Visual FoxPro class library proves to be useful to you, it can substantially reduce your development costs.

Microsoft ships with the Visual FoxPro product several class libraries that are useful as well as instructive. One of these libraries is the WIZARDS.VCX class library. It is full of very interesting classes that define controls, groups of controls, and even special forms. Classes in this library are used by the wizards to create forms. In the Visual FoxPro \VFP\SAMPLES directory there are some fascinating examples of class libraries that you may find useful and illuminating.

The Physical Layout of a Class Library File

Visual class libraries are stored in files with the .VCX extension. A visual class library has no obscure magical format; it is just a DBF table with a .VCX extension. It also has an associated memo file with a .VCT extension. It contains a header record that describes the class library in general. Each one of the other records contains all the definition information for one of the classes in the class library. A record has memo fields that store the class name, base class name, properties, methods, and so on. If you are curious, you can place a VCX file in use (`USE mylib.vcx`) and use the `LIST` or `BROWSE` commands to examine the file's contents. However, you really do not have to concern yourself with the file's structure and composition, since Visual FoxPro automatically maintains class library files with its class library maintenance commands. The two important points for you to remember about a class library file are that it contains a collection of classes and that it is maintained by Visual FoxPro.

Class Library File Maintenance

Class libraries are used in Visual FoxPro to store and access classes that are visually created using the Class Designer. You can add classes to or remove classes from a visual class library by using visual interaction or Visual FoxPro commands. The commands you can use to manipulate or use classes and visual class libraries are summarized in Table 15.1.

Table 15.1. A description of the commands that manipulate VCX visual class libraries.

Commands and Functions	*Description*
`ADD CLASS ClassName [OF ClassLibraryName1] TO ClassLibraryName2 [OVERWRITE]`	Adds a class definition to a VCX visual class library.

continues

Table 15.1. continued

Commands and Functions	*Description*
`CREATE CLASSLIB ClassLibraryName`	Creates a new VCX visual class library file.

`CREATE CLASS ClassName ¦ ?`
`[OF ClassLibraryName2 ¦ ?]`
`[AS cBaseClassName`
`[FROM ClassLibraryName1]]`
	Executes the Visual FoxPro Class Designer so that you can create a new class definition.

`MODIFY CLASS ClassName`
`[OF ClassLibraryName1]`
`[AS cBaseClassName`
`[FROM ClassLibraryName2]]`
`[NOWAIT] [SAVE]`
	Executes the Visual FoxPro Class Designer so that you can modify an existing class definition.

`RELEASE CLASSLIB ClassLibraryName`	Closes a VCX visual class library that contains class definitions.
`REMOVE CLASS ClassName` `OF ClassLibraryName`	Removes a class definition from a specified VCX visual class library.

`RENAME CLASS ClassName1`
`OF ClassLibraryName`
`TO ClassName2`
	Renames a class definition contained in a VCX visual class library.

`SET CLASSLIB TO ClassLibraryName` `[ADDITIVE][ALIAS AliasName]`	Opens a VCX visual class library that contains class definitions. If the `ADDITIVE` keyword is specified, the current visual class libraries remain open.

Creating a VCX Visual Class Library

You can create a class library whenever you save a class, or you can create a class library with the `CREATE CLASSLIB` command. The `CREATE CLASSLIB` command has the following syntax:

```
CREATE CLASSLIB ClassLibraryName
```

`ClassLibraryName` is the name of the VCX visual class library that is created by this command. It automatically overwrites any existing file with the same name unless the `SET SAFETY` command is `ON`. If `SET SAFETY` is `ON`, Visual FoxPro asks if you would like to overwrite the existing class library file.

Adding a Class to a VCX Visual Class Library

You use the ADD CLASS command to add a class definition to a class library or to copy a class definition from one VCX visual class library to another. Here is the syntax of the ADD CLASS command:

```
ADD CLASS ClassName [OF ClassLibraryName1]
     TO ClassLibraryName2 [OVERWRITE]
```

ClassName specifies the name of the class definition to be added to the VCX visual class library, *ClassLibraryName2*. If you specify the optional OF *ClassLibraryName1* clause, Visual FoxPro searches for the class definition (*ClassName*) in the specified visual class library. If you omit the OF *ClassLibraryName1* clause, Visual FoxPro searches for the class definition in any VCX visual class libraries opened with the SET CLASSLIB command. If Visual FoxPro cannot locate the class definition or the class definition already exists in the target visual class library (*ClassLibraryName2*), Visual FoxPro generates an error message.

If you specify a target class library (*ClassLibraryName2*) that does not exist, Visual FoxPro creates the visual class library and adds the class definition to the library.

If you specify the OVERWRITE keyword, Visual FoxPro removes all class definitions from the target visual class library before the class definition is added. If you omit the OVERWRITE keyword, the class definition is added to the target visual class library.

You can also use the Visual FoxPro Program Manager to add a class from one class library to another visual class library. To do this, you add both the source and target visual class libraries to a project. Then you drag classes from the source class library to the target visual class library. Here are example steps for adding classes to a class library:

1. Create a new visual class library, MyClLib.VCX, with the following command:
   ```
   CREATE CLASSLIB MyClLib
   ```
2. Open a project, MyProj.PRJ, from the **F**ile menu **O**pen option or execute the following command from the Command window:
   ```
   MODIFY PROJECT MyProj
   ```
3. Click on the Class Libraries item in the list.
4. Click on the **A**dd button and choose the MyClLib.VCX visual class library from the Open File dialog box.
5. Click on the **A**dd button and choose the visual class library C:\VFP\SAMPLES\CONTROLS\BUTTONS.VCX for the Visual FoxPro sample directory.
6. Click on the plus sign (+) on the Class Libraries item in the list.
7. Click on the plus sign (+) on the Buttons item to open the list. The classes in the BUTTONS.VCX class library, which include cmdCancel, cmdhelp, cmdok, and vcr, display.

8. Drag the `cmdok` class to the `mycllib` visual class library in the list and drop it. Notice that the minus sign (–) changes to a plus sign (+) in front of the `mycllib` item.
9. Click on the plus sign (+) in front of the `mycllib` visual class item. The list opens, revealing the newly added class, `cmdok`, as shown in Figure 15.1.

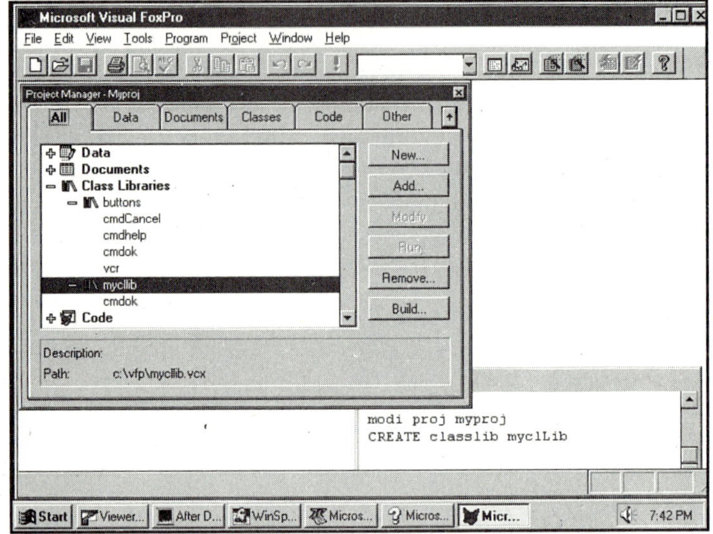

FIGURE 15.1.
Copying classes from one visual class library to another.

NOTE

You cannot add a class definition to a visual class library from a Visual FoxPro program or application (PRG or APP), or from a procedure file. One way you can do this is to re-create your class definition within the Class Designer and manually copy text from the PRG file methods and paste it in the Class Designer event or method window. There is another, easier way. On the CD-ROM that accompanies this book there is a program in \EDC\PrgToVcx.PRG that converts PRG programs to VCX files. This program was contributed by Tom Rettig of Rettig Micro Corporation.

Opening a Visual Class Library

The `SET CLASSLIB TO` command opens a VCX visual class library so that you can have access to the class definition it contains. The `CREATEOBJECT()` function or `ADD OBJECT` statement searches for the class definition for the specified object in the following locations and order:

1. The current program.
2. The VCX class libraries opened with the `SET CLASSLIB` command.

3. Procedure files opened with the `SET PROCEDURE` command.
4. Programs in the Visual FoxPro program calling chain. The search begins with the most recently executed program and continues until the first executed program is encountered.

If Visual FoxPro does not locate the class definition, it gives up and issues the error message Class definition not found.

Here is the syntax of the `SET CLASSLIB TO` command:

```
SET CLASSLIB TO ClassLibraryName
   [ADDITIVE][ALIAS AliasName]
```

The `TO` *`ClassLibraryName`* clause specifies the name of the VCX visual class library file to open. If you do not specify a fully qualified path for the VCX file, Visual FoxPro searches for the visual class library in the following locations and order:

1. The default Visual FoxPro directory. This directory is specified with the `SET DEFAULT` command.
2. The directories in the Visual FoxPro path. The Visual FoxPro search path is defined with the `SET PATH` command.

If you specify the `SET CLASSLIB TO` command without any other arguments, Visual FoxPro closes all open VCX visual class libraries. The `RELEASE CLASSLIB` command can be used to release individual visual class libraries.

If you specify the `ADDITIVE` keyword, the specified visual class library is opened without closing any visual class libraries that are currently open. If you do not specify the `ADDITIVE` keyword, then any visual class libraries that are currently open are closed before the specified visual class library is opened.

You can use an `ALIAS` clause to specify an alias name for a visual class library. You can then refer to the alias name instead of the actual visual class library name. Here is an example:

```
SET CLASSLIB TO MyForms  ALIAS Mine
frmMyNewForm = CREATEOBJECT("Mine.MyNewForm")
```

If you do not specify the name of the `ALIAS` clause, the name of the visual class library is used as the alias. Here is an example:

```
SET CLASSLIB TO MyForms
frmMyNewForm = CREATEOBJECT("MyForms.MyNewForm")
```

Closing an Individual VCX Visual Class Library

You can close an individual visual class library that was opened with the `SET CLASSLIB TO` command with the `RELEASE CLASSLIB` command. Here is the syntax:

```
RELEASE CLASSLIB ClassLibraryName
```

The specified visual class library is closed and removed from memory.

Removing a Class Definition from a Visual Class Library

You can remove from the Project Manager a class definition in a VCX visual class library by selecting the class definition from an open visual class library list and pressing the Remove button. (See Table 15.1.) Also, you can remove a class definition from a visual class library using the `REMOVE CLASS` command. Here is the syntax:

```
REMOVE CLASS ClassName OF ClassLibraryName
```

The specified class (*`ClassName`*) is removed from the named visual class library (*`ClassLibrary`*).

Renaming a Class

You can change the name of a class definition in a VCX visual class library with the `RENAME CLASS` command. Here is the syntax:

```
RENAME CLASS ClassName1 OF ClassLibraryName
   TO ClassName2
```

`ClassName1` specifies the name of the class definition in the VCX visual class library, *`ClassLibraryName`*, that is changed to the class definition name specified by the `TO` *`ClassName2`* clause.

Creating a New Class and Modifying an Existing Class

You can visually create or modify a class in a VCX visual class library using the Class Designer. You can execute the Class Designer from the **F**ile menu **N**ew or **O**pen option from the Project Manager or by executing either the `CREATE CLASS` or `MODIFY CLASS` command from the Visual FoxPro Command window. Here is the syntax of the `CREATE CLASS` command:

```
CREATE CLASS ClassName ¦ ? [OF ClassLibraryName1 ¦ ?]
      [AS cBaseClassName [FROM ClassLibraryName2]]
MODIFY CLASS ClassName ¦ ? [OF ClassLibraryName1 ¦ ? ]
  [AS cBaseClassName [FROM ClassLibraryName2]] [NOWAIT] [SAVE]
```

The *`ClassName`* argument specifies the name of the class definition to create or modify. If you specify a question mark (?), the New Class dialog box displays, as shown in Figure 15.2. Your job is to specify the name of the class definition to create or modify, the class on which you intend to base the class (to be created or modified), and the name of the visual class library in which you plan to store the class definition.

Figure 15.2 shows the first step of an example in which a container class definition named `NavigateBar` that is based on the Visual FoxPro container base class is created and placed in the MyClass.VCX visual class library.

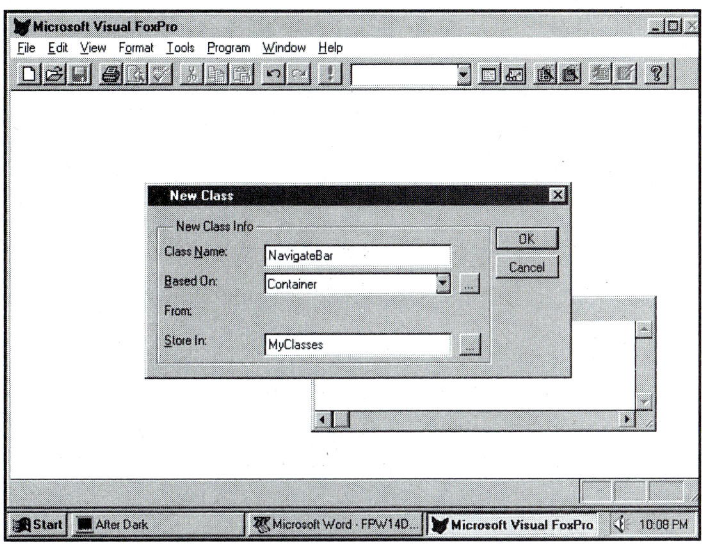

FIGURE 15.2.
The New Class dialog box.

If you do not specify all the information required by the Class Designer, you are required to fill in the missing information in the New Class dialog box. Then the Class Designer appears, as shown in Figure 15.3. The Class Designer window has the same general appearance as the Form Designer window. It contains the same Property window, Form Display window, and Form Controls toolbar. The main difference is that the purpose of the Class Designer is to design class definitions, not forms. Also, the **C**lass menu is added to the systems menu bar, as shown in Figure 15.3. In addition, new menu options are added to the **V**iew and F**o**rmat menus. All the new options for the Class Designer menus are described in Table 15.2.

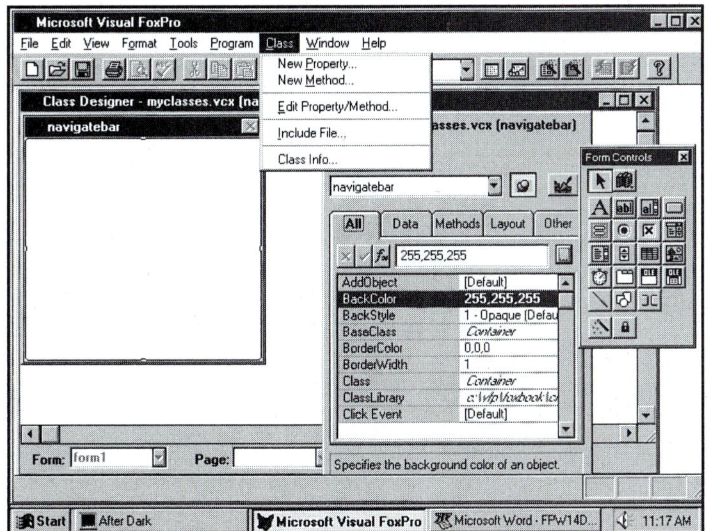

FIGURE 15.3.
The Class Designer window.

Table 15.2. A description of the menus and options used with Class Designer.

Menu	*Option*	*Description*
Edit	Undo, Redo, Cut, Copy, Paste	Editing operations.
View	✓ Design	Places Class Designer in Design mode. If you uncheck the option, the Command window appears.
	Tab Order	Places the Class Designer in Tab Order mode. Displays the Tab Order dialog box, which allows you to change the tab order of the controls. See Chapter 19, "The Form Designer," for more information.
	✓ Properties	Toggles on and off the Properties dialog box, as shown in Figure 15.3.
	✓ Code	Displays a window containing method code. You can choose the control and method from drop-down lists.
	✓ Form Controls Toolbar	Toggles on and off the Form Controls toolbar, which contains the controls that can be placed on the form. The Form Controls toolbar controls are described in Table 15.3. (All of the toolbars described in this table are shown in Figure 15.4.)
	✓ Layout Toolbar	Toggles on and off the Layout toolbar, which contains controls to align and size controls.
	✓ Color Palette Toolbar	Toggles on and off the Color Palette toolbar.
	✓ Grid Lines	Toggles on and off the display of grid lines on the Class Designer form.
	✓ Show Position	Toggles on and off the display of the position and size of form objects on the status bar.
Format	Align, Size, Bring to Front, Send to Back	Same as the controls on the Layout toolbar, which is discussed in detail in Chapter 19.

Menu	*Option*	*Description*
	Horizontal Spacing	This option enables you to control the horizontal spacing between selected controls. From a drop-down menu, you can choose to increase, decrease, or make equal the horizontal spacing between controls.
	Vertical Spacing	This option enables you to control the vertical spacing between selected controls. From a drop-down menu, you can choose to increase, decrease, or make equal the vertical spacing between controls.
	Snap to **G**rid	Toggles the Snap to Grid mode on and off. When you move a control, it moves smoothly across the layout if the Snap to **G**rid option is off. However, if the option is on, the control jumps between the invisible alignment grid lines.
	Set Grid Scale	Changes the size of the cells in the invisible alignment grid used by the Snap to **G**rid option.
Class	New **P**roperty	Displays the Properties window so that you can specify a new property for a class and a description of that property. (See Figure 15.5.) You can also specify whether the property is protected.
	New **M**ethod…	Displays the New Method window so that you can specify the name of a new method for a class and a description of that method. You can also specify whether the method is protected. The new method appears in the Properties dialog box, and the description of the new method appears at the bottom of the Properties window.

continues

Table 15.2. continued

Menu	*Option*	*Description*
	Edit Property/Method	Opens the Property/Method window so that you can edit the name or description of an existing user-defined property or method.
	Include File...	Displays the Include File window so that you can type the name of an Include file or click on the three-dot button to select an existing Include file from the Open File menu. Include files normally have an .H extension.
	Class Info...	Displays the Class Info dialog box, which contains the Class and Members tabs. The Class tab shows the following values, which you can change: The name of the selected class The toolbar icon file The container icon file name The scale units—foxels or pixels A description of the class The Members tab shows a list of all the properties and methods of the class members, their design-time values, a check box indicating whether they are protected, and a check box indicating whether the base class `Init` method executes (`No Init`).

Some of these controls are discussed in the following sections.

The View Menu Show Position Option

The Show Position option toggles the Show Position mode on and off. If you set the Show Position mode to on, a check mark (✓) appears at the left of the option, and the coordinate position of the mouse pointer and the dimensions of selected controls display in the status bar. If you set the Show Position mode to off, the position of the mouse pointer and the dimensions of the selected controls do not display.

The Format Menu Snap to Grid Option

With the Snap to **G**rid option, you can turn the alignment grid on and off. The *alignment grid* is an invisible horizontal and vertical grid. When you move or define a control, it is automatically aligned to (or *snapped to*) the nearest grid line. The alignment grid corresponds to the ruler grid alignment set in the Grid Properties dialog box. A check mark appears to the left of the option when the alignment grid is on. If the alignment grid is off, the control moves freely around the Layout window.

> **TIP**
>
> If you are like me, you find that the Snap to Grid is too restrictive. I like to keep it turned off unless I need it for a specific purpose. To turn it off permanently, open the **T**ools menu Options dialog box Forms tab. Then uncheck the **S**nap To Grid check box. You can save this as a default value by clicking on the Set As Default button.

The Format Menu Set Grid Scale Option

If you choose the **S**et Grid Scale option, the Grid Properties dialog box displays. You can specify the units of measurements for the rulers and grid lines or change the horizontal and vertical grid line spacing.

The Format Menu Bring to Front Option

If you choose the Bring to **F**ront option, the selected control or controls move forward so that they cover the other controls. This option is active only if one or more controls are selected.

The Format Menu Send to Back Option

If you choose the Send to **B**ack option, the selected control or controls move to the bottom of the Class Designer Layout window and are covered by other controls.

The Form Controls Toolbar

You can place controls on the Class Designer Layout window by using the Form Controls toolbar. You click on the control you want and then click someplace on the Layout window, and the control is deposited. You can drag the control to the size you want. The buttons on the toolbar are defined in Table 15.3.

Table 15.3. The Class Designer window Form Controls toolbar.

Icon	*Toolbar Button*	*Description*
	Select Objects	The Select Objects button displays a mouse pointer control that you can use to resize and move other controls. When you create a control, the Select Objects button is automatically selected, unless the Button Lock button is pressed, in which case you can click on a control once and add multiple copies of the control without having to click the toolbar control button again.
	View Classes	The View Classes button brings up a menu that enables you to select and display a registered VCX visual class library. After you select a class, the buttons that represent classes in the selected visual class library display on the toolbar. You can drag and drop class objects the same way you do other controls. However, the selected class cannot be added to container objects, such as grids and page frames, on the form. If you want to add the selected class to a container on the form, simply drag and drop the class picture to an area on the form and then cut and paste the object to the desired container.
A	Label control	This button adds a Label control. The Label control displays static text that cannot be changed by the user. It is used as a caption for other controls.
abl	Text Box control	This button adds a Text Box control The Text Box control displays a text box that holds a single line of text. The user can type new text or change existing text in the text box.

Icon	*Toolbar Button*	*Description*
	Edit Box control	This button adds an Edit Box control. The Edit Box control displays an edit box that contains one or more lines of text. The user can type new text or change existing text in the edit box.
	Command Button control	This button adds a Command Button control. The Command Button control is used to carry out an operation.
	Command Button Group control	This button adds a Command Button Group control. The Command Button Group control displays a group of buttons from which the user can choose to perform an operation.
	Option Button Group control	This button adds an Option Button Group control. An Option Button Group control display multiple options. The user can select only one of the option buttons at a time.
	Check Box control	This button adds a Check Box control. The Check Box control displays a check box that the user can select or clear to indicate if something is true or false. In addition, the user can use check boxes to specify multiple choices, and the user can select or clear more than one check box.
	Combo Box control	This button adds a Combo Box control. The Combo Box control displays either a drop-down combo box or a drop-down list box. The user can select one item from a list of items or enter a value manually.

continues

Table 15.3. continued

Icon	*Toolbar Button*	*Description*
	List Box control	This button adds a List Box control. The List Box control displays a list box from which the user can select an item. The user can scroll the list if it contains more items than can be displayed at one time.
	Spinner control	This button adds a Spinner control. The Spinner control contains numeric input that falls within a given range. The user can click on the arrows to increase or decrease the numeric value or enter a value manually.
	Grid control	This button adds a Grid control. The Grid control displays a spreadsheet-type control similar to a browse window. You can insert columns into a Grid control.
	Image control	This button adds an Image control. The Image control is used to display a graphical image on your form.
	Timer control	This button adds a Timer control. The Timer control is used to trap timer events at set intervals. This control is invisible at runtime.
	PageFrame control	This button adds a PageFrame control. The PageFrame control is used to display multiple, usually tabbed, pages containing controls.
	OLE control	This button adds an OLE control. The OLE control is used to provide object linking and embedding (OLE) from an OLE server into your application.
	OLE Bound control	This button adds an OLE Bound control. The OLE Bound control is used to provide OLE support. However, it is bound to a General data type field.

Icon	Toolbar Button	Description
	Line control	This button adds a Line control. The Line control is used to draw vertical, horizontal, or diagonal lines at design time.
	Shape control	This button adds a Shape control. The Shape control is used to draw a variety of shapes on your form at design time. You can draw a rectangle, rounded rectangle, square, rounded square, oval, or circle.
	Separator control	This button adds a Separator control. The Separator control is used to create an object that places space between controls in a toolbar.
	Builder Lock	The Builder Lock button is used to specify whether a builder is used when a control is added to a form. If you select the Builder Lock button, a control-specific builder opens each time you add a new control to a form. Builders assist you in specifying properties for controls.
	Button Lock	The Button Lock button, if selected, enables you to add multiple controls of the same type without having to click the control button on the toolbar each time you add a control. You can double-click on a control button to achieve the same effect.

An Example Container Class with Table Navigation Buttons

As you can see in Figure 15.3, a window named NavigateBar displays in the Class Designer window. Now, continuing with the development of this example, add six control buttons to the form, as shown in Figure 15.4. Then resize the NavigateBar (container class) window as shown in Figure 15.4. Next, set the values in the Properties window to correspond to the values shown in Table 15.4.

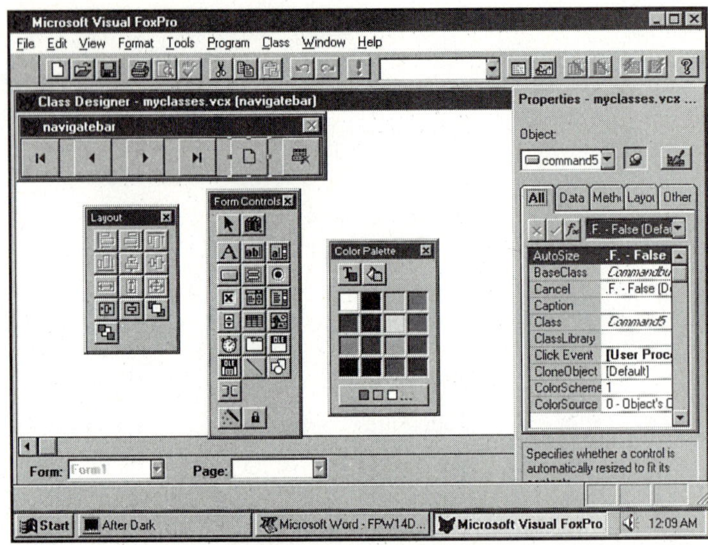

FIGURE 15.4.
The Class Designer window with the `navigatebar` *container class defined.*

TIP

When the Properties window initially displays, it blocks half of the Class Designer window, as shown in Figure 15.3. One of the Visual FoxPro forum contributors, Steven Black of SBC, provides an automated solution for those of you that are tired of manually repositioning and resizing the Properties window when you create a new class or form. You execute a program containing the following code before you use the Form Designer or Class Designer:

```
ON KEY LABEL F9 ZOOM WINDOW Properties ;
     NORM  FROM 0, 0.75*SCOLS() ;
     TO SROWS()*1.08, SCOLS()*1.02
```

Then, when you bring up the Form Designer or Class Designer, you press the F9 key, and the Properties window displays, as shown in Figure 15.4. You may want to adjust the constants in the code for your specific video display. Note that this technique can be extended. You can use the `HIDE WINDOW`, `SHOW WINDOW`, `RELEASE WINDOW`, or `ZOOM WINDOW` commands with any of the toolbars and other windows.

Table 15.4. The properties for `navigatebar` container class controls.

Controls	*Properties*
command1	Caption = "" Picture = frsrec_s.bmp ToolTipText = ("First Record") StatusBarText = ("Go To First Record")
command2	Caption = "" Picture = prvrec_s.bmp ToolTipText = ("Previous Record") StatusBarText = ("Go To Previous Record")
command3	Caption = "" Picture = nxtrec_s.bmp ToolTipText = ("Next Record") StatusBarText = ("Go To Next Record")
command4	Caption = "" Picture = lstrec_s.bmp ToolTipText = ("Last Record") StatusBarText = ("Go To Last Record")
command5	Caption = "" Picture = new_s.bmp ToolTipText = ("Add New Record") StatusBarText = ("Add a New Record")
command6	Caption = "" Picture = remov_s.bmp ToolTipText = ("Delete Record") StatusBarText = ("Add a New Record")

The properties presented in Table 15.4 include `Caption`, `Picture`, `ToolTipText`, and `StatusBarText`. The `Caption` properties are set to null strings since none of the buttons contain text. Each button contains a graphic image represented by a BMP file. A `ToolTipText` property, which is a little message that appears when the mouse pointer hovers over a button, is established for each button. Likewise, the text that displays on the status bar defined by the `StatusBarText` property is established for each button. The next step is to add a new property which defines the alias name of the table. You can do this by first selecting the container class on the Layout form. Then you choose the **C**lass menu New **P**roperty option. The New Property dialog box appears, as shown in Figure 15.5. You type in the name of the new property and a description. The new property will appear in the Properties window. When you select the new property, the description is shown at the bottom of the Properties window.

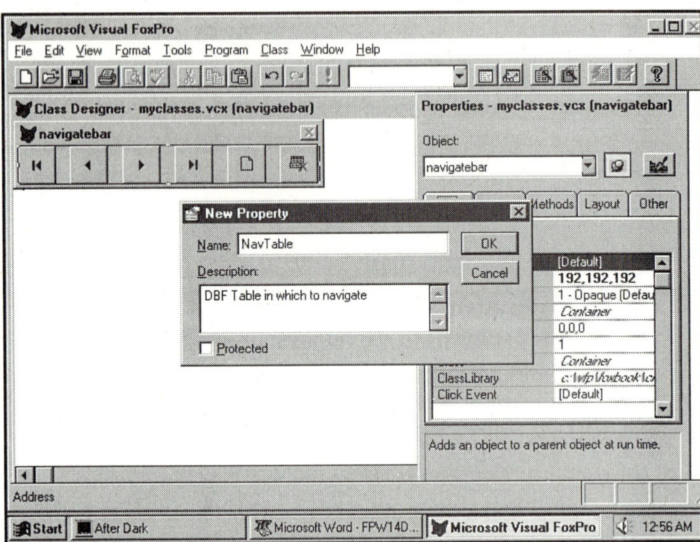

FIGURE 15.5.
The New Property window with the `NavTable` property defined.

When you double-click on one of the controls that you added to the layout, the Code window appears, as shown in Figure 15.6. You enter code to perform some operation for a navigation button event occurrence. The event method code for all six buttons is presented in Table 15.5.

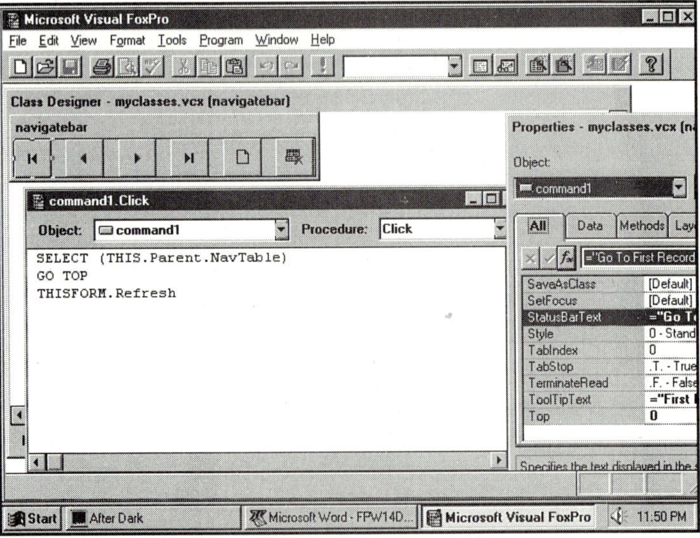

FIGURE 15.6.
The Code window showing the `Command1` button `Click` event method.

Table 15.5. The methods for the `navigatebar` class.

Class	*Event Method Code*	*Comments*
`Command1`	`PROCEDURE Click`	Processes the `Click` event for the `Command1` button.
	`SELECT (THIS.Parent.NavTable)`	Ensures that the table is selected.
	`GO TOP`	Goes to the top of the table.
	`THISFORM.Refresh`	Refreshes the form.
	`ENDPROC`	
`Command2`	`PROCEDURE Click`	Processes the `Click` event for the `Command1` button.
	`SELECT (THIS.Parent.NavTable)`	Ensures that the table is selected.
	`SKIP -1`	Goes to the previous record in the table.
	`IF BOF()` `GO TOP`	Ensures that the record pointer is positioned at the top of the file.
	`ENDIF`	
	`THISFORM.Refresh`	Refreshes the form.
	`ENDPROC`	
`Command3`	`PROCEDURE Click`	Processes the `Click` event for the `Command1` button.
	`SELECT (THIS.Parent.NavTable)`	Ensures that the table is selected.
	`SKIP`	Goes to the top of the table.
	`IF EOF()` `GO BOTTOM`	If the record pointer moved past `EOF`, the record pointer is repositioned to the last record.
	`ENDIF`	
	`THISFORM.Refresh`	Refreshes the form.
	`ENDPROC`	
`Command4`	`PROCEDURE Click`	Processes the `Click` event for the `Command1` button.
	`SELECT (THIS.Parent.NavTable)`	Ensures that the table is selected.

continues

Table 15.5. continued

Class	*Event Method Code*	*Comments*
	`GO BOTTOM`	Goes to the bottom of the table.
	`THISFORM.Refresh`	Refreshes the form.
	`ENDPROC`	
`Command5`	`PROCEDURE Click`	Processes the `Click` event for the `Command1` button.
	`SELECT (THIS.Parent.NavTable)`	Ensures that the table is selected.
	`APPEND BLANK`	Appends a blank record.
	`THISFORM.Refresh`	Refreshes the form.
	`ENDPROC`	
`Command6`	`PROCEDURE Click`	Processes the `Click` event for the `Command1` button.
	`SELECT (THIS.Parent.NavTable)`	Ensures that the table is selected.
	`DELETE`	Deletes the record.
	`THISFORM.Refresh`	Refreshes the form.
	`ENDPROC`	

You have now created a subclass, which contains control buttons, based on the Visual FoxPro container base class. Your subclass will be stored in your MyClasses visual class library. Save your subclass and exit from the Class Designer. Now choose the **T**ools menu **O**ption option. The Options dialog box appears. Choose the Class tab, as shown in Figure 15.7. Now, register your MyClass.VCX visual class library. In this way, you can use your new control on a form.

Using a User-Defined Class from a Visual Class Library

The next step is to create a form that uses your new `NavigateBar` class. To do this, you open the Form Designer either by selecting the **F**ile menu **N**ew option from the Project Manager, or by executing the following command from the Command window:

```
MODIFY FORM NavForm
```

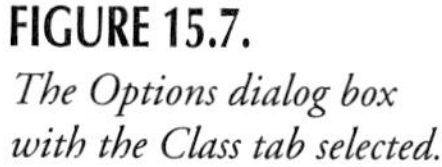

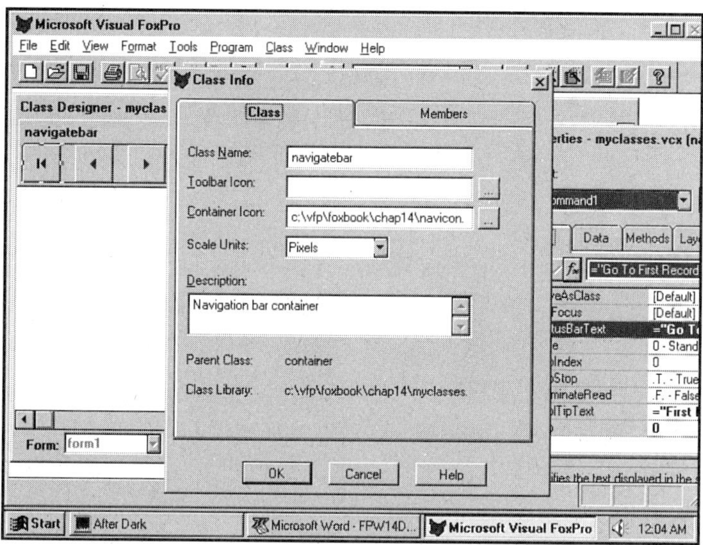

FIGURE 15.7.
The Options dialog box with the Class tab selected.

From the Form Designer window, click on the Views Class button from the Forms Control toolbar. A list pops up that contains an Add option and the names of visual class libraries. Choose the `MyClasses` item from the list. This assumes that you registered your MyClasses.VCX visual class library in the options menu. If you did not, choose the Add... option from the list. An Open File dialog box opens from which you can choose a visual class library. You choose your MyClasses.VCX visual class library at this time. In either case, the buttons for the standard Visual FoxPro visual class library with the `NavigateBar` class button from the MyClasses visual class library are shown in Figure 15.8. Click on the `NavigateBar` button, place your newly designed control on the form layout, and resize the control as shown in Figure 15.8. Next, place a grid on the form using the following steps:

1. Choose the **V**iew menu Data **E**nvironment... option (or right-click on the form and choose the Data **E**nvironment... option), and the Data Environment window appears.
2. Choose the **D**ataEnvironment menu Add... option and add the Address.DBF table to the Data Environment window.
3. Click on the title bar for the Address table window in the Data Environment window and drag it to the form. A grid control will automatically be created.
4. Size and position the grid as shown in Figure 15.8.

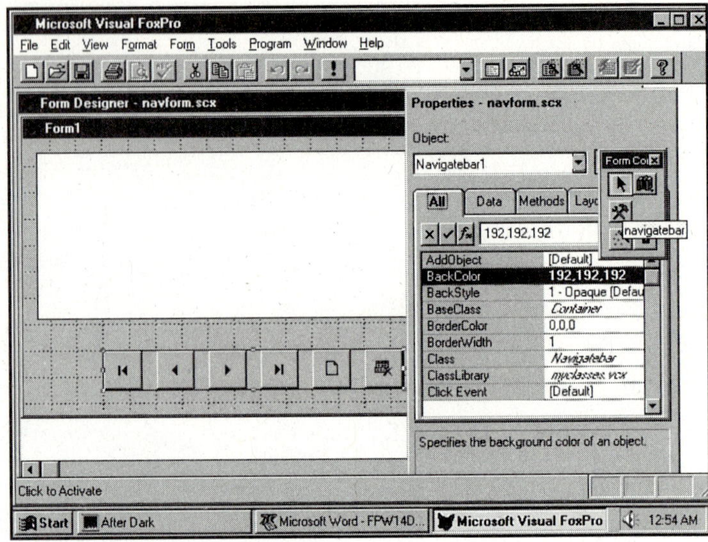

FIGURE 15.8.
The Form Designer window showing the NavForm form.

The next step is for you to set the user-defined property `NavTable` of the `Navigatebar1` subclass to `="Address"`. Also, set the following properties for the `form1` subclass from the Properties window:

Property Setting	*Comments*
`BackColor = RGB(192,192,192)`	Makes background gray
`Caption = "My Navigation Form"`	Adds a custom caption
`AutoCenter = .T.`	Forces the form to be centered in the main window
`ShowTips = .T.`	Allows tips to show in the form

You can execute the form you have created with the following command:

```
DO FORM NavForm
```

The resultant form is presented in Figure 15.9. More information regarding the Forms Designer is presented in Chapter 19.

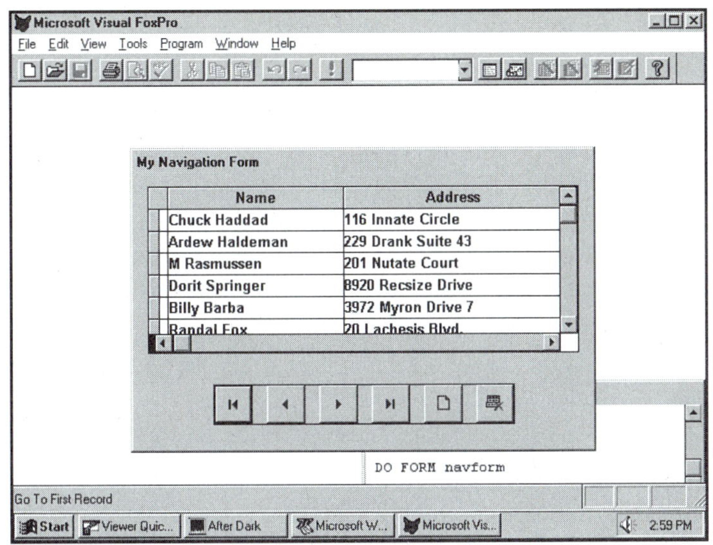

FIGURE 15.9.
The My Navigation Form window.

The Visual FoxPro Class Browser

One of the important object-oriented development environment tools is the *Class Browser*. The Class Browser is shipped with the Visual FoxPro Professional Edition. This tool displays all the elements of a class in a class library and the hierarchical relationship between classes. Visual C++, Borland C++, and SmallTalk all have a Class Browser utility. Visual FoxPro has a Class Browser, too. You use the Class Browser to browse through the classes in a VCX visual class library or a form (SCX) file. You can manage the properties and methods of classes as well as design new subclasses.

Executing the Class Browser

You can execute the Class Browser using the **T**ools menu **C**lass Browser option.

> **NOTE**
>
> The Visual FoxPro Class Browser is a FoxPro application that resides in the same directory as the Visual FoxPro system. It is available with the Visual FoxPro Professional Edition. The **T**ools menu **C**lass Browser option launches the Class Browser by executing the application specified by the `_BROWSER` system memory variable. `_BROWSER` specifies the fully qualified path name of the Class Browser. By default, `_BROWSER` is set to `_BROWSER = HOME() + BROWSER.APP`.

Another way to launch the Class Browser is to execute it from the Command window using the following command:

```
DO (_BROWSER) WITH [<visual class library> ¦ <object reference> ] [, <class name>]]
```

You can specify either *<visual class library>* and a reference to an object (*<object reference>*), or the name of a class (*<class name>*). If you execute the Class Browser and have not specified the WITH clause, the Open File menu displays. Then you select a visual class library file (VCX) or form file (SCX). You can execute multiple instances of the Class Browser. You can even execute multiple instances of the same VCX class library file.

Figure 15.10 is an example of the Class Browser window showing classes from the VFP\SAMPLES\MAINSAMP\LIBS\TSBASE.VCX visual class library. The Class Browser window is in its maximized state.

FIGURE 15.10.
The Visual FoxPro Class Browser window.

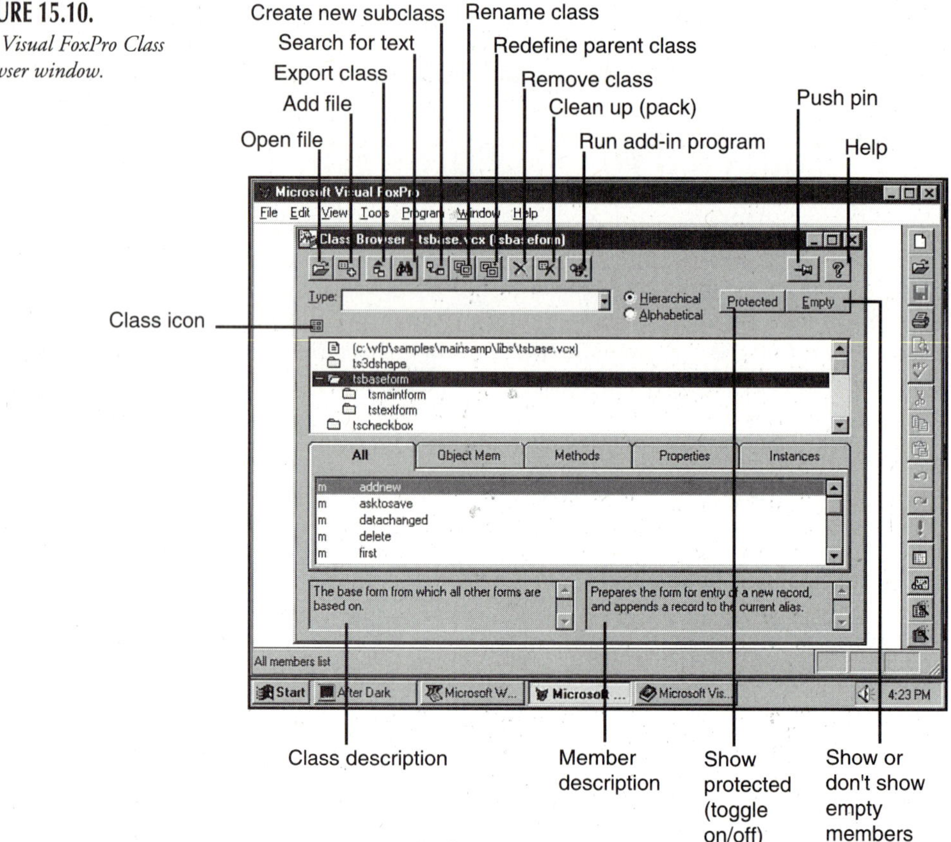

The Class List

In the middle of the Class Browser is the class list. The class list displays the classes in the selected visual class libraries in either hierarchical order or in alphabetical order depending on whether the hierarchical or alphabetical option button is chosen. In hierarchical display mode, class trees can be expanded or collapsed. You click on a class name to select it. You can use the arrow keys to move the cursor up and down the list. If you want to edit a selected class, double-click on the class name, and the Class Designer is launched to modify the selected class.

TECHNICAL NOTE

The class list is a good example of the use of an OLE control. As you recall, the Class Browser is a Visual FoxPro application. It uses the OUTLINE.OCX file OLE control to display the class list in outline form.

Your class hierarchy may span several class libraries. If you double-click on the folder picture next to the class name, the parent class of the specified class displays. If the parent class is located in another directory, the Class Browser launches another instance of itself and automatically selects the parent class in the new Class Browser form.

When a class is selected in the class list, a class picture, a class description, and a class members list display.

The Class Picture

Above the left corner of the class list is the *class picture.* It is a bitmap (BMP) image that represents the base class of the selected class in the class list. You can assign a bitmap image to a class within the Class Designer by selecting the **C**lass menu **C**lass Info... option and setting the Container icon to the desired picture. You can also set the bitmap image of a class in the Class Browser by right-clicking the class picture image. The File Open dialog box appears, and you choose a bitmap file. The bitmap file you choose becomes the class picture, the toolbar icon, and the container icon.

When a class library is registered and you are designing a class with the Class Designer or a form with the Form Designer, you can select that class library from the Forms Control toolbar View Classes button. The class pictures of the classes in that class library appear in the Form Controls toolbar. Then you can drag the class picture and drop it on the form that you are designing. This will add an instance of the selected class.

The Class Description

When you create a class with the Class Designer, you can enter a *class description* from the Class Info dialog box Class tab. When a class is selected, its class description displays in the Class Description edit box at the bottom left corner of the Class Browser window. You can edit the class description in the Class Description window.

When you add a user-defined method or property to a form or class with the Class Designer or Form Designer, you are prompted to enter a description. If you select a method or property in the members list, the member's description displays in the Members/Instance edit box at the bottom right of the Class Browser window. If you select an instance from the members list, the class library, class, base class, and variable scope (public/hidden) of the selected object display. If you select an object, its class name, parent class name, and base class name display.

The Class Members List

The tabbed form pages in the Class Browser window show members and object instances for the selected class. It is referred to as the *class members list.* The class member form pages support the All, Object Members, Methods, Properties, and Instances options. The default members list mode is the All option.

The All Tab

The default tab is the All tab. Select this tab and all members for the selected class display. The members list is ordered alphabetically and by category. The category is represented by a lowercase letter that displays in the first column of the list. If the member is a protected property or method, an asterisk (*) displays between the member category character and the member name.

The Object Members Tab

The Object Members tab list displays objects for the selected class. The object members are created by the `ADD OBJECT` statement. The list is in alphabetical order. The member category is represented by the letter o, which displays in the first column of the list.

The Properties Tab

The Properties tab list displays properties for the selected class. The list is in alphabetical order. The member category is represented by the letter p, which displays in the first column of the list.

The Methods Tab

The Methods tab list displays methods for the selected class. The list is in alphabetical order. The member category is represented by the letter m, which displays in the first column of the list.

The Instances Tab

The Instances tab list displays instances for the selected class. The list is in alphabetical order. The member category is represented by the letter i, which displays in the first column of the list.

Class Type

You can use the Class **T**ype combo box below the toolbar to select a class type or enter a character string to filter the class list. When the Class Type combo box is empty, all classes in the visual class libraries display. Also, you can select other class types, such as Controls, Custom, Form, Formset, and Toolbar. You can also type user-defined class names into the combo box to filter the class list. You can type a wildcard specification in the combo box to represent a range of classes. In addition to the standard wildcard characters (`?` and `*`), you can enclose text in percent signs (`%`), which specify that the enclosed text is included with the user-defined class type entries that display in the class list. You can also supply a list of wildcard specifications in which the wildcard specifications are separated by commas. Here are some examples:

`frm*`	Displays all classes that begin with `frm`
`%fred%`	Displays all classes that contain the text `Fred`
`?md*`	Displays all classes that begin with any character followed by `md`
`grid*,cmd*,frm*`	Displays all classes that begin with `grid`, `cmd`, or `frm`

If the display mode is hierarchical, all classes that satisfy the wildcard specification will display, only if the class that matches the filter is the uppermost class in a tree or all parent classes in the tree match. For example, if the class type filter is `Form*`, a parent class named `BigForm` with a subclass named `Form1` will not display. In alphabetic display mode, all classes and subclasses that begin with `Form` will display.

The Buttons for Filtering

There are three buttons at the top right side of the Class Browser used for filtering class members from the members list. They are labeled **P**rotected, **I**nherited, and **E**mpty.

The **P**rotected command button toggles off and on the protected member filter mode that filters protected members from the members list. The default protected member filter mode is on. The protected member filter mode does not affect the instance list. If the protected members filter mode is on, public members are included and protected members are not included in the members list for the selected class. Otherwise, both public and protected members are included in the members list for the selected class.

The **Inherited** command button toggles on and off the inherited member filter mode, which filters inherited members from the members list. The default inherited member filter mode is off. The inherited member filter mode does not affect the instance list. If the inherited members filter mode is on, declared members are included and inherited members are not included in the members list for the selected class. Otherwise, both inherited and declared members are included in the members list for the selected class.

The **Empty** command button toggles on and off the empty member filter mode. The default empty memory filter mode is off. The empty memory filter mode does not affect the instance list. An example of an empty member might be the `Click` event method for a subclass of the `Form` class when no code is associated with the `Click` event. If the empty member filter mode is on, defined members are included and blank members are not included in the members list for the selected class. If the empty member filter mode is on, both nonblank members and blank members are included in the members list for the selected class.

The Toolbar Buttons

A toolbar spans the top of the Class Browser. The buttons are described in Table 15.6.

Table 15.6. The Class Browser window Form Controls toolbar.

Icon	*Button*	*Description*
	Open File	Opens an existing VCX visual class library or SCX form file or creates a new one.
	Add File	Adds an existing VCX visual class library file or an SCX form file to the Class Browser.
	Export Class	Exports a class definition onto the Clipboard and an edit window.
	Find	Searches for specific text.
	Subclass	Creates a subclass of the selected class.
	Rename	Changes the name of the selected class.
	Redefine	Changes the parent class of the selected class.

Icon	*Button*	*Description*
	Remove	Removes the selected class. If a VCX visual class library file or SCX form file is selected in the class list, the file and its associated memo field file (VCT or SCT) is erased. You should not worry about accidentally pressing this button and losing your file or class, because a confirmation box always displays before the item is actually erased.
	Clean up	Removes records marked for deletion from a VCX or SCX file by executing the `PACK` command.
	Add-ins	Displays the menu of the currently defined add-in programs stored in the BROWSER.DBF table.
	Push pin	This option toggles on and off the always-on-top status of the Class Browser window.
	Help	Displays the Help menu for Class Browser.

As stated in Table 15.7, the Export Class exports a class definition onto the Clipboard. Then an edit window appears containing the generated code for the selected class. At that time the Class Browser is hidden. When you close the edit window, the Class Browser becomes visible again. The edit window, which contains generated code and any changes made to the code, is placed on the Windows Clipboard. If you select the name of a visual class library file in the class list and click the Export button, all classes in the visual class library will be exported. If you select an SCX form filename in the class list and press the Export button, the classes in the SCX form are exported along with header code. The header code creates the proper executable code to create an instance of the form and run it.

Summary

In this chapter, you have learned how to use the Visual FoxPro Class Designer to design classes and subclasses. You have learned all about visual class libraries and how to use controls in a visual class library to create forms in the Class Designer. You have also learned about the Class Browser and how to use it in the process of developing an application.

IV

Rapid Application Development Tools

16

The Visual FoxPro Menu Designer

Few things are harder to put up with than the annoyance of a good example.

—Mark Twain (1835–1910)
Pudd'nhead Wilson

This is the first in a series of chapters dedicated to the Visual FoxPro 3.0 rapid application development (RAD) tools. This chapter teaches you all about the Visual FoxPro Menu Designer.

Visual FoxPro 3.0 introduces object-oriented programming into the Xbase language. You have learned about the visual class objects for containers and controls. You probably would expect that Visual FoxPro would support menu objects, too. This is not the case. Visual FoxPro still uses the FoxPro 2.*x*-type menu definition commands. In a way, this is a good thing because it reduces the number of new things you have to learn if you already know how to program in FoxPro 2.*x*. However, as Visual FoxPro evolves, menu classes will probably be incorporated. You can, however, prepare for the future by always using the Menu Designer to build your user-defined interfaces. Then it will be easier to upgrade your applications when OOP is used to define menu objects.

The hard way to create a menu system is to hand code the menus using the commands you learned about in Chapter 7, "FoxPro Language Elements for Creating Windows and Menu Systems." The easy way to generate a menu interface is to use the Visual FoxPro Menu Designer. The Menu Designer uses "point and shoot" techniques to paint a menu system. Then the Menu Designer generates FoxPro code.

The Visual FoxPro Menu Designer

You may want to use the Visual FoxPro system menu interface as the foundation for everything you do in FoxPro, especially if you're not familiar with the FoxPro command language. Its layout is similar to that of other Windows applications (such as Word for Windows, WordPerfect for Windows, Excel, and Lotus 1-2-3 for Windows). Consequently, the system menu can be the foundation for any FoxPro application you create. You can use the FoxPro Menu Designer to create your own systems menu bar from scratch or by starting with the FoxPro system bar and deleting unwanted menu pads and pop-up options or adding your own menu pads and pop-up menu options. This section describes how to use the FoxPro Menu Designer to create your own custom system menu bar.

For the rest of this discussion, I refer to the FoxPro system menu bar as the SYSMENU. The SYSMENU is normally turned on during the execution of applications. Of course, if you don't want users to access the SYSMENU, you can turn it off with the `SET SYSMENU OFF` command. If you want the SYSMENU to always be available, as it is in the interactive mode, use the `SET SYSMENU AUTOMATIC`.

If you want to have a SYSMENU but you don't want all the pads and options to be displayed, you can create a modified SYSMENU with the FoxPro Menu Designer. This utility enables you to define a custom SYSMENU. Once you've defined your own custom SYSMENU, you can choose the **M**enu menu **G**enerate option, and FoxPro generates a program, with an .MPR extension, that contains all the `DEFINE` commands for your custom SYSMENU. You can execute this menu program using the DO command. You can also incorporate the menu program file into your application. The Menu Designer saves your menu design in a database table with the extension .MNX and an associated memo file with the extension .MNT.

Executing the FoxPro Menu Designer

You can execute the Menu Designer from the SYSMENU, or you can type the CREATE MENU or MODIFY MENU commands into the Command window. To execute the Menu Designer to create a new menu file from the SYSMENU, choose the **F**ile menu **N**ew option, then select the **M**enu option, and the Menu Designer executes.

To execute the Menu Designer using FoxPro commands, execute one of these commands:

```
MODIFY MENU [<expFN> ¦ ? ] [SAVE] [NOWAIT]
   [IN WINDOW <window name1>]
   [IN SCREEN] [WINDOW <window name2>]

CREATE MENU [<expFN> ¦ ? ] [SAVE] [NOWAIT]
   [IN WINDOW <window name1>]
   [IN SCREEN] [WINDOW <window name2>]
```

If you don't supply the filename extension, .MNX is assumed. If the menu file doesn't exist, it is created. If it exists, it is modified. If you specify a question mark instead of a filename, the Open dialog box containing MNX files appears. When you select a name from the menu, the Menu Designer executes and opens the selected menu file for modification. If you don't specify a filename, the filename Untitled is assigned and when you exit the Menu Designer, a Save As dialog box appears, and you can assign the name of the file. Before the Menu Designer exits, it generates the menu file with the .MNX extension. You can choose the **M**enu menu **G**enerate option to create a menu program file with an .MPR extension.

If the NOWAIT keyword is specified, the program executes the Menu Designer, displays its contents, and then continues executing the user program. The Menu Designer window remains on the screen. You can specify the SAVE keyword from within a program to force the Menu Designer to leave its window on the screen when it exits. The WINDOW clause causes the Menu Designer to be drawn inside a previously defined window instead of the Menu Designer window. See Chapter 7 for a description of the DEFINE WINDOW command. The Menu Designer activates the named window on entry, and it occupies the window during processing. The window is deactivated and erased from the screen when the Menu Designer exits. If you specify the optional IN WINDOW clause, the Menu Designer window displays inside the other window.

Elements of the Menu Designer

When the Menu Designer executes, regardless of how it is executed, the Menu Designer window appears on the screen, as shown in Figure 16.1.

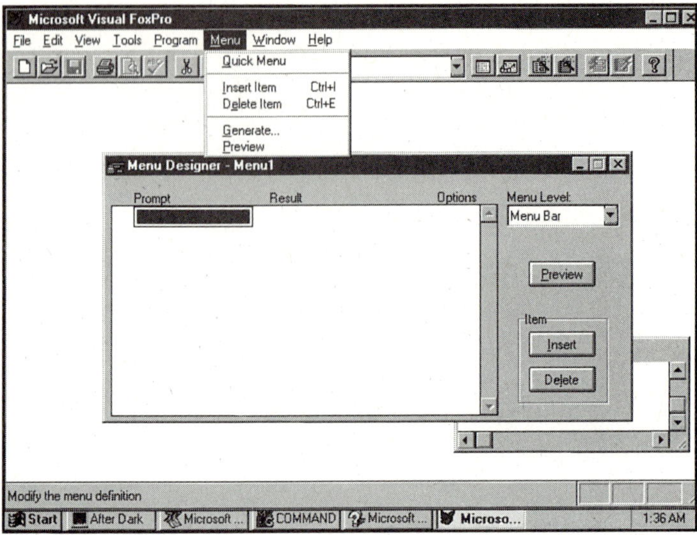

FIGURE 16.1.
The Menu Designer screen.

As you can see, the Menu Designer screen window is rather simple, especially if you compare it to the Form Designer or Report Designer. It contains a three-column list, three push buttons, and a combo box. In addition, when the Menu Designer executes, a **M**enu menu appears on the SYSMENU. (Talk about redundancy—this is like Major Major from *Catch 22.*) The purpose of each menu option is described in Table 16.1. Two additional options appear on the **V**iew menu when the Menu Designer is active. These options are described in Table 16.2.

Table 16.1. The Menu Designer menu.

Menu Option	*Purpose*
Quick Menu	When the Menu Designer executes to create a new menu bar, the menu structure is empty. At that time, you can choose this option and the Menu Designer creates a complete menu structure based in the default FoxPro system menu and displays this structure in the Menu Designer window list, as shown in Figure 16.2.
Insert Item Ctrl+I	Inserts the menu pad or submenu option above the currently highlighted menu item in the Menu Designer window. An Insert push button is also in the Menu Designer window.
D**e**lete Item Ctrl+E	Deletes the menu pad or submenu option that is highlighted in the Menu Designer window. A Delete push button is also in the Menu Designer window.

Menu Option	*Purpose*
Generate...	Once you have defined your custom menu, choose this option and Visual FoxPro generates a program with an .MPR extension that creates your menu. (See the section "Code Generation.")
Preview	With this option you can try out your custom menu. (A **P**review push button is also on the Menu Designer window.) You can view the results of your custom menu system design at any time during the design process. When you choose the Try It push button, your custom menu system displays at the top of the screen, temporarily overwriting the SYSMENU. Simultaneously, the Preview dialog box appears and displays the menu system filename. Whenever you choose a menu pad and submenu option, the selected prompt and the associated command are displayed in the dialog box.

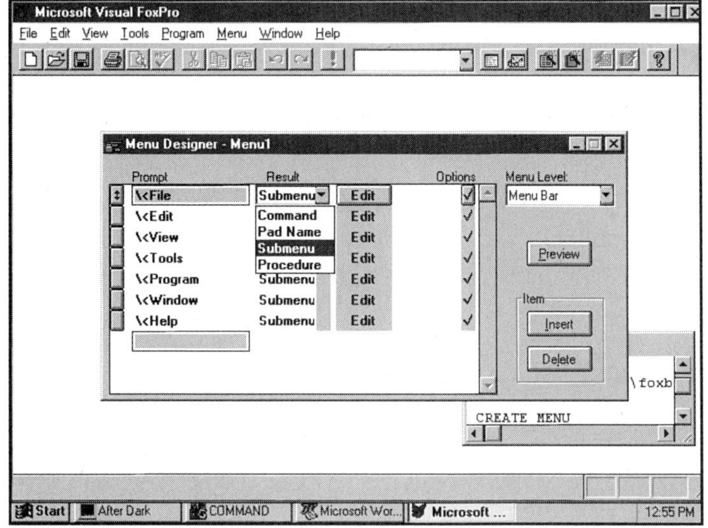

FIGURE 16.2.
The Menu Designer screen with the Quick Menu structure displayed.

Table 16.2. The View menu options for the Menu Designer.

Menu Option	*Purpose*
General Options...	Displays the General Options dialog box. This dialog box contains the following options:
	Procedure: (edit box region)
	This edit box is used to define a procedure that can be executed when any menu pad in the menu system is chosen.
	Edit... (push button)
	This push button displays a program editing window. You enter code in this window for the selected procedure.
	Menu Code:
	Setup... (check box)
	When you select this check box, a program editing window appears in which you enter FoxPro setup code. The setup code executes before menu definition code executes. Once you add setup code, this check box remains checked.
	Cleanup... (check box)
	When you select this check box, a program editing window displays in which you enter cleanup code that executes after menu definition code executes. After you add cleanup code, this check box remains checked.
	Location: (Radio buttons)
	Replace
	Replaces the existing menu system with the new menu system. (This is the default.)
	Append
	Adds the new menu system to the right of the current menu system.

Menu Option	*Purpose*
	Before Displays the menu system before displaying the specified menu pad.
	A**f**ter Displays the menu system after displaying the specified menu pad.
Menu **O**ptions...	Displays the Menu Options dialog box, which contains an edit box. You can enter one or more procedures that can be called to execute whenever any menu pad is chosen. The program creates an `ON SELECTION MENU` command.

NOTE

Using the Menu Designer **Q**uick Menu option is not always the best technique if you are doing something simple, such as adding an option to a SYSMENU pop-up menu. Sometimes it is easier to simply insert a couple of FoxPro commands, such as the following:

```
DEFINE BAR 99 OF _MTOOLS AFTER _mtl_spell;
                        PROMPT "\<Word Count"
                     ON SELECTION BAR 99 OF _MTOOLS WAIT WINDOW NOWAIT;
                        LTRIM(STR(OCCURS(" ", _CLIPTEXT)+1))+ ;
                        " Words in Clipboard"
```

This example counts the number of words in the Clipboard.

NOTE

If you are adding a new menu pad and pop-up to SYSMENU, see the example in Listing 16.1.

The following sections describe the elements of the Menu Designer dialog box.

The Menu Structure Table

As Figure 16.2 illustrates, the menu structure table has three columns: Prompt, Result, and Options. Within this structure table you can create either a menu bar or a pop-up menu. The initial table structure is the SYSMENU menu bar. All other menus are subordinate to SYSMENU. The rows in the table represent either menu pads or pop-up menu bars (options). To create a new menu pad or pop-up option, type the prompt name for a pad or option in the Prompt column. You can specify a hotkey by preceding one of the characters in the name with the \< two-character sequence. For pop-up menus, you can specify a separation bar by using the \- two-character sequence.

Next you specify a result. Under the Result column, specify what happens if the user chooses the named prompt. You choose one of the following options from the result column:

Command	Select this option to define a command for a menu pad or an option. The text box appears. Enter the command in the text box.
Pad Name or Bar#	Pad Name appears when you're defining pads; Bar# appears when you're defining submenu options. The text box appears. Enter the pad name or the bar# in the text box.
Procedure	If you choose this option, you can specify the name of a procedure that executes when the pad, option, or procedure is chosen. A Create button appears to the right of the word Procedure. When you choose the Create push button, the text editing window displays so that you can enter and edit the snippet. A *snippet* is a FoxPro procedure. The Create button label changes to Edit after the procedure is designed.
Submenu	This is the default choice. You use this option to create a submenu for the current pad or option. When you choose Submenu, the Create push button appears to the right of the word Submenu. When you choose the Create push button, a new empty menu structure appears so that you can define the submenu. When you finish designing the new submenu, use the pop-up at the right of the Menu Designer window to return to the parent menu. The Create button label changes to Edit after the submenu is designed.

You can change the order of items in the structure by clicking on the button with the double-headed arrow at the left of the prompt name and dragging the item to the desired location in the list.

The Options column in the table contains a push button for each item in the table. When you choose a button for an item in the table, the Prompt Options dialog box appears. The Prompt Options dialog box contains options that you can establish for the current menu item. These options correspond to the `DEFINE PAD` or `DEFINE BAR` command clauses. You can specify a message that displays on the Windows-style status bar. You can specify a shortcut key, a comment for the generated code, a bar number or pad name, and a `SKIP FOR` condition. The `SKIP FOR` condition disables the menu item if the condition evaluates to a true (`.T.`) value.

The Expression Builder dialog box is launched to let you input a message and `SKIP FOR` expressions. Both the Prompt Options and Expression Builder dialog boxes are shown in Figure 16.3.

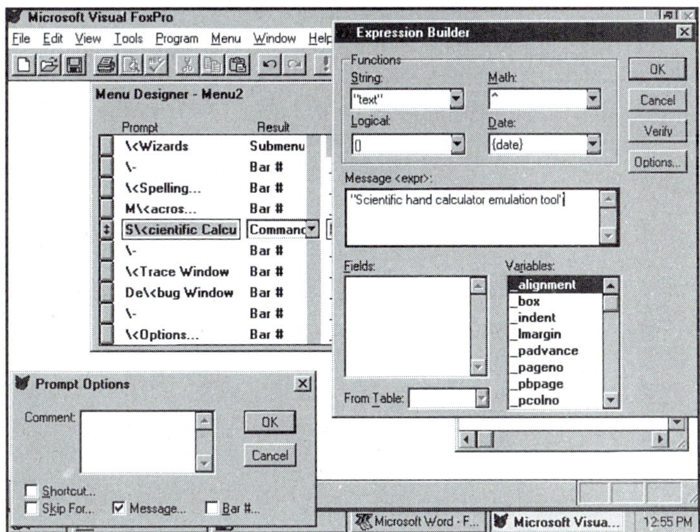

FIGURE 16.3.
The Prompt Options and Expression Builder dialog boxes.

The Menu Selection Combo Box

In the upper-right corner of the Menu Designer dialog box is a combo box. Its options contain the current and higher-level menus. If the structure of a submenu displays in the table, you can choose a higher-level menu or submenu from this pop-up. Then the structure of the higher-level menu displays in this table.

The Menu Design Dialog Box Push Buttons

The Preview, Insert, and Delete push buttons are described in Table 16.1.

Code Generation

After you complete your menu design, you must choose the **M**enu menu **G**enerate... option to generate the menu program (MPR file). When you choose the Ge**n**erate... option, you are given the opportunity to save the current menu design. If you haven't provided a name for the menu design file yet, a Save As dialog box appears and you can choose a drive and directory, and then specify the name of the design file. After the new or modified menu design file (MNX) is saved, the Generate Menu dialog box displays.

The Generate Menu dialog box contains two push buttons, a text box, and a browser (...) button, as shown in Figure 16.4. The text box contains the fully qualified path for the menu program MPR file. It has the same filename as the menu design file, but the filename extension is .MPR. You can change the name in the text box. You can also press the browser push button, and the Save As dialog box appears to assist you in choosing a drive and directory.

The generated code will have comments at the beginning. If you run the Menu Designer from the Project Manager, these comment fields will be filled in with the developer's name, address, and so on, as shown in Listing 16.1. The Project Manager is discussed in Chapter 23, "Building Visual FoxPro Applications."

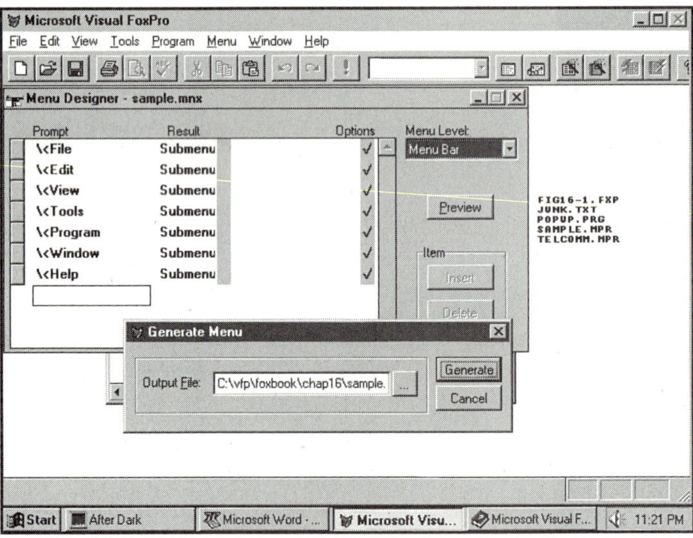

FIGURE 16.4.
The generate and comments dialog boxes.

Finally, you press the Generate button, and the menu program MPR file is generated. Listing 16.1 is an example of a menu program file, this one named SAMPLE.MPR, that was generated by the Menu Designer.

Listing 16.1. Code generated by the Menu Designer.

```
*       ******************************************************
*       *
*       * 01/12/95            SAMPLE.MPR              17:42:52
*       *
*       ******************************************************
*       *
*       * Joe Programmer
*       *
*       * Copyright (c) 1995 Widget Unlimited
*       * 1 Commerce Street
*       * Willowbrook, MD  22222
*       *
*       * Description:
*       * This program was automatically generated by GENMENU.
*       ******************************************************
*       *
*       *                     Menu Definition
*       *
*       ******************************************************
*
SET SYSMENU TO
SET SYSMENU AUTOMATIC

DEFINE PAD _msm_file OF _MSYSMENU PROMPT "\<File" COLOR SCHEME 3 ;
        KEY ALT+F, "" ;
        MESSAGE "Create, open, save, print files or quit FoxPro"
DEFINE PAD _msm_edit OF _MSYSMENU PROMPT "\<Edit" COLOR SCHEME 3 ;
        KEY ALT+E, "" ;
        MESSAGE "Edit text or manipulate OLE objects"
DEFINE PAD _msm_view OF _MSYSMENU PROMPT "\<View" COLOR SCHEME 3 ;
        KEY ALT+V, ""
DEFINE PAD _msm_tools OF _MSYSMENU PROMPT "\<Tools" COLOR SCHEME 3 ;
        KEY ALT+T, ""
DEFINE PAD _msm_prog OF _MSYSMENU PROMPT "\<Program" COLOR SCHEME 3 ;
        KEY ALT+P, "" ;
        MESSAGE "Debug, run, compile, generate and document programs"
DEFINE PAD _msm_windo OF _MSYSMENU PROMPT "\<Window" COLOR SCHEME 3 ;
        KEY ALT+W, "" ;
        MESSAGE "Manipulate windows, display Command and View windows"
DEFINE PAD _msm_systm OF _MSYSMENU PROMPT "\<Help" COLOR SCHEME 3 ;
        KEY ALT+H, "" ;
        MESSAGE "Access information for learning and using FoxPro"
ON PAD _msm_file OF _MSYSMENU ACTIVATE POPUP _mfile
ON PAD _msm_edit OF _MSYSMENU ACTIVATE POPUP _medit
ON PAD _msm_view OF _MSYSMENU ACTIVATE POPUP _mview
ON PAD _msm_tools OF _MSYSMENU ACTIVATE POPUP _mtools
ON PAD _msm_prog OF _MSYSMENU ACTIVATE POPUP _mprog
ON PAD _msm_windo OF _MSYSMENU ACTIVATE POPUP _mwindow
ON PAD _msm_systm OF _MSYSMENU ACTIVATE POPUP _msystem

DEFINE POPUP _mfile MARGIN RELATIVE SHADOW COLOR SCHEME 4
DEFINE BAR _mfi_new OF _mfile PROMPT "\<New..." ;
        KEY CTRL+N, "Ctrl+N" ;
        MESSAGE "Creates a new file"
DEFINE BAR _mfi_open OF _mfile PROMPT "\<Open..." ;
```

continues

Listing 16.1. continued

```
        KEY CTRL+O, "Ctrl+O" ;
        MESSAGE "Opens an existing file"
DEFINE BAR _mfi_close OF _mfile PROMPT "\<Close" ;
        MESSAGE "Closes the current file"
DEFINE BAR _mfi_clall OF _mfile PROMPT "Close All" ;
        MESSAGE "Closes all windows"
DEFINE BAR _mfi_sp100 OF _mfile PROMPT "\-"
DEFINE BAR _mfi_save OF _mfile PROMPT "\<Save" ;
        KEY CTRL+S, "Ctrl+S" ;
        MESSAGE "Saves changes to the current file"
DEFINE BAR _mfi_savas OF _mfile PROMPT "Save \<As..." ;
        MESSAGE "Saves changes to the current file with a new name"
DEFINE BAR _mfi_revrt OF _mfile PROMPT "\<Revert" ;
        MESSAGE "Reverts the current file to the last saved version"
DEFINE BAR _mfi_sp200 OF _mfile PROMPT "\-"
DEFINE BAR _mfi_import OF _mfile PROMPT "\<Import" ;
        MESSAGE "Imports a FoxPro file or a file from "+ ;
                "another application"
DEFINE BAR _mfi_export OF _mfile PROMPT "\<Export" ;
        MESSAGE "Exports a FoxPro file to another application's file"
DEFINE BAR _mfi_sp300 OF _mfile PROMPT "\-"
DEFINE BAR _mfi_setup OF _mfile PROMPT "Page Set\<up..." ;
        MESSAGE "Changes the page layout and printer settings"
DEFINE BAR _mfi_prevu OF _mfile PROMPT "Print Pre\<view" ;
        MESSAGE "Displays full pages as they will be printed"
DEFINE BAR _mfi_print OF _mfile PROMPT "\<Print..." ;
        KEY CTRL+P, "Ctrl+P" ;
        MESSAGE "Prints a text file, contents of the Command "+ ;
                 "window, or contents of the Clipboard"
DEFINE BAR _mfi_sp400 OF _mfile PROMPT "\-"
DEFINE BAR _mfi_quit OF _mfile PROMPT "E\<xit" ;
        MESSAGE "Quits FoxPro"

DEFINE POPUP _medit MARGIN RELATIVE SHADOW COLOR SCHEME 4
DEFINE BAR _med_undo OF _medit PROMPT "\<Undo" ;
        KEY CTRL+Z, "Ctrl+Z" ;
        MESSAGE "Undoes the last command or action"
DEFINE BAR _med_redo OF _medit PROMPT "Re\<do" ;
        KEY CTRL+R, "Ctrl+R" ;
        MESSAGE "Repeats the last command or action"
DEFINE BAR _med_sp100 OF _medit PROMPT "\-"
DEFINE BAR _med_cut OF _medit PROMPT "Cu\<t" ;
        KEY CTRL+X, "Ctrl+X" ;
        MESSAGE "Removes the selection and places it onto the Clipboard"
DEFINE BAR _med_copy OF _medit PROMPT "\<Copy" ;
        KEY CTRL+C, "Ctrl+C" ;
        MESSAGE "Copies the selection onto the Clipboard"
DEFINE BAR _med_paste OF _medit PROMPT "\<Paste" ;
        KEY CTRL+V, "Ctrl+V" ;
        MESSAGE "Pastes the contents of the Clipboard"
DEFINE BAR _med_pstlk OF _medit PROMPT "Paste \<Special..." ;
        MESSAGE "Pastes the Clipboard contents as a linked " + ;
               "object, embedded object, or other object type"
DEFINE BAR _med_sp200 OF _medit PROMPT "\-"
DEFINE BAR _med_slcta OF _medit PROMPT "Select \<All" ;
        KEY CTRL+A, "Ctrl+A" ;
```

```
        MESSAGE "Selects all text or items in the current window"
DEFINE BAR _med_sp300 OF _medit PROMPT "\-"
DEFINE BAR _med_find OF _medit PROMPT "\<Find..." ;
        KEY CTRL+F, "Ctrl+F" ;
        MESSAGE "Searches for specified text"
DEFINE BAR _med_repl OF _medit PROMPT "R\<eplace..." ;
        KEY CTRL+L, "Ctrl+L" ;
        MESSAGE "Replaces specified text with different text"
DEFINE BAR _med_sp400 OF _medit PROMPT "\-"
DEFINE BAR _med_insob OF _medit PROMPT "\<Insert Object..." ;
        MESSAGE "Embeds an object in a General field type"
DEFINE BAR _med_obj OF _medit PROMPT "\<Object..." ;
        MESSAGE "Edits the selected object"
DEFINE BAR _med_link OF _medit PROMPT "Lin\<ks..." ;
        MESSAGE "Opens linked files or changes links"
DEFINE BAR _med_cvtst OF _medit PROMPT "Con\<vert to Static" ;
        MESSAGE "Converts a linked or embedded object into a non-updatable graphic"

DEFINE POPUP _mview MARGIN RELATIVE SHADOW COLOR SCHEME 4
DEFINE BAR _mvi_toolb OF _mview PROMPT "\<Toolbars..." ;
        MESSAGE "Shows, hides, or customizes toolbars"

DEFINE POPUP _mtools MARGIN RELATIVE SHADOW COLOR SCHEME 4
DEFINE BAR 1 OF _mtools PROMPT "\<Wizards" ;
        MESSAGE "Runs the selected wizard"
DEFINE BAR _mtl_sp100 OF _mtools PROMPT "\-"
DEFINE BAR _mtl_spell OF _mtools PROMPT "\<Spelling..." ;
        MESSAGE "Checks spelling"
DEFINE BAR _mst_macro OF _mtools PROMPT "M\<acros..." ;
        MESSAGE "Creates, deletes, or revises a keyboard macro"
DEFINE BAR 5 OF _mtools PROMPT "S\<cientific Calculator" ;
        MESSAGE "Scientific hand calculator emulation tool"
DEFINE BAR _mtl_sp200 OF _mtools PROMPT "\-"
DEFINE BAR _mwi_trace OF _mtools PROMPT "\<Trace Window" ;
        MESSAGE "Displays the Trace window"
DEFINE BAR _mwi_debug OF _mtools PROMPT "De\<bug Window" ;
        MESSAGE "Displays the Debug window"
DEFINE BAR _mtl_sp300 OF _mtools PROMPT "\-"
DEFINE BAR _mtl_optns OF _mtools PROMPT "\<Options..." ;
        MESSAGE "Changes various categories for FoxPro options"
ON BAR 1 OF _mtools ACTIVATE POPUP _mwizards
ON SELECTION BAR 5 OF _mtools DO FORM CALC

DEFINE POPUP _mwizards MARGIN RELATIVE SHADOW COLOR SCHEME 4
DEFINE BAR _mwz_table OF _mwizards PROMPT "\<Table" ;
        MESSAGE "Runs the Table wizard"
DEFINE BAR _mwz_query OF _mwizards PROMPT "\<Query" ;
        MESSAGE "Runs the Query wizard"
DEFINE BAR _mwz_form OF _mwizards PROMPT "\<Form" ;
        MESSAGE "Runs the Form wizards"
DEFINE BAR _mwz_reprt OF _mwizards PROMPT "\<Report" ;
        MESSAGE "Runs the Report wizards"
DEFINE BAR _mwz_label OF _mwizards PROMPT "\<Label" ;
        MESSAGE "Runs the Label wizard"
DEFINE BAR _mwz_mail OF _mwizards PROMPT "\<Mail Merge" ;
        MESSAGE "Runs the Mail Merge wizard"
DEFINE BAR _mwz_pivot OF _mwizards PROMPT "\<PivotTable" ;
```

continues

Listing 16.1. continued

```
        MESSAGE "Runs the PivotTable wizard"
DEFINE BAR _mwz_import OF _mwizards PROMPT "\<Import" ;
        MESSAGE "Runs the Import wizard"
DEFINE BAR _mwz_foxdoc OF _mwizards PROMPT "Fox\<Doc" ;
        MESSAGE "Runs the FoxDoc code formatting wizard"
DEFINE BAR 10 OF _mwizards PROMPT "\<Setup" ;
        MESSAGE "Runs the Setup wizard"
DEFINE BAR 11 OF _mwizards PROMPT "\<Upsizing" ;
        MESSAGE "Runs the Upsizing wizard"
DEFINE BAR _mwz_all OF _mwizards PROMPT "\<All" ;
        MESSAGE "Displays a list of all wizards"

DEFINE POPUP _mprog MARGIN RELATIVE SHADOW COLOR SCHEME 4
DEFINE BAR _mpr_do OF _mprog PROMPT "\<Do..." ;
        KEY CTRL+D, "Ctrl+D" ;
        MESSAGE "Runs a program, application, "+ ;
         "form, report, query, or menu"
DEFINE BAR _mpr_cancl OF _mprog PROMPT "\<Cancel" ;
        MESSAGE "Stops running the current program"
DEFINE BAR _mpr_resum OF _mprog PROMPT "\<Resume" ;
        KEY CTRL+M, "Ctrl+M" ;
        MESSAGE "Resumes running the current suspended program"
DEFINE BAR _mpr_suspend OF _mprog PROMPT "\<Suspend" ;
        MESSAGE "Suspends the currently running program"
DEFINE BAR _mpr_sp100 OF _mprog PROMPT "\-"
DEFINE BAR _mpr_compl OF _mprog PROMPT "Co\<mpile..." ;
        MESSAGE "Compiles the current or selected program"

DEFINE POPUP _mwindow MARGIN RELATIVE SHADOW COLOR SCHEME 4
DEFINE BAR _mwi_arran OF _mwindow PROMPT "\<Arrange All" ;
        MESSAGE "Arranges windows as non-overlapping tiles"
DEFINE BAR _mwi_sp100 OF _mwindow PROMPT "\-"
DEFINE BAR _mwi_hide OF _mwindow PROMPT "\<Hide" ;
        MESSAGE "Hides the active window"
DEFINE BAR _mwi_hidea OF _mwindow PROMPT "Hide All" ;
        MESSAGE "Hides all windows"
DEFINE BAR _mwi_showa OF _mwindow PROMPT "Sh\<ow All" ;
        MESSAGE "Shows all hidden windows"
DEFINE BAR _mwi_clear OF _mwindow PROMPT "Clea\<r" ;
        MESSAGE "Clears text from the application workspace or"+ ;
               " the current output window"
DEFINE BAR _mwi_rotat OF _mwindow PROMPT "\<Cycle" ;
        KEY CTRL+F1, "Ctrl+F1" ;
        MESSAGE "Cycles through all open windows"
DEFINE BAR _mwi_sp200 OF _mwindow PROMPT "\-"
DEFINE BAR _mwi_cmd OF _mwindow PROMPT "\<Command Window" ;
        KEY CTRL+F2, "Ctrl+F2" ;
        MESSAGE "Displays the Command window"
DEFINE BAR _mwi_view OF _mwindow PROMPT "\<View Window" ;
        MESSAGE "Displays the View window"

DEFINE POPUP _msystem MARGIN RELATIVE SHADOW COLOR SCHEME 4
DEFINE BAR _mst_help OF _msystem PROMPT "\<Contents" ;
        KEY F1, "" ;
        MESSAGE "Displays Help table of contents"
DEFINE BAR _mst_hpsch OF _msystem PROMPT "\<Search for Help on..." ;
```

```
        MESSAGE "Searches for Help topics by keyword"
DEFINE BAR _mst_sp100 OF _msystem PROMPT "\-"
DEFINE BAR _mst_techs OF _msystem PROMPT "Technical Support" ;
        MESSAGE "Displays Help on technical support and" + ;
                " common questions for Microsoft Visual FoxPro"
DEFINE BAR _mst_sp200 OF _msystem PROMPT "\-"
DEFINE BAR _mst_about OF _msystem PROMPT "\<About Microsoft Visual FoxPro..." ;
        MESSAGE "Displays information about FoxPro" + ;
                " and the system configuration"
```

You can execute the SAMPLE.MPR menu program by entering the following command in the Command window:

```
DO SAMPLE.MPR
```

You can restore the default SYSMENU using the following command:

```
SET SYSMENU TO DEFAULT
```

Figure 16.5 shows the screen with the custom SYSMENU after SAMPLE.MPR executes. The **T**ools menu is open, revealing its new option, Scientific Calculator. The scientific calculator also displays on the screen. (The scientific calculator was created using the Form Designer and is described in Chapter 19, "The Form Designer.")

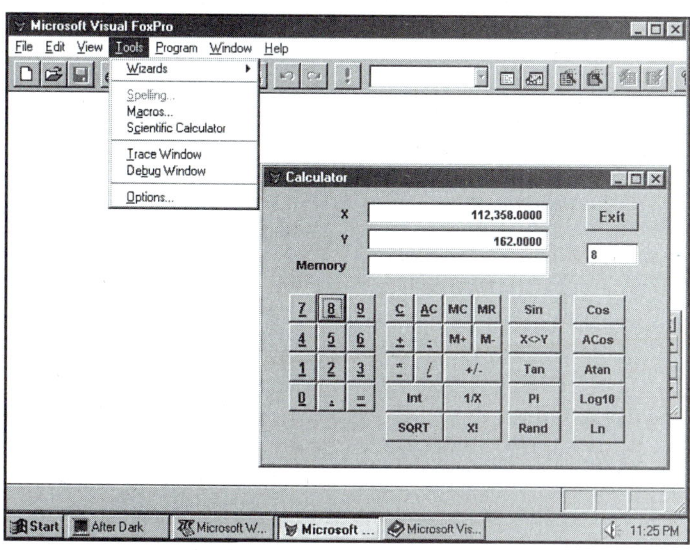

FIGURE 16.5.
The menu bar resulting from executing SAMPLE.MPR.

Using the Menu Designer

Now that you are familiar with the elements of the Menu Designer, you shouldn't have any trouble using it to create your own SYSMENU menu system. This section provides a guided tour through the process of creating a menu for a sample application.

Suppose you want to create an application that supports telecommunications. You design your application so that a new menu pad, named Telcom, is added to the SYSMENU menu bar between the **W**indows and **H**elp menu pads. A pop-up menu associated with the Telcom menu pad contains the following options:

Dial...	Dial a number
Connect	Start or continue communications
Hang Up	Hang up the modem
Transmit...	Transmit a file using various protocols
Receive...	Receive a file using various protocols
Setup...	Set up telecommunications parameters
Quit Telcom	Remove the Te**l**com menu from the system menu bar and exit

Suppose you have written procedures that perform the operations specified by each of the options in the menu. All that remains to be done is to create a new menu pad and pop-up menu. Then you need to indicate that the new menu pad is inserted into SYSMENU following the **W**indow menu pad. Here are the steps you should use:

1. Execute the Menu Designer from the Command window. You can also execute the Menu Designer by choosing the **F**ile menu **N**ew option and choosing a **M**enu file from the New file dialog box. You can also create the menu from the Project Manager by selecting the Menus icon under the Others tab and clicking on the **N**ew button. If you execute the Menu Designer by specifying the Command window, enter the following command:

   ```
   CREATE MENU TELCOMM
   ```

2. From the blank screen shown in Figure 16.1, type the prompt label `Te\<lcom` for the first item in the menu structure table, as shown in Figure 16.6.
3. Choose the **V**iew menu **G**eneral Options... option. Then select the A**f**ter radio button, select Window from the pop-up menu, as shown in Figure 16.6, and choose the OK push button to exit the General Options dialog box.
4. By default, the Result column pop-up option is Submenu. Next to that is the Choose push button. Push it and an empty menu structure table appears on the screen so that you can specify the pop-up menu options. Enter the option labels and separation bars as shown in Figure 16.7.

   For each item in the table, except the separation bars, choose the Command option from the Result column pop-up. Then enter a `DO` command that executes the appropriate procedure when the user chooses the corresponding option. Remember that if the procedure is in a program file with a different name, you must include the `IN` clause with the `DO` command. If the program is not in the current directory, but is in the FoxPro path, you need to specify the fully qualified path of the program file.

FIGURE 16.6.

Inserting the Telcom menu pad after the Windows menu pad.

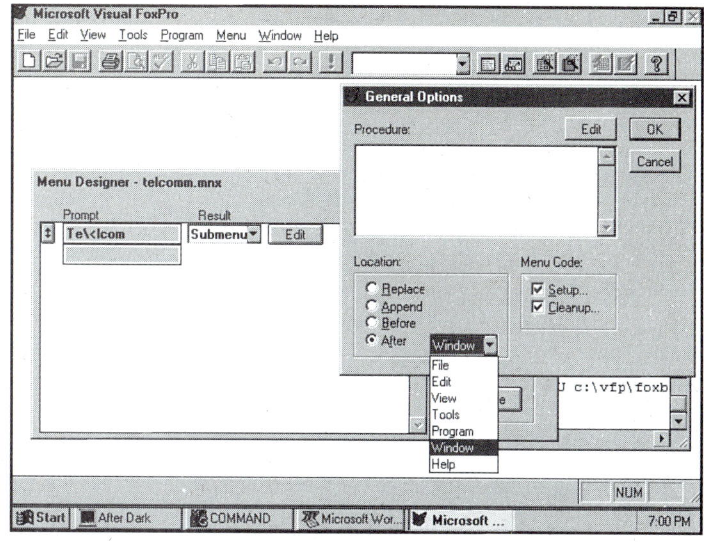

FIGURE 16.7.

Specifying the pop-up menu associated with the Telcom menu pad.

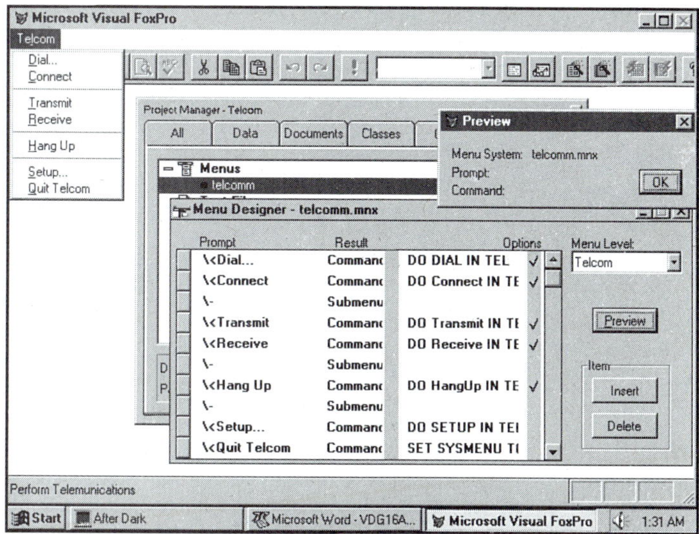

NOTE

At any time during your menu design process, you can press the **P**review button (or Alt+P) to see what your menu will look like. The Preview dialog box is shown in Figure 16.7.

5. Click on the Options column button for each item, and the Prompt Options dialog box displays. Use this dialog box to enter a message that displays on the status bar. When you enter the message into the Expression Builder, don't forget to enclose it in quotes, as shown in Figure 16.3. You can also specify a shortcut key and a conditional `SKIP FOR` clause when appropriate. For example, you might not want the **C**onnect, **R**eceive, **T**ransmit, and Hang Up options in your custom menu to be enabled only when you have established communications.
6. Choose the **G**enerate option in the **P**rogram menu to generate your menu program, TELCOMM.MPR.

That is all there is to it. At the beginning of your application, you can insert the following line of code to establish your new menu pad:

```
DO TELCOMM.MPR
```

At the end of your program, you need to specify the following command to disable the Te**l**com menu pad:

```
SET SYSMENU TO DEFAULT
```

As you can see, little programming is required to build menus. You should practice using the Menu Designer so that you are familiar with all the features of the Menu Designer. You'll find that it is an extremely powerful and useful addition to your programming toolchest.

Summary

This chapter describes how to generate a Visual FoxPro user-defined menu system using the Visual FoxPro Menu Designer.

You can use the Menu Designer presented in this chapter to add a sophisticated, advanced user-defined menu interface to a FoxPro application. Furthermore, this FoxPro user-defined interface is consistent with the rest of the Visual FoxPro user interface as well as with the Windows GUI interface.

17

OLE, OLE 2.0 Controls, DDE, and Operating System Interfaces

The naturalist must consider only one thing: what is the relation of this or that external reaction of the animal to the phenomena of the external world?

—Ivan Petrovich Pavlov (1849–1936)
Scientific Study of So-Called Psychical Processes in the Higher Animals

The bond between the Xbase programming language and its host operating system was strong even before everyone used the Control Program for Microprocessors (CP/M) operating system. Many aspects of Visual FoxPro are backward compatible with older Xbase versions that were designed to allow for deficiencies in older operating systems.

This chapter discusses the language features in Visual FoxPro that you can use to gain access to the host operating system. Some features are largely historical. Some duplicate operating system facilities. Others interface with the Windows graphical environment and are new. In this chapter you'll learn how to run other programs inside Visual FoxPro.

However, the major focus of the chapter is on Visual FoxPro support for object linking and embedding (OLE), OLE 2.0 controls, and dynamic data exchange (DDE). You will learn how to embed OLE objects in a form and link them to other applications. You will be shown how to use the Form Designer to add OLE 2.0 controls to a form.

Historical Holdovers

Files weren't time stamped under CP/M, so dBASE II prompted the user for a date and stored the date of the last update in the DBF header. To maintain compatibility, Visual FoxPro does this too, even though MS-DOS systems record both created and modified time stamps down to the bisecond. CP/M's notion of file size was limited to the number of physical sectors allocated to the file. Therefore, dBASE II wrote an end-of-file sentinel character (1A hex) at the end of all its files to differentiate the *logical* end of the file from the *physical* one. MS-DOS maintains both a logical and physical length for every file, but so does Visual FoxPro, for old time's sake.

Today, Visual FoxPro runs under Microsoft Windows 3.1, NT, and Windows 95. Future versions will run on MS-DOS and the Apple Macintosh. MS-DOS evolved along with the Xbase product line, from MS-DOS Version 1.0, when the IBM PC was introduced, to 2.0, which supported the hierarchical directory structure, to 3.0, which integrates LAN functions and adds a few more. Today, Microsoft offers Windows 3.11, NT, Windows 95, and advanced versions of MS-DOS that take advantage of the protected mode of Intel's 80386, 80486, and Pentium P5 CPU chips and offer the benefits of pre-emptive multitasking. (What in the world does that mean? Sorry, that explanation would require another book.) Visual FoxPro fully supports the capabilities of today's advanced Microsoft operating systems.

Operating System Access

Visual FoxPro provides several functions that allow applications to get information from the operating system. It also provides commands that replace built-in operating system operations.

System Variables

The `DATE()` and `TIME()` functions return the operating system's best guess for the current date and time, which is probably accurate in these days of trickle-charged lithium battery internal clock chips. The system date is returned as a Date type value. The system time is returned as an eight-character string in the form *hh:mm:ss*, based on a 24-hour clock.

To determine the current operating system, you can use the `OS()` function, which returns a character string, such as `DOS 3.3`, `OS/2`, or `UNIX`. The `OS()` function, however, doesn't tell you whether you are running under the Windows graphics environment. Four logical data type system memory constants were added to FoxPro 2.5, which indicate which version of FoxPro is running. A *system memory constant* is a system memory variable with a fixed value. The four system memory constants are `_DOS`, `_WINDOWS`, `_MAC`, and `_UNIX`. For Visual FoxPro, the value of `_WINDOWS` is true, and the other three system memory constants are false.

The `ID()` function returns a character string containing the machine number and machine name when FoxPro is operating in a network environment. The `ID()` function was implemented to provide compatibility with dBASE IV and is identical to the `SYS(0)` function.

The `FILE()` function returns `.T.` if a specified file exists. The file can be specified absolutely or relative to the current subdirectory. In the following examples, the current directory is C:\VFP\MYFILES:

```
? FILE("..\HISFILES\LEDGER.DBF")
? FILE("C:\VFP\BUSINESS\LEDGER.DBF")
```

Both refer to the same file, and if the file exists, both statements return `.T.`. Wildcards aren't supported.

Visual FoxPro has functions that return status information relating to MS-DOS files. The `FSIZE()` function returns the Numeric type value that contains the size of a file in bytes. The `FDATE()` function returns a Date type value that is the MS-DOS file creation date. The `FTIME()` function returns the MS-DOS file creation time as an eight-character string in the form *hh:mm:ss*, based on a 24-hour clock. Here is the syntax:

```
<number>           = FSIZE("<expC>")
<date>             = FDATE("<expC>")
<character string> = FTIME("<expC>")
```

The argument for all three functions is a character expression, `<expC>`, that evaluates to an MS-DOS path and filename. Wildcards aren't supported. Here are a couple examples:

```
? "Size of file in bytes: ", FSIZE(d:\XYZ\YOURFILE)
? "Your file was created on ", FDATE(d:\XYZ\YOURFILE), " at ";
, FTIME(d:\XYZ\YOURFILE)
```

Here is the output:

```
Size of file in bytes:    33311
Your file was created on 12/22/91 at 13:12:01
```

The `DISKSPACE()` function also returns the free space on a disk drive in bytes. Thoughtful application programmers check the amount of free disk space before initiating actions that fail if not enough space exists.

The `MEMORY(<expN>)` function returns the amount of unused memory. The value returned multiplied by 1024 is the number of bytes available. The `SYS(12)` function returns the number of bytes of unused memory. In FoxPro 2.6 a Numeric argument was added to the `MEMORY()` function. This argument, `<expN>`, designates the memory region for which the amount of available memory, in kilobytes, is returned by the `MEMORY()` function. Table 17.1 lists what is returned for each valid value of `<expN>`.

Table 17.1. A list of returned values for the `MEMORY(<expN>)` function.

<expN>	*Returned Value*
0	Total available memory (`MEMORY(3)+MEMORY(6)`).
1	The amount of available memory in the heap. Only a part of this memory is available to FoxPro.
2	The amount of MS-DOS memory available. This is the amount of memory available for running MS-DOS files or BIN files. This value is always 640KB for Visual FoxPro.
3	The amount of available memory that Visual FoxPro can allocate to various processes.
4	0
5	0
6	The amount of memory allocated to the FoxPro buffer manager that can be used by other processes if necessary.
7	0

The following simple example displays all seven modes of the `MEMORY()` function. The computer on which this example was run has 16MB (1600KB) of RAM and a Windows 95 platform:

```
FOR I = 0 TO 7
? "Memory("+STR(I,1)+") = "+ STR(MEMORY(I))+" K"
ENDFOR
```

Here is the resultant output:

```
Memory(0) =      64112 K
Memory(1) =      63055 K
Memory(2) =        640 K
Memory(3) =      63055 K
Memory(4) =          0 K
Memory(5) =          0 K
```

```
Memory(6) =         1056 K
Memory(7) =            0 K
```

Operating system environment variables, a UNIX concept supported by MS-DOS, are powerful configuration devices. The user types the `SET` command (for example, `SET UPDATE=NO`) at the operating system prompt to define variables.

The `HOME()` function returns a character string that lists the directory containing the FoxPro executable file. The `HOME()` function was implemented to provide compatibility with dBASE IV and is identical to `SYS(2004)`.

A Visual FoxPro applications program can ask the operating system for the current value of a variable called `UPDATE` and modify its behavior appropriately. The `GETENV("UPDATE")` function in this case returns the character string `NO`, which the application might interpret to mean Do not allow update during this session.

Just as applications developers were discovering the power of environment variables, they discovered that MS-DOS 2.0 had a severe limitation on the number of environment variables. However, current versions of MS-DOS, NT, and OS/2 support an almost unlimited number of environment variables, so their use in applications will probably increase.

The `NUMLOCK()` and `CAPLOCK()` functions can be used to set the state or return the state of the NumLock and CapLock keys. Both functions return a logical true value (`.T.`) if the key is set. If the key isn't set, they return a false value (`.F.`). If you provide an optional, logical argument for these two functions, the state of the key is set when you provide a true value.

Some forms of the `SET()` function (described in the section "The `SET()` Function" in Chapter 10, "Environment") return certain information about the external hardware and software configuration, such as the amount of memory, the processor type, the printer status, the graphics card in use, the network status, and the path of FoxPro temporary files.

Work-Alike Commands

The Visual FoxPro programming language includes several statements that duplicate built-in operating system commands, such as `CD`, `RM`, `RMDIR`, `MD`, `MKDIR`, `COPY FILE`, `ERASE`, `DIR`, `RENAME`, and `TYPE`. In almost every case, Visual FoxPro makes these commands more useful by adding or suppressing information.

The Visual FoxPro `DIR` command, which can be written also as `DIRECTORY` or `DISPLAY FILES`, is more useful than the operating system version. The Visual FoxPro `DIR` command displays only DBF files and reads enough of the header to provide specific information about each file. The results of the `DIR` command look like this:

```
Database Tables    # Records     Last Update     Size
CUSTMAST.DBF           38         01/28/93       7620
INVENTRY.DBF          588         12/26/92      15112
```

The operating system couldn't possibly know how to find the number of records. The `DIR` command also can function like its operating system analog, because you might be frustrated if Visual FoxPro included commands that looked like operating system commands but behaved differently. Here is an example:

```
DIR f:*.ndx
```

This syntax produces a display similar to the display of the operating system version of `DIR`.

MS-DOS has a cryptic syntax for its `COPY` command:

```
COPY <from_file> <to_file>
```

The Visual FoxPro version of `COPY FILE` is more self-documenting. It is more like the English language, which is the essence of the Xbase language. It has the added virtue of not overwriting an existing file if `SET SAFETY` is `ON`. Here is the Visual FoxPro syntax:

```
COPY FILE <from file> TO <to file>
```

Like its MS-DOS counterpart, `COPY`, or `cp` in UNIX, the `COPY FILE` command produces a byte-for-byte copy of the specified file.

Some might say that the virtue of the Visual FoxPro `ERASE` command (`DELETE FILE` is the same) is that it won't ask whether you're sure if `SET SAFETY` is `OFF`.

The Visual FoxPro version of `RENAME` has the following syntax:

```
RENAME <old name> TO <new name>
```

The Visual FoxPro `TYPE` command is superior to the MS-DOS version. `TYPE <file>` in Visual FoxPro paginates the output, adds a page header consisting of the filename, date, and page number, and it optionally numbers the lines.

The `SET DEFAULT TO` command changes the Visual FoxPro working drive and directory. This command provides MS-DOS functionality for the `<drive>:` command and the `CHDIR <dir>` command. Visual FoxPro also supports the `CHDIR` command. Here is the syntax:

```
SET DEFAULT TO [<expC>]
```

The `<expC>` expression can evaluate to any of the following:

- An MS-DOS drive only (a single letter followed by a colon):
  `SET DEFAULT TO A:.`
  The FoxPro working drive is changed to drive A and the FoxPro working directory becomes the directory last associated with drive A.
- An MS-DOS path consisting only of a series of MS-DOS directory names, separated by a backslash. The special directory names `.` and `..` also can be used here. The last name doesn't require a backslash, but if you specify one, it is accepted:
  `SET DEFAULT TO \Myprogs\New.`

The FoxPro working directory is changed to `\Myprogs\New` and the new directory is associated with the current working drive.

- An MS-DOS drive followed by an MS-DOS directory:

  `SET DEFAULT TO C:\DBASE\Samples.`

  Here is another example:

  ```
  Mydir="C:\Account\System\"
  SET DEFAULT TO (Mydir)
  ```

  In the second example, the working drive becomes drive C, and the working directory becomes `\Account\System`.

The Visual FoxPro working drive and directory are used as defaults when file and directory names are processed. The `SET DEFAULT TO` command also affects the MS-DOS working drive and directory when MS-DOS commands are executed with the `RUN` command.

When Visual FoxPro terminates, it restores the MS-DOS working drive and directory that were active when Visual FoxPro was executed.

MS-DOS Built-in Directory Maintenance Commands

Visual FoxPro 3.0 supports a complete set of MS-DOS directory maintenance commands:

```
CD <path>
CHDIR <path>
MD <path>
MKDIR <path>
RD <path>
RMDIR <path>
```

The `CD` and `CHDIR` commands change the default directory to the specified path, *<path>*, which performs the same function as the `SET DEFAULT TO` command. The `MD` and `MKDIR` commands create the specified disk directory, *<path>*. The `RD` and `RMDIR` commands delete the specified disk directory, *<path>*.

For example, you can change the current directory from a dialog box by using the following statement:

```
CD GETDIR()
```

The `GETDIR()` function displays the Selection Directory dialog box and returns the directory selected by the user.

The *RUN* Command

Visual FoxPro provides several mechanisms for spawning child processes. A *child process* is a program run by another program. When the child process is finished, it returns control to its parent, the program that ran it. Running a child process is called *spawning*.

The RUN command, which also can be entered as ! (which is pronounced *bang*) in the UNIX style, can be used to invoke MS-DOS, spawn other processes (execute other MS-DOS and Windows applications), or drop out to a new shell.

Every built-in MS-DOS command, such as DIR, MKDIR, TYPE, ERASE, and VER, can be executed from Visual FoxPro with the following syntax:

```
!TYPE filename
```

or with this syntax:

```
RUN TYPE filename
```

The ability to issue MS-DOS commands from Visual FoxPro makes the environment seem more friendly. Although Visual FoxPro provides an analog for most operating system commands, sometimes only the MS-DOS (or other operating system) command will do. The freedom to spawn processes, however, carries some responsibility. You could write a program that looks like the following:

```
USE Myfile
!ERASE Myfile.*
```

The results are undefined, but they won't be good. You would probably get a file share error message. If you use the Visual FoxPro ERASE command, it complains that the file is already open.

The ! (RUN) command also can execute any other application that will fit in memory. One use for the RUN command is to execute programs, written in C++ or another language, that act in tandem with a Visual FoxPro application. For example, you can write a program that reads a FoxPro database table (DBF file) and displays the data in an MS-DOS–based spreadsheet program. The Visual FoxPro application that maintains this data offers a menu choice Spreadsheet. When the user chooses Spreadsheet, the spreadsheet program is invoked with the RUN command.

The RUN command can be used to spawn a new DOS shell. The statement

```
RUN COMMAND.COM
```

starts an MS-DOS session in a window or in full-screen mode. It is similar to quitting Visual FoxPro and returning to MS-DOS, except Visual FoxPro is still in memory. Typing EXIT at the MS-DOS prompt returns you to Visual FoxPro. While you are away, any files you opened remain open, and your most recent work might still be buffered and not written to the disk.

Invoking an MS-DOS shell without first issuing a `CLEAR ALL` command is a little risky. Because any MS-DOS process that Visual FoxPro spawns is a child process, it can't modify the environment of its parent (Visual FoxPro). You can't use this mechanism to change environment variables during a session, for instance. There are, however, other ways of communicating; for instance, an MS-DOS child process can create a file for Visual FoxPro to read.

The Visual FoxPro `RUN` command operates slightly differently and the syntax is slightly different from the traditional Xbase `RUN` command. The `RUN` command enables you to run Windows applications as well as MS-DOS programs. Here is the syntax:

```
RUN [/N [<number>]] <filename>
! [/N [<number>]] <filename>
```

You specify `[/N[<number>]]` when you execute a Windows application. For example, to execute Microsoft Word for Windows, you specify the following:

```
RUN /N<number> WINWORD
```

You can specify the optional Numeric value to designate how the Windows application is launched. `<number>` must immediately follow `/N`. Embedded spaces aren't allowed. `<number>` affects how the Windows application opens. Table 17.2 lists allowable values for `<number>` and what the values mean.

Table 17.2. Windows application launch modes for the `RUN` command.

/N<number>	*Application Open Mode*
/N1	Active and normal size
/N2	Active and minimized
/N3	Active and maximized
/N4	Inactive and normal size
/N7	Inactive and minimized

If you execute a Windows application with the `RUN` command, the application behaves as if you opened it using the Windows Program Manager or File Manager.

If you use the `RUN` command to execute an MS-DOS program, the FOXRUN.PIF file must be in the same directory as VFP.EXE. If you don't specify the extension of a program, FoxPro searches the DOS path for the filename of the program with a .PIF (program information file) extension. If the file is found, the program specified by the PIF file is executed using the parameters in the PIF file. If the PIF file isn't found, FoxPro searches the DOS path for an MS-DOS executable file with the name you specified. Then FoxPro uses the FOXRUN.PIF file, which is configured to run the MS-DOS file inside a window. The window is titled FoxPro Run Command. When the MS-DOS program exits, the window title changes to Inactive FoxPro Run Command.

If you aren't satisfied with the current configuration specified by the FOXRUN.PIF parameters, you can change it with the Windows PIF Editor utility. For example, if you want the FoxPro Run Command window to go away when the MS-DOS program finishes editing, you can check the Close Window on Exit check box in the PIF editor. The FOXRUN.PIF file is initially set up to allocate a minimum of 256KB of memory for running an MS-DOS program. If you don't have 256KB of conventional memory available, an MS-DOS alert box appears to announce the bad news. You can either close some open Windows applications to free up additional memory or use the Windows 3.1 PIF Editor, shown in Figure 17.1, to reduce the amount of memory in the KB Required text box.

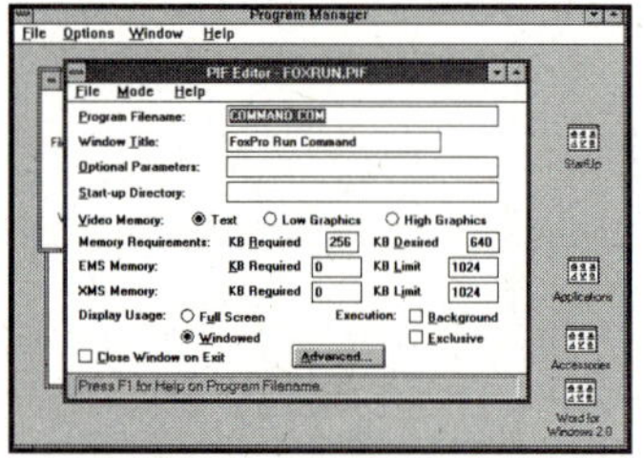

FIGURE 17.1.
The Windows 3.1 PIF Editor with the PIF file FOXRUN.PIF open.

If the external command requires more than 256KB of conventional memory, as initially specified by the FOXRUN.PIF parameters, you are confronted by the dreaded Insufficient Memory error. Again, you can modify FOXRUN.PIF to correct this by increasing the amount of memory specified in the KB Required text box.

If you are using Windows 95, you can run the Explorer. Right-click on the FOXRUN.PIF icon and the shortcut menu appears. Choose the shortcut menu's Properties option to set the memory requirements.

Exchanging Data with Other Applications and OLE 2.0 Controls

Windows supports three mechanisms to interchange data between applications: the Clipboard, object linking and embedding, and dynamic data exchange. These intercommunication mechanisms are discussed in this section.

The Clipboard

You are already familiar with the Clipboard. Any Windows application that works with documents has Cut, Paste, and Copy operations. When you choose the Cu**t** or **C**opy command in the **E**dit menu, the Windows application transfers selected data to the Clipboard. Data can be a variety of types such as text, graphics, spreadsheet cells, and sound. When you choose the **E**dit menu **P**aste option, the application checks to see if the data on the Clipboard is in the format that the program can process. If it is, the application transfers the data from the Clipboard to the program. If the Windows Clipboard contains data in text format, you paste it in a text file. In Visual FoxPro, the Windows Clipboard is used for Cut, Paste, and Copy operations. In addition, you can access the Windows Clipboard data with the `_cliptext` system memory variable. You can also store text data in the Windows Clipboard by storing text in the `_cliptext` system memory variable. Here is an example:

```
STORE "This text is in the Clipboard" TO _ClipText
```

Then you can go to another Windows application and paste the text into a document file.

In Chapter 9, "Full-Screen Data Editing," you learned how to paste objects (pictures, sound, and so forth) generated in other applications into General data type database fields. Here are instructions for transferring a picture from the Clipboard to a General data type field:

1. Execute the Microsoft Paintbrush or Paint application.
2. Draw a picture.
3. Transfer the picture to the Clipboard (Ctrl+C) and exit Paintbrush.
4. Execute or switch to Visual FoxPro.
5. Place a database table in use with a General data type field named `Object` (or any other field name).
6. Execute the `EDIT` command and click on a Gen icon for the `Object` field. (A window appears.)
7. Paste the contents of the Clipboard (the picture) into the window and exit the `EDIT` command.
8. Execute the following program, which covers the screen with pictures of the `Object` field as shown in Figure 17.2:

```
CLEAR
FOR jrow = 0 TO WROWS()-5 STEP 5
   FOR jcol = 1 TO WCOLS()-20 STEP 20
      @ jrow,jcol SAY Object SIZE 5,20 STRETCH
   ENDFOR
ENDFOR
```

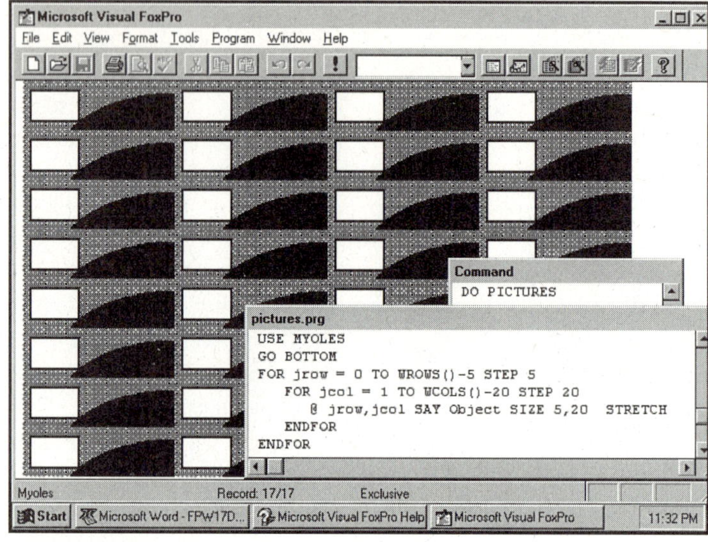

FIGURE 17.2.
An example of the use of the `@...SAY` *command to display pictures created in Microsoft Paint and pasted into a General type database field.*

Object Linking and Embedding

Object linking and embedding (OLE) technology was introduced in Windows 3.1 as another, more powerful, method of transferring and sharing data between Windows applications. You can insert information created in an application into another application. Information can be pictures, text, sound, spreadsheets, and so forth. The information is referred to as an *object.* An object is any information created by a Windows application. When you transfer an object from one application to another, the object is taken from a document referred to as a *source document.* The document into which the object is transferred is referred to as the *destination document.* The process of transferring an object from a source document in one application to a destination document in another is referred to as *object embedding.* The destination document is simply an independent copy of the source document.

When you choose a destination document for editing, the application that created the object opens to edit it. Because the object is embedded, the source document isn't affected. The object that is painted all over the screen in Figure 17.2 was created in the Microsoft Paint application. If you execute the `BROWSE` command and double-click on the Gen icon for the `Object` field, a window appears displaying the picture. Its field name is the same as its title (`MyOLES.Object`). If you click on that window, shown in Figure 17.3, Microsoft Paint opens so you can edit the Paint object from `Object`, which is the FoxPro destination document. When you finish making changes in Paint (or any OLE application that modifies an object), you choose the **E**dit command **U**pdate option, and the embedded object is updated in FoxPro. Then you choose the Paint **F**ile command E**x**it option, and control returns to FoxPro. In Visual FoxPro, OLE objects are embedded (or linked) into General type database fields.

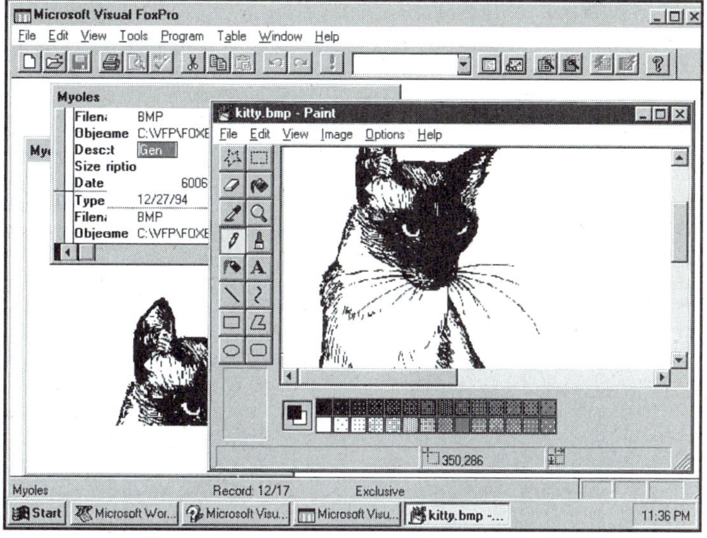

FIGURE 17.3.
An example of editing a General type database field with Microsoft Paint.

The process of *linking* an object involves transferring a reference (or linkage) from the source document to the destination document. In other words, the destination document contains only a link to the source document. When you modify a destination document containing a link, the application that created the object opens and modifies the source document. When you're using linked objects, the shared information always stays current.

The difference between linking and embedding is simply where the information is stored. Linked objects are stored in the source document. Embedded objects are stored in the destination document. If you want to share information among multiple applications and want each application always to have access to current information, use object linking. However, if only one application uses the object, use object embedding.

Applications whose objects can be embedded or linked into other objects are called *servers.* Applications that can accept linked or embedded objects are called *clients.* An application can be both a server and a client if it can export and import linked and embedded objects. Visual FoxPro is a client application because it can accept embedded or linked objects. It isn't a server application because its objects can't be embedded or linked into documents in other applications.

When an object is linked, the location (drive and directory) of the source document is maintained in the destination document. If you move the source document, the linkage is broken. The client no longer knows where the information resides. However, database tables with embedded objects can be moved because the object resides with the database table. The only restriction is that the application that created the object must be available. For example, if you move a FoxPro database table containing embedded Word for Windows objects from one computer to another, Word for Windows must be available on the other computer.

In Visual FoxPro, the Windows Clipboard is used for data interchange. If you use the **E**dit menu **P**aste option, as discussed in the previous section, the object in the Clipboard is embedded. However, if you use the **E**dit menu Paste **S**pecial option, the object is linked. Incidentally, if you paste a new object over an existing object, the original object is overwritten.

An object doesn't have to be on the Clipboard to embed or link. If the general field editing window is open, you can choose the **E**dit menu **I**nsert Object option. The Insert Object dialog box appears, and you can choose the type of OLE object to embed or link. (See Figure 17.4.) You choose the type of object from the list: sound, Paintbrush, Excel, and so forth. Then the corresponding application opens, and you can create a new object or open an existing one. When you save the object and exit from the object's application, the object is automatically embedded into the corresponding general database field.

You can use the Lin**k**s option on the **E**dit menu to open a source document, break a link, fix a broken link, or designate whether the object should be updated manually or automatically.

When an object is linked, if you change it using another Windows application, the new contents are available to FoxPro because only a link (not the contents) is stored in the field. However, if you store (embed) the contents in the FoxPro field, any changes made using the Windows application do not affect the contents of the FoxPro field. Sometimes you have a linked object that you no longer want stored in FoxPro that will change if the source document changes. In other words, you want to convert the linked object to an embedded object; you want to sever the link. You can do this with the **E**dit menu Con**v**ert to Static option. But remember, the process isn't reversible. Once you have destroyed the link, it can't be reestablished.

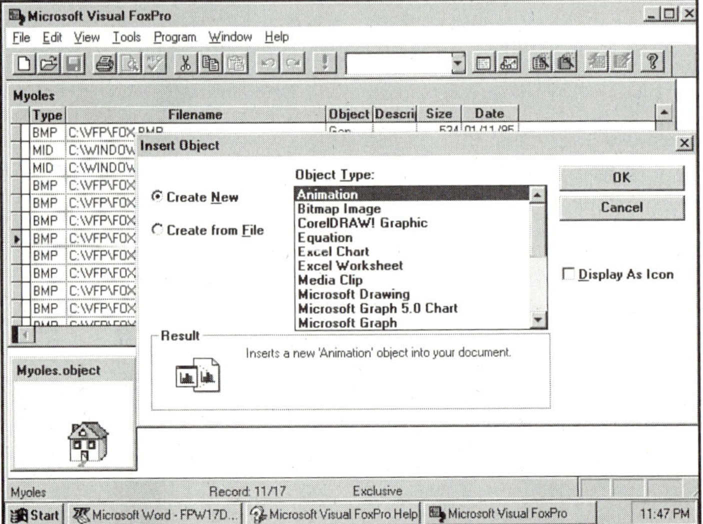

FIGURE 17.4.
The Insert Object dialog box.

You also can create or modify one or more general database fields for the current record using the `MODIFY GENERAL` command. Here is the syntax:

```
MODIFY GENERAL <general field list> [NOMODIFY][NOWAIT]
           [WINDOW  <WindowName1>] [IN [WINDOW] <WindowName2>]
```

This command opens an editing window for a general field with the alias of the field (for example, `MyOles.Object`) displayed as the title. You can insert, edit, or delete linked or embedded objects as discussed earlier.

`<general field list>` can consist of one or more general fields. You can specify the alias name to reference a general field in another work area. Here is an example:

```
MODIFY GENERAL MyOles.Object, Art.picture
```

The `APPEND GENERAL` command imports OLE objects from a file and places them in a General data type field in the current record. If a field already contains an OLE object, the new OLE object overwrites the original. You can either insert (embed) the object into the field, or create a link to the OLE object file and store the link in the general field. Some applications, such as Microsoft Graph, do not support linking. They support only embedding. As a consequence, you can only embed a Microsoft Graph OLE object in a General data type field. Any Windows applications that provide server support for linking, such as Word for Windows and Excel, will let you store a link to the OLE object in a general field. Here is the syntax for the `APPEND GENERAL` command:

```
APPEND GENERAL <general field>  [ FROM <expFN> ]
   [DATA <expC>]
   [LINK] [CLASS <OLE class name>]
```

The `FROM <expFN>` clause specifies the name of the file that contains the OLE object that is inserted into or linked to the specified general field. You must specify the entire filename, including the extension. If the file is not in the current default directory, you must include the full path of the file. The `DATA <expC>` clause specifies a string that is passed to the server application. However, the application must be able to receive and process the string. You specify the `LINK` keyword if you want Visual FoxPro to create a link between the OLE object stored in the general field and the file that contains the object. You can omit `LINK` if you want the OLE object embedded into the general field.

The `CLASS <OLE class name>` clause specifies an OLE class for the specified OLE object. You are required to specify a `CLASS` clause only if the OLE object differs from its default class. For example, you can supply a class name when the file extension for the OLE object's file differs from the default extension for the class. The filename extension for an OLE object file identifies its corresponding OLE server application.

You can determine the class of an OLE object with the Windows 3.1 REGEDIT.EXE application. Once you execute REGEDIT, double-click on a particular OLE object to make the Modify File Type dialog box appear. This dialog box contains a field titled `Identifier` that identifies the class name.

Suppose you want to maintain a catalog of various object files for various OLE server applications, such as Microsoft Word 6 and Excel. Here is a simple starter application for maintaining a catalog of OLE objects. The catalog is maintained in a table, MYOLES.DBF, that contains a General data type field. Here is the structure for table MYOLES.DBF:

```
Structure for table:    C:\VFP\FOXBOOK\CHAP17\MYOLES.DBF
Field  Field Name  Type        Width
    1  TYPE        Character       3
    2  FILENAME    Character     254
    3  OBJECT      General        10
    4  DESCRIPTIO  Character      50
    5  SIZE        Numeric         6
    6  DATE        Date            8
** Total **                      332
```

The form shown in Figure 17.5 was created using the Form Designer.

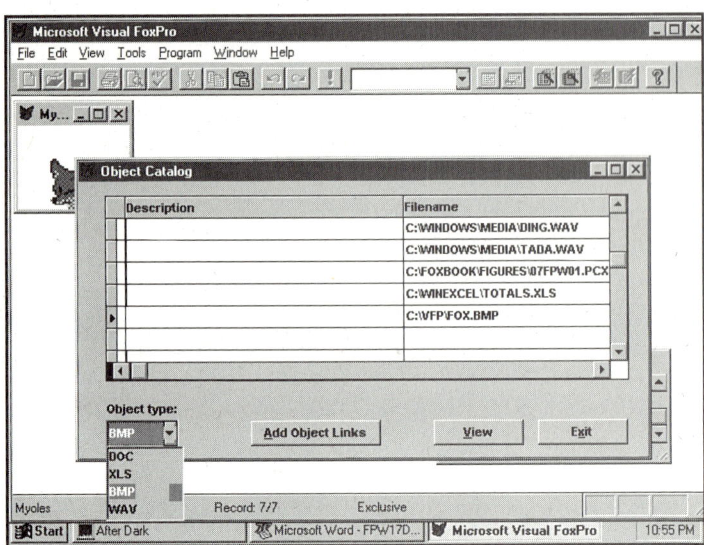

FIGURE 17.5.
A sample form for maintaining a catalog of OLE objects.

The form contains three control buttons, a grid that displays the MYOLES.DBF table, and a combo box. The controls are listed in Table 17.3.

Table 17.3. Form and control classes for the MYDOCS.SCX form.

Name	*Class*	*Caption Property*
`form1`	Form	`Object Catalog`
`command1`	Command button	`Add Object Link`
`command2`	Command button	`View`
`command3`	Command button	`Exit`
`Label1`	Label	`Object type:`

Name	*Class*	*Caption Property*
Grid1	Grid	
column1	Column	
header1	Header	Description
column2	Column	
header2	Header	Filename
combo1	Combo box	

To create this form, execute the `MODIFY FORM MYDOCS` command and perform the following steps:

1. Choose the Data **E**nvironment option from the **V**iew menu, and the Data Environment dialog box appears. Add the MYOLES.DBF and OPTIONS.DBF tables. The OPTIONS.DBF table contains a list of extensions for various OLE objects. Here is the structure:

```
Table: OBJECTS.DBF
Record#        EXTENSION CLASS      DESCRIPTION
1 DOC          Word.Document.6      Microsoft Word 6.0
2 XLS          EXCEL.SHEET          Excel 5.0
3 PCX          PAINTBRUSH           MS Paint Brush
4 WAV          SOUNDREC             Sound Maker
```

2. Add controls as shown in Figure 17.5. Set the properties as shown in Table 17.4.
3. Add the code for the `Click` event for the command1 (**A**dd Object Links) command button, as shown in Listing 17.1.
4. Add code for the `Click` event for the command2 (**V**iew) command button, as shown in Listing 17.2.
5. Add the following statement for the `Click` event for the command3 (E**x**it) command button:

```
RELEASE Thisform
```

Table 17.4. Property settings for the MYDOCS.SCX form.

Object	*Property*	*Setting*
form1	Caption	"Object Catalog"
form1	AutoCenter	.T.
command1	Caption	"\<Add Object Links"
command2	Caption	"\<View"
command3	Caption	"E\<xit"

continues

Table 17.4. continued

Object	Property	Setting
grid	ColumnCount	2
column1	ControlSource	myoles.descriptio
Header1	Caption	"Description"
column2	ControlSource	myoles.filename
column2	ReadOnly	.T.
Header2	Caption	"FileName"
combo1	ControlSource	Objects
combo1	RowSource	Objects.Extension
combo1	RowSourceType	6 - Fields
combo1	Style	2 - Dropdown List
combo1	ColumnCount	1

Listing 17.1. The code for the command1 `Click` event.

```
SELECT MyOles
LOCAL TypeObject
Directory = GETDIR()
NumberFiles = ADIR(FileArray, DIRECTORY+"*." ;
      +Thisform.combo1.value)
IF NumberFiles > 0
    FOR F = 1 TO NumberFiles
       APPEND BLANK
       m.FileName = Directory + FileArray[F,1]
       REPL Type WITH  Thisform.combo1.value, ;
         FileName WITH m.FileName, ;
         Size    WITH  FileArray[F,2],;
         Date    WITH  FileArray[F,3]
       APPEND GENERAL Object FROM (m.FileName) LINK
    ENDFOR
    Thisform.Refresh  && Refresh the form
ELSE
    WAIT "No object files in Directory: " ;
       +Directory  WINDOW AT 12,30
ENDIF
```

Listing 17.2. The code for the command2 `Click` event.

```
LOCAL oOLEbc
IF RECCOUNT("MyOLEs") > 0
    IF Thisform.OutlineIndex > 0
        m.Filename = Thisform.OleControl1.List(Thisform.OutlineIndex)
        SEEK M.FileName IN MyOLEs
        IF FOUND("MyOLEs") AND !EMPTY(MyOLEs.Object)
```

```
            oOLEbc = CREATEOBJECT('oleboundcontrol')
            oOLEbc.ControlSource='MyOLEs.Object'
            oOLEbc.DoVerb(0)    && play
        ENDIF
    ENDIF
ELSE
    This.Enabled = .F.
    WAIT WINDOW AT 15,30 "Empty Object: "+ MyOles.Filename
ENDIF
```

Although this example describes how to build another form, its primary purpose is to demonstrate how to use the `APPEND GENERAL` command. The code presented in Listing 17.1 executes when you click on the Add Object Link button. It first prompts you to select a directory, `GETDIR()`. Then it uses the selected directory and filename extension of the OLE object that is currently selected in the `combo1` control to form a file skeleton. For example, suppose that you select the directory C:\WINWORD\ and that Thisform.combo1.Value happens to be a DOC file. Here is the resulting skeleton:

```
C:\WINWORD\*.DOC
```

Next, the `ADIR()` function fills an array, `FileArray`, with information relating to each of the DOC files in the selected directory. Finally, records are added to the MYOLES.DBF table for each file in the array. After the files are added, the form `Refresh` method (`Thisform.Refresh`) executes to redraw the grid. The user can add a brief description for each file in the grid area.

If you click on the View button, the `Click` method displays the contents of the object linked to the general field in the current record. If the object is a WAV or MID file, the sound is played, and so on. It does this by creating an OLE bound control object and calling the `DoVerb()` method to display the object. If the object is a WAV or MID file, the object is played. Here is the code to do this:

```
LOCAL oOLEbc                              && Object variable
oOLEbc = CREATEOBJECT('oleboundcontrol')  && Create an OLE bound control
oOLEbc.ControlSource='MyOLEs.Object'      && Bind it to the General field, Object
oOLEbc.DoVerb(0)                          && execute OLE object verb
```

The `DoVerb(<expN> ¦ <expC>)` method executes a OLE object verb. The argument can be a number or a character string. The character string (*<expC>*) specifies one of the standard OLE verbs supported by all OLE objects. The number (*<expN>*) is an index of the `ObjectVerbs` properties array for the object. Each OLE object type can have its own set of verbs. However, the values shown in Table 17.5 represent the standard verbs supported by all types of OLE objects.

The View button `Click` event method could have used the following `@...SAY` command to execute the OLE object verb:

```
:@ 1,1 SAY MyOLEs.Object VERB 0
```

Table 17.5. Actions for the `DoVerb()` method arguments.

`<expN>`	*Verb Action*
`0`	This value is the default action for the object.
`1`	The object is activated for editing. If the application that created the object supports in-place activation, the object activates within the OLE container control.
`2`	The object opens in a separate application window. If the application that created the object supports in-place activation, the object activates in its own window.
`3`	The application that creates the object is hidden. This verb is for embedded objects.
`4`	Applications that support in-place activation execute and display any interface tools. If the object does not support in-place activation, an error message is generated.
`5`	This option activates if the OLE object receives focus. It creates a window and prepares the object for editing. If the object does not support single-click activation, an error message is generated.
`6`	You use this option to force an object that is activated for editing to discard all record of changes that the object's application can undo.

OLE 2.0 Controls and Objects

Many of the 16-bit applications you use owe much of their user interface razzle-dazzle to Visual Basic controls. *Visual Basic controls* are dynamic library files, similar to DLLs except that they have a .VBX filename extension. Visual Basic controls, called *VBX files*, are distributed by software vendors to applications developers. VBX files provide support for graphs, editors, fax servers, toolbars, spinners, thermometers, sliders, and other three-dimensional and animated controls. They are marketed as libraries of VBX files by large and small software distributors. Unfortunately, VBX files do not work with 32-bit applications such as Visual FoxPro. The good news is that OLE controls do work with 32-bit applications and are readily available from independent software vendors. 32-bit applications supply a more plentiful variety of powerful interface options than do VBX files. Even better news is that you can extend the power of Visual FoxPro by employing OLE controls to provide your application with more powerful and interesting interface elements. You could not use VBX controls with FoxPro 2.6 for Windows.

An *OLE control* is an encapsulated software package that resides in the Windows\SYSTEM directory and has the filename extension .OCX. However, this control is not called an OCX file—it is called an OLE control. When an application requires the service of an OLE control, it reads the OLE control into memory and executes it. You cannot create OLE controls with Visual FoxPro. You must either buy them from a software supplier or create your own using

C++ development tools, such as Borland C++ Version 4.5 and Microsoft Visual C++ Version 2.1, with the OLE Visual Control Developer's Kit.

There are two OLE icons on the Form Designer form control. You use the OLE bound control to display a general field on a form. It is *bound* to a general field. You use the OLE container control to add OLE objects and OLE 2.0 (OCX) controls to a form.

OLE Bound Controls

Follow these steps to add an OLE bound control to a form:

1. Click on the OLE bound control on the Form toolbar.
2. Click on the form and drag the mouse to size the control.
3. Set Control Source Property to the general field you want to display.

For most applications, you do not need to add any code for methods. Normally, there are no events associated with an OLE bound control that concern you. At runtime, the general field displays on the form. If you double-click on the OLE object on the form, the application associated with the OLE object executes.

Figure 17.6 shows the Form Designer with a big OLE bound control in the center of the form. Listing 17.3 shows the form's properties and methods. This list is created by simply placing the form file, BOUND.SCX, in use and listing the Properties field and the methods. The only object that is important to this example is `oleboundcontrol1`. Notice that the only property that you have to set is `ControlSource`.

FIGURE 17.6.
The Visual FoxPro Form Designer, showing a form containing an OLE bound control.

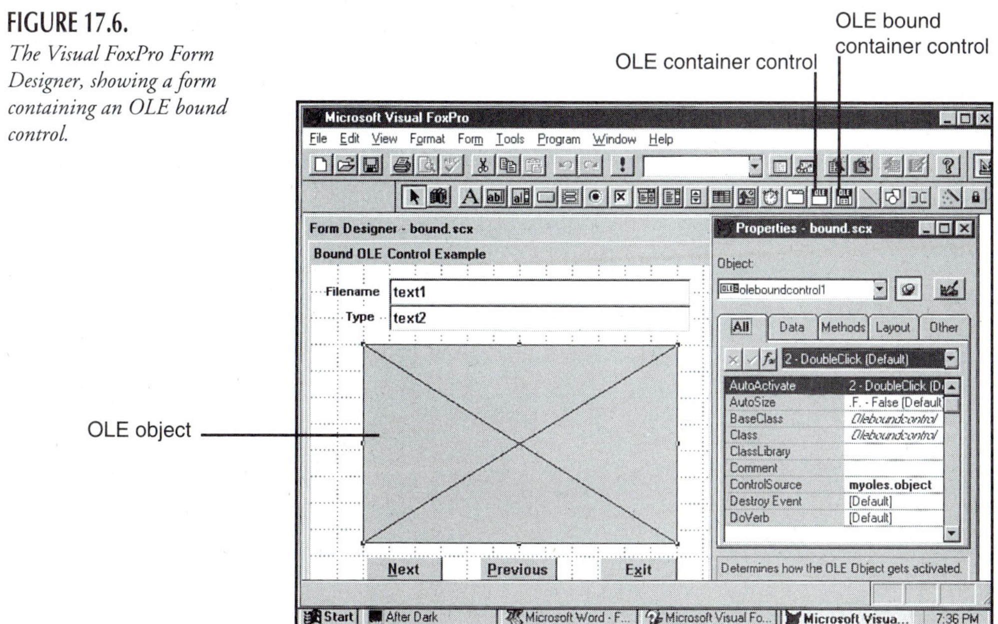

Listing 17.3. A listing of BOUND.SCX form properties and methods.

```
LIST OFF  TRIM(objname),  Properties
Dataenvironment           Left = 17
                          Top = 37
                          Width = 488
                          Height = 192
                          Name = "Dataenvironment"
cursor1                   CursorSource = myoles.dbf
                          Alias = "myoles"
                          Left = 20
                          Top = 10
                          Width = 98
                          Height = 113
                          Name = "cursor1"
  form1                   ScaleMode = 3
                          Caption = "OLE Bound Control Example"
                          FontSize = 8
                          Top = 0
                          Left = 0
                          Height = 296
                          Width = 382
                          Name = "form1"
  oleboundcontrol1        Height = 181
                          Width = 289
                          Top = 72
                          Left = 48
                          ControlSource = "myoles.object"
                          Name = "oleboundcontrol1"
  text1                   Top = 12
                          Left = 72
                          Height = 25
                          Width = 277
                          ControlSource = "myoles.filename"
                          FontSize = 10
                          Name = "text1"
  label1                  Caption = "Filename"
                          Top = 17
                          Left = 14
                          Height = 13
                          Width = 56
                          FontSize = 8
                          Name = "label1"
  label2                  Caption = "Type"
                          Top = 40
                          Left = 32
                          Height = 17
                          Width = 33
                          FontSize = 8
                          Name = "label2"
  text2                   Top = 36
                          Left = 72
                          Height = 25
                          Width = 277
                          ControlSource = "myoles.type"
                          FontSize = 10
                          Name = "text2"
  command1                Caption = "\<Next"
```

```
                                Top = 264
                                Left = 50
                                Height = 25
                                Width = 73
                                Name = "command1"
command2                        Caption = "\<Previous"
                                Top = 264
                                Left = 155
                                Height = 25
                                Width = 73
                                Name = "command2"
command3                        Caption = "E\<xit"
                                Top = 264
                                Left = 265
                                Height = 25
                                Width = 73
                                TerminateRead = .T.
                                Name = "command3"
```

O

```
Object          Method
command1
                PROCEDURE Click
                 IF !EOF() OR RECNO() <> RECCOUNT()
                     SKIP
                     Thisform.refresh
                 ELSE
                     WAIT NOWAIT WINDOW "You are at the end of the
                 table."
                 ENDIF
                 ENDPROC
command2
                PROCEDURE Click
                 IF RECNO()>1
                     SKIP -1
                     Thisform.refresh
                 ELSE
                     WAIT NOWAIT WINDOW "You are at the beginning
                 of the table."
                 ENDIF

                 ENDPROC
command3
                PROCEDURE Click
                 CLEAR EVENTS
                 RELEASE THISFORM
                 ENDPROC
```

You can execute the form with the `DO FORM BOUND` command. The results are shown in Figure 17.7. In the figure, a double-click on the OLE control activated the Microsoft Paint application.

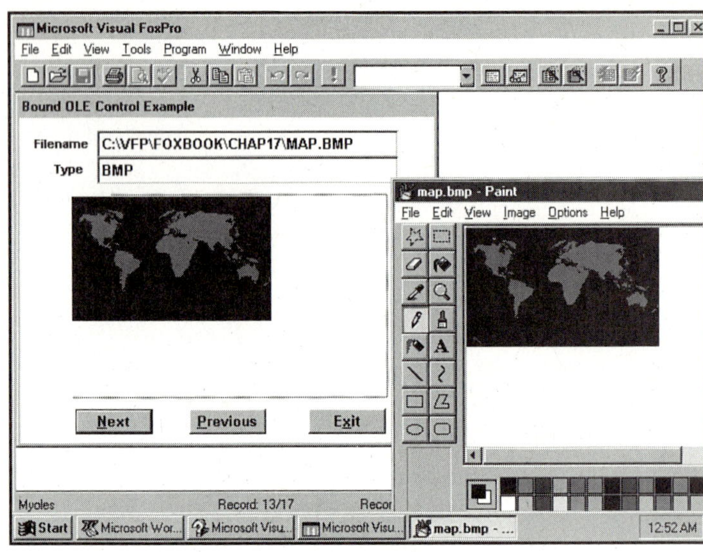

FIGURE 17.7.
An example of the BOUND.SCX form showing an OLE bound control and an associated Microsoft Paint application window.

OLE Container Controls

Visual FoxPro ships with several OLE control (OCX) files that you can add to your form with the Form Designer to provide interesting and powerful extensions to the Visual FoxPro system. These controls are described in Table 17.6.

Table 17.6. A description of the OLE Container controls provided with Visual FoxPro.

OLE Control	*OCX File*	*Description*
MAPI Session	MSMAPI32.OCX	Signs on and establishes a MAPI (Message Application Program Interface) session. Also signs off a MAPI session.
MAPI Message	MSMAPI32.OCX	Allows the user to perform a variety of messaging system functions once a session has been established.
Communications	MSCOMM32.OCX	Adds serial communications to your application. Allows transmission and reception of data through a serial port.
Outline	MSOUTL32.OCX	Displays a list of items in a hierarchical list.

OLE Control	*OCX File*	*Description*
PicClip	PICCLP32.OCX	Selects an area of a source bitmap and displays the image of that area in a form or picture box.

The details relating to properties, methods, and events for the controls listed in Table 17.6 and any other control that might be supplied with future versions of Visual FoxPro can be obtained from the Visual FoxPro help system.

When you install Visual FoxPro, the SETUP program copies OCX controls to the Windows\SYSTEM directory. When you distribute an application that includes OLE controls, you must be sure that any OLE control (OCX) files you use in your application are copied to the customer's Windows\SYSTEM directory.

You can add an OLE 2.0 control or an insertable object to a form. To illustrate this, we will add the OLE 2.0 Outline control described in Table 17.6 to a form. Suppose that you want to replace the grid used in the example, which maintains the list of OLE objects on the MYDOCS.SCX form (shown in Figure 17.5), with an outline control. To accomplish this, we will step through the following procedure:

1. Open the Form Designer to modify the MYDOCS.SCX form with `MODIFY FORM MYDOCS`.
2. Save the file under a new name, `MYDOCS1.SCX`. Choose the **F**ile menu Save **A**s... option to create the new form file (MYDOCS1.SCR).
3. Remove the grid (`grid1`) control by clicking on it and pressing the Delete key.
4. Click on the OLE container control on the Form Controls toolbar.
5. Click on the form and drag the mouse to size the control. The Insert Object dialog box appears, as shown in Figure 17.8. You have the following options:

   Create **N**ew: You can insert a new object into your form. To do this, you just choose the type of object to insert. Then the associated application activates to create the object. Once you are finished, the object is inserted into your form.

   Create from **F**ile: You can insert the contents of a file as an object into your form, in which case, at runtime you can double-click on it to activate its associated application (Excel, Word, Paint, and so on).

   Insert **C**ontrol: You can insert an OLE 2.0 control into your form. This is the route I will pursue. Select this option, as shown in Figure 17.9.

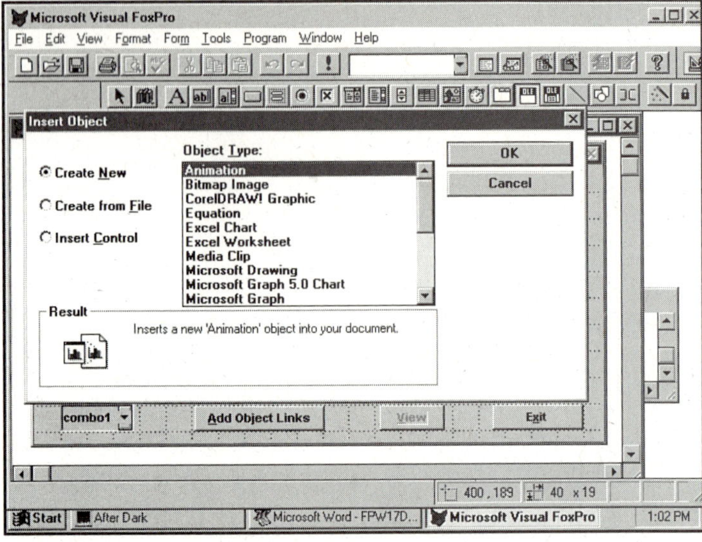

FIGURE 17.8.
The Insert Object dialog box, showing the Create New option.

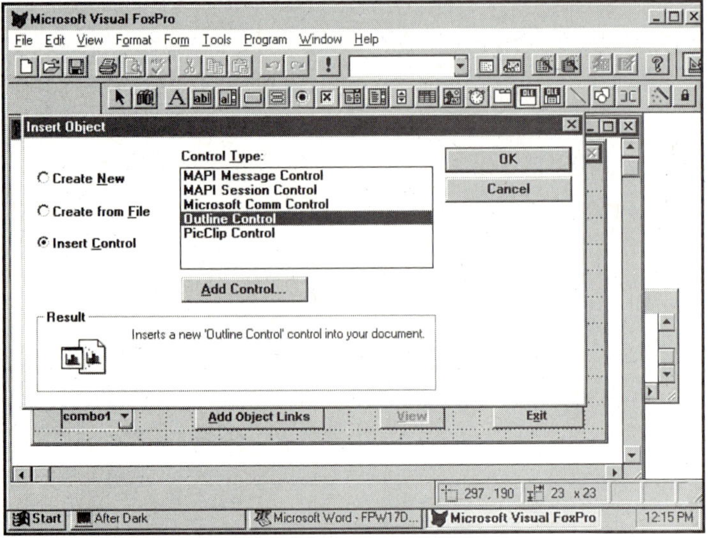

FIGURE 17.9
The Insert Object dialog box, showing available OLE 2.0 controls.

There are five OLE 2.0 controls supplied with Visual FoxPro, as shown in Figure 17.9. I will use the OLE Outline Control to illustrate how to add an OLE 2.0 control. To begin, select the Outline Control item from the Control **T**ype list and click on the OK button. The Outline Control appears on the form, as shown in Figure 17.10.

6. Next, click with the right mouse button on the OLE Outline control, and the shortcut menu shown in Figure 17.10 appears.

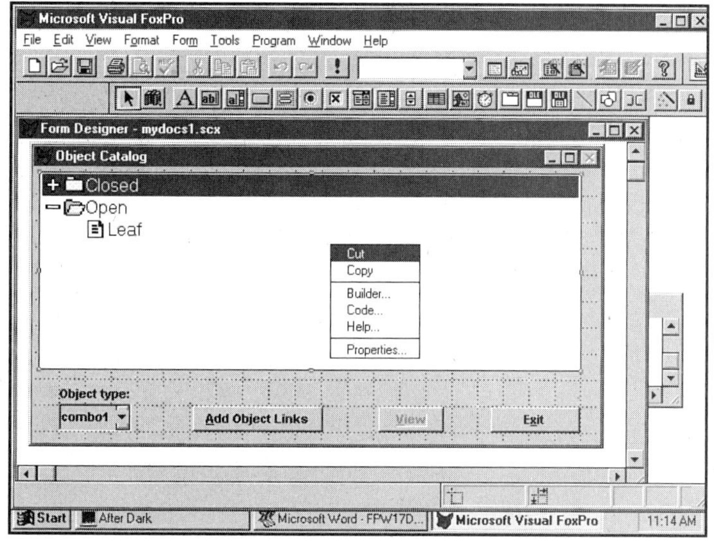

FIGURE 17.10.
The Screen Designer, showing the form containing the OLE Outline control.

7. Choose the Properties... option from the shortcut menu, and the Outline Control Properties dialog box appears, as shown in Figure 17.11. You can set various options in this dialog box. However, in the example being developed, all of the default values for the Outline control are used. Click on the OK button.

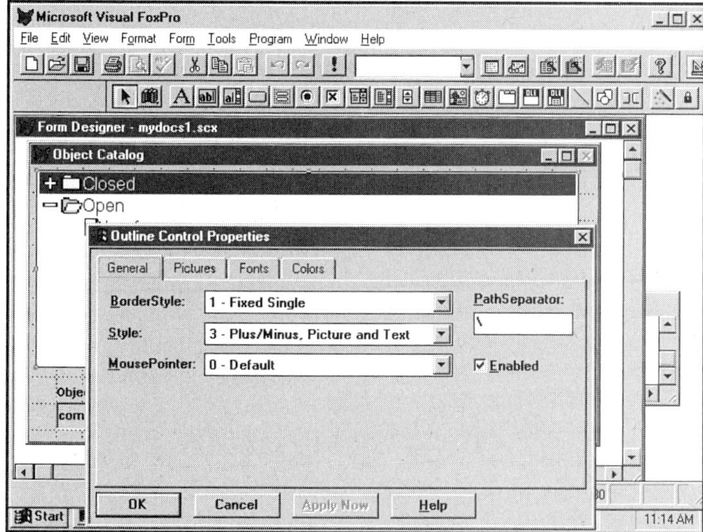

FIGURE 17.11.
The Outline Control Properties dialog box.

NOTE

The Outline Control Properties dialog box is built into the Outline control OCX file. Many OCX files have a built-in Properties dialog box. The dialog box provides a means of establishing specialized properties that pertain to a particular OLE control.

8. Choose the **F**orm menu New Properties option, and add a user-defined property named `OutlineIndex`. Then initialize it in the Properties window.
9. Code the methods as required to build and maintain a hierarchical list as discussed in the following paragraphs. You do not have to set any properties. Figure 17.12 shows the completed MYDOCS1.SCX form in the Form Designer.
10. Click on the standard toolbar Run (!) button to save your form and run it. The resultant form is shown in Figure 17.13.

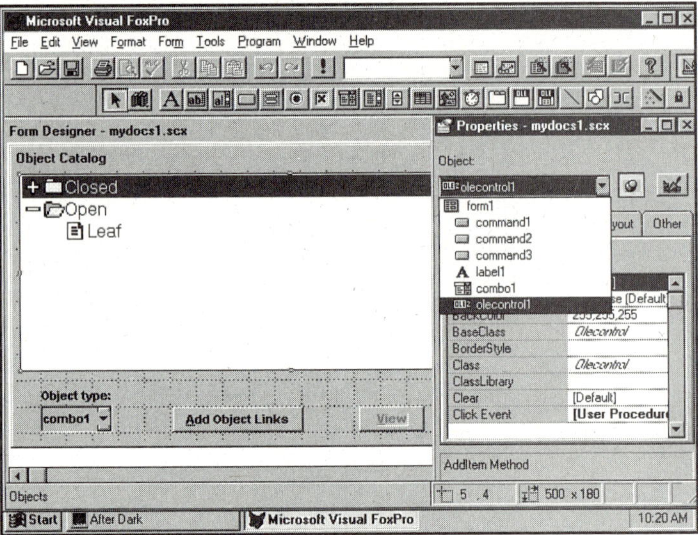

FIGURE 17.12.
The MYDOCS1.SCX form with an outline control.

In Figure 17.12, the Object list box is open, showing all the objects on the MYDOCS1.SCR form. The properties for the form are presented in Listing 17.4. To reduce complexity, superfluous properties have been removed from the listing. The properties for all controls on the form are the same as for the MYDOCS.SCR form (shown in Figure 17.5). Visual FoxPro Help describes many of the properties and methods for the Outline control.

The `Form1.OutlineIndex` property was added to keep track of the currently selected outline item.

Listing 17.4. A listing of the MYDOCS1.SCX form properties set at design time.

```
Object          Property
Dataenvironment
                 InitialSelectedAlias = "myoles"
cursor1          Alias = "myoles"
                 CursorSource = myoles.dbf
                 Order = "filename"
cursor2          Alias = "objects"
                 CursorSource = objects.dbf
form1            Caption = "Object Catalog"
                 AutoCenter = .T.
                OutlineIndex = 0          (User added property)
command1         Caption = "\<Add Object Links"
command2         Caption = "\<View"
                 Enabled = .F.
command3         Caption = "E\<xit"
label1           Caption = "Object type:"
combo1           ColumnCount = 1
                 RowSourceType = 6
                 RowSource = "OBJECTS.Extension"
                 Value = form1.doctype
                 ControlSource = "objects"
                 FirstElement = 1
```

The Outline control (`olecontrol1`) properties that are used at runtime include the following:

Property	*Description*
`Collapse()`	The array used to specify that a list item be collapsed. A list item is collapsed if its subordinate items are not displayed. You specify a true value (`.T.`) to collapse an item. If an item is already collapsed (`.T.`), an error message displays.

`Expand()`	The array used to specify that a list item be expanded. A list item is expanded if its subordinate items are displayed. You specify a true value (`.T.`) to expand an item. If an item is already expanded (`.T.`), an error message displays. You should retrieve the state of the list item before you attempt to expand it. Here is an example:
	`IF !Outline1.Expand(item)`
	`    Outline1.Expand(item)`

`Insert()`	The numeric array used to specify a new insert level for an item. The array contains the indent levels (1, 2, and so on) for each element in the outline list.
`List()`	A character string array used to access the items in the outline list strings.
`ListCount`	The number of items in the list.
`ListIndex`	The currently selected list item.

The methods for the outline control in the MYDOCS1.SCR form are presented in Listing 17.5. The `Init` method for the OLE Outline control (`Olecontrol1`) executes when the form is initialized. Each `Objects.Descript` field (for example, `BMP IMAGE`) from table OBJECTS.DBF is inserted into the outline using the outline's `AddItem()` method. No indent level is specified, so the field is inserted at level 1. Then the filenames of all of the records from the MYOLES.DBF table that correspond to the `Objects.Descript` field (for example, all BMP files) are inserted into the outline using the `AddItem()` method. Then level 2 indentation is specified with the `Indent` property for the filename. The `Indent` property is treated like an array. Each level of indentation is a level of subordination. This process is repeated for all objects in the file. Here is an example:

Outline	*Code*	*Index*	*Indent Level*
`BMP IMAGE`	`This.AddItem("BMP IMAGES")`	`0`	`1`
`C:\IMAGES\CAT.BMP`	`This.AddItem("C:\IMAGES\CAT.BMP")` `This.Indent(1) = 2`	`1`	`2`
`C:\IMAGES\DOG.BMP`	`This.AddItem("C:\IMAGES\CAT.BMP")` `This.Indent(2) = 2`	`2`	`2`
`MS WORD`	`This.AddItem("BMP IMAGES")`	`3`	`2`

The `PictureClick` method responds to a click on the folder picture in the outline. The `Click` method responds to a click anywhere on the outline list item. In either case, the selected item is a filename of an object, its index (`ListIndex`) is stored in the `form1.OutlineIndex` property, that I added with the For**m** menu Add **P**roperty option. If no outline list item is selected or a main category is selected, `OutlineIndex` is set to `0`.

Listing 17.5. A listing of the methods for form MYDOCS1.DOC outline control.

```
************************************************************
* Control Olecontrol1 Methods:
PROCEDURE Init
      SELECT Objects
      SCAN FOR !EOF()
         This.AddItem(Objects.Descript)
         SELECT MYOles
         SCAN FOR !EOF()
            IF Objects.Extension = MyOles.Type
                 This.AddItem(MyOles.FileName)
                 This.Indent(This.ListCount-1)=2
            ENDIF
         ENDSCAN
         SELECT Objects
      ENDSCAN
ENDPROC
*
************************************************************
PROCEDURE Click
      this.PictureClick(this.listindex)
```

```
ENDPROC
*
************************************************************
PROCEDURE  PictureClick
      *** OLE Control Event ***
      Parameters listindex
      IF this.indent(listindex)     = 2          && Filename
           thisform.OutlineIndex     = listindex
           thisform.command2.Enabled = .T.  && Disable View Button
      ELSE
           thisform.OutlineIndex    = 0
           thisform.command2.Enabled = .F.  && Enable View button
      ENDIF
ENDPROC
```

Listing 17.6 presents the methods for the control buttons. When you press the **A**dd Object Links button, the `Click` event method, `command1.Click`, executes. First the Directory dialog box displays. You choose a directory, and the information relating to the object files of the type selected in the Object Type combo box is placed in an array using the `ADIR()` function. The table is sorted by filename using the `ASORT()` function. The file information is appended to the MYOLES.DBF table. The `command1.Click` method also inserts the filenames into the outline. First, it finds the index of the category that corresponds to the filename. Then it uses the `OleControl1.AddItem()` method to add the filenames to the outline list and the `OleControl1.Indent` property to set the indent level to `2`.

Click on the **V**iew control button, and the `Command2.Click` function executes. It, in turn, executes the `MODIFY GENERAL` command to display the currently selected OLE object, as shown in Figure 17.13. You can double-click on the `MODIFY GENERAL` window and the application associated with the OLE object executes, as shown in Figure 17.14. If you double-click on a media clip (AVI) file object, Visual FoxPro will show the movie. If you double-click on a sound (MID or WAV) file object, and you have a sound board, Visual FoxPro will play the sound or song.

Listing 17.6. A listing of the methods for the command button controls for the form MYDOCS1.DOC.

```
************************************************************
* Control command1  Methods:
PROCEDURE  Click
      SELECT MyOles
      LOCAL TypeObject
      IF Thisform.Combo1.ListIndex > 0
         GOTO (Thisform.Combo1.ListIndex) IN Objects ;
         Directory = GETDIR()
         NumberFiles = ADIR(FileArray, DIRECTORY+"*." ;
                       +Thisform.combo1.value)
         IF NumberFiles > 0
            =ASORT(FileArray)
            CurrentIndex = 0
            FOR J = 1 TO Thisform.OleControl1.ListCount
*              Only Look at top level (file extension type) items
               IF ThisForm.OleControl1.Indent(CurrentIndex) = 1
```

continues

Listing 17.6. continued

```
*                  Is the File type we are looking for?
                   IF Objects.Descript = Thisform.OleControl1.List(J-1)
                      CurrentIndex = J
                      EXIT
                   ENDIF
                ENDIF
             ENDFOR
*   Add file information to MYOLES.DBF table
             FOR F = 1 TO NumberFiles
                APPEND BLANK
                m.FileName = Directory + FileArray[F,1]
                REPL Type WITH Thisform.combo1.value, ;
                         FileName WITH m.FileName, ;
                         Size    WITH  FileArray[F,2],;
                         Date    WITH  FileArray[F,3]
                APPEND GENERAL Object FROM (m.FileName) LINK
                ThisForm.OLEControl1.AddItem(m.FileName,CurrentIndex)
                ThisForm.OLEControl1.Indent(CurrentIndex)= 2
                CurrentIndex=CurrentIndex+1
             ENDFOR
             Thisform.Refresh  && Refresh the form
          ELSE
             WAIT "No object files in Directory: " ;
                 +Directory  WINDOW AT 12,30
          ENDIF
       ENDIF
ENDPROC
*
************************************************************
* Control command2  Methods:
PROCEDURE   Click       (Add Object Links)
       IF RECCOUNT("MyOLEs") > 0
           IF Thisform.OutlineIndex > 0
               m.Filename = Thisform.OleControl1.List(Thisform.OutlineIndex)
               SEEK M.FileName IN MyOLEs
               IF FOUND("MyOLEs") AND !EMPTY(MyOLEs.Object)
                    MODIFY GENERAL MyOLEs.Object
               ENDIF
           ENDIF
       ELSE
           This.Enabled = .F.
           WAIT WINDOW AT 15,30 "Empty Object: "+ MyOles.Filename
       ENDIF
ENDPROC
*
************************************************************
* Control command3  Method:   (Exit)
PROCEDURE  Click
       CLEAR EVENTS
       RELEASE THISFORM
ENDPROC
```

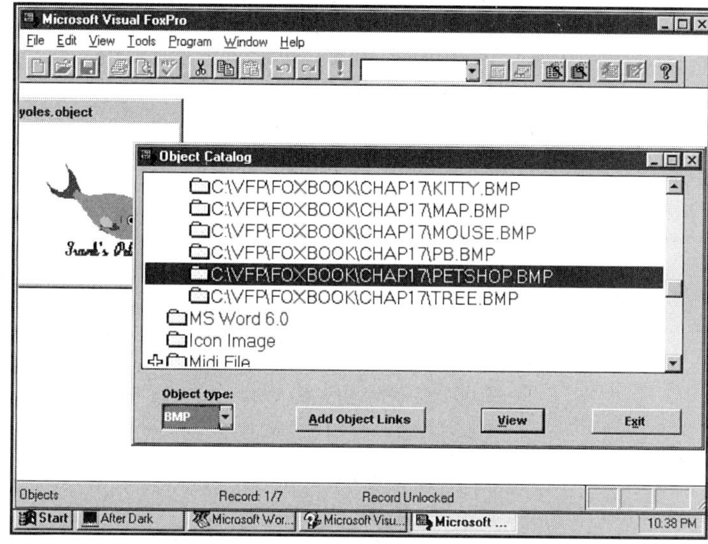

FIGURE 17.13.
The MYDOCS1.SCR form, with the currently selected OLE object displayed.

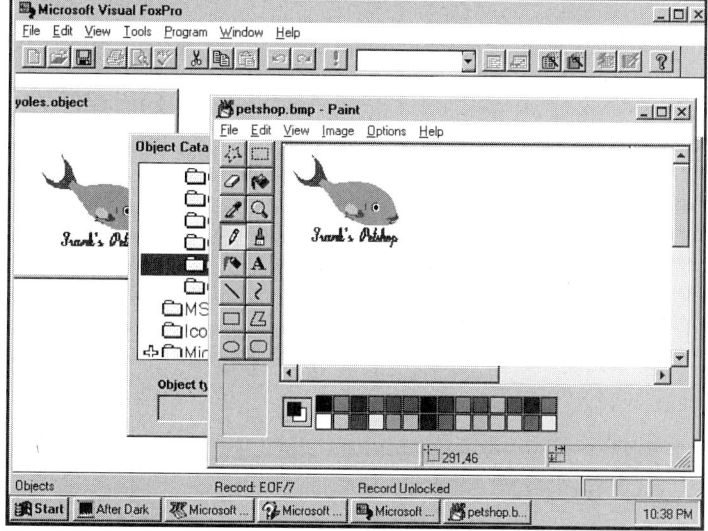

FIGURE 17.14.
The MYDOCS1.SCR form, with the MS Paint application window displayed to edit the currently selected OLE object, which is a BMP image.

Dynamic Data Exchange

Another mechanism for sharing information between Visual FoxPro and other Windows applications is dynamic data exchange. Two Windows applications can sustain DDE communications by passing messages back and forth. One of the applications is the *server* and the other is the *client*. The DDE server is the application that possesses information. The DDE client is the application that obtains that information from the server. Visual FoxPro can be both a server and a client.

The client application broadcasts a message to all currently active Windows applications, requesting the type of required information. The server with access to the required information responds, and the interprocess communication (conversation) begins. Visual FoxPro uses 11 functions to perform DDE interprocess communications with other Windows applications.

Before proceeding with a discussion of these DDE functions, I will discuss the basic DDE terminology. Certain terms are used by all Windows applications that support DDE operations. These terms include *service name*, *topic name*, and *item name*.

Service Names

A *service name* is a name the server responds to when a client attempts to access the server. The default name for Visual FoxPro is `Visual FoxPro`. Not all Windows applications support DDE. Table 17.7 lists a few of the service names for Windows applications that support DDE.

Table 17.7. Some of the DDE service names for FoxPro applications.

Application	*DDE Service Name*
Asymmetric ToolBook	`ToolBook`
Crosstalk for Windows	`Crosstalk`
Microsoft Access	`MSAccess`
Microsoft Excel	`Excel`
Microsoft Visual FoxPro	`Visual FoxPro`
Microsoft Project	`Project`
Microsoft Windows Program Manager	`Progman`
Microsoft Word for Windows	`WinWord`
Polaris PackRat PIM	`PackRat`

Topic Names

The *topic name* specifies a logical set of information. If the information is file based, the topic name is usually a filename. It can even include the path of the file. Other types of information are given application-specific topic names. A client attempting to access a server must specify both the service name of the server and the topic name. Many applications support a general topic name, usually `System`, which is used to request status or other general information from a server application or for sending commands to the server.

Item Names

An *item name* specifies a unit of data that the client requests the server to send. For example, a client could request that Excel send a spreadsheet cell, `R2C3` (row 2, column 3). If data for cell `R2C3` is available, Excel sends it to the client.

Imagine the power this capability provides. From Excel, you can cause FoxPro to execute a program and return results whenever you recalculate a spreadsheet. You can dynamically change fields inserted in a Microsoft Word or WordPerfect document by a DDE interprocess communications operation with FoxPro. From FoxPro, you can carry on a DDE communications session with a Windows telecommunications application such as Crosstalk, access financial data (or any other type of data) downloaded from a telecommunications service, and insert the data in a FoxPro database table. In FoxPro, you can access data from an Excel or 1-2-3 for Windows spreadsheet. The variety of applications you can create using the DDE feature is limited only by your imagination.

There is a downside, however. When two applications use DDE to communicate, they must both be executing. That means that you must have sufficient memory for both applications to be resident at the same time. You will need a comprehensive knowledge of the Visual FoxPro language, and you must know the command language of other Windows applications with which you plan to carry on a DDE communication session.

Summary of DDE Functions

Visual FoxPro supports DDE by providing the functions listed in Table 17.8. These functions violate the Xbase identifier rules. That is, the first four characters of these functions aren't unique, the function names exceed 10 characters, and their function names can't be abbreviated.

Table 17.8. FoxPro DDE functions.

Function	*Usage*
`DDEAbortTrans()`	Cancels an asynchronous DDE transaction.
`DDEAdvise()`	Establishes a warm or hot link to a server application.
`DDEEnabled()`	Sets or returns the DDE status.
`DDEExecute()`	Sends an execute message to a server application.
`DDEInitiate()`	Opens a DDE channel to a server application.
`DDELastError()`	Returns an error code for the last error caused by a DDE function.
`DDEPoke()`	Sends data to a client or server application.
`DDERequest()`	Requests data from a server application.
`DDESetOption()`	Changes or returns DDE settings.

continues

Table 17.8. continued

Function	*Usage*
`DDESetService()`	Adds, removes, or changes the status of services.
`DDESetTopic()`	Associates a topic with a service.
`DDETerminate()`	Closes a DDE channel.

FoxPro as a Client

If you want Visual FoxPro to request data from another Windows application, FoxPro becomes the client. You can write a program to do this. A typical FoxPro program that requests data from another application is composed of code that performs the following steps:

1. Call the `DDEInitiate()` function to establish a link to the server application.
2. If the link is successfully established, call the `DDERequest()` function to request information from the server application. You can call the `DDERequest()` function repeatedly to request additional information.
3. When you finish requesting data, call `DDETerminate()` to terminate the linkage to the server application. You must do this to free up system resources.

These functions establish what is called a *cold link.* When your client initiates all communications between the applications, a cold link is established.

FoxPro as a Server

Visual FoxPro also can be established as a server. The following steps are required for a FoxPro program to behave as a server:

1. Call the `DDESetService()` function to create a service (service name) and specify the type of service.
2. Call the `DDESetTopic()` function to create a service topic and specify the procedure to execute when the topic is specified in a client request.
3. Create the procedure specified in `DDESetTopic()` to accept the parameters passed to the procedure. The procedure is called by a client requesting information. The procedure processes the request and returns the requested information to the client application.

A DDE conversation between applications can be in one of three fundamental modes: cold links, hot links, and warm links. You have already been introduced to cold links. In warm and hot links, the server notifies the client if the data changes. The `DDEAdvise()` function is used to initiate DDE warm and hot link conversations.

For example, suppose you want the server to notify the FoxPro client when any data changes. You can do this using the `DDEAdvise()` function to establish a hot or warm link to the data.

One of the arguments passed to `DDEAdvise()` is the name of a user-defined function (UDF). This UDF is called by the server to notify the client that the data has changed. It is sometimes called a *callback function.* The UDF appropriately processes the changed data. If the link is designated as hot, the server calls the UDF and passes the updated data as soon as it changes. With a warm link, the server notifies the client by calling the callback function. If the client wants the data, the client must request it using the `DDERequest()` function.

The following FoxPro code is used to establish a hot link to Microsoft Excel:

```
Channel = DDEInitiate("Excel","Accounts")
IF Channel = -1   && If Excel is not active…
RUN /N EXCEL     && Execute Excel
Channel = DDEInitiate("Excel","Accounts")
IF Channel <> -1
=DDEAdvise(Channel,"R2C2", HotLink, 1)
…
* Function HotLink is called by Excel if data changes
FUNCTION HotLink
PARAMETER iChannel, sAction, sItem, sR2C2, sFormat, iStatus)
Value = sR2C2  && Fetch changed value
RETURN
```

In the following sections, the syntax and usage of each of the DDE functions supported by Visual FoxPro is described.

The *DDEAbortTrans( )* Function

You use the `DDEAbortTrans()` function to abandon an asynchronous transaction.

If you don't specify a UDF with the `DDEExecute()`, `DDEPoke()`, and `DDERequest()` functions, they wait indefinitely for a server application to respond. If you do specify a UDF with these functions, they return control to the FoxPro program. The FoxPro program continues executing code. When the server application responds, the UDF executes. Both the FoxPro program and the UDF execute asynchronously. Therefore, if you use the `DDEExecute()`, `DDEPoke()`, and `DDERequest()` functions to specify a UDF that executes when data is available, you create an asynchronous transaction. This is the type of transaction that aborts if the `DDEAbortTrans()` function executes. Here is the syntax:

```
DDEAbortTrans(<expN>)
```

If you call the `DDEAbortTrans()` function before the server has processed the request, the UDF won't be called for the transaction.

A logical true value (`.T.`) is returned if the asynchronous transaction is successfully aborted. A logical false value (`.F.`) is returned if the asynchronous transaction can't be aborted. You can use the `DDELastError()` function to determine why the transaction can't be aborted.

The numeric expression *<expN>* specifies the transaction number returned by the `DDEExecute()`, `DDEPoke()`, or `DDERequest()` functions.

The *DDEAdvise( )* Function

You use the `DDEAdvise()` function to specify a warm or hot link to an item name in a server application. When you specify a warm link by calling `DDEAdvise()`, the server application notifies Visual FoxPro that the item name has been modified. If you specify a hot link, the server application notifies FoxPro that the item name has been modified and then passes the new information to FoxPro. You also can use the `DDEAdvise()` function to stop the server from sending notification. Here is the syntax:

```
DDEAdvise(<expN1>, <expC1>, <expC2>, <expN2>)
```

The `DDEAdvise()` function returns `.T.` if it executes successfully; otherwise, it returns `.F.`. Here are the arguments of the `DDEAdvise()` function:

`<expN1>` You specify the channel number in `<expN1>`. The `DDEInitiate()` function returns the channel number if conversation is successfully initiated.

`<expC1>` The `<expC1>` character expression specifies the item name. For example, Microsoft Excel uses row and column notation to refer to cells in a spreadsheet. The item name `R1C1` designates the cell in the first row and column of the spreadsheet.

`<expC2>` The `<expC2>` character expression specifies the UDF that executes when a warm or hot link is established; the item `<expC1>` is modified. When the UDF executes, five parameters are passed to it. These parameters are described in Table 17.9.

`<expN2>` Include a numeric value from 0 to 2 in `<expN2>` to specify the link type. Here is a list of the values and their link types:

`<expN2>`	*Link Type*
`0`	Cold link
`1`	Warm link
`2`	Hot link

You can turn off notification from the server application by specifying 0 in `<expN2>`. If the item changes, the UDF isn't executed. If `<expN2>` is omitted, a warm link is established.

Table 17.9. Parameters passed to a UDF by a server for the `ADVISE` and `TERMINATE` transactions.

Parameter	*Contents*
Channel number	The channel number to the server application.
Action	A character string containing either `ADVISE` or `TERMINATE`.
Item	A character string containing the item name, for example, `R1C1` for an Excel spreadsheet cell.

Parameter	*Contents*
Data	The new data for a hot link or the null string for a warm link.
Advise status	An integer value containing the type of link. Here are the values: 0—cold link 1—warm link 2—hot link

The PARAMETER statement in the UDF should contain five parameters to accept the values passed from the server application. If a warm link is established, the UDF is executed and the null string is passed in the data parameter. At that point, if you want the modified data, you can call the DDERequest() function. If a hot link is established, the UDF executes and the data is passed in the Data parameter. The value returned by the UDF is ignored.

The following short program fragment illustrates how you establish a conversation with Excel to acquire data from a spreadsheet named Accounts. The DDEAdvise() function establishes two links to data in two spreadsheet cells (R2C3 and R2C4). The UDF named NEWDATA executes when data changes in either of the two cells. The UDF tests the item and advise parameters to determine which item changed and the item's link type:

```
channel = DDEInitiate('Excel', 'Accounts')
IF channel != -1    && Is conversation established?
= DDEAdvise(channel, 'R2C3', 'newdata', 1)  && Warm link
= DDEAdvise(channel, 'R2C4', 'newdata', 2)  && Hot link
...
ENDIF

PROCEDURE newdata
PARAMETERS channel, action, item, data, advise

DO CASE
    CASE item = 'R1C1' AND advise = 1  && Warm link
        ...
    CASE item = 'R1C2' AND advise = 2  && Hot link
        ...
ENDCASE
    ...
= DDETerminate(ChannelNo)
```

The *DDEEnabled( )* Function

You use the DDEEnabled() function to enable or disable DDE processing or to return the status of DDE processing. DDE processing can be globally enabled or disabled. You can also enable or disable DDE processing for specific channels. In addition, you can use the DDEEnabled() function to *protect* critical code or disable links for short periods. For example, if you need to make certain modifications to fields accessed by clients, you can disable DDE processing during that period. During the period in which DDE processing is disabled, client requests are queued until DDE processing is enabled. Here is the syntax:

```
DDEEnabled([<expL1> ¦ <expN1> [, <expL2>]])
```

If the `DDEEnabled()` function is issued with none of its optional arguments, the global DDE processing status is returned. If a logical true value (`.T.`) is returned, DDE processing has been globally enabled. If a logical false value (`.F.`) is returned, DDE processing has been globally disabled.

You can globally enable or disable DDE processing by specifying a logical `.T.` or `.F.` value for the value of the optional variable `<expL1>`.

If you want to enable or disable DDE processing for a specific channel, specify the channel number in parameter `<expN1>` and a logical `.T.` or `.F.` value in `<expL2>`.

The *DDEExecute( )* Function

You can use the `DDEExecute()` function to send a command to another application. The problem with this function is that you must be familiar with the command language of the other application because the command you send is for the other application. Like other DDE functions, before you call this function, you must establish a channel to the server application with `DDEInitiate()`.

For example, both Word for Windows and Excel have an extensive set of macro commands (including DDE commands that let you request data from Visual FoxPro from within Excel or Word). If you establish a channel to Excel, you can use the `DDEExecute()` function to send Excel macro commands to Excel from within Visual FoxPro. Here is the syntax:

```
DDEExecute(<expN>, <expC1> [, <expC2> ])
```

If the application to which you send a command successfully executes that command, the `DDEExecute()` function returns a logical true value (`.T.`). If the receiving application can't successfully execute the command or the channel number you include isn't valid, the `DDEExecute()` function returns a logical false value (`.F.`). If you specify the optional asynchronous UDF (`<expC3>`), a transaction number is returned. If an error occurs, `-1` returns. The arguments are defined as follows:

`<expN>`	You specify the channel number in `<expN>`.
`<expC1>`	You specify the command to send to the service name in `<expC1>`. The format of the command can differ from one application to another; consult the application's documentation for the correct syntax.
`<expC2>`	You specify the optional character expression, `<expC2>`, to permit asynchronous command execution requests. If `<expC2>` is omitted, a client waits indefinitely for the server application to execute the command. If you include the name of a UDF in `<expC2>`, client

program execution continues immediately after the command execution request is made. When the server application executes the command, the UDF specified in `<expC2>` executes. The server passes five parameters to the UDF in the order shown in Table 17.10. When you include `<expC2>`, `DDEExecute()` doesn't return a logical value. It returns a transaction number or `-1` if an error occurs.

Table 17.10. Parameters passed to a FoxPro UDF by a server to indicate success or failure of the `DDEExecute()` request.

Parameter	*Contents*
Channel number	The channel number to the server application. The `DDEInitiate()` function returns the channel number if conversation is possible.
Action	An ASCII string that contains one of the following two values: `XACTCOMPLETE` (transaction was successful) or `XACTFAIL` (transaction failed).
Item	The item name (for example, `R2C3` for an Excel spreadsheet cell).
Data	A character string containing the new data (`REQUEST`) or data passed (`POKE` or `EXECUTE`).
Transaction number	The transaction number returned by `DDEExecute()`.

When an error is encountered, you can use the `DDELastError()` function to determine why the transaction failed.

Listing 17.7 presents a sample program that places a Word for Windows document on the Clipboard using DDE communications. For this example, Microsoft Word for Windows is executed using the `RUN` command because an application must be open before you can use the `DDEInitiate()` function to establish a channel to the application. Because the intent is to send WordBasic commands to Word for Windows, the `System` topic name is used. When a valid channel is established, `DDEExecute()` executes to send commands to open a document, select the entire document, and copy selected text to the Clipboard. The memory variable, `Letter`, is assigned the contents of the Clipboard. Finally, a command is sent to exit Word for Windows (to save memory), and the `DDETerminate()` function executes to close the DDE channel.

Listing 17.7. A program that illustrates use of the `DDEExecute()` function.

```
*************************************************************
*     * 11/03/92              DDEEXEC.PRG          06:02:18 *
*************************************************************
```

continues

Listing 17.7. continued

```
*      *                                                  *
*      * Description:                                     *
*      *  Illustrates how to execute commands in other    *
*      *  Windows Applications                            *
**********************************************************
RUN /NI winword
Channel = DDEInitiate("WinWord","system")
IF Channel <> -1
=DDEExecute( Channel, "[AppMaximize]" )
=DDEExecute( Channel, '[FileOpen "f:\winword\letter.doc"]')
=DDEExecute( Channel, "[EditSelectAll]" )
=DDEExecute( Channel, "[EditCopy]" )
Letter = _CLIPTEXT
=DDEExecute( Channel, "[FileExit]" )
=DDETerminate( Channel )
ENDIF
? Letter
```

The *DDEInitiate( )* Function

You use the `DDEInitiate()` function to establish a channel between Visual FoxPro and a DDE server application. After you establish a channel, FoxPro can request information from the server by referencing the channel number in subsequent DDE function calls. Visual FoxPro behaves as the client, requesting information from the server application through the channel. The syntax is this:

```
DDEInitiate(<expC1>, <expC2>)
```

The `DDEInitiate()` function returns the channel number if the DDE conversation is successfully established. Channel numbers begin at 0. The number of channels that you can establish is limited only by your system resources. The `DDEInitiate()` function returns `-1` if the channel can't be established. If the server application isn't open, a dialog box appears asking if you want to open it. If you choose Yes, Visual FoxPro attempts to open the application. You can use the `DDELastError()` function to determine why a channel can't be established. You can close a channel with the `DDETerminate()` function.

The first character expression argument, `<expC1>`, specifies the service name. (See Table 17.7.) The second argument, `<expC2>`, specifies the topic name.

The following example uses `DDEInitiate()` to establish a channel between Visual FoxPro and an Excel spreadsheet named Accounts. `Excel` is the service name and `Accounts` is the topic name. The channel number is stored to a memory variable named `ChannelNo` for use in subsequent DDE functions:

```
ChannelNo = DDEInitiate('Excel', 'Accounts')
IF ChannelNo != -1
...
* Process client actions
...
```

```
= DDETerminate(ChannelNo)  && Close the channel
ENDIF
WAIT WINDOW "DDE Error Number: " + ;
LTRIM(STR(DDELastError()))
ENDIF
```

The *DDELastError( )* Function

The `DDELastError()` function returns an error number for the last DDE function executed. Here is its syntax:

```
DDELastError()
```

When DDE functions don't execute successfully, you can use `DDELastError()` to help determine the cause of the error. If the last DDE function executed successfully, `DDELastError()` returns `0`. If the last DDE function was unsuccessful, `DDELastError()` returns a nonzero value. From the program shown in Listing 17.8, you should have no trouble figuring out the meaning of the DDE error numbers.

Listing 17.8. A program that displays DDE error messages.

```
***********************************************************
*     * 11/03/92              DDEerr.PRG         06:02:18 *
***********************************************************
*     *                                                   *
*     * Description:                                      *
*     *  Function that displays DDE communications error  *
*     *  message.                                         *
***********************************************************
DECLARE DDEerr[26]
ErrNo = DDELastError()
IF ErrNo > 0
DO GetErrs
WAIT WINDOW "DDE Error: " + DDEerr[ErrNo]
RELEASE ALL LIKE DDEerr
ENDIF
RETURN
PROCEDURE GetErrs
IF !FILE ("DDEERR.MEM")
DDEerr[ 1] = "Service busy"
DDEerr[ 2] = "Topic busy"
DDEerr[ 3] = "Channel busy"
DDEerr[ 4] = "No such service"
DDEerr[ 5] = "No such topic"
DDEerr[ 6] = "Bad channel"
DDEerr[ 7] = "Insufficient memory"
DDEerr[ 8] = "Acknowledge time-out"
DDEerr[ 9] = "Request time-out"
DDEerr[10] = "No DDEInitialize"
DDEerr[11] = "Client attempted server transaction identifier"
DDEerr[12] = "Execute time-out"
DDEerr[13] = "Bad parameter"
DDEerr[14] = "Low memory"
DDEerr[15] = "Memory error"
```

continues

Listing 17.8. continued

```
DDEerr[16] = "Connect failure"
DDEerr[17] = "Request failure"
DDEerr[18] = "Poke time-out"
DDEerr[19] = "Could not display message"
DDEerr[20] = "Multiple synchronous transactions"
DDEerr[21] = "Server died"
DDEerr[22] = "Internal DDE error"
DDEerr[23] = "Advise time-out"
DDEerr[24] = "Invalid transaction"
DDEerr[25] = "Unknown"
SAVE ALL LIKE DDEerr TO DDEerr
ELSE
RESTORE FROM DDEerr ADDITIVE
ENDIF
```

The *DDEPoke( )* Function

You use the `DDEPoke()` function to transfer data between client and server applications. The data is sent as a character string to the item name in the application specified by the channel number. Here is the syntax:

```
DDEPoke(<expN>, <expC1>, <exp> [, <expC2> [, <expC3>]])
```

If the poke operation is successful, the `DDEPoke()` function returns a logical true value (`.T.`). If the operation is unsuccessful, a logical false value (`.F.`) is returned. If you specify the optional asynchronous UDF, `<expC3>`, and the operation is successful, `DDEPoke()` returns a transaction number. If the operation is unsuccessful, `-1` is returned. Here is a description of the `DDEPoke()` arguments:

`<expN>` You use the application's channel number, `<expN>`, to specify the application to which the data is sent. If the channel number is a server channel, `DDEPoke()` sends the data in response to a request or a previously established hot link.

`<expC1>` The data is sent to the item name specified by `<expC1>`.

`<exp>` The data sent to the item name is specified by `<exp>`. The format in which the data is sent is specified with `<expC2>`.

`<expC2>` The character expression `<expC2>` specifies the format in which the data is sent. The default format is `CF_TEXT`. In the `CF_TEXT` format, fields are delimited with tabs, and a record is delimited with a carriage return and a line feed.

`<expC3>` You can specify the optional character expression, `<expC3>`, to permit asynchronous data transfer. If `<expC3>` is omitted, a client waits indefinitely for data from the server application. If you include the name of a UDF in `<expC3>`, client program execution continues immediately after the request is made.

When the data is available from the server application, the UDF specified in <expC3> is executed. Five parameters are passed to the UDF in the order specified in Table 17.11.

Table 17.11. Parameters passed to a FoxPro UDF by a server initiated by the `DDEPoke()` and `DDERequest()` functions.

Parameter	*Contents*
Channel number	The channel number to the server application. The `DDEInitiate()` function returns the channel number if conversation is possible.
Action	An ASCII string containing one of the following values: `XACTCOMPLETE` (transaction was successful) or `XACTFAIL` (transaction failed).
Item	The item name (for example `R1C1`, for an Excel spreadsheet cell).
Data	A character string containing the new data for a hot link or the null string for a warm link.
Transaction number	The transaction number returned by `DDEPoke()` or `DDERequest()`.

If the transaction fails, you can use `DDELastError()` to determine the reason for failure.

The *DDERequest( )* Function

The `DDERequest()` function requests data from a server application. Before you can request data, you must establish a channel to the server application with the `DDEInitiate()` function. Here is the syntax:

```
DDERequest(<expN>, <expC1>[, <expC2> [, <expC3>]])
```

If the request for data is successful, the `DDERequest()` function returns the data as a character string. If the request fails, the `DDERequest()` function returns the null string, and the `DDELastError()` function returns a nonzero value. If you specify the optional asynchronous UDF, <expC3>, `DDERequest()` returns a transaction number if the poke operation is successful or `-1` if the operation is unsuccessful. Here is a description for the `DDERequest()` arguments:

<expN> You specify the channel number in <expN>.

<expC1> You use <expC1> to specify the item name. For example, Excel uses row and column notation to refer to cells in a spreadsheet. The item name `R1C1` designates the cell in the first row and column of the spreadsheet.

<expC2>	The character expression <expC2> specifies a format for the data requested. The default format is CF_TEXT. In the CF_TEXT format, fields are delimited with tabs, and a record is delimited with a carriage return and a line feed.
<expC3>	When the data is available from the server application, the UDF specified in <expC3> is executed. Five parameters are passed to the UDF in the order specified in Table 17.11. When you specify the UDF, <expC3>, the DDERequest() function doesn't return the data or the null string. Instead, a transaction number equal to or greater than zero is returned. If the operation fails, -1 is returned.

The following example uses the DDEInitiate() function to establish a channel between Visual FoxPro and an Excel spreadsheet named Accounts. Excel is the service name and Accounts is the topic name. The channel number is stored to a memory variable named ChannelNo for use in subsequent DDE functions.

The DDERequest() function requests the item name R1C1, the data in the first row and column of the Accounts spreadsheet. The source code follows:

```
ChannelNo = DDEInitiate('Excel', 'Accounts')

IF ChannelNo != -1
   ...
   Requestno = DDERequest(ChannelNo, 'R1C1')
   IF !EMPTY(RequestNo) AND DDELastError() = 0  && Successful
     ...
   ENDIF
= DDETerminate(ChannelNo)  && Close the channel
ENDIF
```

The *DDESetOption( )* Function

You can use DDESetOption() to modify or retrieve the DDE settings. Here is the syntax:

```
DDESetOption(<expC> [, <expN> ¦ <expL>])
```

Two options, TIMEOUT and SAFETY, can be specified in <expC>.

You specify TIMEOUT if you want to specify the number of milliseconds that DDE functions wait for the server application to respond before a timeout occurs. The default value is 2000 (2 seconds). If you omit the <expN> argument, the current TIMEOUT value is returned.

If you specify SAFETY for the <expC> argument and use DDEInitiate() to establish a channel to a server application that doesn't respond, a dialog box appears. If you specify .T. or .F. in the <expL> argument, the dialog box display option is enabled or disabled, respectively. If you omit the <expL> argument, the current SAFETY setting is returned.

For example, if you want to specify a timeout elapsed time of three seconds and you want to suppress the display of the SAFETY dialog box, enter the following commands:

```
= DDESetOption("TIMEOUT", 3000)
= DDESetOption("SAFETY", .F.)
```

The *DDESetService( )* Function

Visual FoxPro can behave as a DDE server to send data to client Windows applications. You can use the DDESetService() function to create, release, or modify service names in FoxPro. Using the DDESetTopic() function, you also can create a group of topic names for each service name. You can use the DDESetService() function to retrieve information relating to a service name.

FoxPro has the default service name, Visual FoxPro, which supports requests only at startup. The Visual FoxPro service name has one topic name, SYSTEM. Table 17.12 lists all the item names supported by the SYSTEM topic.

Table 17.12. Item names supported by the SYSTEM topic name.

Item Name	*Item Description*
Topics	A list of available topic names
Formats	A list of supported formats
Status	The current status: BUSY or READY
SysItems	A list of item names

You can use the DDESetTopic() function to modify the FoxPro service name or release it. The information in the next section describes how to use the DDESetTopic() function arguments to manipulate the FoxPro service name. Here is the syntax of the DDESetService() function:

```
DDESetService(<expC1>, <expC2> [, <expL>])
```

The first character expression, <expC1>, specifies the service name that is created, released, or modified. You also can retrieve information relating to the specified service name.

The second character expression, <expC2>, specifies how to operate on the service name. Table 17.13 contains a list of options you can specify for <expC2>, the default values for the options, and a description of each option.

The third argument, <expL>, is optional. It is used to specify the state of the REQUEST, EXECUTE, POKE, or ADVISE options. You specify a logical true value (.T.) in <expL> to enable the option or a false value (.F.) to disable it.

Table 17.13. The `DDESetService()` function options.

Option	*Default Value*	*Description*
`DEFINE`	N/A	Creates a new service name.
`RELEASE`	N/A	Releases an existing service name.
`REQUEST`	`.T.`	Enables or disables requests to the service name.
`EXECUTE`	`.F.`	Enables or disables command execution.
`POKE`	`.F.`	Enables or disables client pokes to the service.
`ADVISE`	`.F.`	Enables or disables client notification of changes to item names.

The options are discussed in further detail in the following sections.

The *DEFINE* Option

When you want to create a new service name, you specify the `DEFINE` option. For example, the following commands create a new service name, `FSERVICE`. If the service name is successfully created, a logical true (`.T.`) is returned; otherwise, a logical false (`.F.`) is returned.

```
IF  DDESetService('fservice', 'DEFINE')
    WAIT WINDOW "The new service name, FSERVICE, was created"
ELSE
    WAIT WINDOW "Operation failed"
ENDIF
```

The *RELEASE* Option

By using too many service names and topic names you can use up system resources. You can release an existing service name with the `RELEASE` option. When you release a service name, all corresponding topic names are also released.

The following example code releases the service name created in the preceding example. If the service name is successfully released, a logical true (`.T.`) is returned; if the service name doesn't exist or can't be released, a logical false (`.F.`) is returned. Here is the example code:

```
IF DDESetService('fservice', 'RELEASE')
    WAIT WINDOW "Service name was successfully released"
ELSE
    WAIT WINDOW "Operation failed"
ENDIF
```

The *REQUEST* Option

You can use the `REQUEST` option to enable or disable client requests for a specified service name or to return the current `REQUEST` status to the service name. You can enable or disable client requests to the service name or specify a logical true or false value. `DDESetService()` returns `.T.` if it is successful. If the operation fails, `.F.` is returned.

You can retrieve the current request status for a service name by omitting the *<expL>* logical expression from the `DDESetService()` function. Then a logical true value is returned if the client requests are enabled for the service name, and a logical false value is returned if client requests are disabled.

The following commands test the enabled status of requests from client applications to the service name, `FSERVICE`. If the requests are enabled, the `REQUEST` option disables the current request status for `FSERVICE`. Here is the sample code:

```
ServName = 'FSERVICE'
Message = "Service Name " + ServName + " is "
IF DDESetService(ServName, 'REQUEST')
    WAIT WINDOW Message + "enabled"
    IF DDESetService('FSERVICE', 'REQUEST', .F.)
        WAIT WINDOW Message + "Disabled"
    ELSE
        WAIT WINDOW "Operation failed"
    ENDIF
ELSE
    WAIT WINDOW Message + "disabled"
ENDIF
```

The *EXECUTE* Option

You can use the `EXECUTE` option to enable or disable command execution requests to a service name or determine the current `EXECUTE` status for a service name. If you want to enable or disable client requests to execute a command, include a logical true (`.T.`) or false (`.F.`) value in *<expL>*. The `DDESetService()` function returns a true value if it is successful; otherwise, a false value is returned.

If you want to retrieve the current command execution status for the service name, omit *<expL>*. A logical true value is returned if client command execution requests are enabled for the service name; otherwise, a logical false value is returned.

The *POKE* Option

You can use the `POKE` option to enable or disable poke requests to a service name or to determine the current `POKE` status for a service name. If you want to enable or disable client poke requests, specify a logical true or false value in *<expL>*. The `DDESetService()` function returns `.T.` if it is successful; otherwise, `.F.` is returned.

If you want to retrieve the current poke status for the service name, omit `<expL>`. A logical true value is returned if client poke requests are enabled for the service name; otherwise, a logical false value is returned.

The *ADVISE* Option

You can use the `ADVISE` option to designate that a client is notified when data changes in an item name or to return the current `ADVISE` status for a service name. Refer to the section "The `DDEAdvise()` Function" for additional information.

If you want to enable or disable client notification, include a logical true (`.T.`) or false (`.F.`) value in `<expL>`. You can retrieve the current client notification status for the service name by omitting `<expL>`. A logical true value is returned if the client notification is enabled for the service name. A logical false value is returned if client notification is disabled.

The *DDESetTopic( )* Function

The `DDESetTopic()` function creates a topic name for a service name or releases the topic name from the service name. Here is the syntax:

```
DDESetTopic(<expC1>, <expC2> [, <expC3>])
```

After a topic name is created, any client requests to the topic name will cause the UDF specified in `<expC3>` to be executed. When the UDF is called, the server passes it a set of parameters whose values are determined by the client request. The value returned by the UDF is passed to the client. The return value is a logical value that indicates whether the topic name is able to provide the service requested by the client.

If the `DDESetTopic()` function successfully creates or releases the topic name, the function returns a logical true value. If the topic name can't be created or released, a logical false value is returned. The arguments are described in the following paragraphs:

`<expC1>`	The first argument (`<expC1>`) specifies the service name. Additional service names can be created with the `DDESetService()` function.
`<expC2>`	The second argument (`<expC2>`) specifies the topic name to create or release. If you specify a UDF in `<expC3>`, the `DDESetService()` function creates the name of the topic in `<expC2>`. If `<expC3>` is omitted, the topic name specified with `<expC2>` is released. If you specify a null string for `<expC2>`, the UDF specified in `<expC3>` executes for any topic name that isn't explicitly declared.
`<expC3>`	The third argument (`<expC3>`) specifies the name of a UDF that executes when a client application makes a request to the topic name. If you omit `<expC3>`, the `DDESetService()` function releases the topic name specified with `<expC2>`. When the UDF executes, it is passed six parameters in the order specified in Table 17.14.

Table 17.14. Parameters passed to a FoxPro UDF by a server.

Parameter	*Contents*
Channel number	The client channel number.
Action	Action can be one of the following: INITIATE, TERMINATE, POKE, REQUEST, EXECUTE, or ADVISE.
Item	The item name. For example, R1C1 for an Excel spreadsheet cell.
Data	Data from the client.
Command	Command from the client.
Advise status	The link type (0 = cold, 1 = warm, 2 = hot).

The values of the item, data, and command parameters depend on the action parameter. Table 17.15 lists the action parameter values and the values contained in the item, data, and command parameters.

Table 17.15. The action parameter values in the item, data, and command parameters.

Action Value	*Item Value*	*Data Value*	*Advise Status*
INITIATE	—	—	—
TERMINATE	—	—	—
POKE	—	—	—
REQUEST	Item name	—	—
EXECUTE	—	New command	—
ADVISE	Item name	—	Link type

If the UDF successfully handles the client request, it should return .T. If the request can't be handled or an error occurs, .F. should be returned. When .F. is returned and the action parameter value is INITIATE, the client topic name request is rejected. The client determines that a request has been ignored if the UDF returns .F., and the action parameter value is POKE, REQUEST, or EXECUTE. A client request is rejected for a warm or hot link if a logical false value is returned by the UDF and the action parameter value is ADVISE.

The *DDETerminate( )* Function

The DDETerminate() function closes a channel established with the DDEInitiate() function. If the channel is successfully closed, the DDETerminate() function returns a logical true value (.T.). If the channel can't be closed, a logical false value (.F.) is returned.

To conserve system resources, it is important that you close channels as soon as they are no longer needed.

All channels are automatically closed if you exit Visual FoxPro by choosing the **File** menu **Exit** option or by executing the `QUIT` command in a program or the Command window. Here is the syntax:

```
DDETerminate(<expN> ¦ <expC>)
```

The argument can be a numeric channel number in `<expN>` or the service name in `<expC>`. If you specify a service name, all channels to the service are closed.

Creating a DDE File Server

As you have already learned, you can add DDE support to your applications so that other Windows applications can access FoxPro data or send commands to your application. Other Windows applications, such as spreadsheets, word processors, and telecommunications, can take advantage of the powerful data retrieval capabilities of Visual FoxPro; but it is not automatic. You must include a DDE server in your application. This section describes how to create a DDE server to provide common DDE services.

After you initialize a DDE server, you can continue normal processing. FoxPro processes any DDE requests using the callback functions you provide to support DDE. Table 17.16 lists DDE services and describes how they are normally supported by DDE servers. The example in this section shows you how to support each of these functions.

Table 17.16. The callback function responses to DDE service actions.

DDE Service Action	*Callback Function Response*
`Initiate`	Opens files relating to a specific topic.
`Request`	Locates data and uses the `DDEPoke()` function to send data back to the requesting application.
`Execute`	Performs the specified FoxPro command.
`Poke`	Updates the specified data item to the value passed.
`Advise`	Uses the `DDEPoke()` function to transmit notification or data to the requesting function.
`Terminate`	Closes files.

The first thing you do when your program executes is initialize your DDE server so Windows applications can access it. You need to do the following:

1. Define the server name (`FoxServ`) using the following command:

```
= DDESetService( "FoxServ", "define" )
```

2. Define the server actions that your server supports. The DDE server accepts `INITIATE`, `TERMINATE`, and `REQUEST` actions by default. However, if you are supporting `ADVISE`, `EXECUTE`, and `POKE` actions, you must supply the following commands:

   ```
   = DDESetService( "FoxServ", "advise", .T. )
   = DDESetService( "FoxServ", "execute", .T. )
   = DDESetService( "FoxServ", "poke", .T. )
   ```

   These commands remain active until you either disable them with another `DDESetService()` function or quit FoxPro. When you get tired of servicing DDE requests, you should release the DDE services to restore memory resources. You do this by executing the following command:

   ```
   = DDESetService( "FoxServ", "release" )
   ```

3. Define the topic names and callback functions. You can specify specific category-related topics as in the following examples:

   ```
   = DDESetTopic( "FoxServ", "SYSTEM", "cbSTopic" )
   = DDESetTopic( "FoxServ", "DATA", "cbDTopic" )
   ```

   If you are going to accept a filename as a topic, you must validate the topic name in the `cbTopic()` callback function and specify a null string as the topic name. Here is an example:

   ```
   = DDESetTopic( "FoxServ", "", "cbTopic" )
   ```

4. Supply the callback functions (UDF). You can have a single generalized callback function or a callback function for each topic. The function must have the parameters described in the section on the `DDESetTopic()` function. Here is an example:

   ```
   FUNCTION  cbTopic
   PARAMETER iChannel, sAction, sItem, sData, sFormat, iStatus
   =DDEEnabled(.F.) && Disable requests during processing
   bReply = .T.     && Success reply
   DO CASE
   CASE sAction = "INITIALIZE"
   ...
   *  Respond to DDE actions
   ...
   =DDEEnabled(.T.) && enable requests
   RETURN bReply
   ```

The majority of the code for a server is the code inside of the callback function that responds to the DDE actions. The following paragraphs discuss how to respond to the various actions.

The *INITIATE* Action

The `INITIATE` action is always the first request. You should write code that initializes any environmental parameters, sets work areas, uses database tables, or performs any other action that prepares the FoxPro environment for subsequent requests. If you are supporting generalized topic names, such as filenames, you must make sure the name is valid. In other words, you need to make sure the file exists. In the following example, suppose that the topic name is a filename:

```
CASE sAction = "INITIALIZE"
sFile = ALLTRIM(sData)
IF FILE(sData + ".dbf") AND LEN(DBF(IChannel+1) ) = 0
USE sData IN IChannel+1  AGAIN
ELSE
bReply = .F.  && Failed
ENDIF
```

The channel number is unique for a DDE session and can be a zero or a positive number. It is used to pick a work area for the database table.

The *TERMINATE* Action

You respond to the `TERMINATE` action by restoring the environment, closing files, and so on. Here is an example:

```
CASE sAction = "TERMINATE"
USE IN IChannel+1
```

The *REQUEST* Action

You respond to the `REQUEST` action by providing whatever data the client requests. You might simply position a database, seek on a key, and return a memory variable or field value. You pass the data back to the client using the `DDEPoke()` function. Here is an example:

```
CASE sAction = "REQUEST"
    IF LEN(DBF(IChannel+1)) > 0
        SELECT IChannel+1
        DO CASE sData
             CASE sData = "TOP"
                 GO TOP
             CASE sData = "BOTTOM"
                 GO BOTTOM
             CASE sData = "NEXT"
                 IF EOF()
                    bReply = .F.
                 ELSE
                    SKIP
                 ENDIF
             CASE sData = "PREVIOUS"
                 IF RECNO() > 1
                    SKIP -1
                 ELSE
                    bReply = .F.
                 ENDIF
             OTHERWISE
                IF !CHKFIELD(sItem) && Correct field name?
                    bReply = .F. && Not a field name
                ELSE
                    * Convert field to string
                    sResults = sCnvFld(sItem)
```

```
                    = DDEPoke(iChannel, sItem, sResults)
                ENDIF
        ENDCASE
    ELSE
        bReply = .F.
    ENDIF
ENDCASE
```

The *EXECUTE* Action

The normal response to the DDE `EXECUTE` action is to execute a command in the server application command language. The command to be executed is passed in the `sData` parameter. Here is an example that illustrates how to respond to the `EXECUTE` action:

```
CASE sAction = "EXECUTE"
    &sData    && Execute FoxPro command
```

This example is ridiculously simplistic. You definitely want to restrict the list of commands that a Windows application can execute.

The *POKE* Action

When a Windows application wants to pass data to FoxPro, it uses the DDE `POKE` action. The normal response in the callback function is to update specified data. You can also use the DDE `POKE` action with a `SYSTEM` topic name to change environmental parameters. In the following example, the `sItem` parameter contains the name of the database field to change, and the `sData` parameter contains the new value for the specified field. Here is the segment of code for the example:

```
CASE sAction = "POKE"
    IF !CHKFIELD(sItem) && Correct field name?
       bReply = .F.  && Not a field name
    ELSE
      REPLACE sItem WITH sData && Update database field
    ENDIF
```

The *ADVISE* Action

When a Windows application wants to set up a hot or warm link, it issues an `ADVISE` action. The server should respond by establishing a mechanism that notifies or transmits data to the client application whenever a specified data item changes. In the following example, a flag, `AdviseFlg`, is set in response to an `ADVISE` action. The `ADVISE` action also turns on and off the link depending on the value of the `iStatus` parameter. If `iStatus` is `0`, the link is established. Here is the segment of code:

```
CASE sAction = "ADVISE"
    If sItem = "Amount"
        AdviseFlg = IIF(iStatus = 0 , .F., .T.)
    ENDIF
```

The procedure in the FoxPro application that is responsible for changing the value of the Amount database field tests the flag whenever it changes the value of the field. If the flag is set, FoxPro transmits the new value to the client application. Here is an example:

```
REPLACE Amount WITH NewValue
IF AdviceFlg
    = DDEPoke(iChannel, sItem, Amount)
ENDIF
```

Of course this simple example focuses on how to establish links and is only used for changing the single field `Amount`. A general form that allows any of the fields in the database to be linked would need a link indicator flag for each data item.

This concludes the instructions for building a FoxPro DDE server as well as the discussion of the extensions to Visual FoxPro to support DDE. The sample programs that accompany Visual FoxPro include an example code for a FoxPro sample DDE server, FOXDATA.PRG. You can find this code in the \VFP\SAMPLES\DDE directory. You can use FOXDATA.PRG as a foundation for your own FoxPro DDE server.

Executing and Quitting Visual FoxPro

You execute Visual FoxPro from Windows either by clicking on the FoxPro icon (the FoxPro fox) or by tabbing to the icon and pressing the Enter key. You can also choose the **F**ile Menu **R**un option. When the Run dialog box appears, enter `VFP.EXE` with the drive and directory prepended. You also can insert the name of the FoxPro program that executes when FoxPro executes. Here is an example:

```
D:\VFP\VFP  MYPROG.PRG
```

Program MYPROG.PRG is executed inside Visual FoxPro.

The syntax for the `QUIT` command has been around since JPLDIS, the first Xbase language developed for the Univac 1108 mainframe. To exit FoxPro, all you need to do is type `QUIT` into the Command window and press the Enter key or include the `QUIT` command in a program. Of course, you can also exit FoxPro by choosing the **F**ile menu E**x**it command.

Final Comments

It seems that the dBASE language has always been in the business of extending the operating system. In the CP/M days, dBASE II provided a last update feature and offered improved disk performance because, unlike CP/M, dBASE II buffered disk reads and writes. Now every modern operating system does these things.

It has always been possible to write applications programs by taking advantage of the facilities operating systems offer. You could write your accounting package in assembly language under

CP/M, for example. This low-level approach, however, not only takes a lot of time and is difficult to do, but is also closely linked to a particular computer and operating system. One of the reasons for the success of dBASE II was that it offered a high-level, system-independent tool for writing applications.

Now that operating systems such as Windows, OS/2, NT, UNIX, and Apple Systems 7 provide all the services an application needs, why should anyone use Visual FoxPro? Besides portability, Visual FoxPro offers a higher-level language. Just as with CP/M, where you didn't want to worry about BDOS calls, FCBs, or extents, the new operating systems are accompanied by plenty of detail. Writing applications in Visual FoxPro means not worrying about device contexts, semaphores, or assembly language. Perhaps the best extension of all is that Visual FoxPro provides a platform-independent application language that takes full advantage of the features of the new operating systems.

So be warned that if you use some of the platform-dependent extensions to Visual FoxPro, such as DDE functions, you will probably have to rewrite parts of your application if you want to move it to another platform (MS-DOS, UNIX, or the Mac).

Summary

This chapter presents language components used to interface with host operating systems. The following functions are discussed: `DATE()`, `DISKSPACE()`, `FDATE()`, `FSIZE()`, `FTIME()`, `GETENV()`, `HOME()`, `ISCOLOR()`, `MEMORY()`, `OS()`, `RUN()`, and `TIME()`, as well as all the DDE functions. In addition, the following commands are described: `?`, `COPY FILE`, `DIR`, `ERASE`, `LOAD`, `RENAME`, and `RUN`.

18

Queries Using SQL and the Query Designer

Gratiano speaks an infinite deal of nothing, more than any man in all Venice. His reasons are as two grains of wheat hid in two bushels of chaff: you shall seek all day ere you find them, and, when you have them, they are not worth the search.

—William Shakespeare (1564–1616) *The Merchant of Venice*

This chapter introduces the Structured Query Language (SQL) and gives an overview of its Visual FoxPro implementation. SQL is the subject of many good books. I cannot discuss SQL in the same depth in just one chapter as I could in a book, but I do present SQL syntax. In SQL you learn about *cursors*, which are temporary database tables that allow host languages, such as the FoxPro language, to read one record at a time from a result table.

SQL commands have their own syntax, keywords, and rules of order. It takes some practice to master the SQL `SELECT` command. Visual FoxPro provides a tool to assist you in learning how to pose a SQL query, the Query Designer. The Query Designer is an interactive tool that guides you through the process of defining a SQL `SELECT` command—all you need to do is point, click, and do a little typing. In this chapter, you learn how to create queries using the Query Designer window.

Background

As discussed in Chapter 2, "Database Management and the FoxPro Language," the relational model of database theory was developed by researchers working for IBM in the 1970s. In the 1980s the Xbase programming language made these concepts accessible to millions of computer owners. FoxPro continues this tradition of taking research out of the lab and making it commercially available.

IBM researchers developed several prototype relational languages in the 1970s. Their concepts were described in published papers (Chamberlin 1976) and implemented in *System R*, a prototype database management project. A company called Relational Software began marketing an implementation called Oracle in 1979, three years before IBM released its version of the Structured Query Language.

Throughout the 1980s SQL became established as the de facto standard in the relational database world (Date 1987). Thanks to the work of the X3H2 database committee, SQL became an official ANSI language standard in February 1987.

SQL enthusiasts did just fine without Xbase. In fact, some have criticized the FoxPro implementation because it is not a full ANSI standard implementation of SQL. It doesn't maintain referential integrity or security. The marketing minds at Ashton-Tate elected to insert a fully compliant ANSI standard SQL into dBASE IV. The result was a two-headed creature, with a wall separating the dBASE IV language from SQL. The designers of FoxPro 2.0 chose to blend some of the SQL commands into the FoxPro language in such a way that the higher-level SQL commands contribute the power of SQL queries to the FoxPro language. A single SQL `SELECT` command can replace many traditional Xbase commands. For example, how many FoxPro commands would you need to retrieve the following information: *List all employees who earn more than their boss.*

It takes only one SQL `SELECT` command to retrieve that information. In any event, because SQL commands were added to FoxPro, hundreds of thousands of hands-on FoxPro practitioners will be exposed to SQL by using Visual FoxPro.

SQL Overview

Before I present the FoxPro SQL commands, I'll provide an introduction to ANSI SQL. SQL is concise. With fewer than 30 verbs, the SQL language is much smaller than the FoxPro language, yet it is more relationally complete. *Relational completeness* is a measure of the selective power of a language. This concept was introduced by E. F. Codd. He stated that a language is said to be relationally complete if its command statements are powerful enough to retrieve any relation definable by means of relational calculus expressions (Codd 1972).

SQL statements are divided into four *data definition language* (DDL) statements—`CREATE`, `ALTER`, `DROP`, and `INSERT`—and about 20 *data manipulation language* (DML) statements, such as `SELECT`, `UPDATE`, and `DELETE`.

SQL is a set-oriented language. A query against one or more data tables produces a result data table. Because the Xbase language and other host languages, such as COBOL and PL/I, are record oriented, the ANSI standard specifies the cursor as a mechanism to provide record-at-a-time access to result tables. Cursors are described in greater detail in the section "Cursors."

A key part of SQL's capability to optimize queries, as well as to control data access by users, is a fully implemented data dictionary. A *data dictionary* is a set of data tables containing *metadata*—that is, data about the data. The *system tables*, which are kept in tables similar to DBF files, list all table names, field names, usernames, access privileges, and other information.

SQL manages one or more data tables in the context of a database, a concept that is foreign to the traditional Xbase. SQL directly supports the relationships between data tables, called *schema*, with information in the data dictionary. A separate data dictionary is grouped with each database in a subdirectory.

Visual FoxPro and SQL share several command verbs, such as `SELECT`, `CREATE`, and `INSERT`, and each applies different semantics to these words. The differences between the syntax of the remaining clauses, however, make it possible for the parser to distinguish them. FoxPro contains the following SQL commands:

`SELECT` — With the SQL `SELECT` command, you can retrieve information from one or more databases. You pose a query with the `SELECT` command, and FoxPro interprets the query and retrieves the designated information.

`CREATE CURSOR` — You use the `CREATE CURSOR` command to create a temporary database defined by a name, type, precision, and scale.

REVISED FOR VISUAL FOXPRO 3

`CREATE TABLE` You use the `CREATE TABLE` command to create a new database. With this command you specify a name, type, precision, and scale for each field in the database to be created.

REVISED FOR VISUAL FOXPRO 3

`INSERT` The SQL `INSERT` command adds a record to the end of an existing database. You supply the data or source of data with the command.

Interactive SQL

You can execute SQL commands in a program file, in a QPR file created by the Query Designer, or one at a time by typing them in the Command window. The latter mode is called *interactive mode.*

Because SQL statements are usually placed on multiple lines for clarity, you can enter a semicolon on each line except the last as you enter lines of a command in the Command window. Here is an example of a SQL statement that you can enter in the Command window:

```
* Example 1
SELECT LName, Salary, LastRaise ;
   FROM Employee ;
   WHERE Salary < 30000   && Last line of a SQL SELECT command
```

Of course, you can do the same thing with any FoxPro command, but traditional FoxPro commands usually are not lengthy.

You can also specify an interactive SQL command using the Query Designer window.

NOTE

Most of the SQL examples discussed in this chapter are included in a program named SQLEXAM.PRG on the disc that accompanies this book.

Embedded SQL

Visual FoxPro supports both *interactive* (Command window) SQL and *embedded* SQL. SQL commands can be mixed in with FoxPro language commands in procedures and functions. These SQL commands are referred to as embedded SQL.

Expression Differences

SQL mode expressions are similar to FoxPro expressions. In fact, dBASE/SQL extends the SQL standard to include most FoxPro functions, as well as user-defined functions.

In addition to FoxPro-style predicates such as the following examples:

```
NAME = "Smith"
```

and

```
Salary > 5000
```

SQL offers the capability to compare values with sets of values, as defined by a nested `SELECT` statement. Here are two examples:

```
Name = ANY (SELECT Name FROM Friends)
```

and

```
Salary >= ANY (SELECT Limit ;
    FROM Charter WHERE Title = Charter.Title)
```

The first SQL example is true if `Name` is found in the Name column in any record of the Friends table. The second example is more complicated. It is true if `Salary` is not greater than the limit found by looking up all records in Charter with a specified title.

`SELECT` is also a clause used with certain predicate operators such as `EXISTS`, `IN`, `SOME`, `NOT`, and `ANY`, which are discussed in the following section.

Here is another example of the SQL-specific relational operator:

```
Name BETWEEN "Jones" AND "Smith"
```

This is equivalent to this FoxPro syntax:

```
Name >= "Jones" AND Name <= "Smith"
```

The SQL version is easier to type and understand but harder to remember.

Databases

As mentioned, a SQL database is a collection of one or more table (DBF) and related files. Chapter 2 describes a database as a collection of data used to model a real-world enterprise, and discusses the relationships and rules between tables in a schema. It is up to the FoxPro programmer to define and enforce integrity rules between DBF files that make up a database.

Indexes

SQL gives you freedom from indexes. You can formulate SQL queries with `ORDER BY` clauses and expect to see the results in whatever order you specify without describing an index file. However, this magic means that SQL has to create temporary indexes "on the fly" to satisfy your request. If you plan to use the same ordering more than a few times, explicitly creating an index can improve the performance of your queries.

When SQL analyzes a query, it uses an optimization procedure to determine the best way to join multiple tables. Sometimes SQL decides that it's faster not to use indexes— if an index tag is not available—than to create an on-the-fly index. In this case, your query might run slower. But if the appropriate index exists, SQL uses it.

When SQL needs an index, it searches through the list of open indexes. However, if SQL opens tables on its own, the only available indexes are structural index tags. Therefore, if you are creating indexes for use with SQL, it is best to create structural index tags.

Simple Queries

Because of the nature of SQL, it makes sense that the most powerful SQL command is the one that selects data to satisfy a query—the `SELECT` command.

In its simplest form, the `SELECT` command behaves like the FoxPro `LIST` command. Here is an example:

```
SELECT <column list>   FROM <table name>   WHERE <expL>
```

This example merely suggests the full power of the `SELECT` command. It is equivalent to the following Visual FoxPro commands:

```
USE <table name> IN 0
BROWSE FOR <expL> FIELDS <column list>
USE
```

The asterisk is a convenient shorthand notation that means all columns. The following example is the same as the preceding FoxPro commands without the `FIELDS` clause:

```
SELECT *   FROM <table name>   WHERE <expL>
```

Joins and Subqueries

One of the most powerful aspects of SQL is its capability to nest `SELECT` clauses—that is, to perform subqueries in support of main queries. In this case, the subquery is performed first and the main query uses the result table. You can also combine, or join, result tables. The `UNION` clause specifies that the result of one selection is joined with the result of another selection.

Nested `SELECT` clauses occur most frequently with comparison operators such as `ANY`, `EXISTS`, and `IN`. Here is an example:

```
* Example 2
SELECT *                           ;
   FROM Employee                    ;
   WHERE EXISTS (SELECT Name FROM HonorLst ;
   WHERE Employee.LName = Name)
```

This example selects full employee records for those employees whose names appear in a separate table, which is called `HonorLst`.

SELECT clauses can be nested quite deeply. More than two or three levels of nesting, however, become difficult to read and slower to execute.

The SQL *SELECT* Command

So far, I've introduced several aspects of the SQL SELECT command. In this section, you'll learn about the semantic elements of the SQL SELECT command supported by Visual FoxPro. Here is an example:

```
SELECT [ALL ¦ DISTINCT]
  [<alias>.]<select_item> [AS <column_name>]
  [, [<alias>.]<select_item> [AS <column_name>] ...]
  ¦ *
  FROM <table> [<local_alias>]
  [, <table> [<local_alias>] ...]
  [[INTO <destination>]
  ¦ [TO FILE <file> [ADDITIVE]
  ¦ TO PRINTER [PROMPT]
  ¦ TO SCREEN]
  [PREFERENCE <expC>]
  [NOCONSOLE] [PLAIN]  [NOWAIT]
  [WHERE <join_condition> [AND <join_condition> ...]
  [AND ¦ OR <filter_condition>
  [AND ¦ OR <filter_condition> ...]]]
  [GROUP BY <groupcolumn>  [, <groupcolumn> ...]]
  [HAVING <filter_condition>]
  [UNION [ALL] <SELECT command>]
  [ORDER BY <order_item>  [ASC ¦ DESC]
  [, <order_item> [ASC ¦ DESC]...]]
```

Don't be intimidated by the complexity of the SQL SELECT command syntax supported by FoxPro. Many of the elements have corresponding counterparts in the Xbase language. Because of that, you should not have much trouble learning the *vocabulary* or the syntax.

The real difficulty in learning to use the SQL SELECT command is learning the rules. The clauses are not as independent as they are in the Xbase language. For example, if you specify a list of tables for a join with the FROM clause, you need to add other clauses to specify how to relate the various tables. Also, if you refer to fields with the GROUP BY clause, you must include the fields in the selected field list. Don't be discouraged, however, because you can use the Query Designer to guide you through the formulation of an SQL SELECT query. The Query Designer is discussed in the section "The Visual FoxPro Query Designer."

Now I'll introduce the elements of the SQL SELECT statement. Table 18.1 provides a brief description of each SQL SELECT clause and keyword.

Table 18.1. A description of the clauses and keywords for the SQL SELECT statement.

Clause or Keyword	*Description*	
All ¦	Includes duplicate rows or records. This is the default.	
DISTINCT	Does not include duplicate rows or records.	
[<*alias*>.]<*select_item*> [AS<*column_name*>],…	Designates output columns. Can be a list of field names or expressions. The AS clause defines column header.	
¦ *	Output columns consist of all fields in source tables specified in a FROM clause.	
FROM <*table*> [<*local_alias*>],…	Specifies a list of table from which data is retrieved for query. <*local_alias*> is the alias name used to reference tables in the rest of the query.	
[	Specifies the destination of the query. If omitted, the query is directed to a BROWSE screen.	
	Here are possible destinations:	
	INTO ARRAY <*array*>]¦	Named array
	INTO CURSOR <*cursor-name*>¦	Temporary table
	INTO DBF <*expFN*>	Named table
	INTO TABLE <*expFN*>	Same as INTO DBF
	TO FILE <*expFN*> [ADDITIVE]¦	List to named text file (LIST)
	TO PRINTER [PROMPT]¦	List to printer (LIST)
	TO SCREEN	List to screen (LIST)
	]	
[PREFERENCE <*expC*>]	The name of the preference attributes for the Browse screen to create or to use if a preference exists. See description of the BROWSE command in Chapter 9, "Full-Screen Data Editing."	
[NOCONSOLE]	Suppresses screen output. Ignored if the INTO clause is specified.	
[PLAIN]	Omits column headings on output. Ignored if the INTO clause is specified.	
[NOWAIT]	Displays the Browse screen and continues program execution.	

Clause or Keyword	*Description*
[WHERE <*join_condition*> [AND <*join_condition*>...] [AND¦OR <*filter_condition*> [AND¦OR <*filter_condition*> ...]]]	Specifies join conditions, such as SET RELATION TO, and specifies filters, such as FOR <*condition*>.
[GROUP BY <*groupcolumn*>, [, <*groupcolumn*> ...]]	Lists output columns that are summarized, or lists group records.
[HAVING <*filter_condition*>]	Designates the filter condition used to eliminate groups from output.
[UNION [ALL] <*SELECT command*>]	Specifies another SELECT command with which to combine results. Duplicates are omitted unless ALL is specified.
[ORDER BY <*order_item*> [ASC ¦ DESC],...	Sorts output in ascending or descending order as specified by the lists of columns used as keys.

The following subtopics focus on each element of the SQL SELECT command. Examples illustrate the use of the elements. The following example illustrates how to use the SELECT command to display the contents of the tables used in the examples:

```
SELECT * FROM students TO FILE examples
SELECT * FROM teachers TO FILE examples ADDITIVE
```

Here is the listing of the file EXAMPLE.TXT:

```
NAME                    STUDNO   CLASSNO   GRADE
Jones                   1122     E301        81
Smith                   4231     E301        86
Newton                  4214     M333        91

NAME                    CLASSNO     SALARY
Murphy                  E301      45444.00
Hughes                  P445      34555.00
Albert                  M333      53889.00
```

Output Columns (The <*select_item*> List)

You always begin a SELECT command by specifying the contents of the result table output columns, which consist of a list of fields and expressions using the following syntax:

```
SELECT [ALL ¦ DISTINCT]
   [<alias>.]<select_item> [AS <column_name>]
   [, [<alias>.]<select_item> [AS <column_name>] ...]
   ¦ *
```

The list of `[<alias>.]<select_item>` elements can be a field from one of the tables specified in the FROM clause. It can be an expression. The expression can include a user-defined function (UDF). If you are specifying a field name and the same name exists in more than one of the tables, you must qualify the field name by preceding the name with an alias name (`<alias>.`). In the following example, the field NAME exists in both the STUDENTS.DBF and TEACHERS.DBF files:

```
* Example 3
SELECT s.name, s.classno, t.name ;
   FROM students s, teachers t ;
   WHERE s.classno = t.classno ;
   TO SCREEN
```

In the preceding example, the s and t are the local alias names for STUDENTS.DBF and TEACHERS.DBF. Here is the output of the result table for the previous example:

```
name_a    classno   name_b
Jones     E301      Murphy
Smith     E301      Murphy*
Newton    M333      Albert
```

For each `<select_item>`, you may use the AS `<column_name>` clause to optionally specify an alternate name. An alternate name is especially useful if you specify an expression. This alternate name is used as the name of the result table column. It must be a valid variable name—that is, it cannot contain characters, such as spaces, that cannot be a field name. The alternate name is used as the field name in the event the results are directed to a new table or cursor. Here is an example of the use of the AS clause:

```
*Example 4
SELECT s.name AS Student, s.classno, t.name AS Teacher;
   FROM students s, teachers t ;
   WHERE s.classno = t.classno ;
   TO SCREEN
```

For the preceding example, the AS clause specified that alternate names appear as headings. The WHERE clause was specified to display students and their corresponding classes and teachers. If I had omitted the WHERE clause, the result table would contain a meaningless outer join. Here is the output of the result table for the above example:

```
Student   classno   Teacher
Jones     E301      Murphy
Smith     E301      Murphy
Newton    M333      Albert
```

If TALK is SET ON and TO SCREEN is specified, the output from the SELECT command is directed either to the main FoxPro window or a window. If the TO or INTO clauses are not specified, a Browse window appears containing the result table.

All rows in query results are displayed unless you specify the DISTINCT keyword, in which case rows with duplicate values are excluded from the results.

If you specify an asterisk (*), all fields from all included tables are sent to the result table. An example is provided earlier in this section.

The SQL SELECT command supports aggregate functions as supported by the FoxPro CALCULATE command. You can specify aggregate functions with the *<select_item>* argument. SQL refers to these functions as *field functions.* The field functions are described in Table 18.2. Incidentally, you cannot nest any of the field functions in a single SELECT command. Here is an example:

```
* Example 5
SELECT AVG(Grade), MIN(grade), MAX(grade) FROM students
```

In the preceding example, all the records in the STUDENTS.DBF table are processed, and the average, minimum, and maximum grades are computed.

Table 18.2. The field functions for the SQL SELECT command.

Field Function	*Description*
AVG(*<select_item>*)	Averages a column of numeric data.
COUNT(*<select_item>*)	Counts the number of *<select_item>* expressions in a column. COUNT(*) counts the number of rows in the query output.
MIN(*<select_item>*)	Determines the smallest value of *<select_item>* in a column.
MAX(*<select_item>*)	Determines the largest value of *<select_item>* in a column.
SUM(*<select_item>*)	Totals a column of numeric data.

You can use almost any FoxPro function, within reason, in a *<select_item>* expression, even a UDF. There are definite benefits in using UDFs, but there are some restrictions. In general, the following is a list of restrictions on the use of UDFs in the *<select_item>* expression:

- A UDF can have a negative impact on the speed of a SELECT command query. If you pose a query that involves the processing of a large number of records, you may find that the use of a UDF so cripples the processing speed of your query that it isn't worth the effort. You might find that a better approach is to use a function written in C or assembly language and incorporated in an API library.
- There is no way for you to know how FoxPro will perform the optimization processing. The method FoxPro uses may vary depending on the number of records and their order in the source tables. As a result, you can make no assumptions about how FoxPro interprets your query. You may not know which work areas are used, the names of current fields being processed, or even the current table. All of the environmental issues depend on precisely where in the optimization process the UDF is invoked. As a result, your UDF cannot depend on the environment.

- Within the UDF, you should never change any of the FoxPro I/O or table environment parameters. If you do, the results can be quite unpredictable.
- Your UDF should only use values passed in the argument list when SELECT calls your UDF. Other values might not be active when your UDF is called.
- As you experiment with the SELECT command, you might discover that your UDF works correctly, even though you violate one or more of the restrictions imposed for UDFs in the SELECT command. Do not use it! There is no guarantee that it will work for all circumstances or will continue to work properly in later revisions of FoxPro. The query optimizer is in a constant state of development and improvement. Who knows what advanced technology will become available in the future.

Source Tables (The *FROM* Clause)

The next clause you specify is the FROM clause. This clause specifies the tables (DBF files) from which data is retrieved for the query. If any tables you specify in the SQL list are open, the SELECT command can find them. If they aren't open and aren't in the current directory or FoxPro path, you must specify the fully qualified filename, including the drive and directory.

You can also supply a local alias name to the right of the filename. This name is useful for referring to the table throughout the SELECT command. The local alias name is only visible within the SELECT command and must be used for referencing the table within the command. It is normal to use a one- to three-character local alias name so you can conveniently refer to the table in a complex SELECT command. Here is the syntax for the FROM clause:

```
FROM <table> [<local_alias>]
  [, <table> [<local_alias>] ...]
```

You must specify all tables (<*table*>) used in the query. If you need to reference the table within a SELECT statement, you must specify the <*local_alias*>. Here is an example:

```
SELECT z.animal ;
  FROM zoo z
```

The previous example displays all animals in the ZOO.DBF table (one field from one table) using the local alias name. The result table displays in a Browse window.

Query Destination (The *INTO* and *TO* Clauses)

The INTO and TO clauses specify a destination for the results of the query. Here is the syntax:

```
[[INTO <destination>]
   ¦ [TO FILE <file> [ADDITIVE]
   ¦ TO PRINTER [PROMPT]
   ¦ TO SCREEN]
```

If you specify the INTO clause, no output is produced and the TO clause is ignored. That is why they are shown as mutually exclusive in the syntax. The query results display in a Browse window if you do not specify the INTO clause. You can specify the TO clause to direct query results to a file, printer, or to the FoxPro or currently active window.

The possible destinations specified with the INTO *<destination>* clause are presented in Table 18.3.

Table 18.3. A description of INTO clause destinations.

INTO Clause	*Description*
INTO ARRAY *<array>*	You can direct query results into an array. If the array exists and is too small to hold the results, the array dimensions are expanded. If the array does not exist, it is created. If the number of records selected by the query is zero, the array is not created.
INTO CURSOR *<cursor>*	You can direct the results of a query into a temporary table, called a *cursor*. If you specify a *<cursor>* that is the name of an open table, FoxPro closes that table and creates a cursor. If the file already exists, it is overwritten. If SET SAFETY is ON, you get a warning. After the SELECT command executes, the temporary cursor remains open, but it is read-only. A cursor file is deleted when it is closed. Cursors may reside on the \SORTWORK drive. Cursors are discussed in more detail in the section "Cursors."
INTO DBF *<table>* ¦ INTO TABLE *<table>*	You can direct the results of a query to a table (*<table>*). If you specify a *<table>* that is the name of an open table, FoxPro closes that table and creates a new table. If the file already exists, it is overwritten. If SET SAFETY is ON, you get a warning. After the SELECT command executes, the temporary cursor remains open. If you don't specify an extension, the table is given a .DBF extension. After the SELECT command completes its execution, the table remains open. The DBF and TABLE keywords are interchangeable.

You can direct the output from query results to an ASCII text file (*<file>*), the printer, or to the main FoxPro window or currently active window by specifying the TO clause. Of course, if the INTO clause is specified, there is no output. If you direct output to an ASCII text file, you can specify the ADDITIVE keyword to append output to existing contents of the text file (<*file*>). If you don't include a TO clause or an INTO clause, query results appear in a Browse window.

In Visual FoxPro, you can specify the optional PROMPT keyword, and before the results are printed, the Printer dialog box appears. From this dialog box you can modify the printer settings. You can specify the number of copies and page numbers to print, and even direct print output to a file. The Windows Printer Setup dialog box can also be opened to adjust additional printer settings.

As indicated, if you specify the AS clause, the result table column name is determined by the AS clause argument. If you do not specify the AS clause, the result table column name is determined by the contents of the <*select_item*> field. If the column contains a table field name, the column name is the same as the field name. If the result table contains more than one field with the same name, an underscore character and a single letter are appended to each name. For a <*select_item*> field with a 10-character name, the name will be truncated to add the underscore and letter. For example, assume both STUDENTS.DBF and TEACHERS.DBF contain NAME fields. You can execute a SELECT command to display the NAME field in both files. Here is an example:

```
* Example 6
SELECT s.name, s.classno, t.name ;
   FROM students s, teachers t ;
   WHERE s.classno = t.classno ;
   TO SCREEN
```

As illustrated in the following output, _A and _B are appended to the NAME fields:

```
Name_a    classno   name_b
Jones     E301      Murphy
Smith     E301      Murphy
Newton    M333      Albert
```

The output column is named EXP when the <*select_item*> argument is an expression. If you specify more than one expression, the output columns are named EXP_1, EXP_2, EXP_3, and so on.

If you specify that the <*select_item*> clause contain a field function such as COUNT(), the output column is named CNT_A. If you specify a field function that has an argument, such as AVG(GRADE), the column output name becomes AVG_GRADE.

In this example, fields from two tables are stored in a third table:

```
SELECT z.name, z.age, a.type ;
   FROM zoo z, animals a ;
   WHERE z.animal_id = a.animal_id ;
   INTO TABLE d:\Zoo\zoo.dbf
```

The *PREFERENCE* Clause

The PREFERENCE clause is used to save the attributes and options of a Browse window for later use. The PREFERENCE state is saved in the resource file. <*expC*> is a name associated with a

PREFERENCE state. When the name is first specified with the BROWSE or SELECT command, it is saved in the resource file (FOXUSER.DBF). From then on, every time the PREFERENCE clause with the same name is specified with BROWSE or SELECT, the Browse window is restored to the saved PREFERENCE state. If you press either Esc or Ctrl+Q to exit the Browse window, the PREFERENCE state is not saved.

The *NOCONSOLE* Keyword

If you specify the NOCONSOLE keyword, the query results aren't displayed in the main FoxPro window or active window. The NOCONSOLE keyword is ignored if the INTO clause is specified.

The *PLAIN* Keyword

You can suppress the display of column headings in query output by specifying the PLAIN keyword.

The *NOWAIT* Keyword

When query results are directed to a Browse window in a program, and you specify the NOWAIT keyword, program execution continues after the Browse window is opened.

When you specify the TO SCREEN clause, output is directed to the main FoxPro window or currently active window. Output continues until the window fills with query results. Then output pauses. When you press any key, the next screen full of query results appears, and so forth. If you specify the NOWAIT keyword, output scrolls off the main FoxPro window without pausing and waiting for a key press.

The *WHERE* Clause

The WHERE clause has a dual purpose. You can use the clause to restrict the records that are included in the query results. Also, you can use the WHERE clause to join files. Here is the syntax of this clause:

```
[WHERE <join_condition> [AND <join_condition>...]
  [AND ¦ OR <filter_condition>
  [AND ¦ OR <filter_condition>...]]]
```

The <*join_condition*> expression specifies fields that link the tables in the FROM clause.

NOTE

With more than one table in a query, you should specify a join condition for every table after the first.

If you are retrieving data from a single table, you can specify a filter expression (<*filter_condition*>) to restrict which records are included in the result table. Here is an example:

```
* Example 7
SELECT * FROM INVOICE WHERE Inv_Date > {10/04/93}
```

If you specify two or more tables in a query and you do not specify a join condition, every record in the first table is joined with every record in the second table as long as the filter conditions are met. This is called an *outer join* and can produce sizable query results.

You should be careful when using the functions shown in Table 18.4, because they allow an optional alias or work area in join conditions. You should not use these functions at all for multiple table queries; to do so can yield unexpected results. SELECT does not use the work areas you specify. It performs an internal equivalent of the USE...AGAIN command. If you do single-table queries that use these functions without an optional <*expWA*> argument, correct results will be generated.

Table 18.4. A list of functions with <*expWA*> arguments.

ALIAS([<*expWA*>])	LOOKUP(<*field1*>, <*exp*>,<*field2*> [,<*expC*>])
BOF([<*expWA*>])	LUPDATE([<*expWA*>])
CDX(<*expN*> [,<*expWA*>])	MDX(<*expN*> [,<*expWA*>])
DBF([<*expWA*>])	NDX(<*expN*> [,<*expWA*>])
DELETED([<*expWA*>])	ORDER([<*expWA*> [,<*expN*>]])
EOF([<*expWA*>])	RECCOUNT([<*expWA*>])
FCOUNT([<*expWA*>])	RECNO([<*expWA*>])
FIELD(<*expN*>[,<*expWA*>])	RECSIZE([<*expWA*>])
FILTER([<*expWA*>])	RELATION(<*expN*>[,<*expWA*>])
FOUND(<*expWA*>)	SEEK(<*exp*> [,<*expWA*>])
FOUND([<*expWA*>])	TAG([<*expC*>,] <*expN*> [,<*expWA*>])
FSIZE(<*expC*>[,<*expWA*>])	TARGET(<*expN*>[,<*expWA*>])
HEADER([<*expWA*>])	USED([<*expWA*>])
KEY([<expC>.]<expN1>[,<expWA>])	

You may run into difficulties if you join a table with empty fields because FoxPro matches empty fields. Use the EMPTY() function to circumvent this problem.

As in the FoxPro `SET RELATION` command, you can specify multiple joins with the `WHERE` clause. You use the logical `AND` operator to separate multiple join conditions. Here is an example that displays only records having an invoice date before 12/15/93:

```
* Example 8
SELECT c.cust_id, c.company, i.porder, i.inv_date ;
   FROM customer c, invoice i ;
   WHERE (c.cust_id = i.cust_id) AND (i.inv_date < {11/15/93})
```

The *<join_condition>* expression can contain field functions and have the following form:

```
<field1> <comparison> <field2>
```

The *<field1>* argument is a field from one table, and *<field2>* is a field from another table. The *<comparison>* operator is one of the operators defined in Table 18.5.

Table 18.5. The `<comparison>` operators used in a `<join_condition>` expression.

<comparison> Operators	*Description*
=	Equal to
<>, !=, #	Not equal to
==	Exactly equal to (Character type only)
>	Greater than
>=	Greater than or equal to
<	Less than
<=	Less than or equal to

The equal operator (=) behaves differently, depending on the setting of the `SET ANSI` command, when it is used to compare character strings. See Chapter 10, "Environment," for a description of the `SET ANSI` command.

You use the *<filter_condition>* expression to specify the criteria records must meet to be included in the query results. You can connect filter conditions with either the `AND` or the `OR` logical operator. Here is an example that displays only records having an invoice date on 11/14/93 or 12/03/93:

```
* Example 9
SELECT c.cust_id, company , i.porder     ;
   FROM customer c , invoice i       ;
   WHERE (c.cust_id = i.cust_id)   AND ;
   (i.inv_date = {11/14/93}  OR ;
   i.inv_date = {12/03/93})
```

In addition, you can use the `NOT` operator to reverse the outcome of a logical expression or use the `EMPTY()` function to check for an empty field. You can compose a *<filter_condition>* expression using any one of the forms described in the following subsections:

<field1> <comparison> <field2>

You can specify selected records by comparing two fields. If the fields are in different `FROM` tables, this form performs a simple join. Here is an example:

```
SELECT FROM students s, teachers s WHERE s.classNo = t.classNo
```

In the following example, four fields from two tables display. The `WHERE` clause establishes the join of the two tables based on the `CUST_ID` field. Local aliases are used. Here is the example:

```
* Example 10
SELECT c.company, c.address1, i.inv_date, i.cost*i.quantity ;
     FROM customer c, invoice i ;
     WHERE c.cust_id = i.cust_id  TO SCREEN
```

Unique data in the specified fields displays in the following example:

```
* Example 11
SELECT DISTINCT a.company, a.cust_id, i.Inv_date, i.cost ;
     FROM customer a, invoice i ;
     WHERE a.cust_id = i.cust_id
```

<field> <comparison> <expression>

You can specify selected records for a query by comparing a field in the `FROM` table with an expression. The expression can contain a UDF, but you should conform to the preceding restrictions:

```
SELECT * FROM students s WHERE s.grade >= 80
```

<field> <comparison> <expression> <field> <comparison> ALL (<subquery>)

If you specify an `ALL` keyword after the *<comparison>* operator in the *<filter_condition>*, the *<field>* must satisfy the comparison condition for all values generated by the subquery before its record is included in the query results. The following example displays any salesman from EMPLOYEE.DBF who earns more than any vice president:

```
* Example 12
SELECT * FROM Employee e ;
     WHERE e.position = 'Salesman' AND ;
     e.salary > ALL (SELECT f.salary FROM Employee f ;
     WHERE f.position = 'VP')
```

A subquery is a `SELECT` command within another `SELECT` command. A subquery must be enclosed in parentheses. You can have multiple subqueries at the same nesting level in the `WHERE` clause. Subqueries can contain multiple join conditions.

<field> <comparison> ANY | SOME (<subquery>)

If you specify an ANY or SOME keyword after the `<comparison>` operator in the `<filter_condition>`, the `<field>` must meet the comparison condition for at least one of the values generated by the subquery to be included in the query results. The following example displays information for any salesman from EMPLOYEE.DBF who earns more than any company vice president:

```
* Example 13
SELECT * FROM Employee e ;
    WHERE e.position = 'Salesman' AND ;
    e.salary > ANY (SELECT f.salary FROM Employee f ;
    WHERE f.position = 'VP')
```

<field> [NOT] BETWEEN <start_range> AND <end_range>

This form of the `<filter_condition>` selects records for inclusion in the query results if `<field>` is within a range of values. The following example displays the names of all employees who are older than 79 and younger than 91:

```
* Example 14
SELECT fname,lname FROM employee WHERE age BETWEEN 80 AND 90
```

[NOT] EXISTS (<subquery>)

This form selects a record for inclusion in the query results if at least one record meets the criteria in the subquery. When you specify the `EXISTS` keyword, the filter condition evaluates to true unless the subquery evaluates to the empty set. The following example displays all companies from the CUSTOMER.DBF table with a `CUST_ID` code that matches a `cust_id` code in the `INVOICE` table:

```
* Example 15
SELECT company FROM customer a WHERE
    EXISTS (SELECT * FROM invoice b  WHERE a.cust_id = b.cust_id)
```

<field> [NOT] IN <value_set>

If you specify the `IN <value_set>` clause, the value of `<field>` must be included in the specified set of values before its record is included in the query results. The following example displays the names of all middle managers, salesmen, and vice presidents from EMPLOYEE.DBF:

```
* Example 16
SELECT fname,lname FROM employee ;
    WHERE position IN ("MM","Salesman","VP")
```

<field> [NOT] IN (<subquery>)

If you specify this form, `<field>` must be part of the set of values returned by the subquery before its record is included in the query results.

```
SELECT *  FROM grocery g  WHERE g.cust_id IN ;
     (SELECT g.cust_id  FROM grocery g  WHERE g.item='Cabbage')
     WHERE c.state NOT
```

<field> [NOT] LIKE <expC>

The `LIKE` filter condition is similar to the FoxPro `LIKE()` function. It searches for each *`<field>`* that matches the specified *`<expC>`*. You can use the wildcard characters `%` (percent) and _ (underscore) as part of *`<expC>`*. The underscore character represents a single unknown character in the string and the `%` character represents a sequence of unknown characters in the string. The _ and `%` characters correspond to the `LIKE()` function wildcard characters `?` and `*`. The following example displays all records from the ZOO.DBF table that have an animal name that begins with a capital letter C and an unknown length:

```
SELECT * FROM ZOO z WHERE z.animal LIKE 'C%'
```

The following example displays all records from the CENSUS.DBF table that have a state that begins with a capital letter N and is followed by one unknown character:

```
SELECT * FROM census c WHERE c.state LIKE 'N_'
```

The `UPPER()`, `VAL()`, `DTOC()`, `PADR()`, `PADL()` and `PADC()` functions can be used in join conditions of the `WHERE` clause.

The *GROUP BY* Clause

You can specify the `GROUP BY` clause to group rows in a query based on values of one or more columns. Here is the syntax of this clause:

```
[GROUP BY <groupcolumn>  [, <groupcolumn>...]]
```

The *`<groupcolumn>`* element can be one of the following:

- A table field
- A SQL field function with table fields as arguments
- A table field that corresponds to a SQL field function

In the following example, the result table contains rows composed of monthly summaries for each customer. The columns are customer, invoice date, quantity, and cost. Here is an example:

```
* Example 17
SELECT customer, CMONTH(inv_date),      ;
        SUM(quantity) , SUM(cost)    ;
        FROM Invoice                 ;
        GROUP BY customer, 2  ;
        ORDER BY customer, inv_date
```

The INVOICE.DBF table presented in Listing 18.1 is processed by the previous `SELECT` statement, and the output consisting of the query result table is shown in Listing 18.2. Notice that the query result table contains a row for each customer and month.

Listing 18.1. The table INVOICE.DBF used in the `GROUP BY` clause example.

CUSTOMER	INV_DATE	QUANTITY	COST
Jones	12/03/92	31	463.45
Smith	12/24/92	51	762.45
Jones	11/22/92	4	59.80
Smith	11/13/92	67	1001.65
Jones	11/02/92	8	119.60
Jones	12/02/92	44	657.80
Smith	12/27/92	23	343.85
Jones	11/14/92	22	328.90
Smith	11/19/92	11	164.45
Jones	11/05/92	88	1315.60

Listing 18.2. The query result table for the `GROUP BY` clause example.

CUSTOMER	EXP_2	SUM_QUANTI	SUM_COST
Jones	November	122	1823.90
Jones	December	75	1121.25
Smith	November	78	1166.10
Smith	December	74	1106.30

Because you cannot have an expression in the `GROUP BY` clause, you need to use the column number to refer to the second query results column in the `GROUP BY` clause. An alternative is to specify the `AS` clause to define a column name for an expression that can be referenced in the `GROUP BY` clause. Here is an example:

```
* Example 18
SELECT customer, CMONTH(INV_DATE) AS month ,     ;
    SUM(quantity) AS Total_qty, SUM(cost) AS Total_cost  ;
    FROM Invoice                    ;
    GROUP BY customer, month         ;
    ORDER BY customer, INV_DATE ;
    TO SCREEN
```

Here are the columns for the result table:

```
CUSTOMER    MONTH          TOTAL_QTY          TOTAL_COST
```

The *HAVING* Clause

You can use the `HAVING` clause to restrict the records that are included in the query results. It is specifically intended for selecting records just before they are included in the result table. You normally specify `[HAVING <filter_condition>]` to determine whether groups are included in the query results. Records are included as long as they meet the conditions for the `<filter_condition>` expression. The `<filter_condition>` expression cannot contain a subquery.

You use the HAVING <*filter_condition*> clause with the GROUP BY clause to specify the criteria that groups must meet to be included in the query results. You can include as many filter conditions with the HAVING clause as you want. You connect them with the AND or OR logical operators. In addition, you can use the NOT logical operator to reverse the outcome of a logical expression.

If you don't specify a GROUP BY clause, the HAVING clause behaves like the WHERE clause. You can use local aliases and field functions in the HAVING clause. For performance reasons, however, you should use a WHERE clause instead of a HAVING clause unless the filter condition contains a field function.

The *UNION* Clause

You use the UNION clause to merge results of one SELECT command with the results of another select command. Here is the syntax of this clause:

```
[UNION [ALL] <SELECT command>]
```

Unless you specify the ALL keyword, duplicate rows in the merged result table are eliminated. If you specify the ALL keyword, duplicate rows are included in the combined results. You can use parentheses to combine multiple UNION clauses.

As with anything in life, there are rules that govern the use of the UNION clause. Here are the rules:

- You can't use the UNION clause to combine subqueries.
- Two SELECT commands joined by a UNION clause must output the same number of columns.
- The data type and width of all the columns of the result table for the two SELECT commands must correspond.
- You can only specify an ORDER BY clause for the final <*SELECT command*>. Furthermore, the ORDER BY clause must refer to output columns by number. The ORDER BY clause affects the order of the entire query result table.

Suppose that you want to generate a phone book containing the names of your friends, customers, and employees. Assume that this information is included in three tables: FRIENDS.DBF, CUST.DBF, and EMPLOYEE.DBF. Suppose also that you want the phone book to be sorted by the first name and then the last name. You can generate this list with the following single (although complicated) SELECT command:

```
* Example 19
SELECT e.fname AS First_Name , e.lname AS Last_Name, ;
       e.phone AS Phone  FROM Employee e;
       ORDER BY 1,2  TO PRINTER;
       UNION  (SELECT f.fname , f.lname, phone FROM Friends f   ;
       UNION SELECT  c.fname, c.lname, c.phone ;
       FROM cust c )
```

A phone list derived from all three files is printed. If you have a friend who is a customer, or an employee who is a friend, their names won't appear multiple times in the phone list because duplicate instances of a row aren't included in the result table when the ALL keyword is not specified.

The first SELECT command selects all the records from the EMPLOYEE.DBF file. The first UNION clause SELECT command selects all records from the FRIENDS.DBF table and includes a UNION clause that selects records from the CUST.DBF table. Records from all three files are combined and sorted. The ORDER BY clause specifies the order of the result table. Notice in the preceding example that numeric values corresponding to column numbers are specified; numeric values must be used.

The *ORDER BY* Clause

The ORDER BY clause specifies the sorting order of the data in the result table. Here is the syntax of the ORDER BY clause:

```
[ORDER BY <order_item>  [ASC ¦ DESC]
       [, <order_item> [ASC ¦ DESC]...]]
```

The ORDER BY clause specifies a list of columns in the result table to be sorted. The *<order_item>* argument specifies the result table column. The most significant sorting order is the *<order_item>* argument specified first in the list. The least significant sorting order is the *<order_item>* argument specified last in the list. Each *<order_item>* can be the name of a field in the FROM table that is also a *<select_item>* in the outermost SELECT command. In other words, it can't refer to a *<select_item>* in a subquery. You can also specify a numeric expression to refer to columns in the result table. To specify the third column, specify 3.

If you want a column to be sorted in descending order, specify the DESC keyword following the *<order_item>* element. The ASC keyword designates ascending order. It is the default sorting order and doesn't need to be specified.

Cursors

A database language, such as SQL, that performs relational operations on tables and produces result tables is conceptually pure but not practical for application programming. Result tables can be as large as the square of the operand tables, and conventional functions and operators aren't prepared to deal with sets of data. So when SQL is embedded in a working language, such as PL /I or COBOL, a device is necessary to allow the host language to read one record at a time from a result table. This mechanism is called a *cursor.*

Using Cursors

Selections and projections (see Chapter 2 for more explanation) produce a result table with rows and columns. FoxPro needs a way to step through a table one record at a time.

A record pointer, called a *cursor*, is associated with a result table. It is created by the `SELECT` command `CURSOR` clause or by the `CREATE CURSOR` command. By default, cursors support read-only access to result tables, but you can also use them to update or delete records.

You can use any FoxPro table editing command to edit a cursor created with the `CREATE CURSOR` command. Cursors created with SQL `SELECT` commands, however, are read-only—you cannot edit them.

The following rules apply to cursors created with the SQL `SELECT` command. They do not apply to cursors created with the `CREATE CURSOR` command.

- Although cursors behave like tables, they are *not* tables. They do not even reside in a disk file. Some cursors don't even have an associated temporary file. If a cursor is stored in a temporary file, it resides on the \SORTWORK drive. (The CONFIG.FPW file `SORTWORK=` command is used to define the drive on which temporary sort files reside. The default is the startup drive.)
- Cursors are sometimes entirely memory resident. This is especially true for queries. Sometimes cursors are merely filtered representations of fields in the table used to create the cursor. (The representations result from the use of the Rushmore technology and the `USE AGAIN` mechanism.)
- Cursors generated by the SQL `SELECT` command are always read-only.
- From within the FoxPro language, you can access a cursor using its alias. After you select a cursor, you can perform all read-only operations.
- Cursors disappear forever once they are closed.
- You cannot use a cursor because it no longer exists after it is closed.
- When `SELECT` creates a cursor, its name becomes the alias name. It is placed in use (even if it is virtual) in an unused work area.
- You can never be sure which work area is home for a cursor. The query optimizer determines which work area is used based on the decisions made during the optimization process.
- In most cases, cursors can be created more quickly than tables.
- You can circumvent the inconvenience, as well as the advantages, of cursors by directing query results into a table (`INTO TABLE` or `INTO DBF` clauses) instead of directing query results into a cursor (`INTO CURSOR` clause). Any tables created by the `SELECT` command are standard FoxPro tables.

- Normally, the values in a cursor are dependent on the values in the source tables. If you change values in the source tables, the values in the cursor may change. If this causes you problems, you can always direct the query results to either a table (INTO DBF or INTO TABLE clauses) or an array (INTO ARRAY clause). An alternative is to not change values in the source tables.
- You can prevent other users from modifying the original tables by either locking the tables used to create the cursor, or by opening the source tables in exclusive mode.

Creating a Table

Chapter 11, "DBF Files and Databases," shows how to use the COPY STRUCTURED EXTENDED, REPLACE, and CREATE FROM commands to create a database table programmatically. As you know, it takes several commands and an existing database table. With the SQL CREATE TABLE command, you can create a database table out of thin air. Furthermore, you use a single command.

A SQL database consists of data tables (DBF files), views based on one or more data tables, and indexes. Tables are simply DBF data files that form part of a SQL database. You can use the traditional Xbase method of creating a DBF file with the Table Designer, or you can use the SQL CREATE TABLE command. Here is the syntax of the SQL CREATE command:

```
CREATE TABLE ¦ DBF <expFN> 1 [NAME  <expTable1> ] [FREE]
        (<field1>  <FieldType> [(<expN1>  [, <expN2> ])
               [NULL ¦ NOT NULL]
               [CHECK <expL1>  [ERROR <expC1> ]]
               [DEFAULT <exp1> ]
               [PRIMARY KEY ¦ UNIQUE]
               [REFERENCES <expTable2> [TAG <tag name1>]
               [NOCPTRANS]]
        [, <field2> ...]])
               [, PRIMARY KEY <exp2> TAG <tag name2>
               ¦, UNIQUE <exp3>  TAG  <tag name3>]
               [, FOREIGN KEY <exp4>  TAG <tag name4>
                    REFERENCES <expTable3>  [TAG <tag name5>]]
               [, CHECK <expL2>  [ERROR <expC2> ]]
        ¦ FROM ARRAY ArrayName
```

The syntax of the CREATE TABLE command is discussed in Chapter 11. In a single CREATE TABLE command you can specify the entire structure of the named table (DBF file). You supply a list of attributes for each field. The attributes for a field consist of its name, data type, precision, and scale. These attributes can be part of the command or can be from an array.

The created table is opened in exclusive mode regardless of the setting of the SET EXCLUSIVE command.

The *TABLE* <expFN> Clause

The TABLE clause, which includes the filename expression, *<expFN>*, specifies the name of the table (DBF file) to create. If you do not specify an extension, .DBF is assumed. A drive and directory can be specified with the TABLE clause. The TABLE and DBF keywords are interchangeable. Either can be specified.

The database table is opened in an unused work area. If a file is in use in the current work area, a new work area is selected. This differs from the FoxPro language CREATE command, which uses the current work area and closes any DBF file already in use in the current work area before it creates the new file.

Specifying Fields

The field specification syntax for the SQL CREATE command is rather cryptic compared to traditional Xbase syntax, but it is more compact. For example, to define two fields, Name and Salary, you specify the following:

```
( Name C(20), Salary N(10,2) )
```

In Xbase terminology, the Name field is a Character (C) data type twenty characters wide. The Salary field is a Numeric (N) data type 10 characters wide with 2 decimal positions. There is a one-to-one correspondence between Xbase and SQL terminology as illustrated here:

Xbase	*SQL*
Name	Name
Data type	Type
Width	Precision
Decimal position	Scale

Consider the following field definition syntax:

```
(<expFld1> <type> [(<precision> [, <scale>] )
[, <expFld2> ... ])
```

The two field name expressions, *<expFld1>* and *<expFld2>*, define the names of fields in the new database table. These names can be literal field names or expressions. All of the following filename expressions are equivalent:

```
"Name"
Name
 (FLD1)   && where FLD1 = "Name"
"Na"+"me"
SUBSTR("name", 1,4)
```

The use of filename and field name expressions doesn't conform strictly to ANSI SQL semantics. This extension, as well as other semantic extensions, results from the blending of FoxPro and SQL.

The <type> argument is a single letter indicating the data type for the field. Type C requires that you specify a field width enclosed in parentheses, (<precision>). For types F and N, you specify a precision (width of field) and scale (number of decimal places) in the form, (<precision>,<scale>). If you omit the <scale> value for N or F types, the <scale> defaults to zero with no decimal places. The <precision> and <scale> arguments are ignored for D, L, M, and P types. The SQL data types and corresponding precision and scale arguments are summarized in Table 18.6.

Table 18.6. SQL data types.

SQL Type	*FoxPro Type*	*Description*	*Length*	*Decimal Position*	*Range*
C(n)		Character	n		n is 1-254
D	D	Date	8		
F(x,y)	F	Float	x+1	y	x is 1-19, y is 0-18
G	G	General	8		
L	L	Logical	1		
M	M	Memo	8		
N(x,y)	N	Numeric	x+1	y	x is 1-20, y is 0-18
P		Picture (SQL only)			

The following example creates a parts list:

```
CREATE TABLE Parts      ;
   (Part_no N(8),       ;
   Recvd D,             ;
   Component L,         ;
   Descript C(30),      ;
   Cost N(9,2),         ;
   PartView P )
```

The *FROM ARRAY* Clause

The FROM ARRAY <array> clause specifies the name of an existing array that contains the name, type, precision, and scale for all fields in the database table to be created. You can use the AFIELDS() function to define the array. The FROM ARRAY clause is used in place of direct specification of the field attributes. Here is an example of how to use the FROM ARRAY clause to create a table. In this example, ONEFILE.DBF is created by ANOTHER.DBF:

```
USE ANOTHER
=AFIELDS(Struct)  && Create array Struct
CREATE TABLE ONEFILE FROM ARRAY Struct
```

NOTE

In Visual FoxPro, a new optional argument was added to the `AFIELDS()` function that lets you specify the work area of the table. The new syntax is `AFIELDS(<array> [,<expWA>] )`.

The *CREATE CURSOR* Command

Unlike the `CREATE TABLE` command, which creates a permanent table, the `CREATE CURSOR` command creates a temporary table. A temporary table exists until it is closed. Then it disappears. Later in this chapter, you will learn that the SQL `SELECT` command creates a cursor, which is a read-only temporary table, that may not even be a file. In other words, you cannot edit a cursor created by the SQL `SELECT` command. On the other hand, a temporary table created with `CREATE CURSOR` can be manipulated like any other table. You can edit, browse, and index a table, and you can add and delete records. A table just disappears when you close it.

The syntax of `CREATE CURSOR` is the same as the `CREATE TABLE` command. Here is the syntax:

```
CREATE CURSOR <expFN>
   (<expFld1> <type> [(<precision> [, <scale>])
   [, <expFld2> ... ]])
   ¦ FROM ARRAY <array>
```

`CREATE CURSOR` selects the lowest available work area and then creates the temporary table. It is open in exclusive mode regardless of the setting of the `SET EXCLUSIVE` command.

You can access the temporary table by selecting its alias name.

Here is an example:

```
CREATE CURSOR supplier ;
      (company  C(25), ;
      compno    C(10), ;
      address   C(30), ;
      city      C(25), ;
      zip       C(5),  ;
      phone     C(13), ;
      Amount    N(8,2),;
      Notes M)
```

The SQL *INSERT INTO* Command

The SQL `INSERT INTO` command adds a new record to the end of an existing table. The new record includes data specified with the `INSERT INTO` command. The data can be entered directly or can be in a specified array or memory variable. Here is the syntax:

```
INSERT INTO <expFN>
      [(<expFld1> [, <expFld2>
      [, ...]])]
      VALUES (<expr1> [, <expr2>
      [, ...]])
```

Although this command is rather cryptic, it is compact. This single command replaces a myriad of FoxPro commands.

The `INTO <expFN>` clause specifies the name of the table to which a record will be added. `<expFN>` is a filename expression. It can be a literal filename or an expression that evaluates to a filename. It can include a drive and directory path.

If the table you specify isn't already open, it is opened in an unused work area in exclusive mode. Then the record is added to the end of the file. The original work area remains selected. The new work area is not selected. If the table you specify is open, the `INSERT INTO` command appends the record to the table. If the table is open in a work area other than the currently selected work area, it isn't selected after the record is appended. The original current work area remains selected.

You can optionally specify a list of fields in the table for which data is assigned in the newly appended record. The field list can be in order. If you do not specify a field list, all of the fields in the table become the field list. The `VALUE` clause contains a list of evaluated expressions (`(<expr1> [,<expr2>[, ...]])`), and the resultant value is stored in the field. You must specify the expressions in the order of the field list or the table structure.

Instead of specifying a `VALUE` clause, you can specify an array using the `FROM ARRAY <array>` clause to supply the values. `<array>` is the name of an existing array containing data for the record to be added. Each element is stored in a table field in the order of the table structure. You can also use the `FROM MEMVAR` clause to specify that you want to assign values to the table fields from memory variables that have the same name as the fields. Data is only assigned to fields that have a corresponding memory variable. Any table fields without a corresponding memory variable are left empty. Here is an example of the use of the `INSERT INTO` command:

```
INSERT INTO Parts ;
   (Part_no,      ;
   Recvd,         ;
   Component,     ;
   Descript,      ;
   Cost,          ;
   VALUES ("Z23-423", 12/12/92, .T., "Green Widget", 53211.23 )

USE FLOWERS
COPY STRUCTURE TO ROSES
SCAN FOR "ROSES"$UPPER( Name )
SCATTER MEMVAR
INSERT INTO ROSES FROM MEMVAR
ENDSCAN
```

The Visual FoxPro Query Designer

One of the powerful features in Visual FoxPro is the relational query-by-example (RQBE) facility, called the Visual FoxPro Query Designer. It is a tool for performing complex interactive query and data organization operations. You can also use the Query Designer to help you learn how to formulate SQL queries. The query-by-example portion of the Query Designer defines the technique it uses to query data. With this technique, you pose a query by filling in example values of desired results in empty selection criteria tables. Visual FoxPro processes your entries and retrieves the information you want. This section describes how to use the Query Designer to retrieve, organize, update, and display information.

Five basic database functions can be performed using the Visual FoxPro Query Designer:

- Selection—A horizontal subset of a FoxPro table is established using a filter to select a group of records.
- Projection—A vertical subset of the fields in a view is selected.
- Join—Two or more database tables are linked to form a result table.
- Sort—The logical or physical order of a table is changed.
- Aggregate operations—Groups of records are summarized.

These five functions can be combined to produce a more complex query.

Using the `CHANGE` or `BROWSE` command normally, you can view data in a table and make changes to the data in any field. Using `CHANGE` or `BROWSE` with the Query Designer alters this slightly because it requires strict adherence to relational view *updateability* rules (rules of the relational model governing the updating of views). In general, it is not always appropriate to update a view. No existing relational DBMS system allows updating of views, because there is no way to determine the nature of the data in the table. The rules for IBM's DB2 DBMS apply to updating views for the Visual FoxPro Query Designer (Chamberlin 1976).

The following views cannot be updated:

- Views with calculated fields. A view might not contain all the fields that make up the calculated field expression. Records cannot be added because no data would be added for the fields not in the view, and the calculated field couldn't be computed. Likewise, the calculated field can't be edited. However, a record can be deleted from this type of view.
- Views with an aggregate operator. Aggregate operators generate records that are a summary of multiple records. Any changes to any of the fields in these summary records don't correspond to an actual record in the original table or files that make up the view.
- Views with more than one table. If a key field is changed in one table, it no longer relates to its counterpart in the other table or to files in the view. Data is lost.

- Views with a sort directive, unless an index is used. If a file is physically reordered, it is sorted to a temporary file, and that file becomes the view. Any changes made to the sorted table aren't reflected in the original file. A view that can't be updated can be viewed in the Browse window, listed in the FoxPro window, reported, or printed. However, no fields can be changed, and no records can be added.

Running the Visual FoxPro Query Designer

There will be times when you want to perform a query too complex to be achieved by viewing the data with the Browse window. You can write a FoxPro program to do your query, or you can use the Query Designer window or the Query Wizard. Wizards are easy to use but are not as versatile. Wizards are discussed in Chapter 24, "Wizards." You can execute a new query by choosing the **F**ile menu **N**ew command and selecting the **Q**uery file type from the New dialog box. Also, you can create a new query from the Project Manager by selecting Queries and clicking on the New button. You are given a choice of using the Query Designer or the Query Wizard to create your query.

Also, you can type the `MODIFY QUERY` or `CREATE QUERY` command into the Command window to execute the Query Designer. Here is the syntax of the two commands:

```
CREATE QUERY [<expFN> ¦ ?] [NOWAIT]
MODIFY QUERY [<expFN> ¦ ?] [NOWAIT] [AS <expN>]
```

If you omit the name of the query file, the Open File dialog box appears, and you choose the name of the existing query file (files with .QPR extensions). If the query file doesn't exist, it is created. If you specify a filename (`<expFN>`) and don't supply a filename extension, .QPR is assumed.

If at least one table is not in use in the current work area, the Open File dialog box appears so that you can choose a table that is referenced in the query.

The optional `AS <expN>` clause specifies the code page of the query. It is used when you want to specify a query with a code page that differs from the current Visual FoxPro code page. Then Visual FoxPro automatically converts the query to the current code page. If you do not specify the `AS` clause, Visual FoxPro performs no code page conversion. Also, you can specify a query's code page from within the Project Container, which keeps track of the query's code page. However, if you use the `MODIFY QUERY` command to open a query outside of the Project Container, you will need to specify the `AS` clause.

It doesn't matter which approach you choose to invoke the Query Designer. When it executes, the Query Designer window displays. Then the Add Table or View window appears on top of the Query Designer window as shown in Figure 18.1. In addition, the **Q**uery menu is added to the FoxPro systems menu bar. The **Q**uery menu is also shown in Figure 18.1.

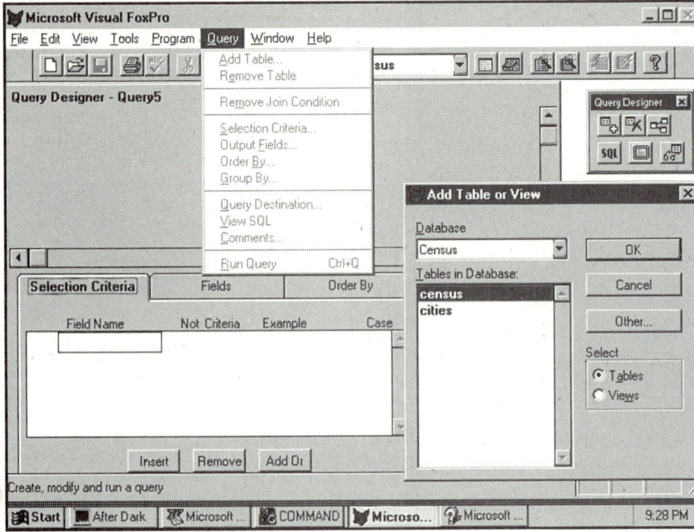

FIGURE 18.1.
The Query Designer window and the Add Table or View window.

You can choose a database to use from the Database combo box. Then you can choose one of the views or tables in the database. As an alternative, you can choose the Other button if you want to use a free table in your query. Remember that a free table is a table that is not associated with a database. You choose a table or view, and the Tables window displays on the top of the Query Designer window, as shown in Figure 18.2.

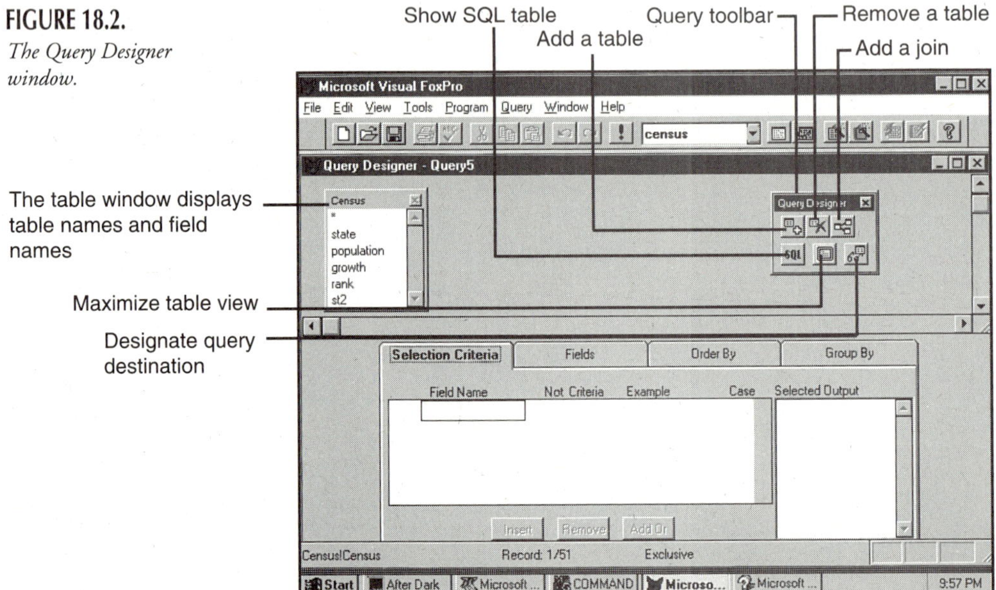

FIGURE 18.2.
The Query Designer window.

The Query Designer window is divided into a top window that displays tables and views that can be used in the query, and a bottom panel that contains four query tabs. Here is a list of the query tabs:

- Selection Criteria—Used to specify record filters
- Fields—Used to select fields that are included in the query results
- Order By—Used to specify the order of the records in the resultant query
- Group By—Used to summarize the results of a query when consolidating a group of associated records into a single result row and performing some calculation based on the group of records

Figure 18.2 shows the name of the table in use, CENSUS.DBF, and the names of the fields in CENSUS.DBF. This table will be used for the first query example.

Your First Query

To generate a query that contains all the fields and records of CENSUS.DBF, click on the Fields tab as shown in Figure 18.3. Then click on the Add All>> button. All of the fields in the Available Fields list box are copied to the Selected Output list box. Also, you can select fields one at a time with the A**d**d>> button. Then you can run the query using one of the following three methods:

- Choose the **Q**uery menu **R**un Query option
- Click on the Run (!) button in the Visual FoxPro standard toolbar
- Press the Ctrl+Q key

Regardless of how you run the query, a Browse window appears containing the query, as shown in Figure 18.3. This is your first query.

Also shown in Figure 18.3 is the QUERY1 (Read Only) window in which the SQL statement for the query displays. You press the Show the SQL button on the Query Designer toolbar or choose the **V**iew SQL option in the **Q**uery pop-up menu to toggle on and off the SQL window display mode. This window contains the SQL statement for the query. The designers of FoxPro must have considered the viewing of the SQL commands to be important—they have provided many ways to activate the SQL command window.

Selecting Fields

Next, you can create a projection by removing two fields from the query output. In the Fields tab, select the `Census.St2` field in the Available Fields list box and press the <**R**emove button. The field is removed. Also remove field `Census.Rank`. Now, execute the query by pressing the standard toolbar Run (!) button again. The resultant query's Browse window displays only the `Census.State`, `Census.Population`, and `Census.Growth` fields, as shown in Figure 18.4.

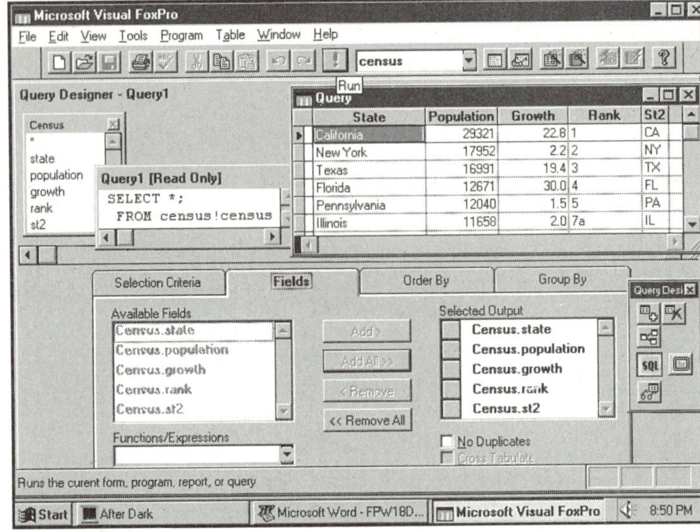

FIGURE 18.3.
Your first query.

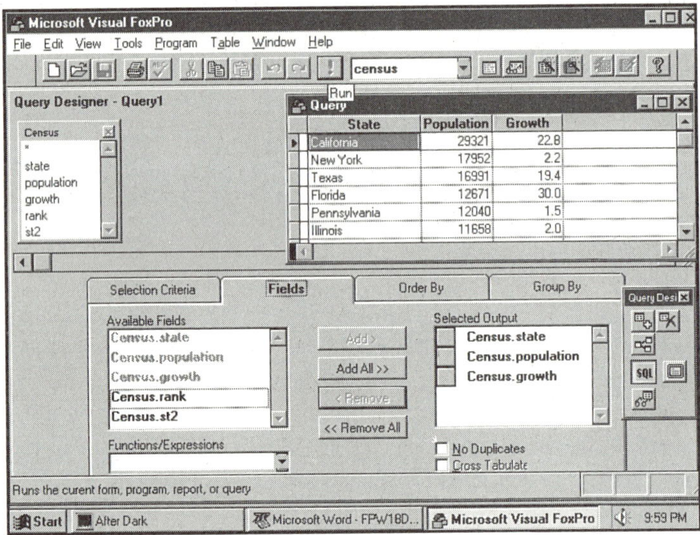

FIGURE 18.4.
The Query Designer and the result table containing `State`, `Population`, *and* `Growth` *fields in the CENSUS.DBF table.*

The SQL window for this example contains the following SQL `SELECT` statement:

```
SELECT Census.state, Census.population, Census.growth;
    FROM census!census
```

NOTE

The exclamation point (!) in the `FROM` clause, which separates the name of the database container file and the table, is the database qualifier operator. It is used to specify the database container file associated with the table being considered. When you specify a table in this manner, the database does not have to be open.

Adding a Filter Condition

In the next example, you will specify a filter condition. The Selection Criteria tab contains a list box with four columns. Select the `Census.State` field from the combo box in the Field Name column. The combo box in the Criteria column, to the right of the NOT push button, contains operators (`Like`, `Exactly Like`, `More Than`, `Less Than`, `Between`, and `In`.) Choose the `Like` operator. Then type the letter C in the Example column. Finally, press the standard toolbar Run (!) button. A Query window appears, as shown in Figure 18.5. Not surprisingly, all records displayed in the Query window begin with the letter C.

TIP

You can drag fields from the table list in the Tables window and drop them into the Field Name column combo box in the Selection Criteria tab.

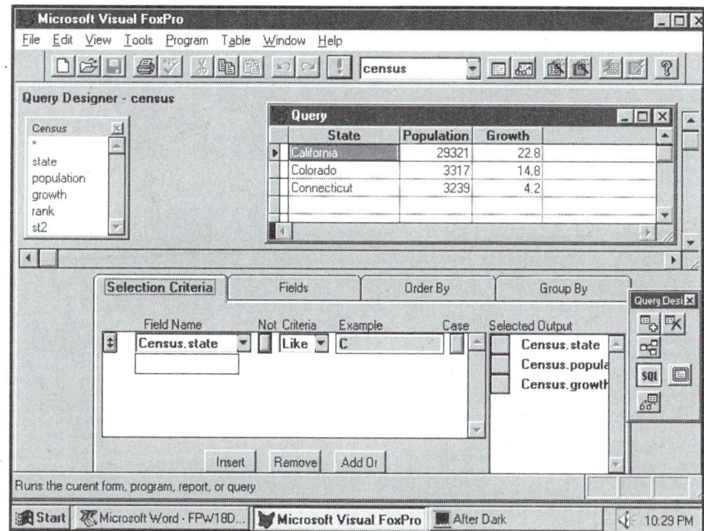

FIGURE 18.5.
A query with a result table containing filtered data.

You can save the query in a file (QPR) and give it a name with the **F**ile menu Save **A**s option. The query shown in Figure 18.5 has been saved and named CENSUS.QPR.

Here is the SQL `SELECT` statement in the SQL window for the example shown in Figure 18.5:

```
SELECT Census.state, Census.population, Census.growth;
   FROM census!census;
   WHERE Census.state = "C"
```

Filtering is the process of selecting a group of records. In relational database theory, this process is called *selecting* a horizontal subset of a table. If you place a constant in the field, it filters records that match the specified value. For example, the expression `Name = "Smith"` filters out those people whose last name is not Smith. Notice that the character string is enclosed in quotation marks.

For each row of the expression there is a column of push buttons under the Not column. If you click on the Not button, the logical meaning of the logical operator is inverted, and a check mark (✓) appears on the button to indicate that the logic is inverted. The preceding example becomes `!(Name = "Smith")`. In the operator column, you can choose an operator from the pop-up list. Operators are described in Table 18.8.

Joining Tables

In the next example, you are going to join the CENSUS.DBF and CITIES.DBF tables. Start by clicking the Add Table button in the Query Designer toolbar. The Add Table or View dialog box appears. Select the CITIES.DBF file from the list of files, as shown in Figure 18.6. The table appears in the Tables window. Also the Query Designer Join Condition dialog box appears, as shown in Figure 18.7. The default join condition displays in the window. The Query Designer figures out the most likely join condition and fills in the window for you. For this example, Query Designer guessed correctly, and the two tables are joined on the `STATE` field as intended. Press the OK push button. If you want to join on another field or you want another join criteria, you can select your choice using the combo boxes in the Join Condition dialog box.

Observe that the CITIES.DBF table now displays in the Query Designer Tables window, and the join condition is represented as a line drawn between the `STATE` fields in the two tables, as shown in Figure 18.8. Now, select the Fields tab and notice that the CITIES.DBF table fields are added to the Available Fields list. Add the `Cities.City` and `Cities.Pop88` fields to the Selected Output list box. You do this by selecting a field in the Available Fields list box. Then press the **A**dd> push button. The selected field from the Available Fields list box is added to the Selected Output list box, as shown in Figure 18.8.

Now press the standard toolbar Run (!) button or just press the Ctrl+Q key to execute the query. The query results are shown in Figure 18.9. The query statistics appear on the status bar for a brief period following the completion of the query processing.

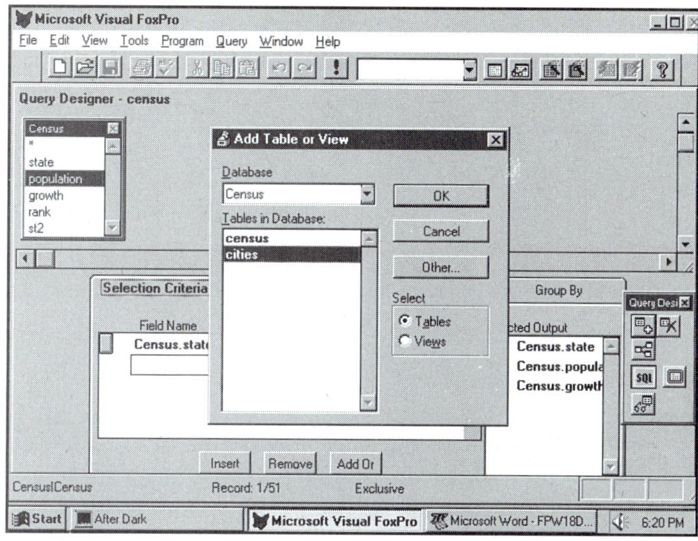

FIGURE 18.6.
The Add Table or View dialog box.

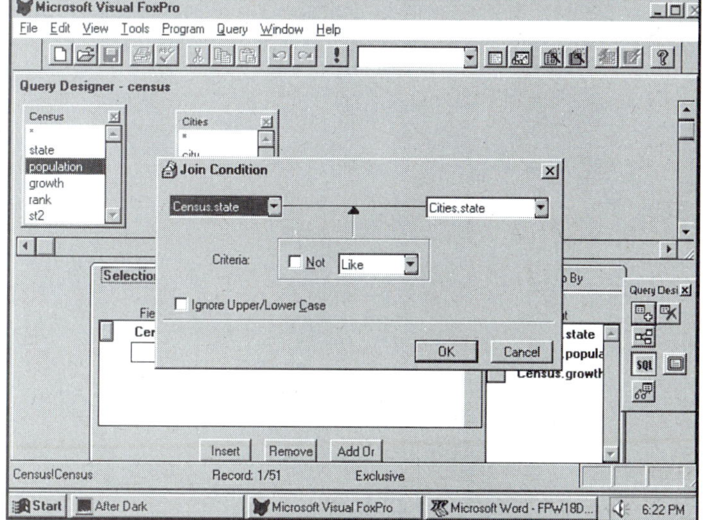

FIGURE 18.7.
The Join Condition dialog box.

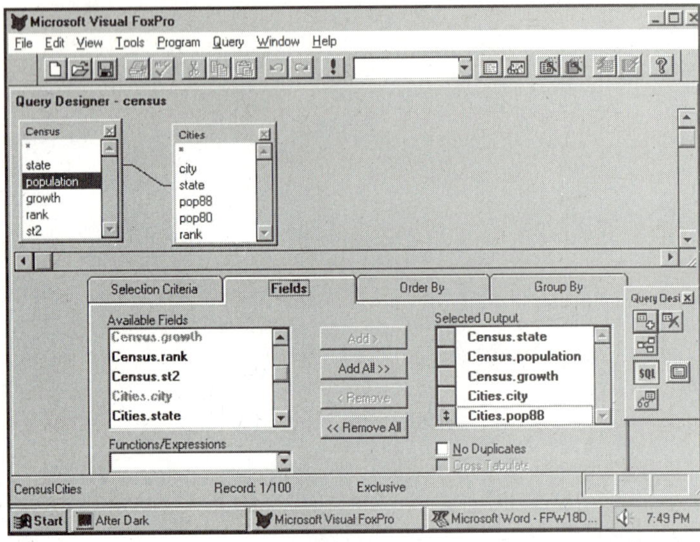

FIGURE 18.8.
The Query Designer window, which shows the join of the CENSUS.DBF and CITIES.DBF files.

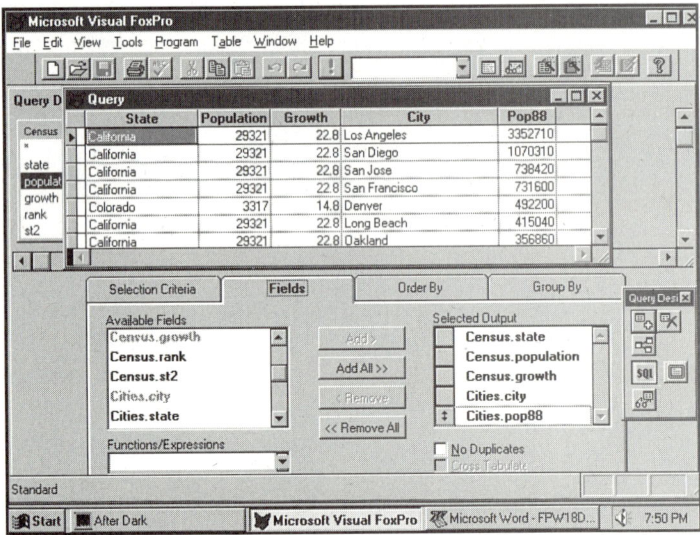

FIGURE 18.9.
The query results, which show the join of the CENSUS.DBF and CITIES.DBF files.

Sorting the Results

Normally, query output is more useful if it is presented in a designated sort order. The next example illustrates how to specify the sorting order of the results. In this example, you will specify that the query output be sorted in descending order by the `Cities.Pop88` field. As you might remember from the description of the SQL `SELECT` command, you designate the order of the result table using the `ORDER BY` clause. When using the Query Designer, you order the query in a similar manner, but visually. Click on the Order By tab, as shown in Figure 18.10.

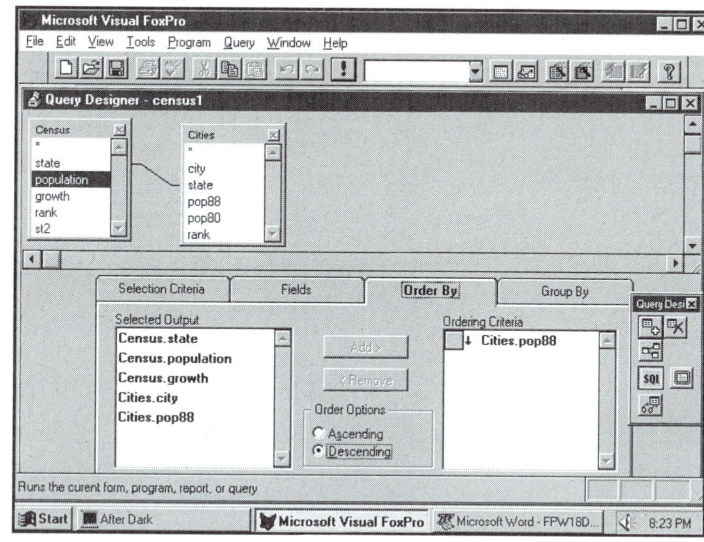

FIGURE 18.10.
The Query Designer Order By tab with descending order sort key, `Cities.pop88`*, selected.*

The Order By tab contains two list boxes: Selected Output and Ordering Criteria. You select (highlight) a field in the Selected Output list box and press the **Add>** button, and the selected field is added to the Ordering Criteria list box. You can repeat the process if you want additional sorting keys. The example, as shown in Figure 18.10, contains only one sort key, `Cities.Pop88`. Next, choose the Descending radio button. Notice the ↓ to the left of the `Pop88` field name in the Outputs Fields panel. The ↓ symbol means that the table is sorted in descending order. If the result table is sorted in ascending order by a key, the ↑ symbol appears instead of the ↓ symbol. If you have more than one keys in the Ordering Criteria list box, the one on the top is the first (major) sort key. You can reorder the sort fields using the column of reordering buttons at the left of the Ordering Criteria list box.

Now press the standard toolbar Run (!) button to execute the query. The query results are shown in Figure 18.11. The records are sorted in descending orer by `Cities.pop88`, the city population field. Here is the `SELECT` statement for this query, which appears in the SQL window:

```
SELECT Census.state, Census.population, Census.growth, Cities.city,;
    Cities.pop88;
    FROM census!census, census!cities;
    WHERE Census.state = Cities.state;
    AND Census.state = "C";
    ORDER BY Cities.pop88 DESC
```

Grouping Data into Summary Records

Now you can proceed to the next example. What if you want to know the average size of cities for each state? From what you learned about SQL earlier in the chapter, you know the `GROUP BY` clause can be specified to summarize output records. You use the Group By tab for this operation. The Group By tab is shown in Figure 18.12. To select a Group By field, select a field from the Available Fields list box. Then press the **A**dd> button, and the selected field appears in the Group By Fields list box. In Figure 18.12, you see that the `Census.State` field is the chosen field in the Group By Fields list box.

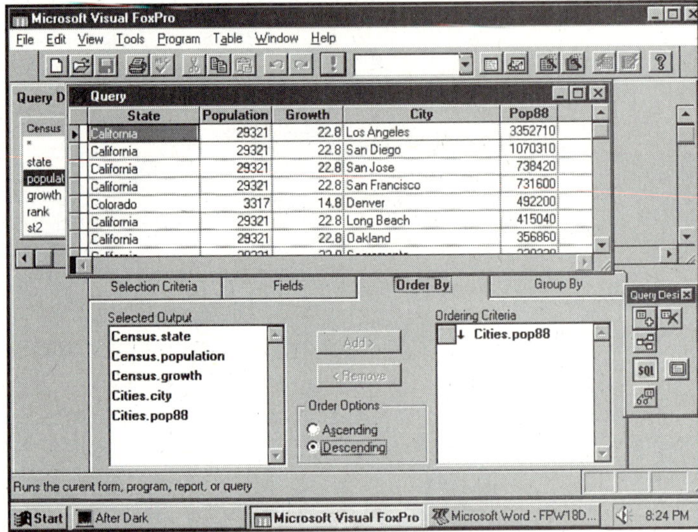

FIGURE 18.11.

An example of an ordered query.

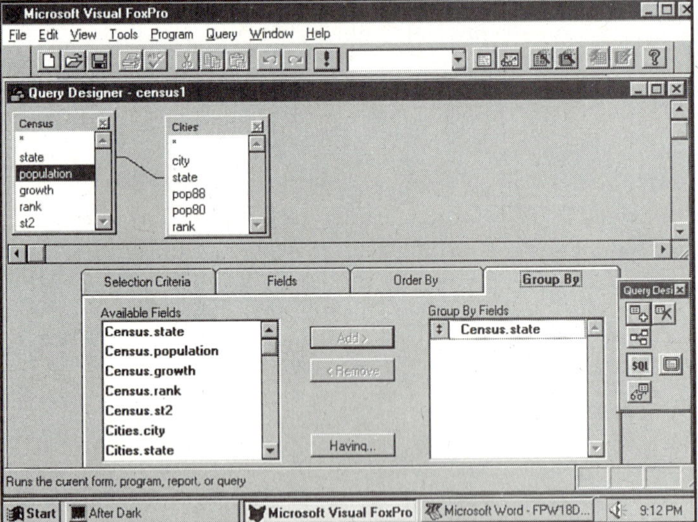

FIGURE 18.12.

The Query Designer Group By tab.

Because you want this query to include all states, you need to delete the condition appearing in the Selection Criteria tab that corresponds to the `Census.State = "C"` condition. Select the row in which the condition appears and press the <**R**emove button at the bottom of the Selection Criteria tab.

Next, click on the Fields tab and remove the `Cities.Pop88` and `Cities.City` fields with the <**R**emove button. Now open the Fields/Expressions combo box. Because you need to average values, select the `AVG()` function as shown in Figure 18.13. A drop-down submenu appears, containing the output fields. Pick the `Cities.Pop88` field (the population of a city for 1988) from the submenu, and the expression `AVG(Cities.Pop88)` appears in the Fields/Expressions combo box.

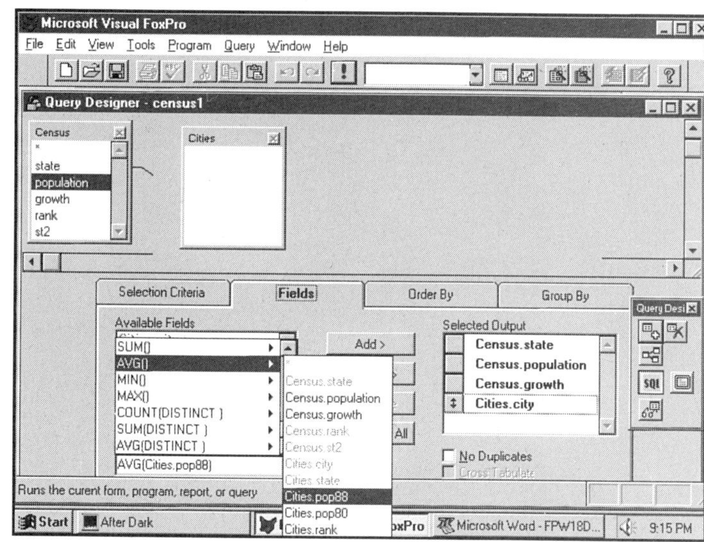

FIGURE 18.13.
The Query Designer Fields tab used to specify the `AVG()` aggregate function as the output field.

Press the **A**dd> button, and the expression moves to the Selected Output list box, as shown in Figure 18.14.

Run the query and view the results. Your results should resemble the query result table shown in Figure 18.14. Now look at the following SQL `SELECT` command from the SQL window:

```
SELECT Census.state, Census.population, Census.growth, AVG(Cities.pop88);
 FROM census!census, census!cities;
 WHERE Census.state = Cities.state;
 GROUP BY Census.state
```

As you can see, the elements of the Query Designer window shown in Figures 18.12 through 18.14 correspond to SQL `SELECT` command clauses. The Query Designer provides an interactive point-and-click alternative to formulating an SQL `SELECT` command by hand. It also enforces the SQL `SELECT` command ordering rules. For example, the Query Designer menus, combo boxes, and lists contain only fields that are allowed in a query.

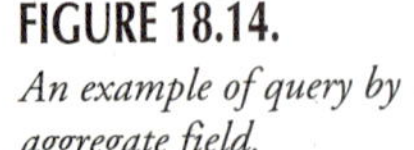

FIGURE 18.14.
An example of query by aggregate field.

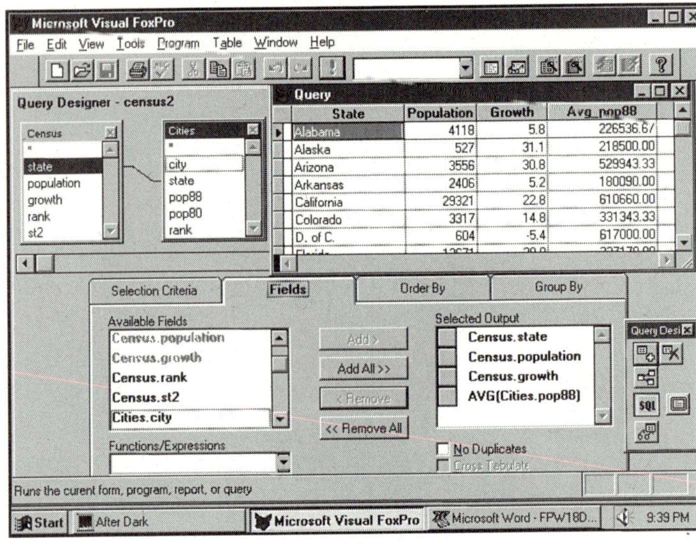

Self-Joining Files

Sometimes a query is posed that involves at least two different records from the same file. The classic example of such a query is "Show me all the employees who earn more than their managers." This type of join is referred to in relational theory as a *self-join.*

You can do a self-join in the Query Designer by adding two instances of the same table to the Query Designer Tables window. For example, consider the table named EMPLOYEE.DBF, which contains the name of the employee, the employee number, the manager's employee number, and the employee's salary, as shown in Listing 18.3.

Listing 18.3. The contents of EMPLOYEE.DBF.

```
LNAME    FNAME    PHONE          EMPNO  SALARY     POSITION   BOSS_ID
Zort     Mort     (818)555-2312  2233   29000.00   Salesman   2222
Johnson  Jane     (818)555-2132  5132   30000.00   Salesman   2222
Altman   Robert   (818)555-6774  2341   27000.00   Engineer   2222
Clinton  Joe      (818)555-1777  2222   28000.00   VP         4122
Smith    Roger    (818)555-1211  4122   78000.00   President     0
```

The classic formulation for the query and the query result table is presented in Figure 18.15. Notice that _a is appended to the name of the second instance of the EMPLOYEE.DBF table. Records in the two files are selected if the field `Employee_a.empno` (the employee number) equals the field `employee.boss_id` (the employee number of the employee's boss) and the employee's salary is more than the boss's salary.

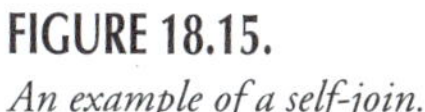

FIGURE 18.15.
An example of a self-join.

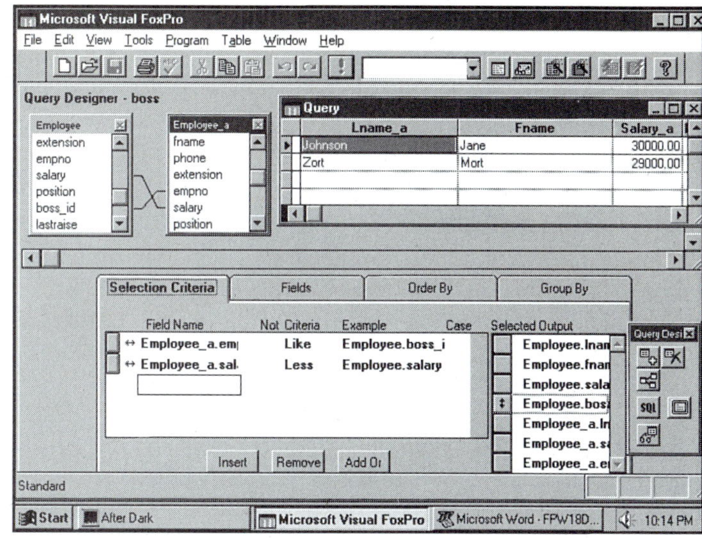

Formulate the query in this manner. From the Command window type the command:

```
MODIFY QUERY BOSS
```

At this point, the Query Designer window appears. Press the Add Table button on the Query Designer toolbar, and the Add Table or View dialog box appears. Choose EMPLOYEE.DBF. Repeat the process to add a second instance of the EMPLOYEE.DBF table. Then the Join Condition dialog box appears. Pick the `Employee_a.salary` field from the left field pop-up menu and the `Employee.boss_id` field from the right field pop-up menu. You want the `Like` operator, which is the default. Press the OK button to confirm the selections.

Next, select the output fields you want to display. Then add a new filter, as shown in Figure 18.14, to the Selection Criteria tab. Run the query. That is all there is to it. The resultant Browse window is shown in Figure 18.15. Here are the contents of the SQL window:

```
SELECT Employee.lname, Employee.fname, Employee.salary, Employee.boss_id,;
        Employee_a.lname, Employee_a.salary, Employee_a.empno;
        FROM employee, employee Employee_a;
        WHERE Employee_a.empno = Employee.boss_id;
        AND Employee_a.salary < Employee.salary
```

Directing Query Designer Output

The material covered so far illustrates how easy it is to compose a complex query. The layout of the window is well organized so that it is not excessively busy, and yet you have access to all the power of the Visual FoxPro Query Designer system. You started out with a simple query, which became progressively more complex as you explored its various features. The design of the final complex query presented in Figure 18.14 is clearly represented in the Query Designer window.

The query design is easily modified, which makes the Query Designer window an ideal environment for formulating queries to play "what if" games. While you are playing these games, you can peruse the query results in the Browse window. When you are satisfied with your query results, you can choose the **Q**uery menu Query Destination option and the Query Destination dialog box appears, as shown in Figure 18.16.

NOTE

Don't forget to right-click. You can right-click on the Query window, and the shortcut menu appears. You can choose the shortcut menu's Output Settings… option to invoke the Query Destination dialog box.

You choose one of seven output options from the Query Destination dialog box. You have the option of outputting results to the printer, a cursor, another table, a text file, the Report or Label Designer, or a graph. If you choose to output the results to a file, you can enter the name of the file; the Query Destination window expands with an additional field that you can use to enter the name of the file.

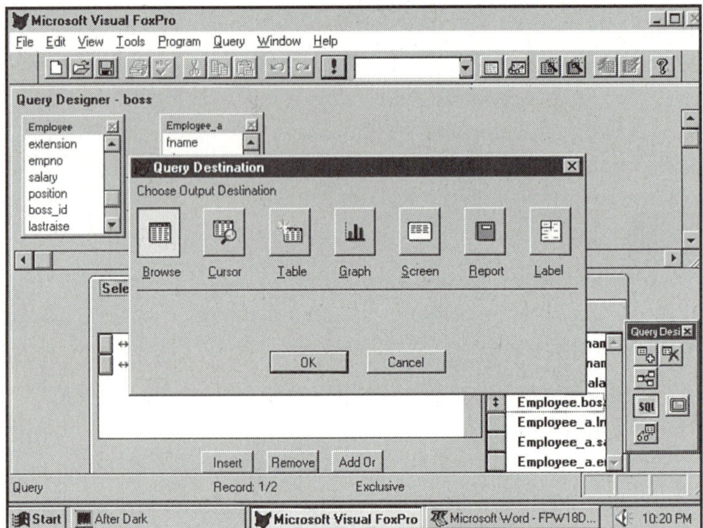

FIGURE 18.16.
The Query Destination dialog box.

Exiting from the Query Designer

You can exit and save your query at any time by pressing Ctrl+W. You can also exit by choosing the **F**ile menu **C**lose option. If you are running Visual FoxPro under Winows 95, you can click on the Close button. If you want to abandon your query, press the Esc key. At any time you can save the current state of a query by choosing the **F**ile menu Save **A**s option and typing a filename, or by choosing the **F**ile menu **S**ave option.

After the Query Designer exits, it leaves the tables and cursors open in various work areas. You can then execute commands that perform various processing operations related to the query, or you can simply clear all work areas with the following command:

```
CLEAR ALL
```

Executing a Query from Within a Program

Once a query is created or modified, you can execute it any time from the Command window or from within a program with the `DO` command. For example, suppose you create a query named WIDGETS.QPR. You can execute the query using the following command:

```
DO WIDGETS.QPR
```

The QPR file is simply the contents of the window that appear when you choose the Query Designer toolbar SQL button. The QPR file consists of a SQL and possibly other commands. For example, if you direct the output to a report, a `REPORT` command is included in the QPR file.

Elements of the Query Designer Window

In the previous sections you were introduced to the Query Designer with a guided tour. Of course, not all of the elements were discussed. This section describes each element of the Query Designer window. Figure 18.17 shows the Query Designer window and menu with each of the window elements.

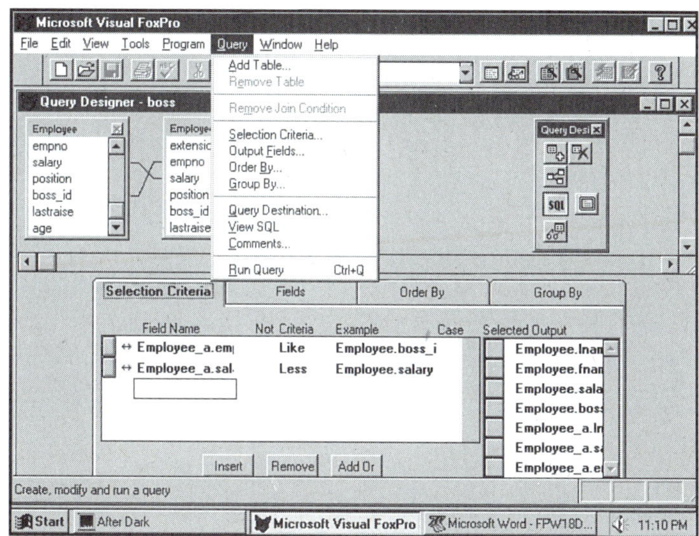

FIGURE 18.17.
The Query Designer window and the Query menu.

The **Q**uery menu options duplicate the options in the Query Designer window and the Query Designer toolbar. There is a reason for providing this dual method of executing options. It provides faster access to the power of Query Designer for those of you who like to use keyboard hotkeys.

There is one **Q**uery menu option that has no counterpart: the **C**omments option. Choose the **C**omments option, and a Comments dialog box appears. You can type in comments, which are placed at the beginning of the current query program (QPR) file.

The View Designer and the Query Designer are very similar. However, the View Designer stores the resultant view in a database container (DBC) file. It also provides certain update options not available under the Query Designer. When you are running the Query Designer, the **A**dvanced Options option appears on the Query menu. You can specify a remote data source with the **A**dvanced Options option. Data sources include local, NetWare SQL, Oracle, and SQLServer tables, and other ODBC data sources. See Chapter 26, "Visual Fox Pro and Client/Server Support."

The Query Designer window is divided into an upper and lower pane. The upper pane shows the tables used in the query. The lower pane is divided up into four page tabs: Selection Criteria tab, Output Fields tab, Order By tab, and Group By tab. Elements in the Tables pane and each of the tab pages are discussed in the following sections.

The Tables Pane

The Tables pane, which I call the Tables window, is a layout area to which you add tables that are used in a query. A table is represented in the Tables window as a small window containing a list of fields and the title bar is the name of the table. If you add a table and one or more tables are already on the layout, the Join Condition dialog box appears, and you can edit the join condition. If a table is in use in the current work area when the Query Designer executes to create a new query, that DBF file initially appears in the Tables window. If you are doing a self-join, you can add a DBF file to the table twice. The second instance of the table name has an underscore and a letter (_a) appended to the name. See Figure 18.15.

The Add Table button on the Query Designer toolbar displays an Add Table or View dialog box from which you can choose a table to include in the query. Once a table is chosen, it is placed in the Tables window. If the table list box contains more than one table, the Query Designer Join Condition dialog box appears, and you can edit the table linkage when the table is placed in the Tables window. Lines are drawn representing the join.

The Remove Table button on the Query Designer toolbar removes the selected (highlighted) table from the Tables window.

The Selection Criteria Tab

The Query Designer Selection Criteria tab page contains one of the most important features of the Query Designer. This tab page helps you specify a selection criteria that filters tables so that only the records that satisfy the criteria appear in the query result table. It uses the same technique to define a filter used in the Query Designer Having dialog box.

The Selection Criteria list box consists of seven columns:

1. A push button used to rearrange rows
2. A push button that activates the Query Designer Join Condition dialog box
3. A Field Name (or `<expression>`) combo box
4. The NOT push button, which inverses the logic of the condition
5. A Filter Condition Operator pop-up menu
6. An example text box
7. The Case check box, which is used to specify whether capitalization of character data is ignored

The purpose and use of each column is discussed in Table 18.7.

Table 18.7. The column options for the Query Designer Selection Criteria list box.

Column	*Description*
Double-headed arrow list	At the left of the existing conditions is a column of double-headed arrows used to rearrange the rows of conditions. You can change the order of items in a list with the double-headed arrows by pressing the Tab key until the item you wish to move is selected. Use the Ctrl+PgUp or Ctrl+PgDn key combination to move the item up or down in the list. You also can click on the double-headed arrow and drag the item to the desired location in the list.
Join condition	Choose this push button, and the Query Designer Join Condition dialog box appears. (See Figure 18.7.) You can modify the join condition for the current column.
Fields	You can enter or choose a field function or expression to establish a comparison. The combo box contains the `<expression>` option. If the `<expression>` option is chosen, the FoxPro Expression Builder appears to help you specify an expression. Here are the field (aggregate) functions in the list: `AVG()` Average value `COUNT()` Count records `MIN()` Minimum value

continues

Table 18.7. continued

Column	*Description*	
	`MAX()`	Maximum value
	`SUM()`	Sum values
	The following aggregate functions will exclude records with duplicate values from the results:	
	`COUNT(DISTINCT)`	Count records
	`SUM(DISTINCT)`	Sum values
	`AVG(DISTINCT)`	Average value
	For each of these functions a submenu appears containing table field names. You select one of the field names, and it becomes the function argument.	
NOT	This push button is normally off. If it is checked, the logic of the condition is inversed.	
Condition	This combo box contains the following operators, which are also described in Table 18.8:	
	`Like`	equal to (=)
	`Exactly Like`	exactly equal to (==)
	`More Than`	greater than (>)
	`Less Than`	less than (<)
	`Between`	between two values `(v1 <= x > v2)`
	`In`	in a list of values
	You choose a conditional operator from the list.	
Example	You enter the text value used in the comparison.	
Case	This push button is used to specify whether capitalization of character data is ignored.	

Each of the condition operators is described in Table 18.8. The `Like` operator is affected by the `SET ANSI` setting. This setting is designed to make the `Like` operator behave as it does in ANSI standard SQL. If `SET ANSI` is `OFF`, which is the default, the `Like` comparisons behave the same as the FoxPro equal (=) operator when comparing character strings. That is, `Like` compares characters in both strings until it reaches the end of one of the strings. At that point, the strings are considered to match if the string on the right is shorter than the string on the left. However, if `SET ANSI` is `ON`, the shorter string is filled with blanks until it is the same length as the longer field. Then the strings are compared character for character. This changes the results. For example, the expression, `"Dog "="Doggy"` is true if `SET ANSI` is `OFF`, and false if `SET ANSI` is

`ON`. Notice that the `SET ANSI` option can be set only in a program or in the Command window using the `SET ANSI ON` or `SET ANSI OFF` command. Furthermore, the `SET ANSI` setting is recognized only by the SQL `SELECT` command. Table 18.8 presents the Selection Criteria tab operators for the Query Designer.

Table 18.8. The Selection Criteria tab operators for the Query Designer.

`Like`	The `Like` operator specifies that the field must match the sample text before the record is included in the query output. For example, if the condition is `Census.State Like T`, all records beginning with the letter T, such as `Texas` and `Tennessee`, are included. The `Like` operator is the default option.
`Exactly Like`	The `Exactly Like` operator specifies that the field must match the example text exactly, character for character, in order for the record to be included in the query output.
`More Than`	The `More Than` operator specifies that the field must be greater than the value in the example text in order for the record to be included in the query output.
`Less Than`	The `Less Than` operator specifies that the field must be less than the value in the example text in order for the record to be included in the query output.
`Between`	The `Between` operator specifies that the field must be greater than or equal to the lower value and less than or equal to the higher value in the example text in order for the record to be included in the query output. The example text must be two values separated by a comma. For example, the condition `students.gdate Between 06/8/93,06/10/93` matches records for the 8th, 9th, and 10th of June 1993, which are to be included in the query results.
`In`	The `In` operator specifies that the field must match one of several comma-delimited examples in the example text in order for the record to be included in the query output. For example, the condition `emp_no IN 2233,3455,7773` matches records if the employee number equals one of the three values 2233, 3455, and 7773.

The bottom of the Selection Criteria tab page contains three push buttons: **I**nsert, **R**emove, and Add **O**r. The **I**nsert push button inserts a new condition above the selected condition. The **R**emove push button deletes the selected condition. The Add **O**r push button creates an `OR` condition.

If you specify a row in the condition list, it is equivalent to setting up a logical expression. When the expression is evaluated, it yields a true or false value. If it creates a false value, a source table record isn't selected. If the logical expression evaluates to a true value, the record is selected. You can combine two expressions with an `AND` or `OR` operator. Unless you specify `OR` with the Add **O**r push button, two rows of the condition list are combined with an `AND` operator. Here is an example:

```
Employee  Like       "Smith"
Age       More Than  40
```

The condition list becomes this:

```
Employee = "Smith" AND (Age > 40)
```

If you choose the Add **O**r push button before you specify the second row of the condition list, the condition list looks like this:

```
Employee  Like       "Smith"
OR
Age       More Than  40
```

The condition list becomes this:

```
Employee = "Smith" OR (Age > 40)
```

If you are unclear how the rows of the condition list are combined, press the View SQL push button on the Query Designer toolbar and look at the SQL `SELECT` command `WHERE` clause.

The Fields Tab

The Fields tab page contains options to add, delete, or rearrange result table output fields. The Available Fields list box contains a list of fields from the tables in the Tables window that can appear in the query output. The Selected Output list box displays the fields to be output in the order they will appear in the query result table.

If you want to rearrange the order of output fields in the list, select the item you want to move. A push button is provided to the left of each item. When you move the mouse pointer to one of the push buttons, a double-headed arrow appears. You can click the mouse on one of the buttons and drag the item to the desired location in the list. You also can change the order of items in a list by pressing the Tab key until the item you wish to move is selected. Then press the Ctrl+PgUp or Ctrl+PgDn key combinations to move the item up or down in the list.

Adding Fields to a Query

To add a field to the Selected Output list box, you can double-click on a field in the Available Fields list box. In addition, you can select a field in the Available Fields list box and press the **A**dd> button to add a field to the Selected Output list box. You can press the A**d**d All> button, and all the fields in the Available Fields list box will be added to the Selected Output list box. You can also drag a field from the fields in the Tables window to the Selected Output list box.

Just click on the field, hold down the mouse button, and drag the field to the Selected Output list box. If you like, you can click on the table name of a table in the Tables window and drag all of the fields in the table to the Selected Output list.

To remove a field, you can select the field in the Selected Output list box and press the <**R**emove button or double-click on the field. The <<Remove **All** button is used to remove all of the fields in the Selected Output list box.

The Query Designer Fields tab enables you to specify fields, functions, and expressions to include in a query. Also, you can adjust the order of field appearance, remove fields, and eliminate duplicate entries using the options described in Table 18.9.

Table 18.9. The controls for the Query Designer Fields tab.

Option	*Description*
Available Fields	The Available Fields list box contains table fields. You can double-click on one of the field names or select a field name and choose the **Add**> push button to move the field to the Selected Output list box.
Selected Output	The Selected Output list box contains fields listed in the order they are output in the query result table. You can double-click on a field or select a field and press the <**R**emove push button to remove the field from the Selected Output list box. You can rearrange the order of items in a list with double-headed arrows at the left of each item name. You point the mouse to the button. Then you click on the double-headed arrow and drag the item to the desired location in the list. You also can change the order of items in a list with double-headed arrows by pressing the Tab key until the item you wish to move is selected. Then use the Ctrl+PgUp or Ctrl+PgDn key combinations to move the item up or down in the list.
Add>	This push button places a selected field from the Available Fields list box into the Selected Output list box.
A**d**d All>>	This push button places all active fields in the Available Fields list box into the Selected Output list box.
<**R**emove	This push button removes a selected field from the Selected Output list box.
<<Remove **All**	This push button removes all the fields from the Selected Output list box.

continues

Table 18.9. continued

Option	*Description*
Functions	This combo box lists aggregate functions that can be included Expressions in the query result output table. Once you choose a function, it appears in the Function text box. To include the function in the output, press the **A**dd> push button. Aggregate functions process records and compute the following commands: `AVG()` Average value `COUNT()` Count records `MIN()` Minimum value `MAX()` Maximum value `SUM()` Sum values The following aggregate functions will exclude records with duplicate values from the results: `COUNT(DISTINCT)` Count records `SUM(DISTINCT)` Sum values `AVG(DISTINCT)` Average value For each of these functions, a submenu appears containing field names. You choose one, and it becomes the function argument. You can also type a function into this combo box to include in the query output, and then push the **A**dd> push button.
No Duplicates	This is a check box. When it is checked, records with all fields matching are not included in the output.
Cross Tabulate	This check box controls the cross-tabulation feature of Microsoft Graph. It can be checked only if the Selected Output list box contains exactly three items. When it is checked, query results are output to Microsoft Graph, a report form, or a table in cross-tabular format. The three items represent the x-axis, the y-axis, and the cell value for the graph.

The Order By Tab: Specifying the Sorting Order of Query Results

Normally, you don't access data in the same order as it appears in the table. Usually, you will want to see the results displayed in a specified order. In the Query Designer, you can specify the order in which fields appear in the query results. You can specify the order by clicking on the Order By tab. The Order By tab appears, as shown in Figure 18.10. You use this tab to specify the order in which records appear in the query results. The Query Designer Order By tab options are described in Table 18.10.

Table 18.10. The controls for the Query Designer Order By tab dialog box.

Option	*Description*
Selected Output	This list box contains the query result output fields. If you double-click on one of these fields, or select one and choose the **A**dd> push button, the field is moved to the Ordering Criteria list box.
Ordering Criteria	This list box contains the sorting fields with the major sort field listed first. You can double-click on a field, or select a field and then choose the **R**emove push button to remove it from the Selected Output list box. You can use the double-headed arrows at the left of the item names to rearrange the list.
Add>	This push button places a selected field from the Selected Output list box into the Ordering Criteria list box.
<**R**emove	This push button removes a selected field from the Ordering Criteria list box.
Ascending Descending	You can select one of these two radio buttons in the Order Option group to specify the ascending or descending sorting button is selected. When you add a new ordering criteria field, the Order Option setting determines whether the order is ascending or descending. You can change the order of an existing ordering criteria field by selecting the field and choosing a different order option.

Group By Tab: Summarizing Data

Sometimes, instead of retrieving all the information in a table, you want to have a summary query table. For example, suppose you have a very simple table of invoice records that looks something like this:

```
Customer  InvNo Amount
Jones      2345  $3,213.11
Jones      2346  $4,234.11
Lambert    2347  $  966.30
Smith      2348  $8,112.41
Smith      2349  $1,231.32
```

Then suppose that you don't want to see all of the records for each individual invoice because all you are interested in is how much each customer owes you. To find this out, you can use the Group By tab to specify that you want to group the records by customer. Your query results will look something like this:

```
Customer       SUM_AMOUNT
Jones          7447.22
Lambert         966.30
Smith          9343.73
```

Of course you also need to order the records properly (using the Order By tab) and add the `SUM()` field function to the query output. The results will show how much Smith and Jones owe you.

To specify a grouping, you select the Group By tab. You use the Query Designer Group By Tab to specify table fields or field functions on which data is summarized. The Group By tab options are described in Table 18.11.

Table 18.11. The options for the Query Designer Group By tab dialog box.

Option	*Description*
Available Fields	This list box contains table fields. You can double-click on one of the fields or select the field name and choose the **A**dd> push button to move the field to the Group By Fields list box.
Group By Fields	This list box contains the Group By fields. You can double-click on one of the fields or select a field and then choose the <**R**emove push button to remove it from the Group By Fields list box. You can use the double-headed arrows at the left of the item names to rearrange the list.
Add>	This push button places the selected field from the Available Fields list box into the Group By Fields list box.
<**R**emove	This push button removes the selected field from the Group By Fields list box.
Having...	Displays the **H**aving... dialog box from which you can specify a filter.

Filtering Group By Query Output

The `WHERE` clause filters records as they are read from the source tables. When you designate Group By fields, you might want to filter out summary records that don't satisfy a condition from the query results. You can't do this with the `WHERE` clause. You can use an example to show how to use the Group By Fields tab. First, consider the sample invoice table used in the discussion of the Group **B**y option that consisted of the following records:

```
Customer     InvNo    Amount
Jones        2345     $3,213.11
Jones        2346     $4,234.11
Lambert      2347     $  966.30
Smith        2348     $8,112.41
Smith        2349     $1,231.32
```

Now, suppose that you didn't want summary records to be included in the query results if the summation of the amount was less than $1000.

As in the previous chapter, records are summarized for each customer. In addition, the **H**aving option is specified to filter out any records with `SUM_AMOUNT < 1000`. Here is the output:

```
Customer        SUM_AMOUNT
Jones           7447.22
Smith           9343.73
```

To specify a group by the Having condition, you click on the **H**aving... push button, and the Having dialog box appears. You use the Query Designer Having dialog box to specify conditions groups must meet to be included in the query output. The Query Designer Having dialog box options are shown in Figure 18.18 and are described in Table 18.12. The Having check box is checked when a Having condition is specified.

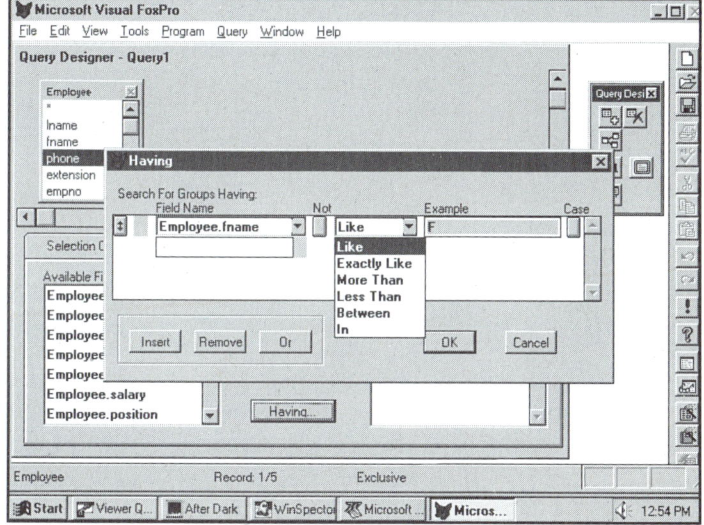

FIGURE 18.18.
The Query Designer Having dialog box.

Table 18.12. The options for the Query Designer Having dialog box.

Option	*Description*
Field Name	You can enter or choose a field function or field to establish a comparison. The combo box list contains the <expression> option. If it is selected, The FoxPro Expression Builder appears to help you specify an expression. Here are the field (aggregate) functions in the list: AVG() Average value COUNT() Count records MIN() Minimum value MAX() Maximum value SUM() Sum values The following aggregate functions will exclude records with duplicate values from the results: COUNT(DISTINCT) Count records SUM(DISTINCT) Sum values AVG(DISTINCT) Average value For each of these functions, a submenu appears, containing table field names. When you select one, it becomes the function argument.
NOT	This push button is normally off. If it is checked, the logic of the condition is inversed.
Condition	This combo box contains the following conditions: Like equal to (=) Exactly like exactly equal to (==) More than greater than (>) Less than less than (<) Between (v1 <= x > v2) between two values In in a list of values You select a conditional operator from the list. See Table 18.8 for more information on conditional operators.
Example	You enter the text value used in the comparison.
Case	This column of push buttons is used to specify whether capitalization of character data is ignored.

Option	Description
Insert	This push button inserts a new condition above the selected condition.
Remove	This push button deletes the selected condition.
Add **O**r	This push button creates an OR condition.
Double-headed arrow lists	To the left of the existing conditions is a column of double-headed arrows used to rearrange the rows of conditions. You can change the order of items in the list with double-headed arrows by pressing the Tab key until the item you wish to move is selected. Press the Ctrl+PgUp or Ctrl+PgDn key combinations to move the item up or down in the list. You also can click on the double-headed arrow and drag the item to the desired location in the list.

One final note: If you don't specify Group By fields, the **H**aving option condition behaves the same as the Selection Criteria option condition.

The SQL Window

When you execute a query, the SQL statements that generate a query appear in the SQL window. You can view this window by clicking on the View SQL button in the Query Designer toolbar or by choosing the **Q**uery menu **V**iew SQL option. The SQL window is a read-only window containing SQL SELECT commands. The SQL window is shown in Figure 18.3.

Output Destination

The **Q**uery Menu **Q**uery Destination option or the Output Destination button in the Query Designer toolbar is used to invoke the Output Destination dialog box shown in Figure 18.16. (You can also use the shortcut menu's Output Settings option.) This dialog box contains options that you use to specify where the query results are output. The options are described in Table 18.13. By default, query results are directed to a Browse window. The Query Destination dialog box merely defines where the output of the query is directed—it does not execute a query. You need to use the **Q**uery menu **R**un Query option or the standard toolbar Run button to execute the query.

Table 18.13. The options for the Output Destination menu.

Option	Destination
Browse	Results are output into a read-only Browse window.
Cursor	Results are output to a temporary table.

continues

Table 18.13. continued

Option	*Destination*
Table/DBF	Results are output into a table that can be browsed, edited, and saved.
Graph	Results are output to the Visual FoxPro Graph Wizard utility, which displays the results in Graphic form and comes with FoxPro.
Screen	Results complete with field headings are output to the screen.
Report	Results are output into a new or existing report form.
Label	Results are output into a new or existing label form.

If you designate that output is directed to a table, cursor, or graph, the dialog box expands to display a Name text box and a Browse button. If you choose the Browse button, the Open dialog box appears. You select a directory and enter a filename. Then the Name text box shows the name of the file that receives the query output. You can also type a filename into the Name text box.

When you choose to direct output to a report or to mailing labels, the Output Destination dialog box expands to allow the display of a number of additional options, as shown in Figure 18.19. These options enable you to format report or label options and set up output destinations. These options are described in Table 18.14.

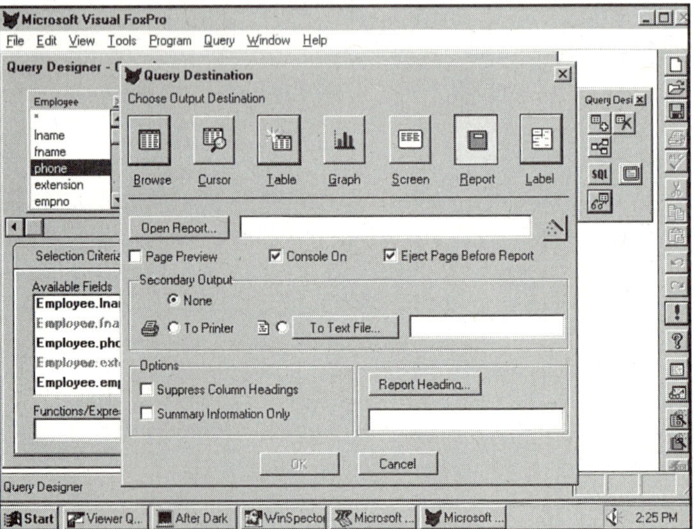

FIGURE 18.19.
The Query Designer Query Destination dialog box with the Report option selected.

Table 18.14. The Query Designer Output Destination dialog box Report option.

Option	*Description*
Open Report...	Either enter the path and filename of the desired report to open in the Report Form text box or push this button to display the Open File dialog box.
Design Report (icon)	Activates the Report Designer to quickly design a report.
Page Preview	When this check box is checked, output for a report is directed to the screen instead of the printer.
Console On	This check box designates whether output is displayed to the screen.
Eject Page Before Report	When this check box is checked, FoxPro outputs a page eject before it prints a report. These three radio buttons determine which options in this dialog box are enabled. They specify the following options: None — Output is directed to the screen. To Printer — Output is directed to the printer. To File — Output is directed to the printer.
To Text File	Type the name of the file to which the output file information is directed or choose the check box to display the Save As dialog box.
Suppress Column Headings	When this check box is checked, headings aren't displayed at the top of each page.
Summary Information Only	When this check box is checked, summary information displays instead of the entire report.
Report Heading...	Enter the heading for the report or select the check box to display Expression Builder and create the heading.

When you choose to direct output to a graph when executing a query, the Visual FoxPro Graph Wizard dialog box appears. It guides you through the process of specifying the graph. The Graph Wizard Step 1 frame is skipped because the source data is the result table. The process begins with Step 2. In Step 2, you specify which field displays on which axis of the graph. You are prompted to drag the field that appears on the horizontal axis to the Axis field. Then you drag the fields that appear in the Data Series (ordinate or vertical axis values) to the list box. This step is shown in Figure 18.20. After you make your choice, press the **N**ext push button, and the Graph Wizard Step 3 frame appears. This frame prompts you to choose the type of graph that you want to plot from a set of picture buttons, as shown in Figure 18.21.

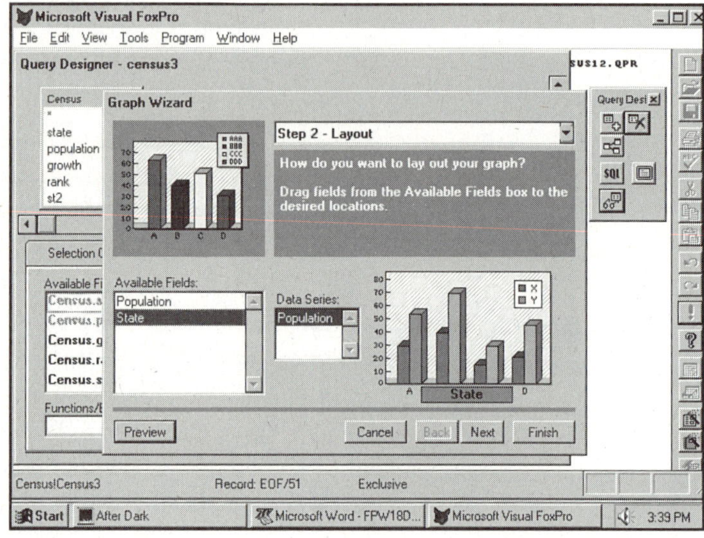

FIGURE 18.20.
The Graph Wizard Step 2 dialog box.

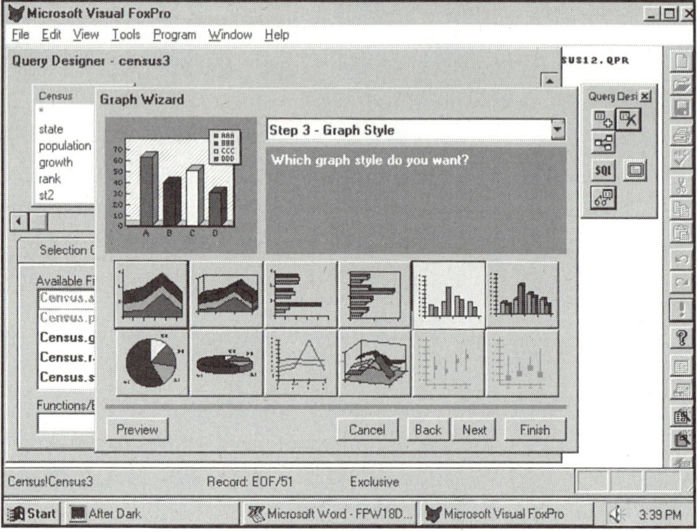

FIGURE 18.21.
The Graph Wizard Step 3 dialog box.

Press the Next push button, and the Graph Wizard Step 4 frame appears, as shown in Figure 18.22. This frame prompts you to enter a graph and legend title. After you have done this, press the Finish button, and the graph is drawn. But first, you are prompted to specify a file name. This file is a DBF table. Your graph is stored in this table as an OLE object. Figure 18.23 shows a sample graph.

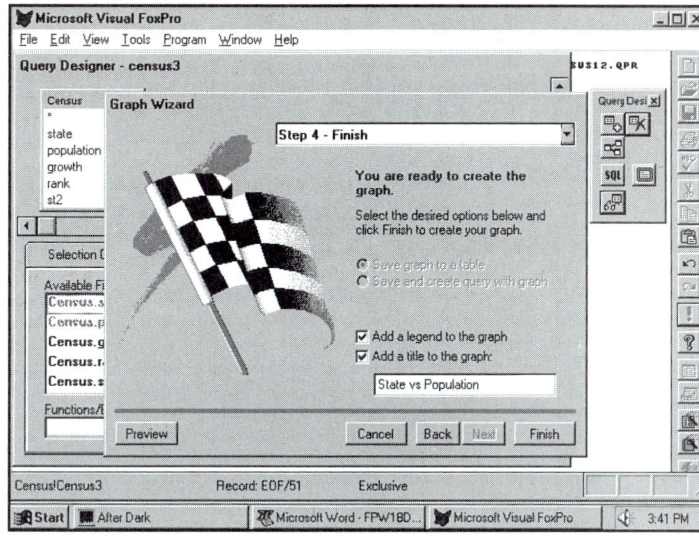

FIGURE 18.22.
The Graph Wizard Step 4 dialog box.

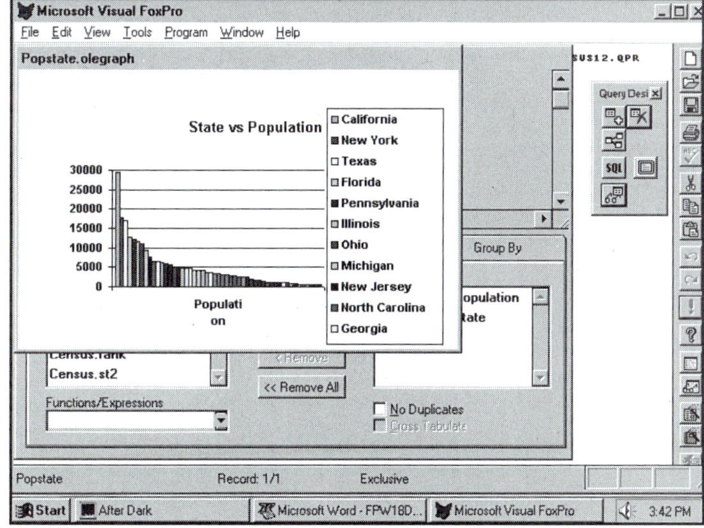

FIGURE 18.23.
An example of a Graph Wizard graph.

Summary

This chapter presents an introduction to the SQL commands supported by Visual FoxPro and an overview of interactive and embedded SQL. The discussion focuses on the SQL SELECT command, which is the FoxPro command that the Visual FoxPro Query Designer uses to do queries. It also gives you a tour of the Query Designer and shows you how to use its powerful features to perform various levels of queries. Finally, it discusses each element of the Query Designer.

Works Cited

Chamberlin, D. D. 1976. "SEQUEL 2: A Unified Approach to Data Definition, Manipulation, and Control." *IBM Journal of Research and Development* Volume 20, Number 6 (November).

Codd, E. F. 1972. "Relational Completeness of Data Base Sublanguages." *Courant Computer Science Symposia Series, Volume 6: Data Base Systems.* Englewood Cliffs, N.J.: Prentice Hall.

Date, C.J. 1987. *A Guide to the SQL Standard.* Reading, Mass.: Addison-Wesley.

19

The Form Designer

A picture is worth
a thousand words.

—Chinese Proverb

A picture shows me at a glance
what it takes dozens of pages of a
book to expound.

—Ivan Sergeyevich Turgenev
(1818–1883)

You have already been introduced to the FoxPro Form Designer. You appreciate its value, and you probably already use it to build interactive interfaces for your applications. In this chapter, you will be provided with a detailed description of the powerful Visual FoxPro Form Designer.

You use the Form Designer to visually create and modify forms and form sets for your applications by pasting controls on a form and arranging these controls until you create your desired form or form set layout. The FoxPro Form Designer goes beyond other form designers because it enables you to create multiple form objects that can be manipulated together. Each form can have a rich variety of complex control objects. Each object has its own vast collection of properties, events, and methods.

Because you have already been introduced to the Form Designer in other chapters, this chapter begins with a description of how to run the Form Designer.

Running the Form Designer

To execute the FoxPro Form Designer and create a form or a set of forms, called a *form set*, either execute the CREATE FORM <*expFN*> command from the Command window or select the **F**ile menu **N**ew command, select the For**m** option button, and enter a filename. To modify an existing form file, choose the **F**ile menu **O**pen command and choose a screen (SCX) file or execute the MODIFY SCREEN <*expFN*> command from the Command window. To create a new form from the Project Manager, you can choose the Form icon in the All or Documents tabs and click on the New button. You can modify an existing form from the Project Manager by clicking on the name of an existing form in the Document tab list box. In either of the cases, the Form Designer screen appears, as shown in Figure 19.1.

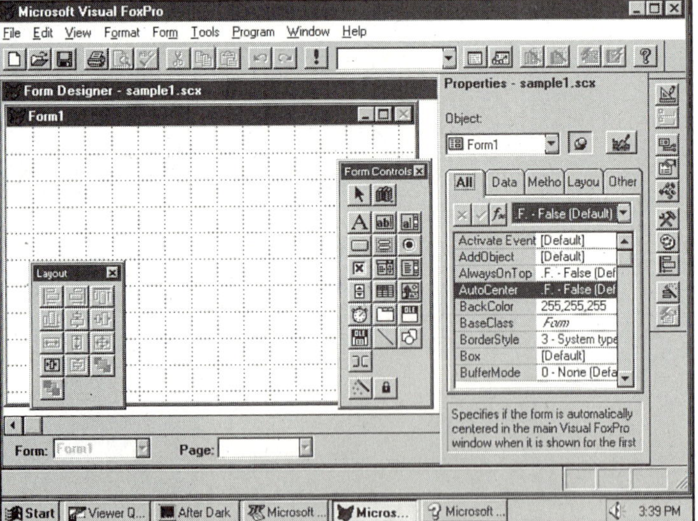

FIGURE 19.1.
The Form Designer screen.

Running Legacy Programs

You can run Legacy screen programs (SPR), developed and run in FoxPro 2.*x*, in Visual FoxPro without any modification. However, when you modify a FoxPro 2.*x* screen (SCX) file, the Form Designer detects that the screen file is a FoxPro 2.*x* SCX file (called a screen file in FoxPro 2.*x*) and executes the Forms Converter application to convert the old FoxPro 2.*x* screen file to a Visual FoxPro form file. The Forms Converter displays the Conversion Options dialog box, as shown in Figure 19.2. When you are confronted with this dialog box, you can either cancel the operation or allow the FoxPro Converter to convert your file.

As you might suppose, the Visual FoxPro 3.0 SCX table is radically different from the FoxPro 2.6 SCX table. The former has a completely different structure since it is based on entirely different objects, which are based on an object-oriented programming model.

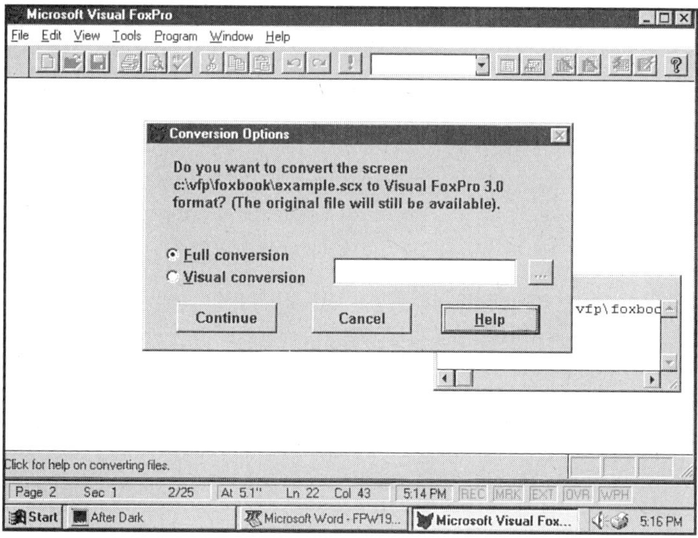

FIGURE 19.2.
The Conversion Options dialog box.

In FoxPro 2.*x*, the Screen Designer generates a screen program with an .SPR extension from the information in the screen SCX file. You execute the FoxPro 2.*x* screen program to display the form (`DO MyScreen.spr`).

There is no screen program file generated by the Visual FoxPro Form Designer. The converter generates a new form file with an .SCX extension and an associated memo (SCT) file. The form file contains everything you need to execute the form. You can execute it with the `DO FORM` command (for example, `DO FORM myform`). All of the executable code, called *methods*, is incorporated in the SCX and SCT files. The converter also creates a new SPR program file that only contains a `DO FORM` command for your convenience.

The converter saves your old FoxPro 2.*x* screen files by changing their filename extensions. It changes the .SCX and .SCT extensions to .S2X and .S2T, respectively.

Once the Form Converter completes its convention process, the Form Designer window displays. Your newly converted FoxPro 2.*x* form appears in the Visual FoxPro Form Designer screen.

The Form Designer Window

When you execute the Visual FoxPro Form Designer, it appears, as shown in Figure 19.1, and the For**m** and F**o**rmat menu pads are added to the FoxPro system menu bar. In addition, options are added to the **V**iew menu. The Save As C**l**ass option is added to the **F**ile menu.

The Form Designer screen contains the Properties window, Form Display window, and Form Control toolbar. The Form Display window contains an initial empty form object named `Form1`. You add controls to this form to build your new form.

There is a Form Designer toolbar that you can activate from the **V**iew menu **T**oolbars… option. The Form Designer toolbar is open in Figure 19.1.

The For**m** menu contains options that affect the entire Form Designer Layout screen. The **U**ndo, Re**d**o, Cu**t**, **C**opy, and **P**aste editing options in the **E**dit menu are available. The F**o**rmat menu contains commands used to align, size, and manipulate controls.

The Form Designer status bar, at the bottom of the Form Designer, contains a Form box and a Page box. You can use the Form box to select a different current form if you have more than one form in the form set. You can use the Page box to select a page if the currently selected object is its page frame container. The Form Designer status bar is shown in Figure 19.1.

The following sections describe the various elements of the Form Designer window, including the system bar menu options and the toolbars.

The File Menu

The **F**ile menu contains the following options, which you can use while designing a form:

Close
Save
Save **A**s…
Save C**l**ass As…
Revert

The Close Option

When you are finished designing a form, you can close it with the **C**lose option. You will be prompted to indicate if you want to save the changes, discard the changes, or cancel the close operation. If you indicate that you want to save the form, the form is saved and the Form Designer exits. You can also press the Ctrl+W key combination to save changes and exit without any prompting. If you want to exit without saving any changes, you can press the Esc key. There is also a Close option on the Close box at the left corner of the screen. If you are running Windows 95, you can press the Close button to save changes and exit.

The Save Option

The **S**ave option saves the current state of the active form in the Form Designer. Suppose that you are working on a complicated form and suddenly you have a power failure—you lose all of your work. If you fear that this can happen, and it does sometimes, it is recommended that you save your work periodically with the **F**ile menu **S**ave option. You can also use the Ctrl+S key combination to execute the **S**ave option. You can also click on the Standard toolbar Save button to execute the **F**ile menu **S**ave option.

The Save As Option

You use the Save **A**s option to save a new form file or to save an existing form file with a different name. When you choose this option, the Save As dialog box appears. You specify a new form file name and it is saved with an .SCX extension.

The Save As Class Option

When the Form Designer is active, the Save **A**s Class option is included on the **F**ile menu. After you have created a form, you can use this option to save a form, the entire form set, or selected controls as a class definition in a visual class library. (See Chapter 15, "The Visual Class Library, the Class Designer, and the Class Browser.") When you choose this option, the Save Class dialog box appears, as shown in Figure 19.3. You do the following:

1. Enter the name of the class.
2. Enter the filename of the visual class library that receives the class.
3. Enter a description of the class. This is optional, but it's recommended.
4. Press the OK button.

In this example, the `Form` class named `CensusForm` is added to the MyLib.VCX class library. Note that if you do not specify an extension, .VCX is assumed.

You can use the `MODIFY CLASS` command to make modifications to the class. You can register your class libraries from the Controls tab of the **T**ools menu **O**ptions option. Then you can select any class library from the Form Controls toolbar View Classes button; your classes will appear as controls on the Form Controls toolbar. You can select them and drag them to the form layout screen as you do any other control.

Your organization can develop a complete set of controls derived from the Visual FoxPro base classes and save them in a visual class (VCX) library. This visual class library can contain commonly used controls, navigation toolbars, and even standard company-specific form templates. You can access these forms and controls from the Form Controls toolbar. The company's visual class library can be maintained by individuals responsible for maintaining interface standards for all applications developed in the organization. If consistency is maintained in this manner, you can reduce the cost of training since users will be familiar with the style of all the forms. Development is made easier since developers can reuse various user interface components. Any organization will benefit by adopting this style of software development methodology because it reduces the cost of development and maintenance of software.

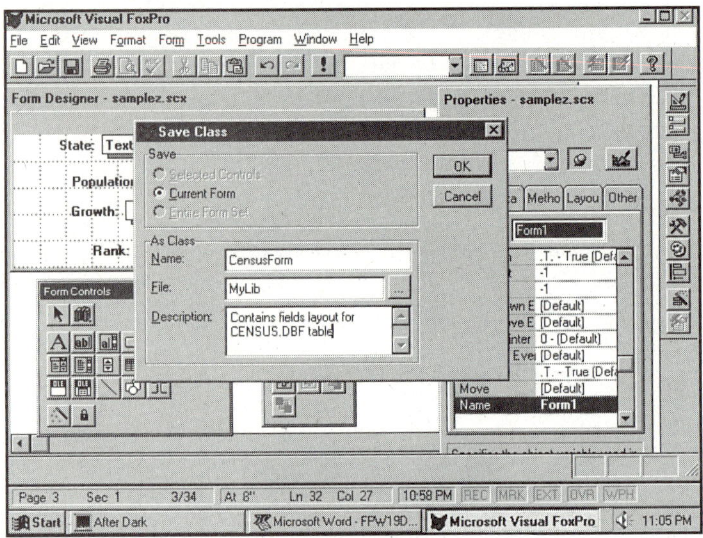

FIGURE 19.3.
The Save Class dialog box.

The Revert Option

The **R**evert option discards changes made to the form since the form was last saved.

The View Menu Options

Table 19.1 describes each of the **V**iew menu options. Figure 19.4 shows the Form Designer with the **V**iew menu open. Each of the open toolbars is also shown in the figure.

Table 19.1. The View Menu used with the Form Designer.

Option	*Description*
✓ **D**esign	This option places the Class Designer in Design mode rather than in Tab Order mode.
Tab **O**rder	This option lets you change the sequence in which controls in a form are selected when the

Option	Description
	user presses the Tab key to move through a form. There are two methods for changing the tab order: interactively and from a list of controls. You use the **T**ools menu Options dialog box to select the tab ordering method. With the interactive method, the form displays. You Shift+click on the boxes next to the controls in the order you want the controls to be selected when the form is used. Numbers appear in the boxes indicating the tab order as shown in Figure 19.5. With the list method, a dialog box appears with a list of controls. You rearrange the list in the desired order you want the controls to be selected when the form is used.
Data **E**nvironment	This option displays the Data Environment Designer so that you can add or remove tables and set relationships.
✓ **P**roperties	This option toggles on and off the Properties dialog box. The Properties dialog box is shown in Figure 19.4.
✓ **C**ode	This option displays a window containing method code. You can choose the control and method from drop-down lists.
✓ Form Contro**l**s Toolbar	This option toggles on and off the Form Controls toolbar, which contains the controls that can be placed on the form. (All of the toolbars described in this table are shown in Figure 19.4.)
✓ Colo**r** Palette Toolbar	This option toggles on and off the Color Palette toolbar. The easiest way to set the foreground and background colors for a control is to use this toolbar.
✓ La**y**out Toolbar	This option toggles on and off the Layout toolbar, which contains the align and size controls.

continues

Table 19.1. continued

Option	Description
✓ Grid Lines	This option toggles on and off the display of grid lines on the class design form.
✓ Show Position	This option toggles on and off the display of the position and size of form objects on the status bar. If Show Position mode is on, a check mark (✓) appears to the left of the option, and the coordinate position of the mouse pointer and the dimensions of selected controls display in the status bar. If you set the mode off, the position and dimensions do not display.

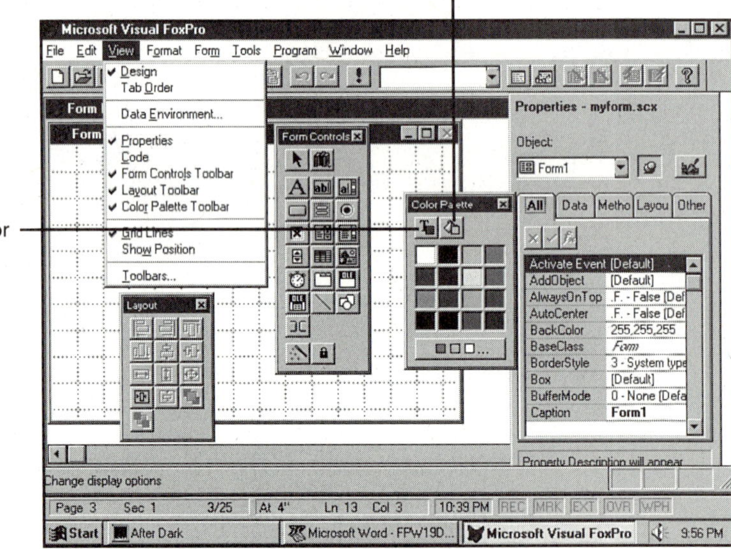

FIGURE 19.4.

The Form Designer with the View menu and toolbars open.

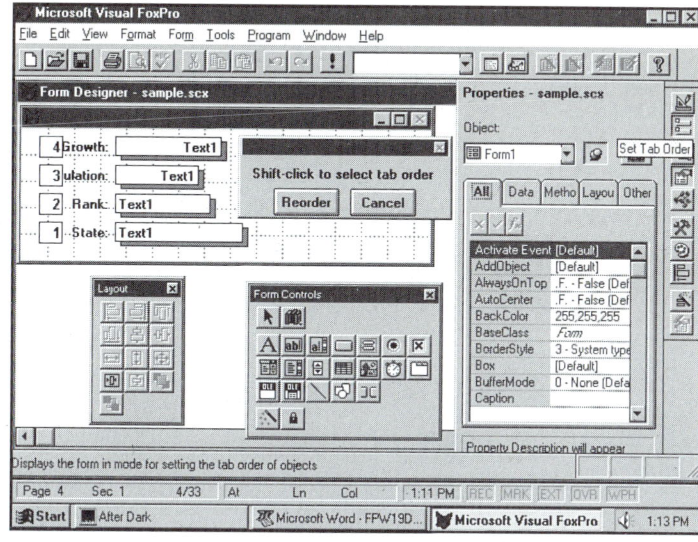

FIGURE 19.5.
Tab reordering using the interactive method.

The Format Menu Options

Figure 19.6 shows the Form Designer with the F**o**rmat menu **A**lign option submenu open. The Layout toolbar is also shown in the figure. Table 19.2 describes each of the F**o**rmat menu options.

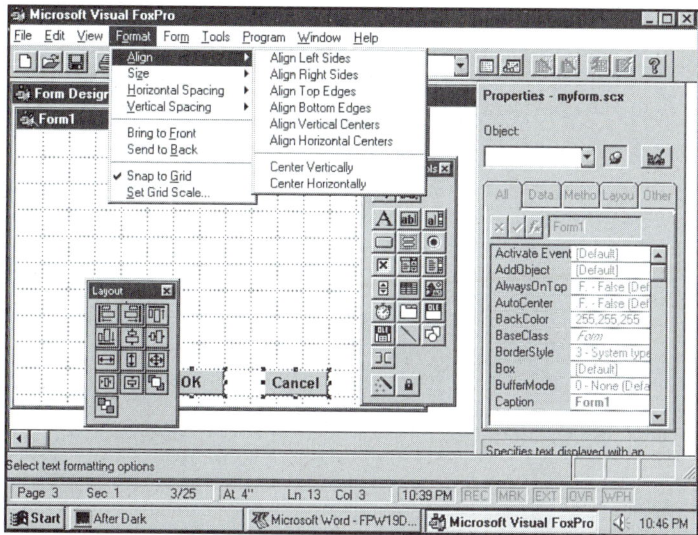

FIGURE 19.6.
The Form Designer with the Format menu open.

Table 19.2. The Format menu used with the Form Designer.

Option	*Description*
Align	This option displays the Align submenu, which corresponds with Layout toolbar buttons. This option includes the following options, align selected controls to the following:
 Left Sides	Left edge of the leftmost control.
 Right Sides	Right edge of the rightmost control.
 Top Edges	Top edge of the topmost control.
 Bottom Edges	Bottom edge of the bottommost control.
 Vertical Centers	Vertical center of the selected controls.
 Horizontal Centers	Horizontal center of the selected controls.
 Center Vertically	Vertical center of the form.
 Center Horizontally	Horizontal center of the form.
Size	This option displays the Size submenu, which contains the following options to size selected controls: To Fit — Sizes the selected controls so that their labels will completely display. To Grid — Resizes the selected controls so that their edges are on alignment with the grid lines. (See View menu Snap to Grid option.)
 To Tallest	Changes the height of the selected controls to the same height as the tallest control.
Ctrl+  To Shortest	Changes the height of the selected controls to the same height as the shortest control.
 To Widest	Changes the width of the selected controls to the same width as the widest control.
Ctrl+  To Narrowest	Changes the width of the selected controls to the same width as the narrowest control.
 (No menu option)	Changes the size of the selected controls to the same size as the largest control.
Horizontal Spacing	This option lets you control the horizontal spacing between the selected controls. A drop-down menu provides you the option to increase, decrease, or make

Option	Description
	the horizontal space equal between two or more controls.
Vertical Spacing	This option lets you control the vertical spacing between the selected controls. A drop-down menu provides you the option to increase, decrease, or make the vertical space equal between two or more controls.
Bring to **F**ront	Choose this option and the selected control or controls move forward so that they cover other controls. This option is active only if one or more controls are selected.
Send to **B**ack	Choose this option and the selected control or controls move to the bottom of the Class Designer Layout window and are covered by other controls.
Snap to **G**rid	This option toggles the Snap to Grid mode on or off. When you move a control, it moves smoothly across the layout if this option is off. However, if it is on, the control jumps between the invisible alignment grid lines. The alignment grid is an invisible horizontal and vertical grid. When you move or define a control, it is automatically aligned to (or *snapped to*) the nearest grid line. The alignment grid corresponds to the ruler grid alignment set in the Grid Properties dialog box. A check mark appears to the left of the option when the alignment grid is on.
Set Grid Scale	This option changes the size of the cells in the invisible alignment grid used by the Snap to **G**rid option. Choose this option and the Grid Properties dialog box displays. You can specify the units of measurements for the rulers and grid lines or change the horizontal and vertical grid line spacing.

TIP

If the Snap to **G**rid mode is on, you can press the Ctrl key while you drag a control and the Snap to Grid mode is disabled. In other words, as long as you hold down the Ctrl key, the control drags smoothly across the Layout window.

The Form Menu

Figure 19.7 shows the Form Designer with the For**m** menu open. Table 19.3 describes each of the For**m** menu options.

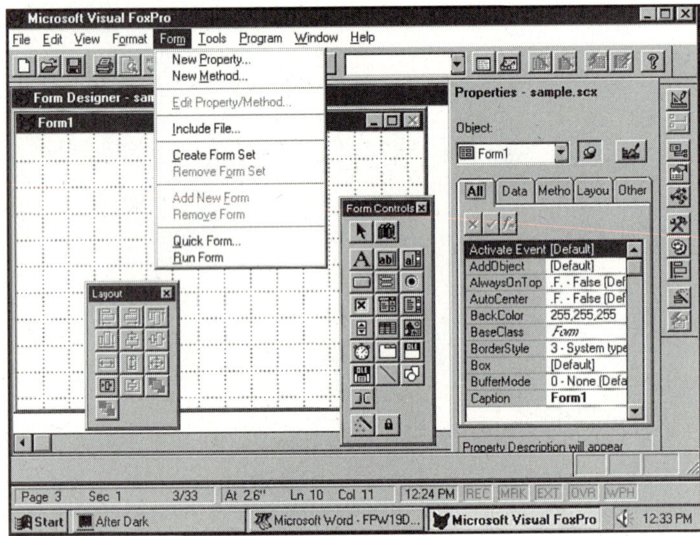

FIGURE 19.7.
The Form Designer with the Form menu open.

Table 19.3. The Form menu used with the Form Designer.

Option	*Description*
New **P**roperty...	This option displays the New Property dialog box so that you can specify a new property for a class and a description of that property. (See Figure 19.8.) You can also specify whether the property is protected. You can add an array property by adding its size and dimensions in the New Property dialog box. For example, you can create a two-dimensional property array with three rows and four columns by typing `MyArray[4,3]` in the Name box. Once you create a new property, it appears in the Property list and you can assign values to it. However, you can assign values to a property array only at runtime.
New **M**ethod...	This option displays the New Method window so that you can specify the name of a new method for a class and a description of that method. (See Figure 19.9.) You can also specify whether the method is

Option	*Description*
	protected. The new method appears in the Properties window with the description appearing at the bottom of the Properties window.
Edit Property/Method...	This option opens the Edit Property/Method dialog box. You can edit the name or description of an existing user-defined property or method.
Include File...	This option displays the Include File window. You can type the name of an include file or click on the three-dot browser button to select an existing include file from the Open File dialog box. Include files normally have an .H extension. The FOXPRO.H header file is an example of an include file.
Create Form Set	This option adds a form set class to the Form Layout window. A form set is a parent class to one or more form classes. You do not have to add a form set if you are working on only a single form. Of course, you can have only one form set.
Remove F**o**rm Set	This option removes a form set from the Form Designer form. You cannot remove a form set unless you only have one form object on the layout. If you have two or more form objects on the Form Layout window, this option is disabled.
Add New **F**orm	This option adds a new form object to the Form Layout window. When a form is initially created, it contains a single form object. Before you add more form objects, you must first create a form set class which is the parent class for the form object. This option is disabled until you create a form set.
Remo**v**e Form	With this option, you can remove a selected form object from the layout. This option is disabled unless you have more than one form on the layout.
Quick Form...	Executes the Form Builder to create a simple form, which you can customize by adding your own controls. The Quick Form... option is discussed in the following section.
Run Form	This option saves the form, exits from the Form Designer, and executes the newly created or modified form. You can also use the Run (!) button on the standard toolbar.

NOTE

Consider this scenario. You have designed a really terrific form and you need a subform. You choose the Create Form Set option to generate a form set. Then you add the new form. There is one drawback. When you add a form set, any existing user-defined properties or methods are deleted. The solution is to manually save the user-defined methods in a program or other text file. List out your user-defined properties. Then add them back to the form set object once you have created it.

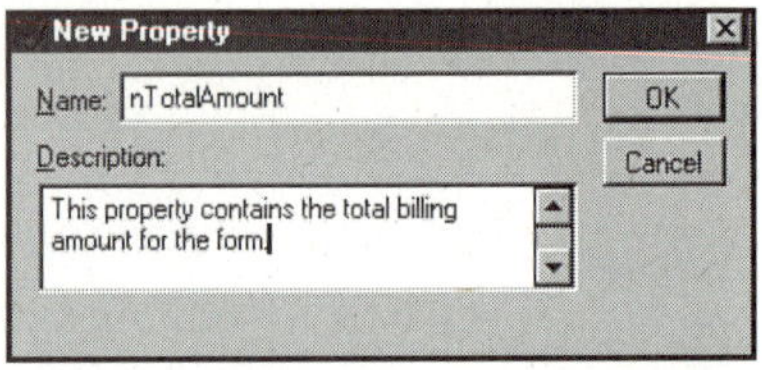

FIGURE 19.8.
The New Property dialog box.

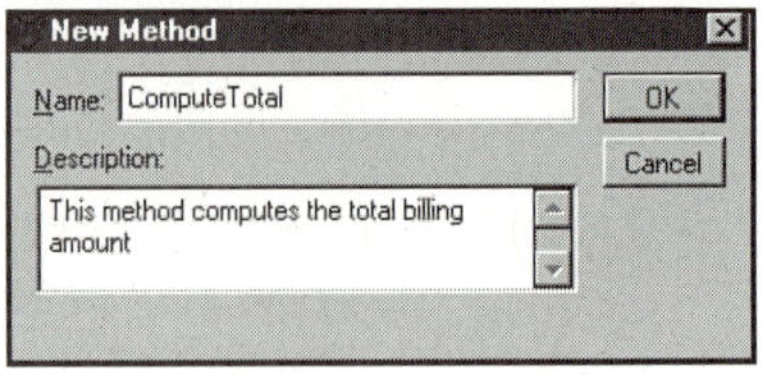

FIGURE 19.9.
The New Method dialog box.

Builders

Visual FoxPro provides tools, called builders, that help you define the options for controls. A *builder* is a tabbed dialog box that leads you through the process of defining the properties for creating and modifying complex controls with a series of tabs. The For**m** menu **Q**uick Form option executes the Form Builder. In addition, you can execute the Form Builder and any other builder using any of the following three techniques:

- You can click the Builder button in the Properties window when a control is selected on the form.
- You can click the Builder Lock button on the Form Controls toolbar. Each time you add a new control to a form, Visual FoxPro displays the appropriate builder.
- You can click the form or a control with the right mouse button to display a shortcut menu. Choose the Builder option.

NOTE

Most of the Visual FoxPro builders let you re-enter the builder to modify previously established settings. This is one feature that Visual FoxPro supports that other products do not support. Builders in other products usually destroy previously established settings when you reenter the builder.

Regardless of the manner in which you execute a builder, the builder's tabbed dialog box displays. You select the options for each tab and then click the OK button to apply the changes.

The Form Builder helps you build a form containing fields. Its tabbed dialog box is shown in Figure 19.10. From the Field Selection tab, you first choose a table and then choose a field to display on the form.

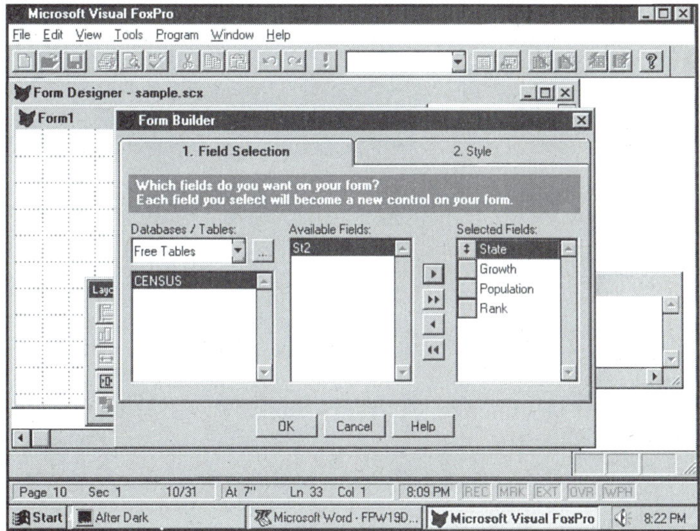

FIGURE 19.10.
The Form Builder dialog box with the Field Selection tab selected.

Next, you select the Style tab and choose a style for the fields in your form, as shown in Figure 19.11. Click on the OK button, and the fields are added to the form. An example form is shown in Figure 19.12.

After you have created an initial form containing fields, you can add any other controls you need, rearrange fields, and perform any other modifications you need to complete your custom form. Each field placed on the screen is actually a container class containing a label object, a text box object, and maybe a shape object. If you want to change the caption, width, or any other property of a display field, choose the label or text box object to be changed from the Options drop-down list on the Properties window. You can also right-click on the container and choose the Edit option. Click on the control and make the appropriate changes.

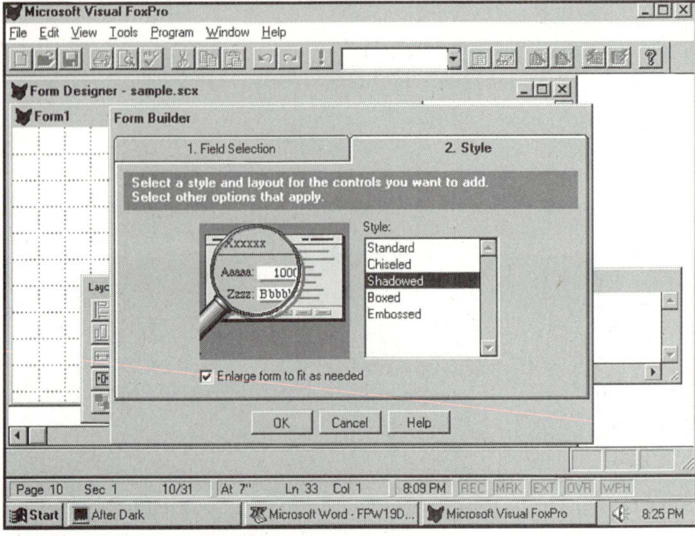

FIGURE 19.11.
The Form Builder dialog box with the Style tab selected.

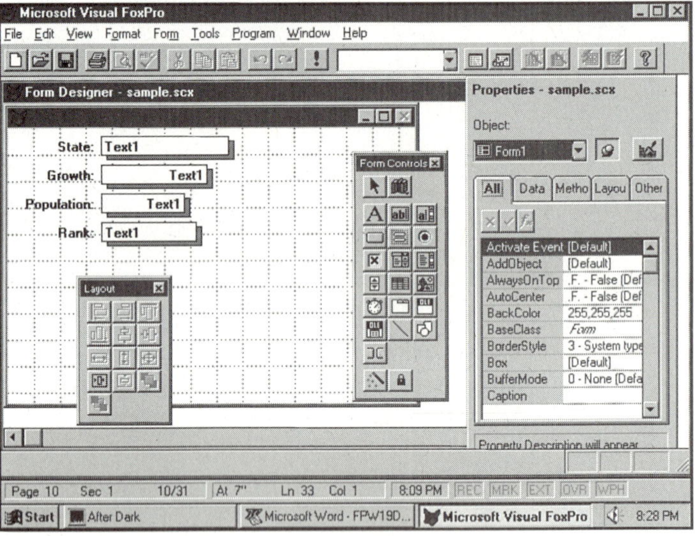

FIGURE 19.12.
A sample form created with the Form Builder.

The bottom button on the vertically displayed Form Designer toolbar to the right of the screen in Figure 19.13 is the AutoFormat Builder button. If you click on it, the AutoFormat Builder displays, as shown in Figure 19.13. You can use this builder to change the appearance of the selected control or controls by selecting the Embossed, Standard, or Professional style from Style list box. When you choose a style, the sample form to the left of the list displays various types of controls in the selected style. This builder automatically establishes the values of some, if not all, of the following properties of the selected control or controls related to the style you select:

```
Alignment          BackColor          BorderStyle
FontBold           FontItalic         FontName
FontSize           FontUnderline      ForeColor
SpecialEffect
```

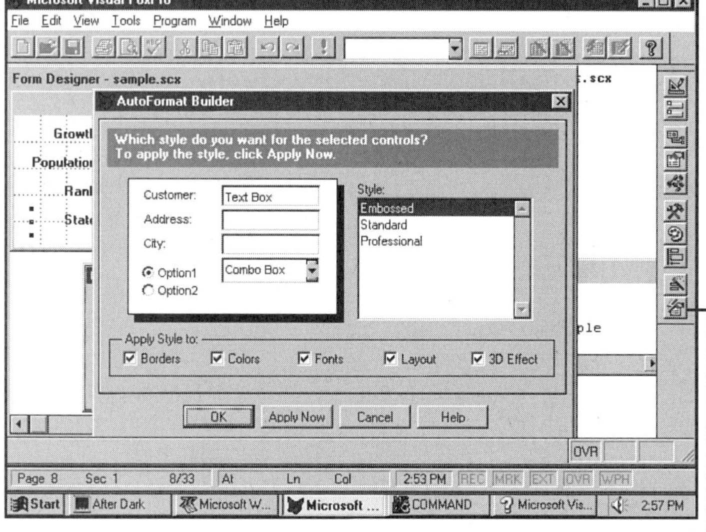

AutoFormat Builder

FIGURE 19.13.
The AutoFormat Builder.

The Form Controls Toolbar

You can place controls on the Form Designer Layout window using the Form Controls toolbar. You click on the control you want, click some place on the Layout window, and the control is deposited. You drag the control to the size you want. The toolbar is shown in Figure 19.14. The buttons on the toolbar are defined in Table 19.4.

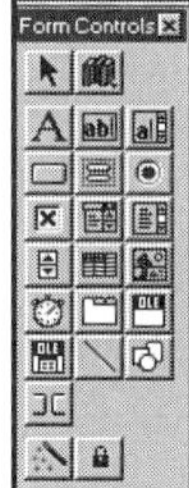

FIGURE 19.14.
The Form Controls toolbar.

Table 19.4. A description of the options on the Form Controls toolbar.

Button	*Description*
Select objects	This mouse pointer control resizes and moves controls. When you create a control, the select objects button is automatically reselected, unless the button lock button is pressed down, in which case, you can keep placing the selected control.
View classes	This button brings up a menu from which you select and display a registered VCX visual class library. After you select a class, the buttons display on the toolbar; they represent classes in the selected visual class library. You can drag and drop the class objects just as you do with other controls. However, the selected class cannot be added to container objects on the form, such as grids and page frames. If you want to add the selected class to a container on the form, simply drag and drop the class picture to an area on the form and then use cut and paste to move the object to the desired container.
Label control	You use the label control to display static text, which cannot be changed by the user. It is used as a caption for the other controls.
Text box control	The text box control holds a single line of text. The user can enter new text or change existing text in the text box.
Edit box control	The edit box control contains one or more lines of text. The user can enter new text or change existing text in the text box.
Command button control	The command button control is used to carry out an operation.
Command button group control	A command button group is a group of command buttons from which the user can choose to perform an operation.
Option button group control	The option button group, or radio buttons, displays multiple options. The user can select only one of the option buttons.

Button	*Description*
Check box control	A check box control displays a box, which the user can select or clear to indicate if something is true or false. In addition, the user can use a check box as a latched command button by setting its `Style` property from `0` (standard) to `1` (graphical).
Combo box control	A combo box control is either a drop-down combo box or a drop-down list box control. In either form, the user can select one item from a list of items. If it is a drop-down combo box, the user can manually enter a value in the text box.
List box control	A list box control displays a list of items from which the user can select an item. You can scroll the list if it contains more items than can be displayed at one time.
Spinner control	A spinner control contains numeric input that falls within a given range. You can click on the arrows to increase or decrease its value or you can enter a number manually.
Grid control	A grid container control is a spreadsheet-type control similar to a Browse window. A grid control contains column controls, which in turn contain header controls and any other type of control.
Image control	An image control displays a graphical bitmap (BMP) image on your form.
Timer control	The timer control is used to trap timer events at set intervals. This control is invisible at runtime.
PageFrame control	A page frame control displays multiple, usually tabbed pages containing controls.
OLE control	An OLE control provides object linking and embedding (OLE) from an OLE server for your application. See Chapter 17, "OLE, OLE 2.0 Controls, DDE, and Operating System Interfaces."
OLE bound control	An OLE bound control provides OLE support. However, it is bound to a General data type field in a table. See Chapter 17.

continues

Table 19.4. continued

Button	Description
Line control	The line control draws vertical, horizontal, or diagonal line styles at design time.
Shape control	The shape control draws a variety of shapes on your form at design time. You can draw a rectangle, rounded rectangle, square, rounded square, oval, or circle.
Separator control	The separator control is used to create an object that places space between controls in a toolbar.
Builder lock	You use the builder lock button to specify whether you want to use a builder when you add a control to the form. When you press down the builder lock button, a control-specific builder opens whenever you add a new control to your form. Builders assist you in specifying properties for controls.
Button lock	If you click on the button lock button, it toggles the button lock mode on and off. When the button mode is on, you can add multiple controls of the same type without having to click the control button on the toolbar each time you add a control. You can turn the button mode on also by double-clicking on a control button.

Adding Controls to a Form

As described in the previous section, you add controls to the Form Designer Layout window by clicking on a control button in the Form Controls toolbar and then clicking some place on the form in the Form Designer window to deposit the control. You can drag the control to the size you want. Next, you drag the control to the desired position on the layout.

TIP

Once an object is selected, little *handles* appear on the sides of the object. You can click on one of the handles and resize the control by dragging the handle to either compress or stretch the control. You can click anywhere on the selected control and drag it to a new location on the screen. This method of sizing and positioning is good for gross operations especially if the Snap to Grid option is on. Another alternative that I use is to select the control (or selected group of controls) and use the control keys to move it one pixel at a time. You can also resize the controls one pixel at a time. You can make the control any of the following options:

- Shorter by pressing Shift+↑
- Taller by pressing Shift+↓
- Narrower by pressing Shift+←
- Wider by pressing Shift+→

Placing a control on the form and sizing it is the easy part. Some of the controls, such as a label, line, and shape objects, are not bound to a table value and normally require you to add any code to process. However, you usually need to establish properties. At the very least, you need to change the `Caption` property for a label. However, you can change the background color (`BackColor`), font type, size, style, and so on. You can click on the Form Designer toolbar AutoFormat Builder button to help you establish properties.

To establish a value for a property manually, you select one of the properties named in the tabbed list in the Properties window. The interface elements of the Properties window are described in the next section. The selected value also appears in the Properties Setting box above the property tabs. For some properties, you can choose one of several values. For example, the `Alignment` property has the following three values:

```
0 - Left
1 - Center
2 - Right
```

You can choose one of these three values from the Properties Setting drop-down list box, or each time you double-click on the property you want to change, it toggles through its options.

Some properties, such as the `BackColor` and `ForeColor` properties, have a *Browser box* (a box with three dots on it) that brings up a dialog box, such as the Colors dialog box. You choose a color, and the color is set. For other properties, you just enter a value or use the Expression Builder to designate a value or expression.

TIP

The easiest way to set the background or foreground colors for a control is to use the Color Palette toolbar as shown in Figure 9.4. Select a control. Then, on the Color Palette toolbar, click on either the Foreground Color or Background Color buttons, and click on the color of your choice. The Foreground Color and Background Color buttons stay pressed until you click on them again.

The Expression Builder activates if you click on the button labeled f_x. The Expression Builder is especially useful for specifying expressions involving constants, variables, and table field values.

Controls that require you to specify table field names to properties, such as `ControlSource` property, have a drop-down list of fields attached to the Properties Settings box if you have already established a data environment. The `ControlSource` property defines a field that is bound to a control. You link a control to its control source. This property tells the control what data to display and possibly where to store the data. For example, if you bind a table field to a text box, the text box displays the value of the field. If the user changes data in the field, the modified value is stored in the table field.

For many types of controls, you will need to add code to support events. For example, you usually need to provide code for the `Click` event for the command buttons. When the user clicks on a command button, the `Click` event method executes.

To add code for methods, you double-click on the control in the Form Designer Layout window. (You can also activate the Code window by choosing the **V**iew menu **C**ode option.) The Code window appears, and you enter the event code. There are two combo box controls on the Code window. One of the combo boxes contains the events and methods for the method code shown in the Code window. The other combo box contains a hierarchical list of the names of the classes for the form set, form, and controls which correspond to the code in the Code window. An example of a Code window is shown in Figure 19.15. The code in the window is for the `Click` event for a command button.

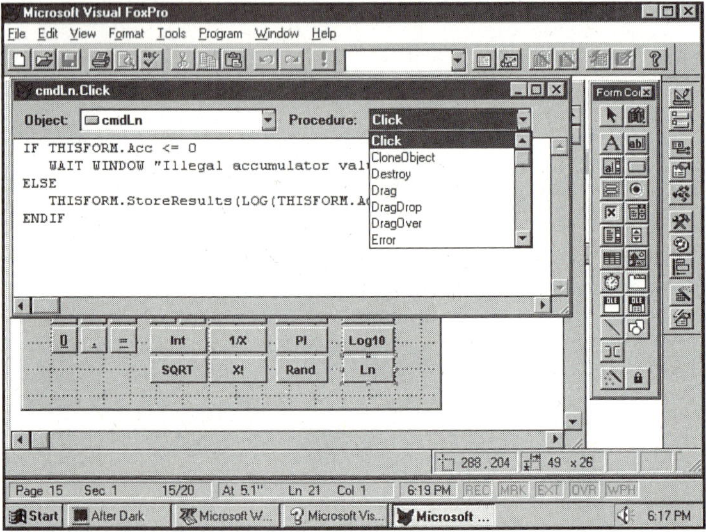

FIGURE 19.15.
The Code window.

The Properties Window

The Properties window is a tool you use to establish the values of a selected form or control. It contains the list of all of the properties and property settings for a selected form or control. You set these properties when you design a form or control. You can also set these properties programmatically.

To establish a property value, you must first open the Properties window. There are a few ways of doing this:

- Choose the **V**iew menu **P**roperties Window option
- Right-click on a control or form and choose the Properties option from the shortcut menu

> **TIP**
>
> You right-click (click with the right mouse button) on an object to open the shortcut menu. Just about every object and element in the Visual FoxPro designers has a shortcut menu with options relevant to the particular object or element. Just for fun, try right-clicking on every object to see what options are available.

- Click on the Properties Window button on the Form Designer toolbar

Once the Properties window is open, it remains open until you close it.

The Properties window components are discussed in the following subsections and are summarized in Table 19.5.

Table 19.5. A summary of the Properties window components.

Element	*Use*
Object: Object list box	Displays and selects control, form, or form set objects.
Push pin button	Controls the properties display state.
Builder button	Runs the builder associated with selected control or form.

continues

Table 19.5. continued

Element	*Use*
All Data Metho Layou Other Tabs	Displays the properties by category for selected control on the form.
All tab	Displays all properties and events.
Data tab	Displays properties related to data binding and related options.
Methods tabs	Displays methods, properties, and associated values. You can double-click an a method, and the Code window appears.
Layout tab	Displays all layout properties and associated values.
Other tab	Displays miscellaneous properties and associated values, including user-defined properties.
Form1 Property Settings box	Allows you to change a value of a property.
Property list	A two-column list with the property names on left and the associated values on the right.
Description panel	Contains text describing the selected property.

The Object List Box

The Object list box contains the name of the currently selected form or control. You click on the arrow to activate the drop-down list. The drop-down list includes a hierarchical list of the current form sets or forms, and all other controls on the form. You can select another form or control on the form. Then you can change the properties for the currently selected form or control.

The Push pin Button

The push pin button toggles on and off the Display on Top mode for the Properties window. When the button is pressed down, which is the default state, the Properties window always remains on top of the other windows, even if the other windows are active. The Properties window does not remain on top if the push pin button is toggled off.

The Builder Button

The Builder button runs the builder associated with the selected control. The builder is a tabbed dialog box that helps you establish values for properties. See the section"Builders" for more information.

The Property Settings Box

You use the Property Settings box to change the value of the property selected in the Property list box. Some of the properties have a set of predefined values. For these, a drop-down arrow appears at the right of the combo box. You click on this arrow and the available values appear. You can also double-click on any property that has multiple selections to change its value. For example, if a property has a true (`.T.`) and false (`.F.`) option, double-clicking on the property will toggle the property setting between `.T.` and `.F.`.

For other types of properties, you are required to enter a value. You can type a value into the Settings box or use the Expression Builder to specify the value or expression for a property.

If the property requires a Character type field (for example, the `Caption` property), you do not need to enclose the value in quotation marks. You can simply type the value into the Property Settings box. For example, if you want the caption to say OK, then simply type `OK`. If you add quotation marks, they will appear in the caption. If you use quote marks, then precede the text with an equal sign (for example, `="OK"`).

The Expression Builder is very useful for establishing a valid expression. It prevents typographic errors. It is especially useful when you specify properties, such as `ControlSource`, that bind a table or cursor field to a property. You execute the Expression Builder by pressing the function button (f_x); the Expression Builder dialog box appears, as shown in Figure 19.16.

FIGURE 19.16.
The Expression Builder.

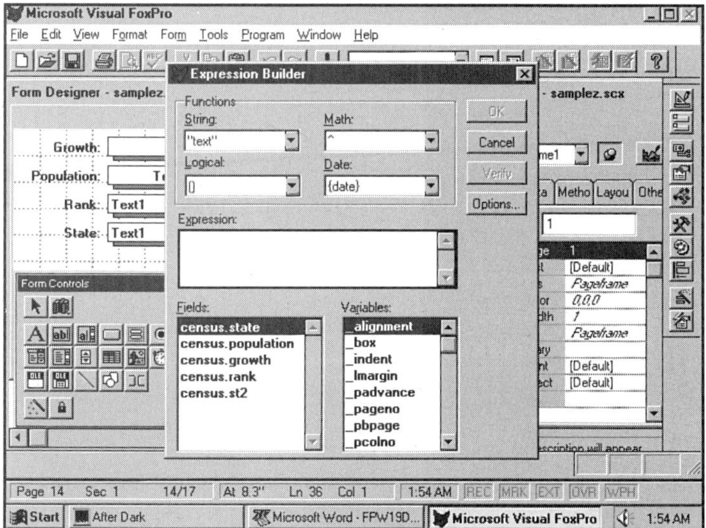

You can use the Expression Builder to specify an expression. You can also specify an expression in the Property Settings box. To do so, you type an equal sign (=) followed by the expression. For example, if you want the `Caption` of a form to be the name of the table in the current work area, type `=DBF()` into the Property Settings box.

When you assign an expression to a property, the expression is evaluated at design time to see if it is valid and at runtime when the object is initialized. If you want to modify a value, you have to do it explicitly (for example, you will need to add code to a method that changes), Suppose that you want to place another table in use when you click on a control button. The `Click` event method might contain the following code:

```
* Click Event method for "Get new Table" control button
ThisForm.TableName=GETFILE("DBF")
USE (ThisForm.TableName)
THISFORM.Caption = THISFORM.TableName
```

The Property List

The Property list is a two-column list. The left column shows property names and the right column shows the current values. The properties in the list are all the properties that can be changed for a selected form or control at design time. There can be other properties for a control, but the other properties can be set only at runtime (that is, when the form displays).

If a property has two predefined choices, such as true (`.T.`) and false (`.F.`), you can toggle between the choices by double-clicking on the property.

You can right-click on a property in the Property list, and a shortcut menu appears. You have the option to return the value of the selected property to its default. The shortcut also contains an option to display the Help menu for the property. This puts help just two clicks away.

Selecting a Control

When you want to move or alter a control on the design screen, you must first select that control. Controls can be selected in several ways, but before you start, be sure that the selection pointer is selected. The selection pointer is selected when the mouse pointer is shaped like an arrow pointing up and to the left. You can choose any of the following methods for selecting controls:

- Click on a control to select the one control
- Press the Shift key when you click on multiple controls to select them
- Drag the *selection marquee* around several controls to select them

NOTE

A *marquee* is a rectangle formed by pointing the mouse pointer to an unoccupied point (anchor) on the design screen. Then you press the left mouse button, hold it down, and drag the cursor to a new location. The rectangle appears on the screen with one corner at the anchor and the opposite corner at the mouse pointer. When you release the left mouse button, the controls inside the rectangle are selected.

After a control is selected, you can resize it, move it, delete it with the Delete key, or modify one of its properties from the Properties window.

Selecting a contained object is a little bit harder. For example, you can select a page of a page frame by performing the following steps:

1. Select a page frame.
2. From the Objects combo box in Properties window, select a page, as shown in Figure 19.17. When you select a page object, the green hash-type border surrounding the page frame appears.

FIGURE 19.17.
Selecting a page of a page frame.

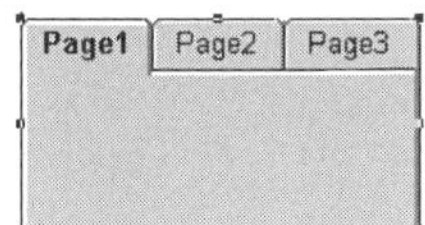

3. Now you can click on any of the pages to select them. (See Figure 19.17A.)

FIGURE 19.17A.
The selected page is indicated by thick border surrounding the page frame.

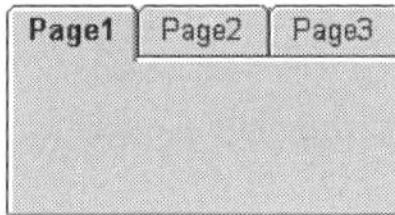

4. Perform operations on the selected page (for example, setting properties, modifying methods, and adding or modifying controls).

Similar steps are required to select a Column object contained by a Grid object.

TIP

The easy way to select an object in a container is to right-click on the container and choose the Edit option from the shortcut menu. When the green border appears, click on the object in the container to select it.

Creating and Editing Event and Method Code

Programmers are not always the best form designers. There are people who never have programmed a line of code who specialize in designing screen layouts. Sometimes, the people who use a form are best qualified to designate what goes on the form, where the form is used, and in what order the data is input. The FoxPro Form Designer is easy for the nonprogrammer to use. It usually takes a programmer, however, to make the form work by writing the appropriate event and method code. Therefore, the screen design can be a cooperative effort involving programmers, interface designers, and users.

To review, events are either user or system actions. Examples of user actions are a mouse click, a modified text box field, and mouse movement. An example of system action is a timer expiration. Methods are procedures that are executed programmatically and perform some task that relates to an object (control or form). For example, list box controls have methods named `AddItem`, `RemoveItem`, and `Clear` that are used for maintaining the contents of a list box control.

How to Use the Code Window

When you want to create or modify events or method code, you activate the Code window using one of the following methods:

- Double-click on a control or form on the Form Designer Layout screen
- Select a control and choose the **V**iew menu **C**ode option
- Select a control and click on the Code Window button on the Form Designer toolbar
- Double-click on the method in the Properties menu
- Right-click on the control and choose the Code... option from the shortcut menu

When the Code window appears, as shown in Figure 19.18, you can start writing the code you want to be executed when the event occurs or the method is called.

In the example shown in Figure 19.18, the Exit command button `Click` event code saves the results in the Windows Clipboard and then releases the form from memory with the following command:

```
RELEASE THISFORM
```

If you want to clear the form from the screen but retain it in memory, you execute the following command instead of the `RELEASE` command:

```
THISFORM.Hide
```

FIGURE 19.18.
The Code window showing the `Click` event for Exit button.

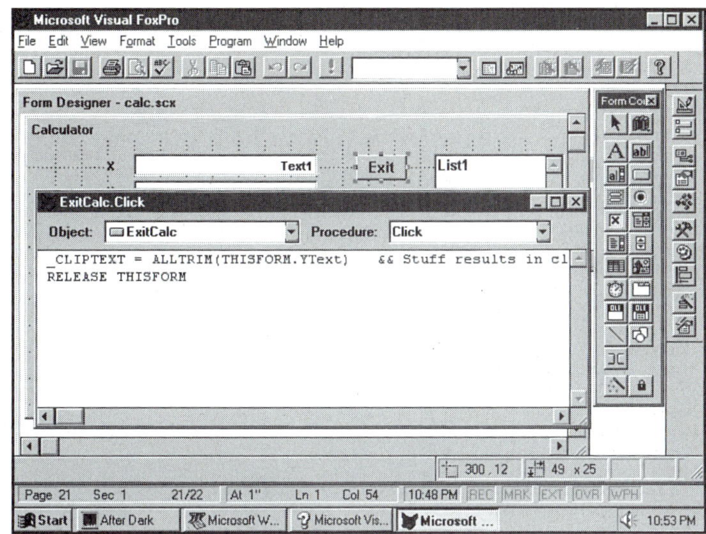

You can move to another event or method procedure by selecting a different event or method from the Procedure box. You can also move between the procedures with the PgUp and PgDn keys. You can edit event or method code for another form or control by selecting another one from the Object box.

Referencing Properties at Runtime

You have considerable latitude in writing code that assigns values to properties at runtime. You can reference properties in one control from another control. To do this, you reference an object in relationship to its container hierarchy. For example, suppose that you have a form set with two forms, `frmInvoice` and `frmNavigate`. Suppose that you want to enable the `cmdBottom` button in the `frmNavigate` form from the `Init` event method in the `frmInvoice` form. Remember that a property is referenced by specifying its object's parent objects, the object, and the property separated by periods. You add the following statement to the `frmInvoice` form's `Init` event code:

```
THISFORMSET.frmNavigate.cmdBottom.Enabled = .T.
```

With this command, the `cmdButton` command button `Enable` method is called. Here is the general syntax for referencing a property or method for an object in the Visual FoxPro container hierarchy:

```
[formset.][form.]control.property = <exp>
[formset.][form.]control.method[(<expression list>)]
```

Table 19.6 lists the properties or keywords you can use to reference an object in its container hierarchy.

Table 19.6. Keywords for referencing objects in a container hierarchy.

Keyword	*Object Referenced*
`ActiveControl`	The control that has focus in the currently active form
`ActiveForm`	The active form
`ActivePage`	The active page on the currently active form
`Parent`	The immediate container of an object
`THIS`	The object, or a procedure or event
`THISFORM`	The form that contains the object
`THISFORMSET`	The form set that contains the object

You can use these keywords to simplify the referencing of properties and methods. For example, code in the `Init` event method to set the `Caption` property can be the following:

```
frmNavigate.cmdTop.Caption = "Top"
```

A simplified form of the same reference using the referencing keywords is this:

```
THIS.Caption = "Top"
```

If you have many references to properties and events, you can use the `WITH...ENDWITH` control structure to further simplify the referencing of properties and events. Here is an example:

```
WITH THISFORMSET.frmNavigate.cmdTop
    .Caption = "Top"
    .FontSize = 8
    .ForeColor = COLOR_BLACK
    .BackColor = COLOR_GRAY
    .SelectOnEntry = .T.
    .Enable
    .SetFocus
ENDWITH
```

In this example, constants defined in the FOXPRO.H include file are used to define colors. You choose the For**m** menu **I**nclude File... option to specify the name of an include file used with the form. Once an include file is specified, you can use any of the constants defined in the file. Listing 19.1 shows the color definitions extracted from the FOXPRO.H include file.

Listing 19.1. The color constants extracted from the FOXPRO.H include file.

```
#DEFINE COLOR_WHITE        16777215
#DEFINE COLOR_BLACK               0
#DEFINE COLOR_GRAY         12632256
#DEFINE COLOR_DARK_GRAY     8421504
```

```
#DEFINE COLOR_RED                255
#DEFINE COLOR_DARK_BLUE      8388608
#DEFINE COLOR_CYAN          16776960
#DEFINE COLOR_DARK_CYAN      8421376
#DEFINE COLOR_GREEN            65280
#DEFINE COLOR_DARK_GREEN       32768
#DEFINE COLOR_YELLOW           65535
#DEFINE COLOR_DARK_YELLOW      32896
#DEFINE COLOR_BLUE          16711680
#DEFINE COLOR_DARK_RED           128
#DEFINE COLOR_MAGENTA       16711935
#DEFINE COLOR_DARK_MAGENTA   8388736
```

The Scientific Calculator Example Form

The simple scientific calculator program presented in Chapter 5, "Expressions," illustrates how to use the functions and expressions in Visual FoxPro. It used traditional FoxPro 2.*x* language elements. Now, a new version of the scientific calculator, as shown in Figure 19.19, will be created using the Form Designer. You will be provided a step-by-step process for creating the calculator form. This version takes full advantage of the Visual FoxPro event model because it is created with the Visual FoxPro Form Designer.

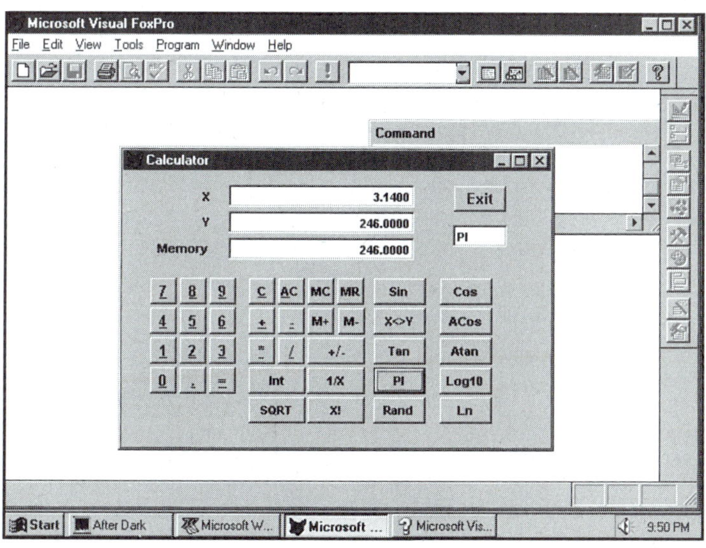

FIGURE 19.19.
The Calculator window created with the Visual FoxPro Form Designer.

To begin, execute the Form Designer. As you know, there are a number of ways to execute the Form Designer. For example, you could execute the Form Designer from the Command window with the following command:

```
CREATE FORM Calc
```

The Form Designer window displays, as shown in Figure 19.1. The calculator designed in this section contains many buttons. I approached this problem by first defining the button for the number 1, named `cmdOne`. Then I pressed Ctrl+C to copy the `cmdOne` control to the Windows Clipboard. Next, I pasted the Clipboard (press Ctrl+V) as many times as required to define all of the number buttons. But first, here are the steps for defining the Form and `cmdOne` button properties and methods:

1. Click on the form and set the following properties in the Properties window for the form:

Property	*Setting*	*Description*
`AutoCenter`	`.T.`	Double-click on property
`BackColor`	`192,192,192`	Click on the browser button and choose light gray from the color palette or use the Color Palette toolbar
`Caption`	`"Calculator"`	Specify the title bar caption
`FontSize`	`8`	Pick from a list of font sizes in the Property Settings box

TIP

The `AutoCenter` property designates whether the form is centered in the Visual FoxPro main window. When the Form Designer executes to edit a dialog box with the setting `AutoCenter=.T.`, the form is initially positioned way to the right and toward the bottom of the Form Designer. You have to click on it and drag it to where you can work with it. To keep this from happening during the development process, you can set `AutoCenter=.F.`. Then it will always be positioned in the upper-left corner of the Form Designer Layout window when the Form Designer executes to modify the form. When you are finished with the development process, you can set `AutoCenter=.T.` again. An alternative is to place the `AutoCenter=.T.` command in the `Init` event method of the form.

2. You will need some variables for the calculator. You create them as user-defined properties. To do this, you choose the For**m** menu New **P**roperty option. After you have added them, assign an initial value to them from the Properties window. The following list shows the variables and their initial settings:

User-Defined Property	*Setting*
`decimal`	`0`
`acc`	`0`
`number`	`0`

```
results                 0
memory                  0
xtext                   =("")
ytext                   =("")
mtext                   =("")
oldoperand              =("+")
```

3. Using the For**m** menu Add New **M**ethod option, you can add the following new user-defined method names: `MemCalc`, `StoreResults`, `StoreAcc`, `ClearAcc`, `Clear`, `Evaluate`, `ShowCalc`, and `vNumber`.

NOTE

In the Visual FoxPro Form Designer, user-defined properties and methods are always added to the top-level container class. If you have a form set, the user-defined properties and methods become members of the form set class. If the form consists of a single form (and no form set), the user-defined properties and methods become members of the form class.

4. Double-click on the form, and the Code window appears. Add code from Listing 19.2 to each of the new user-defined methods added in Step 3. You can use the Procedures box to select the name of the method for which code is added. Do not add the `PROCEDURE` and `ENDPROC` statements. They are automatically added by Visual FoxPro. When you have added the code, press Ctrl+W to close the Code window and save the changes.

NOTE

When you move from one event or method procedure to another in the Code window or when you close the Code window, Visual FoxPro compiles the procedure. If an error is detected, Visual FoxPro displays an error box. You are given the choice of fixing the error or ignoring it. If you elect to fix the error, the Code window remains open so that you can fix the error.

5. Click on the Command Button control button in the Control Layout toolbar. Then click on the Layout form. The button is deposited.
6. Size the button to 26 by 26 pixels.
7. From the Properties window, set the following properties for the `cmdOne` Control Button window:

Property	*Setting*
`Caption`	`\<1`
`Name`	`cmdOne`

8. Double-click on the `cmdOne` command button, and the Code window opens. It is positioned on the `Click` event method. You add the following code (which is shown in Figure 19.20):

```
THISFORM.VNumber(1)
```

Now, use the Ctrl+W key combination to exit the Code window.

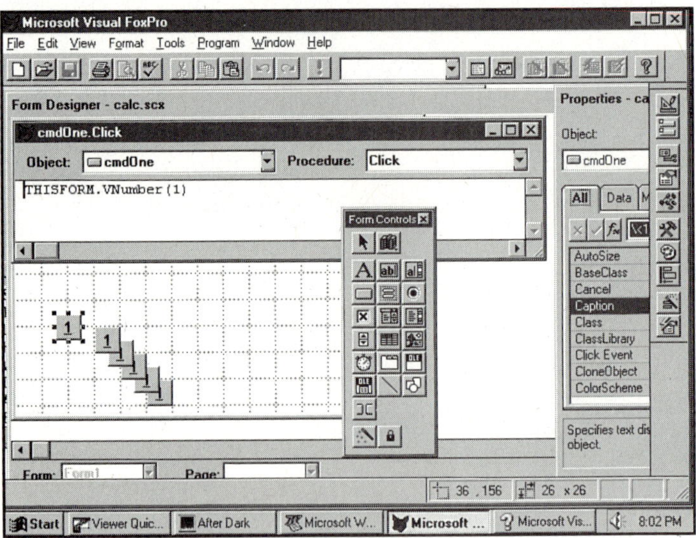

FIGURE 19.20.
The Form Designer, with the Code window showing the `Click` event method for a command button.

9. The `cmdOne` command button is still selected. Press Ctrl+C (or use the **E**dit menu **C**opy option) to copy `cmdOne` to the Clipboard. Next, press Ctrl+V repeatedly, as shown in Figure 19.20, until you have created all 22 of the square buttons you need for the calculator.
10. Paste one more button on the form and stretch it to 55 by 26 pixels. (The size and position of the selected controls are shown on the status bar of the Form Designer.) Copy this button to the Clipboard by pressing Ctrl+V. You will need to paste five of these buttons on the form. In a similar manner, make 11 buttons that are 49 pixels wide and 26 pixels high.
11. Now, drag all of the buttons to the positions shown in Figure 19.21. You can use the Alignment toolbar buttons to assist you in lining up the buttons.

FIGURE 19.21.
The Form Designer with the Calculator form.

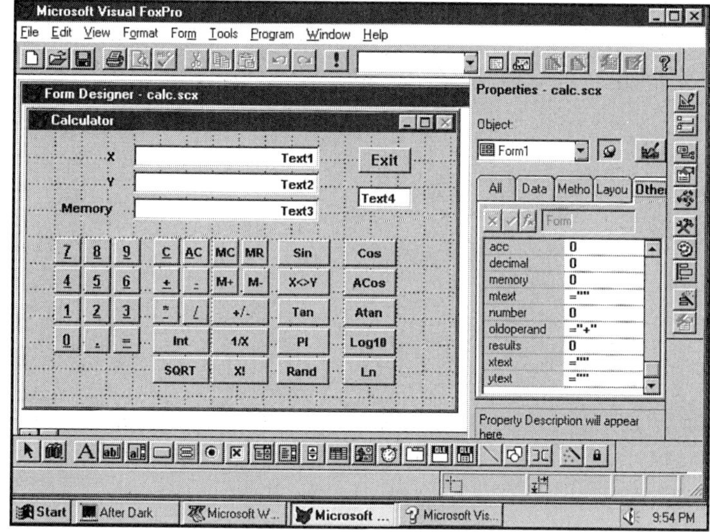

12. From the Properties window, set the `Caption` and `Name` properties for each button as shown in Table 19.7.
13. Add the `Click` event code for all of the buttons as shown in Table 19.7. You can use the Code window Object box to move from the `Click` event procedures for one button to the `Click` event procedures for another button.
14. Add the three label controls, `X`, `Y`, and `Memory`, to the form as shown in Figure 19.21. The `Caption` property for a label control defines the static text. The `FontSize` property for all three label controls is set to `8`. The `BackColor` property for the label controls is set to light gray: `RGB(192,192,192)`.
15. Add the four text box controls to the form as shown in Figure 19.21. The following three properties have common values for all four text controls:

```
FontSize = 8
Alignment = 1
ReadOnly = .T.
```

16. Three of the text box controls are bound to the values of user-defined properties. As a consequence, you set the `ControlSource` property of the `X`, `Y`, and `Memory` text box controls to the following values:

```
ControlSource = "THISFORM.XText"
ControlSource = "THISFORM.YTEXT"
ControlSource = "THISFORM.MText"
```

Listing 19.2 presents the user-defined methods for the Calculator form.

Listing 19.2. User-defined methods for the Calculator form.

```
PROCEDURE vnumber
  PARAMETER Number
  IF THIS.Decimal = 0
     THIS.Acc = THIS.Acc * 10 + Number
  ELSE
     THIS.Acc = THIS.Acc + THIS.Decimal*Number
     THIS.Decimal = THIS.Decimal/10.0
  ENDIF
  THIS.ShowCalc(LTRIM(STR(Number)))
ENDPROC

PROCEDURE showcalc
#DEFINE NFORMAT  "@Z 9999,999,999,999.9999"
  PARAMETER Comment
  THIS.XText =TRANSFORM(THIS.ACC, NFORMAT)
  THIS.YText =TRANSFORM(THIS.Results, NFORMAT)
  THIS.MText =TRANSFORM(THIS.Memory, NFORMAT)
  THIS.Text4.Value = Comment
  THISFORM.Refresh
ENDPROC

PROCEDURE evaluate
  PARAMETER OP   && Operand (+, -, *, /, = )
  THIS.Results = EVALUATE("THIS.Results "+ THIS.OldOperand + " THIS.Acc ")
  IF OP = "="
    THIS.ClearAcc(OP)
    THIS.ShowCalc(OP)
    THIS.OldOperand = "+"
  ELSE
    THIS.ShowCalc(OP)
    THIS.ClearAcc(OP)
    THIS.OldOperand = OP
  ENDIF
ENDPROC

PROCEDURE Clear
  ******************************************************
  * Form1.Clear - Clears accumulator (X) and Results (Y)
  PARAMETER OP
  THISFORM.Acc     = 0  && Clear accumulator
  THISFORM.Decimal = 0  && Reset decimal point
  THISFORM.Results = 0  && Clear Y
  THISFORM.OldOperand = "+"  && Reset operand
  THISFORM.ShowCalc(OP)
ENDPROC

PROCEDURE clearacc
  **********************************************
  * Form1.Clearacc - Clears accumulator (X)
  PARAMETER OP
  THISFORM.Acc     = 0  && Clear accumulator
  THISFORM.Decimal = 0  && Reset decimal point
  THISFORM.ShowCalc(OP)
ENDPROC
```

```
PROCEDURE storeacc
  *****************************************
  * Store value in accumulator
  PARAMETER nValue, OP
  THIS.Acc = nValue
  THIS.ShowCalc(OP)
  THISFORM.OldOperand = "+"
ENDPROC

PROCEDURE memcalc
  PARAMETER MOP
  THIS.Memory = EVALUATE("THIS.Memory "+ MOP + " THIS.Results ")
  THIS.OldOperand = "+"
  THIS.ShowCalc("M"+MOP)
ENDPROC

PROCEDURE storeresults
  *****************************************
  * Store value in Results field
  PARAMETER nValue, OP
  THIS.Results = nValue
  THIS.ClearAcc(OP)
ENDPROC
```

Table 19.7 presents the properties and methods for the Calculator form.

Table 19.7. The properties and methods for the calculator buttons.

Name Property	*Caption Property*	`Click` *Event Method*
cmdZero	"\<0"	THISFORM.VNumber(0)
cmdOne	"\<1"	THISFORM.VNumber(1)
cmdTwo	"\<2"	THISFORM.VNumber(2)
cmdThree	"\<3"	THISFORM.VNumber(3)
cmdFour	"\<4"	THISFORM.VNumber(4)
cmdFive	"\<5"	THISFORM.VNumber(5)
cmdSix	"\<6"	THISFORM.VNumber(6)
cmdSeven	"\<7"	THISFORM.VNumber(7)
cmdEight	"\<8"	THISFORM.VNumber(8)
cmdNine	"\<9"	THISFORM.VNumber(9)
cmdDecimal	"\<."	IF THISFORM.Decimal = 0
		THISFORM.Decimal = .1
		THISFORM.OldOperand = "+"

continues

Table 19.7. continued

Name Property	*Caption Property*	`Click` *Event Method*
		ELSE
		?? CHR(7)
		ENDIF
cmdEquals	"\<="	THISFORM.Evaluate("=")
cmdClear	"\<C"	THISFORM.Clear("C")
cmdAccClear	"\<AC"	THISFORM.ClearAcc("A") && Clear acc
cmdPlus	"\<+"	THISFORM.Evaluate("+")
cmdMinus	"\<-"	THISFORM.Evaluate("-")
cmdMultiply	"\<*"	THISFORM.Evaluate("*")
cmdDivide	"\</"	THISFORM.Evaluate("/")
cmdReverseSign	"+/-"	THISFORM.StoreAcc(-THISFORM.Acc,"+/-")
cmdInverse	"1/X"	THISFORM.StoreAcc(1.0/THISFORM.Acc,"1/X")
cmdSwapXY	"X<>Y"	LOCAL Temp
		Temp = THISFORM.Results
		THISFORM.Results = THISFORM.Acc
		THISFORM.StoreAcc(Temp,"X<>Y")
		THISFORM.OldOperand = "+"
cmdMClear	"MC"	THISFORM.Memory = 0
		THISFORM.ShowCalc("MC")
cmdMRevert	"MR"	THISFORM.StoreAcc(THISFORM.Memory,"MR")
cmdMPlus	"M+"	THISFORM.MemCalc("+") && Add results to memory
cmdMMinus	"M-"	THISFORM.MemCalc("-")
cmdInt	"Int"	THISFORM.StoreResults(INT(THISFORM.Acc),"Int")
cmdSin	"Sin"	THISFORM.StoreResults(SIN(THISFORM.Acc),"Sin")
cmdCos	"Cos"	THISFORM.StoreResults(COS(THISFORM.Acc),"Cos")
cmdACos	"Acos"	

```
IF THISFORM.Acc < -1.0 OR THISFORM.Acc > 1.0
   WAIT WINDOW "Illegal ACOS() argument"
ELSE
   THISFORM.StoreResults(ACOS(THISFORM.Acc),"ACos")
ENDIF
```

Name Property	Caption Property	Click Event Method
cmdATan	"Atan"	`THISFORM.StoreResults(ATAN(THISFORM.Acc),"ATan")`
cmdLog10	"Log10"	
	`IF THISFORM.Acc <= 0`	
	`WAIT WINDOW "Illegal accumulator value"`	
	`ELSE`	
	`THISFORM.StoreResults(LOG10(THISFORM.Acc),"Log10")`	
	`ENDIF`	
cmdTan	"Tan"	`THISFORM.StoreResults(Tan(THISFORM.Acc),"Tan")`
cmdPI	"PI"	`THISFORM.StoreAcc(PI(),"PI")`
cmdSqrt	"SQRT"	
	`IF THISFORM.Acc < 0`	
	`WAIT WINDOW "SQRT of negative value is illegal"`	
	`ELSE`	
	`THISFORM.StoreResults(SQRT(THISFORM.Acc),"Sqrt")`	
	`ENDIF`	
cmdLn	"Ln"	
	`IF THISFORM.Acc <= 0`	
	`WAIT WINDOW "Illegal accumulator value"`	
	`ELSE`	
	`THISFORM.StoreResults(LOG(THISFORM.Acc),"Ln")`	
	`ENDIF`	
cmdFactorial	"X!"	
	`LOCAL Answer, TEMP`	
	`Answer = 0`	
	`IF THISFORM.Acc = 0`	
	`Answer = 1`	
	`ELSE`	
	`IF INT(THISFORM.acc) != THISFORM.ACC`	
	`WAIT WINDOW ;`	
	`"Cannot compute factorial of noninteger"`	
	`RETURN`	

continues

Table 19.7. continued

Name Property	*Caption Property*	`Click` *Event Method*
	`ELSE`	
	`Answer = THISFORM.ACC`	
	`IF THISFORM.acc > 2`	
	`FOR TEMP = THISFORM.ACC-1 TO 2 STEP -1`	
	`Answer = Answer*TEMP`	
	`ENDFOR`	
	`ENDIF`	
	`ENDIF`	
	`ENDIF`	
	`THISFORM.StoreResults(Answer,"X!")`	
`cmdRand`	`"Rand"`	`THISFORM.StoreAcc(RAND(THISFORM.Acc),"Rand")`
`ExitCalc`	`"Exit"`	`CLIPTEXT = ALLTRIM(THISFORM.YText)`
		`RELEASE THISFORM`

The calculator form design is complete. Save the `Calc` form, exit the Form Designer, and run the form. You can run the form using any of the following three methods:

- Execute the `DO FORM Calc` command. This command can be run from the Command window or from within a program.
- In the Program Manager, select the form and press the Run button.
- There's an easy way—You can save the form and run the form from within the Form Designer by pressing the Run (!) button on the standard toolbar.

Now you have completed the design of the calculator. You can use it, add a tally sheet, or whatever you like. In my opinion, it is much easier to create this calculator and get it to work than the one described in Chapter 5.

The Data Environment

The easiest way to define the data environment for a form or form set is to use the Data Environment Designer. With this tool you can visually designate the tables or views with which the form interacts. Once you have established the data environment for the form, it is saved with the form or form set. When the form runs, the tables or views in the data environment open, and the tables or views close when the form is closed or released. When you are designing a form with an established data environment and are setting a value for the `ControlSource` property, the Properties window Settings box contains a list of fields in the data environment from which you can choose a field.

Opening the Data Environment Designer

You open the Data Environment Designer by choosing the **V**iew menu Data **E**nvironment option. Regardless of how you open it, when the Data Environment Designer opens, it appears as a window labeled Data Environment, as shown in Figure 19.22. Notice that the **D**ata Environment menu is added to the system menu bar.

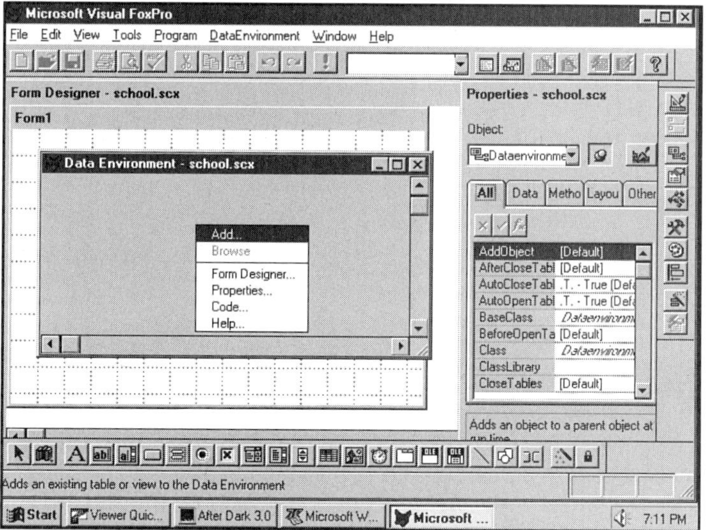

FIGURE 19.22.
The Form Designer and Data Environment Designer.

Adding Tables

The shortcut menu is shown in Figure 19.22. (You can right-click on the Data Environment window to open the shortcut menu.) You can add a table to the window by choosing either the shortcut menu Add... option or the **D**ataEnvironment menu **A**dd... option. In either case, you select a table from the Add Table or View dialog box, and it is added to the Data Environment window, as shown in Figure 19.23. In the figure, the Data Environment window contains three tables, TEACHERS.DBF, STUDENTS.DBF, and CLASSES.DBF, which are associated with the SCHOOLS.DBC database container. Note that you can also add views or free tables.

To delete a table from the Data Environment, just click on the table and press the Delete key.

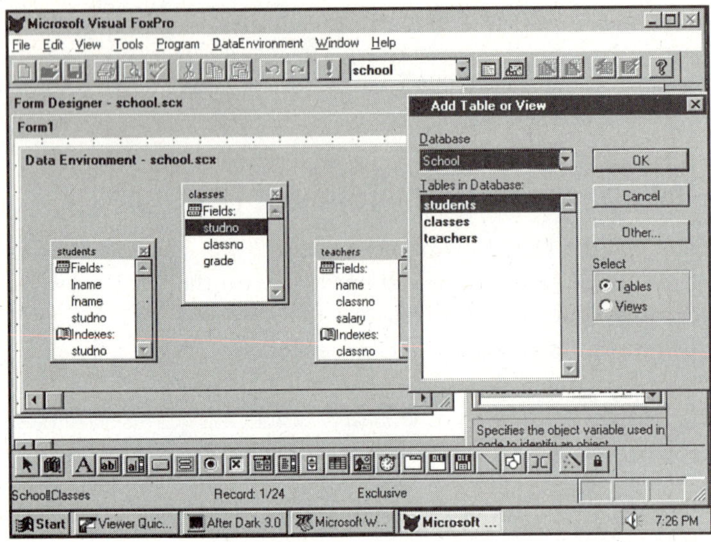

FIGURE 19.23.
Adding tables to the Data Environment Designer.

Establishing Relations

You can establish relations in the Data Environment Designer. If persistent relationships are set in the database, the relationships are automatically added to the data environment. However, in this case, persistent relationships are not set.

You can still establish relations visually with the Data Environment Designer. To set a relation, you drag a field from the primary table onto the matching index in the related table. A relation is automatically established and lines are drawn to visually represent the relation. To create the relations shown in Figure 19.24, drag the `studno` field in the CLASSES.DBF table onto the `studno` index in the STUDENTS.DBF table. Likewise, drag the `classno` field in the TEACHERS.DBF table to the `classno` field in the CLASSES.DBF table.

If you click on one of the lines representing the relation (see Figure 19.24), the line display thickens and the Properties window shows the relation object. The CLASSES.DBF table is related to the STUDENTS.DBF table with a one-to-one relation. The relationship between the TEACHERS.DBF is related to the CLASSES.DBF with a one-to-many relation. The `OneToMany` property determines this. By default, the `OneToMany` property is set to false (`.F.`), indicating that the relation is a one-to-one relation. Obviously, you set it to true (`.T.`) to make it a one-to-many relation. This is equivalent to executing the `SET SKIP TO Classes` command.

If you want the relation to be based on an expression, you can set the `RelationalExpr` property. Initially the `RelationshipExpr` property is set to the name of the primary field for the relation. You can set the field to an expression. For example, if the `classno` field index expression is `UPPER(classno)`, you can change the `RelationshipExpr` property manually from `teachers.classno` to `UPPER(teachers.classno)`.

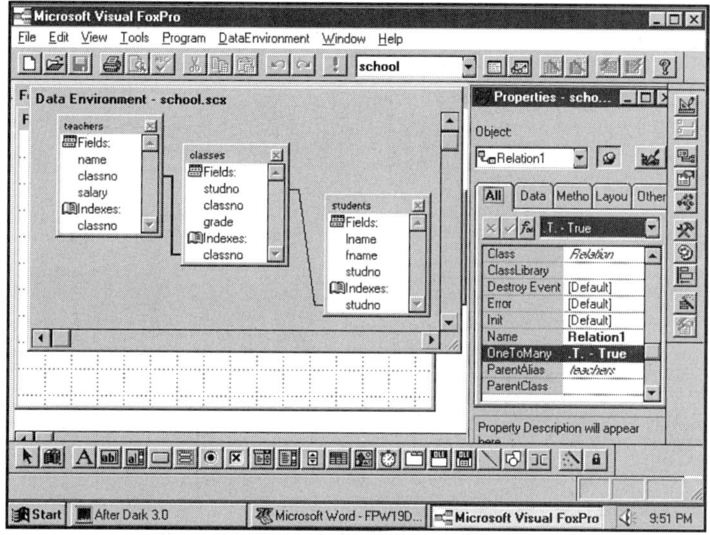

FIGURE 19.24.
The Data Environment Designer with relationships between the tables established.

To delete a relation, click on the relation line, and when it thickens, press the Delete key. Try it, delete a relation, and then put it back. Incidentally, you can also select a table and choose the **D**ataEnvironment menu **R**emove option.

Dragging Fields and Tables

You can drag fields, tables, or views from the Data Environment Designer window to your form to create a form control. To drag a table, you click on the title bar and drag the entire table to the form. Table 19.8 describes what type of control is created when you drag a Database Environment field to a Form Designer form.

Table 19.8. The controls created when an item is dragged from the Data Environment window.

Item Dragged to the Form	*Object Created*
Table	Grid
Logical field	Check box
Memo field	Edit box
General field	OLE bound control
Other fields	Text box

Suppose that you want a form showing information pertaining to a school class. This form will have the teacher's name (`Teachers.Name`), class number (`Classno`), and a grid containing the students' names. To create this form, perform the following steps:

1. Click on the STUDENTS.DBF table title bar and drag the table to the form. A grid appears.
2. Click on the `Teachers.Name` field in the TEACHERS.DBF table and drag it to the form. A text box appears.
3. Click on the `Teachers.Classno` field and drag it to the form. A text box appears.

The form looks like the one shown in Figure 19.25.

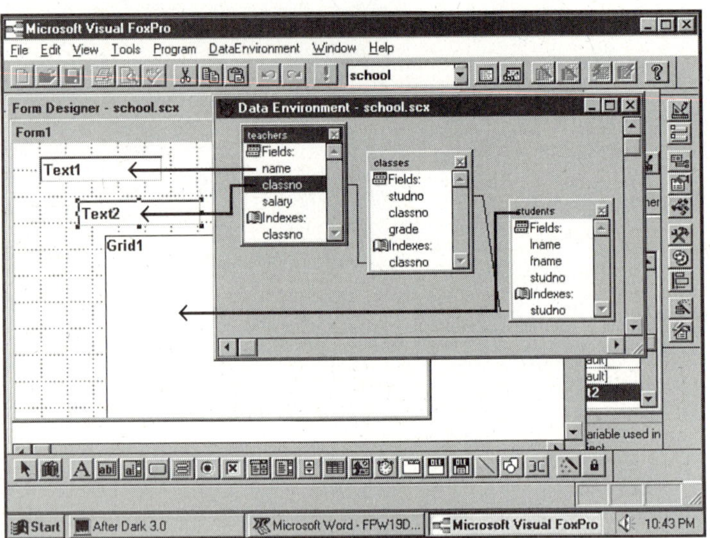

FIGURE 19.25.
An example of dragging a table and fields from the Data Environment Designer to a Database Designer form.

Now rearrange and resize the controls on the form and add label controls to identify the fields using the following steps to make the form appear as it does in Figure 19.26:

1. Add a label control and set the `Caption` property to `Teachers`.
2. Add a label control and set the `Caption` property to `Class #`.
3. Change the `BackColor` property for the form and the label controls to light gray.
4. Add the navigation bar that you created in Chapter 15, "The Visual Class Library, the Class Designer, and the Class Browser," and saved in the visual class library, MYCLASS.VCX, to the form. To do this, use the View Class button on the Form Controls toolbar. Choose the Add… option and add the MYCLASS.VCX class library to the toolbar. Click on the Navigation Bar button on the Forms toolbar and place it on the form as shown in Figure 19.25. You can also drag a class from the Project Manager to the form.

5. Add the following line of code to the `Init` method for the `Navigatebar1` object:

```
THIS.NavTable="Teachers"
```

6. Set the `Form1` form `AutoCenter` property to `.T.` so the form will be centered.

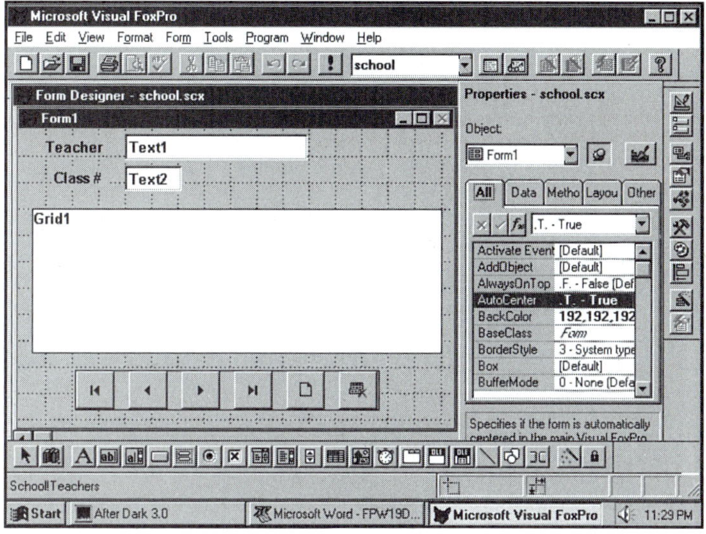

FIGURE 19.26.
The Database Designer with an example school class information form.

Of course you will need to do more work to get the Append and Delete Record buttons on the navigation bar to work properly. You can add a stored procedure and triggers in the database container to handle cascading appends and deletes. I will leave this task as an exercise for you because the object of this example is to demonstrate how to use the Data Environment Designer. I simply disabled the Append and Delete buttons by setting the `Enabled` property for the `Command5` and `Command6` buttons to `.F.`.

> **NOTE**
>
> You can access the `Command5` and `Command6` command buttons using the Objects box in the Properties window to select a command button. Then double-click on the `Enabled` property to change it from true (`.T.`) to false (`.F.`).

Now run the form and it will look like the one shown in Figure 19.27.

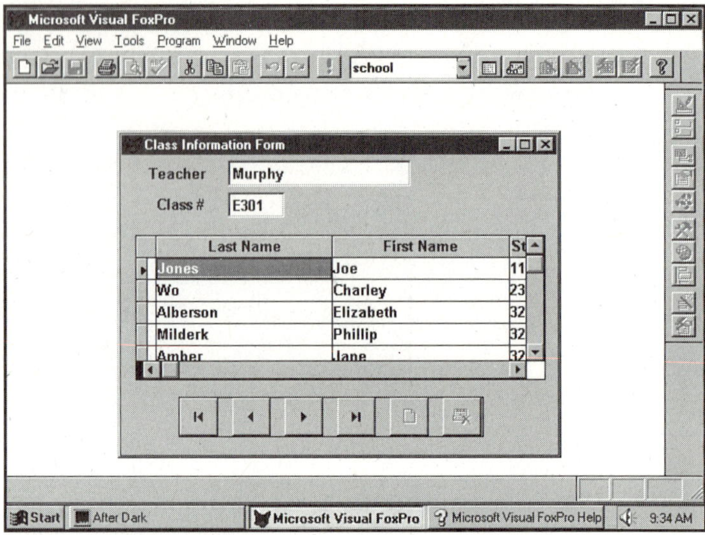

FIGURE 19.27.
A sample school class information form.

Data and Controls

When a user interacts with a control on your form that is bound to data, any value the user changes is stored in the data source. The data source can be a table field, a cursor field, or a variable. You bind a control to a data item by setting its `ControlSource` property. In the case of grid objects, you set the `RecordSource` property. If you do not assign a data source to the `ControlSource` property, the value entered by a user is stored in the control's `Value` property. This section discusses the relationship between the data source and various types of controls.

The Check Box Control

You can set the `ControlSource` property for a check box to a Logical or Numeric field in a table or a variable. The check box is selected if a Logical field has a true (`.T.`) value or a Numeric field contains a nonzero value. A check box is cleared if a Logical field has a false (`.F.`) or `.NULL.` value, or a Numeric field has a `0` or `.NULL.` value.

The Grid and Column Controls

You can bind an entire table or cursor to a grid by setting the `RecordSource` property to the name of the table. When you do this, the number of columns corresponds to the number of fields in the table. Either the field names or, if available, the field captions are used as the column headings. If the `RecordSource` property is not set, a table in the current work area is used as the data source.

If you set `ColumnCount` to a positive number, column objects are added to the grid. You can specify the column `ControlSource` property to a table field for each column if you set the column `Bound` property to true (`.T.`).

If you set the column `Bound` property to false (`.F.`), you can set the `ControlSource` property of a contained control directly.

The Combo Box and List Box Controls

If you assign the `ControlSource` property the name of a memory variable, the value the user chooses in the list is stored in the memory variable. If `ControlSource` is assigned the name of a field in a table, the user-chosen value is stored in the field for the current record. If the value of the table field matches one of the values in the list, the selected value in the list changes when the table's record pointer changes.

If you want the list to contain data from a table, you can set the `RowSourceType` to `2 - Table` in the Properties window. Then set the `RowSource` variable to the field name. The list box or combo box control contains the data values for the designated fields.

If you make a change to the view, such as changing the controlling index (`SET ORDER TO`) or the filtering criteria (`SET FILTER TO`), you can force the list box or combo box control to update its list with new values from the table field specified by the `RowSource` property. You do this by calling the control's `Requery` method.

The Option Button Control

If you set the `ControlSource` property of an option button group to a Character type field or variable, the user-selected option button `Caption` property value is stored in the field. If the value of the Character field corresponds to one of the `Caption` values, that option is initially selected. If you set the `ControlSource` property of an option button group to a Numeric field or variable, the user-selected option button number is stored in the field. The option button numbering begins with 1. If the value of the Numeric field corresponds to an option button number, then that option button is initially selected. The button label or number is stored in the field of the current record only after the user has selected the field.

The Spinner Control

The data source of a spinner control can only be a Numeric field or variable. In other words, the `CountrolSource` property is set to a table field or variable name. The initial value of the field or variable is stored in the spinner. If the user changes the spinner value, the new value is stored in the data source. The `Value` property also contains the spinner value.

The Edit Box and Text Box Controls

The `ControlSource` property can be set to a field or variable. Initially, the value of the field or variable displays. If the user changes the contents of an edit box or a text box control, the new contents are stored in the data source. If you move the record pointer, the new value displays in the edit or text box control. The `Value` property contains the contents of the text box.

Form Properties

There are about 60 properties for the form object that affect the appearance and behavior of the form. However, most of them are rarely used. There is a set of a dozen commonly used form object properties. You will want to consider these properties when you are designing a form. These properties are presented in Table 19.9.

Table 19.9. Commonly used form properties.

Property	*Default*	*Description*
`AlwaysOnTop`	`.F.`	Designates whether or not (`.T.` or `.F.`) the form is always on top of the other forms when it is active.
`AutoCenter`	`.F.`	Designates whether or not (`.T.` or `.F.`) the form is centered in the Visual FoxPro main window when form is initially displayed.
`BackColor`	`255,255,255`	Designates the color of the form window.
`BoderStyle`	`3`	Designates whether the form has no border (`0`), a single line border (`1`), a double line border (`3`) or a system style border (`3`).
`Caption`	`Form1`	Specifies the text displayed in the form's title bar.
`Closable`	`.T.`	Designates whether the user can close the form by double-clicking on the close box, or for Windows 95, clicking on the close button.
`MaxButton`	`.T.`	Designates whether the form has a maximize button.
`MinButton`	`.T.`	Designates whether the form has a minimize button.
`Movable`	`.T.`	Designates whether the form can be moved to a new location on the screen.
`ScaleMode`	`3 - Pixels`	Designates the unit of measurement in the object size and position properties as foxels (`0`) or pixels (`3`). `3` is the recommended default. However, you

Property	*Default*	*Description*
		can set the default to either value from the Forms tab in the **T**ools menu **O**ptions dialog box.
`ShowTips`	`.F.`	Designates whether `ToolTipText` property text displays. When you rest the mouse pointer over a control for a second or two, a little box describing the control appears. But you know that. You define the text in the little box for any control using the `ToolTipText` property. The `ToolTips` text only displays if the `ShowTips` property for its form is `.T.`.
`WindowState`	`0 - Normal`	Designates whether the form is initialized in its minimized (`1`), maximized (`2`), or normal (`0`) state.
`WindowType`	`0 - Modeless`	Designates whether a form is modal (`1`) or modeless (`0`). You must close a modal form before accessing any other elements of your interface for your application.

Page Frames and Pages

A page frame is a container object that contains pages. A page is a container object that contains controls. You can visualize a page frame as a stack of pages, like a book. Only one page can be visible at a time.

You can create a page frame with tabbed pages similar to the Form Designer Properties window, the Project Manager, or the **T**ools menu Options dialog box. You can have pages without tabs and provide some technique for moving from page to page. This is the method used by wizards to move between forms. In this section you will create a form, called the Page Frame Demo program, that will demonstrate both types of page frames.

You can add a page frame to a form by clicking on the Page Frame button on the Form Controls toolbar and dragging it to size in the Form window. Next, you specify the `PageCount` property to designate how many pages you want. Figure 19.28 shows examples of the two page frames. The top page frame has tabs and the bottom one does not have tabs. Each page frame contains four pages.

To review, before you can put controls on a page, you must open the Object drop-down list on the Properties window and then choose the page to which you want to add controls. Notice in Figure 19.28 that the Object drop-down list is open and the `Page1` page is selected. When a page in a page frame is selected, the page frame is surrounded by a thick, green, hashed border.

You can also modify individual pages by right-clicking on the page frame and choosing the Edit option.

NOTE

If the page frame is selected, you can change the top page in the page frame with the Page box in the Form Designer status bar. However, this is all you can do with the Page box. The page is not selected, and you cannot add any controls to the page.

In contrast, the OK button was placed on the form when the `PageFrame1` page frame object was selected. As a result, the OK button always remains visible regardless of the page you select. The OK button `Click` event method contains a `RELEASE THISFORM` command to close the form.

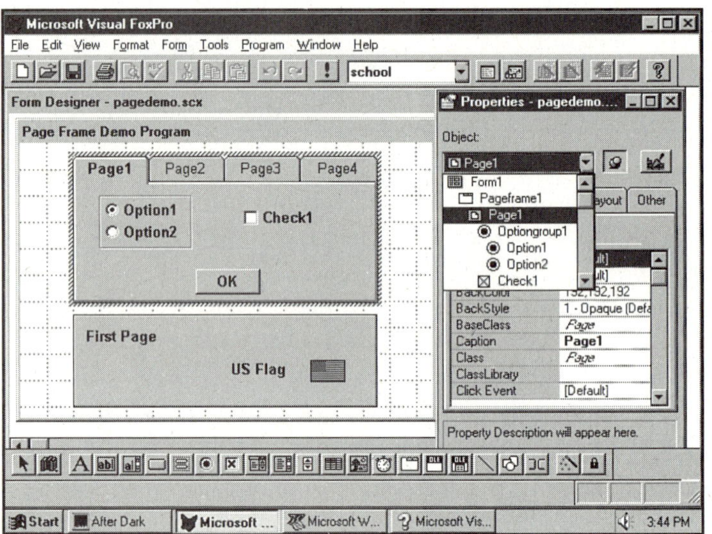

FIGURE 19.28.
Designing the Page Frame Demo Program.

In this example form, PAGEDEMO.SCX, the `Click` event method in the upper page frame contains code to select the same active page number in the bottom page frame as selected in the upper page frame. Here is the code:

```
THISFORM.PageFrame2.ActivePage = THIS.ActivePage
```

The `ActivePage` property is the active page number for a page frame. Figure 19.29 shows the running page demo form with Page 4 selected on both page frames.

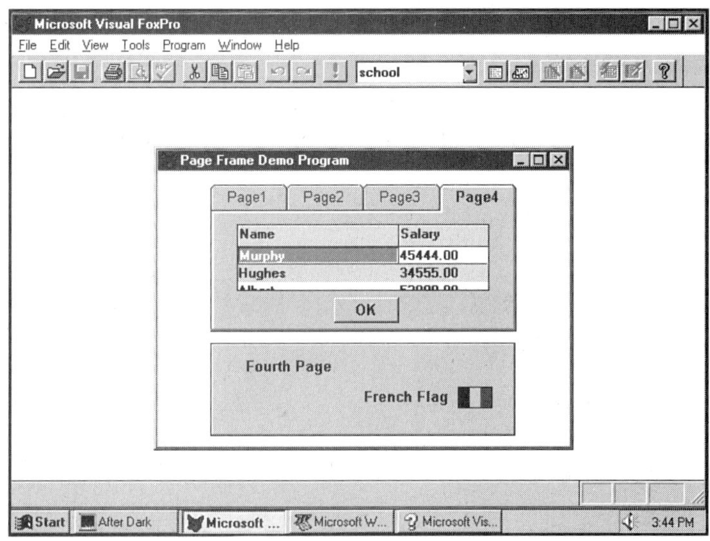

FIGURE 19.29.
A sample page frame demo form.

If you have a large number of pages on a page frame, or if your tab captions on the pages are so wide that they do not fit on the tab, you have two choices. You can clip off the excess caption text, or you can stack the tabs so that all of the captions are visible. You use the `TabStretch` property to designate your choice as shown in Figure 19.30.

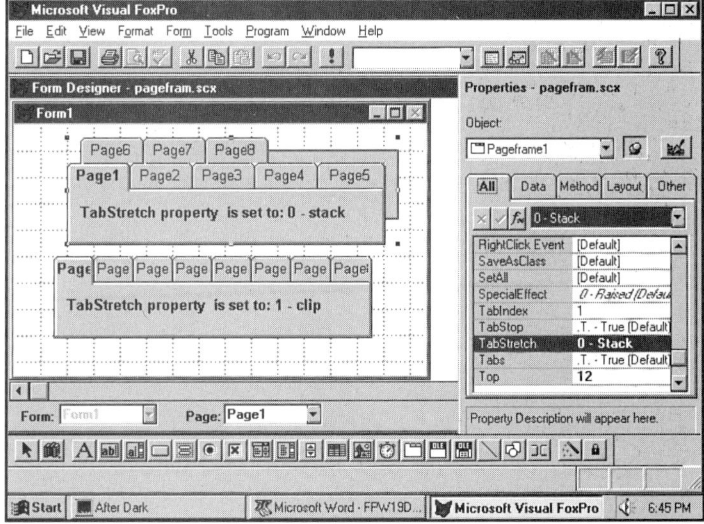

FIGURE 19.30.
The page frame `TabStretch` property.

The Relationship Between Containers and Controls

As you already know, there are two types of objects in Visual FoxPro: containers and controls. A container can be a parent object for other objects. A control can be contained in a container but cannot be a parent object for other objects. The relationship between containers and controls is represented in Table 19.10.

Table 19.10. The relationship between containers and controls.

Container	*What It Can Contain*
Column	Headers and any type of control
Command button group	Command buttons
Form set	Forms and toolbars
Form	Page frames, grids, and any type of control
Grid	Columns
Option button group	Option buttons
Page frame	Pages
Page	Grids and any type of control

Controls

You can utilize the most sophisticated algorithms in your applications and apply the most advanced programming techniques in developing your applications. However, if you do not have an illustrious user interface, you are in trouble. Your work is judged by how easy it is for your customer to interface with the computer and get the work done. With Visual FoxPro control objects as building blocks, you can easily design an excellent advanced user interface that will satisfy your most discriminating customers. An example of all of the available controls is shown in Figure 19.31.

In this section, you will learn how to effectively use the following Visual FoxPro controls:

- Check boxes
- Combo boxes
- Command buttons
- Command button groups
- Edit boxes
- Grid controls
- Image controls
- Labels
- List boxes
- Option button groups
- Shape and line controls
- Spinners
- Text boxes
- Timer controls

OLE Controls are discussed in detail in Chapter 17.

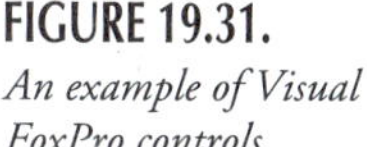

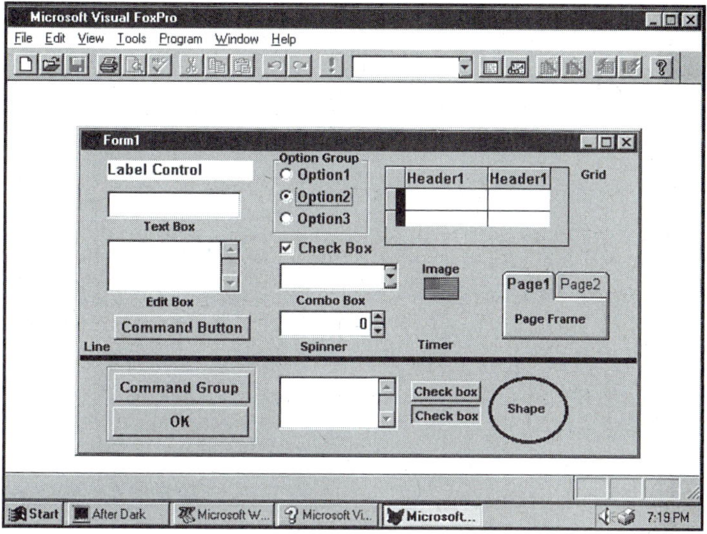

FIGURE 19.31.
An example of Visual FoxPro controls.

The Check Box Control

A check box is most effectively used to represent two-state boolean logic: Yes or No, True or False. The `ControlSource` property for a check box can be a Logical or Numeric field in a table. The check box is selected if a logical field has a true (`.T.`) value, or a numeric field contains a nonzero value. A check box is cleared if the logical field has a false (`.F.`) or `.NULL.` value, or a numeric field has a `0` or `.NULL.` value. When a condition is true, an X appears in the check box.

You use the `Caption` property to specify the text that appears next to a check box.

There is a third state you can represent with a check box—a disabled state. This state can represent an option for which it is not appropriate for the user to make a choice. You represent this third state through disabling the check box by setting the `Enabled` property to false (`.F.`).

If you set the `Style` property to `0`, the check box is a *standard check box*. However, you can set the `Style` property to `1`, and the check box becomes a command button with a latch, such as the Control Lock or Builder Lock buttons on the Form Controls toolbar, or the push pin buttons. It is then called a *graphics check box*. An example of two graphics check boxes is at the bottom of Figure 19.31. The lower one is latched or *checked*. You can use the `Picture` property to place a graphics bitmap (BMP) file on a control. If you specify both the `Caption` and `Picture` properties for a graphics text box control, the `Caption` text is centered at the bottom of the check box control.

The Combo Box and List Box Controls

List box and combo box controls provide a variety of types of scrollable lists from which the user can select an item. Multiple options are always visible for a list box control. However, only one option is always visible for a combo box control. But when you open a combo box control by clicking on the down button, all of the options display in a scrollable drop-down list box control. You normally use a list box control instead of a combo box control when you have sufficient space on the form to display a list box control, and you want to accentuate the choices. In contrast, you use a combo box control if you want to conserve space, and you want to accentuate the currently selected value.

When you design either of these two controls, you may want to use the respective builder to help you set the various properties. To execute the builder, you can click on the Builder button on the Properties window or right-click and choose the Builder option from the shortcut menu. You can also set the Builder Lock button on the Form Controls toolbar; the builder executes when you place a control on a form. When you execute the builder, it displays as shown in Figure 19.32. You designate what you want in the list box control. If you want values from a table, you can choose a table and fields from the table.

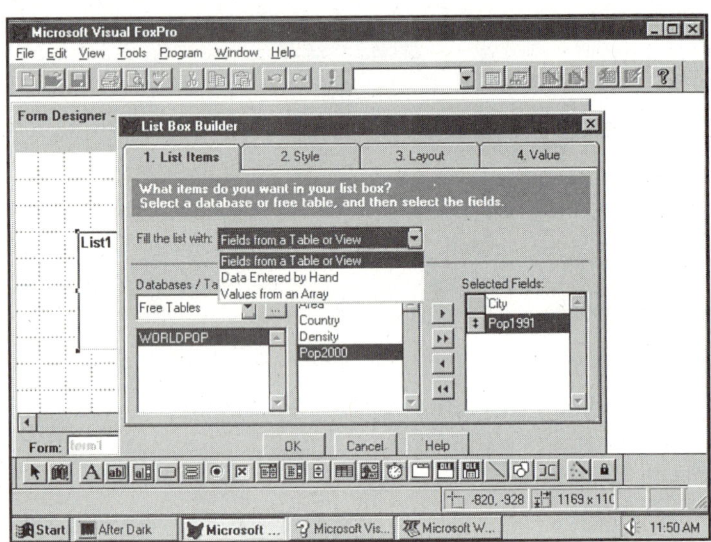

FIGURE 19.32.
The List Box Builder with the List Items tab selected.

When you are finished specifying which fields you want to display, choose the Style tab and specify the type of style you want for your list box control, as shown in Figure 19.33. From an interface design point of view, it is important that you use the same style throughout your application.

Next, you choose the Layout tab to adjust the manner in which columns display in the heading, as shown in Figure 19.34.

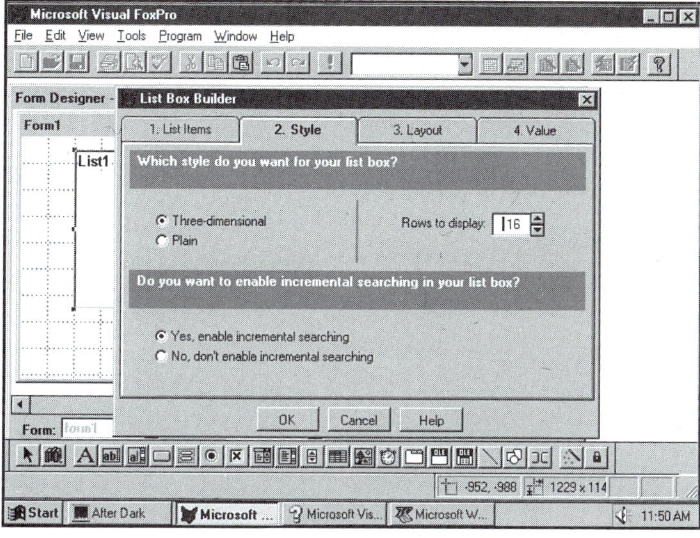

FIGURE 19.33.
The List Box Builder with the Style tab selected.

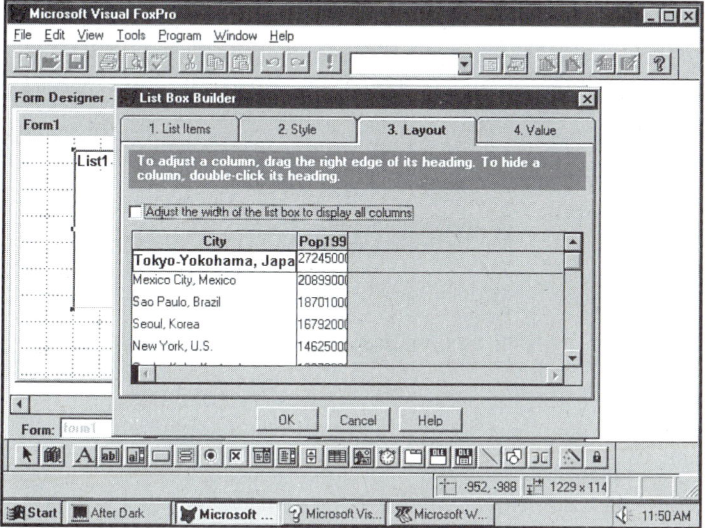

FIGURE 19.34.
The List Box Builder with the Layout tab selected.

Finally, you choose the Value tab to select which value is returned, as shown in Figure 19.35. And that is it. The builder has helped you set properties. Using a builder is a good way to initialize a list box control or most any complex control. However, there are properties that are not handled by the builder: You might need to add event code, set some properties, and call some methods.

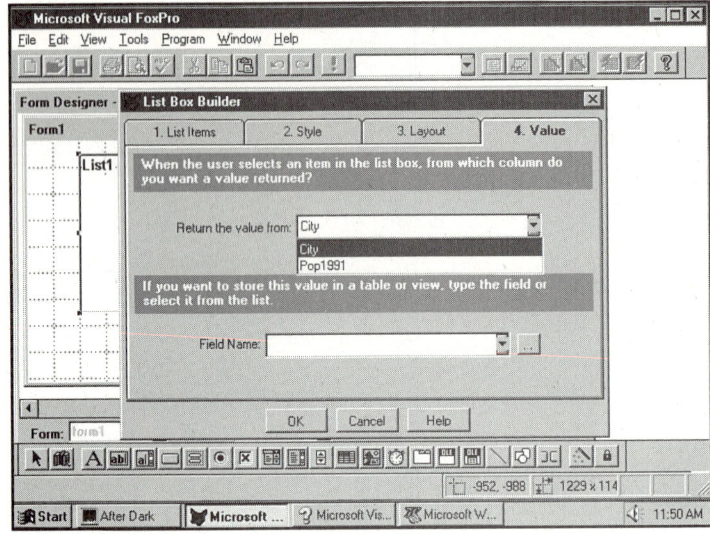

FIGURE 19.35.
The List Box Builder with the Value tab selected.

The `Style` property is specified with the combo box control and is not used by the list box control. If you set the `Style` property to `2`, it becomes a drop-down list box. With the exception that you must open it before you can see the list, it behaves like a list box control. If you set the `Style` property to `0`, which is the default, the combo box control becomes a drop-down combo box control. It includes a drop-down list combined with a text box. The user can select a value from the list or can enter text in the edit area.

Table 19.11 lists the properties that are typically used by both the list box and combo box controls.

Table 19.11. Typically used list box and combo box properties.

Property	*Default*	*Description*
`ColumnCount`	`-1`	Specifies the number of columns in the list.
`ControlSource`		You specify where the selected value is stored.
`IncrementalSearch`	`.T.`	Designates whether or not (`.T.` or `.F.`) the incremental search is enabled. If it is, the control attempts to track an item in the list as the user types characters. An example of incremental search is the Help system Search option.
`MoverBars`	`.F.`	Designates whether or not (`.T.` or `.F.`) the mover bars are displayed in the list so that the user can easily rearrange the items in the list. An example of mover bars can be found in the Database Designer, which lets you rearrange the fields in the structure.

Property	Default	Description
`MultiSelect`	`.F.`	Determines whether or not (`.T.` or `.F.`) the user is allowed to select more than one item in the list at a time. It is done while pressing the Ctrl key while clicking the item.
`RowSource`	-	Specifies the source of the values that display in the list.
`RowSourceType`	`0`	Specifies the type of source of data used in a list. It can be any of the following:

RowSourceType	Source of List Items
`0 - None`	Programmatically adds items to list. You use the `AddItem` and `AddListItem` methods to add items to list.
`1 - Value`	Specifies a list of multiple values (for example, `RowSource="One, Two,Three"`).
`2 - Alias`	Specifies one or more table fields. Use the `ColumnCount` property to specify how many fields to display.
`3 - SQL`	Specifies the SQL statement to select items (for example, `RowSource = ;    "SELECT * FROM myfile INTO CURSOR temp"`).
`4 - Query`	Specifies the query (.QPR) file (for example, `RowSource="XYZ.QPR"`).
`5 - Array`	Specifies the name of the array with items.
`6 - Fields`	Specifies the field or comma delimited list of fields (for example, `RowSource="Name,Account"`).
`7 - Files`	Specifies the file skeleton (for example, `RowSource="*.DBF"`).
`8 - Structure`	Specifies the table for the structure to be displayed.
`9 - Popup`	Specifies the `DEFINE POPUP` name. Included for compatibility with earlier versions of FoxPro.

continues

Table 19.11. continued

Property	*Default*	*Description*
`Style`	`0`	Designates whether the combo box control is a drop-down combo box (`0`) or a drop-down list box (`1`). Not available for list box controls.

Each of the `RowSourceType` property settings will be discussed in detail later in this chapter. First, I will examine an example of the use of the list box and combo box controls. In this example, tables containing information on the population of the largest cities in the world, WORLDPOP.DBF and COUNTRY.DBF, are used as the data sources for a form, CITIES.SCX. The resultant form is shown in Figure 19.36.

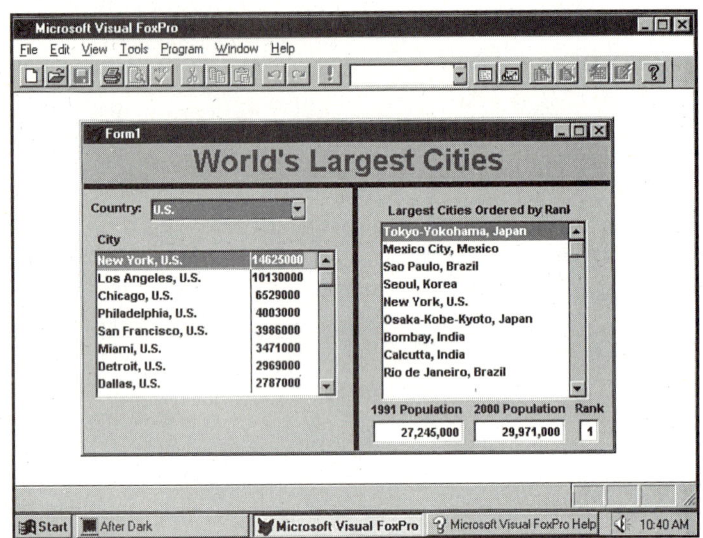

FIGURE 19.36.
An example program that illustrates the use of the list box and combo box controls.

Here are the steps to design the example form shown in Figure 19.36 using the Visual FoxPro Form Designer:

1. Right-click on the form and choose the Data Environment option from the shortcut menu.
2. Add the WORLDPOP.DBF and COUNTRY.DBF tables to the data environment. Exit from the Data Environment Designer.
3. Set the following properties for the form:

Property	*Description*
`AutoCenter = .T.`	Center in the Visual FoxPro window
`BackColor = 192,192,192`	Set the background to light gray

Add the following code to the `Load` event method:

```
PUBLIC Zcountry
ZCountry = ""
```

The public variable `ZCountry` is used in the SQL `SELECT` statement assigned to the `RowSelect` property for one of the list box controls.

4. Add a combo box control (`Combo1`) to the form and size it as shown in the figure. Then, set the following properties in the Properties window:

Property	*Description*
`FontSize = 8`	
`RowSourceType = 6`	List contains fields
`RowSource = "country.country"`	Name of the field
`Style = 2`	Drop-down list box

5. Add the list box control (`List1`) below the combo box control and size it. Then set the following properties in the Properties window:

Property	*Description*
`FontSize = 8`	
`ColumnCount = 2`	There are two columns
`ColumnWidths = "140,65"`	Width of the two columns
`RowSourceType = 3`	Source is SQL statement
`RowSource = "SELECT City,Pop1991 FROM WorldPop WHERE ZCountry = WorldPop.Country INTO CURSOR Temporary"`	
`Width = 225`	Width of list box

When `RowSourceType` is set to `3`, you are required to set `RowSource` to a SQL `SELECT` statement. This specific SQL `SELECT` statement selects the `City` and `Pop1991` fields from the CITIES.DBF table for the country that matches the specified country (`ZCountry`). The results are used as the two columns in the list box control. The `INTO CURSOR Temporary` clause is needed. If it is omitted, Visual FoxPro brings up the selected data in a Browse window. In other words, the `INTO` clause is needed only to suppress the Browse window.

6. Add the second list box control (`List2`) at the right of the form and size it as shown in the figure. Set the following properties in the Properties window:

Property	*Description*
`FontSize = 8`	
`RowSourceType = 2` open table	Alias—Displays the first field in
`RowSource = "worldpop.city"`	Specifies the field to display

7. Add a text box below the `list2` list box control and size it as shown in the figure. Then set the following properties:

Property	*Description*
`FontSize = 8`	
`Alignment = 1`	Right aligns in the field
`InputMask = ("999,999,999")`	Template for display of numeric values Same as the `PICTURE` clause on the `@...SAY` statement

   The data source (`ControlSource`) is not established for this text box because it is set programmatically in the `Click` event method for the `List2` list box control.

8. Select the text box from Step 4 and press Ctrl+C to copy the text box to the Clipboard. Then press Ctrl+V twice to paste two more text boxes on the form. They will have the same properties as the original text box. Position and size the two new text boxes as shown in Figure 19.36.
9. Add the label controls to the form as shown in the figure. Note that the `Caption`, `FontSize`, and `BackColor` properties need to be set.
10. Add the line controls, as shown in the form, to divide the form. The `BorderWidth` property defines the width of the line. In this form, the `BorderWidth` property is set to `5`.
11. Now add the methods shown in Table 19.12. The `PROCEDURE` and `ENDPROC` statements are automatically added by the Code window system. You must not add them to the Code window. They are provided here as a reference.

Table 19.12. Event methods for the CITIES.SCX form.

Procedure	*Description*
`PROCEDURE Form1.Load` `    PUBLIC ZCountry`	Add public Variable used in the SQL `select` command to designate the country for which city data is retrieved from WORLDPOP.DBF table. It is placed before any controls are loaded so that it will be in scope when the `List1` list box control loads.
`    Zcountry = ""`	Forces the variable to be a Character type.
`ENDPROC`	
`PROCEDURE Combo1.Init` `    GO TOP IN Country`	Combo box control `Init` event method. Makes sure that the `Country` field in the first record is selected in the combo box control when the form displays.

Procedure	*Description*
`THIS.Value=Country.Country`	Establishes the data source for the `Value` property.
`ZCountry = THIS.Value`	Saves the value in the public variable so that it can be used by the SQL statement defined by the `RowSource` property for the List1 list box control.
`ENDPROC`	
`PROCEDURE Combo1.Click`	Combo box `Click` event method.
`ZCountry = THIS.Value`	Stores the name of the country currently selected in the combo box control in a memory variable.
`THISFORM.List1.Requery`	Forces the `List1` list box control to refresh its list from the data source which, in this case, is the WORLDPOP.DBF table because the filter has changed.
`THISFORM.Refresh`	Refreshes the entire form.
`ENDPROC`	
`PROCEDURE List2.Init`	`List1` list box control `Init` event method.
`GO TOP`	
`THIS.Value = City`	Forces the `Click` event method to display values in text boxes for the first record.
`THIS.Click`	
`ENDPROC`	
`PROCEDURE List2.Click`	`List2` list box control `Click` event method. Positions the WORLDPOP.DBF table to the record that corresponds to current selection in the `List2` list box control.
`LOCATE for THIS.VALUE=Worldpop.CITY`	
`THISFORM.Text3.Value = RECNO()`	Establishes order ranking
`THISFORM.Text1.Value = Pop1991`	value in the `Text3` text box.
`THISFORM.Text2.Value = Pop2000`	Establishes 1991 population and 2000 population values in the text boxes.
`THISFORM.Refresh`	Repaints all controls. When you modify the contents of one control from another, you need to call the `Refresh` method.
`ENDPROC`	

This example shows how to add list box and combo box controls to a form. You also learned that Tokyo and Mexico City are the two largest cities by population. Now, it is time to examine the `RowSource` types.

List Items Defined Programmatically (*RowSourceType = 0*)

If you set the `RowSourceType` property to `0`, you are required to set the data source programmatically. You can use the `AddItem` and `AddListItem` methods to add items to a list. You use the `RemoveItem` method to remove an item from a list. For example, you might put the following code in the form's `Init` event method to add items to a list box control named `lstBaudRate`:

```
THISFORM.lstBaudRate.RowSourcetype = 0
THISFORM.lstBaudRate.AddItem("1200 Baud")
THISFORM.lstBaudRate.AddItem("2400 Baud")
THISFORM.lstBaudRate.AddItem("4800 Baud")
THISFORM.lstBaudRate.AddItem("9600 Baud")
THISFORM.lstBaudRate.AddItem("14400 Baud")
THISFORM.lstBaudRate.AddItem("19200 Baud")
```

You can remove an item from the list with the `RemoveItem` method. For example, to remove the fifth item in the above list (`"14400 Baud"`), use the following statement:

```
THISFORM.lstBaudRate.AddItem(5)
```

A List Containing a Specified Item (*RowSourceType = 1*)

If you set the `RowSourceType` property to `1`, you establish a set of item values by assigning a character string containing a comma delimited list of items to the `RowSource` property. For example, if you want to specify the same items defined in the previous section, assign the following text to the `RowSource` property in the Properties window:

```
1200 Baud,2400 Baud,4800 Baud,9600 Baud,14400 Baud,19200 Baud
```

or this:

```
="1200 Baud,2400 Baud,4800 Baud,9600 Baud,14400 Baud,19200 Baud"
```

If you define the `RowSource` property programmatically, enclose the text in quotes, as shown in the follow example:

```
RowSource = "1200 Baud,2400 Baud,4800 Baud," + ;
            "9600 Baud,14400 Baud,19200 Baud"
```

In addition, you can use the `List` property to specify values. The `List` property is an array of character strings. Each element defines the text for an item. You can cause a bitmap (BMP) graphics image to be placed at the beginning of an item in a list box control. You do this with the `Picture` property. For a list box and combo box control, the `Picture` property is an array of character strings. Each character string specifies the name of the BMP graphics image file. Figure 19.37 shows a form with a list box control populated with pictures of flags for different countries. To create this list box control, a list box control is added to a form and the following code is placed in the `Init` event method for the list box control:

```
THIS.RowSourceType = 1
THIS.LIST(1) = "  Australia"
THIS.LIST(2) = "  France"
THIS.LIST(3) = "  Japan"
THIS.LIST(4) = "  Sweden"
THIS.LIST(5) = "  United Kingdom"
THIS.LIST(6) = "  United States"
THIS.Picture(1) = "FLGASTRL.BMP"
THIS.Picture(2) = "FLGFRAN.BMP"
THIS.Picture(3) = "FLGJAPAN.BMP"
THIS.Picture(4) = "FLGSWED.BMP"
THIS.Picture(5) = "FLGUK.BMP"
THIS.Picture(6) = "FLGUS.BMP"
```

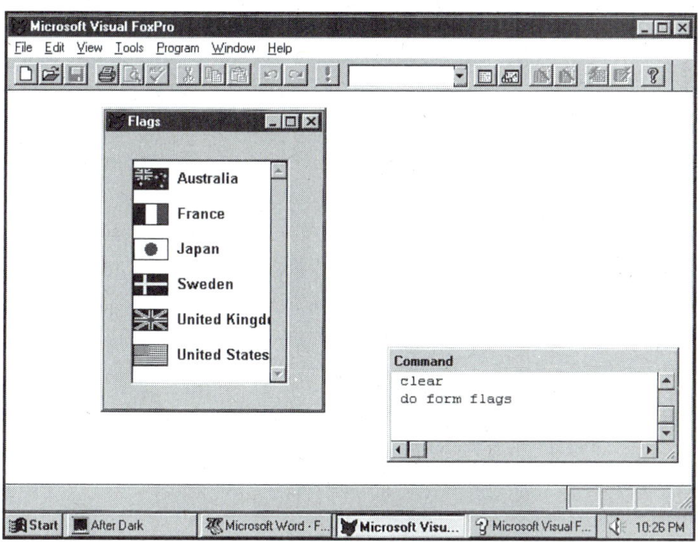

FIGURE 19.37.
A sample program that illustrates the use of the list box control `DataSourceType` *set to* `1`.

A List Containing Fields from a Table (*RowSourceType* = 2)

If you set the `RowSourceType` property to `2`, you include one or more fields from the table in use in the active work area as multiple columns in the list box control. The first field of the table displays in a single column if the `ColumnCount` property has a value of `0` or `1`. The `ColumnCount` specifies the number of columns in the list box control. If you set the `ColumnCount` property to `4`, the list box control will contain the first four fields of the table. This is not especially useful if you want to specify a different order for the fields. If this is the case, set `RowSourceType` to `5` or `6`.

List Items Defined by a SQL Statement (*RowSourceType = 3*)

If you set the `RowSourceType` property to `3`, the items that fill a list box or a combo box control consists of one or more columns of data from the results of an SQL query. You assign a character string to the `RowSource` property containing an SQL `SELECT` statement. For example, the following statement specifies that the list contains multiple columns containing data from the fields table, INVOICE.DBF:

```
RowSource = "SELECT * FROM Invoice INTO CURSOR Temporary"
```

The `INTO` clause is specified to prevent Visual FoxPro from displaying a Browse window containing the results table. The `INTO` clause has no other purpose. The example shown in Figure 19.36 illustrates the use of this type of `RowSource`.

List Items Defined by a Query (*RowSourceType = 4*)

If you set the `RowSourceType` property to `4`, you can assign the name of a query file (QPR) to the `RowSource` property. If you do not specify an extension, QPR will be assumed. The results of the query are used to populate the list box control. If you have more than one field in the results, the list will contain multiple columns. Here is an example:

```
RowSource = "Customers.qpr"
```

List Items Defined from Array Elements (*RowSourceType = 5*)

If you set the `RowSourceType` property to `5`, you can populate the list with array elements. The array can be a standard array or it can be a property array.

You must make sure that the scope of the array extends throughout the lifetime of the form because Visual FoxPro uses the array to refresh the list box control as needed. For example, when the list box control scrolls, it retrieves values to display from the data source. As a consequence, if you declare a local array in the same method you establish the `RowSource` property, the array is gone when the method exits and the list box control no longer works. For best results, add a property array to the form or form set. You create a property array using the For**m** menu New **P**roperty option to specify the new property with array dimensions. For example, assign an array with 10 rows and 3 columns:

```
MyArray[10,3]
```

Then assign value to the array in one of the project methods. In the following example, values are assigned to the array in the `Form1` form `Init` event method:

```
PROCEDURE Form1:Init
        FOR i=1 TO 3
          FOR j=1 TO 10
               THISFORM.MyArray[j,i] = "MyArray["+str(j,2)+","+str(i,2)+"]"
          ENDFOR
        ENDFOR
ENDPROC
```

Now place a list box control (`List1`) on the form and size it as shown in Figure 19.38.

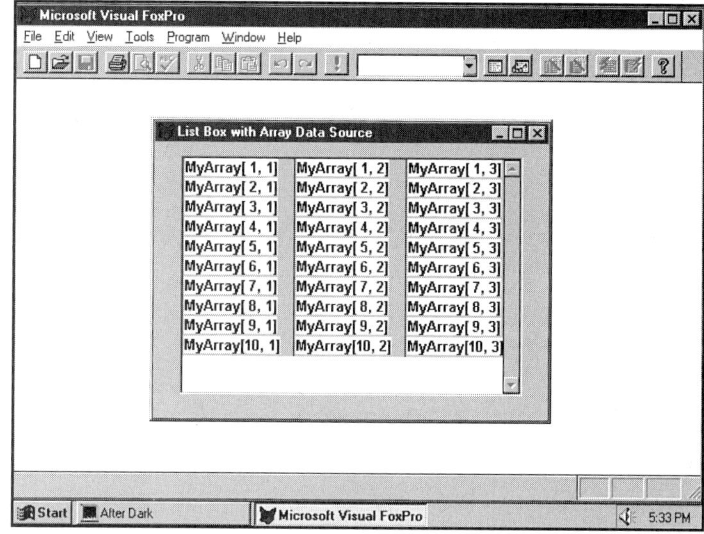

FIGURE 19.38.
A sample program that illustrates the use of the list box control with an array as a data source.

In the Properties window set the properties for the list box control, `List1`, as indicated in Table 19.13. Any other property settings are unimportant to this example.

Table 19.13. Sample list box control properties using an array as a data source.

Property	*Setting*	*Description*
`ColumnCount`	`3`	The number of columns in the array to display. The array has three columns so all three array columns are displayed.
`ColumnWidths`	`"100,100,100"`	Specifies the width of each column. Note that the width of the list box control in Figure 19.38 is 315.
`RowSourceType`	`5`	Specifies that the data source is an array.
`RowSource`	`"THISFORM.myarray"`	Name of the array containing data to populate the list box control.

The properties listed in Table 19.14 are extremely useful when you need them.

Table 19.14. Commonly used list box properties.

Property	*DataType*	*Description*
`ListCount`	N	Returns the number of items in the list portion of a combo box or list box control. *
`MultiSelect`	0	Designates whether or not (`.T.` or `.F.`) a user is allowed to select multiple items in a list box control.
`List`	C	Character string array used to access the items in a combo box or list box control.*
`ListItem`	C	Character string array used to access the items in a combo box or list box control by item ID.*
`ListItemID`	N	Specifies the unique ID number for the selected item in a control.*
`NewItemID`	N	Designates item ID of the item most recently added to a combo box or list box control.*
`Picture`	C	Character string array used to specify the bitmap (BMP) file, icon (ICO) file, or general field to be displayed on each combo box or list box control item.*
`Selected`	L	Logical array that specifies whether an item is selected in a combo box or list box control for each item.*
`TopItemID`	N	Specifies the item ID of the item that appears in the topmost position in a list.*

*Available at runtime only.

If the `MultiSelect` property is set to `.T.`, the user can select multiple items in a list box control. You can use the `Selected` property array to determine which items are selected. For example, the following method code displays a Wait window for every item selected in the `List1` list box control:

```
FOR I=1 TO ListCount
   IF THISFORM.List1.Selected(I)
       WAIT WINDOW TIMEOUT 1 THISFORM.List1.LIST(I)+" was selected"
    ENDIF
ENDFOR
```

A List Containing Field Data (*RowSourceType = 6*)

If you set the `RowSourceType` property to `6`, you specify the name of a field or a comma-delimited list of field names to the `RowSource` property. Here are some examples of what you can assign to the `RowSource` property in the Properties window:

```
Animals
Animals,cost,quantity
Zoo.Animals,Zoo.Cost,Zoo.Quantity
```

Of course, if you assign the value of the `RowSource` property in a method, you enclose it in quotes. Here is an example:

```
RowSource = "Animals,cost,quantity"
```

The example shown in Figure 19.36 illustrates this type of list box control data source.

A List Containing Filenames (*RowSourceType = 7*)

If you set the `RowSourceType` property to `7`, the list is filled with filenames in the current directory. Options are available that let you choose another drive and directory. The example shown in Figure 19.39 shows a list box control containing the names of tables in the current work area. The figure also shows a drop-down menu containing drive selections. Here are the property settings for the list box control to define this type of list box control:

Property	*Description*
`RowSourceType = 7`	Displays files in the current directory
`RowSource = "*.DBF "`	Specifies a file skeleton and displays DBF table files

This form also displays a list box control populated with the names of the fields of the table selected in the file list. When you click on a DBF table filename, the `Click` event method executes. This methods replaces the contents of the `Text1` text box with the name of the selected table, places the selected file in use, and forces the field list's list box control to reread the table structure. Here is the file display list box control `Click` event method:

```
PROCEDURE List1.Click
   THISFORM.Text1.Value = THIS.Value
   USE (THIS.Value)
   THISFORM.List2.Requery
   THISFORM.Refresh
ENDPROC
```

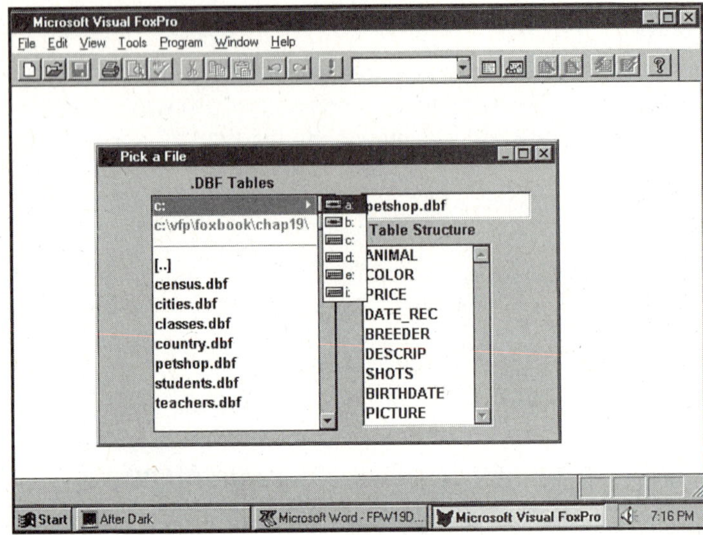

FIGURE 19.39.
A sample program that illustrates the use of the list box control with the files in a directory as the data source.

A List Containing a Table Structure (*RowSourceType = 8*)

If you set the `RowSourceType` property to `8`, the list box control is filled with the field names of the table in use in the current work area or specified with the `RowSource` property. Figure 19.39 shows an example of this type of list.

A List with *DEFINE POPUP* Items (*RowSourceType = 9*)

If you set the `RowSourceType` property to `9`, you can populate the list from a previously defined pop-up. As you remember from Chapter 7, "FoxPro Language Elements for Creating Windows and Menu Systems," you can define a pop-up using the antiquated `DEFINE POPUP` command. You assign the name of the defined pop-up to the `RowSource` property. This type of list is included to retain compatibility with earlier versions of FoxPro.

The Command Button Control

As you read this book, you become more experienced at placing command buttons on forms and writing `Click` event code. Therefore, I assume that you are already aware of what a command button control is and how to use it. Table 19.15 is a list of commonly used command button control properties.

Table 19.15. Frequently used command button control properties.

Property	*Default*	*Description*
`Caption`	`"Command1"`	Specifies the text displayed on the button.
`Cancel`	`.F.`	Designates whether or not (`.T.` or `.F.`) a command button control is the Cancel button. If it is, when the user presses the Esc key, the button's `Click` event fires. The form will not exit unless the code in the `Click` event method causes it to exit.
`DisablePicture`	`""`	Specifies the name of the bitmap (BMP) file displayed on the control when the control is disabled (`Enabled=.F.`).
`DownPicture`	`""`	Specifies the name of the bitmap (BMP) file displayed on the control when the mouse button is pressed on the control. This picture also displays when the `Value` property equals `1`, which indicates that you have toggled a value on.
`Enabled`	`.T.`	Designates whether or not (`.T.` or `.F.`) a command button control is enabled.
`Picture`	`""`	Specifies the name of the bitmap (BMP) file displayed on the control. The `Caption` property displays below picture as shown in Figure 19.40.

Figure 19.40 shows three instances of the BUTTON.SCX form showing the buttons in different states. A check box control is used to illustrate the contrast of appearance between a check box and command button control when both are toggled on and off. A check box control latches and unlatches when you click on it. A command button control remains depressed only as long as the mouse button is pressed down.

The check box control toggles the enabled state of the Happy Button picture button on and off. When it is on, the Happy Button button is enabled, as shown in the second and third instances of the form.

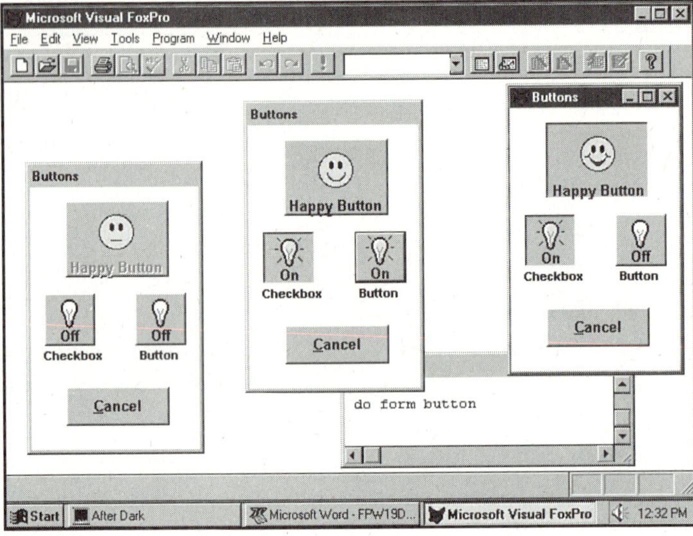

FIGURE 19.40.
A sample program with picture buttons using command button and check box controls.

Two controls contain a light bulb that can be turned on and off. One is a check box and the other is a command button. The `Picture` and `DownPicture` properties are set to show the states of the light bulbs. The `Style` property of the check box control (`Check1`) is set to `1` to indicate that the check box has a graphics style. Here are the relevant properties of the check box control:

```
Picture = lightoff.bmp
DownPicture = lighton.bmp
Caption = "Off"
Style = 1
```

The following check box control `Click` event method contains code to change the `Caption` property to `On` or `Off` and to enable or disable the Happy Button picture button:

```
PROCEDURE Check1.Click
   IF THIS.Value = 1   && Checked
     THIS.Caption = "On"
     THISFORM.Button.Enabled = .T.  && Enable Happy Button
   ELSE
     THIS.Caption = "Off"
     THISFORM.Button.Enabled = .F.  && Disable Happy Button
   ENDIF
ENDPROC
```

The Happy Button picture button displays three different faces for each of the three states: enabled (`face02.bmp`), disabled (`face01.bmp`), or clicked (`face03.bmp`). The Happy Button button for the instance of the Buttons form on the right was depressed when Figure 19.40 was created. To prevent the smiling face from toggling on and off, the picture button's `Click` event method consists of the following statement:

```
THIS.Value = 0
```

Here are the pertinent properties for the Happy Button button:

```
Picture = face02.bmp
DownPicture = face03.bmp
DisabledPicture = face01.bmp
Caption = "Happy Button"
Enabled = .F.
```

Notice that the Happy Button button is initially disabled.

The `Cancel` property for the Cancel button is set to true (`.T.`) so that if the user presses the Esc key, the `Click` event of this button executes. The `Caption` property is set to `\<Cancel`. As you probably already know, the two characters `\<` denote that the following character (in this case, C) is the access key.

Here are the pertinent properties for the `Command2` command button control:

```
CommandPicture = lightoff.bmp
DownPicture = lighton.bmp
Caption = "Off"
Name = "Command2"
```

The command button control has no `Value` property. I needed a way to determine whether the command button was toggled on or off, so I added a user-defined property, `Toggle`. I did not bother to initialize it because it defaults to a logical false (`.F.`) value. The following command button control `Click` event method contains code to change the `Caption` property to `On` or `Off` and to enable or disable the Happy Button picture button:

```
PROCEDURE Command2.Click
     IF THISFORM.Toggle && Checked?
          THIS.Caption = "On"
          THISFORM.Button.Enabled = .T.  && Enable Happy Button
     ELSE
          THIS.Caption = "Off"
          THISFORM.Button.Enabled = .F.  && Disable Happy Button
     ENDIF
     THISFORM.Toggle = !THISFORM.Toggle
ENDPROC
```

The `Click` event method for the Cancel button consists of the following code:

```
PROCEDURE Command1.Click
     IF MessageBox("Are you absolutely sure you want to  exit?",;
               4+32, "Cancel" ) = 6  && Yes
          RELEASE THISFORM
     ENDIF
ENDPROC
```

The Command Button Group Control

The command group control is a container that contains command button controls. The important properties of this container are the `ButtonCount` and `Caption` properties. You set the `ButtonCount` properties to define the number of command button controls in the group. Because you need to change the captions for each individual button, you need to select the button from the Object drop-down combo box in the Properties window (or do the right-click thing). Then change its properties. You can control the buttons from the command group `Click` event method. For example, if you have three buttons in the group, you can add the following example code to the group's `Click` event method:

```
DO CASE
    CASE THIS.VALUE = 1
        *  Do some action for first button
    CASE THIS.VALUE = 2
        *  Do some action for second button
    CASE THIS.VALUE = 3
        *  Do some action for third button
ENDCASE
```

If you add `Click` event code to a button in a group and click on the button, the code for that button executes and the code for its button group's `Click` event is not executed.

The Edit Box Control

The edit box control is a complete word processor with the ability to select, cut, paste, and copy text; to word wrap automatically; and to move through text with the arrow keys. You can edit long character strings and memo fields in an edit box control. Table 19.16 presents a list of properties typically used with an edit box control.

Table 19.16. Typical properties used with an edit box control.

Property	*Default*	*Description*
`AllowTabs`	`.F.`	Specifies the text displayed on the button.
`HideSelection`	`.T.`	Designates whether or not (`.F.` or `.T.`) the selected text in the edit box is visible when the edit box is not selected.
`ReadOnly`	`.F.`	Designates whether or not (`.T.` or `.F.`) the selected text in the edit box is read-only (can be viewed but not be edited).
`ScrollBars`	`.T.`	Designates whether or not (`.T.` or `.F.`) the edit box contains vertical scrollbars.

If you want to edit a memo field, set the `ControlSource` property to the name of the memo field to edit. If you have a memo field named `Abstract` in a table named ARTICLES.DBF, you set the `ControlSource` property to `ARTICLES.Abstract`.

The following example illustrates how to edit a file with an edit box control, as shown in Figure 19.41. This form, EDITOR.SCX, transfers a file to a memo field, lets the user edit it with an edit box control, and transfers the file back to the memo field.

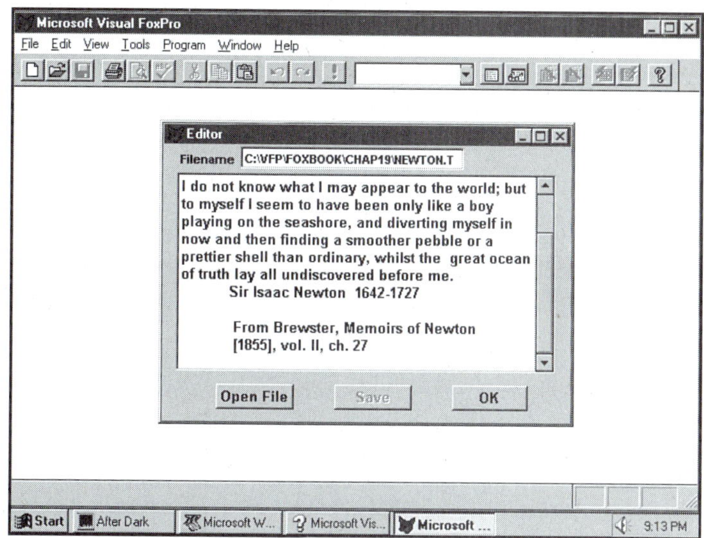

FIGURE 19.41.
A sample form that illustrates the use of an edit box control.

The form `Load` event method creates a cursor with a memo field. This must be done before the controls are loaded because the `Temp1.TextFile` field is assigned to the `ControlSource` property for the `Edit1` edit box control. The form `Load` event method consists of the following line of code:

```
CREATE CURSOR Temp1 (TextFile M)
```

The form `Init` event occurs after the controls are loaded but are yet to be displayed. The event code appends a blank record to the cursor and calls the `Click` method for the `cmdOpenFile` button with the following code:

```
PROCEDURE Init
   SELECT Temp1
   APPEND BLANK
   THISFORM.cmdOpenFile.Click    && Open a file
ENDPROC
```

The `cmdOpenFile` button `Click` event code calls the `GETFILE()` function to display the File Open dialog box, which lets the user choose the name of a text file to edit. Next, this method uses the `APPEND MEMO` command to transfer the contents of the named file to the memo field. Finally, the form's refresh method is called to redraw all of the controls. Here is the code for the `cmdOpenFile` button `Click` event:

```
PROCEDURE cmdOpenFile.Click
  IF THISFORM.cmdSave.Enabled    && Save file already open
      THISFORM.cmdSave.Click
  ENDIF
  THISFORM.cFileName = GETFILE("TXT")   && Open File Dialog
  SELECT Temp1
  IF !Empty(THISFORM.cFileName)
      APPEND MEMO TextFile FROM (THISFORM.cFileName)
```

```
        THISFORM.Refresh
        THISFORM.Text1.Value = THISFORM.cFileName
    ENDIF
ENDPROC
```

If any text is changed in the `Edit1` edit box control by the user, the `InteractiveChange` event occurs. If this event occurs, the following method is called to enable the `cmdSave` button:

```
PROCEDURE Edit1:InteractiveChange
   IF !THISFORM.cmdSave.Enabled
       THISFORM.cmdSave.Enabled = .T.
   ENDIF
ENDPROC
```

If the user clicks on the Save button and it is enabled, the `cmdSave.Click` event occurs and the following code executes to save the file with the `COPY MEMO` command:

```
PROCEDURE cmdSave.Click
   IF !EMPTY(THISFORM.cFileName)
      COPY MEMO TextFile TO (THISFORM.cFileName)
      THISFORM.cmdSave.Enabled = .F.
   ENDIF
ENDPROC
```

If the user clicks on the OK button, the `cmdOK.Click` event occurs and the following code executes to save the text in the memo field to the file, if the text in the `Edit1` edit box changed, by calling the `cmdSave.Click` method:

```
PROCEDURE cmdOK.Click
   IF THISFORM.cmdSave.Enabled AND ;
      MESSAGEBOX("Save the file?", 4+32, "Save") =6
          THISFORM.cmdSave.Click     && Save the file
   ENDIF
   RELEASE THISFORM
ENDPROC
```

Table 19.17 lists all the relevant properties for the EDITOR.SCX form.

Table 19.17. Relevant property settings for the EDITOR.SCX form.

Control	*Property*	*Description*
`Form1`	`cFileName`	User-defined property to contain the filename.
`Edit1`	`ControlSource="Temp1.Textfile"`	Source of data for edit box.
`cmdOpenFile`	`Caption = "Open File"`	Text that appears on the button.
	`Name = "cmdOpenFile"`	Name of the button.
`cmdSave`	`Caption = "Save"`	Text that appears on the button.

Control	Property	Description
	`Enabled = .F.`	Initially, the Save button is disabled.
	`Name = "cmdSave"`	
`cmdOK`	`Caption = "OK"`	Text that appears on the button.
	`Cancel = .T.`	Executes this method if the user presses the Esc key.
	`Name = "cmdOK"`	Text that appears on the button.

The Grid Control

The grid control is one of the most powerful controls in Visual FoxPro. It is similar to a Browse window, except that it is much more complicated; the Browse window is a simple grid control. In this section, you will learn about the powerful capabilities of the grid control.

Remember that a grid control is a container that contains column controls. Column controls contain a header control and any other type of control used to display columns of data. In fact, a column control can even contain another grid control.

You can easily create a simple grid. All you have to do is drag a table to the Form Designer layout window from the Data Environment Designer, the Program Manager, or the Database Designer. You might have to add better column headings if you do not use a database table with long field names.

Properties Frequently Used with Grid Controls

When you add a grid control to a form, the first thing you normally do is to set the `ColumnCount` property to the number of columns. When columns are created, they are named `Column1`, `Column2`, and so on. Each of these column containers has a header, named `Header1`, and a text field, named `Text1`. For example, if you add a grid to a form, you can programmatically reference the properties, the header, and the text field for `Column3` from the grid `Init` event method using the following statements:

```
THIS.Column3.Header1.Caption = "Invoice Number"
THIS.Column3.Column1.Text1.ControlSource = "Invoice.InvNo"
```

If you want a different type of control for the column, you can add it using the following statements:

```
THIS.Column1.AddObject("lstAccounts","LISTBOX")
THIS.Column2.AddObject("cmdPushMe","COMMANDBUTTON")
THIS.Column4.AddObject("spnAccounts","SPINNER")
*
* You must make the added controls visible
THIS.Column1.lstAccounts.Visible = .T.
THIS.Column2.cmdPushMe.Visible   = .T.
THIS.Column4.spnAccounts.Visible = .T.
*
* You need to designate the current control for the column
THIS.Column1.CurrentColumn = "lstAccounts"
THIS.Column2.CurrentColumn = "cmdPushMe"
THIS.Column4.CurrentColumn = "spnAccounts"
*
*  Set the Sparse property for the cmdPushMe
THIS.Column2.Sparse = .T.
```

In the previous code, a list box, command button, and spinner control were added to the columns. You must make these controls visible.

You can add multiple controls to a column. However, only one of them can be active. The `CurrentControl` property designates which control in a column is active. Unless you want the text box (`Text1`) control to be the initially active control, you need to set the `CurrentColumn` property.

You can set the column's `Sparse` property to true (`.T.`) if you want the added control designated by the `CurrentControl` property in a grid column to appear only when the cell is selected. Unselected cells in the column display the data value in the text box. However, if you set the `Sparse` property to false (`.F.`), the control designated by the `CurrentColumn` displays for all rows in the column. In this example, the command button (`cmdPushMe`) control displays for every single row for Column 2 since the `Sparse` property is set to false (`.F.`) The default for the `Sparse` property is true (`.T.`). Therefore, the other controls display only when the user selects a cell in the respective column.

TIP

If you want to use the `InputMask` property to define a display format (for example, `InputMask= "$999,999.99"`) and you want it to affect all of the rows of a grid, set the `Sparse` property to false. If it is set to true, only the selected cell is affected by the `InputMask` setting.

The `Columns` property is an array of references to columns. For example, `Columns(1)` refers to `Column1`. The following example illustrates the use of the `Column`, `InputMask`, and `Sparse` properties to augment a grid for which the number of columns is unknown at design time.

This example also illustrates how to build a form that automatically sets the currency type display formats for every Currency data type field in a grid. Here are the steps required to create the form:

1. Execute the Form Designer.
2. Open the Data Environment Designer and add a table with at least one Currency data type field.

TIP

A table is two clicks away. Remember that you can right-click on the form and choose the Data Environment option from the shortcut menu window to execute the Data Environment Designer. Then right-click on the Data Environment Designer window and choose the Add option from the shortcut menu to choose a table from the Add Table or View dialog box.

3. Drag the table to the form. A grid is automatically created.

NOTE

In Step 3 you create a grid with a default setting of `-1` for the `ControlCount` property. The number of columns is automatically determined when the grid is loaded, based on the number of fields in the table.

4. Size the form and the grid as shown in Figure 19.42.
5. In the Grid `Init` event method, add the following code:

```
FOR nColumn = 1 TO THIS.ColumnCount
   IF TYPE(THIS.Columns(nColumn).ControlSource) = "Y"
        THIS.Columns(nColumn).Text1.InputMask = "###,###,###.99"
       THIS.Columns(nColumn).Text1.Alignment = 1  && right adjust
THIS.Columns(nColumn).Sparse = .F.
   ENDIF
ENDFOR
```

6. Save the grid and run it.

Using these steps, you create the sample form BUDGET.SCX. The resultant form is shown in Figure 19.42. Note that the fields were manually sized so that all of the fields are visible. You can add code to specify the size of each of the currency fields.

Several grid properties, such as `RecordSourceType`, `RecordSource`, `ChildOrder`, and `LinkMaster`, are sometimes set when a form is designed. The `RecordSourceType` and `RecordSource` properties are discussed in the section "Data and Controls." The `ChildOrder` property specifies the foreign key of the child table that is joined with the primary key of the parent table. The `LinkMaster` property specifies the name of the parent table for child records displayed in the grid.

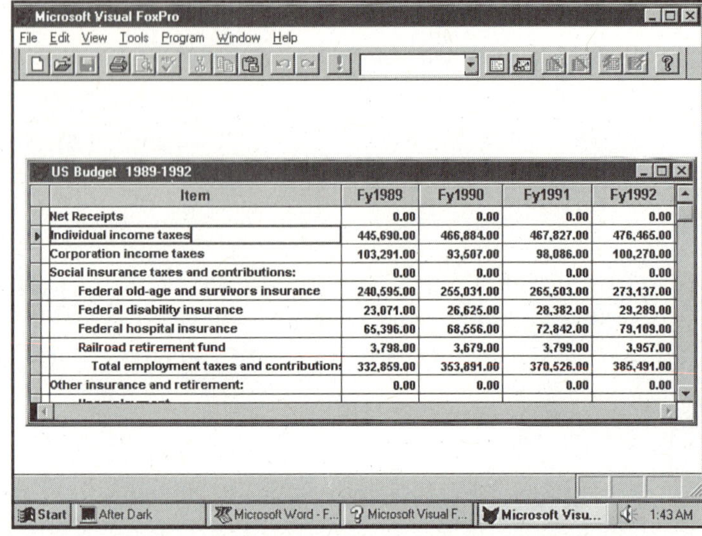

FIGURE 19.42.
A sample form that illustrates the use of the `Columns`, `InputMask`, and `Sparse` properties with a grid.

TIP

If you want a grid to be resized to fill its form when the size of the form changes (the same way the Browse grid is resized), add the following two lines of code to both the `Resize` and the `Init` event methods of the form containing a grid named `Grid1`:

```
THISFORM.Grid1.Height = THIS.Height
THISFORM.Grid1.Width = THIS.Width
```

Of course if you have other controls in the form, you will have to make appropriate `Height` and `Width` property adjustments.

Designing a Grid Visually

The best way to learn how to use grid controls is to work through an example of the design of a more complicated grid, step by step. In this example, we will step through the process required to design the form shown in Figure 19.43. Table 19.18 shows the structure for the ACMEAUTO.DBF table and the types of controls that display columns in the Automobile Sales form.

Table 19.18. The structure of the ACMEAUTO table, which displays in the Automobile Sales form.

Field	*Field Name*	*Type*	*Width*	*Column*	*Control*	*Headings*
	(none)			1	CommandButton	Details
1	`MAKE`	Character	8	2	TextBox	Make

Field	*Field Name*	*Type*	*Width*	*Column*	*Control*	*Headings*
2	`MODEL`	Character	12	3	TextBox	Model
3	`PRICE`	Numeric	11,2	4	TextBox	Price
4	`AC`	Logical	1	6	CheckBox	A/C
5	`AIRBAGS`	Logical	1			
6	`ENGINE`	Character	2	7	ComboBox	Engine
7	`PS`	Logical	1			
8	`AS_BRAKES`	Logical	1			
9	`QUANTITY`	Numeric	3	5	Spinner	Quantity
Total			41			

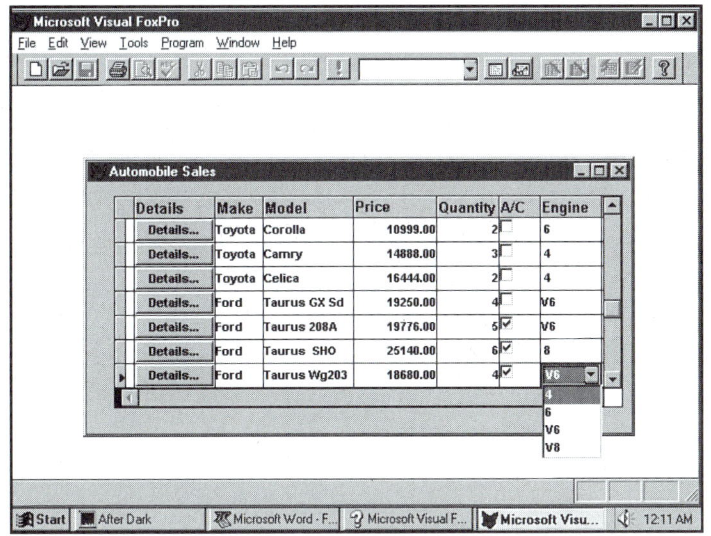

FIGURE 19.43.
A sample form that illustrates the use of a grid control with the various control types used in the columns.

Now I will step through the procedures to visually create the form shown in Figure 19.43. This application is not exactly a form. It is a form set consisting of two forms. One form contains the grid that is the primary focus of this exercise. The second form displays all of the fields in the ACMEAUTO.DBF table as text box and check box controls. The second form displays when you press one of the command buttons in the first column of the grid.

Execute the Form Designer to create the GRID.SCR form and perform the following tasks:

1. With the form selected, change the `Caption` property to `Automobile Sales`, the `AutoCenter` property to `.T.`, and the `BackColor` property to light gray.

2. Place a new grid on the `Form1` form. Click on the grid button in the Form Controls toolbar and then click on the form.
3. Change the `ColumnCount` property to `7`, and the `RecordSourceType` property to `6 - Fields`.
4. Select `Column1` from the Object box drop-down list in the Properties window. Notice the thick green outline that appears around the grid control as shown in Figure 19.44.

TIP

The quickest and easiest way to select `Column1` is to right-click on one of the rows below the `Column1` heading on the form. Choose the Edit option from the shortcut menu.

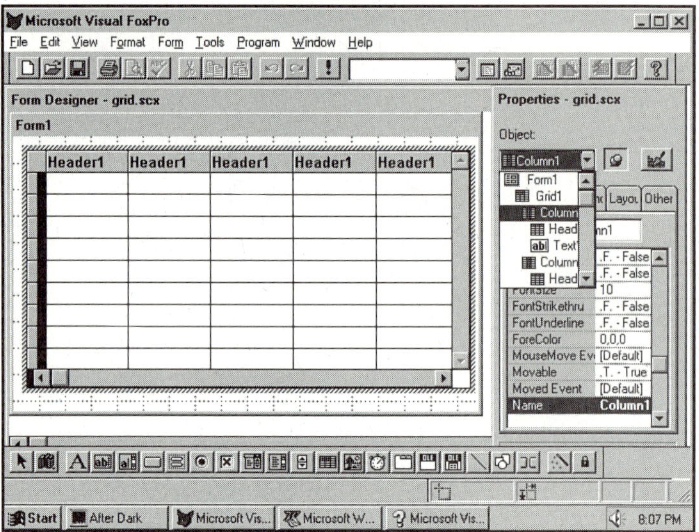

FIGURE 19.44.
Selecting Column 1 of the grid.

5. Change the `Sparse` property to `.F.` because, in this example, you want the command button to appear on every row, no matter which row is selected.
6. With `Column1` still selected, click on the Command Button tool on the Form Controls toolbar. Then click on any row in Column 1. A little square symbol appears.
7. The `Command1` object should still be selected. If it is not, select it from the Object box drop-down list on the Properties window.
8. The `Command1` control should still be selected in the Properties window. Change the `Caption` property to `Details` for the `Command1` control.

9. In the `Click` event of the `Command1 CommandButton` control, type the following:

```
THISFORMSET.Form2.Show(1)
```

   This line of code displays the `Form2` form as a modal form.

10. Select the `CurrentControl` property of the `Column1` column and select `Command1` from the Object box drop-down list.
11. Add the ACMEAUTO.DBF table to the data environment.
12. Change the widths of the grid columns so that they roughly correspond to the widths of the columns in Figure 19.43.

NOTE

You can change grid column widths visually by clicking on the vertical line between the headings. The mouse pointer changes to a double-headed arrow. Drag the vertical line to the desired column width.

13. Select `Column2`, set the `ControlSource` property to `acmeauto.make` using the Object box drop-down list of fields. At the same time, set the `ControlSource` properties for the other columns. Here is a list of the `ControlSource` properties for each column:

Column	`ControlSource` *Property*
`Column3`	`acmeauto.model`
`Column4`	`acmeauto.price`
`Column5`	`acmeauto.quantity`
`Column6`	`acmeauto.engine`

14. Select `Column4` and change the `Sparce` property to `.F.` and the `InputMask` property to `$99,999.99`.
15. Select the `Column5` column and add a spinner control in the same manner that you added the `Command1` button. (See Step 6.)
16. Select the `CurrentControl` property of the `Column5` column and select `Spinner1` from the Object box drop-down list on the Properties window.
17. Add a check box control to Column 6. Change the `Caption` property for `Checkbox1` to blanks.
18. Select the `CurrentControl` property of the `Column6` column and select `CheckBox` from the Object box drop-down list on the Properties window.
19. Repeat Step 14 to add a combo box control to Column 7. Change its `RowSourceType` property to `1 - Value` and its `RowSource` property to `4,6,V6,V8`.
20. Select the `CurrentControl` property of the `Column7` column and select `ComboBox` from the Object box drop-down list on the Properties window.

21. Select the `Heading1` objects for each column and change the `Caption` property to reflect the headings shown in Figure 19.43.
22. Now, you will create a form set and a second form, Form2. Choose the Form menu Create Form Set option to create a form set object.
23. Choose the Form menu Add New Form option to add a new form, `Form2`.
24. Choose the Form menu Quick Form… option to execute the Form Builder. Select all fields from the ACMEAUTO.DBF table in the order shown in Figure 19.45.
25. Choose the Shadowed style from the Style tab and press OK.
26. Arrange the fields and modify the field captions as shown in Figure 19.45. Change the form's `BackColor` property to light gray.
27. Add an OK button and add the following statement to the `Click` event method:

```
RELEASE THISFORMSET
```

28. Save the form and run it.

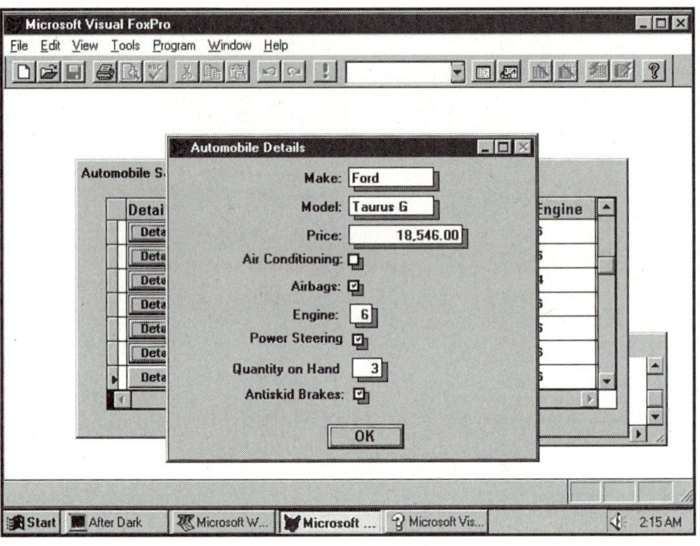

FIGURE 19.45.
A sample form initially created with the Form Builder.

If you make a mistake and need to delete a control, you can do so by following these steps:

1. Select the control you want to delete from the Object drop-down list in the Properties window.
2. Click on the title bar of the form to select the form.
3. Press the Delete key.

The *SetAll* Method

You can use the `SetAll` method to assign property settings to some or all of the objects in a container object. The grid container class is no exception. You can set the properties for all of a grid's columns with a single call to the `SetAll` method. For example, if you want to set the `BackColor` property for all of the column objects in a grid control to blue, add the following line of code to the grid's `Init` event method:

```
Form1.Grid1.SetAll('BackColor', RGB(0, 0, 255), 'Column')
```

In addition, you can assign property settings for objects contained by other objects within a container. For example, you can set the color of the text of all the column headers for a grid object to red by inserting the following statement in the `Init` event method for the grid:

```
Form1.Grid1.SetAll('ForeColor', RGB(255, 0, 0), 'Header')
```

The following steps set the color of every odd row in the grid to green, like on a ledger sheet:

1. Modify the BUDGET.SCX form that was created earlier in this chapter.
2. Place the following code in the `Init` event method of the grid:
   ```
   cExpression = 'IIF(MOD(RECNO("Budget"),2) = 0, 16777215, 65280 )'
   THIS.SetAll('DynamicBackColor', cExpression, 'Column')
   ```
3. Save the form and run it.

There is nothing mysterious about the two numbers in the above statements. It is more efficient to use the actual numbers that represent the color than to call the `RGB()` function every time a row displays. These numbers were taken from the FOXPRO.H include file constant definitions:

```
#DEFINE COLOR_WHITE        16777215
#DEFINE COLOR_GREEN           65280
```

The resultant form is shown in Figure 19.46.

The Image Control

You can add a bitmap (BMP), icon (ICO), or general field graphics picture to a form using an image control. Image controls are not just for displaying pictures. They have many of the same properties, events, and methods that other controls, such as a command button, possess. The typical properties supported by the image control are presented in Table 19.19.

Table 19.19. Typical properties used with the image control.

Property	*Default*	*Description*
`Picture`	""	Specifies the name of a bitmap (BMP) file displayed on the image control.

continues

Table 19.19. continued

Property	*Default*	*Description*
`BorderColor`	`0,0,0`	Specifies the color of the border for the image.
`BorderStyle`	`.T.`	Designates whether or not (`.F.` or `.T.`) there is a visible border for the image.
`BackStyle`	`1 - Opaque`	Specifies whether anything behind the control is visible (`0`), or the control is opaque (`1`), in which case the control's `BackColor` property obscures anything behind the control. See Figure 19.47.
`Stretch`	`0 - Clip`	Designates how an image is sized to fit inside a control. See Figure 19.47. `0 - Clip`—Does not stretch the image. It does not display any portion of the image that extends beyond the borders of the Image control. `1 - Stretch`—Stretches the image to fit the control but does not retain its original proportions. `2 - Zoom`—The image resizes to fit the control while maintaining its original proportions.
`Visible`	`.T.`	Designates whether or not (`.T.` or `.F.`) the image control is visible.

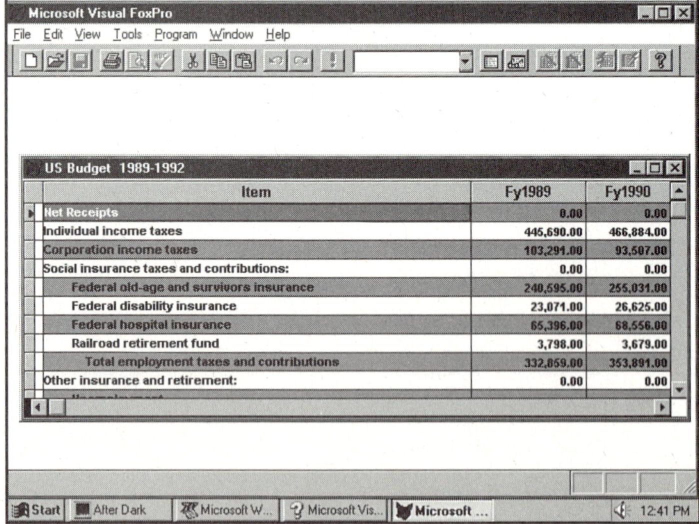

FIGURE 19.46.
A sample of the use of the `SetAll` *method with a grid object.*

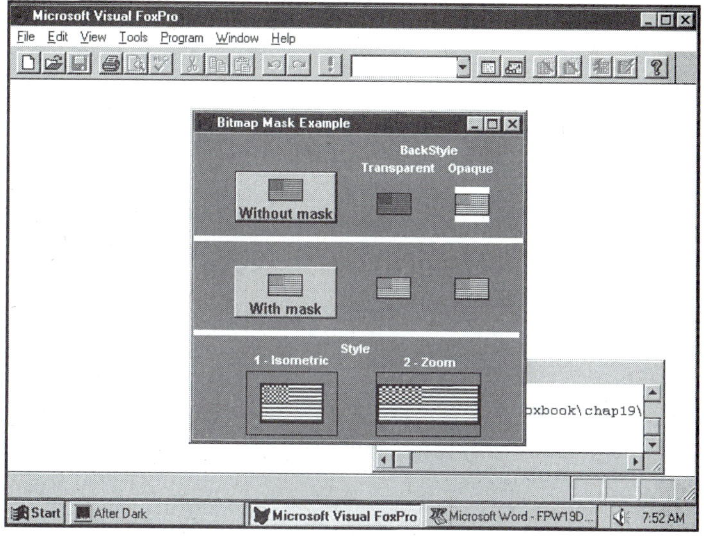

FIGURE 19.47.
A sample form that illustrates the use of an image control.

A bitmap image often has white space surrounding the little picture when it displays on an image, command button, or graphical check box control. The white pixels make the picture look bad because they do not match the background color. To remedy this, Visual FoxPro creates a mask in which white pixels are effectively made transparent. However, the mask does not always work because sometimes the white pixels are part of the image. You can rectify this problem by providing a mask file with the same root name as the BMP or ICO file and the extension .MSK. For example, FLGUS1.BMP is a bitmap file and FLGUS1.MSK is its corresponding mask. The mask file has black pixels that correspond to pixels in the BMP file that you want to display, and white pixels for any pixel that you want to be transparent. When Visual FoxPro looks for a bitmap (BMP) or icon (ICO) file, it also looks for a corresponding mask (MSK) file. If it does not find a corresponding mask (MSK) file, Visual FoxPro uses its own default mask.

For an image control, you have a choice. You can set the `BackStyle` to either opaque or transparent. If you set it to transparent, Visual FoxPro uses the mask (MSK) file, if it is available, when drawing the image control.

Look at the top row of American flags on the command button and the image controls in Figure 19.47. There is no mask (MSK) file and, as a result, the white part of the flag is gray. In the middle panel, a mask file is available, and the stars and alternate stripes are white.

A mask file must have the same dimensions as its corresponding BMP or ICO file. You can create a mask file using the following steps:

1. Open the BMP file in ImageEdit, PaintBrush, or another bitmap utility.
2. Blacken all portions of the picture that should be displayed exactly as in the bitmap (BMP) file.

3. Set the color of any portion of the picture that you want to be transparent to white.
4. Save the file in the same directory with the same filename, but change the extension to .MSK.

The Label Control

Label controls display static text on a form. It is Visual FoxPro's interpretation of the FoxPro `@...SAY` command. There is no data source for a label control, and you cannot edit data. However, you can programmatically change the `Caption` property which changes its displayed text.

Like for all other controls, you can assign an access key (hotkey) using the `\<` character sequence. (See the section "Access Keys.") In addition, you can include a label control in the form's tab order. The label control's access key activates the next active control in the tab order.

You can disable a label control using the `Enabled` property. When a label control is disabled, the access key is inactive, the same as it is for the other controls.

Table 19.20 describes the properties frequently used with the label controls.

Table 19.20. Typical properties used with the label control.

Property	*Default*	*Description*
`Caption`	`"Label1"`	Specifies the text displayed by the label control.
`AutoSize`	`.T.`	Designates whether or not (`.T.` or `.F.`) the width of the label is automatically adjusted to the length of the caption.
`BackStyle`	`1 - Opaque`	Specifies whether anything behind the control is visible (`0`), or the control is opaque (`1`), in which case the control's `BackColor` property obscures anything behind the control.
`DisabledBackColor`	`255,255,255`	Designates the background color displayed when a control is disabled.
`DisabledForeColor`	`0,0,0`	Designates the foreground color displayed when a control is disabled.
`TabIndex`	-	Specifies the tab order of controls on a page and the tab order of a form object in a form set.
`WordWrap`	`.T.`	Designates whether or not (`.T.` or `.F.`) text displayed on the label can wrap to additional lines.

You can also display text on a form using a text box or edit box control with the `ReadOnly` property set to true.

The Option Button Group Control

An option button group is a container group that contains option buttons. You use option buttons to provide the user with a predefined set of options so that the user cannot specify invalid information.

After you place an option group on the form, you need to designate how many option buttons you have by setting the `ButtonCount` property. Interface studies indicate that a group of options should not be more than seven. It is better to use a list box control if you have a large number of options.

You will need to set properties for the individual buttons. Use the Object box in the Properties window to select individual option buttons or right-click and choose the Edit option. At the very least, you need to set the `Caption` property of each option button. You can also set properties of individual option buttons by specifying the names at runtime. For example, to set the `Caption` properties at runtime for the option buttons in the option group `opgParity`, you can specify the following code:

```
THISFORM.opgParity.Option1.Caption = "Odd"
THISFORM.opgParity.Option2.Caption = "Even"
THISFORM.opgParity.Option3.Caption = "None"
```

You can accomplish the same thing using the `Buttons` property for the group option buttons control. Here is an example:

```
THISFORM.opgParity.Buttons(1).Caption = "Odd"
THISFORM.opgParity.Buttons(2).Caption = "Even"
THISFORM.opgParity.Buttons(3).Caption = "None"
```

You can use the `SetAll` method of the group option buttons control to set a property of all of the option buttons in the group. For example, suppose that you wanted to set the background color of all of the buttons for `opgParity` group to light gray. Use the following line of code:

```
THISFORM.opgParity.SetAll("BackColor", COLOR_GRAY, "OptionButton")
```

This example assumes that you used the For**m** menu **I**nclude File option to include the FOXPRO.H header file which contains the `COLOR_GRAY` definition.

You can determine which option button of a group of option buttons is selected by examining the `Value` property of the option button group. The `Value` property contains a numeric value that designates which button is selected. For example, if you have four buttons in a group and the third button is selected, then `Value` equals `3`. If no buttons are selected, the `Value` property is `0`. Suppose that you have a group (`opgTwenty`) of three option buttons with `Animal`, `Vegetable`, and `Mineral` captions. You can display the caption of the selected button when it changes by placing the following statements in the `Click` event method for the `opgTwenty` group:

```
WAIT WINDOW "You Selected button: "+THIS.Buttons(THIS.Value).Caption
```

The `Value` property of the option button group is initially set to `0` (no buttons selected); as indicated previously, it returns the number of the selected button. If you set the `Value` property to the `Caption` property of a button, then that button will be initially selected. If you set the `Value` property to an empty string, no button will be initially selected. Also, when an option button is selected, a character string containing the `Caption` of the option button is returned. In the above example, you can set `Value = ""` and use the following code to display the `Caption` property:

```
WAIT WINDOW "You Selected button: "+THIS.Value
```

This dual role of the `Value` property can be illustrated with the following example `Click` event method for the `OptionGroup1` control in the CONTROLS.SCX example shown in Figure 19.31:

```
IF  TYPE("THIS.Value")="C"   && Is Value property Character data type?
    WAIT WINDOW TIMEOUT 1 THIS.Value + ;
       " (Value is Character type)"
       THIS.Value = 0
ELSE
    IF  TYPE("THIS.Value")="N"   && Is Value property Numeric data type?
        WAIT WINDOW TIMEOUT 1 ;
           THIS.Buttons(THIS.VALUE).Caption +" (Value is Numeric)"
           THIS.Value = ""
    ENDIF
ENDIF
```

This silly example illustrates the different values the `Value` property can have depending on its data type.

As discussed earlier in this chapter, the `ControlSource` property of both the option group control and the option button can be bound to a field or variable.

The Spinner Control

The spinner control, as shown in Figure 19.31, is used to "spin" through numeric values. You set the range of allowed values with the `KeyboardHighValue`, `SpinnerHighValue`, `KeyboardLowValue`, and `SpinnerLowValue` properties.

A spinner control has a text box in which you can enter a number. It also has an up and down arrow. If you click on the up arrow, the value in the associated text box increases by the value of the `Interval` property. If you click on the down arrow, the value in the associated text box decreases by the value of the `Interval` property. The `Interval` property defaults to `1`. However, it can have any nonzero positive or negative value. Table 19.21 lists the properties that are typically used with a spinner control.

Table 19.21. Typical properties used with the spinner control.

Property	*Default*	*Description*
`DisabledBackColor`	`255,255,255`	Designates the background color displayed when a control is disabled.
`DisabledForeColor`	`0,0,0`	Designates the foreground color displayed when a control is disabled.
`Interval`	`1`	Specifies how much to increment or decrement the value each time the user clicks on one of the spinner control's arrow keys.
`KeyboardHighValue`	`100`	Designates the highest value that can be entered using the keyboard.
`KeyboardLowValue`	`0`	Designates the lowest value that can be entered using the keyboard.
`SelectedBackColor`	`255,255,255`	Designates the background color displayed when a control is selected.
`SelectedForeColor`	`0,0,0`	Designates the foreground color displayed when a control is selected.
`SpinnerHighValue`	`100`	Designates the highest value that can be entered by clicking on the arrows.
`SpinnerLowValue`	`0`	Designates the lowest value that can be entered by clicking on the arrows.

The Text Box Control

A text box is an uncommon standard control in Visual FoxPro. You use it to add or edit data in nonmemo fields and memory variables. When you set a `ControlSource` property for a text box to a field of a table or cursor, the value of that field displays in the text box control and the `Value` property is set to that value. You can programmatically assign a new value to the `Value` property, and the value displays in the text box control and is stored in the field. Table 19.22 lists properties commonly used with the text box control.

Table 19.22. Typical properties used with the text box control.

Property	*Default*	*Description*
ControlSource	" "	Specifies the nonmemo field in a table, cursor, or memory variable to be edited.
InputMask	" "	A character string that designates the data entry rule each character entered must follow. It is similar to a FORMAT clause on an @...GET statement. The characters in the mask are defined as follow: 9—Digits and signs (+ and -). #—Digits, blanks, and signs. $—Displays currency symbol. *—Displays asterisks to the left of the value. .—(period) Specifies decimal point position. ,—(comma)Separates digits. Y—For logical character type, this allows you to type T, F, Y, N, t, f, y, or n.
DisabledBackColor	255,255,255	Designates the background color displayed when a control is disabled.
DisabledForeColor	0,0,0	Designates the foreground color displayed when a control is disabled.
PasswordChar	" "	Designates whether characters entered by a user or placeholder characters are displayed in a text box; if you specify a character, such as "*", the character becomes a placeholder and displays in the field as you type. This hides what you actually type.
TabStop	.T.	Designates whether or not (.T. or .F.) the user can tab to the control. A text box control can also be selected by the user clicking on it.

The following code shows examples of how to use the `InputMask` property to control the values that can be typed into a text box.

```
InputMask="999,999.99" Displays example:  3,456.32
InputMask="$999,999.99" Displays example: $3,456.32
InputMask="###-##-####" Displays example: 123-345-3333
InputMask="***,***.99" Displays example: **3,456.32
InputMask="999,999.99" Displays example: 123,456.32
```

You can provide a visual indication of the current field by changing the colors of a text box control or any other control. You do this by setting the `ForeColor` and `BackColor` properties in the `GotFocus` event method. Then you can restore the original colors in the `LostFocus` event method.

The Timer Control

You can place a timer control on your form and then program the timer to perform a designated action at regular time intervals. You might use it to schedule tasks to be run at a certain time, to time a process to make sure it is successfully completed, to animate controls, or simply to place a special clock on a form. You can place multiple timers on a form to schedule multiple processes.

There are really only two properties that are important to the timer control: the `Interval` and the `Enabled` properties. The `Enabled` property turns the timer on (`.T.`) and off (`.F.`). The default setting for the `Enabled` property is `.T.`. If you do not want the timer to be on when the form loads, you set the `Enabled` property to `.F.` when you design the form. Then you can turn it on and off, as required, at runtime.

The `Interval` property specifies the approximate number of milliseconds between events. When the specified interval expires, the `Timer` event code executes. The `Interval` property does not specify how long—it specifies how often the `Timer` event code executes. The `Timer` event continues to trigger at each interval until you turn it off by setting the `Enabled` property to `.F.`.

You should be aware of the limitations of the `Interval` property when you are programming a timer. Here are the limitations:

- The `Interval` property can be set between 0 and 2,147,483,647 (2^{31}-1) or about 24.9 days or 596.52 hours.
- There is no guarantee that the `Timer` event will fire precisely on time. To get an accurate time, you should retrieve the time from the system clock with the `TIME()` function.
- The computer system clock generates a systems timer interrupt 18 times a second; although the `Interval` property is measured in milliseconds, the actual precision is no better than $^1/_{18}$ of a second.
- If the computer performing intensive calculations or processing I/O interrupts, the interval between `Timer` events may vary even more than $^1/_{18}$ of a second.

The following simple example, the CLOCK.SCX form, illustrates how to use the timer control. In this example, you add the timer control to the form the same way you would any other control. The timer control displays on the form in the Form Designer, as shown in Figure 19.48. However, the timer control is invisible when you run the form, as shown in Figure 19.49. The CLOCK.SCX form has a couple of text box controls: `txtDate` and `txtTime`. `txtTime` is an option group with six buttons, a spinner, an Exit button, and two timer controls. The `FontSize` property for `txtTime` is set to `72`.

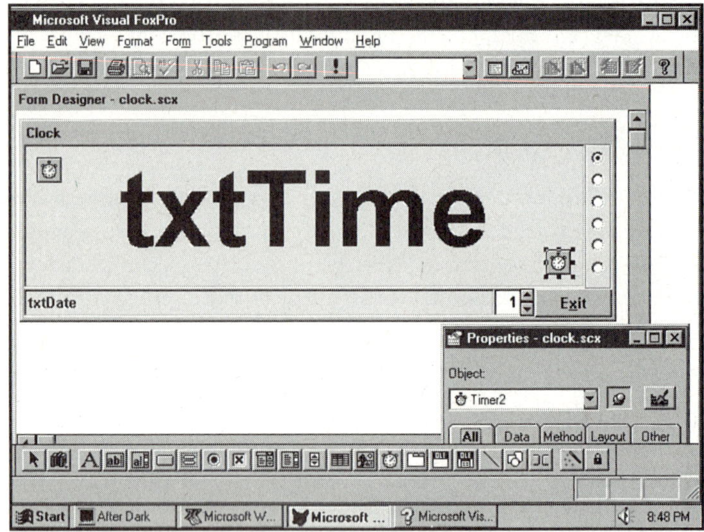

FIGURE 19.48.
A sample form that illustrates the use of a timer control.

The first timer control, `Timer1`, displays the time and date whenever the `Timer` event occurs. The `Interval` property is set to 500 milliseconds (1/2 second). If the `Interval` property is set for 1 second (1000), it misses a second occasionally. It is best to always set the `Interval` property to one-half of the shortest period you want to distinguish. In this case, it is best to have the `Timer` event code execute every second. Sometimes the display is updated with the same time twice. If the display updates too often, you might experience a flickering display. If you do, you can add code which tests to see if the time changes before you update the display. Here is the code for the `Timer` event:

```
cTime = Time()
IF WMINIMUM(THISFORM.Name)  && Is Form minimized?
   THISFORM.Caption = "Clock    " + cTime    && Show Time on Title bar
ELSE
   THISFORM.Caption = "Clock "
   * Place Date in TextBox in the form:  Month dd, yyyy
   THISFORM.txtDate.Value = CDOW(date())+" "+ ;
      CMONTH(date())+" "+ ;
      ALLTRIM(STR(DAY(date())))+", " ;
      +ALLTRIM(STR(YEAR(date())))
   * Place Time in TextBox in the form:  HH:MM:SS am/pm
```

```
    nHour = VAL(SUBSTR(cTime,1,2))
    IF nHour > 12
       cTime = ALLTRIM(STR(nHour - 12)) ;
             + SUBSTR(cTime,3,6) + " pm"
    ELSE
       cTime = cTime + "am"
    ENDIF
    THISFORM.txtTime.Value = cTime
ENDIF
```

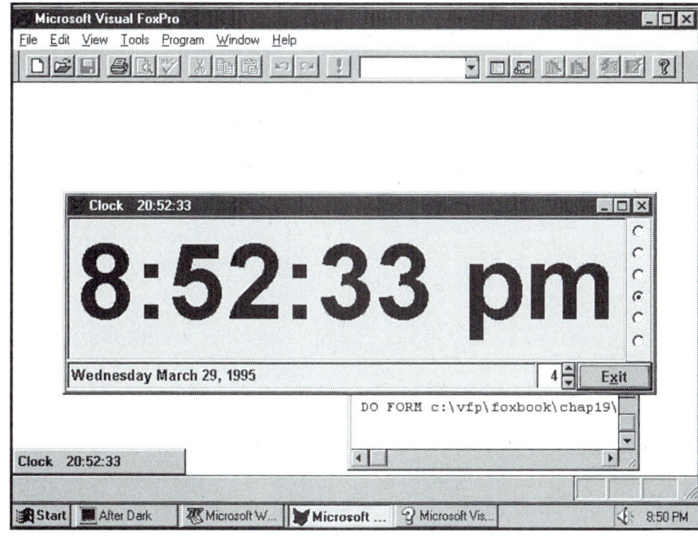

FIGURE 19.49.
A sample execution of the CLOCK.SCX form that illustrates types of uses for timer controls.

The second timer control demonstrates simple animation. Each time the `Timer` event occurs, the next option control in the option group is selected using the following line of code in the `Timer` event method for the `Timer2` control:

```
THISFORM.OptionGroup1.Value =  MOD(THISFORM.OptionGroup1.Value,6)+1
```

A spinner control changes the `Interval` property for the `Timer2` control. When the user changes the control, the `InteractiveChange` event occurs which executes the following event code:

```
IF THIS.Value = 0
   THISFORM.Timer2.Enabled = .F.    && Turn off Timer2
ELSE
   THISFORM.Timer2.Interval = THIS.Value*500
   THISFORM.Timer2.Enabled = .T.    && Turn on Timer2
ENDIF
```

The Shape and Line Controls

You can use shape and line controls to group forms together and to divide the form into logical panels to enhance readability.

A line control is a simple line that displays horizontally, vertically, or diagonally. The line control property that you are most likely to change is the `BorderWidth` property. This property specifies the width of the line in pixels. In Figure 19.47, the `BorderWidth` property for the lines are set to 5 pixels wide.

The `LineSlant` property designates which way the line slants when it is not vertical or horizontal. You can specify `(/)` or `(\)`, to instruct the Form Designer how you want the line to slope, in a rectangle that appears only when you size a line control.

You can use the shape control to display a box, circle, or ellipse. The properties that are often set for the shape control are presented in Table 19.23.

Table 19.23. Typical properties used with the shape control.

Property	*Default*	*Description*
`Curvature`	`0`	Specifies the curvature of the shape with values between `0` and `99`. Examples are shown in Figure 19.50.
`FillStyle`	1	Specifies whether a shape is solid, transparent, or has a fill pattern, as shown in Figure 19.50.
`BorderStyle`	1	Specifies the border style of an object. Styles are shown in Figure 19.50. Applies only if `BorderWidth` is greater than 1 pixel. Applies to lines and shapes.
`BorderWidth`	1	Specifies the width in pixels of the border for the shape. Applies to lines and shapes.
`SpecialEffects`	1	Specifies whether the shape control is plain or in 3-D. This property only applies when the `Curvature` property equals `0`.

The line and shape controls normally are not changed directly at runtime. However, both controls possess many of the same properties, events, and methods other controls have. Both controls can respond to events such as `Click`, `DblClick`, and `DragOver` and can be changed at runtime.

You can draw graphics objects on the form using the following form methods:

Method	*Object Drawn on a Form*
`Circle`	Circular figure or arc
`Cls`	Clears graphics and text
`Line`	Line

`Pset`	Sets a point on a form to a specific color
`Print`	Prints a character string on a form

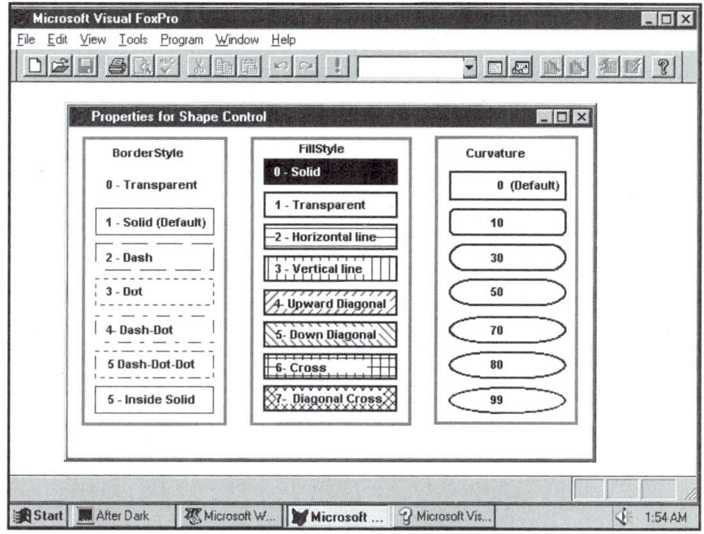

FIGURE 19.50.
An example that illustrates the `FillStyle`, `BorderStyle`, *and* `Curvature` *properties for the shape control.*

Form properties, such as `DrawWidth`, `DrawStyle`, `DrawMode`, `FillColor`, `FillStyle`, and `ForeColor`, define properties of objects drawn on the form.

Special Control Features

You can make a better user interface if you take advantage of some of the special features that are available in Visual FoxPro. These special features include access keys, tool tip text, status bar messages, and drag-and-drop operations. Each of these features have been mentioned in other previous sections. However, this section focuses in more detail on each of these special features.

Access Keys

You can define an *access key* (or *hotkey*) to a control by placing the `\<` character sequence immediately in front of the character that you want to be the access key. For example, to have the letter a be the access key for a C**a**ncel control button, set the `Caption` property to `C\<ancel`.

When the caption displays, the access key is underlined. When you run the form, you can press Alt+<*access key*> to move the focus to that control. Incidentally, if one form in a form set has focus and you press an access key for a control on another form of the same form set, the other form becomes active and the control with the access key receives focus.

Tool Tips and Status Bar Messages

Each control has a `ToolTip` property that defines a text message which displays after the mouse pointer rests on the control for a couple of seconds. Picture buttons are handy, but sometimes they do not provide a clue as to their function. You should provide a tool tip message for each of your picture buttons. It is easy to do. Just set the `ToolTip` property at design time. Also, set the `ShowTips` property in the form or form set property list to `.T.`. It must be set to true (`.T.`) or else the tool tip text will not display.

You can set the `StatusBarMsg` property to specify a longer reminder message which appears on the Visual FoxPro status bar when you move the mouse pointer over the control.

Drag and Drop

As you have developed applications in Visual FoxPro, you have probably already discovered that you can drag fields and tables from the Data Environment Designer, Project Manager, and Database Designer to a form or report. You have dragged controls from the Form Controls toolbar to a form or a report. But did you know that you can add the drag-and-drop feature to your application? You can drag objects from any form to any other form in your application. You can respond to a drag event from any control in your application.

You can specify a cursor (CUR) file that displays as the dragged object moves. If you do not specify one, a mouse cursor changes to a gray rectangle outline which is visible as long as the user drags the object.

When the user drops an object on a control, the `DragDrop` event fires and the `DragDrop` event code executes. For example, consider the BUTTON.SCX form shown in Figure 19.40. Suppose that you were to modify this form to allow yourself to drag the Cancel button, light bulb button, or light bulb check box onto the Happy Button button, at which time the Happy Button button eats the dragged button.

The `DragMode` property controls the drag mode. The default mode is the manual drag mode (`DragMode = 0`) in which you are required to call the control's `Drag` method when you want to begin, end, or cancel a drag operation. The other drag mode is automatic drag mode (`DragMode = 1`). When the `DragMode` property is set to automatic mode, you can click on the control and drag it. However, other access to the control is suspended: For example, you cannot click on it—the `Click`, `DblClick`, and other user interaction events do not fire when the `DragMode` property is set to automatic mode.

Since you want to use the buttons for control, you do not want to initially set the `DragMode` property to automatic. You can add an option to toggle the drag mode on and off. The user can activate this option by double-clicking on the form. To make this work, add the following code to the form's `DblClick` event method:

```
*************************************************
* Double-click on the form to toggle DragMode
* property between 1 (Manual) and 2 (Automatic)
LOCAL lNewMode
IF THISFORM.Check1.DragMode = 1
   lNewMode = 0
   THISFORM.Caption = "Buttons"
ELSE
   lNewMode = 1
   THISFORM.Caption = "Drag Buttons"
ENDIF
THISFORM.Check1.DragMode = lNewMode
THISFORM.Command2.DragMode = lNewMode
THISFORM.Command1.DragMode = lNewMode
```

This code toggles the `DragMode` property between manual and automatic modes for the `Check1` check box and the `Command1` and `Command2` buttons. It also changes the form's title to indicate when you can drag the controls.

Now you add code to the Happy Button button's `DragDrop` event method to make the Happy Button button gobble up the control buttons when you drop them. It also gobbles up the label controls below the control. Here is the code:

```
PROCEDURE Button.DragDrop
Parameters oSource, nXCoord, nYCoord, nState
Wait window nowait "Gobbled up "+oSource.Name timeout 2
oSource.Visible = .F.
oSource.Enabled = .F.
DO CASE
   CASE oSource.Name = "Command2"
        oSource.Parent.Label2.Visible = .F.
   CASE oSource.Name = "Check1"
        oSource.Parent.Label1.Visible = .F.
ENDCASE
ENDPROC
```

When the user drags a control (the source) over the Happy Button button (the target) and drops it (releases the mouse button), the Happy Button button's `DragDrop` event fires and Visual FoxPro calls the `DragDrop` event method and passes it three arguments. The `oSource` parameter is a reference to the object being dragged. The `nXCoord` and `nYCoord` parameters are coordinates of the mouse pointer within the target's coordinate system. The `nIndex` parameter is a number that uniquely identifies a control if it is a control array. The `DragDrop` event method controls what occurs after a drag operation is finished. You can use it to delete, copy, print, or move a file.

Notice how the program references other objects in the form. For example, the label control is hidden using the following statement:

```
oSource.Parent.Label2.Visible = .F.
```

The `Parent` property is a reference to the form containing the object referenced by `oSource`. This way you can create multiple instances of the Button form, drag a control from one instance to the Happy Button of another instance, and drop the control; the `Label2` control on the same form instance as the drag-and-dropped control is hidden. Try it.

The `DragOver` event is used to provide a visual representation of what will happen when an object is dropped on a control. When a cursor moves over a form or control, the form or control's `DragOver` event occurs. You can change the cursor when it is dragged over a control to provide a visual clue as to what will happen if you drop the object. You add this code to the control's `DragOver` event method. In the following example, the Happy Button button's `DragOver` event contains the following code which changes the cursor shape when an object is dragged over the Happy Button button:

```
PROCEDURE Button.DragOver
Parameters oSource, nXCoord, nYCoord, nState
DO CASE
   CASE nState = 0    && Enter control
      THISFORM.cSaveIcon = oSource.DragIcon  && Save icon
      oSource.DragIcon = "Danger.CUR"
   CASE nState = 1    && Leave control
      oSource.DragIcon = THISFORM.cSaveIcon
ENDCASE
```

When the mouse pointer initially moves over the control, the `DragOver` event is called with the `nState` parameter set to `0`. When the mouse pointer moves off of a control, Visual FoxPro calls the `DragOver` event method with the `nState` parameter set to `1`. In this example, a cursor, warning the user of danger, displays while the mouse cursor is over the Happy Button button. As you remember, the dragged object is in danger because if the user drops the object, the Happy Button button eats it. You also need to define the `Form1.cSaveIcon` property using the For**m** menu New **P**roperty option.

Oh yes, one other thing: The `DragIcon` properties for the controls are assigned the names of cursor (CUR) files as indicated in the following list:

Control	`DragIcon` *Property Cursor File*
`Command1`	Lighton.CUR
`Check1`	Lighton.CUR
`Command2` (Cancel)	Cancel.CUR

If you want to manually control drag operations (`DragMode=0`), you can call the `Drag` method for the control being dragged and pass it an optional argument. If you omit the argument, a value of `1` is assumed. Here are the values for the `Drag` method argument:

Call Example	*Purpose*
`THISFORM.Control.Drag(0)`	Cancels the drag operation and restores the original position of the control. Also, the `DragDrop` event method is *not* called.

`THISFORM.Control.Drag(1)`	Begins the drag operation of the control. This is the default.
`THISFORM.Control.Drag(2)`	Ends the drag operation of the control. In other words, drops the control.

Here is the typical technique for doing manual drag-and-drop operations:

1. Add code to the `MouseDown` event method, which calls the `Drag(1)` method to start the drag operation.
2. Add code to the `MouseUp` event method to either drop (`Drag(1)`) the object or cancel (`Drag(0)`) the drag operation.

For example, suppose that you want to drag a button named `cmdDragMe` to the Happy Button button (`Button` control). Before you do this, you must create a new form named DRAG.SCX from the BUTTON.SCX form. One way to do this is to modify the BUTTON.SCX form. Then, use the **F**ile menu Save **A**s button to save the form as DRAG.SCX. To modify the DRAG.SCX form perform the following steps:

1. Add a new control button, name it `cmdDragMe`, and set its `Caption` property to `DragMe`.
2. Add the following line of code to the `MouseDown` event method:
   ```
   THIS.Drag(1)&& Start Dragging cmdButton
   ```
3. Add the following line of code to the `MouseUp` event method:
   ```
   THIS.Drag(2)&& End Dragging operation
   ```
4. Click on the Standard toolbar's Run (!) button to run the form.

You can drag the `DragMe` button to the Happy Button button and drop it. The Happy Button button will gobble up the button just as it gobbles the other buttons.

Finally, here is a summary of the principal drag-and-drop properties, events, and methods:

- The `DragMode` property enables automatic and manual drag mode.
- The `DragIcon` property defines the cursor shape displayed during the dragging operation.
- The `DragDrop` event occurs when an object is dropped on a control.
- The `DragOver` event occurs when the mouse pointer moves over a control.
- The `Drag` method is called to control manual drag-and-drop operations to start and stop the operation.

Animation

You can use the timer control to control animation. Each time the timer event fires, you can perform the next phase of an animation process.

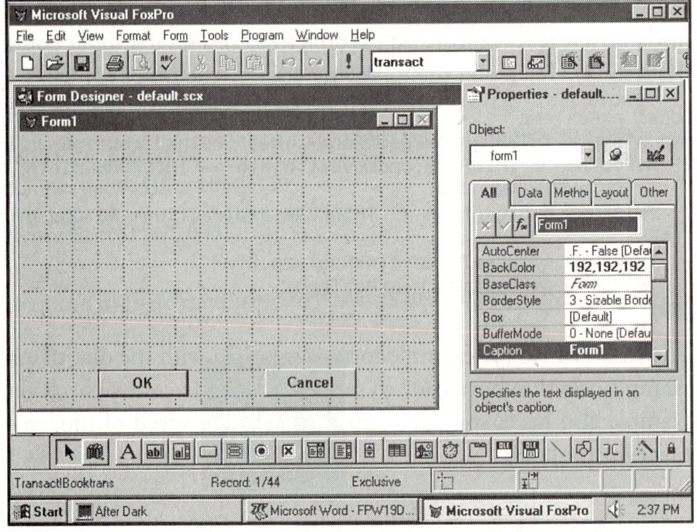

FIGURE 19.53.
A custom form template.

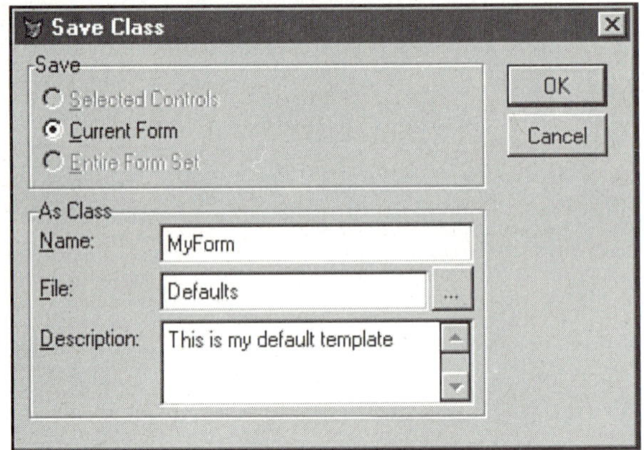

FIGURE 19.54.
The Save Class dialog box.

Choose the **T**ools menu **O**ptions option, and the Options dialog box appears. From the Options dialog box Forms tab, you can register your custom form template. Check the Form check box. When the Open dialog box appears, select the DEFAULTS.VBX visual class library. Your custom form `MYFORM` class becomes the registered form template, as indicated in Figure 19.55.

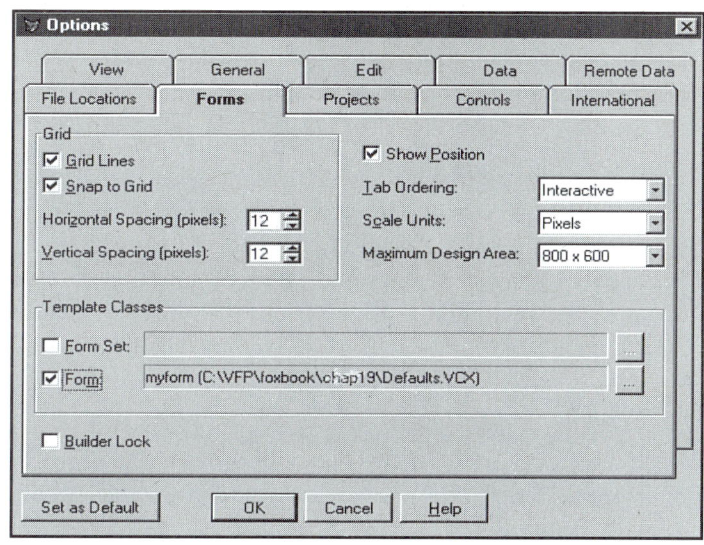

FIGURE 19.55.
The Options dialog box Forms tab.

Now, whenever you execute the Form Designer to create a new form, a form is created based on your custom template form, as shown in Figure 19.56. When you add another form to a form set, it is based on your custom template form.

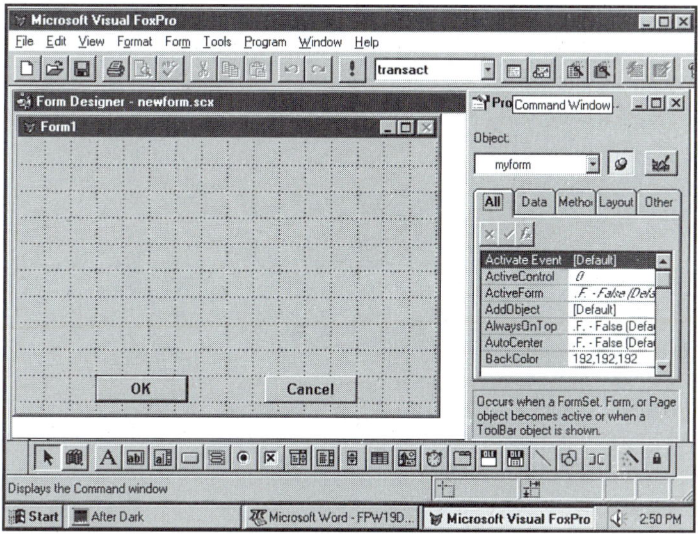

FIGURE 19.56.
The Form Designer using a custom form template.

You can do the same thing with the form set that you did for the form. Then each time you create a new form set, a form set is created which is based on your custom form set. If you have registered a form template, a form is created based on your custom form.

Summary

The approach I have taken in writing this book is to provide you with an understanding of the Visual FoxPro language before you are formally introduced to the FoxPro development tools. Because of that, you read this chapter armed with the knowledge of how to write Visual FoxPro code and the fundamentals of OOP. As a result, you understand the significance of each of the objects. You weren't intimidated by events and methods, and you already knew the value of properties.

In this chapter you have learned about all the elements of the Form Designer and the Data Environment Designer. You have learned how to use each of the controls and containers and how to create forms, form sets, and templates.

20

Report and Label Designers and Wizards

Reporting facts is the refuge of those who have no imagination.

—Luc, Marquis de Vauvenargues (1715–1747)

The capability of generating reports is an important part of any database management system. The Visual FoxPro Report Designer is easy to use, powerful, flexible, and fun to operate. Visual FoxPro also supports a variety of Report Wizards that are even easier to use to create reports. The Report Wizards are presented in Chapter 24, "Wizards."

The Visual FoxPro Report Designer supports the following types of reporting:

- One-keystroke quick report layouts
- Complex tabular reports
- Tabular reports with multiple columns
- Fill-in forms (such as invoice forms)
- Mailing labels using predefined forms

Two basic functions are associated with the Report Designer: designing a report and printing a report. For this discussion, creating a new report from scratch and redesigning an existing report are considered the same task. Printing a report involves generating a report and directing the output to the printer or a file. Figure 20.1 shows a sample Report Designer window.

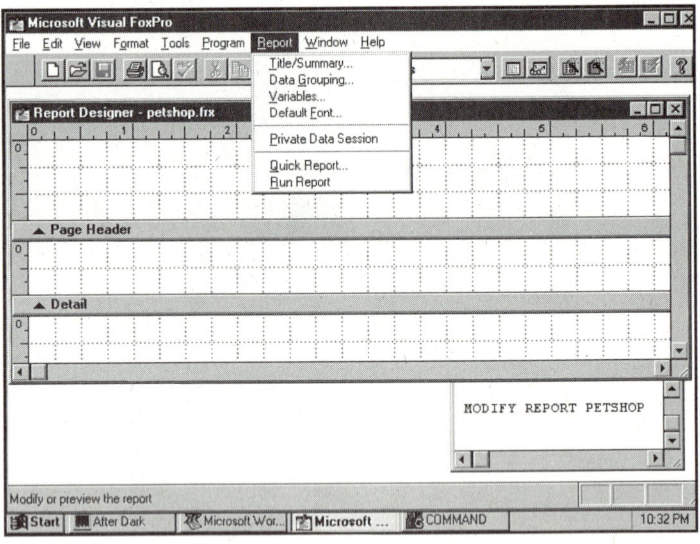

FIGURE 20.1.
The Report Designer window.

Designing a report involves placing controls on the work surface. The controls consist of the following:

- Fields from the active database table or view
- Special calculated fields created for the report
- Text that you can type anywhere on the work surface
- Boxes with square and rounded corners
- Lines

After you create or generate a report, you use the REPORT command to print it. Chapter 8, "Input and Output," describes the REPORT command.

As Figure 20.1 shows, the Report Designer window is similar to the Form Designer window, except that the former doesn't have bands, the toolbar doesn't have as many buttons, and you cannot place any active controls on the Report Designer Layout window. The components of a report (header, detail, subtotals, and so forth) are subdivided into separate areas on the workspace, which are called *bands.*

There are many ways to execute the Report Designer to create a new report. You can choose the **F**ile menu **N**ew or **O**pen option. From the Project Manager, you can select the report icon and click on the New button. You can execute the Report Wizard. You can execute the CREATE REPORT or MODIFY REPORT command from the Command window. This is the syntax of the CREATE REPORT and MODIFY REPORT commands:

```
CREATE REPORT [<expFN> ¦ ?] [NOWAIT] [SAVE]
   [[WINDOW <window1>]
   [IN [WINDOW] <window2> ¦ IN SCREEN]]
MODIFY REPORT [<expFN> ¦ ?] [[WINDOW <window1>]
   [IN [WINDOW] <window2>  ¦ SCREEN]]
   [NOENVIRONMENT] [NOWAIT] [SAVE]
```

If you don't supply the filename extension, .FRX is assumed. A file with an .FRT extension is also generated. Executing this command creates the report form file if it does not already exist. If it exists, this command processes it. If you specify a question mark (?) instead of a filename or if you specify no filename at all, the Open File dialog box appears, containing FRX (or FoxBASE+ FRM) files. The file you select from this menu is processed. When you exit from the CREATE REPORT or MODIFY REPORT command, the FRX file is saved. The [NOENVIRONMENT] keyword is left over from earlier versions of FoxPro. It is not used in Visual FoxPro except when you first modify a FoxPro 2.*x* report form. You can also display the Report Designer in a user-defined window. See Chapter 7, "FoxPro Language Elements for Creating Windows and Menu Systems," for a description of user-defined windows and all of the rest of the keywords and clauses.

The Report Designer also generates mailing labels. However, when you want to create a label form, you don't execute the Report Designer directly with the CREATE REPORT command; you execute the CREATE LABEL command. You can execute the Report Designer to create or modify a label form by choosing the **F**ile menu **N**ew or **O**pen option or by executing the CREATE LABEL or MODIFY LABEL command from the Command window. This is the syntax:

```
CREATE LABEL  [<expFN> ¦ ? ]
MODIFY LABEL  [<expFN> ¦ ? ]
```

If you don't supply the filename extension, .LBX is assumed. When this command executes, the label form file is created if it doesn't already exist. If it exists, this command processes it. If you specify a question mark (?) instead of a filename or if you specify no filename at all, the Open File dialog box appears, containing LBX files. The file you select from this menu is processed. When you exit from the CREATE LABEL or MODIFY LABEL command, the LBX file is saved.

I'll further discuss using the Report Designer to generate labels later in this chapter, but first I'll focus on the elements and usage of the Report Designer.

The Toolbars

You can place, move, size, align, and delete controls on the report layout form the same way you place form controls on the Form Designer layout window. There are three toolbars used with the Report Designer: the Report Controls, Layout, and Color Palette toolbars. You can turn them on or off from the View menu. The Layout menu contains a selection pointer button and picture buttons representing report controls identified in Figure 20.2.

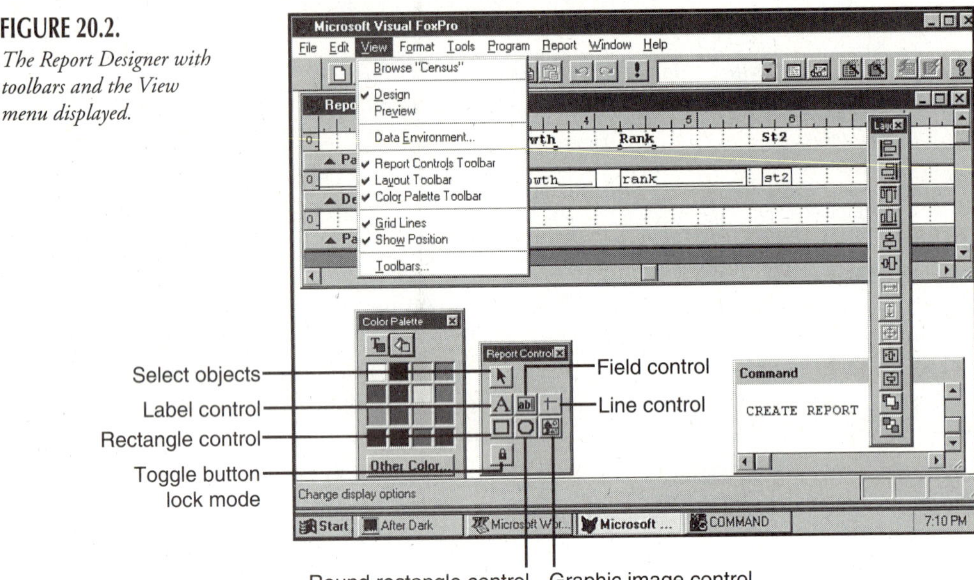

FIGURE 20.2.
The Report Designer with toolbars and the View menu displayed.

The Layout toolbar buttons that perform the alignment and sizing operations on selected controls are shown in Table 20.1.

Table 20.1. Layout toolbar controls.

Control	*Alignment for the Selected Control*
	Left edges
	Right edges
	Top edges
	Bottom edges

Control	*Alignment for the Selected Control*
	Horizontal centers
	Vertical centers
Control	*Size for the Selected Control*
	Same width as widest selected control
	Same height as tallest selected control
	Same height and width as largest control
Control	*Other Layout Toolbar Button*
	Centers one or more selected controls in the form horizontally
	Centers one or more selected controls in the form vertically
	Positions the selected controls in front of all the other controls
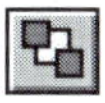	Positions the selected controls behind all the other controls

TIP

You can press the Ctrl key when you click on a Layout toolbar size control button; the selected controls will be resized to the size of the smallest button. Pressing the Ctrl key when you click on an alignment control also affects its operation. The alignment controls align the controls to the edge of the control closest to the direction the controls will move during the align process. However, if the Ctrl key is pressed when you click on an alignment control, the alignment will be on the edge of the control that is farthest from the direction the controls move during the alignment process.

Adding Controls to a Report Layout Form

Click a control in the Report Controls toolbar, point the mouse pointer to a spot on the Report Layout window and click. You can size the line, rectangle, rounded corner, and field controls by dragging the mouse pointer until you obtain the desired size. A single click of the mouse places other report controls on the Report Layout window.

NOTE

If you want to place more than one report control of the same type on the Report Layout window, click on the button lock control and you can place multiple controls on the Report Layout window without clicking the control each time. When you finish creating controls of the same type, click on the button lock control or click on the selection pointer.

When you choose the field or picture control, a dialog box opens in which you can define the control properties. In addition, you can activate a control dialog box for any control by double-clicking a control. Also, you can click on a control with the right mouse button and choose the Properties option from the shortcut menu.

Selecting Controls

The Visual FoxPro interface is consistent. You select one or more controls in the Report Designer the same way you do using the Form Designer.

To select a control, click the selection pointer button and then click the control. You can include multiple controls in a selection either by pressing the Shift key while you click multiple controls or by dragging a marquee around several controls.

You can associate multiple controls for more than one operation by identifying them as a *group*. Then you can move, cut, paste, delete, or copy them as a single object. To do this, select the controls that you want to treat as a group and choose the F**o**rmat menu Grou**p** option. At any time, you can disassociate controls in a group so that they become individual controls by selecting the group and choosing the F**o**rmat menu **U**ngroup option.

When you select a control, you can move it or resize it. You can change the font, font size, or font style from the F**o**rmat menu F**o**nt option. You can change the background or foreground color for one or more selected controls using the Color Palette toolbar.

NOTE

In FoxPro 2.6, there was a Rep**o**rt menu and an **O**bject menu, which contained all of the options needed for the Report Designer. The menu structure was changed in Visual FoxPro to be more consistent with other Windows applications. Options that relate to the Report Designer are spread out across the system menus. For example, you can define the report layout using the **F**ile menu Page Set**u**p option; you can change the font, size, and alignments from the F**o**rmat menu; and you can establish the data environment, open Report Designer toolbars, and set options from the **V**iew menu.

Moving a Control

You can move a control by clicking it and dragging it to a new location. You keyboard aficionados can select a control and use the arrow keys to move it to a new location. When you move a control, it moves smoothly across the layout if the F**o**rmat menu Snap to **G**rid option is off. However, if it is on, the control jumps between the invisible alignment grid lines.

Sizing a Control

When a control is selected, small rectangles appear on its sides and corners. These rectangles are called *handles*. You can resize a control by clicking one of these handles and dragging it until it reaches the desired size. The sizing operation also depends on the Snap to **G**rid setting.

NOTE

You can override the Snap to **G**rid setting by pressing the Ctrl key while you size a control with the mouse. You can resize a control with the keyboard using the arrow keys while pressing the Shift key.

Placing or Editing a Label Control on the Report Layout Window

To add a new label control, or to edit text in an existing label control, click the label control and click the spot on the Report Layout window where you want to add it or edit text. The shape of the mouse cursor turns into a blinking vertical bar. Type new text or edit existing text.

Drawing a Line

You can draw a vertical or horizontal line by clicking the line control and clicking the spot on the Report Layout window where you want to place one end of the line. Then drag the mouse to another spot on-screen where you want to place the other end of the line. You can always click a line to select it. Then you can move or resize it, or modify its properties (`Fill`, `Pen`, and `Color`).

Drawing a Box

You can draw a rectangular box by clicking the rectangle control, or you can draw a rectangular box with rounded corners by clicking the rounded rectangle control. Click the spot on the Report Layout window where you want one corner of the box and drag the mouse pointer to another spot on the Report Layout window where you want the other corner of the box. You can also click the borders of the line to select it. Then you can resize or move it, or you can use the F**o**rmat menu option to change its pen (size, type, and color) and fill (type and color).

If you double-click a rounded rectangle, the Round Rectangle dialog box appears, as shown in Figure 20.3. You can choose the shape of a rounded rectangle from an elliptical to a slightly rounded shape and specify some other options. Some options in this dialog box specify what happens to the rounded rectangle if the band in which it resides stretches. Table 20.2 describes the Round Rectangle dialog box options.

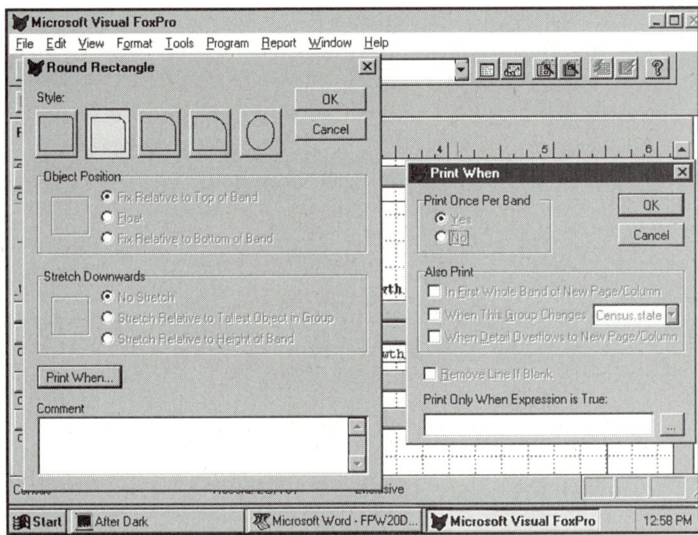

FIGURE 20.3.
The Round Rectangle and Print When dialog boxes.

Table 20.2. A description of the Round Rectangle dialog box options.

Option	*Description*
Style	This option consists of picture push buttons. Click your favorite picture.
Object Position	Three radio buttons enable you to specify what happens to a rounded rectangle when its report band stretches.
Fix Relative to Top of Band	When you select this option, the box remains positioned relative to the top of the band.
Float	When you select this option, the top of the box remains positioned relative to the top of the band, the bottom of the box remains positioned relative to the bottom of the band, and the sides stretch.
Fix Relative to Bottom of Band	When you select this option, the box remains positioned relative to the bottom of the band.

Option	Description
No stretch	The box does not change its size.
Stretch Relative to Tallest Object in Group	Use this option if you are displaying a field with a variable number of lines and you want the rectangle to stretch to contain all of the lines.
Stretch Relative to Height of Band	This is used if you have a varied number of lines but the box can extend beyond multiple field controls.
Print When...	If you select this button, the Print When dialog box displays, as shown in Figure 20.3 and as described in Table 20.3.
Comment...	If you choose this push button, the Comment dialog box displays. It contains an edit box into which you can type comments.

If you double-click on a line or a rectangle control, the Line/Rectangle dialog box displays. It contains all the options that the Round Rectangle dialog box contains except the Style picture buttons.

The Print When dialog box provides options used to suppress the printing of repeated values of a control. Figure 20.3 shows this dialog box and Table 20.3 describes its options.

Table 20.3. The Print When dialog box description.

Option	Description
Print Once Per Band	This option contains two radio buttons used to suppress the printing of repeated values.
In First Whole Band of New Page/Column	You can mark this check box if you want the field name to show in the first complete band of a new page or column.
When This Group Changes	This check box is enabled for a field in a group band. You can mark this check box and choose a field name from a list to designate that you want the control to print when the chosen field changes.

continues

Table 20.3. continued

Option	*Description*
When **D**etail Overflows to New Page/Column	If you select this check box, the control is printed when the detail overflows to a new page or column.
Print Only When **E**xpression is True...	If you select this check box, the Expression Builder dialog box appears and you specify a logical expression. When the report prints, FoxPro evaluates the logical expression and, if it is true, the corresponding control is printed.
Remove Line If Blank	If you select this check box, the printing of blank lines is suppressed.

Placing a Field or an Expression on the Report Layout Window

You can place a field or an expression on the Report Layout window by clicking the field control and clicking the spot on the Report Layout window where you want the left side of the field to display. If you click and hold down the left mouse button when you place a field on-screen, you can drag the mouse pointer to define the size of the newly defined field.

After you place a field on-screen, the Report Expression dialog box appears, as shown in Figure 20.4. This dialog box is similar to the dialog box for other controls, with the addition of the Expression and Format text boxes and associated push buttons.

You can either type a field or expression to the right of the Expression push button or you can press the button and the Expression Builder dialog box displays, as shown in Figure 20.4. With this dialog box, you can choose a field or compose an expression. You can use the Verify push button to validate your expression so that you can make sure you composed it correctly.

You can specify the format that your expression or field displays either by typing a `FUNCTION` display code (preceded by an `@` sign) into the text box to the left of the Format push button or by pressing the Format push button, which displays the Format dialog box shown in Figure 20.5. This dialog box has different editing options depending on the data type of the specified field or expression.

You can use the Calculations push button to specify statistical calculations. The section "Group Bands" discusses this further.

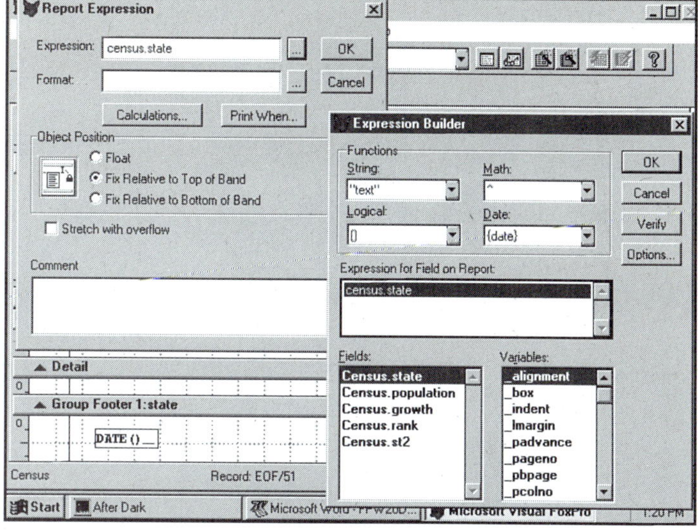

FIGURE 20.4.
The Report Expression and Expression Builder dialog boxes.

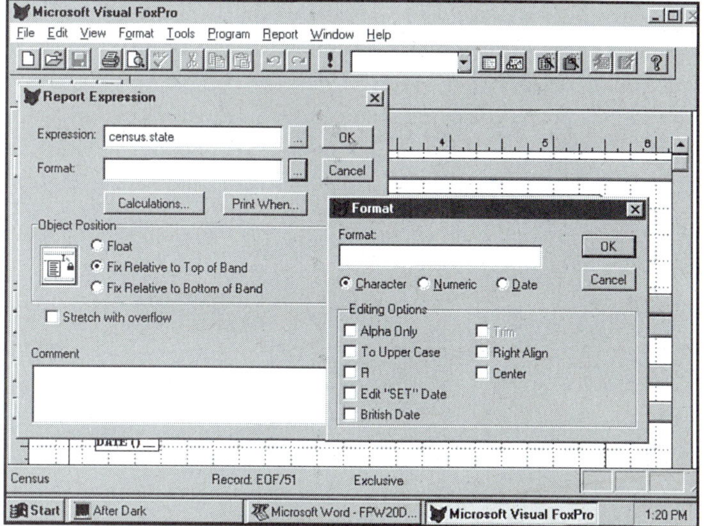

FIGURE 20.5.
The Report Expression and Format dialog boxes.

Placing a Picture on the Report Layout Window

You can place a picture on the Report Layout window by clicking the picture control and clicking the spot on the Report Layout window where you want one corner of the picture frame. Then you drag the mouse pointer where you want the opposite corner of the picture frame. When you release the mouse button, the Report Picture dialog box appears, as shown in Figure 20.6.

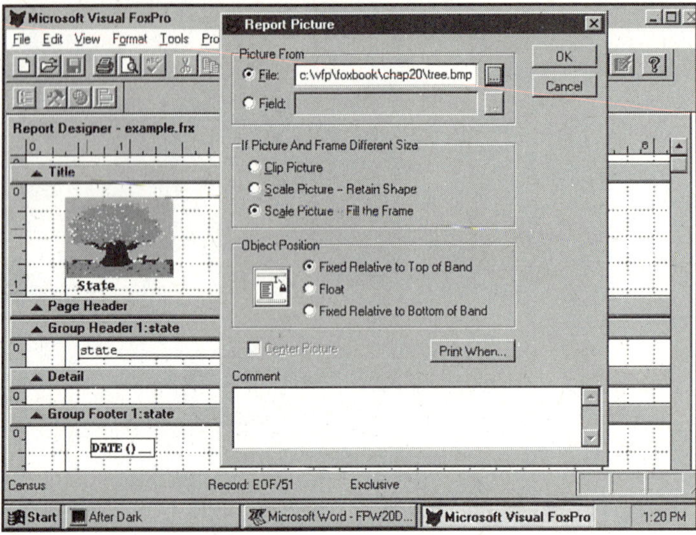

FIGURE 20.6.
The Report Picture dialog box.

You can enter the name of a General type database field or choose a bitmap picture that will appear on the report. Indicate your choice by selecting either the **F**ile or F**i**eld radio buttons. If you decide to specify a bitmap file, you can either type the name of a bitmap (BMP) file in the text box to the left of the Fil**e** push button, or you can push the Fil**e** push button that displays the Picture dialog box. The Open dialog box, shown in Figure 20.7, is similar to the standard Open File dialog box, except it has a window that previews your picture. When you pick an existing bitmap (BMP) file and press the OK push button, the Picture dialog box closes and the file you picked appears in the Fil**e** text box.

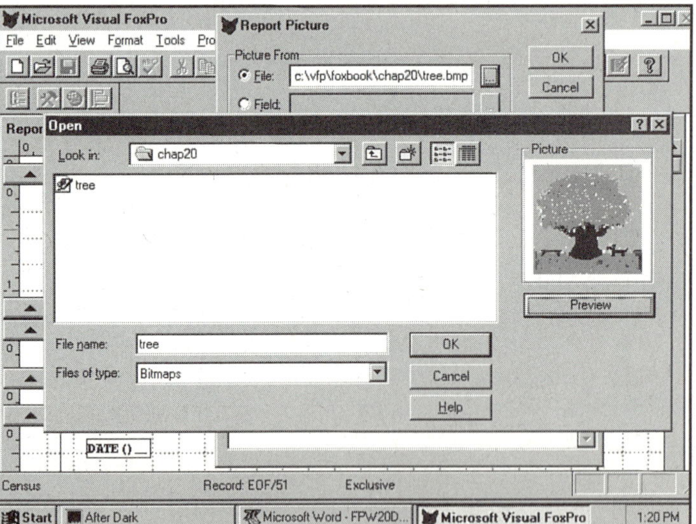

FIGURE 20.7.
The Report Picture and Open dialog boxes.

If you want to enter the name of a General type database field that contains a bitmap file, you can either type the name of the field to the left of the Field push button, or you can press the Field push button, and the Choose Fields/Variables dialog box appears.

The Report Picture dialog box has several options you can use to specify how the picture displays within the picture frame. Table 20.4 describes these.

Table 20.4. The Report Picture dialog box description.

Option	*Description*
Clip Picture	Three radio buttons specify how a picture displays if its size differs from the size of the picture frame. You can clip it or scale it. You can either scale the picture to fill the frame or scale the picture isometrically, which means that the picture grows or shrinks without losing its proportions.
	The Clip Picture radio button trims any portion that extends past the edges of the frame and preserves the original dimensions of the picture. The top-left corner of the picture is anchored at the top-left corner of the picture frame. The parts of the picture, if any, hanging off the right and bottom of the picture, are clipped. If this omits some part of the picture you wanted to view and you do not want to scale the picture, you can increase the size of the frame or use Microsoft Paint Brush or some other bitmap editing utility to edit the bitmap for your needs; then you can save it in a new file.
Scale Picture - Retain Shape	This radio button isometrically expands or shrinks the picture to fill the frame. This means that the bitmap picture is resized but its proportions are retained. Use this scale option when you don't want any horizontal or vertical distortion.
Scale Picture - Fill The Frame	This radio button stretches or shrinks the picture horizontally and vertically to fill the frame.
Center Picture	If you select this check box, the picture is smaller than the frame, and it is not scaled; it is centered in the frame. Otherwise, the picture is placed in the top-left corner of the frame.

What Are Bands?

The report work surface contains special objects called bands. A *band* is a discrete region of the work surface bounded by a unique band marker bar that extends across the Report Layout window. The *band marker bar* identifies a band and represents its level of organization in the report structure. On the left side of the band marker bar is the name of the band. Initially, you have bands named Page Header, Detail, and Page Footer. Additional bands are added when you add groups to a report. You can also add bands for a report header page and a summary page. You can place display controls inside a band. You can add or remove lines in the various bands by clicking and dragging the push button that is to the left of a band marker.

As Figure 20.8 illustrates, there are seven types of bands, if you include group bands and report header and report summary bands. You can add group bands by choosing the Report Menu Data Grouping option, which opens the Data Grouping dialog box. Information within each band maps to a section of a report.

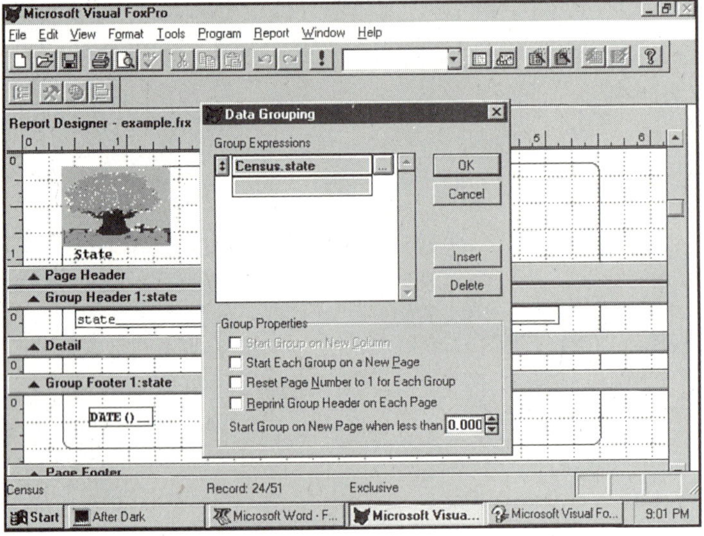

FIGURE 20.8.
The Data Grouping dialog box.

You might notice that most bands appear in pairs, and the pairs are nested. In Figure 20.9, pairs of bands appear on different rectangles representing a different nesting level. The only band not paired is the Detail band.

The Page Header and Page Footer bands also come in pairs. These bands, however, are controlled by page breaks rather than by changes in some data value.

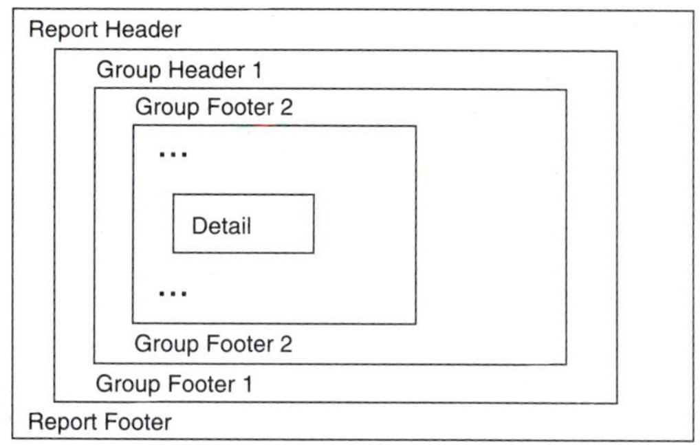

FIGURE 20.9.
A representation of Report Designer band pairs.

The Page Header Band

Controls placed in the Page Header band appear at the top of each page of the report. Typically, controls indicate column headings and report page identification information. Only one Page Header band appears per report.

The Page Footer Band

The controls placed in the Page Footer band appear at the bottom of each page of the report. This band is optional. Only one Page Footer band appears per report.

The Title Band

The Title band contains information that appears at the beginning of a report. It is typically used to provide a report with a cover sheet describing the information in the report. Only one Title band appears per report. This band is optional and if you want it, you must add it using the Rep**o**rt menu **T**itle/Summary... option.

Group Bands

Group bands come in pairs. The Group Header band contains information displayed before a group of detail lines are printed. You can use it to display column heading information, for example. The Group Footer band contains information displayed after a group of detail lines are printed and can be used to display group totals and subtotals. You can have up to 20 group levels of group bands.

Suppose you want multiple levels of report control breaks (subtotals). For example, you might want to generate subtotals on the corporate departments, the facility, and the division. You can add groups by choosing the Data G**r**ouping option in the Rep**o**rt menu.

A change in a data value or expression can trigger a control break. The Group Summary band can compute and display statistical information based on the data in the records of the group. Here is how you add a statistical calculation field to the layout for a group band:

1. Place a field or expression control on a Group Footer band layout, and the Report Expression dialog box appears.
2. Specify a field or expression.
3. Click on the Calculations push button and the Subtotal or Calculate Field dialog box appears, as shown in Figure 20.10.
4. Choose a type of statistical calculation.
5. Specify when the calculations are reset. For example, you can reset a calculation when a data value changes, at the end of a page or column, or at the end of a report.

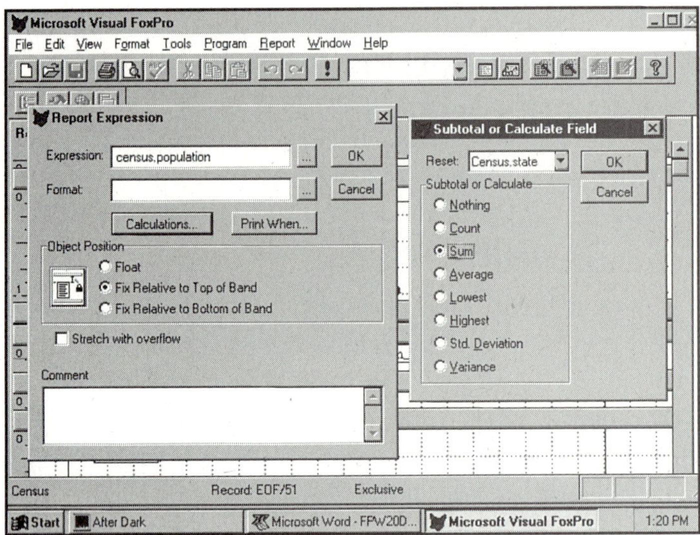

FIGURE 20.10.
The Subtotal or Calculate Field and Report Expression dialog boxes.

The Calculate functions are the same functions used with the `CALCULATE` command: Average, Count, Maximum, Minimum, Sum, Standard Deviation, and Variance. For example, to obtain a total on a report column consisting of the `AMOUNT` database field, place the `SUM(AMOUNT)` calculated field on a Group Summary band. An example column might look like this:

```
AMOUNT          Header Band
334.56          Detail Band
2,000.00
1,000.00
- - - - -       Summary Band containing SUM(AMOUNT)
3,334.56
```

The Detail Band

The Detail band displays the data in the records from the active database table or view. The information defined on the report layout surface of the Detail band displays for each record. The information in the Detail band can result in the display of a row of tabular columns or pages of a form.

The Summary Band

The Summary band contains information that appears at the end of a report. This is a good place for report summary information or grand totals. Only one Summary band appears on each report. This band is optional, and if you want it, you must add it using the **R**eport menu **T**itle/Summary option.

The Report Menu

When the FoxPro Report Designer window is open, the **R**eport menu is added to the FoxPro system menu. Moreover, additional options are added or enabled on other system menus. The **R**eport menu contains options that globally affect the report. This section describes the **R**eport menu options.

The Title/Summary Option

When you choose the **T**itle/Summary option, the Title/Summary dialog box appears, which contains check boxes that enable you to add or remove a Title band and a Summary band. Initially, the Report Layout window does not contain these bands. A single Title band appears for a report, and it is printed before the report printing begins. It is normally used to define a cover sheet for the report. A single Summary band is also printed after the report has finished printing. It is normally used to print report summary information, such as grand totals. In addition, the Title/Summary dialog box contains options to start a new page after the information in the Title band prints and before the information in the Summary band prints.

The Data Grouping Option

The Data **G**rouping option is used to add a new Group band to the report layout. It is described in the section "Group Bands."

Variables

Choose the **V**ariables option, and the Report Variables dialog box displays, as shown in Figure 20.11. The dialog box contains the options described in Table 20.5. You can place these variables on the Report Layout window or use them in various report expressions.

You can specify a memory variable name and either an initial value or an expression to assign it. Options are available to reset this variable at control-break points and to release this variable when the report is completed.

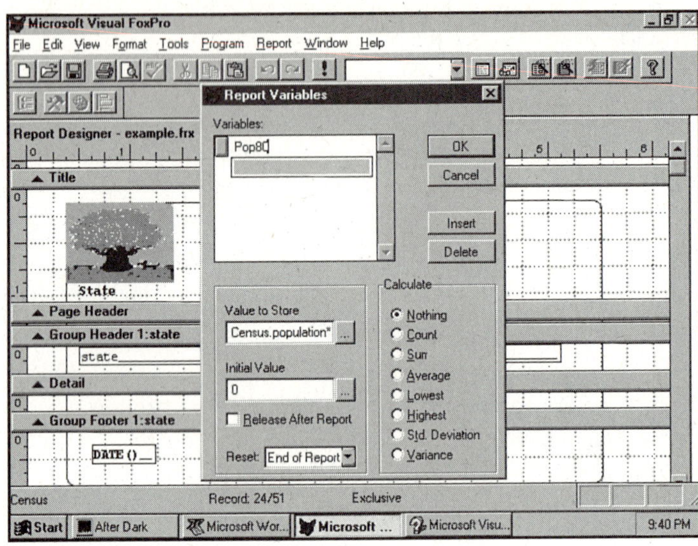

FIGURE 20.11.
The Report Variables dialog box.

Table 20.5. The Report Variables dialog box description.

Option	*Description*
Variables:	This option is a list of report memory variables in the order in which they are evaluated. You can rearrange the order of items in the list by clicking the double-headed arrow and dragging the item to the desired location in the list. You can also press Ctrl+PgUp or Ctrl+PgDn to move the selected item up or down in the list.
Insert	You can press this push button to add a new memory variable in the list before the variable currently selected.
Delete	You can delete a selected variable by pressing this push button.
Value to Store	You can type an expression into this text box or press the associated push button, and the Expression Builder displays so you can build an expression to compute the value to store in the memory variable.
Initial Value	You can specify an initial value for the currently selected memory variable. You can type the initial value or expression into this text box or press the associated push button, and the Expression Builder

Option	Description
	displays so you can build an expression to compute the initial value to store in the memory variable. The memory value is set to the initial value before the report begins processing detail records. If the Reset control is established, the memory variable is reset to the initial value during the specified control break.
Release After Report	If you check this control, the selected memory variable is released after the report is completed.
Reset:	You can choose a control break from this list control. Then the selected memory variable is reset to its initial value at control-break points. Control breaks that you can choose include end of page, end of report, end of column, and data grouping control breaks.
Calculate	The Calculate option group specifies what type of calculation you want a variable to perform while processing records. This variable is initially set to its initial value, and then its value is continually calculated until it is reset to its initial value at a control break. The remaining items in this table are Calculate options. You may choose one of them:
Nothing	No calculations will be made on this variable. The value remains set to its initial value.
Count	Counts number of records.
Sum	Computes the summation of the values of the variable.
Average	Computes the arithmetic mean of the values of a variable.
Lowest	Displays the minimum value that occurred in a variable.
Highest	Displays the maximum value that occurred in a variable.
S**t**d. Deviation	Returns the square root of the variance for the values of a variable.
Variance	Measures the degree to which individual values vary from the average of all the values.

The Default Font Option

With the Default **F**ont option you can specify a font that is used by default for all text in a report. You can still define the font of individual controls. When you choose this option, the Font dialog box appears and you select a font name, size, and style. The selected font becomes the default font for the report.

The Private Data Session Option

A data session is a complete and separate data environment. It describes the work area, cursors in the work area, their indexes, and relations. When you start Visual FoxPro, the Global data session, data session 1, is active. If you want to generate a report without affecting your current environment, you can specify when you design the report that the report should have its own private data session. You do this by choosing the **P**rivate Data Session option. A check mark appears at the left of this option indicating that it is active. You also must define a data environment for the report.

A new data session is created when the report starts and is closed when the report is finished.

The Quick Report Option

When you choose the **Q**uick Report option, the Quick Report dialog box displays, as shown in Figure 20.12. This option automatically places the following controls in the report layout:

- Selected fields in the Detail band
- Field headings in the Page Header band
- Date and page numbering in the Page Footer band

Now you can move them around, and add some text and perhaps some graphics to complete the report design. The **Q**uick Report option is very useful for creating an initial form that you can modify as needed. This option is enabled only when the Detail band of the Report Layout window is empty.

The Quick Report dialog box contains two picture buttons. As you can see from Figure 20.12, the picture button selected is a column layout. The other picture button is a form layout button. In a *column layout*, fields are displayed from left to right across the page in the Detail band, as shown in Figure 20.13. If you choose the *form layout* picture button, fields are displayed one below the other in the Detail band.

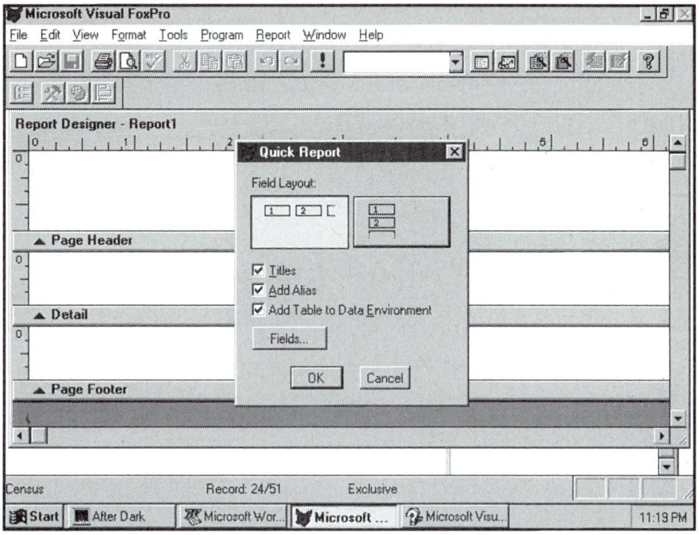

FIGURE 20.12.
The Quick Report dialog box.

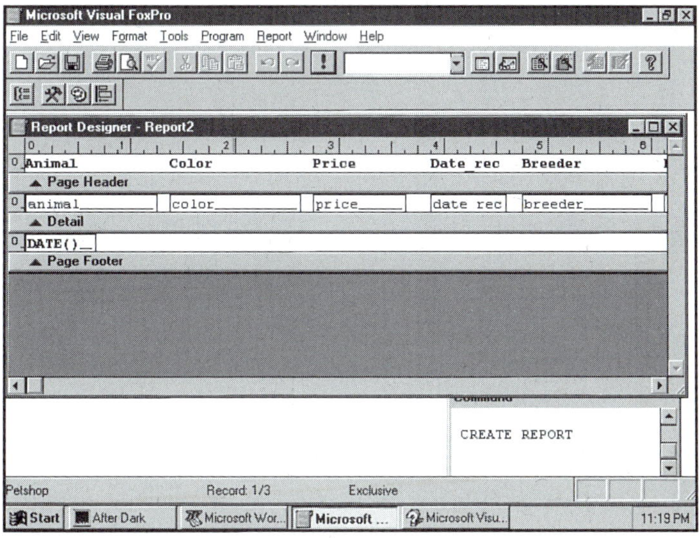

FIGURE 20.13.
An example column layout created by the Quick Report option.

When you mark the **T**itles check box, field names are displayed as titles above (column layout) or to the left of (form layout) the corresponding field. Most of the time, you can just drop all the fields in the Detail band and delete all the fields you don't need. However, sometimes you have too many fields in the database table, which makes this scheme impractical. This dialog box includes an option to choose a list of fields from the database table to be automatically placed in the Detail band. To do this, check the Fields push button, and the Field Picker dialog box appears. You can specify fields to include in the quick report.

It is always a good idea to let the quick report add alias names to the fields it places on the report layout. However, if you do not want the alias name to be included with the field names, you can uncheck the **A**lias check box and an alias will not be inserted with the fields in the report.

If you want your report to establish a data environment, check the Add Table to Data **E**nvironment control.

The Run Report Option

The Run **R**eport option performs the same function as the `REPORT` command. You have the option of directing a report to the printer or to a file. There are many ways in Visual FoxPro to print a report, including the following:

- Use the **R**eport menu **R**un Report option executed from within the Report Designer.
- Press the Ctrl+P key combination while you're in the Report Designer.
- Use the **F**ile menu **P**rint option.
- Use the Run (!) button on the Visual FoxPro standard toolbar.
- Use the Print control on the standard Visual FoxPro toolbar.
- Use the `REPORT` command.

The **R**un Report option displays the Print dialog box to print the report currently being designed. You are provided with the options discussed in the following sections.

The Type Combo Box

Generally, you can choose the type of file to print with the **T**ype combo box. However, in this case Report is selected because you are going to print a report.

The File Text Box and the Browse Button

For printing reports, the **F**ile text box contains the name of a temporary file to print. You do not need to change this. However, in general, you can type the name and path of another file you want to print. You can use the Browse button to display the Print File dialog box. Then you can select a file to print by searching through directories to find it.

The Line Numbers Check Box

If you check the **L**ine Numbers option, Visual FoxPro prints line numbers in the left margin. This option is not available for reports and labels.

The Page Eject Before Check Box

If you check the Page Eject **B**efore option, Visual FoxPro advances the printer to the top of the next page before printing the report. This option is available for all file types.

The Page Eject After Option

The Page Eject **A**fter option is not available for reports or labels. For other file types, if you check this option, Visual FoxPro advances the printer to the top of the next page after printing the file.

The Restore Environment Option

If you check the **R**estore Environment option and you have changed the environment settings during the printing of a report or label, Visual FoxPro returns the environment to the previously saved environment. This option is available only for reports and labels.

The Print Setup Option

The **P**rint Setup option displays the Windows Print Setup dialog box so you can select a printer and change printer settings.

The Options Option

The **O**ptions option displays the Print Options dialog box, which lets you set a filter and scope for the records in the view or table to be printed. In particular, you can specify a `FOR` or `WHILE`, `NEXT`, `REST`, `RECORD`, or `ALL` clauses. `ALL` is the default.

Other System Menu Options Relating to the Report Designer

The Report Menu contains only a few of the options that you need to use when designing a report. Options are spread throughout the system menu that relate to the Report Designer. These options are described in Table 20.6.

Table 20.6. The menu options you use when designing a report.

Menu	*Option*	*Usage*
File	Page Set**u**p	Defines page layout.
	Print Pre**v**iew	Displays report on the screen.
	Print…	Prints the report (same as **R**eport menu **R**un Report option).
Edit	**U**ndo, Re**d**o, Cu**t**, **C**opy, **P**aste	Editing operations.
View	✓ **D**esign	Displays the Report Designer.
	Pre**v**iew	Displays the Preview window.
	Data **E**nvironment…	Displays the Database Environment Designer so that you can visually

continues

Table 20.6. continued

Menu	*Option*	*Usage*
		establish a data environment for the report. You can add tables, indexes, and views, and you can establish relationships. (See Chapter 11, "DBF Files and Databases.")
	✓ Report Control**s** Toolbar	Toggles on and off the Report Controls toolbar.
	✓ La**y**out Toolbar	Toggles on and off the Layout toolbar.
	✓ Colo**r** Palette Toolbar	Toggles on and off the Color Palette toolbar.
	✓ **G**rid Lines	Toggles on and off the display of grid lines on the report form.
	✓ Sho**w** Position	Toggles on and off the display of the position and size of form objects on the status bar.
F**o**rmat	**A**lign, Si**z**e, Bring to **F**ront, Send to **B**ack	Same as the controls on the Layout toolbar.
	Horizontal Spacing	This option lets you control the horizontal spacing between selected controls. A drop-down menu provides you the option to increase, decrease, or make the horizontal space equal, usually between more than two controls.
	Vertical Spacing	This option lets you control the vertical spacing between selected controls. A drop-down menu provides you the option to increase, decrease, or make the vertical space equal, usually between more than two controls.
	Grou**p**	Using this option, you can associate multiple controls for more than just one operation by identifying them as a *group*. Then you can move, cut, paste, delete, or copy them as a

Menu	*Option*	*Usage*
		single object. Select multiple controls and choose this option.
	Ungroup	Disassociates a group of controls so that they can be operated on separately.
	Snap to **G**rid	Toggles the Snap to Grid mode on or off. When you move a control, it moves smoothly across the layout if the Snap to **G**rid option is off. However, if it is on, the control jumps between the invisible alignment grid lines.
	Set Grid Scale	Changes the size of the cells in the invisible alignment grid used by the Snap to **G**rid option.
	F**o**nt	Changes the font name, size, and style of selected controls.
	Text Alignment	Left, center, or right aligns text in a control.
	F**i**ll	Changes the fill pattern for selected rectangular and rounded rectangular controls.
	P**e**n	Changes pen styles and types for selected line, rectangle, or round rectangle type controls.
	Mode	Changes transparent or opaque mode of a control.

Some of these controls are discussed in the following sections.

The File Menu Page Setup Option

Choose this option, and the Page Setup dialog box displays as shown in Figure 20.14. You can set the number and width of columns, space between columns, and left margin width of your report. In addition, you can designate whether the report is oriented as a report or as labels. The Page Layout dialog box also displays a pictorial representation of a page of the report that displays column and margin settings. Table 20.7 describes the options for this dialog box.

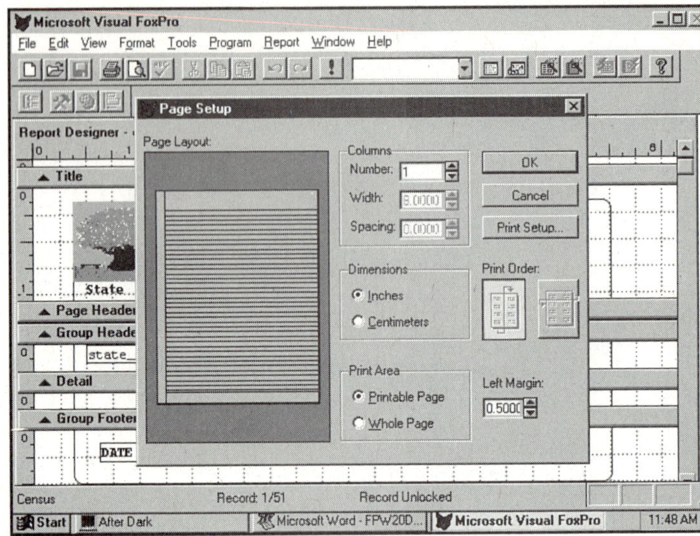

FIGURE 20.14.
The Page Setup dialog box.

Table 20.7. The Page Setup dialog box description.

Option	*Description*
Columns:	Specifies the following report column parameters:
Number	Use this spinner to specify the number of columns in the report. You can have up to 50 columns.
Width	Use this spinner to specify the width of a column in specified units.
Spacing	Use this spinner to specify the space between columns in specified units.
Dimensions:	Defines the following page dimension options:
Inches **C**entimeters	The dimensions of the page parameters as shown in spinners are given in either inches or centimeters. You can select which units you want to use by selecting one of the two radio buttons.
Print Area:	Defines the following Page Print area options:
Printable Page **W**hole Page	You can choose to print your report to allow for margins (Printable Page) or to print on the entire page (Whole Page) by choosing one of these two push buttons.

Print Order:	Defines the following Print Order options:
Report (icon) Label (icon)	You can specify your report as *report-oriented* or *label-oriented* by choosing one of two picture buttons. In report orientation, the columns are filled with detail lines from the top to the bottom of the first column, the second column is filled from top to bottom, and so forth. In label orientation, rows are filled from left to right, starting from the top of the page. Tabular reports and phone book listings are examples of report orientation. Multicolumn mailing labels are examples of label orientation.
Print **S**etup...	This push button opens the Windows Print Setup dialog box.

The Page Layout option plays an important role in defining the appearance of your report. Visual FoxPro enables you to do things that could never have been done using an MS-DOS based Xbase. Here is an example of a multiple column report that displays breeds of cats and dogs. In this example, Figure 20.15 shows three columns.

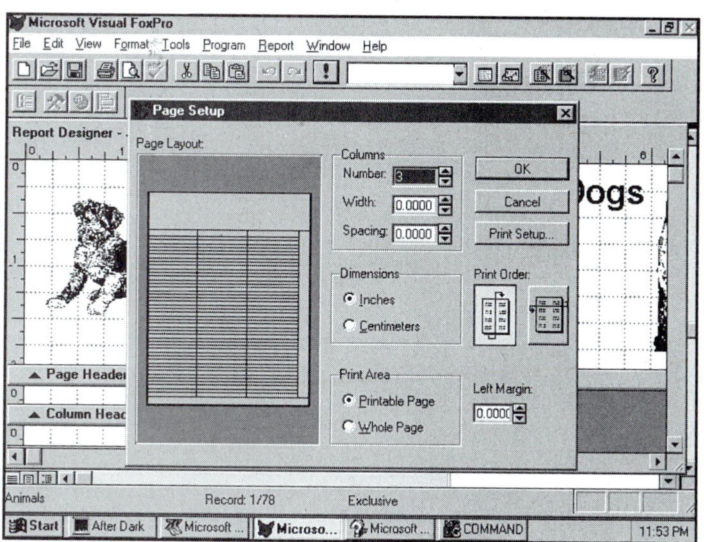

FIGURE 20.15.
The Page Setup dialog box showing a three-column example.

The database table ANIMALS.DBF contains several fields, but only two are used in the report: `Animals.Animal` and `Animals.Type`. The `Animals.Animal` field is placed in the Detail band. The `Animals.Type` field is used as a control-break field, as shown in Figure 20.16. Notice that when a record is encountered with a different value of Type, the different value begins printing on a new column. This value change occurs only once, because there are only two values for the `Animals.Type` field, `Dog` and `Cat`.

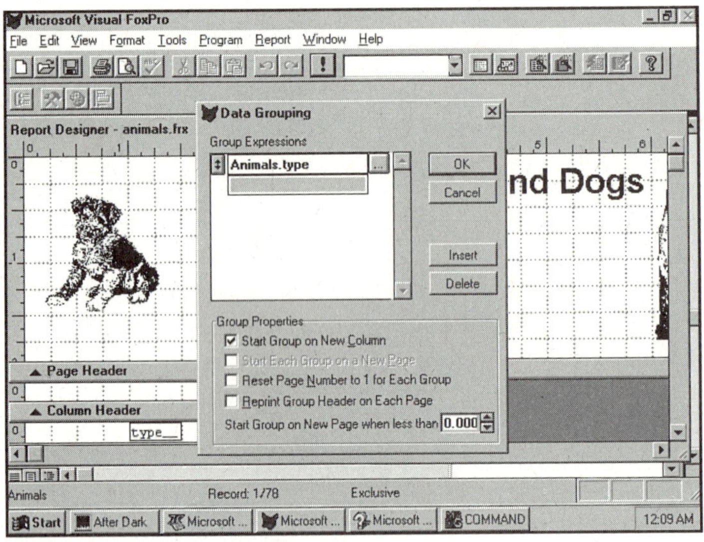

FIGURE 20.16.
A data grouping showing the control break on the `Animals.Type` field.

The Page Header band contains a label control and a couple pictures. The label control is a header, `Breeds of Cats and Dogs`, displayed in 24-point type. The header is surrounded by two picture controls that are bitmap files, DOGGY.BMP and KITTY.BMP. That is all you need to design this report. Save the report to the filename ANIMALS.FRX, and exit from the Report Designer.

If you want to print the report, you can choose the **R**eport menu **R**un Report option, or the **F**ile menu **P**rint command, or you can execute the following commands in the Command window:

```
USE Animals
REPORT FORM Animals TO PRINTER
```

When this command executes, the Windows Print dialog box appears, asking how many copies of the report you want and what pages of the report you want printed. After you respond, output from the report is directed to the printer and to the main FoxPro window, as shown in Figure 20.17.

FIGURE 20.17.
The output from the report ANIMALS.FRX.

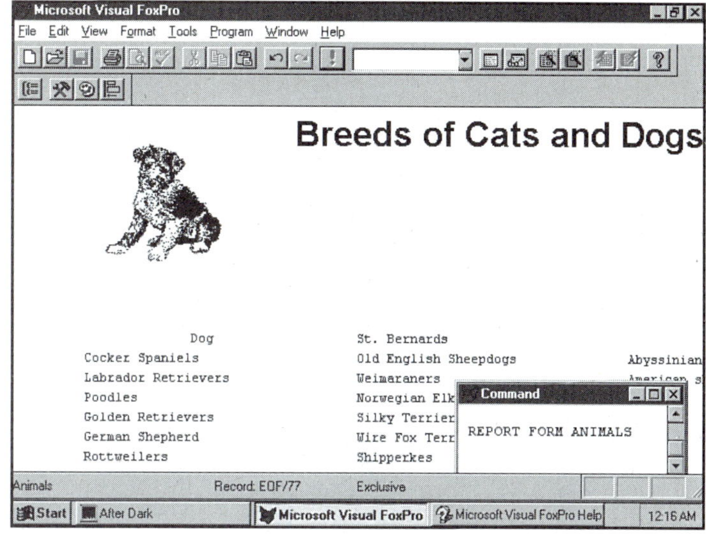

The Page Preview Option

You can also access the Page Preview dialog box from the **File** menu Print Pre**v**iew option, the Visual FoxPro main toolbar Preview control, or by choosing the Pre**v**iew option from the **V**iew menu. You can also execute the `REPORT` command from a program or from the Command window with the `PREVIEW` keyword specified.

When the Page Preview window appears, it contains a miniature scale model of the first page of your report and the Page Preview toolbar as shown in Figure 20.18. The Page Preview toolbar contains buttons for the following preview operations:

- Go to first page.
- Go to previous page.
- Go to specified page (displays the Go To dialog box for you to enter a page number).
- Go to next page.
- Go to last page.
- Zoom drop-down box. (The Zoom drop-down box lets you select the size you want your preview document to appear in the preview window as a percentage of its normal size. You can select one of the page size options shown in Figure 20.18.)
- Exit from preview.

The **Z**oom option in the Zoom drop-down box displays a full-page representation of a section of your report (Initial display). If you click on the preview window, the display toggles between its zoom size and the size you selected in the Zoom drop-down box.

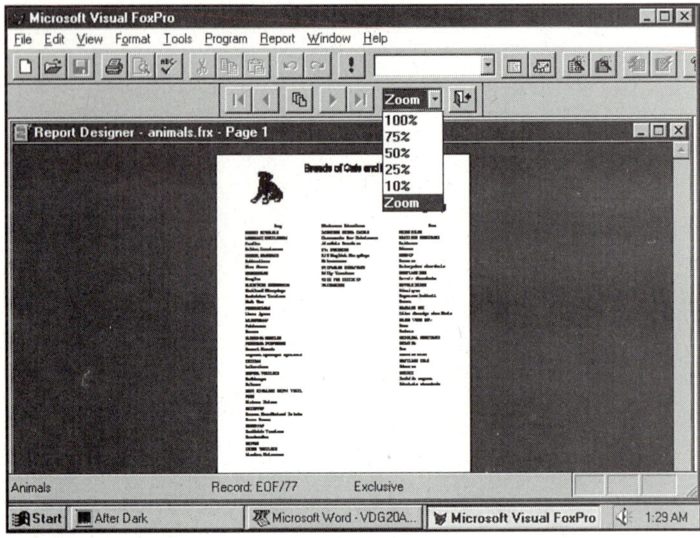

FIGURE 20.18.
The Page Preview dialog box.

The Data Environment Option

The Data Environment option displays the Database Environment Designer dialog box so that you can visual establish a data environment for the report. You can add tables, indexes, and views, and establish relationships. You can click on a table in the Data Environment dialog box and drag it to the Report Layout form; the field controls corresponding to fields in the table are created, as shown in Figure 20.19. In addition, you can click on individual fields in a table in the Data Environment dialog box and drag them to any bands of the Report Layout form.

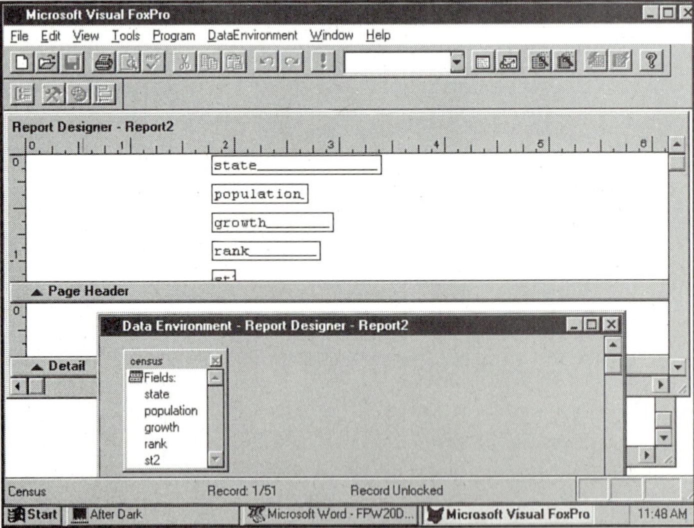

FIGURE 20.19.
The Report form with field controls resulting from dragging the table from the Data Environment dialog box.

The View Menu Grid Lines Option

You can turn on or off the display of grid lines on the Report Layout window with the Grid Lines option.

The View Menu Position Option

The Show **P**osition option toggles the Show Position mode on and off. If the Show Position mode is set on, a check mark (✓) appears at the left of the option, and the coordinate position of the mouse pointer and the dimensions of selected controls are displayed in the status bar. If you set the mode off, the position and dimensions are not displayed.

The Format Menu Snap to Grid Option

With the Snap to **G**rid option, you can turn the *alignment grid* on and off. The alignment grid is an invisible horizontal and vertical grid. When you move or define a control, it is automatically aligned to (or *snapped to*) the nearest grid line. The alignment grid corresponds to the ruler grid alignment set in the Ruler/Grid dialog box. A check mark appears to the left of the option when the alignment grid is on. If the alignment grid is off, the control moves freely around the Report Layout window.

The Format Menu Set Grid Scale Option

If you choose the **S**et Grid Scale option, the Ruler/Grid dialog box displays, as shown in Figure 20.20. You can use this to specify the units of measurement for the rulers and grid lines or change the horizontal and vertical grid line spacing.

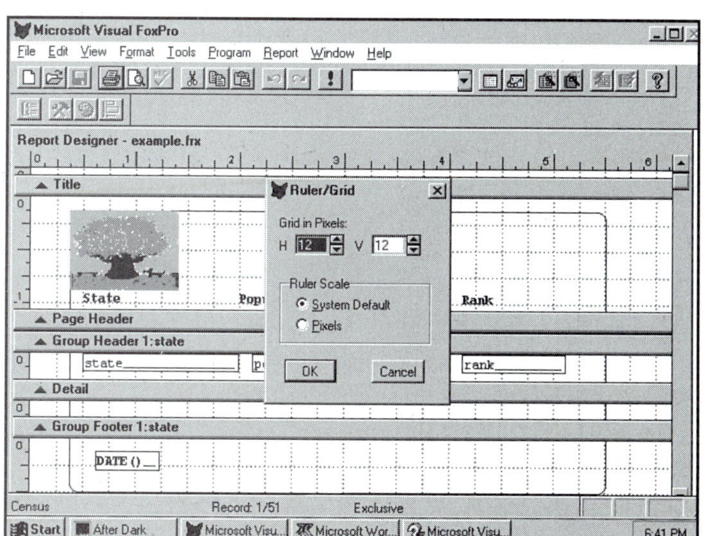

FIGURE 20.20.
The Ruler/Grid dialog box.

The Format Menu Bring to Front Option

Choose the F**o**rmat menu Bring to **F**ront option or press Ctrl+G, and the selected control or controls move forward so that they cover other controls. This option is active only if one or more controls are selected.

The Format Menu Send to Back Option

If you choose the Send to **B**ack option or press Ctrl+J, the selected control or controls move to the bottom of the Report Layout window and are covered by other controls.

The Format Menu Group Option

This option has nothing to do with group bands. It is used to group display controls together. If more than one control is selected and you choose this option, the controls are grouped together as a single control. For example, if you have a box surrounding some fields and some text and you want to treat the whole group of controls as a single control, you can select all the controls you want to include in the group and choose the Grou**p** option. From then on, you can treat the grouped controls as a single control that you can move, cut, copy, and paste. However, you cannot change the size, font attributes, fill, pen, fill color, or pen color of a grouped control.

The Format Menu Ungroup Option

You can choose the **U**ngroup option to separate previously grouped controls so that they can be individually grouped. This option is disabled unless the selected control is a grouped control.

The Format Menu Font Option

Choose the F**o**nt option, and the Font dialog box appears for you to change the font, font size, and style for the text in the selected control or controls. (See Figure 19.2 in Chapter 19, "The Form Designer.")

The Format Menu Text Alignment Option

If a label control is selected, you can choose the **T**ext Alignment option, and a submenu appears containing the text alignment options described in Table 20.8.

Table 20.8. A description of text alignment options.

Option	*Description*
Left	This option aligns the selected text to the left.
Center	This option centers the selected text in the report layout window.
Right	This option aligns the selected text to the right.
Single space	This option displays the selected text with no blank lines between lines of text. In other words, you can single-space lines of text.
1 1/2 space	This option displays the selected text with one and a half blank lines separating lines of text.
Double space	This option displays selected text with two blank lines separating lines of text. In other words, you can double-space lines of text.

The Format Menu Fill Option

If one or more rectangle or round rectangle type controls are selected, you can choose this option, and a submenu appears with pictures of fill patterns. You can choose a fill pattern for the control. Figure 9.3 in Chapter 9, "Full-Screen Data Editing," shows fill patterns to illustrate PATTERN clause options.

The Format Menu Pen Option

If one or more line, rectangle, or round rectangle type controls are selected, you can choose this option and a submenu appears containing pen styles and types. (See Table 9.6 in Chapter 9.) You can choose a pen type or style for the control. The cascading submenu contains the options described in Table 20.9.

Table 20.9. A description of pen styles and types.

Option	*Outline Width of Selected Control*
Hairline	1-pixel outline width.
1 Point	1-point outline width. (Note that the actual size depends on the resolution of the display monitor.)
2 Point	2-point outline width.
4 Point	4-point outline width.

continues

Table 20.9. continued

Option	*Outline Width of Selected Control*
6 Point	6-point outline width.
None	No outline.
Dotted	Dotted line outline for a specified width.
Dashed	Dashed line outline for a specified width.
Dash-dot	Outline composed of alternating dashes and dots.
Dash-dot-dot	Outline composed of alternating dashes and two dots.

The Format Menu Mode Option

If one or more controls are selected, you can choose this control, and a submenu appears with options to display the control or controls in Transparent or Opaque mode.

Building a Report

Now that you have learned about the components of the Visual FoxPro Report Designer, it is time to use the Report Designer to create a report. In this section, I'll guide you through the creation of a relatively complicated report form that generates invoices.

To begin, you use a database consisting of three tables. The first table, CLIENTS.DBF, contains client information such as the following:

- The client's name (`Name`)
- The client's address (`Address`)
- The client number (`Client_ID`)
- Other fields that are not used in this invoice report

The second table, TRANSACT.DBF, contains information about each transaction, such as the following:

- Inventory number of an item purchased (`Inv_no`)
- The number of items purchased (`Quantity`)
- Date of purchase (`Trans_date`)
- The client number of the client who made the purchase (`Client_No`)

The third table, ITEM.DBF, contains information relating to each stock item (things that are sold) consisting of the following items:

- Price of one item (`Unit_Price`).

- Item inventory number (`Inv_No`). (This field is used to relate this file to the transaction.)
- Description of item (`Descrip`).

Listing 20.1 provides the structures of the three tables.

Listing 20.1. The structures of the tables CLIENTS.DBF, TRANSACT.DBF, and ITEM.DBF.

```
Structure for table: f:\foxpro\inven\clients.dbf
Number of data records: 3
Date of last update:    11/17/92
Field  Field Name  Type        Width     Dec     Index
1      CLIENT_ID   Character   5                Asc
2      NAME        Character   20
3      ADDRESS     Character   30
4      CITY        Character   15
5      STATE       Character   2
6      ZIP         Character   5
7      AREACODE    Character   3
8      PHONE       Character   8
9      EXTENSION   Character   5
10     STARTBAL    Numeric     8         2
11     BALDATE     Date        8
** Total **                      110

Structure for table: f:\foxpro\inven\transact.dbf
Number of data records: 44
Date of last update:    11/17/92
Field  Field Name  Type        Width     Dec     Index
1      TRANS_DATE  Date        8
2      AMT         Numeric     8         2
3      CLIENT_ID   Character   5                 Asc
4      INV_NO      Character   5
5      QUANTITY    Numeric     6
** Total **                       33

Structure for table: f:\foxpro\inven\item.dbf
Number of data records: 20
Date of last update:    11/17/92
Field  Field Name  Type        Width     Dec     Index
1      UNIT_PRICE  Numeric     8         2
2      DESCRIP     Character   30
3      INV_NO      Character   6                 Asc
** Total **                      45
```

Table TRANSACT.DBF has an index tag on field `Client_ID` so that you can relate the CLIENTS.DBF table to it. Likewise, table ITEM.DBF has an index tag on field `Inv_No` so that you can relate the TRANSACT.DBF table to it. The next step is to establish a view for the invoice example. To do this, place each of the three tables in use in a different work area, specify ordering, and establish relations. Save the view in the view file named TRANSACT.VUE. Listing 20.2 shows the commands for establishing this view. Study them carefully to ensure that you understand what each of them does.

Listing 20.2. The commands that establish the view for the invoice example.

```
***************************************************************
*      * 12/94               INVEN.PRG                        *
***************************************************************
*      * Author's Name: Jeb Long                              *
*      *                                                      *
*      * Description:                                         *
*      * This program is used to set up the inven database    *
*      *                                              *       *
***************************************************************
SET SAFETY OFF
CLOSE DATA
CLEAR ALL
CLEAR ALL
CLOSE DATA
OPEN DATABASE Orders

USE Clients  IN 0
USE Item     IN 0 ORDER Inv_No
USE Transact IN 0 ORDER Client_ID
SET RELATION TO Inv_No    INTO Item     IN Transact
SET RELATION TO Client_ID INTO Transact IN Clients
SET SKIP TO Transact     && Establish one to many relation
CREATE VIEW TRANSACT FROM ENVIRONMENT   && Save the view
SELECT Clients
```

After you establish the view, you can browse the view to make sure everything is in order. For example, the `BROWSE` command shown in Figure 20.21 is as follows:

```
BROWSE FIELDS Clients.Name, ;
Transact.trans_date,;
Transact.quantity,  ;
Item.unit_price, ;
Item.descrip
```

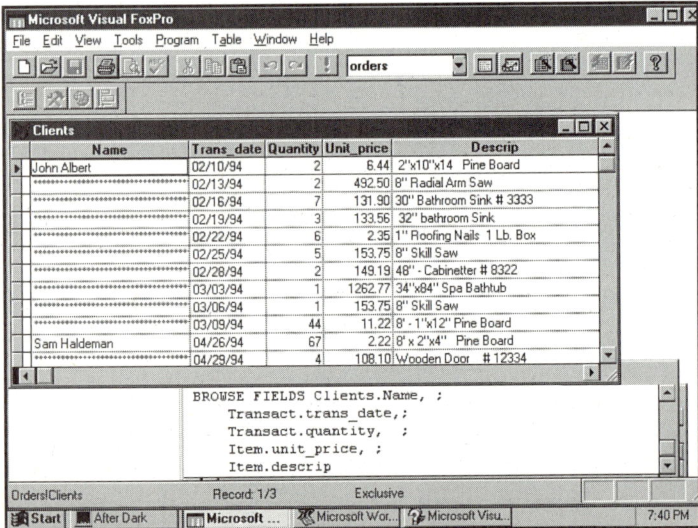

FIGURE 20.21.
A Browse window displaying some of the fields in the example's view.

As you know, an invoice form usually contains one instance of the client's information and a list of transactions. This arrangement suggests that you can create a Group band with a control break on the client, and that the Detail band can contain transaction information. Furthermore, the Group Header band should then contain the client's name and address. The Group Footer should contain the total amount resulting from a summation of the item costs over all the transactions for a client.

Now you are ready to begin designing the report. First, execute the Report Designer with the following command:

```
CREATE REPORT Transact
```

The Report Designer window appears, as shown in Figure 20.1. As the first order of business, open the Data Environment dialog box and add the file to the data environment as shown in Figure 20.22.

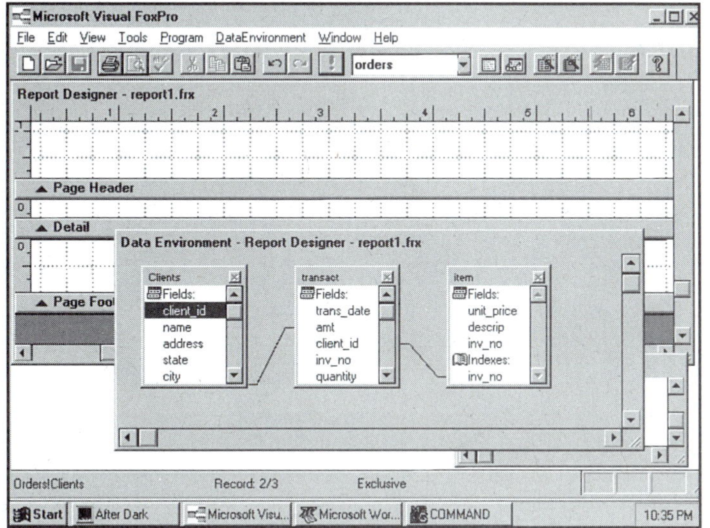

FIGURE 20.22.
The Report Layout window for the sample invoice report with the Data Environment dialog box displayed.

Next, add a Group band. To do this, choose the **R**eport menu Data **G**rouping option, and the Data Grouping dialog box appears as shown in Figure 20.23. Use the Group Expressions browser button and select the field `Clients.client_ID` as the field on which to group. Then check the Start Each Group on a New **P**age check box. Press the OK push button to return to the Report Layout window. Expand all the bands so that they look like the ones in Figure 20.23.

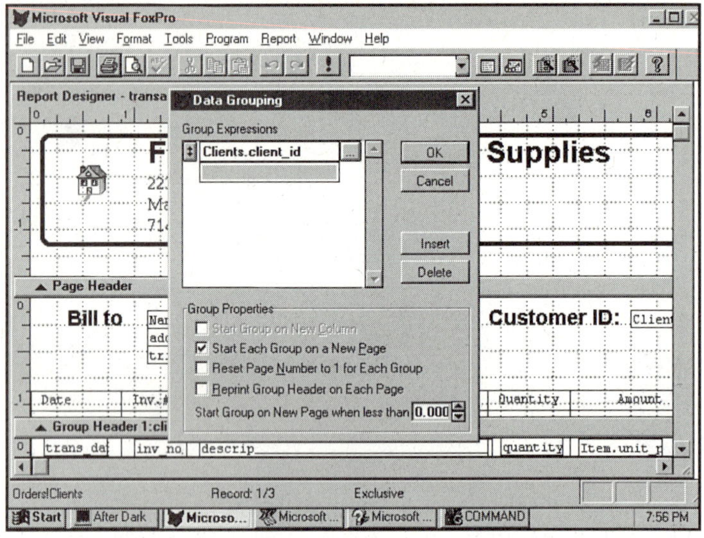

FIGURE 20.23.
The Report Layout window for the sample invoice report with the Data Grouping dialog box open.

The next step is to start adding controls to the bands so that they resemble the example shown in Figure 20.24. Use the controls in the Report Controls toolbar to add the following controls to the Page Header band:

```
Label controls
  Company name and address
  The word "Invoice"
  Rounded rectangle control with a 4 point outline
  Picture Control representing the company logo
```

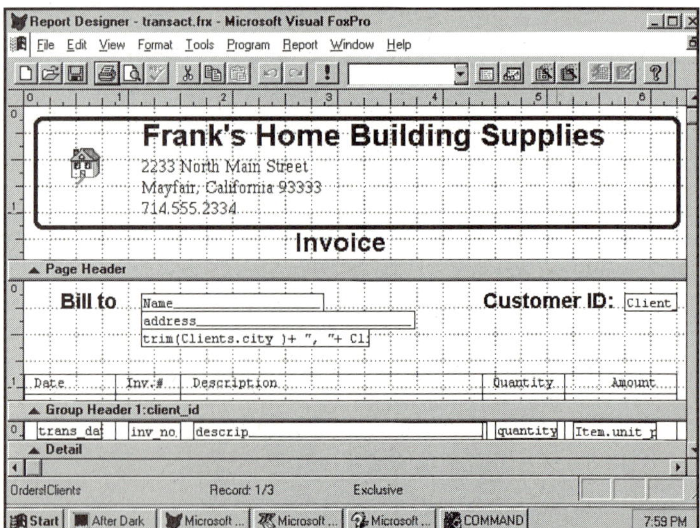

FIGURE 20.24.
The Report Layout window for the example invoice report.

Next, add the following information to the Group Header band:

```
Label controls
  Bill To
  Customer ID:
  Date
  Inv. #
  Description
  Quantity
  Amount
Field/Expression Controls
  Clients.Name
  Clients.Address
  TRIM(Clients.City)+", "+Clients.State+Zip
  Client_ID
```

Add the following controls to the Detail band:

```
Field/Expression Controls
  Transact.Trans_date
  Transact.Inv_no
  Item.Descrip
  Item.Unit_Cost * Transact.Quantity  (Format: @$ 999,999.00)
```

Use the rectangle control to draw a rectangle starting in the Group Header band and extending below the word Total: in the Group Footer box, as shown in Figure 20.25. Similarly, use the Line control to draw vertical lines separating the fields.

Add the following controls to the Group Footer band:

```
Label control
  Total:
  Field/Expression Controls
  Item.Unit_Cost * Transact.Quantity  (Format: @$)
```

When you place a Field control in the Report Layout window, the Report Expression dialog box always activates. For the expression that you place in the Group Footer band, it is not enough to simply specify the expression and format. You also need to click on the Calculations button to activate the Subtotal or Calculate Field dialog box, as shown in Figure 20.25. You must select the **S**um radio button so that the total will be computed. You also need to specify that you want the calculation to be reset to zero when the value of the `Client.Client_ID` (the control break) changes. This is how you indicate that you want to compute a new total for each client.

Finally, add the friendly comment `Thank you for your order` to the Group Footer band as a label control.

Now you need to save the report. Press Ctrl+W (or Ctrl+End) to save your report form and exit. At any time during the process of creating or modifying your form, you can save its current state by choosing the **F**ile menu **S**ave command or pressing Ctrl+S.

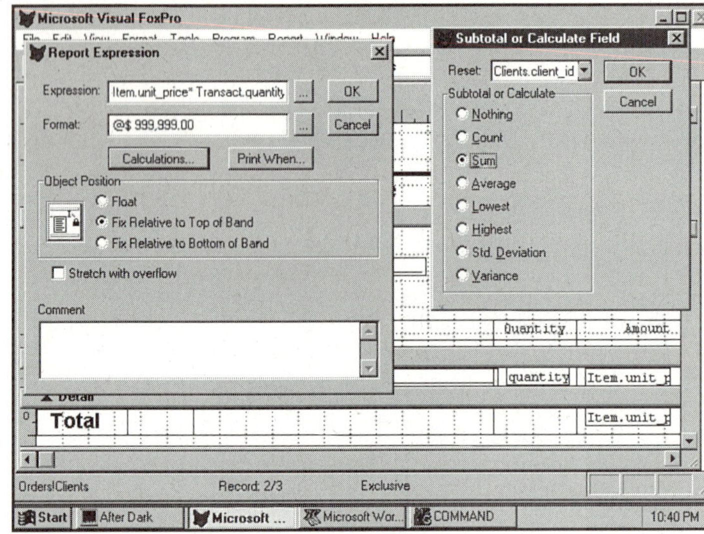

FIGURE 20.25.
The Report Layout window for the example invoice report, with the Report Expression and Subtotal or Calculate Field dialog boxes open.

The first time you save your report form, you are prompted to type a name for your report.

Now preview your report. You can do this by using the `REPORT` command or by clicking on the standard Visual FoxPro toolbar preview control (the control with a magnifying glass). The Print Preview window showing the first page of the report is shown in Figure 20.26.

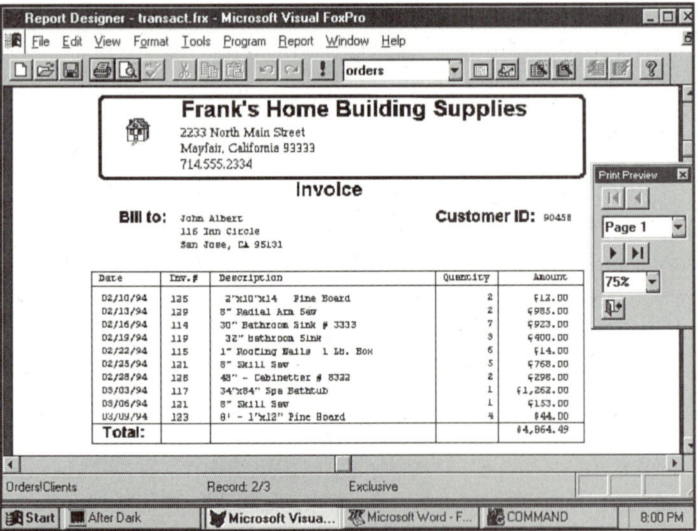

FIGURE 20.26.
The sample output from the Report Form invoice.

The following command could be used to print the report:

```
REPORT FORM INVOICE ENVIRONMENT
```

All the FoxPro commands shown in Listing 20.2 could have been replaced with the following single SQL `SELECT` command:

```
SELECT * FROM clients c,transact t , item i;
   WHERE t.client_id=  ANY (select x.client_id from clients x) ;
   AND t.inv_no = i.inv_no ;
   ORDER by c.client_id    ;
   INTO CURSOR Trans
   REPORT FORM Transact1
```

Instead, I used the FoxPro commands in this example to make it clearer which fields are associated with which tables. If you refer to fields using the cursor, all fields come from the same table. However, in general, the use of the SQL `SELECT` command is an exceptionally efficient method of selecting records for reports and labels. However, you must output your SQL `SELECT` query into some type of table (a database table, an array, or a cursor) that the `REPORT` or `LABEL` command can reference.

Designing Labels

A facility for generating mailing labels has been included in every version of Xbase since dBASE II. With each new product, the Label Designer has become easier to use and has been given more power. Visual FoxPro is equipped with the most powerful Label Designer currently available. Your labels can contain fancy text, bitmap pictures, and graphics figures. It is even easier to create mailing labels using the Labels Wizard, which is described in Chapter 24.

When you learned how to use the Visual FoxPro Report Designer, you also learned how to use the Label Designer. The only difference is that when you execute a command to create a label form, the New Label dialog box appears, as shown in Figure 20.27. Choose one of the available predefined label options from the New Label menu. All of the available options are listed in Table 20.10. The options specify an Avery label order number and the dimensions of a label, including height, width, and how many labels are printed across the page.

FIGURE 20.27.
The New Label dialog box.

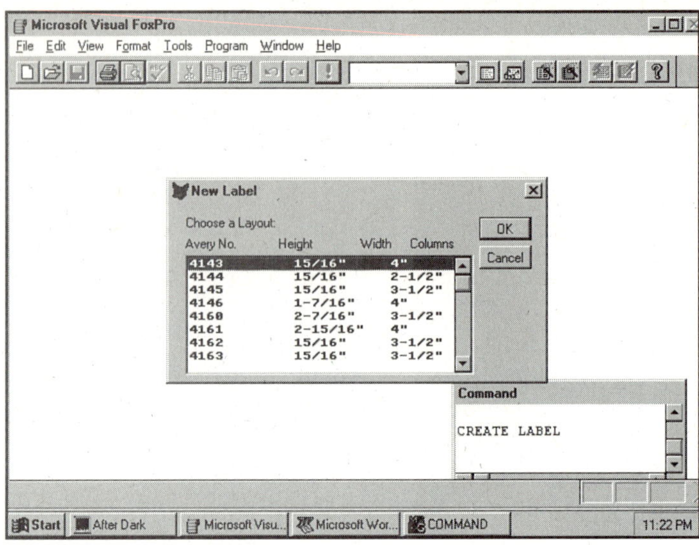

Table 20.10. The available label forms and corresponding Avery label order numbers.

Avery Number	*Height*	*Width*	*Number of Columns*
4143	$\frac{15}{16}$"	4"	2
4144	$\frac{15}{16}$"	$2\frac{1}{2}$"	3
4145	$\frac{15}{16}$"	$3\frac{1}{2}$"	1
4146	$1\frac{7}{16}$"	4"	1
4160	$2\frac{7}{16}$"	$3\frac{1}{2}$"	1
4161	$2\frac{15}{16}$"	4"	1
4162	$\frac{15}{16}$"	$3\frac{1}{2}$"	1
4163	$\frac{15}{16}$"	$3\frac{1}{2}$"	1
4166	3"	5"	1
4167	$3\frac{1}{2}$"	6"	1
4168	$2\frac{1}{6}$"	4"	1
4169	3"	5"	1
4240	$1\frac{1}{4}$"	$4\frac{3}{4}$"	1
4241	$2\frac{3}{4}$"	$2\frac{3}{4}$"	1
4249	$\frac{15}{16}$"	$3\frac{1}{2}$"	1
4250	$\frac{15}{16}$"	$3\frac{1}{2}$"	1
4251	$\frac{15}{16}$"	$3\frac{1}{2}$"	1

Avery Number	*Height*	*Width*	*Number of Columns*
4253	15/16"	3 1/2"	1
4254	15/16"	3 1/2"	1
4255	7/16"	3 1/2"	1
4256	7/16"	3 1/2"	1
4257	7/16"	3 1/2"	1
4258	7/16"	3 1/2"	1
4259	7/16"	3 1/2"	1
4266	7/16"	3 1/2"	1
5095	2 1/2"	3 3/8"	2
5096	2 3/4"	2 3/4"	3
5097	1 1/2"	4"	2
5160	1"	2 5/8"	3
5161	1"	4"	2
5162	1 1/3"	4"	2
5163	2"	4"	2
5164	3 1/3"	4"	2
5165	8 1/2"	11"	1
5196	2 3/4"	2 3/4"	3
5197	1 1/2"	4"	2
5198	1 2/3"	3 1/2"	2
5199-F	1 5/6"	3 1/16"	2
5199-S	2/3"	5 13/16"	1
5260	1"	2 5/8"	3
5261	1"	4"	2
5262	1 1/3"	4"	2
5266	2/3"	3 7/16"	2
5267	1/2"	1 3/4"	4
5383	2 1/6"	3 1/2"	2
5384	3"	4"	2
5385	2 1/6"	4"	2
5386	3"	5"	1

continues

Table 20.10. continued

Avery Number	*Height*	*Width*	*Number of Columns*
5388	3"	5"	1
5389	4"	6"	1
5395	$2^{1}/_{2}$"	$3^{3}/_{8}$"	2
5660	1"	$2^{5}/_{6}$"	3
5662	$1^{1}/_{3}$"	$4^{1}/_{4}$"	2
5663	2"	$4^{1}/_{4}$"	2
5883	$2^{1}/_{6}$"	$3^{1}/_{2}$"	2
5895	$2^{1}/_{3}$"	$3^{3}/_{8}$"	2
5896	$2^{3}/_{4}$"	$2^{3}/_{4}$"	3
5897	$1^{1}/_{2}$"	4"	2
EAL 04	37mm	89mm	1
L7160	38.10mm	63.50mm	3
L7161	46.56mm	63.50mm	3
L7162	33.87mm	99.06mm	2
L7163	38.10mm	99.06mm	2
L7164	71.97mm	63.50mm	2
L7165	67.73mm	99.06mm	2
L7166	93.13mm	99.06mm	2
L7167	289.05mm	199.60mm	1
L7562	33.87mm	99.06mm	2
L7563	38.10mm	99.06mm	2
OML 101	24mm	102mm	1
OML 102	37mm	102mm	1
OML 103	49mm	102mm	1
OML 104	37mm	127mm	1
OML 105	49mm	127mm	1
OML 202	37mm	102mm	2
OML 203	49mm	102mm	2
Tab1 102.36	36.1mm	120mm	1
Tab1 107.23	23.4mm	107mm	1
Tab1 107.36	36.1mm	107mm	1

Avery Number	*Height*	*Width*	*Number of Columns*
Tab1 107.49	48.8mm	107mm	1
Tab1 89.23	23.4mm	89mm	1
Tab1 89.36	36.1mm	89mm	1
Tab2 107.23	23.4mm	107mm	2
Tab2 107.36	36.1mm	107mm	2
Tab2 89.23	23.4mm	89mm	2
Tab2 89.36	36.1mm	89mm	2

After you decide which label you want and choose one, the Report Designer Layout window opens, as shown in Figure 20.28. If you don't find a label that is the size you need, choose one that is close. When the Report Designer Layout window appears, choose the **F**ile menu Page Set**u**p option and make the necessary adjustments. The Detail band layout area is the size of a single label. You can use any of the controls in the Report Controls toolbar to place controls in this layout area. In Figure 20.28, `name`, `address`, `city`, `state`, and `ZIP` code fields were placed in the layout area, and a rounded rectangle with a 2-point outline was added. The Expression Builder was used to build an expression that contains the city, state, and ZIP fields for the third line of the label. Here is the resultant expression:

```
RTRIM(Clients1.city)+", "+ Clients1.state+" "+ Clients1.zip
```

You can preview your labels by selecting the **V**iew menu Pre**v**iew option as shown in Figure 20.29. A miniature representation of a page of labels appears in the Page Preview window.

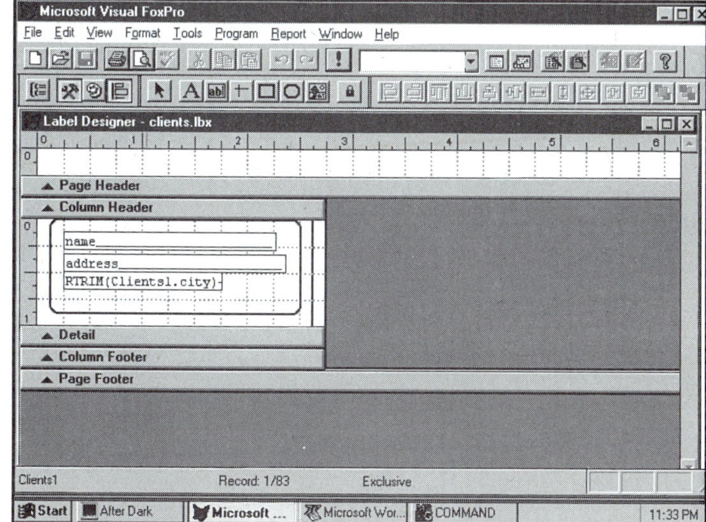

FIGURE 20.28.
The Report Layout window used to design a label.

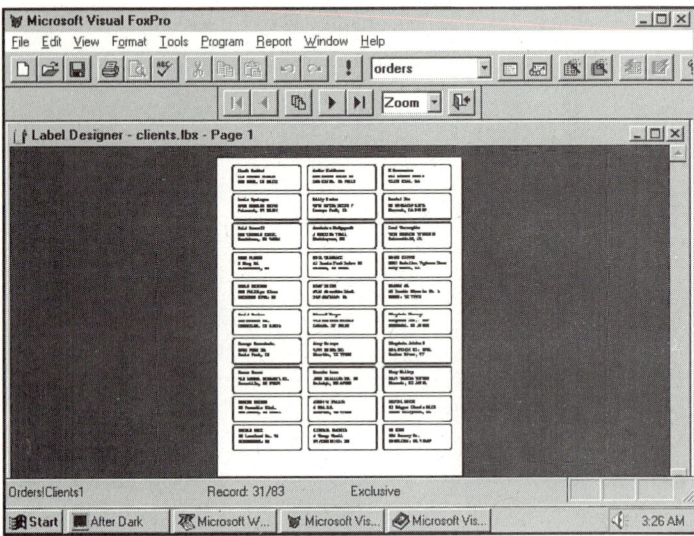

FIGURE 20.29.
A preview of sample labels.

You can buy mailing labels with your company name, address, and logo already printed on them. On the other hand, you can print a professional looking presentation of your company information on the label when you print your mailing labels with the Visual FoxPro Label Designer. In the example Report Layout window shown in Figure 20.30, the mailing labels contain the mailer's company name, address, and logo (bitmap file), as well as the fields for the client's name and address. Figure 20.31 shows the Print Preview window displaying sample labels. Notice that the option to display the labels at 75% of their actual size was selected. You can print the actual labels with the LABEL command. You can also print labels by choosing the **F**ile menu **P**rint option, which displays the Print dialog box. You choose the Label file type, and the Open File dialog box opens. Choose a Label Form file, and the Run Label dialog box appears. Specify whether you want to preview or print the specified labels.

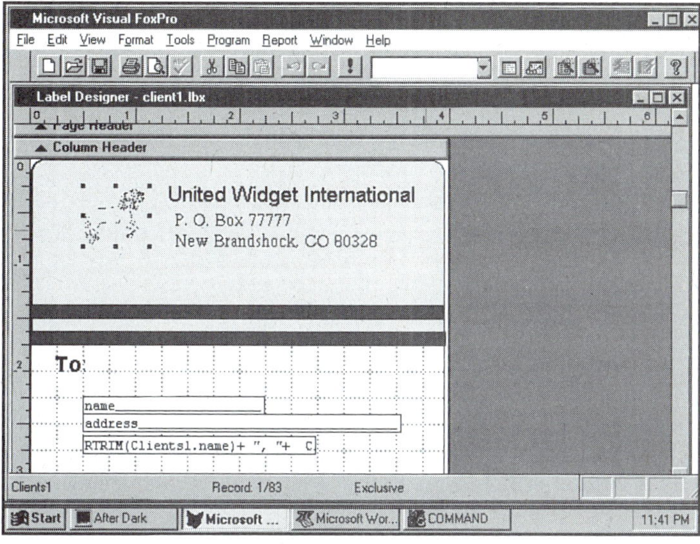

FIGURE 20.30.
The Report Layout window used to design a custom label.

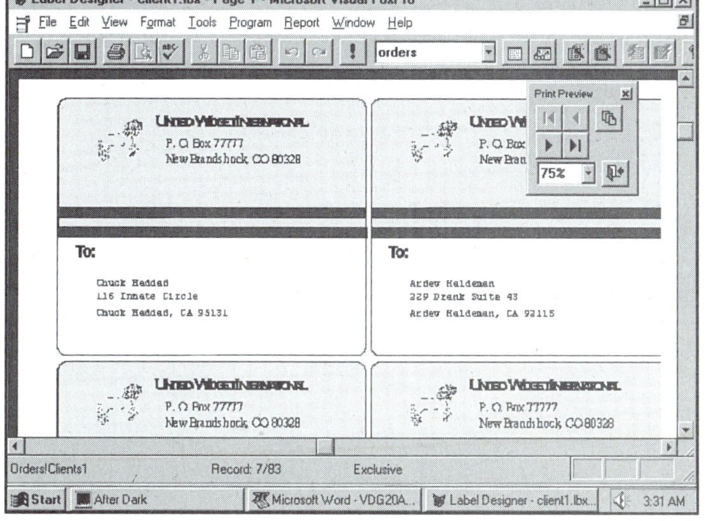

FIGURE 20.31.
The Print Preview window showing sample custom labels.

Summary

You might have mastered the art of using FoxPro to gather, manipulate, organize, analyze, and view data, but you cannot be considered a FoxPro authority until you have become proficient in the creation of useful and well-organized reports. In most cases, reports are the only portal through which others can view your creation. I once knew a programmer who spent a large portion of his programming development effort designing his reports. He felt that reports printed by his programs were the only tangible product by which managers could measure the quality of his work. His attitude was admirable, but with the Visual FoxPro Report Designer you can really dazzle your managers and it doesn't take much time at all.

There was a time when programmers spent a considerable amount of time writing tedious code to generate reports. With the highly versatile and powerful Visual FoxPro Report Designer, Label Designer, and Report and Label Wizards you can quickly and easily design and develop sophisticated reports and labels that will satisfy most, if not all, of your reporting requirements.

Everybody is a report designer. To make matters worse, reports tend to have a wider readership than even input forms. When you show the design of your report to your customers, everyone has a suggestion for improvement. Then, after you develop the program and show reports with real data, the user community has even more suggestions. This is no surprise; it is a normal and expected phenomenon. You usually need to modify reports during the user test phase of a development effort. If you code your reporting modules by hand, you normally have a substantial amount of reprogramming work to do during this phase. However, if you use the Visual FoxPro Report Designer, you can make changes to a report (or labels) quickly and with minimal effort.

In this chapter, you learned how to use the Report Designer to create the following types of reports:

- Simple tabular reports
- Tabular reports with multiple grouping levels
- Tabular reports with multiple columns
- Fill-in forms (such as invoice forms)
- Complex reports containing tabular and fill-in forms
- Mailing labels using predefined forms

You have learned that you can add text in a variety of fonts, font sizes, and styles, and that you can add graphical controls including lines, rectangles, rectangles with rounded corners, ellipses, and bitmapped pictures.

21

Extending the Visual FoxPro Language

There is nothing in this world constant, but inconsistency.

—Jonathan Swift (1667–1745)
A Critical Essay Upon the Facilities of the Mind

You can extend Visual FoxPro in a system-dependent manner by means of its facility to use `SET LIBRARY TO` on FoxPro API library modules. The information in this chapter is at a high level technically; you can skip it unless you want to use some of the power to extend FoxPro's functionality.

Traditional Xbase Extendability

In traditional MS-DOS Xbase programs, named binary modules, which contain code written in C or assembly language, can be loaded into memory, released from memory, and called using the `LOAD`, `CALL`, and `RELEASE` commands, respectively. Although Visual FoxPro supports the `LOAD` and `CALL` commands, more powerful techniques are available to extend Visual FoxPro. I discuss these techniques later in this chapter. You don't need to read this section unless you want to write assembly language routines to be called from Visual FoxPro programs. You also do not have to read the next section unless you want information about an antiquated method of executing an external program. I am not going to say that by the end of the chapter you will be able to write DLL-type executable programs and load them with the `SET LIBRARY TO` command because coding in C++ is a complicated endeavor. However, if you are a C++ programmer, you will learn how to create Visual FoxPro FLL libraries.

Named modules can be loaded into memory, released from memory, and called with parameters. Parameters are passed by reference or by value; binary modules return values by changing passed parameters or returning a value. A binary module, in MS-DOS parlance, is a COM file with an ORG set at 0 instead of 100H. That means it is a binary image, rather than an EXE file. COM files are limited to a total of 65500 bytes. Visual FoxPro executes the module by reading the entire file into memory and jumping to the first byte. The code must not allocate or use memory that is not part of the binary image and must preserve the CS and SS registers.

The `LOAD` command loads binary routines from disk into memory. Sixteen files (up to 64KB each) can be loaded into memory at one time.

```
LOAD <file> [SAVE] ¦ [NOSAVE]
```

The filename, exclusive of extension, becomes the module name. If you don't provide an extension, Visual FoxPro assumes .BIN. When you call a binary routine, the extension should be omitted. If the loaded file (`<file>`) has the same filename and a different extension than one previously loaded, the new file overwrites the previously loaded file.

You can specify the `SAVE` keyword with both the `LOAD` and `CALL` commands. If you specify the `SAVE` keyword, FoxPro copies the current contents of video RAM into FoxPro's desktop upon return from the binary routine (assuming that the binary routine is writing directly into video RAM). In other words, FoxPro is aware of anything written by the binary routine and FoxPro

an FLL function in memory, you use less of your valuable memory resources when an FLL or DLL function is used. The entire Windows system is composed of DLLs. All the device drivers are DLLs. The Windows systems files—GDI32.DLL, USER32.DLL, KERNEL32.EXE, and ADVAPI32.DLL—are DLLs.

Windows systems have two types of executable modules: application modules and DLL modules. Application modules are the executable (EXE) files for an application. A DLL module normally has a .DLL file extension as well, but it can have an extension such as .DRV, .EXE, or .FON.

An executable (EXE) application actively performs a task. When it executes, it actively processes messages, creates windows, interacts with the user, and generates output. In contrast, a DLL library function is passive and serves only as a function that can be called on by an active application to perform some operation. With very few exceptions, DLL modules are as passive as any other library function.

When an application is loaded, it is given its own stack in local memory. A DLL module doesn't have its own stack. It uses the stack of the task that called it.

Both an application and a DLL module type can import a DLL function if either needs to use that function. *Import a function* means to create a dynamic link to that function. You can dynamically import a DLL module during execution of a Visual FoxPro application by using the `SET LIBRARY TO` command. However, in FoxPro, the filename extension for DLL files is .FLL, for Fox Link Library. The default filename extension for the `SET LIBRARY TO` command is .FLL. You can still execute DLL files, however, but you must specify the .DLL filename extension.

An application can import a DLL module while the application is executing. This is called a *dynamic import.* When a DLL is successfully imported, the application can call a function in the DLL module.

When an application calls a DLL function, Windows is responsible for finding the function and loading it in memory. It searches the same directories that it searches when it loads your application. The directory search order is the following:

1. Current directory
2. Windows directory (containing WIN.COM)
3. Windows systems directory (containing KERNEL32.EXE)
4. Directories specified in the MS-DOS path environmental variable
5. Network directories

Registering 32-Bit Dynamic Link Libraries

Dynamic link libraries are the foundation of the Windows system. DLLs enable programs to share functions that are loaded at runtime. The `DECLARE` command can be used to register a function residing in an external 32-bit DLL. In fact, you must execute the DECLARE command before you can call any 32-bit DLL functions. One type of DLL library is the Windows API 32-bit DLL library. You can find more information about the Windows API 32-bit DLL functions by referring to the documentation included with the *Microsoft Win32 Programmer's Guide.*

You can release all registered 32-bit DLLs from memory with the CLEAR DLLS or CLEAR ALL commands. The DISPLAY STATUS and LIST STATUS commands list all of the DLL functions in memory.

If you want to call a 16-bit DLL function, you can use the FOXTOOLS.FLL library, which is discussed in the next section. Microsoft still supports FOXTOOLS.FLL in Visual FoxPro to provide backward compatibility support for old 16-bit DLL libraries. However, Microsoft encourages you to use the DECLARE command for calling Windows 32-bit DLL functions. This is probably because they want to get out of the business of supporting two methods of providing the same functionality.

The syntax for the DECLARE command for registering a 32-bit DLL library function is

```
DECLARE [cFunctionType] FunctionName IN LibraryName [AS AliasName]
           [cParamType1 [@] ParamName1, cParamType2 [@] ParamName2, ...]
```

You specify the cFunctionType parameter to designate whether the 32-bit Windows DLL has a return value. If you do not specify cFunctionType, the function does not have a return value. If you specify cFunctionType, it denotes the data type of the return value. It can have any of the following values:

cFunctionType	*Description*
INTEGER	32-bit integer
SINGLE	32-bit floating point
DOUBLE	64-bit floating point
STRING	Character string

The FunctionName parameter designates the name of the 32-bit Windows DLL function that the DECLARE command registers. This name is different from FoxPro names because it is case-sensitive. For example, you must specify the Windows DLL GetActiveWindow() function as GetActiveWindow and not as GETACTIVEWINDOW. However, when you use the function in Visual FoxPro, you no longer need to honor case-sensitivity; you treat it as you would any other Visual FoxPro name identifier. For example, to register the Windows DLL GetActiveWindow() function and call it, you use the following commands:

```
DECLARE INTEGER GetActiveWindow IN win32api
nActiveWindow = GETACTIVEWINDOW()
? nActiveWindow
```

If a 32-bit Windows DLL function has the same name as a Visual FoxPro function, you use FunctionName to specify its actual name and the AS AliasName clause to specify an alias name. For example, Visual FoxPro has a function called MESSAGEBOX(), and so does the Windows API.

You can specify the following statement and refer to the Windows API function as `MB()` when you call it:

```
#INCLUDE "FOXPRO.H"
DECLARE INTEGER  MessageBox IN USER32 AS mb ;
         INTEGER, STRING, STRING, INTEGER
Answer = MB(0,"Do you know?","Question", MB_YESNO + MB_ICONQUESTION )
```

NOTE

The Windows 32 API system provides support for applications distributed worldwide. To support this market, Microsoft provides support for international character sets. Some of the 32-bit Windows DLL functions might have a letter (W for UNICODE or A for ASCII) appended to the end of their name. For example, the `MessageBox` function should be named `MessageBoxA` (for single-byte ASCII character sets) and `MessageBoxW` (for UNICODE character sets). However, the `DECLARE` command automatically adds the letter to the end of the function name when required.

You also use the `AS AliasName` clause to specify an alias name if the 32-bit Windows DLL function is not a legal Visual FoxPro name.

You are required to specify the `IN LibraryName` clause, which identifies the name of the external Windows DLL that contains the Windows 32-bit DLL function that you specify with the `FunctionName` parameter. All of the Windows API 32-bit DLL functions are stored in one of the four DLL files: kernel32.DLL, gdi32.DLL, user32.DLL, or advapi.DLL.

If you look through all of the Windows 32 API documents, both hard copy and CD-ROM, you'll have trouble figuring out which API functions are in which DLL file. Consequently, you can specify `IN Win32API`, and Visual FoxPro searches through all four libraries for the 32-bit API function specified with `FunctionName`. The following is an example of the use of the `DECLARE` command, which is used to call the Windows API `MessageBeep()` function:

```
DECLARE MessageBeep IN win32api INTEGER
=MessageBeep(1)  && Sound the Bell with Windows API functions
```

You are also required to specify a parameter list (`cParameterType1 [@] ParamName1, cParameterType2 [@] ParamName2, ...`), which represents the arguments that the 32-bit DLL function expects. You supply a data type for each parameter, which can be one of the following keywords:

ParameterType1	*Description*
`INTEGER`	32-bit integer
`SINGLE`	32-bit floating point
`DOUBLE`	64-bit floating point
`STRING`	Character string

Visual FoxPro generates an error if the parameters are not of the type that the Windows 32-bit DLL function expects.

If you are required to pass a parameter by reference when you call the function, you must include the `@` character after the parameter type, `cParameterType`. If you omit the `@` after `cParameterType` in the `DECLARE` command, in the calling function, or in both, the parameter is passed by value.

If you want to remind yourself what a parameter does or improve readability, you can add the optional `ParamName` elements to the parameter list to suggest its purpose. However, they are not used by Visual FoxPro. They are not used by the Windows 32-bit DLL function. `ParamName` elements are simply and strictly ignored. In the following example, the `ParamName` elements' names do make it easier to remember what arguments you need to specify when you call the function:

```
DECLARE INTEGER  MessageBox IN USER32 AS mb ;
         INTEGER  nWindowHandle, ;
         STRING   cMessageText, ;
         STRING   cTitleBarText, ;
         INTEGER  nDialogBoxType
= MB( 0, "This is message text", "Title Bar Text", 16 );
```

The example presented in Listing 21.2 illustrates how to call a 32-bit Windows API function. This example first fetches the handle of the active window, which in this case happens to be the Visual FoxPro main window. The program then retrieves the title bar text from the active window, which is Microsoft Visual FoxPro.

Listing 21.2. A program that illustrates how to call a 32-bit Windows API function.

```
*********************************************************************
* Program: GETWIND.PRG
* Purpose: Illustrates how to call 32-bit Windows API functions
*********************************************************************
* Register Windows API functions:
DECLARE INTEGER GetActiveWindow IN USER32
DECLARE INTEGER GetWindowText IN USER32 AS GWT INTEGER,STRING,INTEGER
*  Call API functions:
nActiveWindow=GETACTIVEWINDOW()
? "Active Window Handle: ", nActiveWindow
Buffer = SPACE(80)
? "Length of Text:       ", GWT( nActiveWindow,  @Buffer, LEN(Buffer))
? "Active Window Title:  ",BUFFER
CLEAR DLLS  && Release DLL functions from memory
```

Example output from executing the program GETWIND.PRG is as follows:

```
Active Window Handle:     3456
Length of Text:             23
Active Window Title:   Microsoft Visual FoxPro
```

Just because all the examples in this section call Windows 32-bit API functions does not mean that the only 32-bit DLL library functions are Windows API functions. In addition, you can use the `DECLARE` command to register functions in 32-bit DLL libraries that you purchase from any third-party developer. You can also develop your own using Visual C++ Version 2.*x*, Borland C++ Version 4.5, or any other compiler that creates 32-bit DLL libraries.

Using Windows API DLLs in FoxPro Applications

This section describes a FoxPro API library named FOXTOOLS.FLL that allows access to Windows API functions. The FOXTOOLS.FLL file is supplied with the Visual FoxPro product. It resides in the \VFP directory.

You can open the FOXTOOLS.FLL file using the `SET LIBRARY TO` command. Then you can call API library functions from your Visual FoxPro programs to call any Windows API function with simple scalar values including integers, longs, floats, doubles, character strings, and buffers. In addition, the function must return either an integer, a long, float, double, or string value. You might be surprised at how many of the Windows API functions meet these criteria.

Of course, to be able to generate calls to Windows API functions, you must know what the Windows API functions are, what arguments they have, and how to call them. You can obtain this knowledge by acquiring a Microsoft SDK document and a copy of a C language windows.H header file. Armed with these tools, some imagination, and initiative, you can do some incredible things with Windows API functions.

The FoxPro FoxTools API library contains three major functions:

Function	*Description*
`RegFn32()`, `RegFn()`	Register a function and its arguments
`CallFn()`	Calls a registered function

The functions are described in the following sections.

RegFn32() and *RegFn()*: Registering a Windows API Function

You must call the `RegFn()` function to get a DLL function register number. This number is used as an argument for the `CallFn()` function. The syntax is

```
RegFn(FunctionName, ArgTypes, ReturnType [, DLLName] )
RegFn32(FunctionName, ArgTypes, ReturnType [, DLLName] )
```

`RegFN()` is used with Windows 3.1, and `RegFN32` is used with the 32-bit operating environment (Windows 95 and Windows NT). The arguments are defined as follows:

Argument	*Description*
`FunctionName`	A character string containing the name of the function to be registered. Most DLL library functions are referenced by name. However, some are referred to by an ordinal value. If the DLL function is identified with an ordinal value, you must specify an integer value for this argument instead of a name. Windows doesn't ignore case as FoxPro does. For example, `GetWindowDirectory` must be specified with `G`, `W`, and `D` in uppercase, and everything else in lowercase.
`ArgTypes`	A character string containing one character for each argument the function accepts. The following values are allowed: `I`—Integer `L`—Long `C`—String of characters, by value `S`—String of characters, by reference (can be modified) `F`—Floating-point number `D`—Double-precision, floating-point number The arguments are assumed to be passed by value unless you precede a type character with an `@` character, in which case the argument is passed by reference. `ArgTypes` cannot contain any embedded or trailing spaces. The number of arguments is derived from the number of characters in the string. For example, the value of `ArgTypes` for a DLL function with two character arguments followed by two integer arguments is `CCI@I`. The last integer argument is passed by reference because it's preceded with an `@` character.
`ReturnType`	A character string containing one character. For example, if the function returns a floating point number, specify the character string `"F"`.
`[,<DLLName>]`	This optional argument is a character string that is the name of the DLL to use. You must supply the filename extension. If the DLL resides in a directory that is along the search path, you don't need to specify the path. This argument is optional if the function name is supplied as the first

argument. In this case, previously loaded DLL libraries are searched in reverse order for the function name. If it is not found, standard Windows libraries are searched for the function. If the DLL library can't be opened, the `RegFn()` function returns `-1`. An error message box, which cannot be disabled, also displays.

If this argument is omitted, the `RegFn()` function automatically searches the following libraries:

WIND32: KERNEL32.DLL
GDI32.DLL
USER32.DLL
ADVAPI.DLL
WIN32S: KERNL386.DLL
GDI.EXE
USER.EXE

The `RegFn32()` function returns a numeric value, which is used with the `CallFn()` function to do the actual Windows API function call. The `RegFn()` function returns `-1` if the function cannot be found. It also displays an error message box.

FoxTools is loaded with many other functions that Microsoft uses internally and for which it does not provide technical support. However, many FoxPro developers use these functions anyway. They are described in Table 21.1.

Table 21.1. Other FOXTOOLS.FLL functions.

Function	*Description*

`ADDBS(<expC>)`	Returns `<expC>` with a backslash appended, if needed. Here are some examples:
	`? ADDBS("C:")` returns: `C:\`
	`? ADDBS("C:\")` returns: `C:\`

`CLEANPATH(<expC>)`	Returns a "best guess" corrected filename for an invalid filename. It removes spaces, invalid characters, duplicate backslashes, and so forth. For example, `? CLEANPATH("C:D:\\THISISALONGFILE ")` returns `D:\THISISAL`.
`DRIVETYPE(<expC>)`	Returns a numeric value that indicates the type of drive specified with `<expC>`. The returned values are as follows: `0`—No type `2`—Floppy disk

continues

Table 21.1. continued

Function	*Description*
	3—Hard disk 4—Removable / network drive For example, `? DRIVETYPE("C:")` returns `3`.
`DEFAULTEXT(<expC1>,<expC2>)`	Returns *<expC1>* with a new extension, if it does not already have one. *<expC1>* specifies a filename with or without an extension. *<expC2>* specifies an extension. For example, `? DEFAULTEXT("C:\BIN\COMPRESS.COM", "BIN")` returns `C:\BIN\COMPRESS.COM`.
`FORCEEXT(<expC1>,<expC2>)`	Returns a string with the old extension replaced with a new extension. *<expC1>* specifies a filename with or without an extension. *<expC2>* specifies an extension without a period. For example, `? FORCEEXT ("C:\FX\CUSTOMER.XXX", "DBF")` returns `C:\FX\CUSTOMER.DBF`.
`FORCEPATH(<expC1>,<expC2>)`	Returns *<expC1>* with its path changed to *<expC2>*. *<expC1>* specifies the filename with or without a path. *<expC2>* specifies the replacement path. For example, `? FORCEPATH("C:\DOS\FOO.EXE", "C:\FX")` returns `C:\FX\FOO.EXE`.
`FOXTOOLVER()`	Returns the version number of the FOXTOOLS.FLL library.
`JUSTDRIVE(<expC>)`	Returns the drive letter from a complete path, as in the following example: `? JUSTDRIVE("C:\BIN\LS.EXE")` returns `C:`.
`JUSTEXT(<expC>)`	Returns the three-letter extension from a complete path, as in the following example: `? JUSTEXT("C:\FX\FOO.TXT")` returns `TXT`.
`JUSTFNAME(<expC>)`	Returns a string with the filename from a complete path, as in the following example: `? JUSTFNAME(("C:\FX\FOO.TXT")` returns `FOO.TXT`.
`JUSTPATH(<expC>)`	Returns a string with the pathname from a complete path, as in the following example: `? JUSTFNAME(("C:\FX\FOO.TXT")` returns `C:\FX`. Here's another example: `? JUSTPATH("C:\FOXPROW\FOXPROW.EXE")` returns `C:\FOXPROW`.

Function	*Description*
JUSTSTEM(<*expC*>)	Returns a string with the first eight characters of a filename from a complete path, as in the following example: ? JUSTFNAME(("C:\FX\FOO.TXT") returns FOO.
MAINHWND()	Returns a Windows handle (HWND) to the main FoxPro window.
NEXTWORD(<*expC1*>,<*expN*> [,<*expC2*>])	Returns the next word in <*expC1*>, beginning at character <*expN*> and ending just before any character in the optional <*expC2*> or the end of the <*expC1*> string. The default value for <*expC2*> is space, a tab, and a carriage return, as in the following example: ? NEXTWORD("This is a test of Foo", 12) returns est.
REDUCE(<*expC1*>,<*expC2*>)	Removes repetitive values in a string. It is usually used to remove a group of spaces in a string and replace it with one space. <*expC1*> specifies a character string to change. <*expC2*> specifies characters for which to search, as in the following example: ? REDUCE("This has.....spaces", " ") returns This has spaces.
STRFILTER(<*expC1*>,<*expC2*>)	Returns only characters specified in <*expC2*>. This function is case sensitive. <*expC1*> specifies a character string for which to search. <*expC2*> specifies characters for which to search, as in the following example: ? STRFILTER("The Thing", "T") returns TT.
VALIDPATH(<*expC1*>)	Returns a logical true (.T.) value if the MS-DOS filename and path syntax is valid. Note that this function is not perfect. It sometimes thinks a file has a valid name when it doesn't. However, it will not reject as invalid a valid name. This function does not check whether the filename exists.
WORDNUM(<*expC1*>, <*expN*>[,<*expC2*>])	Returns the <*expN*> word in <*expC*>, delimited by any character in the optional <*expC2*>. The default for <*expC2*> is a space, a tab, and a carriage return, as in the following example: ? WORDNUM("This is the fourth word", 4) returns fourth.

continues

Table 21.1. continued

Function	*Description*
`WORDS(<expC1>[,<expC2>])`	Returns the number of words in `<expC>`, delimited by any character in the optional `<expC2>` field. The default for `<expC2>` is a space, a tab, and a carriage return. `? WORDS("This has four word")` returns `4`.

The following Clipboard functions, shown in Table 21.2, correspond to Windows SDK functions that are similarly named. You should definitely not use these functions unless you know exactly what you're doing! Microsoft recommends that you use the `_CLIPTEXT` system memory variable to access the Windows Clipboard.

Table 21.2. FOXTOOLS.FLL Clipboard functions.

Function	*Description*
`CLOSECLIP()`	Closes the Clipboard that was previously opened using the `OPENCLIP()` function. If successful, this function returns `.T.`.
`COUNTCLIPF()`	Retrieves the number of different data formats currently in the Clipboard.
`EMPTYCLIP()`	Empties the Clipboard and frees handles to data in the Clipboard. It then assigns ownership of the Clipboard to the window that currently has the Clipboard open. It returns a logical value.
`ENUMCLIPFM(<expN>)`	Enumerates the formats found in a list of available formats that belong to the Clipboard. Each call to this function specifies a known available format; the function returns the format that appears next in the list.

`GETCLIPDAT(<expN>)`	Retrieves a handle of the current Clipboard data having a specified format in `<expN>`. `<expN>` contains the following definitions:
	`cf_Text = 1`
	`cf_Bitmap = 2`
	`cf_MetaFilePict = 3`
	`cf_SYLK = 4`
	`cf_DIF = 5`
	`cf_TIFF = 6`
	`cf_OEMText = 7`
	`cf_DIB = 8`
	`cf_Palette = 9`

Function	Description
`GETCLIPFMT(<expN>)`	Retrieves the name of a registered Clipboard format.

`ISCLIPFMT(<expN>)`	Returns a true (`.T.`) value if data exists in the Clipboard for the specified format (`<expN>`). Formats are defined as follow:
	`cf_Text = 1`
	`cf_Bitmap = 2`
	`cf_MetaFilePict = 3`
	`cf_SYLK = 4`
	`cf_DIF = 5`
	`cf_TIFF = 6`
	`cf_OEMText = 7`
	`cf_DIB = 8`
	`cf_Palette = 9`
	For example, the following command returns true if there is text on the Clipboard:
	`? ISCLIPFMT(cf_Text)`

`OPENCLIP(<expN>)`	Opens the Clipboard. Other applications cannot modify the Clipboard until the `CLOSECLIP` function is called. `<expN>` is the handle of the window and `0` is acceptable. Most of the other Clipboard functions rely on this function. Here's an example: `? OPENCLIP(0).`
`REGCLIPFMT(<expC>)`	Registers a new Clipboard format and returns a numeric value that indicates the newly registered format. If the identical format name has been registered before, even by a different application, the format's reference count is incremented (that is, increased by one) and the same value is returned as when the format was originally registered. The return value is `0` if the format cannot be registered. The registered format can be used in subsequent Clipboard functions as a valid format in which to render data, and it will appear in the Clipboard's list of formats. `<expC>` is a string that names the new format, as in the following example: `? REGCLIPFMT("MyRegClip")`
`SETCLIPDAT(<expN>, <expC>)`	Stores the data (`<expC>`) in the Clipboard and returns a true (`.T.`) value if successful, as in the following

continues

Table 21.2. continued

Function	*Description*
	example: `? SETCLIPDAT(1, "Test")` returns `.T.`.

There are other functions in FoxTools.FLL that begin with `ED` and `W`. These correspond to the Visual FoxPro API functions described in the FoxPro 2.5 Library Construction Kit (LCK). The LCK is part of the Professional Edition Visual FoxPro product. You use it to write your own libraries using C or C++.

The same Windows API function can be registered more than once to allow functions to take different arguments.

The `RegFn32()` function returns a numeric value, which is used with the `CallFn()` function to do the actual Windows API function call. The `RegFn()` function returns `-1` if the function cannot be found. It also displays an error message box.

CallFN(): Calling a Windows API Function

The `CallFN()` function calls a Windows API function. It returns the integer value returned by the Windows API function. The syntax is

```
CallFN(FnNum, Arg1, Arg2, ....)
```

This function requires at least one argument, which is the function register number from the previous call to `RegFn()`. You must pass the same number of arguments that were declared with the `ArgTypes` argument to `RegFn()` or an error message box displays and the Windows API function is not called.

All arguments, by default, are passed by value except for the `S` type, which must be passed by reference. As you may remember, when you pass a variable by reference, you precede the variable name with the `@` character. All arguments must match their declared type. `F` and `D` types must be a floating-point number. `I` and `L` types must be an integer value. `S` must be a string passed by reference.

Examples of the FOXTOOLS.FLL Function Usage

Many Windows applications display an hourglass during some time-consuming operations. The following example program illustrates the use of the FoxTools library to call Windows cursor shape change functions to display an hourglass-shaped cursor. In the example shown in Listing 21.3, when you create an `HourGlass` object, an hourglass-shaped cursor displays. The reference to the `HourGlass` object is stored in the memory variable `Changer`. The hourglass cursor displays for the lifetime of the `Changer` memory variable. When the program

HOURGLAS.PRG exits, `Changer` is released and the cursor changes back to its original form.

When the `HourGlas` object is created, the `HourGlass.Init` method is automatically called. In this method, the FoxTools.FLL library is loaded. Then the Windows API functions are called using the `RegFN32()` function to change the shape of the cursor to an hourglass.

When the object is released, the `HourGlass.Destroy()` function is automatically called, which restores the cursor to its original shape and releases the FoxTools.FLL library.

Listing 21.3. The HOURGLAS.PRG program, which illustrates how to use FoxTools to change the shape of the cursor.

```
*******************************************************
*    Program: HourGlas.PRG shows you how to change the  *
*    cursor to an hourglass and then back again         *
*******************************************************
* these are the predefined cursor shapes (from WINDOWS.H)
#define IDC_ARROW       (32512)
#define IDC_IBEAM       (32513)
#define IDC_WAIT        (32514)
#define IDC_CROSS       (32515)
#define IDC_UPARROW     (32516)
#define IDC_SIZE        (32640)
#define IDC_ICON        (32641)
#define IDC_SIZENWSE    (32642)
#define IDC_SIZENESW    (32643)
#define IDC_SIZEWE      (32644)
#define IDC_SIZENS      (32645)
***********************************************
LOCAL Changer
Changer = CreateObject("HourGlass")
* Hourglass displays during processing
FOR I = 1 TO 100
? i
ENDFOR
RETURN
****************************************************
DEFINE CLASS HourGlass AS Custom
PROTECTED OldCursor, SetCursor

   PROTECTED PROCEDURE Init
   LOCAL LoadCursor

   set library to sys(2004)+"foxtools.fll" additive
   LoadCursor = regfn32("LoadCursor", "IL", "I")
   This.SetCursor  = regfn32("SetCursor", "I", "I")
   This.OldCursor = callfn(This.SetCursor, callfn(LoadCursor, 0, IDC_WAIT))
   ENDPROC
**************************************************************
* DESTROY event occurs when an instance of object is released.
**************************************************************
   PROTECTED PROCEDURE DESTROY
   =callfn(This.SetCursor, This.OldCursor)
```

continues

Listing 21.3. continued

```
   release library sys(2004)+"foxtools.fll"
   ENDPROC
ENDDEFINE
```

The example shown in Listing 21.4 illustrates how to retrieve the Windows directory. It calls the Windows API `GetWindowDirectory()` function. You can determine the calling sequence for the `GetWindowsDirectory()` function or any other Windows API function by looking at Windows C compiler documentation. This function has two arguments. The first is a reference to a character buffer large enough to hold the directory. The second argument is an integer that specifies the size of the character string. The function returns an integer that is the size of the actual Windows directory. It also transfers the directory path into the character string. The GETWDIR.PRG program fetches the Windows directory and displays in a wait window.

Listing 21.4. The source code of a program that uses the FOXTOOLS.FLL library to fetch the Windows directory.

```
***************************************************************
*      * 12/94               GetWDir.prg                 *
*      * Description:                                    *
*      *  GetMdir.PRG  illustrates how to use FOXTOOLS.FLL      *
*            to call a typical Windows API function         *
*            Specifically, this program gets the Windows        *
*            directory                                          *
*   It calls the Windows API function:                          *
*     UINT GetWindowsDirectory(lpszWinPath, cchWinPath) *
*     where:  LPTSTR lpszWinPath;    Address of buffer for      *
*                                    Windows directory          *
*             UINT cchWinPath;       Size of directory buffer   *
*     The GetWindowsDirectory function retrieves the path       *
*     of the Windows directory.                          *
*     Returns: Length of path                                   *
***************************************************************
*  First load the FOXTOOLS.FLL library
SET LIBRARY TO SYS(2004)+"foxtools.fll" ADDITIVE
*  Next register the function and specify it has two arguments
*    @C - LPTSTR lpszWinPath
*    I  - Size of character buffer
*  It returns an I - type
getwdir = RegFn32("GetWindowsDirectory", "@CI", "I")
bigstr = REPLICATE(CHR(0), 144)    && set up a big string
* Now call the GetWindowsDirectory() function
retlen = CallFn(getwdir, @bigstr, 144)
WAIT WINDOW "The Windows directory is " + left(bigstr, retlen)
RELEASE LIBRARY SYS(2004)+"foxtools.fll"
```

The following example loads and calls the Windows API `MessageBox()` function, which performs the following operations:

- Draws a box
- Displays a question mark icon
- Displays a query message
- Displays Yes and No push buttons
- Returns user response

If you refer to Windows API documentation, you'll see that the `MessageBox` function call has the following syntax:

```
int MessageBox( HWndParent, lptext, lpCaption, wType )
HWndParent - Handle to parent window (msgboxRN)
lptext     - Text in box
lpCaption  - Message box window title
wType      - Specifies icon and type of buttons OR'ed
together.
```

The first argument for the `MessageBox()` function is a handle to the parent window. It is an integer value. In the example shown in Listing 21.5, the Windows main window is the parent window and, consequently, `HWndParent` is assigned a zero value. The second argument is a string (`C`), which specifies the text displayed in the message box. The third argument is a string that specifies the text that appears in the title bar. The last argument is an integer (`I`) that designates which icon displays in the message box.

In the example shown in Listing 21.5, FoxTools is loaded using the `SET LIBRARY TO` command. Next, the `RegFn()` function is called to register the `MessageBox` function. Because the function has three arguments, the `ArgTypes` string has a value of `ICCI`. The `int` in the `MessageBox` function syntax indicates that the `MessageBox` function returns an integer (`I`) value. The `ReturnType` argument is therefore assigned a value of `I`.

Listing 21.5. The source code of a program that uses the FOXTOOLS.FLL library.

```
****************************************************************
*     *  ShowMBox.PRG illustrates how to use FOXTOOLS.FLL       *
*           to call a typical Windows API function             *
****************************************************************
* The #define statements came from the windows.h header
* file that comes with C compilers. The following statements
* define combinations of push buttons that are produced by
* the MessageBox function:
#define MB_OK                0
#define MB_OKCANCEL          1
#define MB_ABORTRETRYIGNORE  2
#define MB_YESNOCANCEL       3
#define MB_YESNO             4
#define MB_RETRYCANCEL       5

* Following #defines available Icons that can be used
```

continues

Listing 21.5. continued

```
#define MB_ICONHAND          16
#define MB_ICONQUESTION      32
#define MB_ICONEXCLAMATION   48
#define MB_ICONASTERISK      64

SET LIBRARY TO (SYS(2004)+"FOXTOOLS")   && Load CALLDLLS.DLL Library

msgboxRN = RegFn32( "MessageBox",  "ICCI","I" )
*************************************************************
* Syntax for Windows API MessageBox() function
*    int Messagebox( HWndParent, lptext, lpCaption, wType )
*     HWndParent - Handle to parent window (msgboxRN)
*     lptext - Text in box
*     lpCaption - Message box window title
*     wType     - Specifies icon and type of buttons OR'ed
*                together.
*************************************************************
result = CallFn(msgboxRN, 0, "Do you want to answer",;
    "Ask The User", MB_YESNO + MB_ICONQUESTION)

WAIT WINDOW "User says: " + iif(result = 6, "Yes", "No")
* ...
RETURN
```

Windows has more than 400 API functions. Many of them can be called using the technique shown in Listing 21.6.

Listing 21.6. A sample program for creating a Visual FoxPro FLL file.

```
#include "pro_ext.h"
void Tst(ParamBlk FAR *parm) {
  _Execute("wait window 'executes'");
}

void Load(void) {
  _Execute("wait window 'load'");
}

void Unload(void) {
  _Execute("wait window 'unload'");
}


FoxInfo myFoxInfo[] ={
    {"TST" , (FPFI) Tst, 0, ""},
    {"LOAD"  , (FPFI) Load  , CALLONLOAD, ""},
    {"UNLOAD", (FPFI) Unload, CALLONUNLOAD, ""}
};

FoxTable _FoxTable ={
    (FoxTable FAR *) 0, sizeof(myFoxInfo)/sizeof(FoxInfo), myFoxInfo
};
```

Compressing Those Memo Fields

Visual FoxPro is rich in features. It has about every feature you can imagine that takes full advantage of the Microsoft Windows environment. However, Visual FoxPro does not have the capability to compress data in memo fields. This section presents a program that maintains a database table containing compressed documents. It packs a file and inserts the compressed file in a memo field. It also decompresses memo fields. This program makes use of the edilzssa.dll compression library for Windows. The edilzssa.dll library contains functions that perform file-to-file compression and decompression operations. This library is a shareware program provided by Eschalon Development, Inc., (Eschalon Development Inc., 110-2 Renaissance Square, New Westminster, BC, V3M 6K3 Canada, Tel: (604) 520-1543.) and is included on the CD-ROM that accompanies this book. As with all shareware, if you find this library useful, you can send a check to the vendor to register the software and, in appreciation, the developer will send you an improved version of the DLL library. This DLL library was created for general use and can be accessed only within Visual FoxPro using the FOXTOOLS.FLL library. The library consists of two functions: `LZSSPackFile()` compresses a file, and `LZSSUnPackFile()` decompresses a file.

NOTE

The edilzssa.DLL library uses an enhanced form of the LZSS compression algorithm. The LZSS algorithm is an improved variant of the dictionary-based compression LZ77 algorithm developed by Jacob Ziv and Abraham Lempel.

These are the structure of DOCUMENT.DBF is shown in Listing 21.7. It contains a memo field in which the compressed file is stored and various document description fields. The purpose of the form file DOCUMENT.SCX is to maintain the DOCUMENT.DBF database table and to compress and decompress the memo fields as required. Listing 21.8 and 21.9 show the methods for the DOCUMENT.SCX form file.

Listing 21.7. The structure for DOCUMENT.DBF used in the data compression example.

```
Structure for table:     c:\vfp\book\document.dbf
Number of data records: 5
Date of last update:     01/13/95
Memo file block size:    64
Field   Field Name   Type          Width  Dec
1      TITLE        Character      40
2      DATE         Date            8
3      KEYWORDS     Character      50
4      FILENAME     Character      40
5      DOCUMENT     Memo           10
** Total **                       148
```

You execute the DOCUMENT.SPX form file with the following command:

```
DO FORM Document
```

When DOCUMENT.SPX executes, it displays a dialog box that enables you to edit fields in the database table. (See Figure 21.1.) The form also contains push buttons that you can use to designate which database table maintenance operation you want to perform. The DOCUMENT.SPX form file was created using the Visual FoxPro Form Designer.

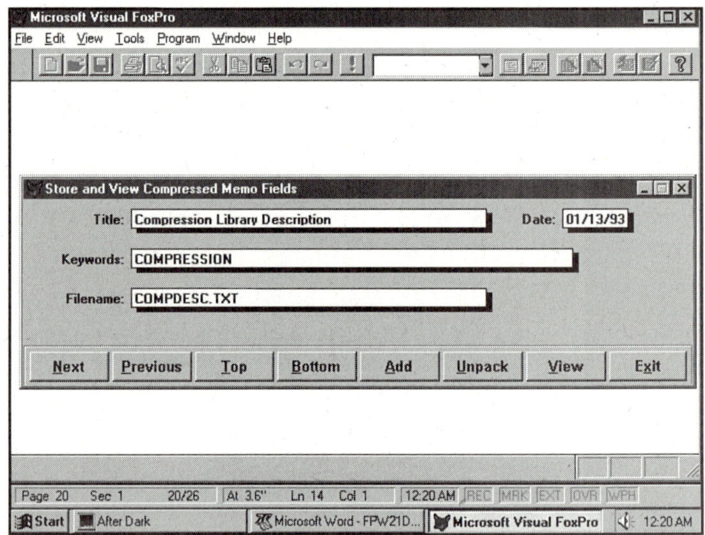

FIGURE 21.1.
The Store and View Compressed Memo Fields dialog box.

These are the steps to create the form with the Form Designer:

1. Add the DOCUMENT.DBF file to the database environment.
2. Add to the form a control button group consisting of eight control buttons. The control buttons are defined as follows:

Next	Move to the next record.
Previous	Move to the previous record.
Top	Move to the first record in the database table.
Bottom	Move to the last record in the database table.
Add	Add a new record. An Open File dialog box appears and you choose a file. The file is compressed using the `LZSSPackFile()` function and placed in the memo field of the new record. The current date is used. Finally, you can edit the new record and add descriptive data.

UnPack	The DOCUMENT memo field for the current record is transferred to a temporary file (crunch.TMP). LZSSUnPackFile() is called to decompress the crunch.tmp file and write the decompressed document into the file designated by the filename field for the current record.
View	The DOCUMENT memo field is decompressed (like UnPack) into the file VIEW.TMP. Then VIEW.TMP displays in an edit window.
Exit	The program DOCUMENT exits.

3. Add the Document.Title, Document.Date, Document.Keywords, and Document.Filename text boxes to the form. Also add the labels and shadowbox.
4. Use the Form menu New Methods option to add the names of the AddNewDoc, Compress, Decomp, and FileSize methods.
5. Double-click on the form to bring up the Methods edit box. Add the code shown in Listing 21.8 to the Form1 methods.
6. Add the code for the CommandGroup1 container Click event method shown in Listing 21.9.

The LZSSPackFile() and LZSSUnPackFile() library functions are called using functions in the FOXTOOLS.FLL library. The RegFn() function is called to register either function.

NOTE

The compression library is a 16-bit DLL. For 32-bit DLLs, use the FOXTOOLS.FLL RegFn32() function.

Because the function has two arguments, the ArgTypes string will have a value of CC. Both functions return an integer error code. Therefore, the ReturnType argument is assigned a value of I. Finally, you assign "edilzssa.dll" to the DLLName string.

When either of the edilzssa.DLL library functions are called and have successfully performed their duty, a dialog box appears that reminds you to register the shareware by sending money to the vendor. The dialog box does not appear in the registered version.

Listing 21.8. Methods for the Form1 Form object.

```
***************************************************************
*  Method: Form1.Init - Loads FOXTOOLS.FLL library
PROCEDURE Form1.Init
  SET LIBRARY TO (SYS(2004)+"FOXTOOLS") ADDITIVE
ENDPROC

***************************************************************
* Procedure AddNewDoc - Compresses document file and adds it to
*                       to a memo field
```

continues

Listing 21.8. continued

```
PROCEDURE Form1.AddNewDoc
  docfile = GETFILE() && Open file dialog box
  IF EMPTY(docfile) AND THISFORM.COMPRESS(docfile)
       APPEND BLANK
       REPL filename with docfile
       REPLACE DATE WITH DATE()
       APPEND MEMO Document FROM crunch.txt
       DELETE FILE crunch.txt
  ENDIF

ENDPROC

***************************************************************
* Method: Compress(Source)  - Compresses Source file
*
PROCEDURE Form1.compress
  PARAMETER NameFile
  Regno = RegFN( "LZSSPACKFILE",  "CC", "I", "edilzssa.dll" )
  Success = .F.
  IF Regno = -1
     WAIT WINDOW "Unable to register edilzssa.dll file"
  ELSE
  *************************************************************
  * LZSSPackFile(Source, Destination)  - Compresses source file
  *                                      and writes compressed
  *                                      destination file
  *
     DELETE FILE crunch.txt
     ErrCode = CallFN(Regno, NameFile, "crunch.txt" )
     IF ErrCode = 0
        WAIT WINDOW  STR(100-(100*form1.FileSize("crunch.txt") ;
           /form1.FileSize(NameFile) ),5,2);
           +"% Compression"  TIMEOUT 10
         Success = .T.
     ELSE
          WAIT WINDOW "Error Number "+LTRIM(STR(ErrCode));
            +"... Compression not performed"
     ENDIF
  ENDIF
  RETURN Success
ENDPROC

**************************************************************
* Procedure: DECOMP
* LZSSUnPackFile(Source, Destination)  - Decompresses source file
*                                        and writes destination file
*
PROCEDURE Form1.Decomp
  PARAMETER Target
  Regno = RegFN( "LZSSUnPACKFILE",  "CC", "I","EDILZSSA.DLL" )
  IF FILE(Target)
      WAIT WINDOW Target+" already exists."
  ELSE
      Regno = RegFN( "LZSSUnPACKFILE",  "CC", "I","EDILZSSA.DLL" )
      IF Regno = -1
        WAIT WINDOW "Unable to register edilzssa.dll file"
```

```
      ELSE
        ErrCode = CallFN(Regno, "crunch.txt", Target )
        IF ErrCode <> 0
            WAIT WINDOW "Error Number "+LTRIM(STR(ErrCode));
                        +" Occurred"
        ENDIF
      ENDIF
  ENDIF
  ERASE crunch.txt
ENDPROC

****************************************************************
* Procedure: FileSize(<file>) - Returns size of <file> in bytes
*    If you don't pass it any parameters, it returns -2.
*    If the file cannot be found, the UDF returns -1.
*    (This function was derived from FSEEK() HELP example.)
*
PROCEDURE Form1.FileSize
  PARAMETERS cfile          && File to be checked
  PRIVATE mhandle,fsize

  IF PARAMETERS( ) = 0
        RETURN -2           && Return -2 if no parameter passed
  ELSE
        IF !FILE(cfile)
            RETURN -1  && Return -1 if file does not exist
        ENDIF
  ENDIF
  mhandle = FOPEN(cfile)      && Open file
  fsize = FSEEK(mhandle,0,2)  && Determine file size
  =FCLOSE(mhandle)            &&  Close file
  RETURN fsize                &&  Return file size
ENDPROC
```

Listing 21.9. The code for the CommandGroup1 container class Click event method.

```
***************************************************************
* File positioning functions consist of code that handles
*   click events for all eight command buttons.
***********************************************************
PROCEDURE CommandGroup1.Click
   Choice = This.Value
   DO CASE
        CASE Choice = 1  && NEXT
           IF RECNO() < RECCOUNT()
               SKIP
           ENDIF
        CASE Choice = 2  && PREVIOUS
           IF RECNO()>1
              SKIP -1
           ENDIF
        CASE Choice = 3  && TOP (First record)
           GO TOP
        CASE Choice = 4  && BOTTOM (Last record)
           GO BOTTOM
```

continues

Listing 21.9. continued

```
        CASE Choice = 5  && Add new memo
           Thisform.AddNewDoc
        CASE Choice = 6  && Unpack a memo
           COPY MEMO Document TO crunch.txt
           Thisform.DECOMP( Filename )
           RETURN .T.
        CASE Choice = 7  && VIEW
           ERASE crunch.txt
           COPY MEMO Document TO crunch.txt
           RELEASE WINDOW VIEW.TMP
           ERASE VIEW.TMP
           ThisForm.DECOMP("VIEW.TMP")
           IF ".BMP"$upper(filename)
             DEFINE WINDOW BITMAP FROM 20,1 TO 40,20
             FILL FILE VIEW.TMP
             SHOW WINDOW BITMAP
             WAIT WINDOW
             RELEASE WINDOW BITMAP
           ELSE
             MODI FILE VIEW.TMP NOWAIT
           ENDIF
        CASE Choice = 8
           RELEASE Thisform
                   CLEAR EVENTS
           RETURN
   ENDCASE
   Thisform.Refresh
ENDPROC
```

Creating Your Own Visual FoxPro Libraries

You can create your own Visual FoxPro libraries. However, you need to purchase the Visual FoxPro Professional Edition. It contains the Library Construction Kit and the libraries for the Microsoft Visual C++ 2.0 compiler. You can write a program in C or C++, compile it, and link it as a Fox link library (FLL). Then you open your custom library with the `SET LIBRARY TO` command and call your library functions as you would call any other FoxPro system function.

When you create your library, you need to write a C or C++ program. The form of the function has the same basic structure regardless of what the function does. As a result, there is a standard form or *template* for building Visual FoxPro library functions. Listing 21.10 presents a sample C/C++ language template to create a Visual FoxPro library.

Listing 21.10. A sample C and C++ language template for creating a Visual FoxPro library.

```
#include <pro_ext.h >
//  (Any other #include files)

void Internal_Name( ParamBlk *param )
```

```
{
//     Insert your function code here
}
FoxInfo myFoxInfo[] = {
    ("FUNC_NAME" , (FPFI) Internal_Name, 0, ""),
};
#if defined(_cplusplus)
        extern "C" {
#endif
    FoxTable _FoxTable = {
       (FoxTable *) 0, sizeof(myFoxInfo)/sizeof(FoxInfo), myFoxInfo
    };
#if defined(_cplusplus)
}
#endif
```

You must have the PRO_EXT.H file for all Visual FoxPro API libraries. This file has all of the typedefs, structs, and function declarations that are used in Visual FoxPro API.

Visual FoxPro determines the function name, the number of parameters, and the type of each parameter from the FoxInfo structure. The FoxTable pointer is a linked list that keeps up with the FoxInfo structures.

Visual FoxPro communicates with a library function through the FoxInfo structure. You define an array of FoxInfo structures with each element defining a function. For example, if you have three functions, the FoxInfo structure might be like this:

```
FoxInfo myInfo[] = {
     {"FuncOne", (FPPI) myfunc1, 2, "IC" },
     {"FuncTwo", (FPPI) myfunc2, 4, "CDN.C" },
     {"FuncThree", (FPPI) myfunc3, 3, "CCC" }
};
```

`FuncOne`, `FuncTwo`, and `FuncThree` are the names that are used to reference the functions from Visual FoxPro. These names can be up to 10 characters. `myfunc1`, `myfunc2`, and `myfunc3` are the internal names of the three functions and are case sensitive. The numbers `2`, `4`, and `3` are the number of parameters. The types of each parameter are `"IC"`, `"CDN.C"`, and `"CCC"`. Each character represents the data type shown in Table 21.3 for one of the parameters.

Table 21.3. Visual FoxPro API parameter data types.

Value	*Description*	*Value*	*Description*
`""`	No parameters	`"L"`	Logical type
`"?"`	Any data type	`"N"`	Numeric type
`"C"`	Character type	`"R"`	Reference
`"D"`	Numeric type	`"T"`	DateTime type
`"I"`	Integer	`"Y"`	Currency type

Precede a character with a period to indicate that the parameter is optional.

Visual FoxPro API functions are available to use with a library. These functions are listed in help. They provide access to all levels of Visual FoxPro internal functionality. Here are examples of categories of API functions that are supported:

Debugging	Memo field I/O	Editing functions
Dialogs	String operations	Statements
Expressions	Memory management	Input/Output
Error handling	Arrays	Table I/O
File I/O	Menu	Window operations

When you purchase the Visual FoxPro Professional Edition, the Help system contains help for each Visual FoxPro API function and examples of how to use them. Listing 21.11 contains the help for the Visual FoxPro API `_Evaluate()` function.

Listing 21.11. Example provided with Visual FoxPro help for the Visual FoxPro API `_Evaluate()` function.

```
The following example has the same functionality as
the Visual FoxPro EVALUATE( ) function.

Visual FoxPro Code

SET LIBRARY TO EVALUATE
? XEVAL("2 + 3")
? XEVAL("'a' + 'b'")
? XEVAL("SIN(PI()/2))")


C Code

#include <pro_ext.h>

FAR EvaluateEx(ParamBlk FAR *parm)
{
   char FAR *expr;
   Value result;

//  Null terminate character string
if (!_SetHandSize(parm->p[0].val.ev_handle,
      parm->p[0].val.ev_length + 1))
      {
      _Error(182); // "Insufficient memory"
      _HLock(parm->p[0].val.ev_handle);
       expr = (char FAR *) _HandToPtr(parm->p[0].val.ev_handle);
       expr[parm->p[0].val.ev_length] = '\0';
       Evaluate(&result, expr);
      _RetVal(&result);
      _HUnLock(parm->p[0].val.ev_handle);
       }
    FoxInfo myFoxInfo[] = {
        {"XEVAL", (FPFI) EvaluateEx, 1, "C"},
```

```
};
FoxTable _FoxTable = {
      (FoxTable FAR *) 0, sizeof(myFoxInfo)/sizeof(FoxInfo), myFoxInfo
};
```

After you have coded your C or C++ library functions, you use Microsoft Visual C++ Version 2.0 (or 2.1) (32-bit version) to compile and link your library as a DLL. Then you rename it so that it has an .FLL extension. If you do not rename it, you have to include the extension when you use the `SET LIBRARY TO` command.

Summary

This chapter discusses how to provide extended functionality to Visual FoxPro. You have learned how to use the `LOAD` and `CALL` binary modules. In addition, you have learned how to use the `SET LIBRARY TO` command to open FoxPro API library modules. Finally, you were shown how to use a sample DLL library to call Windows API library functions.

22

Project Management and Building Applications

Intelligence is the faculty of making artificial objects, especially tools to make tools.

—Henri-Louis Bergson (1859–1941) *L'Evolution Créatrice*

This book has focused on the individual trees instead of the forest; it's time to focus on the forest. When you create an application, it consists of a whole menagerie of files. You have program files, screen files, bitmap files, report files, and so on. You have so many files to keep track of that you may feel you are becoming a tool of the tools. That is not necessary because Visual FoxPro has another tool that does the work of keeping up with the files—Project Manager. The good news is that it's very easy to use. This chapter describes how to use Project Manager to build an application.

Project Files

A *project* is a specialized database table that maintains a list of all files required to create an application. These files include the following:

- Program files (PRG)
- Screen program files (SPR) (from FoxPro 2.6)
- Class library files (VCX)
- Menu program files (MPR)
- Database container files (DBC)
- Database tables (DBF)
- Memory variable files (MEM)
- Screen files (SCX)
- Menu files (MNX)
- Query files (QRY)
- Report form files (FRX)
- Label form files (LBX)
- Library files (FLL)
- Format files (FMT)

The project also maintains all references to each of the files, the dependencies, and the interrelationships. A project file has a .PJX extension and an associated memo file with a .PJT extension. It is the programmer's responsibility to specify all the components of a project that are necessary for the final application. Project Manager then ensures that the generated application is based on the latest source files. For example, when you modify one of the program files in a project and you build an application, Project Manager recompiles each file, if necessary, before it includes it in the application.

Creating and Modifying Project Files

You create a project in the same way that you create any other file. You can choose the **File** menu **New** option and choose the project file type, and the project dialog box appears, as shown in Figure 22.1. As you can see, it contains page frames showing all of the components of an application. Each page frame contains an outline list containing the component type icon and the names of associated files that make up the project. There are also six push buttons. The Pr**o**ject menu is placed on the Visual FoxPro System menu bar.

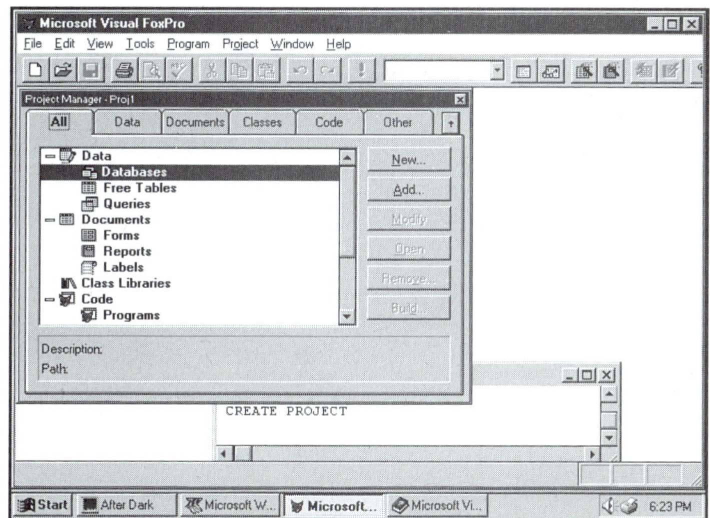

FIGURE 22.1.
The project dialog box.

You can click on the Add push button, and the Open dialog box appears, as shown in Figure 22.2. You can select a file and click on the OK push button (or double-click on the filename), and Project Manager adds it to the project. You keep adding files until all the files in your application appear in the Project window. You can select a file and press the Remove push button to remove it from the project. You can select a file and click on the Modify push button to modify a file using one of the designers or the editor if the file is a program. You can select an item in the outline and click on the New push button to create a new file. You are given the choice of creating the file with a wizard or the appropriate designer.

TIP

If a database container file is in a project and the Project Manager file is open, the database is open. You cannot close the database with the `CLOSE DATABASE` command or menu equivalent as long as the Project Manager remains open.

FIGURE 22.2.
The Open dialog box.

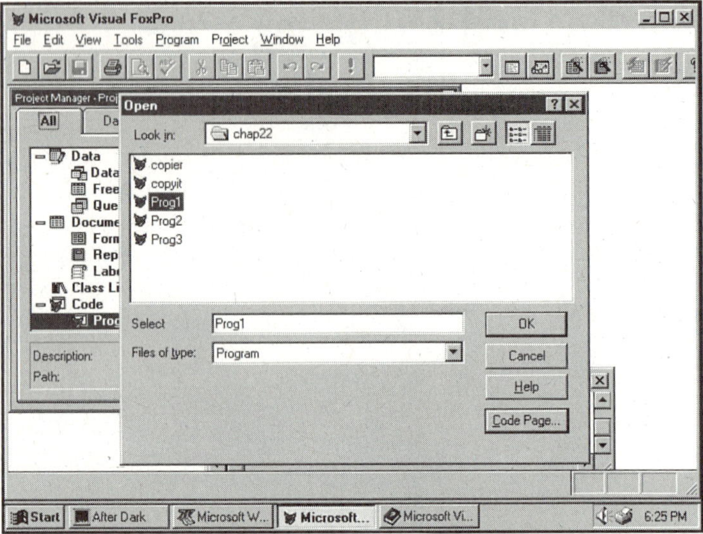

Project Manager determines which file is the main program and places a bullet symbol to the left of its file type. If you add a program that references other programs, you don't need to add the other programs to the project because the Project Manager automatically searches for references to other program files and adds those it finds to the project when you do a project build.

All you need to do to build a project is click on the Build push button and the Build Options dialog box appears, as shown in Figure 22.3. If you haven't supplied a project name, the Save As dialog box displays, and you supply a filename. Project Manager compiles all the programs and determines various dependencies and relationships between the files. The relationship between the various components of an application can become complicated. Project building is covered in more detail later in this chapter.

The fourth push button from the top changes its function and its caption depending on which file type is selected, as indicated in Table 22.1.

Table 22.1. Captions for the Project Manager Run push button.

File Type	*Caption*	*Project Menu Option*	*Function*
Database icon	**O**pen	**O**pen File	Opens a database
Database (DBC)	Cl**o**se	Cl**o**se File	Closes the database
Table	**B**rowse...	**B**rowse File	Browses the table
Program	R**u**n	R**u**n File	Executes the program
Form	R**u**n	R**u**n File	Executes the form

File Type	Caption	Project Menu Option	Function
Query	Run	Run File	Executes a query
Labels	Preview...	Preview File	Previews labels
Report	Preview...	Preview File	Previews report
Other files	Run	Run File	Disabled
No selection	Run	Run File	Disabled

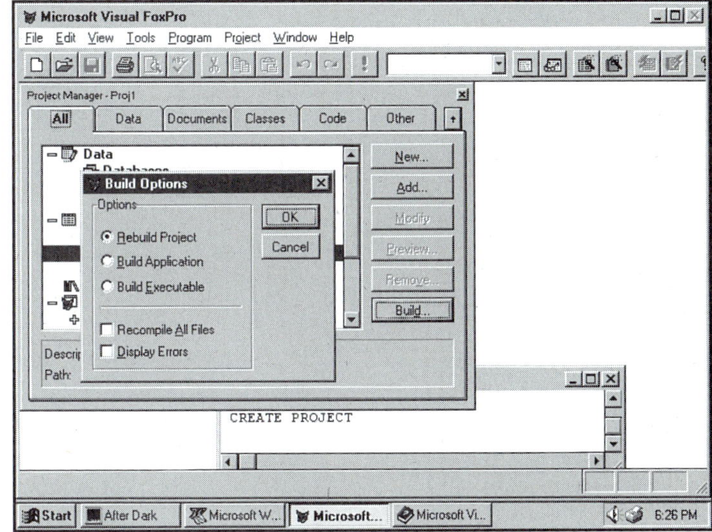

FIGURE 22.3.
The Build Options dialog box.

You can also activate a Project window to create or modify a file with the `MODIFY PROJECT` or `CREATE PROJECT` commands. Both commands do the same thing and have the same keywords and clauses, as illustrated in the following syntax:

```
CREATE PROJECT [<expFN> ¦ ?]
   [NOWAIT]  [SAVE]
   [WINDOW <window name1>]
   [IN [WINDOW] <window name2>
   ¦ IN SCREEN]

MODIFY PROJECT [<expFN> ¦ ?]
   [NOWAIT] [SAVE]
   [[WINDOW <window name1>]
   [IN [WINDOW] <window name2>
   ¦ SCREEN]]
```

The keywords and clauses for these two commands are described in Table 22.2.

Table 22.2. Definitions of clauses and keywords for the `MODIFY PROJECT` and `CREATE PROJECT` commands.

Clause and Keyword	*Description*
`<expFN> ¦ ?`	This option specifies the name, `<expFN>`, of a project file to be created or modified. If you don't supply the filename extension, the .PJX extension is assumed. If the project file does not exist, it is created. If the project file exists, it is modified. If you don't specify a filename with the `CREATE PROJECT` command, a new project dialog box appears. The filename of `UNTITLED.PJR` is assigned to the project. When you close the Project window, a Save As dialog box appears and you can give the project a different name. If you omit the filename with the `MODIFY PROJECT` command, the Open File dialog box appears. If you specify a question mark (`?`) instead of a filename, an Open dialog box appears, containing project (PJX) files. When you select one of the files, the specified project file dialog box opens.
`NOWAIT`	If you don't specify this option when a Project window opens, program execution pauses until the Project window is closed. If you specify the `NOWAIT` option, program execution continues on the program line immediately following this command—the program does not pause until the Project window closes.
`SAVE`	If you specify this keyword, the Project window remains open after another window is activated. The `SAVE` keyword is ignored if this command is executed from the Command window. You can close a Project window opened with the `SAVE` keyword specified by pressing Ctrl+W, Ctrl+End, Ctrl+Q, or Esc, or by clicking on the close box or choosing the **C**lose option from the **F**ile menu.
`WINDOW <window name1>`	If this clause is executed, the project dialog box adopts the characteristics of the specified window.
`IN [WINDOW] <window name2>`	If this clause is specified, the Project window opens in the specified parent window.
`IN SCREEN`	If you specify the `IN SCREEN` clause, the Project window displays in the main Visual FoxPro window instead of inside of a user-defined window.

You can programmatically create a project with the BUILD PROJECT command. It automatically creates a project database consisting of the list of files specified with the FROM clause. The BUILD PROJECT command opens and processes the specified files and adds them to the project file. The processing involves any required code generation, program compilation, and any other processing that ensures the newly created project file is based on the latest source files. This is the syntax of the BUILD PROJECT command:

```
BUILD PROJECT <expFN1> [FROM <file list>]

<file list> ::= <expFN2> [,<expFN3> [ ,...]
```

The <*expFN1*> argument is the name of the project file to be created.

You use the FROM clause to specify the list of files that are included in an application. A file can be a program, menu, report, label, screen, or library file. You can execute the BUILD PROJECT file without the FROM clause to refresh an existing project file.

As Project Manager creates a project from the BUILD PROJECT command, all program file references that include a path are processed using only the filename portion. The BUILD PROJECT command searches for the program in the default directory and, if it's not found there, it searches along the Visual FoxPro path. For example, suppose Project Manager is processing a program and it encounters the following line of code:

```
DO C:\VFP\MYAPP\PROG97.PRG
```

Program Manager searches for a program named PROG97.PRG in the default directory. If the program isn't found in the default directory, the Program Manager searches for PROG97.PRG along the Visual FoxPro path. If PROG97.PRG is still not found, the Program Manager issues an error message.

If the Program Manager encounters a program, menu, or screen file during the project build operation, it searches for its compiled file, compares its time stamp to that of the matching PRG file, and recompiles the source code if necessary.

Each project file contains a time stamp that is refreshed when you make changes to the file in the project or when dependencies change. This helps ensure that any applications created from a project file always use the most recent source.

When errors are reported during execution of the BUILD PROJECT command, the process continues and a project file is built. The occurrence of any unresolved references and other errors does not prevent creation of the project file. As a result, you can build a project even though all the required components are not actually created or available at the time the project is built. When you've resolved the errors, you can rebuild the project. You can also use the MODIFY PROJECT command to modify information stored in the project file to resolve errors. You can view errors by choosing the Pr**o**ject menu **E**rror option.

Modifying Components Within a Project File

When you develop an application, you are continually adding new components and changing existing components. When an application becomes complicated, you have numerous names to remember. However, if you use Project Manager to keep track of your files in your application, you have a list of all the files in the project. If you want to edit one of them, all you need to do is select one of the files in the list and click on the Edit push button or double-click on the filename. If the file is a program file, the Text Editor window opens so you can edit the selected file. If the file is a screen file, the Screen Builder opens so you can modify the screen file. Regardless of the object you choose to edit, the appropriate object editor is activated to edit your object.

You may find it useful to keep a Project dialog box open while you develop an application, so that all your file-editing operations are just a double-click away.

You can collapse the Project Manager window into a toolbar by clicking on the push button with the up arrow at the upper-right corner of the window. The collapsed toolbar is shown in Figure 22.4. To *tear off* a tab, you click on one of the tabs and drag the page frame off the Project Manager. In Figure 22.4, the Data tab frame has been separated from the toolbar. You can expand the collapsed Project Manager toolbar by clicking on the push button with the down arrow at the right of the toolbar.

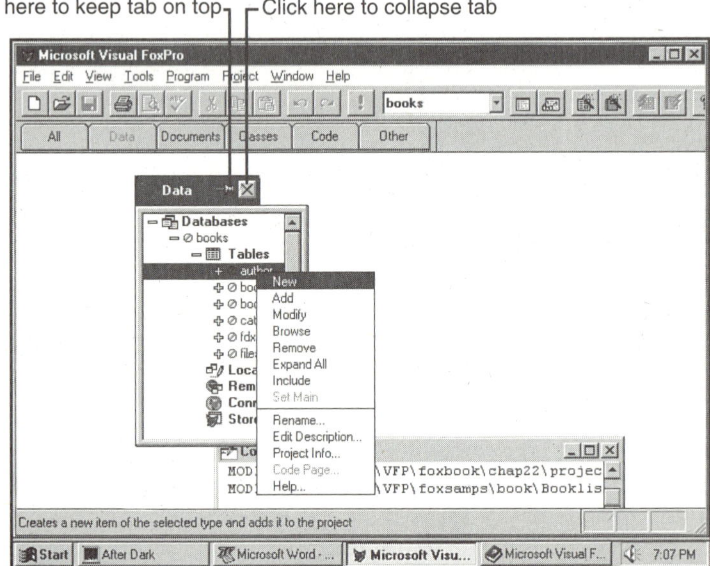

FIGURE 22.4.
A collapsed Project Manager and torn off Data tab.

TIP

If you right-click on an item in the Project Manager file list, the shortcut menu appears. It is also shown in Figure 22.4. The shortcut menu is a quick and convenient way to access Project menu options.

You can dock Project Manager by first collapsing Program Manager, and then dragging it to the top or the bottom of the main FoxPro window. When the Project Manager is docked, its title bar disappears and the tab buttons look like toolbar buttons, as shown in Figure 22.4.

The Project Menu

The Pr**o**ject menu contains options that have a global effect on the project as opposed to operations that are performed on individual files. Figure 22.5 shows the Pr**o**ject menu.

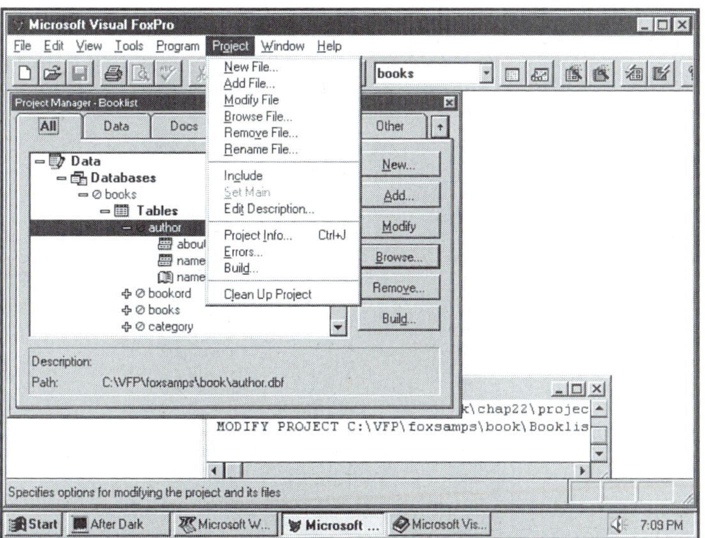

FIGURE 22.5.
The Project menu.

New File...

You can create a new file and add it to Project Manager by selecting an item in the outline and choosing the **N**ew File option. If you plan to create a table, form, report, or label, you use the dialog box that asks if you want to use a wizard or a designer to generate the file.

NOTE

Incidentally, the **N**ew File option does the same thing as the **N**ew push button in the Project Manager dialog box. You need this option as you need some other Pr**o**ject menu options when the Project Manager is collapsed.

Add File...

You can add an existing file to the Project Manager by selecting an item in the outline and choosing the **A**dd File option. The **O**pen File dialog box appears, and you select a file. (This does the same thing as the Project Manager **A**dd push button.)

Modify File

You can modify one of the Project Manager files with the **M**odify File option. First, select a file in the Project Manager outline and choose the **M**odify File option. If you are creating a table, form, report, or label, the corresponding designer activates. (This does the same thing as the Project Manager **M**odify push button.)

Run File, Browse File, and Preview File

You can execute a form, application, query, or program with the R**u**n File option. Just select a file and choose the R**u**n File option. The menu option also executes other types of files, but it has a different caption. The caption changes depending on the type of file you select, as shown in Table 22.1. (This option does the same thing as the Project Manager R**u**n push button.)

Remove File...

You can remove one of the files in the Project Manager by selecting the file you want to remove and choosing the Remo**v**e File option. (This option does the same thing as the Project Manager Remo**v**e... push button.)

Rename File...

You can rename one of the files in the Project Manager by selecting the file you want to rename and choosing the **R**ename File option. Then the Rename File dialog box appears. You type in a new name and the file is renamed. (This option does the same thing as the Project Manager **R**ename push button.)

Include/Exclude

When you create an application (APP) file from the files in a project file, you normally want to include only files that are never edited. You obviously don't want a database table or an index (unless it is a read-only database table, such as a report form FRX file) included in an application. You can have a program or screen that is shared by several applications. You might want to keep a program separate from an application so that you can make changes to the program without having to re-create the application (APP) file.

In any event, you can specify which files are included in an application file by using the Include/Exclude option. The option's prompt is In**c**lude when the selected file is marked as excluded and Ex**c**lude when a selected file is not marked as excluded. The exclude mark is a circle with a diagonal bar through it that appears to the right of the filename in the Project window list. For example, in Figure 22.5, the tables (author, bookord, books, and category) are marked as excluded.

When you select a file, this option reflects its current include or exclude state. If you choose this option, the state is toggled. If an application needs an excluded file, it must be distributed with the application.

Set Main

Normally, Project Manager can determine which program file is the main program. If it chooses the wrong file for some reason, you can specify the main program by selecting the actual main program and choosing the **S**et Main option. A bullet appears to the left of the main program in the outline.

Errors...

When you build a project, build errors do not normally display. The error count, however, displays on the status bar. If you have any build errors, you can choose the **E**rrors option to display a window that contains the build errors found during the project build.

Edit Description

A filename path and description display in a status window at the bottom of the Project Manager window that corresponds to the selected file. Initially, the Description field is blank. However, you can add a description. Its purpose is to provide some helpful information relating to the file. You can add or change the description for a selected file with the Edi**t** Description option. This option opens a Description window and you type a new description into a text box or edit the existing description.

Cleanup Project

The Cleanup Project option permanently removes all records marked for deletion in the project file database and reduces the size of its associated memo file. It performs a PACK command.

Project Info

The Project Info option displays the Project Information dialog box. It has two tabs. The Project tab is shown in Figure 22.6. You use it to specify options that affect generated code. You can specify comments for program headers, debug mode, encryption mode, the home directory for the project, and an icon for the executable program. In addition, it displays the number of files in the project and the date the application was last built.

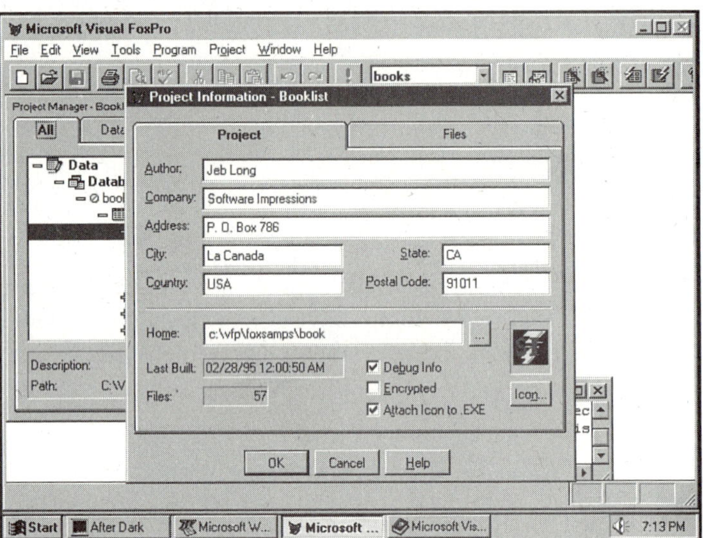

FIGURE 22.6.
The Project Information dialog box with the Project page frame showing.

The debug mode specifies whether you want debug information saved in the application. Normally, during debugging operations you want debugging information in the generated application. However, after you have debugged your application, you turn off the debugging mode and the debugging information is omitted. As a result, the size of your application is substantially reduced. You can also set a mode to encrypt your application to protect it from user examination.

The second tab is the Files tab (shown in Figure 22.7). It lists the type, name, date and time last modified, and the code page (when it applies) for all the files in the project. It also specifies whether a file is included in the built application. You can change the sorting order of the list by clicking on the header of the column by which you want the list to be ordered. If you want the list sorted by name, click on the header for the Name column.

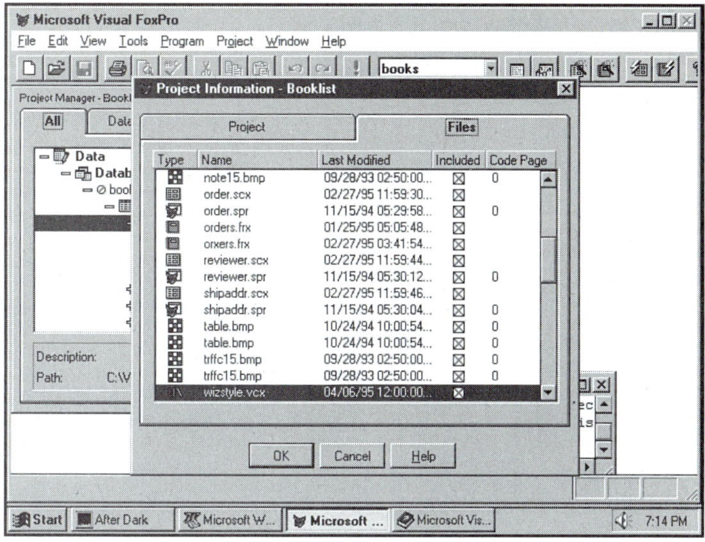

FIGURE 22.7.
The Project Information dialog box with the Files page frame showing.

Tools Menu Options

The **O**ptions option is presented in the section "The Options Dialog Box Projects Tab" in Chapter 10, "Environment." You can specify whether or not the Project Manager displays the New File dialog box. The New File dialog box lets you decide whether you want to create the new file using a wizard or a designer. If you specify that you do not want to use wizards and then press the New button, the appropriate designer runs to create your new file.

You can also specify whether the project runs a file or modifies it when you double-click on its entry in the Project Manager file list. When you are developing an application, it might be more convenient to set this option so that when you double-click on a file, it is modified. However, if you primarily run applications, you might find the alternate option more convenient.

Resolving Undefined External References

When you build a project, Project Manager reads each program file to determine which files are a part of the project. It searches for commands such as `DO`, `SET LIBRARY TO`, and `REPORT` to look for the names of files that are referenced.

When you refer to a filename in a program and specify a literal name, the Program Manager has no trouble interpreting it, as in the following example:

```
DO MYPROG
REPORT FORM TALLYHO
DO MYMENU.MPR
```

However, when you indirectly designate a filename with a filename expression or by a program macro (&) substitution, Program Manager has no way to know its name, as in the following example:

```
Prog="MYPROG"
DO &Prog
filter = "NOT 'GREEN'$UPPER(Descript)"
REPORT FORM Apple FOR &filter
DO (Prog)
```

The Project Manager does not process any command that contains a macro substitution. In the preceding example, the Project Manager does not process the REPORT command and cannot locate the Apple report file in the command.

NOTE

You should use a name expression instead of macro substitution whenever possible because macro substitution slows down processing and your programs run more slowly.

It is a good idea to include all the required files in a project when the project is built. The Program Manager also tracks arrays and must be informed if an array was created in another procedure. You can inform the Project Manager that a file was referenced in a program, even if it was referenced indirectly (as a filename expression or in macro substitution) by using the EXTERNAL command.

Only Project Manager recognizes the EXTERNAL command. It is used to search for references to files and arrays. The command is ignored by the compiler. In fact, if you don't use Project Manager to maintain your applications, you never need the EXTERNAL command. This is the syntax of the EXTERNAL command:

```
EXTERNAL ARRAY <array names>

EXTERNAL LABEL ¦ LIBRARY ¦ MENU ¦ PROCEDURE
   ¦ REPORT ¦ SCREEN  <filename list>
```

The EXTERNAL command specifies files and arrays that are referenced within a program so Project Manager can resolve undefined references in a project. Files specified by EXTERNAL are included in a project by Project Manager. You must include one of the LABEL, LIBRARY, MENU, PROCEDURE, REPORT, or SCREEN keywords before the filenames to tell Project Manager the type of files to include in the project. You can specify a list of names for each keyword, however. The keywords are described in Table 22.3.

Table 22.3. Definitions of clauses and keywords for the EXTERNAL command.

Keyword	*Description*
ARRAY	You use this keyword to specify the name of an array used in a program if the array is created in a higher-level program. (The EXTERNAL ARRAY statement is specified in the lower-level program.)
LABEL	You use this keyword in a program that refers to a label definition file using an indirect file reference or macro substitution.
LIBRARY	You use this keyword in a program that refers to a library (FLL) file using an indirect file reference or macro substitution.
MENU	You use this keyword in a program that refers to a menu definition file using an indirect file reference or macro substitution.
PROCEDURE	You use this keyword in a program that refers to an external procedure using an indirect file reference or macro substitution, or uses a UDF in an expression.
REPORT	You use this keyword in a program that refers to a report definition file using an indirect file reference or macro substitution.
SCREEN	You use this keyword in a program that refers to a screen definition file using an indirect file reference or macro substitution.

In the following example, the EXTERNAL commands are provided to designate that a file and an array are referenced by the program. When an array is passed to a UDF or procedure, you are required to identify the array name referenced in the user-defined function (UDF) (AINVERT). Here is the code for the example:

```
*    Create an array
DIMENSION AnArray[5]
*    Name of array used in the UDF
EXTERNAL ARRAY AryTable
EXTERNAL PROGRAM Program1
SET TALK OFF
AnArray[1] = 5
AnArray[2] = 4
AnArray[3] = 3
AnArray[4] = 2
AnArray[5] = 1
ZFile = "Program1"
DO (ZFile)

*    Pass array by reference to a UDF
= AINVERT(@MyArray)
```

```
FUNCTION AINVERT
PARAMETER AryTable
Top = ALEN(AryTable)
Middle = Int(Top/2)
FOR I = 1 TO Middle
    Temp = AryTable[Top]
    AryTable[Top] = AryTable[I]
    AryTable[I] = Temp
    Top = Top - 1
ENDFOR
RETURN
```

Building Applications

You can use Project Manager just to keep up with your files in your project. In that case, you never use Project Manager to compile an application file. If you want all your files in the project compiled into a single file that can be executed, however, you can request that Project Manager build an application (APP) file for you. To build an application, press the **B**uild push button in the Project dialog box and the Build Options dialog box appears, as shown in Figure 22.8. Then select the **B**uild Application radio button and press the OK push button. Project Manager does the rest. It creates an application file containing all enabled files in the project.

TIP

Before you build an application, be aware of the debug mode setting in the Project Information dialog box shown in Figure 22.6. When you are debugging a program, you want debugging information in the generated application. However, after you have debugged your application, turn off the debugging mode, and the debugging information is omitted. As a result, the size of your application is substantially reduced. You can also set a mode to encrypt your application to protect it from user examination.

You can also build an application programmatically using the `BUILD APP` command. This is the syntax:

```
BUILD APP <expFN> FROM <project>
```

The `<expFN>` element specifies the name of an application file to create. If you don't supply the filename extension, the .APP extension is assumed. If the application file doesn't exist, it is created. If it exists, it is overwritten. The `FROM <project>` clause specifies the name of the project from which the application is built.

When you set up a project file in preparing to create an application, be sure that only read-only files are included in the application. When you build a project, Project Manager guesses which files are read-only and which files are editable. Project Manager then includes read-only files and excludes the others. Obviously, database tables and indexes associated with the project are editable.

However, Program Manager considers all other files read-only, and they are included. You can manually exclude files that you don't want to include in the application by using the Project Menu Exclude option. If a circle with a diagonal line appears to the right of the filename for an item listed in the Project dialog box, the file is excluded and is not included in the application.

FIGURE 22.8.
The Build Options dialog box.

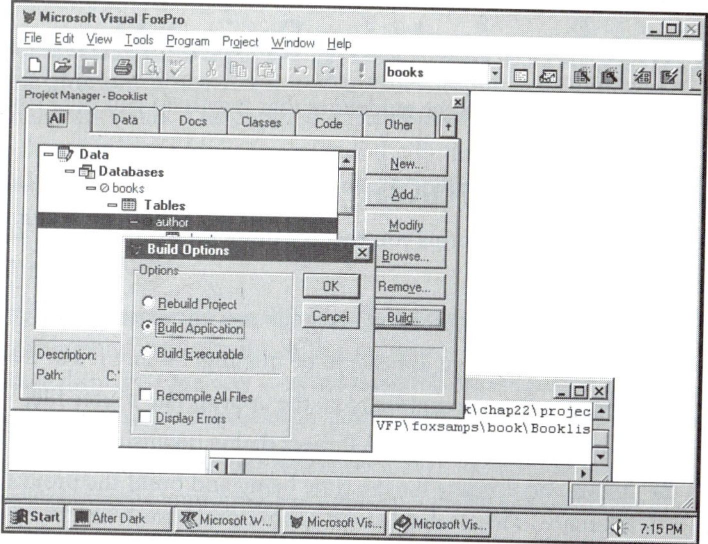

In Figure 22.8, you see a third radio button, Build Executable. This option enables you to build an EXE file that you can execute from Windows, as you can any other Windows application. However, this option is disabled. You must purchase the Professional Edition of Visual FoxPro, which contains the Visual FoxPro Distribution Kit, to take advantage of this option. This kit enables you to distribute an application as a standalone executable, and the customer doesn't need a copy of Visual FoxPro. Several other options are available when you build an application with the Distribution Kit.

The simplest option is the *runtime application*. You develop a runtime application by creating an APP application file and distributing a runtime package. This package consists of your APP file, any editable files (normally database table and index files), the runtime support library files, and the runtime loader program, FOXR.EXE.

You may use the Build Executable option in the Build Options dialog box to create a *compact executable* (EXE) file. The size of the EXE file is slightly larger than its corresponding APP application file. You can execute compact executable files from Windows, but you still need to distribute the runtime support library files to the customer along with the EXE file and the editable files.

The principal advantage of compact executable and runtime applications is that your license gives you limitless distribution of your application to users in your organization. Microsoft rules for runtime distribution do not require you to charge a fee for distribution.

23

Building Visual FoxPro Applications

When schemes are laid in advance, it is surprising how often the circumstances fit in with them.

—Sir William Osler (1849–1919)

Nothing great was ever achieved without enthusiasm…

—Ralph Waldo Emerson (1803–1882) *Essays: First Series*

This chapter discusses how to approach building a Visual FoxPro application from both business and technical standpoints. If you use Visual FoxPro to build a simple address book application for your boss, you don't need any complex development process. However, if you are developing a complex multiuser inventory tracking system and you manage a team of programmers, writers, and testers, you need to adopt proven software engineering procedures to achieve your goals. This chapter provides an overview of accepted software methodology. Many excellent software engineering books cover this topic in detail, such as *Peopleware*, by Tom DeMarco and Timothy Lister; *Software Engineering, A Practitioner's Approach*, by Pressman; and *Software Engineering*, by Jensen and Tonies. In your quest to improve your software development skills, you should read some of these books. Consult your local technical libraries and bookstores for more information.

This chapter also discusses types of programming errors that occur. In addition, I introduce the Visual FoxPro integrated programming environment, including the Program Editor, compiler, and interactive debugger.

The Business Side of an Application

Congratulations! You have won the contract to build a FoxPro database application for a client. Now the pressure is on you, and it's time for you to go to work. This section is an overview of accepted procedures for developing an application from a business standpoint. The business part of a project is important. When a software development project fails, it is usually because of people problems, not technical problems.

The Interview

When you negotiated your contract to develop a database management system, you probably dealt with members of upper management, who have little or no hands-on interaction with your final creation.

The first thing you need to do is determine the scope of the system you are building. You do this by finding out what the people who use the system want. You must interview each person who either contributes to the data in the system or uses data from the system. This doesn't mean only the managers of the user organizations. You must interview the people who actually enter information into the system, the people who collect and provide the data that is entered into the system, and the people who actually look at the output. Basically, you must interview all the people who have any involvement with the system.

These interviews are not only important as a way for you to solicit data input and reporting requirements, but they are equally important in order to gain the commitment of everyone involved in the operation so the project will be an overall success. You'll discover that most users are cooperative if they feel you listen to their needs and you project a feeling that you truly appreciate and value their contribution. Be sure to politely listen to what users say. People like to feel they have the power to influence changes that affect their environment, so you won't encounter much difficulty in gaining the user's cheerful participation in planning exercises.

The interview is also a means by which you can develop a good working relationship with the users. You should maintain a good relationship through the entire development cycle so that you can continue to receive important feedback. You can maintain a good relationship if you are always polite, always listen, and are always responsive.

Strong communications skills are an important factor in gathering the information you need to design the database application. You might find that some people don't comprehend the potential of a computerized system. Others might not understand the importance of providing detailed information regarding their needs. Others may be too lazy to dwell on the details necessary to define all the input and output data items. Still others provide no input because they feel threatened by the introduction of a new computerized system; they know how to do their job now and don't want to be inconvenienced by learning something new. You have to listen closely to what your potential users say and do not say. You must be sensitive to the circumstances, encourage the weak, explain the advantages to the doubters, motivate the uncommitted, and calm the fears of the apprehensive.

As you proceed with the interviews, you must gain an understanding of your audience. This is another critical factor in the success of your database system because it drives many of the aspects of your design and implementation. As you talk to a user, you should keep in mind the following questions:

- How much does the user know about computers?
- What information would be useful to the user?
- In what manner should the information be presented?
- How much work is the user willing to do to access information?
- How often will the user need to access information?
- When information is required, does the user need it immediately or does the user want to read a report?
- What information can the user supply as input?

A technique that can prove extremely beneficial is to use the Form Designer and Report Designer to create prototype input forms and reports from preliminary data you've gathered, which enables you to have the users look at real windows. You might even be able to make changes to the forms while you are conducting interviews. Some users who previously could not visualize the potential benefits of a system become strong advocates when this technique is employed.

The interview questions I have suggested represent the type of questions that you can use to focus on information you can use during the design process. When doing this exercise, try to identify everything possible about the subject and the data input/output requirements.

During your interviews, you should gather a list of input data items and report requirements. You might even have enough information to proceed to the next step in the design process, the specifications.

Project Management

You manage software development just like you do any other project. You divide the system into subtasks, assign the responsibility for each subtask to a knowledgeable person, establish a schedule for completing each task or objective, and monitor each task. These are the major subtasks:

- Estimating
- Design
- Implementation
- Testing
- Documentation
- Site installation
- Training
- Customer support

The software is written during the implementation phase. This task is further divided into subtasks. The software system is divided into modular subsystems, each subsystem is assigned to a programmer, and each subsystem development task is scheduled and monitored.

The system must be designed before the implementation and documentation phases begin, and the implementation phase must be complete before the testing phase begins. However, you can do unit testing, in which you test each module as it is developed. After testing is complete and the customer officially approves the system, you can perform the site installation and training phases.

The Design Phase

From a technical perspective, the design process involves specifying the tables, the relationships between the tables, the input forms, the reports, and the various support systems. However, this section focuses on the design from a business perspective. During the design process, you should communicate with the users to gain their feedback and nurture their continued commitment. Good communication between you and the users is essential to the success of the design phase of the project. A successful design substantially reduces the amount of time required to implement the system, because any design flaw identified during implementation results in expensive and time-consuming recoding of flawed programs during the implementation phase.

Your design should contain a written description of the system, including databases and tables, and relationships between tables, input forms, and reports. You should use the Form Designer and Menu Designer to create prototype input forms and menus. The design should contain schedules for each phase of the development process including implementation, testing, product installation, and training. You should present a design review to the user community. Because you've maintained good communications with the users, the design review should be an extremely smooth process. After your customer has accepted and approved your design, you can proceed with system implementation.

Testing

Testing is divided into three general phases. The first phase, *unit testing*, occurs during implementation. It takes place when a software subsystem is completed, to ensure that the subsystem operates as advertised. After you've completed the implementation phase, you combine the system and make sure that the entire system operates properly. This phase is called *integration testing*. Errors are identified and reported, and the programmer repairs the defect. It is always a good idea to have a person other than the programmer test the software. After you are convinced that the software is properly tested, you should install the software for your customer's users so they can perform the third phase of testing: *acceptance testing*. If you've done your job well, the acceptance testing phase is simply a formality. When your customer formally approves the software, you have completed the testing phase and are ready to install the final software and train the users.

Client-Requested Changes

Invariably, when customers start using their new information system, they discover that they need some additional features. Some changes are trivial and can be made on an informal basis. Some changes, however, are so involved that they change the scope of the task. You should have some provision in your contract to account for client-requested changes. You can specify an hourly rate for making unforeseen changes to the system, or you can specify that you will submit an estimate for such changes.

The design of a database application is never finished. Customers always want to add some new feature, and customer requirements change. The customer might expand his business, new regulations might be imposed, tax structures might change, or new hardware might become available. Before you start, you should plan for client-requested changes. In addition, you should design and implement your database application so that extended features can be added easily.

User Documentation

You should provide the customer with user documentation for the new software system. The documentation should provide clear, concise instructions written to the level of the audience using the database application. The documentation should also explain how to use every feature of the system. Good documentation reduces training and support costs over the life of the product. You should begin writing documentation during the design phase and complete it during the implementation phase.

Site Installation and Training

You've completed the acceptance testing phase and the users are familiar with their new database management application. The hardware is installed and is operational. Everything is ready. It is now time to initiate the site installation phase of the development effort. In this phase, you install the final software system on the customer's hardware and supply the final documentation.

If there is a pre-existing system, you should run your new system and the user's pre-existing system in parallel as a final check to be sure your new system is fully operational. After your customer is satisfied with the operation of your new system, use of the old system can be suspended.

At this point, you begin the final phase: *customer training*. During this phase, the cooperative alliance that you have built between yourself and the users really pays off. In many cases, your users will already know how to use the system. In any event, when all the users are comfortable with their new system and some person with authority places a final stamp of approval on the system, your task is almost completed.

Customer Support

Your contract with your customer should have some provision for customer support. You will probably provide a warranty for the software system for a certain period (for example, 30 days, 3 months, or 6 months). You will probably also include a provision to supply customer support for a certain hourly rate after the warranty expires. It is essential that the customer be able to obtain customer support whenever it's needed.

The Technical Side of an Application

This section covers software development methodology and the phases of the software development life cycle analysis, design, implementation, and maintenance. This chapter also covers debugging methodology and how to debug programs.

Software Methodology

In the relatively brief history of software development, techniques for developing software (software methodology) have been created to improve the success rate of a software development project. Your local technical library has an abundance of literature dedicated to this subject. The elements of the software development process (software development life cycle) are discussed in this section. These are the elements:

- Analysis
- Design
- Implementation
- Maintenance
- Testing and debugging

Analysis

During the analysis stage of development, information is gathered to determine the feasibility of a software project. This also might be referred to as the cost/benefit phase. During this period, the analyst and user compare objectives, goals, functions, priorities, and time requirements. The systems analyst collects data, comes to conclusions, and makes observations about the project. Note that a good working relationship with the user is a necessity. In fact, the interface between the analyst and the user is more important than any other single factor in the software development process.

Before you undertake a project, all parties involved need to agree on what the software should accomplish. The systems analyst examines objectives, functions, goals, and constraints.

Finally, functional specifications are produced. These documents tell what the software does. The specifications contain descriptions of the software being produced, user input, file data structures, and report formats.

Design

In the next phase of software development, a plan is constructed that satisfies software requirements. This step involves everything except the coding: writing program narratives, task steps, input and output requirements, and designing objects. This is also the time for defining algorithms.

Note that if you generate good design documentation, the actual coding time is reduced, as is the time spent debugging.

If possible, distribute your design to a group of your peers and ask them to review it. Next, convene a design review meeting to go over the design with others. The feedback from this review is extremely valuable.

Implementation

Adequate program design makes the implementation phase go smoothly. Most likely, you have your own programming style. I don't intend to tell you how to code; a few basic suggestions, however, might prove helpful.

What's Wrong with Top-Down Development?

The traditional approach to application development is a top-down methodology. This concept involves developing high-level control programs that control the functionality of lower-level modules. Each module performs an independent and precise task and is controlled from the high-level program. This approach involves developing a main program with a control structure that can execute all the various functions; dummy modules are written that execute each of the functions. Next, the main program is tested to ensure that all the paths are operating correctly. Finally, the code is developed and tested for each of the functions.

This approach might seem reasonable. However, the "do this, now do that" process of developing a design is no longer adequate to deal with the event-driven world of a modern interactive interface. Such a design becomes so complex that mere humans become quickly bogged down. You might think it is easier to be in control of each step your program executes, and you feel comfortable writing procedural code to anticipate every user response. However, the complexity can quickly become overwhelming. Customers are demanding applications that are more powerful and have a more interactive user interface. Furthermore, debugging, upgrading, and maintenance become more difficult as programs sprout more complex path structures inherent in procedural programs. There is a better object-oriented design.

Object-Oriented Programming

The objective of object-oriented design is to unravel complexity. Object-oriented programming (OOP) is an approach to programming that focuses on the data rather than the actions. Instead of designing a system based on how data is manipulated, OOP design is based on the object being manipulated. In contrast to a top-down design, object-oriented design focuses on the type of data forms that are to be processed and the hierarchical structure of the various classes of data. Data and methods (procedures and functions) are combined, and methods perform actions on the associated data in response to the occurrence of some event to define the data's behavior. You design classes that specify the objects used in the application, determine the elements and methods needed to manipulate the data, and program and test all the classes in an application. When you have accurately defined all the required classes, you can proceed with the task of designing the program that uses the objects associated with the classes. This process is the reverse of top-down design because, with OOP, you first design the low-level elements and then proceed with the high-level program organization.

Documenting Code

When you are writing code, add plenty of comments defining the functionality, input, and output for each module. When you change a module, be sure to change the comments appropriately. You might think this is extra work, but it pays off when you need to make changes to the code a year later. It's a good practice to add a preamble to each function that describes its use, calling sequence, external dependencies, and so forth. One technique for improving code readability is to indent levels of control structures. Code that is easy to read is easy to follow.

In addition to self-documented code, you should create system documentation. In many cases, organizations and clients require that system documentation be provided as part of the task deliverables. This is one of the most tedious programming tasks the programmer must do. You're in luck, however, because you can create programming documentation using the Visual FoxPro Documenting Wizard. You provide some fundamental information about your application, such as the name of the main program, and the Documenting Wizard locates all the files associated with the application and automatically generates system documentation for your application.

To execute the Documenting Wizard, choose the **T**ools menu **W**izard option. Then choose the **D**ocumenting (FoxDoc) Wizard. In either case, the FoxDoc Wizard dialog box has six steps (as shown in Figures 23.1a, 23.1b, and 23.1c) to specify the system documentation you want for your application.

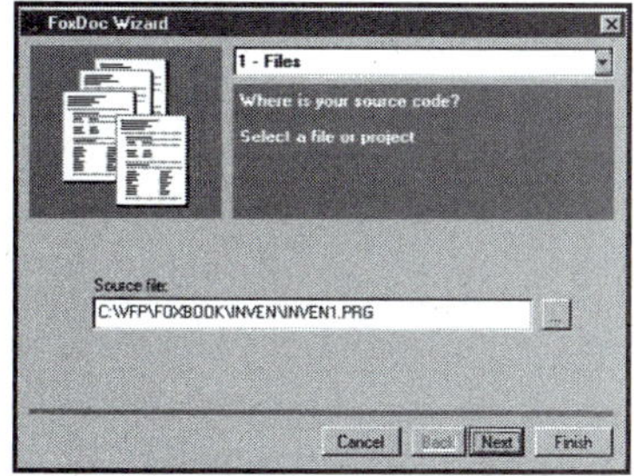

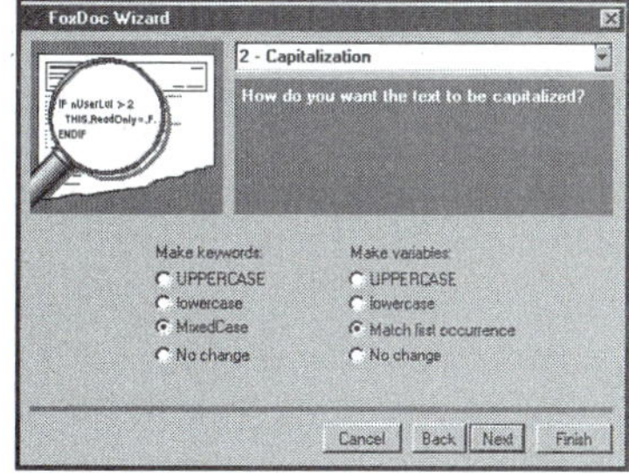

FIGURE 23.1A.
Step 1 and Step 2 of the FoxDoc Wizard.

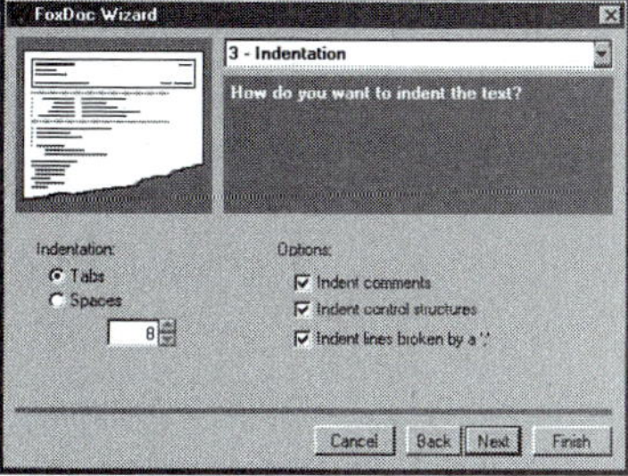

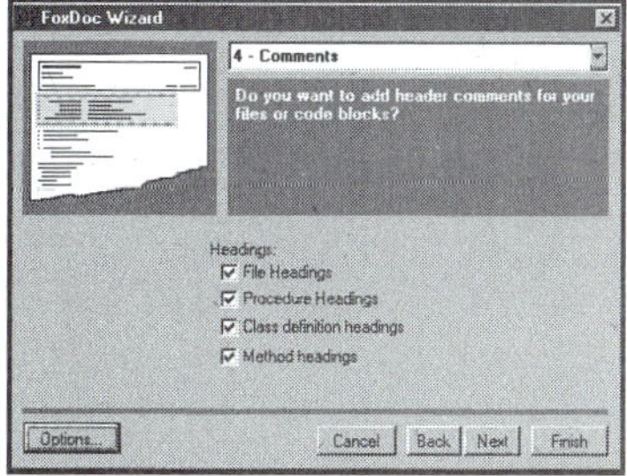

FIGURE 23.1B.
Step 3 and Step 4 of the FoxDoc Wizard.

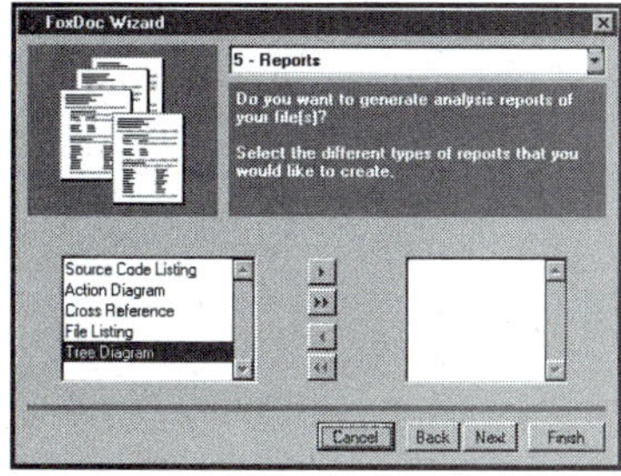

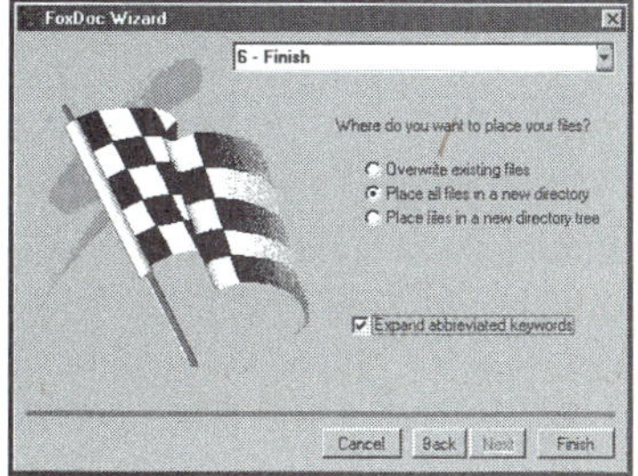

FIGURE 23.1C.
Step 5 and Step 6 of the FoxDoc Wizard.

The FoxDoc Wizard leads you through the following six steps so that you can specify the system documentation you want for your application and rules for creating it:

1. Specify the Project Manager file for the application to be documented.
2. Specify capitalization rules for variables and keywords.
3. Specify indentation rules for control structures, comments, and continuation lines.
4. Specify rules for automatically adding headers for procedures, functions, methods, and class definitions.
5. Specify which of the following reports you want: Source Code Listing, Action Diagram, Cross Reference, File Listing, or Tree Diagram.
6. Specify the directory in which you want the reports and the beautified source code.

The FoxDoc Wizard generates system documentation for all the components of your application. The FoxDoc Wizard offers the option of activating the Beautify utility to reformat each of the source files in your application and, if you want, add headers to each source file, function, and method in your application.

Adhering to the Programming Style Guidelines

You will benefit if you follow some programming style guidelines. It doesn't matter which guidelines you follow if you're consistent. Here are some sample guidelines designed to make a program more readable:

- Add an identification block of comments in front of each procedure and function that describes its use.
- Add a change log. A *change log* is a block of comments with a line containing the date that a change was made, who made it, and the purpose of the change.
- Indent each level of a structure.
- Specify keywords in all uppercase.
- Specify variable names and other identifiers in lowercase or mixed case.
- Place a blank line between groups of related statements.

Programming style is optional. However, if you conform to a style, your code is much more readable for others who work with your code, and for you when you perform code maintenance months later.

Visual FoxPro supplies the Beautify utility that is built into the Documenting Wizard. It reformats a program file so that it corresponds to a consistent style. To execute the Documenting Wizard, you choose the **T**ools menu **W**izard option. Then choose the **D**ocumenting option.

Keeping Procedures Small

Keep all methods, procedures, and functions as small and concise as possible. Long procedures are hard to understand, debug, and maintain. It is always best to divide large, complex procedures into several smaller procedures.

Minimizing Coupling

One of the advantages of OOP is that each object is encapsulated (that is, self-contained as a unit of program logic). Therefore, by design, the number of interfaces between class objects is minimized. Consequently, the class objects are more independent and easier to debug, test, and maintain. If you have too much coupling between procedures, a change to one procedure usually requires you to change all associated procedures. A small change to one procedure can cause other coupled procedures to malfunction. This makes testing, debugging, and maintaining of traditional procedural code more difficult.

For example, assume that many modules share access to a public memory variable. If you make a change in one module that affects the public memory variable, you must examine the impact of the change in all modules that reference the public variable and then make any required changes. All the modules that reference the public variable are coupled.

Reuse Procedures

Whenever possible, don't reinvent the wheel. Develop class objects that inherit properties and methods from other classes. You can build a class library of commonly used classes and use them in other applications. When you develop traditional Xbase functions, you can build a library of useful procedures. Trade them with other programmers and you will save many programming hours. The Wizard class library, WIZSTYLE.VBX, is a good example of a class library. You can use the class browser, BROWSER, to examine a class library in order to find useful classes from which to derive your own classes.

Maintenance

During this phase of the software development cycle, you have to fix bugs, add new features, and so on. This process can be complex; the better the code is written, however, the easier this task will be. Well-documented software that has plenty of comments is also helpful.

The following pointers might be beneficial:

- Understand how the system does or does not work.
- Determine modifications.
- Try to determine how modifications will affect the current system.
- Enact and test the modifications.

Testing and Debugging

It is rare for a computer program to work the first time you run it. The program will contain errors, and the more complex the program is, the more bugs it will contain. The errors must be detected, isolated, and corrected. This process is debugging. Correcting an error is usually the easiest step; detecting an error is usually the most difficult step. Debugging is a skill you develop as you gain more experience. You isolate a bug, correct the bug, recompile the program, and test the program. You repeat this process until a correctly working program emerges.

Testing is the process of identifying software defects. Testing is vital, as you know if you've heard horror stories about how a customer ran into some bug that caused hideous data loss. The testing and debugging processes are interleaved with the implementation process, as shown in Figure 23.2.

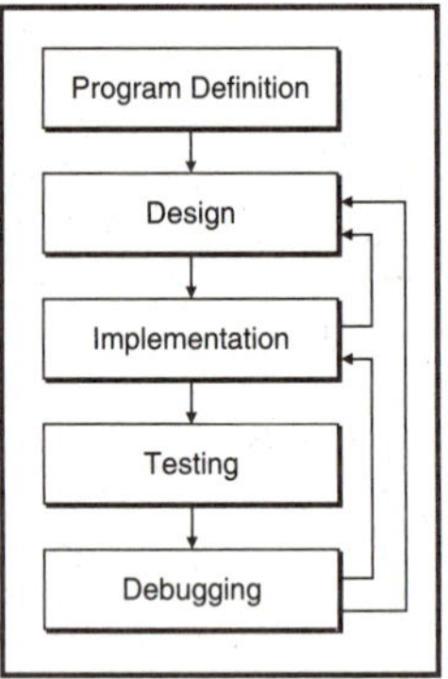

FIGURE 23.2.
Development processes.

Testing begins during development. The first level of testing is unit testing, which is the process of testing each procedure independently as soon as it's developed and before it's integrated with the rest of the system. Most, if not all, paths through the logic of a procedure should be tested during the unit testing phase.

The next phase of testing is integration testing. During integration testing, each interface path between the modules is tested.

Then functional testing is performed to determine whether the overall system operates according to design specifications. Performance testing is also undertaken to ensure that the algorithms are efficient enough to provide the user with acceptable response times.

You can't debug until a bug is found through testing. After a bug is identified, the programmer must locate the cause of the bug and correct it. The debugging process can range from correcting simple syntax errors to rewriting entire algorithms. If any changes are made that affect the design, the design specifications have to be changed also.

Types of Errors

This section discusses the four types of errors encountered in FoxPro programs: syntax, logic, regression, and dormant.

Syntax and Control Flow Errors

These are the easiest errors to fix because the compiler detects and isolates them. Some of the most common errors appearing in Xbase programs are the following:

- Missing space between keywords and variables
- Missing delimiters
- Misspelled keywords, variable names, and filenames
- Memory variables not initialized
- Database operations performed on the wrong file
- Wrong syntax for the command
- Data type mismatch errors in expressions and function arguments
- Control flow nesting errors
- One of a pair of control flow statements missing (for example, a missing `ENDIF` statement)
- Invalid loops

The first seven errors in the preceding list are syntax errors. The other errors listed are control flow errors. The FoxPro compiler makes it easy to correct some of these errors because it opens the text editing window so you can fix the error when the compiler encounters it. You must correct all the errors before the program will compile correctly. After you correct all the errors, you recompile or attempt to re-execute the program.

Logic Errors

Because the compiler cannot detect logic errors, or logic bugs, they are harder to isolate. The program can compile with no syntax errors or warnings and still yield the wrong results. Don't panic. The tester is responsible for detecting bugs and reporting them to the programmer. The programmer is responsible for finding the origin of the bug, and then isolating and correcting the bug. Isolating the problem is usually the most difficult phase of debugging a logic error; however, the correction is usually easy. The Visual FoxPro Debugger can help you with this phase.

Regression Errors

A regression error is one that you create in an attempt to correct a logic error. Whenever you correct an error, you must thoroughly test the correction to be sure that it fixes the bug you are correcting and does not result in another error. Regression errors are common, but they are easy to isolate and correct. A general principle to follow when debugging is that a bug is probably caused by the last code you touched.

Dormant Errors

The most embarrassing errors are dormant errors, the ones that stay hidden in the back halls of your program and don't reveal themselves until after you deliver the program to your customers. These bugs are hard to detect, but easy to isolate and correct. Customers usually use real-world data, whereas internal testing organizations usually use contrived data. Real-world data is the data that customers use in their daily work environment. Many software development companies send out beta test versions of the program to a sampling of customers so that the program can be tested with real-world data.

Debugging During Design

Software reliability is designed into a program. You can design your program so that it is easier to program, debug, and maintain. Most tasks can be divided into subtasks. A class definition normally contains the definition for all of the data and methods for a subtask. It is important that you encapsulate subsets of logic data into a class object. When you define functional modules, you can design each method (procedure) so that its variables and properties are protected (private). This helps reduce the side effects resulting from an interaction between properties (variables) in other parts of the program. You can control variable interaction by communicating between objects using passed arguments.

One of the major advantages of OOP design is that your program is easier to debug than traditional procedural programs, because it is easier to isolate and correct a bug as a result of the interaction between properties (program variables) in objects being minimized.

Programmers often write scaffolding programs (or software drivers) to test the logic paths of an individual object before it is incorporated with the rest of the application. The scaffolding software is not part of the program and is either discarded or retained for maintenance. Software debugging is simpler if you can separately debug each function, procedure, or object.

The best recommendation I can make is that you design your program to be a modular class object. Each object can be coded and tested separately from the rest of the program. Then, if you detect an error, it's easier to isolate and correct the error because you have fewer lines of code to inspect.

Visual FoxPro Integrated Development Tools

This section discusses how you can use the Visual FoxPro integrated development system tools to create, compile, and debug a program. These are the most fundamental tools used by a programmer for developing programs in Visual FoxPro. They consist of the Program Editor, compiler, and debugger.

The Program Editor

You could not have read this far in this book without knowing about the Visual FoxPro text editor. Because it is one of the major components used in any software development environment, however, I chose to review it in this section.

Visual FoxPro has a built-in Windows-style editor that you use for creating and editing your FoxPro programs and class methods. If you know how to use any editor in Windows, you can use the FoxPro Program Editor. When you want to edit a program, you can execute the `MODIFY COMMAND` command, or choose either the **F**ile menu **N**ew option or **F**ile menu **O**pen option and specify the name of a program file to create or open. If you are using the Project Manager, you can double-click on a program filename in the Project Manager program list to activate the Program Editor. When you use the text editor to edit a program, it is referred to as the Program Editor. After you exit from the editor while editing a method in the Visual FoxPro Form Designer, Visual FoxPro compiles the method. If an error is encountered, the Program Editor window remains open and a system error box displays the error. The line of code containing the error is highlighted.

When a program is executing and an error occurs, the Program Editor window opens and displays the program in which the error occurred. The line of code containing the error is highlighted. You can fix the error, save the changes, and re-execute your program.

The help system fully supports the Program Editor. If you forget the syntax of a command, select the name of the command, press F1 to activate help, and help is provided. You can reposition the windows so that you can view the Help window while you type in the command.

When you edit your program or method, you can use the control keys or the mouse to move through text and perform editing operations. Table 23.1 is a summary of the Program Editor control keys. Table 23.2 describes how to select text using the mouse. You can change the text editor edit options by choosing the **T**ools menu **O**ptions option Edit tab.

Table 23.1. Control key usage for the Program Editor.

Key	*Usage*
Right arrow	Move one character to the right.
Left arrow	Move one character to the left.
Up arrow	Move up one line.
Down arrow	Move down one line.
PgUp	Move up one window of text.
PgDn	Move down one window of text.
Home	Move to beginning of current line.
End	Move to end of current line.

continues

Table 23.1. continued

Key	*Usage*
Ctrl+right arrow	Move one word to the right.
Ctrl+left arrow	Move one word to the left.
Ctrl+Home	Move to beginning of text.
Ctrl+End	Move to end of text.
Shift+left arrow	Select the character at the left of the cursor and move the cursor left one character.
Shift+right arrow	Select the character at the right of the cursor and move the cursor right one character.
Shift+up arrow	Select the current line and move the cursor down one line.
Shift+down arrow	Select the current line and move the cursor up one line.
Shift+up/down arrow	Select one line at a time.
Shift+Ctrl+left/right arrow	Select from cursor to beginning/end of a word.
Shift+Ctrl+End	Select from cursor to end of text.
Shift+Ctrl+Home	Select from cursor to beginning of text.
Ctrl+A	Select all text.
Backspace	If nothing is selected, deletes the character to the left of the cursor. If text is selected, deletes selection.
Ctrl+Backspace	Deletes the word in which the cursor is positioned. If the cursor is positioned on the blank space following a word, the space and previous word are deleted.
Delete	If nothing is selected, deletes the character the cursor is on. If text is selected, deletes the selection.
Insert	Pressing Insert toggles between insert and overtype modes. The cursor looks like a flashing underscore when you are in insert mode. Typing a character in insert mode inserts it at the cursor location to the right of existing text. In overtype mode, the cursor is a solid flashing box. Each character you type replaces the character that the cursor is on. In general, when text is selected, typing any characters (except editor control characters) replaces the selected text with the typed text.

Key	*Usage*
‘	To insert a control character, press the ‘ (left single quote) key followed by the letter that would normally follow Ctrl. For example, Ctrl+Q is inserted into a file by typing ‘Q. To enter ‘ itself, you must type ‘ twice.
Alt+ddd	High-bit characters used to create boxes and other graphics can be entered directly in editor files. You hold down the Alt key and type the (decimal) key code of the desired character.
Ctrl+X	Cut; removes selected text for placement in a different location.
Ctrl+C	Copy; duplicates selected text for use in another location.
Ctrl+V	Paste; places cut or copied text into a file at the cursor location.
Ctrl+F	When you want to find and replace a word or phrase that appears throughout a text file, program file, memo field, or the Command window, choose the appropriate find-and-replace command from the **E**dit menu.
Ctrl+G	Find next.
Ctrl+E	Replace and find again.

Table 23.2. Text selection operations using the mouse.

Operation	*Mouse Action*
Select text	Position the pointer on the character where you want selection to begin, drag to the right by holding down the mouse button and moving the mouse, and then release the mouse button. Drag down to highlight entire lines of text.
Select a word	Position the pointer on the word and double-click.
Select a line	Position the pointer on a line and triple-click.
Select text word by word	Double-click on a word and drag.

continues

Table 23.2. continued

Operation	*Mouse Action*
Select text line by line	Triple-click on a line and drag.
Select a segment of text	Point the mouse cursor at one location and click. Then Shift+click at another location to select from the original cursor location to the Shift+click location.
Drag and drop	Select some text. Then position the selected text and drag it to the new location. You can also select text and drag a copy of it to the new location. Hold down the Ctrl key as you drag the copy of the selected text to its new location.

You can save your file using the **F**ile menu **S**ave or Save **A**s options. You can exit from a text editing window by one of the following methods:

- Choose the **F**ile menu **C**lose option.
- Choose the Close menu box **C**lose option.
- Press Escape (abandon changes and exit).
- Press Ctrl+W or Ctrl+End (the traditional Xbase save-and-exit key).

If you want to use your own editor, you can still use the `CONFIG.FPW TEDIT=` command to define its name.

To edit any text file, program, or memo field when the Program Editor is open, you can choose the **T**ools menu **S**pelling option and the Spelling dialog box appears. FoxPro uses the dictionary specified in the MS Proofing Tools section of your WIN.INI file.

The Compiler

Visual FoxPro has a built-in compiler. The compiler translates command lines and expressions into internal pseudocode that the FoxPro interpreter subsequently recognizes and executes. Input to the compiler can be a command line from the Command window or lines of code in an ASCII file called a program file. The compiler can compile command lines and expressions from internal sources also (for example, the commands dispatch when you choose a FoxPro system menu bar option).

These are the limitations of the compiler:

- A compiled procedure is limited to 65528 bytes.
- The maximum number of nested `DO` commands is 32.

- The maximum number of nested structured program commands is 65.
- The maximum number of procedure parameters is 24.
- The maximum number of source program lines is unlimited.
- The maximum number of procedures per file is unlimited.

The compiler is another Visual FoxPro software tool. FoxPro automatically compiles source files before it executes them. If the `SET DEVELOPMENT` flag is `ON` and a program is executed, FoxPro compares the creation dates of the source and object modules. (The `SET DEVELOPMENT` command is described in Chapter 10, "Environment.") If the object module is older, FoxPro deletes the object module and automatically recompiles the source module. This operation is performed whenever you use `DO`, `DO FORM`, `SET FORMAT TO`, `SET VIEW TO`, `SET PROCEDURE TO`, or `SET CLASSLIB TO`, or close a Code window in the Class or Form Designer. When `SET DEVELOPMENT` is `OFF`, date checking is not done. The `SET DEVELOPMENT` command differentiates between compilation during application development and compilation during application use. When an application is being developed, the flag is set `ON`. When the application is delivered to the customer, the flag is set `OFF` because none of the object files should change.

The object modules are not like class objects; they are files that contain compiled code. The filename extension of the source file determines the filename extension of the generated object file. The following list shows the filename extensions of the source file and its corresponding object module file for different types of programs:

Program Type	*Source File Extension*	*Object Module Extension*
2.6 form code	.SPR	.SPX
3.0 form code	.SPX*	.SPX*
Class library	.VCX*	.VCX*
Stored procedures	.DBC*	.DBC*
Local and remote	.DBC*	.DBC*
Views		
Format	.FMT	.PRX
Menu	.MPR	.MPX
Program	.PRG	.FXP
Query	.QPR	.QPX

*Source and object code is stored in memo fields in a DBF-type file.

The compiler checks the syntax of all language components in the source module. It also detects control structure nesting errors. Whenever the compiler detects a fatal error, it displays an error message and continues compiling the remaining lines of source code, but it does not generate an object file. If the `SET LOGERROR` command is `ON`, compilation errors are output to an error file whose root name is the same as the program being compiled, with an .ERR extension.

Because programs are automatically compiled as they are being executed, the `COMPILE` command is not required for normal development operations. It was added to the language to support the following:

- Preliminary syntax checking
- Production module compilation (the `NODEBUG` and `ENCRYPT` keywords)
- Compilation of source files by the Program Manager

This is the syntax for the `COMPILE` commands:

```
COMPILE <filename> [NODEBUG] [ENCRYPT] [AS <nCodePage>]x
COMPILE FORM <filename>
COMPILE DATABASE <DBC filenames>
```

You can compile the form objects using the `COMPILE FORM` command. You can compile stored procedures in database container (DBC) files with the `COMPILE DATABASE` command. The `<filename>` clause is the name of the source module to be compiled. You can also specify wildcard characters `*` and `?` in the filename to compile a group of files. For example, if you want to compile all the program files, execute the following command:

```
COMPILE *.PRG
```

If you specify the `NODEBUG` keyword, the resulting object files are smaller because they contain no debugging information. If you specify the `ENCRYPT` keyword, your resulting object file is encrypted so that nosy people cannot access your source code by disassembling the object file. The `AS <nCodepage>` clause specifies the code page for which the program is compiled.

In the following example, a program with errors is compiled:

```
TYPE bad.prg NUMBER
COMPILE bad


bad.prg 12/23/92
1
2 * Main procedure
3 PROCEDURE BAD
4
5    * Set up database environment
6    DO Set_env
7    SET COLOR TO Z/Z
8    STORE "" TO part_id, part_name, descrip, vendor_id, commnt
9    STORE 0  TO price, cost, qty_onhand, qty_2order, lead_time
10    discontinu = .F.
11    dbf       = "GOODS"           && Standard report available
12    mlist     = NOT APPLICABLE"   && No mailing list available
13    cust_rpt = "N/A"              && No custom reports available
14    STORE "m->part_id" TO key, key1
15    STORE "NONE" TO key2, key3
16    list_flds = "PART_ID, PART_NAME, QTY_ONHAND"
```

```
17
18     SELECT
19     USE Goods ORDO Part_id
20     GO TOP   This is bad syntax
21     * Define popup menus
22     DO Bar_def
23
24     * Activate main popup menu_execute user choices
25     SET COLOR TO &c_popup.
26     ACTIVATE POPUP main_mnu
27     *
28     PROCEDURE BAD
29     DO Filt_ans
30     DO WHILE .T. This is bad syntax
31     IF choice = "Y"
32        * Start process of choosing filter condition
33        IF "" = TRIM(mvendorid)
34      filters_on = .F.
35        ELSE
36         GO record_num
37      ENDIF
38     ENDDO
39 RETURN

SET COLOR TO Z/Z
Error in line 7: Syntax error.
mlist     = NOT APPLICABLE"
Error in line 12: Syntax error.
SELECT
Error in line 18: Syntax error.
USE Goods ORDO Part_id
Error in line 19: Unrecognized phrase/keyword in command.
GO TOP   This is bad syntax
Error in line 20: Unrecognized phrase/keyword in command.
ENDDO
Error in line 38: Nesting error.
Error in line 40: If/else/endif mismatch.
```

Compiler Directives

Visual FoxPro supports compiler directives. Compiler directives are instructions to the compiler that are processed before the program is compiled. They can appear anywhere in a program file and are not part of the program. They are typically used to suppress the compilation of portions of the file, which makes the program easy to change and recompile in different environments.

A compiler directive begins with a pound sign (#) followed by the directive. Some directives are followed by a name, `<directive name>`, which can consist of up to 10 letters, numbers, and underscore characters. The first character must be a letter or underscore. You should adopt a standard naming convention for directive names so that your code is readable and easy to debug and maintain. This is the syntax of the compiler directives:

```
#DEFINE <directive name> <expr>
#UNDEF <directive name>
```

```
#IF <expN1> ¦ <expL1>
   <statements>
[#ELIF <expN2> ¦ <expL2>
    <statements>
   ...
#ELIF <expNn> ¦  <expLn>
   <statements>]
[#ELSE
   <statements>]
#ENDIF
#INCLUDE <filename>
```

The `#DEFINE` and `#UNDEF` preprocessor directives are used to create compile-time constants in programs. By creating constants with `#DEFINE` instead of using system memory variables, you can reduce memory consumption, increase performance, and simplify programs. You can create a constant by specifying the `#DEFINE` directive. You specify the name of the directive with the *`<directive name>`* field and the directive value with the *`<expr>`* field. When you compile a program, any occurrence of the directive name is replaced by the directive value. It is a direct text substitution operation. For example, when the following code is compiled, the directive name `HUNDRED` is replaced with the text `(100)`:

```
#DEFINE HUNDRED (100)
FOR JX = 1 TO HUNDRED
   ? HUNDRED - JX
ENDFOR
```

You can remove a `#DEFINE` directive from the system and consequently stop the substitution for the directive name with the `#UNDEF` directive. A `#DEFINE` directive name has program scope starting only at the line following its `#DEFINE` statement and continuing until the end of the program or until an `#UNDEF` statement for the directive name is encountered. The directive name is available only to the program in which it's defined.

WARNING

Never use FoxPro keywords as directive names. Do not use system memory variables as directive names because the keywords in the code would be replaced by the directive value.

You can use the `#IF...#ENDIF` preprocessor directives to conditionally include source code in a compiled program. For instance, if you use `#IF...#ENDIF` directives to conditionally compile platform-specific code in an application, you can improve the source code readability, reduce compiled program size, and improve performance. This is because you don't have to include platform-dependent code for all versions of your program. This is the syntax of the conditional directives:

```
#IF <expN1> ¦ <expL1>
     <statements>
 [#ELIF <expN2> ¦ <expL2>
     <statements>
```

```
    ...
#ELIF <expNn> ¦  <expLn>
     <statements>]
 [#ELSE
     <statements>]
#ENDIF
```

When a program that contains `#IF...#ENDIF` directive structures is compiled, successive logical or numeric expressions within the structure are evaluated. The evaluation results determine which set of FoxPro statements are included in the compiled code, as in the following example:

```
#DEFINE VERSION  .T.
#IF VERSION
     ? "VERSION is .T."
#ELSE
     ? "VERSION is .F.
#ENDIF
```

The numeric expressions (`<expN1>`, `<expN2>`, and so on) or logical expressions (`<expL1>`, `<expL2>`, and so on) are evaluated. If an expression specified with the `#IF` or `#ELIF` directives is numeric and evaluates to a nonzero value or the expression is logical and evaluates to true (`.T.`), the statements immediately following the `#IF` directive are included in the compiled code. Then the `#IF...#ENDIF` structure is exited, and the first program line following `#ENDIF` is compiled.

If the expression following the `#IF` directive is numeric and it evaluates to `0` or logical, which evaluates to a false (`.F.`) value, the statements immediately following `#IF` are not included in the compiled code. In this case, any following `#ELIF` directives are evaluated. If the `#IF` expression evaluates to `0` or false, the `#ELIF` directives are then evaluated. If the `#ELIF` expressions evaluate to `0` or false, the `#ELSE` statements are compiled.

The expressions are evaluated at compile time. Therefore, they must be constant expressions. The expressions cannot contain memory variables, field names, or even system memory variables. System memory variables are not evaluated until runtime. The expressions can, however, contain constant functions such as `OS()` or `VERSION()`.

The following example illustrates how the `#IF...#ENDIF` directives are evaluated:

```
#DEFINE VALUE <constant number value>
#IF VALUE=1
     ? " Compile this code only if VALUE = 1"
#ELIF VALUE = 2
     ? "Compile this code only if VALUE = 2"
#ELIF VALUE = 3
     ? "Compile this code only if VALUE = 3"
#ELSE
     ? "Compile this code if VALUE is not equal 1,2, or 3"
#ENDIF
? "Always compile this line of code"
```

Notice that in the preceding code, if the `#ELSE` directive is omitted, no program statements between `#IF` and `#ENDIF` are included in the compiled code. In the following example, the `#IF...#ENDIF` directive structure determines which version of FoxPro compiles the program and displays a message indicating on which platform the program is compiled:

```
#IF 'WINDOWS' $ UPPER(VERSION())
     ? 'This program was compiled using Visual FoxPro'
#ELIF 'MAC' $ UPPER(VERSION())
     ? 'This program was compiled using FoxPro for Mac'
#ELIF 'UNIX' $ UPPER(VERSION())
     ? 'This program was compiled using FoxPro for UNIX'
#ELSE
     ? 'This program was compiled using FoxPro for DOS'
#ENDIF
```

The `#INCLUDE` statement instructs the preprocessor to insert a *header file* into the source file. A header file is a text file containing comments, `#DEFINE...#UNDEF` and `#IF...#ENDIF`, and preprocessor statements. The compiler compiles the text in the header as though the source program contained the text.

This is the syntax of the include command:

```
#INCLUDE "<filename>"
```

`<filename>` specifies the filename of the header file. Note that it must be enclosed in double quotes. If you specify a path with the filename, Visual FoxPro looks for the header file in the specified directory. However, if you specify the filename without a path, Visual FoxPro looks for the header file in the default Visual FoxPro directory. The default Visual FoxPro directory is defined by the `SET PATH` command. Here are some examples:

```
#include "foxpro.h"
#include "CONSTANT.H"
#include "C:\INVOICE\FINANCE.H"
```

Normally, header files used in languages such as C and C++ have the filename extension .H. This tradition has been extended to Visual FoxPro header files so that most Visual FoxPro header files you encounter will have the filename extension .H. It is suggested that you adopt this convention to make it easier for you to identify header files.

Many of the constants used in Visual FoxPro have been defined in a file named FOXPRO.H. This file has been shipped as part of the Visual FoxPro product. It contains a variety of compile-time constants used in Visual FoxPro. It resides in the Visual FoxPro home directory.

Listing 23.1 shows an example header file that contains three `#DEFINE` directives that create compile-time constants. The program file GOODNESS.PRG, shown in Listing 23.2, contains an `#INCLUDE` directive that inserts the GOODNESS.H header file into the source file when the file is compiled. The three defined compile-time constants in the header file are available to the program.

Listing 23.1. The source listing of a header file.

```
*** This is a Header file GOODNESS.H ***
#DEFINE IS_GOOD        1
#DEFINE IS_BETTER      2
#DEFINE IS_BEST        3
```

Listing 23.2. The source listing of a program that includes a header file.

```
*******************************
*** Program file SHOWGOOD.PRG ***
#INCLUDE "GOODNESS.H"

FUNCTION ShowGood
PARAMETER GoodCode
  DO CASE
    CASE GoodCode = IS_GOOD
      WAIT WINDOW "This is a good thing"
    CASE GoodCode = IS_BETTER
      WAIT WINDOW "This one is better"
    CASE GoodCode = IS_BEST
      WAIT WINDOW "This is the best of all "
  ENDCASE
RETURN
```

The Visual FoxPro Interactive Debugger

When you've finished writing a program and you've located and repaired all the errors reported by the compiler, you're ready to begin the real debugging phase by tracking down and repairing logic bugs. Many logic bugs are easy to locate, but some are elusive. You need a debugger to locate hard-to-find bugs. A powerful, interactive debugger is built into Visual FoxPro. This debugger enables you to step through the program a line at a time while you view various program parameters.

The Debugger contains the various elements that you use during the debugging process. These include the following:

- The **T**ools and **P**rogram menus, which contain options that can be used to initiate debugging.
- The Trace window, which shows the source code and current executing command.
- The Debug window, which displays variables and expressions during debugging.

The Program and Tools Menus

The **P**rogram and **T**ools menus have options dedicated to the FoxPro Debugger. **P**rogram menu options are described in Table 23.3 and **T**ools menu options are described in Table 23.4. To use the Debugger, choose the **T**ools menu **T**race Window option, or type `ACTIVATE WINDOW TRACE` in the Command window, and the Trace window appears. The Trace window is described in the next section.

Table 23.3. The Program menu options.

Option	*Description*
Do (Ctrl+D)	Executes a FoxPro program.
Cancel	Cancels the execution of a program that was paused using the `SUSPEND` command.
Resume (Ctrl+M)	Resumes the execution of a program that was paused using the `SUSPEND` command.
Suspend	Suspends the execution of an executing program.
Co**m**pile...	Creates an executable version of a program. Actually, if you choose the **D**o option, it compiles a program (if required) before it executes. However, you may compile without executing it with this menu option.

Table 23.4. The Tools menu options for the Debugger.

Option	*Description*
De**b**ug Window	Displays the FoxPro Debug window. You can enter program variables or expressions in the Debug window, and their corresponding values display as the program executes.
Trace Window	Displays the FoxPro Trace window. You can execute a program and its source displays on the Trace window. You can execute the program a line at a time and the line that executes is highlighted. The Trace window is shown in Figure 23.3 and its menu bar is described in Table 23.5.

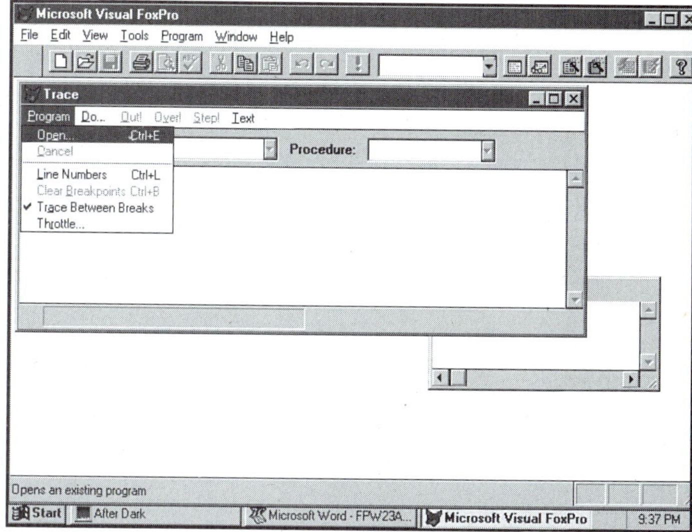

FIGURE 23.3.
The Trace window.

The Trace Window

The Trace window is the principal element of the Debugger. It is the window that contains the source listing of the program you are debugging. The line of code that is about to execute is highlighted to help you follow the program logic. The Trace window enables you to see your program as it runs.

To use the Debugger to debug your program, choose the Trace option, and the Trace window appears, as shown in Figure 23.3. You can also activate the Trace window by executing either `SET ECHO ON` or `SET STEP ON` from the Command window.

HISTORICAL FOOTNOTE

You might wonder why you can initiate the Trace window in so many strange ways. The `SET ECHO` and `SET STEP` commands are historical holdovers that date back to Vulcan, the predecessor to dBASE II. These commands were used for primitive debugging operations. In earlier Xbase dialects, the `SET ECHO` command displays the command line as it executes, and the `SET STEP` command executes a command and suspends execution so that you can display values. Now we have an advanced interactive debugger in FoxPro and the original meaning of these commands is lost to technological antiquity.

The Trace window contains its own menu bar, as described in Table 23.5. The Program menu pad contains a pop-up menu. The rest of the menu pads execute a debugging operation when you choose them.

Table 23.5. The Trace window menu bar description.

Menu Pad	*Option*	*Description*
Program	Op**e**n...	Choose this option and the Open File dialog box appears. You pick a program to debug.
	Cancel	Choose this option to terminate the execution of a suspended program.
	Line Numbers	Use this option to toggle on and off the display of program line numbers in the Trace window. The line numbers display to the left of the program text in the Trace window.
	Clear **B**reakpoints	Choose this option to clear all breakpoints you have set in the program.
	Tr**a**ce Between Breaks	This option is used to toggle the display and highlight every line of program code as it executes.
	Th**r**ottle...	If you choose this option, the Execution Throttle dialog box displays, which contains options to specify the execution speed of programs. When you are debugging a program, it is often convenient to slow down the execution so you can see the values change in the Debug window.
Do...		Displays the **D**o dialog box to open a program.
Resume!		Suspends program execution on the first executable line. After

Menu Pad	*Option*	*Description*
		you choose a program, **D**o… toggles to Resume to continue program execution.
Out!		If you choose this menu program, execution continues from the statement following the line that the called procedure is currently executing.
O**v**er!		If you choose this option, menu and program execution continues without displaying the executed lines of a called subprocedure and stops executing at the line of code following the line that called the subprocedure. O**v**er is short for *skip over procedure call.*
Step!		If you choose this menu, the current line of the program executes and then execution pauses. Step is short for *take a single step.*
Text		This pop-up, as associated with this menu, contains options to change the font size of the program displayed in the window.
Object		This is a drop-down combo box that displays class objects. If you open this combo box, it displays a hierarchical display of class objects.
Procedure		This is a drop-down combo box that displays the name of the executing class method that displays in the Trace window.

When the Trace window first opens, it is empty. You choose the Trace window Program menu Open option, and the Open File dialog box appears and displays program (.PRG) files. You open a program file, and it displays in the window. In Figure 23.4, the program SORT.PRG displays in the Trace window. The first line of the program is highlighted. You can begin debugging.

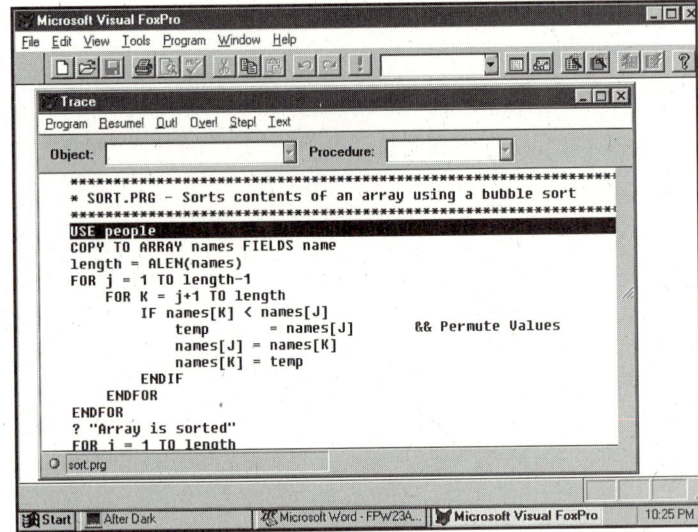

FIGURE 23.4.
The Trace window with the SORT.PRG file displayed.

NOTE

The exclamation points to the right of menu pad items in Figure 23.4 are a commonly used clue in Windows interfaces to indicate that no pop-up menu is associated with the menu pad.

Another way to open a program file is to choose the Trace window Do menu; the Do dialog box appears, and you then choose a program to debug.

Debug a Program

It's time to debug a simple program. Choose the Do menu and select a file to debug. In this example, I chose the file SORT.PRG, which displays in the Trace window, as shown in Figure 23.4.

Notice that the executable line in the trace program is highlighted. Execution is suspended at the first line of code. Also notice that the name of the program (SORT.PRG) appears in the Trace window status bar. The stage is set for debugging.

If you choose the **S**tep! menu, the highlighted line executes and execution pauses at the next line.

You can open the Debug window by choosing the Debug option from the Program menu on the FoxPro System menu bar. The Debug window displays, as shown in Figure 23.5. If you enter variable names or expressions in the left column of the Debug window, the right column shows corresponding values. As you can see in Figure 23.5, the variables `J`, `K`, `names[J]`, and `names[K]` have been typed into the Debug window. Values are not shown in the Debug window because the variables are not yet defined.

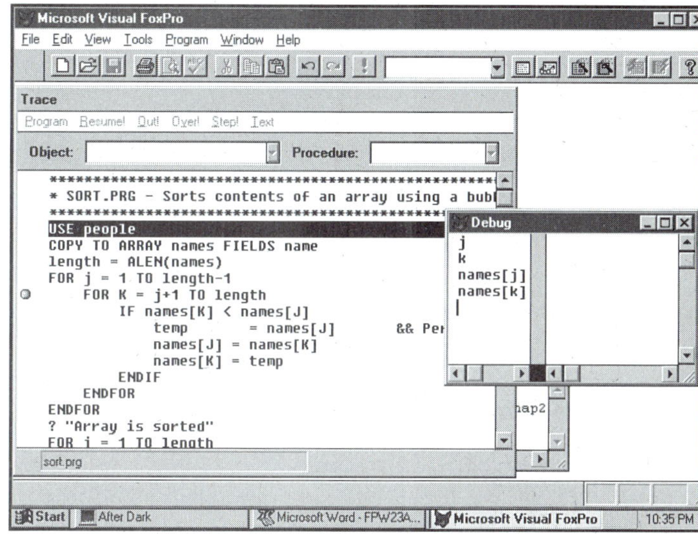

FIGURE 23.5.
The Trace and Debug windows.

To the left of the second `FOR` statement is a small symbol that resembles a sphere. This is a breakpoint indicator. You place or remove a breakpoint symbol by clicking on a line of code in the Trace window. Notice that another breakpoint symbol is on the status bar to indicate that a breakpoint is set somewhere even if its line is not currently displayed.

If you choose the **R**esume! menu pad, the program starts executing lines of code until the program exits or reaches a line of code marked with a breakpoint indicator, in which case execution is suspended. In this example, if you press the **R**esume! menu pad, execution stops at the second `FOR` statement, which is the line with the breakpoint symbol (as shown in Figure 23.6). Notice that values for the variables are displayed in the Debug window.

You might notice that each line of code is highlighted as it is executed. You can speed up the display with the **P**rogram menu Thr**o**ttle option. If you don't want to watch the lines slowly execute one at a time between instances of breakpoints, you can turn off the **P**rogram menu Tr**a**ce option between breaks option.

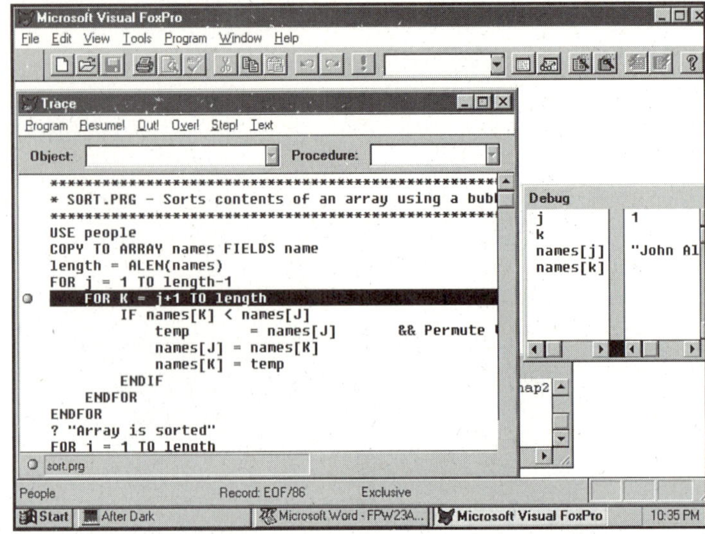

FIGURE 23.6.
The SORT.PRG program execution is suspended at a breakpoint.

The object of the bubble sort is for `name[1]` to end up with the smallest value in the table following a pass through the `FOR K=J+1 TO Length-1` loop. The array element `name[2]` should contain the second smallest value in the table. However, as you'll soon determine by debugging, the program sorts the program in descending order. As an exercise, you are to figure out where the bug is in SORT.PRG and fix it.

Other options that I need to comment on are the Over! and **O**ut! menu pads. Consider the following example. Assume that program execution is suspended at line 5, as shown in Figure 23.7. If you choose **S**tep!, `Prog2` is called and execution is suspended at line 5 of program `Prog2`. If you choose O**v**er!, `Prog2` is called and executed, and execution is suspended at line 6 of `Prog1`. If you are not at a line of code that calls another procedure or function, O**v**er! operates like **S**tep!. If you are stepping through the lines of code in `Prog2` and choose **O**ut!, the program execution continues until it reaches line 6 of `Prog1` and execution is suspended.

If you want to pass parameters to a program to be debugged, you can use the following procedure to execute the FoxPro debugger:

1. Choose the **P**rogram menu Tr**a**ce option to open the Trace window.
2. From the Trace window Program menu, choose the Op**e**n option and choose the program or application.
3. Set a breakpoint on the first executable line of the program.
4. From the Command window, execute the `DO` command and include the `WITH` clause.

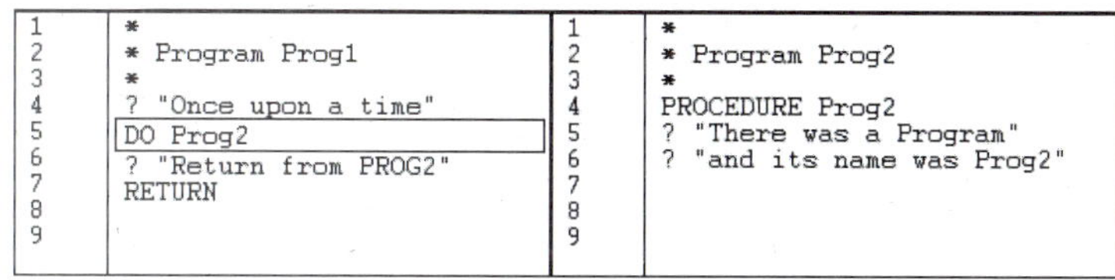

```
*
* Program Prog1
*
? "Once upon a time"
DO Prog2
? "Return from PROG2"
RETURN
```

```
*
* Program Prog2
*
PROCEDURE Prog2
? "There was a Program"
? "and its name was Prog2"
```

FIGURE 23.7.
An example that demonstrates the use of the Over! and Out! menus.

Debugging a Form

You can debug a form in the Trace window. You execute the form just as you execute a program. That is, you open the Trace window and use the Trace window **P**rogram menu Op**e**n option and choose a form (SCX) file.

Consider the sample program \VFP\SAMPLES\CONTROLS\MAIN.PRG that is distributed with Visual FoxPro. First, set the default directory to its directory using either the Options dialog box or the following command:

```
SET DEFAULT TO \VFP\SAMPLES\CONTROLS
```

Next, open the Trace window and execute the following sample program by choosing the Trace window **P**rogram menu Op**e**n option and then selecting the file:

```
\VFP\SAMPLES\CONTROLS\MAIN.PRG
```

The main program, like most OOP main programs, is simple and consists of the following code, which appears in the Trace window:

```
DO FORM MAIN
READ EVENTS
```

Start by stepping through this program by clicking on the **S**tep! menu pad until the sample program's Using FoxPro Controls form appears, as shown in Figure 23.8.

Next click on the **R**un Example control button, and the `Click` method for the `cmdrun` object appears, as shown in Figure 23.9. Notice that the method name appears in the Procedure drop-down list. The object name appears in the Object drop-down list. If you click on the Object drop-down list, the hierarchical structure displays showing the controls in the form as shown in Figure 28.10. You'll find that tracing through this sample case will help you understand how forms and OOP operate. Moreover, you will gain the experience and knowledge you need when you debug your own forms.

The FoxPro Debugger is not only powerful, it's easy to use. As you trace through a program or form, you can observe which paths are taken, and you can watch variables and expressions change. With a little practice, you quickly learn how to track down even the most obscure bugs using the Visual FoxPro interactive Debugger.

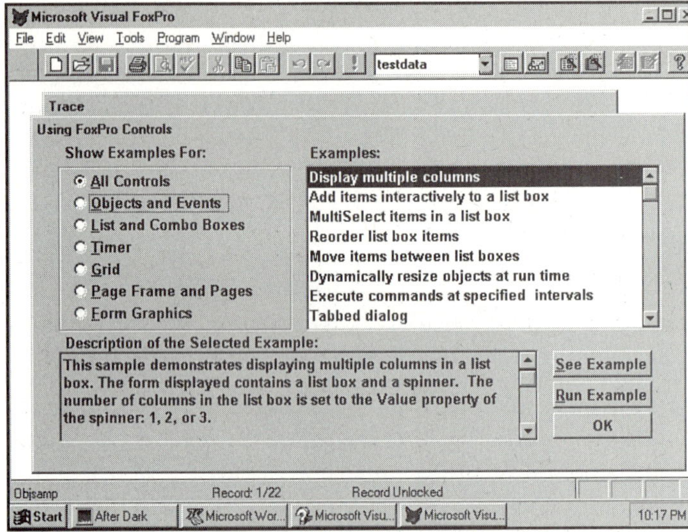

FIGURE 23.8.
The sample form MAIN.SCX, used in the trace example.

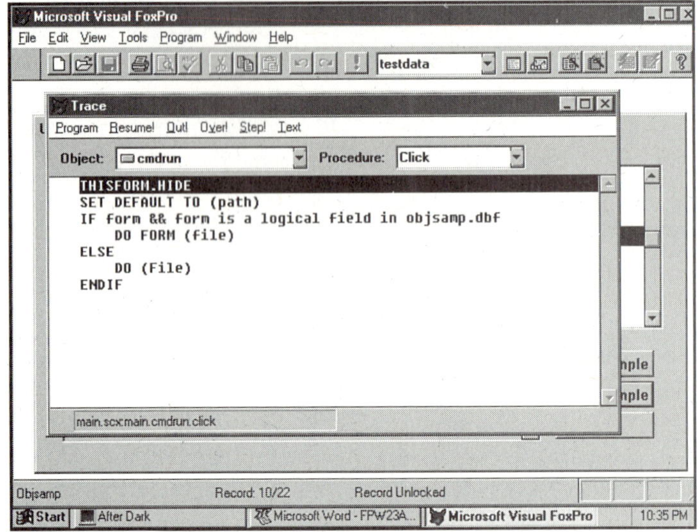

FIGURE 23.9.
The sample form MAIN.SCX with the `Click` *method displayed.*

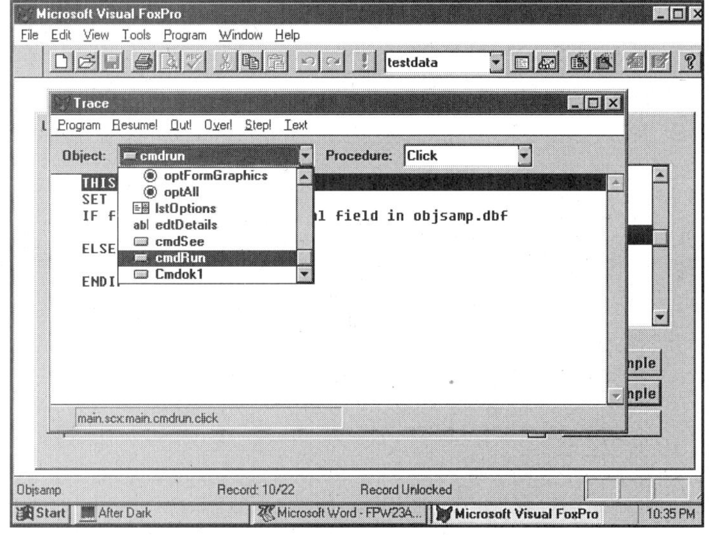

FIGURE 23.10.
The Trace window with the Object drop-down combo box open, showing visual objects.

Summary

This chapter introduces time-proven software development methodology that is an essential tool for any developer. It provides an approach for building Visual FoxPro applications from both business and technical points of view.

You have also learned about types of programming errors that you can encounter and how to use the Visual FoxPro integrated programming tools to develop FoxPro programming language applications. These tools include the Program Editor, the compiler, the Class Browser, and the interactive Debugger.

In this book, you have journeyed through the powerful and complex world of the Visual FoxPro database management system. It is the first Xbase that transcends platforms. Versions of Microsoft's FoxPro operate in Windows, MS-DOS, UNIX, and the Apple Macintosh platforms. With Visual FoxPro, you can develop an application for one platform and run it on all the other platforms with little or no changes.

24

Wizards

Any sufficiently advanced technology is indistinguishable from magic.

—Arthur C. Clarke

Visual FoxPro Wizards

What could be simpler to use than a good software installation program? You just move between the install windows while you follow instructions and answer questions. When the install program determines that you have satisfactorily answered all the questions, it installs some software. Well, FoxPro wizards are like a good installation program, except that a FoxPro wizard provides you with instructions concerning database operations and asks you to provide database-related answers. Then the wizard performs some database operation.

Wizards were introduced to FoxPro 2.6 for Windows to help low-end users take advantage of the power of FoxPro. New wizards were added to Visual FoxPro, and old wizards were made even more powerful. A *wizard* is a software tool that helps you quickly and easily perform a database management operation. It provides you with instructions, asks you questions, and performs its appointed task based on your answers. This chapter discusses what the following Microsoft Visual FoxPro wizards do and how to use them:

- The Table Wizard—Creates a new table containing the fields you specify.
- The Query Wizards

  The Cross-Tab Wizard—Displays query data in spreadsheet format.

  The Graph Wizard—Creates a graph in Microsoft Graph that displays data from a table.

  The Local View Wizard—Creates a view using local data.

  The Query Wizard—Creates a query from one or more tables.

  The Remote View Wizard—Creates a view using remote data.
- The Form Wizard—Creates a data-entry form from a single table.
- The One-To-Many Form Wizard—Creates a data-entry form from two related tables, and displays fields from the child table in a grid on the form.
- The Report Wizards

  The Group/Total Report Wizard—Creates a summary report that provides optional totaling for groups of records.

  The One-To-Many Report Wizard—Creates a report that groups records from a parent table with records from a child table.

  The Report Wizard—Creates a formatted report from a single table.
- The Label Wizard—Creates mailing labels for standard Avery formats.
- The Mail Merge Wizard—Creates a data source that your favorite word processor can use in a mail merge.
- The PivotTable Wizard—Sends data from Visual FoxPro to an Excel PivotTable and optionally creates a form that contains the embedded Excel PivotTable.

- The Import Wizard—Transfers data from other applications into a new or an existing Visual FoxPro table.

The following wizards are supplied with the Microsoft Visual FoxPro Professional Edition:

- The Documenting Wizard (See Chapter 23, "Building Visual FoxPro Applications.") —Generates program documentation, code listings, and cross-referencing lists, and beautifies source code.
- The Setup Wizard—Prepares an application for distribution on disks. (See Chapter 22, "Project Management and Building Applications.")
- The Upsizing Wizard—Moves local databases, tables, and views in a local prototype to a remote SQL server. (See Chapter 26, "Visual FoxPro and Client/Server Support.")

Interoperability

Both the PivotTable Wizard and the Mail Merge Wizard demonstrate the power of Visual FoxPro to interoperate with other Windows applications through OLE automation. With the PivotTable Wizard, you can summarize a Visual FoxPro table into an Excel PivotTable, which is automatically passed to Excel so that you can do analysis. The Mail Merge Wizard controls Microsoft Word to create and edit a mail merge form and to generate mail merge output.

Executing Wizards

There are several ways to execute wizards. Ominous sounding, is it not? Perhaps it would have been better if the computer terminologists had picked a kinder and gentler term, such as *start*, *run*, or *do*. Here are the ways to execute a wizard:

- You can execute a wizard from the Project Manager while creating a new table, query, form, report, or label.
- If you choose the **T**ools menu **W**izards option, a drop-down window appears, containing a list of wizards. If you choose any of the wizards in the list, the selected wizard executes. If you choose **A**ll, the FoxPro Wizards dialog box appears, as shown in Figure 24.1. It contains a list of all the wizards. You choose the wizard you want to execute.
- If you execute the **F**ile menu **N**ew option, the New dialog box appears. You have the choice of using a designer or a wizard to create certain files. Click on the Wizard button and Visual FoxPro executes a wizard to create the file.
- You can execute a wizard with the `DO \VFP\WIZARD` statement from the Command window.
- You can click on the New Local View button in the Database Designer toolbar. You are given the choice of executing either the Local View Wizard or the View Designer.

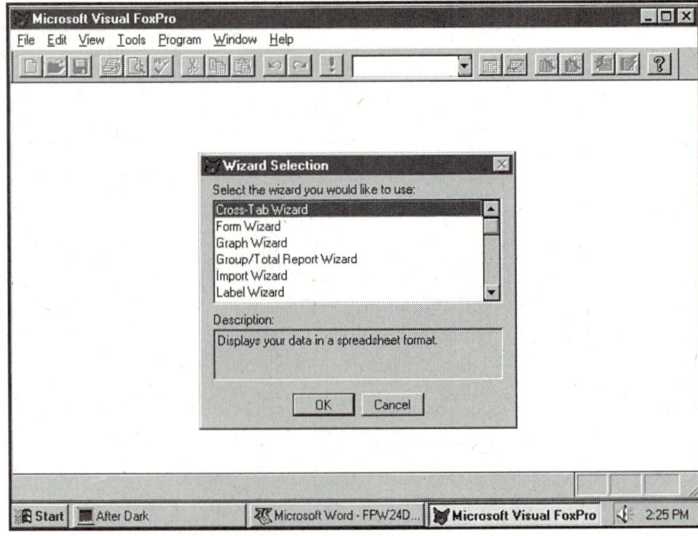

FIGURE 24.1.
The FoxPro Wizards Selection dialog box.

NOTE

FoxPro wizards are written in the Visual FoxPro language. You can execute a FoxPro wizard with the `DO WIZARDS\WIZARD.APP` command. The fact that the wizards were written graphically using FoxPro illustrates that highly sophisticated and attractive applications can be developed using the Visual FoxPro language. You can write your own wizards. In addition, there is a visual class library file (WIZSTYLE.VCX) that contains classes defining various visual objects used by wizards to create forms in the \VFP\WIZARDS directory. You can use this visual class library to design your own forms.

When you execute a wizard, the first Wizard dialog box appears. It is referred to as the Wizard Step 1 form. If one or more tables are already in use, they appear in a list in the Database/ Tables section of the Wizard Step 1 form, as shown in Figure 24.2. However, if you execute a wizard and no table is in use, you must select a table by clicking on the *browser button*, which is the button with three dots on it. The Open Table dialog box appears, and you select a table on which to operate. Next you choose fields to operate on from the Available Fields list box. As you select a field, it is moved to the Selected Fields list box. You can press the double arrow to move all the fields to the Selected Fields list box. You can use the single-right-arrow button to move the fields one at a time. You can use the buttons in the Selected Fields list box to reorder the fields. This Step 1 form is used by most of the wizards.

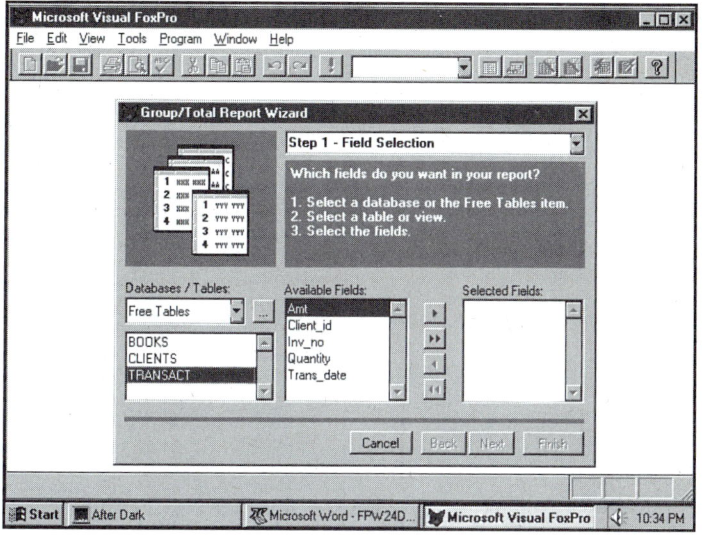

FIGURE 24.2.
The Group/Total Report Wizard—Step 1 dialog box.

When a wizard starts executing, you read the instructions and answer the questions in a Wizard dialog box and choose the Next button when you are ready to proceed to the next Wizard dialog box. You can always press the Back button to return to a previous Wizard dialog box.

When you reach the last Wizard dialog box and are ready to let the wizard complete its operations, choose the Finish button.

How to Modify a Wizard-Created Item

You cannot use a wizard to modify tables, queries, forms, reports, and labels created by a wizard. However, you can use their associated designers to modify them. For example, when you are using the Project Manager, you select the object created by a wizard in the Project Manager file list and press the Modify button. Then the appropriate designer will open so that you can modify the file.

The Microsoft Visual FoxPro wizards are discussed in the remaining sections.

The Table Wizard

The Table Wizard assists you in establishing a new FoxPro table. The Table Wizard window contains a list of typical tables with typical sample fields frequently used in databases. Each of these fields has a typical data type and field width. All you have to do is select the fields you want, and they are added to your new table. If you like, you can use them as they are or rename them and change the data types and field widths as needed. You can also set the sort order of the data in the table. The whole process is very intuitive. It consists of four easy steps.

Step 1: Select the Fields

The Table Wizard steps you through three dialog boxes to create a new table. You use the Step 1 dialog box, as shown in Figure 24.3, to select fields.

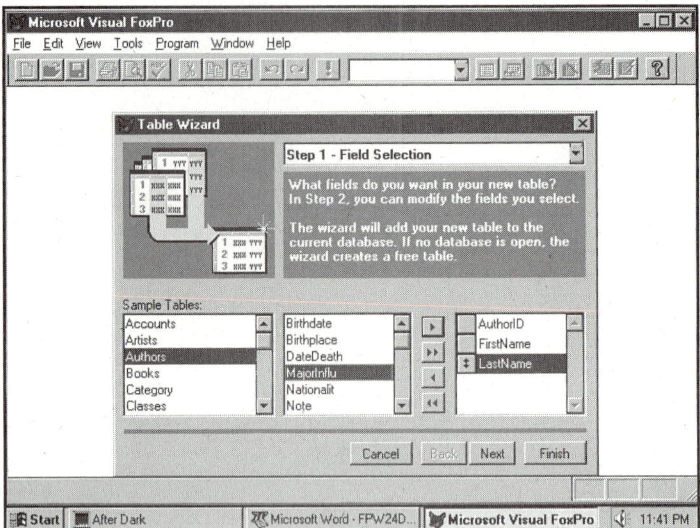

FIGURE 24.3.
The Table Wizard—Step 1 dialog box.

You select a sample table from the Tables list box. Fields associated with the selected table appear in the Fields list box. You select fields for your new table from the Fields list box and move them to the Selected Field list box, which represents the table you are going to create. The buttons between the Fields list box and the Selected Fields list box perform the following operations:

- ▶ Moves the selected field from the Fields list box to your table.
- ▶▶ Moves all fields in the Fields list box to your table.
- ◀ Removes the selected field from your table. You can also remove a field from the Selected Fields list box by double-clicking on the field.
- ◀◀ Removes all fields from your table.
- ↕ Reorders fields in the Selected Fields list box. Click on the button and drag a field up or down the list.

Step 2: Modify Field Properties

You use the Step 2 dialog box, as shown in Figure 24.4, to change the name, type, or width of a field. You can add a log field name (caption) if a database container (DBC) file is open.

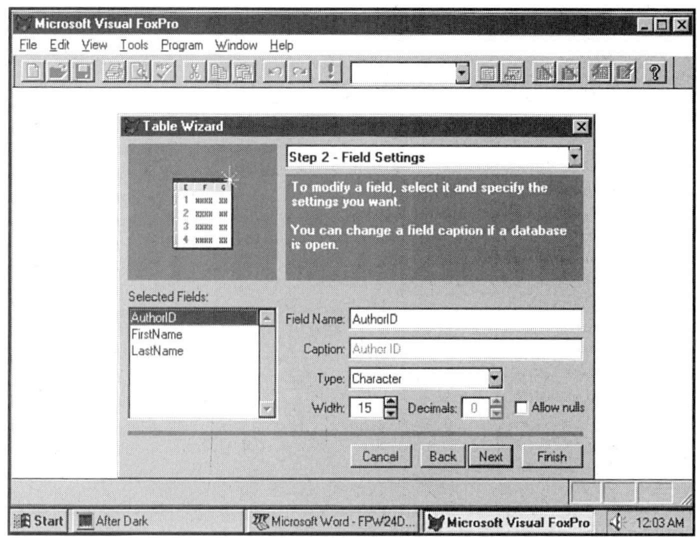

FIGURE 24.4.
The Table Wizard—Step 2 dialog box.

Step 3: Specify Indexes

You use the Step 3 dialog box, as shown in Figure 24.5, to specify which fields are indexed in your new table by placing a check mark to the left of the field name.

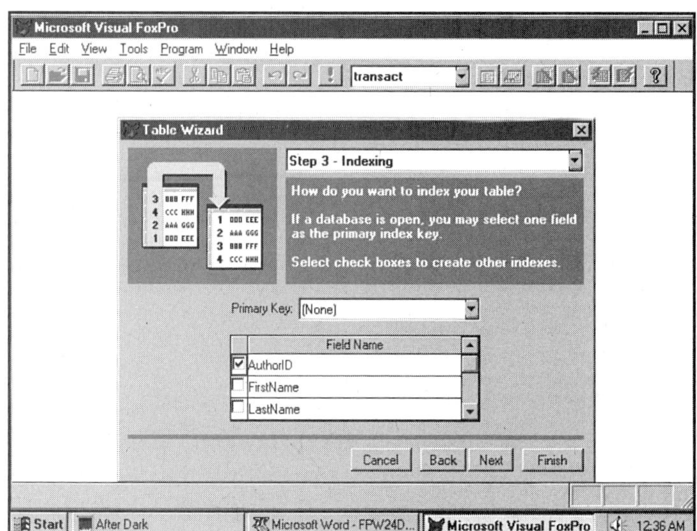

FIGURE 24.5.
The Table Wizard—Step 3 dialog box.

Step 4: The Final Step

You use the Step 4 dialog box, as shown in Figure 24.6, to designate the action you want to take once the table is created.

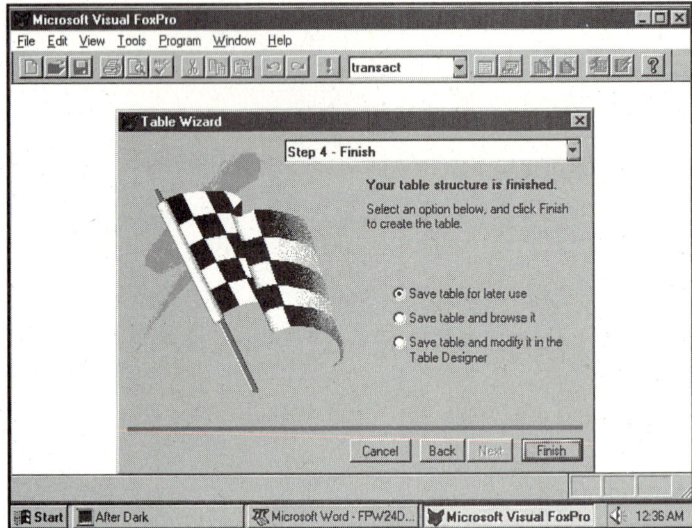

FIGURE 24.6.
The Table Wizard—Step 4 dialog box.

Choose one of the three options shown in Figure 24.6. Then choose the Finish button, and the wizard will complete the table creation process. Here are the three options:

- Save table for later use

  This option displays the Save As dialog box. You enter a name, and FoxPro saves the DBF table structure. The same save table operation is performed for the other three options before other operations are executed.

- Save table and browse it

  This option saves the table and displays it in a Browse window. You can add, edit, or view records.

- Save table and modify it in the Table Designer

  This option saves the table. Then it displays the Table Designer. You can modify the structure as required.

The Form Wizard

The Form Wizard leads you through four steps to create an attractive FoxPro form, which you can use to manage the information in your table. You can view and edit data. There is a set of buttons at the bottom of the form. You use these buttons to navigate through the table and perform various database management operations. The buttons can have text labels or pictures representing their function, as shown in Figure 24.7.

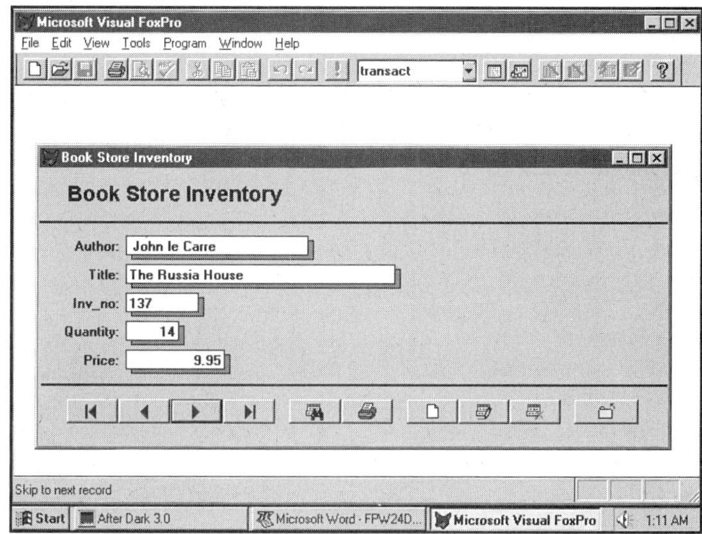

FIGURE 24.7.
A sample form created by the Form Wizard.

Now you can begin creating the form shown in Figure 24.7 using the Form Wizard. The Step 1 dialog box is discussed earlier in the section "Executing Wizards." Using the Step 1 dialog box, you can select a table and select fields for inclusion in your form.

Step 2: Choose the Style of Your Form

You use the Step 2 dialog box (shown in Figure 24.8) to select from the Style list box the style for the form and its push buttons. The styles in the list include Standard, Chiseled, Shadowed, Boxed, and Embossed. The picture at the top of the form illustrates the appearance of the style highlighted in the list. The Shadowed style was selected for the form shown in Figure 24.7.

Next, select which type of push button you want. The push buttons are placed across the bottom of the Form. You can have text captions on the buttons, picture buttons, or even no buttons at all.

Step 3: Designate the Sort Order

You use the Step 3 dialog box, shown in Figure 24.9, to specify the sort order. You designate which fields are to be sorted by selecting fields from the Available Fields list box and moving them to the Selected Fields list box. The fields are concatenated in the order they appear in the Selected Fields list box to form a single index key. The Form Wizard skips this step if the data source for your form is a query.

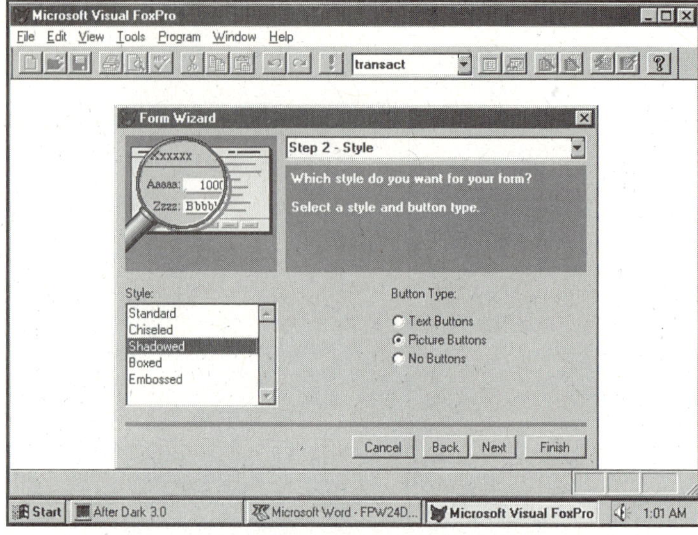

FIGURE 24.8.
The Form Wizard—Step 2 dialog box.

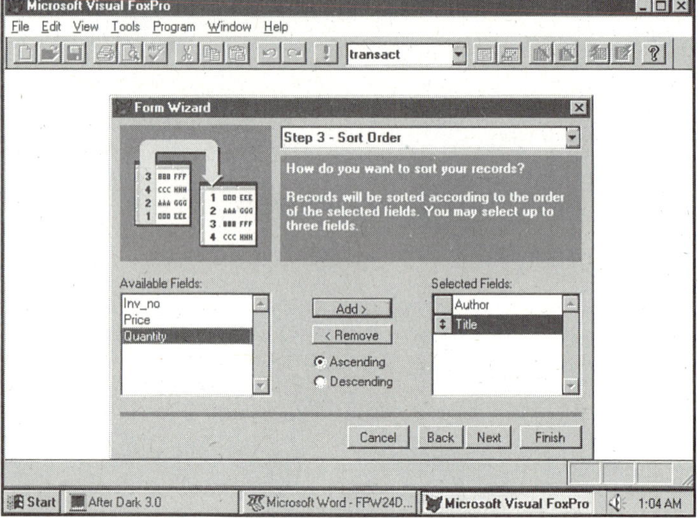

FIGURE 24.9.
The Form Wizard—Step 3 dialog box.

Step 4: The Final Step

The dialog box for the final step, Step 4, is shown in Figure 24.10. You enter a title that will appear at the top of the new form. Then you select one of the three options for saving the form and choose the Finish button. The Project Manager places the name of your newly created form in the Documents table list under the form icon.

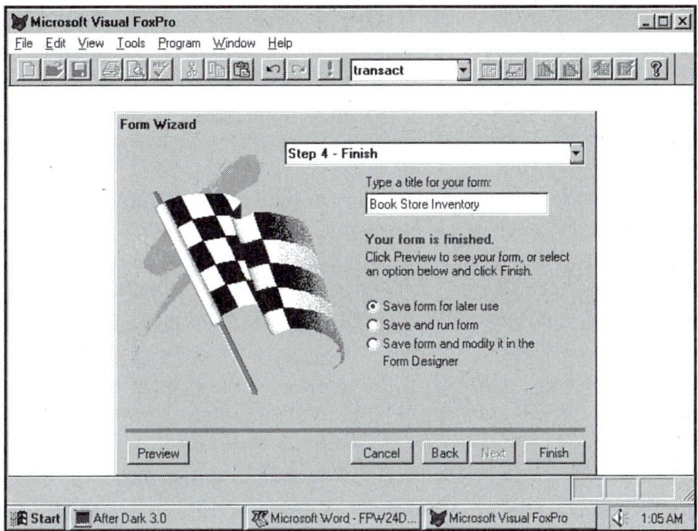

FIGURE 24.10.
The Form Wizard—Step 4 dialog box.

The three save options are defined as follow:

- Save form for later use

  You select this option if you want only to create a form (SCX) file. Later on, you can use the form file to generate and then run the form.

- Save and run form

  You select this option if you want the Form Wizard to create, generate, and display the form. When the form displays, you can add, edit, view, and print records.

- Save form and modify it in the Form Designer

  You select this option if you want to save the form and make custom changes with the Form Designer window (`MODIFY FORM` command).

Regardless of the option you choose, the Form Wizard displays the Save As dialog box. You supply a name for the form, and the Form Designer window appears so that you can make custom changes.

The third option is often useful because the Form Wizard has to guess at the width of the display fields and does not allow for custom property settings. Many times you will need to make refinements to your form.

If you press the Preview button, the Form Wizard generates a temporary form and displays it on the screen. The only difference is that there is a big Return to Wizard! button on the form, as shown in Figure 24.11. You can return to the wizard and make additional changes to the form as you like.

At the bottom of the form is a row of buttons. These buttons are described in Table 24.1.

FIGURE 24.11.
An example form created by the Form Wizard.

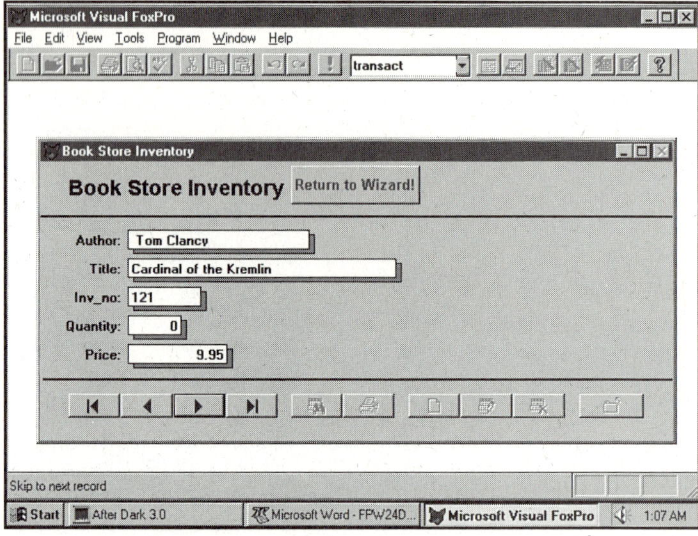

Table 24.1. The buttons in the form created by the Form Wizard.

Picture	*Button*	*Operation*
	Top	Positions to the first record in the table.
	Previous	Positions to the previous record in the table.
	Next	Positions to the next record in the table.
	Bottom	Positions to the last record in the table.
	Find	This button displays the Browse window.
	Print	This button displays a print dialog box. You have the option of printing the current record or all of the records in the table. The Report Wizard executes to create a report with the same name as the form. You have the option of printing or previewing the generated report.
	Add	This button adds a new record to the table. While a record is being added, the Add button changes to Save, and the Edit button changes to Revert. You can choose the Save button to save a new record or the Revert button to discard a new record.

Picture	Button	Operation
	Edit	Use this button to make changes to the currently displayed record. While a record is being edited, the Add button changes to Save, and the Edit button changes to Revert. You can choose the Save button to save an edited record or the Revert button to discard changes.
	Delete	This button deletes the current record.
	Revert	This button abandons the new record changes or the changes made during editing. This button is present only when a record is being added or edited.
	Save	This button saves the new record in the table or saves the changes made during editing. This button is only present when a record is being added or edited.
	Exit	This button closes the Form window and exits the form.

The One-To-Many Form Wizard

The One-To-Many Form Wizard leads you through six steps to create an impressive data entry form from two related tables. The fields in the child table display in a grid on the form. You can use this form to manage the information in both related tables. You can view and edit data. The set of buttons at the bottom of the form is the same as the buttons generated by the Form Wizard.

Suppose you want to create an invoice form for clients of a book distributor and that you have a Clients file, CLIENTS.DBF, with the following structure:

```
Structure for table:    C:\VFP\FOXBOOK\CHAP24\CLIENTS.DBF
Number of data records: 4
Date of last update:    04/05/95
Code Page:              1252
Field  Field Name       Type                 Width    Dec   Index   Collate Nulls
    1  CLIENT_ID        Character                5            Asc   Machine    No
    2  NAME             Character               20            Asc   Machine    No
    3  ADDRESS          Character               30                             No
    4  CITY             Character               15                             No
```

```
     5  STATE           Character          2                   No
     6  ZIP             Character          5                   No
     7  AREACODE        Character          3                   No
     8  PHONE           Character          8                   No
     9  EXTENSION       Character          5                   No
    10  STARTBAL        Numeric            8     2             No
    11  BALDATE         Date               8                   No
** Total **                              110
```

The TRANSACT.DBF table contains the monthly transactions for each client. You want the Clients table (parent) to be related to the transaction table (child) with a one-to-many relationship so that all of the invoice items for the month will appear on the invoice. Here is the structure of the TRANSACT.DBF table:

```
Structure for table:     C:\VFP\FOXBOOK\CHAP24\TRANSACT.DBF
Number of data records: 44
Date of last update:     04/05/95
Code Page:               1252
Field  Field Name      Type               Width   Dec   Index   Collate Nulls
    1  TRANS_DATE      Date                   8           Asc   Machine    No
    2  AMT             Numeric                8     2                      No
    3  CLIENT_ID       Character              5           Asc   Machine    No
    4  INV_NO          Character              5           Asc   Machine    No
    5  QUANTITY        Numeric                6                            No
** Total **                                  33
```

You can create this invoice form with the One-To-Many Form Wizard. Incidentally, both of these tables are associated with a database container file, TRANSACT.DBC.

The first thing to do is to open the Database Container. Next, execute the One-To-Many Form Wizard.

Step 1: Select the Parent Table and Fields

The One-To-Many Form Wizard steps you through five dialog boxes to create a new form. You use the Step 1 dialog box, as shown in Figure 24.12, to select fields from the parent table. Note that this dialog is the same one used as the first step for most wizards. The fields in the Selected Fields list box display in text boxes on the form. Now press the Next button to proceed to the next step.

Step 2: Select the Child Table and Fields

For Step 2, you designate which table you want to be the child table as shown in Figure 24.13. In this example, TRANSACT.DBF was selected. You choose fields for the Selected Fields table. These fields will appear in the grid on the form. Now press the Next button to proceed to the next step.

Step 3: Establish Relationship

In this step, you choose a matching field in each of the two tables that designates how the fields are related. See Figure 24.14. The One-To-Many Form Wizard figures out the most likely related matching fields by determining which field in the child table is indexed and has either the same field name or one that closely resembles the field in the parent table. If the One-To-Many Form Wizard guesses wrong, you can choose the correct fields from the drop-down list. Now press the Next button to proceed to the next step.

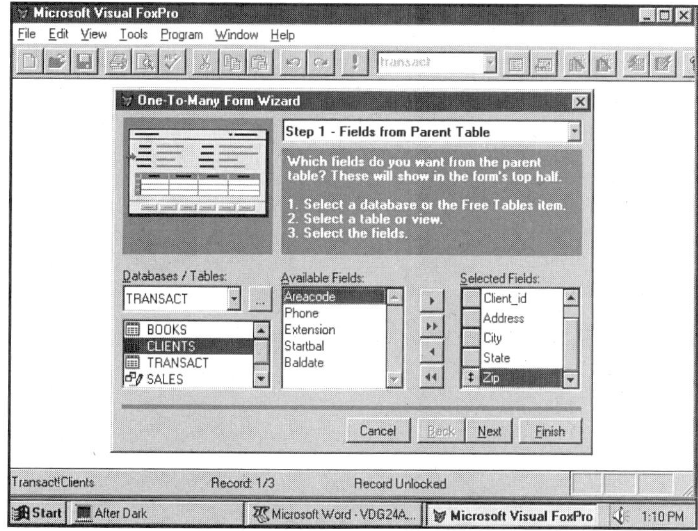

FIGURE 24.12.
The One-To-Many Form Wizard—Step 1 dialog box.

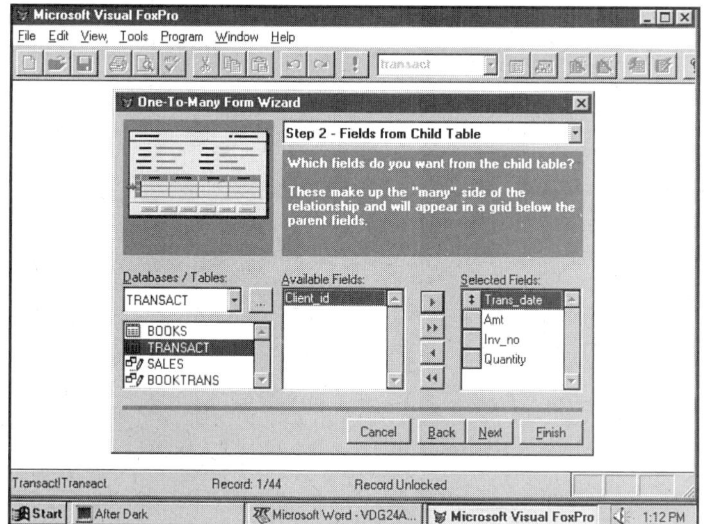

FIGURE 24.13.
The One-To-Many Form Wizard—Step 2 dialog box.

Step 4: Choose the Form's Style

This step sets the style of the form. It is identical to the Form Wizard Step 2 dialog box, as shown in Figure 24.8. Specify your favorite style and press the Next button to proceed to the next step.

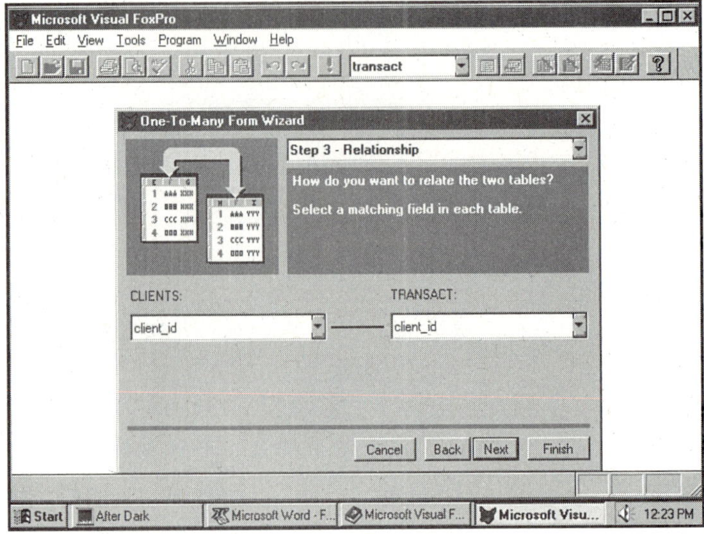

FIGURE 24.14.
The One-To-Many Form Wizard—Step 3 dialog box.

Step 5: Designate Sorting Order

This step sets the sorting order of the parent table for the form. It is identical to the Form Wizard Step 3 dialog box, as shown in Figure 24.9. Tell the One-To-Many Form Wizard that you want the form to be sorted by name and press the Next button to proceed to the next step.

NOTE

The same Step 3—Sort Order frame is used in many wizards. In this case, as in other cases, I will refer you to the figure for another wizard rather than repeating instructions over and over. Also, the instructions on the Step 3—Sort Order frame are so clear, readable, and understandable that you probably do not have to refer to the other figure anyway.

Step 6: The Final Step

This is the final step. It is identical to the Form Wizard Step 4 dialog box, as shown in Figure 24.10. Add a title such as `Customer Invoice`. Now press the Preview button and your preview form should resemble the form shown in Figure 24.15.

If you find that there are problems with the form, you can press the Back button to return to the previous steps and rectify the problem. When you are satisfied with the previewed form, select the option Save the form and modify it in the Form Designer and press the Finish button to exit the wizard.

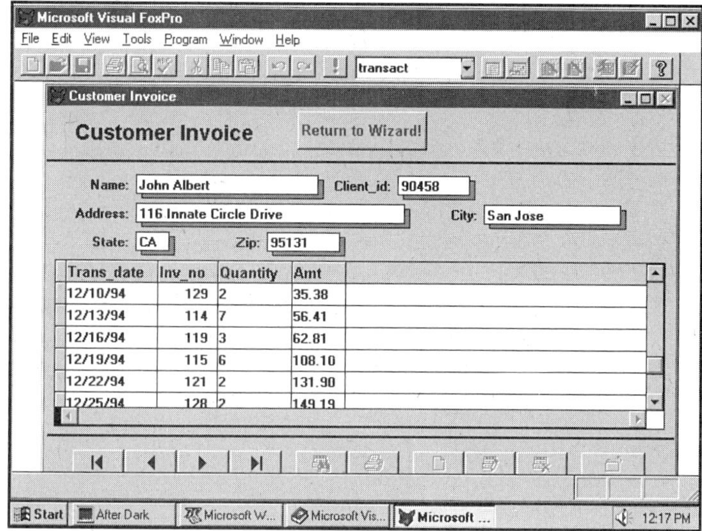

FIGURE 24.15.
A preview of a form created by the One-To-Many Form Wizard.

The preview form is well laid out for a first cut. First you need to make a list of things that need to be changed on the form with the Form Designer. Here is a sample list:

1. Make better headings in the grid
2. Add total field (`Transact.Quantity*Transact.Amt`)
3. Fix the poor display of currency values by setting the `Column4` column Alignment property to 1 to right adjust the numbers in the text field

Next, from the Objects box in the Properties window choose the `Heading1` object from the `Column1` column and change the heading from `Trans_Date` to `Date`. Likewise, change the `Amt` heading to `Unit Cost` and the `Inv_no` heading to `Item #`.

Now add another column. Set the `ColumnCount` property for the grid to 5. Set the properties for Column 5 to the following values using the visual techniques you learned in Chapter 19, "The Form Designer":

```
Column5.Heading1 = "Total"
Column5.ControlSource = TRANSFORM(transact.quantity * ;
                                  transact.amt,   ;
                                  '###,###.##')
Column5.Sparse    = .F.        (Force InputMask displays in for rows)
Column5.Alignment = 1            (Right adjust the value of Total in the field)
Column5.Text1.InputMask = "#,###.99"
```

Next, click on the lines separating the headings and resize the fields. The resultant form should appear something like the form in Figure 24.16.

Now click on the Run (!) button on the standard toolbar to run the form. It should appear as it does in Figure 24.17.

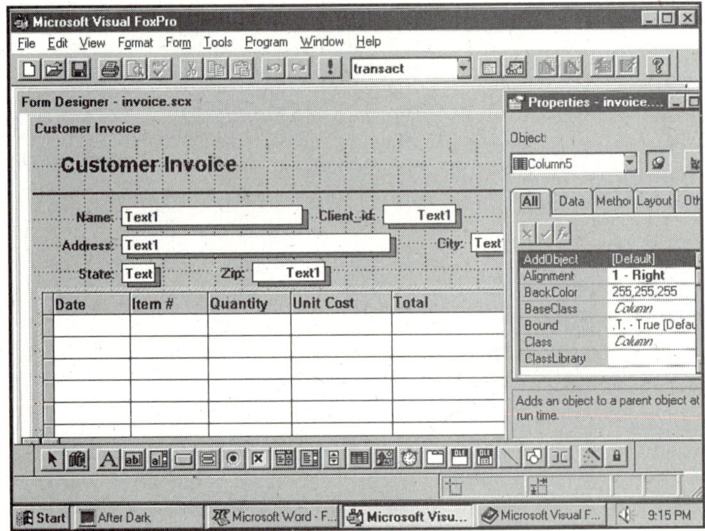

FIGURE 24.16.
Adding a new field to the INVOICE.SCX form.

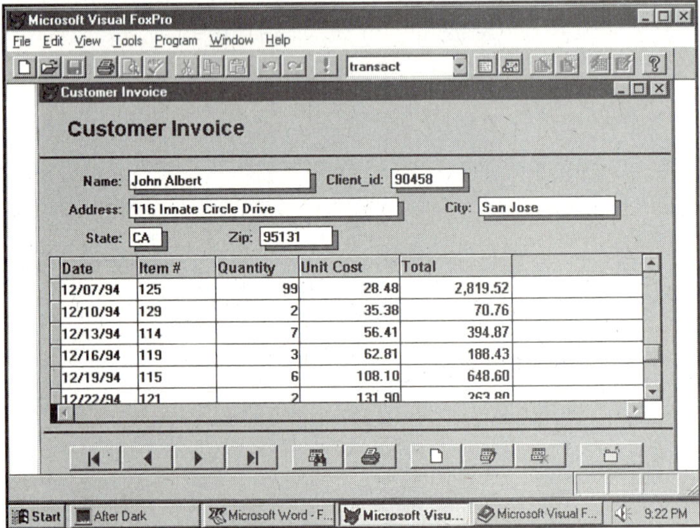

FIGURE 24.17.
The modified INVOICE.SCX form.

Report Wizards

When you execute a Report Wizard option, the Report Wizards dialog box displays, and you can choose from the following three Report Wizards:

- The Group/Total Report Wizard
- The One-To-Many Report Wizard
- The Report Wizard

The Group/Total Report Wizard guides you through the creation of a report form that sorts records into up to three groupings and optionally provides subtotals and totals for numeric fields. The One-To-Many Report Wizard guides you through the creation of a report that groups records from a parent table with records from a child table. The Report Wizard guides you through the generation of a simple report form with one, two, or three columns. The steps required for all three of the reports are fairly simple and straightforward. In this section, you will be shown how to use the Report Wizard.

Step 1: Select the Table and Fields

To begin, you use the Step 1 dialog box (shown in Figure 24.3) to choose a table as the data source. Your next mission is to select fields that you want to include in your report. You choose fields from the list of available fields, which contains the fields in the selected table. You select fields just as you did for the Form Wizard. When you are finished choosing fields, you press the Next button to proceed to Step 2.

Step 2: Specify the Report Style

As you can see in Figure 24.18, you choose one of the three available styles for your new report in Step 2. The graphic at the top of the dialog box changes to illustrate how the selected style will appear. Notice in Figure 24.18 that the picture illustrates what the Ledger style looks like.

Step 3: Specify the Layout

You specify how many columns you want in your new report. You can have one, two, or three columns in your report.

In addition, you are asked to select the report layout. You can select horizontal layout if you want the field names to appear at the top of the columns of data as column titles. You can select vertical layout if you want the report to appear like a form with field titles running down the left side of each report column.

You are treated to a graphical representation of a multicolumn report, which reflects the number of columns you selected, as shown in Figure 24.19.

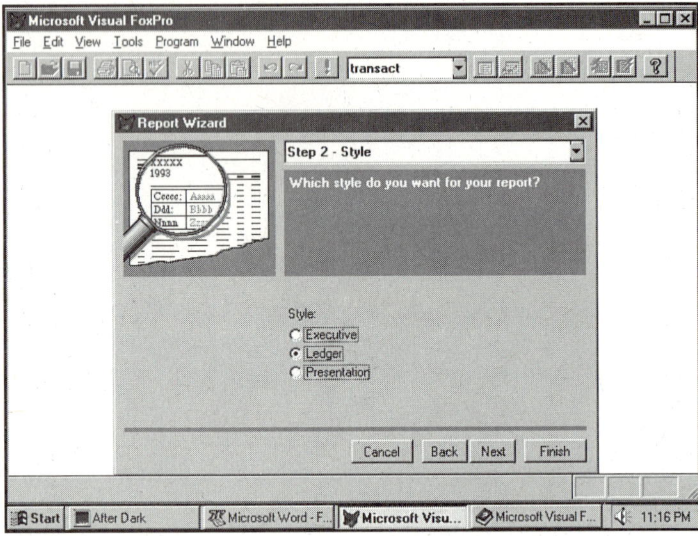

FIGURE 24.18.
The Report Wizard—Step 2 dialog box.

Also, you can specify whether you want a column or row layout and whether you want portrait or landscape orientation for your report.

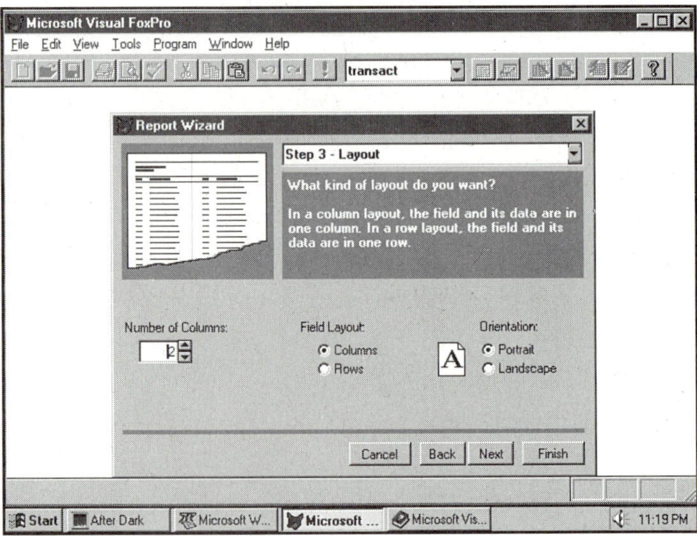

FIGURE 24.19.
The Report Wizard—Step 3 dialog box.

Step 4: Designate Sorting Order

You use the Step 4 dialog box, as shown in Figure 24.20, to specify the sort order. This step is identical to the Form Wizard Step 3 dialog box. This step is skipped if the data source for your report is a query.

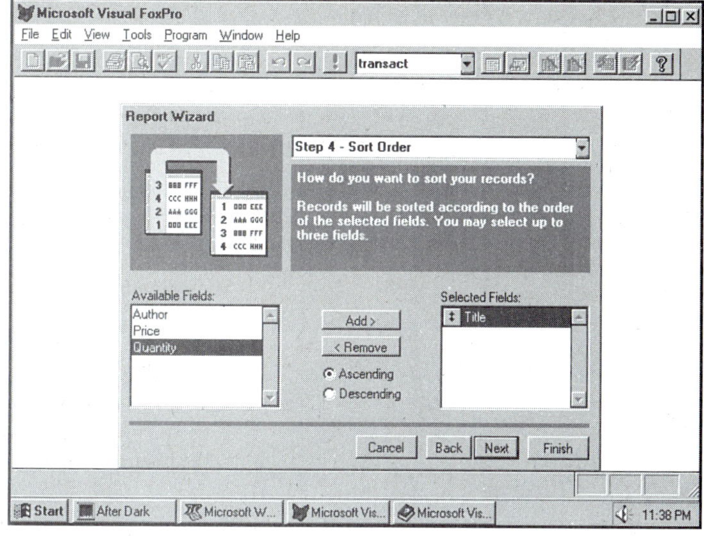

FIGURE 24.20.
The Report Wizard—Step 4 dialog box.

Step 5: The Final Step

Now you have reached the last step, Report Wizard Step 5, as shown in Figure 24.21. At this point, your report is defined. All you have to do is enter a title for your report and specify whether you want fields that do not fit on the line to be wrapped. If you like, you can preview your report by pressing the Preview button. The Preview window appears, containing a representation of your report, as shown in Figure 24.22. As demonstrated in Figure 24.23, the Preview window provides you with options for zooming the report to different sizes so that you can view its overall layout or study its details.

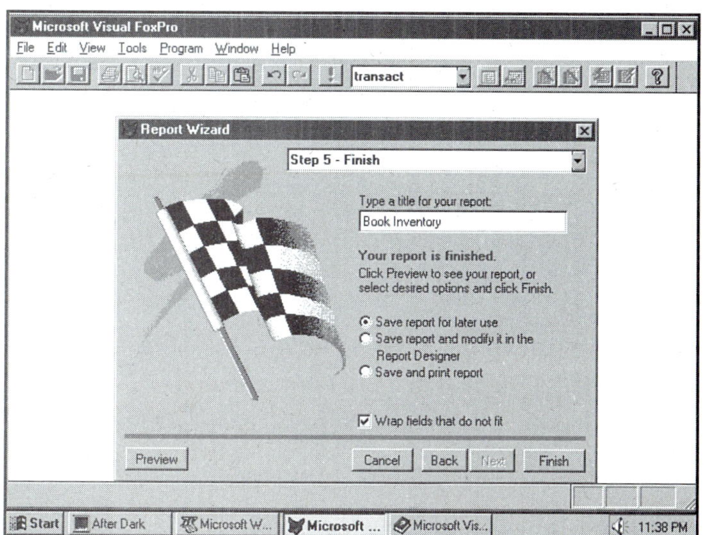

FIGURE 24.21.
The Report Wizard—Step 5 dialog box.

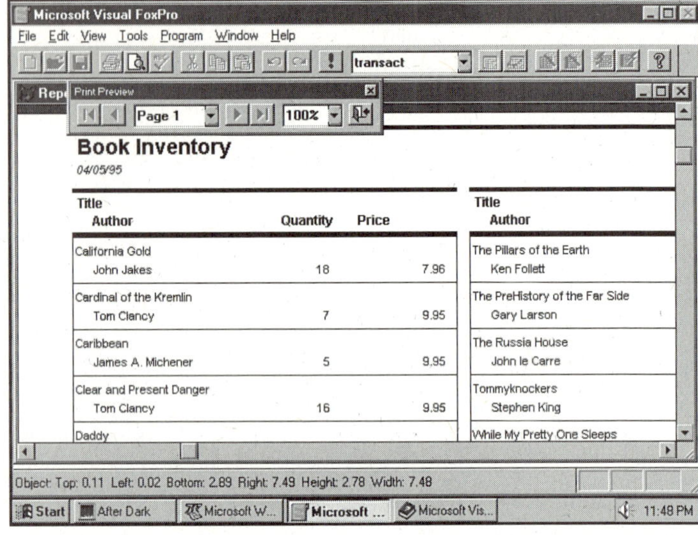

FIGURE 24.22.
A sample Report Wizard Page Preview window.

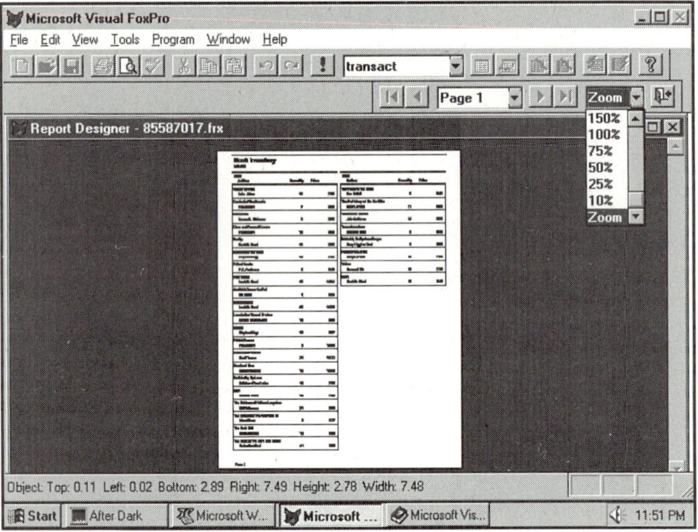

FIGURE 24.23.
Zooming a sample report page in the Preview window.

You have the same choices for saving and exiting in the Report Wizard that you have for the other wizards. The three save options are defined as follows:

- Save report for later use

  You select this option if you want only to create a report (FRX) file. Later on you can use the report file to generate and print the report.

- Save and print report

  You select this option if you want the Report Wizard to create, generate, and print the report. First, the Save As dialog box appears, and you supply a name for the report. Then the Report Wizard saves the report. Finally, the Print dialog box displays. You select the appropriate print options, and the report prints.

- Save report and modify it with the Report Designer

  You select this option if you want to save the report form and make custom changes with the Report Designer (`MODIFY REPORT` command).

Regardless of the option you choose, the Report Wizard displays the Save As dialog box. You supply a name for the report, and the Report Designer window appears so that you can make custom changes.

The Report Wizards quickly and easily create attractive reports. However, there is a trade-off. The wizards make assumptions about things, such as the width of display fields, that may not be acceptable. Furthermore, you might require custom picture templates and display function codes. However, there is a solution. The third option allows you to save the report and invoke the FoxPro Report Designer so that you can make your own refinements to your report.

The One-To-Many Report Wizard

When you create a report with the One-To-Many Report Wizard, you step through six dialog boxes. The first four are identical to the first four steps in the One-To-Many Form Wizard. The last two are almost identical to the last two steps in the standard Report Wizard. The only difference is that a One-To-Many Report Wizard can only create a single column report. Here are the six steps:

1. Choose fields from the parent (main) table
2. Choose fields from the related table
3. Establish relationship
4. Designate sort order
5. Define layout
6. Preview, save, and exit

If you supply the One-To-Many Report Wizard with the same responses supplied to the One-To-Many Form Wizard when you created the form shown in Figure 24.14, you will get a report similar to the one shown in Figure 24.24. Notice that the field caption properties from the database container were used by the One-To-Many Report Wizard as report headings.

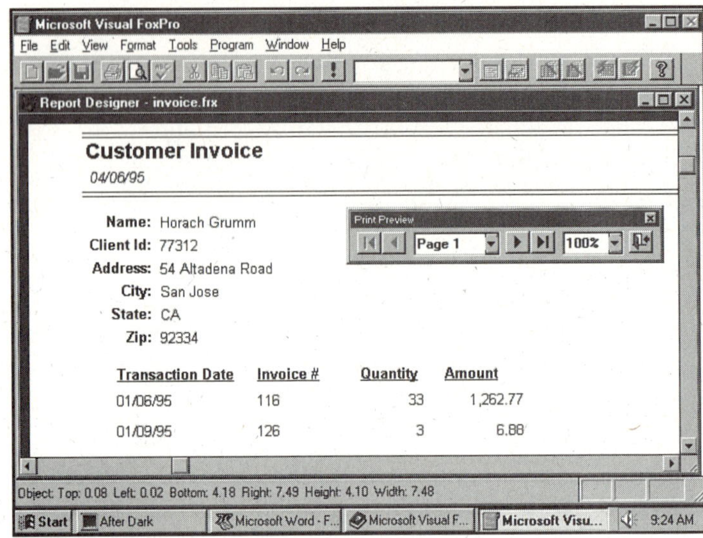

FIGURE 24.24.
An example report preview created using the One-To-Many Report Wizard.

Group/Total Report Wizard

The Group/Total Report Wizard is very similar to the Report Wizard. The Group/Total Report Wizard guides you through the creation of a report form that sorts records. There are two differences between the two wizards:

- The Group/Total Report Wizard does not allow you to build multiple column reports and has no layout step.
- The Group/Total Report Wizard lets you enter up to three groupings and optionally provides subtotals and totals for numeric fields.

The Group/Total Report Wizard has five steps:

1. Select the table or field
2. Select the report style
3. Specify three-level grouping
4. Specify sort order
5. Finish up

The frame for Step 3 is the only one that is different from the Report Wizard. This frame lets you specify up to three levels of grouping. There are three drop-down list boxes; each one represents a level of grouping. You choose one of the fields from the drop-down list to specify the field that will be used for a group level.

You can specify also whether you want report totals and group-level subtotals. Totals will be printed for each numeric field selected for the report.

The remaining process is identical to the Report Wizard process.

Query Wizards

If you are a Query Designer expert, you probably will not need to use the Query Wizards. They do not provide the same full functionality provided by the Visual FoxPro Query Designer. However, if you are a first-time user, the Query Wizards will provide you with an invaluable tool for searching multiple tables for records that match some criteria. The Query Wizards use a simple step-by-step procedure that leads you through the process of creating a query. The Query Wizards also help you learn SQL queries without being overwhelmed by the complexity of the Visual FoxPro Query Designer.

When you execute the Query Wizard, the Wizard Selection dialog box displays as shown in Figure 24.25. You are asked to specify which of the Query Wizards you want to use. Here is a list of the Query Wizards and a brief description of what they do:

- The Query Wizard—Creates a query from one or more tables
- The Cross-Tab Wizard—Displays summarized data in a spreadsheet format
- The Local View Wizard—Creates a view using local data
- The Remote View Wizard—Creates a view using remote data

The Local View Wizard, Remote View Wizard, and Query Wizard are almost identical. If you learn one, then you have learned all three. Therefore, I will give you a tour of the Query Wizard. In addition, you will be shown how to use the Cross-Tab Wizard.

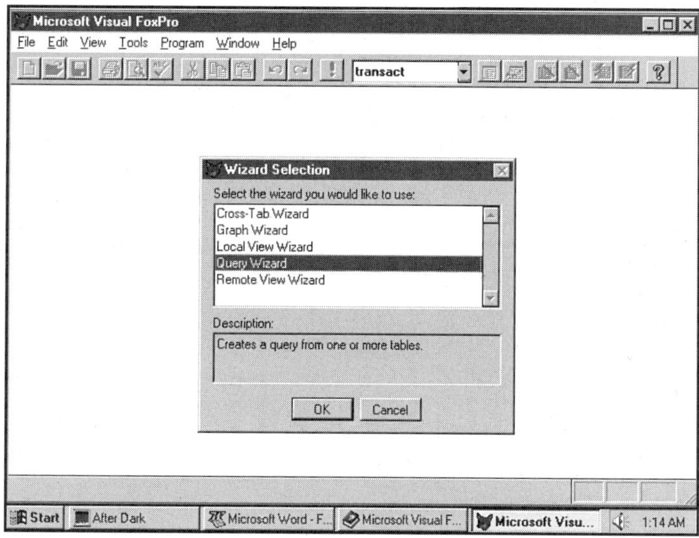

FIGURE 24.25.
The Query Wizard Selection dialog box.

The Query, Local View, and Remote View Wizards

The Query Wizard searches one or more tables for records that match a specified criterion. This wizard creates an updatable query file with a .QPR extension. Then when you run your query, a data set, which reflects the query specifications, is made available for you to edit. The changes you make to the query results records will be reflected in the original tables on which the query is based. This is the same type of query created when you use the Visual FoxPro Query Designer.

The Local View Wizard is almost identical to the Query Wizard. The only difference is that the Local View Wizard stores the query results in the currently active database container (DBC) file. A database must be in use before you can use the Local View Wizard. The Query Wizard stores its results in a query (QPR) file. The step for creating the query for both Wizards is identical.

If you have established a connection to remote data, you can use the Remote View Wizard. The steps for creating a query are the same as for the Query and Local View Wizards. The resultant query is stored in the currently active database container (DBC) file.

You can use FoxPro aggregate functions (such as `AVG`, `COUNT`, `MAX`, `MIN`, or `SUM`) in your queries, and the query results are read-only. You use a read-only query result in a browse operation or incorporate them into a report. However, you cannot update the records.

Both the Query Wizard and Local View Wizard lead you through five steps to create a query. Each of these steps is discussed in the following sections. Here is a list of the steps:

1. Select tables and fields to be used in the query
2. Establish relationships
3. Establish the sort order of records (optional)
4. Add filtering to specify which records are received
5. Browse and save the query

Step 1: Select the Table and Fields

The first thing you do is to use the Step 1 dialog box, as shown in Figure 24.26, to select fields from tables or views. You select the tables and fields the same way you do for the other wizards. The only difference is that you can choose fields from more than one table. You choose a table and then move the fields from the Available Fields list box to the Selected Fields list box. Fields in the Selected Fields list box will be included in the query results.

When you use tables or views from a database, you can use only tables that are in the currently active database. Notice in Figure 24.26 that there are three tables and a local view named Sales.

Three fields, `Trans_date`, `Quantity`, and `Amt`, were chosen from the Transact.DBF table. Now the `Title` and `Author` fields will be chosen from the Books.DBF table. All five fields will appear in the query results. When you are finished choosing fields, press the Next button to display the next step.

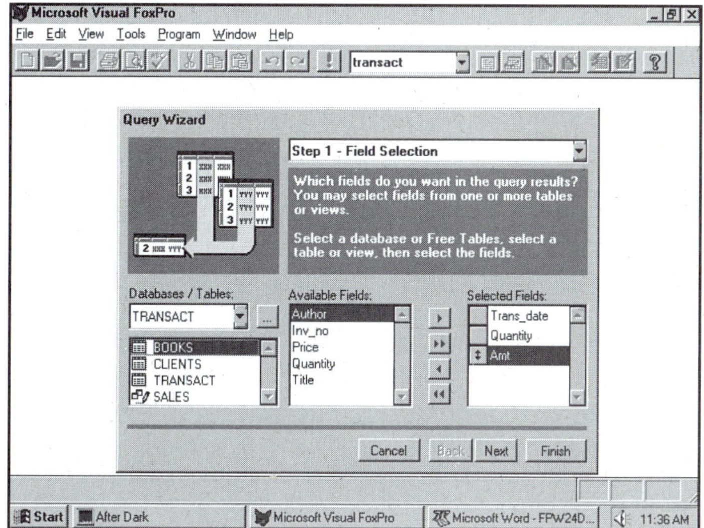

FIGURE 24.26.
The Query Wizard—Step 1 dialog box.

Step 2: Establish Relationships

If you select more than one table in Step 1, the Step 2 dialog box appears, as shown in Figure 24.27. You use this dialog box to specify the relationship between the tables. In other words, you *join* the tables. You select matching fields from a parent table and a child table using the combo boxes and then press the Add button.

In this example, you established a join between the Transact table and the Books table. The tables are related on fields `Transact.Inv_No` and `Books.Inv_No`.

All you have to do to delete the relationship between two tables is select the relationship and press the Remove button.

Step 3: Designate Sorting Order

In the next step, Step 3, you specify how the records retrieved by the query are sorted. You can select up to three fields from the Available Fields list box to establish the order of the result table. Figure 24.28 shows the Step 3 dialog box.

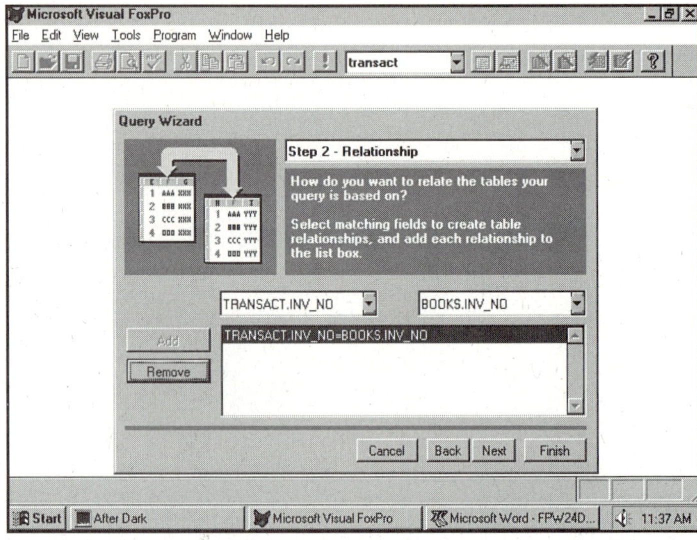

FIGURE 24.27.
The Query Wizard—Step 2 dialog box.

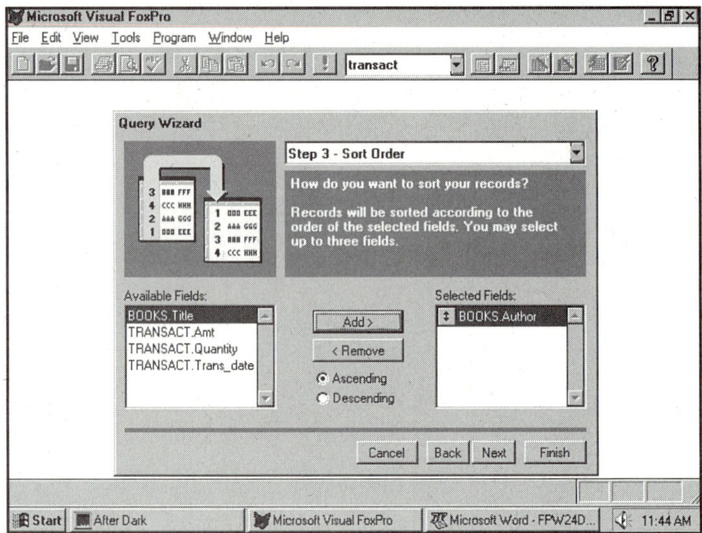

FIGURE 24.28.
The Query Wizard—Step 3 dialog box.

This example shows that the result table will be sorted on the `Books.Author` field.

Step 4: Filtering

Figure 24.29 displays the Step 4 dialog box.

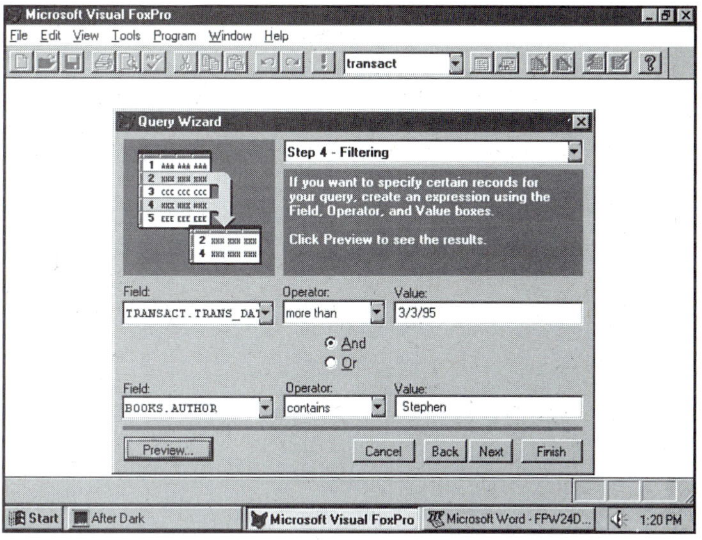

FIGURE 24.29.
The Query Wizard—Step 4 dialog box.

In this dialog box, you have the option of adding an optional expression to further limit the records retrieved by the query. Records that satisfy the expression are included in the query result. The expression consists of a field name, an operator, and example text. For example, the expression

```
Field          Expression      Example Text
Trans_Date     More Than       3/11/95
```

designates that all records for all transactions that initiated data after the 11th of March 1995 will be included in the query results. The comparison operators are selected from a drop-down list, as presented in Table 24.2.

Table 24.2. Query Wizard comparison operators.

Operator	*Description*
Equals	Designates that the field must match the example text.
Not Equals	Designates that the field must not match example text.
More Than	Specifies that the field must be greater than the value in the example text.
Less Than	Specifies that the field must be less than the value in the example text.
Is Blank	Specifies that the field must contain blank characters.

continues

Table 24.2. continued

Operator	*Description*
Contains	Specifies that the text must contain the value in the example text.
Between	Specifies that the field must be greater than or equal to the lower value and less than or equal to the higher value in the example text. The two values in the example text are comma delimited. (`INVOICES.IDATE Between 05/10/95,05/12/95` would match records for the 10th, 11th, and 12th of May 1995.)
In	Specifies that the field must match one of several comma-delineated examples in the example text.

You can use the Step 4 Expression Builder to formulate the most complex filter expression.

You can add more expressions, and when you do, they are combined with an `AND` operator. This means that all expressions must evaluate to a Logical true value if a record is to be included in the results. Here is an example:

```
    CITY = 'Boston'
AND
    LASTNAME = "Hubbell"
```

The preceding expression designates that all data from Boston and for people with the last name Hubbell will be included in the query results.

If you want all records to be included in the results that match either expression but not both, you can press the OR button or add the `OR` operator between the expressions. For example, if you want all data from Boston and Los Angeles to be included in the results, specify the following:

```
    CITY = 'Boston'
OR
    CITY = "Los Angeles"
```

You can also add parentheses around an expression to ensure that the expressions are evaluated correctly. In the example shown in Figure 24.29, it is requested that the result table contain records with a transaction date after 3/11/95 for an author whose name contains Stephen.

You have the option to preview the query based on the current choices. Just press the Preview button and a Browse window displays like the one shown in Figure 24.30

Step 5: The Final Step

Now you have reached the last step of the Query Wizard, which is shown in Figure 24.31.

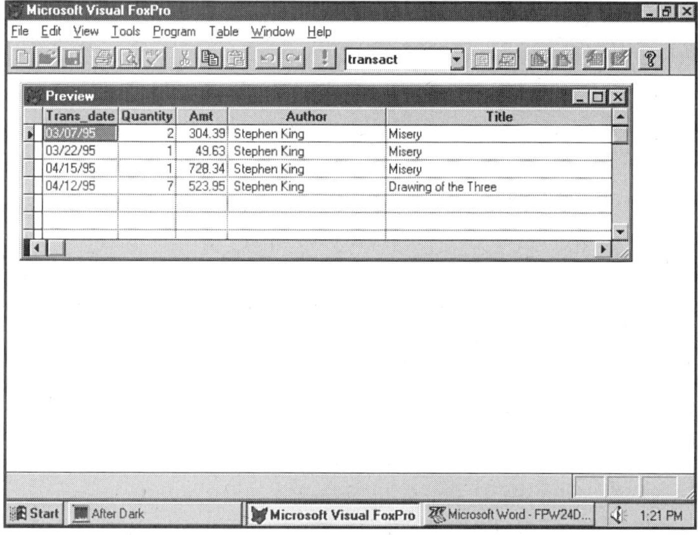

FIGURE 24.30.
A preview of the query results.

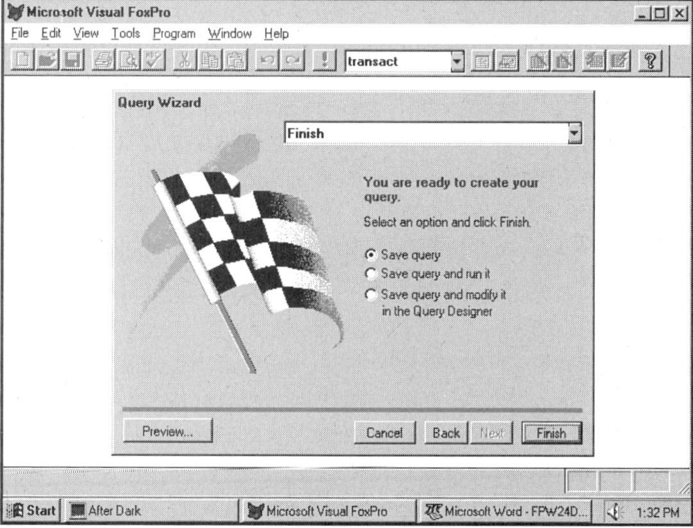

FIGURE 24.31.
The Query Wizard—Step 5 dialog box.

At this point, your query is defined. All you have to do now is to enter a name, and save and run your query. If you like, you can preview your query by pressing the Preview… button, and a Browse window containing the query results appears as shown in Figure 24.30. If you are satisfied with the previewed results, select one of the following options and choose the Finish button:

- Save query

  You select this option if you want only to create and save a FoxPro query (QPR) file. Later you can run the query file.

- Save query and run it

  You select this option if you want the Query Wizard to save the query and display it in a Browse window. First, the Save As dialog box appears, and you supply a name for the query. Then the query is saved, and the Browse window displays.

- Save query and modify it in the Query Designer

  You select this option if you want to save the query and make additional changes with the Query Designer.

The Local and Remote View Wizards have similar save options. Instead of specifying the name of a QPR file, you specify the name of the view.

The Cross-Tab Wizard

The Cross-Tab Wizard steps you through the process of creating a query that summarizes data in a spreadsheet format. Suppose that you have a table containing the types of toys manufactured by your company and the number of toys purchased by different age groups. You can create a cross-tab query showing how many toys are purchased by different age groups. You place the `AgeGroup` field in the row heading column and the `TypeofToy` field in the column header field. You place the `NumberSold` field in the grid. You also can have a total or summary column.

The example presented in the following subsections steps you through the simple process of creating a cross-tab query on a table containing monthly stock quotes for various companies. The table contains the following fields, which will be used in the query.

Field	*Description*
`Name`	A character field containing a symbol for the name of the company
`Month`	A character field containing the year and month stored in the form *YYYY* month
`Last`	A numeric field containing the closing stock quote for the first business day of the month

Step 1: Select the Table and Fields

The first step is to choose a table and at least three fields from the table to be used in the cross-tab query. If you are playing what-if games, you may want to choose more than three fields so you can try different fields in the cross-tab query. Figure 24.32 shows the Step 1 dialog box. In this example, the company symbol (`Name`) field, the month of the stock quote (`Month`) field, and the closing stock quote for the first business day of the month (`Last`) field were chosen.

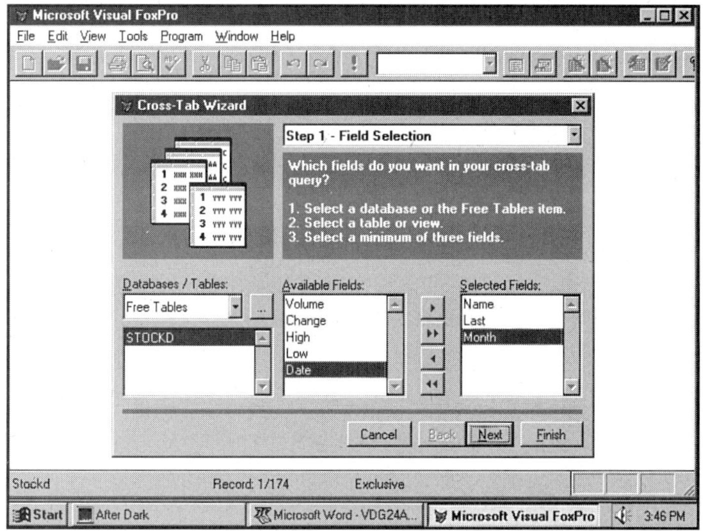

FIGURE 24.32.
The Cross-Tab Query Wizard—Step 1 dialog box.

Step 2: Specify the Layout

In this step, you drag a field from the Available Fields list box to the layout form. In this case, the `Name` field is the row heading column and the `Month` field is the column heading field. Values of the `Last` field are displayed in the grid cells. Figure 24.33 shows the Step 2 dialog box after the fields are dragged to their respective places in the layout.

This is not a great example since the whole purpose of the Cross-Tab Wizard is to summarize data. This example does not illustrate that if you have multiple values for a grid cell, they are summed. The STOCKD.DBF table has only one item for each company and each month. Of course, a summation of stock prices does not make sense.

Step 3: The Total Column

Step 3 provides you with the option of having a Totals column at the right of the spreadsheet grid. You are provided with the following options:

- Sum of data—Displays the summation of the values in a row for each row
- Number of cells containing data—Displays a count of the number of cells in the grid row that contain data
- Percentage of the table total—Displays a percentage of the total value that the sum of the values in a single row represent
- None—Does not display the Totals column at the right of the spreadsheet

Figure 24.34 shows the Step 3 dialog box.

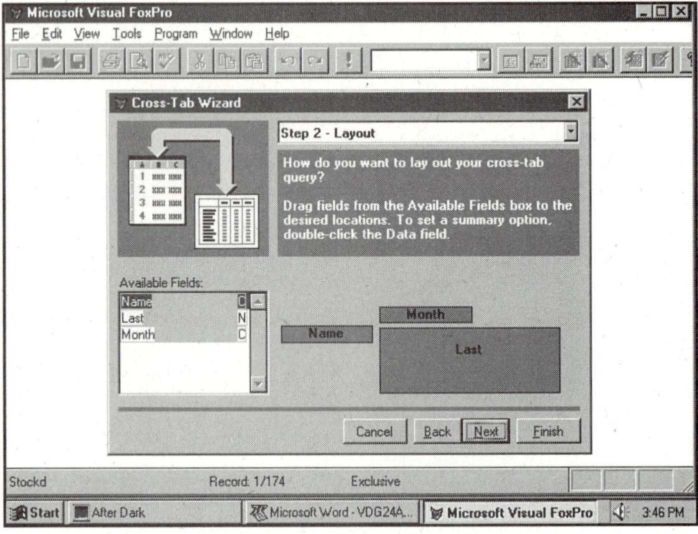

FIGURE 24.33.
The Cross-Tab Query Wizard—Step 2 dialog box.

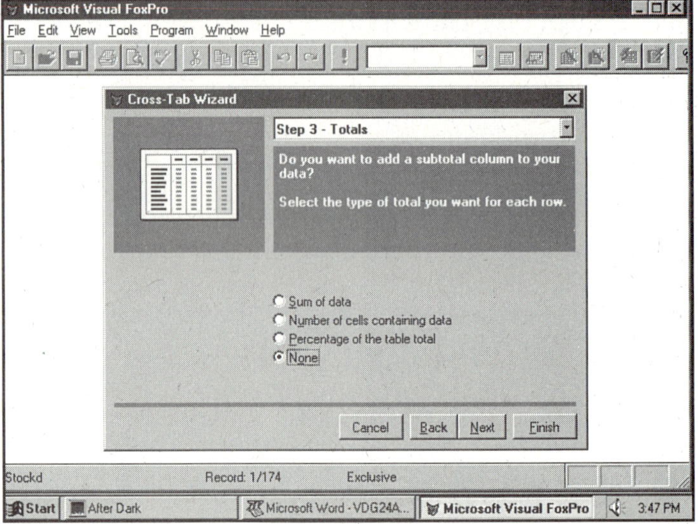

FIGURE 24.34.
The Cross-Tab Query Wizard—Step 3 dialog box.

Step 4: The Final Step

Step 4 contains the same options for saving your cross-tab query as the other Query Wizards. It also has a Preview button that lets you review the results of your cross-tab query. Figure 24.35 shows a preview of the cross-tab query. The Browse window in Figure 24.35 shows the monthly value of the various stocks.

FIGURE 24.35.
A preview of the cross-tab query.

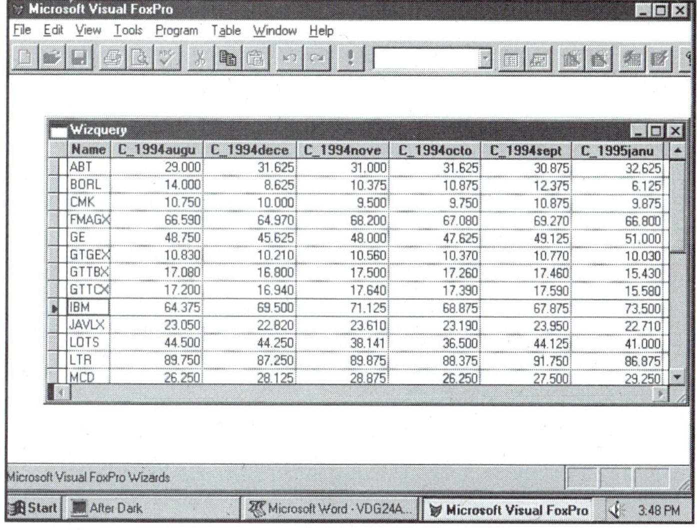

Name	C_1994augu	C_1994dece	C_1994nove	C_1994octo	C_1994sept	C_1995janu
ABT	29.000	31.625	31.000	31.625	30.875	32.625
BORL	14.000	8.625	10.375	10.875	12.375	6.125
CMK	10.750	10.000	9.500	9.750	10.875	9.875
FMAGX	66.590	64.970	68.200	67.080	69.270	66.800
GE	48.750	45.625	48.000	47.625	49.125	51.000
GTGEX	10.830	10.210	10.560	10.370	10.770	10.030
GTTBX	17.080	16.800	17.500	17.260	17.460	15.430
GTTCX	17.200	16.940	17.640	17.390	17.590	15.580
IBM	64.375	69.500	71.125	68.875	67.875	73.500
JAVLX	23.050	22.820	23.610	23.190	23.950	22.710
LOTS	44.500	44.250	38.141	36.500	44.125	41.000
LTR	89.750	87.250	89.875	88.375	91.750	86.875
MCD	26.250	28.125	28.875	26.250	27.500	29.250

Notice that during this six-month period the value of Borland International (BORL) and Lotus (LOTS) stock went down, whereas the value of IBM stock went up. Also, stock in Abbot Labs (ABT), a pharmaceutical firm, went up in value with the demise of the national health care program. MacDonald's stock went up also.

The Graph Wizard

The Graph Wizard steps you through the process of creating a graphical representation of data in a table. In this example, a table containing IBM stock prices, ranging over a six-month period, will be plotted.

Step 1: Select the Table and Fields

The first step for the Graph Wizard is exactly like the first step for the other Query Wizards and is shown in Figure 24.36. You choose a table and field in the table to plot. In the example, the `High`, `Low`, `Last`, and `Date` fields from table IBM.DBF are chosen. Here is a description of the selected fields:

Selected Field	*Description*
`Date`	Date of stock trading
`High`	Highest stock price for the day
`Low`	Lowest stock price for the day
`Last`	Closing stock price for the day

Figure 24.36 shows the Step 1 dialog box.

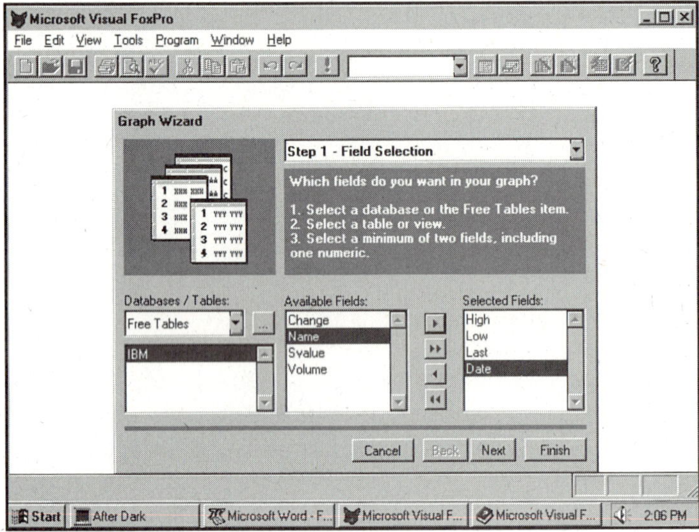

FIGURE 24.36.
The Graph Wizard—Step 1 dialog box.

Step 2: Specify the Graph Layout

In Step 2, shown in Figure 24.37, you specify which field will appear as the axis of the graph and which fields will be plotted on the ordinate (Data Series). You drag a field from the Available Fields list box to the appropriate place. As you can see, the `Date` field has been dragged to the Axis box. The other fields were dragged to the Data Series list box.

Step 3: Select a Graph Style

Figure 24.38 shows the Step 3 dialog box. In this step, you choose one of the pictures, which represents the style of the graph that will be plotted.

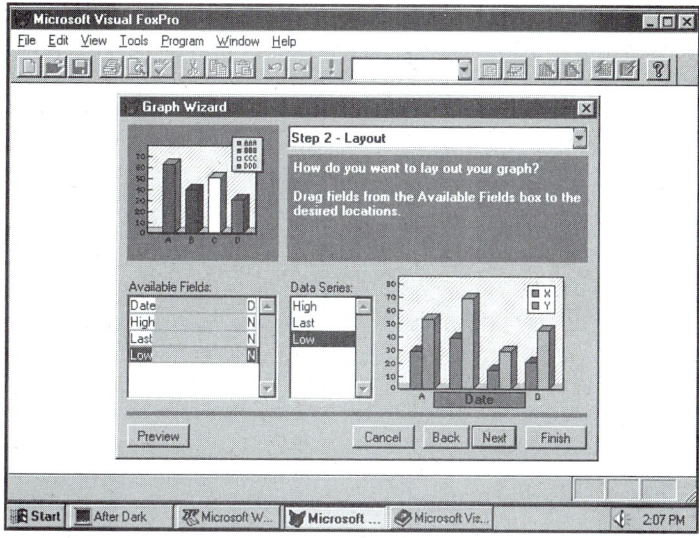

FIGURE 24.37.
The Graph Wizard—Step 2 dialog box.

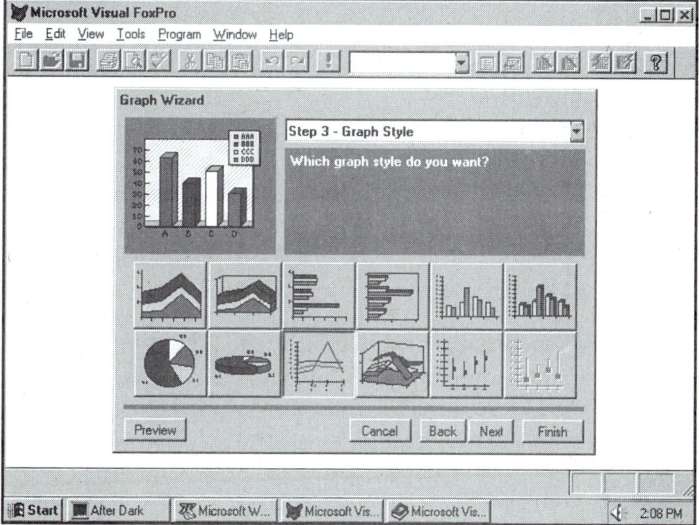

FIGURE 24.38.
The Graph Wizard—Step 3 dialog box.

Step 4: The Final Step

Step 4 is the final step. You can save your graph definition information in a memo field table. Other than that, the save options are the same as for the other Query Wizards. The final step has a Preview button that lets you review the results of your graph. Figure 24.39 shows the resultant graph Preview window. It displays a plot for the high, low and closing prices for IBM stock over a six-month period.

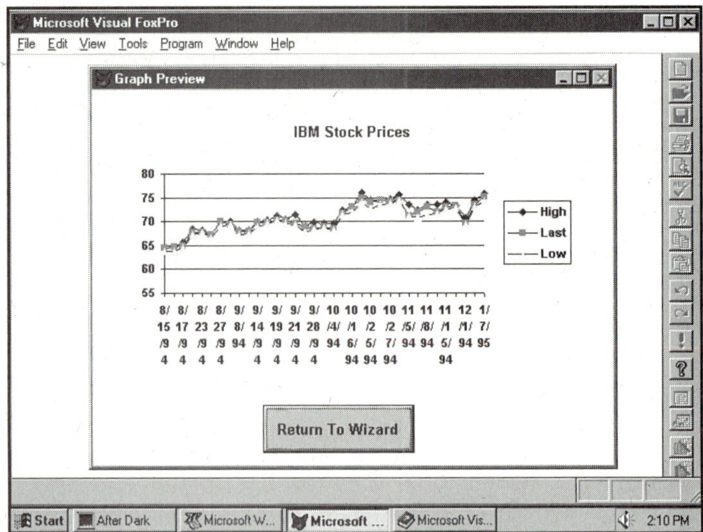

FIGURE 24.39.
An example of the Graph Wizard Preview window.

The Label Wizard

The Label Wizard leads you through the process of creating mailing labels. You can create mailing labels for a variety of Avery label types in English or metric label sizes. When you execute the Label Wizard, the Step 1 dialog box appears. You choose a table or view as the data source. You can choose a free table, or a table or view from a database. Then you press the Next button and proceed to the Step 2.

Step 2: The Label Type

The Step 2 dialog box (shown in Figure 24.40) displays, and you specify an Avery label type. You have the option of viewing labels in either English or metric dimensions. You select from the list the Avery label that you want to use for your mailing labels.

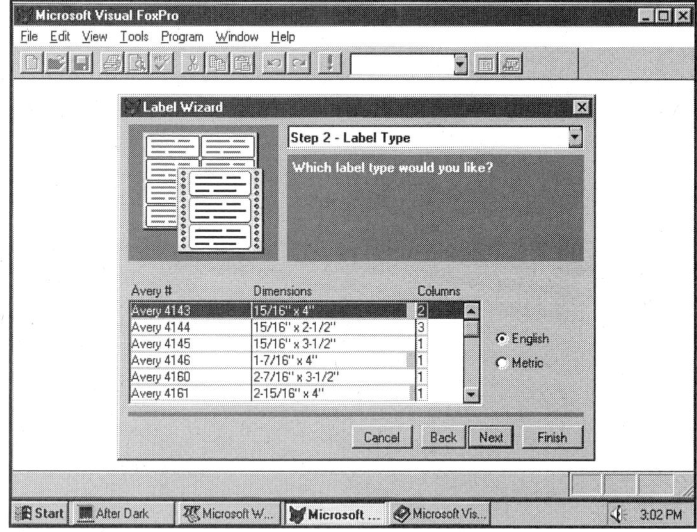

FIGURE 24.40.
The Label Wizard—Step 2 dialog box.

Step 3: The Layout

In the next step, Step 3, you select fields in the order you want them to appear on the mailing label. (See Figure 24.41.) You can either double-click the field name or select the field name and choose the right-arrow button to select a field just as you select a field for the Form Wizard.

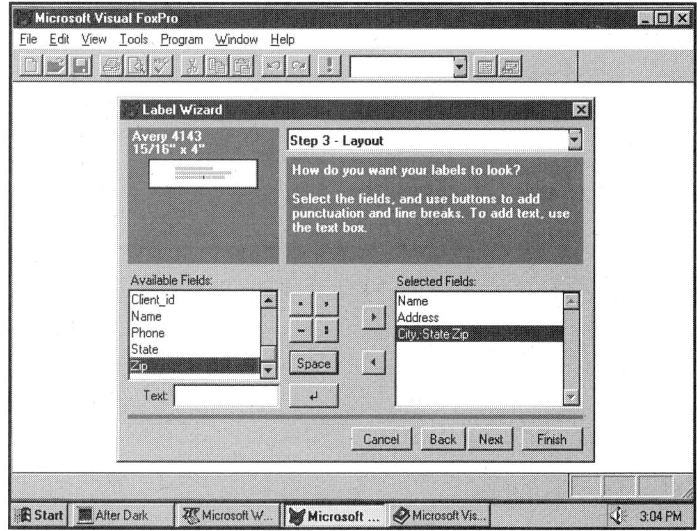

FIGURE 24.41.
The Label Wizard—Step 3 dialog box.

You choose the Enter button to start a new line. The Enter button is the button beneath the Space button. If you want to place more than one field on the same line, follow these steps:

- Add the first field
- Press the Space button or one of the punctuation buttons
- Add the next field. For example, you can specify `City, State` with the following steps:
  Select the `City` field
  Press the comma (,) button
  Press the Space button
  Select the `State` field

You can find out whether the label contents will fit on the label by viewing the picture at the top of the dialog box. This picture is a miniature representation of your label. You can see if the fields are wider than the mailing label or if you have too many text lines for the label.

Step 4: Designate Sorting Order

The Step 4 dialog box prompts you to define the sort order of the labels. This dialog box is exactly like the Form and Report Wizard Sort Order dialog boxes.

Step 5: The Final Step

You have reached the last step, Step 5, which is shown in Figure 24.42. At this point, your labels are defined. If you like, you can preview your labels by pressing the Preview… button. The Preview window contains a representation of how your labels will look when printed. (See Figure 24.43.)

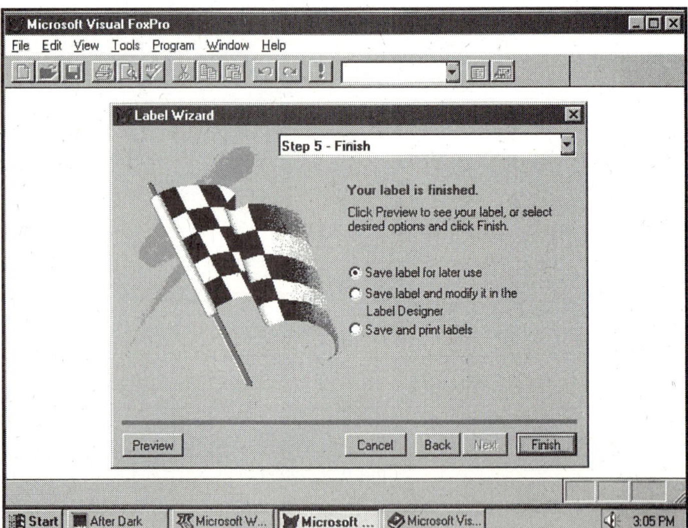

FIGURE 24.42.
The Label Wizard—Step 5 dialog box.

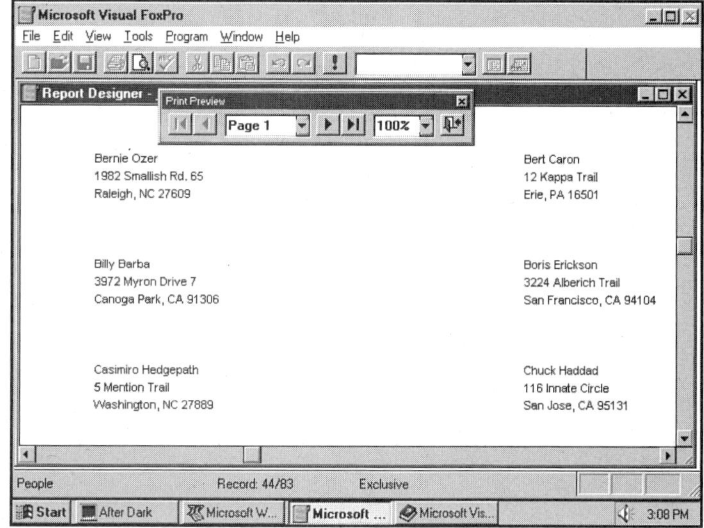

FIGURE 24.43.
A sample Label Wizard Print Preview window.

The three save options are defined as follow:

- Save labels for later use

  You select this option if you want only to create a FoxPro label (LBX) file. Later you can use the label file to generate and print labels.
- Save label and modify it in the Label Designer

  You select this option if you want to save the label form and make custom changes to it with the Label Designer (`MODIFY LABEL` command).
- Save and print labels

  You select this option if you want the Label Wizard to create, generate, and print the labels. First, the Save As dialog box appears, and you supply a name for the labels. Then the labels are saved. Finally, the Print dialog box displays, you select the appropriate print options, and the wizard prints the labels.

For all three options, the Label Wizard displays the Save As dialog box. You supply a name for the label form, and the Report Layout window appears so that you can make custom changes.

The Label Wizard asks you a few questions, as do all the wizards, and then automatically creates mailing labels. However, there is a trade-off. The Label Wizard makes assumptions about things such as formatting fields. You might only want to use part of a field in a label, or you might require custom display templates and display codes. (See the discussion of the `@...SAY` command `PICTURE` and `FUNCTION` clauses in Chapter 9, "Full-Screen Data Editing.") There is a solution. With the third option, you can save the label file and invoke the FoxPro Report Layout window so that you can make refinements to your label forms.

The Mail Merge Wizard

The Mail Merge Wizard uses a Visual FoxPro table as a data source and translates data into a form that can be used by word processors. The word processor merges information in each record with a single main document. The main document can be any document with references to data in the data source file, such as a form letter, a label, or an envelope. If you are using Microsoft Word 2.0 or 6.0 for Windows, the Mail Merge Wizard executes Word to complete the mail merge process.

If you are using Microsoft Word 6.0 for Windows, before you begin, you must make sure that the FoxPro table is not opened in exclusive mode. You can use the Catalog Manager Settings dialog box to set the exclusive flag to the Off position. If the exclusive flag is set to the On position, a File in Use error occurs during the mail merge operation.

The Mail Merge Wizard procedure is composed of five very simple steps:

1. You are prompted to provide a data source (table) for the mail merge. You specify the table or view and selected fields from it to be included in the mail merge operation.
2. Specify your word processing program. (See Figure 24.44.)
3. If you are using Microsoft Word for Windows, select an existing main document or create a new one for the mail merge operation. (See Figure 24.45.)
4. If you are using Microsoft Word 6.0, select the type of main document you want to create (form letter, label, envelope, or catalog). (See Figure 24.46.)
5. If you are using Microsoft Word 2.0 or 6.0 for Windows, Word executes when you choose the Finish button so that you can continue with the mail merge process. (See Figure 24.47.)

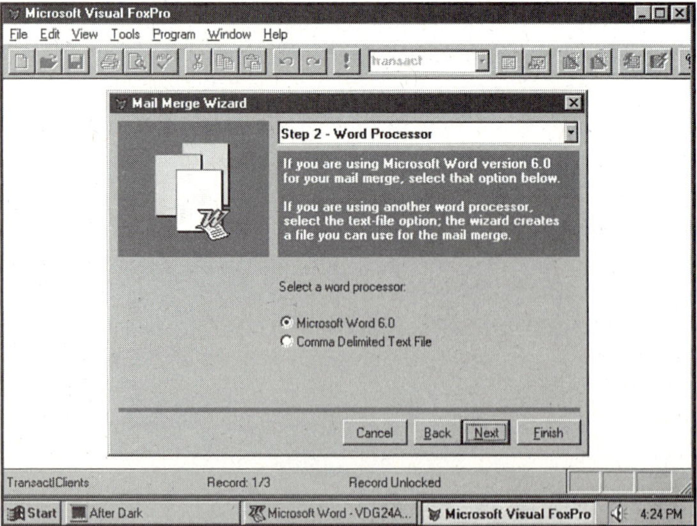

FIGURE 24.44.
The Mail Merge Wizard—Step 2 dialog box.

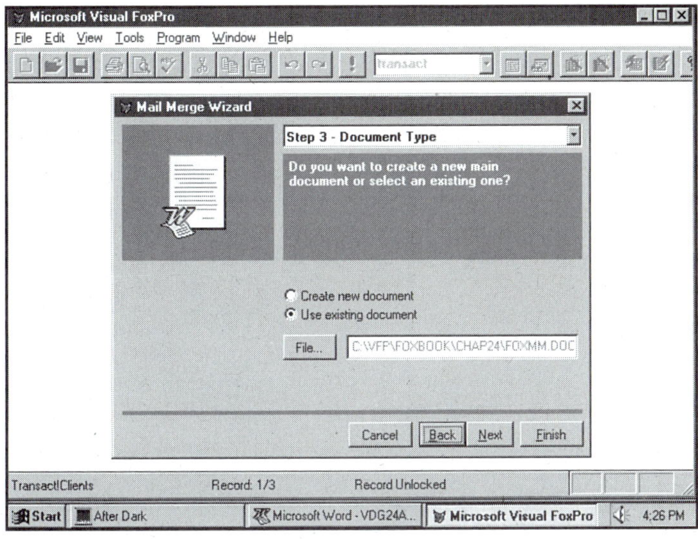

FIGURE 24.45.
The Mail Merge Wizard—Step 3 dialog box.

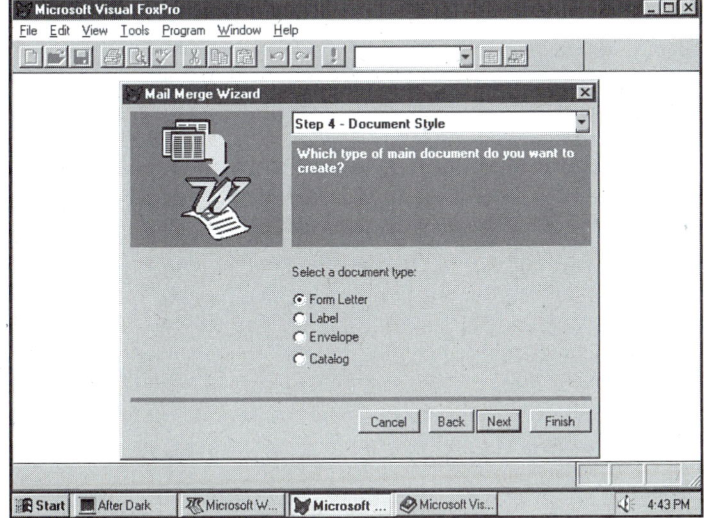

FIGURE 24.46.
The Mail Merge Wizard—Step 4 dialog box.

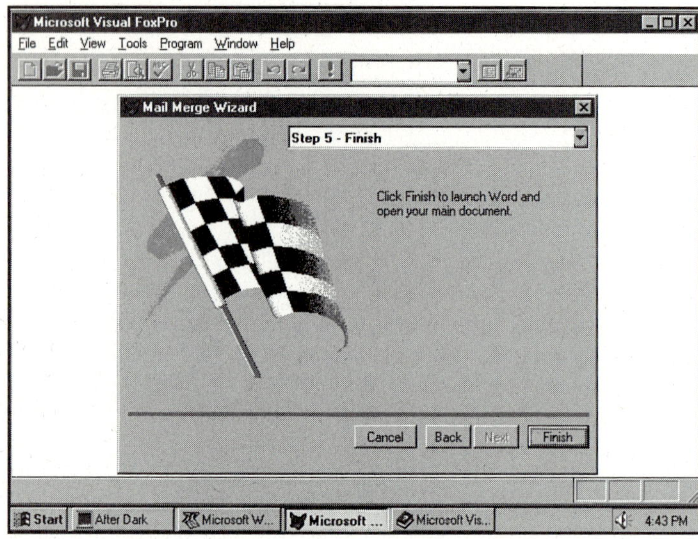

FIGURE 24.47.
The Mail Merge Wizard—Step 5 dialog box.

For Step 5, if you are not using Microsoft Word 6.0, when you press the Finish button, the Save As dialog box displays. The Mail Merge Wizard saves the source data as a comma delimited text file to be used by the word processor for mail merge processing.

If you are using Microsoft Word 2.0 or 6.0 for Windows, the Mail Merge Wizard executes Word to do the mail merge operation. Figure 24.48 shows a Word 6.0 for Windows screen with the mail merge template attached. This example also shows a main document named FOXMM.DOC. If you press the Insert Merge Field… button, a dialog box containing a list of the data fields appears. You choose a field, and it is inserted into the document. The text `<<FIRSTNAME>>` refers to the corresponding data field in the source data and is an example of a field that was inserted into the main document.

If you press the button to the right of the check mark button on the Mail Merge toolbar, Word 6.0 executes the mail merge operation and saves the results in a document. The resultant document is shown in Figure 24.49.

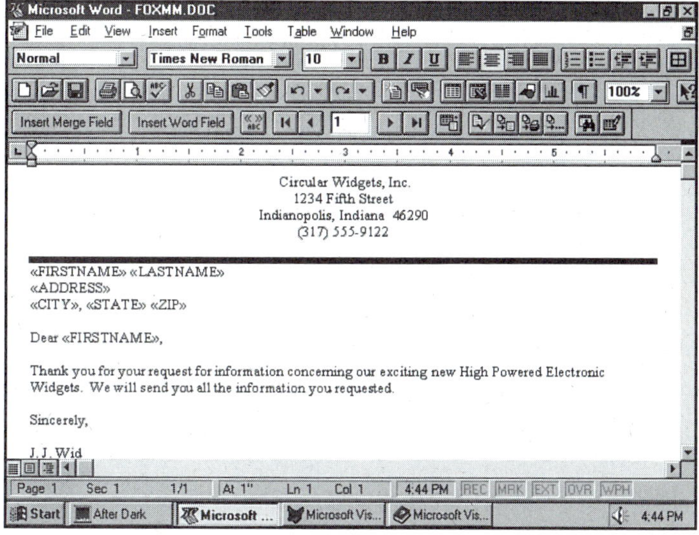

FIGURE 24.48.
The Word 6.0 for Windows screen with the mail merge main document displayed.

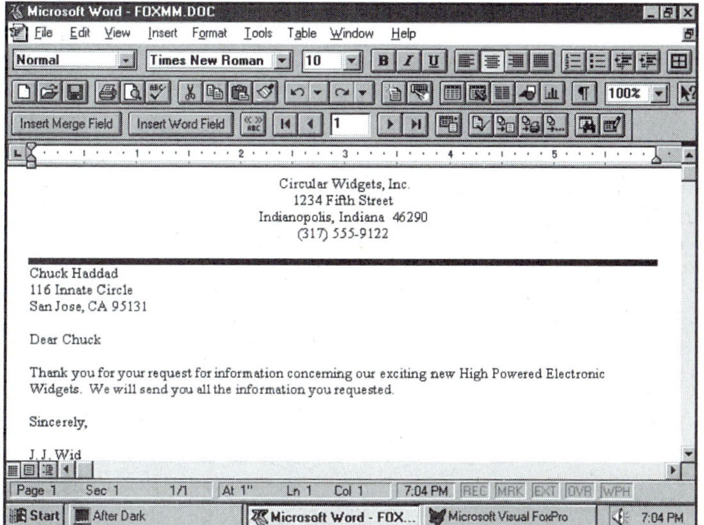

FIGURE 24.49.
The Word 6.0 for Windows screen with mail merge results displayed.

The PivotTable Wizard

The PivotTable Wizard builds either an Excel PivotTable or a Visual FoxPro form containing a PivotTable. A PivotTable is an interactive table that summarizes data from some data source such as an Excel database or a Visual FoxPro table or view. The Visual FoxPro PivotTable Wizard leads you through a simple three step procedure to create a PivotTable.

Step 1 is the same as it is for most other wizards. You choose a free table, or a table or view from a database. Then you select at least three fields.

In Step 2, as shown in Figure 24.50, you specify the layout for your PivotTable the same way you specify the layout for a cross-tab table. You drag fields from the Available Fields list box to the labeled areas on the PivotTable layout form. The labeled areas are defined as follows:

Row	Specifies a field whose values display as row labels
Column	Specifies a field whose values are used to display column headings
Data	Specifies a field whose values are summarized in the spreadsheet grid
Page	Specifies a field whose value is displayed on each page of the PivotTable

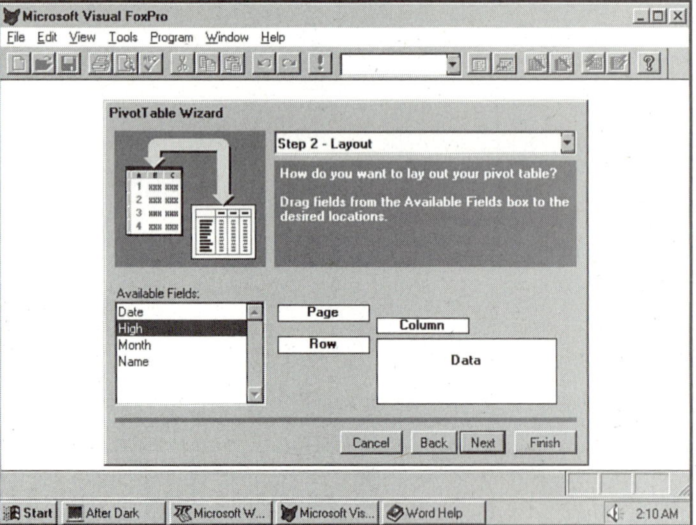

FIGURE 24.50.
The PivotTable Wizard—Step 2 dialog box.

For example, suppose that you have a table containing national sales information. The table contains the following fields:

Field	*Drag to Layout Field*
`State`	Page
`Year`	Row
`Sales`	Data
`Salesman`	Column

These specifications will yield a pivot table with a page for each `State` field, and each page will have data similar to the following example:

```
Texas
        Smith    Jones    Amil     Total
1992    2,345    3,333    1,234    6,874
1993    9,311    6,112    5,512   20,935
1994    8,313    9,531    6,331   24,175
Total  19,969   18,976   13,077   51,984
```

The third and final step lets you choose the type of pivot table created by the PivotTable Wizard. You can create an Excel PivotTable or a form containing a PivotTable grid.

You can also choose whether you want grand row totals and grand column totals. When you are ready to generate the PivotTable, just press the Finish button.

The Import Wizard

The Import Wizard asks you a few questions, as do all the wizards, and then transfers data from a file created by other applications into a new or an existing Visual FoxPro table. The Import Wizard supports a variety of formats, including the following:

- Text files (TXT)
- Microsoft Excel 2.0 through 5.0 (XLS)
- Lotus 123 Version 1-A (WKS)
- Lotus 123 Version 2.*x* (WK1)
- Lotus 123 Version 3.*x* (WK3)
- Paradox 3.5, 4.0, 4.5 (DB)
- Symphony (WR1 and WRK)
- Multiplan 4.1 (MOD)
- RapidFile (RPD)

Step 1: Specify the File to Be Imported

In the Step 1 dialog box, you specify the following:

- The type of file being imported
- The name of the file being imported
- Whether you want to create a table or append imported records to an existing file
- The name of the table that receives imported data

Step 1a: Specify the Options

The Import Wizard Step 1a dialog box appears if you are importing a text file. It shows imported data in a grid, as shown in Figure 24.51. If you are satisfied with the way the data appears in the grid, click on the Next button and proceed to Step 2. Otherwise, click on the Options... button, and the Options dialog box appears, as shown in Figure 24.52.

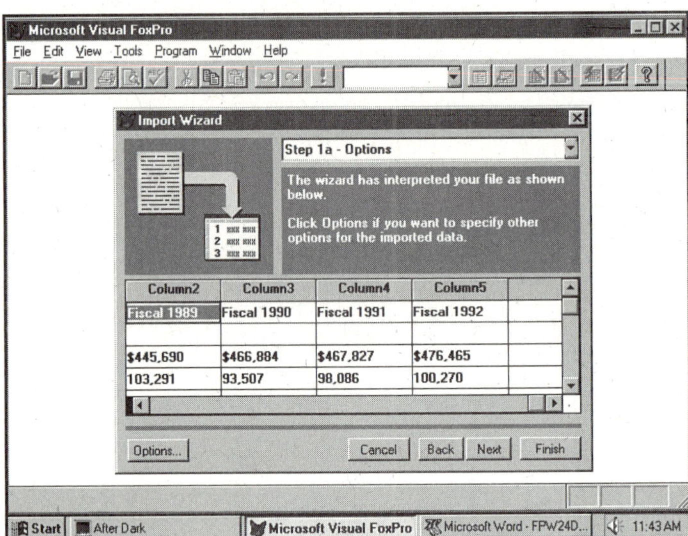

FIGURE 24.51.
The Import Wizard—Step 1a dialog box.

Step 2: Specify the Field Settings

In Step 2, you specify field names, field types, and the widths of the fields. The Step 2 dialog box shows data in the grid and text boxes to specify field attributes for the selected field. You click on a field column in the grid to select it and then modify its settings, as shown in Figure 24.53.

FIGURE 24.52.
The Import Wizard Options dialog box.

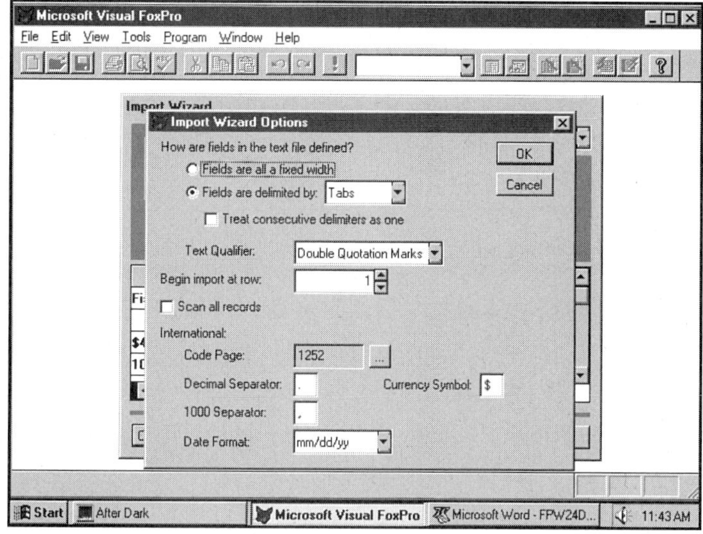

FIGURE 24.53.
The Import Wizard—Step 2 dialog box.

It would be nice if during the importing operation Visual FoxPro would ignore currency symbols and commas while converting text to numeric values. But it does not. One way to remedy this situation is to leave the field with currency values as Character fields. Then, after you have imported the data, use the `STRTRAN()` function to remove all the commas and currency symbols. Here is an example:

```
USE BUDGET
REPLACE ALL FY1989 WITH STRTRAN(FY1989, ",")  , ;
            FY1989 WITH STRTRAN(FY1989, "$" )
MODIFY STRUCTURE
```

Then modify the structure and change the `FY1989` field from Character to Numeric.

After you are finished changing field settings, click on the Next button and proceed to the final step, Step 3. The only choice you have in Step 3 is to cancel the whole wizard operation or to finish the operation. Click on the Finish button and the import operation is performed.

Using Wizards

When you are developing a complex application for a customer that involves hundreds of specialized screens, reports, and forms, you probably do not have much use for wizards. Sometimes you might use wizards to create an initial form, a report, a mailing label, or a mail merge report. Then you can create the initial object with a designer. Wizards are especially useful for performing one-time operations such as importing data, prototyping, and analyzing data. In this section, you will see how to perform a simple analysis of temperature conditions.

Here is the scenario. The boss comes into the analyst's office and says, "I hate this L.A. weather. The climate is too bland. The temperature is always in the 70s. It never snows. I am going to move this business to someplace with real weather. Find me the city in the United States with the most extreme temperature ranges. We will move there."

After the analyst finishes her résumé and letter of resignation, she brings up the Microsoft Bookshelf, and searches the *World Almanac* for a table containing temperatures of U.S. cities. She discovers a table of extreme temperatures of U.S. cities. She copies the table into Word 6.0 for Windows, and saves it as a text file. The text file is named WEATHER.TXT and starts out like this:

```
Alabama    Mobile      61   41   91   73   104    3   64.64
Alabama    Montgomery  57   36   92   72   105    0   49.16
Alaska     Juneau      27   16   64   47    90  -22   53.15
...
```

Next, the analyst uses the Import Wizard, as shown in Figure 24.54, to create a table from the text file. The resultant table is named EXTREME.DBF and contains the following fields:

```
Structure for table:     C:\VFP\FOXBOOK\CHAP24\EXTREME.DBF
Number of data records: 71
Date of last update:     04/14/95
Code Page:               1252
Field  Field Name       Type      Width    Dec
    1  STATE            Character    13
    2  STATION          Character    19       Weather station city
    3  JAN_HIGH         Numeric       5       Normal high temperature in January
    4  JAN_LOW          Numeric       4       Normal low temperature in January
    5  JULY_HIGH        Numeric       4       Normal high temperature in July
    6  JULY_LOW         Numeric       4       Normal high temperature in July
    7  MAXIMUM          Numeric       4       Maximum recorded temperature
    8  MINIMUM          Numeric       3       Minimum recorded temperature
    9  RAIN             Numeric       5       Average annual rainfall
** Total **                          62
```

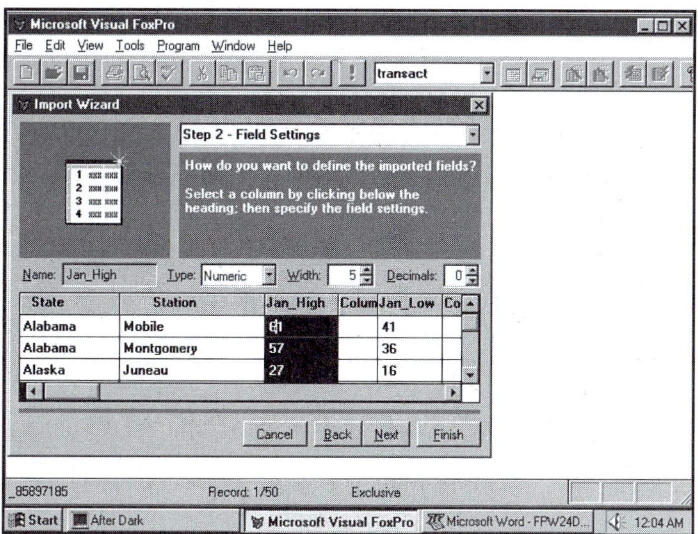

FIGURE 24.54.
The Import Wizard, used to import temperature table, EXTREME.DBF.

The Query and Local View Wizards are useful for doing what-if studies. The analyst uses the Local View Wizard to pick cities with high and low temperatures. The query filter, shown in Figure 24.55, reduces the number of choices to nine cities. The view results are shown in Figure 24.56.

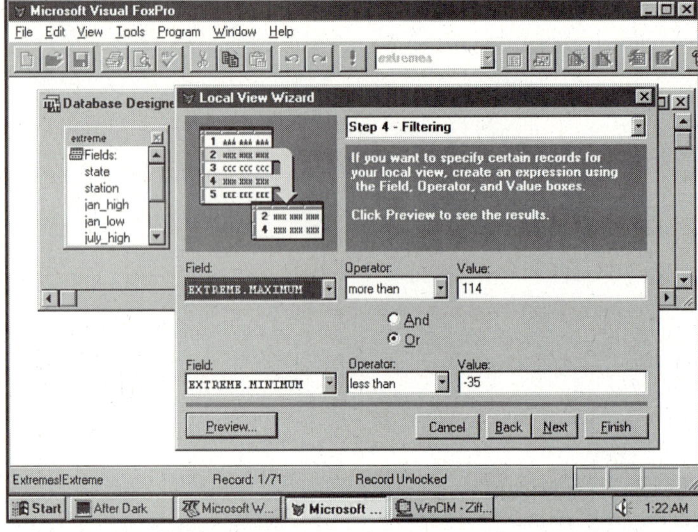

FIGURE 24.55.
The Local View Wizard, used to pick cities with the most extreme temperatures.

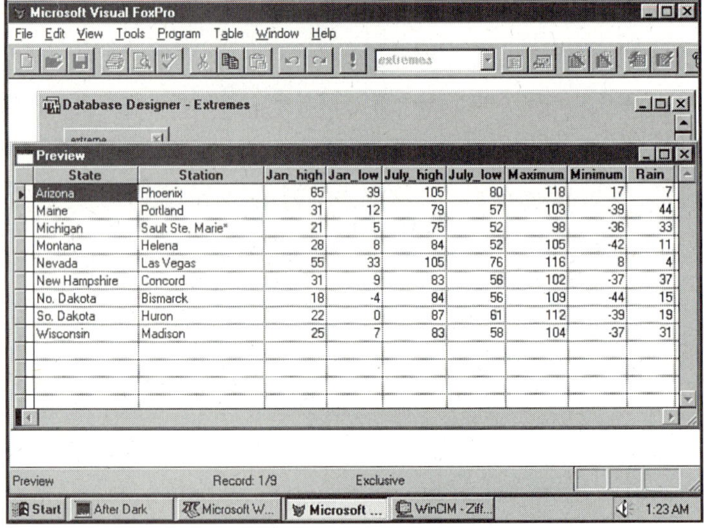

State	Station	Jan_high	Jan_low	July_high	July_low	Maximum	Minimum	Rain
Arizona	Phoenix	65	39	105	80	118	17	7
Maine	Portland	31	12	79	57	103	-39	44
Michigan	Sault Ste. Marie*	21	5	75	52	98	-36	33
Montana	Helena	28	8	84	52	105	-42	11
Nevada	Las Vegas	55	33	105	76	116	8	4
New Hampshire	Concord	31	9	83	56	102	-37	37
No. Dakota	Bismarck	18	-4	84	56	109	-44	15
So. Dakota	Huron	22	0	87	61	112	-39	19
Wisconsin	Madison	25	7	83	58	104	-37	31

FIGURE 24.56.
U.S. cities with the highest and lowest recorded temperatures.

Next, the analyst uses the Graph Wizard to prepare a graph representing the Local View Wizard results shown in Figure 24.56. The resultant graph is shown in Figure 24.57. Notice that Bismarck, North Dakota has the largest temperature deviation. The normal annual temperature varies 88 degrees Fahrenheit.

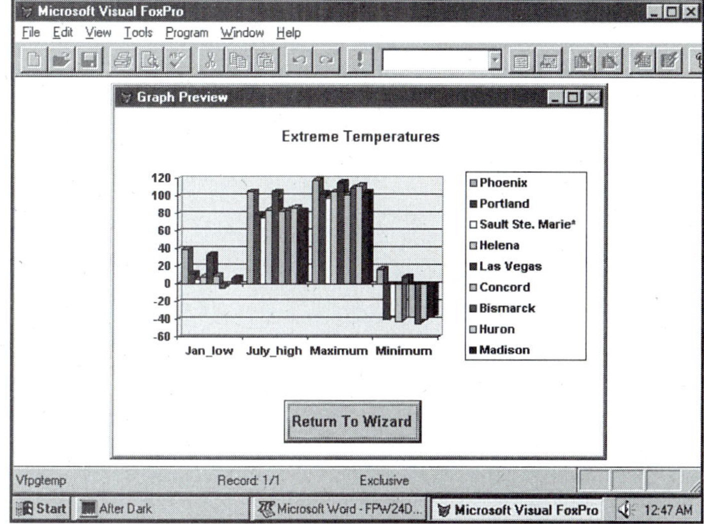

FIGURE 24.57.
A graph of U.S. cities with the highest and lowest recorded temperatures.

Summary

In this chapter you were introduced to the Visual FoxPro wizards. These wizards were added so that new users can quickly and easily benefit from the power of FoxPro. Experienced users can benefit by using wizards to quickly create an initial form, query, or report. Then they can add advanced features using the designers. The Import Wizard is especially useful to all levels of users.

V

Visual FoxPro Connectivity

25

Multiuser Considerations

Of course the music is a great difficulty. You see, if one plays good music, people don't listen, and if one plays bad music, people don't talk.

—Oscar Wilde (1854–1900)
The Importance of Being Earnest

This chapter focuses on the various FoxPro multiuser language features. First, I'll acquaint you with network and multiuser terms. FoxPro supports locking that is both explicit and automatic (implicit). These concepts are the subject of the section on concurrency control presented later in this chapter. Shared read-only access leads to a discussion of various change-detection functions. I continue the chapter by presenting FoxPro flexible network printer controls. Next, I discuss a new innovation in Visual FoxPro 3.0: buffered access to data. Finally, I conclude the chapter by presenting transaction processing.

The capability of a database management language to share data files among multiple users of the same system is becoming increasingly important. FoxPro 2.0 consists of a single-user and a multiuser product. Visual FoxPro comes with single- and multiuser capabilities combined in a single package and enables multiple users to share access to the same database tables.

Visual FoxPro can optionally perform automatic file and record locking. To ensure that the `BROWSE` or `EDIT` command displays the latest data, you can set FoxPro to refresh the screen at specified intervals.

Multiuser considerations do not necessarily involve only access to database tables on a network. The users share other network resources such as the network printers. This chapter also discusses FoxPro commands for routing output to a printer.

Local Area Networking

Local area networks (LANs) are useful for sharing data files and system resources such as printers. Any workstation (or node) on the LAN can access DBF files on a central file server, and programs such as FoxPro work with the network management software so several workstations can access the data at the same time without difficulty.

The International Standards Organization (ISO) has developed a seven-layer protocol for implementing a LAN, as shown in Figure 25.1. The bottom layers (1 and 2) represent the hardware that connects each workstation. Successive layers provide more intelligence. For example, one layer institutes a mechanism to detect or avoid situations in which more than one computer is "talking" on the wire at the same time. Higher still in this hierarchy (layer 6) is software that allows one workstation to access disk files on the server of another workstation. Application programs such as FoxPro stand at the highest level of this protocol; the details of the implementation of layers 1 through 6 are purposely hidden from them.

Because the details of the network are unimportant to FoxPro (and to other applications), the same copy of FoxPro can work on many different network configurations. Whether your wiring has a ring or a star topology, and whether you use IBM, Novell, 3Com, AT&T, Ungermann-Bass, or some other network software, the details and differences barely concern FoxPro. Actually, some differences do matter. FoxPro is prepared to detect and talk to only a finite number of different software packages. In theory, however, an application program such as FoxPro deals logically with the network software and does not need to concern itself with the hardware implementation.

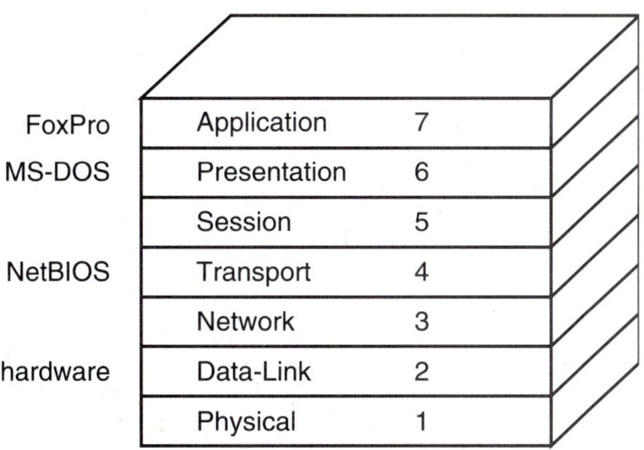

FIGURE 25.1.
The ISO Open Systems Interconnection reference model.

A LAN permits various workstations to share data files that can include the FoxPro executable files. Although the workstations can share the same central copy of FoxPro, a copy of it is loaded into the memory of each workstation. This is important because if each workstation merely communicated with one central FoxPro, the software could more easily detect conflicts between users and enforce security constraints. Instead, each copy of FoxPro software on each workstation must work hard to avoid conflicts without knowing how many other copies of FoxPro are running on the same network. This situation is called a *peer LAN*, because no copy of FoxPro has more authority than another. (See Figure 25.2.)

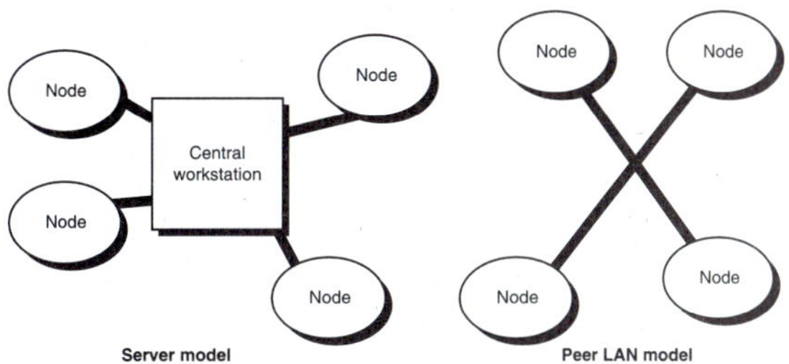

FIGURE 25.2.
The central server model versus the peer LAN model.

Central software that controls access by many users is called a *database server*; an example is the Sybase SQL Server marketed by Microsoft. A server offers centralized conflict resolution and integrity control. These capabilities can be important enough to justify the overhead of having each workstation communicating with the central server. Because the server is inherently multitasking (it keeps track of multiple users), it can perform tasks in the background. For example, suppose a workstation issues a command such as this:

```
LIST ALL FOR City = "Dallas"
```

Whether you are on the central server or on the peer LAN, FoxPro must look at every record. On a peer LAN, FoxPro must request every record from the network file server in order to look at it. A true database server, however, can minimize network traffic considerably by sending FoxPro only those records that match the condition. That is, the server reduces network traffic by performing a central selection.

In cases of *high selectivity*—when only two records out of thousands have `City = "Dallas"`—you can save an enormous amount of time. The following command illustrates the worst-case behavior:

```
LIST ALL
```

Each record must be sent over the network. This operation is no slower for a server than for a peer LAN.

A downside to the server approach is that servers that perform background selection are voracious users of processor time and memory. When a server runs on a microcomputer with a mere 50MHz, Intel 486-based microprocessor, for example, the apparent speed of every workstation depends on how many background selections are processing.

NOTE

Servers are practical when central control is more important than speed of throughput or when they are implemented on mainframes, minicomputers, or microcomputers with high-speed 100MHz, Intel Pentium microprocessors.

Locks

Network software provides a way to lock files and portions of files so that different copies of FoxPro running on different workstations can share data files without conflicts.

Supporting locks by the network software itself is vital, because application programs such as FoxPro can't do it alone. Imagine that before writing a DBF record you agree that FoxPro should look at the delete flag. If the flag contains FFH, it means that another copy of FoxPro software is updating the record and you should wait. If it isn't FFH, you should set it to FFH to warn any other copies of FoxPro and proceed to write the record. What could possibly go wrong in this case? This is a classic example of a race condition.

A *race condition* occurs when two programs compete for the same resource; the one that gets the resource first wins. The problem with this approach is that two copies of FoxPro software could be checking the flag at nearly the same time. Both read the flag and see that it is not FFH, so both try to set the flag to FFH. One is a little faster and does it first, but because the other has already checked the flag, it does not check it again. Next, both write to the same record, with disastrous results. A separate problem is that other programs might also be accessing this particular DBF file record, and these third-party programs do not know that they are supposed to check the delete flag.

The solution is a central locking facility in the network software. One call to the network handles the "if it is not FFH, set it to FFH" logic. Therefore, only one workstation tests each byte at a time, and the race condition is avoided. Furthermore, because the network is the guardian, third-party applications cannot accidentally overwrite records that FoxPro has locked.

Collision

When one workstation asks for a lock on a record that is already locked by another copy of FoxPro on the network, the result is a collision. Two solutions are possible. The user can give up and try again later, or the user can keep trying, realizing that the other user won't have the record locked forever. FoxPro offers a flexible mechanism (described in the next section) that enables the user to specify how long to keep trying for a lock before giving up.

Degree of Concurrency

If your application collides with another, as described previously, you must wait for a lock. This inhibits the performance of your application. If another user locks a record and goes to lunch or on vacation, your application will seem to stop altogether.

The *degree of concurrency* of a system measures the extent to which application programs release locks as soon as possible. A system has higher concurrency when the average time spent waiting for a lock is kept to a minimum. Conversely, a system has much lower concurrency when it locks records in case they might be updated and holds locks while waiting for user input. The following is pseudocode representing the logic for both low and high concurrency systems:

Low Concurrency	*Higher Concurrency*
Lock the record	Read the record
Read the record	Display the current contents of the record
Display the current record	Allow full-screen edit of the record
Allow full-screen edit	Okay to save changes (Y/N)?
Okay to save changes (Y/N)?	If okay:
	Lock the record
	Save the changes
	Unlock the record
If okay:	
Save changes	
Unlock the record	

When very high concurrency is important, a FoxPro application might use a temporary local file and change records in the central file in batches. How long locks are held must be balanced against how often locks are requested in a particular system.

Locking Granularity

Another way to increase concurrency is to lock the minimum number of bytes required. An application that locks the entire file before updating a single record stops other applications from updating any other record. The speed of other applications is improved by locking only the single record, which improves the granularity of the lock.

Visual FoxPro supports both file and record locking; the latter is generally the best choice for concurrency. Network software typically supports locking of any arbitrary byte range, so a program can conceivably lock a field at a time instead of a record at a time. The marginal increase in concurrency, however, is probably not worth the trouble.

Deadlock

Another classic problem occurs when two applications need more than one resource each. Each acquires the first resource but can't get the second because the other application has it. Both applications wait for each other and nothing happens for a long time. This is called *deadlock*, or *deadly embrace*. Here is an example:

Application 1	*Application 2*
Try to lock record 5	Try to lock record 3
Try to lock record 3	Try to lock record 5
If lock fails, wait	If lock fails, wait
Wait, wait, wait	Wait, wait, wait

This problem has several solutions. One is to be sure that resource requests always occur in the same order. In this example, if Application 2 tries to lock the records in the same order as Application 1, Application 2's first lock request fails, forcing it to wait until Application 1 finishes. This solution does not work for a general-purpose program such as FoxPro, because all users sharing a DBF file might not be using the same application. A database server might use this solution, but Visual FoxPro cannot.

FoxPro avoids deadlock by not waiting forever for a lock and by releasing previous locks when a lock request ultimately times out after attempting to lock a record for a predetermined number of times. Here's a replay of the example:

Application 1	*Application 2*
While not successful	While not successful
Lock record 5, 3	Lock record 3, 5
Proceed	Proceed

In this case, each application must wait until both resources are available, which effectively avoids deadlock. Although the application program "waits forever," FoxPro internally locks the first record and makes a finite number of attempts at locking the second record. If the second record is not successfully locked, the lock on the first record is released before control returns to the application. The application programmer still retains enough control to force a deadlock.

Concurrency Control

FoxPro provides several tools for controlling concurrent access to the same data by multiple users. In addition to explicit file and record locks, FoxPro can automatically lock data during modification. Generally, explicit locks designed into an application program offer finer granularity, and thus greater concurrency, for the system as a whole.

In a network situation, certain FoxPro commands require more than a record lock. For instance, the following commands require that the DBF file in question be opened for exclusive, rather than shared, use:

```
ALTER TABLE
INDEX
INSERT [BLANK]
MODIFY STRUCTURE
PACK
REINDEX
ZAP
```

You can select exclusive file access in two ways:

- By using the `EXCLUSIVE` keyword of the `USE` command, which opens a DBF file exclusively.
- By using the `SET EXCLUSIVE ON` command, which makes all subsequent `USE` commands exclusive.

If the current DBF file is not opened in exclusive mode, the commands in the preceding list report the error Exclusive open of file is required.

Other FoxPro commands perform automatic file locks for the duration of the command. These are the commands:

```
ALTER TABLE
APPEND
DELETE
RECALL
REPLACE
UPDATE
```

If you do not specify a scope clause or if the scope is `RECORD n` or `NEXT 1`, FoxPro performs an automatic record lock rather than a file lock. An automatic record lock also occurs in the `EDIT` and `BROWSE` commands whenever a user presses a key that modifies the data. If the record is successfully locked, the data is first updated so that the modifications affect the latest version of the record.

Commands such as `INDEX`, `REINDEX`, `APPEND FROM`, and `PACK` can take considerable time to execute. During the execution, you must have exclusive use of the DBF file and any associated files. During this time, no other user can access the file. You should plan your applications so that the execution of these commands can be performed when it will not inconvenience other users. A better way is to devise some alternate technique. For example, you can reuse deleted records instead of always using `APPEND BLANK` to add records and then to routinely pack the database with the `PACK` command. In the following example, assume that the database has an index tag (`DELETED`) with a key `DELETED()`:

```
*********************************************************
*   Name:     Recycler
*   Purpose:  Illustrates how to recycle deleted records
*
SET REPROCESS TO AUTOMATIC
SET DELETED OFF  && Make sure deleted records are accessed
USE Register
INDEX ON DELETED() TAG DELETED
SET ORDER TO
SET DELETED ON  && Now ignore deleted records
...
*
**** Add a record
DO WHILE LASTKEY() <> 27
   SCATTER MEMVAR BLANK
   @ 1,1 SAY  "Enter Last Name:" GET M.LNAME
   @ 2,6 SAY       "First Name:" GET M.FNAME
   @ 3,13 SAY             "ID#:" GET M.ID
   READ
   IF UPDATED()
*       Code for validating the user's input
*       before committing the record goes here.
*       If input is valid, use the following code:
      SET ORDER TO DELETED
      SEEK .T.
      IF FOUND()
         IF LOCK()
            RECALL
            GATHER MEMVAR && Recycle deleted record
            UNLOCK
         ELSE
            ? "Unable to save record"
         ENDIF
      ELSE
         USE Register EXCLUSIVE
         APPEND BLANK  && You only have to do this
                       && if no deleted records exist
         GATHER MEMVAR && Recycle deleted record
         USE Register
      ENDIF
      SET ORDER TO
   ENDIF
ENDDO
RETURN
```

Because `REPROCESS` is set to `AUTOMATIC`, the locks will be attempted forever, or until the user presses the Esc key. Notice that REGISTER.DBF was placed in exclusive use before the `APPEND BLANK` was executed. If the database runs out of deleted records during the work day and too many users are adding records, the system really slows down. In the morning, before any other users sign on, run a program that checks how many deleted records are available. If too few deleted records exist, you can add some more. For example, if users add no more than 100 records during the work day, run the following code in the morning before users start adding records:

```
USE Register EXCLUSIVE INDEX DELETED
SET DELETED OFF
COUNT FOR DELETED() TO NDelete
IF NDelete < 100
       FOR I = NDelete TO 100
              APPEND BLANK
              DELETE
       ENDFOR
ENDIF
```

You may recall from Chapter 12, "Data Set Operations," that the `SCATTER MEMVAR BLANK` command creates memory variables with the same name as the database fields and fills them with blank values. Then when the data is entered and validated, you can transfer these memory variables to a data record with the `GATHER MEMVAR` command.

The read-only commands listed in Table 25.1 cause an automatic file lock if `SET LOCK` is `ON`. `SET LOCK OFF` improves concurrency (which translates to better system performance), but data integrity is not guaranteed. The result of a `COUNT` command might not be accurate with respect to the state of the DBF file, either at the start of the command or at the end, if other users are modifying records while you are counting. For this reason, `SET LOCK` defaults to `ON`. The commands affected by `SET LOCK` command are shown in Table 25.1.

Table 25.1. How commands are affected by autolocking.

	Item(s) Locked			
Command	*Table*	*Header*	*Record*	*Records*
`ALTER TABLE`	✓			
`APPEND`	✓			
`APPEND BLANK`		✓		
`APPEND FROM`	✓			
`APPEND FROM ARRAY`		✓		
`APPEND MEMO`			✓	
`BLANK`			✓	
`BROWSE`			✓	1
`CHANGE`			✓	1
`DELETE`			✓	
`DELETE NEXT 1`			✓	

continues

Table 25.1. continued

		Item(s) Locked		
Command	*Table*	*Header*	*Record*	*Records*
`DELETE RECORD n`			✓	
`DELETE` (of more than one record)	✓			
`DELETE` (SQL)			✓	
`EDIT`			✓	1
`GATHER`			✓	
`INSERT`	✓			
`INSERT` (SQL)		✓		
`MODIFY MEMO`			✓	2
`READ`			✓	1
`RECALL`			✓	
`RECALL NEXT 1`			✓	
`RECALL RECORD n`			✓	
`RECALL` (of more than one record)	✓			
`REPLACE`			✓	1
`REPLACE NEXT 1`			✓	1
`REPLACE RECORD n`		✓[3]		
`REPLACE` (of more than one record)	✓[4]			
`SHOW GETS`			✓	1
`TABLEUPDATE()`	✓			
`UPDATE`	✓			
`UPDATE (SQL)`	✓			

[1]The current record and all records from aliased fields in related tables once editing of a field begins.

[2]The record is locked when editing starts.

[3]Record `n` and all records from aliased fields.

[4]The entire table and all files from aliased fields are locked.

On a LAN, locking is the only way to prevent collisions between users of the same data files. A user can lock an entire file—which slows down the applications of other users—or a single record. FoxPro provides several ways for programmers to lock both records and files, and failing that, it locks records and files automatically.

TIP

In terms of overall system performance, the best applications explicitly lock records only when necessary.

A system that supports lock requests must provide for the failure of those requests. Typically, an application program makes a request when it needs to continue a lock. If the lock request fails, continuing with the application is futile. The following sections provide some suggestions for handling lock request contingency problems.

The *SET REPROCESS* Command

Rather than forcing the user to give up, programmers should design application programs to keep trying. How many times a lock request is reprocessed depends on the nature of the system. An airline reservations program might conclude that because the other workstations lock records so briefly, a lock request that isn't satisfied after a few tries indicates that something is seriously wrong. A management information systems tool that is preparing a cumulative report while other managers add to the data might wait a long time before giving up.

In Visual FoxPro, the `SET REPROCESS` command allows an application program to tune the system behavior. You can use `SET REPROCESS` in four ways:

```
SET REPROCESS TO <expN> [SECONDS]
SET REPROCESS TO 0
SET REPROCESS TO -1
SET REPROCESS TO AUTOMATIC
```

In the first case, `SET REPROCESS TO <expN>`, the application sets the number of times the system will retry a lock request before reporting a failure. The value of `<expN>` ranges from 1 to 32000. (Sometimes, when a number such as 32000 or 64000 is mentioned, the writer probably does not realize that limits in a binary computer are more likely to be an exact power of 2, minus 1. When you see 32000, you might believe that the real limit is 32767. In this case, however, the limit is set at 32000.) You can specify the optional `SECONDS` keyword, and `<expN>` designates how many seconds the system waits following an unsuccessful lock attempt before it retries a record lock operation. The airline reservations program just described might set `REPROCESS` to `10` or to `20`.

The second case, `SET REPROCESS TO 0`, is the default. When no `ON ERROR` procedure has been specified, this method displays the following message: Please wait, another user has locked this record or file. It then retries the lock request until it is successful or the user presses Esc.

In the third case, `SET REPROCESS TO -1` tells FoxPro to keep trying until the lock request is successful. This approach is problematic because, while FoxPro waits for the lock, it appears to hang or freeze, which can resemble a system crash. For this reason, you cannot set `REPROCESS` to `-1` in CONFIG.FPW. The low-priority MIS report described earlier might use `SET REPROCESS TO -1`. It may take all night, but when it finally is possible to lock the file, the seemingly frozen application will pounce, lock the file, and do its work.

The argument is an integer value, ranging from `-2` to `32000`. The `-1` value directs the system to continually reprocess the operation to infinity. The default value is `0` and suppresses the reprocess. If you specify the optional `SECONDS` keyword, *<expN>* designates how many seconds the system waits following an unsuccessful lock attempt before it retries a record lock operation.

If you specify a numeric value of `-2`, or specify the `SET PROCESS TO AUTOMATIC` clause, the system attempts to lock a record or file repeatedly until the lock is successful or until you press the Esc key. While attempting to lock a record, FoxPro displays the following system message: Attempting to lock...Press Esc to cancel.

When you press the Esc key and an `ON ERROR` command is active, it executes. If no `ON ERROR` procedure is active, an alert box appears containing the following message: Record is in use by another.

Error Recovery

Unless you use the second or third `REPROCESS` methods, a LAN application must be prepared for a lock request to fail. When no `ON ERROR` procedure is defined, a lock failure results in the error File in use by another or Record in use by another.

When you specify an `ON ERROR` procedure, control branches there in case of lock failure. A lock failure is considered a recoverable error because you can write an application to correct the problem (by waiting for the lock to be freed, or by revealing the name of the user currently holding the lock and leaving the user to find his or her own solution). The `ERROR()` function returns the number of the error that caused the invocation of the `ON ERROR` function. This error won't always be a lock error, but when it is, it will be one of three values:

ERROR()	*Message*
108	File is in use by another
109	Record is in use by another
130	Record is not locked

The `ON ERROR` command can return, which continues the program at the line after the command that caused the error. With lock errors in particular, however, it's best to issue the `RETRY` command, which continues the program by re-executing the command that caused the error.

Locking Granularity

As mentioned, an application program used on a LAN should perform explicit locking, rather than expecting FoxPro to perform automatic file and record locking. Applications should strive for maximum granularity, as well, which means that you should lock records rather than files whenever possible.

In Visual FoxPro, the `FLOCK()` function locks files and the `RLOCK()` function locks records. (For compatibility with earlier versions, `LOCK` is a synonym for `RLOCK`.) The `FLOCK()` function locks the DBF file in the current work area or in a specified work area. If the file is related to other files, they are automatically locked as well.

Unlike most FoxPro functions, `FLOCK()` and `RLOCK()` perform operations as if they were commands; they don't merely calculate or return a value. They return `.T.` if the operation is successful or `.F.` if it is not. If `NETWORK()` is `.F.`, all lock requests succeed.

NOTE

The `NETWORK()` function is not very informative. In Visual FoxPro, it always returns a true (`.T.`) value if you are executing FoxPro. It returns a false (`.F.`) value only if you are running a single-user version of FoxPro 2.0. For example, if you are writing code to be run on both a single-user FoxPro 2.0, you can add the following code to your application so that files are used in exclusive mode when running in FoxPro 2.0:

```
IF NETWORK()
    SET EXCLUSIVE OFF
ENDIF
```

In its simplest form, the `RLOCK()` function locks the current record in the current work area. As an alternative, you can specify a different work area using its number or alias, as in `RLOCK(2)` or `RLOCK("ACCTG")`.

You can lock the header of a table by specifying `RLOCK(0)`. This makes it possible for you to prevent other users from adding new records to the table while it is locked.

You'll often find it necessary to lock several records at one time. By default, `SET MULTILOCKS` is `OFF`, and you can lock only a single record with the `RLOCK()` and `LOCK()` functions. However, if `SET MULTILOCKS` is `ON`, you can specify a character string as the first argument of the two record-locking functions. The character string contains a list of records to be locked, as in the following example:

```
? RLOCK("2, 4, 6, 8, 10", 2)
```

This example attempts to lock records 2, 4, 6, 8, and 10 in the DBF file in work area 2. The command fails if any one of the records cannot be locked. For instance, if another user locks record 8, this function locks records 2, 4, and 6 and fails to lock record 8. The function then automatically unlocks records 2, 4, and 6 and returns the error Record is in use by another. RETRY attempts the entire command again, not just the lock on record 8.

When explicit locks are successfully applied, they must be explicitly removed as well. Application programs that use FLOCK() and RLOCK() must also use the UNLOCK command. This is the syntax of the UNLOCK command:

```
UNLOCK [IN <expWA>  ¦ ALL ] [RECORD <expN> ]
```

The UNLOCK command removes all locks granted in the current work area or all work areas on records, on the file, or on both. You might use the IN clause with UNLOCK to specify a different work area. Issuing an UNLOCK ALL command releases locks in all work areas. You can also unlock a single record with the UNLOCK RECORD command. Remember that system performance depends on locking as few records as possible for as short a time as possible, so use UNLOCK quickly. Here is an example of the use of the UNLOCK command:

```
IF FLOCK()                  && Bad concurrency
     GOTO 28
     IF Amount > 3200
          REPLACE Overpaid WITH .T.
     ENDIF
ENDIF
* …Other stuff…
* …I almost forgot…
UNLOCK
GOTO 28                     && Good concurrency
IF Amount > 3200
     IF RLOCK()
          REPLACE Overpaid WITH .T.
          UNLOCK
     ENDIF
ENDIF
```

This example works for a system that seems to perform much faster than the system in the first example, because it unlocks the record as soon as possible.

After you perform an explicit lock of a file or one or more records, you can release the lock in several ways. You can use the UNLOCK command to unlock a file or record in the current or specified work area. You can release a lock for all locked records and files in all work areas using the UNLOCK ALL command. If SET MULTILOCKS is OFF, you unlock a locked record when you issue another record lock function, RLOCK(). If you issue the SET MULTILOCKS command, it releases all record locks for all work areas. In other words, all records are unlocked. If you issue a FLOCK() function to lock a database, any locked records in that database are unlocked. Finally, when you close a file, all record and file locks are released. The commands listed in Table 25.2 will unlock tables and records.

Table 25.2. Commands that unlock records and tables.

Command	*Unlocking Operation*
`CLOSE`	Release all record and file locks
`CLOSE ALL`	Release all record and file locks
`END TRANSACTION`	Release automatic locks
`FLOCK()`	Release all record locks in the affected file, and then lock the file
`QUIT`	Release all record and file locks
`SET MULTILOCKS OFF`	Enable the automatic release of the current lock as the new lock is secured
`TABLEUPDATE()`	Release all locks before updating the table
`UNLOCK`	Unlock record and file locks in the current work area
`UNLOCK ALL`	Release all locks for all work areas
`USE`	Release all record and file locks

How to Avoid a Deadlock Condition

The capability of the `RLOCK()` function to lock more than one record at a time in an all-or-nothing fashion is the best way to avoid a deadlock. Whenever an application acquires a lock on one resource and requests a second lock, deadlock is a possibility because another application may be holding the second resource and waiting for the first one.

Inconsistent Analysis

Inconsistent analysis occurs when an application tries to improve concurrency by not locking an entire file before calculating an aggregate across a DBF table. The sum of a particular field is different before and after another user replaces a single record, but either way, `SUM` is consistent. Inconsistent analysis describes the case in which the other user is replacing two records, moving a quantity from one record to another, which should not affect `SUM`. Depending on the timing, however, the first user's `SUM` may include the second user's subtraction but not the second user's addition, making the result inconsistent. When consistent results are important, the lesson is clear: Lock the entire file. In fact, if `SET LOCK` is `ON`, FoxPro locks the file for you to avoid inconsistent analysis.

The Lost Update Problem

The lost update problem occurs when a user updates a record that another user has already updated, as in the following example:

First User	*Second User*
Reads record 28	Reads record 28
	Locks record 28
	Changes it
	Unlocks it
Locks record 28	
Changes it	
Unlocks it	

In this example, the second user's changes are lost. To avoid this problem in the `EDIT` and `BROWSE` commands, FoxPro automatically rereads the record when it's locked. If the contents have changed, the system displays this message: Data in record has changed. Press Esc to abandon and any other key to continue.

Application programs must be sensitive to the problem of lost updates by detecting changed records before locking.

Shared Read-Only Access

FoxPro 2.0 removed a significant restriction that FoxBASE+ and dBASE III PLUS multiusers faced: When one user locks a record in FoxBASE+ or dBASE III PLUS, no other user can read the record until the first user unlocks it. The capability of one workstation to read a DBF file while it is being updated by several other workstations is significant for many applications. This capability is called *shared access*, and Visual FoxPro supports it. The reads are called *dirty reads*. This can be dangerous because the data is changing. (See the section "Inconsistent Analysis.")

Because Visual FoxPro operates in a peer LAN environment rather than as a central database server, no one workstation can ever detect the actions of another workstation. Therefore, a user cannot detect a changed record except by constantly rereading the record and comparing it to a previous copy.

To support dirty reads, Visual FoxPro possesses the capability to automatically update the displays of other workstations and possesses a means for application programs to detect records that have changed since the last read.

The Automatic Refresh Feature

You can't help but be impressed the first time you see the automatic refresh feature in Visual FoxPro. To experience this phenomenon, execute a `BROWSE` screen on multiple microcomputers with each browsing the same database base, modify one field of a record on one computer, and almost instantaneously the displays on the other workstations are silently modified to reflect the change.

With the SET REFRESH command, the user can specify how often FoxPro checks for changes to data being displayed by the EDIT, CHANGE, or BROWSE commands. The specified value is the number of seconds—from 1 to 3600 (one hour)—that the system will wait between refreshes. If the interval is 0 (which is the default), no refresh occurs.

A portion of the data is buffered in the local memory of the workstation. You can specify the second optional numeric argument (<*expN2*>) to designate how often the local buffers are updated. The value can range from 0 to 3600 seconds. The default is 0. If <*expN2*> is set to 1, the local buffers refresh every second. The example shown in Figure 25.3 simulates a multiuser environment by executing Visual FoxPro twice. In each instance the following code is executed from the Command window:

```
USE Register SHARE
SET REFRESH TO 1    && Refresh every second
BROWSE
```

When you edit a field in the Browse Window in one instance of Visual FoxPro and move off the record, the record is updated. The value of the same updated field is refreshed in the Browse window in the second instance of Visual FoxPro. The value shown on the screen for any other user in a multiuser environment who is viewing the same data and has the SET REFRESH parameter set to something other than 0 updates in the same manner.

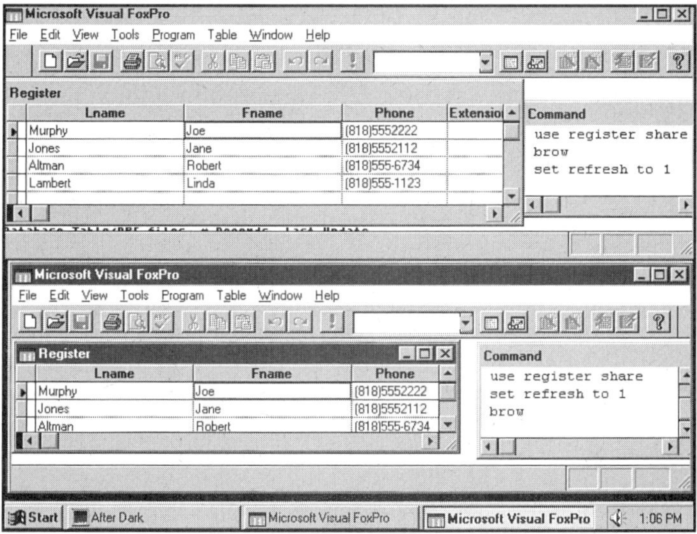

FIGURE 25.3.
An example of the use of the SET REFRESH TO *command.*

Buffering Access in a Multiuser Environment

Visual FoxPro 3.0 introduced *buffering*, a really neat new way to protect your data during update operations. You have two modes of buffering: table buffering and record buffering. You can do any kind of data maintenance operations in a buffer in a multiuser environment and Visual

FoxPro automatically takes care of testing for conflicts, locking, and releasing records or tables. Here is the way it works:

1. You instruct Visual FoxPro to perform record or table buffering using the `CURSORSETPROP()` function. Buffering remains in effect until you explicitly disable buffering or close the table.
2. Visual FoxPro automatically transfers data from the record to a buffer. The buffer is maintained in memory or disk. Note that other users can access the original data and make changes to it while you are working with the data.
3. You make changes to a record in the buffer.
4. You move to another record, programmatically make changes to another record, or issue a call to the `TABLEUPDATE()` function.
5. Visual FoxPro attempts to lock the record, and if no other user made a change to the record, Visual FoxPro writes the edited record to the file.
6. If changes were made to the record by other users, you resolve whatever conflicts are involved before Visual FoxPro transfers buffered data to the original table.

The precise details of buffer operations depend on the type of buffering and locking method you specify.

Buffering Methods

Visual FoxPro supports record buffering and table buffering. The type of buffering you use depends on the application. If you want to access, edit, and write a single record at a time, you should choose record buffering. It provides the most effective method of providing validation with the least impact on other users. However, it is effective only when you are editing a single record at a time.

If you are going to update several records at one time, you should choose table buffering. It is also the best choice if you are editing child records in one-to-many relationships.

If you want the best protection for your existing data, you should use Visual FoxPro transaction processing, which is discussed in the section "Transaction Management."

Buffering Locking Modes

In addition to choosing record or table buffering types, you need to choose the best buffering locking mode for your application. The two types of buffering locking modes are *pessimistic* and *optimistic*. This is not a half-empty, half-full choice. Your decision about which to use depends on the type of multiuser environment in which your application is operating and the requirements of a particular application. The type of locking mode determines when and how record locks are released.

If you use pessimistic buffering, other users in a multiuser environment are prohibited from accessing a particular record or table while you are making changes to it. Pessimistic buffering provides the most secure environment. The bad news is that the pessimistic buffering slows down operations. The rule is this: If you don't need it, don't use it.

When you want the most efficient method of updating records in a multiuser environment, you use optimistic buffering because locking takes place only at the time the record is written. This reduces the time that any one user monopolizes the data in a multiuser environment.

Specifying Buffering and Locking Methods

You specify which buffering and locking technique you want to use with the `CURSORSETPROP()` function. There are many forms of this function. Most of them are used for specifying options for remote connections. This is the syntax of this function for setting the buffering mode:

```
CURSORSETPROP("Buffering",<expN> [,<expWA>])
```

The second argument (<expN>) specifies the locking or buffering mode. It is described in Table 25.3.

Table 25.3. The buffering and locking methods.

<expN>	*Buffering Mode Enabled*
1	Sets record and table buffering off. This method of record locking and data writing is identical to that of earlier FoxPro versions.
2	Sets pessimistic record buffering on. The current record is immediately locked and transferred to a buffer. Specifically, Visual FoxPro attempts to lock the record, and if successful, transfers the contents of the record to a buffer and permits the user to edit it. If the record pointer is moved or the `TABLEUPDATE()` function is executed, the buffer is written to the original table and the lock is released.
3	Sets optimistic record buffering on. Initially, Visual FoxPro transfers the record at the current record pointer to a buffer and permits editing. When the record pointer moves or the `TABLEUPDATE()` function executes, Visual FoxPro attempts to lock the record. If successful, Visual FoxPro compares the contents of the record in the table with the original contents of the buffer. If the values are the same, Visual FoxPro writes the buffer to disk and releases the lock. On the other hand, if the contents differ, it indicates that the record has been updated by another user and Visual FoxPro generates an error condition.

continues

Table 25.3. continued

<expN>	*Buffering Mode Enabled*
4	Sets pessimistic table buffering on. The table is immediately locked and the contents of the records are copied to buffers. The buffer of records is written to the original table and the record is unlocked when the `TABLEUPDATE()` function executes.
5	Sets optimistic table buffering on. When the `TABLEUPDATE()` function executes, Visual FoxPro attempts to lock the table. If it is successful, Visual FoxPro compares the contents of the records with the contents of the original (unedited) buffer of records. If the contents are the same, the updated buffer of records is written to the original table and the table lock is released. If the comparison operation indicates that another user has updated a record, Visual FoxPro generates an error condition.

You must set `MULTILOCKS` to `ON` for all buffering modes except `1`, in which case it is set to `OFF`. The default buffering method is `1` for operating on tables and `5` for operating on views.

Updating Buffers

After you establish the buffering and locking method with the `CURSORSETPROP()` function, you can begin updating operations.

You can write edits to an original table using the `TABLEUPDATE()` function. You use `TABLEREVERT()` to cancel a failed update to a table even if table buffering is not enabled. This is the syntax for these functions:

```
TABLEUPDATE(lAllRows [, lForce] [,<expWA> ])
TABLEREVERT([lAllRows]  [,<expWA> ])
```

If you call the `TABLEUPDATE()` function with the `lAllRows` parameter set to true (`.T.`) and table buffering is enabled, all records in the buffer are written to the original table. If you specify a false value (`.F.`) for the first argument, only the changes made to the current record are written to the original file.

If you call `TABLEREVERT()` with the `lAllRows` parameter set to true (`.T.`) and table buffering is enabled, all changes made to the records in the buffer are discarded. If you specify a false value (`.F.`) for the first argument or omit it and table buffering is enabled, the changes made to the current record are discarded. The `TABLEREVERT()` function ignores the value of `lAllRows` if record buffering is enabled and the changes made to the current record are discarded.

If you specify the second argument (`lForce`) as a true (`.T.`) value, and if changes were made by another user in a multiuser environment, those changes are overwritten by the contents of the buffer. If you specify a false (.F.) value, Visual FoxPro transfers records from the buffer to the original table starting with the first record and continuing until either the last record is written or a record that was modified by another user is encountered, in which case an error condition is generated.

The optional third argument (<*expWA*>) specifies the work area for the table on which the TABLEUPDATE() and TABLEREVERT() functions operate. If omitted, the functions operate on the table or cursor in the current work area.

The TABLEUPDATE() function returns a true (.T.) value if all the changed records were successfully written to the original table. If the TABLEUPDATE() function is unable to commit all the changes to the original table, it returns a false (.F.) value and the record pointer is positioned at the record that has changes that could not be committed. Incidentally, you can use the AERROR() function to determine why the record was not committed.

The TABLEREVERT() function returns the number of records with changes that were discarded.

When you define a class, you normally place code to initialize the data environment in the Load or Init event methods for the form or formset. For example, the following code can be placed in the Load event method for the form:

```
PROCEDURE Form1.Load
    OPEN DATABASE myDB
    USE myTable
    =CURSORSETPROP("Buffering", 2)  && Set pessimistic locking
ENDPROC                             && and record buffering
```

The code to check whether a record has changed is placed at the appropriate place. For example, if you are editing data in a Grid object, you can place code in the BeforeRowColChange event. Here is an example:

```
PROCEDURE Grid1.BeforeRowColChange
    PARAMETER nColIndex  && Index of newly active row or column
    IF RECNO() # THISFORM.OldRecordNumber  && Record Changed?
        * Yes, Check for change in a field
        THISFORM.OldRecordNumber = RECNO()
        IF "2" $ GETFLDSTATE( -1 )  && Did any fields change?
            nAnswer = MESSAGEBOX("Field Changed. Save?", ;
                      4+32+256, "Data Changed" )  && Yes/No box
           IF nAnswer = 7  && Is it No?
            * If the user does not want to save data, revert it
                TABLEREVERT( .F. )  && Get original values
            ENDIF
        ENDIF
    ENDIF
    * Now, make sure change is written
    SKIP   && Repositions record which writes record
    IF EOF()
       SKIP -1
    ENDIF
    THISFORM.Refresh   && Refresh the form
ENDPROC
```

The `GETFLDSTATE()` function used in the preceding example is used after an update operation to determine whether a field changed. This is the syntax:

```
GETFLDSTATE( cFieldName ¦ nFieldNumber [,<expWA>])
```

For the first argument, you can enter either a field name, a field number, or `-1`. The optional second argument specifies the work area of the table and if omitted, this function operates on the table or cursor in the current work area.

If you enter a field name or number, the `GETFLDSTATE()` function returns one of the numbers shown in Table 25.4.

Table 25.4. The values returned by the `GETFLDSTATE()` function.

Return Value	*Meaning*
1	Field or deletion status has not changed.
2	Field value has changed or deletion status has not changed.
3	Field in an appended record has not been edited or the record deletion status has not changed.
4	Field has been edited in an appended record or the record deletion status has changed.

If you specify `-1` for the `nFieldNumber` argument, the `GETFLDSTATE()` function returns a character string with a deletion and edit status value from Table 25.4 for all of the fields in the table or cursor. For example, if a table has three fields and only the second field is edited, the `GETFLDSTATE()` function returns a character string, `"1121"`.

The `GETFLDSTATE()` function operates on both buffered and unbuffered data. However, it is most effective when it is used with record buffering because it gives you the option to check for changes, and if data changes, you can apply validation rules. As a result, you can either commit or discard data. You can use the `GETFLDSTATE()` function in the `Click` event methods of record navigation buttons to detect change so that you can take some action before you reposition the record pointer.

The `CURVAL()` and `OLDVAL()`functions are used to detect changed values for a buffered field. These functions generate an error condition if buffering mode is not enabled. The `CURVAL()` function returns the value of a field directly from the original table. The `OLDVAL()` function returns the original field value for a field that has been buffered. In other words, the `OLDVAL()` function returns the value of a field right after it is buffered but before it is edited.

If a field was not changed by another user in a multiuser environment, the values returned by the `CURVAL()` and `OLDVAL()` are the same. If another user changes the value of a field, `CURVAL()` and `OLDVAL()` return different values. This is the syntax of these functions:

```
CURVAL( cFieldName, [<expWA>])
OLDVAL( cFieldName, [<expWA>])
```

The `cFieldName` argument specifies the name of the field whose value is returned. The optional second argument specifies the work area of the table containing the field. If omitted, the current work area is assumed.

The example presented in Listing 25.1 illustrates how you can use the `OLDVAL()` function to retrieve the original value of a field in a buffered table. It also illustrates the use of the `CURVAL()` function. Note that because this is a single user example, `CURVAL()` and `OLDVAL()` always return the identical values. If this example is run in a multiuser environment and another user changes the value of a field, the values returned by the `CURVAL()` and `OLDVAL()` functions will differ.

A free table named ANIMALS.DBF is created using the `CREATE TABLE` command. The SQL `INSERT` command is used to insert a record into the table and assign a value of `Dog` into the `Animal` field. The `SET MULTILOCKS` parameter is set to `ON` as required for table buffering. Then the `CURSORSETPROP(5)` function sets the mode to optimistic table buffering. Next, the `REPLACE` command modifies the value of the `Animal` field. The value of `Animal` and the value returned by the `CURVAL()` and `OLDVAL()` functions are displayed before and after the `REPLACE` command executes. Next, the buffer containing the modified record is transferred to the table using the `TABLEUPDATE()` function. After the update, the value of the `Animal` field and the values returned by the two functions are again the same as shown in the listing.

Listing 25.1. An example illustrating the use of the `CURVAL()` and `OLDVAL()` functions.

```
Code                                                       Results
***************************************************
* Program: VALTEST.PRG
* Purpose: Illustrates use of CURVAL() and OLDVAL()
CREATE TABLE Animals (Animal C(10))
APPEND BLANK
INSERT INTO Animals (Animal) VALUES ("Dog")
SET MULTILOCKS ON
? CURSORSETPROP("Buffering", 5 )                                            .T.
CLEAR
? "Original Animal value: ", Animal                        Original Animal value:  Dog
REPLACE Animal WITH "Cat"
? "Modified Animal value: ", Animal                        Modified Animal value:  Cat
? "Returned by OLDVAL():  ", OLDVAL("Animal")              Returned by OLDVAL():   Dog
? "Returned by CURVAL():  ", CURVAL("Animal")              Returned by CURVAL():   Dog
= TABLEUPDATE(.T.)
? "New Updated Values:"                                    New Updated Values:
? "   Value of Animal:        ", Animal                    Value of Animal:        Cat
? "   Returned by OLDVAL( ): ", OLDVAL("Animal")           Returned by OLDVAL( ):  Cat
? "   Returned by CURVAL( ): ", CURVAL("Animal")           Returned by CURVAL( ):  Cat
```

If you have enabled table buffering and you want to know which records in a table buffer are modified, you can use the `GETNEXTMODIFIED()` function. This function is especially useful in an error-recovery procedure when you attempt to commit records in a table buffer with the `TABLEUPDATE()` command and an error occurs. This error usually indicates that one of the modified records in the buffer could not be written to disk because it was changed by another user in a multiuser environment. You use the `GETNEXTMODIFIED()` function to find out which modified record in the buffer did not get written to the original table.

This is the syntax of the function:

```
GETNEXTMODIFIED(nRecordNumber [, <expWA>])
```

The `nRecordNumber` argument specifies which record to start searching for the next modified record. But be careful—you need to specify a value for `nRecordNumber` that is one record before the one you want to begin the search with. For example, if you specify `0`, the search begins with the first record in the table. The search continues until either a modified record is found or the end of the table is encountered.

The optional second argument specifies the work area for the table on which the search is performed. If the argument is omitted, the current work area is used.

If the `GETNEXTMODIFIED()` function returns `0`, there are no modified records in the table buffer after the current record. If the `GETNEXTMODIFIED()` function encounters a modified record, the search stops and the `GETNEXTMODIFIED()` function returns the record number of the modified record. A record is considered to be modified if any fields in the record are modified or the deletion status is changed.

Note that `GETNEXTMODIFIED()` returns an error condition if you attempt to use it on a table or cursor that does not have table buffering enabled.

The GNMText.PRG program presented in Listing 25.2 illustrates the operation of the `GETNEXTMODIFIED()` function. In this example, table buffering is enabled for the Employee.DBF table. Then record 3 is modified with the `REPLACE` command. The `GETNEXTMODIFIED()` function is executed to find a modified record. It finds record 3. Then the `TABLEREVERT()` function discards all of the changes in the table buffer. When `GETNEXTMODIFIED()` is executed again, it finds no modified records.

Listing 25.2. An example illustrating the operation of the `GETNEXTMODIFIED()` function.

```
*************************************************************************
*  Program: GNMTest.PRG
*  Purpose: Illustrates operation of GETNEXTMODIFIED() function
*************************************************************************
CLEAR ALL
CLEAR
SET MULTILOCKS ON                    && Necessary for table buffering
```

```
USE Employee
? CURSORSETPROP("Buffering", 5 )     && Enable table buffering
SKIP 2                               && Move record pointer to the third record
REPLACE LName with "Mealey"          && Change last name
? GETNEXTMODIFIED(0)                 && Returns 3, third record was modified
= TABLEREVERT(.T.)                   && Discard all table changes
? GETNEXTMODIFIED(0)                 && Returns 0, since no records are modified
```

Adding Records to a Buffered Table

When you enable table buffering, you can add records to the buffer or delete them. When you add a new record with the `APPEND`, `APPEND BLANK`, or SQL `INSERT` command, the `RECNO()` function returns a negative record number. `RECNO()` returns `-1` for the first record you add, `-2` for the second record you add, and so forth.

You can use the `DELETE` command to mark for deletion any records that you add to the buffer. However, when you use the `TABLEUPDATE()` command to commit the buffer to the original table, the records marked for deletion are added to the table. If you want to remove an added record, you can use the `TABLEREVERT()` function to remove the record before you execute the `TABLEUPDATE()` function.

Listing 25.3 presents an example of what happens when you add records to and delete records from a table buffer. The following list describes each step performed in the listing:

1. The table ANIMALS.DBF is created.
2. Three records are added.
3. The file is placed in use.
4. Table buffering is enabled.
5. Two new records are added. Notice that `RECNO()` returns `-1` through `-2` for the appended records.
6. The record pointer is positioned to the first appended record with the `GO -1` command. Notice that `GO 4` also positions you to the same record.
7. The first appended record is deleted. Notice that the record is marked for deletion.
8. The record is removed from the table buffer using the `TABLEREVERT(.F.)` function. The `.F.` argument specifies that only the current record is to be removed. Notice that the function returns `1`, indicating that one "changed record" was removed from the table buffer. You can remove all the appended records from the table buffer by executing the `TABLEREVERT(.T.)` function.
9. Now the table is updated. Notice that the table has been updated and the normal record numbering is restored.

Listing 25.3. Appending and deleting records in table buffers.

```
Code                                               Results (comments)
CLEAR ALL
CREATE TABLE Animals FREE (Animal C(20))           && (1)
INSERT INTO Animals (Animal) VALUES ("Lion")       && (2)
INSERT INTO Animals (Animal) VALUES ("Tiger")
INSERT INTO Animals (Animal) VALUES ("Elephant")
USE Animals  && (3)
? CURSORSETPROP("Buffering", 5 )  && (4) .T.
LIST RECNO(),Animal                                Record#  RECNO()    ANIMAL
                                                         1           1 Lion
                                                         2           2 Tiger
                                                         3           3 Elephant

INSERT INTO Animals (Animal) VALUES ("Aardvark")   && (5)
INSERT INTO Animals (Animal) VALUES ("Monkey")
LIST RECNO(),Animal                                Record#  RECNO()    ANIMAL
                                                         1        1 Lion
                                                         2        2 Tiger
                                                         3        3 Elephant
                                                         4       -1 Aardvark
                                                         5       -2 Monkey
GO -1                                              && (6)
DISPLAY RECNO(),Animal                             Record#  RECNO()    ANIMAL
                                                         4         -1 Aardvark
GO 4
DISPLAY RECNO(),Animal                             Record#  RECNO()    ANIMAL
                                                         4         -1 Aardvark
DELETE  && (7)
LIST RECNO(),Animal                                Record#  RECNO()    ANIMAL
                                                         1        1 Lion
                                                         2        2 Tiger
                                                         3        3 Elephant
                                                         4 *     -1 Aardvark
                                                         5       -2 Monkey
? TABLEREVERT(.F.)                                 && (8) Remove record  1
LIST RECNO(),Animal                                Record#  RECNO()    ANIMAL
                                                         1        1 Lion
                                                         2        2 Tiger
                                                         3        3 Elephant
                                                         4       -2 Monkey
? TABLEUPDATE(.T.)                                 && (9)      .T.
LIST RECNO(),Animal                                Record#  RECNO()    ANIMAL
                                                         1        1 Lion
                                                         2        2 Tiger
                                                         3        3 Elephant
                                                         4        4 Monkey
```

Transaction Management

Transaction management is one of the more advanced features of Visual FoxPro. Mainframe systems have supported this important concept for years, but now Visual FoxPro supports the notion of atomic update integrity.

This section explains transactions and the Visual FoxPro commands that implement the concepts. It describes restrictions placed on the rest of the language during a transaction. To write applications that seem to magically pick up the pieces after disaster strikes, you need to know the details of the logging and rollback process. This chapter also contains a sample program that uses transactions.

What Is Atomic Update Integrity?

What in the world is atomic update integrity? Although it sounds vaguely reminiscent of Cold War nuclear strategy, the term describes a database management system that ensures that the data will always be in a stable state. For example, when you change a data record with the REPLACE command, Visual FoxPro guarantees that the record will be left as it was or that it will be changed as you specified. If the REPLACE command reports an error, you can be confident that the original contents of the record still remain.

This is an important idea: It must not be possible to leave a data record in limbo or perform only half a REPLACE command. Visual FoxPro provides this security automatically, without requiring any special transaction programming commands. REPLACE and other commands that change data are all-or-nothing. Classic DBMS theory extends this notion to whole databases by asserting that it must not be possible to leave a database in an indeterminate state. To make this assertion a reality, you need transactions.

A transaction is a unit of work, some sequence of Visual FoxPro commands that must happen in an all-or-nothing fashion to maintain database integrity. For example, consider a general ledger database. One table, LEDGER.DBF, forms the ledger and is created using the following code:

```
OPEN DATABASE LEDGER
CREATE TABLE LEDGER  (Acct_no   C(6) ) , (Balance   N( 9,2 ))
```

Another table, TRANSFER.DBF, holds checks and deposits, and is created using the following command:

```
CREATE TABLE Transfer
    ( From_acct C(6)   ),
    ( To_acct   C(6)   ),
    ( Tdate     D(8)   ),
    ( Amount    N(9,2) )
```

To record a payment by a client requires changing two accounts. The balance of the client's account ($626.00, for example) is reduced by the amount of the payment, and the balance of the cash in the account ($1.00) is increased. The Visual FoxPro code might look like the following:

```
USE Transfer
APPEND BLANK
REPLACE From_acct WITH 626.00, To_acct WITH 1.00, ;
   Tdate WITH DATE(), Amount WITH M.Amt
```

If something goes wrong with the REPLACE command, the worst that can happen is that a blank record is added to the transfer file. The application program can ignore blank records and preserve integrity.

But consider the following code, which uses the transaction file to update the ledger itself. This code results in a dangerous update that might leave the database in an undefined state:

```
USE Transfer IN 2
USE Ledger
DO WHILE !EOF("TRANSFER")
     SEEK TRANSFER.From_acct
     REPLACE Balance WITH Balance - TRANSFER.Amount
     SEEK TRANSFER.To_acct
     REPLACE Balance WITH Balance + TRANSFER.Amount
     SKIP IN "TRANSFER"
ENDDO
CLOSE DATABASES
```

If something goes wrong—a power failure or a hard disk crash, for example—you could take the money from From_acct without adding it to To_acct. This would wreck the integrity of the ledger table. When the power came back on or when the hard disk was fixed, you couldn't be sure that the accounts balanced.

This is an example of the need for an atomic update. You must update both the From_acct record and the To_acct record in one fell swoop to be sure that the update happens in its entirety or that nothing happens. You want to explain this need to the system by saying the following:

```
*  I am beginning an atomic update
SEEK From_acct
REPLACE
SEEK To_acct
REPLACE
* Yea.. I am done; if I got here, I am okay
```

If you get an error of some kind, you want to be able to put the system back exactly as it was before the SEEK command in the previous example.

Because all types of complicated commands can occur between the I am beginning an atomic update and I am done statements, supporting atomic updates is what computer programmers refer to with mock mathematical precision as a *nontrivial task*. The user's view of a programmer's nontrivial task is merely that the program seems to run slowly.

The *BEGIN TRANSACTION, END TRANSACTION,* and *ROLLBACK* Commands

Although supporting the full generality of atomic updates in Visual FoxPro involves a lot of behind-the-scenes work, it is necessary to add only a few new commands to implement transactions. This is the syntax of these commands:

```
BEGIN TRANSACTION
END TRANSACTION
ROLLBACK
```

You tell Visual FoxPro that you are beginning a transaction with the `BEGIN TRANSACTION` command. The examples in the DBMS literature usually indicate `I am done` with a `COMMIT` command, but in Visual FoxPro `END TRANSACTION` was used. To tell Visual FoxPro to put the system back as it was, you use the `ROLLBACK` command.

These new commands can be executed from the Command window as in programs; `ROLLBACK` is particularly useful in `ON ERROR` procedures. A `CANCEL` command during a transaction automatically issues a `ROLLBACK` command for you. However, there are some restrictions on transactions. Transactions are supported only for tables in databases. Inversely, free tables are not supported by transactions.

You save modifications that you make and terminate the transaction by issuing the `END TRANSACTION` command. If the transaction fails or if you issue `ROLLBACK`, the file or files in the transaction are restored to their original state. Various factors can make a transaction fail, such as a power failure, a server failure, a computer crash, or exiting Visual FoxPro without committing the transaction by executing an `END TRANSACTION` command. Here are the rules that pertain to transactions:

- An `END TRANSACTION` statement that is not preceded by a `BEGIN TRANSACTION` statement generates an error.
- A `ROLLBACK` statement that is not preceded by a `BEGIN TRANSACTION` statement generates an error.
- After a transaction begins, it remains in effect until it encounters an `END TRANSACTION` or `ROLLBACK` command. It continues to execute across procedures and functions.
- If the application exits while a transaction is in effect, a `ROLLBACK` is initiated.
- A transaction works only in a database container.
- You cannot use the `INDEX` command in an index if it overwrites an existing index or if the production index file is open.
- Within a transaction, Visual FoxPro performs a lock as soon as a command requests it. However, unlocks are cached (that is, saved in a buffer) and not performed until an `END TRANSACTION` or `ROLLBACK` command executes.
- If you execute an `FLOCK()` or `RLOCK()` function within a `TRANSACTION`, the `END TRANSACTION` will not release the lock. You must explicitly perform an `UNLOCK` operation within the transaction.

Transactions can be nested up to five levels deep. Updates made within a nested transaction are not committed until the outermost `END TRANSACTION` executes. In nested transactions, the `END TRANSACTION` always refers to the previously executed `BEGIN TRANSACTION` and a `ROLLBACK` command only operates on the previously executed `BEGIN TRANSACTION` command.

For example, the following code shows transactions nested two levels deep:

```
OPEN DATABASE dbx
USE xyFile
BEGIN TRANSACTION
   REPLACE y WITH y - 1     && Level 1
   REPLACE x WITH x - 1
   BEGIN TRANSACTION && level 2 nested transaction
       REPLACE y WITH y + 1
       REPLACE x WITH x + 1
   END TRANSACTION      && Ends level 2 nested transaction
END TRANSACTION         && Ends level 1 nested transaction
                        &&   and commits changes for all transactions
```

In a set of nested transactions, an update within the innermost transaction has precedence over all other updates in the same block of nested transactions. In the previous example, the REPLACE commands in the level 2 nested transaction overwrite the changes made by the REPLACE statements made in the level 2 nested transaction.

If you want the entire relation scan to be an atomic transaction, write code similar to the following example:

```
OPEN DATABASE Example
USE Example
BEGIN TRANSACTION               && Legal, but not ideal
 SCAN WHILE ! EOF()
     REPLACE x WITH y
     REPLACE z WITH y
ENDDO
END TRANSACTION
```

If, on the other hand, you want the REPLACE commands to be atomic (a good approach, which breaks a large transaction into many smaller transactions), rearrange it like this:

```
OPEN DATABASE PF
USE Employee
SCAN  WHILE .NOT. EOF()
    BEGIN TRANSACTION     && Smaller transactions are better
       REPLACE x WITH y
       REPLACE z WITH y
    END TRANSACTION
    SKIP
ENDDO
```

It is bad programming practice to include too many commands between BEGIN TRANSACTION and END TRANSACTION, because too much work will be lost if a ROLLBACK becomes necessary. Furthermore, when you are operating in a multiuser environment and other users on the network try to access records you have modified, they must wait until you execute an END TRANSACTION command to end your transaction. While the other users wait, they are confronted with an alert box that displays the message Record not available...please wait. This is another reason for keeping the length of the transaction to a minimum or conducting the transaction during times when others do not need access. In this way, you can contribute to corporate tranquillity. You should use BEGIN TRANSACTION and END TRANSACTION to bracket two or three commands at a time that must be executed in an all-or-nothing fashion.

The example shown in Listing 25.4 demonstrates how to effectively use nested transactions. In this example, buffered table updates are used. If a buffered table update fails, a recovery process is applied to resolve updating problems.

Listing 25.4. An example that demonstrates the effective use of nested transaction processing.

```
*************************************************
* Procedure: Trans2.prg
* Purpose: Illustrates effective use of nested
*          transactions to resolve concurrency
*          and database updating conflicts
*
CLOSE DATABASES
SET MULTILOCKS ON  && Needed for table buffering
SET EXCLUSIVE OFF
OPEN DATABASE PF
USE Employee
=CURSORSETPROP("buffering",5 ) && Optimistic table buffering
*  Give everybody a 10% raise.
lErrorFound = .F.          && Set error indicator flag
ON ERROR DO ReplaceError   && Set error condition trap
REPLACE ALL Employee.Salary with 1.1*Employee.Salary
IF lErrorFound    && If error was found, Exit
     RETURN
ENDIF
ON ERROR
BEGIN TRANSACTION
    Good = TABLEUPDATE( .T. ) && Update entire table
    IF NOT Good               && Problem with updates?
       ROLLBACK               && If so, undo all of the changes
       =AERROWS(ArrErrors) && Array of errors
       TheError = ArrErrors[1,1]
       DO CASE

             CASE TheError = 1585
                * Record was changed by another user
                *  Find the record that was modified
                nNextModifiedRecord = GetNextModified(0)
                DO WHILE nNextModifiedRecord <> 0
                     GO nNextModifiedRecord
                     =RLOCK() && Lock the record
                     * Did other user change the salary field?
                     nSalary = Salary && Get salary field value
                     IF OLDVAL("Salary") <> CURVAL("Salary")
                        =MESSAGEBOX("Other user changed Salary "+;
                        "for "+LName+" To: "+STR(CURVAL("Salary"))
                     ENDIF
                     = TABLEREVERT(.F.) && Revert the record
                     * Overwrite salary field
                     REPLACE Salary WITH nSalary
                     UNLOCK RECORD nNextModifiedRecord
                     nNextModifiedRecord = ;
                     GetNextModified(nNextModifiedRecord)
                 ENDDO
```

continues

Listing 25.4. continued

```
                BEGIN TRANSACTION     && Translation level 2
                   =TABLEUPDATE(.T.,.T.)  && Force record updates
                END TRANSACTION
            CASE TheError = 1700
               * Record is in use by another user
            CASE TheError = 1583
               * Record level rule was violated
               * (There are no record rules, here)
            CASE TheError = 1584
               * Unique index violation
               *  (There is no unique index, here)
             OTHERWISE
                =MESSAGEBOX("Unknown error #"+STR(TheError)
        ENDCASE
    ELSE
        END TRANSACTION
    ENDIF
CLOSE ALL
CLEAR ALL
RETURN
FUNCTION ReplaceError
lErrorFound = .T.
=AERROWS(ArrErrors) && Array of errors
TheError = ArrErrors[1,1]
DO CASE
        CASE TheError = 1539
           * Handle trigger errors
        CASE TheError = 1581
           * Attempt to add null value field
        CASE TheError = 1582
           * Field rule (salary > 50000) was violated
           * ( Don't give them raise if it would give
              them more than 50K )
           = TABLEREVERT(.F.) && Restore original value
        OTHERWISE
            =MESSAGEBOX("Unknown error #"+STR(TheError)
ENDCASE
RETURN
```

The *TXTLEVEL()* Function

The TXTLEVEL() function returns the transaction nesting level. It returns a numeric value between 0 and 5. A value of 0 denotes that a transaction is not in progress. Of course, because a transaction nesting level cannot exceed five levels, the maximum value returned by the TXTLEVEL() function is 5.

The operation of the TXTLEVEL() function is illustrated in the following example, which shows transactions nested two levels deep:

```
*****************************************************************
* Procedure: Trans1.prg
* Purpose: Illustrates use of TXNLEVEL() function
CLOSE DATABASES
OPEN DATABASE PF
USE Employee
BEGIN TRANSACTION
    ? "Transaction level: ", TXNLEVEL()  && Transaction level: 1
    BEGIN TRANSACTION
      ? "Transaction level: ", TXNLEVEL() && Transaction level: 2
    END TRANSACTION
END TRANSACTION
CLOSE ALL
CLEAR ALL
? "Transaction level: ", TXNLEVEL()    && Transaction level: 0
```

The `TXNLEVEL()` function is useful for determining whether all of the previously executed transaction groups have successfully executed. For example, following an `END TRANSACTION` statement, you can add the following statements to undo or rollback updates that are made in an uncompleted transaction:

```
IF TXNLEVEL() > 0
    ROLLBACK
ENDIF
```

Commands That Cannot Be Used in Transactions

The following commands are not supported during a transaction:

```
APPEND PROCEDURES    CREATE CONNECTION          MODIFY DATABASE
CLEAR ALL            CREATE DATABASE            MODIFY PROCEDURE
CLOSE ALL            CREATE TRIGGER             MODIFY VIEW
CLOSE DATABASES      CREATE VIEW                DELETE TRIGGER
CLOSE TABLES         CREATE SQL VIEW            DELETE VIEW
COPY INDEXES         DELETE CONNECTION          MODIFY CONNECTION
COPY PROCEDURES      DELETE DATABASE
```

None of the following commands and functions can be executed for a table that participates in a transaction:

```
ALTER TABLE          INSERT                     SETCURSORPROP()
CREATE TABLE         MODIFY STRUCTURE           TABLEREVERT()
DELETE TAG           PACK                       ZAP
INDEX                REINDEX
```

There are few, if any, real-world uses of database management systems in which integrity is not important. But for many Visual FoxPro programmers, transaction management is something new, and new concepts must be learned. Also, systems run more slowly with transaction management. These objections will gradually be overcome by the overarching need for database integrity.

Network Resources

Besides sharing data files, you can use a LAN to share central resources such as printers or other output devices. FoxPro supports redirection of output devices with the SET PRINTER command.

On many LANs, you can redirect printer output using network software so that all programs, including FoxPro, automatically print on a central device. Using the SET PRINTER command from FoxPro, you can accomplish the same effect more flexibly. For example, application programs written in FoxPro can offer users a choice of shared or local printers.

The syntax varies based on the LAN software. For example, on an IBM PC network, IBM Token Ring network, or Ungermann-Bass network, the syntax is this:

```
SET PRINTER TO [\\<computer name>]\<printer name>=LPT#
```

On a Novell network, you use the SPOOL or CAPTURE commands before starting FoxPro to establish a shared printer as LPT2, for example. The syntax in FoxPro is simply this:

```
SET PRINTER TO LPT2
SET PRINTER TO LPT2
```

By default, printer output is sent to the MS-DOS PRN device. To direct output to a local printer (or a network printer that has been set up to look like a local printer), use the following syntax:

```
SET PRINTER TO LPT<#>
SET PRINTER TO COM<#>
```

You can use usual output devices—for example, plotters, displays (as in signs), and FAX machines—as if they are printers by configuring them so that application programs such as FoxPro look like printers. You can also specify network printer parameters such as the title of a banner page, form numbers, and number of copies. Chapter 10, "Environment," describes the SET PRINTER options in detail.

Summary

This chapter covers a lot of ground, from network hardware to concurrency. It explains several important multiuser terms and FoxPro's place in the ISO protocol model.

The discussion of file and record locking led to concurrency issues, multiuser pitfalls, shared read-only access, and changed record detection.

In addition, this chapter describes three new commands and a function added to Visual FoxPro to support atomic update integrity, or (in the less formal terminology) transaction processing.

The chapter then covers network resources, including how Visual FoxPro lets application programs switch easily from local printers to network printers.

26

Visual FoxPro and Client/Server Support

To know yet to think that one does not know is best; Not to know yet think that one knows will lead to difficulty.

—Lao-Tzu (6th Century B.C.)

Client/server is a system that consists of a server, which manages databases, and a client (or *front end*), which requests data from the server. This centralized method of managing databases is ideal for databases that have a large number of users who require remote access to information in the database. The client does not manipulate the data; the client passes a SQL request over the network to the server, and the server performs the query and returns the requested data to the client.

The traditional FoxPro multiuser solution distributes tables on the network server and allows multiple users to access these tables. Interaction is controlled with record and file locking. Every time you request data from the client, you have to examine all of the data on the remote computer and select the information you want to use; all of the data is transferred across the network from the server to the client. This type of operation puts a considerable load on the network. If you have many users accessing data, it can really slow down the network response. Consider what happens when you index a table on the server. All the records in a table on the server are transferred across the network to the client's computer so that the index can be created. Then the index blocks are transferred back to the server. This is the way traditional FoxPro works. On the other hand, when you are using a SQL database server and you want to create an index on a table, you transmit a single command to the server, and the database server creates the index.

In the recent past, microcomputer-based database applications were limited to relatively small- and medium-sized databases. Large corporate databases were still maintained on large minicomputers and mainframes. Now that network servers have become more powerful and SQL database servers have become available, more and more large companies are moving their large corporate database to a microcomputer client/server environment. They use terms such as "downsizing" and "rightsizing," but some corporations still have not made the switch to the client/server environment. Eventually, the client/server environment will become the dominant database management solution for corporations. As this happens, database management systems that provide a client front end to these powerful database servers will also become dominant.

The Microsoft SQLServer for Windows NT, Oracle, and other servers have become very popular because they are powerful, offer excellent security, and can handle a huge number of transactions. They provide server (or *back-end*) support.

Regardless of which back-end database engine you use, you still need a client, or front-end, software package to provide users with access to server data.

Database management front-end packages, such as PowerBuilder by Powersoft and Microsoft's Access, have been gaining market share in the database sector because they provide access to SQL servers. Many organizations have given up on available front-end products because of the products' limitations and lack of programmability. These organizations are writing their own custom front ends in C and C++. Visual FoxPro is an excellent choice for a front end because of its excellent performance, its rich object-oriented development environment, and its seamless connectivity.

Visual FoxPro supports two modes of connectivity. You can create views and work with server tables in much the same way that you work with local Visual FoxPro tables. Or you can use a technique know as *SQL pass-through* (*SPT*). When you use the SQL pass-through method, you send a SQL command that is native to the back-end server, and the server returns the results to Visual FoxPro.

You can develop a powerful client/server application that uses views to access remote data. You can use Visual FoxPro remote views to select the data you want from the remote server and then place the data in a Visual FoxPro cursor. You can use this cursor to process the information and update the remote data.

One of the outstanding features of Visual FoxPro is that you can create a complete application using local views to build a local prototype of the application. Then you can use the Upsizing Wizard to transform the local views to remote views. However, the Upsizing Wizard only works if you use the Microsoft SQLServer for Windows NT as your server.

The Open Database Connectivity Standard

The first thing you do when you want to access remote data is to create a connection. You connect to an alien remote environment that does not maintain data in the same way the Visual FoxPro database engine stores and maintains data. However, this is not a problem because Visual FoxPro connects to a remote server by utilizing the open database connectivity (ODBC) standard. ODBC drivers are available for most all database servers. You must have an ODBC driver for the server to which you want to connect. ODBC drivers provide a totally seamless and independent system interface between the client and the server.

The ODBC driver passes commands and data between Visual FoxPro and the remote server. The server ODBC driver converts Visual FoxPro data into data that can be interpreted by the server and visa versa. The data types handled by the ODBC driver are also standardized. By default, Visual FoxPro converts the data type of each standard ODBC field received from a remote ODBC connection into an equivalent Visual FoxPro data type. This is shown in Table 26.1. You can change the default types using the `DBSETPROP()` function. Servers have their own translation rules, which they use to translate standard ODBC fields to their native format.

Table 26.1. ODBC field data types and their equivalent Visual FoxPro data types.

ODBC Data Type	*Equivalent Visual FoxPro Data Type*

`SQL_CHAR`
`SQL_VARCHAR`
`SQL_LONGVARCHAR`
	The values are converted into a Visual FoxPro Character field unless the width of the Character field is less than the value of the `UseMemoSize` cursor property; otherwise, values are converted into a Memo field

`SQL_BINARY`	Memo

continues

Table 26.1. continued

ODBC Data Type	*Equivalent Visual FoxPro Data Type*
SQL_LONGVARBINARY	Memo
SQL_VARBINARY	Memo
SQL_DECIMAL SQL_NUMERIC	Numeric or Currency; if the server field is a SQL Money data type, the field becomes a Visual FoxPro Currency data type
SQL_BIT	Logical
SQL_TINYINT	Integer
SQL_SMALLINT	Integer
SQL_INTEGER	Integer
SQL_BIGINT	Character
SQL_REAL	Double
SQL_FLOAT	Double
SQL_DOUBLE	Double
SQL_DATE	Date
SQL_TIME	DateTime (the date becomes 1/1/1990, for example)
SQL_TIMESTAMP	DateTime

When you pass Visual FoxPro cursor data to a remote server, the ODBC driver translates the Visual FoxPro fields to standard ODBC data types, as shown in Table 26.2.

Table 26.2. The conversion of Visual FoxPro field data types to ODBC standard field data types.

Visual FoxPro Data Type	*Equivalent ODBC Data Type*
Character	SQL_CHAR (width < 255 characters)
	SQL_LONGVARCHAR (width > 254 characters)
Currency	SQL_DECIMAL
Date	SQL_DATE (for all servers except SQLServer for which data fields are translated into SQL_TIMESTAMP types)
DateTime	SQL_TIMESTAMP
Double	SQL_DOUBLE
General	SQL_LONGVARBINARY
Logical	SQL_BIT
Memo	SQL_LONGVARCHAR
Numeric	SQL_DOUBLE

You cannot access remote data until you install an ODBC driver on the client computer and establish an ODBC data source. In other words, until you install an ODBC driver, you cannot create remote views and you cannot use SQL pass-through.

Microsoft supplies a variety of ODBC drivers with Visual FoxPro, including drivers for the following:

- FoxPro version 2.*x* database files
- Microsoft Access database files
- Paradox version 3.*x* and 4.*x* tables
- dBASE III and IV files
- Btrieve tables
- SQLServer database files
- Microsoft Excel spreadsheets
- Fixed-width and delimited-text files
- Oracle7 database files

When installing Visual FoxPro, if you choose the Complete Install option, ODBC drivers for all of the applications in the previous list are installed. If you want to install specific drivers, choose the Custom Install option and select the ODBC Support option on the Options list. Once the appropriate driver is installed, you can add a data source for the ODBC driver. You can do this by following these steps:

1. Choose the ODBC Administrator icon from either the Windows Control Panel or the Visual FoxPro program group, and the Data Source dialog box appears.
2. Click on the Add button in the Data Source dialog box, and the Add Data source dialog box appears.
3. Select the driver you want from the Installed ODBC Drivers list box, click on the OK button, and the ODBC Setup dialog box appears.
4. Establish the appropriate options in the ODBC Setup dialog box. Note that there is a Help button in the ODBC Setup dialog box to help you make decisions about the options. When you are finished, click on the OK button. That is it.

Now all you have to do is set up your server on the network, and you will be ready to go. Just execute Visual FoxPro and get connected.

The Connection

The first step for accessing data from a remote server is to establish a connection. To do this, you specify three or four parameters, depending on the type of connection. For a standard ODBC connection, you specify the data source name, your user ID, and your password.

Alternatively, you can specify a *connection string* for some types of server connections and the name of the database to use.

Visual FoxPro lets you store the connection in a database. This makes it easier to reference the name of the connection when you want to create a remote view. To create a named connection, you open a database (OPEN DATABASE <*cDatabase*>) and then create a connection with the CREATE CONNECTION <*connection name*> command. Here is an example:

```
OPEN DATABASE MyDatabase
CREATE CONNECTION MyConnection
```

The Connection Designer opens for you to define the connection, as shown in Figure 26.1. You can also create a connection in the Project Manager by selecting the Connections icon in the Databases list box; you click on the **N**ew button to open the Connection Designer.

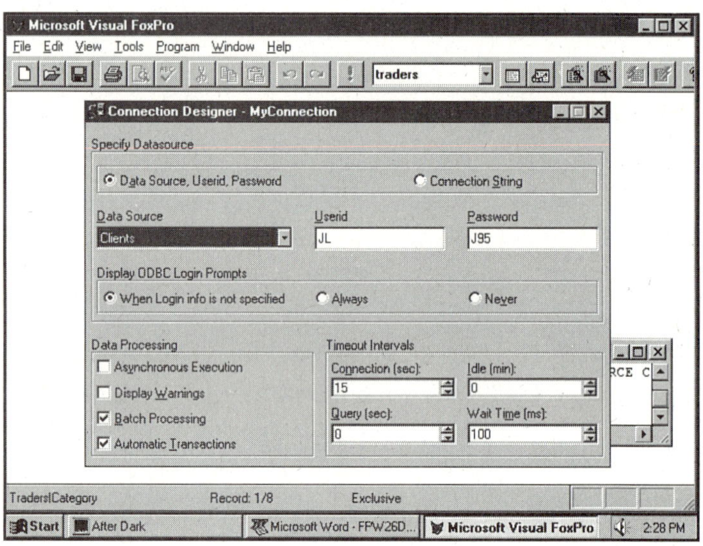

FIGURE 26.1.
The Connection Designer.

Remember that you cannot use the Connection Designer unless a database is open. You use the Connection Designer to create or modify a named connection. The Connection Designer dialog box might appear complicated, but it is fundamentally simple. You should focus mainly on the Data Source, User ID, and Password boxes. Your job is to choose a data source from the list of installed ODBC data sources. If the data source requires a user ID and password, you must enter them. That is all you need to do unless you are setting other options to optimize the performance. When you close the Connection Designer, the connection is established. The other options in the Connection Designer are described in Table 26.3.

Table 26.3. The other Connection Designer options.

Option	*Description*
Always	Specifies that Visual FoxPro always prompts the user with the ODBC data source login dialog box. This enables the user to use a login ID and password that are different from the ones stored in the named connection.
Never	Specifies that Visual FoxPro never prompt the user with the ODBC data source login dialog box. This option ensures higher security.
	Data Processing Group
Asynchronous Execution	Use this check box to specify whether a connection is asynchronous or synchronous. This option corresponds to the `Asynchronous` connection property. This check box and other check boxes in the Data Processing group correspond to the connection properties you can establish with the `DBSETUP()` function.
Display Warnings	Use this check box to specify that you want nontrappable warnings to be displayed. This option corresponds to the `DispWarnings` connection property.
Batch Processing	Use this check box to specify that the connection operates in batch mode. This option corresponds to the `BatchMode` connection property.
Automatic Transactions	Use this check box to indicate that you want transaction processing to be handled automatically. This option corresponds to the `Transactions` connection property.
	Timeout Interval Group
Connection (sec)	Connection time-out interval in seconds. This option corresponds to the `ConnectTimeout` connection property. This and other spinner controls in the Timeout Intervals group are used to specify time-out intervals, which also can be set with the `DBSETPROP()` function.
Query (sec)	Query time-out interval in seconds. This option corresponds to the `QueryTimeout` connection property.
Idle (min)	Idle time-out interval in minutes. Active connections are deactivated after the specified time interval. This option corresponds to the `IdleTimeout` connection property.
Wait Time (ms)	Execution wait time. This option designates the amount of time in milliseconds that elapses before Visual FoxPro determines that the SQL statement has completed executing. This option corresponds to the `WaitTime` connection property.

You can always return to the Connection Designer to modify the connection by executing the MODIFY CONNECTION command from the Command window or by selecting the connection name in the Project Manager Database list box and clicking on the Modify button.

You do not have to create a connection visually. You can create a connection without the aid of the Connection Designer by executing either the DATASOURCE or CONNSTRING clause with the CREATE CONNECTION command. Here is the syntax:

```
CREATE CONNECTION [<Connection Name> | ?]
       [ DATASOURCE <cDataSourceName>
       [ USERID <cUserID>] [ PASSWORD <cPassWord>]
     | CONNSTRING <cConnectionString>]
```

Note that in this syntax, you either specify the CONNECTION, DATASOURCE, and USERID clauses or you specify the CONNSTRING clause. The *<Connection Name>* clause specifies the name of the connection to create and insert in the active database. If you specify a question mark, Visual FoxPro displays the Connection Designer, from which you can create and name the connection when you save it.

The DATASOURCE *<cDataSourceName>* clause specifies the name of the ODBC data source for the connection. USERID *<cUserID>* specifies your user identification for the ODBC data source. PASSWORD *<cPassWord>* specifies your password for the ODBC data source.

The CONNSTRING *<cConnectionString>* clause specifies a character string containing a *connection string* for the ODBC data source. You can use the connection string instead of explicitly including the ODBC data source, the user identification, and the password.

The CREATE CONNECTION command creates the connection and adds your connection to the active database. You can remove a connection from the active database with the DELETE CONNECTION command. The following example opens the database, named MyDataBase, and then creates a connection, called MyConnection, to the ODBC data source, named SQLNT, with the user ID jl and the password Glibble:

```
CLOSE DATABASES
OPEN DATABASE MyDatabase
CREATE CONNECTION MyConnection  DATASOURCE "SQLNT" ;
     USERID "jl" PASSWORD "Glibble"
RENAME MyConnection TO MYCon1   && Rename the newly created connection
DISPLAY CONNECTIONS             && Displays named connections in the database
DELETE CONNECTION Mycon1        && Removes the connection just renamed
```

You can use the CONNSTRING clause to create a connection, as illustrated in the following example:

```
CLOSE DATABASES
OPEN DATABASE MyDatabase
CREATE CONNECTION MyConnection  CONNSTRING "DSN=SQLNT; UID=jl; PWD=Glibble"
DISPLAY CONNECTIONS             && Displays named connections in the database
DELETE CONNECTION Mycon1        && Removes the newly created connection
```

In the `CONSTRING` clause, there can be no spaces before or after the equal sign or before the semicolon. The `DSN` keyword specifies the data source, the `UID` keyword specifies the user ID, and the `PWD` keyword specifies the password.

You connect SQL pass-through (SPT) commands by executing the `SQLCONNECT()` and `SQLSTRINGCONNECT()` functions. There are three ways to establish an SPT connection, as illustrated in the following examples.

The following command launches the Select Connection or Datasource dialog box, as shown in Figure 26.2. You choose a data source, and a SQLServer login dialog box appears so that you can choose a connection. This is the command:

```
nHandle = SQLCONNECT()
```

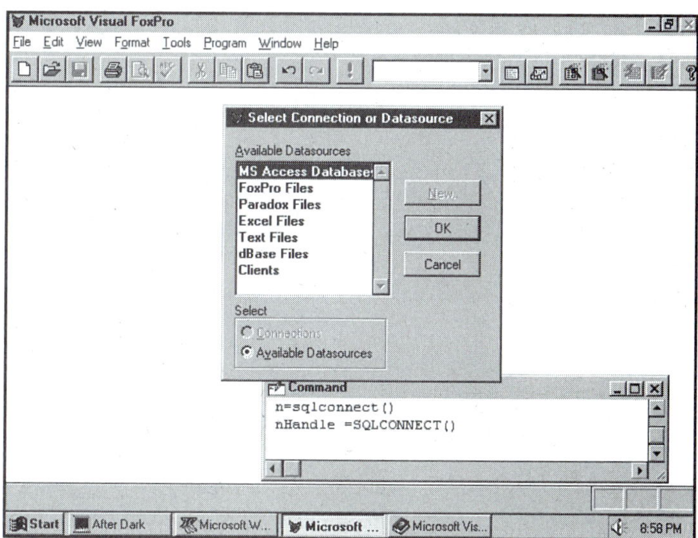

FIGURE 26.2.
The Select Connection or Datasource dialog box.

The standard method of creating an SPT connection is to specify a data source, a user ID, and if required, a password. Here is an example of the standard form of a `SQLCONNECT()` function call:

```
nHandle =  SQLCONNECT("SQLNT", "jl")
IF nHandle <= 0
   = MESSAGEBOX("Cannot make connection", 16, "SQL Connect Error")
ELSE
   = MESSAGEBOX("Connection made", 48, "SQL Connect Message")
   = SQLDISCONNECT(nHandle)
ENDIF
```

Note that the `SQLDISCONNECT()` function is used to close a connection.

You can also use a connection string with the `SQLSTRINGCONNECT()` function as illustrated with the following example:

```
nHandle =  SQLCONNECT("DSN=SQLNT; UID=jl; PWD=Glibble; DATABASE=Students")
IF nHandle <= 0
   = MESSAGEBOX("Cannot make connection", 16, "SQL Connect Error")
ELSE
   = MESSAGEBOX("Connection made", 48, "SQL Connect Message")
   = SQLDISCONNECT(nHandle)
ENDIF
```

The value returned by the `SQLCONNECT()` and `SQLSTRINGCONNECT()` functions, `hHandle`, is used as an argument for the other SPT functions to reference this connection. Now that you have established a connection, you are ready to query the server.

Accessing Data from the Remote Server

Once you are connected, you can query remote databases on a server. You can transfer selected data from the server to a Visual FoxPro cursor. Using SPT functions, you can pass a command to a server, and the server processes the command and transmits the resultant data back to the Visual FoxPro client. Normally, the command is a Transact SQL `SELECT` statement and the resultant data is in the form of a Visual FoxPro cursor.

TIP

Here are some things to remember when you are requesting data from a server. When accessing a vast store of data, keep the result set as small as possible. Let the server summarize the data, and request only the information you need. You can create a view consisting of remote data and local data. Keep local copies of large, infrequently changed tables, such as lookup tables.

There are two methods of querying the server tables. One way is to use remote views that are maintained within database container files. The second way is to use the SQL pass-through `SQLEXEC()` function. Both methods create a SQL statement and pass it to the server, which returns a Visual FoxPro cursor. However, the mechanisms for the two methods are considerably dissimilar.

Remote Views

Once you have a valid data source or a named connection, you can create a remote view. The process is very similar to creating a local view. The only difference is that you add a connection or data source instead of a Visual FoxPro table or cursor when you create a local view. Use the following steps to create a remote view:

1. Select a database in the Project Manager.
2. Select the Remote Views icon, which is shown in Figure 26.3.
3. Click on the **N**ew button.
4. You can use the View Designer or the Remote View Wizard to create a remote view.

You create the view the same way you create a local view, except the data is remote.

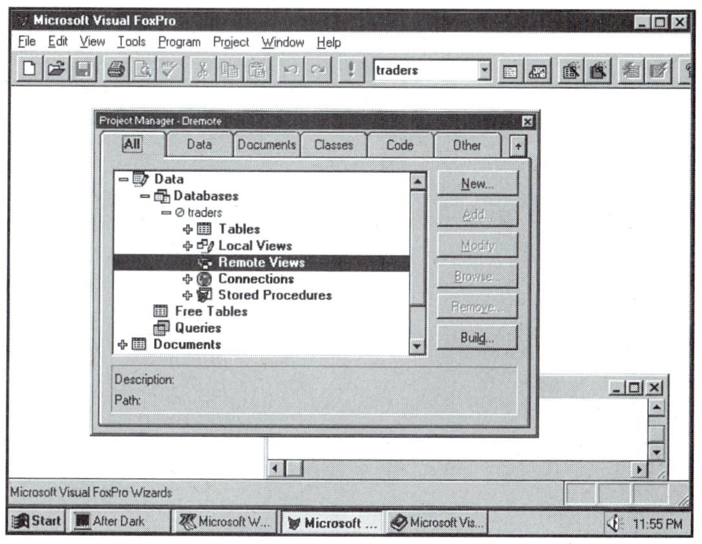

FIGURE 26.3.
The Project Manager with the Remote Views icon selected.

You can create a remote view programmatically using the `CREATE SQL VIEW` command and specifying the `CONNECTIONS` clause. For example, if you want to create a remote view, called `Products`, in the `Trader` database, which is based on a products table that resides on the remote server, you can use the following statements:

```
OPEN DATABASE Trader
CREATE SQL VIEW Products CONNECTION MyConnection;
     AS SELECT * FROM products
```

You can also specify the `REMOTE` keyword instead of the `CONNECTION` keyword with the `CREATE SQL VIEW` command in the above example. A dialog box appears from which you select a connection or a data source. Here is an example:

```
OPEN DATABASE Trader
CREATE SQL VIEW Products REMOTE ;
     AS SELECT * FROM products
```

Whether you create a view with the View Designer or the `CREATE SQL VIEW` command, it is advisable to limit the number of records in the resultant cursor. This is especially true if the server contains a massive amount of data. To filter the data in the View Designer, add a filter to the Selection Criteria tab, as shown in Figure 26.4.

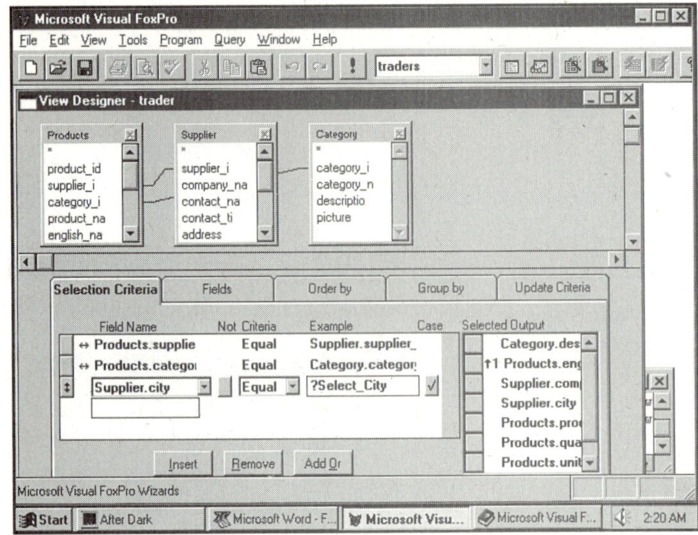

FIGURE 26.4.
The View Designer with a record filter.

This filter makes use of a neat new feature in Visual FoxPro that allows you to filter records in a view without creating a separate view for each subset of records. This feature is called a *parameterized view*. A parameterized view contains a parameter preceded with a question mark (?) character in the example field (`?Select_City`). Choose the **Q**uery menu View **P**arameter… option, and the View Parameter dialog box appears, as shown in Figure 26.5.

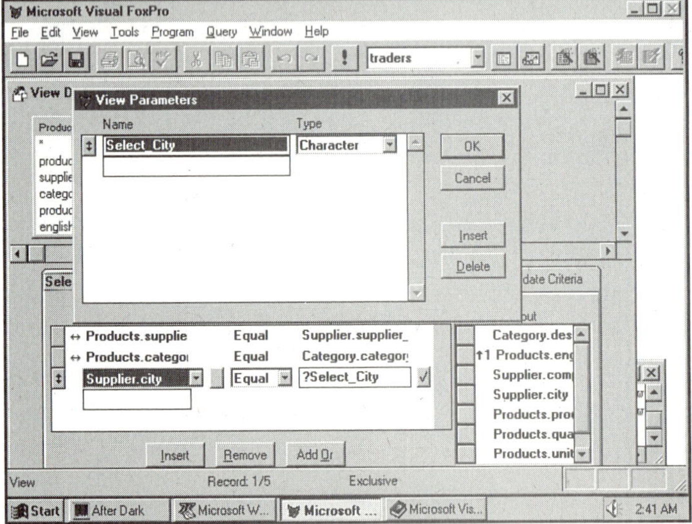

FIGURE 26.5.
The View Designer with the View Parameters dialog box.

When you run the query, the parameter you supply is evaluated as a Visual FoxPro expression. If the evaluation fails, Visual FoxPro prompts you for the parameter value. In this case, each time you run the parameterized query, you are prompted to enter a value, as shown in Figure 26.6. The records that are downloaded are limited to those records that match the parameter value. In this case, only records with a `Supplier.Cities` field that begin with `Mel`, such as `Melborne`, `Melrose`, `Melvindale`, are included in the resultant cursor.

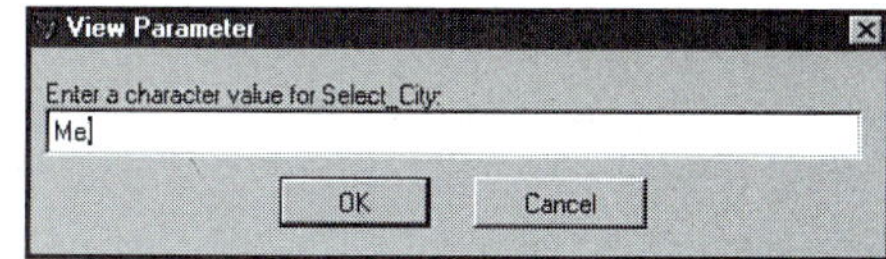

FIGURE 26.6.
The View Parameters dialog box, which prompts you for a value of the parameter.

You can programmatically add a filter to the `SELECT` statement in the `CREATE SQL VIEW` command to limit the scope of records. You can also specify a parameterized view with a `CREATE SQL VIEW` command. You can limit the scope of records to those records that match the parameterized value. If the search fails, you are prompted to enter a new value. You specify a parameterized view with the `WHERE` clause, which is added to the `CREATE SQL VIEW` command. In the following example, a view is created and the Browse window contains only records for `Chicago`:

```
Select_City = "Chicago"
OPEN DATABASE Trader
CREATE SQL VIEW Products CONNECTION MyConnection;
     AS SELECT * FROM products WHERE products.City = ?Select_City
BROWSE
```

Once the view is created, you can use it again and again for different cities. In the following example, the resultant Browse window contains records for `London`:

```
Select_City="London"
USE Trader!Products
BROWSE
```

TIP

Normally, a parameter is a simple identifier. However, a parameter can be an expression. If it is, enclose the parameter expression in parentheses, so that the entire expression is evaluated as part of the parameter.

The process is the same for local and remote views. You can combine local tables and connections in a remote view. The connectivity is seamless.

SQL Pass-Through Queries

You use the `SQLEXEC()` function to perform queries. The `SQLEXEC()` function creates a local Visual FoxPro cursor. Here is an example of a parameterized query:

```
Select_City="Chicago"
nHandle = SQLCONNECT("MyQuery")
IF nHandle <= 0
   = MESSAGEBOX("Cannot make connection", 16, "SQL Connect Error")
ELSE
   nCount = SQLEXEC(nHandle, "SELECT * FROM Products ;
      WHERE Products.Cities = ?Select_City", "MyQuery" )
   = SQLDISCONNECT(nHandle)
ENDIF
```

In this example, the `SQLEXEC()` function passes a SQL statement to the server. The server processes the statement and returns the resultant records for `Chicago`. Then Visual FoxPro creates a cursor named `MyQuery` containing the records. If you do not specify a name for the cursor, `SQLRESULT` is used. You can examine error conditions by calling `AERROR()` immediately after the error occurs.

The SPT functions used to execute and control queries include the `SQLCANCEL()`, `SQLEXEC()`, `SQLMORERESULTS()`, `SQLCOMMIT()`, and `SQLROLLBACK()` commands. The `SQLCANCEL()` function cancels an executing SQL query. The `SQLMORERESULTS()` function puts another result set into a cursor. It returns the number of records in the result set or returns `0` if the statement creating the result set is still executing. You use the `SQLCOMMIT()` function to request a transaction commitment and the `SQLROLLBACK()` function to request a transaction rollback.

If the `SET ESCAPE` command is `ON` and the connection is in synchronous mode, you can press the Esc key or issue the `SQLCANCEL()` function to cancel the execution of the `SQLEXEC()`, `SQLMORERESULTS()`, `SQLTABLES()`, and `SQLCOLUMNS()` functions. The other SPT functions are not interruptable.

You can retrieve a list of column names for a specified SQL table and information about each column with the `SQLCOLUMNS()` function. The information is returned to a Visual FoxPro cursor. You can retrieve a list of names of tables in the data source. The names are placed in a Visual FoxPro cursor.

The `SQLGETPROP()` function retrieves a connection property from an active connection. You can set a property of an active connection with the `SQLSETPROP()` function.

NOTE

Using SPTs is the best technique for creating read-only cursors and for passing SQL-type statements to the remote server. For example, you can use SPTs to perform data definition operations, manipulation and execution of remote stored procedures, and similar tasks. On the other hand, it is easy to create remote views with the Database

Designer, the View Designer, and the Remote View Wizard. Views provide automatic buffering and update capabilities. As a result, views are best suited for general database management operations.

Prototyping

Visual FoxPro contains development tools that make rapid application development possible; it is easy to create views, forms, and reports. Visual FoxPro is probably the best development environment for developing prototype applications that are destined to run in a client/server environment. Many times, a Visual FoxPro developer finds it most productive and convenient to develop an application using local views and then *upsize* to the server once the application has been tested and debugged. On the other hand, if remote access is available, you might want to develop an application using the remote data source. Here is the nice part: Both methods are easy to do.

A local prototype for a Visual FoxPro client/server application is a totally operational application that uses local views to access local tables. Your local tables are copies of all the tables or a portion of the tables on a server. Your local views and tables imitate views and tables on the server. Of course, the format of Visual FoxPro tables are physically different. But because you access remote data through ODBC drivers, there will be no difference in the data.

You will need to understand the architecture of the database on the server so that you can properly mimic it using local Visual FoxPro tables and views. Also, you will not need massive amounts of data on your local computer to develop the application. Small tables will do nicely. Once you have established a local data environment that mimics the server's database, you probably will have achieved the optimum application development environment. During the development process, the objective is to minimize the differences between local views and remote views so that once you are ready to deploy the prototype on the server, the transition will be effortless.

Once you have completed the implementation, testing and debugging all of the forms, reports, queries, and other components of your prototype application, you can integrate all of the components and perform end-to-end testing and debugging. When you have completed the end-to-end testing and all of the interested parties have determined that the prototype is complete, bug free, and meets all of the design objectives, then it is time to upsize the prototype. You can upsize the prototype manually, or you can use the Upsizing Wizard to simplify the job if you use the Microsoft SQLServer for Windows NT as your server.

You might also find it beneficial to perform the upsizing operation on local views early in the prototyping process to make sure that your application can achieve your performance objectives. You need to use remote views with the same real data that your users will be working with. Prototyping on local views is convenient, but it does not simulate the actual client/server environment in which your users will be operating. Once you are convinced that you are on the right track, you can continue the process of developing your prototype using local views.

The Upsizing Process

Before you can use the Upsizing Wizard, there are a number of things you must do.

Preparing the Server

The following checklist contains all of the tasks you have to complete to prepare the server for upsizing:

- Make sure the server has enough disk space to hold the data for the new application.
- Make sure you have all of the necessary permissions on the SQLServer to which you plan to upsize. The Upsizing Wizard must be permitted to complete its tasks without encountering any attempted access violations.
- Make estimates of the server database and device size because the Upsizing Wizard will request this information. For example, if you want to create a new database on the server, the size of the new database must be at least 2MB since that is the minimum database size allowed by the Microsoft SQLServer.

Preparing the Client

Before you upsize your prototype, you must prepare your client computer by establishing access to the server through an ODBC data source or named connection.

In addition, you should back up all components of your application and database. Although it is always good practice to periodically back up your hard drives, it is particularly important to back up the DBC, DBT, and DBX files before upsizing, because the Upsizing Wizard changes these files. If you need to revert the files, you will have to do it from your backup files. If you do not back up these files, you will have no way to restore them.

The last step is to close all of the tables in the database to be upsized. The Upsizing Wizard opens all tables in the database exclusively. If the Upsizing Wizard detects any files open in shared mode, it will close them and then open them exclusively. If the Upsizing Wizard cannot open a table exclusively, it displays a message that tells you which tables are not available for upsizing.

The Upsizing Wizard

To execute the Upsizing Wizard, choose the **T**ools Menu **W**izards option. Then choose the Wizards menu **U**psizing option. The Upsizing Wizard appears, as shown in Figure 26.7.

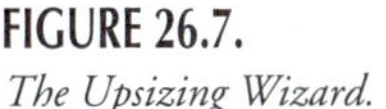

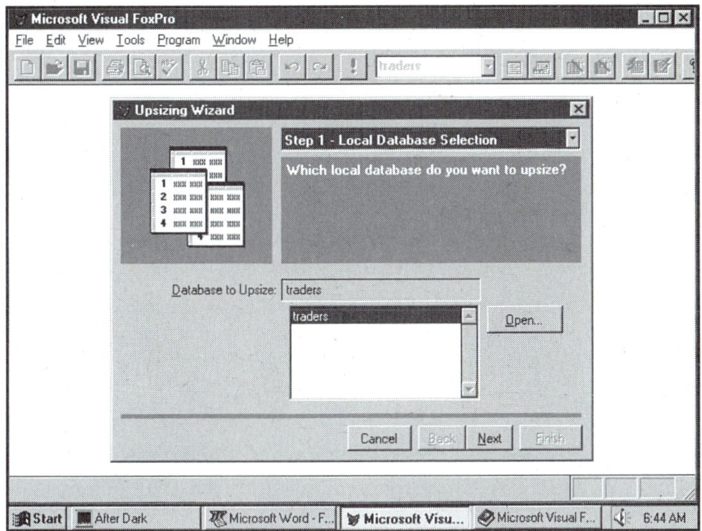

FIGURE 26.7.
The Upsizing Wizard.

Follow the instructions presented by the Upsizing Wizard screens. When you have preceded to the 9th and final screen and have specified the appropriate options, click on the Finish button, and the Upsizing Wizard will do the rest.

The upsizing operation can be a great consumer of time. It all depends on the size of your tables, the network loading, and how busy the database server is. If you have large tables, the Upsizing Wizard might require as long as two or three hours to finish the upsizing process.

Although the Upsizing Wizard is slow, it is thorough and rather clever. It creates a SQLServer database that, for all practical purposes, duplicates the functionality of Visual FoxPro database. The following section describes each of the Upsizing Wizard steps.

Step 1: Select a Local Database

If a database is not active or the wrong database is active, you can choose the Open button and the Open dialog box displays. You can choose a DBC database file.

Step 2: Select a Data Source

In this step you select the ODBC SQLServer data source or the named connection you want to use. If you use a named connection to access your data source, the Upsizing Wizard associates the named connection with any remote views it creates during the upsizing operation.

If you use a data source name rather than a connection name to log on to the data source and you choose to have the Upsizing Wizard create remote views, the Upsizing Wizard makes up its own name (`Upsize`) for the named connection. If more than one named connection exists, the wizard appends a number to the name (`Upsize2`, `Upsize3`, and so on).

When you choose the Next button, the Upsizing Wizard displays the ODBC Login dialog box. If you used a named connection with a saved password, the Upsizing Wizard automatically logs you on to the SQLServer you have selected.

Step 3: Choose a Target Database

If you want to add Visual FoxPro tables to an existing SQLServer database, you can upsize to an existing database and the Upsizing Wizard skips to Step 6. If you choose to create a new remote database, you enter its name. The name can be up to 30 characters long and can include letters, digits, and the symbols `#`, `$`, and _ (underscore). Spaces are not allowed.

Step 4: Select the Database Device (SQLServer)

In Step 4, you select the size and device for your database. You can choose from a list of existing devices or you can create a new device. The size of a new database must be at least 2MB because that is the minimum size allowed by the SQLServer.

Step 5: Specify the Log Device (SQLServer)

The SQLServer creates a transaction log for your database. You can use this log to reconstruct the database in the event of a serious system problem.

It is best if the database and the log are placed on separate physical disk devices. You must create the devices prior to executing the Upsizing Wizard. This is because the wizard creates all new devices on the same physical drive on which the master database device resides.

You should place the database and its log on separate devices if you have only one physical disk. This is so you can use the SQLServer `DUMP TRANSACTION` command.

Step 6: Specify the Tables to Be Upsized

It is essential that other users not change any data in the tables to be upsized. To prevent this from happening, the wizard attempts to open all of the tables exclusively that are in the database you have selected to be upsized. The wizard closes any tables that are opened in shared mode and reopens them exclusively. This can cause you to lose any temporary relations. Temporary relations are those that are established with the `SET RELATION` or `SET SKIP` commands.

If the wizard is unable to open any tables in exclusive mode, the table will not be available to be upsized.

Step 7: Establish Field Data Types

In this step, you can change the default mapping of a field from Visual FoxPro data types to the ODBC standard data types. The default data types are presented in Table 26.2.

However, you cannot change the default mapping for a key field to a data type that prevents the field from being indexed. You can change the default mapping of a field that is part of an index key if you choose a data type that can be indexed. You must make sure that the data types for all fields that make up a key match. Visual FoxPro warns you if you change the default data type mapping for a field that is not a key field but is used in a Visual FoxPro index.

You can click on the **R**eset button to restore all the data types to the default settings.

Step 8: Establish Upsizing Options

By default, the Upsizing Wizard exports the structure of a table and its data. You can also export field names, data types, indexes, defaults, relationships (referential integrity constraints), and validation rules.

Visual FoxPro indexes and defaults become SQLServer indexes and defaults. If you request that validation rules be exported, the Upsizing Wizard attempts to export field-level and row-level validation rules and table relationships to SQLServer, where they become stored procedures called from SQLServer triggers.

Always update indexes if you export table relationships or you might experience mediocre performance.

Step 9: Finishing Up

You have reached the final step. The Upsizing Wizard provides you with the following three save options:

- Upsize without generating SQL code
- Only generate SQL code for upsizing
- Upsize and generate SQL code

You can only choose the first and third options if you have permission to use the `CREATE TABLE` command on the SQLServer. All the SQL code generated by the Upsizing Wizard is stored on your hard disk if you choose an option that saves SQL code.

A Final Word About Upsizing

The Upsizing Wizard makes the process of upsizing simple. However, there is still some unfinished business. You should make sure that the upsized tables you want to edit are still updatable. You need to restore the permissions on the server database so that users can update the objects they need. You also need to make sure your newly upsized database is recoverable. To do this you must schedule regular backups for your database. Last but not least, you must begin testing and debugging your application on the server.

Summary

This chapter covers Visual FoxPro's seamless connectivity support. You have learned how to create a connection to a remote server, how to query remote databases, and how to create remote views. Also, you learn how to develop a local prototype application and how to use the Upsizing Wizard to convert the application's local views to remote views.

It was best said by the English author Samuel Butler, "Don't learn to do, but do to learn." The best way to learn Visual FoxPro is to try it, use it, stumble, fall, get up, and try again. The more you work with it, the more you gain experience and knowledge. Visual FoxPro is a wonderful and powerful system that, in my opinion, is the best tool on the market today for solving database management problems.

I hope you have enjoyed our journey together through the many facets of Visual FoxPro as much as I have enjoyed presenting it to you and as much as I enjoyed writing this book. Now it is time for you to continue the voyage on your own. But feel free to revisit this book anytime you have a need since this book is also a great reference. Good luck.

VI

Appendixes

```
<opN> ::=              + ¦ - ¦ * ¦ / ¦ ** ¦ ^ ¦ ==

<primaryC> ::=         (<expC>)  ¦ <functionC> ¦ <array element>
                       ¦<fieldC> ¦ <fieldM>    ¦ <memvarC>
                       ¦<quoted string>

<primaryL> ::=         (<expL>) ¦ <functionL> ¦ <array element>
                       ¦ <fieldL> ¦ <memvarL> ¦ .T. ¦ .t. ¦ .F.
                       ¦ .f. ¦ .Y. ¦ .y. ¦ .N. ¦ .n.
```

NOTE

`.Y.` (yes) and `.N.` (no) are language specific; that is, Y and N in English, S and N in Spanish, and so on.

```
<primaryN> ::=           ( <expN> ) ¦ <functionN> ¦ <array element>
                         ¦ <fieldN> ¦ <fieldF>    ¦ <integer>
                         ¦ <float> ¦ <expD> - <expD>

<secondaryL> ::=         <expN> <opL> <expN>   ¦ <expC> <opL> <expC>
                         ¦ <expD> <opL> <expD> ¦ <primaryL>

<expSTYLE> ::=           <expC> (which evaluates to <Style_chars>)

<Style_char> ::=          B ¦ I ¦ N ¦ O ¦ S ¦ - ¦ T ¦ U

<expFUNC> ::=            <expC> (which evaluates to a <Func_chars>)

<expPIC>  ::=            <expC>(which evaluates to a <picture>)

<picture> ::=            [@<Func_chars><space>][<picture symbol>]

<stringPIC> ::=          <dbl_quote_strPIC>¦<single_quote_strPIC>

<picture symbol> ::=     ! ¦ # ¦ $ ¦ * ¦ + ¦ - ¦ , ¦
                         . ¦ 9 ¦ A ¦ L ¦ N ¦ X ¦ Y ¦
                         <other symbols>

<other symbols> ::=      Overrides the data character for
                         character type data

<Func_chars> ::=         <Func_char> [<Func_char>]...

<Func_char> ::=          ! ¦ ^ ¦ ( ¦ $ ¦ A ¦
                         B ¦ C ¦ D ¦ E ¦ I ¦ J ¦
                         K ¦ L ¦ M <string> ¦ R ¦
                         S<digits> ¦ T ¦ X ¦ Z ¦

<color character> ::=    B ¦ G ¦ I ¦ N ¦ R ¦
                         U ¦ W ¦ X ¦ * ¦ +

<termL> ::=              [.NOT.] <secondaryL>
```

Other Language Components

Here is the BNF for other language components used in the definition of commands and functions:

```
<array> ::=                <identifier> referring to an array of <memvars>

<array element> ::=        <array> '[' <expN> [, <expN> ] ']'
```

> **NOTE**
>
> Quoted square brackets (`'['`) are literal in this instance.

```
<border string> ::=         up to 8 <expC> (delimited by
                            commas) specifying the
                            character to use for top,
                            bottom, left, right, top
                            left, top right, bottom
                            left, and bottom right, in
                            that order.

<browse field list> ::=     <field name1> [:R] [:<column width>]
                            [:V = <expL1> [:F] [:E = <expC1>]]
                            [:P = <expC2>]
                            [:B = <exp1>, <exp2> [:F]]
                            [:H = <expC3>]
                            [:W = <expL2>]
                            [, <field name2> [:R]  ... ]
                            ¦  <calculated field exp>
                            [, <field name> [:R] [:<column width>]  ¦
                            <calculated field exp>]...]

<calculated field exp> ::= <field name> = <exp>

<calcFunc> ::= AVG(<expN>)  ¦ CNT() ¦ MIN(<exp>) ¦MAX(<exp>)
                            ¦ NPV(<expN>, <fieldN> [, <expN>])
                            ¦ STD(<expN>) ¦ SUM(<expN>) ¦ VAR(<expN>)

<color> ::=                 B ¦ G ¦ I ¦ N ¦ R ¦ U ¦ W ¦ X ¦ * ¦ + [<color>]

<color pair> ::=            <color> [ / <color> ]
<column width> ::=          <positive integer>
<column> ::=                <expN> (evaluates to screen col position)
<row> ::=                   <expN> (evaluates to screen row position)
<coord> ::=                 <row>, <column>
<DOS command> ::=           any command that is meaningful to the
                            host operating system

<field> ::=                 <identifier> referring to a DBF file field
```

```
<field list> ::=        <field> [/R] ¦ <calc field exp>
                        ¦ ALL  [ LIKE <skeleton> ] [ EXCEPT <skeleton> ]

<function> ::=          <procedure> referring to a user-defined
                                    function

<index> ::=             <expFN> ¦ [TAG] <expTN> [OF <expFN>]

<key label> ::=         F1...F10 ¦ Ctrl-F1...Ctrl-F10
                        ¦ Shift-F1...Shift-F9 ¦ Alt-0...Alt-9
                        ¦ Alt-A...Alt-Z ¦ LEFTARROW
                        ¦ RIGHTARROW ¦ UPARROW ¦ DNARROW
                        ¦ Home ¦ End ¦ PgUp ¦ PgDn ¦ Del
                        ¦ BACKSPACE ¦ Ctrl-LeftArrow
                        ¦ Ctrl-RightArrow ¦ Ctrl-Home
                        ¦ Ctrl-End ¦ Ctrl-PgUp ¦ Ctrl-PgDn
                        ¦ INS ¦ TAB ¦ BACKTAB
                        ¦ Ctrl-A...Ctrl-Z

<keyword> ::=           FoxPro 2.5 for Windows keyword

<macro> ::=             <identifier> referring to a recorded
                         keystroke macro

<memvar> ::=            <identifier> referring to a memory
                                     variable

<menu> ::=              <identifier> referring to a user-defined menu

<module> ::=            name of binary object file

<output> ::=            TO PRINT [PROMPT] ¦ TO FILE <expFN>

<pad> ::=               <identifier> referring to a pad of a
                                     user-defined menu

<path> ::=              Operating system specific reference to a
                        particular subdirectory

<popup> ::=             <identifier> referring to a user-defined
                                     popup

<procedure> ::=         <identifier> referring to a procedure, a
                                     PRG file, or a DBO file

<scope> ::=             <scope clause> [FOR <expL>] [WHILE <expL>]

<scope clause> ::=      ALL ¦ NEXT <expN> ¦ RECORD <expN> ¦ REST

<skeleton> ::=          <identifier> with wild cards * and ?

<unquoted character string> ::=    literal characters

<variable> ::=          <field> ¦ <memvar>

<window> ::=            <identifier> referring to a user-defined window
```

Commands

Here is the BNF for FoxPro 2.5 commands:

```
[<memvar>]  = <exp1> [, <exp2> ...]

\ ¦ \\ <text line>

!    [/N [K]] <DOS command>  ¦ <program name>

? ¦ ?? [<exp1> [PICTURE <expPIC>] [FUNCTION <expFUNC>]
       [AT <expN>] [STYLE <expSTYLE>]  [, <exp2>]] ...

??? <expC>

@ <row, column>
   [SAY <exp1>
   [BITMAP [CENTER]]
   [ISOMETRIC ¦ STRETCH]
   [VERB <expN1> ¦ <expC1>]
   [FUNCTION <expFUNC>]
   [PICTURE <expPIC>]
   [SIZE <expN2>, <expN3>]
   [FONT <expC4> [, <expN4>]] [STYLE <expSTYLE>]
   [COLOR SCHEME <expN5>
   ¦ COLOR <color pair list1>
   ¦ COLOR RGB (<color value list1>)]]
   [GET <memvar> ¦ <field>
   [FUNCTION <expFUNC>]
   [PICTURE <expPIC>]
   [FONT <expC8> [, <expN6>]]
   [STYLE <expSTYLE>]
   [DEFAULT <exp2>]
   [ENABLE ¦ DISABLE]
   [MESSAGE <expC10>]
   [[OPEN]  WINDOW <window>]
   [RANGE [<exp3>] [, <exp4>]]
   [SIZE <expN7>, <expN8>]
   [VALID <expL1> ¦ <expN9> [ERROR <expC11>]]
   [WHEN <expL2>]
   [COLOR SCHEME <expN10>
   ¦ COLOR <color pair list2>
   ¦ COLOR RGB (<color value list2>)]]
```

(List Control)

```
@ <row, column> GET <variable> ¦ <field>
   [FUNCTION <expFUNC>] ¦ [PICTURE <expPIC>]
   FROM <array>
   [RANGE <expN1> [, <expN2>]]  ¦ POPUP <popup>
   [FONT <expC3> [, <expN3>]] [STYLE <expSTYLE>]
   [DEFAULT <exp>]
   [SIZE <expN4>, <expN5>]
   [ENABLE ¦ DISABLE]
   [MESSAGE <expC5>]
   [VALID <expL1>]
   [WHEN <expL2>]
```

```
   [COLOR SCHEME <expN6>
   ¦ COLOR <color pair list>
   ¦ COLOR RGB (<color value list>)]
```

(Pop-up Control)

```
@ <row, column> GET <variable>
   FUNCTION <expFUNC> ¦ PICTURE <expPIC>
   [FONT <expC3> [, <expN1>]] [STYLE <expSTYLE>]
   [DEFAULT <exp>] [FROM <array>]
   [RANGE <expN2> [, <expN3>]]
   [SIZE <expN4>, <expN5>] [ENABLE ¦ DISABLE]
   [MESSAGE <expC5>]
   [VALID <expL1>]
   [WHEN <expL2>]
   [COLOR SCHEME <expN6> [, <expN7>]
   ¦ COLOR <color pair list>
   ¦ COLOR RGB (<color value list>)]
```

(Push Button and Radio Button Control)

```
@ <row, column> GET <variable>
   FUNCTION <expFUNC> ¦ PICTURE <expPIC>
   [FONT <expC3> [, <expN1>]] [STYLE <expSTYLE>]
   [DEFAULT <exp>]
   [SIZE <expN2>, <expN3> [, <expN4>]]
   [ENABLE ¦ DISABLE]
   [MESSAGE <expC5>]
   [VALID <expL1>]
   [WHEN <expL2>]
   [COLOR SCHEME <expN5>
   ¦ COLOR <color pair list>
   ¦ COLOR RGB (<color value list>)]
```

(Spinner Control)

```
@ <row, column>  GET <variable> SPINNER <expN1>
   [, <expN2> [, <expN3>]]
   [PICTURE <expPIC>] [FUNCTION <expFUNC>]
   [FONT <expC3> [, <expN4>]] [STYLE <expSTYLE>]
   [SIZE <expN5>, <expN6>]  [DEFAULT <expN7>]
   [ENABLE ¦ DISABLE]  [MESSAGE <expC5>]
   [RANGE [<expN8>] [, <expN9>]]
   [VALID <expL1> ¦ <expN10> [ERROR <expC6>]]
   [WHEN <expL2>]
   [COLOR SCHEME <expN11>
   ¦ COLOR <color pair list>
   ¦ COLOR RGB (<color value list>)]
```

```
@ <row, column> EDIT <variable>
   [FUNCTION <expFUNC>]
   [FONT <expC2> [, <expN1>]] [STYLE <expSTYLE>]
   [DEFAULT <exp>]
   SIZE <expN2>, <expN3> [, <expN4>]
   [ENABLE ¦ DISABLE]
   [MESSAGE <expC4>] [VALID <expL1> [ERROR <expC5>]]
   [WHEN <expL2>]
   [NOMODIFY]
   [SCROLL]
```

```
   [TAB]
   [COLOR SCHEME <expN5>
   ¦ COLOR <color pair list>
   ¦ COLOR RGB (<color value list>)]

@ <row1, column1>, <row2, column2>  BOX [<expC>]

@ <row1, column1> [CLEAR  ¦ CLEAR TO <row2, column2>]

@ <row1, column1> FILL TO <row2, column2>
   [COLOR SCHEME <expN>
   ¦ COLOR <color pair list>
   ¦ COLOR RGB (<color value list>)]

@ <row, column> MENU <array>, <expN1> [, <expN2>]
   [TITLE <expC>] [SHADOW]

@ <row, column> PROMPT <expC1>
   [MESSAGE <expC2>]

@ <row1, column1> TO <row2, column2>
   [DOUBLE ¦ PANEL  ¦ <border string>]
   [PATTERN <expN1>]  [PEN <expN2> [, <expN3>]]
   [STYLE <expC>]
   [COLOR SCHEME <expN4>
   ¦ COLOR <color pair list>
   ¦ COLOR RGB (<color value list>)]

ACCEPT [<expC>] TO <memvar>

ACTIVATE MENU <menu> [NOWAIT] [PAD <pad>]

ACTIVATE POPUP <popup> [AT <row>, <column>]
   [BAR <expN>] [NOWAIT] [REST]

ACTIVATE SCREEN

ACTIVATE WINDOW [<window1> [, <window2> ... ]] ¦ ALL
   [IN [WINDOW] <window3> ¦ SCREEN]
   [BOTTOM ¦ TOP ¦ SAME] [NOSHOW]
```

NEW FOR VISUAL FOXPRO 3

```
ADD CLASS <class name> FROM <expFN1> TO  <expFN2>  OVERWRITE

ADD TABLE <expFN> ¦ ? [NAME <expC>]
```

REVISED FOR VISUAL FOXPRO 3

```
ALTER TABLE <expTable1>

        [ADD ¦ ALTER [COLUMN] <field1>
               <FieldType> [(<expN1>  [, <expN2> ]])
               [NULL ¦ NOT NULL]
               [CHECK <expL1>  [ERROR <expC1>1]]
               [DEFAULT <exp1>]
               [PRIMARY KEY ¦ UNIQUE]
               [REFERENCES <expTable2> [TAG <tag name1> ]]
               [NOCPTRANS]]
        [ALTER [COLUMN] <field2>
               [SET DEFAULT <exp2>]
               [SET CHECK <expL2> [ERROR <expC2>]]
```

```
              [DROP DEFAULT]
              [DROP CHECK]]
        [DROP [COLUMN] <field3>]
        [SET CHECK <expL3> [ERROR <expC3>]]
        [DROP CHECK]
        [ADD PRIMARY KEY <exp3> TAG <tag name2>
        [DROP PRIMARY KEY]
        [ADD UNIQUE <exp4> TAG <tag name3>]
        [DROP UNIQUE TAG <tag name4>]
        [ADD FOREIGN KEY [<exp5>] TAG <tag name4>
              REFERENCES <expTable2> [TAG <tag name5>]]
        [DROP FOREIGN KEY TAG <tag name6> [SAVE]]
        ¦
        [RENAME COLUMN <field4> TO <field5>]
        [NOVALIDATE]

APPEND [BLANK] [IN <expWA>]

APPEND FROM <expFN> ¦ ? [FIELDS <field list>] [FOR <expL>]
   [[TYPE] [DELIMITED [WITH TAB ¦ WITH <delimiter> ¦ WITH BLANK]
   ¦ DIF ¦ FW2 ¦ MOD ¦ PDOX ¦ RPD ¦ SDF ¦ SYLK
   ¦ WK1 ¦ WK3 ¦ WKS ¦ WR1  ¦ WRK ¦ XLS ¦ XL5 [SHEET <expC>]]]
   [AS <expN>]


APPEND FROM ARRAY <array> [FOR <expL>] [FIELDS <field list>]

APPEND GENERAL <general field> >  [ FROM <expFN> ¦ MEMO <Picture Field Name> ]
   [ DATA <expC> ]
   [LINK] [CLASS <ole class>]

APPEND MEMO <memo field> FROM <expFN> [OVERWRITE] [AS <expN>]

APPEND PROCEDURE FROM <expFN> [AS <expN>] [OVERWRITE] ASSIST

AVERAGE [<exp list>] [<scope>] [FOR <expL1>] [WHILE <expL2>]
   [TO <memvar list>  ¦ TO ARRAY <array>]
   [NOOPTIMIZE]

BEGIN TRANSACTION

BLANK [FIELDS <field list>] [<scope>] [NOOPTIMIZE]

BROWSE [FIELDS <browse field list>]
   [FOR <expL1>]  [FORMAT] [FREEZE <field>]
   [KEY <exp1> [, <exp2>]] [NAME <object reference>]
   [LAST]  [LEDIT] [REDIT] [LOCK <expN2>]
   [LPARTITION] [NOAPPEND] [NOCLEAR] [NODELETE]
   [NOEDIT ¦ NOMODIFY] [NOLGRID] [NORGRID]
   [NOLINK] [NOMENU] [NOOPTIMIZE] [NOREFRESH]
   [NORMAL] [NOWAIT] [PARTITION <expN3>]
   [PREFERENCE <expC3>] [REST] [SAVE]
   [TIMEOUT <expN4>] [TITLE <expC4>]
   [VALID [:F] <expL2> [ERROR <expC5>]]  [WHEN <expL3>]
   [WIDTH <expN5>] [[WINDOW <window1>]
   [IN [WINDOW] <window2> ¦ IN SCREEN]]
   [COLOR SCHEME <expN6>
   ¦ COLOR <color pair list>
   ¦ COLOR RGB (<color value list>)]
```

```
BUILD APP <.app file> FROM <project>

BUILD EXE <.exe file> FROM <project> [STANDALONE] [EXTENDED]

BUILD PROJECT <.pjx file> FROM
   <program> ¦ <menu> ¦ <report>  ¦ <label> ¦ <screen>
   ¦ <library>  [, <program> ¦ <menu> ¦ <report>
   ¦ <label>  ¦ <screen> ¦ <library>] ... ]

CALCULATE <calcFunc> [<scope>]  [FOR <expL1>] [WHILE <expL2>]
   [TO <memvar list> ¦ TO ARRAY <array>]
   [NOOPTIMIZE]

CALL <expFN> [WITH <expC> ¦ <memvar>] [SAVE ¦ NOSAVE]

CANCEL
```

NEW FOR VISUAL FOXPRO 3

```
CD ¦ CHDIR  <path>

CHANGE [FIELDS <browse field list>]
   [<scope>] [FOR <expL1>] [WHILE <expL2>]
   [FONT <expC1> [, <expN1>]] [STYLE <expSTYLE>]
   [FREEZE <field>] [KEY <exp1> [, <exp2>]]
   [LAST] [LEDIT] [REDIT]  [LPARTITION]
   [NOAPPEND] [NOCLEAR] [NODELETE] [NOEDIT ¦ NOMODIFY]
   [NOLINK] [NOMENU] [NOOPTIMIZE] [NORMAL] [NOWAIT]
   [PARTITION <expN1>]  [PREFERENCE <expC3>]
   [REST] [SAVE] [TIMEOUT <expN2>]
   [TITLE <expC4>]  [VALID [F:] <expL3> [ERROR <expC5>]]
   [WHEN <expL4>] [WIDTH <expN3>]
   [[WINDOW <window1>]
   [IN [WINDOW] <window2> ¦ IN SCREEN]]
   [COLOR SCHEME <expN4>
   ¦ COLOR <color pair list>
   ¦ COLOR RGB (<color value list>)]

CLEAR
```

REVISED FOR VISUAL FOXPRO 3

```
CLEAR ALL ¦ EVENTS ¦ FIELDS ¦ GETS ¦ MACROS ¦ MEMORY ¦ MENUS
   ¦ POPUPS ¦ PROGRAM ¦ PROMPT ¦ READ ¦ TYPEAHEAD ¦ WINDOWS
```

REVISED FOR VISUAL FOXPRO 3

```
CLOSE ALL ¦ ALTERNATE ¦ DATABASES ¦ FORMAT
   ¦ INDEXES ¦ PROCEDURE ¦ TABLES
   ¦ MEMO <memo field1>  [, <memo field2> ... ] ¦ ALL

COMPILE <expFN> ¦ <skeleton> [ENCRYPT] [NODEBUG]
```

NEW FOR VISUAL FOXPRO 3

```
COMPILE DATABASE <expFN>

COMPILE FORM <expFN> ¦ <skeleton> [ALL]

CONTINUE

COPY FILE <expFN1> TO <expFN2>

COPY INDEXES <index file list> ¦ ALL  [TO <.cdx file>]
```

```
COPY MEMO <memo field> TO <expFN> [ADDITIVE] [AS <expN>]
```

REVISED FOR VISUAL FOXPRO 3

```
COPY PROCEDURE TO <expFN> [AS <expN>] [ADDITIVE]

COPY STRUCTURE TO <expFN> [FIELDS <field list>]
   [WITH] CDX ¦ [WITH] PRODUCTION]]
```

NEW FOR VISUAL FOXPRO 3

```
COPY TO <expFN> STRUCTURE EXTENDED [FIELDS <field list>] [AS <expN>]
```

REVISED FOR VISUAL FOXPRO 3

```
COPY TAG <tag name> [OF <.cdx file>]  TO <index file>

COPY TO <expFN> [FIELDS <field list>]
   [<scope>] [FOR <expL1>] [WHILE <expL2>]
   [[WITH] CDX] ¦ [[WITH] PRODUCTION]
   [NOOPTIMIZE]
   [TYPE] [FOXPLUS ¦ DIF ¦ MOD  ¦ SDF ¦ SYLK ¦ WK1 ¦ WKS
   ¦ WR1 ¦ WRK ¦ XLS ¦ XL5 [SHEET <expC>] ¦ DELIMITED
   [WITH <delimiter> ¦ WITH BLANK ¦ WITH TAB]]
   [AS <expN>]
```

REVISED FOR VISUAL FOXPRO 3

```
COPY TO ARRAY <array> [FIELDS <field list>]
   [<scope>] [FOR <expL1>]  [WHILE <expL2>]
   [NOOPTIMIZE]

COUNT [<scope>] [FOR <expL1>] [WHILE <expL2>]
   [TO <memvar>] [NOOPTIMIZE]

CREATE [<expFN> ¦ ?]

CREATE CLASS  CREATE CLASS <expFN> ¦ ? [OF <ClassLibraryName1> ¦ ?]
      [AS <expN> [FROM <ClassLibraryName2>]]
```

NEW FOR VISUAL FOXPRO 3

```
CREATE CLASSLIB <ClassLibraryName>
```

NEW FOR VISUAL FOXPRO 3

```
CREATE COLOR SET <color set name>

CREATE CONNECTION [<expFN> ¦ ?]  [DATASOURCE <expC1>   [ USERID <expC2>] [
PASSWORD <expC3>]  ¦ CONNSTRING <expC4>]
```

NEW FOR VISUAL FOXPRO 3

```
CREATE CURSOR <expFN>
   (<fname1> <FieldType> [(<precision> [, <scale>])
   [, <fname2> ... ]])
   ¦ FROM ARRAY <array>

CREATE [<expFN1>] FROM [<expFN2>]

CREATE DATABASE [<expFN> ¦ ?]
```

NEW FOR VISUAL FOXPRO 3

```
CREATE FORM [<expFN> ¦ ?] [NOWAIT] [SAVE]
   [[WINDOW <window1>]
   [IN [WINDOW] <window2> ¦ IN SCREEN]]
```

NEW FOR VISUAL FOXPRO 3

```
CREATE LABEL [<expFN> ¦ ?] [NOWAIT] [SAVE]
   [[WINDOW <window1>]
   [IN [WINDOW] <window2> ¦ IN SCREEN]]

CREATE MENU  [<expFN> ¦ ?] [NOWAIT] [SAVE]
```

```
   [[WINDOW <window1>]
   [IN [WINDOW] <window2> ¦ IN SCREEN]]

CREATE PROJECT [<expFN> ¦ ?] [NOWAIT] [SAVE]
   [WINDOW <window1>]
   [IN [WINDOW] <window2> ¦ IN SCREEN]

CREATE QUERY [<expFN> ¦ ?]

CREATE REPORT [<expFN> ¦ ?] [NOWAIT] [SAVE]
   [[WINDOW <window1>]
   [IN [WINDOW] <window2> ¦ IN SCREEN]]

CREATE REPORT <expFN1> ¦ ?  FROM <expFN2>
   [FORM ¦ COLUMN] [FIELDS <field list>] [ALIAS]
   [NOOVERWRITE] [WIDTH <expN>]

CREATE SCREEN [<expFN> ¦ ?] [NOWAIT] [SAVE]
   [[WINDOW <window1>]
   [IN [WINDOW] <window2> ¦ IN SCREEN]]

CREATE SCREEN <expFN1> ¦ ?  FROM <expFN2>
   [ROW ¦ COLUMN] [FIELDS <field list>] [ALIAS]
   [NOOVERWRITE]  [SIZE <expN1>, <expN2>]
   [SCREEN]]
```

REVISED FOR VISUAL FOXPRO 3

```
CREATE SQL VIEW [ <ViewName> ] [REMOTE]
        [CONNECTION <ConnectionName> [SHARE]
        ¦ CONNECTION <DataSourceName>]
        [AS <SQLSELECTStatement>]
```

REVISED FOR VISUAL FOXPRO 3

```
CREATE TABLE ¦ DBF <expFN> 1 [NAME  <expTable> ] [FREE]
        (<field1>  <FieldType> [(<expN1>  [, <expN2> ])
               [NULL ¦ NOT NULL]
               [CHECK <expL1>  [ERROR <expC1> ]]
               [DEFAULT <exp1> ]
               [PRIMARY KEY ¦ UNIQUE]
                       [REFERENCES <expTable2> [TAG <tag name1>]
               [NOCPTRANS]]
        [, <field2> ...]])
               [, PRIMARY KEY <exp2> TAG <tag name2>
               ¦, UNIQUE <exp3>  TAG  <tag name3>]
               [, FOREIGN KEY <exp4>  TAG <tag name4>
                       REFERENCES <expTable3>  [TAG <tag name5>]]
               [, CHECK <expL2>  [ERROR <expC2> ]]
        ¦ FROM ARRAY ArrayName
```

NEW FOR VISUAL FOXPRO 3

```
CREATE TRIGGER ON <expTable> FOR DELETE ¦ INSERT ¦ UPDATE  AS <exp>
CREATE VIEW <expFN>

DEACTIVATE MENU <menu1> [, <menu2> ... ] ¦ ALL

DEACTIVATE POPUP <popup1> [, <popup2> ... ] ¦ ALL

DEACTIVATE WINDOW <window1> [, <window2> ... ] ¦ ALL

DECLARE <array1> (<expN1> [, <expN2>])
   [, <array2> (<expN3> [, <expN4>])] ...
```

NEW FOR VISUAL FOXPRO 3

```
DECLARE [cFunctionType] FunctionName IN LibraryName [AS AliasName]
        [cParamType1 [@] ParamName1,
               cParamType2 [@] ParamName2, ...]
```

```
#DEFINE <constant name> <exp>
```

```
#UNDEF <constant name>
```

REVISED FOR VISUAL FOXPRO 3

```
DEFINE BAR <expN1> ¦ <System option name>
   OF <popup> PROMPT <expC1>
   [BEFORE <expN2>  ¦ AFTER <expN2>]
   [KEY <key label> [, <expC2>]]
   [MARK <expC3>] [MESSAGE <expC4>] [SKIP [FOR <expL>]]
   [FONT <expC5> [, <expN2>]] [STYLE <expSTYLE>]
   [COLOR <color pair list>
   ¦ COLOR SCHEME <expN2>
   ¦ COLOR RGB (<color value list>)]
```

```
DEFINE BOX FROM <column1> TO <column2>
   HEIGHT <expN1> [AT LINE <expN2>]
   [SINGLE ¦ DOUBLE ¦ <border string>]
```

NEW FOR VISUAL FOXPRO 3

```
DEFINE CLASS <ClassName1> AS <cBaseClass>
        [[PROTECTED <PropertyName1>, <PropertyName2> ...]
               <PropertyName> = <exp> ...]
        [ADD OBJECT [PROTECTED] <ObjectName> AS <ClassName> [NOINIT]
               [WITH <cPropertylist>]]...
        [[PROTECTED] FUNCTION ¦ PROCEDURE <cProcedureName>
               <cStatements>
        [ENDFUNC ¦ ENDPROC]]...
ENDDEFINE
```

REVISED FOR VISUAL FOXPRO 3

```
DEFINE MENU <menu> [BAR [AT LINE <expN1>]]
   [IN [WINDOW] <window> ¦ IN SCREEN]
   [KEY <key label>] [MARK <expC1>] [MESSAGE <expC2>]
   [NOMARGIN]
   [FONT <expC5> [, <expN2>]] [STYLE <expSTYLE>]
   [COLOR <color pair list>
   ¦ COLOR SCHEME <expN2>
   ¦ COLOR RGB (<color value list>)]
```

REVISED FOR VISUAL FOXPRO 3

```
DEFINE PAD <pad> OF <menu> PROMPT <expC1>
   [AT <row>, <column>]  [BEFORE <pad>
   ¦ AFTER <pad>]  [KEY <key label> [, <expC2>]]
   [MARK <expC3>] [SKIP [FOR <expL>]] [MESSAGE <expC4>]
   [FONT <expC5> [, <expN2>]] [STYLE <expSTYLE>]
   [COLOR <color pair list>
   ¦ COLOR SCHEME <expN>
   ¦ COLOR RGB (<color value list>)]
```

REVISED FOR VISUAL FOXPRO 3

```
DEFINE POPUP <popup>
   [FROM <row1>, <column1>] [TO <row2>, <column2>]
   [IN [WINDOW] <window> ¦ IN SCREEN]
   [FOOTER <expC1>] [KEY <key label>]
   [MARGIN] [MARK <expC2>] [MESSAGE <expC3>]
   [MOVER] [MULTISELECT]
   [PROMPT FIELD <exp>
```

```
  ¦ PROMPT FILES [LIKE <skeleton>]
  ¦ PROMPT STRUCTURE]
  [RELATIVE] [SCROLL] [SHADOW] [TITLE <expC4>]
  [FONT <expC5> [, <expN2>]] [STYLE <expSTYLE>]
  [COLOR SCHEME <expN>
  ¦ COLOR  <color pair list>
  ¦ COLOR RGB (<color value list>)]

DEFINE WINDOW <window1>
   FROM <row1, column1> TO <row2, column2>
   ¦ AT <row3, column3> SIZE <row4, column4>
   [IN [WINDOW] <window2> ¦ IN SCREEN ¦ IN DESKTOP]
   [FONT <expC1> [, <expN1>]]   [STYLE <expSTYLE>]
   [FOOTER <expC3>] [TITLE <expC4>] [HALFHEIGHT]
   [DOUBLE ¦ PANEL ¦ NONE ¦ SYSTEM ¦ <border string>]
   [CLOSE ¦ NOCLOSE] [FLOAT ¦ NOFLOAT] [GROW ¦ NOGROW]
   [MDI ¦ NOMDI] [MINIMIZE] [SHADOW] [ZOOM ¦ NOZOOM]
   [ICON FILE <expC5>] [FILL <expC6> ¦ FILL FILE <bmp file>]
   [ COLOR SCHEME <expN2>
   ¦ COLOR <color pair list>
   ¦ COLOR RGB (<color value list>)]
```

REVISED FOR VISUAL FOXPRO 3

```
DELETE [<scope>] [FOR <expL1>] [WHILE <expL2>] [NOOPTIMIZE] [IN <expWA>]

DELETE CONNECTION <connection name>
```

NEW FOR VISUAL FOXPRO 3

```
DELETE DATABASE <expFN> ¦ ?  [DELETETABLES]

DELETE FILE [<expFN> ¦ ?]
```

NEW FOR VISUAL FOXPRO 3

```
DELETE TAG <tag name1> [OF <.cdx file1>]
   [, <tag name2> [OF <.cdx file2>]] ... [IN <expWA>]

DELETE TAG ALL [OF <.cdx file>]  [IN <expWA>]
```

NEW FOR VISUAL FOXPRO 3

```
DELETE TRIGGER ON <expTable> FOR DELETE ¦ INSERT ¦ UPDATE

DELETE VIEW <expFN>
```

NEW FOR VISUAL FOXPRO 3

```
DIMENSION <array1> (<expN1> [, <expN2>])
   [, <array2> (<expN3> [, <expN4>])] ...

DIR ¦ DIRECTORY [[ON] <drive:>] [[LIKE] [<path>] [<skeleton>]]
   [TO PRINTER [PROMPT] ¦ TO FILE <expFN>]

DISPLAY [[FIELDS] <field list>]
   [<scope>] [FOR <expL1>] [WHILE <expL2>]
   [OFF]  [TO PRINTER [PROMPT] ¦ TO FILE <expFN>]
   [NOCONSOLE] [NOOPTIMIZE]
```

NEW FOR VISUAL FOXPRO 3

```
DISPLAY CONNECTIONS
   [TO PRINTER [PROMPT] ¦ TO FILE <expFN>] [NOCONSOLE]
```

NEW FOR VISUAL FOXPRO 3

```
DISPLAY DATABASE
   [TO PRINTER [PROMPT] ¦ TO FILE <expFN>] [NOCONSOLE]

DISPLAY FILES [ON <drive>] [LIKE <skeleton>]
   [TO PRINTER [PROMPT] ¦ TO FILE <expFN>] [NOCONSOLE]
```

```
DISPLAY MEMORY [LIKE <skeleton>]
   [TO PRINTER [PROMPT] ¦ TO FILE <expFN>] [NOCONSOLE]

DISPLAY OBJECTS [LIKE <skeleton>]
   [TO PRINTER [PROMPT] ¦ TO FILE <expFN>] [NOCONSOLE]

DISPLAY PROCEDURES
   [TO PRINTER [PROMPT] ¦ TO FILE <expFN>] [NOCONSOLE]

DISPLAY STATUS
   [TO PRINTER [PROMPT] ¦ TO FILE <expFN>] [NOCONSOLE]

DISPLAY STRUCTURE  [IN <expWA>]
   [TO PRINTER [PROMPT]  ¦ TO FILE <expFN>] [NOCONSOLE]

DISPLAY TABLES
   [TO PRINTER [PROMPT] ¦ TO FILE <expFN>] [NOCONSOLE]

DISPLAY VIEWS
   [TO PRINTER [PROMPT] ¦ TO FILE <expFN>] [NOCONSOLE]

DO <expFN> [WITH <parameter list>] [IN <expFN>]

DO CASE
   CASE <expL1>
      <statements>
   [CASE <expL2>
      <statements>
   ...
   CASE <expLN>
      <statements>]
   [OTHERWISE
      <statements>]
ENDCASE

DO FORM <expFN> ¦ ? [NAME <memvar>]
     [WITH <parameter list>] [NOREAD]

DO WHILE <expL>
   <statements>
   [LOOP]
   [EXIT]
ENDDO

EJECT

EJECT PAGE

END TRANSACTION

ERASE <expFN> ¦ ?

ERROR <expN> [,<message text1>]  ¦ <message text2>

EXIT
```

```
EXPORT TO <expFN>
   [FIELDS <field list>
   [<scope>] [FOR <expL1>] [WHILE <expL2>]
   [NOOPTIMIZE]
   [TYPE] DIF ¦ MOD ¦ SYLK ¦ WK1 ¦ WKS ¦ WR1 ¦ WRK ¦ XLS ¦ XL5 [SHEET <expC>]

EXTERNAL ARRAY ¦ LABEL ¦ LIBRARY
   ¦ MENU ¦ PROCEDURE ¦ REPORT ¦ SCREEN
   <expFN> ¦ <array names>

FILER [LIKE <skeleton>] [NOWAIT]
   [IN [WINDOW] <window> ¦ SCREEN]

FIND <char string>

FLUSH

FOR <memvar> = <expN1> TO <expN2>   [STEP <expN3>]
   <statements>
   [EXIT]
   [LOOP]
ENDFOR ¦ NEXT

FUNCTION <function name>

GATHER FROM <array> ¦ MEMVAR ¦ NAME <object name>
    [FIELDS <field list>] [MEMO]

GETEXPR [<expC1>] TO <memvar>  [TYPE <expC2> [; <expC3>]]
   [DEFAULT <expC4>]

GO [RECORD] <expN1> [IN <expN2> ¦ <expC>]

GO TOP ¦ BOTTOM [IN <expN2> ¦ <expC>]

GOTO [RECORD] <expN1> [IN <expN2> ¦ <expC>]

GOTO TOP ¦ BOTTOM  [IN <expN2> ¦ <expC>]

[ic:revised]HELP [IN [WINDOW] <window> ¦ SCREEN] [<topic>] [NOWAIT]

HIDE MENU <menu1> [, <menu2> ... ]  ¦ ALL [SAVE]

HIDE POPUP <popup1> [,<popup2> ... ] ¦ ALL [SAVE]

HIDE WINDOW [<window1>
   [, <window2>] ... ] ¦ ALL
   [IN [WINDOW] <windowN>
   ¦ SCREEN]
   [SAVE]

#IF <expN1> ¦ <expL1>
   <statements>
[#ELIF <expN2> ¦ <expL2>
   <statements>
   ...
[#ELIF <expNn> ¦ <expLn>
   <statements>]
```

```
[#ELSE
   <statements>]
#ENDIF

IF <expL>
   <statements1>
[ELSE
   <statements2>]
ENDIF
```

REVISED FOR VISUAL FOXPRO 3

```
IMPORT FROM <expFN> [TYPE] FW2 ¦ MOD ¦ PDOX
   ¦ RPD ¦ WK1 ¦ WK3 ¦ WKS ¦ WR1 ¦ WRK ¦ XLS ¦ XL5 [SHEET <expC>]
```

NEW FOR VISUAL FOXPRO 3

```
#INCLUDE <filename>
```

REVISED FOR VISUAL FOXPRO 3

```
INDEX ON <exp> TO <.idx file> ¦ TAG <tag name> [OF <.cdx file>]
   [FOR <expL>] [COMPACT] [ASCENDING ¦ DESCENDING]
   [UNIQUE] [ADDITIVE] [CANDIDATE]

INPUT [<expC>] TO <memvar>

INSERT [BEFORE] [BLANK]

[ic:new]INSERT INTO <expFN>  [(<file name1> [, <file name2> [, ...]])]
   VALUES (<exp1> [, <exp2> [, ...]])

INSERT INTO <.dbf file> FROM ARRAY <array>  FROM MEMVAR

JOIN WITH <expWA>  TO <expFN>
   FOR <expL> [FIELDS <field list>] [NOOPTIMIZE]

KEYBOARD <expC> [PLAIN] [CLEAR]

LABEL [FORM <expFN1> ¦ ?] [ENVIRONMENT]
   [<scope>] [FOR <expL1>]  [WHILE <expL2>]
   [NOCONSOLE] [NOOPTIMIZE] [PREVIEW] [SAMPLE]
   [TO PRINTER [PROMPT] ¦ TO FILE <expFN2>]
   [PDSETUP]

LIST  [FIELDS <exp list>]
   [<scope>] [FOR <expL1>] [WHILE<expL1>]
   [OFF] [NOCONSOLE] [NOOPTIMIZE]
   [TO PRINTER [PROMPT] ¦ TO FILE <expFN>]

[ic:new]LIST CONNECTIONS
   [TO PRINTER [PROMPT] ¦ TO FILE <expFN>] [NOCONSOLE]

[ic:new]LIST DATABASE
   [TO PRINTER [PROMPT] ¦ TO FILE <expFN>] [NOCONSOLE]

LIST FILES  [ON <drive>] [LIKE <skeleton>]
   [TO PRINTER [PROMPT]  ¦ TO FILE <expFN>]

LIST MEMORY [LIKE <skeleton>] [NOCONSOLE]
   [TO PRINTER [PROMPT] ¦ TO FILE <expFN>]
```

```
LIST OBJECTS [LIKE <skeleton>] [NOCONSOLE]
   [TO PRINTER [PROMPT] ¦ TO FILE <expFN>]

LIST PROCEDURES
   [TO PRINTER [PROMPT] ¦ TO FILE <expFN>] [NOCONSOLE]

LIST STATUS  [NOCONSOLE]
   [TO PRINTER [PROMPT] ¦ TO FILE <expFN>]

LIST TABLES
   [TO PRINTER [PROMPT] ¦ TO FILE <expFN>] [NOCONSOLE]

LIST VIEWS
   [TO PRINTER [PROMPT] ¦ TO FILE <expFN>] [NOCONSOLE]

LIST STRUCTURE [NOCONSOLE]
   [TO PRINTER [PROMPT] ¦ TO FILE <expFN>]

LOAD <expFN> [SAVE] [NOSAVE]

LOCAL <memvar list>

LOCAL [ARRAY] <Array1> (Rows1 [, <Col1>])   [, <Array2> (<Rows2> [, <Col2>])] ...

LOCATE FOR <expL1> [<scope>] [WHILE <expL2>] [NOOPTIMIZE]

LPARAMETERS <parameter list>

MD ¦ MKDIR <path>

MENU BAR <array1>, <expN1>

MENU <expN2>, <array2>, <expN3> [, <expN4>]

MENU TO <memvar>

MODIFY CLASS <class name> [OF <ClassLibraryName1>]
        [AS <cBaseClassName> [FROM <ClassLibraryName2>]]

MODIFY COMMAND <expFN> ¦ MODIFY FILE [<expFN>]
   [NOEDIT] [NOWAIT] [RANGE <expN1>, <expN2>]
   [[WINDOW <window1>]
   [IN [WINDOW] <window2> ¦ SCREEN]]
   [SAME] [SAVE]

MODIFY CONNECTIONS <connection name> ¦ ?

MODIFY DATABASE [<database name> ¦ ?] [NOWAIT]

MODIFY FORM [<expFN> ¦ ? ] [NOWAIT]

MODIFY GENERAL <general field>

MODIFY LABEL [<expFN> ¦ ?] [[WINDOW <window1>]
   [IN [WINDOW] <window2> ¦ IN SCREEN]]
   [NOENVIRONMENT] [NOWAIT] [SAVE]
```

```
MODIFY MEMO <memo field1> [, <memo field2> ... ]
   [NOEDIT] [NOWAIT]  [RANGE <expN1>, <expN2>]
   [[WINDOW <window1>] [IN [WINDOW] <window2>
   ¦ SCREEN]] [SAME] [SAVE]

MODIFY MENU [<expFN> ¦ ?] [[WINDOW <window1>]
   [IN [WINDOW] <window2>
   ¦ IN SCREEN]] [NOWAIT] [SAVE]

MODIFY PROCEDURE
```

NEW FOR VISUAL FOXPRO 3

```
MODIFY PROJECT [<expFN> ¦ ?]
   [[WINDOW <window1>]
   [IN [WINDOW] <window2> ¦ SCREEN]]
   [NOWAIT] [SAVE]
```

REVISED FOR VISUAL FOXPRO 3

```
MODIFY QUERY [<expFN> ¦ ?] [NOWAIT] [AS <expN>]

MODIFY REPORT [<expFN> ¦ ?] [[WINDOW <window1>]
   [IN [WINDOW] <window2>  ¦ SCREEN]]
   [NOENVIRONMENT] [NOWAIT] [SAVE]

MODIFY SCREEN [<expFN> ¦ ?] [[WINDOW <window1>]
   [IN [WINDOW] <window2> ¦ IN SCREEN]]
   [NOENVIRONMENT] [NOWAIT] [SAVE]

MODIFY STRUCTURE
```

NEW FOR VISUAL FOXPRO 3

```
MODIFY VIEW <expFN> [REMOTE]

MODIFY WINDOW <window> ¦ SCREEN
   FROM <row1, column1>  TO <row2, column2>
   ¦ AT <row3, column3>  SIZE <row4, column4>
   [FONT <expC1> [, <expN1>]]  [STYLE <expSTYLE>]
   [TITLE <expC3>]  [HALFHEIGHT]
   [DOUBLE ¦ PANEL ¦ NONE  ¦ SYSTEM]
   [CLOSE ¦ NOCLOSE] [FLOAT ¦ NOFLOAT] [GROW ¦ NOGROW]
   [MDI ¦ NOMDI] [MINIMIZE] [ZOOM ¦ NOZOOM]
   [ICON FILE <expC4>]
   [FILL FILE <bmp file>]
   [COLOR SCHEME <expN2>
   ¦ COLOR <color pair list>
   ¦ COLOR RGB (<color value list>)]
```

NEW FOR VISUAL FOXPRO 3

```
MOUSE [CLICK ¦ DBLCLICK] [AT nRow1, nColumn1]
   ¦ DRAG TO nRow2, nColumn2, nRow3, nColumn3 ...]
   [BUTTON LEFT ¦ BUTTON MIDDLE ¦ BUTTON RIGHT]
   [SHIFT][CTRL][ALT]

MOVE POPUP <popup> TO <row>, <column>
   ¦ BY <expN1>, <expN2>

MOVE WINDOW <window> TO <row>, <column>
   ¦ BY <expN1>, <expN2>
   [CENTER]

NOTE [<comments>]
   * [<comments>]
   && [<comments>]
```

```
ON BAR <expN> OF <expC> [<command>]     (New in FoxPro 2.6)

ON BAR <expN> OF <popup1>
   [ACTIVATE POPUP <popup2> ¦ ACTIVATE MENU <menu>]

ON ERROR [<command>]

ON ESCAPE [<command>]

ON EXIT BAR <expN> OF <expC> [<command>]

ON EXIT MENU <expC2> [<command>]

ON EXIT PAD <expC1> OF <expC2> [<command>]

ON EXIT POPUP <expC1> [<command>]

ON KEY [<command>]

ON KEY [ = <expN>] [<command>]

ON KEY [LABEL <key label>] [<command>]

ON MENU <expC> [<command>]

ON MOUSE [<command>]

ON PAD <pad> OF <menu1>
   [ACTIVATE POPUP <popup>
   ¦ ACTIVATE MENU <menu2>]

ON PAD <expC1> OF <expC2> [<command>]

ON PAGE [AT LINE <expN> <command>]

ON POPUP <expC> [<command>]

ON READERROR <command>

ON SELECTION BAR <expN> OF <popup> [<command>]

ON SELECTION MENU <menu> ¦ ALL  [<command>]

ON SELECTION PAD <pad> OF <menu> [<command>]

ON SELECTION POPUP <popup>  ¦ ALL [BLANK] [<command>]
```

NEW FOR VISUAL FOXPRO 3

```
OPEN DATABASE  [<expFN> ¦ ?]
        [EXCLUSIVE ¦ SHARED]
        [NOUPDATE]
        [VALIDATE]

PACK [MEMO] [DBF]
```

```
PACK DATABASE

PARAMETERS <parameter list>

PLAY MACRO <macro name> [TIME <expN>]

POP KEY [ALL]

POP MENU <menu> [TO MASTER]

POP POPUP <popup>

PRINTJOB <statements>
ENDPRINTJOB

PRIVATE <memvar list>

PRIVATE ALL [LIKE <skeleton> ¦ EXCEPT <skeleton>]

PROCEDURE <procedure name>

PUBLIC <memvar list>

PUBLIC [ARRAY] <array1> (<expN1>
   [, <expN2>]) [, <array2>"("<expN3> [, <expN4>] ")"  ] ...

PUSH KEY [CLEAR]

PUSH MENU <menu>

PUSH POPUP <popup>

QUIT
```

```
RD ¦ RMDIR  <path>

READ  [CYCLE] [EVENTS]
   [ACTIVATE <expL1>] [DEACTIVATE <expL2>]
   [MODAL] [WITH window title list]  [SHOW <expL3>]
   [VALID <expL4 ¦ expN1>]  [WHEN <expL5>]
   [OBJECT <expN2>]  [TIMEOUT <expN3>]
   [SAVE] [NOMOUSE] [LOCK ¦ NOLOCK]
   [COLOR <color pair list>
   ¦ COLOR SCHEME <expN4>
   ¦ COLOR RGB (<color value list>)]

READ MENU BAR TO <memvar1>, <memvar2> [SAVE]

READ MENU TO <memvar> [SAVE]

RECALL [<scope>] [FOR <expL1>] [WHILE <expL2>] [NOOPTIMIZE]

REGIONAL <memvar list>

REINDEX [COMPACT]
```

```
RELEASE <memvar list>

RELEASE ALL [EXTENDED] [LIKE <skeleton> ¦ EXCEPT <skeleton>]

RELEASE BAR <expN> OF <popup>  ¦ RELEASE BAR ALL OF <popup>
RELEASE CLASSLIB <ClassLibraryName>

RELEASE LIBRARY <library name>

RELEASE MENUS [<menu list> [EXTENDED]]

RELEASE PAD <pad> OF <menu>
   ¦ RELEASE PAD ALL OF <menu>

RELEASE POPUPS [<popup list> [EXTENDED]]

RELEASE PROCEDURES <expFN>

RELEASE WINDOWS [<window list>]

RELEASE MODULE <expFN>

REMOVE CLASS <ClassName> OF <ClassLibraryName>

REMOVE TABLE  <expTable> ¦ ? [DELETE]

RENAME <expFN1> TO <expFN2>

RENAME CLASS <ClassName1> OF <ClassLibraryName> TO <ClassName2>

RENAME CONNECTIONS <connection name1> TO <connection name2>

RENAME TABLE <expFN1> TO <expFN2>

RENAME VIEW <expFN1> TO <expFN2>

REPLACE <field1> WITH <exp1> [ADDITIVE]
   [, <field2> WITH <exp2> [ADDITIVE]] ...
   [<scope>] [FOR <expL1>] [WHILE <expL2>]  [NOOPTIMIZE]

REPORT [FORM <expFN1> ¦ ?]  [ENVIRONMENT]
   [<scope>] [FOR <expL1>] [WHILE <expL2>] [HEADING <expC>]
   [NOEJECT] [NOCONSOLE] [NOOPTIMIZE] [PLAIN] [PREVIEW]
   [TO PRINTER [PROMPT]  ¦ TO FILE <expFN2>]
   [SUMMARY]  [PDSETUP]

RESTORE FROM <expFN> ¦ FROM MEMO <memo field>  [ADDITIVE]

RESTORE MACROS  [FROM <expFN> ¦ FROM MEMO <memo field>]

RESTORE SCREEN [FROM <memvar>]

RESTORE WINDOW <window list> ¦ ALL
   FROM <expFN> ¦ FROM MEMO <memo field>

RESUME

RETRY
```

```
RETURN  [<exp> ¦ TO MASTER  ¦ TO <program name>]

ROLLBACK
```

NEW FOR VISUAL FOXPRO 3

```
RUN [/N [K]] <DOS command>  ¦ <program name>

SAVE MACROS TO <expFN>  ¦ TO MEMO <memo field>

SAVE SCREEN [TO <memvar>]

SAVE TO <expFN>  ¦ TO MEMO <memo field>
   [ALL LIKE ¦ EXCEPT <skeleton>]

SAVE WINDOW <window list> ¦ ALL  TO <expFN>
   ¦ TO MEMO <memo field>

SCAN [NOOPTIMIZE] [<scope>] [FOR <expL1>] [WHILE <expL2>]
   [<statements>]
   [LOOP]
   [EXIT]
ENDSCAN

SCATTER [FIELDS <field list>] [MEMO]  TO <array>
   ¦ TO <array> BLANK
   ¦ MEMVAR ¦ MEMVAR BLANK
   ¦ NAME <object name>
```

REVISED FOR VISUAL FOXPRO 3

```
SCROLL <row1, column1>, <row2, column2>,  <expN1> [, <expN2>]

SEEK <exp>

SELECT <expWA>

SELECT [ALL ¦ DISTINCT]
   [<alias>.]<select_item> [AS <column_name>]
   [, [<alias>.]<select_item> [AS <column_name>] ...]
   FROM <table> [<local_alias>]
   [, <table> [<local_alias>] ...]
   [[INTO <destination>]  ¦ [TO FILE <expFN>  [ADDITIVE]
   ¦ TO PRINTER [PROMPT] ¦ TO SCREEN]
   [PREFERENCE <name>]
   [NOCONSOLE]
   [PLAIN]
   [NOWAIT]
   [WHERE <joincondition> [AND <joincondition> ...]
   [AND ¦ OR  <filtercondition>
   [AND ¦ OR  <filtercondition> ...]]]
   [GROUP BY <groupcolumn> [, <groupcolumn> ...]]
   [HAVING <filtercondition>]
   [UNION [ALL] <SELECT command>]
   [ORDER BY <order_item> [ASC ¦ DESC]
   [, <order_item> [ASC ¦ DESC]...]]
```

REVISED FOR VISUAL FOXPRO 3

```
SET

SET ALTERNATE ON ¦ OFF
```

SET ALTERNATE TO [<*expFN*> [ADDITIVE]]

NEW FOR VISUAL FOXPRO 3

SET ANSI ON ¦ OFF

SET AUTOSAVE ON ¦ OFF

SET BELL ON ¦ OFF

REVISED FOR VISUAL FOXPRO 3

SET BELL TO [<*frequency*>, <*duration*>] ¦ <*WAV filename*>,<*duration*>]

SET BLINK ON ¦ OFF

SET BLOCKSIZE TO <*expN*>

SET BORDER TO [SINGLE ¦ DOUBLE ¦ PANEL ¦ NONE
¦ <*border string1*> [, <*border string2*>]]

SET BRSTATUS ON ¦ OFF

SET CARRY ON ¦ OFF

SET CARRY TO [<*field list*> [ADDITIVE]]

SET CENTURY ON ¦ OFF

NEW FOR VISUAL FOXPRO 3

SET CLASSLIB TO <*ClassLibraryName*> [ADDITIVE] [ALIAS <*AliasName*>]

SET CLEAR ON ¦ OFF

SET CLOCK ON ¦ OFF ¦ STATUS

SET CLOCK TO [<*row*>, <*column*>]

NEW FOR VISUAL FOXPRO 3

SET COLLATE TO [<*expC*>]

SET COLOR OF NORMAL ¦ MESSAGES ¦ TITLES ¦ BOX ¦ HIGHLIGHT
¦ INFORMATION ¦ FIELDS TO [<*standard*>]

SET COLOR OF SCHEME <*expN1*> TO [[<*color pair list*>]
¦ [SCHEME <*expN2*>]]

SET COLOR SET TO [<*color set name*>]

SET COLOR TO [[<*standard*>] [, [<*enhanced*>] [, [<*border*>]]]]

SET COMPATIBLE FOXPLUS ¦ DB4 ¦ ON ¦ OFF [PROMPT ¦ NOPROMPT]

SET CONFIRM ON ¦ OFF

SET CONSOLE ON ¦ OFF

NEW FOR VISUAL FOXPRO 3

SET CPCOMPILE TO <*expN*>

]SET CPDIALOG ON ¦ OFF

NEW FOR VISUAL FOXPRO 3

SET CURRENCY TO [<*expC*>]

SET CURRENCY LEFT ¦ RIGHT

SET CURSOR ON ¦ OFF

SET DATE [TO] AMERICAN ¦ ANSI ¦ BRITISH ¦ FRENCH ¦ GERMAN
¦ ITALIAN ¦ JAPAN ¦ USA ¦ MDY ¦ DMY ¦ YMD

SET DATABASE TO *<expFN>*

NEW FOR VISUAL FOXPRO 3

SET DATASESSION TO *<expN>*

SET DEBUG ON ¦ OFF

SET DECIMALS TO [*<expN>*]

SET DEFAULT TO [*<expC>*]

SET DELETED ON ¦ OFF

SET DELIMITERS ON ¦ OFF

SET DELIMITERS TO *<expC>* ¦ TO DEFAULT

SET DEVELOPMENT ON ¦ OFF

SET DEVICE TO SCREEN ¦ TO PRINTER [PROMPT]
¦ TO FILE *<expFN>*

SET DIRECTORY TO *<expC>*

SET DISPLAY TO CGA ¦ COLOR ¦ EGA25
¦ EGA43 ¦ MONO ¦ VGA25 ¦ VGA50

SET DOHISTORY ON ¦ OFF ¦ TO *<expFN>* [ADDITIVE]

REVISED FOR VISUAL FOXPRO 3

SET ECHO ON ¦ OFF

SET ESCAPE ON ¦ OFF

SET EXACT ON ¦ OFF

SET EXCLUSIVE ON ¦ OFF

SET FDOW TO *<expN>*

NEW FOR VISUAL FOXPRO 3

SET FIELDS ON ¦ OFF [GLOBAL ¦ LOCAL]

SET FIELDS TO [*<field list>* ¦ ALL]
[LIKE *<skeleton>*] [EXCEPT *<skeleton>*]

REVISED FOR VISUAL FOXPRO 3

SET FILTER TO [*<expL>*]

SET FIXED ON ¦ OFF

SET FORMAT [TO [*<expFN>* ¦ ?]]

SET FULLPATH ON ¦ OFF

SET FUNCTION *<expN>* ¦ *<key label>* TO [*<exp>*]

```
SET FWEEK TO [<expN>]

SET HEADING ON ¦ OFF

SET HELP ON ¦ OFF

SET HELP TO [<expFN>]

SET HELPFILTER [AUTOMATIC] TO [<expL>]

SET HOURS TO [12 ¦ 24]

SET INDEX TO [<index file list> ¦ ?
   [ORDER  <expN>  ¦ <.idx file>
   ¦ [TAG] <tag name> [OF <.cdx file>]
   [ASCENDING ¦ DESCENDING]]  [ADDITIVE]

SET INTENSITY ON ¦ OFF
```

```
SET KEY TO [<exp>1 ¦ RANGE <exp> [, <exp>]]
   [IN <expWA>]

SET KEYCOMP TO DOS ¦ WINDOWS

SET LIBRARY TO  [<expFN> [ADDITIVE]]

SET LOCK ON ¦ OFF

SET LOGERRORS ON ¦ OFF

SET MACKEY TO [<expC>]

SET MARGIN TO <expN>

SET MARK OF MENU <menu> TO <expC1> ¦ <expL1>

SET MARK OF PAD <pad> OF <menu> TO <expC2> ¦ <expL2>

SET MARK OF POPUP <popup>  TO <expC3> ¦ <expL3>

SET MARK OF BAR <expN> OF <popup> TO <expC4>  ¦ <expL4>

SET MARK TO [<expC>]

SET MEMOWIDTH TO <expN>

SET MESSAGE TO [<expC>]

SET MESSAGE TO [<expN>  [LEFT ¦ CENTER ¦ RIGHT]]

SET MESSAGE WINDOW [<window>]

SET MOUSE ON ¦ OFF

SET MOUSE TO [<expN>]

SET MULTILOCKS ON ¦ OFF
```

SET NEAR ON ¦ OFF

SET NOCPTRANS TO [FieldName1 [, FieldName2 ...]]

NEW FOR VISUAL FOXPRO 3

SET NOTIFY ON ¦ OFF

SET NULL ON ¦ OFF

SET OLEOBJECT ON ¦ OFF

NEW FOR VISUAL FOXPRO 3

SET ODOMETER TO [<*expN*>]

SET OPTIMIZE ON ¦ OFF

SET ORDER TO [<*expN1*> ¦ <*.idx index file*>
¦ [TAG] <*tag name*> [OF <*.cdx file*>]
[IN <*expN2*> ¦ <*expC*>] [ASCENDING ¦ DESCENDING]]

REVISED FOR VISUAL FOXPRO 3

SET PALETTE ON ¦ OFF

NEW FOR VISUAL FOXPRO 3

SET PATH TO [<*path*>]

SET POINT TO [<*expC*>]

SET PRINTER FONT <*font name*> [, <*font size*>] [STYLE <*font style*>]

NEW FOR VISUAL FOXPRO 3

SET PRINTER ON [PROMPT] ¦ OFF

SET PRINTER TO [<*expFN*> [ADDITIVE] ¦ <*port*>]

SET PRINTER TO [\\<*machine name*> \<*printer name*> = <*dest*>]

SET PRINTER TO [\\SPOOLER [\NB]
[\F = <*expN*>] [\B = <*banner*>]
[\C = <*expN*>] [\P = <*expN*>]]
[\S = <*server*>] [\Q = <*queue*>]

SET PROCEDURE TO [<*expFN1*>][, <*expFN2*>,...] [ADDITIVE]

REVISED FOR VISUAL FOXPRO 3

SET READBORDER ON¦OFF

SET REFRESH TO <*expN1*> [, <*expN2*>]

SET RELATION TO [<*exp1*> INTO <*expWA*>
[, <*exp2*> INTO <*expWA*> [, ...]] [ADDITIVE]] [IN <*expWA2*>]

REVISED FOR VISUAL FOXPRO 3

SET RELATION OFF INTO <*expWA*> [IN <*expWA2*>]

REVISED FOR VISUAL FOXPRO 3

SET REPROCESS TO <*expN*> [SECONDS] ¦ TO AUTOMATIC

SET RESOURCE ON ¦ OFF

SET RESOURCE TO [<*expFN*>]

SET SAFETY ON ¦ OFF

SET SCOREBOARD ON ¦ OFF

NEW FOR VISUAL FOXPRO 3

```
SET SECONDS ON ¦ OFF

SET SEPARATOR TO [<expC>]

SET SHADOWS ON ¦ OFF

SET SKIP TO [<expWA1> [, <expWA2>] ... ]

SET SKIP OF MENU <menu> <expL>

SET SKIP OF PAD <pad>  OF <menu> <expL>

SET SKIP OF POPUP <popup> <expL>

SET SKIP OF BAR <expN> ¦ <System option name>
   OF <popup> <expL>

SET SPACE ON ¦ OFF

SET STATUS ON ¦ OFF

SET STATUS TIMEOUT TO <expN>

SET STATUS BAR ON ¦ OFF

SET STEP ON ¦ OFF

SET STICKY ON ¦ OFF
```

NEW FOR VISUAL FOXPRO 3

```
SET SYSFORMATS ON ¦ OFF

SET SYSMENU ON ¦ OFF ¦ AUTOMATIC
   ¦ TO [<popup list>]
   ¦ TO [<menu pad list>]
   ¦ TO [DEFAULT] ¦ SAVE ¦ NOSAVE

SET TALK  ON ¦ OFF ¦  WINDOW [<window>] ¦ NOWINDOW

SET TEXTMERGE [ON ¦ OFF] [TO [<expFN>] [ADDITIVE]]
   [WINDOW <window>] [SHOW ¦ NOSHOW]

SET TEXTMERGE DELIMITERS  [TO <expC1> [, <expC2>]]

SET TOPIC TO [<expC> ¦ <expL>]
```

NEW FOR VISUAL FOXPRO 3

```
SET TOPIC ID TO <expN>

SET TRBETWEEN ON ¦ OFF

SET  TYPEAHEAD TO <expN>

SET UDFPARMS TO VALUE ¦ REFERENCE

SET UNIQUE ON ¦ OFF

SET VIEW ON ¦ OFF
```

```
SET VIEW TO <expFN> ¦ ?

SET WINDOW OF MEMO TO <window>

SHOW GET <variable> [, <expN1> [PROMPT <expC>]]
   [ENABLE ¦ DISABLE] [LEVEL <expN2>]
   [COLOR <color pair list>
   ¦ COLOR SCHEME <expN3>
   ¦ COLOR RGB (<color value list>)]

SHOW GETS [ENABLE ¦ DISABLE]
   [LEVEL <expN1>]  [OFF ¦ ONLY]
   [WINDOW <window>]  [LOCK]
   [COLOR <color pair list> ¦ COLOR SCHEME <expN2>
   ¦ COLOR RGB (<color value list>)]

SHOW MENU <menu1> [, <menu2> ... ] ¦ ALL
   [PAD <pad>]  [SAVE]

SHOW OBJECT <expN1>
   [ENABLE ¦ DISABLE]
   [LEVEL <expN2>]
   [PROMPT <expC>]
   [COLOR <color pair list>
   ¦ COLOR SCHEME <expN3>
   ¦ COLOR RGB (<color value list>)]

SHOW POPUP <popup1> [, <popup2> ... ] ¦ ALL  [SAVE]

SHOW WINDOW <window1>  [, <window2> ... ] ¦ ALL
   [IN [WINDOW] <windowN>  ¦ IN SCREEN]
   [REFRESH]  [TOP ¦ BOTTOM ¦ SAME]   [SAVE]

SIZE POPUP <popup>  TO <expN1>, <expN2>
   ¦ BY <expN3>, <expN4>

SKIP [<expN1>]  [IN <expN2> ¦ <expC>]

SORT TO <expFN>  ON <field1>  [/A] [/D] [/C]
   [, <field2>  [/A] [/D] [/C] ... ]
   [ASCENDING ¦ DESCENDING]
   [<scope>]  [FOR <expL1>] [WHILE <expL2>]
   [FIELDS <field list>]  [NOOPTIMIZE]

STORE <exp> TO <memvar list> ¦ <array>
   <memvar> ¦ <array> = <exp>

SUM  [<exp list>]  [<scope>] [FOR <expL1>] [WHILE <expL2>]
   [TO <memvar list> ¦ TO ARRAY <array>]   [NOOPTIMIZE]

SUSPEND

TEXT
   <text lines>
ENDTEXT

TOTAL TO <expFN> ON <exp> [FIELDS <field list>]
   [<scope>] [FOR <expL1>] [WHILE <expL2>] [NOOPTIMIZE]
```

```
TYPE <expFN1>  [TO PRINTER [PROMPT] ¦ TO FILE <expFN2>]
   [NUMBER] [AUTO] [WRAP]
```

REVISED FOR VISUAL FOXPRO 3

```
UNLOCK [IN <expWA>  ¦ ALL ] [ RECORD <expN> ]

UPDATE ON <key field> FROM <expWA>
   REPLACE <field1> WITH <exp1>
   [, <field2> WITH <exp2> ... ] [RANDOM]
```

REVISED FOR VISUAL FOXPRO 3

```
USE [<expFN> ¦ ?] [IN <expWA> ¦ 0]  [AGAIN]
   [INDEX <index list> ¦ ? [ORDER [<expN>
   ¦ <.idx index file>
   ¦ [TAG] <tag name>  [OF <.cdx file>]
   [ASCENDING ¦ DESCENDING]]]]
   [ALIAS <expWA>] [EXCLUSIVE] [SHARED] [NOUPDATE] [NOREQUERY]

VALIDATE DATABASE VALIDATE DATABASE   [RECOVER]   [NOCONSOLE]   [TO PRINTER
[PROMPT] ¦ TO FILE <expFN>]
```

REVISED FOR VISUAL FOXPRO 3

```
WAIT [<expC>] [TO <memvar>] [WINDOW [NOWAIT]]
   [TIMEOUT <expN>] [CLEAR]  [ AT <row>,<col> ]
```

NEW FOR VISUAL FOXPRO 3

```
WITH <object name>
  [.statements]
ENDWITH
```

REVISED FOR VISUAL FOXPRO 3

```
ZAP   [IN <expWA> ]

ZOOM WINDOW <window>
   MIN [AUTO] ¦ MAX ¦ NORM
   [AT <row1, column1>   ¦ FROM <row1, column1>
   [SIZE <row2, column2> ¦ TO <row2, column2>]]
```

Functions

Functions return a value of a particular type for use in expressions. In the following list, the letter in the left column indicates the return type of each function. A ? in the left column indicates that the return type varies depending on the type of the function's parameters.

NEW FOR VISUAL FOXPRO 3 (ACLASS, ACOPY); NEW FOR VISUAL FOXPRO 3 (ADATABASES, ADBOBJECTS)

```
<expN1> % <expN2>
N    & <memvar> [. <expC>] <expC1> $ <expC2>
N    ABS(<expN>)
N    ACLASS(<array>, <object> )
N    ACOPY(<array1>, <array2> [, <expN1> [, <expN2>
          [, <expN3>]]])
N    ACOS(<expN>)
N    ADEL(<array>, <expN> [,2])
N    ADIR(<array>  [, <expC1> [, <expC2>]])
N    ADATABASES(<array>)
N    ADBOBJECTS (<array>, <expC>)
N    AELEMENT(<array>, <expN1> [, <expN2>])
N    AERROR(<array>)
```

```
N    AFIELDS(<array> [,<expWA>])
L    AFONT(<array> [,<expC> [,<expN>]])
N    AINS(<array>, <expN> [,2])
N    AINSTANCE(<array> , <expC>)
N    ALEN(<array> [, <expN>])
C    ALIAS([<expWA>])
C    ALLTRIM(<expC>)
N    AMEMBERS(<array>, <object name> [, 1 ¦ 2 ] )
C    ANSITOOEM(<expC>)
N    APRINTERS(<array>)
N    ASC(<expC>)
N    ASCAN(<array>, <exp> [, <expN1>[, <expN2>]])
N    ASELOBJ(<array> [,1])
N    ASIN(<expN>)
N    ASORT(<array> [, <expN1> [, <expN2> [, <expN3>]]])
N    ASUBSCRIPT(<array>, <expN1>, <expN2>)
N    AT(<expC1>, <expC2> [, <expN>])
N    ATAN(<expN>)
N    ATC(<expC1>, <expC2> [, <expN>])
N    ATCLINE(<expC1>, <expC2>)
N    ATLINE(<expC1>, <expC2>)
N    ATN2(<expN1>, <expN2>)
N    AUSED(<array>[, <expN>])
N    BAR()
N    BARCOUNT([<expC>])
C    BARPROMPT(<expN> [, <expC>])
L    BETWEEN(<exp1>, <exp2>, <exp3>)
N    BITAND(<expN1>,<expN2>)
N    BITCLEAR (<expN1>,<expN2>)
N    BITLSHIFT (<expN1>,<expN2>)
N    BITNOT(<expN1>,<expN2>)
N    BITOR(<expN1>,<expN2>)
N    BITRSHIFT(<expN1>,<expN2>)
N    BITSET(<expN1>,<expN2>)
N    BITTEST (<expN1>,<expN2>)
N    BITXOR(<expN1>,<expN2>)
L    BOF([<expWA>])
L    CANDIDATE ([<index number>][,<Expwa>] )
L    CAPSLOCK([<expL>])
C    CDOW(<expD>)
C    CDX(<expN1> [, <expN2> ¦ <expC>])
N    CEILING(<expN>)
C    CHR(<expN>)
L    CHRSAW([<expN>])
C    CHRTRAN(<expC1>, <expC2>, <expC3>)
C    CMONTH(<expD>)
N    CNTBAR(<expC>)
N    CNTPAD(<expC>)
N    COL()
N    COMPOBJ(<expC1>,<expC2>)
N    COS(<expN>)
C    CPCONVERT(<expN1>,<expN2>,<expC>)
C    CPCURRENT ( 1 ¦ 2)
C    CREATEOBJECT(<expC>,  <expC1>,<expC2>,...)
```

```
X     CURSORGETPROP(<expC>  [,<expWA>] )
L     CURSORSETPROP(<expC> [,<exp>] [,<expWA>] )
X     CURVAL(<field>,<expWA>)
D     CTOD(<expC>)
T     CTOT(<expC>)
C     CURDIR([<expC>])
-     CURVAL(<field1>[, <expWA>])
D     DATE()
D     DATETIME()
N     DAY(<expD>)
C     DBC()
C     DBF([<expWA>])
-     DBGETPROP(<expC1>,<expC2>,<expC3>)
-     DBSETPROP(<expC1>,<expC2>,<expC3>,<expC4>)
L     DBUSED(<expC>)
L     DDEAbortTrans(<expN>)
L     DDEAdvise(<expN1>, <expC1>, <expC2>, <expN2>)
L     DDEEnabled([<expL1> ¦ <expN1> [, <expL2>]])
L     DDEExecute(<expN>, <expC1> [, <expC2> [, <expC3>]])
N     DDEInitiate(<expC1>, <expC2>)
N     DDELastError()
L/N   DDEPoke(<expN>, <expC1>, <expC2> [, <expC3> [, <expC4>]])
C/N   DDERequest(<expN>, <expC1> [, <expC2> [, <expC3>]])
L/N   DDESetOption(<expC> [, <expN> ¦ <expL>])
L     DDESetService(<expC1>, <expC2> [, <expC3> ¦ <expL>])
C     DDESetTopic(<expC1>, <expC2>  [, <expC3>])
L     DDETerminate(<expN> ¦ <expC>)
L     DELETED([<expC> ¦ <expN>])
L     DESCENDING([[<expFN>,]<expN>[,<expWA>]])
N     DIFFERENCE(<expC1>, <expC2>)
N     DISKSPACE()
C     DMY(<expD>)
N     DOW(<expD>¦<expT> [,<expN>]))
C     DTOC(<expD> [,1])
N     DTOR(<expN>)
C     DTOS(<expD>)
C     DTOT(<expT>)
L     EMPTY(<exp>)
L     EOF([<expWA>])
N     ERROR()
?     EVALUATE(<expC>)
N     EXP(<expN>)
N     FCHSIZE(<expN1>, <expN2>)
L     FCLOSE(<expN>)
N     FCOUNT([<expWA>])
N     FCREATE(<expC> [, <expN>])
D     FDATE(<expFN>)
L     FEOF(<expN>)
N     FERROR()
L     FFLUSH(<expN>)
C     FGETS(<expN1> [, <expN2>])
C     FIELD(<expN1> [, <expN2> ¦ <expC>])
L     FILE(<expC>)
C     FILTER([<expWA>])
C     FKLABEL(<expN>)
N     FKMAX()
L     FLOCK([<expWA>])
N     FLDCOUNT([<expWA>])
```

```
C    FLDLIST([<expN>])
N    FLOOR(<expN>)
N    FONTMETRIC(<expN1> [,<expC1> ,<expN2> [,<expC2>]])
N    FOPEN(<expC> [, <expN>])
N    FOR([[<expN>[,<expWA>]]])
L    FOUND([<expWA>])
N    FPUTS(<expN1>, <expC> [, <expN2>])
C    FREAD(<expN1>, <expN2>)
N    FSEEK(<expN1>, <expN2> [, <expN3>])
N    FSIZE(<expC1> [, <expN> ¦ <expC2>])
N    FSIZE(<expFN>)                        (SET COMPATIBLE DB4)
C    FTIME((<expFN>)                                                    NEW FOR VISUAL FOXPRO 3
C    FULLPATH(<expFN1> [, <expN> ¦ <expFN2>])
N    FV(<expN1>, <expN2>, <expN3>)
N    FWRITE(<expN1>, <expC> [, <expN2>])
N    GETBAR(<expC>, <expN>)
N    GETCOLOR([<expN>])                                                 NEW FOR VISUAL FOXPRO 3
N    GETCP(<expN>,<expC>,<expC>)
C    GETDIR([<expC1> [, <expC2>]])
C    GETENV(<expC>)
C    GETFILE([<expC1>] [, <expC2>] [, <expC3>] [, <expN>)
N    GETFLDSTATE( <expC> ¦ <expN> [, <expWA> ] )                        NEW FOR VISUAL FOXPRO 3
C    GETFONT()
N    GETNEXTMODIFIED(<expN>[,<expWA>])
O    GETOBJECT(<expFN>[,<expC>])
N    GETPAD(<expC>, <expN>)
C    GETPICT(<expC1> [,<expC2] [,<expC3>])                              NEW FOR VISUAL FOXPRO 3
C    GETPRINTER()
D    GOMONTH(<expD>, <expN>)
N    HEADER([<expWA>])
C    HOME()
N    HOUR(<expT>)                                                       NEW FOR VISUAL FOXPRO 3
C    ID()
C    IDXCOLLATE(<expC>[,<expN1>[,<expWA>]])
?    IIF(<expL>, <exp1>, <exp2>)
L    INDBC()                                                            NEW FOR VISUAL FOXPRO 3
N    INKEY([[<expN>] [, <expC>]])
N    INLIST(<exp1>, <exp2> [, <exp3> ... ])
L    INSMODE([<expL>])
N    INT(<expN>)
L    ISALPHA(<expC>)
L    ISBLANK(<exp>)
L    ISCOLOR()
L    ISDIGIT(<expC>)
L    ISEXCLUSIVE([ <expWA> ])                                           NEW FOR VISUAL FOXPRO 3
L    ISLOWER(<expC>)
L    ISMOUSE()
L    ISNULL(<exp>)                                                      NEW FOR VISUAL FOXPRO 3
L    ISREADONLY([<expWA>])
L    ISUPPER(<expC>)
C    KEY([<.cdx file>,] <expN1> [, <expN2> ¦ <expC>])
L    KEYMATCH(<exp>[,<expN1>[,<expWA>]])
N    LASTKEY()
C    LEFT(<expC>, <expN>)
N    LEN(<expC>)
L    LIKE(<expC1>, <expC2>)
N    LINENO([1])
C    LOCFILE([<expFN>] [,<expC1>] [, <expC2>] [, <expC4>])
```

```
L     LOCK([<expN1> ¦ <expC1>] ¦ [<expC2>, <expN2> ¦ <expC3>])
N     LOG(<expN>)
N     LOG10(<expN>)
?     LOOKUP(<field1>, <search exp>, <field2> [, <expC>])
C     LOWER(<expC>)
C     LTRIM(<expC>)
D     LUPDATE([<expWA>])
N     MAX(<exp1>, <exp2> [, <exp3> ... ])
N     MCOL([<expC>])
N     MDOWN()
L     MDX(<expN1> [, <expN2> ¦ <expC>])
C     MDY(<expD>)
N     MEMLINES(<memo field>)
N     MEMORY()
C     MENU()
C     MESSAGE([1])
N     MESSAGEBOX(<expC1> [,<expN> [,<expC2>]])
CDN   MIN(<exp1>, <exp2> [, <exp3> ... ])
N     MINUTE(<expT>)
C     MLINE(<memo field>, <expN1> [, <expN2>])
N     MOD(<expN1>, <expN2>)
N     MONTH(<expD>)
L     MRKBAR(<expC>, <expN>)
L     MRKPAD(<expC1>, <expC2>)
N     MROW([<expC>])
N     MTON(<expY>)
C/L   MWINDOW([<window>])
C     NDX(<expN1> [, <expN2> ¦ <expC>])
L     NETWORK()
C     NORMALIZE(<expC>)
Y     NTOM(<expN>)
L     NVL(<expC1>,<expC2>)
L     NUMLOCK([<expL>])
N     OBJNUM(<variable> [, <expN>])
O     OBJREF(<expC>)
N     OBJTOCLIENT(<expC>,<expN>)
C     OBJVAR(<expC>,<expN>)
N     OCCURS(<expC1>, <expC2>)
-     OEMTOANSI(<expC>)
-     OLDVAL(<field1>[, <expWA>])
C     ON(<expC1> [, <expC2>])
C     ORDER([<expN1> ¦ <expC>[, <expN2>]])
C     OS()
C     PAD()
C     PADL(<exp>, <expN> [, <expC>])
C     PADR(<exp>, <expN> [, <expC>])
C     PADC(<exp>, <expN> [, <expC>])
C     PADPROMPT(<expC1> [, <expC2>])
N     PARAMETERS()
N     PAYMENT(<expN1>, <expN2>, <expN3>)
N     PCOL()
N     PCOUNT()
N     PI()
C     POPUP()
L     PRIMARY( <expN> [, <expWA> ])
L     PRINTSTATUS()
C     PRMBAR(<expC>, <expN>)
C     PRMPAD(<expC1>, <expC2>)
```

```
C      PROGRAM([<expN>])
C      PROMPT()
C      PROPER(<expC>)
N      PRTINFO(<expN>)
N      PROW()
C      PUTFILE([<expC1>] [, <expFN>] [, <expC2>] )
N      PV(<expN1>, <expN2>, <expN3>)
N      RAND([<expN>])
N      RAT(<expC1>, <expC2> [, <expN>])
N      RATLINE(<expC1>, <expC2>)
N      RDLEVEL()
N      READKEY([<expN>])
N      RECCOUNT([<expWA>])
N      RECNO([<expWA>])
N      RECSIZE([<expWA>])
N      REFRESH([<expN1>[,<expN2>]] [,<expWA>])
C      RELATION(<expN1>[, <expN2> ¦ <expC>])
C      REPLICATE(<expC>, <expN>)
L      REQUERY([<expWA>])
N      RGB(<expN1>,<expN2> ,<expN3>)
C      RGBSCHEME(<expN1>[,<expN2>])
C      RIGHT(<expC>, <expN>)
L      RLOCK([<expN1> ¦ <expC1>] ¦ [<expC2>, <expN2> ¦ <expC3>])
N      ROUND(<expN1>, <expN2>)
N      ROW()
N      RTOD(<expN>)
C      RTRIM(<expC>)
C      SCHEME(<expN1> [, <expN2>])
N      SCOLS()
N      SEC(<expT>)
N      SECONDS()
L      SEEK(<exp> [, <expWA>][,<expN> ¦ <expFN> ¦ <expC>])
N      SELECT( [ 0 ¦ 1 ] ¦ <expWA> ])
C/N    SET(<expC> [,1])
-      SETFLDSTATE(<expC> ¦ <expN>, <expN> [, <expWA> ])
N      SIGN(<expN>)
N      SIN(<expN>)
L      SKPBAR(<expC>, <expN>)
L      SKPPAD(<expC1>, <expC2>)
C      SOUNDEX(<expC>)
C      SPACE(<expN>)
N      SQLCANCEL(<expN>)
N      SQLCOLUMNS(<expN>,<expC1> [,FOXPRO ¦ NATIVE] [,<expC2>]))
L      SQLCOMMIT(<expN>)
N      SQLCONNECT(<expC1>,<expC2>,<expC3>)
N      SQLDISCONNECT(<expN>)
N      SQLEXEC(<expC1>,<expC2> [,<expC3>])
N      SQLGETPROP(<expN>¦<expC>, <expC>)
N      SQLMORERESULTS(<expN>)
L      SQLROLLBACK(<expC>)
N      SQLSETPROP((<expN>¦<expC>, <expC>[,<exp>])
N      SQLSTRINGCONNECT(<expC>)
N      SQLTABLES(<expN>[,<expC1>] [,<expC2>])
N      SQRT(<expN>)
N      SROWS()
C      STR(<expN1> [, <expN2> [,<expN3>]])
C      STRTRAN(<expC1>, <expC2> [, <expC3>] [, <expN1>][, <expN2>])
C      STUFF(<expC1>, <expN1>, <expN2>, <expC2>)
```

```
C      SUBSTR(<expC>, <expN1> [, <expN2>])
N      SYSMETRIC(<expN>)
C      SYS(<expN> [,<expN>] )
N      TABLEREVERT([<expL>] [,<expWA>])
L      TABLEUPDATE([<expL>] [,<expWA>])
C      TAG([<.cdx-file>,] <expN1>[, <expN2> ¦ <expC>])
N      TAGCOUNT([<expFN>[,<expWA>]])
N      TAGNO([<expC>[,<expFN>[,<expWA>]]])
N      TAN(<expN>)
C      TARGET(<expN1>[, <expN2> ¦ <expC>])
C      TIME([<expN>])
C      TRANSFORM(<exp>, <expC>)
C      TRIM(<expC>)
C      TTOC(<expT> [,1])
D      TTOD(<expD>)
N      TXNLEVEL()
N      TXTWIDTH(<expC1> [, <expC2>, <expN> [, <expC3>]])
C      TYPE(<expC>)
C      UNIQUE([[<expFN>,]<expN>[,<expWA>]])
L      UPDATED()
C      UPPER(<expC>)
L      USED([<expWA>])
N      VAL(<expC>)
C      VARREAD()
C      VERSION()
L      WBORDER([<window>])
C/L    WCHILD([<window1> ¦ <expN1>])
N      WCOLS([<window>])
N      WEEK(<expD>¦<expT> [,<expN>][,<expN>]))
L      WEXIST(<window>)
C/L    WFONT(<expN> [, <window>])
C      WINDOW()
C/L    WLAST([<window>])
N      WLCOL([<window>])
N      WLROW([<window>])
L      WMAXIMUM([<window>])
L      WMINIMUM([<window>])
C/L    WONTOP([<window>])
C/L    WOUTPUT([<window>])
C      WPARENT([<window>])
L      WREAD([<window>])
N      WROWS([<window>])
C      WTITLE([<window>])
L      WVISIBLE(<window>)
N      YEAR(<expD>)
```

C

Glossary

386 enhanced mode One of three Windows 3.*x* operating modes. This mode runs on the x86 (80386, 80486, Pentium P5, and Pentium P6) microprocessors with access to extended memory and support for non-Windows (DOS) applications. Standard and 386 enhanced mode run in protected mode.

8087 family of math coprocessors Processors that perform high-speed floating calculations and binary-coded-decimal (BCD) calculations. This refers to the 8087, 80287, and 80387 coprocessors. (Most 80486 and Pentium P5 microprocessors have a built-in math coprocessor.)

active window The window on the screen to which the next output is directed. The active window has a highlighted title bar and border.

aggregate function A function that performs numeric operations. It is used with the `CALCULATE` command and RQBE and SQL operations. Aggregate functions include `SUM()`, `AVG()`, `MIN()`, `MAX()`, `COUNT()`, `STD()`, and `VAR()`.

alert A window containing a warning or error message. Some people consider the bell to be an alert also.

alias A name assigned to a work area when a table is placed in use.

alternate index A candidate index that has been chosen as the primary index.

`AND` A logical binary operator that produces a true result if both of its operands have a true value. It produces a false value if either or both of its operands are false.

ANSI (American National Standards Institute) The organization responsible for developing voluntary national technical standards.

API (Application Programming Interface) A set of routines and functions that provides an interface between an application and the operating system for operations such as input, output, file management, and graphics output. Examples are the Microsoft Windows API and the FoxPro API.

application A file (with an .APP extension) composed of Visual FoxPro programs, forms, menus, reports, and files compiled in a single file.

argument A value passed to a function or a procedure.

arithmetic conversion An operation that converts information from a numeric value to another type, as in the conversion from a character type string to a number, which is performed by the `STR()` function.

arithmetic expression An expression consisting of numbers, numeric variables, functions, and numeric operators. An example of an expression is `X*3 + SQRT(Y)`.

arithmetic operator A symbol that represents an operator that performs an arithmetic operation on numeric operands.

array A collection of data elements organized according to an arrangement. Each element of an array can be referenced with a numeric index. In FoxPro, an array can have one or two indexes.

ASCII (American Standard Code for Information Interchange) A commonly accepted set of 255 character codes that represent numbers, characters, and special symbols.

assembler A processor that translates a program written in a symbolic assembly language into an object form that a computer can execute.

assembly language A low-level computer language in which the symbolic code has a one-to-one correspondence with the actual machine language instructions executed by a computer.

attached A table (DBF file) that is associated with a database container but is outside the database container. You can open an attached table only if its associated database container is active.

back-end data Any data that exists outside of Visual FoxPro in a form supported by OLE. Examples of back-end data sources include Paradox, Microsoft Access, and SQLServer.

base class In Visual FoxPro, a base class is a class internally defined in FoxPro that you use as a basis for deriving user-defined classes. For example, you can derive your own graphics object class from FoxPro form and control base classes.

basic optimizable expression The most rudimentary form of a logical expression that Rushmore technology can optimize. It consists of a constant expression, a logical operator, and an index expression. (See Chapter 13, "Data Ordering," for more information.)

binary A two-state, on/off logic. A binary number notation system that uses ones and zeros to represent values.

binary file A file that is not a text file. It contains values other than text characters. Examples are EXE, BMP, and OBJ files. In FoxPro, a binary (BIN) file contains executable code and can be loaded into memory with the `LOAD` command and executed with the `CALL` command.

binary format Data stored directly from memory to a disk file without any translation. Numeric numbers are represented as binary values in binary format as opposed to as a series of ASCII numbers.

binary mode A way to directly access files without performing any translations.

binary resource file A file output from the Resource Compiler with an .RES extension. A binary resource file contains compiled Windows bitmap, icon, dialog, or cursor resource data.

bit A binary digit or ⅛ of a byte. A bit has a value of either 0 or 1. A bit is the smallest unit that a computer handles.

bitmap An array of bits representing pixels in a graphic image stored in a file with a .BMP extension.

bitmapped font A font in which an array of bits represents each character as opposed to a set of equations. Windows TrueType fonts are defined with a set of equations.

bitwise operators Operators that act on individual bits of a value rather than on an entire value. In FoxPro, the bitwise operators are `AND`, `OR`, `XOR`, and `NOT`.

BOF (beginning of file) When a database file is positioned to physical record 1, the record is said to be at the beginning of the file, and if there is no controlling index, the `BOF()` function returns a true value.

boolean Data represented as true/false or yes/no. Logical data types are boolean data.

bound control A control on a form that derives its value from a particular field value of a table or query. For example, a text box containing the city field value for the current record is a bound control.

browse To view data in a tabular form. You browse data when you view information in a Browse table. (See information on the `BROWSE` command in Chapter 9, "Full-Screen Data Editing.")

buffer The portion of a computer's memory reserved for data currently being processed. For example, during input/output operations, the buffer temporarily holds data.

builder A Visual FoxPro tool that can help you set up properties for a particular control. Another type of builder is the Expression Builder, which can help you build an expression.

byte An 8-bit unit used for accessing addresses in memory. A byte is the unit of measure for memory and disk space size. 1 byte contains 1 ASCII character.

.C The filename extension for a C source file.

calculated value An identifier that resembles a read-only variable. A calculated value is associated with an expression. When you refer to a calculated value, its expression is evaluated and the results are returned. A calculated value can be specified in a `BROWSE` or `CHANGE` field list.

candidate index An index that can be used as a primary index because it contains no nulls or duplicate values.

caption A title of a form or the name beside or on a control. For example, Cancel is the `Caption` property on a cancel button control.

case sensitivity A state that indicates whether an uppercase letter is treated as having the same value as its corresponding lowercase letter. C and UNIX are case sensitive. FoxPro, Xbase, and MS-DOS are not case sensitive.

char A Character data type variable.

character An alphanumeric symbol (for example, A, 1, B, 2, z).

character expression An expression that consists of character strings, Character type operators, functions, and Character data type variables and fields.

character field A type of field in a data table (database file) that can be up to 254 characters and can contain any ASCII character.

character string A sequence of bytes treated as ASCII characters (letters, numbers, and other symbols). In FoxPro, a character string is often enclosed in single quotation marks, double quotation marks, or square brackets (for example, `"string"`, `'strong'`, `[Strum]`).

check box A menu control item that is a small square box followed by a text label or picture. You can toggle on and off a check box by clicking on it. When it is on, an X displays inside the box. When it is off, the box is empty.

child table The related table in a one-to-one or one-to-many relationship. A parent (or primary) table relates to a child table.

class A template that defines the properties of an object and defines how an object should look and behave.

clause A language element that follows the command verb in FoxPro. A clause can be a single keyword, or it can be a keyword followed by some other language element, such as an expression or a variable.

click To press and quickly release one of the mouse buttons while the mouse points to an object on the screen. The left mouse button is used most frequently.

client-server application An application with a local (client) user interface that accesses data from a remote server. Work is distributed between the client and server.

Clipboard A temporary storage buffer for text. The Clipboard is used to cut, paste, and copy text.

code page A table used by an operating system to define a character set. A character is stored in memory as a numeric value. When Windows displays a numeric value, it uses a particular code page to map the numeric value to a specific character set. Different countries use different code pages.

code snippet A procedure, a user-defined function (UDF), or an expression associated with a menu or some global action, such as initialization and cleanup operations, that relates to a menu system. You can specify code snippets in the Menu Designer and FoxPro 2.5 Screen Builder.

code symbol An address of a procedure or function.

command A statement the user submits to the computer that results in the computer performing some kind of action. In the FoxPro language, a command consists of a verb and usually some additional clauses. You can place commands in a program, or you can type a command into the FoxPro Command window. In Windows, a menu option is often called a command.

command keyword An element of a command that specifies some action. Some keywords stand alone, and other keywords introduce clauses.

comments Program statements that are not executed. Comments usually provide some information about what the program does. In FoxPro, text following the `&&` delimiter is a comment. If the first nonblank character on a code line is an asterisk, the entire code line contains comments. The compiler ignores comments. In the C programming language, comments are delimited by `/*` and `*/`.

compact single-entry index An index (IDX) file that contains only one index. You must explicitly open this file to use it, and it must be active for it to be updated.

compile The process of translating a programming language source into executable code.

compiler A computer program that translates source code into executable code. FoxPro contains a built-in compiler that compiles program files written in the FoxPro language into pseudocode, which the FoxPro interpreter can execute.

compiler directive A special command, used in a program, that is processed before the program is compiled. A compiler directive is sometimes called a *preprocessor directive.* The first character of a compiler directive is a pound sign (`#`). See *directive.*

compound index file An index (CDX) file that contains multiple indexes called *tags.* A structural compound index file is similar to the compound index file except that it is opened when its associated table is placed in use.

concatenate To join or chain two objects. In FoxPro, the concatenation operator (`+`) combines strings into a single string. In computer terminology, concatenate usually refers to joining strings and files.

conditional expression A language expression that evaluates to a true (`.T.`) or false (`.F.`) value.

configuration file A file (CONFIG.FPW) that contains all FoxPro initial environmental settings.

constant A value that doesn't change during execution. `345.33`, `"This is a constant"`, and `{12/12/94}` are examples of constants.

constant expression An expression that evaluates to a constant.

constraints An expression associated with a field or record that designates data entry rules. Constraints can be used to provide Visual FoxPro with data integrity checking. Field-level constraints (or field-level rules) for a field are evaluated when you move to the next field to make sure the data entered is valid. A record-level constraint (or row-level rule) is checked when you move to a new record.

container classes Visual FoxPro base classes that group together other classes.

control A graphical object with a simple input and output function. Examples are push button controls, edit boxes, labels, lines, grids, and text boxes.

control array A group of controls that share the same name, properties, and event procedures. Each control has a unique index. When one of the controls responds to an event, it calls the event procedure to which it passes its unique index value.

control character A nonprinting ASCII character used to edit control or shortcut keys. To enter a control character, you hold down the Ctrl key plus a character key. The notation for a control key sequence is Ctrl+<*character*>. For example, Ctrl+C.

controlling index One of the active indexes, sometimes called the master index, that controls the order in which data records are accessed.

coprocessor See *8087 family of math coprocessors.*

CPU Central processing unit.

criteria A set of limiting conditions used in a query or filter to designate a set of records.

.CUR The filename extension for a cursor resource object.

curly braces Punctuation marks ({}) used as delimiters for date fields in FoxPro programs.

cursor (1) A thin blinking line or other representation that indicates the location of typed input or mouse action. (2) A temporary read-only table that is not saved in a file (database).

custom control A user-created control based on one or more of the FoxPro base classes.

Data Definition Language (DDL) Computer language used to specify the database structure to the database management system.

Data Manipulation Language (DML) A computer language used to instruct the database management system to perform database management operations on a database.

data type A term used to define the method by which data is stored and maintained in FoxPro. The seven data types in FoxPro are Character, Float, Numeric, Logical, Date, Memo, and General.

database A collection of related data and objects.

Database Container The Visual FoxPro container tool that manages tables, queries, forms, fields, persistent relations, and index tags.

date field A field in a database that represents a date in the form *mm/dd/yyyy.* A date field takes up 8 bytes. A date is actually stored in *yyyymmdd* form.

DBMS (database management system) Software used to organize, analyze, store, retrieve, and edit information.

DDE (dynamic data exchange) Established protocol that exchanges data between Windows applications. If two cooperative Windows applications are running, they can exchange data using cut and paste operations.

debugger A development tool program, such as the FoxPro Debugger, used to detect bugs.

declaration A language construct that associates a name with other attributes, such as type, or values.

decrement To count backward (for example, 7, 6, 5, 4).

default A value or response that is not specified, but rather assumed by a program. For example, a computer uses a *default value* if you don't specify a value.

default control In a group of controls (radio buttons, push buttons, and so on), the default control is the one that is preselected. If you press Enter without selecting any control, the default control is chosen.

definition A language construct that specifies and initializes memory requirements for a variable or specifies attributes of a function.

delimiter A character that marks the beginning or end of a unit of data. A unit of data is an associated sequence of characters such as numbers or keywords. Single quotation marks, double quotation marks, or square brackets are delimiters for a string constant (for example, `"Aardvark"`).

design time The period of time in which you create an application. During design time, you build components and set properties. Some properties can be set at design time. Others can be set at *runtime.*

desktop The FoxPro main window that is the workspace on which all FoxPro systems, user-defined windows, and other objects display.

detail band A region on a report normally used to display information relating to each record in a database.

dialog box An impermanent window that displays program information or prompts the user for input.

dialog box controls Controls within a dialog box.

dimension The number of array subscripts.

directive An instruction to the preprocessor to perform some operation on the source code prior to compilation.

disable To cause an object to be unavailable for use; for example, a disabled menu option in a Windows program. These menu options are usually displayed in a dimmed intensity and cannot be chosen.

DLL (dynamic link library) A special library that lets applications share resources and functions. DLL files developed for FoxPro for Windows are called Fox-linked library (FLL) files.

docked An object that is fixed to the top, side, or bottom of the FoxPro main window. Toolbars and database containers are examples of dockable objects.

double-click To press and quickly release one of the mouse buttons twice in rapid succession while the mouse points to an object on the screen. The left mouse button is usually used.

double precision A floating-point numeric value that occupies 8 bytes of memory. Double precision values are accurate to 15 or 16 significant places.

DPMI (MS-DOS Protected Mode Interface) A program, called a *server*, that makes extended or expanded memory available to programs. Examples of DPMI servers include the MSDPMI processor for DOS sessions. This server allows programs to take advantage of the 32-bit architecture of the 80386 microprocessor. The Microsoft C/C++ 7 compiler is a 32-bit program. It cannot run under DOS unless MSDPMI is operating. It can run in a DOS session under Windows also.

drag To move the mouse while holding down the mouse button. When you reach the desired position, release the mouse button and the drag operation stops.

drag and drop An operation in which you drag an object onto another object to perform an operation.

dynamic data exchange See *DDE.*

dynamic link library See *DLL.*

dynamic linking The act of performing a link operation for an application at runtime.

EGA (enhanced graphics adapter) A color video display device for IBM PCs and compatibles that can display in 64 colors, and up to 16 colors simultaneously.

element An individual member of an array.

embed A term used in OLE to indicate that a copy of an object from one application is inserted into another application with no further association. Changes made to the copy are not reflected in the original object.

emulator A software package that simulates math coprocessor operations.

encapsulation A mechanism for hiding the internal workings of a module to support abstraction.

environment variable A variable stored in the MS-DOS environment table that contains information relating to the software environment. An environment variable is most often used to store information to assist in file location.

EOF (end of file) A code that signifies the end of a file.

escape sequence A combination of characters preceded by a code-extension character (also called an *escape character*). The code-extension character indicates that the succeeding characters are interpreted differently. Escape sequences are normally used to control printed or displayed output. The Esc key is sometimes used as an escape character.

event An action, such as a mouse click, that is recognized by an object. Event code executes when an event occurs.

event code Code executed when an event occurs.

event driven A condition in which an action is triggered by the occurrence of some event, such as a mouse click or a keypress.

.EXE The filename extension for an executable application file.

executable file A program, containing machine language instructions, that is ready to be run by the operating system.

execute To perform instructions in a software program.

expanded memory Memory above 640KB that can be used by real-mode programs and is controlled through paging by an expanded memory manager.

expression An operand or a combination of operands and operators. When evaluated, an expression yields a single value.

Expression Builder The Visual FoxPro tool used to build an expression by picking fields, variables, operations, and functions from a dialog box.

expression list An expression or a sequence of expressions separated by commas.

extended memory Memory above either 640KB or 1MB that is made available to protected-mode programs on computers with at least an 80286 microprocessor. Extended memory is used by Windows in standard mode or 386 enhanced mode.

extension See *filename extension.*

field A data unit in a record. A record is made up of one or more fields. One or more records make up a table (database file).

field-level rule Constraints bound to a field used for data validation. When a field value is inserted or changed, field-level rules are evaluated to ensure that data is valid.

field object A field or memory variable placed on a report or screen.

file handle An integer value returned when a file is opened and used to reference that file for any of the I/O operations. A file handle is used with FoxPro and C language low-level file I/O operations.

file type The category of a file used by FoxPro; the filename extensions usually denote the type. For example, .PRG indicates a program file, .APP indicates an application file, .DBF indicates a database file, .CDX indicates a compound index file, .IDX indicates a single index file, and so on.

filename The name used to reference a file consisting of a base name and an extension. The base name optionally can be followed by a period and have a filename extension of up to three characters. In MS-DOS and Windows 3.1, the base name can be up to eight characters. In Windows 95, the filename can be longer and can include spaces.

filename extension An extension to a filename that consists of up to three characters preceded and separated from the filename by a period. Filename extensions normally represent a file type. For example, the extension .EXE in FOXPROW.EXE indicates that the file is an executable file.

filter A set of criteria used to select a subset of records for processing.

FLL (Fox-linked library) See *DLL*.

floating point A Float data type. A technique for storing numbers with a decimal point in which a set of digits is added that keeps track of the location of the radix point. For example, 1.345E+04.

font A complete set of characters in a given typeface, weight, and size.

foreign key A value of a field or combination of fields that is used to match a primary key in some other table.

form A Visual FoxPro container class that consists of one or more page forms. A form behaves like a window or dialog box.

form page A Visual FoxPro container class that is a single page of a form. A form page contains controls. Only one form page can be active within a form.

form set A Visual FoxPro container class that is a collection of one or more associated forms.

free table A table that is not attached to a database container. A free table cannot have extended attributes such as default values and field-level rules.

function A program code section that performs a specific task. FoxPro system functions are built into FoxPro. Programmers can write user-defined functions (UDFs). A call or reference to a function can be an element in an expression because it takes zero or more arguments and returns a single value.

function call A statement that passes control to a function. A function call also passes arguments. The function returns a single value to the function call.

General field A field in a database that stores binary data, which can represent a picture, sound, or other objects.

generate code An operation performed by the Menu Designer that translates user-defined screens and menus into FoxPro language code. Code generated by the Menu Designer is stored in a menu program (MPR) file.

global variable A variable that is visible throughout an entire program. In FoxPro, database fields and public memory variables are global symbols.

graphic object A line or box used in reports or screens.

Group band A pair of regions on the Report Designer desktop in which report objects are placed. These objects display on the report if certain criteria are met. You add a Group band to the report by choosing the **R**eport menu Data G**r**ouping option.

Group Footer band A report Group band into which report objects are placed to print each time a group criterion changes. Group Footer bands usually contain calculated fields.

Group Header band A report Group band into which report objects are placed to print each time a group criterion changes after a group footer band prints. Normally, Group Header bands contain band identification information that precedes the printing of detailed information.

hexadecimal A base 16 number represented by characters 0 through 9 and A through F. The letters A through F correspond to decimal values 10 through 15. For example, 3E9F is a hexadecimal number.

hide To make a window disappear without deactivating it.

hotkey An underlined key in a menu pad or option that indicates the letter to press in combination with the Alt key to choose a menu item.

I/O (input/output) The exchange of data; for example, the keyboard is an input device and the terminal screen is an output device. File I/O means reading and writing files.

.ICO The filename extension for an icon resource file.

icon A small graphic image in a graphical user interface that represents a program file, a data file, or some other computer entity. An icon displays when an application window is minimized.

identifier The name of a variable, constant, macro, function, or data type. The name is contrived by the programmer.

.IDX The filename extension for a FoxPro independent index file that contains a single index. An IDX file cannot contain the same name as its associated database DBF file. It must be explicitly opened for a database file, whereas a structural CDX file is opened automatically when its associated database file opens.

increment To count forward (for example, 6, 7, 8, 9).

index A file or compound index tag that controls the order in which database file records are accessed. The sequence is determined by key fields. An IDX file contains a single index. A CDX file contains multiple index tags.

indexed database file A database file whose access order is determined by an index.

inheritance An object-oriented programming term that denotes the ability of a subclass to receive the characteristics of the class on which it is based. If the parent class characteristics change, the subclass inherits the changed characteristics. For example, if you add a new property to a class, the new property is available to any subclass based on that class.

initialize The process by which a variable is assigned a value when it is created. For example, `STORE 3 to X`.

input focus The state of a Windows object that is activated to receive input. After a user clicks on or tabs to an application's window object, that window has input focus.

input mask A property of a field that controls the format of user input. Input masks are equivalent to FoxPro 2.5 `FORMAT` statements.

insert mode A text-editing state in which any typed character is inserted at the cursor position, and text to the right of the cursor moves to the right. This mode is in contrast to the *overtype mode.*

instance An object-oriented programming term that denotes any single object created from a class. A class is a definition of an object only while an instance of an object exists and can be used to perform operations.

integer A whole number that has no fractional or decimal part.

invisible button A screen control that is invisible. Its operation can be defined by a program control.

join condition A condition that designates the relationship between two database files based on fields in both tables.

key A field or expression used to identify a record.

keyboard shortcut key A keystroke combination that you can use to choose menu options instead of using a mouse. For example, the Ctrl+F shortcut key chooses the **E**dit menu **F**ind option.

keyword A term in the FoxPro language that has a predefined meaning and provides instructions to the compiler. Examples of keywords are `COPY`, `ALL`, and `SDF`.

lifetime Processing period in which a variable exists. A private variable exists from the time it is created until the function or procedure in which it is defined returns. A public variable exists from the time it is created until the program exits.

link A term used in object linking and embedding (OLE) that denotes a connection between a source document and a destination document. A linked object is a reference to the object for the destination file. When the source file changes, the destination object changes.

linker A software program that combines object modules to generate an executable module. Object files contain relocatable addresses. These object modules can be user defined or extracted from a library. The linker loads into memory the object modules needed to build the executable module and then replaces the relocatable addresses with absolute addresses. This process continues until all external references are resolved; then the linker creates an executable module.

linking An operation performed by the *linker*.

literal A character specified as a constant part of a format, such as the slash used in data formats. A literal is also used to designate a type of specification, as in *literal filename*, which means that you can enter the actual filename in contrast to entering a constant character string.

local alias A temporary name used with the SQL `SELECT` command to refer to a table. A local alias is defined in the `FROM` clause.

local data Data existing in the client. It is not FoxPro data.

local variable A variable accessible only within a function or a procedure. Global variables can be accessed across functions and procedures.

lock A process by which you can prevent other users from modifying a file, database file, or record.

logical field A database field that accepts only true (`.T.`) or false (`.F.`) values. The width of a character field in a table is one character.

logical operator An operator that combines logical expressions to produce a complex logical expression. `AND` and `OR` are logical operators.

loop A program construct that repeats.

low-level language A programming language that is close to machine code in its complexity. Assembly language is a low-level language.

machine code The native language of a computer that consists of binary computer instructions, which a computer interprets to execute a program.

macro (1) A sequence of characters emitted when a key is pressed. You define a macro for a keystroke by pressing the Ctrl+F10 key combination. (2) A constant identifier that is equated to an expression using a `#define` compiler directive. The preprocessor substitutes every occurrence of the identifier with the characters to which the identifier is equated before the source file is compiled.

macro substitution (1) The act of replacing an ampersand, followed by a character type memory variable, in a command line with the contents of the memory variable. This process is performed before a command executes. (2) The act of replacing a constant identifier, equated to an expression, by using a `#define` compiler directive in a program before the program is compiled.

main FoxPro window The window beneath all system and user-defined windows in FoxPro.

main program The program with which program execution begins.

maximize To cause a window to expand to fill the screen or its parent window.

medium model A memory model with one data segment and one or more code segments.

memo field A database field used to store large amounts of information. A memo field can hold any type of data, including documents and binary data. In the database (DBF) file, the field width of a memo field is 10 bytes, which is the address of the data in a tightly associated memo file that has the same root name and an .FPT extension.

memory variable A location in memory where data is stored and manipulated. A memory variable, sometimes called a *memvar,* has an identifier, a type, and a value. The identifier is used to reference the variable. The type of a memory variable can be Character, Date, Currency, DateTime, Numeric, or Logical, or it can be an array. Its type is determined when a variable is stored to it. See *public* and *private.*

memvar A memory variable.

menu A list of items that appears when you choose a menu title from a menu bar. This is also referred to as a *pop-up menu.*

menu bar The bar at the top of a window, below the title bar, which is used to display menus.

menu name Text or icon on the menu bar that specifies a menu.

menu option An item on a menu that performs a designated action when chosen. A menu option is sometimes called a *menu command,* because when you select a menu option, some action occurs.

menu pad A region on the menu bar with a menu name.

menu system A combination of the menu bar, menu pads with associated pop-up menus, and the pop-up menu options.

method An object-oriented programming term that denotes an action that an object can perform.

minimize To reduce a window to its icon.

modal A characteristic of a window, form, or dialog box object. When a modal window, form, or dialog box is active, no other window can be activated until the modal object is dismissed or closed. For example, an error box is a modal window.

modeless A characteristic of a window or dialog box object. When a modeless window or form is active, other windows can be activated without closing the modeless window. For example, the Debug, Trace, Command, and Project windows are modeless.

multiple instances Several objects created from the same class. Each class has its own properties and private data. However, all the instances share the same code.

name expression A character expression that evaluates to a name. A name expression, in its simplest form, is a memory variable enclosed in parentheses. If you don't specify the parentheses, the memory variable is treated as a literal name.

native data Data stored in Visual FoxPro DBF files.

nested loop The structure of one loop within another loop.

nonmodal A characteristic of a window or dialog box that allows other windows to be brought forward while the nonmodal window is active. For example, the Command window is a nonmodal window.

normalize The act of removing duplicate information from relational database files through an efficient database design.

null Having no assigned value. A null value is not equivalent to blank or zero or any other value.

null character A character with a zero value, `'\0'`, that marks the end of a string.

numeric field A database field that stores numeric values used in Numeric expressions. The field data value can contain numbers, a sign, a decimal point, and if needed, an exponent.

object An instance of a class. It combines both data and procedures.

object file A file containing object code; its filename extension is .FXP. The linker translates object files and object modules from a library into an executable program.

object linking and embedding (OLE) A protocol that defines the sharing of data between two applications. An object, such as a document, graph, or picture in a source (or object) application, can be linked or embedded in a destination (container) document such as a report.

object module An object file created by a compiler. The compiler translates a source program to an object module.

ODBC See *open database connectivity.*

OLE automation The ability to control OLE in one application from another application programmatically.

OLE 2.0 control A prepackaged OLE 2.0 object that is unlike other OLE objects. It is used as a control in a 32-bit application the same way a VBX control is used in a 16-bit application. OLE controls have events and can be subclassed to create other controls. OLE controls have a file type of OCX and can be created using the Microsoft OLE Custom Control Developer's Kit provided with Microsoft Visual C++ 2.1.

one-to-many relationship A relationship between tables in which one record in a primary table can be related to many records in a related table.

one-to-one relationship A relationship between tables in which one record in a primary table can be related to only one record in a related table.

open database connectivity (ODBC) Standard protocol for database servers. You must install the appropriate database server driver to connect FoxPro to the server and access remote data.

operand A value manipulated inside an expression.

operator One or more characters that designate how one or more operands of an expression are operated on. For example, the `+` operator in the expression `1 + 2` designates that the two operands are added.

optimize To cause some process to operate as efficiently as possible. For example, the statement "Rushmore technology optimizes data access" means that Rushmore makes data access more efficient. In other words, it speeds up data access.

overtype mode A text editing state the opposite of insert mode. When you type a character while in overtype mode, the character at the cursor is overwritten. Also called *overwrite mode.*

pack To permanently remove records in a database file that are marked for deletion.

Page Footer band The region at the bottom of each page of a report in which specified text is printed. The contents of the report Footer band are printed in this region.

Page Header band The region at the top of each page of a report in which specified text is printed. The contents of the report Header band are printed in this region.

parameter An identifier that receives a value passed to a function.

parent table A primary table in a one-to-one or one-to-many relationship.

pass by reference A method of passing a variable to a user-defined function (UDF). The calling program passes the address of a variable to the UDF or procedure. The UDF or procedure uses that address to retrieve or modify the value of the variable. Arrays are passed by reference. Obviously, expressions are always passed by value. You can use the `SET UDFPARAMS` command to specify that arguments are passed to a UDF or procedure by reference or by value. As a consequence, the passed variable is changed.

pass by value A means of passing a variable to a user-defined function (UDF). A copy of a variable is created and passed to the UDF. The UDF can modify the copy without affecting the original variable. When the UDF returns, the copy is discarded. See *pass by reference.*

paste To insert the contents of the Clipboard at the insertion point.

pathname The full name of a file that specifies the storage location of a file or directory. A path can contain a drive name, directory names, and a filename. For example, C:\VFP\SAMPLES\MYFILE.DBF.

pixel The smallest element that can be displayed on a screen or printer.

point (1) A unit of measure for type. Twelve points equal 1 pica, and 6 picas (or 72 points) equal approximately 1 inch. (2) To position the mouse pointer at a location on the screen.

polymorphism An object-oriented programming term that denotes methods that have the same name but different behavior, depending on the type of object that uses the method.

pointer An arrow on the screen that follows the movement of the mouse.

pop-up control A rectangle with an underlined arrow in a gray box to its right. Click on the arrow and a list of items appears. The user can select one of the items in the list. It is called a combo box control in Visual FoxPro.

pop-up menu A list of options that appears when you choose a pop-up control in a dialog box.

precedence A term that refers to the position an operation occupies in a precedence table. Operators with high precedence levels are evaluated before operators with low precedence levels.

preprocessor A processor, attached to the compiler, that modifies the source code in accordance with directives before the compiler processes the source code.

primary key A field or group of fields whose value uniquely identifies a record.

primary table A table whose columns are referenced by other tables in a one-to-one or one-to-many relationship.

private variable A variable that exists from the time it is defined until the procedure or function in which it is defined returns control to its calling program. A private variable is visible from within its procedure and any called procedures.

procedure A set of instructions that acts as a unit. One procedure can execute statements in another procedure, which executes its instructions and returns control to the first procedure.

programming language A collection of symbols and the associated rules and syntax used to write a program.

project A special table with a .PJX extension that keeps track of all files needed to construct an application. The types of files that can be included in a project are program, screen, menu, report, label, library, query, and format files.

property An attribute of a field, control, or database object. You set a property to define one of the characteristics of the object or an aspect of the object's behavior. For example, the `Enabled` property affects whether a control object is enabled at runtime.

protected mode One of the operating modes of x86 (286, 386, 486, Pentium P5, and Pentium P6) family of processors in which programs running simultaneously cannot invade each other's memory space or directly access input/output devices, preventing system failures during a multitasking operation. The other mode is *real mode.* The Windows standard and enhanced operating modes run under protected mode.

D

Resources

This appendix provides a repository for additional sources of Visual FoxPro information. It includes a list of magazines, training, and online services that support Visual FoxPro.

Magazines

FoxPro Advisor Magazine
4010 Morena Blvd., Suite 200
San Diego, CA 92117
(800)336-6060

This monthly magazine focuses on Visual FoxPro. I consider this magazine to be the best centralized source of current Visual FoxPro information available.

Data Based Advisor Magazine
4010 Morena Blvd., Suite 200
San Diego, CA 92117
(800)336-6060

This monthly magazine focuses on a variety of database management systems and client/server products and services.

DBMS Magazine
411 Borel Ave.
San Mateo, CA 94402
(800)456-2859

This monthly magazine focuses on database servers.

Fox Talk
Pinnacle Publishing, Inc.
PO Box 888
Kent, WA 98035-9912
(800)231-1293

This is a monthly newsletter and companion disk.

The Pinter FoxPro Letter
P.O. Box 10349
Truckee, CA 96162-10349
(800)995-2797

Training

Many colleges and universities across the country offer Visual FoxPro classes. In addition, there are numerous commercial firms that offer seminars and scheduled classes in cities across the country. They usually provide hands-on training. This means that each student has a computer to work on as the class proceeds. Here are just a few of the companies that offer classes:

APPtitude Seminars
5001 Baum Blvd., Suite 530
Pittsburgh, PA 15217
(800)832-2450

APPtitude offers hands-on Visual FoxPro training programs and has permanent classrooms in Pittsburgh, New York, and Washington, DC. It offers regularly scheduled classes nationally and internationally.

Applications Developers Training Company
7151 Metro Blvd., Suite 100
Minneapolis, MN 55439
(800)578-2062

This company offers nationwide hands-on Visual FoxPro training seminars.

The Flash Consultant
Flash Creative Management, Inc.
1060 Main Street
River Edge, NJ 07661
(201)489-2500
Fax: (201)489-6750

This company offers nationwide five-day training sessions.

The Information Management Group
720 North Franklin, Suite 300
Chicago, IL 60610
(800)922-2019
Fax: (312)280-8108

This company offers monthly training classes in Chicago. It is an authorized Microsoft technical education center that has been offering training on database products since 1986. It offers Visual FoxPro classes with hands-on instruction.

ISResearch, Inc.
2 Crowne Point Court, Suite 260
Cincinnati, Ohio 45241-4312
(513)772-4636 ext. 1530
Fax: (513)772-5779

ISResearch offers five-day training courses in the eastern United States. They also offer on-site training.

ISResearch, Inc.
2 Crowne Point, Suite 260
Cincinnati, Ohio 45241-5412
(513)772-4636

This company offers nationwide five-day, hands-on Visual FoxPro training programs.

MicroMega Systems, Inc.
832 Baker Street
San Francisco, CA 94115
(415)346-5757
Fax: (415)346-6804

This company offers training and courseware.

Micro Endeavors, Inc.
3150 Township Line Road
Drexel Hill, PA 19026
(800)331-9434
Fax: (215)449-4757

This company offers nationwide hands-on Visual FoxPro training programs.

Microsoft FoxPro Training Centers
1 Microsoft Way
Redmond, WA 98052
(800)426-9400

Microsoft will refer you to a Microsoft Visual FoxPro certified trainer in your area. Also, they will provide you with the name of a certified Microsoft solution provider who can provide Visual FoxPro consulting and training or can develop custom applications for your organization.

PROSOFT Systems International, Inc.
(800)PRO-FOX1

This company offers nationwide one-day, hands-on Visual FoxPro training seminars in July.

Online Services

You can keep up with the latest up-to-the-minute information on Visual FoxPro by accessing electronic online services.

The Internet offers a variety of information for FoxPro users through World Wide Web sites, newsgroups, and mailing lists.

One of the most interesting and up-to-date sites is Colin's FoxPro Page on the World Wide Web at the address `http://www.state.sd.us/people/colink/fox_page.htm`. Colin's page offers such items as FoxPro News, FoxPro Tip-of-the-UTP, Talking FoxPro on IRC, and Internet FoxPro Resources, including WWW FoxPro Sites, FoxPro FTP sites, mailing lists, and newsgroups.

Another good World Wide Web site for FoxPro information is the FoxPro Resources page at `http://www.hop.man.ac.uk/staff/mpitcher/foxpro/resource.html`.

If you don't have access to the World Wide Web, here are some FTP sites on the Internet for FoxPro information and resources:

Site: `lenti.med.umn.edu`
IP Address: `128.101.81.1`
Directory: /pub/halfdan/foxpro
Admin: Gerald Skerbitz (`gsker@lenti.med.umn.edu`)

Site: `nstn.ns.ca`
IP Address: `137.186.128.11`
Directory: /pub/pc-stuff/foxpro
Admin: Paul Russell (`russell@atl.sofkin.ca`)

Site: `ftp.microsoft.com`
IP Address: `198.105.232.1`
Directory: /developr/fox
Admin: Microsoft (`csftpad@microsoft.com`)

Site: `mercurio.univr.it`
IP Address: `157.27.1.2`
Directory: /pub/msdos/foxpro
Admin: Germano Rossi (`germano@chiostro.univr.it`)

Site: `ftp.hop.man.ac.uk`
IP Address: `130.88.76.100`
Directory: /ftp/foxpro
Admin: Malcolm Pitcher (`mpitcher@fs1.ho.man.ac.uk`)

You will meet many friendly, well-informed people on CompuServe who can answer any Visual FoxPro question you can contrive. You sign on to CompuServe and use the following electronic addresses to access further information:

Forum	*Forum Address*
Data Based Advisor Magazine	`GO DBA`
Microsoft FoxPro Forum	`GO FOXFORUM`
Microsoft Fox Users Forum	`GO FOXGANG`
Microsoft Fox Users Forum	`GO FOXUSER`

The FoxPro Forum is a place to go if you need to ask questions and get the latest specific Visual FoxPro-related information. The Fox Users Forum is a place for users to go to socialize and discuss topics related to FoxPro and Visual FoxPro products. It includes a want ad library and a third-party developer section for people to discuss third-party add-ons for FoxPro and Visual FoxPro.

If you are not now a CompuServe user, but have a modem attached to your computer and you'd like to become a CompuServe user, contact CompuServe to establish a new account:

CompuServe Services
5000 Arlington Centre Blvd.
P.O. Box 20212
Columbus, OH 43220
(800)544-4005

There are several third-party software packages that will facilitate communications with CompuServe. The WinCIM CompuServe package operates with Windows. It was developed by CompuServe to automate electronic mail. To find out more about WinCIM, type `GO WINCIM` at any CompuServe ! prompt. You will probably find out about WinCIM when you sign up for CompuServe. I received in the mail a free CD-ROM from CompuServe that contained WinCIM. TAPCIS completely automates CompuServe mail and operates under MS-DOS. You can find out more about TAPCIS by calling (800)872-4768 or typing `GO TAPCIS` at any CompuServe ! prompt.

Other online services have areas dedicated to database management systems:

America Online
8619 Westwood Center Drive
Vienna, VA 22182-2285
(703)448-8700

GEnie
GE Company Information Services Division
401 North Washington Street
Rockville, MD 20850
(800)638-9636

Prodigy Services
(800)PRODIGY

Index

Symbols

A

B

C

D

E

G

L

N

P

Q

S

W

X–Z

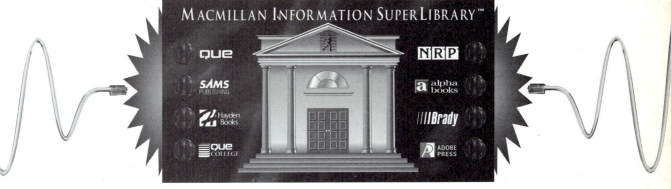

Add to Your Sams Library Today with the Best Books for Programming, Operating Systems, and New Technologies

The easiest way to order is to pick up the phone and call

1-800-428-5331

between 9:00 a.m. and 5:00 p.m. EST.

For faster service please have your credit card available.

ISBN	Quantity	Description of Item	Unit Cost	Total Cost
0-672-30453-8		Access 2 Developer's Guide, Second Edition (book/disk)	$44.95	
0-672-30496-1		Paradox 5 for Windows Developer's Guide, Second Edition (book/disk)	$49.99	
0-672-30643-3		Develop a Professional Visual FoxPro 3 Application in 14 Days (book/CD-ROM)	$35.00	
0-672-30565-8		FoxPro 2.6 for Windows Developer's Guide, 2nd Edition (book/disk)	$45.00	
0-672-30538-0		FoxPro 2.6 for Windows Unleashed (book/disk)	$35.00	
0-672-30198-9		dBASE 5 for Windows Developer's Guide (book/disk)	$39.99	
0-672-30467-8		SYBASE Developer's Guide (book/disk)	$40.00	
0-672-30488-0		Teach Yourself Access 2 in 14 Days, Second Edition	$24.95	
0-672-30494-5		Access 2 Unleashed (book/disk)	$34.95	
0-672-30512-7		DB2 Developer's Guide, Second Edition	$59.99	
0-672-30700-6		Developing SYBASE Applications (book/CD-ROM)	$39.99	
❑ 3 ½" Disk		Shipping and Handling: See information below.		
❑ 5 ¼" Disk		TOTAL		

Shipping and Handling: $4.00 for the first book, and $1.75 for each additional book. Floppy disk: add $1.75 for shipping and handling. If you need to have it NOW, we can ship product to you in 24 hours for an additional charge of approximately $18.00, and you will receive your item overnight or in two days. Overseas shipping and handling adds $2.00 per book and $8.00 for up to three disks. Prices subject to change. Call for availability and pricing information on latest editions.

201 W. 103rd Street, Indianapolis, Indiana 46290

1-800-428-5331 — Orders   1-800-835-3202 — FAX   1-800-858-7674 — Customer Service

Book ISBN 0-672-30653-0

Installing Your CD-ROM

What's on the CD

The CD contains code and sample programs created by the author, Jeb Long, as well as third-party applications and utilities that work with Visual FoxPro.

Software Installation Instructions

1. Insert the CD into your CD-ROM drive.
2. From File Manager or Program Manager, choose Run from the File menu.
3. Type `<drive>SETUP` and press Enter. (`<drive>` corresponds to the drive letter of your CD-ROM drive. For example, if your CD-ROM is drive D:, type `D:SETUP` and press enter.)
4. Follow the on-screen instructions in the installation program. Files will be installed to the Visual FoxPro directory, \VFP, under a subdirectory called Foxbook, unless you choose a different directory during installation.
5. The setup program will also create a new group within the Program Manager called Visual FoxPro Developer's Guide.
6. Be sure to read the README text file that appears within the Program Manager group Visual FoxPro Developer's Guide for more detailed information about the programs installed on your hard drive, and any special instructions for running applications.
7. The author has created a program called SAMPLES.SCX that acts as a catalog for all the files and sample programs on the CD. Open SAMPLES.SCX to view files and launch certain programs directly from the catalog.